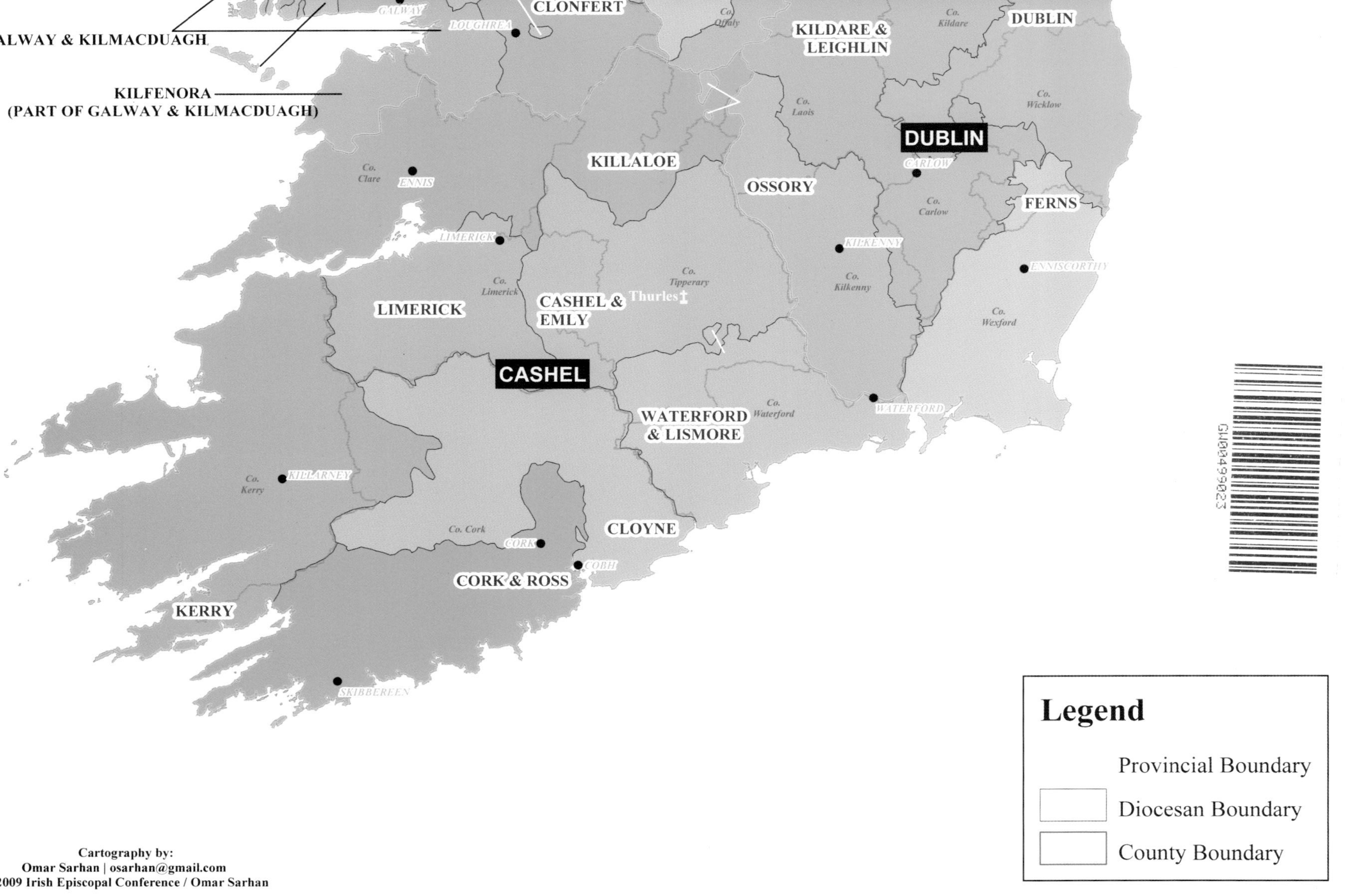


Cartography by:
Omar Sarhan | osarhan@gmail.com

# IRISH CATHOLIC DIRECTORY 2012

**BENEDICT XVI**
BISHOP OF ROME
Vicar of Jesus Christ

Successor of the Prince of the Apostles, Supreme Pontiff of the Universal Church, Primate of Italy, Archbishop and Metropolitan of the Roman Province, Sovereign of the State of the Vatican City.

Servant of the Servants of God, Joseph Ratzinger, born at Marktl am Inn, Germany on 16 April 1927; ordained priest on 29 June 1951, ordained Archbishop of Munich and Freising on 25 March 1977; created Cardinal on 27 June 1977. He was elected Pope on 19 April 2005 and inaugurated on 24 April.

# IRISH CATHOLIC DIRECTORY 2012

PUBLISHED BY AUTHORITY
FOR THE HIERARCHY OF IRELAND

This publication
has been supported
by the generous
sponsorship
of

VERITAS

Published for the Hierarchy by
Veritas Publications
7–8 Lower Abbey Street
Dublin 1
Ireland
publications@veritas.ie
www.veritas.ie





ISBN 978 1 84730 326 4

Cover design: Colette Dower, Veritas Publications
Design & Typesetting: Colette Dower, Veritas Publications
Printed in the Republic of Ireland
by Hudson Killeen Ltd, Dublin

*Veritas books are printed on paper made from the wood pulp of managed forests.
For every tree felled, at least one tree is planted, thereby renewing natural resources.*

# PREFACE

This is the twenty-second edition of the *Irish Catholic Directory*. Information for this edition was collected between August 2011 and November 2011. In general, all information comes from the organisation or community concerned.

Veritas has made every effort to ensure the accuracy and completeness of the information in the *Directory*. However, this information can only be as good as that supplied to us.

We would like to express our gratitude to all the bishops, diocesan secretaries, priests, brothers, sisters and lay people who have over the years supplied information, answered queries, chased details and checked proofs.

We are also indebted to the advertisers and sponsors, without whose support this publication would not be possible.

Finally, it may be appropriate to remind readers that the *Directory* is simply an orderly listing of personnel in the Church and related organisations. Our task is to make this listing as easy to use as possible. The *Directory* is not a statement of Church policy, nor an expression of precedence, and should not be taken as such.

# CONTENTS

## ALL IRELAND STD DIALLING

All STD numbers in this *Directory* are listed with both the number and the local area code.

Callers from the Irish Republic to Northern Ireland simply **need to dial 048 followed by the 8-digit local number.**

# 2011 REVIEW OF THE PASTORAL ACTIVITIES OF THE IRISH EPISCOPAL CONFERENCE, ITS AGENCIES, COUNCILS AND INITIATIVES details on www.catholicbishops.ie

**JANUARY**

On 2 January, Cardinal Seán Brady, Archbishop of Armagh and Primate of All Ireland, presided and preached the homily at a Mass in Saint Patrick's Cathedral Armagh to mark both the first anniversary of the death of Cardinal Cahal Daly and a special day of prayer for renewal of the faith in the Church in Ireland.

*Share the Good News* – the first National Directory for Catechesis in Ireland – was formally launched at a media conference on 5 January in the Mater Dei Institute of Education, Dublin. Cardinal Brady, Archbishop Diarmuid Martin, Archbishop of Dublin and Primate of Ireland, Bishop William Murphy, Bishop of Kerry and Chairman of the Episcopal Council for Catechetics participated in the launch along with writer and editor Rev Dr Gareth Byrne. *Share the Good News* is a ten year plan for evangelisation, for catechesis and for religious education in the Catholic Church in Ireland. It is available in Veritas shops throughout Ireland and online at *www.veritas.ie*.

As part of the Service of the Apostolic Visitation to the Archdiocese of Armagh, a 'Service of Penitence and Healing' was held on 23 January in Saint Patrick's Cathedral, Armagh. Cardinal Cormac Murphy-O'Connor, Archbishop Emeritus of Westminster and Apostolic Visitor to the Archdiocese of Armagh preached the homily, and Cardinal Brady and Sheila Baroness Hollins, Consultant Psychiartist and assistant to Cardinal Cormac Murphy-O'Connor for the Visitation, both gave addresses.

On 27 January, Bishop Brendan Kelly, Bishop of Achonry and Chair of the Council for Education of the Irish Episcopal Conference, celebrated Mass to launch Catholic Schools Week 2011. This Mass was transmitted by RTÉ1 television from its Donnybrook studio. The choir for the Mass was provided by the pupils of St Clare's Primary School, Harold's Cross Road, Dublin. Prior to the broadcast of this Mass, Cardinal Brady introduced a short televised documentary highlighting the value and contribution that Catholic schools make to our parish communities. CSW 2011 ran from 31 January to 6 February.

**FEBRUARY**

On 4 February, 'Towards Healing', the new counselling and support service for survivors of abuse by clergy or religious, was launched. It can be contacted by free-phone 1800 0303416 (ROI) and 08000963315 (Northern Ireland and UK). The new service replaced the Faoiseamh Counselling Service, which had been in operation since 1997, and which provided face-to-face counselling to nearly 4,000 persons during that time, as well as helpline support to over 15,000 survivors of abuse by clergy and religious. The new Towards Healing service was set up following consultation between the Irish Episcopal Conference, the Conference of Religious or Ireland, the Irish Missionary Union and Faoiseamh, and with survivor groups, and is designed to ensure that survivors of abuse receive counselling and other support services in a more holistic manner than heretofore.

On 6 February, the feast day of Saint Mel, the patron saint of the Diocese of Ardagh and Clonmacnois and of the Cathedral in Longford, the media launch of the announcement of the design team for the restoration of Saint Mel's Cathedral took place in Bishop's House, Longford. The Saint Mel's design team included the doyen of church architects, Dr Richard Hurley, as the design architect for this major project of restoration. Bishop Colm O'Reilly, Bishop of Ardagh and Clonmacnois, said: 'It is my hope that this immense challenge that we face will offer us an important opportunity for renewal, not only renewal of a destroyed Cathedral but renewal of a sense of community and creation of an understanding of the purpose that a cathedral fulfils. It is in faith that all of us must set out on the journey towards restoration of Saint Mel's Cathedral knowing that we will not walk alone, for God is with us.'

On 10 February, Bishop John Buckley, Bishop of Cork and Ross and Bishop Noël Treanor, Bishop of Down and Connor, jointly called for prayers for those who were killed and injured in the plane crash at Cork airport.

On 11 February, ACCORD, the Catholic marriage care service, announced a 6 per cent increase in the number of couples booking their marriage preparation courses online for the first six weeks in 2011. In 2010 the online bookings figure was 1183 compared to 1255 for the same period in 2011.

On Sunday 20 February, a Liturgy of Lament and Repentance for the sexual abuse of children by priests and religious was held in Saint Mary's Pro-Cathedral, within the framework of the Apostolic Visitation of the Archdiocese of Dublin. The liturgy asked the forgiveness of God and of all survivors for the failure of those Church leaders and many others in the family of the Church to respond with love, integrity, honesty, understanding and compassion to the pain and distress of survivors. During the liturgy which has been prepared principally by survivors, Cardinal Sean O'Malley and Archbishop Diarmuid Martin washed the feet of a group of people who have suffered in various ways through abuse.

At a media conference on 21 February in the Capuchin Day Centre in Dublin's Bow Street, the Council for Justice and Peace of the Irish Episcopal Conference launched *From Crisis to Hope: Working to achieve the Common Good.* The document addressed the considerable financial turmoil that we face individually and collectively and the associated disaffection throughout Irish society. The document called for the protection of the poorest and most vulnerable in our society as a core element of any measures aimed at addressing the current political, social and economic crises.

On 21 February, the Northern Ireland Catholic Council on Social Affairs, which is chaired by Cardinal Brady, assisted by Bishop Treanor, with a membership of mostly lay Catholics, called for the unanimous support for the retention of the current '50:50' special recruitment provisions for the Police Service of Northern Ireland.

On 24 February, the Holy Father, Pope Benedict XVI, published his 2011 Lenten Message. The text has as its title a passage with a theme from Colossians: 'You were buried with him in baptism, in which you were also raised with him.' (cf. Col 2: 12)

**MARCH**

The Spring General Meeting of the Irish Bishops' Conference concluded on 2 March in the Columba Centre in Saint Patrick's College, Maynooth. The following issues were discussed by the bishops during their meeting: New *Roman Missal*; Lent and preparation for Easter; *Share the Good News*; Safeguarding Children; Prayers for the people of New Zealand, North Africa and Southern Sudan; *Pastoral Letter of Pope Benedict XVI to the Catholics of Ireland*; The 50th International Eucharistic Congress in Ireland in 2012; the Meeting of the Commission for Worship, Pastoral Renewal and Faith Development and representatives of the Association of Catholic Priests; The Solemnity of St Patrick, General Election in the Republic of Ireland; Policing in Northern Ireland; and the Beatification of John Paul II on Divine Mercy Sunday 1 May, 2011.

On the 7 March Cardinal Brady and Archbishop Martin launched the 50th International Eucharistic Congress 2012 in the Royal Dublin Society, Ballsbridge, Dublin. Cardinal Brady and Archbishop Martin called for volunteers and for prayer for the success of the Congress in Ireland. The media launch also included the commissioning of the Congress Bell which will start a pilgrimage to the 26 dioceses of Ireland and return to the RDS ahead of the start of the International Eucharistic Congress on 10 June 2012. The theme of the 2012 Congress is 'The

Eucharist: Communion with Christ and one another'. The Eucharistic Congress is one of the largest liturgical events and opportunities for pilgrimage throughout the universal Catholic Church. It is hosted by a different country every four years. The main events of the Congress next year will take place in the RDS, Dublin. Over the week 10–17 June, a programme of liturgical and cultural events, workshops and daily celebration of the Eucharist will culminate in an open air Mass and closing ceremony in Croke Park, Dublin.

To coincide with the first anniversary of the Pastoral Letter of Pope Benedict XVI to the Catholics of Ireland on 19 March, Irish bishops published their pastoral response *Towards Healing and Renewal*. Cardinal Brady encouraged everyone to read this short pastoral response to key issues raised by the Holy Father's *Pastoral Letter* of March 2010. *Towards Healing and Renewal* outlines the commitment of the Church in Ireland to healing and renewal and the steps on this journey pointed out by survivors of abuse and their representatives. *Towards Healing and Renewal* outlines initiatives to enhance the personal, pastoral, spiritual and practical support available to survivors of abuse. The launch of the bishops' pastoral response included the following detail:

- €10m co-funding over the next five years for 'Towards Healing', the expanded counselling service for survivors
- Meetings and dialogue between bishops and survivors of abuse to continue
- Pope Benedict's 2010 *Pastoral Letter* prompted the reflections of over 3,000 people on renewal in the Church in Ireland.

Importantly, *Towards Healing and Renewal* also mentions ways in which parishes can play a part in assisting the process of healing for survivors of abuse.

*Towards Healing and Renewal* represents part of a wider response and longer journey by the Church in Ireland offering its support to survivors of abuse on their journey to healing and peace, and in committing itself to renewal.

## APRIL

Cura, the crisis pregnancy agency of the Catholic Church, held its 34th annual conference on 1 and 2 April in Athlone, Co Westmeath. Bishop Gerard Clifford, President of Cura and Auxiliary Bishop of Archdiocese of Armagh, addressed the conference which was attended by 150 Cura members. The 2011 conference focused on the strategic review and planning process which is currently being undertaken by the agency. The objective of this process is to evaluate how effectively Cura has been delivering support and help to clients facing an unplanned pregnancy and to identify ways to improve the agency's effectiveness in delivering these services to our clients in the future.

On 13 April, the Diocese of Limerick announced the appointment of its first Director of Safeguarding Children to oversee all aspects of child protection in Church related activities throughout the Diocese. Mr Ger Crowley, a former Head Social Worker and Director of Child Care Services in the statutory child protection services, commenced the role in early March. Limerick Diocese, after the Archdiocese of Dublin, is only the second diocese to make such an appointment.

On 14 April, Archbishop Martin, together with the staff of the Archdiocese's Child Safeguarding and Protection office launched the Diocesan Policy for Child Safeguarding and Protecting Children. This Policy brings together a series of long established practices and procedures in the Archdiocese to safeguard children, in compliance the National Church policy *Safeguarding Children*.

On 25 April, Easter Sunday, six students from the Pontifical Irish College, Rome, were ordained deacons. The ordination ceremony, celebrated by Bishop Seamus Hegarty, Bishop of Derry, was held in the Church of Santa Maria sopra Minerva, Rome. Two of the new deacons, Brendan Collins and Patrick Lagan, come from the Diocese of Derry, whilst Philip John Harris is from the Diocese of Waterford and Lismore; Ryan McAleer from the Archdiocese of Armagh; Conor McGrath from the Diocese of Down and Connor; and Milan Tomaga from the Diocese of Banska-Bystrica in Slovakia.

On 28 April, Cardinal Brady celebrated Mass commemorating the 40th anniversary for 1,100 Irish pilgrims of the Irish Pilgrimage Trust at the Marian Shrine in Lourdes. Cardinal Brady said: 'I have thought long and hard to discover the common chord, the bond that unites the three big events of the week: this pilgrimage; the Royal wedding; and the Papal Beatification. They all have in common ... the bond of love. The love in our hearts that responds to God's love that is given to us.'

On 21 April, bishops throughout the country celebrated the Mass of Chrism with their priests and people. Bishop Leo O'Reilly, Bishop of Kilmore, said 'Today is a day to thank God for our priests, for the quiet work they do day in day out, year in year out in parishes, schools, hospitals and communities.'

## MAY

To mark the Beatification of Blessed John Paul II by the Holy Father Pope Benedict XVI on Divine Mercy Sunday 1 May, the first Sunday after Easter, Cardinal Brady and Archbishop Martin celebrated Masses of Thanksgiving for Irish pilgrims in Rome and for parishioners in Dublin.

On 5 May, Archbishop Martin delivered the homily for the Annual 1916 Commemoration Mass in the Church of the Sacred Heart, Arbour Hill, Dublin. Archbishop Martin said: 'As each generation of history emerges, Ireland needs new generations of young men and women who have the vision to dream and the courage to realise their dreams.'

Cardinal Brady opened the plenary meeting of the structured dialogue between the Irish Government and Church, Faith Communities, philosophical and non-confessional organisations at the Office of the Taoiseach, Dublin, on 19 May. In his address Cardinal Brady said: 'The Churches, faith communities and organisations represented here contribute immensely to the life of local communities in pastoral, charitable and volunteer activities. They represent a vital source of social capital and an essential part of the common good.'

Bishop John McAreavey, Bishop of Dromore and co-chair of the Bishops' Council for Communications, welcomed the publication by the Congregation for the Doctrine of the Faith of new guidelines in cases of sexual abuse on 16 May. Bishop McAreavey said: 'I wholeheartedly welcome today's important initiative by the Congregation. These new guidelines offer assistance on preventing sexual abuse and on reporting allegations to the police.'

## JUNE

The June issue of *Intercom* magazine, the Irish Episcopal Conference's pastoral and liturgical resource for people in ministry, included a wide-ranging interview with Fr Federico Lombardi SJ, Director of the Holy See Press Office on his life and ministry.

As part of the preparations for the 50th International Eucharistic Congress in Dublin in June 2012, a meeting of International Delegates and the Pontifical Committee for the International Eucharistic Congress is taking place in Dublin from 1–3 June. Cardinal Brady and Archbishop Martin addressed the meeting of the Pontifical Council for the International Eucharistic Congress on the preparations for next year's Congress in Ireland. Details of both the online registration for 2012, and details for the National Eucharistic Congress in Knock on 25 June 2011 were also announced at this meeting.

On 5 June, the Universal Catholic Church celebrated the 45th World Communications Day on the theme 'Truth, proclamation and authenticity of life in the digital age'. The theme was chosen by Pope Benedict XVI and he reflected on it in his traditional message for World Communications Day.

On 6 June, a statement was issued from the Vatican in relation to the conclusion of the first phase of the Apostolic Visitation which was first announced by the Holy Father in his *Pastoral Letter to the Catholics of Ireland* of March 2010. The statement said: 'The Visitation to the four metropolitan archdioceses, the seminaries and the religious institutes has been very useful, thanks to the cooperation of everyone who took part in this initiative. The Holy Father's sincere thanks goes to them, especially to the four Metropolitan Archbishops. As far as the Irish dioceses and seminaries are concerned, the Congregation for Bishops and the Congregation for Catholic Education do not envisage further Apostolic Visitations. By early 2012, the Holy See will publish an overall synthesis indicating the results and the future prospects highlighted by the Visitation, not least with a view to the nationwide Mission announced in the above mentioned Letter of the Holy Father.'

The Summer General Meeting of the Irish Bishops' Conference concluded in Maynooth on 15 June. Topics discussed by the bishops included: Pope Benedict XVI, National Board for Safeguarding Children in the Catholic Church, the forthcoming National and separately the 50th International Eucharistic Congress in Ireland, and the new translation of the *Roman Missal*.

Pope Benedict XVI sent a special Apostolic Blessing on the occasion of the National Eucharistic Congress which took place at the National Marian Shrine in Knock on 25 and 26 June. The text of the Blessing read: 'The Holy Father was pleased to learn of the celebration of the Irish National Eucharistic Congress and he sends his warm and prayerful best wishes to you and to the Bishops, priests, religious and lay faithful of Ireland.'

On 28 June, the Bishops' Council for Justice and Peace issued a statement opposing cuts to Sunday premium payments and criticising the bonus culture. Chair of the CJP Bishop Raymond Field said: 'The proposal to cut Sunday premium payments is a prime example of a decision that would prioritise economic considerations at the expense of the well-being of citizens and the good of society.'

The 29 June, Feast day of the Apostles Saints Peter and Paul, marked the 60th anniversary of the ordination of Pope Benedict XVI to the priesthood. Congratulating the Holy Father Cardinal Brady said: 'On behalf of the Catholics of Ireland I offer to His Holiness, Pope Benedict, our wholehearted congratulations and good wishes on the momentous occasion of the sixtieth anniversary of his ordination to priesthood, today 29 June. I express gratitude for all the graces and blessings which God has chosen to give through His Holiness and through his ministry, as priest, bishop and most especially as Supreme Pastor of the Church to so many people in so many places, through six decades of tireless service.'

**JULY**

The Archdiocese of Armagh hosted a three day festival of prayer called *Spiritfest 2011* from Friday 1 to Sunday 3 July. International keynote speakers such as Fr Lawrence Freeman and Monica Brown were joined by Bishop Richard Clarke, Rev Ruth Patterson, Fr Paschal McDonnell, and Professor Rev Eamon Conway for a weekend of workshops, prayer and a special performance by The Priests. Cardinal Brady said: 'I hope that Spiritfest can offer an opportunity, a pause on the journey, towards next year's International Eucharistic Congress, for prayer and reflection.'

The 42nd annual summer school of the Irish Church Music Association opened on 4 July at Saint Patrick's College, Maynooth. The 2011 theme was 'The Mystery of Faith' and it looked towards the introduction of the new translation of the *Roman Missal* on the first Sunday of Advent on 27 November and the celebration of Ireland hosting the 50th International Eucharistic Congress in June 2012.

On 13 July, Archbishop Dermot Clifford, Apostolic Administrator of the Diocese of Cloyne, held a media conference in Cork following the publication of the Commission of Investigation report by Chairperson Judge Yvonne Murphy into the Diocese of Cloyne. Archbishop Clifford said: 'I accept the findings of the Commission of Investigation into the handling by Church and State authorities of allegations and suspicions of child sexual abuse against a number of clerics in the Diocese of Cloyne. I wish to thank the members of the Commission on the completion of their very thorough investigation. This is the first time that the survivors of child sexual abuse in the Diocese of Cloyne have had an opportunity to have their stories heard publicly.' Cardinal Brady and Archbishop Martin led responses by bishops to issues raised by the Cloyne Report.

On 20 July, the United Nations declared a famine in parts of Somalia as 13 million people in Somalia, Kenya and Ethiopia were at risk of starvation. Collections were held in parishes across Ireland on the weekend of 23 and 24 July in response to the Catholic Church's emergency appeal for the region. Mr Justin Kilcullen, the director of Trócaire, the Irish Church's overseas aid agency, visited some of the worst affected areas in east Africa and he led awareness raising in Ireland of this international humanitarian crisis.

Following the announcement on 26 July of Fr Gregory Collins OSB's election as Abbot of Dormition Abbey in Jerusalem, Bishop Noël Treanor said: 'I warmly welcome the election of Fr Gregory Collins OSB as the sixth Abbot of Dormition Abbey in Jerusalem. I send him my congratulations and those of the people of Belfast, the city he was born in. I send him my good wishes and blessings as he takes up his appointment in Jerusalem – the sacred land in which Our Lord walked during his time on earth.'

On 31 July, the annual Reek Sunday pilgrimage took place on Croagh Patrick, Co Mayo, led by Archbishop Michael Neary, Archbishop of Tuam. In his homily on the summit Archbishop Neary said: 'In a time when the Church in Ireland is shaken by wrongdoing, we have come to this place where Christian hopes, as a people, first were raised.' An estimated 20,000 pilgrims climbed Croagh Patrick on Reek Sunday, most of whom received the sacraments of the Eucharist and Reconciliation at the summit.

**AUGUST**

ACCORD's *Annual Report 2010* was launched at a press conference on 11 August, and new figures released showed an 8 per cent increase in demand by couples for the agency's marriage counselling service during 2010. Since 2008, there has been a 20 per cent increase in the demand for marriage counselling in ACCORD centres throughout Ireland.

On 21 August, RTÉ1 television broadcast the closing Mass for World Youth Day, live from Madrid. Live commentary and translation were provided by Fr Thomas McCarthy, OP, and Yanira Romero. RTÉ coverage included a video package reflecting the experience of pilgrims since the arrival of the Holy Father in Madrid.

Twenty-two men began their studies for priesthood on 29 August at Ireland's national seminary, Saint Patrick's College, Maynooth. This group includes a chartered surveyor, a pub manager, several mature students and at least one school-leaver. The average age of the new entrants was 25 years old, and they come from 14 of the 26 dioceses of Ireland. After an introductory month, 18 students commenced their academic formation in Maynooth and the remaining four began their studies at Saint Malachy's College, Belfast.

**SEPTEMBER**

On 3 September, Mgr Ettore Balestrero, the Holy See's Under-Secretary for Relations with States, met with Ms Helena Keleher *Chargé d'Affaires* of the Embassy of Ireland to the Holy See, and conveyed the Holy See's Response to the *Cloyne Report* to the Irish Government. This Response was prepared arising from a meeting on 14 July, following the publication of the Report of the Commission of Investigation into the Diocese of Cloyne, where Mr Eamon Gilmore TD, Tánaiste and Minister for Foreign Affairs and Trade, in the course of a meeting with the Apostolic Nuncio in Ireland, Archbishop Giuseppe Leanza, requested him to convey to the Holy See a copy of the *Cloyne Report* together with the Irish Government's views on the matters raised, to which the Minister requested a Response. On 3 September, the Response of the Holy See was published: 'Recognising the seriousness of the crimes detailed in the Report, which should never have happened within the Church of Jesus Christ, and wishing to respond to the Irish Government's request, the Holy See, after carefully examining the *Cloyne Report* and considering the many issues raised, has sought to respond comprehensively.' Cardinal Brady and Archbishop Martin welcomed the Response of the Holy See.

On 8 September, Fr Ciarán O'Carroll was appointed as Rector of the Pontifical Irish College in Rome. Prior to his appointment, Fr O'Carroll had been the Episcopal Vicar for Evangelisation in the Archdiocese of Dublin and Administrator of the Catholic University Church on St Stephen's Green, Dublin. Fr O'Carroll succeeded Mgr Liam Bergin from the Diocese of Ossory, who was Rector of the Irish College from 2001.

On Sunday 11 September, a significant step in the journey towards the full use of the new edition of the *Roman Missal* was taken as changes to some of the people's responses and prayers at Mass were introduced in parishes across the country this weekend. Missalettes with the changes included, and/or Congregational Cards with the new texts, were made available to Mass-goers.

From the 27 November next, the first

Sunday of Advent, congregations and priests will use the full text of the new edition of the *Roman Missal* for the celebration of the Mass. A number of text and video resources have been prepared and made available to help the faithful prepare for the introduction of the new translation on www.catholicbishops.ie.

On 14 September, five members of the Irish Episcopal Conference, led by Cardinal Brady and five bishops of the Church of Ireland, led by Archbishop Michael Jackson, spent a day in prayer, fellowship and discussion. This historic meeting came about as a result of the request from the International Anglican/Roman Catholic Commission for Unity and Mission that Roman Catholic and Anglican bishops in individual countries should meet from time to time to develop their fellowship and to discuss matters of common concern. The bishops reflected together on the Sacrament of Baptism not only on a liturgical level but in terms of the life to which the baptised are called in today's world.

On 15 September, Pope Benedict XVI appointed Archbishop Giuseppe Leanza, Apostolic Nuncio to Ireland, as the new Apostolic Nuncio to the Czech Republic.

On 21 September, Archbishop Martin hosted an evening with 25 young leaders from different Christian Churches, arising from his participation in the 'Breathing Spaces' programmes of Irish Peace Centres. Discussion centred on the challenges the leaders experience within their own denominations and across denominations as well as their reflections on the contribution of individual Christians and of the Christian Churches, working together for the construction of the future of Irish society.

As part of the preparations for the 50th International Eucharistic Congress in 2012, the Congress took part in the National Ploughing Championships in Athy, Co Kildare, from 20–22 September and was located at the 'Ecumenical Stand' – a joint initiative between the Catholic Archdiocese of Dublin, the Church of Ireland and the Methodist Church in Ireland who came together to share space and invite people to come together to pray. The International Eucharistic Congress Bell was also present during the Championships.

On 25 September, Archbishop Martin celebrated Mass at the Knock Shrine for the annual pilgrimage of the Legion of Mary. Archbishop Martin said: 'The fundamental equality within God's people is about the call to be holy, which is sown in the gift of baptism and addressed to each one of us. Anyone, inside or outside the Church, has the right to criticise the Church; reform and renewal will only come through those who truly live the life and holiness of the Church.'

**OCTOBER**

October was designated as Mission Month by the Catholic Church, the theme being *Together in Faith*. World Missions Ireland – the work of the Pontifical Mission Societies – brings the prayers, solidarity and financial help of the Church in Ireland to Christian communities in other parts of the world, especially those in greatest need. In his message for Mission Sunday on 23 October, Pope Benedict declared that 'Missionary activity renews the Church, revitalises faith and Christian identity, and offers fresh enthusiasm and new incentive. Faith is strengthened when it is given to others! It is in commitment to the Church's universal mission that the new evangelisation of Christian peoples will find inspiration and support.'

On 2 October, the Catholic Church in Ireland celebrated our annual Day for Life with the theme 'A call to solidarity and hope in difficult times'. Day for Life 2011 reflected what it means to lead a full and happy life. It took as its starting point the words of the Holy Father during his recent visit to the United Kingdom: 'Happiness is something we all want, but one of the great tragedies in this world is that so many people never find it, because they look in the wrong places. The key to it is very simple – true happiness is to be found in God.'

On 3 October, Bishop McAreavey and Bishop Brennan of the Episcopal Council for Communications welcomed the theme chosen by Pope Benedict for the World Day of Social Communications 2012: 'Silence and word: path of evangelisation'. The full text of the WDSC message is published annually on 24 January, Feast of Saint Francis of Sales, patron saint of journalists.

Archbishop Martin celebrated Votive Mass of the Holy Spirit to mark the start of the Michaelmas Law term on 3 October. In his homily in Saint Michan's Church in Halston Street, Dublin, Archbishop Martin said: 'the fundamental role of faith for the building of societies, which are truly pluralist, should not be overlooked. These are difficult times, but they are perhaps going to be among the more creative times for our society in Ireland. At this moment, we require a wise, enlightened and broad vision of juridical culture which asserts its legitimate independence from political power and influence and is governed not by the fashion of the day.'

Bishop Michael Smith, Bishop of Meath, described priesthood as a 'radical option' in today's world during the ordination Mass for Fr Kevin Heery (28). The ordination took place on 9 October in the Cathedral of Christ the King, Mullingar, Co Westmeath, and was attended by hundreds of parishioners from Mullingar as well as by local, national and international media. In preparation for the ordination parishioners conducted a 24 hour prayer vigil and fast.

On 9 October, Bishop Christopher Jones, Bishop of Elphin, presided at Mass in Saint Cuan's Church in the Parish of Ahascragh and Caltra to welcome Fr Kevin Reynolds back to the parish. Bishop Jones said: 'We are all truly delighted to welcome Fr Kevin Reynolds back home to the parish of Ahascragh today. We welcome also Fr Anthony Chantry, the Superior General of the Mill Hill Community from London and also Fr Michael Corcoran, Regional Representative of the Mill Hill Missionaries in Ireland, who both accompany Fr Kevin today. When I offered Mass with you and for you on Saturday evening 28 May last, I appealed for prayers that all investigations would be carried out quickly so that the truth regarding the allegations which RTÉ had broadcast about Fr Kevin might be ascertained. RTÉ has now accepted that all of the allegations which it broadcast against Fr Kevin are baseless and without any foundation whatsoever, and that Fr Kevin is entirely innocent.'

The Catholic Schools Partnership published research on school patronage in the Republic of Ireland on 10 October. Fr Michael Drumm, CSP Executive Chairperson, launched the research in Saint Ciarán's Catholic National School, Hartstown, in Dublin.

About 1,600 pilgrims – including 200 young people – attended 'Come and See' the Meath Diocesan Eucharistic Congress over the 14, 15 and 16 October. Among the speakers were Fr Kevin Doran, Secretary General of the International Eucharistic Congress 2012; Fr John Harris OP; Fr Declan Hurley Administrator of St Mary's Parish Navan; Fr Kevin Heery; Sister Consilio Rock; Footballer Ger Brennan; Baroness Nuala O'Loan; GAA Tyrone Manager Mr Mickey Harte; Dr Andrew O'Connell and Pat Reynolds. Net Ministries and Elation Ministries guided young people in prayer and discussion in preparation for the Sacrament of Reconciliation. RTÉ Radio 1's new *Saturday with Charlie Bird* programme broadcast live from the Congress in Navan, and the hour-long show included an audience of lay and clergy who discussed their experience of the Catholic Church and their hopes for the future.

On 17 October, Bishop Donal McKeown, Auxiliary Bishop of Down and Connor and Chair of the Council for Vocations of the Episcopal Conference launched a new 'vocations app' which has been designed to inform and promote vocations to the priesthood in Ireland. The APP is available to download free from the Apple iPhone app store.

On 25 October, Archbishop Martin appointed Fr Kieran McDermott as the new Episcopal Vicar for Evangelisation and Ecumenism for the Archdiocese of Dublin. He succeeds Fr Ciaran O'Carroll, recently appointed Rector of the Pontifical Irish College in Rome.

On 31 October, Cardinal Brady sent a personal letter of congratulations, prayers and good wishes to Mr Michael D. Higgins and his family on his election as the ninth President of Ireland. In his letter Cardinal Brady spoke of his confidence in the ability of the people of Ireland, North and South, to meet the challenges facing them at this time. Cardinal Brady offered his prayers for Mr Higgins as he seeks to give shape to that future in his role as President of Ireland.

**NOVEMBER**

On 2 November, the Holy See Press Office Director Fr Federico Lombardi SJ responded to Ireland's Department of Foreign Affairs and Trade announcement that it was to close, for economic reasons, its embassy in the Holy See: 'The Holy See takes note of the decision by Ireland to close its embassy in Rome to the Holy See. Of course, any State which has diplomatic relations with the Holy See is free to decide, according to its possibilities and its interests, whether to have an ambassador to the Holy See resident in Rome, or resident in another country. What is important are diplomatic relations between the Holy See and the States, and these are not at issue with regard to Ireland.'

Cardinal Brady said on 3 November: 'I wish to express my profound disappointment at this decision which means that Ireland will be without a resident ambassador to the Holy See for the first time since diplomatic relations were established and envoys were exchanged between the two States in 1929. I know that many others will share this disappointment.'

On 10 November, Veritas, the publisher and retailer of the Irish Episcopal Conference, announced plans to open a new store in 2012 in the town of Lourdes, France. The Lourdes store will be the eleventh retail outlet in the Veritas retail network and the first to be located outside the island of Ireland.

Cardinal Brady celebrated the 31st anniversary Mass on 19 November in Saint Mary's Pro Cathedral in Dublin in commemoration of the Servant of God, Frank Duff, Founder of the Legion of Mary. Cardinal Brady said, 'As Frank Duff reminds us, it was Christ Himself who chose to build that Church on the rock of Peter's faith. And Christ does not contradict Himself or the truths he has entrusted to us. As Catholics, the bonds which unite us to the See of Peter are very ancient and precious, very precious … those bonds are to be preserved and strengthened as an integral part of our beliefs.'

On 23 November, Pope Benedict XVI accepted the resignation of Bishop Séamus Hegarty, Bishop of Derry. Following the retirement of Bishop Hegarty the Diocesan College of Consultors met on 25 November and elected Mgr Eamon Martin as Diocesan Administrator for the Diocese of Derry. On accepting election, Mgr Martin said: 'I thank the College of Consultors for the trust they have shown in electing me as Diocesan Administrator for the Diocese of Derry. It is my prayer that I will live up to that trust. In thanking Bishop Hegarty for his seventeen years of ministry as bishop in the Diocese of Derry, I pray for him in his retirement, in particular for his health.'

On 26 November, Pope Benedict XVI appointed the Rt Rev Mgr Charles John Brown as the Apostolic Nuncio to Ireland. Mgr Charles John Brown was born in New York, United States of America, on 13 October 1959. He was ordained priest for the Archdiocese of New York in Saint Patrick's Cathedral on 13 May 1989. Mgr Brown served as curate in the Parish of Saint Brendan, in the Bronx, New York, from 1989 to 1991. From 1994 Mgr Brown has been attached to the Congregation for the Doctrine of the Faith in Rome. He was appointed Chaplain to His Holiness on 6 May 2000. Mgr Brown was appointed Assistant Secretary to the International Theological Commission in September 2009.

On 26 November, the annual joint meeting of the Irish Catholic Bishops' Council for Justice and Peace with the Northern Ireland Catholic Council for Social Affairs took place in the Ballymascanlon House Hotel near Dundalk, Co Louth. Addressing the meeting were Bishop Noël Treanor, chair of the Bishops' Commission for International and Social Affairs; Police Service of Northern Ireland Chief Constable Matt Baggott who spoke on faith and policing; Fr Seán Healy and Sister Brigid Reynolds of Social Justice Ireland who discussed fairness/justice and the common good; and Bishop Field, Chair of the Council for Justice and Peace.

On 27 November – the First Sunday of Advent and the beginning of the new Church year – parishes across the island of Ireland prayed for the first time the prayers of the Mass using the full version of the new translation of the *Roman Missal*.

Also on 27 November, the Council for Marriage and the Family of the Irish Episcopal Conference published resources to assist families in their spiritual preparation during Advent and Christmas 2011. Commenting on the resources Bishop Jones, Chair of the Council for Marriage and the Family, said: 'The family home is called the domestic Church because it is the place where children learn the message of Christ for the first time. These prayers and blessings for the home for Advent and Christmas are offered as opportunities for families to pause, to take time out together and to reflect on the true meaning of Christmas during this Advent Season, when we prepare for the celebration of the Nativity of Jesus. I ask parishes around the country to support the promotion of these prayerful resources which have been specially designed for use by families.'

In its pre-budget message to Minister Frances Fitzgerald on 29 November, ACCORD asked that government funding for the agency be retained at 2011 levels or that cuts deemed necessary by the Minister be minimal. ACCORD findings indicate that two thirds of almost 4,000 couples who sought help in the first six months of 2011 had financial concerns. A further 30 per cent of clients said that finance was a serious issue for them.

On 30 November, the first six reviews of safeguarding practice in dioceses were released by the respective bishops in the Dioceses of Ardagh and Clonmacnois, Derry, Dromore, Kilmore, Raphoe and Tuam. These reviews had been undertaken by the National Board for Safeguarding Children in the Catholic Church in Ireland. Copies of each review are available from the respective diocesan websites and also from the website of the National Board www.safeguarding.ie. The National Board has started into its next round of reviews which will include a number of religious congregations as well as dioceses.

**DECEMBER**

On 1 December, Mgr Joseph Quinn, the much loved and popular Parish Priest of the National Marian Shrine in Knock, died.

On 6 December, the well-known and highly respected architect Dr Richard Hurley died.

Veritas unveiled its annual moving crib at their flagship store on Lower Abbey Street, Dublin 1, on 7 December, ahead of the popular Feast of the Immaculate Conception on 8 December.

The Winter General Meeting of the Irish Episcopal Conference concluded in Maynooth on 7 December. The following issues were discussed by bishops: the appointment of the new Apostolic Nuncio, Mgr Charles Brown; Advent and the Sacrament of Reconciliation; A Bible in every home; (i) the Government's Budget for 2012; and (ii) *Hope in Challenging Times* – reflection for Christmas 2011; safeguarding children in the Catholic Church; publication of *Living Communion – Vision and Practice for Parish Pastoral Councils in Ireland today*; Trócaire's Christmas 2011 'Global Gift' campaign; 50th International Eucharistic Congress in Ireland in 2012; and, the retirement of Bishop Séamus Hegarty as Bishop of Derry.

On 12 December, leaders of the four largest Irish Christian Churches travelled together to London to express their grave concern over the impact of proposed welfare reforms on the most vulnerable in Northern Ireland. The Church leaders had a private meeting with Minister for Welfare Reform, Lord David Freud, who was accompanied by Secretary of State for Northern Ireland, Mr Owen Patterson MP. Following the meeting with Lord Freud the Church leaders travelled to the Palace of Westminster where they met other Members of Parliament and the House of Lords involved in debating the Welfare Reform Bill as it passes through its final stages in the Houses of Parliament.

On Christmas Day, Bishop Thomas Finnegan (86), Bishop Emeritus of Killala, died. Thomas Anthony Finnegan was Bishop of Killala from 1987 to 2002.

Cardinal Brady led the bishops of Ireland in their Christmas reflections for 2011, which were widely publicised. Cardinal Brady said: 'This is my hope and my prayer for Christmas 2011, that each of us will rediscover the simplicity, hope and joy of that first Christmas. I pray that Ireland as a country will become a gentler, kinder, more compassionate, more caring and more neighbourly place. May Christ, and His life and goodness, be born in each of us and in our country this Christmas and may we find in Him our greatest hope in challenging times.'

*For further details please visit www.catholicbishops.ie*

# THE ROMAN CURIA

## SECRETARIAT OF STATE

*Secretary of State:*
Cardinal Tarcisio Bertone (SDB)

**First Section: General Affairs**
*Sostituto:*
Archbishop Giovanni Angelo Becciu
Palazzo Apostolico Vaticano,
Città del Vaticano 00120
Tel 66988-3913 Fax 66988-5255

**Second Section: Relations with States**
*Secretary:*
Archbishop Dominique Mamberti
Palazzo Apostolico Vaticano,
Città del Vaticano 00120
Tel 66988-3913 Fax 66988-5255

## CONGREGATIONS

**Congregation for the Doctrine of the Faith**
*Prefect:* Cardinal William Joseph Levada
*Secretary:* Archbishop Luis Francisco Ladaria Ferrer (SJ)
Piazza del S. Uffizio 11, 00193 Roma
Tel 66988-3357/3413
Fax 66988-3409

**Congregation for the Oriental Churches**
*Prefect:*
Cardinal Leonardo Sandri
*Secretary:*
Archbishop Cyril Vasil (SJ)
Palazzo del Bramante,
Via della Conciliazione, 34, 00193 Roma
Tel 66988-4282 Fax 66988-4300

**Congregation for Divine Worship and the Discipline of the Sacraments**
*Prefect:*
Cardinal Antionio Cañizares Llovera
*Secretary:* Archbishop Joseph Augustine Di Noia (OP)
Palazzo delle Congregazioni,
Piazza Pio XII, 10, 00193 Roma
Tel 66988-4316/4318
Fax 66988-3499

**Congregation for the Causes of Saints**
*Prefect:* Cardinal Angelo Amato (SDB)
*Secretary:* Archbishop Marcello Bartolucci
Palazzo delle Congregazioni,
Piazza Pio XII, 10, 00193 Roma
Tel 66988-4247 Fax 66988-1935

**Congregation for Bishops**
*Prefect:* Cardinal Marc Ouellet (PSS)
*Secretary:*
Archbishop Manuel Monteiro de Castro
Palazzo delle Congregazioni,
Piazza Pio XII, 10, 00193 Roma
Tel 66988-4217 Fax 66988-5303

**Pontifical Commission for Latin America**
*President:*
Cardinal Marc Ouellet (PSS)
*Vice President:*
Archbishop José Octavio Ruiz Arenas
00120 Città del Vaticano, 00153 Roma
Tel 66988-3131/3500 Fax 66988-4260

**Congregation for Clergy**
*Prefect:*
Cardinal Mauro Piacenza
*Prefect Emeritus:*
Cardinal Cláudio Hummes (OFM);
Cardinal José Tómas Sánchez
Palazzo delle Congregazioni,
Piazza Pio XII, 3, 00193 Roma
Tel 66988-4151 Fax 66988-4845

**Congregation for the Evangelisation of Peoples**
*Prefect*: Archbishop Fernando Filoni
*Secretary:*
Archbishop Savio Hon Tai-Fai (SDB)
*SAC Official:*
Archbishop Pierguiseppe Vacchelli
Palazzo di Propaganda Fide, Piazza di Spagna, 48, 00187 Roma
Tel 66987-9299 Fax 66988-0118

**Congregation for the Institutes of Consecrated Life and for Societies of Apostolic Life**
*Prefect:* Archbishop João Bráz de Aviz
*Secretary:* Archbishop Joseph William Tobin (CSsR)
Palazzo delle Congregazioni,
Piazza Pio XII, 3, 00193 Roma
Tel 66988-4128 Fax 66988-4526

**Congregation for Catholic Education**
*Prefect:* Cardinal Zenon Grocholewski
*Secretary:*
Archbishop Jean-Louis Bruguès (OP)
Palazzo delle Congregazioni, Piazza Pio XII, 3, 00193 Roma
Tel 66988-4167 Fax 66988-4172

## TRIBUNALS

**Apostolic Penitentiary**
*Major Penitentiary:*
Cardinal Fortunato Baldelli
*Official:*
Bishop Gianfranco Girotti (OFM Conv)
Palazzo della Cancelleria,
Piazza della Cancelleria, 1, 00186 Roma
Tel 66988-7526/7523 Fax 66988-7557

**Supreme Tribunal of the Apostolic Signatura**
*Prefect:* Cardinal Raymond Leo Burke
*Secretary:*
Bishop Frans Daneels (OPraem)
Palazzo della Cancelleria,
Piazza della Cancelleria, 1, 00186 Roma
Tel 66988-7520 Fax 66988-7553

**Tribunal of the Roman Rota**
*Dean:*
Bishop Antoni Stankiewicz
Palazzo della Cancelleria,
Piazza della Cancelleria, 1, 00186 Roma
Tel 66988-7502 Fax 66988-7554

## PONTIFICAL COUNCILS

**Pontifical Council for the Laity**
*President:* Archbishop Stanislaw Rylko
*Secretary:* Bishop Josef Clemens
00120 Città del Vaticano, 00153 Roma
Tel 66988-7322/7141 Fax 66988-7214

**Pontifical Council for Promoting Christian Unity**
*President:* Cardinal Kurt Koch
*Secretary:* Bishop Brian Farrell (LC)
Via dell'Erba, 1, 00193 Roma
Tel 66988-3072/4271
Fax 66988-5365

**Pontifical Council for the Family**
*President:* Cardinal Ennio Antonelli
*Secretary:* Bishop Jean Laffitte
Piazza S. Calisto, 16, 00153 Roma
Tel 66988-7243 Fax 66988-7272

**Pontifical Council for Justice and Peace**
*President:* Cardinal Peter Kodwo Appiah Turkson
*Secretary:* Bishop Mario Toso (SDB)
Città del Vaticano, 00153 Roma
Tel 66987-9911 Fax 66988-7205

**Pontifical Council 'Cor Unum'**
*President:* Cardinal Robert Sarah
00120 Città del Vaticano, 00153 Roma
Tel 66988-9411 Fax 66988-7301

**Pontifical Council for the Pastoral Care of Migrants and Itinerant People**
*President:*
Archbishop Antonio Maria Vegliò
*Secretary Emeritus:*
Archbishop Agostino Marchetto;
Archbishop Francesco Gioia
00120 Città del Vaticano, 00153 Roma
Tel 66988-7193/7242 Fax 66988-7111

**Pontifical Council for Pastoral Assistance to Healthcare Workers**
*President:*
Archbishop Zygmunt Zimowski
*Secretary:* Mgr Jean-Marie Mate Musivi Mpendawatu
Via della Conciliazione, 3, 00193 Roma
Tel 66988-4720/3138 Fax 66988-3139

**Pontifical Council for Legislative Texts**
*President:*
Archbishop Francesco Coccopalmerio
*Secretary:*
Bishop Juan Ignacio Arrieta Ochoa de Chinchetru
Palazzo delle Congregazioni, Piazza Pio XII, 10, 00193 Roma
Tel 66988-4008 Fax 66988-4710

**Pontifical Council for Inter-Religious Dialogue**
*President:* Cardinal Jean-Louis Tauran
*Secretary:* Archbishop Pier Luigi Celata
Via dell'Erba, 1, 00193 Roma
Tel 66988-4321
Fax 66988-4494

**Pontifical Council for Culture**
*President:*
Cardinal Gianfranco Ravasi
*Secretary:*
Bishop Barthélemy Adoukonou
00120 Città del Vaticano, 00153 Roma
Tel 66989-3811 Fax 66988-7368

**Pontifical Council for Social Communications**
*President:*
Archbishop Claudio Maria Celli
*Secretary Emeritus:*
Bishop Pierfranco Pastore
Palazzo S. Carlo,
00120 Città del Vaticano
Tel 66989-1800 Fax 66989-1840

## OFFICES

**Apostolic Chamber**
*Chamberlain of the Holy Church:*
Cardinal Tarcisio Bertone (SDB)
*Vice-Chamberlain:*
Archbishop Santos Abril y Castelló
Palazzo Apostolico,
00120 Città del Vaticano
Tel 66988-3554/2139

**Administration of the Patrimony of the Apostolic See**
*President:*
Archbishop Domenico Calcagno
*Secretary:* Mgr Luigi Mistò
Palazzo Apostolico,
00120 Città del Vaticano
Tel 66989-3403 Fax 66988-3141

**Prefecture for the Economic Affairs of the Holy See**
*President:* Archbishop Giuseppe Versaldi
*Secretary:* Fr Lucio Ángel Vallejo Balda
Palazzo delle Congregazioni,
Largo del Colonnato, 3, 00193 Roma
Tel 66988-4263 Fax 66988-5011

**Synod of Bishops**
*Secretary General:*
Archbishop Nikola Eterović

**Prefecture of the Papal Household**
*Prefect:*
Archbishop James Michael Harvey
*Official:* Bishop Paolo De Nicolò
00120 Città del Vaticano
Tel 66988-3114 Fax 66988-5863

**Office of Papal Charities**
*Almoner of His Holiness:*
Archbishop Félix del Blanco Prieto
00120 Città del Vaticano
Tel 66988-3135 Fax 66988-3132

**International Theological Commission**
*President:*
Cardinal William Joseph Levada
Palazzo delle Congr. per la Dottrina della Fede, Piazza del S. Uffizio, 11,
00193 Roma
Tel 66988-4727

**Pontifical Ecclesiastical Academy**
*President:* Archbishop Beniamino Stella,
Piazza della Minerva, 74, 00186 Roma
Tel 6688201 Fax 66880-1274

**Vatican Library**
*Librarian:* Cardinal Raffaele Farina (SDB)
Cortile del Belvedere,
00120 Città del Vaticano
Tel 66987-9411 Fax 66988-4795

**Vatican Secret Archives**
*Prefect:* Bishop Sergio Pagano (B)
*Archivist:* Cardinal Raffaele Farina (SDB)
00120 Città del Vaticano
Tel 66988-3314 Fax 66988-5574

## COMMISSIONS AND COMMITTEES

**Pontifical Commission for the Cultural Heritage of the Church**
*President:*
Cardinal Gianfranco Ravasi
Palazzo della Cancelleria Apostolica,
Piazza della Cancelleria, 1,
00186 Roma
Tel 66988-7617/7556 Fax 66988-7556

**Pontifical Commission 'Ecclesia Dei'**
*President:*
Cardinal William Joseph Levada
Palazzo delle Congr. per la Dottrina della Fede, Piazza del S. Ufficio, 11,
00193 Roma
Tel 66988-5213/5494 Fax 66988-3412

**Pontifical Biblical Commission**
*President:*
Cardinal William Joseph Levada
Palazzo delle Congr. per la Dottrina della Fede, Piazza del S. Uffizio, 11, 00193 Roma
Tel 66988-4682

**Pontifical Commission for Sacred Archaeology**
*President:* Cardinal Gianfranco Ravasi
Via Napoleone III, 1, 00185 Roma
Tel 6446-5610 Fax 6446-7625

**Pontifical Committee for International Eucharistic Congresses**
*President:* Archbishop Piero Marini
Palazzo San Calisto,
00120 Città del Vaticano,
Tel 66988-7366 Fax 66988-7154

## INSTITUTIONS CONNECTED WITH HOLY SEE

**L'Osservatore Romano**
*Editor-in-Chief:*
Prof. Giovanni Maria Vian
00120 Città del Vaticano
Tel 66988-3461 Fax 66988-3252

# APOSTOLIC NUNCIATURE

*Address:* The Apostolic Nunciature, 183 Navan Road, Dublin 7
Tel 01-8380577 Fax 01-8380276

*Papal Nuncio:* His Excellency Archbishop Charles John Brown, Titular Archbishop of Aquileia
Born 13 October 1959, New York, USA
Ordained priest 13 May 1989
Appointed Titular Archbishop of Aquileia 26 November 2011
Episcopal Consecration 6 January 2012
Appointed Apostolic Nuncio to Ireland 26 November 2011

*Secretary:* Reverend Juan Antonio Cruz Serrano

# THE IRISH EPISCOPATE

## THE HIERARCHY

**Archbishops**

His Eminence Seán Cardinal Brady DCL, DD
Archbishop of Armagh
Primate of All Ireland
Ara Coeli, Armagh BT61 7QY
Tel 028-37522045 Fax 028-37526182
Email admin@aracoeli.com

Most Rev Diarmuid Martin DD
Archbishop of Dublin and Primate of Ireland, Archbishop's House,
Drumcondra, Dublin 9
Tel 01-8373732 Fax 01-8369796

Most Rev Dermot Clifford DD
Archbishop of Cashel and Emly
Archbishop's House, Thurles,
Co Tipperary
Tel 0504-21512 Fax 0504-22680
Email office@cashel-emly.ie

Most Rev Michael Neary DD
Archbishop of Tuam
Archbishop's House, Tuam, Co Galway
Tel 093-24166 Fax 093-28070
Email archdiocesetuam@eircom.net

**Retired Archbishops**

His Eminence Desmond Cardinal Connell DD
Retired Archbishop of Dublin
29 Iona Road, Glasnevin, Dublin 9
Tel 01-8373732 Fax 01-8369796

Most Rev Joseph Cassidy DD
Retired Archbishop of Tuam
The Presbytery, Moore,
Ballydangan, Athlone, Co Roscommon
Tel/Fax 0905-73539

**Bishops**

Most Rev Philip Boyce DD
Bishop of Raphoe
Ard Adhamhnáin, Letterkenny,
Co Donegal
Tel 074-9121208 Fax 074-9124872
Email raphoediocese@eircom.net

Most Rev Denis Brennan DD
Bishop of Ferns
Bishop's House, Summerhill, Wexford
Tel 053-9122177 Fax 053-9123436
Email adm@ferns.ie

Most Rev John Buckley DD
Bishop of Cork and Ross,
Diocesan Office, Bishop's House,
Redemption Road, Cork
Tel 021-4301717 Fax 021-4301557
Email secretary@corkandross.org

Most Rev Dermot Clifford DD
Archbishop of Cashel and Emly
Apostolic Administrator Diocese of Cloyne,
Cloyne Diocesan Centre, Cobh, Co Cork
Tel 021-4811430
Email cloyne@indigo.ie

Most Rev Gerard Clifford DD
Titular Bishop of Geron and Auxiliary Bishop of Armagh
Annaskeagh, Ravensdale,
Dundalk, Co Louth
Tel 042-9371012 Fax 042-9371013
Email gcliffrd@indigo.ie

Most Rev Martin Drennan DD
Bishop of Galway
Mount St Mary's, Taylor's Hill, Galway
Tel 091-563566 Fax 091-528536
Email galwaydiocese@eircom.net

Most Rev Anthony Farquhar DD
Titular Bishop of Ermiana, Auxiliary Bishop of Down and Connor
24 Fruithill Park, Belfast BT11 8GE
Tel 028-90624252
Email ajf@downandconnor.org

Most Rev Raymond Field DD
Titular Bishop of Ard Mor and Auxiliary Bishop of Dublin
3 Castleknock Road,
Blanchardstown, Dublin 15
Tel 01-8209191 Fax 01-8209191
Email rf6275@eircom.net

Most Rev John Fleming DD, DCL
Bishop of Killala
Bishop's House, Ballina, Co Mayo
Tel 096-21518 Fax 096-70344
Email bishop@killaladiocese.org

Most Rev Séamus Freeman (SCA) DD
Bishop of Ossory
Sion House, Kilkenny
Tel 056-7762448 Fax 056-7763753
Email bishop@ossory.ie

Most Rev Christopher Jones DD
Bishop of Elphin, St Mary's, Sligo
Tel 071-9162670/9162769
Fax 071-9162414
Email elphindo@eircom.net

Most Rev Brendan Kelly DD
Bishop of Achonry; Bishop's House,
Ballaghaderreen, Edmondstown,
Co Roscommon
Tel 094-9860021 Fax 094-9860921
Email bishop@achonrydiocese.org

Most Rev John Kirby DD
Bishop of Clonfert
St Brendan's, Coorheen, Loughrea,
Co Galway
Tel 091-841560 Fax 091-841818
Email clonfert@iol.ie

Most Rev William Lee, DD, DCL
Bishop of Waterford and Lismore
Bishop's House, John's Hill, Waterford
Tel 051-874463 Fax 051-852703
Email waterfordlismore@eircom.net

Most Rev John McAreavey DD, DCL
Bishop of Dromore
Bishop's House, 44 Armagh Road, Newry,
Co Down BT35 6PN
Tel 028-30262444 Fax 028-30260496
Email bishopofdromore@btinternet.com

Most Rev Liam MacDaid DD
Bishop of Clogher
Bishop's House, Monaghan
Tel 047-81019 Fax 047-84773
Email diocesanoffice@clogherdiocese.ie

Most Rev Donal McKeown DD
Titular Bishop of Killossy and Auxiliary Bishop of Down and Connor,
73 Somerton Road, Belfast BT15 4DE
Tel 028-90776185 Fax 028-90779377

Most Rev William Murphy DD
Bishop of Kerry
Bishop's House, Killarney,
Co Kerry
Tel 064-6631168 Fax 064-6631364
Email bishopshouse@eircom.net

Most Rev Colm O'Reilly DD
Bishop of Ardagh and Clonmacnois
St Michael's, Longford,
Co Longford
Tel 043-3346432 Fax 043-3346833
Email ardaghdi@iol.ie

Most Rev Kieran O'Reilly (SMA) DD
Bishop of Killaloe, Westbourne,
Ennis, Co Clare
Tel 065-6828638 Fax 065-6842538
Email office@killaloediocese.ie

Most Rev Leo O'Reilly DD
Bishop of Kilmore, Bishop's House,
Cullies, Co Cavan
Tel 049-4331496 Fax 049-4361796
Email bishop@kilmorediocese.ie

Most Rev Michael Smith DD, DCL
Bishop of Meath
Bishop's House,
Dublin Road, Mullingar,
Co Westmeath
Tel 044-9348841/9342038
Fax 044-9343020
Email bishop@dioceseofmeath.ie

Most Rev Noël Treanor DD
Bishop of Down and Connor
Lisbreen, 73 Somerton Road,
Belfast, Co Antrim BT15 4DE
Tel 028-90776185 Fax 028-90779377
Email dccuria@downandconnor.org

Most Rev Eamonn Walsh DD, VG
Titular Bishop of Elmham and
Auxiliary Bishop of Dublin
Naomh Brid, Blessington Road,
Tallaght, Dublin 24
Tel/Fax 01-4598032
Email elmham@eircom.net

**Retired Bishops**

Most Rev Eamonn Casey DD
Retired Bishop of Galway
Beagh, Co Galway

Most Rev Brendan Comiskey DD
Retired Bishop of Ferns
PO Box 40, Summerhill, Wexford

Most Rev Edward Daly DD
Retired Bishop of Derry, Gurteen,
9 Steelstown Road,
Derry BT48 8EU

Most Rev Joseph Duffy DD
Retired Bishop of Clogher
Bishop's House, Monaghan,
Co Monaghan

Most Rev Thomas Flynn DD
Retired Bishop of Achonry
St Michael's, Cathedral Grounds,
Ballaghaderreen,
Co Roscommon

Most Rev Laurence Forristal DD
Retired Bishop of Ossory
Molassy, Freshford Road,
Kilkenny

Most Rev Seamus Hegarty DD
Retired Bishop of Derry
Bishop's House, St Eugene's Cathedral,
Derry BT48 9AP

Most Rev Francis Lagan DD
Retired Titular Bishop of Sidnascestre
and Auxiliary Bishop of Derry
9 Glen Road, Strabane,
Co Tyrone BT82 8BX

Most Rev John Magee DD
Retired Bishop of Cloyne
Cloyne Diocesan Centre, Cobh, Co Cork

Most Rev James Moriarty DD,
Retired Bishop of Kildare and Leighlin,
Bishop's House, Carlow

Most Rev Donal Murray DD
Retired Bishop of Limerick,
Kilmoyle, North Circular Road, Limerick

Most Rev Fiachra Ó Ceallaigh DD
Retired Titular Bishop of Tre Taverne &
Retired Auxiliary Bishop of Dublin,
19 St Anthony's Road, Rialto, Dublin 8

Most Rev Dermot O'Mahony DD
Titular Bishop of Tiava and Retired
Auxiliary Bishop of Dublin
19 Longlands, Swords, Co Dublin
Tel 01-8401596 Fax 01-8403950

Most Rev Patrick J. Walsh DD
Retired Bishop of Down and Connor
6 Waterloo Park North, Belfast BT15
5HW
Tel 028-90778182

Most Rev William Walsh DD
Retired Bishop of Killaloe, Westbourne,
Ennis, Co Clare

## MITRED ABBOTS

Rt Rev Dom Mark Patrick Hederman (OSB)
Glenstal Abbey, Murroe, Co Limerick
Tel 061-386103

Rt Rev Dom Augustine McGregor (OCSO)
Mount Melleray Abbey,
Cappoquin, Co Waterford
Tel 058-54404

Rt Rev Dom Peter Garvey (OCist)
Bolton Abbey, Moone, Athy, Co Kildare
Tel 0507-24102

Rt Rev Dom Celsus Kelly (OCSO)
Our Lady of Bethlehem Abbey,
11 Ballymena Road, Portglenone,
Ballymena, Co Antrim BT44 8BL
Tel 028-25821211 Fax 028-25822310

Rt Rev Dom Richard Purcell (OCSO)
Mount St Joseph Abbey, Roscrea,
Co Tipperary
Tel 0505-21711

Fr Laurence McDermott, Superior
Mellifont Abbey, Collon, Co Louth
Tel 041-9826103

Rt Rev Charles J. White (CRL)
Apartment 3, 52 Castle Avenue,
Clontarf, Dublin 3
Tel 01-8333229

## THE IRISH EPISCOPAL CONFERENCE

*President*
His Eminence Seán Cardinal Brady
*Vice President*
His Grace Most Rev Diarmuid Martin
*Episcopal Secretary:* Most Rev William Lee
*Finance Secretary:* Most Rev John Fleming
*Executive Secretary*
Rev Gearóid Dullea
Columba Centre, Maynooth, Co Kildare
Tel 01-5053000 Fax 01-6292360
Email ex.sec@iecon.ie
*Communications Director*
Mr Martin Long
Columba Centre, Maynooth, Co Kildare
Tel 01-5053000 Fax 01-6016401
Email mlong@catholicbishops.ie
*Executive Administrator of the Commissions & Agencies of the Episcopal Conference:* Mr Harry Casey
Columba Centre, Maynooth, Co Kildare
Tel 01-5053000 Fax 01-6016401
Email harry.casey@iecon.ie

**Standing Committee**
His Eminence Seán Cardinal Brady; His Grace Most Rev Diarmuid Martin; His Grace Most Rev Dermot Clifford; His Grace Most Rev Michael Neary; Most Rev William Lee; Most Rev John Fleming; Most Rev Christopher Jones; Most Rev Seamus Freeman; Most Rev Denis Brennan; Most Rev Brendan Kelly; Most Rev Leo O'Reilly; Most Rev Noël Treanor

## THE FIVE EPISCOPAL COMMISSIONS OF THE IRISH EPISCOPAL CONFERENCE

*An Episcopal Commission advises or makes proposals/recommendations to the Standing Committee and Plenary Assembly of the Irish Episcopal Conference. Councils and Agencies assist the Episcopal Commissions, and the Episcopal Conference itself, in attaining their objectives. An Advisory Group/Body/ Committee to a Council of the Irish Episcopal Conference advises the relevant Council.*

**Episcopal Commission for Catholic Education and Formation**
*Chaired by Most Rev Leo O'Reilly DD*

**Episcopal Commission for Pastoral Care**
*Chaired by Most Rev Christopher Jones DD*

**Episcopal Commission for Planning, Communications and Resources**
*Chaired by His Grace Most Rev Dermot Clifford DD*

**Episcopal Commission for Social Issues and International Affairs**
*Chaired by Most Rev Noël Treanor DD*

**Episcopal Commission for Worship, Pastoral Renewal and Faith Development**
*Chaired by Most Rev Seamus Freeman DD*

*The Councils and Agencies of the Irish Episcopal Conference are clustered in five Departments corresponding to the five Episcopal Commissions. Details of several bodies which are linked to the Episcopal Conference are placed in square brackets and provided for your information.*

## DEPARTMENT OF CATHOLIC EDUCATION AND FORMATION

*Executive Secretary to the Episcopal Commission/Department*
Rt Rev Mgr James Cassin
Tel 01-5053014 Email jim.cassin@iecon.ie

## COUNCIL FOR CATECHETICS OF THE IRISH EPISCOPAL CONFERENCE

*Members of the Council*
Most Rev William Murphy DD *(Chairman)*
Most Rev Denis Brennan DD, Mr Brendan O'Reilly *(Executive Secretary)*, Rt Rev Mgr Dermot A Lane, Ms Maura Hyland, Rev Joseph McCann, Ms Sharon Haughey, Sr Anne Codd, Mr Gerry O'Connell, Sr Marie McNamara, Ms Marie Therese Canavan, Ms Patricia Kieran, Rev Michael McGrath

*National Director:* Mr Brendan O'Reilly
Columba Centre, Maynooth, Co Kildare
Tel 01-5053140 Fax 01-6016401
Email brendan.oreilly@iecon.ie

## COUNCIL FOR DOCTRINE OF THE IRISH EPISCOPAL CONFERENCE

*Members of the Council*
Most Rev Michael Neary DD *(Chairman)*;
Most Rev Philip Boyce DD;
Most Rev Martin Drennan DD
The Council for Doctrine works with the Theological Committee and the Bioethics Consultative Group on matters relating to faith and morals.

*Members of the Theological Committee*
Most Rev Michael Neary DD *(Chairman)*
Dr Mette Lebech; Rev Brendan Leahy; Rev Seamus O'Connell; Mgr Dermot Lane; Rev Fintan Lyons (OSB); Rev Bede McGregor (OP); Rev Jim Corkery (SJ); Sr Vera Donnelly (OP); Dr John Murray
Columba Centre, Maynooth, Co Kildare
Tel 01-5053000

**Bioethics Consultative Group**
Columba Centre, Maynooth, Co Kildare
Tel 01-5053000

## COUNCIL FOR ECUMENISM (AND DIALOGUE) OF THE IRISH EPISCOPAL CONFERENCE

*Members of the Council*
Most Rev Anthony Farquhar DD *(Chairman)*;
Most Rev Gerard Clifford DD;
*Secretary:* Vacant
Columba Centre, Maynooth, Co Kildare
Tel 01-5053000

**Advisory Committee on Ecumenism**
*Secretary:* Very Rev Kieran McDermott PP
'Emmaus', Main Street, Dundrum, Dublin 14
Tel 01-2984348

Advises the hierarchy on ecumenical affairs in Ireland and maintains contact with the Secretariat for Promoting Christian Unity, Rome. The council has a membership of approximately 35, including the episcopal members, a priest representative from each diocese, and people chosen for their competence and experience in the ecumenical field.

## COUNCIL FOR EDUCATION OF THE IRISH EPISCOPAL CONFERENCE [WITH NORTHERN IRELAND COUNCIL FOR CATHOLIC EDUCATION (NICCE)]

The Council for Education articulates policy and vision for Catholic Education in Ireland, north and south, on behalf of the Episcopal Conference. It has responsibility for the forward planning necessary to ensure the best provision for Catholic Education in the country. It liaises with other Catholic Education Offices, the Department of Education and Skills and the Department of Education, Northern Ireland. The Council advises the Conference on all government legislation as applied to education. It responds to and acts as spokesperson for the Episcopal Conference on issues related to the work of education. It seeks also to develop long-term strategies in education for the Episcopal Conference

*Members of the Council for Education*
Most Rev Brendan Kelly *(Chairman)*
Most Rev Leo O'Reilly DD
Most Rev Donal McKeown DD
Rt Rev Mgr Dan O'Connor
Rt Rev Mgr Dermot Lane
Fr Michael Drumm
Ms Eileen Flynn
Sr Elizabeth Maxwell
Mr Ferdia Kelly
*Executive Secretary*
Rt Rev Mgr James Cassin
Council for Education of the IEC,
Columba Centre, Maynooth, Co Kildare
Tel 01-5053014
Email education@iecon.ie
*Administrative Assistant:* Ms Ann Maertens
Tel 01-5053027
Email ann.maertens@iecon.ie

*Northern Ireland Council for Catholic Education (NICCE)*
Until 2005, there was no central body seeking to offer leadership across the Catholic education sector in NI. The 500+ 'Maintained' schools (nursery, primary and non-selective post-primary) were managed by CCMS (a statutory body) while the 32 Voluntary Grammar schools had a considerable degree of independence. The Northern Ireland Council for Catholic Education (NICCE) was set up in 2005 by the Trustees in order to provide co-ordination of the Catholic sector in a time of rapid change.

*Members of the Council for Education Northern Ireland (NICCE)*

*Diocesan Trustees*
Most Rev Donal McKeown DD *(Chair)*
Most Rev John McAreavey DD
Most Rev Noël Treanor DD

*Nominees from Religious and Lay Trusts*
Br Patrick Collier (FSC)
Sr Eithne Woulfe (SSL)
Prof Muredach Dynan

*In attendance*
Most Rev Patrick Walsh DD
Mr Gerry Lundy
Fr Timothy Bartlett
Br Patrick Collier
Mgr Jim Cassin

Northern Ireland Council for Catholic Education
1 Killyman Road, Dungannon BT71 6DE
Tel 028-87751500
Email info@catholiceducation.org
Website info@catholiceducation-ni.com

**Catholic Education Service (CES)**
The Catholic Education Service (CES) is a national education service inspired by the gospel of Jesus Christ in support of the mission of Catholic education. CES was set up by the Irish Episcopal Conference (IEC) in association with the Conference of the Religious of Ireland (CORI).

The Catholic Education Service is a charity created by Deed of Trust. The Trustees of the CES are four Catholic Bishops who are Ordinaries of Catholic dioceses in Ireland and each representing one of the four ecclesiastical provinces of Ireland (Most Rev Leo O'Reilly DD, Most Rev John Buckley DD, Most Rev Seamus Freeman DD, Most Rev Brendan Kelly DD) and two Religious appointed by CORI (Sr Elizabeth Maxwell, IPVM, Fr David Corrigan, SM). The trustees of the CES are ex officio members of Catholic Education Service Committee (CESC)

**The Catholic Education Services Committee (CESC)** is a service incorporating a number of bodies as follows:

**The Catholic Schools' Partnership (CSP)** serves first and second level Catholic schools and colleges in the Republic of Ireland.

**The Trustee Support Service (TSS)** will serve Catholic schools and colleges in Northern Ireland.

CESC serves the formal education system at all levels as well as the non-formal and informal sectors. It aims to support a vibrant Catholic education sector in response to changing social, economic and political conditions in Ireland.

*Members of the Catholic Education Services Committee (CESC)*
Most Rev John Buckley DD; Most Rev Seamus Freeman DD; Most Rev Brendan Kelly DD; Most Rev Donal McKeown DD; Most Rev Diarmuid Martin DD; Most Rev Leo O'Reilly DD; Fr David Corrigan SM; Sr Noelle Corscadden IBVM; Sr Miriam Hennessy RSC; Br Francis Manning FSC; Fr Brian Moore CM; Sr Elizabeth Maxwell IPVM
*Executive Secretaries:* Sr Eithne Woulfe; Rt Rev Mgr James Cassin
Catholic Education Service
Columba Centre, Maynooth, Co. Kildare
Tel 01-5053014
Email education@iecon.ie

**Catholic Schools Partnership (CSP)**
Catholic Schools Partnership was established in 2009 by the Irish Bishops Conference in co-operation with CORI. It aims to provide support for all the partners in Catholic education at first and second level in the Republic of Ireland. This includes patrons/trustees, management bodies including boards of management and teachers in Catholic schools.

The Partnership is overseen by a Council with thirty-three members drawn from various stakeholders. The members of the Council are: Fr Michael Drumm (Chairperson), Ms Kathleen Bradley, Mr P.J. Callanan, Sr Marie Carroll, Mgr Jim Cassin, Br Patrick Collier, Fr David Corrigan, Mrs Mairead Darcy, Fr Tom Deenihan, Sr June Fennelly, Sr Thomasina Finn, Ms Eileen Flynn, Mr John Hayden, Sr Margaret Mary Healy, Most Rev Brendan Kelly, Mr Ferdia Kelly, Mr Gerry Lundy, Ms Anne McDonagh, Most Rev Donal McKeown, Fr Denis McNelis, Ms Maeve Mahon, Mr Paul Meany, Mr Noel Merrick, Sr Maighread Ní Ghallchobhair, Mgr Lorcan O'Brien, Mr Brendan O'Reilly, Most Rev Leo O'Reilly, Sr Anne Marie Quinn, Sr Ena Quinlan, Mr Paul Scanlan, Mrs Maria Spring, Ms Anne Walsh.
New House, St Patrick's College, Maynooth, Co Kildare
Tel 01-5053161
Email office@catholicschools.ie

**Association of Trustees of Catholic Schools (ATCS)**
The Association of Trustees of Catholic Schools (ATCS) was established in September 2009. ATCS is a representative body for the 'Catholic Trustee Voice' in Irish education at primary and post-primary level. Its membership includes members of the Irish Episcopal Conference, representatives of various religious congregations, representatives of the recently established lay trusts, as well as the trustees of a number of other Catholic schools.

*ATCS Board*
Mr Gerry Bennett (PP), Sr Marie Carroll (P), Fr Tom Deenihan (PP)(Chairperson), Dr Eilís Humphreys (PP) (Secretary), Ms Anne Kelleher (PP), Bishop Brendan Kelly (PP), Ms Anne McDonagh (PP), Fr John O'Boyle (P), Sr Ena Quinlan (P), Sr Anne Marie Quinn (P), Mr Paul Scanlan (PP)
[P=Primary,PP=Post Primary]
*Contact details:*
*Secretary:* Dr Eilís Humphreys, c/o Le Chéile Schools Trust, St Mary's, Bloomfield Avenue, Donnybrook, Dublin 4
Email eilis@lecheiletrust.ie
*Chairperson:* Fr Tom Deenihan
Email secretary@corkandross.org

**[Association of Management of Catholic Secondary Schools (AMCSS)**
**Joint Managerial Body (JMB)**
**Secretariat of Secondary Schools**
Emmet House, Milltown, Dublin 14
Tel 01-2838255 Fax 01-2695461
Email info@secretariat.ie
Website www.jmb.ie
*President:* Mr Noel Merrick
*General Secretary:* Mr Ferdia Kelly
*Assistant General Secretary*
Ms Bernadette Kinsella
*Directory of Education*
Mr Michael Redmond
*Director of Financial Support Services*
Mr Fergus Dunne

The Association of Management of Catholic Secondary Schools (AMCSS) represents the interests of Boards of Management, Managers and Principals of Voluntary Secondary Schools. It negotiates on behalf of those schools with the Department of Education and Skills and with the ASTI. It is available through its Secretariat as a resource to the Council for Education of the Irish Episcopal Conference and the Conference of Religious in Ireland. The Secretariat of Secondary Schools is the administrative office of AMCSS and of the Joint Managerial Body (JMB), which represents all denominational schools in certain matters.

**Catholic Primary School Management Association (CPSMA)**
*Chair:* Mrs Maria Spring
Tel 087-2597004
*General Secretary:* Ms Eileen Flynn
*Assistant General Secretary*
Ms Margaret Gorman
*Office Manager:* Ms Linda Gorman
New House, St Patrick's College, Maynooth, Co Kildare
Tel 01-5053192/1850-407200
Fax 01-5053195
Email info@cpsma.ie
Website www.cpsma.ie

The association represents the boards of management of all Catholic primary schools. Its standing committee has close links with the Episcopal Commission for Education.]

## DEPARTMENT OF PASTORAL CARE

*Executive Secretary to the Episcopal Commission/Department*
Rev Peter Murphy
Tel 01-5053107 Email peter.murphy@iecon.ie

## COUNCIL FOR MARRIAGE AND THE FAMILY OF THE IRISH EPISCOPAL CONFERENCE

*Members of the Council for Marriage and Family of the Irish Episcopal Conference*
Most Rev Christopher Jones DD *(Chair)*
Most Rev Seámus Freeman DD
Most Rev Colm O'Reilly DD
Most Rev Liam MacDaid DD
Rev Peter Murphy (Secretary), Rev Tim Bartlett, Mr Stephen Cummins, Mr Eoin O'Mahony, Ms Brenda Drumm, Ms Barbara Gilroy, Mr Gerry Mangan, Ms Breda McDonald, Rev Michael McGinnity, Sr Anne Codd, Ms Deirdre O'Rawe, Ms Trish Conway and Mr Andrew O'Callaghan
Columba Centre, Maynooth, Co Kildare
Tel 01-5053000 Fax 01-6016401
Email columbacentre@iecon.ie

The purpose of the Council for Marriage and the Family is to assist the Bishops in their mission, specifically as it relates to marriage, families and family life.

## ACCORD

**Catholic Marriage Care Service**
*President:* Most Rev Christopher Jones DD
*Vice President:* Most Rev Liam MacDaid DD
*National Director:* Ms Ruth Barror
*National Chaplain:* Rev Peter Murphy
*Central Office:* Columba Centre, Maynooth, Co Kildare
Tel 01-5053112 Fax 01-6016410
Email admin@accord.ie
www.accord.ie
www.gettingmarried.ie

ACCORD, Catholic Marriage Care Service, is an Agency of the Irish Catholic Bishops' Conference. It has 60 Centres located throughout the dioceses of Ireland. Its ministry is primarily concerned with supporting the sacrament of marriage by helping couples as they prepare for marriage and offering support to them in their marriage relationship. ACCORD's aim is to promote a better understanding of Christian marriage and to help couples initiate, sustain and enrich their commitment to one another and to family life. ACCORD's core services include Marriage Preparation and Marriage Counselling, Fertility Awareness and Wellbeing, Marital Sex Therapy, Marriage Enrichment and Schools Programmes. For further information phone your local ACCORD Centre or ACCORD Central Office or visit *www.accord.ie* or *www.gettingmarried.ie*.

## CURA

**Pregnancy Counselling Service**
*President:* Most Rev Gerard Clifford DD
*National Co-ordinator:* Ms Louise Graham
*National Office*
Columba Centre, Maynooth, Co Kildare
Tel 01-5053040 Fax 01-6292364
Email curacares@cura.ie
Website www.cura.ie

CURA is an agency of the Catholic Church and was established in 1977 as a caring service for those for whom their pregnancy is or has become a crisis.

Services provided:
- Unplanned/Crisis pregnancy support and counselling
- Pregnancy testing
- Post-abortion counselling support
- School Awareness Programme
- Support to mothers and fathers of a new baby

National Helpline: 1850-622626
All services are Free, Confidential and Non-Judgemental. Services are also available to men and other family members.

## COUNCILS FOR EMIGRANTS AND IMMIGRANTS OF THE IRISH EPISCOPAL CONFERENCE

### EMIGRANTS (IECE)

The Irish Episcopal Council for Emigrants (IECE) seeks to respond to the needs of Irish emigrants prior to and following departure. It is particularly committed to addressing the needs of our most vulnerable emigrants, especially the elderly Irish emigrant community, the undocumented in the United States and Irish prisoners overseas. Working in conjunction with the host Church, our apostolates and sister organisations, the IECE seeks to respond to the needs of the Irish as an emigrant community.

*Members of the Council for Emigrants*
Most Rev John Kirby *(Chair)*
Most Rev Donal McKeown DD; Rev Paul Byrne OMI, Rev Alan Hilliard, Sr Marianne O'Connor OSU and Rev Gerry French
*Acting Director of IECE:* Mr Harry Casey
*Administrator:* Ms Bernadette Martin
Columba Centre, Maynooth, Co Kildare
Tel 01-5053155 Fax 01-6292363
Email bernie.martin@iecon.ie
immigrants@iecon.ie
Website www.catholicbishops.ie

**Irish Council for Prisoners Overseas is an outreach of IECE**
The Irish Council for Prisoners Overseas (ICPO) is currently the only organisation working on behalf of Irish prisoners overseas and their families. Established in 1985, the Irish Council for Prisoners Overseas (ICPO) promotes social justice and human dignity for Irish people in prisons overseas and for their families. ICPO provides information, support and advocacy to Irish prisoners wherever they are: it makes no distinction in terms of religious faith, the nature of the prison conviction or of a prisoner's status. Casework, family support, prison visits and policy work comprise core components of this work.

*Staff Maynooth:* Ms Joanna Joyce, Ms Catherine Jackson, Sr Anne Sheehy
*Volunteers Maynooth:* Sr Agnes Hunt, Ms Eileen Boyle, Ms Joan O'Cléirigh and Sr Mary Whyte
*Staff London:* Rev Gerry McFlynn, Ms Liz Power, Ms Breda Power, Mr Declan Ganly, Mr Russel Harland
*Volunteers London:* Sr Maureen McNally, Rev Stephen McKenna, Ms Sara Thompson Sr Agnes Miller, Ms Kathleen Walsh
*Maynooth Office:* Columba Centre, Maynooth, Co Kildare
Tel 01-5053156 Fax 01-6292363
Email icpo@iecon.ie
Website www.catholicbishops.ie
*London Office:* 50-52 Camden Square, London NW1 9XB
Tel 0044-2074824148 Fax 0044-2074824815

**[The Irish Chaplaincy in Britain**
*Director:* Mr Eugene Dugan
Tel 0044-207-4825528 Fax 0044-207-4824815
Email prisoners@irishchaplaincy.org.uk
Website www.irishchaplaincy.org.uk]

### IMMIGRANTS (IECI)

The Irish Episcopal Council for Immigrants (IECI) develops and fosters initiatives for the pastoral care of immigrants among the dioceses and parishes of Ireland. It identifies immigrant communities within a local setting, recognises their needs and develops pastoral outreach strategies to engage with, support and integrate immigrant communities into dioceses and local parishes.

*Members of the Council for Immigrants*
Most Rev Eamonn Walsh DD (Chair), Sr Julie Doran, Mr Gerard Forde, Sr Anne Hayes, Rev Lazurus Iwueke, Rev Jaroslaw Maszkiewicz, Sr Moira McDowall, Rev Brian McLaughlin, Sr Louise O'Connell, Rev Patrick O'Hagan, Rev William Purcell
*Field Officer:* Dr Helen Young
Columba Centre, Maynooth, Co Kildare
Tel 01-5053009
Email helen.young@iecon.ie

## CATHOLIC HEALTHCARE COMMISSION

*Episcopal Members*
Most Rev John Buckley *(Chairman)*; Most Rev Raymond Field; Mr Joe Fallon *(Chairperson)*
*Representatives of CORI*
Sr Pat O'Donovan; Sr Anna Corcoran; Sr Margaret Cashman; Sr Marianne O'Connor, Director General CORI
*Representative of NAHC*
Ms Margaret Mulcaire
Sr Marianne O'Connor
*Co-opted:* Sr Helena O'Donoghue
*Secretary:* Ms Danielle Browne
Catholic Healthcare Commission, c/o CASS, PO Box 10858, Blackrock, Co Dublin
Tel 01-2782693
Email danielle_cass@ireland.com
www.catholicbishops.ie/healthcare

The Catholic Healthcare Commission believes that healthcare ministry is an essential component of the healing mission of Jesus Christ. The Commission works to support life and to promote healthcare for all in a spirit of Christian love and compassion, respecting the dignity and rights of every person.

## IRISH BISHOPS' DRUGS INITIATIVE

*Chair:* Ms Patricia Conway
*Vice Chair:* Most Rev Eamonn Walsh DD
*National Co-ordinator:* Mr John Taaffe
*Community Development Worker:* Mr Darren Butler
*Committee Members:* Sr Kathleen Kelleher, Fr Eamon Treanor, Mr Chris Murphy, Mr David Conway, Ms Gwen McKenna and Ms Marion Rackard
Columba Centre, Maynooth, Co Kildare
Tel 01-5053044/086-8611531
Email ibdi@iecon.ie

The Irish Bishops' Drugs Initiative was established in 1997 as a Church response to the growing problem of drug/alcohol misuse in Ireland. Its vision is to enable parishes to use a pastoral response in partnership with other service providers to respond to the primary and secondary prevention of drug/alcohol harms in parish communities.

## OUTREACH TO PRISONERS

*Irish Prison Chaplains Team*
*Episcopal Liaison*
Most Rev Eamonn Walsh DD
*Coordinator of the National Prison Chaplains:* Rev Ciarán Enright
Arbour Hill Prison, Dublin 7
Tel 01-6732990/6719333

There are at present twenty full-time and five part-time chaplains working in Irish prisons. The vision of the chaplaincy is one that affirms the dignity of the person and seeks to be a voice for those deprived of their freedom. It is a vision that urges us to take a prophetic stance on issues of social justice and to continue the exploration of Restorative Justice as a valid alternative to imprisonment.

## [CHAPLAINCY FOR DEAF PEOPLE

Rev Gerard Tyrrell *(Director)*
The National Chaplaincy for Deaf People
40 Lower Drumcondra Road, Dublin 9
Tel/Voice/TDD 01-8305744
Fax 01-8600284
Email gerard@ncdp.ie or office@ncdp.ie]

## DEPARTMENT OF PLANNING, COMMUNICATIONS AND RESOURCES

*Executive Secretary to the Episcopal Commission/Department*
Rev Timothy Bartlett
Tel 01-5053000
Email tim.bartlett@iecon.ie

## COUNCIL FOR COMMUNICATIONS OF THE IRISH EPISCOPAL CONFERENCE

*Members of the Council*
Most Rev Denis Brennan DD *(Co-Chairman)*
Most Rev John McAreavey DD *(Co-Chairman)*
His Eminence Seán Cardinal Brady DD
Rev Gearóid Dullea *(Executive Secretary)*
Mr Martin Long
Rev Timothy Bartlett
*Secretary:* Ms Maura Hyland
Veritas Company,
7/8 Lower Abbey Street, Dublin 1
Tel 01-8788177 Fax 01-8786507

**Catholic Communications Office**
*Director:* Mr Martin Long
*Communications Officers*
Ms Brenda Drumm
*Editor of Intercom*
Mr Francis Cousins
*Communications Assistant*
Ms Marie Purcell
Columba Centre,
Maynooth, Co Kildare
Tel 01-5053000 Fax 01-6016413
Email info@catholicbishops.ie
www.catholicbishops.ie
Twitter @CatholicBishops
Facebook Irish Catholic Bishops' Conference

**Veritas Communications**
*President:* Most Rev Joseph Duffy DD
Most Rev Dermot Clifford DD
*Chairman:* Very Rev Martin Clarke
*Deputy Chairman:* Sr Nano Brennan
*Director:* Ms Maura Hyland

Veritas advises the Episcopal Commission on Communications on matters related to communications. It has the following divisions:

*Veritas Company Ltd*
7-8 Lower Abbey Street, Dublin 1
Tel 01-8788177 Fax 01-8744913
Email sales@veritas.ie
Unit 309, Blanchardstown Centre, Dublin 15
Tel 01-8864030 Fax 01-8864031
Email blanchardstownshop@veritas.ie
Veritas at DRC Bookshop,
St Patrick's School Building,
193-195 Donegall Street, Belfast BT1 2FL
Tel 028-90236249 Fax 028-90236250
Email enquiries@drcbookshop.com
Carey's Lane, Cork
Tel 021-4251255 Fax 021-4279165
Email corkshop@veritas.ie
20 Shipquay Street, Derry BT48 6DW
Tel 028-71266888 Fax 028-71365120
Email derryshop@veritas.ie
83 O'Connell Street, Ennis, Co Clare
Tel 065-6828696 Fax 065-6820176
Email ennisshop@veritas.ie
13 Lower Main Street, Letterkenny, Co Donegal
Tel 074-9124814 Fax-074-9122716
Email letterkennyshop@veritas.ie
16-18 Park Street, Monaghan
Tel 047-84077 Fax 047-84019
Email monaghanshop@veritas.ie
Sallins Road, Naas, Co Kildare
Tel 045-856882 Fax 045-856871
Email naasshop@veritas.ie
Adelaide Street, Sligo
Tel 071-9161800 Fax 071-9160121
Email sligoshop@veritas.ie
*Veritas UK:* Veritas Warehouse,
14 Rosemount Business Park,
Ballycoolin, Dublin 11, Ireland
Tel 01926-451730 Fax 01926-451733
Email warehouse@veritas.ie

*Veritas Publications*
7-8 Lower Abbey Street, Dublin 1
Tel 01-8788177 Fax 01-8786507
Publishers of general religious books, liturgical texts in Irish and English, and catechetical texts.
*Director:* Maura Hyland
*Manager of Publications:* Caitriona Clarke
*Commissioning Editor:* Donna Doherty
*Intercom Magazine*
Catholic Communications Office,
Columba Centre, Maynooth, Co Kildare
Tel 01-5053000 Fax 01-6016401
*Editor:* Mr Francis Cousins
Email fcousins@catholicbishops.ie
*Subscriptions:* Mr Ross Delmar
Tel 01-8788177 Fax 01-8786507
Twitter @IntercomJournal

## COUNCIL FOR RESEARCH AND DEVELOPMENT OF THE IRISH EPISCOPAL CONFERENCE

*Members of the Council*
Most Rev Dermot Clifford DD *(Chairman)*
Most Rev Kieran O'Reilly DD;
Dr Darach Turley; Ms Louise McCann;
Ms Ann Morash; Dr Brian Conway

**Council for Research and Development**
*Social Researcher:* Mr Eoin O'Mahony
Tel 01-5053024 Fax 01-6016401
Email eoin.omahony@iecon.ie

The Council supervises and assists in research projects approved or requested by the Episcopal Conference, its Agencies and Commissions; the social researcher of the Council devises research programmes to explore and identify developmental needs and possibilities in relation to the Church in Ireland; it offers a consultancy service and acts as an information resource to members of the Conference.

## COUNCIL FOR FINANCE AND GENERAL PURPOSES OF THE IRISH EPISCOPAL CONFERENCE

*Episcopal Members of the Council*
Most Rev John Fleming *(Chairman)*;
Most Rev Seamus Hegarty
Most Rev Michael Smith
*Financial Controller:* Mrs Anne Young
Columba Centre, Maynooth, Co Kildare
Tel 01-5053000 Fax 01-6292360
Email finance@iecon.ie

The Finance and General Purposes Council is composed of three Episcopal members and three lay persons. The Council provides central administrative and accounting services for all the commissions and acts in an advisory capacity to the Episcopal Conference.

## COUNCIL FOR GOVERNANCE

*Members of the Council*
Most Rev William Lee DD *(Chairman)*
Most Rev John Fleming DD
Columba Centre, Maynooth, Co Kildare
Tel 01-5053000 Fax 01 6016401
Email ex.sec@iecon.ie

## DEPARTMENT OF SOCIAL ISSUES AND INTERNATIONAL AFFAIRS

*Executive Secretary to the Episcopal Commission/Department*
Mr Harry Casey
Tel 01-5053000
Email harry.casey@iecon.ie

## COUNCIL FOR EUROPEAN AFFAIRS OF THE IRISH EPISCOPAL CONFERENCE

*Members of the Council on European Affairs*
Most Rev Noël Treanor DD *(Chairman)*;
Most Rev Diarmuid Martin DD

**COMECE**
19 Square de Meeûs, 1050 Bruxelles, Belgium
Tel 32-(0)-22350510 Fax 0032-2-2303334
Email comece@comece.eu
Website www.comece.org

COMECE is a Commission of the Episcopal Conferences of the member countries of the European Community, with an office in Brussels. Rev Prof Dr Piotr Mazurkiewicz is General Secretary.

## COUNCIL FOR JUSTICE AND PEACE OF THE IRISH EPISCOPAL CONFERENCE

*Members of the Council*
Most Rev Raymond Field DD (Chair)
Most Rev John Kirby DD
Most Rev Noël Treanor DD
*Research Co-ordinator:* Dr Nicola Rooney
Columba Centre, Maynooth, Co Kildare
Tel 01-5053000 Fax 01-6016401
Email cjp@iecon.ie

The Council's role is to assist the Church in responding to the challenges facing it in the areas of human rights, social justice in Ireland and internationally, peace, including peace education, and world development. Its main activities are in research, education and information.

## COUNCIL FOR THE MISSIONS OF THE IRISH EPISCOPAL CONFERENCE

*Episcopal Members of the Episcopal Council*
Most Rev Colm O'Reilly DD *(Chairman)*
Most Rev Kieran O'Reilly DD

**National Mission Council**
*Chairman:* Most Rev Colm O'Reilly DD
*Secretary:* Rev Eamon Aylward (SSCC)
IMU, St Paul's Retreat, Mount Argus, Lower Kimmage Road, Dublin 6W
Tel 01-4923326/4923325 Fax 01-4923316
Email executive@imu.ie

**World Missions Ireland (Pontifical Mission Societies)**
*National Director:* Rev Gary Howley
64 Lower Rathmines Road, Dublin 6
Tel 01-4972035
Email director@wmi.ie

Co-ordinates the activities of all national missionary bodies and acts as a forum for discussion on matters related to national mission policy.

## TRÓCAIRE

The Catholic Agency for World Development

*Board of Trustees*
His Eminence Seán Cardinal Brady
His Grace Most Rev Diarmuid Martin
His Grace Most Rev Dermot Clifford
His Grace Most Rev Michael Neary
Most Rev Noël Treanor
Most Rev John Kirby
*Executive Committee*
Most Rev John Kirby *(Chairman)*
Most Rev Colm O'Reilly
*Director:* Justin Kilcullen
*Deputy Director and Head of Communications and Education*
Eamonn Meehan
*Head of International Department*
Caoimhe De Barra
*Lenten Campaign Coordinator*
Karen Casey
*Press and Communications*
Catherine Ginty
Maynooth, Co Kildare
Tel 01-6293333 Fax 01-6290661
Email info@trocaire.ie
Website http://www.trocaire.org
*Offices and Resource Centres:*
50 King Street, Belfast BT1 6AD
9 Cook Street, Cork
12 Cathedral Street, Dublin 1

Trócaire, the Catholic Agency for World Development, was established by the Irish bishops in 1973 to express the Church's concern for the needs and problems of the people of the developing nations. Trócaire's long-term development projects and emergency relief programmes in Africa, Asia and Latin America tackle the injustice of global poverty. In Ireland, through its education programmes and campaigning, Trócaire works to raise awareness about development issues and the principles of social justice involved.

## DEPARTMENT OF WORSHIP, PASTORAL RENEWAL AND FAITH DEVELOPMENT

*Executive Secretary to the Episcopal Commission/Department*
Sr Anne Codd
Tel 01-5053025
Email anne.codd@iecon.ie

## COUNCIL FOR PASTORAL RENEWAL AND ADULT FAITH DEVELOPMENT OF THE IRISH EPISCOPAL CONFERENCE

*Members of the Council*
Most Rev Seamus Freeman DD *(Chairman)*
Most Rev Donal McKeown DD;
Most Rev William Murphy DD;
Representatives of: Regional networks of Diocesan personnel for pastoral renewal and adult faith development; Ecclesial Movements and Associations of Lay Faithful; CORI and IMU; Lay Pastoral Workers; Ministry with youth and young adults and Centres of theological and pastoral education and training.

*Executive Staff of the Council*
*Resource person:* Sr Anne Codd (pbvm)
Email anne.codd@iecon.ie
Tel 01-5053029
*Research Assistant:* Ms Julieann Moran
Email julieann.moran@iecon.ie
Columba Centre, Maynooth, Co Kildare
Tel 01-5053025
Email pastoralrenewal@iecon.ie

The Council supports ongoing dialogue and reflection on current, relevant topics between all groups and agencies represented by its members. The Council brings to the Episcopal Commission for Worship, Pastoral Renewal and Faith Development the fruits of these dialogues and reflections, for crafting into recommendations and presentation to the Episcopal Conference. On behalf of Conference, the Council promotes frameworks and processes which are aimed at ongoing development of shared vision as well as pastoral priorities and strategies at national level.

Areas for research, reflection and supportive action by the Council include evangelisation, adult faith development, parish development, lay discipleship and ministry, and the young Church.

**National Committee of Diocesan Youth Directors (NCDYD)**
Most Rev Donal McKeown DD *(Chairman)*
96 Downview Park West, Belfast BT15 5HZ
Tel 028-90781642
Rev Jim Caffrey *(Secretary)*
Director of Catholic Youth Care (CYC)
Arran Quay, Dublin 7
Tel 01-8725055
Email jcaffrey@cyc.ie

## COUNCIL FOR LITURGY OF THE IRISH EPISCOPAL CONFERENCE

*Episcopal Members of the Council for Liturgy*
Most Rev Martin Drennan DD *(Chairman)*
Most Rev Brendan Kelly DD
Most Rev John McAreavey DD
*Secretary:* Rev Patrick Jones
National Centre for Liturgy, St Patrick's College, Maynooth, Co Kildare
Tel 01-7083478 Fax 01-7083477
Email liturgy@spcm.ie
www.liturgy-ireland.ie

**National Centre for Liturgy**
St Patrick's College, Maynooth, Co Kildare
Tel 01-7083478 Fax 01-7083477
*Director:* Rev Patrick Jones
Email liturgy@spcm.ie
www.liturgy-ireland.ie

The National Centre, relocated at Maynooth in 1996, houses the National Secretariat for Liturgy, offers programmes in liturgical formation at the Centre and elsewhere and provides an advisory service on liturgical matters.

**Advisory Committee on Church Music**
*Chairperson:* Prof Gerard Gillen
*Secretary:* Sr Moira Bergin
National Centre for Liturgy, St Patrick's College, Maynooth, Co Kildare
Tel 01-7083478 Fax 01-7083477
Email moira.bergin@spcm.ie

**Advisory Committee on Sacred Art and Architecture**
*Chairperson:* Mr Alexander White
*Secretary:* Rev Patrick Jones
National Centre for Liturgy, St Patrick's College, Maynooth, Co Kildare
Tel 01-7083478 Fax 01-7083477
Email patrick.jones@spcm.ie

**Coiste Comhairleach um an Liotúirge i nGaeilge**
*Cathaoirleach*
An Mgr Pádraig Ó Fiannachta
*Rúnaí:* An Canónach Seán Terry
Baile an Londraigh,
Cluain Uamha, Co Chorcai
Fón 021-4646779
Ephost jterry@eircom.net

**Schola Cantorum**
*Director:* Mr Gerard Lillis
St Finian's College, Mullingar,
Co Westmeath
Tel 044-9342906/086-2528029
Email scholacantorum@eircom.net
Website www.scholacantorum.ie

Established by the hierarchy in 1970 to provide specialised training in music for boys and girls within the framework of their general post-primary education.

Scholarships are awarded to students of good general and musical ability.

## COUNCIL FOR VOCATIONS OF THE IRISH EPISCOPAL CONFERENCE

*Members of the Council*
Most Rev Donal McKeown DD *(Chairman)*
Most Rev Seamus Freeman DD
*National Co-ordinator for Vocations*
Rev William Purcell
Email info@vocations.ie

## COUNCIL FOR RELIGIOUS OF THE IRISH EPISCOPAL CONFERENCE

*Members of the Council for Religious of the IEC*
Most Rev John McAreavey DD *(Chairman)*
Most Rev Seamus Freeman DD
Most Rev Diarmuid Martin DD

## COUNCIL FOR CLERGY OF THE IRISH EPISCOPAL CONFERENCE

*Episcopal Members of the Council*
Most Rev Philip Boyce DD *(Chairman)*
Most Rev Donal McKeown DD

*Consultors*
Very Rev Dan Bollard
Rev Oliver Treanor
Very Rev Stephen Farragher
Mrs Marie Hogan
Fr Leon Ó Giolláin SJ
Sr Consilio Rock RSM

**National Training Authority for the Permanent Diaconate**
Columba Centre, Maynooth, Co Kildare
Tel 01-5053000 Fax 01-6016401

## [NATIONAL BOARD FOR SAFEGUARDING CHILDREN IN THE CATHOLIC CHURCH IN IRELAND

*Chairman:* Mr John B Morgan
Chief Executive Officer: Mr Ian Elliott
*Director of Safeguarding*
Ms Teresa Devlin
*Director of Professional Standards*
Sr Colette Stevenson
*Administrator:* Ms Ann Doyle
*Assistant Administrator:* Ms Imelda Ashe
National Board for Safeguarding Children in the Catholic Church in Ireland
New House, St Patrick's College,
Maynooth, Co Kildare
Tel 01-5053124 Fax 01-5053026
Email admin@safeguarding.ie

The National Board for Safeguarding Children in the Catholic Church in Ireland was established in 2006 in order to provide best practice advice and to monitor the safeguarding of children in the Catholic Church.

Over recent years there has been an increasing recognition of the existence of child abuse and growing acceptance of the potential risks to children from others working in positions of trust. Greater attention, therefore, has been paid to how church organisations ensure that the children with whom they are in contact are kept safe from harm.]

# ARCHDIOCESES AND DIOCESES OF IRELAND

Ireland is divided into four provinces: Armagh, Dublin, Cashel and Tuam, named from metropolitan sees. The areas covered by each province and diocese are described at the beginning of the entry for each diocese; a map of the ecclesiastical areas is printed on the front endpaper of this directory.

For ease of reference, the four archdioceses appear at the beginning of this section in the traditional order, but the individual dioceses appear in full alphabetical order regardless of province. Thus Achonry, from the Province of Tuam, starts the section, followed by Ardagh and Clonmacnois from the Province of Ardagh and so on.

The provinces and their suffragan sees are as follows:

**Province of Armagh**
Metropolitan See: Armagh
Suffragan Sees: Dioceses of Ardagh & Clonmacnois, Clogher, Derry, Down & Connor, Dromore, Kilmore, Meath, Raphoe.

*The Archbishop of Armagh is Primate of All Ireland.*

**Province of Dublin**
Metropolitan See: Dublin
Suffragan Sees: Dioceses of Ferns, Kildare & Leighlin, Ossory.

*The Archbishop of Dublin is Primate of Ireland.*

**Province of Cashel**
Metropolitan See: Cashel
Suffragan Sees: Dioceses of Cloyne, Cork & Ross, Kerry, Killaloe, Limerick, Waterford & Lismore.

**Province of Tuam**
Metropolitan See: Tuam
Suffragan Sees: Dioceses of Achonry, Clonfert, Elphin, Galway & Kilmacduagh with Kilfenora*, Killala.

**Kilfenora is in the Province of Cashel, but the Bishop of Galway and Kilmacduagh is its Apostolic Administrator.*

# ARCHDIOCESE OF ARMAGH

PATRONS OF THE ARCHDIOCESE
ST MALACHY, 3 NOVEMBER; ST PATRICK, 17 MARCH;
ST OLIVER PLUNKETT, 1 JULY

SUFFRAGFEN SEES: ARDAGH AND CLONMACNOIS, CLOGHER, DERRY, DOWN AND CONNOR, DROMORE, KILMORE, MEATH, RAPHOE

INCLUDES ALMOST ALL OF COUNTIES ARMAGH AND LOUTH
APPROX HALF OF COUNTY TYRONE
AND PARTS OF COUNTIES DERRY AND MEATH

**His Eminence Cardinal Seán Brady DCL, DD**
Archbishop of Armagh; Primate of All Ireland; born 1939; ordained priest 22 February 1964; ordained Coadjutor Archbishop 19 February 1995; installed Archbishop of Armagh 3 November 1996; created Cardinal 24 November 2007.

Residence: Ara Coeli,
Cathedral Road,
Armagh BT61 7QY
Tel 028-37522045 Fax 028-37526182
Email admin@aracoeli.com
www.archdioceseofarmagh.com

## ST PATRICK'S CATHEDRAL, ARMAGH

The building of the new St Patrick's Cathedral lasted from St Patrick's Day 1840, when the foundation stone was laid, until its solemn consecration in 1904. There were occasional intermissions of the work, and one of the longest gaps occurred because of the Great Famine. Primate Crolly, who had initiated the building, became a victim of famine cholera, and, at his own wish, his body was laid to rest under the sanctuary of the unfinished cathedral.

For five years the low outline of the bare walls remained, but with the translation of Dr Paul Cullen to the See of Dublin, work was resumed under Primate Dixon. On Easter Monday 1854, tarpaulins and canvas covers were drawn from wall to wall to allow Mass to be celebrated in the unfinished building.

During the Famine cessation the original architect, Thomas J. Duff, died. The architect to take over from Duff's original Perpen-dicular Gothic design was J. J. McCarthy, destined to become one of the famous architects of the nineteenth century. In his anxiety to achieve a greater degree of classical purity, McCarthy drew up a continuation design in the old fourteenth-century Decorated Gothic. While critics may debate the wisdom of such a radical change when the building had reached a relatively advanced stage, the effect was undoubtedly to create an overall impression of massive grandeur.

The final impetus to complete the building came when Dr McGettigan was appointed (1870) to Armagh, and the solemn dedication took place in 1873.

Dr Logue, following Primate McGettigan's death, was to achieve the splendid interior decoration and the addition of the Synod Hall. He travelled to Rome and Carrara in search of precious marble for the reredos, pulpit and altar, and it was he also who achieved the decoration of the interior with mosaic. Under him, stained-glass windows were commissioned from Meyer in Germany. Cardinal Vanutelli represented Pope Pius X at the solemn consecration in 1904. A grand carillon was installed in 1924.

Vatican II's decree on Sacred Liturgy stressed the participation of the laity and hence greater visibility had to be afforded to the congregation. For this reason all the architects who submitted designs based their plans on the removal of the 1904 marble screens, which hindered visibility of the sanctuary from the sides. By raising, enlarging and opening the sanctuary area, the cathedral has, to a large extent, been restored to its original form.

With the removal of the rood screen, a new crucifix had to be placed at the sanctuary, and a specially commissioned 'Cross of Life' by Imogen Stuart was affixed to the right of the sanctuary.

The rededication took place in 1982, and a portion of St Malachy's relics from France, together with a relic of St Oliver Plunkett, was placed in the new altar. And so, the mortal remains of two of Armagh's most celebrated *comharbaí Phádraig* were carried back to the scene of their labours in more troubled times.

A unique, but now also an historical feature of the primatial cathedral, is the Cardinals' Hats. They are no longer conferred on new Cardinals. They were hung here and went deliberately untended so that their decay would represent the end of all earthly glory. The most recently hung (and last to be presented) is that of Cardinal Conway. Beside it are Cardinal Logue's and Cardinal O'Donnell's, while on the opposite side are the hats of Cardinals D'Alton and MacRory.

**Most Rev Gerard Clifford DD**
Titular Bishop of Geron and Auxiliary Bishop to the Archbishop of Armagh; born 1941; ordained priest 18 June 1967; ordained Bishop 21 April 1991
Residence: Annaskeagh, Ravensdale, Dundalk, Co Louth
Tel 042-9371012 Fax 042-9371013
Email gcliffrd@indigo.ie

## CHAPTER

*Dean:* Rt Rev Colum Curry VG
*Archdeacon:* Rt Rev Francis Donnelly
*Canons:* Most Rev Gerard Clifford VG
Very Rev Tomás Ó Sabhaois
Very Rev Michael Ward
Very Rev Patrick McDonnell
Rt Rev Christopher O'Byrne
Rt Rev Raymond Murray
Very Rev James Clyne
Very Rev Michael Crawley
Rt Rev James Carroll

## ADMINISTRATION

**Vicars General**
Most Rev Gerard Clifford DD
Annaskeagh, Ravensdale, Dundalk, Co Louth
Tel 042-9371012 Fax 042-9371013
Email gcliffrd@indigo.ie
Rt Rev Dean Colum Curry PP
4 Circular Road, Dungannon, Co Tyrone BT71 6BE
Tel 028-87722775

**Vicars Forane**
Very Rev Gerard Campbell PP, Kilkerley
Rt Rev Mgr James Carroll PP, Drogheda
Very Rev Paul Clayton-Lea PP, Clogherhead
Very Rev Malachy Conlon PP, Cooley
Very Rev Kevin Cullen PP, Cullyhanna
Rt Rev Dean Colum Curry PP, VG, Dungannon
Very Rev Benedict Fee PP, Clonoe
Very Rev John Gates PP, Magherafelt
Very Rev Patick Hannigan PP, Killeeshil
Very Rev Patrick McEnroe PP, Darver & Dromiskin
Very Rev Dermot Maloney PP, Dromintee
Very Rev Peter Murphy PP, Ardee & Collon
Very Rev Richard Naughton PP, Cloghogue
Very Rev Michael O'Dwyer PP, Portadown
Rev Seán O'Neill PP, Termonmaguirc
Very Rev Patrick Rushe Adm, Holy Redeemer, Dundalk
Very Rev Eugene Sweeney Adm, Armagh
Very Rev Gerard Tremer PP, Cookstown

**Chancellor**
Very Rev Michael C. Toner PP
Ara Coeli, Cathedral Road, Armagh BT61 7QY
Tel 028-37522045 Fax 028-37526182
Email mtoner@aracoeli.com
diocesansecretary@aracoeli.com

**Diocesan Curia**
Very Rev Michael C. Toner PP
Diocesan Secretary
Email mtoner@aracoeli.com
diocesansecretary@aracoeli.com
Mr John McVey
Financial Administrator
Email jmcvey@aracoeli.com
Ara Coeli, Cathedral Road, Armagh BT61 7QY
Tel 028-37522045 Fax 028-37526182

**Archives**
*Director:* Mr Roddy Hegarty
Cardinal Tomás Ó Fiaich Memorial Library and Archive,
15 Moy Road, Armagh BT61 7LY
Tel 028-37522981 Fax 028-37511944
Email roddy.hegarty@ofiaich.ie

## CATECHETICS EDUCATION

**Catholic Primary School Managers' Association**
*Secretary:* Very Rev Malachy Conlon PP
Parochial House, Top Rath, Carlingford, Co Louth
Tel 042-9376105
Email malachykilkerley@eircom.net

**Council for Catholic Maintained Schools**
*Senior Management Officer*
Mr Stephen Walsh
1 Killyman Road, Dungannon
Co Tyrone BT71 6DE
Tel 028-87752116 Fax 028-87752783
Email stephen.walsh@ccmsschools.com

**Diocesan Advisers for Religious Education**
*Primary Schools*
Sr Elizabeth Wall
La Verna, St Clare's Convent, Newry, Co Down BT34 1PR
Tel 028-30253887
Email marylizwall@btinternet.com
*Post-Primary Schools*
Rev Declan O'Loughlin
Parochial House, 30 Newline, Killeavy, Newry, Co Down BT35 8TA
Tel 028-30889609
Email decoloughlin@yahoo.co.uk

## PASTORAL

**Accord**
*Drogheda Chairperson*
Mrs Sharon Duggan-Meehan
Verona, Cross Lane, Drogheda, Co Louth
Tel 041-9843860
Email accorddrogheda@eircom.net

*Armagh Chairperson*
Mr Denis Bradley
1 Tavanagh Avenue, Portadown, Co Armagh BT62 3AJ
Tel 028-38334781
Email armagh@accordni.com

*Dundalk Chairperson*
Mrs Mary McDonnell
St Patrick's, Roden Place, Dundalk, Co Louth
Tel 042-9331731
Email accorddundalk@eircom.net

**Apostolic Work Society**
*Diocesan President:* Ms Jean Hanratty
13 College Street, Armagh BT61 9BT
Tel 028-37522781

**Armagh Diocesan Pastoral Centre**
*Director:* Sr Rhoda Curran (RSM)
*Assistant Director:* Mr Joseph Purcell
The Magnet, The Demesne, Dundalk, Co Louth
Tel 042-9336393 Fax 042-9336432

**Armagh Diocesan Pastoral Council**
*Acting Chairperson:* Mr Pat Logue
Cleevehill, Coolfore, Monasterboice, Co Louth
Email plogue@aibp.ie
*Secretary:* Mrs Sheila McEneaney
Ashridge, Brackley, Markethill, Co Armagh BT60 1SE
Tel 028-37552056
Email sheila.mceneaney@hotmail.com

**Charismatic Renewal**
Rt Rev Dean Colum Curry PP, VG
Parochial House, 4 Circular Road, Dungannon, Co Tyrone BT71 6BE
Tel 028-87722775

**Chokmah**
*Co-ordinator:* Rev Thomas Hamill
'Shekinah', 25 Wynnes Terrace, Dundalk, Co Louth
Tel 042-9331023
Email tomhamill@eircom.net

**Communications**
*Diocesan Officer:* Vacant

**CURA**
17 Jocelyn Street, Dundalk, Co Louth
Tel 042-9337533
*Co-ordinator:* Ms Kathleen Coburn

**Diocesan Safeguarding Committee**
*Chairperson:* Sr Loretto McKeown (RSM)
Convent of Mercy, Catherine Street, Newry, Co Down BT35 6JG
Tel 028-30257095
*Designated Officer:* Mr Pat McGlew
Tel 028-37525592

**Diocesan Safeguarding Office**
*Director of Safeguarding:* Mr Pat McGlew
*Admin Officer:* Mr Pierce Fox
Archdiocese of Armagh, Catheral Road, Armagh BT61 7QY
Tel 028-37525592
Email pfox@archdioceseofarmagh.com

**Ecumenism**
Very Rev Pádraig Murphy PP
Email pplordship@live.ie
Parochial House, Ravensdale, Dundalk, Co Louth
Tel 042-9371327 Fax 042-9371327
Very Rev Seán Dooley PP
Email seandooleyfriesian@btconnect.com
Parochial House, Tullyallen, Co Louth

**Fr Mathew Union**
*Diocesan Chairman*
Very Rev Seamus Rice PE, AP
Parochial House, 89 Derrynoose Road, Derrynoose, Co Armagh BT60 3EZ
Tel 028-37531222
Email seamusrice@live.co.uk

**Historic Churches Advisory Committee**
(Armagh, Clogher and Kilmore)
*Chair:* Most Rev Gerard Clifford VG
Annaskeagh, Ravensdale,
Dundalk, Co Louth
Tel 042-9371012 Fax 042-9371013
Email gcliffrd@indigo.ie

**Knock Pilgrimage**
*Director:* Rev Benedict Fee PP, VF
Parochial House, Magheralanfield,
140 Mountjoy Road, Coalisland,
Co Tyrone BT71 5DY
Tel 028-87738381
Email frbennyfee@hotmail.com

**Legion of Mary**
*Armagh Curia President*
Ms Dympna McNamee
16 Springfield Crescent, Mullaghmore,
Dungannon, Co Tyrone BT70 1QU
Tel 028-87724178
*Drogheda Curia President*
Ms Elizabeth Molony
194 Meadow View, Drogheda, Co Louth
Tel 041-9830617
*Dundalk Curia President:* Mrs Alice Keeley
Carnalogue, Louth Village, Co Louth
Tel 042-9384768

**Liturgy Commission**
*Chair:* Sr Mairead Ní Fhearáin
St Clare's Convent, 42 Madden Row,
Keady, Co Armagh BT60 3RW
Tel 028-37531252

**LMFM Community Radio**
Very Rev Canon James Carroll PP, VF
Parochial House, 9 Fair Street,
Drogheda, Co Louth

**Lourdes Pilgrimage**
*Director:* Very Rev Eamonn McCamley PP
Parochial House, 17 Eagralougher Road,
Loughgall, Co Armagh BT61 8LA
Tel 028-38891231

**Marriage Tribunal**
(See Marriage Tribunals section.)

**Pastoral Renewal & Family Ministry**
*Director:* Dr Tony Hanna
Email tonyhann@indigo.ie
Armagh Diocesan Pastoral Centre,
The Magnet, The Demesne,
Dundalk, Co Louth
Tel 042-9336649

**Pioneer Total Abstinence Association**
*Diocesan Director*
Very Rev Seamus Rice PE, AP
Parochial House, 89 Derrynoose Road,
Derrynoose, Co Armagh BT60 3EZ
Tel 028-37531222

**Polish Chaplaincy**
Rev Daniel Glocko (SChr) CC
Parochial House, 6 Circular Road,
Dungannon, Co Tyrone BT71 6BE
Tel 028-87722631
Email danijjel@gmail.com

**Pontifical Mission Societies**
*Diocesan Director*
Very Rev Vincent Darragh PE
81 Mullinahoe Road, Ardboe,
Dungannon, Co Tyrone BT71 5AU
Tel 028-86735774
Email vdarragh@aol.com

**Seminarian Liaison**
Very Rev Joseph McKeever PP
9 Newry Road, Crossmaglen, Newry,
Co Down BT35 9HH
Tel 028-30861208
Email jmckeever02@googlemail.com

**Senate of Priests**
*Chairman*
Rt Rev Dean Colum Curry PP, VG
Parochial House, 4 Circular Road,
Dungannon, Co Tyrone BT71 6BE
Tel 028-87722775
Email ccurry@btinternet.com

**SPRED**
*Co-ordinator:* Ms Patricia Lennon
19 The Glen, Newry, Co Down BT35 8BS
Tel 028-30265353

**Travellers**
*Co-ordinator:* Rev Aloysius MacCourt CC
Parochial House, 55 West Street,
Stewartstown, Dungannon,
Co Tyrone BT71 5HT
Tel 028-87738252

**Vocations Commission**
*Vocations Director*
Very Rev Peter McAnenly PP
10 Killymeal Road, Dungannon,
Co Tyrone BT71 6DP
Tel 028-87722906
Email p.mcanenly@btinternet.com

**Youth Commission (ADYC)**
*Chairperson:* Rev Brian White CC
Parochial House, Grianán Mhuire,
Main Street, Blackrock, Dundalk,
Co Louth
*Director:* Mr Dermot Kelly
*Admin Officer:* Mr Pierce Fox
Archdiocese of Armagh, Cathedral Road,
Armagh BT61 7QY
Tel 028-37523084
Email armaghyouth@yahoo.co.uk

## PARISHES

*Mensal parishes are listed first. Other parishes follow alphabetically. Historical names are given in parentheses. Church titulars are in italics.*

**ARMAGH**
*St Patrick's Cathedral, St Malachy,* Irish Street, *St Colmcille's,* Knockaconey
*Immaculate Conception,* Tullysaran
Email armaghparish@btconnect.com
Very Rev Eugene Sweeney Adm, VF
Email esweeney64@btconnect.com
Rev Rory Coyle CC
Email rory_coyle@hotmail.com
Rev John McKeever CC
Email john_mckeever@yahoo.com
Rev Victor Onwukeme (MSP) CC
Email onwukeme2006@yahoo.com
Parochial House, 42 Abbey Street,
Armagh BT61 7DZ
Tel 028-37522802 Fax 028-37522245
Rev Kevin Donaghy *(Priest in residence)*
Parochial House, 86 Maydown Road,
Artasooley, Tullysaran, Benburb,
Co Armagh BT71 7LN
Tel 028-37548210

**DUNDALK, ST PATRICK'S**
*St Patrick's, Roden Place*
*St Nicholas's, Church Street*
www.stpatricksparishdundalk.org
Very Rev Mark O'Hagan Adm
Email ohagan.mark@gmail.com
Rev Séamus Dobbin CC
Rev Magnus Ogbonna (MSP) CC
Email doziemsp@yahoo.com
Rev Garrett Campbell CC
Email garrett.campbell@btinternet.com
St Patrick's Presbytery, Roden Place,
Dundalk, Co Louth
Tel 042-9334648 Fax 042-9336355
Email mensalparish@eircom.net

**DUNDALK, HOLY REDEEMER**
*Holy Redeemer*
www.redeemerparish.ie
Very Rev Patrick Rushe Adm, VF
Email revpicard1@eircom.net
Rev Paul Montague CC
Email revpaulmontague@eircom.net
Ard Easmuinn, Dundalk, Co Louth
Tel 042-9334259 Fax 042-9329073
Email holyredeemer@eircom.net

**DUNDALK, ST JOSEPH'S**
*St Joseph's*
Very Rev Michael Cusack (CSsR) Adm
Rev Eamon Hoey (CSsR) CC
Email nedhoey@gofree.indigo.ie
Rev Patrick Sugrue (CSsR) CC
Email dundalkoffice@redemptorists.ie
St Joseph's, St Alphonsus Road,
Dundalk, Co Louth
Tel 042-9334042 Fax 042-9330893

**DUNDALK, HOLY FAMILY**
*Holy Family*
Very Rev James O'Connell (SM) Adm
Email jimhoconnell@yahoo.co.uk
Rev Patrick Stanley (SM) CC
Rev Francis Corry (SM) CC
Holy Family Parish,
Dundalk, Co Louth
Tel 042-9336301 Fax 042-9336350
Email theholyfamily@eircom.net

**DROGHEDA**
*St Peter's, West Street*
*Our Lady of Lourdes, Hardman's Gardens*
www.saintpetersdrogheda.ie
Email stpetersadmin1@eircom.net
Rt Rev Mgr James Carroll PP, VF
Parochial House,
9 Fair Street, Drogheda, Co Louth
Tel 041-9838537 Fax 041-9841351
Email jcarlpp@eircom.net
Very Rev Canon Patrick McDonnell PE
Very Rev Martin Kenny PE
Email martin.kenny34@gmail.com
Rev Emlyn McGinn CC
Email emlynmcginn@yahoo.com
Our Lady of Lourdes Presbytery,
Hardman's Gardens, Drogheda, Co Louth
Tel 041-9831899
Rev Piotr Delimat CC
Email pieetro@wp.pl
Rev Sean Ryan (SMA) CC
St Peter's Presbytery, 10 Fair Street,
Drogheda, Co Louth
Tel 041-9838239
Email sean.ryan@sma.ie

**DUNGANNON (DRUMGLASS, KILLYMAN AND TULLYNISKIN)**
*St Patrick's, Dungannon,*
*St Malachy's Edendork,*
*St Brigid's, Killyman,*
*Sacred Heart, Clonmore*
www.parishofdungannon.com
Rt Rev Dean Colum Curry PP, VG
4 Circular Road, Dungannon,
Co Tyrone BT71 6BE
Tel 028-87722775
Email ccurry@btinternet.com
Rev Aidan Dunne CC
Email fadunne@googlemail.com
Rev Séamus White CC
Rev Daniel Glocko (SChr) CC
Email danijjel@gmail.com
Parochial House, 6 Circular Road,
Dungannon, Co Tyrone BT71 6BE
Tel 028-87722631
*Parish Office:* 4 Killyman Road,
Dungannon, Co Tyrone BT71 6DH
Tel/Fax 028-87726893
Email parishofdungannon@lycos.com

**ARDBOE**
*Blessed Sacrament, Mullinahoe*
*Immaculate Conception, Moortown*
Very Rev Seán McCartan PP
Parochial House, Moortown, Cookstown,
Co Tyrone BT80 0HT
Tel 028-86737236
Email seancmccartan@googlemail.com
Very Rev Vincent Darragh PE
81 Mullinahoe Road, Ardboe,
Dungannon, Co Tyrone BT71 5AU
Tel 028-86735774
Email vdarragh@aol.com

**ARDEE & COLLON**
*Nativity of Our Lady, Ardee*
*St Catherine's, Ballapousta*
*Mary Immaculate, Collon*
Website www.ardeeparish.com
Email ardee.collon@gmail.com
Very Rev Peter Murphy PP, VF
Tel 041-6850920 Fax 041-6850922
Very Rev Thomas McGeough PE, AP
Tel 041-6850920 Fax 041-6850922
Email tmgeough12@gmail.com
Rev Anselm Emechebe (MSP) CC
Tel 041-6860080
Parochial House, Hale Street,
Ardee, Co Louth
Rev William Mulvihill CC
Parochial House, Collon, Co Louth
Tel 041-9826106

**AUGHNACLOY (AGHALOO)**
*St Mary's, Aughnacloy,*
*St Brigid's, Killens,*
*St Joseph's, Caledon*
Rev John McGoldrick (in residence)
Parochial House, 56 Minterburn Road,
Laireakean, Caledon, Co Tyrone BT68 4XH
Tel 028-37568288
Email minterburn@hotmail.com

**BALLINDERRY**
*St Patrick's*
Very Rev Peter Donnelly PP
Parochial House,
130 Ballinderry Bridge Road, Coagh,
Cookstown, Co Tyrone BT80 0AY
Tel 028-79418244

**BALLYGAWLEY (ERRIGAL KIERAN)**
*St Matthew's, Garvaghy, St Mary's,*
*Dunmoyle, Immaculate Conception,*
*Ballygawley, St Malachy's, Ballymacilroy*
Very Rev Michael Seery PP
Parochial House, 115 Omagh Road,
Ballygawley, Co Tyrone BT70 2AG
Tel 028-85568208
Email errigalciarog@aol.com
Very Rev Brian Hackett PE, AP
Parochial House, 31 Church Street,
Ballygawley, Co Tyrone BT70 2HA
Tel 028-85568219
Email brianhackett04@aol.com

**BERAGH**
*Immaculate Conception, Beragh,*
*St Malachy's, Seskinore,*
*St Patrick's, Drumduff*
Very Rev Séamus McGinley PP
Parochial House, Beragh, Omagh,
Co Tyrone BT79 OSY
Tel 028-80758206
Email smcginley01@btinternet.com

**BESSBROOK (KILLEAVY LOWER)**
*SS Peter and Paul, Bessbrook,*
*St Malachy, Camlough, Sacred Heart, Lislea,*
*Immaculate Conception, Lissummon*
*Road, Newry, Good Shepherd,*
*Cloughreagh*
Rev Seán Larkin PP
Parochial House, 11 Chapel Road,
Bessbrook, Newry, Co Down BT35 7AU
Tel 028-30830206 Fax 028-30838154
Email larkinseanj@aol.com
Rev Phelim McKeown CC
Parochial House, 9 Chapel Road,
Bessbrook, Newry,
Co Down BT35 7AU
Tel 028-30830272
Email frphelim@eircom.net
Very Rev Robert McKenna PE, AP
Parochial House, 26 Newtown Road,
Camlough, Newry,
Co Down BT35 7JJ
Tel 028-30830237 Fax 028-30837273
Email robert.mckenna3@btinternet.com

**CARLINGFORD AND CLOGHERNY**
*St Michael's, Carlingford*
*St Lawrence's, Omeath*
www.carlinnparish.com
Very Rev Brian MacRaois PP
Parochial House, Chapel Hill,
Carlingford, Co Louth
Tel 042-9373111 Fax 042-9373131
Email cairlinnparish@eircom.net
Very Rev James Shevlin PE, AP
Parochial House, Omeath, Co Louth
Tel 042-9375198
Email jamesshevlin@eircom.net

**CLOGHERHEAD**
*St Michael's, Clogherhead,*
*SS Peter and Paul, Walshestown*
www.clogherhead.com
Very Rev Paul Clayton-Lea PP, VF
Tel 041-9822438
Email clogherheadparish@hotmail.com
Very Rev William Murtagh PE, AP
Tel 041-9822224
Parochial House, Clogherhead,
Drogheda, Co Louth

**CLOGHOGUE (KILLEAVY UPPER)**
*Sacred Heart, Cloghogue, St Joseph's,*
*Meigh, St Michael's, Killean*
Very Rev Richard Naughton PP, VF
Mountain Lodge, 132 Dublin Road,
Newry, Co Down BT35 8QT
Tel 028-30262174 Fax 028-30262174
Very Rev Canon S. James Clyne PE, AP
24 Chapel Road, Killeavy, Newry,
Co Down BT35 8JY
Tel 028-30848222
Email clyne@eircom.net

**CLONOE**
*St Patrick's, Clonoe, St Columcille's,*
*Kingsland, St Brigid's, Brockagh*
Email clonoeparish@tiscali.co.uk
Very Rev Benedict Fee PP, VF
Parochial House, Magheralanfield,
140 Mountjoy Road, Coalisland,
Co Tyrone BT71 5DY
Tel 028-87738381 Fax 028-87738048
Email frbennyfee@hotmail.com
Very Rev Kieran MacKeone PE, AP
Parochial House, 132 Washing Bay Road,
Coalisland, Dungannon,
Co Tyrone BT71 4QZ
Tel 028-87740376
Email kieran.mckeone@btinternet.com
Rev John McCallion CC
Parochial House, 18 Annaghmore Road,
Coalisland, Dungannon,
Co Tyrone BT71 4QZ
Email revtrad@btinternet.com

**COAGH**
*Our Lady's, Coagh*
*SS Joseph and Malachy, Drummullan*
Very Rev Oliver Breslan PP
Parochial House, Hanover Square,
Coagh, Cookstown, Co Tyrone BT80 0EF
Tel 028-86737212
Email coaghparish@aol.com

**COALISLAND**
*Holy Family, Coalisland*
*St Mary & St Joseph, Coalisland,*
*St Mary's, Stewartstown*
Email coalislandparish@yahoo.co.uk
Very Rev Paul Byrne PP
Parochial House, 31 Brackaville Road,
Coalisland, Co Tyrone BT71 4NH
Tel 028-87740221 Fax 028-87746449
Email pauldbyrne@yahoo.co.uk
Rev Gregory Carvill CC
5 Plater's Hill, Coalisland,
Co Tyrone BT71 4JZ
Tel 028-87740302
Email greg.carvill@gmail.com
Rev Aloysius McCourt CC
55 West Street, Stewartstown,
Dungannon, Co Tyrone BT71 5HT
Tel 028-87738252
Email almaccourt@btinternet.com

**COOKSTOWN (DESERTCREIGHT AND DERRYLORAN)**
*Holy Trinity, Cookstown, Sacred Heart,*
*Tullydonnell, St John's, Slatequarry,*
*St Laurán's, Cookstown*
Very Rev Gerard Tremer PP, VF
Parochial House, 1 Convent Road,
Cookstown, Co Tyrone BT80 8QA
Tel 028-86763370 Fax 028-86763370
Email
fr.gerard.tremer@cookstownparish.com

Rev Cathal Deveney CC
Parochial House, 3 Convent Road,
Cookstown, Co Tyrone BT80 8QA
Tel 028-86763293 Fax 028-86763490
Email cdeveney@me.com
Rev John Flanagan (SPS) CC
Parochial House, 6 Tullydonnell Road,
Dungannon, Co Tyrone BT70 3JE
Tel 028-87758224

**COOLEY**
*St James's, Grange*
*Our Lady, Star of the Sea, Boher*
*St Anne's, Mullaghbuoy*
Very Rev Malachy Conlon PP, VF
Top Rath, Cooley, Carlingford, Co Louth
Tel 042-9376105 Fax 042-9376075
Email malachykilkerley@eircom.net
Rev Thomas McNulty CC
Parochial House, Grange,
Carlingford, Co Louth
Tel 042-9376577
Email tommymcnulty37@gmail.com

**CROSSMAGLEN (CREGGAN UPPER)**
*St Patrick's, Crossmaglen,*
*St Brigid's, Glassdrummond,*
*Sacred Heart, Shelagh*
Email uppercreggan@googlemail.com
Very Rev Joseph McKeever PP
9 Newry Road, Crossmaglen,
Newry, Co Down BT35 9HH
Tel 028-30861208 Fax 028-30860163
Email jmckeever02@googlemail.com
Rev Liam McKinney CC
Parochial House, 9a Newry Road,
Crossmaglen, Newry, Co Down BT35 9HH
Tel 028-30868698 Fax 028-30860163
Email ltpmckinney@yahoo.com
Rev Bernard King (SM) CC
Parochial House, Glassdrummond,
Crossmaglen, Newry, Co Down BT35 9DY
Tel 028-30861270
Email baking@btinternet.com

**CULLYHANNA (CREGGAN LOWER)**
*St Patrick's, Cullyhanna*
*St Michael's, Newtownhamilton*
*St Oliver Plunkett's, Dorsey*
Very Rev Kevin Cullen PP, VF
Parochial House, Tullinavall Road,
Cullyhanna, Newry, Co Down BT35 OPZ
Tel 028-30861235

**DARVER AND DROMISKIN**
*St Peter's, Dromiskin, St Michael's, Darver*
Very Rev Patrick McEnroe PP, VF
Darver, Readypenny, Dundalk, Co Louth
Tel 042-9379147
Email patrickmmcenroe@eircom.net
Very Rev Liam Pentony CC
Parochial House, Dromiskin,
Dundalk, Co Louth
Tel 042-9382877
Email frliampentony@gmail.com

**DONAGHMORE**
*St Patrick's, Donaghmore*
*St John's, Galbally*
Very Rev Gerard McAleer PP
Parochial House, 63 Castlecaulfield Road,
Donaghmore, Dungannon,
Co Tyrone BT70 3HF
Tel 028-87761327
Email
donaghmoreparish@btinternet.com

Very Rev Patrick Breslan PE, AP
Parochial House, 55 Dermanaught Road,
Galbally, Dungannon, Co Tyrone BT70
2NR
Tel 028-87758277

**DROMINTEE**
*St Patrick's, Dromintee*
*Sacred Heart, Jonesboro*
Very Rev Dermot Maloney PP, VF
Parochial House, 40 The Village,
Jonesboro, Newry, Co Down BT35 8HP
Tel 028-30849345
Email drominteeparish@btinternet.com

**DUNLEER**
*St Brigid's, Dunleer,*
*St Finians's Dromin,*
*St Kevin's, Philipstown*
www.dunleerparish.ie
Very Rev G. Michael Murtagh PP
Parochial House, Old Chapel Lane,
Dunleer, Co Louth
Tel 041-6851278
Email gmmurtagh@eircom.net

**EGLISH**
*St Patrick's*
Very Rev Peter McAnenly PP
10 Killymeal Road, Dungannon,
Co Tyrone BT71 6DP
Tel 028-87722906
Email p.mcanenly@btinternet.com
parishofeglish@gmail.com

**FAUGHART**
*St Brigid's, Kilcurry,*
*Most Holy Rosary, Brid-a-Crinn,*
*St Joseph's, Castletown*
Very Rev Christopher McElwee (IC) PP
Rev Bernard Hughes (IC) CC
Rev James Pollock (IC)
St Brigid's, Kilcurry, Dundalk, Co Louth
Tel 042-9334410/9333235

**HAGGARDSTOWN AND BLACKROCK**
*St Fursey's Haggardstown*
*St Oliver Plunkett's, Blackrock*
Very Rev Pádraig Keenan PP
Parochial House, Chapel Road,
Haggardstown, Dundalk, Co Louth
Tel 042-9321621
Email pkredeemer@eircom.net
Rev Brian White CC
Grianán Mhuire, Main Street, Blackrock,
Dundalk, Co Louth
Tel 042-9322244 Fax 042-9322244
Email roadbowler@hotmail.com

**KEADY (DERRYNOOSE)**
*St Patrick's, Keady, St Joseph's,*
*Derrynoose, St Joseph's, Madden*
Very Rev Canon Michael Crawley PP
Parochial House, 34 Madden Row, Keady,
Co Armagh BT60 3RW
Tel 028-37531242 Fax 028-37539627
Email parishofkeady@btinternet.com
Rev Malachy Murphy CC
Parochial House, St Patrick Street, Keady,
Co Armagh BT60 3TQ
Tel 028-37531246 Fax 028-37530850
Email malomurphy@googlemail.com
Very Rev Séamus Rice PE, AP
Parochial House, 89 Derrynoose Road,
Derrynoose, Keady, Co Armagh BT60 3EZ
Tel 028-37531222 Fax 028-37539397
Email seamusrice@live.co.uk

**KILDRESS**
*St Joseph's, Killeenan*
*St Mary's, Dunamore*
Very Rev Patrick Hughes PP
Parochial House, 10 Cloughfin Road,
Kildress, Cookstown, Co Tyrone BT80 9JB
Tel 028-86751206
Email patrickhughes309@btinternet.com

**KILKERLEY**
*Immaculate Conception*
Very Rev Gerard Campbell PP, VF
Parochial House, Kilkerley,
Dundalk, Co Louth
Tel 042-9333482
Email gerryw.campbell@gmail.com

**KILLCLUNEY**
*St Patrick's, Baile Mhic an Aba,*
*St Michael's, Cladaí Móra,*
*St Mary's, Grainseach Mhór*
Very Rev Peter Kerr PP
Parochial House,
194 Newtown Hamilton Road,
Ballymacnab, Armagh BT60 2QS
Tel/Fax 028-37531641
Rev Eugene O'Neill *(Priest in residence)*
4 Ballymacnab Road, Co Armagh BT60 2QS
Tel 028-37531620
Email freoneill@btopenworld.com

**KILLEESHIL**
*Assumption, Killeeshil, St Patrick's,*
*Aughnagar, St Joseph's, Ackenduff*
Very Rev Patrick Hannigan PP, VF
Parochial House, 65 Tullyallen Road,
Dungannon, Co Tyrone BT70 3AF
Tel 028-87761211
Email killeeshilparish@yahoo.co.uk

**KILMORE**
*Immaculate Conception, Mullavilly,*
*St Patrick's, Stonebridge*
www.parishofkilmore.com
Very Rev Michael C. Toner PP
Parochial House, 114 Battlehill Road,
Richhill, Co Armagh BT61 8QJ
Tel 028-38871661
Email parishofkilmore@googlemail.com

**KILSARAN**
*St Mary's, Kilsaran*
*St Nicholas, Stabannon*
Very Rev Eamon Treanor PP
Parochial House, Kilsaran,
Castlebellingham, Dundalk, Co Louth
Tel 042-9372255
Email treanoret@eircom.net

**KNOCKBRIDGE**
*St Mary's, Knockbridge*
Very Rev Gerard McGinnity PP
Parochial House, Knockbridge,
Dundalk, Co Louth
Tel 042-9374125
Email m.gmc@hotmail.com

**LISSAN**
*St Michael's*
Very Rev Patrick Hughes Adm
Parochial House, 10 Cloughfin Road,
Kildress, Cookstown, Co Tyrone BT80 9JB
Tel 028-86751206
Email patrickhughes309@btinternet.com
Rev Charles McCann AP
Parochial House, 2 Tullynure Road,
Cookstown, Co Tyrone BT80 9XH
Tel 028-86763674
Email frmccann1@verizon.net

**LORDSHIP (AND BALLYMASCANLON)**
*St Mary's, Ravensdale*
*St Mary's, Lordship*
*Our Lady of the Wayside, Jenkinstown*
www.lordship-ballymascanlon.org
Very Rev Pádraig Murphy PP
Parochial House, Ravensdale,
Dundalk, Co Louth
Tel/Fax 042-9371327
Email pplordship@live.ie
Very Rev Patrick Larkin, PE, AP
Parochial House, Jenkinstown,
Dundalk, Co Louth
Tel 042-9371328

**LOUGHGALL**
*Our Lady of Peace, Maghery*
*St Peter's, Collegeland*
*St Patrick's, Loughgall*
*St John's, Tartaraghan*
Very Rev Eamonn McCamley PP
Parochial House, 17 Eagralougher Road,
Loughgall, Co Armagh BT61 8LA
Tel 028-38891231 Fax 028-38891827
Email loughgall@gmail.com

**LOUTH**
*Our Lady of Immaculate Conception, Louth*
*Our Lady of the Snows, Stonetown*
Very Rev Seán Quinn PP
Parochial House, Louth Village, Dundalk,
Co Louth
Tel 042-9374285
Email louthparish@dna.ie

**MAGHERAFELT AND ARDTREA NORTH**
*Assumption, Magherafelt*
*St John's, Milltown*
*St Patrick's Castledawson*
Email magherafeltparish@btinternet.com
www.magherafeltparish.org
Very Rev John Gates PP, VF
Parochial House, 30 King Street,
Magherafelt, Co Derry BT45 6AS
Tel 028-79632439
Email jgatesbrack@btconnect.com
Rt Rev Mgr Canon Christopher O'Byrne PE, AP
Parochial House, 12 Aughrim Road,
Magherafelt, Co Derry BT45 6AY
Tel 028-79634038
Very Rev Arthur McAnerney PE, AP
Parochial House, 10 Aughrim Road,
Magherafelt, Co Derry BT45 6AY
Tel 028-79632351
Email arthur.mcanerney@btinternet.com

**MELL**
*St Joseph's*
Very Rev John McAlinden (CSsR) Adm
Parochial House, Slane Road, Mell,
Drogheda, Co Louth
Tel 041-9838278
Email johnmcalinden@oceanfree.net

**MELLIFONT**
*Our Lady of the Assumption, Tullyallen*
Very Rev Seán Dooley PP
Parochial House, Tullyallen,
Drogheda, Co Louth
Tel 041-9838520
Email seandooleyfriesian@btconnect.com
Very Rev Laurence Caraher PE, AP
The Ravel, School Lane, Tullyallen,
Drogheda, Co Louth
Tel 041-9834293
Email lacaraher@gmail.com

**MIDDLE KILLEAVY**
*St Mary's, Dromalane,*
*St Malachy's, Carnagat*
www.middlekilleavy.com
Email assumptionnewry@gmail.com
Very Rev Lawrence Boyle PP
'Glenshee', Dublin Road,
Newry, Co Down BT35 8DA
Tel 028-30262376
Email lorcanboyle@gmail.com
Rev Francis Coll CC
Parochial House, 17 Carnmore Drive,
Newry, Co Down BT35 8SB
Tel 028-30269047
Rev Fergus Breslan CC
Hospital Road, Newry,
Co Down BT35 8DL

**MIDDLETOWN (TYNAN)**
*St John's, Middletown*
*St Joseph's, Tynan*
Very Rev Seán Moore PP
Parochial House, 290 Monaghan Road,
Middletown, Co Armagh BT60 4HS
Tel 028-37568406
Email
middletowntynanparish@hotmail.co.uk

**MONASTERBOICE**
*Immaculate Conception, Tenure,*
*Nativity of Our Lady, Fieldstown*
Very Rev Stephen Duffy PP
Parochial House, Monasterboice,
Drogheda, Co Louth
Tel 041-9822839
Email fatherduffy@eircom.net
Rev Michael Hickey (CSSp) CC
Parochial House, Tenure,
Dunleer, Co Louth
Tel 041-6851281
Email michaelhickey01@eircom.net

**MONEYMORE (ARDTREA)**
*SS John and Trea, Moneymore*
*St Patrick, Loup*
Very Rev Martin McArdle PP
Parochial House, 10 Springhill Road,
Moneymore, Magherafelt,
Co Derry BT45 7NG
Tel 028-86748242
Email ardtrea@btinternet.com
Rev Harry Coyle *(Priest in residence)*
Lisieux, 99 Loup Road,
Ballynenagh, Moneymore,
Co Derry BT45 7ST
Tel 028-79418235

**MOY (CLONFEACLE)**
*St John the Baptist, Moy*
*St Jarlath's, Clonfeacle*
www.clonfeacleparish.com
Very Rev John Connolly PP
75 Clonfeacle Road, Blackwatertown,
Dungannon, Co Tyrone BT71 7HP
Email connollyjm@btinternet.com
Very Rev John Hughes PE, CC
Parochial House, Benburb Road, Moy,
Dungannon, Co Tyrone BT71 7SQ
Tel 028-87784240
Email revjhughes@tiscali.co.uk

**MULLAGHBAWN (FORKHILL)**
*St Mary's, Mullaghbawn*
*Our Lady, Queen of Peace, Aughanduff*
St Oliver Plunkett, Forkhill
Very Rev John Heagney PP
Parochial House, Mullaghbawn,
Newry, Co Down BT35 9XN
Tel 028-30888286 Fax 028-30888370
Email heagneyjh@aol.com

**NEWBRIDGE**
*St James, Newbridge*
Very Rev John Fox PP
Parochial House, 153 Aughrim Road,
Toomebridge, Antrim BT41 3SH
Tel 028-79468277 Fax 028-79468277
Email
newbridgechurch@googlemail.com

**POMEROY**
*Assumption, Pomeroy,*
*Immaculate Conception, Altmore*
www.pomeroyparish.homestead.com
Very Rev Martin McVeigh PP
Parochial House,
9 Cavanakeeran Road, Pomeroy,
Dungannon, Co Tyrone BT70 2RD
Tel 028-87758329
Email pomeroyparish@hotmail.com

**PORTADOWN (DRUMCREE)**
*St John the Baptist's, Garvaghy Road*
*St Patrick's, William Street*
www.drumcreeparish.com
Very Rev Michael O'Dwyer PP, VF
Parochial House, 15 Moy Road,
Portadown, Co Armagh BT62 1QL
Tel 028-38350610
Email modppvf@fsmail.net
Rev Michael Sheehan CC
Parochial House, 11 Moy Road,
Portadown, Co Armagh BT62 1QL
Tel 028-38332218
Email frmichaelpsheehan@eircom.net

**TALLANSTOWN**
*St Malachy's, Reaghstown,*
*St Medoc's, Clonkeen,*
*SS Peter and Paul, Tallanstown*
Very Rev Peter Clarke PP
Parochial House, Tallanstown,
Dundalk, Co Louth
Tel 042-9374197
Email tallanstownparish@eircom.net

**TANDRAGEE (BALLYMORE AND MULLAGHBRACK)**
*St James's, Tandragee*
*St Patrick's, Ballyargan*
*St Joseph's, Poyntzpass*
*St James's, Markethill*
Very Rev Michael Woods PP
Parochial House, 40 Market Street,
Tandagree, Co Armagh BT62 2BW
Tel 028-38840442
Email parish57@btinternet.com

**TERMONFECHIN**
*Immaculate Conception, Termonfechin*
*The Assumption, Sandpit*
Very Rev Aidan Murphy PP
Parochial House, Termonfechin,
Drogheda, Co Louth
Tel 041-9822121
Email termonfechinparish@eircom.net

**TERMONMAGUIRC (CARRICKMORE, LOUGHMACRORY & CREGGAN)**
*St Colmcille's, Carrickmore*
*St Oliver Plunkett, Creggan*
*St Mary's, Loughmacrory*
Email termonmaguircparish@gmail.com
Rev Sean O'Neill PP, VF
Parochial House, 1 Rockstown Road,
Carrickmore, Omagh,
Co Tyrone BT79 9BE
Tel 028-80761207 Fax 028-80760938
Email oneillsean@btinternet.com
Very Rev Thomas Mallon PE, AP
Parochial House, 170 Loughmacrory
Road, Omagh, Co Tyrone BT79 9LG
Tel 028-80761230 Fax 028-80761131
Email mallontv@aol.com

**TOGHER**
*St Columcille, Togher*
*St Finnian, Dillonstown*
*St Borchill, Dysart*
*St Mary's, Drumcar*
http://homepage.eircom.net
/~togherparish/
Very Rev Thomas Daly PP
Parochial House, Boicetown, Togher,
Drogheda, Co Louth
Tel 041-6852110
Very Rev Sean Quinn PE, AP
Parochial House, Dillonstown,
Dunleer, Co Louth
Tel 041-6863570

**WHITECROSS (LOUGHILLY)**
*St Teresa's, Tullyherron*
*St Malachy's, Ballymoyer*
*St Brigid's, Carrickananney*
*St Laurence O'Toole, Belleeks*
Very Rev Michael Rogers PP
Parochial House, 25 Priestbush Road,
Whitecross, Co Armagh BT60 2TP
Tel 028-37507214
Email rogers228@freeuk.com

## INSTITUTIONS AND CHAPLAINCY SERVICES

**Aiken Military Barracks**
Barrack Street, Dundalk, Co Louth
Rev Bernard McCay-Morrissey OP
Tel 042-9332295

**Community School**
Ardee, Co Louth
Mr Seán Moran
Tel 041-6853313

**Cuan Mhuire**
Armagh Road, Newry, Co Down
Tel 028-30262429
(Bessbrook Parish Clergy)

**Dundalk Institute of Technology**
Dundalk, Co Louth
Rev Clem McManus (CSsR)
Dundalk Institute of Technology,
Dublin Road, Dundalk, Co Louth
Tel 042-9370224

**Our Lady of Lourdes Hospital**
Drogheda, Co Louth
Rev Thomas Hogan CSsR
Our Lady of Lourdes Hospital,
Drogheda, Co Louth
Tel 041-9837601

**St Paul's High School**
Bessbrook, Co Armagh
Very Rev Dermot Maloney PP, VF
Parochial House, 40 The Village,
Jonesboro, Newry, Co Down BT35 8HP
Tel 028-3084945 (H) 028-30830309 (S)
Email maloney750@btinternet.com

*The following hospitals are served by parochial clergy:*
**Armagh Community Hospital**
Armagh
Tel 028-37522802 (Chaplain)

**Longstone Special Care Hospital**
Armagh
Tel 028-37522802 (Chaplain)

**Louth County Hospital**
Dundalk, Co Louth
Tel 042-9334648 (Chaplain)

**Mid-Ulster Hospital**
Magherafelt, Co Derry
Tel 028-79632351

**St Brigid's Hospital**
Ardee, Co Louth
Tel 041-6850920 (Chaplain)

**St Joseph's Hospital**
Ardee, Co Louth
Tel 041-6853313 (Chaplain)

**St Luke's Psychiatric Hospital, Armagh**
Armagh
Tel 028-37522802 (Chaplain)

**St Oliver Plunkett's Hospital**
Dundalk, Co Louth
Tel 042-9334259 (Chaplain)

**South Tyrone Hospital**
Dungannon, Co Tyrone
Tel 028-87722631 (Chaplain)

## PRIESTS OF THE DIOCESE ELSEWHERE

Rev Dominic Mallon
13 Richview Heights, Keady,
Co Armagh BT60 3SW
Rev Andrew McNally
c/o 8 Moneymore Road, Magherafelt,
Co Derry BT45 6AD
Email andymacs@mac.com
Rev David Moore
1a Rockstown road, Carrickmore,
Omagh, Co Tyrone BT79 9BE
Tel 028-80760433
Email d.moore2323@btinternet.com
Very Rev John O'Leary
175 Adams Street, 11E Brooklyn,
NY 11208 USA
Tel 718-5107111
Email jpolear7@aol.com

## RETIRED PRIESTS

Very Rev John Bradley PE
8 Killymeal Road, Dungannon,
Co Tyrone BT71 6BE
Tel 028-87722183
Rev Desmond Corrigan
c/o Ara Coeli, Armagh BT61 7QY
Very Rev James Crowley PE
Parochial House, 60 Aughnagar Road,
Ballygawley, Dungannon,
Co Tyrone BT70 2HP
Tel 028-85568399
Rt Rev Archdeacon Francis Donnelly PE
64 Meadow Grove,
Dundalk, Co Louth
Tel/Fax 042-9353264
Very Rev John Finn PE
Moorehall Lodge Nursing Home,
Hale Street, Ardee, Co Louth
Tel 041-6871942
Very Rev James Grimes PE
61 Castlecaulfield Road,
Donaghmore, Co Tyrone BT70 3HF
Tel 028-87767727
Very Rev Seán Hegarty PE
1a Convent Road, Cookstown,
Co Tyrone BT80 8OA
Tel 028-86769629
Email dshegarty@btinternet.com
Very Rev Terence Kelly PE
3 Cranagh, Ballinderry Bridge Road,
Coagh, Cookstown,
Co Tyrone BT80 0AS
Very Rev Kieran MacOscar PE
Parochial House, 10 Mullavilly Road,
Tandragee, Co Armagh BT62 2LX
Tel 028-38840840
Email revmacoscar@btinternet.com
Very Rev Patrick J. McCrory PE
Parochial House, Sixemilecross,
Omagh, Co Tyrone BT79 9NF
Tel 028-80758344
Email patrick.mccrory@btinternet.com
Very Rev Patrick McGuckin PE
79 Reclain Road, Galbally, Dungannon,
Co Tyrone BT70 2PQ
Tel 028-87759692
Email frpmcguckin@hotmail.com
Very Rev Brendan McHugh PE
Parochial House, Mullanhoe,
Ardboe, Dungannon,
Co Tyrone BT71 5AU
Tel 028-86737338
Very Rev Brendan McNally PE
Parochial House, Reaghstown,
Ardee, Co Louth
Tel 041-6855117
Very Rev James McNally PE
14 Derrygarve Road, Castledawson,
Co Derry BT45 8HA
Tel 028-79469998
Email sainttrea@btinternet.com
Rt Rev Mgr Raymond Murray PE
60 Glen Mhacaha, Cathedral Road,
Armagh BT61 8AS
Tel 028-37510821
Email raylmurray@tiscali.co.uk

Very Rev Christopher O'Brien PE
Haroldstown, Tobinstown,
Tullow, Co Carlow
Tel 059-9161633
Very Rev Owen O'Donnell PE
Parochial House, Dunamore,
Cookstown, Co Tyrone
Tel 028-86751216
Very Rev Canon Tomás Ó Sabhaois PE
Avila Nursing Home, Convent Hill,
Bessbrook, Newry,
Co Down BT35 7AW
Very Rev Canon Michael Ward PE
6 Augherainey Close,
Donaghmore, Dungannon,
Co Tyrone BT70 3HF
Tel 028-87761847

## RELIGIOUS ORDERS AND CONGREGATIONS

### PRIESTS

**AUGUSTINIANS**
St Augustine's Priory, Shop Street,
Drogheda, Co Louth
Tel 041-9838409 Fax 041-9831847
*Sub-Prior:* Rev Malachy Loughran (OSA)
Email focal@eircom.net

**CISTERCIANS**
Mellifont Abbey, Collon, Co Louth
Tel 041-9826103 Fax 041-9826713
Email mellifontabbey@eircom.net
*Prior:* Br Joseph Ryan
*Superior:* Rev Laurence McDermott

**DOMINICANS**
St Magdalen's, Drogheda, Co Louth
Tel 041-9838271 Fax 041-9832964
*Prior:* Very Rev Dermot Brennan (OP)

St Malachy's Priory, Dundalk, Co Louth
Tel 042-9334179/9333714
Fax 042-9329751
*Prior:* Very Rev Bede McGregor (OP)

**JESUITS**
Iona, 211 Churchill Park,
Portadown, Co Armagh BT62 1EU
Tel 028-38330366 Fax 028-38338334
*Superior:* Rev Brendan MacPartlin (SJ)
Email iona@jesuit.ie

**MARISTS**
Cerdon, Marist Fathers,
St Mary's Road, Dundalk, Co Louth
Tel 042-9334019
*Superior:* Rev Kevin Cooney (SM)

St Mary's College, Dundalk, Co Louth
Tel 042-9339984
*Principal:* Mr Con McGinley

(See also under parishes – Dundalk, Holy Family)

**REDEMPTORISTS**
St Joseph's, Dundalk, Co Louth
Tel 042-9334042/9334762
Fax 042-9330893
*Superior*
Very Rev Michael Cusack (CSsR) PP
Email redsdalk@iol.ie
*Vicar-Superor:* Rev Eamonn Hoey (CSsR)

(See also under parishes – Dundalk, St Joseph's)

**ROSMINIANS**
See under parishes – Faughart

**SERVITES**
Servite Priory, Benburb, Co Tyrone
Tel 028-37548241
Retreat, conference and youth centre
*Prior:* Very Rev Chris O'Brien (OSM)
*Provincial*
Very Rev Bernard Thorne (OSM)

### BROTHERS

**DE LA SALLE BROTHERS**
Dundalk, Co Louth
Tel 042-9334439 Fax 042-9330870
*Superior:* Br Raymond McKeever
Community: 4

De La Salle College,
Dundalk, Co Louth
Tel 042-9331179 Fax 042-9330870
*Principal:* Mr Martin Brennan

**SAINT JOHN OF GOD NORTH EAST SERVICES**
St Mary's, Drumcar, Dunleer, Co Louth
Tel 041-6851211 Fax 041-6851529
Email admin.northeast@sjog.ie
*Director:* Mrs Bernadette Shevlin
*Community Superior*
Br Ronan Lennon (OH)
Community: 3
*School Principal:* Mr Kevin Toale
Residential and day services for children and adults with varying degrees of intellectual disability.

Domus Services, Drogheda, Dundalk
Tel 041-9873044
Drumcar Park Enterprises
Tel 041-6851112

Saint John of God Day Centre,
Hilltop, Dundalk, Co Louth
Tel 042-9334663

### SISTERS

**CONGREGATION OF THE SISTERS OF MERCY**
Mill Street, Dundalk, Co Louth
Tel 042-9334200
*Leader:* Sr Regina McGeown
Community: 14

Mile End, Avenue Road,
Dundalk, Co Louth
Tel 042-9330410
Community: 3

Bethany, 34 Point Road,
Dundalk, Co Louth
Tel 042-9331602

15 Cypress Gardens, Bay Estate,
Dundalk, Co Louth
Tel 042-9329315

6 Newry Road,
Dundalk, Co Louth
Tel 042-9339285

Convent of Mercy,
Ardee, Co Louth
Tel 041-6853359
Community: 11

Dun Mhuire,
29 Convent Hill, Bessbrook,
Newry, Co Down BT35 7AW
Tel 028-30830258
*Leader:* Sr Kathleen O'Connor
Community: 4

58 Fairhill Road, Cookstown,
Co Tyrone BT80 8AG
Tel 028-86763363
Community: 5

Convent of Mercy, Dungannon,
Co Tyrone BT71 6AR
Tel 028-87722623
Community: 5

Sisters of Mercy,
90 Church View, Bessbrook,
Newry, Co Down BT35 78T
Tel 028-30837140

115 Oaklawns,
Dundalk, Co Louth
Tel 042-9334569

Convent Lodge, Ein Karim,
Hale Street, Ardee, Co Louth
Tel 041-6857852

**DAUGHTERS OF CHARITY OF ST VINCENT DE PAUL**
St Vincent's Retreat and Holiday Centre
Termonfeckin, Drogheda, Co Louth
Tel 041-9822115
*Superior:* Sr Louise Coughlan
Community: 3
Pastoral work, Retreat & Holiday Centre

**DOMINICAN CONTEMPLATIVES**
Monastery of St Catherine of Siena,
The Twenties, Drogheda, Co Louth
Tel 041-9838524
Email siena@eircom.net
www.dominicannuns.ie
http://dominicannunsireland.blogspot.com
*Prioress:* Sr M. Breda Carroll (OP)
Community: 21

**FRANCISCAN MISSIONARIES OF THE DIVINE MOTHERHOOD**
Franciscan Friary, Laurence Street,
Droghega, Co Louth
Tel 041-9838554
Fax 041-9832535
Community: 3

**FRANCISCAN MISSIONARY SISTERS FOR AFRICA**
Franciscan Convent, Mount Oliver,
Dundalk, Co Louth (Motherhouse)
Tel 042-9371123 Fax 042-9371159
Email fmsamto@eircom.net
*Sister-in-Charge*
Sr Patricia McConvey (FMSA)
Community: 39

**HOLY FAMILY OF BORDEAUX SISTERS**
1-2 Wesleyan Mews, Church Street,
Magherafelt, Co Derry BT45 6NZ
Tel 028-79632529
*Contact:* The Sisters
Community: 2
Parish and pastoral work, art and retreat work

**MEDICAL MISSIONARIES OF MARY**
Motherhouse, Beechgrove,
Drogheda, Co Louth
Tel 041-9837512 Fax 041-9839219
Email beechgroveadm@eircom.net
*Leader:* Sr Ursula Sharpe

MMM Nursing Facility
Áras Mhuire, Beechgrove,
Drogheda, Co Louth
Tel 041-9842222
Email arasmhuire@eircom.net

Greenbank, Mell,
Drogheda, Co Louth
Tel 041-9831028
Email mmmgreenbankmell@eircom.net
Community: 5

13-14 Ashleigh Heights,
Drogheda, Co Louth
Tel 041-9830779/041-9830778
Email mmmashleigh@eircom.net
Community: 5

**MISSIONARIES OF CHARITY**
19A Cathedral Road,
Armagh BT61 7QX
Tel 04837-528654
*Superior:* Sr M. Cleopha (MC)
Community: 4
Hostel for men

**NOTRE DAME DES MISSIONS (OUR LADY OF THE MISSIONS)**
Pine Cottage, Dublin Road,
Dundalk, Co Louth
Community: 4
Pastoral work

**PRESENTATION SISTERS**
Greenhills, Drogheda, Co Louth
Tel 041-9831420
Community: 4
School ministry
Our Lady's College, Greenhills
Tel 041-9831786 Fax 041-9832809
Email greenhillsconvent@yahoo.com

Primary Convent Primary School,
Ballymakenny Road,
Drogheda, Co Louth
Tel 041-9837119
Fax 041-9839425
Email presdrogheda.ias@eircom.net

103 Thomas Street, Portadown,
Co Armagh BT62 3AH
Tel 028-38332220
Email presentation103@hotmail.com
Community: 4
Cross community and pastoral ministry

28 Garvaghy Park,
Portadown, Co Armagh BT62 1HB
Tel 028-38335964
Email evetere1234@yahoo.com
Community: 4
School and pastoral ministry

**SACRED HEART SOCIETY**
2 Convent Road, Armagh BT60 4BJ
Tel 028-37522046 Fax 018-3751864
Community: 5
Education and pastoral work

*Linked with 2 Convent Road*
Gate Lodge, 4 Convent Road
Armagh BT60 4BG
Email sr.nora.smyth@googlemail.com
Pastoral work and writing

2B Callan Crescent, Armagh BT61 7RH
Community: 2
Tel/Fax 028-37528473
Email nandolo21@hotmail.com
Neighbourhood projects

**SISTERS OF ST CLARE**
St Clare's Convent, Keady,
Co Armagh BT60 3RW
Tel 028-37531252
*Contact Person*
Sr Vera Kelly
Community: 8

St Clare's Convent,
4 The Brambles, Stewartstown Road,
Coalisland, Co Tyrone BT71 4SN
Tel 028-37746418
Community: 3

**ST JOHN OF GOD SISTERS**
3 Tudor Grove, Mullaharlin Road,
Dundalk, Co Louth
Tel 042-9336422
Community: 1

**ST LOUIS SISTERS**
266B Monaghan Road, Tynan,
Co Armagh BT60 4SQ
Tel 028-37568498
Community: 9

75 Hanslough Road, Middletown,
Co Armagh BT60 4HN
Tel 028-37568033
Community: 1

Dún Lughaidh, Dundalk, Co Louth
Tel 042-9335786
Community: 10
Dún Lughaidh Post-Primary School
Tel 042-9334474
Pupils: 700

137 Cedarwood Park,
Cox's Demesne, Dundalk, Co Louth
Tel 042-9339816
Community: 1

2 Mill Road, Dundalk, Co Louth
Tel 042-9335773
Community: 4

## EDUCATIONAL INSTITUTIONS

**Coláiste Rís**
Chapel Street, Dundalk, Co Louth
Tel 042-9334336 Fax 042-9338380
*Principal:* Mr Pádraig Hamill

**St Patrick's Academy**
37 Killymeal Road, Dungannon,
Co Tyrone BT71 6DS
Tel 028-87722668
Fax 028-87722745
*Principal:* Mr Fintan Donnelly

**St Patrick's Grammar School**
Cathedral Road, Armagh BT61 7QZ
Tel 028-37522018 Fax 028-37525930
*Headmaster:* Rev Kevin Donaghy
*Priests on Staff*
Rev John McGoldrick
Tel 028-37568288

**St Joseph's Convent Grammar School**
58 Castlecaulfied, Donaghmore,
Co Tyrone BT70 3HF
Tel 028-87761227
*Principal:* Mr Enda Cullen

**EDMUND RICE SCHOOLS TRUST**
St Joseph's Secondary School,
Newfoundwell, Drogheda, Co Louth
Tel 041-9837232
*Principal:* Mr David Madden

St Joseph's Primary School,
Sunday's Gate, Drogheda, Co Louth
Tel 041-9833620
*Principal:* Mr Frank Bradley

**EDMUND RICE SCHOOLS TRUST NORTHERN IRELAND**
Christian Brothers' Primary School,
Greenpark, Keady Road,
Armagh BT60 4AB
Tel 028-37524354
Fax 028-37522308
*Principal:* Mr Nial P. Smyth

## CHARITABLE AND OTHER SOCIETIES

**Aras Mhuire**
Shambles Lane, Dungannon,
Co Tyrone BT70 1BW
Tel 028-87726852
Oratory and bookshop

**Avila Nursing Home**
Convent of Mercy, Convent Hill,
Bessbrook, Co Armagh BT35 7AW
Tel 028-30838969

**Armagh Diocesan Family Care Society**
Under the patronage and immediate direction of the Archbishop and clergy executive committee.
*Secretary:* Mr John McVey
Ara Coeli, Armagh BT61 7QB
Tel 028-37522045

**Cuan Mhuire**
132 Armagh Road, Newry, Co Down
Tel 028-30269121
Alcohol counselling

**Family of God Community**
The Oratory, Carroll's Village,
Dundalk, Co Louth
Tel 042-9335851 Fax 042-9335566

**Pioneer Shop**
30 Thomas Street, Armagh BT61 7QB
Tel 028-37523586

*also*

Holy Family Church, Coalisland,
Co Tyrone BT71 4LS
Tel 028-87749046

**St Mary's Drumcar**
Residential and Day Training Centre
St Mary's, Drumcar, Co Louth
Tel 041-6851211/6851264

**SOS Prayer**
The Oratory, Carroll's Village,
Dundalk, Co Louth
Tel 042-9339888

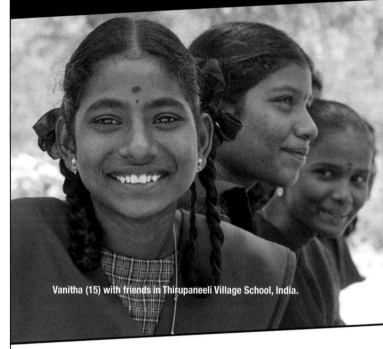

# ARCHDIOCESE OF DUBLIN

PATRONS OF THE ARCHDIOCESE
ST KEVIN, 3 JUNE; ST LAURENCE O'TOOLE, 14 NOVEMBER

SUFFRAGFEN SEES: KILDARE AND LEIGHLIN, FERNS, OSSORY

INCLUDES CITY AND COUNTY OF DUBLIN, NEARLY ALL OF COUNTY WICKLOW AND PORTIONS OF COUNTIES CARLOW, KILDARE, LAOIS AND WEXFORD

**Most Rev Diarmuid Martin DD**
Archbishop of Dublin and Primate of Ireland
Born 8 April 1945; ordained priest 25 May 1969; ordained bishop by Pope John Paul II 6 January 1999; elevation to Dignity of Archbishop and Apostolic Nuncio March 2001; appointed Coadjutor Archbishop of Dublin 3 May 2003; Canonical/Liturgical Reception as Coadjutor 30 August 2003; succeeded as Archbishop of Dublin 26 April 2004

Residence: Archbishop's House, Drumcondra, Dublin 9
Tel 01-8373732 Fax 01-8369796

## ST MARYS PRO-CATHEDRAL, DUBLIN

Though Catholic Dublin has not possessed a cathedral since the Reformation, for almost two hundred years now St Mary's Pro-Cathedral has served as the Mother Church of the Dublin arch-diocese. In that time it has won a special place in the hearts of the Dublin people, to whom it is known affectionately as 'The Pro'.

The Pro-Cathedral was born of the vision of Archbishop John Thomas Troy and brought to fruition thanks to the unstinting labours of its second administrator, Archdeacon John Hamilton. The parish of Saint Mary's, straddling the Liffey, was established in 1707 and a chapel dedicated to St Mary was opened in 1729. In 1797 Archbishop Troy successfully petitioned the Holy See to allow him take St Mary's as his *mensal* parish. He thereupon set about raising funds to build a 'dignified, spacious church' in a central location in the parish.

The site chosen was a building on Marlborough Street, opposite Tyrone House. Formerly the town house of the Earl of Annesley, it was purchased for £5,100 and a deposit was paid in 1803. However, it was not until 1814 that designs were publicly invited for the new church. A design of uncertain authorship, marked only with the letter 'P', for a church in the form of a Grecian Doric temple, was chosen as the winner. The only substantial alteration to the design was the erection of a dome.

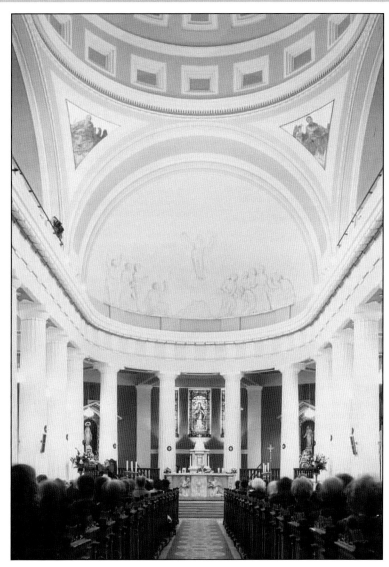

The foundation stone was laid by Archbishop Troy in 1815. On the feast of St Laurence O'Toole in 1825, Archbishop Murray celebrated High Mass, to mark the dedication of the church to the 'Conception of the Virgin Mary', to a packed congregation, which included Daniel O'Connell. After the dedication, the interior embellishment of the church continued. Highlights included the alto relief representation of the Ascension by John Smyth; the high altar carved by Peter Turnerelli, and the marble statues of Archbishops Murray and Cullen by Thomas Farrell. Stained-glass windows, depicting Our Lady flanked by St Laurence O'Toole and St Kevin, were installed behind the sanctuary in 1886. The high point of liturgical embellishment was the generous benefaction by Edward Martyn, who endowed the Palestrina choir for male voices in 1902.

**Emeritus Archbishop**
**His Eminence Desmond Cardinal Connell**
born in Dublin 24 March 1926; ordained priest 19 May 1951; ordained Archbishop of Dublin 6 March 1988; created Cardinal 21 February 2001
*Address:* Archbishop's House, Drumcondra, Dublin 9
Tel 01-8373732 Fax 01-8369796

**Most Rev Eamonn Walsh DD, VG**
Titular Bishop of Elmham;
Auxiliary Bishop of Dublin; ordained Bishop 22 April 1990
*Residence:* Naomh Brid, Blessington Road, Tallaght, Dublin 24
Tel/Fax 01-4598032

**Most Rev Raymond Field DD, VG**
Titular Bishop of Ard Mor;
Auxiliary Bishop of Dublin; ordained Bishop 21 September 1997
*Residence:* 3 Castleknock Road, Blanchardstown, Dublin 15
Tel/Fax 01-8209191

**Most Rev Dermot O'Mahony DD**
Titular Bishop of Tiava; former Auxiliary Bishop of Dublin; ordained Bishop 13 April 1975
*Residence:* 19 Longlands, Swords, Co Dublin
Tel 01-8401596 Fax 01-8403950

**Most Rev Fiachra Ó Ceallaigh DD**
Titular Bishop of Tre Taverne; former Auxiliary Bishop of Dublin; ordained Bishop 17 September 1994
*Residence:* 19 St Anthony's Road, Rialto, Dublin 8
Tel 01-4537495 Fax 01-4544966

**Episcopal Vicar with responsibility for the deaneries of Howth, Fingal South East and Fingal South West**
Rt Rev Mgr John Fitzpatrick PP
3 Glencarraig, Church Road, Sutton, Co Dublin
Tel 01-8323147

**Episcopal Vicar with responsibility for the deaneries of Bray, Donnybrook, Dun Laoghaire and Wicklow**
Rt Rev Mgr Enda Lloyd
Cluain Mhuire, Killarney Road, Bray, Co Wicklow

**Episcopal Vicar with responsibility for the deaneries of Cullenswood, North City Centre and South City Centre**
Rt Rev Mgr Dermot Clarke PP
Parochial House, 34 Aughrim Street, Dublin 7
Tel 01-8386571

**Vicar General**
Rt Rev Mgr Lorcan O'Brien VG
Archbishop's House, Drumcondra, Dublin 9
Tel 01-8373732

**Vicar for Priests**
Rev John Hughes (OSA)
Archbishop's House, Dublin 9
Tel 01-8379253

**Vicar for Evangelisation and Ecumenism**
Very Rev Kieran McDermott
Diocesan Offices, Archbishop's House, Dublin 9
Tel 01-8373732

## CHAPTER

*Dean:* Most Rev Dermot O'Mahony DD
*Precentor:* Most Rev Eamon O. Walsh VG
*Chancellor:* Rt Rev Mgr James Ardle Canon MacMahon
*Treasurer:* Rt Rev Mgr Owen Canon Sweeney
*Archdeacon of Dublin*
Ven Archdeacon Macarten Brady PE
*Archdeacon of Glendalough:*
Ven Archdeacon Kevin Lyon CC
*Prebendaries*
*Cullen:* Very Rev John Canon Battelle PE
14 Pine Valley, Grange Road, Dublin 16
*Kilmactalway:* Vacant
*Swords:* Vacant
*Yago:* Very Rev James Canon Loughran PE
Maryfield Nursing Home, Chalepizod, Dublin 20
*St Audoen's*
Very Rev Bernard Canon Brady
61 Glasnevin Hill, Dublin 9
*Clonmethan*
Very Rev Walter Canon Harris PE
151 Clonsilla Road, Blanchardstown, Dublin 15
*Wicklow*
Very Rev Erill D. Canon O'Connor
14 Clare Road, Drumcondra, Dublin 9
*Timothan:* Very Rev Patrick Canon Fagan PE
The Presbytery, Ballyboughal, Co Dublin
*Malahidert*
Very Rev Raymond T. Canon Molony
Presbytery No. 2, Thormanby Road, Howth, Co Dublin
*Castleknock:* Vacant
*Tipper:* Rev John Canon Piert PC
The Presbytery, Johnstown, Arklow, Co Wicklow
*Tassagard*
Very Rev Maurice Canon O'Moore PE
6 Richmond Avenue, Monkstown, Co Dublin
*Dunlavin:* Rev Patrick Canon Dowling
Holy Family Residence, Roebuck Road, Dundrum, Dublin 14
*Maynooth:* Vacant
*Howth:* Very Rev John Canon Flaherty, Moderator, Parochial House, Sperrin Road, Drimnagh, Dublin 12
*Rathmichael*
Very Rev Brendan Canon Carbery
Elmhurst, Hampstead Avenue, Glasnevin, Dublin 11
*Monmahenock*
Rt Rev Mgr Andrew P. Canon Boland PE
13 Griffith Avenue, Dublin 9
*Stagonilly:* Vacant
*Tipperkevin, 1a pars*
Very Rev John Canon Fitzgibbon PE
The Presbytery, Chapel Road, Lusk, Co Dublin
*Tipperkevin, 2a pars*
Very Rev James A. Canon Randles PE
Sacred Heart Residence, Sybil Hill Road, Killester, Dublin 5
*Donaghmore, 1a pars*
Very Rev John Canon MacMahon PE
Holy Family Residence, Roebuck Road, Dundrum, Dublin 14
*Donaghmore, 2a pars*
Very Rev Michael D. Canon Supple
Holy Family Residence, Roebuck Road, Dublin 14

**Deaneries and Vicars Forane**
*Bray*
Very Rev Laurence Behan *(Moderator)* VF
Parochial House, St Fergal's, Killarney Road, Bray, Co Wicklow
Tel 01-2768191
*Dun Laoghaire*
Rt Rev Mgr Dan O'Connor PP, VF
St Michael's Parochial House, 4 Eblana Avenue, Dun Laoghaire, Co Dublin
Tel 01-2801505
*Wicklow:* Very Rev Kevin Rowan Adm, VF
Parochial House, Ashford, Co Wicklow
Tel 0404-40540
*Donnybrook:* Very Rev Martin Clarke PP, VF
Parochial House, Stillorgan Road, Dublin 4
Tel 01-2838311
*South City Centre*
Very Rev John Gilligan Adm, VF
47 Westland Row, Dublin 2
Tel 01-6765517
*North City Centre*
Very Rev Donal Neary (SJ) PP, VF
Presbytery, Upper Gardiner Street, Dublin 1
Tel 01-8363411
*Cullenswood*
Very Rev John Flaherty *(Moderator)*
Parochial House, Sperrin Road, Dublin 12
Tel 01-4556103
*South Dublin:* Very Rev Martin Noone, Moderator & Co-PP, VF
St Mary's Presbytery, Willbrook Road, D 14
Tel 01-4954554
*Tallaght:* Very Rev David Brough PP
85 Tymon Crescent, Old Bawn, Dublin 24
Tel 01-4627080
*Blessington*
Very Rev Gerard Tanham PP, VF
Parochial House, 1 Stanhope Place, Athy, Co Kildare
Tel 059-8631781
*Fingal North:* Very Rev Eugene Taaffe PP, VF
29 Westbrook Rise, Balbriggan, Co Dublin
Tel 01-6903391
*Finglas*
Very Rev Liam McClarey (SCA) PP, VF
Parochial House, Corduff, Blanchardstown, Dublin 15
Tel 01-8213596
*Maynooth:* Rev John Hassett CC, VF
127 Castlegate Way, Adamstown, Lucan, Co Dublin
Tel 01-6812088
*Fingal South-East*
Very Rev Peter Finnerty PP, VF
2 Maypark, Malahide Road, Dublin 5
Tel 01-8313722
*Fingal South-West*
Very Rev Pat Carroll Co-PP, VF
124 New Cabra Road, Dublin 7
Tel 01-8385244
*Howth:* Very Rev Eoin McCrystal PP, VF
2 Grangemore Grove, Donaghmede, Dublin 5
Tel 01-8474652

**College of Consultors**
Most Rev Eamonn Walsh DD, VG
Most Rev Raymond Field DD, VG
Rt Rev Mgr Lorcan O'Brien VG
Rt Rev Mgr John Fitzpatrick, EV
Rt Rev Mgr Enda Lloyd EV
Very Rev Mgr Dermot A. Clarke PP, EV
Rev Gareth Byrne, Council of Priests
Very Rev John Hughes (OSA) EV for Priests
Very Rev Kieran McDermott EV for Evangelisation and Ecumenism
Very Rev Donal Neary (SJ) PP

## ADMINISTRATION

**Moderator of the Curia**
Rt Rev Mgr Lorcan O'Brien VG
Office of the Moderator,
Holy Cross College, Clonliffe, Dublin 3
Tel 01-8379347

**Chancellor**
Rt Rev Mgr John Dolan LCL
The Chancellery,
Archbishop's House, Dublin 9
Tel 01-8379253 Fax 8571650

**Ecclesiastical Censor**
Rt Rev Mgr John Dolan
The Chancellery, Archbishop's House,
Dublin 9
Tel 01-8379253

**Diocesan Archivist**
Ms Noelle Dowling
Diocesan Offices, Archbishop's House,
Dublin 9
Tel 01-8379253

**Vicar for Religious**
Sr Elizabeth Cotter
Archbishop's House, Dublin 9
Tel 01-8379253

**Financial Administrator**
Mr Kieran O'Farrell
Finance Secretariat, Archbishop's House,
Drumcondra, Dublin 9
Tel 01-8379253 Fax 01-8368393

**Master of Ceremonies to the Archbishop**
Rev Damian McNeice
Diocesan Liturgical Resource Centre,
Holy Cross College, Clonliffe, Dublin 3
Tel 01-8379253 Ext 238

**Archbishop's Secretary**
Very Rev Mgr Paul Callan
Archbishop's House, Drumcondra, Dublin 9
Tel 01-8373732 Fax 01-8369796

***Vicar for Evangelisation and Ecumenism***
Very Rev Kieran McDermott
Diocesan Offices,
Archbishop's House, Dublin 9
Tel 01-8373732
***Child Protection Service***
Tel 01-8360314 Fax 01-8842599
Email cps@dublindiocese.ie
Website www.cps.dublindiocese.ie
*Director:* Mr Andrew Fagan
Tel 01-8842590
*Victim Support Person*
Mr Joseph McDonagh
Tel 01-8842591
*Priest Delegate:* Rev Desmond Doyle
***Child Protection Training Co-ordinator***
Rev Paddy Boyle
Email p.boyle@dublindiocese.ie
***Communications Office***
*Director:* Ms Annette O'Donnell
Tel 01-8360723 Fax 01-8360793
Email annetteodonell@dublindiocese.ie
Website www.dublindiocese.ie

***Diocesan Office for Public Affairs***
*Director:* Vacant
***Education***
*Director:* Ms Anne McDonagh
Tel 01-8379253 Fax 01-8368393
Email amcdonagh@dubcated.org
*Senior Education Specialists*
Ms Catherine Hennessy
Email chennessy@abhouse.org
Mr Bill Lowe
Email blowe@dubcated.org
***Finance***
Mr Kieran O'Farrell
Email k.ofarrell@abfinance.org
Mr Seamus Leahy
Email sleahy@abfinance.org
Ms Keava Lyons
Email klyons@abfinance.org
Ms Ide Finnegan ACMA
Email i.finnegan@abfinance.org
Mr James Frain
Email james.frain@abfinance.org
***Diocesan Liturgical Resource Centre***
*Director:* Rev Pat O'Donoghue
Email pod@dublindiocese.ie
***50th International Eucharistic Congress***
*President:* Most Rev Diarmuid Martin
*Secretary General:* Rev Kevin Doran
*General Manager:* Ms Anne Griffin
Sandymount Building, RDS,
Simmonscourt Road, Dublin 4
Tel 01-2349900 (English language)
01-2349900 (Gaeilge, Francais, Italiano)
Email info@iec2012.ie

## DIOCESAN COMMITTEES

**Clerical Fund Society**
Diocesan Offices, Archbishop's House,
Dublin 9
Tel 01-8379253
*President:* The Archbishop of Dublin
*Vice-Presidents:* The Vicars General

**Standing Committee**
*Chairman:* Most Rev Eamonn Walsh DD
*Secretary:* Mr Kieran O'Farrell

**Commission on Parish Boundaries**
c/o Archbishop's House,
Drumcondra, Dublin 9
Tel 01-8379253
*Chairman:* Mr Willie Soffe
*Secretary:* Ms Anne Donnellan

**Common Fund Executive Committee**
Diocesan Offices,
Archbishop's House, Dublin 9
Tel 01-8379253
*Chairman:* Very Rev Anthony Reilly
*Secretary:* Mr Kieran O'Farrell

**Finance Committee**
Diocesan Offices,
Archbishop's House, Dublin 9
Tel 01-8379253
*Chairman:* Mr Leo O'Donnell
*Joint Secretaries:*
Ms Ide Finnegan
Mr Kieran O'Farrell

## CATECHETICS EDUCATION

**Diocesan Advisers for Religious Education in Primary Schools**
Education Secretariat,
Archbishop's House, Drumcondra, Dublin 9
Tel 01-8379253 Fax 01-8368393
Ms Cathy Burke, Ms Fiona Crotty, Ms
Sonya Murray, Sr Anne Neylon
*All at the Education Secretariat*

**Diocesan Advisors for Religious Education in Post Primary Schools**
Mr Gary Abrahamian

## LITURGY

**Liturgy Commission**
Appointments pending

**Commission for Sacred Music**
Appointments pending

**Commission for Sacred Art and Architecture**
Appointments pending

**Historical Churches Advisory Commission**
Appointments pending

## PASTORAL

**Accord**
Ms Barbara Gilroy (Dublin Director)
35 Harcourt Street, Dublin 2
Tel 01-4780866 Fax 01-4750462
Email admin@dublin.accord.ie

**Catholic Guides of Ireland**
*Diocesan Chaplain:* Vacant

**CROSSCARE**
**Catholic Social Service Conference**
*Director:* Mr Conor Hickey
Holy Cross College, Clonliffe, Dublin 3
Tel 01-8360011/5

**Catholic Men & Women's Society (formerly Catholic Young Men's Society of Ireland)**
2A Irishtown Road, Dublin 4
*Contacts:* Patrick Carroll Tel 01-4960393
Brendan Moran Tel 01-6689905
*Secretry:* Betty Barry
Tel 01-6602650 (h)/6684507 (w)

**Catholic Youth Care**
*Director:* Rev Jim Caffrey
20/23 Arran Quay, Dublin 7
Tel 01-8725055 Fax 01-8725010

**Chaplaincy for Deaf People**
*Chaplain:* Rev Gerard Tyrrell
40 Lower Drumcondra Road, Dublin 9
Tel 01-8305744 Fax 01-8600284
Email office@ncdp.ie
Website www.ncdp.ie

**Committee for the Continuing Formation of Priests**
c/o Archbishop's House, Dublin 9
Tel 01-8375107
Email john@abhouse.org

**Council of Priests**
*President:* Most Rev Diarmuid Martin DD
*Chairman:* Very Rev Aquinas Duffy PP
*Secretary:* Vacant

**CÚNAMH**
30 South Anne Street, Dublin 2
Tel 01-6710598

**Dublin Roman Catholic Diocesan Hospital Chaplains Conference**
*Chairman of Committee:* Rev Gerard Byrne
Chaplain, Blackrock Clinic
Tel 01-2832222

**Emigrants**
*Contact:* Yvonne Fleming
1A Cathedral Street, Dublin 1
Tel 01-8732844/8726171 Fax 01-8727003
Email info@emigrantadvice.ie
Website www.emigrantadvice.ie

**Ecumenism**
*Chairman and Secretary:*
Rev Brendan Leahy
St Patrick's College, Maynooth, Co Kildare

**Knock Diocesan Pilgrimage**
*Director:* Very Rev David Lumsden PP
83 Tonlegee Drive, Edenmore, Dublin 5
Tel 01-8480917

**Legion of Mary**
*Diocesan Chaplain:* Vacant

**Lourdes Diocesan Pilgrimage**
*Director:* Rev John Gilligan
Lourdes Pilgrimage Office,
Holy Cross College, Clonliffe, Dublin 3
Tel 01-8376820

**Marriage Tribunal**
(See Marriage Tribunals section)

**Permanent Diaconate**
*Diocesan Director*
Rev Kevin Doran
Holy Cross Docesan Centre,
Clonliffe Road, Dublin 3
Tel 01-8087531

**Pontifical Mission Societies**
*Diocesan Director*
Very Rev Patrick Carroll PP
124 New Cabra Road, Dublin 7
Tel 01-8385244

**Social Service Centre**
Crosscare Housing and Welfare
Tel 01-8726775 Fax 01-8727003
Crosscare Migrant Project
Tel 01-8732844 Fax 01-8727003
1 Cathedral Street, Dublin 1

**Travellers**
*Ministry to the Travelling People (Dublin Diocese):* Very Rev Derek Farrell PP
*Office:* St Laurence House,
6 New Cabra Road, Phibsboro, Dublin 7
Tel 01-8388874/087-2573857 Fax 01-8388901
Email partravs@iol.ie

**Vocations**
*Co-ordinator:* Rev Eamonn Bourke
Holy Cross College, Clonliffe, Dublin 3
Tel 01-8379253

## PARISHES

*Mensal parishes are listed first. Other parishes follow alphabetically. Church titulars are in italics.*

**PRO-CATHEDRAL**
*St Mary's (Immaculate Conception) Marlborough Street, Dublin 1*
Very Rev Damian F. O'Reilly Adm
Rev Patrick O'Donoghue CC
Rev Denis Laverty PC
*Parish Sister:* Sr Anne Killeen (DC)
*Supply:* Charbel Al Daccache
Pro-Cathedral House,
83 Marlborough Street, Dublin 1
Tel 01-8745441 Fax 01-8742406
Email procath@dublindiocese.ie
Website www.procathedral.ie
*Supply:* Rev Francis Walsh
The Arlington Hotel, 23-25 Bachelors Walk, O'Connell Bridge, Dublin 1

**WESTLAND ROW**
*St Andrew's, Westland Row, Dublin 2*
Very Rev John Gilligan Adm, VF
Tel 01-7005268(w)/8368746(h)
Email john.gilligan@dcu.ie
Rev Anthony Asare PC
47 Westland Row, Dublin 2
Tel 085-2778177
Rev Egidijus Arnasius
48 Westland Road
Tel 01-6761030/087-7477554
Email arnasius@gmail.com
*Parish Office:* Tel 01-6761270 Fax 01-6763544
Email westlandrow@dublindiocese.ie
Website www.saintandrewsparish.ie

**CITY QUAY**
*Immaculate Heart of Mary, Dublin 2*
Very Rev Paul St John (SVD) Adm
Rev John Owen (SVD) CC
The Presbytery, City Quay, Dublin 2
*Parish Office:* Tel 01-6773073
Website cityquay@dublindiocese.ie

**SEAN MCDERMOTT STREET**
*Our Lady of Lourdes, Sean McDermott Street, Dublin 1*
Very Rev Timothy Wrenn (SDB) Adm
Tel 01-8363358
Rev Hugh O'Donnell (SDB) CC
*Supply:* Rev Peter Joe Previnth
24 Killarney Street, Dublin 1
*Parish Office:* Tel 01-8551259/086-8382631
Email seanmcdermott@dublindiocese.ie

**ARDLEA**
*St John Vianney, Ardlea Road, Artane, Dublin 5*
Very Rev Robert Mann (SCJ), (*Moderator*)
Rev David Marsden (SCJ)
Rev Liam Rooney (SCJ)
Rev Marian Szalwa (SCJ)
Parochial House, St John Vianney, Ardlea Road, Dublin 5
Tel 01-8474173
*Parish Sister:* Sr Nellie Barron (SJG)
*Parish Office:* Tel 01-8474123
Email st.jvianney@yahoo.ie

**ARKLOW**
*(Grouped with the parish of Castletown) SS Mary and Peter, Arklow, Co Wicklow*
*Chapel of Ease: St David's, Johnstown, Co Wicklow*
Very Rev Martin Cosgrove PP
Parochial House, Arklow, Co Wicklow
Tel/Fax 0402-32294
Email mfc53@indigo.ie
Rev Michael Murtagh CC
2 St Mary's Terrace, Arklow, Co Wicklow
Tel 0402-41505
Very Rev John Canon Piert PC
The Presbytery, Johnstown, Arklow, Co Wicklow
Tel 0402-31112
Rev Binoy Mathew Kombanathottathil (SVD) CC
Presbytery No. 2, St Mary's Terrace, Arklow, Co Wicklow
*Parish Office:* Tel/Fax 0402-31716
Email parking5@eircom.net
www.arklowparishcouncil.homestead.com

**ARTANE**
*Our Lady of Mercy, Brookwood Grove, Dublin 5*
Very Rev Peter O'Connor PP
12 Brookwood Grove, Artane, Dublin 5
Tel 01-8312390
Rev Peter Healy CC
16 Brookwood Grove, Artane, Dublin 5
Tel 01-8377337
*Parish Office:* Tel 01-8314297 Fax 01-8314054
Email ourladyofmercy.church@gmail.com

**ASHFORD**
*Church of the Most Holy Rosary, Co Wicklow*
Rev Kevin Rowan Adm
The Parochial House, Ashford, Co Wicklow
Tel/Fax 0404-40540
Email revkev@eircom.net

**ATHY**
*St Michael's, Co Kildare*
Very Rev Gerard Tanham PP
Parochial House, 1 Stanhope Place, Athy, Co Kildare
Tel 059-8631781/087-2311947
Email gerardtanham@eircom.net
Rev Paul O'Driscoll CC
3 Stanhope Place, Athy
Tel 0402-32196
Email paul.odriscoll@oceanfree.net
Very Rev Philip Dennehy PE
4 Stanhope Place, Athy
Tel 059-8631696
Email pdenn@eircom.net
Aine Egan PPW
5 Abbey Court, Properous Road, Clane, Co Kildare
*Parish Office*: Tel 059-8638391
Email athyparishrc@eircom.net
Website www.stmichaelsathy.net

**AUGHRIM**
*The Most Sacred Heart, Co Wicklow*
Very Rev Edward Barry Adm
The Presbytery, Most Holy Rosary, Ashford, Co Wicklow
Tel 0404-40224

**AUGHRIM STREET**
*The Holy Family, Dublin 7*
Very Rev Mgr Dermot Clarke PP
Parochial House,
34 Aughrim Street, Dublin 7
Tel 01-8386571
Rev Martin Ryan (CSsR) CC
Presbytery No 3, Most Sacred Heart Parish,
St Joseph's Road, Dublin 7
Rev Michael Simpson CC
Presbytery No. 2, Holy Family Parish,
St Joseph's Road, Dublin 7
Tel 01-8339177
Mairin Keegan PPW
4 College Green, Maynooth, Co Kildare

**AVOCA**
*SS Mary and Patrick, Co Wicklow*
Very Rev Eamonn Crosson PP
Parochial House, Avoca, Co Wicklow
Tel 0402-35156
Email eamonncrosson@eircom.net
Rev Thomas Coughlan (*Assistant Priest*) PC
The Presbytery, Avoca, Co Wicklow
Tel 059-8624109
*Parish Offices:* Avoca Tel 0402-35156
Templerainey Tel 0402-31943
Email Avoca avpar@eircom.net
Templerainey stjoseph@eircom.net

**AYRFIELD**
*St Paul's, Dublin 13*
Very Rev Tom Colreavy PP
28 Glentworth Park,
Ard-na-Gréine, Dublin 13
Tel/Fax 01-8484836
Email tomcolreavy@eircom.net
Rev Patrick Gleeson CC
8 Slademore Close, Ard-na-Gréine,
Dublin 13
Tel 01-6081260(w)/6767316(h)
*Parish Office*: Tel 01-8160984
Email parishofficeayrfield@eircom.net
Website www.stpaulsparishayrfield.com

**BALALLY**
*Church of the Ascension of The Lord, Dublin 16*
Very Rev Dermot A. Lane DD, PP
162 Sandyford Road, Dublin 16
Tel 01-2956165
Email dalane@eircom.net
Rev Paddy Moran CC
1 Cedar Road, Wedgewood Estate,
Balally Dublin 16
Tel 01-8380170
Email padmoran@gmail.com
*Supply:* Rev Santosh Kumar (SAC)
Pallottine Fathers, Sandyford Road,
Dublin 16
*Parish Office*: Tel 01-2954296
Email parishofbalally@eircom.net
Website www.balallyparish.ie

**BALBRIGGAN**
*SS Peter and Paul, Balbriggan, Co Dublin*
Very Rev Eugene Taaffe PP
c/o The Presbytery Parish of SS Peter &
Paul, Dublin Road, Balbriggan, Co Dublin
Tel 01-8202544
Rev Padraig O'Sullivan CC
Apt 1 The Presbytery, Balbriggan, Co Dublin
Tel 01-8491250
Rev Aloysius Zuribo
16 Ashfield Drive, Balbriggan, Co Dublin
Tel 01-8020602
*Parish Pastoral Worker*: Niamh Morris
Tel 085-9365767
*Parish Office:* Tel 01-8412116 Fax 01-6904834
Email balbrigganparishoffice@gmail.com

**BALCURRIS**
*St Joseph's, Ballymun*
Rev Val Kyne (SSC) PP
Tel 01-8423865
Very Rev John Chute (SSC) CC
Rev Gerry French (SSC)
St Joseph's, Balcurris, Ballymun, Dublin 11
Tel 01-8423865
*Parish Office:* Tel 01-8423865

**BALDOYLE**
*SS Peter and Paul, Dublin 13*
Very Rev Francis Desmond Dooley PP
The Presbytery, Baldoyle, Dublin 13
Tel 01-8322060
Rev Ronald Dunne CC
91 Grange Road, Baldoyle, Dublin 13
Tel 01-8323046
*Parish Office:* Tel 01-8324313
Email info@baldoyleparish.ie
Website www.baldoyleparish.ie

**BALLINTEER**
*Ballinteer parish is now under the Team Ministry of Dundrum/Ballinteer/ Meadowbrook*
*St John the Evangelist, Ballinteer Avenue, Dublin 16*
Very Rev Richard M. Behan, VF
*(Moderator)*
Presbytery No 1, Ballinteer Avenue,
Dublin 16
Tel 01-4944448
Email rmfb@eircom.net
Very Rev Patrick Battelle PE
14 Pine Valley, Grange Road,
Rathfarnham, Dublin 16
Tel 01-4935962
Gerald Byaruhanga *(Team Assistant)*
Presbytery No 2, Ballinteer Avenue,
Ballinteer, Dublin 16
*Parish Office*: Tel 01-4994203
Email
parishoffice@ballinteer.dublindiocese.ie
Website www.ballinteer.dublindiocese.ie

**BALLYBODEN**
*Our Lady of Good Counsel, Dublin 16*
Very Rev Pádraig Daly (OSA) PP
Rev John Lyng (OSA) CC
Tel 01-4543356
Rev Michael Brennock (OSA) CC
St Augustine's, Taylors Lane,
Ballyboden, Dublin 16
*Parish Office:* Tel 01-4944966
Website www.ballybodenparish.com

**BALLYBRACK-KILLINEY**
*SS Alphonsus and Columba, Co Dublin*
Very Rev Alex Conlan PP
Parochial House, Ballybrack, Co Dublin
Tel 01-2826404
Email alexconlan_ie@yahoo.com
Rev James Tormey CC
130 Churchview Road, Ballybrack, Co Dublin
Tel 01-2851919
*Parish Offices*: St Alphonsus & Columba
Tel 01-2820788
St Stephens Tel 01-2854512
Church of the Apostles Tel 01-2024804
Website www.ballybrack-killiney-parish.org

**BALLYFERMOT**
*Our Lady of the Assumption, Dublin 10*
Rev Richard Delahunty (CSsR) PP &
Coordinator
Rev Cornelius Kenneally (CSsR) CC
Rev Winfried Pauly (CSsR) CC
197 Kylemore Road, Ballyfermot, Dublin 10
*Parish Office:* Tel 01-6264691

**BALLYFERMOT UPPER**
*St Matthew, Blackditch Road, Dublin 10*
Very Rev Seamus Ryan PP
No 1 Presbytery, Blackditch Road, Dublin 10
Tel 01-6265695 Fax 01-6230654
Email seamusoriain09@gmail.com
Rev Joseph Ryan CC
11 Palmerstown Court, Dublin 20
Tel 01-6268772
Email josephry@indigo.ie
*Parish Office:* Tel 01-6265695 Fax 01-6230654
Email seamusoriain09@gmail.com
Website www.stmatthewsballyfermot.com

**BALLYGALL**
*Our Mother of Divine Grace, Ballygall Road East, Dublin 11*
Very Rev Brendan Quinlan PP
41 Cremore Heights, St Canice's Road,
Glasnevin, Dublin 11
Tel 01-8573776
Email quinlanbt@gmail.com
Rev Harry Gaynor CC
112 Ballygall Road East, Glasnevin, Dublin 11
Email ringo11@eircom.net
*Parish Office*: Tel 01-8369291
Email omdgballygallchurch@eircom.net
Website www.ballygallparish.ie

**BALLYMORE EUSTACE**
*Immaculate Conception, Naas, Co Kildare*
Rt Rev Mgr John Wilson Adm
Parochial House, Ballymore Eustace,
Naas, Co Kildare
Email jacw@gofree.indigo.ie
Rev James Prendiville CC
The Presbytery, Hollywood (via Naas),
Co Wicklow
Tel 045-864206
*Parish Office*: Tel 045-864114
Email hwparishoffice@gmail.com

**BALLYMUN**
*Church of the Virgin Mary, Ballymun, Dublin 9*
Rev Gerard Corcoran CC *(Moderator)*
The Presbytery, Shangan Road, Ballymun,
Dublin 9
Tel 01-8421551/8421451
Email moelitreacha@eircom.net
Rev Expedit Gnoumou PC
Presbytery, Silloge Road, Ballymun,
Dublin 11
*Parish Office*: 01-8421551/087-6606870
Website moelitreacha@eircom.net

**BALLYMUN ROAD**
*Our Lady of Victories, Ballymun Road, Dublin 9*
Very Rev Colm Kenny Adm
137 Ballymun Road, Dublin 11
Tel 01-8341051
Rev Fintan Gavin PC
97 Ballymun Road, Dublin 9
Tel 01-6761322
Rev Patrick Sweeney PC
13 Home Farm Road, Drumcondra, Dublin 9
Tel 01-6264639
*Parish Office*: Tel 01-8420346
Email ourladyofvictoriesparish@eircom.net

**BALLYROAN**
*Ballyroan Parish is now under the Team Ministry of Rathfarnham/Churchtown/Ballyroan*
*Church of the Holy Spirit, Marian Road, Dublin 14*
Very Rev Brendan Madden PP
67 Anne Devlin Park, Ballyroan, Dublin 14
Tel 01-4037536
*Parish Office*: Tel 01-4947303
Email ballyroanparish@gmail.com
Website www.ballyroanparish.ie

**BAWNOGUE**
*Church of the Transfiguration, Bawnogue, Clondalkin, Dublin 22*
Very Rev Joseph Beere (CSSp) PP
Tel 01-4592273/087-6952153
Email transfig2000@eircom.net
Rev Marino Nguekam (CSSp) CC
Email rnguekam@yahoo.fr
Presbytery, Bawnogue, Clondalkin, Dublin 22

**BAYSIDE**
*Church of the Resurrection, Bayside, Dublin 13*
Very Rev Paul Ward PP
Parochial House, Bayside Square North, Sutton, Dublin 13
Tel 01-8323150
Email wardp@iol.ie
Rev Joe Kelly CC
5 Bayside Square East, Sutton, Dublin 13
Tel 01-8322305
Email gradyjoe1@eircom.net
Rev Christopher Sheridan CC
7 Bayside Square East, Sutton, Dublin 13
Tel 01-8730700(w)/8745441(h)
*Parish Office*: Tel 01-8323083
Email baysidercchurch@eircom.net
Website www.baysideparish.ie

**BEAUMONT**
*(Grouped with the parishes of Larkhill, Whitehall, Santry & Kilmore Road West)*
*Church of Nativity of Our Lord, Dublin 5*
Very Rev Gerard Deegan Adm
Tel 01-8473209
Rev Dan An Nguyen CC
Presbytery, Montrose Park, Beaumont, Dublin 5
*Parish Office:* Tel 086-8134445 Fax 01-8473209

**BEECHWOOD AVENUE**
*Church of the Holy Name, Dublin 6*
Rev Bernard Kennedy MA, MSc, Adm
67 Edenvale Road, Dublin 6
Tel 01-4972165
Email b.kennedy@esatclear.ie
Rev Paul Freeney PE
Parochial House, 43 Beechwood Avenue Upper, Ranelagh, Dublin 6
Tel 01-4972687
*Supply:* Inimabasi Macjoe Akpan
St Patrick's, Leeson Park, Dubin 6
*Parish Office:* Tel 01-4967449
Email info@beechwoodparish.com
Website info@beechwoodparish.com

**BERKELEY ROAD**
*St Joseph's, Dublin 7*
Very Rev Christopher Clarke (OCD) PP
Email chrisfpclarke@hotmail.com
Rev Patrick Keenan (OCD) CC
Tel 01-8306356/8306336
Rev David Donnellan (OCD) CC
Rev Patrick Beecher (OCD) CC
The Presbytery, Berkeley Road, Dublin 7
*Parish Office*: Tel 01-8302071

**BLACKROCK**
*St John the Baptist, Blackrock, Co Dublin*
Very Rev Edward Conway PC
1 Maretimo Gardens West, Blackrock, Co Dublin
Tel 01-2882248
Email eddieconway@ireland.com
Rev John Delany Adm
24 Barclay Court, Blackrock, Co Dublin
Tel 01-8375440
*Parish Office*: Tel 01-2882104
Email saintjohnthebaptist@eircom.net

**BLAKESTOWN**
*Blakestown Parish is now under the Team Ministry of Blakestown/Hartstown/Huntstown/Mountview*
*St Mary of the Servants, Dublin 15*
Very Rev Liam Ó Cuív Co-PP
The Presbytery Blakestown, Clonsilla, Dublin 15
Tel 01-8210874
Email liamocuiv@yahoo.com
*Parish Office:* Tel 01-8210874 Fax 01-8210650
Email blakestownparish@dublindiocese.ie

**BLANCHARDSTOWN**
*St Brigid's*
Very Rev John Jones PP
Parochial House, Blanchardstown, Dublin 15
Tel 01-8213660
Email jj36297@hotmail.com
Rev John Casey (CSsR), CC
28 Broadway Road, Blanchardstown, Dublin 15
Tel 01-8213716
Email johnffcasey@eircom.net
Rev Patrick Guckian CC
44 Woodview Grove, Blanchardstown, Dublin 15
Tel 01-8341894
Kevin Mullaly PPW
8 Finglaswood Road, Finglas West, Dublin 11
*Chaplain:* Alan Hilliard
19 Springlawn Close, Blanchardstown, Dublin 15
Tel 01-5053055
*Parish Office*: Tel 01-8238354

**BLESSINGTON**
*(Grouped with the parish of Valleymount)*
*Church of Our Lady*
Very Rev Timothy Murphy PP
The Presbytery, Main Street, Blessington, Co Wicklow
Tel 045-865442
Email office@blessington.info
*Our Lady of Mercy, Crosschapel*
Rev Kevin Lyon CC
Parochial House, Crosschapel, Blessington, Co Wicklow
Tel 045-865215
Email lyonk@indigo.ie
*St Brigid's Church, Manor Kilbride*
Rev Paraic McDermott (CSSp) CC
The Presbytery, Manor Kilbride, Blessington, Co Wicklow
Tel 01-4582154
Rev Edward Downes CC
Parochial House, St Joseph's Parish Cross, Valleymount, Co Wicklow
Tel 01-2826895
*Parish Office*: Tel/Fax 045-865327
Email office@blessington.info
Website www.blessington.info

**BLUEBELL**
*Bluebell Parish is now under the Team Ministry of Inchicore (Mary Immaculate & St Michael's) & Bluebell*
*Our Lady of the Wayside, Dublin 12*
Very Rev Tomas Koscinski (OMI) Co-PP
Rev R. Warren (OMI)
Oblate Fathers House of Retreat, Inchicore, Dublin 8
Tel 01-4541117
*Parish Office*: Tel 01-4501040
Website www.oblateparishesindublin.ie

**BOHERNABREENA**
*St Anne's, Dublin 24*
Very Rev David Brough PP, VF
85 Tymon Crescent, Oldbawn, Dublin 24
Tel/Fax 01-7168543(w)/2605582(h)
Email david.brough@ucd.ie
*Parish Office*: Tel 01-4510986
Email bohernabreenaparish@eircom.net

**BONNYBROOK**
*St Joseph's, Bonnybrook, Dublin 17*
Very Rev Kevin Moore, *(Moderator)*
122 Greencastle Road, Dubin 17
Tel 01-8487657
Rev Frank Duggan CC
Parochial House No 2, Bonnybrook, Dublin 17
Tel 01-8485194
*Parish Office*: Tel 01-8485262

**BOOTERSTOWN**
*Church of the Assumption*
Rt Rev Mgr Seamus Conway PP
Parochial House, Booterstown, Co Dublin
Tel 01-2882889
*Parish Office*: Tel/Fax 01-2831593
Email info@booterstownparish.ie
Website www.booterstownparish.ie

**BRACKENSTOWN**
*St Cronan's*
Very Rev Barry Murphy Adm
Parochial House, Brackenstown Road, Swords, Co Dublin
Tel 01-8020602
Rev Tony Pazhayakalam (CST) PC
Parochial House, Brackenstown Road, Swords, Co Dublin
*Parish Office*: Tel 01-8401188
Email cronanc@gofree.indigo.ie
Website www.brackenstown.dublindiocese.ie

**BRAY (BALLYWALTRIM)**
*St Fergal's, Bray, Co Wicklow*
Rev Laurence Behan *(Moderator)*
Tel 01-2882162
Rev Hugh O'Donnell (OFM) *(Assistant)*
St Fergal's, Killarney Road, Bray, Co Wicklow
*Parish Office:* Tel 01-2860980
Fax 01-2768196
Email stfergal@iol.ie
Website www.stfergalsbray.ie

**BRAY**
*Holy Redeemer, Main Street, Bray, Co Wicklow*
Rt Rev Mgr Enda Lloyd Co-PP, EV
Cluain Mhuire, Killarney Road, Bray, Co Wicklow
Email padreenda@hotmail.com
Very Rev Robert Colclough Co-PP
'Shirley', Sidmonton Road, Bray, Co Wicklow
Tel 01-2868413
Workineh Tessema *(Team Assistant)*
Godfrey Kalema *(Team Assistant)*
Presbytery, Herbert Road, Bray, Co Wicklow
Leonard Kaye PPW
25 Oaktree Road, Stillorgan, Co Dublin
Tel 087-2904964
*Parish Office*: Tel 01-2868413
Email admin@holyredeemerbray.ie
Website www.holyredeemerbray.ie

**BRAY, PUTLAND ROAD**
*Our Lady Queen of Peace*
Very Rev Joseph Whelan Co-PP
Tel 01-2988746
Rev Jean-Marie Mbombo Mukaya (CICM) *(Assistant)*
Tel 01-2865723
Parochial House, Putland Road, Bray, Co Wicklow
*Sacristy*: 01-2867303
Email secretary@queenofpeace.ie
*Parish Office*: Tel 01-2745497
*Villa Pacis – Parish Centre*: 01-2760045
Email villafas1@hotmail.com

**BRAY, ST PETER'S**
*St Peter's, Little Bray, Co Wicklow*
Very Rev Ben Mulligan PP
42 Corke Abbey, Little Bray, Co Wicklow
Tel 01-2720224
Rev Robert Walwa PC
15 Connawood Drive, Bray, Co Wicklow
*Parish Office*: Tel 01-2829467
Email stpeterslittlebray1@eircom.net
Website http://homepage.eircom.net/~stpeterslittlebray

**BROOKFIELD**
*St Aidan's, Brookfield Road*
Very Rev Hugh Kavanagh Co-PP
1 Brookfield Road, Tallaght, Dublin 24
Email aodh@eircom.net
Martin Hughes *(Team Assistant)*
The Presbytery, St Aidan's Parish, Brookfield Road, Tallaght, Dublin 24
Tel 01-4624410

**CABINTEELY**
*St Brigid's, Dublin 18*
Rev Arthur O'Neill Adm
1B Willow Court, Druid Valley, Cabinteely, Dublin 18
Tel 01-4508432
Rt Rev Mgr Conor Ward *(Assistant)*
17 Prospect Lawn, The Park, Cabinteely, Dublin 18
Tel 01-2898656

**CABRA**
*Cabra Parish is now under the Team Ministry of Cabra/Cabra West/Phibsboro*
*Christ the King, Dublin 7*
Rev Patrick F. Carroll Co-PP
124 New Cabra Road, Dublin 7
Tel 01-2838311
Email pat47@eircom.net
Rev Thomas F. O'Shaughnessy *(Team Assistant)*
73 Annamoe Road, Dublin 7
Tel 01-8385626
*Parish Office:* Tel 01-8680804
Email christthekingchurch@eircom.net

**CABRA WEST**
*Cabra West Parish is now under the Team Ministry of Cabra/Cabra West/Phibsboro*
*Church of the Most Precious Blood, Dublin 7*
Very Rev John Greene *(Moderator)*
No 3 Presbytery, Dunmanus Court, Cabra West, Dublin 7
Tel 01-6275663
Very Rev Neil Dargan Co-PP
Presbytery No. 4, Dunmanus Road, Dublin 7
Tel 01-8380181
*Parish Office*: Tel 01-8384418

**CASTLEDERMOT**
*The Assumption, Castledermot, Co Kildare*
Very Rev Brendan Cantwell PP
Parochial House, Castledermot, Co Kildare
Tel 059-9144164/086-2528545
*Parish Office:* Tel/Fax 059-9144888
Email parishoffice@cabrawestparish.com
Website www.cabrawestparish.com

**CASTLEKNOCK**
*Our Lady Mother of the Church*
*Castleknock, Dublin 15*
Very Rev Maurice O'Shea PP
6 Beechpark Lawn, Castleknock, Dublin 15
Tel 01-8212967
Email ciaranos@eircom.net
Rev Denis O'Connor (CSsR) CC
32 Auburn Drive, Dublin 15
Tel 01-8214003
*Supply:* Bollineni Bala Kumar
27 Leinster Road, Rathmines, Dublin 6

**CASTLETOWN**
*(Grouped with the parish of Arklow)*
*St Patrick's, Castletown, Co Wexford*
Very Rev Martin Cosgrove PP
Parochial House, Arklow, Co Wicklow
Tel/Fax 01-4556103
Email mfc53@indigo.ie

**CELBRIDGE**
*St Patrick's, Celbridge, Co Kildare*
Very Rev Paul Taylor PP
Tel 01-6275874
*Supply:* Soosai Manickam
Parochial House, Main Street, Celbridge, Co Kildare
Rev Kevin Doherty CC
Parochial House, Celbridge, Co Kildare
Rev Douglas Zaggi PC
The Presbytery, St Brigid's Parish, Straffan, Co Kildare
Tel 01-6012197
Rev Brian McKittrick CC
The Presbytery, Celbridge, Co Kildare
*Parish Office*: Tel 01-6288827
Email celbridgeparishoffice@gmail.com

**CHAPELIZOD**
*Nativity of the BVM, Chapelizod, Dublin 20*
Very Rev Martin J. Daly PP
Parochial House, Chapelizod, Dublin 20
Tel 01-2832302
Rev James Somers (SDB) CC
The Presbytery, Chapelizod, Dublin 20
Tel 01-6264656

**CHERRY ORCHARD**
*Most Holy Sacrament*
*Parish Team:* Rev Patrick Reynolds (CSsR) PP
Email patcssr@yahoo.com
Rev Sean Duggan (CSsR) CC
The Presbytery, 103 Cherry Orchard Avenue, Dublin 10
Rev Gerard O'Connor (CSsR) CC
52 Elmdale Park, Dublin 10
Tel 01-6263813

**CHURCHTOWN**
*Churchtown Parish is now under the Team Ministry of Rathfarnham/Churchtown/Ballyroan*
*The Good Shepherd*
Very Rev Dermot Nestor Co-PP
Parochial House, Nutgrove Avenue, Dublin 14
Tel 01-2985916
Rev Gerard Young Co-PP
23 Oakdown Road, Dublin 14
Tel 01-8339666
*Emergencies*: Tel 087-2402585
*Parish Office*: Tel 01-2984642
Email info@goodshepherdchurchtown.ie
Website www.goodshepherdchurchtown.ie

**CLOGHER ROAD**
*Clogher Parish is now under the Team Ministry of Crumlin/Mourne Road/Clogher Road*
*St Bernadette's*
Rev Melvyn Mullins Co-PP, Adm
192 Sundrive Road, Dublin 12
Tel 01-4023307(w)/6777480(h)
Email mullins.melvyn@gmail.com
*Parish Office:* Tel 01-4733109
*Sacristy:* Tel 01-4535099
Email clogherroadparish@eircom.net
Website www.clogherroad.ie

**CLONDALKIN**
*Immaculate Conception, Dublin 22*
Website www.clondalkin.dublindiocese.ie
Very Rev John Wall PP
St Columba Parish House, New Road, Clondalkin, Dublin 22
Tel 01-4640441
Email johnswall@gofree.indigo.ie
Rev Damian Farnon CC
St Cecilia's, New Road, Clondalkin, Dublin 22
Tel 01-4592665

*Clonburris, Our Lady Queen of the Apostles*
Rev Shan O'Cuiv PC
c/o The Presbytery
Clondalkin, Dublin 22
Tel 01-4573440
*Parish Office*: Tel 01-4640706

*Knockmitten*
Rev Desmond Byrne (CSSp) CC
45 Woodford Drive, Monastery Road, Clondalkin, Dublin 22
Tel 01-4592323
Rev James McCaffrey (CSSp) CC
The Presbytery, St Mary's, New Road, Clondalkin, Dublin 22
Tel 01-4526514
Peter Siney PPW
Flat 6, 218 Clonliffe, Dublin 3
*Parish Office*: Tel 01-4640706

**CLONSKEAGH**
*Immaculate Virgin Mary of the Miraculous Medal, Bird Avenue, Dublin 14*
Rev Kevin Bartley Adm
14 Rosemount Crescent,
Roebuck Road, Clonskeagh, Dublin 14
Tel 01-8322396/087-2755413
James Larkin *(Assistant)*
*Supply:* Charles Light Nyarwa
72 Bird Avenue, Clonskeagh, Dublin 14
*Parish Office*: Tel/Fax 01-2837948
Email parishoffice@clonskeagh.org
Website www.clonskeaghparish.ie

**CLONTARF, ST ANTHONY'S**
*St Anthony, Clontarf, Dublin 3*
Rev Thomas McCarthy
119 The Stiles Road, Dublin 3
Tel 01-8384325
*Parish Office*: Tel 01-8333459
Email
saintanthonysclontarf@dublindiocese.ie
Website www.stanthonysclontarf.ie

**CLONTARF, ST JOHN'S**
*St John the Baptist, Clontarf Road, Dublin 3*
Rev Laurence White Co-PP
186 Clontarf Road, Dublin 3
Tel 01-2862346
Rev Martin Hogan Co-PP
187 Clontarf Road, Clontarf, Dublin 3
Tel 01-8338575(h)/087-9721213
*Parish Office*: Tel 01-8334606
Email sjtbclontarf@eircom.net
Website stjohnsclontarf.dublindiocese.ie

**CONFEY**
*St Charles Borromeo, Leixlip, Co Kildare*
Rev Anthony O'Shaughnessy Adm
73 Newtown Park, Leixlip, Co Kildare
Tel 01-4931057
Rev Peter Clancy CC
75 Newtown Park, Leixlip, Co Kildare
Tel 01-8386231
*Parish Office*: Tel/Fax 01-6247410
Email confeyparish@gmail.com

**COOLOCK**
*St Brendan's, Coolock Village, Dublin 5*
Rev John Hand (SM) *(Moderator)*
Email johnohand@eircom.net
*Superior:* Rev John Harrington (SM) PC
Rev Patrick G. Byrne (SM) PC
The Presbytery, Coolock Village, Dublin 5
Tel 01-8484799
*Parish Office*: Tel 01-8480102/01-8484799
*Parish Mobile:* 087-2269887
Email malachy@stbrendanscoolock.org
Website www.stbrendanscoolock.org

**CORDUFF**
*St Patrick's, Corduff, Blanchardstown, Dublin 15*
Very Rev Liam McClarey (SCA) PP
Parochial House, Corduff
Blanchardstown, Dublin 15
Email liammcclarey@eircom.net
Rev Joseph McLoughlin (SCA) CC
The Presbytery, Corduff,
Blanchardstown, Dublin 15
Email loughlinmc@hotmail.com

**CRUMLIN**
*Crumlin Parish is now under the Team Ministry of Crumlin/Mourne Road/ Clogher Road*
*St Agnes*
Very Rev Mgr John F. Deasy *(Team Assistant)*
55 St Agnes' Road, Crumlin, Dublin 12
Tel 01-4550955
Rev Michael Kelly Co-PP
94 Old County Road, Crumlin Dublin 12
Tel 01-4542308
Rev Paul Tyrrell Co-PP
41 St Agnes Road, Crumlin, Dublin 12
Tel 01-6600075
Rev Peter Coffey (SDB) Co-PP
Tel 01-4555605
Rev John Foster (SDB) *(Team Assistant)*
Tel 01-4555605
Salesian House, St Teresa's Road
Crumlin, Dublin 12
*Parish Pastoral Worker:* Gráinne Prior
c/o Parish Office
Tel 085-7197941
*Parish Office*: Tel 01-4555383
Fax 01-4652500
Email crumlinparish@eirccom.net
Website www.crumlinparish.ie

**DALKEY**
*Assumption of BVM*
Very Rev Patrick Devitt Adm
No 1 Presbytery, Castle Street,
Dalkey, Co Dublin
Tel 01-8373869
Email paddy.devitt@materdei.dcu.ie
Rev Declan Gallagher CC
No 3 Presbytery, Castle Street,
Dalkey, Co Dublin
Tel 01-2692052
*Parish Office*: Tel 01-2859418
Email office@dalkeyparish.org

**DARNDALE-BELCAMP**
*Our Lady Immaculate, Dublin 17*
Very Rev Leo Philomin (OMI) PP
The Presbytery, Darndale, Dublin 17
Tel 01-8474547
Rev Peter Daly (OMI) CC
Rev Edward Quinn (OMI) CC
The Presbytery, Darndale, Dublin 17
Email nedqnn@gmail.com
*Parish Office*: Tel 01-8474599
Email parish@darndaleparish.ie
Website www.darndalebelcamp.ie

**DEANSRATH**
Very Rev Daithi Kenneally (CSSp) PP
St Ronan's Presbytery, Deansrath,
Clondalkin, Dublin 22
Tel 01-4125222
Email stronansdeansrath@hotmail.com

**DOLLYMOUNT**
*St Gabriel's, St Gabriel's Road, Dublin 3*
Rev Gareth Byrne PC
107 Mount Prospect Avenue,
Clontarf, Dublin 3
Tel 01-8339301
Rev Dermot Mansfield (SJ) *(Team Assistant)*
Manresa House, Clontarf Road, Dublin 3
Tel 01-8057209/087-6942844
Rev Patrick McManus *(Moderator)*
34 Dollymount Grove, Clontarf, Dublin 3
Tel 01-2889879/087-2371089
Email frpatmcmanus@eircom.net
*Parish Pastoral Worker*: Deirdre McDermott
Tel 087-6942844
*Parish Office*: Tel 01-333602
Email stgabrielschurch@eircom.net

**DOLPHIN'S BARN**
*(Grouped with the parish of Rialto)*
*Our Lady of Dolours, Dublin 8*
Very Rev Gerard Fleming (SCA) CC
437 South Circular Road, Rialto, Dublin 8
Tel 01-4533490
Email dolphinsbarn@dublindiocese.ie
Rev Diarmuid Byrne Adm
18 St Anthony's Road, Rialto, Dublin 8
Tel 01-4534469
Rev Gobezayehu Yilma Getachew
287 South Circular Road, Rialto, Dublin 8
*Parish Office*: Tel 01-4547271
Email dolphinsbarn@dublindiocese.ie

**DOMINICK STREET**
*St Saviour's, Dublin 1*
Very Rev Gregory Carroll (OP) PP
Tel 01-8897610
Email stsaviours@eircom.net
Rev Marek Grubka (OP) CC
Tel 01-8897610
Rev Cezary Binkiewicz (OP) CC
St Saviour's, Upper Dorset Street, Dublin 1
*Parish Office*: Tel 01-8897610
Email stsaviours@eircom.net
Website www.saintsavioursdublin.ie

**DONABATE**
*St Patrick's*
Rev Patrick Reilly (OPraem) CC
13 Seaview Park, Portrane, Co Dublin
Tel 01-8436099
Rev Patrick Hannon PC
St Mary's, Donabate, Co Dublin
*Parish Office:* Tel/Fax 01-8434574 (9.30-12.00 noon)
Email stpatricksrcdonabate@gmail.com
Website www.donabateparish.ie

**DONAGHMEDE – CLONGRIFFIN – BALGRIFFIN**
*Church of the Holy Trinity*
Very Rev Eoin McCrystal PP
*Supply:* Enoch Usifo
Rev Raymond Kondowe
12 Grangemore Grove, Donaghmede, Dublin 13
Tel/Fax 01-8476392
Email epmcc@eircom.net
Rev Gary Darby (OS Cam) CC
41 Grangemore Grove, Donaghmede, Dublin 13
Tel 01-8301122/8032000(w)/8032239/8032411(w direct line)
Email garrydarby@eircom.net
*Parish Office*: Tel 01-8479822
Email donaghmede@dublindiocese.ie
Website www.holytrinityparish.ie

**DONNYBROOK**
*Church of the Sacred Heart, Dublin 4*
Very Rev Martin Clarke PP
No. 1 Presbytery, Stillorgan Road, Dublin 4
Tel 01-2802130/087-2208044
Rev Conor Harper (SJ) CC
Jesuit Community, Milltown Park, Sandford Road, Ranelagh, Dublin 6
Tel 01-2180244
Rev John Boyers PC
16 'Wilfield', Sandymount Avenue, Ballsbridge, Dublin 4
Tel 01-2888149
*Parish Office*: Tel 01-2693903
Email mclarke@donnybrookparish.ie
Website www.donnybrookparish.ie

**DONNYCARNEY**
*Our Lady of Consolation, Dublin 5*
Very Rev Peter Finnerty PP, VF
2 Maypark, Malahide Road, Dublin 5
Tel 01-8404162
Rev John Ennis CC
1 Maypark Road, Dublin 5
Tel 01-4599018
*Parish Office*: Tel 01-8316016
*Emergency Sick Calls Only:* 087-2506786
Email info@donnycarneyparish.ie
Website www.donnycarneyparish.ie

**DONORE AVENUE**
*St Teresa of the Child Jesus, Dublin 8*
Very Rev Edwin McCallion (SM) PP
Email edwinmcc@hotmail.com
Very Rev Sean McArdle (SM) CC
Rev Robert Kelly (SM) CC
Email rfksm@eircom.net
The Presbytery, Donore Avenue, Dublin 8
Tel 01-4542425/4531613
Email donoreavenue@dublindiocese.ie

**DRUMCONDRA**
*Corpus Christi, Home Farm Road, Dublin 9*
Rev William King PP
23 Clare Road, Drumcondra, Dublin 9
Tel 01-8378552
Email williamking58@eircom.net
Rt Rev Mgr Lorcan O'Brien VG
4 Walnut Ave., Drumcondra, Dublin 9
Tel 01-8379253(w)/01-8372496(h)
Email obrienlorcan@eircom.net
Rev Stephen Ifeanyi Ezenwegbu PC
23 Clare Road, Drumcondra, Dublin 9
Tel 01-8378552
*Parish Office*: Tel 01-8360085
Email corpuschristi@eircom.net
Website www.drumcondra.dublindiocese.ie

**DUBLIN AIRPORT** *see* **SWORDS**

**DUNDRUM**
*Holy Cross, Dublin 14*
Very Rev Kieran McDermott Co-PP
Emmaus, Main Street, Dundrum, Dublin 14
Tel 01-2984348
Email kieranjmcdermott@gmail.com
Rev Brian Edwards Co-PP
3 Sweetmount Drive, Dundrum, Dublin 14
Tel 01-2952869
Very Rev Mgr Donal O'Doherty PE
Holy Cross, Upper Kilmacud Road, Dundrum, Dublin 14
Tel 01-2985264
Email 32donalodoherty@eircomm.net
*Parish Pastoral Worker*
Geraldine O'Keeffe
2 Marley Walk, Marley Estate, Rathfarnham, Dublin 16
Tel 087-1211795
*Parish Office*: Tel 01-2983494
*Emergency Calls*: Tel 087-2561418
Email parishofficedundrum@eircom
Website www.holycrossdundrum.org

**DUN LAOGHAIRE**
*St Michael's, Co Dublin*
Rt Rev Mgr Daniel J. O'Connor PP, VF
St Michael's Parochial House, 4 Eblana Avenue, Dun Laoghaire, Co Dublin
Tel 01-2801505/087-7425862
Rev Patrick Monahan CC
'Renvyle', Corrig Avenue, Dun Laoghaire, Co Dublin
Tel 01-2802100
Rev Aidan Carroll CC
'Carraig Donn', 23 Glenageary Woods, Dun Laoghaire, Co Dublin
Tel 01-4972816
*Parish Office:* Tel 01-2804969
Email stmichdl2@eircom.net
Website www.dunlaoghaireparish.ie

**DUNLAVIN**
*St Nicholas of Myra, Dunlavin, Co Wicklow*
Rev Douglas Malone Adm
The Presbytery, Dunlavin, Co Wicklow
Tel 045-401227
Rev Eamonn McCarthy CC
The Presbytery, Donard, Co Wicklow
Tel 045-404614
*Parish Office*: Tel 045-407871
Website www.dunlavinparish.ie

**EADESTOWN**
*The Immaculate Conception, Naas, Co Kildare*
Very Rev Miceal Comer PP
The Presbytery, Eadestown, Naas, Co Kildare
Email eadestownparish@gmail.com

**EAST WALL – NORTH STRAND**
*St Joseph's, Church Road, Dublin 3*
Very Rev Peter J. Reilly PP
Parochial House, St Joseph's Parish, East Wall, Dublin 3
Tel 01-8742320
Email pjreilly@eircom.net
Rev Pius Biamse PC
Tel 01-8745317
80 St Mary's Road, East Wall, Dublin 3
*Parish Office*: Tel 01-8560980
Email stjosephsparish1941@gmail.com

**EDENMORE**
*(Grouped with the parish of Grange Park)*
*St Monica's, Dublin 5*
Very Rev David Lumsden PP
83 Tonlegee Drive, Raheny, Dublin 5
Tel 01-4592665
Rev Patrick Boyle PC
29 Glenayle Road, Edenmore, Dublin 5
Tel 01-6765517(w)
Rev Paul Dunne CC
60 Grange Park Grove, Dublin 5
Tel 01-4519416/087-6902246
Rev Anthony Power CC
35 Grange Park Avenue
Tel 01-8480244
*Parish Office*: Tel 01-8471497
Email stmonicaedenmore@eircom.net

**ENNISKERRY**
*Immaculate Heart of Mary, Enniskerry, Co Wicklow*
Very Rev John Sinnott PP
Parochial House, Enniskerry, Co Wicklow
Tel 01-2863506
Email jmpsinnott@eircom.net
Rev Pearse Walsh CC
The Presbytery, Kilmacanogue, Bray, Co Wicklow
Tel 01-4780616
*Parish Office Enniskerry:* Tel 01-2760030 (10 am-1 pm, Mon-Fri)
*Parish Office Kilmacanogue*
Tel 01-2021882 (10 am-1 pm, Mon-Fri)
Email stmochonogs@eircom.net

**ESKER-DODDSBORO-ADAMSTOWN**
*Esker-Dodsboro-Adamstown Parish is now under the Team Ministry of Lucan/Esker-Dodsboro-Adamstown/Lucan South*
*St Patrick's*
Rev John Hassett VF *(Moderator)*
127 Castlegate Way, Adamstown, Co Dublin
Tel 01-6812088
Email hassettorama@gmail.com
Rev Michael Drumm *(Team Assistant)*
47 Westbury Drive, Lucan, Co Dublin
Tel 01-8376027(w)/8328396(h)
*Parish Office*: Tel 01-6281018
Email stpatrickschurchesker@eircom.net
Website www.stpatrickslucan.ie

**FAIRVIEW**
*Church of the Visitation of BVM, Dublin 3*
Very Rev Joseph Connick (OFM Conv)
Rev Patrick Griffin (OFM Conv) CC
Rev Antony Nallukunnel (OFM Conv) PP
Rev Ciprian Budau (OFM Conv) CC
Friary of the Visitation,
Fairview Strand, Dublin 3
Tel 01-8376000 Fax 01-8376021
*Parish Office*: Tel 01-8376000

**FINGLAS**
*St Canice's, Dublin 11*
Very Rev Pádraig O'Cochláin PP
The Presbytery, 5 The Lawn,
Finglas, Dublin 11
Rev Gabriel O'Dowd CC
The Presbytery, St Margaret's,
Finglas, Dublin 11
Tel 01-8341009
Rev Michael Shiels CC
Tel 087-8180097
Rev Severinus Ndugwa PC
The Presbytery 2, St Canice's Parish,
Finglas, Dublin 11
*Parish Office:* Tel 01-8343110
Email stcanices2@eircom.net

**FINGLAS WEST**
*Church of the Annunciation, Dublin 11*
Rev Eamonn Cahill Adm
7 Cardiffcastle Road, Finglas West,
Dublin 11
Tel 01-2956317
Rev Piaras MacLochlainn CC
Rev Rustico Tinkasiimire PC
10 Finglaswood Road, Finglas West,
Dublin 11
John Graham PPW
37 Old Fair Green, Dunboyne, Co Meath
Tel 087-2211963
*Parish Office*: Tel 01-8341284

**FIRHOUSE**
*Our Lady of Mount Carmel, Dublin 24*
Rev Padraig B. Coleman (OFM) PC
Presbytery No 2, Ballycullen Avenue,
Firhouse, Dublin 24
Tel 01-4599899
Very Rev Patrick Madden PP, VF
Presbytery 1, Ballycullen Avenue,
Firhouse, Dublin 24
Tel 01-4599855
Email maddenp1@eircom.net
*Parish Office:* Tel 01-4524702
Email
ourladyofmountcarmelchurch@eircom.net

**FOXROCK**
*Our Lady of Perpetual Succour*
(All certs available 10.30 am–11.30 am)
Rev Frank Herron Adm
11 Foxrock Court, Foxrock, Dublin 18
Tel 01-4513109
Rev Derek Smyth PhD CC
2 Kill Lane, Foxrock, Dublin 18
Tel 01-2894734
*Parish Office:* Tel 01-2893492/01-2898879
Email secretary@foxrockparish.ie
Website www.foxrockparish.ie

**FRANCIS STREET**
*St Nicholas of Myra, Dublin 8*
Rev Martin Dolan Adm *(pro-tem)*
The Presbytery, Francis Street, Dublin 8
Tel 01-4544861
*Parish Office*: Tel 01- 4542172
Email franciss@francisstreetparish.ie
Website www.francisstreetparish.ie

**GARDINER STREET**
*St Francis Xavier, Dublin 1*
Very Rev Donal Neary (SJ) PP, VF
Rev William Reynolds (SJ) CC
The Presbytery, Upper Gardiner Street,
Dublin 1
Tel 01-8363411
Email sfx@jesuit.ie
Website www.gardinerstparish.ie

**GARRISTOWN**
*Garristown Parish is now under the Team Ministry of Rolestown/ Garristown/The Naul*
*Church of the Assumption, Co Dublin*
Rev Thomas McGowan Co-PP
Parochial House, Garristown, Co Dublin
Tel/Fax 01-8412932

**GLASNEVIN**
*Our Lady of Dolours, Dublin 9*
Rev Eamonn Bourke PC
25 The Haven, Dublin 9
Tel 083-3318910
Very Rev Sean Mundow PP
77 Botanic Avenue, Dublin 9
Tel 01-8373455
Email smundow@tinet.ie
*Parish Office*: Tel 01-8379445

**GLASTHULE**
*St Joseph's, Glasthule, Co Dublin*
Very Rev William Farrell CC
Parochial House, St Joseph's,
Glasthule, Co Dublin
Tel 0404-40540
Rev Denis Kennedy (CSSp) CC
St Joseph's Presbytery, Glasthule, Co Dublin
Tel 01-2800403
*Parish Office*: Tel 01-6638604/5
Sacristy: 01-2800182
*Emergencies*: Tel 087-2620480
Email stjosephsglasthule@gmail.com
Website www.glasthuleparish.com

**GLENDALOUGH**
*St Kevin's, Co Wicklow*
Very Rev Oliver Crotty Adm
Parochial House, Glendalough, Co Wicklow
Tel 0404-46214
*Parish Office*: Tel 0404-45777
Email glendalough2007@eircom.net
Website www.glendalough.dublindiocese.ie

**GRANGE PARK**
*(Grouped with the parish of Edenmore)*
*St Benedict's, Grange Park View, Dublin 5*
Very Rev David Lumsden PP
83 Tonlegee Drive, Raheny, Dublin 5
Tel 01-4592665
Rev Paul Dunne CC
60 Grange Park Grove, Raheny, Dublin 5
Tel 01-4519416/087-6902246
Email stmonicaedenmore@eircom.net

**GREENHILLS**
*Church of the Holy Spirit, Dublin 12*
Very Rev Myles Healy (CSSp) PP
55 Fernhill Road, Greenhills, Dublin 12
Rev Roddy Curran (CSSp) CC
104 St Joseph's Road, Greenhills,
Dublin 12
Rev Richard Eneji (CSSp) CC
Kimmage Manor, Whitehall Road,
Dublin 12
*Parish Office:* Tel 01-4509191 Fax 01-4605287
Email greenhillsparish@eircom.net
Website holyspiritparishgreehills.ie

**GREYSTONES**
*Church of the Holy Rosary, Co Wicklow*
Very Rev Liam Belton PP, VF
Parochial House, La Touche Road,
Greystones, Co Wicklow
Tel 01-2819252
Rev Denis Quinn CC
The Presbytery, Kimberley Road,
Greystones, Co Wicklow
Tel 01-2877025
Rev Owen Lynch CC
The Presbytery, Blacklion, Co Wicklow
Paul Thornton PPW
23 Blackthorn Green, Sandyford,
Dublin 16
*Parish Office*: Tel 01-2874025
Email office@greystonesparish.com

**HADDINGTON ROAD**
*St Mary's, Dublin 4*
Very Rev Mgr Patrick Finn PP
St Mary's, Haddington Road, Dublin 4
Tel 01-6643295/086-3848432
Email frpfinn@stmaryshaddingtonroad.ie
Rev Eoin G. Cassidy PC
Tel 01-6688135
Rev Michael Collins CC
Tel 01-2983557/087-6970061
The Presbytery, Haddington Road,
Dublin 4
Rev Pat Claffey (SVD) CC
3 Pembroke Road, Dublin 4
Email info@stmaryshaddingtonroad.ie
Website stmaryshaddingtonroad.ie

**HALSTON STREET AND ARRAN QUAY**
*St Michan's, Halston Street, Dublin 7*
Very Rev Bryan Shortall (OFM Cap) PP
Capuchin Friary, Church Street,
Dublin 7
Email halstonst@irishcapuchin.com
Rev Angelus O'Neill (OFM Cap) CC
Capuchin Friary, Church Street,
Dublin 7
Tel 01-8474469

**HAROLD'S CROSS**
*Our Lady of the Rosary, Dublin 6W*
Very Rev Gerry Kane PP
213B Harold's Cross Road, Dublin 6W
Tel 01-4947303
Email gkane@ireland.com
*Parish Office*: Tel 01-4965055
Email enquiries@hxparish.ie
Website www.hxparish.ie

**HARRINGTON STREET**
*St Kevin's, Dublin 8*
Very Rev Paul Kenny Adm
Parochial House,
Harrington Street, Dublin 8
Tel 01-4542172
Very Rev Gerard Deighan CC
The Presbytery, Harrington Street,
Dublin 8
Tel 01-2107858

**HARTSTOWN**
*Hartstown Parish is now under the Team Ministry of Blakestown/Hartstown/ Huntstown/Mountview*
*St Ciaran's, Dublin 15*
Rev Joseph Coyne *(Moderator)*
St Ciaran's, 36 Ashfield Lawn,
Huntstown, Dublin 15
Tel 01-8249695
Email pchuntstown@eircom.net
*Parish Office*: Tel 01-8249651/01-8204777
Website www.st-ciarans-parish.ie

**HOWTH**
*Church of the Assumption Howth, Co Dublin*
Right Rev Mgr Brendan Houlihan PP
Parochial House, Mount Saint Mary's,
Thormanby Road, Howth, Dublin 13
Tel 01-8322036
Email assumptionhowth@eircom.net
Rev Kilian Brennan CC
Presbytery No 1, Thormanby Road,
Howth, Co Dublin
Tel 01-8451902
Email kilianbrennan@eircom.net
Email assumptionhowth@eircom.net

**HUNTSTOWN**
*Sacred Heart of Jesus, Dublin 15*
Rev George P. Begley Co-PP
257 Pace Road, Littlepace, Dublin 15
Tel 01-2868413(w)/2862955(h)
*Parish Pastoral Worker:* Mr Clinton Maher
7 The Avenue, Dunboyne Castle,
Dunboyne, Co Meath
Tel 01-8218910

**INCHICORE, MARY IMMACULATE**
*Inchicore Mary Immaculate Parish is now under the Team Ministry of Inchicore, (Mary Immaculate & St Michael's) & Bluebell*
*Mary Immaculate, Tyrconnell Road, Dublin 8*
Very Rev Michael O'Connor (OMI) *(Moderator)*
Rev Michael Guckian (OMI)
Oblate Fathers, House of Retreat,
Inchicore, Dublin 8
Tel 01-454111
Website www.oblateparishesindublin.ie

**INCHICORE, ST MICHAEL'S**
*St Michael's, Emmet Road, Dublin 8*
Rev Tomasz Koscinski (OMI) Co-PP
Rev Dermot Mills (OMI) Co-PP
Tel 01-4501040
Parochial House, 118 Naas Road, Dublin 12
Rev Louis McDermott (OMI) Co-PP
52a-52b Bullfin Road
Rev Bernard Halpin Co-PP
52b Bullfin Road
Website www.oblateparishesindublin.ie

**IONA ROAD**
*St Columba's, Dublin 9*
Very Rev James F. Caffrey PP
'Marmion', 87 Iona Road, Dublin 9
Tel 01-8305651(parish)/8725055 (CYC)
Rev Peter Kilroy CC
74 Iona Road, Dublin 9
Tel 01-8308257 Fax 01-8309824
Email saintcolumba@eircom.net
Website www.ionaroadparish.ie

**JAMES'S STREET**
*St James's Church, Dublin 8*
Very Rev John Collins *(Moderator)*
The Presbytery,
James' Street, Dublin 8
Tel 01-4534921
Email roseo9@eircom.net
*Parish Office:*
Tel 01-4531143/087-1445888
Email jamesstreet@dublindiocese.ie

**JOBSTOWN**
*St Thomas the Apostle*
Rev Derek Doyle Co-PP
The Presbytery, St Thomas the Apostle
Parish, Jobstown, Tallaght, Dublin 24
Tel 01-2819253

**JOHNSTOWN-KILLINEY**
*Our Lady of Good Counsel, Killiney, Co Dublin*
Very Rev Peadar Murney PP
56 Auburn Road, Killiney, Co Dublin
Tel 01-2856660 Fax 01-2852509
Email pmurney@eircom.net
Rev Joseph McDonald CC
59 Auburn Road, Dun Laoghaire,
Co Dublin
Tel 01-2852509
*Parish Office*: Tel 01-2351416
Email johnstownparish@gmail.com
Website www.johnstownparish.org

**KILBARRACK-FOXFIELD**
*St John the Evangelist, Greendale Road, Kilbarrack, Dublin 5*
Very Rev Paul Lavelle PP
123 Foxfield Grove, Dublin 5
Very Rev Declan Doyle PC
56 Foxfield Saint John, Dublin 5
Tel 01-8144340
Email dec_doyle@eircom.net
Very Rev Cathal Price CC
54 Foxfield St John, Dublin 5
Tel 01-8323683
Email cathalprice@gmail.com
*Parish Office*: Tel 01-8390433
Email info@kilbarrackfoxfieldparish.ie
Website www.kilbarrackfoxfieldparish.ie

**KILBRIDE AND BARNDARRIG**
*St Mary's, Barndarrig, Co Wicklow*
Very Rev Michael Vincent Dempsey PP
The Presbytery, Barndarrig,
Co Wicklow
Rev Joseph Doran CC
The Presbytery, Brittas Bay,
Co Wicklow

**KILCULLEN**
*Sacred Heart and St Brigid, Kilcullen*
Very Rev Michael Murphy PP
Parochial House, Kilcullen, Co Kildare
Tel 045-481230
Email mclm@eircom.net
*Parish Pastoral Worker:* Miss Hannah Evans
Clongowney, Mullingar, Co Westmeath
Tel 045-480727/087-9365767
Email hannah.evans@dublindiocese.ie
*Parish Office:* Tel 045-480727
Email kilcullenparish@eircom.net
Website www.kilcullenparish.net

**KILLESTER**
*St Brigid's, Howth Road, Dublin 5*
Rt Rev Mgr Alex Stenson PP
126 Furry Park Road, Dublin 5
Tel 01-6286220
Rev Michael O'Grady CC
264 Howth Road, Killester, Dublin 5
Tel 01-4508432
*Parish Office*: Tel 01-8332974
Website www.killester.dublindiocese.ie

**KILLINARDEN**
*Church of the Sacred Heart, Killinarden, Tallaght, Dublin 24*
Very Rev Manus Ferry (MSC) PP
Rev John Finn (MSC) CC
The Presbytery, Killinarden, Tallaght,
Dublin 24
Email sacredheartparish@eircom.net

**KILL-O'-THE-GRANGE**
*Holy Family, Kill Avenue, Dun Laoghaire, Co Dublin*
Very Rev John D. Killeen PP
20 Abbey Court, Abbey Road,
Blackrock, Co Dublin
Tel 01-2982282
Rev Michael O'Connor (CSSp) CC
Presbytery No 2, Church Grounds,
Kill Avenue, Dun Laoghaire, Co Dublin
Tel 01-2140863

**KILMACANOGUE** *see* **ENNISKERRY**

**KILMACUD-STILLORGAN**
*(Grouped with the parish of Mount Merrion)*
*St Laurence, Co Dublin*
Rev Tony Coote Adm *(Kilmacud & Mount Merrion)*
79 The Rise, Mount Merrion, Co Dublin
Tel 01-7162100 (w)/2839290 (h)
Rev Conleth Meehan CC *(Kilmacud & Mount Merrion)*
6 Allen Park Road, Stillorgan, Co Dublin
Tel 01-2880545
*Parish Office*: Tel 01-2884009
Email kilmacudparish@eircom.net
Website www.kilmacudparish.com

**KILMORE ROAD WEST**
*St Luke the Evangelist, Dublin 5*
Rev Patrick Littleton Adm
St Luke's, Kilbarron Road,
Kilmore West, Dublin 5
Tel 01-8486806
*Parish Office*: Tel 01-8488149

**KILNAMANAGH-CASTLEVIEW**
*St Kevin's, Dublin 24*
Very Rev Philip Curran PP
Presbytery No 1, Treepark Rd,
Kilnamanagh, Dublin 24
Tel 01-8378552/086-2408188
Email pcurran@dublindiocese.ie
Rev Colin Rothery CC
43 Chestnut Grove, Ballymount Road,
Tallaght, Dublin 24
*Parish Office*: Tel 01-4515570

**KILQUADE**
*St Patrick's, Kilquade, Co Wicklow*
Very Rev Liam Belton PP, VF
Parochial House, La Touche Road,
Greystones, Co Wicklow
Tel/Fax 01-2819252
Email liam.belton@gmail.com
Rev Eamonn Clarke CC
The Presbytery, Kilcoole, Co Wicklow
Tel 01-2876207
Rev Sean Smith CC
The Presbytery,
Newtownmountkennedy, Co Wicklow
Paul Thornton PPW
23 Blackthorn Green, Sandyford,
Dublin 16
*Parish Office:* Tel 01-2819658
Email kilquadeparish@eircom.net
Website www.kilquadeparish.com

**KIMMAGE MANOR**
*Church of the Holy Spirit, Kimmage Manor, Whitehall Road, Dublin 12*
Very Rev Patrick Doody (CSSp) PP
66 Rockfield Avenue, Dublin 12
Email pdoody68@aol.com
*Parish Office:* Tel 01-4064377

**KINSEALY**
*(Grouped with the parishes of Malahide, Yellow Walls & Portmarnock)*
*St Nicholas of Myra, Malahide Road, Co Dublin*
Very Rev Martin O'Farrell PE
'Aghadoe', Kinsaley Lane, Malahide,
Co Dublin
Tel 01-8461767

**KNOCKLYON**
*St Colmcille, Idrone Avenue, Dublin 16*
Very Rev James Murray (OCarm) PP
Tel 01-4941204
Rev Michael Morrissey (OCarm) CC
Rev Sean MacGiollarnáth (OCarm) CC
Carmelite Presbytery, Idrone Avenue,
Knocklyon, Dublin 16
Email presbytery@knocklyonparish.com
Website www.knocklyonparish.com

**LARKHILL-WHITEHALL-SANTRY**
*(Grouped with the parishes of Kilmore Road West & Beaumont)*
*Holy Child, Thatch Road, Dublin 9*
Very Rev Michael Carey Adm
151 Swords Road, Whitehall, Dublin 9
Tel 01-8374887
Email athairmichael@eircom.net
Rev Bernard Collier CC
2 Knightswood, Coolock Lane,
Santry, Dublin 9
Tel 01-4540811
Rev Thomas Kearney CC
137 Shantalla Road, Whitehall, Dublin 9
Tel 01-8313806
Rev Damian McNeice PC
149 Swords Road, Whitehall, Dublin 9
Tel 01-8372521
Conor McCann PPW
Ashtree House, 29 Cluain Ard, Kilmead,
Co Kildare
*Parish Office:* Tel 01-8375274 Fax 01-7979606
Website www.whitehall.dublindiocese.ie

**LAUREL LODGE-CARPENTERSTOWN**
*St Thomas the Apostle, Castleknock, Dublin 15*
Very Rev Michael Cullen PP
The Presbytery, Church Grounds,
Laurel Lodge, Castleknock, Dublin 15
Tel 01-8379253(w)/8484800(h)
Email mcullen@laurellodgeparish.ie
Rev Dan Joe O'Mahony (OFM Cap)
The Oratory, Blanchardstown Dublin 15
Email danjoe2006@gmail.com
*Parish Office*: Tel 01-8208112
Website www.laurellodgeparish.ie

**LEIXLIP**
*Our Lady's Nativity, Co Kildare*
Rev John McNamara Adm
Parochial House, Old Hill, Leixlip,
Co Kildare
Tel 01-8401661
Rev Noel Watson CC
No 1 Presbytery, 4 Old Hill,
Leixlip, Co Kildare
Tel 01-6243718
Email noelwatson@hotmail.com
Rev Nobert Ngussa Jipandile PC
Rev Eladius Leonard Mutunzi PC
Presbytery No 2, 6 Old Hill, Leixlip,
Co Kildare
*Parish Office:* Tel 01-6243673/01-6245159
Email leixlip.parish@oln.ie
Website www.oln.ie

**LITTLE BRAY** *see* **BRAY, ST PETER'S**

**LOUGHLINSTOWN**
*St Columbanus, Dun Laoghaire*
Very Rev Edward Griffin PP
10 The Oaks, Loughlinstown Drive,
Dun Laoghaire, Co Dublin
Tel 086-2395706/01-8480917
Email loughlinstownparish@eircom.net
*Parish Office*: Tel 01-2824085

**LUCAN**
*Lucan Parish is now under the Team Ministry of Lucan/Esker- Dodsboro-Adamstown/Lucan South*
*St Mary's, Lucan, Co Dublin*
Very Rev Peter O'Reilly Co-PP
231 Beech Park, Lucan, Co Dublin
Tel 01-6281756
Very Rev Thomas Kennedy Co-PP
14 Roselawn, Lucan, Co Dublin
Tel 01-2882162
*Parish Pastoral Worker:* Colette Kavanagh
Tel 087-7952330
*Parish Office*: Tel 01-6217041
Email parishoffice@stmarysparishlucan.ie
Website www.stmarysparishlucan.ie

**LUCAN SOUTH**
*Lucan South Parish is now under the Team Ministry of Lucan/Esker- Dodsboro-Adamstown/Lucan South*
*Church of Divine Mercy, Balgaddy*
Very Rev Donal Roche PP
Parochial House, Foxdene Avenue,
Lucan, Dublin 22
Tel 01-4056858
Email donaljroche@gmail.com
Rev Francis Oladipo PC
32 Earlsfort Road, Lucan, Dublin 22
*Parish Office*: Tel 01-4572900
Email churchdivinemercy@eircom.net
Website lucansouthparish.net

**LUSK**
*St MacCullin's, Lusk, Co Dublin*
Very Rev Paul Hampson PP
Parochial House, St MacCullin Parish
Chapel, Lusk, Co Dublin
Tel 087-2452161
*Parish Office*: Tel 01-8438421
Email luskparish@eircom.net
Website www.luskparish.ie

**MALAHIDE**
*(Grouped with the parishes of Yellow Walls, Kinsealy & Portmarnock)*
*St Sylvester's, Malahide, Co Dublin*
Rev Peter Briscoe Adm
12 The Warren, Malahide, Co Dublin
Tel 01-6684265
Rev Paul Thornton CC
146 Seapark, Malahide, Co Dublin
Email pauljthornton@gmail.com
Rev Frank Reburn CC
11 Millview Court, Malahide, Co Dublin
Tel 01-8338575
Email freburn@hotmail.com
*Parish Office:* Tel 01-8451244 Fax 01-8168539
Email stsylvesters@eircom.net
Website www.malahideparish.ie

**MARINO**
*St Vincent de Paul, Griffith Avenue, Dublin 9*
Very Rev Thomas Noone PP
69 Griffith Avenue, Dublin 9
Tel 01-2694522(w)/8367904(h)
Rev Kevin Doran PC
IEC General Seretary, c/o International
Eucharistic Congress 2012, Sandymount
Tel 0404-45140
Email kevin.doran@dublindiocese.ie
Rev John Aikoye PC
c/o The Sacristy, St Vincent de Paul Church,
Griffith Avenue, Dublin 9
Tel 01-8332772
*Supply:* Athnas Kerketta (MSFS)
St Vincent de Paul Church, Marino, Dublin 3
*Parish Office:* Tel 01-8332772/087-2506786
Email info@marinoparish.ie
Website www.marinoparish.ie

**MARLEY GRANGE**
*The Divine Word, 25/27 Hermitage Downs, Rathfarnham, Dublin 16*
Rev Colm McGlynn (OSM) PP
Tel 01-8210874
Rev Camillus McGrane (OSM) CC
25/27 Hermitage Downs,
Marley Grange, Rathfarnham, Dublin 16
Email divine_word@ireland.com
*Parish Office:* Tel 01-4944295 Fax 01-4941042
Email divine_word@ireland.com
Website www.marleygrangeparish.com

**MAYNOOTH**
*St Mary's, Maynooth, Co Kildare*
Very Rev Liam Rigney PP
Parochial House, Moyglare Road
Tel 01-8556474
Email liamrigney@eircom.net
Rev David Halpin CC
The Presbytery, 18 Straffan Way, Maynooth, Co Kildare
Tel 01-4415001
*Parish Office*: Tel 01-6293885
Email maynoothparishoffice@eircom.net
www.maynoothparish.dublindiocese.ie

**MEADOWBROOK**
*Meadowbrook Parish is now under the Team Ministry of Dundrum/Ballinteer/ Meadowbrook*
*St Attracta's Oratory, Dublin 16*
Very Rev John Ferris Co-PP
75 Ludford Drive, Dublin 16
Tel 01-8405948
*Parish Office*: Tel 01-2980471
Email info@meadowbrookparish.ie
www.meadowbrookparish.ie

**MEATH STREET AND MERCHANTS QUAY**
*St Catherine of Alexandria, Dublin 8*
*Church of the Immaculate Conception (popularly known as Adam and Eve's)*
*4 Merchant's Quay, Dublin 8*
Rev Niall Coghlan (OSA) PP
Tel 01-4944966
Rev Michael Mernagh (OSA) CC
St John's Priory, Thomas Street, Dublin 8
Rev Richard Goode (OSA) CC
The Presbytery, Meath Street, Dublin 8
Br Niall O'Connell (OFM) *(Guardian)*
Adam and Eve's, Merchant's Quay, Dublin 8
Tel 01-6771128 Fax 01-6771000

**MERRION ROAD**
*Our Lady Queen of Peace, Dublin 4*
Very Rev Fergus O'Connor (Opus Dei) PP
Email fergusoconnor@eircom.net
Rev Charles Connolly (Opus Dei) CC
31 Herbert Avenue, Merrion Road, Dublin 4
Email ppapers@eircom.net
*Parish Office*: Tel 01-2691825
Email queenofpeacemerrion@eircom.net
Website www.merrionroadchurch.ie

**MILLTOWN**
*SS Columbanus and Gall, Dublin 6*
Rev Phillip Bradley, Adm
67 Ramleh Park, Milltown, Dublin 6
Tel 01-6280205
Rev Alan Mowbray (SJ) PC
Gonzaga Jesuit Community, Sandford Road, Dublin 6
Tel 01-4972943 ext 208
*Parish Office*: Tel 01-2196740/ 01-2680041/087-9500334
Email milltownparishcentre@eircom.net
Website www.milltownparish.ie

**MONKSTOWN**
*St Patrick's, Carrickbrennan Road*
Very Rev Michael Coady PP
Parochial House, Carrickbrennan Road, Monkstown, Co Dublin
Tel 01-6684192
Email clovis78@eircom.net
*Parish Office*: Tel 01-2807854
Website www.monkstownparish.ie

**MOONE**
*Church of the Blessed Trinity*
Very Rev Francis McEvoy PP, VF
Parochial House, Crookstown, Athy, Co Kildare
Tel 059-8624109
Email mcevoyf@eircom.net
Rev Colm O'Siochru CC
The Presbytery, SS Mary & Laurence Parish, Kilmead, Athy Co Kildare
Te 0507-26117
*Parish Office*: Tel 059-8623154
Wesbite www.narraghmoreparish.org

**MOUNT ARGUS**
*St Paul of the Cross, Harold's Cross, Dublin 6W*
Very Rev Frank Keevins (CP) PP
Rev Ignatius Watters (CP)
Rev Kenneth Brady (CP) CC
St Paul's Retreat, Mount Argus, Dublin 6W
Email secretary@mountargusparish.ie
Website www.mountargusparish.ie

**MOUNT MERRION**
*St Therese, Mount Merrion, Co Dublin*
Very Rev Tony Coote Adm
79 The Rise, Mount Merrion, Co Dublin
Tel 01-7162100(w)/2839290(h)
Email tony.coote@gmail.com
Rev John Bracken CC
83 The Rise, Mount Merrion, Co Dublin
Tel 01-2895780
Rev Conleth Meehan CC
6 Allen Park Road, Stillorgan, Co Dublin
Tel 01-2880545
Rev Patrick J. O'Byrne CC
188 Lower Kilmacud Road, Kilmacud, Co Dublin
Tel 01-8436011
*Parish Office:* Tel 01-2881271/01-2783804
Email mountmerrionparishoffice@eircom.net
Website www.mountmerrionparish.ie

**MOUNTVIEW**
*Mountview Road Parish is now under the Team Ministry of Blakestown/ Hartstown/ Huntstown/ Mountview*
*St Philip the Apostle, Blanchardstown, Dublin 15*
Rev Patrick O'Byrne Co-PP
No 2 The Presbytery, Mountview, Blanchardstown, Dublin 15
Tel 01-4510986
Email pat.obyrne@yahoo.com
Email mountview@dublindiocese.ie
Website www.stphilipsmountainview.ie

**MOURNE ROAD**
*Mourne Road Parish is now under the Team Ministry of Crumlin/Mourne Road/ Clogher Road*
*Our Lady of Good Counsel, Dublin 12*
Very Rev John Canon Flaherty *(Team Moderator)*
Parochial House, Sperrin Road, Drimnagh, Dublin 12
Rev David Brannigan Co.PP
89 Sperrin Road, Drimnagh, Dublin 12
Tel 01-8412116
Email copp@mourneroad.ie
*Parish Pastoral Worker*: Gráinne Prior
8 Castletown, Leixlip, Co Kildare
Tel 085-7197941
*Parish Office:* Tel 01-4556105 Fax 01-4550133
Email mourneroadparish@eircom.net
Website www.mourneroad.ie

**MULHUDDART**
Very Rev Eugene McCarthy (CP) PP
24 The Court, Mulhuddart Wood, Mulhuddart, Dublin 15
Tel 01-8128941
*Parish Office*: Tel 01-8205480
Email mulhudoffice@gmail.com
Website www.mulhuddartparish.com

**NARRAGHMORE**
*(Grouped with the parish of Moone)*
*SS Mary and Laurence, Co Kildare*
Very Rev Frank McEvoy PP, VF
Parochial House, Crookstown, Athy, Co Kildare
Rev Colm R. Ó Siochrú CC
The Presbytery, Kilmead, Athy, Co Kildare
Tel 0507-26117
Email mcevoyf@eircom.net
Website www.narraghmoreparish.org

**NAUL**
*The Naul Parish is now under the Team Ministry Rolestown/Garristown/The Naul*
*St Canice's, Damastown, Co Dublin*
*The Nativity of BVM, Naul*
*The Assumption of BVM, Ballyboughal*
Very Rev Denis M. Delaney *(Moderator)*
Parochial House, The Naul, Co Dublin
Tel 01-8401514
Very Rev Patrick Canon Fagan PE
The Presbytery, Ballyboughal, Co Dublin

**NAVAN ROAD**
*Our Lady Help of Christians, Dublin 7*
Rev John O'Brien Adm
Parochial House, 199 Navan Road, Dublin 7
Tel 01-2768191
Rev Paul Coyle CC
194 Navan Road, Dublin 7
Tel 01-6290553
*Parish Office*: Tel 01-8380265
Email navanroadparish@eircom.net

**NEILSTOWN**
*St Peter the Apostle, Dublin 22*
Very Rev Donal Toal (SMA) PP
Rev Paul Monahan (SMA) CC
The Presbytery, Neilstown, Clondalkin, Dublin 22
Tel 01-4573546

**NEWCASTLE**
*(Grouped with the parishes of Saggart, Rathcool & Brittas)*
*St Finian's, Co Dublin*
Very Rev Enda Cunningham PP
St Mary's Parochial House, Saggart, Co Dublin
Rev Aidan Kieran CC
No 1 the Glebe, Peamount Road, Newcastle Lyons, Co Dublin
Tel 01-2852509

**NEWTOWNPARK**
*The Guardian Angels, Blackrock, Co Dublin*
Very Rev Dermot Leycock PP
64 Newtownpark Avenue,
Blackrock, Co Dublin
Tel 01-8333793
Rev Seamus Toohey CC
7 Avondale Court, Blackrock, Co Dublin
Tel 01-2884043
Rev William Fortune CC
32 Newtownpark Avenue,
Blackrock, Co Dublin
Tel 01-2100337
*Parish Office*: Tel 01-2832988
Email newtownparkparish@eircom.net
Website www.newtownparkparish.com

**NORTH WALL-SEVILLE PLACE**
*St Laurence O'Toole's (North Wall), Dublin 1*
Rev Declan Blake Adm
Parochial House, 49 Seville Place,
Dublin 1
Rev Fearghus O'Fearghail PC
St Laurence O'Toole's Presbytery,
49 Seville Place, Dublin 1
Tel 01-8740796
Pauline O'Shea PPW
54 Cherry Avenue, River Valley, Swords,
Co Dublin
*Parish Office:* Tel 01-8744236

**NORTH WILLIAM STREET**
*St Agatha's, Dublin 1*
Very Rev Brian Lawless Adm
Presbytery, North William Street,
Dublin 1
Tel 01-6244568
Email frbrian@stagathasparish.ie
Rev Anthony Scully CC
89 Ballybough Road, Dublin 3
Tel 01-8363451
*Parish Office*: Tel 01-8554078
Email office@stagathasparish.ie
Website www.stagathasparish

**OLD BAWN (*see* TALLAGHT, OLDBAWN)**

**PALMERSTOWN**
*St Philomena's, Dublin 20*
Very Rev Anthony Reilly PP
Parochial House, Palmerstown,
Dublin 20
Tel 01-6249323
Email reillya48@gmail.com
Rev Vincent O'Connell (CSSp) PC
Hospital Chaplain, Hermitage Medical
Centre, Old Lucan Road, Lucan,
Dublin 20
*Parish Office*: Tel 01-6260900/01-6266241

**PHIBSBORO**
*Phibsboro Parish is now under the Team Ministry of Cabra/Cabra West/Phibsboro*
*St Peter's, Dublin 7*
Very Rev Paschal Scallon (CM) Co-PP
Rev Eamon Devlin (CM) Co-PP
St Peter's, Phibsboro, Dublin 7
Tel 01-8389708 Fax 01-8389950
*Parish Pastoral Worker*: Natasha Curran
St Judes, Ballycarney, Green Road,
Carlow, Co Carlow
Email info@stpetersphibsboro.ie
Website www.stpetersphibsboro.ie

**PORTERSTOWN-CLONSILLA**
*St Mochta's, Porterstown, Dublin 15*
Very Rev John Daly PP
St Mochta's, Porterstown, Dublin 15
Tel 01-8213218
Email frjohn@stmochtasparish.ie
Website www.stmochtasparish.ie

**PORTMARNOCK**
*(Grouped with the parishes of Malahide, Yellow Walls & Kinsealy)*
*St Anne's, Portmarnock, Co Dublin*
Rt Rev Mgr Peter Briscoe Adm
12 The Warren, Malahide, Co Dublin
Tel 01-6684265
Rev John Murphy CC
St Anne's, Strand Road,
Portmarnock, Co Dublin
Tel/Fax 01-2697754
Rev Niall McDermott CC
12 Blackberry Rise, Portmarnock, Co Dublin
Tel 01-8361398
Email niallmcd@clearwire.ie
Rev Bryan Nolan PC
21 Wheatfield Grove Dublin 9
Tel 01-8038970
Email bynolan@hotmail.com
*Parish Office:* Tel 01-8461561 Fax 01-8169802
Email stannes@portmarnockparish.ie
Website www.portmarnockparish.ie

**PRIORSWOOD**
*St Francis of Assisi, Dublin 17*
Very Rev Patrick Flynn (OFM Cap) PP
*(Guardian)*
Rev Seán Kelly (OFM Cap) CC
*Parish Office*: Tel 01-8474469/01-8474358
Fax 01-8487296
Email priorswoodparish@yahoo.ie

**RAHENY**
*Our Lady Mother of Divine Grace, Howth Road, Dublin 5*
Rt Rev Mgr Martin O'Shea PP
5 St Assam's Road West, Raheny, Dublin 5
Tel 01-8313806
Rev Patrick O'Rourke (LC) CC
24 Watermill Road, Raheny, Dublin 5
*Parish Office*: Tel 01-8313232

**RATHDRUM**
*SS Mary and Michael, Co Wicklow*
Very Rev Brian O'Reilly PP
Parochial House, Rathdrum, Co Wicklow
Tel 01-4599899
Email froreilly@gmail.com
Rev Nayagiam Arockia Doss PC
Parochial House, Rathdrum, Co Wicklow
*Parish Office*: Tel 01-0404 46517
Website www.rathdrumparish.com

**RATHFARNHAM**
*Rathfarnham Parish is now under the Team Ministry of Rathfarnham/ Churchtown/Ballyroan*
*The Annunciation, Dublin 14*
Very Rev Martin G. Noone PP
*(Moderator)*
St Mary's Presbytery, Willbrook Road,
Rathfarnham, Dublin 14
Tel 01-4954554
Email martin.noone@dublindiocese.ie
Rev Desmond Hayden *(Assistant Priest)*
St Mary's Presbytery, Willbrook Road,
Rathfarnham, Dublin 14
Tel 01-8338424
*Parish Pastoral Worker*: Margaret Drew
15 Castlemanor, Sea Road, Newcastle,
Co Wicklow
Tel 01-4952695
*Parish Office:* Tel 01-4958695 Fax 01-4958696
Email rathfarnhamparish1@eircom.net

**RATHGAR**
*Church of the Three Patrons, Rathgar Road, Dublin 6*
Rev Joseph Mullan PP
49 Rathgar Road, Dublin 6
Tel 01-4970039/087-2326254
Rev Francis Sammon (SJ) CC
156b Rathgar Road, Dublin 6
Tel 01-4966042
Rev Gerry Moloney (CSsR) PC
Redemptorist Community, Marianella,
Orwell Road, Rathgar, Dublin 6
*Parish Office*: Tel 01-4972215
Email 3patrons@eircom.net
Website www.rathgarparish.ie

**RATHMINES**
*Mary Immaculate, Refuge of Sinners, Rathmines, Dublin 6*
Very Rev Richard Sheehy PP, VF
52 Lower Rathmines Road, Dublin 6
Tel 01-4975958
Rev John Galvin CC
Rev Patrick McCafferty PC
Tel 01-4976148
48 Lower Rathmines Road, Dublin 6
Frank Brown PPW
14 Old Court Avenue, Ferncourt,
Ballycragh, Dublin 24

**RIALTO**
*(Grouped with the parish of Dolphin's Barn)*
*Our Lady of the Holy Rosary of Fatima, Rialto, Dublin 8*
Very Rev Gerard Fleming (SAC) CC
437 South Circular Road, Dublin 8
Tel 01-4533490
Email dolphinsbarn@dublindiocese.ie
Rev Diarmuid Byrne Adm
18 St Anthony's Road Dublin 8
Tel 01-4534469
Rev Gobezayehu Yilma Getachew PC
287 South Circular Road, Dublin 8
*Parish Office*: Tel 01-4539020
Website www.rialtoparish.com

**RINGSEND**
*St Patrick's, Dublin 4*
Very Rev Ivan Tonge PP
St Patrick's, 2 Cambridge Road,
Dublin 4
Tel 01-8744236/8741625
Rev Fergal MacDonagh CC
The Presbytery, 1A St Patricks Parish,
Irishtown Road, Dublin 4
Tel 01-6684724
*Parish Office*: Tel 01-6697429
Email
stpatrickschurchringsend@eircom.net

**RIVERMOUNT**
*St Oliver Plunkett, St Helena's Drive, Dublin 11*
Very Rev Seamus Ahearne (OSA) PP
The Presbytery, 60 Glenties Park, Finglas South, Dublin 11
Tel 01-8343722/087-6782746
Email seamus.ahearne@gmail.com
Rev Noel Hession (OSA)
Parochial House, St Helena's Drive South, Dublin 11
Email hessionn@eircom.net
Rev Paddy O'Reilly (OSA)
Parochial House, St Helena's Drive, Dublin 11
Email paddyforeilly@eircom.net

**RIVER VALLEY**
*St Finian's, Swords, Co Dublin*
Very Rev Niall Mackey PP
Parochial House, 1 River Valley Heights, Swords, Co Dublin
Tel 01-8403400
Email mackeyniall@mac.com
Rev Peter McCarron CC
The Presbytery, 2 River Valley Heights, Swords, Co Dublin
Tel 01-8404162
Email peteremccarron@eircom.net
Website www.rivervalley.dublindiocese.ie

**ROLESTOWN–OLDTOWN**
*Rolestown parish is now under the Team Ministry of Rolestown Garristown/The Naul*
*St Brigid's, Rolestown, Co Dublin*
Very Rev John F Keegan Co-PP
Parochial House, Rolestown, Swords, Co Dublin
Tel 01-2826404
Rev John Carey Co-PP
The Presbytery, Oldtown, Co Dublin
Tel 01-8433133
Email parishrolestown@gmail.com

**ROUNDWOOD**
*St Laurence O'Toole, Co Wicklow*
Very Rev Paul Kelly PP
The Presbytery, St Laurence O'Toole Parish, Roundwood, Co Wicklow
Tel 01-2818149
*Parish Office:* Tel 01-2818384 (mornings)
Email roundwoodparish@eircom.net

**ROWLAGH & QUARRYVALE**
*Immaculate Heart of Mary, Clondalkin, Dublin 22*
Rev John Dunphy Adm
30 Wheatfields Close, Clondalkin, Dublin 22
Tel 01-6263920
Email johnmdunphy@eircom.net
Rev Asif Imran Malik PC
32 Wheatfields Close, Clondalkin, Dublin 22
*Parish Office:* Tel/Fax 01-6261010
Email parishofrowlagh@eircom.net

**RUSH**
*St Maur's, Rush, Co Dublin*
Very Rev Kieran Coghlan PP
The Presbytery, Chapel Green, Rush, Co Dublin
Tel 01-8438024
Email kcoghlan@eircom.net
Rev Rossa Doyle CC
Sandyhills, South Shore Road, Rush, Co Dublin
Tel 01-8430973
Email rossadoyle@hotmail.com
Mary Kirk PPW
44a Hayestown, Rush, Co Dublin
Email rushparish@dublindiocese.ie
Website www.rushparish.dublindiocese.ie

**SAGGART/RATHCOOLE/BRITTAS**
*(Grouped with the parish of Newcastle)*
*Nativity of the BVM, Co Dublin*
Rev Michael Shortall PC
Tel 01-4587187
Very Rev Enda Cunningham PP
St Mary's Parochial House, Saggart, Co Dublin
Rev Aidan Kieran CC
No 1 the Glebe, Peamount Road, Newcastle Lyons, Co Dublin
Tel 01-2852509
Rev Michael McGowan PC
7 St Patrick's Crescent, Rathcoole, Co Dublin
Tel 01-4589210
*Parish Pastoral Worker*: Sean O'Rourke
36 Dodder Park Road, Rathfarnham, Dublin 14
Tel 087-0540695

**SALLYNOGGIN**
*Our Lady of Victories, Co Dublin*
Very Rev Henry Nevin (SDS) PP
Rev Eric Powell (SDS) CC
Tel 01-2854653/2854667
Rev Liam Talbot (SDS) CC
St Kevin's Presbytery, Pearse Street, Sallynoggin, Co Dublin
*Parish Office*: Tel 01-2854667
Email sallynogginparish@eircom.net

**SANDYFORD**
*St Mary's, Dublin 18*
Very Rev Andrew O'Sullivan *(Moderator)*
Parochial House, St Mary's, Sandyford Village, Dublin 18
Tel 045-481222
Very Rev Fergus McGlynn Co-PP
10 Bearna Park, Sandyford, Dublin 18
Very Rev Gerard Moore Co-PP
The Presbytery, St Mary's, Sandyford Village, Dublin 18
Tel 01-8316219
Rev Linus Ubale PC (*Nigeria*) *(Team Assistant)*
58 Ticknock Park, Ticknock Hill, Sandyford, Dublin 18
Rev Peter Byrne (LC) PC *(Team Assistant)*
c/o Legionaires of Christ, Leopardstown, Foxrock, Dublin 18
*Pastoral Worker:* Sr Angela O'Connor (SHCJ)
Kilmuire, Military Road, Co Dublin
Tel 085-9365769
*Parish Office*: Tel 01-2956414
Email office@sandyfordparish.org
Website www.sandyfordparish.org

**SANDYMOUNT**
*St Mary's Star of the Sea, Dublin 4*
Very Rev John McDonagh Adm
Stella Maris, 15 Oswald Road, Sandymount, Dublin 4
Tel 01-2857773
Rev Peter O'Connor CC
10 Cranfield Place, Sandymount, Dublin 4
Tel 01-6676438
*Parish Office:* Tel 01-6683316
Fax 01-6683894
Email sandymountparish@eircom.net

**SHANKILL**
*St Anne's, Co Dublin*
Very Rev John O'Connor (SAC) PP
St Benin's Parish, Dublin Road, Shankill, Co Dublin
Tel 01-2824425
Email johnhoconnor@hotmail.com
Rev Michael O'Dwyer (SAC) CC
Rev Rory Hanly (SAC) CC
Email roryhanly@yahoo.co.uk
9 Seaview Lawn, Shankill, Co Dublin
*Supply:* Jose Maria Recondo
St Benin's, Dublin Road, Shankill, Co Dublin
*Parish Office*: Tel 01-2822277
Email st.annes-parishoffice@yahoo.ie

**SILLOGE**
*Holy Spirit, Silloge Road, Dublin 11*
*Virgin Mary, Shangan Road, Dublin 9*
Very Rev Gerard Corcoran *(Moderator)*
The Presbytery, Parish of the Virgin Mary, Shangan Road, Dublin 9
Tel 01-8421551/8421451
Email moelitreacha@eircom.net
Rev Expedit Gnoumou PC
Presbytery Holy Spirit Parish, Silloge Road, Ballymun, Dublin 11
*Parish Office*: Tel 01-8620586

**SKERRIES**
*St Patrick's, Co Dublin*
Very Rev Richard Hyland PP
42 Strand Street, Skerries, Co Dublin
Rev Richard Shannon CC
42A Strand Street, Skerries, Co Dublin
*Parish Office*: Tel 01-8106771
Email stpatrickschurchskerries@gmail.com

**SPRINGFIELD**
*St Mark's, Maplewood Road, Tallaght, Dublin 24*
Rev Patrick McKinley *(Moderator)*
68 Maplewood Road, Springfield, Tallaght, Dublin 24
Tel 01-8421551
Rev Gerard Doyle Co-PP
70 Maplewood Road, Tallaght, Dublin 24
Tel 01-4628336
Saule Cameron (PPW)
67 Rheban Manor, Athy, Co Kildare
*Parish Office*: Tel 01-4620777
Email stmarkschurch@eircom.net
Website www.stmarksspringfield.com

**SRULEEN**
*Sacred Heart, St John's Drive, Clondalkin, Dublin 22*
Rev Pearse Mullen (SSCC) Adm
Rev Eamon Aylward (SSCC) PC, CC
*Parish Office*: Tel 01-4570032
Email pb2000@eircom.net

**SUTTON**
*St Fintan's, Greenfield Road, Dublin 13*
Rt Rev Mgr John V. Fitzpatrick PP, EV
3 Glencarraig, Church Road, Sutton, Dublin 13
Tel 01-8323147
Email jvf@eircom.net
Rev Liam Lacey CC
8 Greenfield Road, Sutton, Dublin 13
Tel 01-4627080
Email liamflacey@gmail.com
*Parish Pastoral Worker*: James Daly
Email james.daly@dublindiocese.ie
Tel 01-8392001/086-8701217
*Parish Office:* Tel 01-8392001
Email office@stfintansparish.ie
Website www.stfintansparish.ie

**SWORDS**
*St Colmcille's, Co Dublin*
*(Dublin Airport Church, Our Lady Queen of Heaven is in this parish)*
Very Rev Cyril Mangan PP
5 Lissenhall Park, Seatown Road, Swords, Co Dublin
Tel 01-8403378
Rev James Sheeran CC
The Presbytery, 18 Aspen Road, Kinsealy Court, Swords, Co Dublin
Tel 01-8187908
Rev Desmond G. Doyle PC
Chaplain's Residence, Dublin Airport, Co Dublin
Tel 01-8144340
*Parish Office*: Tel 01-8407277
Email stcolmcilleschurch@eircom.net
Website www.swordsparish.com

**TALLAGHT, DODDER**
*St Dominic's, Dublin 24*
Rev Laurence Collins (OP) Adm
Rev Tom Jordan (OP) *(Priest in residence)*
Presbytery, St Dominic's Road, Tallaght, Dublin 24
Tel 01-4510620 Fax 01-4623223
*Parish Office:* Tel 01-4510620
Fax 01-4623223
Website www.stdominicsparishtallaght.ie

**TALLAGHT, OLDBAWN**
*St Martin de Porres, Dublin 24*
Very Rev David Brough PP, VF
85 Tymon Crescent, Old Bawn, Dublin 24
Tel 01-7168543(w)/2605582(h)
Email davidbrough@eircom.net
Rev David Fleming CC
The Presbytery, St Martin de Porres Parish, Bohernabreena, Tallaght, Dublin 24
Tel 01-4555794
Email davg@eircom.net
*Pastoral Worker:* Breda Carroll
Blackhall, Calverstown, Kilcullen, Co Kildare
Tel 085-1329895
Email stmartinsparish@eircom.net
*Parish Office:* Tel/Fax 01-4510160
Email stmartinsparish@eircom.net

**TALLAGHT, ST MARY'S**
*St Mary's, Tallaght Village, Dublin 24*
Rev Donal Sweeney (OP) Adm
Rev Robert Regula (OP) CC
St Mary's Priory, Tallaght, Dublin 24
Tel 01-4048100 Fax 01-4596784

**TALLAGHT, TYMON NORTH**
*St Aengus's, Castletymon Road, Dublin 24*
Very Rev Benedict Moran (OP) PP
The Presbytery, St Aengus's, Balrothery, Tallaght, Dublin 24
Tel 01-4513757
Email benmoran@indigo.ie.
Rev Albert Leonard (OP) CC
Tel 01-4513757
Email aldleonard@yahoo.com
*Parish Office*: Tel 01-4624038
Email staenguschurch@eircom.net.
Website www.staengusparishtallaght.ie

**TEMPLEOGUE**
*St Pius X, College Drive, Dublin 6W*
Tel 01-4905284
Very Rev Aquinas T. Duffy PP
22 Wainsfort Park, Terenure, Dublin 6W
Tel 01-8842592
Email frduffy@eircom.net
Rev Karl Fortune CC
23 Wainsfort Grove, Terenure, Dublin 6W
*Parish Office:* Tel 01-4905284/087-9672258
Email info@stpiusx.ie
Website www.stpiusx.ie

**TERENURE**
*St Joseph's, Dublin 6*
Very Rev Francis McDonnell PP
Parochial House, 83 Terenure Road East, Dublin 6 Tel 0404-67196
Email fkmcdonnell@eircom.net
Rev Tom Dooley (SM) CC
4 Greenmount Road, Dublin 6
Tel 01-4904959
*Parish Office*: 01-4921755
Email stjosephterenure@eircom.net

**TRAVELLING PEOPLE**
*Chapel of Ease, St Oliver's Park, Clondalkin, Dublin 22*
Very Rev Derek Farrell PP
6 New Cabra Road, Phibsboro, Dublin 7
Tel 087-2573857/4628441
Email derek@ptrav.ie
*Parish Pastoral Worker*
Georgina Jameson
20 Halpin Court, Wicklow Town
*Parish Office:* St Laurence House, 6 New Cabra Road, Phibsboro, Dublin 7
Tel 01-8388874 Fax 01-8388901
*Urgent messages:* Tel 087-2573875
Email into@ptrav.ie. www.ptrav.ie
Recommended Websites:
www.exchangehouse.ie
www.paveepoint.ie
www.stpetersphibsborough.com

**UNIVERSITY CHURCH**
*Our Lady, Seat of Wisdom, St Stephen's Green, Dublin 2*
Very Rev Ciarán O'Carroll Adm, EV
87A St Stephen's Green, Dublin 2
Tel 01-4589002
Rev Shoba Nyambe PC
87B St Stephen's Green, Dublin 2
*Parish Office*: Tel 01-4759674
Website www.universitychurch.ie

**VALLEYMOUNT**
*(Grouped with the parish of Blessington)*
*St Joseph's, Valleymount*
*Our Lady of Mount Carmel, Lacken*
Very Rev Tim Murphy PP
The Presbytery, Main Street, Blessington, Co Wicklow
Tel 045-865442
Rev Edward Downes CC
Parochial House, Cross, Vallymount, Co Wicklow
Tel 01-2826895

**WALKINSTOWN**
*Assumption of the BVM, Dublin 12*
Very Rev John Jacob Adm
12 Walkinstown Road, Dublin 12
Tel 01-4501372
Rev Patrick J. Healy (SDB) CC
162 Walkinstown Road, Dublin 12
Tel 01-4501372
*Parish Sacristy*: Tel 01-4502649

**WHITEFRIAR STREET**
*Our Lady of Mount Carmel, Whitefriar Street, Dublin 2*
Very Rev Charles Hoey (OCarm) PP
Tel 01-8062846
Rev Desmond Kelly (OCarm) CC
Carmelite Priory, 56 Aungier Street, Dublin 2
Tel 01-4758821
Email whitefriars@eircom.net

**WICKLOW**
*St Patrick's, Wicklow, Co Wicklow*
Very Rev Timothy Hannon PP
The Abbey, Wicklow, Co Wicklow
Tel 0404-46229
Email bal.tor@hotmail.com
Rev Denis Nolan CC
The Presbytery, Rathnew, Co Wicklow
Tel 0404-67488/087-2389594
Email drnolan@eircom.net
Rev James McPartland CC
St Patrick's Road, Wicklow Town, Co Wicklow
Tel 01-4540534
Email jmcpart@gofree.indigo.ie
*Parish Office:* Tel 0404-61699
Email parishofficewicklow@eircom.net
Website See http://www.carmelites.ie/Ireland/irelandtoday.htm and click on the Whitefriar Street link

**WILLINGTON**
*St Jude the Apostle, Orwell Park, Dublin 6W*
Very Rev Gregory O'Brien PP
2 Rossmore Road, Templeogue, Dublin 6W
Tel 01-8385244
*Parish Office*: Tel 01-4600127
Email judesparishoffice@eircom.net

**YELLOW WALLS, MALAHIDE**
*(Grouped with the parishes of Malahide, Kinsealy & Portmarnock)*
*Sacred Heart Church, Eastuary Road, Malahide, Co Dublin*
Very Rev Peter Briscoe Adm PP
12 The Warren, Malahide, Co Dublin
Tel 01-6684265

Rev Frank Reburn CC
11 Millview Court, Malahide, Co Dublin
Tel 01-8338575
Email fdreburn@hotmail.com
Rev Paul Thornton CC
146 Seapark, Malahide, Co Dublin
Email thorntonpaul@eircom.net
Email yellowwallsparish@gmail.com
Website www.yellowwallsparish.ie

## INSTITUTIONS AND THEIR CHAPLAINS

### COLLEGES

**Coláiste Mhuire Marino**
Griffith Avenue, Dublin 9
*Chaplain:* Vacant

**Dublin Institute of Technology**
**Co-ordinator of Chaplaincy Team at DIT:**
Sr Mary Flanagan
*Office:* 143-149 Rathmines Road, Dublin 6
Tel 01-4023307 Fax 01-4023449
Email mary.flangan@dit.ie

**Dublin Institute of Technology at Bolton Street**
Tel 01-4023000 Fax 01-4023999
*Chaplain:* Rev Alan Hilliard
Office Tel 01-4023618

**Dublin Institute of Technology at Kevin Street**
Ms Fionnuala Walsh
Tel 01-4024568 Fax 01-4024999
Email fionnuala.walsh@dit.ie

**Dublin Institute of Technology at Mounjoy Square**
Tel 01-4023000 Fax 01-4024298
Contact Co-ordinator of Chaplaincy

**Dublin Institute of Technology at Cathal Brugha Street**
Tel 01-4023000 Fax 01-4024499
*Chaplain:* Mr Finbarr O'Leary
Tel 01-4024308

**Dublin Institute of Technology at Aungier Street**
Tel 01-4023000 Fax 01-4023003
*Chaplain:* Sr Mary Flanagan
Office Tel 01-4023050
Email mary.flanagan@dit.ie
*Residence:* 14 Heather Lawn,
Marlay Wood, Dublin 16
Tel 01-4942324

**Dublin Institute of Technology at Rathmines Road**
Tel 01-4023000 Fax 01-4023499
Contact Co-ordinator of Chaplaincy

**Dublin Institute of Technology at Adelaide Road**
Tel 01-4023000
Contact Co-ordinator of Chaplaincy

**Dublin City University**
Rev Joe Jones
InterFaith Centre, Dublin 9
Tel 01-7005268 Fax 01-7005663
*Residence:* 30 Willow Park Crescent
Glasnevin, Dublin 11
Email joe.jones@dcu.ie

**Institute of Technology**
Tallaght, Dublin 24
Tel 01-4042000
Sr Bernadette Purcell

**Mater Dei Institute of Education**
Tel 01-8376027
Mr Barrie McEntee

**National College of Art and Design**
100 Thomas Street, Dublin 8
*Chaplain:* Vacant

**St Patrick's College, Drumcondra**
Dublin 9
Tel 01-8842000
Rev Sean Farrell (CM)

**National University of Ireland, Maynooth (NUIM)**
Chaplaincy Service,
NUI Maynooth, Co Kildare
Tel 01-7083588
*Chaplains:* Mr Shay Claffey
Tel 01-7083588
Email seamus.claffey@nuim.ie
*Executive Assistant:* Ms Susan Caldwell
Tel 01-7083320
Email susan.caldwell@nuim.ie

**Trinity College, Dublin 2**
Rev Patrick Gleeson
Tel 01-6081260
48 Westland Row, Dublin 2
Rev Peter Sexton (SJ)
House 27 Trinity College, Dublin 2
Tel 01-8961260

**University College, Dublin**
Chaplains' Room, UCD, Belfield, Dublin 4
Tel 01-7068317
Rev John McNerney Tel 01-2600715
Rev John Callanan (SJ) Tel 01-7167408
Rev Leon Ó Giollain (SJ)
*Chaplains' Residence:* St Stephen's, UCD
Belfield, Dublin 4 Tel 01-7161971

### DEFENCE FORCES

**Department of Defence**
Colaiste Caoimhin, Glasnevin, Dublin 9
Tel 01-8379911 ext 3197 Fax 01-8379928

**Head Chaplain**
Rt Rev Mgr Eoin Thynne HCF
Tel 01-8042270
*Administrative Secretary:* Sgt John Kellett

**McKee Barracks**
Dublin 7
Tel 01-8388614
Rev Patrick Mernagh

**McKee Barracks and St Bricin's Hospital**
Dublin 7
Tel 01-6778502
Rt Rev Mgr Eoin Thynne HCF

**Cathal Brugha Barracks**
Rathmines, Dublin 6
Tel 01-8046493
Rev David Tyndall

**Casement Aerodrome**
Baldonnel, Co Dublin
Tel 01-4592497
Rev Jerry Carroll

**International Military Pilgrimage to Lourdes**
(Pelerinage Militaire Internationale)
*Director:* Defence Forces HQ, Dublin 9
Tel 01-8042271

**KFOR**
Irish Transport Company, KFOR
BSPO 559, London, England

### HOSPITALS

**Adelaide and Meath Hospital**
*(Incorporating National Children's Hospital)*
Tallaght, Dublin 24
Tel 01-4142000/4142480
*Chaplains:* Rev John Kelly,
Ms Eden dela Cruz, Ms Catherine Shirley,
Ms Kathleen Graham

**Baggot Street Hospital**
Baggot Street, Dublin 4
Vacant

**Beaumont Hospital**
Beaumont Road, Dublin 9
Tel 01-8377755
*Direct Line:* 01-8092815/8093229
Rev Eoin Hughes Tel 01-8477573
Rev Denis Sandham (OSCam)
Rev Kevin Kiernan (OFMCap)
Ms Jenny Cuypers

**Beaumont Convalescent Home**
Tel 8379186
Vacant

**Blackrock Clinic**
Blackrock, Co Dublin
Tel 01-2832222
Rev Gerard Byrne

**Blackrock Hospice**
Sweetman's Avenue, Blackrock, Co Dublin
Tel 01-2064000
Sr Ann Purcell

**Bloomfield**
Donnybrook, Dublin 4
Tel 01-4950021
Carmelite Fathers, Avila,
Morehampton Road, Dublin 4
Tel 01-6683155/6683091

**Bon Secours Hospital**
Glasnevin, Dublin 9
Tel 01-8065300
Rev William Ryan (OFMCap), Sr Goretti Spillane, Ms Fionnuala Prunty, Ms Patricia Nolan, Ms Eileen Kavanagh

**Cappagh National Orthopaedic Hospital**
Cappagh, Dublin 11
Tel 01-8341211
Appointment Pending

**Central Mental Hospital**
Dundrum
Tel 01-2989266
Rev Desmond O'Grady (SJ)

**Cherry Orchard Hospital**
Ballyfermot
Tel 01-6264702
Rev Seamus Fleming (CSSp)
St Mary's Presbytery, Lucan, Co Dublin
Tel 086-8903864

**Children's Hospital**
Temple Street
Tel 01-8748763
Sr Julie Buckley

**Clonskeagh Hospital**
Vergemount, Dublin 6
Tel 01-2697877
Appointment Pending

**Coombe Women's and Infant's University Hospital**
Dolphin's Barn, Dublin 8
Tel 01-4085200
Ms Catherine Dilworth, Sr Gina Chua

**Connolly Hospital**
Blanchardstown, Dublin 15
Tel 01-8213844
Rev Martin Geraghty (OSCam)
Rev Anthony O'Riordan (SVD)
Tel 01-6465168
Ms Caroline Mullen

**Hermitage Medical Centre**
Old Lucan Road, Lucan, Co Dublin
Tel 01-6459000
Rev Vincent O'Connell (CSSp)
Kimmage Tel 01-4928561

**Leopardstown Park Hospital**
Tel 01-2955055
Sr Annette Byrne
Ms Miriam Molan

**Mater Hospital**
Eccles Street, Dublin 7
Tel 01-8301122
Rev Vincent Xavier Kakkadampallil (OSCam), Rev John Philip Kakkarakunnel, Ms Catherine Ingoldsby, Ms Maire Breathnach, Sr Mary Flynn, Ms Margaret Sleator

**Mater Private Hospital**
Dublin 7
Tel 01-8858888
Rev Kieran Dunne

**Mount Carmel Hospital**
Tel 01-4922211
Rev Pat Horgan (CSSp)
Marianella, 75 Orwell Road, Rathgar, Dublin 6
Tel 01-4922688

**National Maternity Hospital**
Holles Street, Dublin 2
Tel 01-6373100
Sr Marion Ryan
Ms Eithne O'Reilly

**National Rehabilitation Hospital**
Rochestown Avenue,
Dun Laoghaire, Co Dublin
Tel 01-2854777
Rev Michael Kennedy (CSSp)
Sr Catherine O'Neill

**Newcastle Hospital**
Tel 01-2819001
Rev Sean Smith CC
The Presbytery, Newtownmountkennedy, Co Wicklow
Tel 01-2819253

**Orthopaedic Hospital**
Castle Avenue, Clontarf
Tel 01-8332521
Rev Míceál Hastings

**Our Lady's Hospice**
Harold's Cross
Tel 01-4972101
Rev Brendan McKeever CP
Ms Elizabeth Coyle
Sr Rose Gallagher

**Our Lady's Children's Hospital**
Crumlin, Dublin 12
Tel 01-4096100
Rev Anthony Conlan, Ms Katherine McElwee, Ms Maria McGee

**Peamount Hospital**
Newcastle, Co Dublin
Tel 01-6010300
Rev Jim Byrnes (CSSp)

**Rotunda Hospital**
Parnell Street, Dublin 1
Tel 01-8730700
Ms Anne Charlton
Tel 01-8745441

**Royal Hospital Donnybrook**
Morehampton Road, Dublin 4
Tel 01-4972844
Appointment Pending

**Royal Victoria Eye and Ear Hospital**
Adelaide Road, Dublin 12
Tel 01-6785500
*Chaplain:* Vacant

**St Brendan's Hospital**
Upper Grangegorman, Dublin 7
Tel 01-8693000
Rev Piaras Ó Duill (OFMCap)
Tel 01-8730599

**St Bricin's Military Hospital**
Infirmary Road, Dublin 8
Tel 01-6776112
Rt Rev Mgr Eoin Thynne (HCF)

**St Columcille's Hospital**
Loughlinstown, Co Dublin
Tel 01-2825800
Rev Desmond Farren (MSC)
Ms Marianne Quinn

**St Francis Hospice**
Raheny, Dublin 5
Tel 01-8327535
Rev Eustace McScweeney (OFMCap)
Capuchin Friary, Raheny, Dublin 5
Tel 01-8313886
Sr Marian Gribbin, Sr Anna Kennedy, Sr Maire Brady

**St Ita's, Portrane**
Tel 01-8436337
Very Rev Joseph Connolly PP
Parochial House, Donabate, Co Dublin
Tel 01-8436011

**St James's Hospital**
James's Street, Dublin 8
Tel 01-4103000
Direct Line 01-4103659/4162023
Rev Brian Gough, Rev Jim Stapleton (CSSp), Sr Joyce Cullinane, Sr Anne Kelly

**St John of God Hospital**
Stillorgan, Co Dublin
Tel 01-2881781
Rev Hugh Gillan (OH)

**St Joseph's Hospital**
Clonsilla
Tel 01-8217177
*Chaplain:* Vacant

**St Joseph's Hospital**
Springdale Road, Raheny, Dublin 5
Tel 01-8478433
Appointment Pending

**St Loman's Hospital**
Ballyowen, Palmerstown, Dublin 20
Tel 01-6264077
Rev Jeremiah Lambe (CSSp)

**St Luke's Hospital**
Highfield Road, Rathgar, Dublin 6
Rev Patrick O'Brien (OSCam)
Tel 01-4065000 Res 01-2882873

**St Mary's Hospital**
Phoenix Park, Dublin 20
Tel 01-6250300
Rev Linus Mbajo (CSSp)
Rev John Agbaragba (CSSp)
Rev Azenda Ikyegh (CSSp)

**St Michael's Hospital**
Lower George's Street, Dun Laoghaire
Tel 01-2806901
Rev Thomas McDonald (CSSp)
Sr Margaret Hilliard

**St Patrick's Hospital**
James Street, Dublin 8
Tel 01-6775423
*Chaplain:* Vacant

**St Paul's (Autistic Children)**
Beaumont
Tel 01-8377673
Very Rev Gerard Deegan Adm
Tel 01-8477740

**St Vincent's Hospital**
Athy, Co Kildare
Tel 059-8643000
Dominican Fathers Athy
Tel 059-8631573

**St Vincent's University Hospital**
Elm Park, Dublin 4
Tel 01-2214000
Direct Line 01-2094325
Rev Jim MacDonnell (CSSp), Rev Liam Cuffe

**St Vincent's Private Hospital**
Tel 01-2638000
Rev John O'Keeffe (SJ), Rev Brendan Staunton (SJ), Sr Jacinta Forde, Ms Niamh Brennan

**St Vincent's, Fairview**
Tel 01-8375101
Mr Jim Owens

**Stewart's Hospital, Palmerstown**
Tel 01-6264444
Rev Linus Mbajo (CSSp)
Rev John Agbaragba (CSSp)
Rev Azenda Ikyegh (CSSp)

**St Colman's, Rathdrum**
Tel 0404-46109
Very Rev Brian O'Reilly PP
Tel 0404-46229

## PRISONS

**Arbour Hill Prison**
Ard na Gaoithe, Arbour Hill, Dublin 7
Rev Ciaran Enright
Email ccenright@irishprisons.ie
*Prison General Office:* Tel 01-6719333

**Clover Hill Remand Centre**
Cloverhill Road, Clondalkin, Dublin 22
Rev John O'Sullivan (MSC)
Tel 01-6304586
Email jjosullivan@irishprisons.ie
Sr Carmel Miley (CP)
Tel 01-6304585
Email cjmiley@irishprisons.ie
Sr Margaret O'Donovan (DC)
Tel 01-6304584
Email mmodonovan@irishprisons.ie
*Prison General Office:* Tel 01-6304531/2

**Dóchas Centre Mountjoy Women's Prison**
North Circular Road, Dublin 7
Sr Mary Mullins Tel 01-8858920
Email mtmullins@irishprisons.ie
Prison General Office 01-8858987

**Mountjoy Prison**
North Circular Road, Dublin 7
Mrs Ruth Breen
Tel 01-8062843
Email rabreen@irishprisons.ie
Mark Davis
Tel 01-8062843
Sr Gráinne Haslam (RSM)
Tel 01-8062846
Rev Jimmy Kelly (OSM)
Tel 01-8062843
*Prison General Office:* Tel 01-8062800

**Saint Patrick's Institution**
North Circular Road, Dublin 7
Tel 01-8062894
Miss Ruth Comerford
Email rmcomerford@irishprisons.ie
*General Office:* Tel 01-8062906

**Shelton Abbey**
Arklow, Co Wicklow
Sr Patricia Egan (RSCJ)
Tel 0402-42321
*General Office:* Tel 0402-42300

**Training Unit**
Glengariff Parade, Dublin 7
Sr Mairead Gahan LCM
Tel 01-8309612
Email gahanmairead@eircom.net
*Prison General Office:* Tel 01-8062881

**Wheatfield Prison**
Cloverhill Road, Clondalkin, Dublin 22
Sr Esther Murphy (RSC) Tel 01-6209447
Email esmurphy@irishprisons.ie
Sr Imelda Wickham (PBVM)
Tel 01-6209466
Email imwickham@irishprisons.ie
Sr Joan Kane (OSU) Tel 01-6209446
Email jakane@irishprisons.ie
Sr Kathleen Cunningham (DC)
Tel 01-6209466/7
*Prison General Office:* Tel 01-6209400

## PRIESTS ELSEWHERE IN THE DIOCESE

Rev Patrick Desmond
Apostolic Nunciature, *Res:* The Lodge, Mount Sackville, Chapelizod, Dublin 20
Tel 01-8214004
Rev Patrick Jones, Director
National Centre for Liturgy,
St Patrick's College, Maynooth, Co Kildare
Tel 01-7083478
Rev Brendan Leahy
St Patrick's College, Maynooth, Co Kildare
Rev Dermod McCarthy
RTÉ, Donnybrook, Dublin 4
Tel 01-2083237/087-2499719 Fax 01-2083974
Email mccartd@rte.ie
Rev Peter Murphy
Accord Catholic Marriage Care Service,
Columba Centre, Maynooth, Co Kildare

## PRIESTS WORKING OUTSIDE THE DIOCESE

Rev Seamus Connell
c/o St Columban's, Dalgan Park,
Navan, Co Meath
Rev Adrian Crowley
Instituto de Idiomas Maryknoll Padres,
Casilla 550, Cochabamba, Bolivia
Rev Ian Evans
Chaplain, England
Rev John Kennedy (Congregation for the Doctrine of the Faith)
Via del Mascherino 12, 00193 Roma, Italy
Rev Eoin Murphy
St Joseph's Church, 109 Linden Street,
Saint John's, MI48879, USA
Rev Seamus O'Brien
c/o Diocese of Monterey,
580 Fremont Street, Monterey,
CA 93943-3216, USA
Very Rev Ciaran O'Carroll
Rector, Pontifical Irish College,
Via dei SS Quattro 1, 00184, Roma
Rev Desmond O'Reilly
St Charles Borromeo Parish,
7584 Center Parkway, Sacramento,
California 95823, USA
Rt Rev Mgr Paul Tighe
Secretary of the Pontifical Council for Social Communications, Vatican City

## RETIRED PRIESTS

Very Rev John Canon Battelle PE
14 Pine Valley, Grange Road, Dublin 16
Very Rev Denis T. Bergin
76 Trintonville Road,
Sandymount, Dublin 4
Rt Rev Mgr Andrew P. Canon Boland PE
13 Griffith Avenue, Dublin 9
Very Rev Bernard Canon Brady
61 Glasnevin Hill, Dublin 9
Ven Archdeacon Macarten Brady PE,
Sacred Heart Residence, Sybil Hill Road,
Killester, Dublin 5
Rev Noel Campbell
Ballysmutlan, Manor Kilbride,
Blessington, Co Wicklow
Very Rev Brendan F. Canon Carbury
Elmhurst, Hampstead Avenue,
Glasnevin, Dublin 11
Very Rev Patrick Carmody
16 Hazelgrove, Ardfert, Co Kerry
Rev Denis Carroll
85 Hillcrest Drive, Esker, Lucan, Co Dublin
Very Rev Seamus Cassidy
Tavis, Kilmainham Wood, Kells, Co Meath
Rev Myles Christy
c/o Elmhurst Nursing Home, Hampstead Avenue, Glasnevin, Dublin 9
Rev Diarmuid Connolly
4 Summerfield Lawn, Blanchardstown,
Dubin 15
Rev Michael Connolly
54 Wyattville Park,
Loughlinstown, Co Dublin
Very Rev Philip Corcoran
c/o Archbishop's House
Rev Edward Corry
Presbytery No. 2, Treepark Road,
Kilnamanagh, Dublin 24
Very Rev Patrick J. Culhane
138 Lucan Road, Chapelizod, Dublin 20
Rev Seamus F. Cullen
2 Ceol na Mara, Lower Main Street,
Rush, Co Dublin
Tel 01-8438024
Email scullen1@eircom.net
Very Rev Hugh Daly PE
St Mary's, 50 Cremore Road,
Glasnevin, Dublin 11
Rev Aidan D'Arcy
Little Sisters of the Poor, Sybil Hill,
Raheny, Dublin 5
Rev Philip Dennehy
4 Stanhope Place, Athy, Co Kildare
Rev Cornelius Dowling
St Anthony's, 13 Richmond Grove,
Monkstown, Co Dublin
Tel 01-2800789
Email dowcpb@eircom.net
Rev Patrick Canon Dowling
Holy Family Residence, Roebuck,
Dundrum, Dublin 14
Rev Tom Early
23 Estuary Road, Malahide
Tel 01-8450122
Very Rev Patrick Fagan PE
The Presbytery, Ballyboughal, Co Dublin
Rev James Fingleton
279 Howth Road, Raheny, Dublin 5
Very Rev John Canon Fitzgibbon PE
The Presbytery, Chapel Road,
Lusk, Co Dublin
Very Rev Denis Foley
32 Walkinstown Road, Dublin 12
Very Rev Desmond Forristal
St Joseph's Centre, Crinken Lane,
Shankill, Co Dublin
Very Rev Paul Freeney PE
Parochial House,
43 Upper Beechwood Avenue,
Ranelagh, Dublin 6
Very Rev Mgr Colm Gallagher
594 Howth Road, Raheny, Dublin 5
Very Rev J. Anthony Gaughan
56 Newtownpark Avenue, Blackrock,
Co Dublin

Rev Michael Geaney
7 Rockliffe Terrace, Blackrock Road, Cork
Very Rev Walter Canon Harris PE
151 Clonsilla Road, Blanchardstown, Dublin 15
Very Rev Mícheál Hastings
103 Mount Prospect Drive, Clontarf, Dublin 3
Tel 01-8335255/087-2358634
Very Rev Liam Hickey
St Ciaran's, 1 Cherryfield Park, Hartstown, Dublin 15
Very Rev Ciaran Holahan
11 Foxrock Court, Foxrock, Dublin 18
Rev Cecil Johnston
8 Corrig Park, Dun Laoghaire, Co Dublin
Tel 01-285594
Rev Bert Kelly
Presbytery No 1, Rathdrum, Co Wicklow
Tel 0404-46214
Very Rev James J. Kelly PE
Parochial House, Clogher Road, Dublin 12
Very Rev Thomas V. Kelly
Castlebar Road, Westport, Co Mayo
Very Rev Eugene Kennedy
7 Riverwood Vale, Castleknock, Dublin 15
Email ekennedy@laurellodgeparish.ie
Very Rev James Canon Loughran PE
Maryfield Nursing Home, Chapelizod, Dublin 20
Rev John Lynch
2 Cooleen Avenue, Beaumont, Dublin 9
Rt Rev Mgr James Ardle Canon MacMahon
Queen of Peace Centre,
6 Garville Avenue, Rathgar, Dublin 6
Very Rev John Canon MacMahon
Holy Family Residence, Roebuck, Dundrum, Dublin 14
Rev Christopher J. Madden, Lisieux
196 Oakcourt Avenue, Palmerstown, Dublin 20
Very Rev Patrick J. Mangan PE
Dun Mhuire, 44 Upper Beechwood Avenue, Ranelagh, Dublin 6
Very Rev Val Martin
c/o Archbishop's House
Rev Colm Mathews
47 Old Court Manor, Dublin 24
Very Rev Eugene McCarney
Parochial House, Castletown, Gorey, Co Wexford
Rev Padraig McCarthy
14 Blackthorn Court, Sandyford, Dublin 16
Rev Cornelius McGillicuddy
Sacred Heart Residence, Sybil Hill Road, Killester, Dublin 5
Rt Rev Mgr John J. Moloney PE
50 Rathgar Road, Dublin 6
Rev Raymond Canon Molony
Presbytery No 2, Thormanby Road, Howth, Co Dublin
Tel 01-8222092
Very Rev Patrick B. Moore PE
25 Thomastown Road, Dun Laoghaire, Co Dublin
Very Rev Seamus Moore
8 Herbert Avenue, Dublin 4
Rev John F. Moran
192 Navan Road, Dublin 7
Very Rev Benedict Mulligan
42 Corke Abbey, Little Bray, Co Wicklow
Very Rev Patrick Mulvey
Our Lady's Manor, Dalkey, Co Dublin
Very Rev Thomas Murphy
17 Glencorp Road, Larkhill, Dublin 9
Rev James Murray
9 Hillcrest Manor, Templeogue, Dublin 6W
Very Rev Liam Murtagh
33 Grace Park Road, Drumcondra, Dublin 9
Tel 087-2408416
Very Rev Ronald Neville PE
213a Harold's Cross Road, Dublin 6
Rev Sean Noone
The Presbytery, Pollathomas, Co Mayo
Rev James O'Brien
Sacred Heart Residence, Sybil Hill Road, Killester, Dublin 5
Very Rev John O'Connell PE
53 Ardmore Wood, Herbert Road, Bray, Co Wicklow
Canon Erill O'Connor
14 Clare Road, Dublin 9
Tel 01-8372677
Very Rev Donal O'Doherty PE
Holy Cross, Upper Kilmacud Road, Dundrum, Dublin 14
Rev Philip O'Driscoll
23 Barclay Court, Blackrock, Co Dublin
Very Rev Thomas O'Keeffe
20 Glen Avenue, The Park, Cabinteely, Dublin 18
Very Rev Maurice O'Moore PE
6 Richmond Avenue, Monkstown, Co Dublin
Very Rev Sean O'Neill PE
'Iona', 3 St Colmcille's Park, Swords, Co Dublin
Rev Sean O'Rourke
15 Seaview Park, Shankill, Co Dublin
Rev Padraig O'Saorai
12 Ashville, Athy, Co Kildare
Rev Brian O'Sullivan
The Cottage, Glengara Park, Glenageary, Dun Laoghaire, Co Dublin
Rev John K. O'Sullivan
97 Kincora Avenue, Clontarf, Dublin 3
Rev Sean O'Toole
Presbytery, Sea Road Arklow
Tel 0402-32153
Email seanotoole@eircom.net
Rev Sean Quigley
The Presbytery, 48 Aughrim Street, Dublin 7
Very Rev Leo Quinlan
'Carrefour', Jarretstown, Dunboyne, Co Meath
Very Rev James A. Canon Randles PE
Sacred Heart Residence, Sybil Hill Road, Killester, Dublin 5
Rev Henry Regan
Presbytery No. 1, Church Grounds, Kill Avenue, Dun Laoghaire, Co Dublin
Very Rev Denis Ryan PE
Parochial House House,
1 Rossmore Road, Dublin 6W
Very Rev Patrick G. Ryan
Mounthaven Lodge Nursing Home, Kilcock, Co Kildare
Rt Rev Mgr Richard Sherry PE
Presbytery No 2, Stillorgan Road, Donnybrook, Dublin 4
Very Rev Patrick Shiel
74 Mount Drinan Avenue, Kinsealy Downs, Swords, Co Dublin
Very Rev Mgr Thomas Stack PE
Apt 4, Maple Hall (adjoining church), SS Columbanus and Gall, Milltown, Dublin 6
Very Rev John Stokes
44 Carlton Court, Swords, Co Dublin
Tel 01-8138566
Rev Michael D. Supple
Holy Family Residence, Roebuck Road, Dublin 14
Rt Rev Mgr Owen Sweeney
54 Seabury, Sydney Parade Avenue, Dublin 4
Rev Jeremiah Threadgold
Sacred Heart Residence, Sybil Hill Road, Raheny, Dublin 5
Rev Michael Wall
Sacred Heart Residence, Sybil Hill Road, Killester, Dublin 5
Rev John M. Ward
1 Chestnut Grove, Ballymount Road, Dublin 24

## PERSONAL PRELATURE

**OPUS DEI**
Harvieston, Cunningham Road, Dalkey, Co Dublin
Tel 01-2859877 Fax 01-2305059
*Vicar for Ireland:*
Rev Justin Gillespie DD

## RELIGIOUS ORDERS AND CONGREGATIONS

## PRIESTS

**AUGUSTINIANS**
St Augustine's, Taylor's Lane, Ballyboden, Dublin 16
Tel 01-4241000 Fax 01-4939915
Email www.augustinians.ie
*Provincial:* Rev Gerry Horan (OSA)
*Prior:* Rev John Lyng (OSA)

St John's Priory, Thomas Street, Dublin 8
Tel 01-6770393/6770415/6770601
Fax 01-6713102/6770423
*Prior:* Rev Tony Egan (OSA)

Orlagh Retreat Centre
Old Court Road, Dublin 16
Tel 01-4930932/4933315/4931163
Fax 01-4930987
Email orlagh@augustinians.ie
*Prior:* Rev John Byrne (OSA)

(See also under parishes – Ballyboden, Meath Street and Rivermount)

**BLESSED SACRAMENT CONGREGATION**
Blessed Sacrament Chapel,
20 Bachelors Walk, Dublin 1
Tel 01-8724597 Fax 01-8724724
Email sssdublin@eircom.net
*Superior:* Rev James Campbell (SSS)

**CAMILLIANS**
St Camillus, South Hill Avenue,
Blackrock, Co Dublin
Tel 01-2882873 Fax 01-2833380
*Superior:* Rev Denis Sandham

St Camillus,
11 St Vincent Street North, Dublin 7
Tel 01-8300365

**CAPUCHINS**
Provincial Office
12 Halston Street, Dublin 7
Tel 01-8733205 Fax 01-8730294
Email capcurirl@eircom.net
*Provincial Minister*
Very Rev Desmond McNaboe (OFMCap)

St Mary of the Angels, Church Street,
Dublin 7
Tel Parish 01-8730925
Tel Friary 01-8730599/Fax 01-8730250
*Guardian:* Rev Bryan Shortall (OFMCap)

Capuchin Friary (Immaculate Heart of Mary), Raheny, Dublin 5
Tel 01-8313886/8312805
*Guardian* and *Definitor*
Rev John Wright (OFMCap)

(See also under parishes – Halston Street and Priorswood)

**CARMELITES (OCARM)**
Provincial Office, Gort Muire,
Ballinteer, Dublin 16
Tel 01-2984014 Fax 01-2987221
*Provincial*: Rev Martin Kilmurray (OCarm)

Whitefriar Street Church,
56 Aungier Street, Dublin 2
Tel 01-4758821 Fax 01-4758825
Email whitefriars@eircom.net
*Prior*: Rev David Weakliam (OCarm)
*Parish Priest:* Rev Charles Hoey (OCarm)

Terenure College, Terenure, Dublin 6W
Tel 01-4904621 Fax 01-4902403
Email admin@terenurecollege.ie
*Prior/Manager:* Rev Michael Troy (OCarm)
*Sub-Prior:* Rev Eoin Moore (OCarm)
*Principal (Senior School):*
Rev Eanna Ó hÓbáin (OCarm)
*Principal (Junior School):*
Rev Michael Troy (OCarm)

(See also under parishes – Knocklyon and Whitefriar Street)

**CARMELITES (OCD)**
53 Marlborough Road, Donnybrook,
Dublin 4
Tel 01-6617163 Fax 01-6683752
Email jnoonan@ocd.ie
Website www.ocd.ie
*Provincial:* Rev James Noonan (OCD)

St Teresa's, Clarendon Street, Dublin 2
Tel 01-6718466/6718127
*Prior:* Rev Christopher Clarke (OCD)

Avila, Bloomfield Avenue,
Morehampton Road, Dublin 4
Tel 01-6430200 Fax 01-6430281
Email avila@ocd.ie
*Prior:* Rev Michael McGoldrick (OCD)

Karmel Vocation Centre,
53/55 Marlborough Road, Dublin 4
Tel 01-6601832
*Prior:* Rev Edward Smyth (OCD)

St Joseph's, Berkeley Road, Dublin 7
Tel 01-8306356/8306336
*Prior:* Rev David Donnellan (OCD) PP

**CISTERCIANS**
Bolton Abbey, Moone, Co Kildare
Tel 059-8624102 Fax 059-8624309
Email info@boltonabbey.ie
Website www.boltonabbey.ie
*Abbot:* Rt Rev Dom Peter Garvey (OCSO)

**COMBONI MISSIONARIES**
8 Clontarf Road, Dublin 3
Tel/Fax 01-8330051
Email combonimission@eircom.net
*Superior:* Rev Antonio Benetti (MCCJ)

**CONGREGATION OF THE PRIESTS OF THE SACRED HEART OF JESUS**
Fairfield, 66 Inchicore Road, Dublin 8
Tel 01-4538655
Email scjdublin@eircom.net
House of Formation
*Superior and Formation Director:*
Rev John Kelly (SCJ)

(See also under parishes – Ardlea)

**CONGREGATION OF THE SACRED HEARTS OF JESUS AND MARY (SACRED HEARTS COMMUNITY)**
*Provincialate:* Coudrin House,
27 Northbrook Road, Dublin 6
Tel 01-6604898
Email ssccdublin@eircom.net
Website www.sacredhearts.ie
Community 01-6686584 Fax 01-6686590
*Provincial*: Very Rev Derek Laverty (SSCC)

Sacred Heart Presbytery,
St John's Drive, Clondalkin, Dublin 22
Tel 01-4570032

(See also under parishes – Sruleen)

**DIVINE WORD MISSIONARIES**
3 Pembroke Road, Dublin 4
Tel 01-6680904
*Praeses:* Rev Albert Escoto
Email albert_escoto2000@yahoo.com

133 North Circular Road, Dublin 7
Tel 01-8386743
Email provincial@svdireland.com
*Provincial:* Rev Patrick Byrne
*Praeses:* Rev John Feighery

Maynooth, Co Kildare
Tel 01-6286391/2 Fax 01-6289184
Email dv.twomey@may.ie
*Rector:* Rev D. Vincent Twomey

(See also under parishes – City Quay)

**DOMINICANS**
Provincial Office, St Mary's,
Tallaght, Dublin 24
Tel 01-4048118/4048112 Fax 01-4515584
Email provincialop@eircom.net
*Provincial:* Very Rev Pat Lucey (OP)

St Mary's Priory, Tallaght, Dublin 24
Tel 01-4048100 Fax 01-4596784
Parish 01-4048188
*Prior:* Very Rev Donal Sweeney (OP) PP
Email dsyop@eircom.net

St Saviour's,
Upper Dorset Street, Dublin 1
Tel 01-8897610 Fax 01-8734003
Email stsaviours@eircom.net
*Prior:* Very Rev Gregory Carroll (OP) PP

St Dominic's,
Athy, Co Kildare
Tel 059-8631573 Fax 059-8631649
*Prior:* Very Rev Joseph O'Brien (OP)

Dominican Community,
47 Leeson Park, Dublin 6
Tel 01-6602427
*Superior:* Very Rev Bernard Treacy (OP)

(See also under parishes – Dominick Street and three of the Tallaght parishes)

**FRANCISCANS (OFM)**
Provincial Office, Franciscan Friary,
4 Merchant's Quay, Dublin 4
Tel 01-6742500 Fax 01-6742549
Email greccio@eircom.net
*Provincial:* Rev Hugh McKenna (OFM)
Email hughmck@gmail.com

Adam and Eve's, Merchant's Quay,
Dublin 8
Tel 01-6771128 Fax 01-6771000
*Guardian:* Br Niall O'Connell (OFM)

Franciscan House of Studies,
Dún Mhuire, Seafield Road,
Killiney, Co Dublin
Tel 01-2826760 Fax 01-2826993
Email dmkilliney@eircom.net
*Guardian:* Rev Kieran Cronin (OFM)

(See also under parishes – Merchant's Quay)

**FRANCISCANS: ORDER OF FRIARS MINOR**
Conventual (Greyfriars) (OFMConv)
The Friary of the Visitation of the BVM,
Fairview Strand, Fairview, Dublin 3
Tel 01-8376000 Fax 01-8376021

(See also under parishes – Fairview)

**HOLY SPIRIT CONGREGATION**
Holy Spirit Provincialate, Temple Park,
Richmond Avenue South, Dublin 6
Tel 01-4977230/4975127 Fax 01-4975399
Email secretaryspiritan@irishspiritans.ie
*Provincial Leadership Tam*
Rev Brian Starken (CSSp), Rev Peter Conaty (CSSp), Rev Seán O'Leary (CSSp)

Holy Spirit Education Office,
(Des Places Educational Association Ltd),
Kimmage Manor, Dublin 12
Tel 01-4997610
www.desplaces.ie
Awareness Education Office
Rev Tony Byrne (CSSp)
Tel/Fac 01-8388888
Email info@awarenesseducation.org

Holy Spirit Missionary College,
Kimmage Manor,
Whitehall Road, Dublin 12
Tel 01-4064300 Fax 01-4920062
*Community Leader*
Rev Michael Kilkenny (CSSp)
Development Studies Centre
Tel 01-4064386 Fax 01-4064388
*Director:* Mr Patrick Reilly

Spiritan House – SPIRASI Project,
Spiritan Asylum Services Initiative,
213 North Circular Road, Dublin 7
Tel 01-8389664
*Director:* Mr Greg Straton

Blackrock College, Blackrock, Co Dublin
Tel 01-2888681 Fax 01-2834267
Email info@blackrockcollege.com
*Community Leader*: Rev Tom Nash (CSSp)
*Principal:* Alan MacGinty

Willow Park
Tel 01-2881651 Fax 01-2783353
Email admin@willowparkschool.ie
*Principal Senior School:* Mr Donal Brennan
*Principal Junior School:* Mr Jim Casey

St Mary's College, Rathmines, Dublin 6
Tel 01-4998760 Fax 01-4972621
Junior School Tel 01-4995721
Email junsec@stmarys.ie
Senior School Tel 4995700 Fax 01-4972574
Email sensec@stmarys.ie
*Community Leader*
Rev John B. Doyle (CSSp)
*Principal Secondary School*
Mr Denis Murphy
*Principal Junior School*
Mrs Mary O'Donnell

St Michael's College,
Ailesbury Road, Dublin 4
Tel 01-2189400 Fax 01-2698862
Email stmcoll@indigo.ie
*Community Leader*
Rev Patrick Dundon (CSSp)
*Principal:* Tim Kelleher
*Principal Junior School:* Lorna Heslin

Kimmage Development Studies Centre,
Kimmage Manor, Dublin 12
Tel 01-4064386 Fax 01-4064388
www.kimmagedsc.ie
*Director:* Mr Patrick Reilly

Templeogue College,
Templeville Road, Dublin 6W
Tel 01-4903909 Fax 01-4920903
*Communty Leader:* Rev John Byrne (CSSp)
*Principal:* Ms Aoife O'Donnell
Info@templeoguecollege.ie

(See also under parishes – Bawnogue, Greenhills and Kimmage)

**JESUITS**
Irish Jesuit Provincialate
Milltown Park, Sandford Road, Dublin 6
Tel 01-4987333 Fax 01-4987334
Email curia@jesuit.ie
*Provincial:* Rev Tom Layden (SJ)
*Assistant Provincial:* Rev Noel Barber (SJ)

Jesuit Communication Centre
Irish Jesuit Provincialate,
Milltown Park, Sandford Road, Dublin 6
Tel 01-4987347/01-4987348
*Manager:* Ms Pat Coyle
Email coylep@jesuit.ie

Jesuit Curia Community, Loyola House,
Milltown Park, Sandford Road, Dublin 6
Tel 01-2180276
Email loyola@jesuit.ie
*Superior:* Rev Noel Barber (SJ)
*Minister:* Rev Michael Drennan (SJ)

Belvedere College, Dublin 1
Tel 01-8586600 Fax 01-8744374
*Rector:* Rev Bruce Bradley (SJ)
Secondary day school
*Headmaster:* Gerard Foley

Milltown Park, Sandford Road, Dublin 6
Tel 01-2698411/2698113 Fax 01-2600371
Email milltown@jesuit.ie
*Rector:* Rev Conall O Cuinn (SJ)

Milltown Institute of Theology and Philosophy, Milltown Park, Dublin 6
Tel 01-2776300 Fax 01-2692528
Email info@milltown-institute.ie
*Acting President:* Rev Finbarr Clancy (SJ)

Lay Retreat Association of St Ignatius,
Milltown Park, Dublin 6
Tel 01-2951856
*Spiritual Director*: Rev Fergus O'Keefe (SJ)

25 Croftwood Park,
Cherry Orchard, Dublin 10
Tel 01-6267413

Gonzaga College,
Sandford Road, Dublin 6
Community Tel 01-4972943
Email gonzaga@s-j.ie
(College) Tel 01-4972931 Fax 01-4967769
Email (College) office@gonzaga.ie
Fax (Community) 01-4960849
Email (Community) gonzaga@jesuit.ie
*Rector:* Rev Myles O'Reilly (SJ)
*Minister:* Rev Kennedy O'Brien (SJ)
*Headmaster:* Mr Kevin Whirdy

Manresa House, Dollymount, Dublin 3
Tel 01-8331352 Fax 01-8331002
Email manresa@jesuit.ie
*Rector:* Rev Joseph Dargan (SJ)

Dominic Collins' House, Residence,
129 Morehampton Road, Dublin 4
Tel 01-2693075 Fax 01-2698462
*Vice-Superior:* Rev David Coghlan (SJ)

John Sullivan House, 56/56a Mulvey Park,
Dundrum, Dublin 14
Tel 01-2983978
Email sullivan@jesuit.ie
*Superior:* Rev Gerard Clarke (SJ)
Tel 2986424
*Minister:* Rev Fergus O'Keefe (SJ)

35 Lower Leeson Street, Dublin 2
Tel 01-6761248 Fax 01-7758598
*Superior:* Rev Brian Grogan (SJ)

Campion House, Residence,
28 Lower Hatch Street, Dublin 2
Tel 01-6383990 Fax 01-6762805
Email campion@jesuit.ie
*Superior:* Rev John O'Keeffe (SJ)

Jesuit Community,
27 Leinster Road, Rathmines, Dublin 6
Tel 01-4970250
Email leinster@jesuit.ie
*Vice-Superior:* Rev James Corkery (SJ)

(See also under parishes – Gardiner Street)

**LEGIONARIES OF CHRIST**
Leopardstown Road, Foxrock, Dublin 18
Tel 01-2955985/2955902
Email ireland@legionaries.org
*Superior:* Rev Anthony Bannon (LC)

Clonlost Retreat and Youth Centre
Killiney Road, Killiney, Co Dublin
Tel 01-2350064
*Chaplain:* Rev Feargal O'Duill (LC)

Dublin Oak Academy
Kilcroney, Bray, Co Wicklow
Tel 01-2863290 Fax 01-2865315
Email secretary@dublinoakacademy.com
*Director:* Rev Francisco Cepeda (LC)
*Chaplain:* Rev Steven Kwon (LC)

Woodlands Academy
Wingfield House, Bray, Co Wicklow
Tel 01-2866323 Fax 01-2864918
*Chaplain:* Rev Steven Kwon (LC)

Faith and Family Centre,
Dal Riada House, Avoca Avenue,
Blackrock, Co Dublin
Tel 01-2889317
Email faithandfamilycentre@arcol.org
*Director:* Rev Michael Mullan (LC)

**MARIANISTS**
St Columba's, Church Avenue,
Ballybrack, Co Dublin
Tel 01-2858301
*Director:* Br James Contadino (SM)

St Laurence College, Loughlinstown,
Shankill PO, Co Dublin
Tel 01-2826930 Fax 01-2821878
*Principal:* Mr John Carr

**MARIST FATHERS**
Mount St Mary's, Milltown, Dublin 14
*Regional Superior:* Rev David Corrigan (SM)
Tel 01-2698100
*Superior:* Rev Brendan Bradshaw (SM)
Tel 01-2697322 (Residence)

Catholic University School,
89 Lower Leeson Street, Dublin 2
Tel 01-6762586/6760247
*Superior:* Rev Martin Daly (SM)

Chanel College, Coolock, Dublin 5
Tel 01-8480896/8480655
*Superior:* Rev Kieran Butler (SM)

(See also under parishes – Coolock and Donore Avenue)

**MILL HILL MISSIONARIES**
St Joseph's House, 50 Orwell Park,
Rathgar, Dublin 6
Tel 01-4127700 Fax 01-4127781
Email josephmhm@eirccom.net
*Regional Superior*
Rev Michael Corcoran (MHM)
Tel 086-2239051
*Rector:* Rev Patrick Molloy (MHM)
*Vice Rector:* Rev Patrick O'Connell (MHM)
*Bursar:* Rev Patrick Murray
Email millhill@iol.ie

**MISSIONARIES OF AFRICA**
Provincialate, Cypress Grove Road,
Templeogue, Dublin 6W
Tel 01-4992346
Email provirl@indigo.ie
*Delegate Superior*
Rev P. J. Cassidy (MAfr)

Cypress Grove,
Templeogue, Dublin 6W
Tel 01-4055263/4055264
Email provirl@indigo.ie
*Superior:* Vacant

**MISSIONARIES OF THE SACRED HEART**
Provincialate,
65 Terenure Road West, Dublin 6W
Tel 01-4906622 Fax 01-4920148
Provincial Leader
Rev Joseph mcGee (MSC)

Woodview House, Mount Merrion
Avenue, Blackrock, Co Dublin
Tel 01-2881644
*Leader:* Rev David Smith (MSC)

(See also under parishes – Killinarden)

**OBLATES OF MARY IMMACULATE**
Provincial Residence,
Oblates of Mary Immaculate House of
Retreat, Tyrconnell Road,
Inchicore, Dublin 8
Email omisec@eircom.net
*Provincial*
Very Rev William Fitzpatrick (OMI)

Oblate House of Retreat,
Inchicore, Dublin 8
Tel 01-4534408 Fax 01-4543466
*Superior:* Rev Anthony Clancy (OMI)

170 Merrion Road,
Ballsbidge, Dublin 4
Tel 01-2693658 Fax 01-2600597

Oblate Scholasticate, St Anne's,
Goldenbridge Walk, Inchicore, Dublin 8
Tel 01-4540841 Fax 01-4731903

(See also under parishes – Bluebell, Darndale and the two Inchicore parishes)

**PALLOTTINES**
Provincial House, 'Homestead',
Sandyford Road, Dundrum, Dublin 16
Tel 01-2956180
*Provincial:* Rev Jeremiah Murphy (SAC)
*Rector:* Rev Michael Irwin (SAC)
Email motherofdivinelove@gmail.com

(See also under parishes – Corduff and St Anne's)

**PASSIONISTS**
St Paul's Retreat,
Mount Argus, Dublin 6W
Tel 01-4992000 Fax 01-4992001
Email passionistsmtargus@eircom.net
*Provincial:* Rev Pat Duffy (CP)

(See also under parish – Mount Argus)

**REDEMPTORISTS**
Liguori House,
75 Orwell Road, Dublin 6
Tel 01-4067100 Fax 01-4922654
Email provincial@redemptorists.ie
*Provincial:* Rev Michael G. Kelleher (CSsR)

Marianella,
75 Orwell Road, Dublin 6
Tel 01-4067100 Fax 01-4929635
*Superior:* Rev Con J. Casey (CSsR)

(See also under parishes – Ballyfermot and Cherry Orchard)

**ROSMINIANS**
Clonturk House, Ormond Road,
Drumcondra, Dublin 9
Tel 01-6877014
*Provincial:* Rev David Myers (IC)
Rector: Rev Matt Gaffney (IC)

**ST COLUMBANS MISSIONARY SOCIETY**
St Columban's, Grange Road,
Donaghmede, Dublin 13
Tel 01-8476647
*Contact Person:* Rev Patrick Crowley (SSC)

*House of Studies:* St Columban's,
67-68 Castle Dawson, Rathcoffey Road,
Maynooth, Co Kildare
Tel 01-6286036
*Priest-in-Charge:* Rev William Curry (SSC)

(See also under parishes – Balcurris)

**ST PATRICK'S MISSIONARY SOCIETY**
21 Leeson Park, Dublin 6
Tel 01-4977897 Fax 01-4962812
*House Leader:* Rev Danny Gibbons (SPS)

**SALESIANS**
*Provincialate:* Salesian House,
45 St Teresa's Road, Crumlin, Dublin 12
Tel 01-4555787 Fax 01-4558781
Email (secretary) tdunnesdb@gmail.com
*Provincial:* Very Rev Michael Casey (SDB)
Email ruanet@ireland.com
michael_casey@eircom.net
*Novitiate:* Tel 01-4555605
*Rector:* Rev Michael Ross (SDB)

Salesian College, Maynooth Road,
Celbridge, Co Kildare
Tel 01-6275058/6275060 Fax 01-6272208
*Rector:* Rev Daniel Carroll (SDB)
Secondary School Tel 01-6272166/6272200

Don Bosco House
12 Clontarf Road, Dublin 3
Tel 01-8336009/8337045
Rev Val Collier *(Priest-in-charge)*
Students' Residence

Rinaldi House
72 Seán Mac Dermott Street, Dublin 1
Tel 01-8363358 Fax 01-8552320
*Rector:* Rev Val Collier (SDB)

(See also under parishes – Sean McDermott Street)

**SALVATORIANS**
Our Lady of Victories,
Sallynoggin, Dun Laoghaire, Co Dublin
Tel 01-2854667 Fax 01-2847024
Email sallynogginparish@eircom.net
*Superior:* Rev Henry Nevins (SDS)

**SERVITES**
Servite Priory, St Peregrine,
Kiltipper Road, Tallaght, Dublin 24
Tel 01-4517115
*Prior:* Rev Tim Flynn (OSM)

Servite Oratory,
Rathfarnham Shopping Centre,
Dublin 14
Tel 01-4936300
*Director:* Rev Timothy M. Flynn (OSM)

Divine Word, Marley Grange,
25-27 Hermitage Downs, Rathfarnham,
Dublin 16
Tel 01-4944295
*Prior*: Very Rev Colm McGlynn (OSM) PP

**SOCIETY OF AFRICAN MISSIONS**
SMA House, 82 Ranelagh Road,
Ranelagh, Dublin 6
Tel 01-4968162/3 Fax 01-4968164
*Rector:* Rev John O'Brien (SMA)

(See also under parishes – Neilstown)

**SOCIETY OF ST PAUL**
St Paul's House, Moyglare Road,
Maynooth, Co Kildare
Tel 01-6285933 Fax 01-6289330
Email book@stpauls.ie
*Superior & Rector of Scholasticate*
Rev Pius Nechikattil (SSP)

**SONS OF DIVINE PROVIDENCE**
Sarsfield House, Sarsfield Road,
Ballyfermot, Dublin 10
Tel 01-6266233/6266193
Email don-orion@clubi.ie
*Superior:* Rev Michael Moss (FDP)

**VINCENTIANS**
Provincial Office: St Paul's, Sybill Hill,
Raheny, Dublin 5
Tel 01-8510840/8510842 Fax 01-8510846
Email cmdublin@iol.ie
*Provincial:* Very Rev Brian Moore (CM)

11 Iona Drive, Glasnevin, Dublin 9
Tel 01-8305238
*Superior*
Very Rev Stephen Monaghan (CM)

St Joseph's, 44 Stillorgan Park,
Blackrock, Co Dublin
Tel 01-2886961
*Superior*
Very Rev Colm McAdam (CM)

All Hallows Institute for Mission and
Ministry, Drumcondra, Dublin 9
Tel 01-8373745/6 Fax 01-8377642
Email info@allhallows.ie
*President*
Very Rev Patrick J. McDevitt (CM)
*Superior:* Very Rev Joseph McCann (CM)
Ministry to Priests,
Missions and Retreat: Tel 01-8373745

St Vincent's College,
Castleknock, Co Dublin
Tel 01-8213051
*President/Superior*
Very Rev Peter Slevin (CM)

St Paul's College, Raheny, Dublin 5
Tel 01-8314011/2 Fax 01-8316387
Email rmccm@eircom.net
Tel 01-8318113 (Community)
*Superior:* Very Rev Eamon Flanagan (CM)

(See also under parishes – Phibsboro)

## BROTHERS

**ALEXIAN BROTHERS**
47 Upper Drumcondra Road, Dublin 9
Tel 01-8375973
*Contact:* Br John Moran
Community: 4

**CHRISTIAN BROTHERS**
Province Centre, Marino,
Griffith Avenue, Dublin 9
Tel 01-8073300 Fax 01-8073366
Email cbprov@edmundrice.ie
*Province Leader:* Br J. K. Mullan
Community: 8

St Helen's, York Road,
Dun Laoghaire, Co Dublin
Tel 01-2801214/2841656 Fax 01-2841657
*Community Leader*: Br Mark McDonnell
Community: 7

Christian Brothers' House,
Woodbrook, Bray, Co Wicklow
Tel 01-2821510
*Community Leader*: Br Pat Gaffney
Community: 6

Christian Brothers' House,
Drimnagh Castle, Walkinstown, Dublin 12
Tel 01-4501567 Fax 01-4508930
*Community Leader*: Br T. A. Earley
Community: 6

Christian Brothers' House, Oatlands,
Mount Merrion, Co Dublin
Tel 01-2889510 Fax 01-2109511
*Community Leader:* Br John Hearne
Community: 9

Christian Brothers; House,
Synge Street, Dublin 8
Tel 01-4751292/4755798 Fax 01-4761015
*Community Leader:* Br Declan Power
Community: 9

Community Education Centre
D8CEC, 108 James' Street,
Digital Hub, Dublin 8
Tel 01-5424130
Email info@d8cec.com
*Director:* Marie Mulvihil

Christian Brothers' House,
46 Westland Row, Dublin 2
Tel 01-6762112
*Community Leader:* Br Seamus Nolan
Community: 7

Christian Brothers' House,
10 Rosmeen Gardens, Dun Laoghaire,
Co Dublin
Tel 01-2802105
*Community Leader:* Br Colm Griffey
Community: 10

42 Glasnevin Avenue, Dublin 11
Tel 01-8623564
Community: 3

Christian Brothers' Residence,
St David's Park, Artane, Dublin 5
Tel 01-8317833
*Community Leader:* Br John Ledwidge
Community: 5

Artane School of Music
Tel 01-8318929
*Administrator:* Joe Edge
*Musical Director:* Ronan O'Reilly
Email artaneschooofmusic@eircom.net

Oratory of the Resurrection,
Artane, Dublin 5
Tel 01-8327168
*Director:* Br John Ledwidge

St Patrick's, Baldoyle, Dublin 13
Tel 01-8391287
Retirement home for brothers
*Community Leader:* Br Ferdi Foley
Community: 40

Christian Brothers' Monastery,
St Declan's, Nephin Road, Dublin 7
Tel 01-8389560
*Community Leader:* Br Dermot Ambrose
Community: 5

Clareville, 89A Finglas Road,
Finglas, Dublin 11
Tel 01-8309811
Community: 5

Marino Institute of Education,
Griffith Avenue, Dublin 9
Tel 01-8057700 Fax 01-8335290
*President:* Dr Anne O'Gara

Christian Brothers, St Joseph's Community,
Marino Institute of Education,
Griffith Avenue, Marino, Dublin 9
Tel 01-8057790
*Community Leader:* Br Chris Glavey
Community: 8

242 North Circular Road, Dublin 7
Tel 01-8680454
*Community Leader:* Br Paddy McShane
Community: 6

Edmund Rice House,
North Richmond Street, Dublin 1
Tel 01-8556258 Fax 01-8555243
*Community Leader:* Br Leo Judge
Community: 5

Emmaus Retreat Centre, Lissenhall,
Swords, Co Dublin
Tel 01-8401399/8402450 Fax 01-8408248
*Community Leader:* Br D. D. Young
Community: 4
Retreat Centre with Holy Faith Sisters
and Oblate Fathers

Mainistir Aodhain,
Collins Avenue West, Whitehall, Dublin 9
Tel 01-8379953
*Community Leader:* Br Kieran Walsh
Community: 6

Christian Brothers, 8 Croftwood Grove,
Cherry Orchard, Ballyfermot, Dublin 10
Community: 2
Tel 01-6208920

Education Inclusion Initiative,
17 Synge Street, Dublin 8
Tel 01-4053868
*Co-ordinator:* Br Michael Murray
Email mmurray32@hotmail.com

The Life Centre,
57 Pearse Square, Dublin 2
Tel 01-6718894 Fax 01-6709179
Email lifecentre57@yahoo.ie
*Director:* Br Paul Hendrick

Cherry Orchard Life Centre, 61 Elmdale
Crescent, Cherry Orchard, Ballyfermot,
Dublin 10
Tel 01-6235832
*Director:* Helen Dowling
Email cherryolife@gmail.com

**DE LA SALLE BROTHERS**
Provincialate, 121 Howth Road, Dublin 3
Tel 01-8331815 Fax 01-8339130
Email province@iol.ie
*Superior:* Br Pius McCarthy
Community: 5

Beneavin College, Beneavin Road,
Finglas East, Dublin 11
Tel 01-8341410
*Headmaster:* Mr Joe Twomey

Mount La Salle, Ballyfermot, Dublin 10
Tel 01-6264408
*Superior:* Br Christopher Commins
Community: 10
Scoil Iosagain Mhuire
*Principal:* Mr Patrick Deeley
Scoil Mhuire Sheosaimh
*Principal*: Ms Naomi Plant
Tel 01-6267527 Schools
Tel 01-6262696 Staff Room
Tel 01-6234829 Home/School Liaison
Fax 01-6236021

Ard Scoil La Salle, Raheny Road, Dublin 5
Tel 01-8480055 Fax 01-8480082
*Principal:* Mr Gerard Lynch

Benildus House,
160A Upper Kilmacud Road, Dublin 14
Tel 01-2981110
*Superior:* Br Ciarán Creedon
Community: 3

Benildus Pastoral Centre,
160A Upper Kilmacud Road, Dublin 14
Tel 01-2694195 Fax 01-2694168
*Director:* Ms Michelle Sinnott

St Benildus College, Upper Kilmacud
Road, Blackrock Co Dublin
Tel 01-2986539 Fax 01-2962710
*Headmaster:* Mr Sean Mulvihill

Hazelwood House,
160 Upper Kilmacud Road, Dublin 14
Tel 01-2985670
*Superior:* Br Thomas Durnin
Community: 4

St John's Monastery,
Le Fanu Road, Dublin 10
Tel 01-6260867
*Superior:* Br Martin Breen
Community: 4

Secondary School
*Principal:* Ms Ann Marie Leonard
Tel/Fax 01-6264943

De La Salle College, Wicklow Town
Tel 0404-67581 Fax 0404-66661
*Headmaster:* Ms Marie Carroll

**FRANCISCAN BROTHERS**
49 Laurleen Estate,
Stillorgan, Co Dublin
Email franciscanbrs@eircom.net

**MARIST BROTHERS**
Marian College, Lansdowne Road,
Ballsbridge, Dublin 4
Tel 01-6683740
*Superior:* Br John Hyland
Community: 4
Secondary School

Moyle Park College,
Clondalkin, Dublin 22
Tel 01-4574837
*Superior:* Br Nicholas Smith
Community: 4
Secondary School

**PATRICIAN BROTHERS**
Patrician College, 35 Cardiffcastle Road,
Finglas West, Dublin 11
Tel 01-8342811
*Superior:* Br Dermot Dunne (FSP)
Community: 2

**PRESENTATION BROTHERS**
Provincial House, Glasthule, Co Dublin
Tel 01-2842228
*Contact:* Br Ray Dwyer (FPM)
Community: 6

**SAINT JOHN OF GOD BROTHERS**
Provincial Curia,
Granada, Stillorgan, Co Dublin
Tel 01-2771495 Fax 01-2831274
Email provincial@sjog.ie

Saint John of God Hospital Ltd,
Stillorgan, Co Dublin
Tel 01-2771400 Fax 01-2881034
*Chief Executive:* Ms Emma Balmaine
*Superior:* Br Kilian Keaney (OH)
Community: 8
Private psychiatric hospital

Cluain Mhuire,
Community Mental Health Services,
Newtownpark Avenue, Blackrock, Co Dublin
Tel 01-2172100 Fax 01-2833886
Email cms@sjog.ie
*Director:* Mr Pat Conroy

Saint John of God Kildare Services,
St Raphael's, Celbridge, Co Kildare
Tel 01-6288161 Fax 01-6273614
Email admin.kildare@sjog.ie
*Director:* Ms Claire Dempsey
*Superior:* Br Charles Somers (OH)
School Principal: Mrs Kathy Waldron
Community: 2
Residential and day centre for children
and adults with varying degrees of
intellectual disability

Saint John of God, Carmona Services,
Dunmore House,
111 Upper Glenageary Road,
Dun Laoghaire, Co Dublin
Tel 01-2852900 Fax 01-2851713
email admin.carmona@sjog.ie
*Director:* Ms Philomena Gray
*School Principal:* Ann Campbell
Incorporating residential, day &
enterprise services for people with
intellectual disability.

St Augustine's School, Obelisk Park,
Carysfort Avenue, Blackrock, Co Dublin
Tel 01-2881771 Fax 01-2834117
Email staugustines@sjog.ie
*Director:* Ms Teresa Mallon
*Principal:* Mr John Kingston
Special School

Saint John of God Lucena Clinic Services,
59 Orwell Road, Rathgar, Dublin 6
Tel 01-4923596 Fax 01-4928388
Email admin.lucena@sjog.ie
*Superior:* Br Gregory McCrory (OH)
*Director:* Mr Patrick Conroy
*School Principal:* Mr John Condon
Community: 2
Psychiatric service

Saint John of God Menni Services,
St John of God Centre,
Islandbridge, Dublin 8
Tel 01-6741500 Fax 01-6703829
Email admin.menni@sjog.ie
*Director:* Ms Annamarie McGill
*School Principal:* Ms Rita McCabe
Incorporating Menni Day Services Menni
Residential Services (Tel 01-4731474) and
Menni Enterprises (Tel 01-4569320)

Suzanne House, 6 Main Road,
Tallaght, Dublin 24
Tel 01-4521966 Fax 01-4525504
Email andrew.heffernan@sjog.ie
*Director:* Mr Andrew Heffernan
Respite service for multiple handicapped
and sick children

STEP, 30 Carmanhall Road,
Sandyford Industrial Estate, Dublin 18
Tel 01-2952379 Fax 01-2952371
Email step@sjog.ie
*Director:* Ms Teresa Mallon
Training centre and supported
employment

City Gate, 30 Carmanhall Road,
Sandyford Industrial Estate, Dublin 18
Tel 01-2952379 Fax 01-2952371
Email citygate@sjog.ie
*Director:* Ms Teresa Mallon
Housing Service

St Joseph's Centre,
Crinken Lane, Shankill, Co Dublin
Tel 01-2823000 Fax 01-2823119
email stjosephs@sjog.ie
*Director:* Ms Emma Balmaine
Residential day service for older people

Genil Community,
17 Laurleen, Blackrock, Co Dublin
*Superior:* Br Finnian Gallagher (OH)
Community: 2

## SISTERS

**BLESSED SACRAMENT SISTERS**
91 Seabury Crescent, Malahide, Co Dublin
Tel 01-8451878
Community: 3

**BON SECOURS SISTERS (PARIS)**
Sisters of Bon Secours, Sacre Coeur,
1 Beechmount, Glasnevin Hill, Dublin 9
Tel 01-8065353
Community: 2
Hospital Ministry

Bon Secours Convent,
Glasnevin, Dublin 9
*Co-ordinator:* Sr Veronica Norton
Tel 01-8375111 Fax 01-8571020
Community: 12
Hospital Ministry, Outreach Ministry

'Le Chéile', 9 St David's Terrace,
Glasnevin, Dublin 9
Tel 01-8370018
Community: 2
Hospital Ministry

Sisters of Bon Secours, 9 Abbeyvale,
215 Botanic Avenue, Drumcondra,
Dublin 9
Tel 01-8373209
Community: 1
Hospital Ministry

Sisters of Bon Secours,
119 Esker Lawns, Lucan, Co Dublin
Tel 01-6217158
Community: 1
Parish Ministries

**BRIGIDINE SISTERS**
5 Sycamore Drive, Dundrum, Dublin 16
Tel 01-2988130
*Contact:* Sr Theresa Kilmurray
Community: 2
Clinical Pastoral Education, Parish Ministry

7 Sycamore Drive, Dublin 16
Tel 01-2966449
Community: 1
*Contact:* Sr Loretto Ryan
Community Work

2 Dartmouth Road, Dublin 6
Tel 01-6603027
Community: 4
Pastoral Work, Spiritual Direction,
Hospital Catering

15 Gortmore Drive, Rivermount,
Finglas, Dublin 11
Tel 01-8642440
*Contact:* Sr Rita Minehan
Community: 1
Parish, Counselling

94 Moyville, Ballyboden, Dublin 16
Tel 01-7941596
Contact: Sr Anna Hennessy
Community: 1
Education

163 Park Drive Avenue, Castleknock,
Dublin 15
Tel 01-8200482
*Contact:* Sr Mary Slattery
Community: 1
Counselling

**CARMELITES**
Carmelite Monastery of the Immaculate
Heart of Mary, Delgany, Greystones,
Co Wicklow
Email
contact@carmelitemonasterydelgany.ie
*Prioress:* Sr Monica Lawless
Community: 8
Contemplatives, Mass & greeting cards,
candles and hermitage facilities.

Carmelite Monastery of St Joseph,
Upper Kilmacud Road, Stillorgan, Co Dublin
Email contact@kilmacudcarmel.ie
www.kilmacudcarmel.ie
*Prioress:* Sr Mary Brigeen Wilson
Community: 12
Contemplatives, altar breads

Carmelite Monastery of St Joseph,
Seapark, Malahide, Co Dublin
Email community@malahidecarmelites.ie
*Prioress:* Sr Rosalie Burke
Community: 9
Contemplatives
www.malahidecarmelites.ie

Carmelite Monastery of the Assumption,
Firhouse, Dublin 24
Tel 01-4526474
Email
firhousecarmel.firhouse@gmail.com
*Prioress:* Sr M. Veronica O'Connell
Community: 8
Contemplatives, needlework, scapulars,
cards and candles

Carmelite Monastery of the Immaculate
Conception, Roebuck, Dublin 14
Tel 01-2884732 Fax 01-2870145
Altar Breads Fax 01-2835037
www.roebuckcarmel.com
Email carmel@roebuckcarmel.com
*Prioress:* Sr Teresa Whelan
Community: 7
Contemplatives; altar breads supplied

**CARMELITE SISTERS FOR THE AGED AND INFIRM**
Our Lady's Manor, Bullock Castle,
Dalkey, Co Dublin
Tel 01-2806993 Fax 01-2844802
Email ourladysmanor1@eircom.net
*Superior:* Sr Therese Eileen Mulvaney
Email sistereileen@eircom.net
*Administrator:* Sr Bernadette Murphy
Community: 7

**CHARITY OF JESUS AND MARY SISTERS**
11 Mount Shannon Road,
Kilmainham, Dublin 8
Tel 01-4531503

**CHARITY OF NEVERS SISTERS**
91 Cherrywood, Loughlinstown Drive,
Dun Laoghaire, Co Dublin
Tel 01-2824204
Email scnmkelly@eircom.net

76 Cherrywood, Loughlinstown Drive,
Dun Laoghaire, Co Dublin
Tel 01-2720453

66 Verschoyle Court, Dublin
Tel 01-6624815

17 Stephen's Place, Dublin
Tel 01-6768159
Email sisternoradowney@eircom.net

29 Hazelgrove Court, Tallaght, Dublin 24
Contact person: Sr Rosaleen Cullen
Email rosaleencullen@upcmail.ie

**CHARITY OF ST PAUL THE APOSTLE SISTERS**
St Paul's Convent, Greenhills, Dublin 12
Tel 01-4505358 Fax 01-4505132
Email marylyons2010@gmail.com
*Contact:* Sr Mary Lyons
Community: 7
Primary and secondary schools; parish
work; chaplaincy

**CLARISSAN MISSIONARY SISTERS OF THE BLESSED SACRAMENT**
Our Lady of Guadalupe Residence for
Students, 28 Waltersland Road,
Stillorgan, Co Dublin
Tel/Fax 01-2886600
Email misclaridub@hotmail.com
www.guadaluperesidence.com
*Superior:* Sr Gabriela Luna

**CONGREGATION OF THE SISTERS OF MERCY**
'Rachamim', 13/14 Moyle Park,
Convent Road, Clondalkin, Dublin 22
Tel 01-4673737 Fax 01-4673749
Email mercy@csm.ie
Website www.sistersofmercy.ie
*Congregational Leader:* Sr Coirle McCarthy

Mercy International Centre
64A Lower Baggot Street, Dublin 2
Tel 01-6618061
Email director@mercyinternational.ie
*Director:* Sr Mary Reynolds
Heritage tours, school tours, conference
facilities and pilgrimages to the tomb of
Ven. Catherine McAuley
Website www.mercyworld.org

*South Central Province*

*The Sisters of Mercy minister throughout the diocese in pastoral and social work, community development, counselling, spirituality, education and health care, answering current needs.*

St Mary's Convent, Arklow, Co Wicklow
Tel 0402-32675
Community: 2

1 & 2 Church Crescent, Athy, Co Kildare
Tel 059-8631361 Fax 059-8638180
Community: 9

2 Oak Lawn, Carlow Road,
Athy, Co Kildare
Tel 059-8638209
Community: 2

12 Park Avenue, Athy, Co Kildare
Tel 059-8634220
Community: 2

21 Shamrock Drive, Athy, Co Kildare
Tel 059-8632908
Community: 1

101/102 Rockfield Green,
Maynooth, Co Kildare
Tel 01-6291992 Fax 01-6016896
Community: 5

Mercy Convent, Beaumont, Dublin 9
Tel 01-8376741/8379186
Fax 01-8372770
Community: 15

18 Beverley Crescent,
Knocklyon, Dublin 16
Tel 01-4941232
Community: 2

St Ann's, Booterstown, Co Dublin
Tel 01-2882140 Fax 01-2782047
Community: 14
Province Archives

Flat 339 St Teresa's Gardens,
Donore Avenue, Dublin 8
Tel 01-4530498
Community: 2

St Brendan's Drive, Coolock, Dublin 5
Tel 01-8486420
Community: 12

26 Myrtle Park, Dun Laoghaire,
Co Dublin
Tel 01-2803181 Fax 01-2300040
Community: 3

Our Lady of Lourdes Hospital,
Rochestown Avenue, Dun Laoghaire,
Co Dublin
Tel 01-2851804 Fax 01-2355163
Community: 10

23-26 The Paddocks, Kilmainham,
Dublin 8
Tel 01-4737234
Community: 8

81 Mackintosh Park,
Dun Laoghaire, Co Dublin
Tel-2851707
Community: 3

13 Emmet Crescent, Inchicore, Dublin 8
Tel 01-4163275
Community: 2

19 Emmet Crescent, Inchicore, Dublin 8
Tel 01-4163890
Community: 2

47 Emmet Crescent, Inchicore, Dublin 8
Tel 01-4538196
Community: 1

Mater Misericordiae,
Eccles Street, Dublin 7
Tel 01-8301122 Fax 01-8309070
Community: 23

8-9 Leo Street, Dublin 7
Tel 01-8858593 Fax 01-8300464
Community: 2

1 Oatfield Grove, Rowlagh, Clondalkin,
Dublin 22
Tel 01-6261114
Community: 4

Stella Maris, Convent Lane,
Rush, Co Dublin
Tel/Fax 01-8437347
Community: 4

St Michael's, Dun Laoghaire, Co Dublin
Tel 01-2805557 Fax 01-2805470
Community: 17

1 Rossfield Grove, Brookfield, Tallaght,
Dublin 24
Tel 01-4510444
Community: 2

40 Hillcourt Road, Glenageary, Co Dublin
Tel 01-2854729
Community: 3

14 Coolatree Close, Beaumont, Dublin 9
Tel 01-8377023
Community: 3

12 Cremore Lawn, Glasnevin, Dublin 11
Tel 01-8644045
Community: 3

63 Kenilworth Park, Harolds Cross,
Dublin 6W
Tel/Fax 01-4928191
Community: 3

65 Kenilworth Park, Harolds Cross,
Dublin 6W
Tel/Fax 01-4929414
Community: 2

Glencree, 60 Knocklyon Road,
Templeogue, Dublin 16
Tel 01-4933027
Community: 4

90/91 The Park, Beaumont Woods,
Dublin 9
Tel 01-8570741 Fax 01-7979966
Community: 4

McAuley House, Beaumont, Dublin 9
Tel 01-8379186 Fax 01-8373503
Community: 19

83/85 Silloge Park, Ballymun, Dublin 11
Tel/Fax 01-8547611
Community: 2

6 Butterfield Avenue, Rathfarnham,
Dublin 14
Tel 01-4943169 Fax 01-4947234
Community: 3

40 Gilford Road, Sandymount, Dublin 4
Tel/Fax 01-2601081
Community: 3

Sisters of Mercy, 14 Walnut Avenue,
Courtlands, Drumcondra, Dublin 9
Tel 01-8377602 Fax 01-8570684
Community: 4

Sisters of Mercy,
1 Charlemont, Griffith Avenue, Dublin 9
Tel 01-8571246 Fax 01-8368149
Community: 3

Sisters of Mercy, 25 Cork Street, Dublin 8
Tel 01-4535262
Community: 6

11 Grangemore Road, Donaghmede,
Dublin 13
Tel 01-8482242
Community: 2

2 Charlemont, Griffith Avenue, Dublin 9
Tel 01-4425896
Community: 2

Cuan Mhuire, Athy, Co Kildare
Tel 059-8631493
Community: 2

Sunnybank, Laragh East,
Glendalough, Co Wicklow
Tel 0404-45791
Community: 3

**CROSS AND PASSION CONGREGATION**
Cross and Passion Sisters,
3-5 Carberry Road, Glandore Road,
Dublin 9
Tel 01-8377256
Community: 5
Education, pastoral ministry

Cross and Passion Convent
22 Griffith Avenue, Marino, Dublin 9
Tel 01-8336381
*Sister in Charge:* Sr Nora Horan
Community: 17
Nursing, pastoral ministry, care of elderly

Cross and Passion Convent,
41 Alderwood Green, Springfield,
Tallaght, Dublin 24
Tel 01-4511850 Fax 01-4624416
Community: 4
Pastoral ministry, prison chaplaincy,
retreat work

Cross and Passion Convent,
13 Clare Road, Drumcondra, Dublin 9
Tel 01-8375511 Fax 01-8375500
Community: 4
Community development, pastoral
ministry, formation

25 Stanford, Harlech Grove,
Clonskeagh, Dublin 14
Tel 01-2104833
Community: 1
Parish work

**DAUGHTERS OF CHARITY OF ST VINCENT DE PAUL**
Provincialate, St Catherine's Provincial
House, Dunardagh, Blackrock,
Co Dublin
Tel 01-2882669/2882896 Fax 01-2834485
*Local Superior:* Sr Carmel McArdle
Community: 26
Administration and retreats

Rickard House, Dunardagh, Blackrock,
Co Dublin
Tel 01-2833900/2833933
*Superior:* Sr Nuala Dolan
Community: 25
House for retired sisters

St Vincent's Centre, Navan Road, Dublin 7
Tel 01-8384304
*Superior:* Sr Stella Bracken
Community: 6
Care, training and education of people
with intellectual disability

St Vincent's, North William Street,
Dublin 1 Tel 01-8552998
*Superior:* Sr Bridget O'Connor
Community: 6
Primary schools, parish and social work
Social Housing Project, Rendu Apartments

77 Kilbarron Park, Kilmore West, Dublin 5
Tel 01-8470648
*Superior:* Sr Anna Kennedy
Community: 4
Social and pastoral ministry

3 St Assam's Drive, Raheny, Dublin 5
Tel 01-8312859
*Superior:* Sr Margaret Joyce
Community: 3
House of Residence for Sisters involved in St Francis Hospice and child and family services

St Louise's, Drumfinn Road, Ballyfermot, Dublin 10
Tel 01-6264921
*Superior:* Sr Claire Sweeney
Community: 7
Education and parish work

St Joseph's Hospital, Clonsilla, Co Dublin
Tel 01-8217177
*Superior:* Sr Zoe Kileen
Community: 10
Residential centre for women with intellectual disability

St Louise's, Glenmaroon, Chapelizod, Dublin 20
Tel 01-8216166 Fax 01-8211991
Residential centre for girls with intellectual disability.

St Michael's School for children with learning difficulties.
Glen College Training Centre
Tel 01-8215866/8217169 Fax 01-8211991

10 Henrietta Street, Dublin 1
Tel 01-8732771
*Superior:* Sr Frances Mulloy
Community: 22
House of residence

St Vincent's Trust, 8/9 Henrietta Street, Dublin 1
(Specialised second chance education for young people and adults)
Community Services
Tel 01-8874100 Fax 01-8723486

109 Mount Prospect Avenue, Clontarf, Dublin 3
Tel 01-8338508
*Superior:* Sr Angela Doyle
Community: 14
House for retired sisters

3 Shanliss Drive, Santry, Dublin 9
Tel 01-8423951
*Superior:* Sr Patricia Walsh
Community: 3
Chaplaincy and pastoral services

St Teresa's, Temple Hill, Blackrock, Co Dublin
Tel 01-2788205 Fax 01-2886915
*Superior:* Sr Bernadette McGinn
Community: 10
House of Residence

St Rosalie's, Portmarnock, Co Dublin
Tel 01-8460132
Residential centre for people with intellectual disability

St Catherine's, Knockmore Avenue, Killinarden, Tallaght, Dublin 24
Tel 01-4516320
*Superior:* Sr Louise O'Connell
Community: 5
Teaching, parish and social work, after care, chaplaincy

Seton House, 25 Northbrook Road, Dublin 6
Tel 01-6687300
*Superior:* Sr Bridget Callaghan
Community: 8
House of residence

7 Belvedere Road, Dublin 1
Tel 01-8556719
*Superior:* Sr Geraldine Henry
Community: 3
House of residence for sisters involved in child and family services, refugee centre, mission development

166 Navan Road, Dublin 7
Tel 01-8383801
*Superior:* Sr Marie Fox
Community: 3
House of residence, pastoral work, prison ministry, services for prople with intellectual disability

St Louise's, 16 Dalymount, Phibsboro, Dublin 7
Tel 01-8680308
*Superior:* Sr Aine Cahalan
Community: 4
House of residence for sisters involved in parish work, work with refugees, prison visiting, services for people with intellectual disability

25 Killarney Street, Dublin 1
Tel 01-8366487
*Superior:* Sr Nora O'Sullivan
Community: 4
House of residence for sisters involved in parish work, day care, prison chaplaincy, child and family services

**DAUGHTERS OF THE CROSS OF LIÈGE**
Beech Park Convent, Beechwood Court, Stillorgan, Co Dublin
Tel 01-2887401/2887315 Fax 01-2881499
Email beech@eircom.net
*Superior:* Sr Anne Kelly
Community: 18

**DAUGHTERS OF THE HEART OF MARY**
St Joseph's, Tivoli Road, Dun Laoghaire, Co Dublin
Tel 01-2801204. Community: 8
Email heartofmary@eircom.net
Parish work; teaching; social work, prayer groups
St Joseph's Primary School
Principal's Office: Tel 01-2803504

32 Brackenbush Road, Killiney, Co Dublin
Tel 01-2750917

**DAUGHTERS OF THE HOLY SPIRIT**
88 Foxfield Road, Raheny, Dublin 5
Tel 01-8312795
Community: 3
*Contact person:* Sr Teresa Buckley DHSp
Email tbuckley1929@yahoo.co.uk

9 Walnut Park, Drumcondra, Dublin 9
Tel 01-8371825
Community: 3
Pastoral ministry

**DAUGHTERS OF JESUS**
17 Marino Green, Marino, Dublin 3
Tel 01-8335530
*Contact:* Sister-in-charge

**DAUGHTERS OF MARY AND JOSEPH**
65 Iona Road, Glasnevin, Dublin 11
Tel 01-8305640
Community: 6
Administration, pastoral, education

142 Chapelgate, St Alphonsus' Road, Dublin 9
Tel 01-8827740
*Contact person:* Sr Brigid Devane
Community: 1
Pastoral

37 Bancroft Road, Tallaght, Dublin 24
Tel 01-4515321
Community: 4
Pastoral

10 Moynihan Court, Tallaght, Dublin 24
*Contact person:* Sr Mary Doyle
Community: 1
Pastoral

Flat 7, 116 North Circular Road, Dublin 7
Tel 01-8380525
*Contact person:* Sr Peggy McArdle
Community: 1
Community Development

109 Botanic Avenue, Dublin 9
Tel 01-8367107
*Contact person:* Sr M. Fintan Curran
Community: 1
Pastoral

**DAUGHTERS OF OUR LADY OF THE SACRED HEART**
Provincial House, 14 Rossmore Avenue, Templeogue, Dublin 6W
Tel 01-4903200 Tel/Fax 01-4903113
Email olshprov@eircom.net
*Provincial:* Sr Vianney Murray
Community: 3

50 Maplewood Road, Springfield, Tallaght, Dublin 24
Tel 01-4512183
*Superior:* Sr Juliana O'Donoghue
Community: 2

**DAUGHTERS OF WISDOM**
20 Grace Park Meadows, Drumcondra, Dublin 9
Tel 01-8316508
Community: 2

**DISCIPLES OF THE DIVINE MASTER**
Divine Master Convent, Newtownpark Avenue, Blackrock, Co Dublin
Tel 01-2114949 *(community)*
01-2886414 *(Liturgical Centre)*
Fax 01-2836935
Email pddmdublin@eircom.net
*Sister in Charge:* Sr Kathryn Williams
Community: 6
Contemplative-apostolic, perpetual adoration, Liturgical apostolate, distributors and producers of high-quality Liturgical art, vestments, church goods, private retreats, prayer groups.

**DOMINICAN SISTERS**
Generalate, 5 Westfield Road, Dublin 6
Tel 01-4055570/1/2/3 Fax 01-4055682
Email domgen@eircom.net
*Congregation Prioress:* Sr Helen Mary Harmey
Community: 4
*Congregaton Bursar:* Sr Brighde Vallely
*Congregation Archivist:* Sr Mary O'Byrne

Region Offices, Mary Bellew House, Dominican Campus, Cabra, Dublin 7
Tel 01-8299700 Fax 01-8299799
Email regionop@gmail.com
*Region Prioress:* Sr Elisabeth Healy
Community: 10

Novitiate, 71 Bancroft Park, Tallaght, Dublin 24
Tel 01-4515130
Email domban@eircom.net
*Prioress:* Sr Margaret Mary Ryder
Community: 6

Dominican Convent, 9 Elgin Road, Ballsbridge, Dublin 4
Tel 01-4055570
*Contact person:* Sr Edel Murphy

St Mary's, Rectory Green, Riverston Abbey, Cabra, Dublin 7
Tel 01-8683041
Email domcab1@eircom.net
*Prioress:* Sr Carmel Finnegan
Community: 7

St Mary's, Cabra, Dublin 7
Tel 01-8380567 Fax 01-8682050
Email domcabra@eircom.net
*Prioress:* Sr Maria Maguire
Community: 18
Secondary School
Tel 01-8385282 Fax 01-8683003
Primary and secondary schools, Schools for hearing-impaired, blind/deaf girls and boys (day and boarding) Special schools for emotionally disturbed children. Parish work

Dominican Convent, Sion Hill, Blackrock, Co Dublin
Tel 01-2886831/2/3
Email siondoms2002@yahoo.com
*Prioress:* Sr Darina Hosey
Community: 20
Froebel. Tel 01-2888520
Secondary School. Tel 01-2886791

St Mary's, 47 Mount Merrion Avenue, Blackrock, Co Dublin
Tel 01-2888551
Email stmarysblackrock@yahoo.ie
Community: 5
Education and parish work

Matt Talbot Community, 'Cana'
40 St Laurence Road, Chapelizod, Dublin 20
Tel 01-6202769
Email scmhndom@indigo.ie
Community: 1
Adult education

Dominican Convent, Convent Road, Dun Laoghaire, Co Dublin
Tel 01-2801379 Fax 01-2302209
Email dldoms@eircom.net
*Prioress:* Sr Dympna O'Shaughnessy
Community: 11
Primary School. Tel 01-2809011
Education, pastoral ministry

Dominican Convent, 204 Griffith Avenue, Dublin 9
Tel 01-8379550 Fax 01-8571802
Email dsisters@gofree.indigo.ie
*Prioress:* Sr Marie Cunningham
Secondary School. Tel 01-8376080
Community: 13

Dominican Sisters, 52 Newtownpark Ave, Blackrock, Co Dublin
Tel 01-2833964
Email galldoms@eircom.net
Community: 1

Dominican Convent, Muckross Park, Donnybrook, Dublin 4
Tel 01-2693018/2693707 Fax 01-2604041
Email muckrossconvent@eircom.net
*Prioress:* Sr Caitriona Geraghty
Community: 16
Secondary school. Tel 01-2691096

St Catherine's, 2 Heather View Road, Aylesbury, Tallaght, Dublin 24
Tel 01-4523462 Fax 01-4625636
Email domabury2@eircom.net
Community: 6
Education; pastoral ministry

1 Avonbeg Road, Tallaght, Dublin 24
Tel 01-4514627
Email avonbeg@dominicansisters.com
Community: 2
Pastoral

2 Croftwood Crescent, Cherry Orchard, Ballyfermot, Dublin 10
Tel 01-6231127
Email cherrydom@eircom.net
Community: 2
Education, pastoral ministry

93 Nephin Road, Cabra, Dublin 7
Tel 01-8682054
Email domsis@gofree.indigo.ie
Community: 4
Education

Dominican Sisters, Santa Sabina House, Cabra, Dublin 7
Tel 01-8682666 Fax 01-8682667
Email santasabina@dominicansisters.com
*Prioress:* Sr Joan Looby
Community: 31

St Dominic's, St Mantan's Road, Wicklow
Tel 0404-67148
Email opwicklow@eircom.net
Community: 5
Education

An Clochán Retreat Centre, Glendalough, Co Wicklow
Tel 0404-45137 Fax 0404-45962
Email anclochan@eircom.net
Community: 1

Dominican Sisters, St Mary's Convent, Wicklow
Tel 0404-67328 Fax 0404-65054
Email ecenw@eircom.net
Community: 4

Dominican Sisters, St Mary's, 63 Annamoe Road, Phibsboro, Dublin 7
Tel 01-8385541
Email annamoe63@eircom.net
Community: 3

Dominican Sisters, 62 Ashington Avenue, Navan Road, Dublin 7
Tel 01-8386304
Community: 3

**FRANCISCAN MISSIONARIES OF THE DIVINE MOTHERHOOD**
Emohruo, 2 Fonthill Abbey, Ballyboden Road, Rathfarnham, Dublin 14
Tel/Fax 01-4934275
Community: 3

St Francis Convent, 3/4 Fonthill Abbey, Ballyboden Road, Rathfarnham, Dublin 14
Tel 01-4932537 Fax 01-4954846
Community: 4

**FRANCISCAN MISSIONARIES OF MARY**
St Francis Convent, The Cloisters, Mount Tallant Avenue, Terenure, Dublin 6W
Tel 01-4908549
Email fmmcloisters@eircom.net
*Superior:* Sr Josephine McGlynn
Community: 8
House of studies, pastoral work

Assisi, 36 Grange Abbey Drive, Donaghmede, Dublin 13
Tel 01-8470591
*Superior:* Sr Mary Dunne
Community: 5
Social, pastoral work

97 St Lawrence Road, Clontarf, Dublin 3
Tel 01-8332683/8332181
Email fmmclontarf@yahoo.co.uk
*Superior:* Sr Elizabeth O'Hagan
Community: 9
Pastoral, hospitality for missionary sisters

St Joseph's Convent, Old Road,
Hayestown, Rush, Co Dublin
Tel 01-8439308
*Superior*: Sr Mary Teresa Hoey
Community: 17
Care of elderly sisters

FHM, 4 Muckross Drive,
Perrystown, Dublin 12
Tel 01-4562028
*Superior:* Sr Mary Dornan
Community: 4
Youth ministry

**FRANCISCAN MISSIONARIES OF ST JOSEPH**
St Joseph's, 16 Innismore,
Crumlin Village, Dublin 12
Tel 01-4563445
*Superior:* Sr Johanna Kelly
Community: 4

**FRANCISCAN MISSIONARY SISTERS FOR AFRICA**
Generalate, 34A Gilford Road,
Sandymount, Dublin 4
Tel 01-2838376 Fax 01-2602049
Email fmsagen@iol.ie
*Congregational Leader*
Sr Miriam Duggan (FMSA)
Community: 5

34 Gilford Road,
Sandymount, Dublin 4
Tel 01-2691923
*Contact person:* Sr Mary Ryan (FMSA)
Community: 8

Regional House
142 Raheny Road, Raheny, Dublin 5
Tel 01-8473140 Fax 01-8481428
Email fmsanar@iol.ie
*Contact person Regional*
Sr Eilish Costello (FMSA)
Community: 5

**FRANCISCAN SISTERS**
3 St Andrew's Fairway,
Lucan, Co Dublin
Tel 01-6108756
Email citaearls@yahoo.com
Community: 3

**FRANCISCAN SISTERS OF THE IMMACULATE CONCEPTION**
Franciscan Sisters, 97/99 Riverside Park,
Clonshaugh, Dublin 17
Tel 01-8474214
Community: 2
Administration, pastoral ministry, nursing

**FRANCISCAN SISTERS MINORESS**
St Anthony's Convent,
1 Cabra Grove, Dublin 7
Tel 01-8380185
*Superior:* Sr Barbara Flynn
Community: 4
Pastoral ministry

**GOOD SHEPHERD SISTERS**
245 Lower Kilmacud Road, Goatstown,
Dublin 14
Tel 01-2982699
Email rgsdublin@eircom.net
www.goodshepherdsireland.com
Community: 3
Provincialate

65 Taney Crescent, Goatstown, Dublin 14
Tel 01-2960235
Email rgstaney@gmail.com
Community: 3
Social work, apostolate

**HANDMAIDS OF THE SACRED HEART OF JESUS**
St Raphaela's, Upper Kilmacud Road,
Stillorgan, Co Dublin
Tel 01-2889963 Fax 01-2889536
*Superior*: Sr Patricia Lynch
Email trishaci@yahoo.com
Community: 8
Primary School. Tel 01-2886878
Secondary School. Tel 01-2888730
Students' residence. Tel 01-2887159
Fax 01-2889536

**HOLY CHILD JESUS, SOCIETY OF THE**
1 Stable Lane, Off Harcourt Street,
Dublin 2
Tel 01-4754053
Email stablelane@shcj.org
Community: 10

21 Grange Park Avenue, Raheny, Dublin 5
Tel 01-8488961
Email shcjdub@gofree.indigo.ie
Community: 2

Convent of the Holy Child Jesus,
Kilmuire, Military Road, Killiney,
Co Dublin
Tel 01-2823089
Community: 5
Secondary School. Tel 01-2823120

Holy Child Community School,
Sallynoggin, Co Dublin
Tel 01-2855334

**HOLY FAITH SISTERS**
Generalate, Aylward House,
Glasnevin, Dublin 11
Tel 01-8371426 Fax 01-8377474
Email aylward@eircom.net
*Superior General:* Sr Vivienne Keely

*Regional Superior:* Sr Rosaleen Cunniffe
68 Iona Road, Dublin 9
Tel 01-8301404 Fax 01-8303530
Email ionahfs@eircom.net

Main Street, Celbridge, Co Kildare
Tel 01-6288267
Community: 4
Ministries, Primary school

25 Clare Road, Drumcondra, Dublin 9
Tel 01-8373569
Community: 3
Social work, prayer ministry

183 Clontarf Road, Dublin 3
Tel 01-8336076
Community: 6
Holy Faith Secondary School
Tel 01-8332754
*Principal:* Ms Deirdre Gogarty
Parish ministry

Star of the Sea,
182 Clontarf Road, Dublin 3
Community: 4
Social work, faith development, prison ministry

The Coombe, Dublin 8
Tel 01-4540244. Community: 10
Primary and Secondary Education, Parish Centre, Pastoral, Miltown Institute, NUI Maynooth, Counselling

St Brigid's Primary School
Tel 01-4547734
*Principal:* Ms Deirdre Early
Home-school link; Parish Centre;
Counselling; Parish sister, Whitefriar Street

11 Drumcairn Green, Fettercairn,
Tallaght, Dublin 24
Tel 01-4513951
Community: 2
Counselling, parish work

12 Finglaswood Road, Dublin 11
Tel 01-8641551
Community: 2
Counselling

13/14 Wellmount Parade, Dublin 11
Tel 01-8640874
Community: 2
Congregational house; prayer ministry, justice work

St Michael's Secondary School
Tel 01-8341767
*Principal:* Mr John Barry
St Brigid's School
Senior School. Tel 01-8342416
*Principal:* Ms Martha Savage
Infant School. Tel 01-8342416
Principal: Mrs Carmel Lillis

Holy Faith Sisters,
144 Cappagh Road, Finglas, Dublin 11
Tel 01-8643205
Community: 1
Ministry to Travellers

Glasnevin, Dublin 11
Tel 01-8373427
*Resident Co-ordinator:* Sr Maura Keogh
Community: 32
St Mary's Secondary School Tel 01-8374413
*Principal:* Mrs Margaret Lennon
St Brigid's Primary School Tel 01-8376653
*Principal:* Mrs Evelyn O'Brien
Mother of Divine Grace Primary School
Tel 01-8344000
*Principal:* Ms Alice Bermingham
Pastoral ministries; social work;
secondary and primary education
Marian House Nursing Home
Tel 01-8376165
*Care Team:* Sr Eileen Holton &
Sr Maureen Ferguson

Greystones, Co Wicklow
Tel 01-2874081
Community: 5
Prayer, parish ministry
St David's Co-educational Secondary School Tel 01-2874800/2874802
*Principal:* Mary O'Doherty
St Brigid's Primary School. Tel 01-2876113
*Principal:* Sr Kathleen Lyng

Credo, 2 Fairways Grove,
Griffith Road, Dublin 11
Tel 01-8348015
Community: 2
St John's Education Centre,
Mater Dei lecturer

Regional House, 68 Iona Road, Dublin 9
Tel 01-8301404/8305668
*Regional Leader:* Sr Rosaleen Cunniffe
Community: 2
Regional administration

Kilcoole, Co Wicklow
Tel 01-2874229
Community: 2
Parish ministry, faith development, Justice, Luisne Spirituality Centre
Primary Schools
Tel 01-2874649

St Brigid's Road, Killester, Dublin 5
Tel 01-8310009
Community: 8
Primary school, library work, pastoral work

6 St Mary's Road, Dublin 4
Tel 01-6681124
Community: 8
Parish ministry, prayer ministry
St Brigid's Primary School
Tel 01-6681155
*Principal:* Ms Ann-Marie Hogan

18 Church Street, Skerries, Co Dublin
Tel 01-8491203
Community: 5
Pastoral work, Emmaus Retreat Centre

14 Main Road, Tallaght, Dublin 24
Tel 01-4515904
Community: 2
Spiritual direction, faith development, retreat ministry

81 Naas Road, Dublin 12
Tel 01-4551142
Community: 2
Parish work and administration

11 Aylward Green, Finglas, Dublin 11
Tel 01-8646401
Community: 2
Parish work, club for people with disabilities

11 Johnstown Park, Ballygall Road East, Dublin 11
Tel 01-864640
Commun ity: 4
Parish ministry

178-180 Clontarf Road, Dublin 3
Community: 9
Secondary education, Spiritual Direction, pastoral, healing remedies, prayer network, congregational website, art therapy, social justice, St John's Education Support Centre, Third-level education

5 Dargan Court, Meath Road,
Bray, Co Wicklow
Counselling, pastoral

Joseph's Cottage, Kippure East,
Manor Kilbride, Co Wicklow
Tel 0404-4507
Conservation work, parish work

105 Tyrconnel Park, Inchicore,
Dublin 8
Pastoral work

30 Convent Court, Delgany,
Co Wicklow
Primary school education

**HOLY FAMILY OF BORDEAUX SISTERS**
11 Arran Road, Drumcondra, Dublin 9
Tel 01-8370922
*Contact:* Sr Bernadette Deegan *(Regional Superior)*
Community: 3
Hospitality and pastoral work

Holy Family of Bordeaux Sisters,
Irishtown, Clane, Co Kildare
Tel 01-6288459
*Contact person:* The Superior
Community: 4
Parish work, chaplaincy, adult Religious education, literacy and pastoral work

**INFANT JESUS SISTERS**
Provincial House, 56 St Lawrence Road,
Clontarf, Dublin 3
Tel 01-8338930
*Provincial:* Sr Rosemary Barter
Email rbarterijs@eircom.net
Tel 01-8339577
Community: 2

121 Tonlegee Road, Dublin 5
Tel 01-8472926
Community: 3
Pastoral ministry

140 Carrickhill Rise, Portmarnock,
Co Dublin
Tel 01-8461647
Community: 2
Pastoral ministry

211 Clontarf Road, Dublin 3
Tel 01-8331700
Community: 6
Pastoral ministry

16 Ard na Meala, Ballymun, Dublin 11
Tel 01-8426534
Community: 3
Pastoral ministry, youth ministry, social work

2 Carrig Close, Poppintree,
Ballymun, Dublin 11

1 Eccles Court, Dublin 7
Tel 01-8309004
Pastoral ministry

**JESUS AND MARY, CONGREGATION OF**
Provincialate, 'Errew House',
110 Goatstown Road, Dublin 14
*Provincial Offices:* Tel 01-2993130
*Direct line:* Tel 01-2969150
*Bursar's Office:* Tel 01-2993140
*Provincial Superior:* Sr Mary Mulrooney
Tel 01-2969150
Email mulrooney.mary@gmail.com
*Local superior:* Sr Pauline Caffrey
Tel 01-2966059
Community: 5

Our Lady's Grove Community,
110 Goatstown Road, Dublin 14
Community: 7
Convent. Tel 01-2966104
Primary School. Pupils: 433
Secondary School. Pupils: 370

Home Farm Community, 'Errew House',
110 Goatstown Road, Dublin 14
Tel 01-2993665
*Superior:* Sr Anna Dyar
Community: 4

**LA RETRAITE SISTERS**
77 Grove Park, Rathmines, Dublin 6
Tel 01-4911771
*Contact:* Sr Barbara Stafford
Email barbarastaffordlr@eircom.net
Community: 3

**LA SAINTE UNION DES SACRES COEURS**
Teallach Mhuire, 41 Broadway Road,
Blanchardstown, Dublin 15
Tel 01-8214459
Community: 4
Pastoral work, student counsellor, group facilitation consultation

9 Tandy's Hill, Lucan, Co Dublin
Tel 01-6218863
*Contact:* Sr Rosemarie Madden
Parish work

126 Malahide Road, Clontarf, Dublin 3
Tel 01-8332778
Community: 3
Pastoral work, literacy

14 Glenshane Grove,
Brookfield, Tallaght, Dublin 24
Tel 01-4527684
Community: 2
Teaching, pastoral work, travellers, counselling

**LITTLE COMPANY OF MARY**
Provincialate, Cnoc Mhuire,
29 Woodpark, Ballinteer Avenue,
Dublin 16
Tel 01-2987040 Fax 01-2961936
*Province Leader:* Sr Teresa Corby

40 Braemor Park,
Churchtown, Dublin 14
Tel 01-4904755/4904692/4904794/4904795
Community: 22

14 Heather Lawn,
Marlay Wood, Dublin 16
Tel 01-4942324
Apostolic Community: 1
Province Resource Centre

16 Heather Lawn,
Marlay Wood, Dublin 16
Tel 01-4947205
Apostolic Community: 1

Little Company of Mary,
81 Mountain View Park,
Rathfarnham, Dublin 14
Tel 01-2986854
Apostolic Community: 1

Little Company of Mary,
12 The Avenue, Grange Manor,
Lucan, Co Dublin
Tel 01-6109360
Apostolic Community: 1

Little Company of Mary
2 Esker Wood Grove, Lucan, Co Dublin
Tel 01-6210474
Apostolic Community: 1

Little Company of Mary,
64 Templeroan Avenue, Knocklyon,
Dublin 16
Tel 01-4957130
Apostolic Community: 1

Little Company of Mary, 45 Priory Way,
Kimmage, Dublin 12
Tel 01-4907763
Community: 1

Little Company of Mary,
62 West Priory, Navan Road, Dublin 7
Tel 01-8386325
Community: 1

**LITTLE SISTERS OF THE ASSUMPTION**
Provincial House, 42 Rathfarnham Road,
Terenure, Dublin 6W
Tel 01-4909850 Fax 01-4925740
Email pernet42@eircom.net
*Provincial:* Sr Mary Keenan
Sisters work in nursing, social work and family care, and with local community development groups

12 Convent Lawns, Ballyfermot,
Dublin 10
Tel 01-6230898

155 Swords Road, Whitehall,
Dublin 9
Tel 01-8374894
Email lsas.155@gmail.com

11 The Covert, Woodfarm Acres,
Palmerstown, Dublin 20
Tel 01-6268556
Email littlesisters@eircom.net

8 Owendore Crescent,
Rathfarnham, Dublin 14
Tel 01-4931147

Patrickswell Place, Finglas,
Dublin 11
Tel 01-8342592
Email fagefinglas@yahoo.co.uk

Mount Argus, Assumption Convent,
Mount Argus Road, Dublin 6W
Tel 01-4977038

4 Oakdale, Oakton Park,
Ballybrack, Co Dublin
Tel 01-2821143

5-6 Grange Crescent, (off Pottery Road),
Dun Laoghaire, Co Dublin
Tel 01-2853961

41 Liscarne Court, Rowlagh,
Clondalkin, Dublin 22
Tel 01-6263077
Email lsarow@gofree.indigo.ie

14 Forestwood Avenue, Santry Avenue,
Dublin 9
Tel 01-8428016
Email lsacomm@oceanfree.net

**LITTLE SISTERS OF THE POOR**
Sacred Heart Residence,
Sybil Hill Road, Raheny, Dublin 5
Tel 01-8332308
*Provincial:* Sr Christine Devlin
*Superior:* Sr Monica
Email msraheny@eircom.net
Community: 25
Nursing home for the elderly

Holy Family Residence,
Roebuck Road, Dublin 14
Tel 01-2832455
*Superior:* Sr Jacinta
Community: 16
Nursing home for the elderly

St Brigid's Novitiate,
Roebuck Road, Dublin 14
Tel 01-2832536

**LORETO (IBVM)**
Provincialate, Loreto House,
Beaufort, Dublin 14
Tel 01-4933827
Email lorprovbeaufort@eircom.net
*Provincial:* Sr Noelle Corscadden

Abbey House, Loreto Terrace,
Grange Road, Rathfarnham, Dublin 14
Tel 01-4932807
*Superior:* Sr Marie Carr
Community: 32
Primary School, Secondary Day School, pastoral work

Loreto College and Junior School,
53 St Stephen's Green, Dublin 2
Tel 01-6618179/6618181

Loreto Community,
Nos 3, 6, 8, 9 Fort Ostman,
Old County Road, Crumlin, Dublin 12
Community: 4
*Superior:* Sr Mary O'Dwyer
Loreto Secondary School. Tel 01-4542380
Senior Primary School. Tel 01-4541669
Junior Primary School. Tel 01-4541746
Loreto Centre Apartments, Crumlin Road
Tel 01-4541078
Community: 7
Personal and community development

Loreto Community, Bray, Co Wicklow
Tel 01-2862021
Email loretoconventbray@eircom.net
*Superior:* Sr Miriam Doran
Community: 11
Primary and secondary schools; pastoral work

Nos 29/30 The Courtyard
Vevay Crescent
*Superior:* Sr Josephine Keegan
Community: 2

Loreto Abbey, Dalkey, Co Dublin
Tel 01-2804331/2804416
Email lorcomdalkey@eircom.net
*Superior:* Sr Estelle McGoldrick
Community: 9
Primary and secondary schools; pastoral work

Teach Muire, Leslie Avenue,
Dalkey, Co Dublin
Tel 01-2800495
Email lorlesliedalkey@eircom.net
*Superior:* Sr Estelle McGoldrick
Community: 5
Educational and pastoral work

Loreto Community,
Balbriggan, Co Dublin
Tel 01-8412796
*Superior:* Sr Maureen Thornton
Community: 16
Secondary school; pastoral work

Loreto Education Trust,
Foxrock, Dublin 18
Tel 01-2899956
Education and offices

Loreto Hall, 77 St Stephen's Green,
Dublin 2
Tel 01-4781816
*Superior:* Sr Denise Harvey
Community: 13
Pastoral work

The Apartments,
77 St Stephen's Green, Dublin 2
*Community Leader:* Sr Clair Dillon
Community: 6

Loreto, 13 Carrigmore Place, City West,
Saggart, Co Dublin
Tel/Fax 01-4589918
Also, 15 Carrigmore Place, City West,
Saggart, Co Dublin
Tel 01-4580780

Loreto, 22 Brookdale Drive,
River Valley, Swords, Co Dublin
*Superior:* Sr Josephine Keegan
Community: 6
Tel 01-8405982
Secondary School, River Valley, Swords
Social and pastoral work

Loreto, 5 Greenville Road, Blackrock,
Co Dublin
Tel 01-2843171
*Superior:* Sr Josephine Keegan
Community: 3
Education, social and pastoral work

Loreto, 20 Herberton Park,
Rialto, Dublin 8
Tel 01-4535048
Email lorialto@hotmail.com
*Superior:* Sr Mary O'Dwyer
Community: 3
Social and pastoral work

265 Sundrive Road, Dublin 12
Tel 01-4541509
*Superior:* Sr Mary O'Dwyer
Community: 4
Education and pastoral work

7/8/9/10 Stonepark Orchard,
Stonepark Abbey
Tel 01-4952110/4952111/4951444/4950155
Community: 10
Education and pastoral work

175, 176, 178, 184, 185 Prior's Gate,
Greenhills Road, Tallaght, Dublin 24

9, 11, 50, 52 New Bancrost Hall,
Tallaght Main Street, Dubin 24

64, 66, 68 Griffith Hall,
Glandore Road, Dublin 9

10 Loreto, Crescent, Rathfarnham,
Dublin 14

21, 30, 30 The Croft,
Parc na Silla Avenue, Loughlinstown,
Dublin 18

**MARIE AUXILIATRICE SISTERS**
7 Florence Street,
Portobello, Dublin 8
Tel 01-4537622
*Contact Person:* Sr Máire Nally
Community: 4
Spiritual direction, social outreach,
education

Marie Auxiliatrice Sisters
130 Upper Glenageary Road,
Dun Laoghaire, Co Dublin
Tel 01-2857389
*Contact Person:* Sr Eileen Cartin
Email eileencartin@marieaux.org
Community: 2
Spiritual direction, social outreach,
counselling, prison ministry

**MARIE REPARATRICE SISTERS**
29 Brackenstown Village,
Swords, Co Dublin
Tel 01-8406321
Email smrbtown@eircom.net
*Superior:* Sr Eileen Carroll
Community: 3
Hospital chaplaincy, spiritual direction/
retreats. House of welcome to parish
groups

9 St Andrew's Grove, Malahide,
Co Dublin
Tel 01-8455113
Email smrmal@eircom.net
*Superior:* Sr Elizabeth Dunne
Community: 2
Parish ministry, spiritual direction/
retreats

**MARIST SISTERS**
Provincialate, 51 Kenilworth Square,
Rathgar, Dublin 6
Tel 01-4972196
Email secirl@eircom.net
*Leader – Ireland:* Sr Brigid M. McGuinness
Community: 5

10 Cambridge Terrace,
Dartmouth Square, Dublin 6
Tel 01-6605332
Email maristcambridge@yahoo.ie
Community: 3
Justice, education

Sundrive Road, Crumlin, Dublin 12
Tel 01-4540778
Email sundrivesm@eircom.net
*Superior:* Sr Eleanor Keaney
Community: 16
Primary school
Social work, youth work, health care,
adult education, Marist laity

185 Killarney Park, Bray, Co Wicklow
Tel 01-2863396
Email smbray@wickloowtoday.com
Community: 4
Education, social work, parish ministry,
retreat work

27 Grange Park Grove, Raheny, Dublin 5
Tel 01-8480232
Email raheny27@yahoo.ie
*Superior:* Sr Mary Brennan
Community: 4
Parish Ministry, chaplaincy

**MEDICAL MISSIONARIES OF MARY**
Congregational Centre,
Rosemount, Rosemount Terrace,
Booterstown, Co Dublin
Tel 01-2882722 Fax 01-2834626
Email rcsmmm@eircom.net

MMM Communications Department,
Rosemount Terrace, Booterstown,
Co Dublin
Tel 01-2887180/086-1019826
Fax 01-2834626
Email mmm@iol.ie

*European Area Leader*
Sr Dervilla O'Donnell
3 Danieli Road, Artane, Dublin 5
Tel 01-8316469
Email dervillaod@eircom.net

Réalt na Mara, 11 Rosemount Terrace,
Booterstown, Co Dublin
Tel 01-2832247
Email mmmrealtnamara@eircom.net
Community: 6

26 Malahide Road, Artane, Dublin 5
Tel 01-8310427
Email mmmartane@eircom.net
Community: 4

52 St Agnes Road, Crumlin, Dublin 12
Tel 01-4552692
Email mmmcrumlin@eircom.net
Community: 3

33 Templeville Drive
Templeogue, Dublin 6W
Tel 01-4991803
Email mmm.templeogue@upcmail.ie
Community: 3

177 Philipsburgh Avenue,
Marino, Dublin 3
Tel 01-8376336
Email mmmmarino@eircom.net
Community: 3

1 The Grange, Laurel Place,
Terenure Road West, Dublin 6W
Tel 01-4925263
Email mmmtv@gofree.indigo.ie
Community: 6

The Lodge, 1A School Avenue,
Killester, Dublin 5
Tel 01-8187552

Hillview, St Margaret's Avenue,
Raheny, Dubin 5
Tel 01-8324221
Email mmmraheny@eircom.net

**MISSIONARIES OF CHARITY**
223 South Circular Road, Dublin 8
Tel 01-4540163
*Superior:* Sr M. Imelda (MC)
Community 4
Hostel For Men

**MISSIONARY FRANCISCAN SISTERS OF THE IMMACULATE CONCEPTION**
Assisi House, Navan Road, Dublin 7
Tel 01-8682216
Community: 3
*Contact:* Sr Philomena Conroy

**MISSIONARY SISTERS OF THE HOLY ROSARY**
Generalate, 23 Cross Avenue,
Blackrock, Co Dublin
Tel 01-2881708/9 Fax 01-2836308
Email mshrgen@indigo.ie
*Superior General:* Sr Maureen O'Malley
Community: 7

Regional House, Drumullac,
42 Westpark, Artane, Dublin 5
Tel 01-8510010 Fax 01-8187494
Email mshrreg@eircom.net
*Regional Superior:* Sr Conchita McDonnell
Community: 3

Holy Rosary Convent, Brookville,
Westpark, Artane, Dublin 5
Tel 01-8480603/8481216
*Superior:* Sr Madeleine Aiker
House for sisters on leave from mission.
Pastoral, health care
Community: 12

Holy Rosary Convent, 48 Temple Road,
Dartry, Dublin 6
Tel 01-4971918/4971094
*Superior:* Sr Teresa Stapleton
Pastoral, education, care of the elderly
Community: 25

Holy Rosary Sisters, Glankeen,
9 Richmond Avenue South, Dartry,
Dublin 6
Tel 01-4977277
Pastoral, health care, care of elderly
Community: 9

Holy Rosary Sisters (Community)
11 Dalymount, Phibsboro, Dublin 7
Tel 01-8680381
Pastoral, educational, health care
Community: 7

Holy Rosary Sisters, 2 Grange Abbey
Cresent, Baldoyle Dublin 13
Tel 01-8476219
Pastoral, health care, education
Community: 4

Holy Rosary Sisters, 72 Grange Park,
Baldoyle, Dublin 13
Tel 01-8390291
Regional administration, counselling
Community: 3

Holy Rosary Sisters,
140 Brookwood Avenue, Artane, Dublin 5
Tel 01-8187672
Community: 4

Holy Rosary Sisters, Greenfields,
Greenfield Road, Sutton, Dublin 13
Tel 01-8392005/8392070 Fax 01-8392025
*Superior:* Sr Angela Morgan
Regional administration, pastoral
Community: 16

Holy Rosary Sisters, 'Greenacres',
Upper Kilmacud Road, Dublin 14
*Superior:* Sr Brenda Kelly
Community: 7

Holy Rosary Sisters,
25/26 Rathfarnham Wood,
Rathfarnham, Dublin 14
Community: 6

**MISSIONARY SISTERS OF OUR LADY OF APOSTLES**
70b Shellbourne Road,
Ballsbridge, Dublin 4
Tel 01-6685796
Email olasrsdub@eircom.net
No. of sisters: 5
House of studies

**MISSIONARY SISTERS OF ST COLUMBAN**
St Columban's Convent,
Magheramore, Wicklow
Tel 0404-67348 Fax 0404-67364
Email colsrsww@eircom.net
*Community Leader:* Sr Ita McElwain
Community: 44
Motherhouse, congregational nursing
home for sick and retired members

St Agnes Road, Crumlin, Dublin 12
Tel 01-4555435
Community: 9
Mission awareness

85 Eglinton Road, Donnybrook, Dublin 4
Tel 01-2695936
Community: 8
House of studies

Apt C14, Killarney Street, Dublin 1
Tel 01-6577339
Community: 2
Parish ministry, work with migrants

2 Seskin View Park, Tallaght, Dublin 24
Tel 01-4940392
Community: 3
Hospital ministry and Parish ministry

Columban Sisters,
Parish House No. 1, Holy Spirit Parish,
Silloge, Ballymun, Dublin 11
Tel 01-8423696
Community: 3

*Contact Person for above five houses*
Sr Patricia McGuinness
85 Eglinton Road, Donnybrook, Dublin 4

**MISSIONARY SISTERS OF ST PETER CLAVER**
Our Lady of the Angels
81 Bushy Park Road/PO Box 22881,
Terenure, Dublin 6
Tel 01-4909360 Fax 01-4920918
*Superior:* Sr Lucyna Wisniowska
Email claver4@hotmail.com
Community: 4
Assist needy missions, especially those in
Africa

**MISSIONARY SISTERS SERVANTS OF THE HOLY SPIRIT**
Regional House,
143 Philipsburgh Avenue,
Fairview, Dublin 3
Tel 01-8369383
Email sspsfairview@yahoo.com
*Community Leader:* Sr Carmen Lee
Community: 4

98 Foxfield Road,
Raheny, Dublin 5
Tel 01-8319011
*Community Leader:* Sr Renata Sistemich
Community: 2

**NOTRE DAME DES MISSIONS**
Upper Churchtown Road, Dublin 14
Tel 01-2983308
Email ntrdame@hotmail.com
*Leader:* Sr Carmel Looby
Email mlooby1@hotmail.com
Community: 18
Community for retired sisters

Sisters of Our Lady of the Missions
5 Griffeen Glen Park, Griffeen Valley,
Lucan South, Co Dublin
Tel 01-6219088
Shared Leadership
Community: 2
Education, pastoral work

**OUR LADY OF THE CENACLE**
3 Churchview Drive, Killiney, Co Dublin
Tel 01-2840175
Email cenacledublin@eircom.net
*Contact:* Cenacle Sisters
Community: 3
Retreats, spiritual direction, hospital
chaplain, facilitation days/ evenings of
prayer, pastoral work

**OUR LADY OF CHARITY SISTERS**
Regional House,
63 Lower Sean McDermott Street,
Dublin 1
Tel 01-8711109 Fax 01-8366526

Beechlawn Complex, High Park,
Grace Park Road, Drumcondra, Dublin 9
Services to women, the elderly and
various ministries
Nursing Home Tel 01-8369622

72 Clonshaugh Road,
Dublin 17
Tel 01-8479088
Varied ministries

206 Grace Park Road,
Dublin 9
Tel 01-8572677
Varied ministries

**OUR LADY OF SION SISTERS**
127 Griffith Avenue,
Drumcondra, Dublin 9
Tel 01-8573130 Fax 01-8573189
Website www.sistersofsion.org

**POOR CLARES**
St Damian's, Simmonscourt Road,
Ballsbridge, Dublin 4
Fx 01-6685464
Email pccdamians@mac.com
Website www.pccdamians.ie
*Abbess/Contact:* Sr M. Brigid
Community: 9
Contemplatives
Daily community periods of Exposition
are shared with the public
Evening Prayer and Benediction on
Sundays and First Fridays at 4.30 pm
Mass Monday-Saturday 7.30 am, Sundays
and Bank Holidays 9.00 am

**POOR SERVANTS OF THE MOTHER OF GOD**
St Mary's Convent, Manor House,
Raheny, Dublin 5
Tel/Fax 01-8317626

St Mary's Convent, 2 St John's,
Castledermot, Athy, Co Kildare
Tel 059-9144152
Community: 2

St Mary's Convent, Manor House,
Raheny, Dublin 5
Tel 01-8313652 Fax 01-8313299
Community: 10
Education, pastoral ministry

Maryfield Convent, Chapelizod,
Dublin 20
Tel 01-6264684/6265402 Fax 01-6233673
Community: 13
Home for elderly

216 Tonlegee Road, Dublin 5
Tel 01-8478566
Community: 4
Care of the elderly, pastoral ministry

Providence, 2 Creighton Street,
Dublin 2
Tel 01-6713130
Community: 2
Pastoral Ministry

Croí Mhuire, 120 Lucan Road,
Chapelizod, Dublin 20
Fax/Tel 01-6233734
Community: 2
Elderly and pastoral work

St Gabriel's Home, Glenayle Road,
Cameron Park, Dublin 5
Tel 01-8474339 Fax 01-8486610
Community: 4
Home for elderly and community care service

39 Glenayle Road, Dublin 5
Tel 01-8770700
Community: 4
Pastoral Ministry

Kairos Spirituality Centre,
125 Castlegate Way, Adamstown, Lucan,
Co Dublin
Tel 01-6822079
Community: 1
Pastoral Ministry

Cuan Mhuire, Old Mill,
Viccanstown Road, Athy, Co Kildare
Tel 059-8631090
Community: 1
Councelling Ministry

**CONGREGATION OF THE SISTERS OF NAZARETH**
Nazareth House,
Malahide Road, Dublin 3
Tel 01-8338205 Fax 01-8330813
Email nazarethdublin@eircom.net
*Superior*: Sr Hannah O'Connor
Community: 15
*Regional Superior:* Sr Cataldus Courtney
Tel 01-8332024 Fax 01-8334988
Home for elderly. Beds: 73

**PRESENTATION SISTERS**
Lucan, Co Dublin
Tel 01-6280305
Community: 5
Home for missionaries on home leave
Mission Office Tel/Fax 01-6282467
*Contact:* Sr Josephine Murphy
Email pbvmmo@gofree.indigo.ie

69 Fortlawn Drive, Mountview,
Blanchardstown, Dublin 15
Tel 01-8119430
Email presfortlawn@eircom.net
*Contact:* Sr Mary Byrne
Interprovincial Community: 2
School and pastoral work

*Northern Province:*
George's Hill, Dublin 7
Tel 01-8746914
Community: 10
Presentation Convent Primary School
Tel/Fax 01-8733061
Email presghill@eircom.net
School and pastoral ministry

2/3 Castlebridge Estate,
Maynooth, Co Kildare
Tel 01-6289952
*Community Leader:* Sr Eithne Cunniffe
Community: 7
Scoil Mhuire Primary School
Tel 01-6280056 Fax 01-6282611
School and pastoral ministry

Apartment 2, Riverforest Court, Leixlip,
Co Kildare
Tel 01-6242538
Email presleixlip1@eircom.net
Community: 3

*South-East Province:*
Provincialate, 27 Wainsfort Drive,
Terenure, Dublin 6W
Tel 01-4929588 Fax 01-4929590
Email secretary@presprose.com
*Provincial:* Sr Frances Murphy
Community: 2

Presentation Convent of the Immaculate
Conception, Clondalkin, Dublin 22
Tel 01-4592656
*Local Leader:* Sr Concepta O'Brien
Community: 13
Scoil Mhuire Primary School,
Convent Road, Clondalkin, Dublin 22
Tel 01-4592986
Scoil Ide Primary School,
New Road, Clondalkin, Dublin 22
Tel 01-4592973
Scoil Aine Primary School
Tel 01-4591645
Coláiste Bríde Secondary School,
New Road, Clondalkin, Dublin 22
Tel 01-4592900

Presentation Convent,
Warrenmount, Dublin 8
Tel 01-4543358
*Local Leader:* Sr Teresa Ryan
Community: 13
Primary. Tel 01-8788852
Post Primary. Tel 01-4547520
Warrenmount CED Centre Ltd
Tel 01-4542622

7B Oliver Bond House, Dublin 8
Tel 01-6776702
*Contact Person:* Sr Brigid Phelan
Community: 2

17A South Earl Street, Dublin 8
*Contact:* Sr Imelda Wickham
Tel 01-4532239
Community: 1

41 O'Curry Road, Dublin 8
Tel 01-4542806
*Contact:* Sr Carmel Daly
Community: 3

335 Dolphin House,
Dolphin's Barn, Dublin 8
*Contact:* Sr Mary Flynn
Tel 01-4540499
Community: 2

5 Foxdene Green, Balgaddy,
Lucan, Co Dublin
Tel 01-4574533
Community: 3

2 The Weavers, Meath Place, Dublin 8
*Contact:* Sr Bernadette Flanagan
Community: 1

27 Mayfield Park, Watery Lane, Dublin 22
Tel 01-4037316
*Contact:* Sr Kathleen Barrett
Community: 2

Block G, 176 The Tramyard,
Spa Road, Inchicore, Dublin 8
*Contact:* Sr Bernadette Purcell
Community: 1

42 Temple Hill,
Terenure Road West, Dublin 6W
Tel 086-3422227
*Contact:* Sr Una Trant
Community: 1

9A Kilmahuddrick Walk, Clondalkin,
Dubin 22
Tel 01-4576441
*Contact:* Sr Mary Brennan
Community: 2

25 Weaver Court, Neilstown, Dublin 22
Tel 087-2624140
*Contact:* Kathleen Meagher

**REDEMPTORISTINES**
Monastery of St Alphonsus,
St Alphonsus Road, Dublin 9
Tel 01-8305723 Fax 01-8309129
*Superior:* Sr Gabrielle
Email gabrielle.fox@redemptorists.ie
Community: 15
Contemplatives

**RELIGIOUS OF CHRISTIAN EDUCATION**
Provincial Office, 3 Bushy Park House,
Templeogue Road, Dublin 6W
Tel 01-4901668 Fax 01-4901101
*Provincial leader:* Sr Rosemary O'Looney

Community Residence,
4/5 Bushy Park House,
Templeogue Road, Dublin 6W
Tel 01-4905516
*Superior:* Sr Rosemary O'Looney

13 Oriel Street Lower, Dublin 1
Tel 087-6359057
Counselling

Our Lady's School,
Templeogue Road, Dublin 6W
Secondary School. Tel 01-4903241
*Principal:* Ms Graínne Friel

**RELIGIOUS OF SACRED HEART OF MARY**
Cormaria, 7 Bancroft Road,
Tallaght, Dublin 24
Tel 01-4515674
Community: 5
Ministry in local area

13/14 Huntstown Wood,
Mulhuddart, Dublin 15
Tel 01-8223566
Community: 3
Pastoral ministry, addiction, HIV counselling

70 Upper Drumcondra Road, Dublin 9
Tel 01-8379898
Community: 4
Education, pastoral

72 Upper Drumcondra Road, Dublin 9
Tel 01-8368331
Community: 4
Spiritual direction, ministry in local area

**RELIGIOUS SISTERS OF CHARITY**
Generalate, Caritas, 15 Gilford Road,
Sandymount, Dublin 4
Tel 01-2697833/2697935

Provincialate, Provincial House,
Our Lady's Mount, Harold's Cross,
Dublin 6W
Tel 01-4973177

Marmion House, St Mary's,
185 Merrion Road, Dublin 4
Tel 01-2027223
Various Apostolic Ministries

Overseas Office, Naomh Brid,
28/38 Belvedere Place, Dublin 1
Tel/Fax 01-2604826

St Anne's, 29 Thornville Drive,
Kilbarrack East, Dublin 5
Tel 01-8321112/8321114
Various Apostolic Ministries

St Mary's, Stanhope Street, Dublin 7
Tel 01-6779183
Various Apostolic Ministries

Stanhope Lodge,
Stanhope Green, Dublin 7
Tel 01-6704016
Various Apostolic Ministries

Convent of the Assumption,
76 Upper Gardiner Street, Dublin 1
Tel 01-8746431
Various Apostolic Ministries

Sisters of Charity, 3C Liberty House,
Railway Street, Dublin 1
Tel 01-8364269
Various Apostolic Ministries

St Monica's, Belvedere Place, Dublin 1
Tel (Community) 01-8552317
Various Apostolic Ministries

Naomh Bríd Community,
28/38 Belvedere Place, Dublin 1
Tel 01-8557647
Various Apostolic Ministries

Our Lady of the Nativity, Lakelands,
Sandymount, Dublin 4
Tel 01-2692076/2603362
Various Apostolic Ministries

St Mary's, Donnybrook, Dublin 4
Tel 01-2600315/2600818
Various Apostolic Ministries

Mary Aikenhead House, St Mary's,
Donnybrook, Dublin 4
Tel 01-2693258
Various Apostolic Ministries

Sisters of Charity, Our Lady's Mount,
Harold's Cross, Dublin 6W
Ard Mhuire Community
Tel 01-4961488
Maranatha Community
Tel 01-4961423
Shandon community
Tel 01-4982614
Heritage Centre
Tel 01-4910041
Various Apostolic Ministries

4 Telford House, St Mary's,
Merrion Road, Dublin 4
Tel 01-2605495
Various Apostolic Ministries

Stella Maris Convent, Baily, Co Dublin
Tel 01-8322228 Fax 01-8063469
Various Apostolic Ministries

St Agnes' Convent, Armagh Road,
Crumlin, Dublin 12
Tel 01-4555591
Various Apostolic Ministries

Our Lady Queen of Ireland,
Walkinstown, Dublin 12
Tel 01-4503491
Various Apostolic Ministries

Sisters of Charity,
Seville Place, Dublin 1
Tel 01-8744179
Various Apostolic Ministries

Sisters of Charity, 95/97 Richmond Road,
Fairview, Dublin 3
Tel 01-8376874
Various Apostolic Ministries

Sisters of Charity,
1 Temple Street, Dublin 1
Tel 01-8745778/8745779

Presbytery 2, Dunmanus Road,
Cabra West, Dublin 7
Tel 01-8687231
Various Apostolic Ministries

26 Park Avenue, Sandymount, Dublin 4
Tel 01-2604659
Various Apostolic Ministries

28 Park Avenue, Sandymount, Dublin 4
Tel 01-2604654
Various Apostolic Ministries

Providence,
St Mary's, Merrion Road, Dublin 4
Tel 01-2693450
Various Apostolic Ministries

Shalom
St Mary's, Merrion Road, Dublin 4
Tel 01-2602775
Various Apostolic Ministries

386 Clogher Road, Crumlin, Dublin 12
Tel 01-4169016/4169622
Various Apostolic Ministries

Sisters of Charity, 2 Carrickmore Place,
Saggart, Co Dublin
Tel 01-4133841

**ROSMINIANS (SISTERS OF PROVIDENCE)**
104a Griffith Court, Fairview, Dublin 3
Tel 01-8375021
Email teresamolloy@eircom.net
*Contact Person:* Sr Teresa Molloy
Community: 3

**SACRED HEART SOCIETY**
76 Home Farm Road,
Drumcondra, Dublin 9
Tel 01-8375412 Fax 01-8375542
Email rscjirs@gmail.com
*Provincial Superior:* Sr Aideen Kinlen
Email aideenkinlen@eircom.net

6 Achill Road, Drumcondra, Dublin 9
Tel 01-8360866 Fax 01-8360112
Email 6achill@eircom.net
Community: 4. Administration;
Adult education and pastoral work;
youth and pastoral ministry.

*Linked with Achill Road:*
49 Philipsburgh Terrace, Marino, Dublin 3
Tel 01-8554018
Email lawlesse@hotmail.com

9 Clonshaugh Drive, Priorswood, Dublin 17
Tel 01-8474244 Fax 01-8488940
Email tdeasy@eircom.net
Community: 3
Parish work

10 Walnut Rise, Dublin 9
Fax 01-8844547
Email phil.sinnott@upcmail.ie
Community: 3
Pastoral ministry

7 Merrion View Avenue, Dublin 4
Tel 01-2602533
Email dairne@eircom.net
almcs@eircom.net
Community: 3
Facilitation; English teaching; refugees and asylum seekers; Religious Formation Ministry Programme

Linked with Merrion View Avenue:
5 Redcourt Oaks, Seafield Road East,
Clontarf, Dublin 3
Educational Trusteeships and voluntary work

23 Castlelands Grove, Dalkey, Co Dublin
Historical research; part-time university teaching

Sacred Heart Schools Network Ltd
Mount Anville Day Secondary School 634 pupils. Tel 01-2885313/4
Mount Anville Junior and Montessori School 467 pupils. Tel 01-2885313/4
Mount Anville Primary School,
Lower Kilmacud Road,
Stillorgan, Co Dublin
Pupils: 420
Tel 01-2831148 Fax 01-2836395

Cedar House, Provincial Infirmary,
35 Mount Anville Park, Dublin 14
Tel 01-2831024/5 Fax 01-2831348
Community: 21

36 Mount Anville Park, Dublin 14
Tel 01-2880739 Fax 01-2104826
Community: 3
Work in Ceder House

37/38 Mount Anville Park, Dublin 14
Tel 01-2880708 Fax 01-2780673
Community: 6
Work in parish; translation

96 Mount Anville Wood,
Lower Kilmacud Road, Dublin 14
Tel 01-2880786 Fax 01-2789119
Email sshdublin@eircom.net
Community: 6
Work in Mount Anville and other schools; administration' spiritual ministry; prison chaplaincy; research

201 Lower Kilmacud Road,
Stillorgan, Co Dublin
Tel 01-2834832 Fax 01-2104825
Community: 3
Work in Mount Anville, Cedar House and parish

107 Beechwood Lawn, Rochestown Avenue, Dun Laoghaire, Co Dublin
Tel 01-2354933
Community: 2
Email silemac@eircom.net
Pastoral Ministry

67 Clonard Park, Sandyford, Dubin 16
Tel 01-2999989
Email rbk@eircom.net
Pastoral ministry

**SACRED HEARTS OF JESUS AND MARY (PICPUS) SISTERS**
Sector House, 11 Northbrook Road,
Ranelagh, Dublin 6
Tel 01-4910173 (Co-ordinator)
Tel 01-4974831 (Community)
Fax 01-4965551
Community: 6
*Contact:* Mary McCloskey (SSCC)

Aymer House, 11 Northbrook Lane,
Ranelagh, Dublin 6
Tel 01-4975614
Community: 4

**SALESIAN SISTERS OF ST JOHN BOSCO**
Provincialate, 203 Lower Kilmacud Road,
Stillorgan, Co Dublin
Tel 01-2985188
*Provincial Superior:* Sr Mary Doran
Convent Tel 01-2985908
*Superior:* Sr Moira O'Sullivan
Community: 6
Parish ministry, provincial administration

38 Morehampton Road,
Donnybrook, Dublin 4
Tel 01-6684643
Community: 3
Mission promotion, working in resource centre, President APTS

40 Morehampton Road,
Donnybrook, Dublin 4
Tel 01-6680012
*Superior:* Sr Jennifer Perkins
Community: 4
Art therapy, hospital ministry, facilitators' training course for youth retreats

91-95 Ashwood Road, Bawnoge,
Clondalkin, Dublin 22
Tel 01-4571792
*Superior:* Sr Mary McCormack
Community: 5
Teaching and related activities

36 Glenties Park, Finglas South, Dublin 11
Tel 01-8345777
*Superior:* Sr Máire O'Byrne
Community: 4
Social and parish work

28 Hazelwood Crescent, Greenpark,
Clondalkin, Dublin 22
Tel 01-4123928
Superior: Sr Cathering Kelly
Community: 5
Teaching and related activities, parish work

**SISTERS OF ST CLARE**
St Clare's Convent,
Tel 01-4995100
63 Harold's Cross Road, Dublin 6W
*Contact:* Sr Dominic Savio Ward
Community: 11
Primary School

**ST JOHN OF GOD SISTERS**
34 Dornden Park, Booterstown, Co Dublin
Tel 01-2698898
Community: 4
Community Project residence

39 St David's Wood, Malahide Road,
Artane, Dublin 5
Community: 2

**SISTERS OF ST JOSEPH OF CHAMBERY**
St Joseph's Convent,
Springdale Road, Raheny, Dublin 5
Tel 01-8478351 Fax 01-8485764
*Superior:* Sr Mary Peter Raleigh
Email mpraleigh@eircom.net
Community: 6
Care of the sick and pastoral activity

St Joseph's Convent, 5 Kincora Grove,
Clontarf, Dublin 3
Tel 01-8337866
*Regional Superior:* Sr Eileen Silke
Email esilke10@eircom.net
Tel 01-8337866
Community: 4

**SISTERS OF ST JOSEPH OF CLUNY**
Mount Sackville Convent,
Chapelizod, Dublin 20
Tel 01-8213134
Email clunyprov@sjc.ie
Website www.sjc.ie
*Provincial Superior:* Sr Rowena Galvin
Tel 01-8213134
*Superior:* Sr Louis Marie O'Connor
Tel 01-8213134
Community: 43
Primary school; secondary day school; nursing home

St Joseph of Cluny Convent,
Ballinclea Road, Killiney, Co Dublin
Tel 01-2851038
*Superior:* Sr Clare Little
Community: 9
Junior and secondary schools

Cluny House, 1 Beechwood Park,
Rathmines, Dublin 6
Tel 01-4971641
*Superior:* Sr Peggy McLoughlin
Community: 3

Parslickstown Drive,
Mulhuddart, Dublin 15
Tel 01-8217339
*Superior:* Sr Ignatius Davis
Community: 3
Education and pastoral ministry

47/49 Cruise Park Drive, Tyrrelstown,
Dublin 15
Tel 01-8856391 Fax 01-8856395
*Superior:* Sr Agnes Reilly
Community: 3
Parish work

**SISTERS OF ST JOSEPH OF LYON**
3 St Margaret's Avenue,
Raheny, Dublin 5
Tel 01-8325896
Email sistersofjoseph@oceanfree.net
*Contact Person:* Sr Marie Kiernan

**ST JOSEPH OF THE SACRED HEART SISTERS**
St Joseph's Convent, 6 Farmleigh Avenue,
Stillorgan, Co Dublin
Tel 01-2781228 Fax 01-2782139

Sisters of St Joseph of the Sacred Heart,
25 Nutley Square, Donnybrook,
Dublin 4
Tel 01-2602306

Sisters of St Joseph of the Sacred Heart, 27 Castlerosse View, Baldoyle, Dublin
Tel 01-8324508

Sisters of St Joseph, 11 The Courtyard, Vevay Crescent, Bray, Co Wicklow
Tel 01-2761288

Sisters of St Joseph, 48 Seatown Villas, Swords, Co Dublin
Tel 01-8907345

**ST LOUIS SISTERS**
St Louis Generalate, 3 Beech Court, Ballinclea Road, Killiney, Dublin
Tel 01-2350304/2350309 Fax 01-2350345
*Institute Leader:* Sr Donna Hansen

St Louis Convent,
Charleville Road, Dublin 6
Tel 01-4975467
Community: 28
St Louis High School, Rathmines
Tel 01-4975458. Pupils: 750
St Louis Primary School, Rathmines
Tel 01-4976098. Pupils: 400
St Louis Infant School, Rathmines
Tel 01-4972188. Pupils: 300

Blakestown Road,
Mulhuddart, Dublin 15
Tel 01-8217432
Community: 8
Varied apostolates

7 Grosvenor Road, Rathgar, Dublin 6
Tel 01-4965485
Community: 6
Varied apostolates

8 Grosvenor Road, Rathgar, Dublin 6
Tel 01-4966631
Community: 7
Varied apostolates

St Louis Mission House,
1 Grosvenor Road, Rathgar, Dublin 6
Tel 01-4960538
Community: 3

38 Bushy Park Road, Terenure, Dublin 6
Tel 01-4900043
Community: 2
Varied apostolates

130 Beaufort Downs,
Rathfarnham, Dublin 16
Tel 01-4934194
Community: 4
Varied apostolates

17 Kilclare Crescent, Jobstown,
Tallaght, Dublin 24
Tel 01-4526344
Community: 1
Education

49 Moynihan Court,
Main Road, Tallaght Village, Dublin 24
Tel 01-4628386
Community: 4
Varied apostolates

**ST MARY MADELEINE POSTEL SISTERS**
35 Charlemont, Griffith
Avenue, Dublin 9
*Regional Superior:* Sr M. Luke Minogue
Tel 01-8373931
Community: 1

**ST PAUL DE CHARTRES SISTERS**
Queen of Peace Centre, Garville Avenue, Rathgar, Dublin 6
Tel 01-4975381/4972366 Fax 01-4964084
Email spcqueen@eircom.net
*Regional Superior*
Sr Rose Margaret Nuval
Community: 6
Residences for the elderly

**URSULINES**
Generalate, 17 Trimleston Drive,
Booterstown, Co Dublin
Tel 01-2693503
*Congregational Leader*
Sr Mary McHugh

Ursuline Sisters, 24 Shrewsbury Wood,
Cabinteely, Dublin 18
Tel 01-2853706
Email urscab@eircom.net
Community: 3

St Ursula's, Sandyford, Dublin 18
Tel 01-2956881
*Contact Person:* Sr Finbarr Muckley
Community: 4
Pastoral ministry

**URSULINES OF JESUS**
26 The Drive, Seatown Park,
Swords, Co Dublin
Tel 01-8404323
Email ujswords@eircom.net
*Contact Person:* Sr Mary McLoughney
Community: 3
Parish ministry, reflexology and aromatherapy.

## EDUCATIONAL INSTITUTIONS

**Holy Cross College,**
Clonliffe, Dublin 3
Tel 01-8375103/4 Fax 01-8371474

**All Hallows College**
Drumcondra, Dublin 9
Tel 01-8373745/8373746 Fax 01-8377642
*President*
Rev Patrick McDevitt (CM) PhD
(See Seminaries and Houses of Study section)

**Kimmage Mission Institute at Milltown**
Milltown Institute, Dublin 6
Tel 01-2698388 Fax 01-4928506
*Department Head*
Rev Patrick Roe (CSSp)

**Marino Institute of Education**
Griffith Avenue, Dublin 9
Tel 01-8057700

**Mater Dei Institute of Education**
Clonliffe Road, Dublin 3
Tel 01-8376027/8/9 Fax 01-8370776
Email info@materdei.deu.ie
Website www.materdei.ie
*President:* Very Rev Dermot Lane
*Director:* Dr Andrew McGrady PhD

**The Milltown Institute of Theology and Philosophy**
Milltown Park, Dublin 6
Tel 01-2698388
*President:* Rev Brian Grogan (SJ)
(See Seminaries and Houses of Study section)

**St Patrick's College**
Drumcondra, Dublin 9
Tel 01-8376191
*President:* Dr Padraic Travers

**St Patrick's College**
Maynooth, Co Kildare
Tel 01-6285222 Fax 01-7083959
*President:* Rt Rev Mgr Hugh Connolly
(See Seminaries and Houses of Study section)

**EDMUND RICE SCHOOLS TRUST**
Ardscoil Chaoimhin,
Christian Brothers Secondary School,
Coolgreaney Road, Arklow, Co Wicklow
Tel 0402-32564/39176 Fax 0402-32565
*Principal:* Mr Peter Somers

St Brendan's College, Woodbrook, Bray, Co Wicklow
Tel 01-2822317 (Principal)
Tel 01-2822800 (Staff) Fax 01-2822616
Email stbrendanscollege@hotmail.com
*Principal:* Mr John Taylor

Colaiste Eanna, Ballyroan, Dublin 16
Tel 01-4931767 Fax 01-4933489
Staff Tel 01-4932821
Email secretary@colaiste.enna.ie
Principal: Mr Brendan McCauley

Clonkeen College, Clonkeen Road,
Blackrock, Co Dublin
Tel 01-2892709/2892790 Fax 01-2898260
Email clonkeenrec@eircom.net
*Principal:* Mr Dom Twomey

Edmund Rice Schools Trust
Meadow Vale, Clonkeen Road,
Blackrock, Co Dublin
Tel 01-2897511
*CE:* Mr Gerry Bennett

Christian Brothers Primary School,
Armagh Road, Crumlin, Dublin 12
Tel 01-4562622 Fax 01-4550766
Email scoilcolm.ias@eircom.net
*Principal:* Ms Claire Keenan

Christian Brothers Primary School,
Drimnagh Castle, Walkinstown,
Dublin 12
Tel 01-4552066 (Principal)
Tel 01-4516049 (Staff)
Email drimnaghcastle.ias@eircom.net
*Principal:* Mr Eugene Duffy

Meánscoil Iognáid Rís, Drimnagh Castle, Walkinstown, Dublin 12
Tel 01-4518316 (Principal)
Tel 01-4500805 (Staff) Fax 01-4505401
Email dch@eircom.met
*Principal:* Mr Ray Walsh

Scoil San Séamus, Basin Lane, Dublin 8
Tel 01-4534321 Fax 01-4730382
Email jamesst@eircom.net
*Principal:* Ms Deirdre Brennan

Christian Brothers Secondary School, James's Street, Dublin 8
Tel 01-4547756 Fax 01-4547856
*Acting Principal*: Mr John Devilly
Website www.jambo.com

Scoil Mhuire Primary School, Oatlands, Mount Merrion, Co Dublin
Tel 01-2887108
Email oatlandsprimary@eircom.net
*Principal:* Ms Ber O'Sullivan

Oatlands College, Mount Merrion, Co Dublin
Tel 01-2888533/2880662
Email oatlands@iol.ie
*Principal:* Mr Keith Ryan

Coláiste Eoin, Bóthar Stigh Lorgan, Baile an Bhóthair, Carraig Dubh, Co Atha Cliath
Tel 01-2884002/2884029 Fax 01-2836896
Email coleoin@iol.ie
*Principal:* Finian Martin

Coláiste Íosagáin, Stillorgan Road, Booterstown, Co Dublin
Tel 01-2884028
*Principal:* Fiona Uí Uiginn

Scoil Iosagáin, Aughavannagh Road, Dublin 12
Tel 01-4541821 Fax 01-4169930
*Principal:* Ms Mairead Fanning

St Teresa's Primary School, Donore Avenue, Dublin 8
Tel 01-4541899
Email scoiltreasa@hotmail.com
*Principal:* Ms Annmarie Spillane

Bunscoil Sancta Maria, Synge Street, Dublin 8
Tel 01-4784316 Staff Tel 01-4781705
Fax 01-4784316
Email bscoilsynge.eircom.net
Website www.syngestreet.com
*Principal:* Pádraig Ó Néill

St Paul's Secondary School, Synge Street, Dublin 8
Tel 01-4783998 Staff Tel 01-4782327
Fax 01-4784154
Email syngestoffice@eircom.net
Website www.syngestreet.com
*Principal:* Mr Michael Minnock

Christian Brothers Primary School, Francis Street, Dublin 8
Tel 01-4531800
Email francisstcbs.ias@eircom.net
*Acting Principal:* Ms Fiona Collins

Christian Brothers Secondary School, Cumberland Street, Dublin 2
Tel 01-6614143 Fax 01-6763653
Email westlandcbs@eircom.net
*Principal:* Ms Kate Byrne

CBC Junior School, Monkstown Park, Dun Laoghaire, Co Dublin
Tel 01-2805854 Fax 01-2805907
Email cbcadmin@indigo.ie
*Principal:* Mr D. Molloy

Christian Brothers College, Monkstown Park, Dun Laoghaire, Co Dublin
Tel 01-2805854/2809314 Fax 01-2805907
Email cbcadmin@indigo.ie
*Principal:* Dr Gerard Berry

Coláiste Phádraig, Ballydowd, Lucan, Co Dublin
Tel 01-6282299 Fax 01-6282713
Email lucancbs@iol.ie
*Principal:* Mr Brian Murtagh

St David's Secondary School
Tel 01-8315322
*Principal:* Mr Padraic Kavanagh

Scoil Chiaráin Primary School, Collins Avenue East, Dublin 5
Tel 01-8313072
*Principal:* Mr Martin Troy

St Fintan's High School, Sutton, Dublin 13
Tel 01-8324632/8324595
*Principal:* Ms Mary Fox

St Kevin's College, Ballygall Road East, Dublin 11
Tel 01-8371423/8375318
*Principal:* Mr Ciaran O'Hare

St Declan's Secondary School, Nephin Road, Dublin 7
Tel 01-8381531
*Principal:* Ms Miriam Marsh

Gaelscoil Choláiste Mhuire, 4 Cearnóg Pharnell, Baile Átha Cliath 1
Tel 01-8729131
*Príomhoide:* An tUas S. Feiritéar

Coláiste Mhuire, Bothar Ráth Tó, Baile Átha Cliath 7
Tel 01-8688996 Fax 01-8688998
*Príomhoide:* Tomás O'Mhurchú

St Vincent's Primary School, Glasnevin, Dublin 11
Tel 01-8302328
*Principal:* Mr Peter Molumby

St Vincent's Secondary School, Glasnevin, Dublin 11
Tel 01-8304375/8304748
*Principal:* Mr John Horan

Scoil Mhuire, Griffith Avenue, Dublin 9
Tel 01-8338294/8336421
*Principal:* Mr Ben Dorney

Scoil Iosef, Fairview, Dublin 3
Tel 01-8336127
*Principal:* An tUsal P. Ó Fainín

St Joseph's Secondary School, Fairview, Dublin 3
Tel 01-8339779
*Principal:* Mr Gerry Cullen

Ard Scoil Ris, Griffith Avenue, Marino, Dublin 9
Tel 01-8332633/8332172
*Principal:* Mr Brian O'Dwyer

St Paul's Primary School, North Brunswick Street, Dublin 7
Tel 01-8722167
*Principal:* Mr Donal Ó Suibhne

St Paul's Secondary School, North Brunswick Street, Dublin 7
Tel 01-8720781/8722472
*Principal:* Mr Michael Blanchfield

O'Connell Primary School, North Richmond Street, Dublin 1
Tel 01-8557517
*Principal:* Mr Patsy O'Keeffe

O'Connell Secondary School, North Richmond Street, Dublin 1
Tel 01-8748307
*Principal:* Mr Gerry Duffy

St Laurence O'Toole Primary School, Seville Place, Dublin 1
Tel 01-8363490
Principal: Mr Mark Candon

Coláiste Choilm, Swords, Co Dublin
Tel 01-8401420
*Principal:* Mr David Neville

St Aidan's Secondary School, Collins Avenue West, Dublin 9
Tel 01-8377587/8379869
*Principal:* Mr James Reynolds

## CHARITABLE AND OTHER SOCIETIES

*Adoption Societies*

**CÚNAMH**
30 South Anne Street, Dublin 2
Tel 01-6779664
*Administrative Secretary:* Mr Jim Dwan
*Senior Social Worker:* Ms Julie Kerins

**St Brigid's Orphanage**
Holy Faith Convent, The Coombe, Dublin 8
Tel 01-4542917/4540244
*Sister in Charge*
Sr M. Benignus McDonagh

**St Louise Adoption Society**
Park House, North Circular Road, Dublin 7
Tel 01-8387122

**St Patrick's Guild**
203 Merrion Road, Dublin 4
Tel 01-2196551
*Director:* Sr Francis Fahy

*Travellers Family Care*

**Derralossary House**
Roundwood, Co Wicklow
Tel 01-2818355
Residential home for girls
Ballyowen Meadows
Tel 01-6235735
Exchange House Youth Service
61 Great Strand Street, Dublin 1
Tel 01-4546488
Training and employment programme and youth work

*Hostels*

**Don Bosco House**
57 Lower Drumcondra Road, Dublin 9
Tel 01-8360696
Salesian hostel for homeless boys.
Priest in Charge: Rev V. Collier (SDB)
**Homeless Girls' Hostel**
Sherrard House,
19 Upper Sherrard Street, Dublin 1
Tel 01-8743742

**Iveagh Hostel**
Bride Road, Dublin 8
Tel 01-4540182

**Home Again**
22 Newtown Avenue, Blackrock, Co Dublin
Tel 01-2882295
*Director:* Mr John Molloy
Residential home for boys

**Morning Star Hostel**
Morning Star Avenue,
Brunswick Street, Dublin 7
Tel 01-8723401

**Regina Coeli Hostel**
Morning Star Avenue,
Brunswick Street, Dublin 7
Tel 01-8723142

**St Brigid's Hostel**
8/9/10 Henrietta Street, Dublin 1
For girls
Tel 01-8732580/8727469

**St Vincent de Paul Night Shelter**
Back Lane, Dublin 8
Tel 01-4542181

*Housing*

**Catholic Housing Aid Society**
Grenville Street, Dublin 1
Tel 01-8741020
*Secretary:* Mrs Valerie Power
Flats for the aged

**Mother Mary Aikenhead Social Services Centre**
Mount St Anne's, Milltown, Dublin 6
Tel 01-2698995
Provides flats at a nominal rent for young married couples

**Threshold**
21 Stoneybatter, Dublin 7
Tel 01-6353600/6786090
Website www.threshold.ie

*Other*

**CROSSCARE Catholic Social Care Agency**
Holy Cross College, Clonliffe, Dublin 3
Tel 01-8360011
*Chairman:* Mr Frank O'Connell
*Director:* Mr Conor Hickey

**Conference of St Philip Neri (SVP)**
91-92 Sean McDermott Street, Dublin 1
Tel 01-8550022
Prison visitation and aid to discharged prisoners

**Cuan Mhuire**
Athy, Co Kildare
Tel 059-8631493 Fax 059-8638765
Rehabilitation centre for alcoholics and those with allied problems

**Irish School of Evangelisation (ISOE)**
9A Wyattville Park, Dun Laoghaire, Co Dublin
*Contact:* Joe O'Callaghan
Tel 01-2827658
Email isoe@esatclear.ie
www.esatclear.ie/~isoe

**Our Lady's Choral Society**
(The Archdiocesan Choir)
*Director:* Rev Paul Ward
*Hon Secretary:* Lois Jarvis
Tel 01-2819363

**Society of St Vincent de Paul**
Dublin Office,
91-92 Sean McDermott Street, Dublin 1
Tel 01-8550022 Fax 01-8559168

**Specialists in Church Refurbishments:**

- Upholstery of church kneeler boards and seating
- Sand and varnishing of church pews
- Refurbishment of Stations of The Cross
- Woodworm treatment of church timbers

- Roofing and gutter cleaning and repair
- Lightning conductor maintenance
- Stone cleaning and pointing
- Cleaning, restoration and storm glazing of church windows
- Internal and external painting
- Tailored maintenance packages and quotations arranged free of charge
- **Fully insured for all height work**

All Ireland and UK Coverage

Ranks Church Contractors:
117 Ardanlee, Culmore, Derry City

Office Phone/Fax: UK 028 71358315 • Eire 048 71358315
Mobile 0851216237 • Email rankscc@hotmail.co.uk

# ARCHDIOCESE OF CASHEL AND EMLY

PATRON OF THE ARCHDIOCESE
ST AILBE, 12 SEPTEMBER

SUFFRAGEN SEES: CLOYNE, CORK AND ROSS, KERRY, KILLALOE, LIMERICK, WATERFORD AND LISMORE

INCLUDES MOST OF COUNTY TIPPERARY AND PARTS OF COUNTY LIMERICK

**Most Rev Dermot Clifford PhD, DD**
Archbishop of Cashel and Emly; born 1939; ordained priest 22 February 1964; ordained Coadjutor Archbishop 9 March 1986; installed Archbishop of Cashel and Emly 12 September 1988; appointed Apostolic Administrator of Cloyne 7 March 2009

Residence: Archbishop's House, Thurles, Co Tipperary
Tel 0504-21512 Fax 0504-22680
Email office@cashel-emly.ie
Website www.cashel-emly.ie

## CATHEDRAL OF THE ASSUMPTION, THURLES

The Cathedral of the Assumption stands on the site of earlier chapels. The first church on this site was part of the Carmelite priory, which dates from the early fourteenth century.

Some time before 1730 George Mathew, Catholic proprietor of the Thurles Estate, built a chapel for the Catholics of Thurles beside the ruins of the Carmelite priory. It was known as the Mathew Chapel. In 1810 Archbishop Bray consecrated the new 'Big Chapel', which was more spacious and ornate than its humble predecessor.

Soon after his appointment as archbishop in 1857, Dr Patrick Leahy revealed his plan to replace the Big Chapel with 'a cathedral worthy of the archdiocese'. Building commenced in 1865, and the impressive Romanesque cathedral, with its façade modelled on that of Pisa, was consecrated by Archbishop Croke on 21 June 1879. The architect was J. J. McCarthy. Barry McMullen was the main builder, and J. C. Ashlin was responsible for the enclosing walls, railing and much of the finished work.

The cathedral has many beautiful features, including an impressive rose window, a free-standing baptistry and a magnificent altar. The prize possession of the cathedral is its exquisite tabernacle, the work of Giacomo dello Porta (1537–1602), a pupil of Michelangelo. This tabernacle, which belonged to the Gesú (Jesuit) Church in Rome, was purchased by Archbishop Leahy and transported to Thurles.

The cathedral was extensively renovated and the sanctuary sympathetically remodelled on the occasion of its first centenary in 1979.

The most recent extensive conservation and renewal of the Cathedral, during 2001–2003, has restored the building to its original splendour.

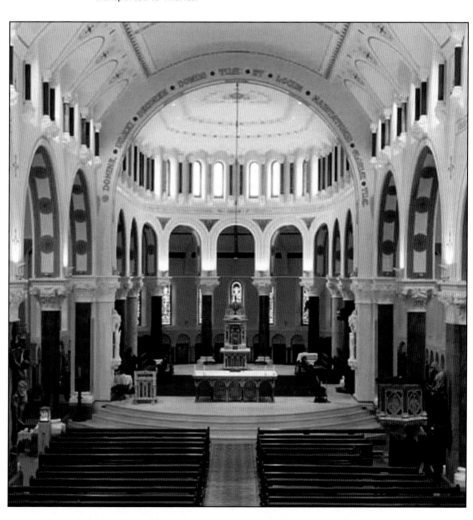

## CHAPTER

*Dean*
Rt Rev Mgr Christy O'Dwyer VG
*Archdeacon*
Venerable Matthew McGrath VG
Tipperary
*Chancellor:* Vacant
*Precentor:* Vacant
*Treasurer:* Vacant
*Penitentiary:* Very Rev Canon Conor Ryan
Hospital
*Theologian*
Very Rev Canon Liam McNamara
Ballybricken, Grange,
Kilmallock, Co Limerick
*Prebendaries*
*Newchapel:* Very Rev Canon Thomas J. Ryan, Murroe
*Lattin:* Vacant
*Killennellick:* Very Rev Canon Liam Ryan
Killenaule

## ADMINISTRATION

**College of Consultors**
Rt Rev Mgr Christy O'Dwyer PP, VG
Venerable Matthew McGrath PP, VG
Rev Nicholas J. Irwin
Very Rev John J. O'Rourke PP
Rev Celsus Tierney

**Vicars General**
Rt Rev Mgr Christy O'Dwyer PP, VG
Cashel, Co Tipperary
Tel 062-61127
Venerable Matthew McGrath PP, VG
St Michael Street, Tipperary Town
Tel 062-51536

**Vicars Forane**
Very Rev Canon Thomas J. Ryan
Very Rev Canon Conor Ryan
Very Rev Canon Liam Ryan
Very Rev Canon Thomas F. Breen
Very Rev Canon Eugene Everard
Very Rev Canon John O'Neill

**Diocesan Planning Finance Committee**
*Secretary*
Venerable Matthew McGrath PP, VG
Tel 062-51536
Very Rev George Bourke PP
Tel 0504-44227
Very Rev Conor Hayes PP
Parochial House, Kilteely, Co Limerick
Tel 061-384213
Rev Nicholas J. Irwin CC
Borrisoleigh, Thurles, Co Tipperary
Tel 0504-51230
Rev John O'Keefe CC
Birdhill, Killaloe, Co Tipperary
Tel 061-379172

**Diocesan Archivist**
Rt Rev Mgr Christy O'Dwyer PP, VG
Cashel, Co Tipperary
Tel 062-61127

**Diocesan Secretary/Chancellor**
Rev Nicholas J. Irwin
Archbishop's House, Thurles, Co Tipperary
Tel 0504-21512

## CATECHETICS EDUCATION

**Adult Religious Education**
Rev Thomas Dunne CC
Templemore, Co Tipperary
Tel 0504-32890

**Catechetics**
*Director:* Rev Patrick Coffey
Lisgaugh, Doon, Co Limerick
Tel 061-380247
*Assistant Director*
Very Rev Michael Kennedy PP
The Parochial House, New Inn,
Cashel, Co Tipperary
Tel 052-62395

**Boards of Management of Primary Schools**
*Education Secretary*
Rev John O'Keefe CC
Birdhill, Killaloe, Co Tipperary
Tel 061-379172/087-2421678

## LITURGY

**Liturgical Commission**
*Secretary*
Very Rev Canon Eugene Everard PP
The Parochial House, Templemore,
Co Tipperary
Tel 0504-31684

## PASTORAL

**Accord**
Accord House, Cathedral Street,
Thurles, Co Tipperary
Tel 0504-22279
*Diocesan Director:* Rev Patrick Coffey CC
Doon, Co Limerick
Tel 061-380247

**Adoption Society**
*Director:* Rev Celsus Tierney
Holy Cross Abbey, Holy Cross,
Thurles, Co Tipperary
Tel 0504-43118

**Charismatic Renewal**
*Adviser*
Very Rev Canon Denis Talbot PP, VF
Galbally, Co Tipperary
Tel 062-37922

**Child Protection Delegate**
Mr Bill Meagher
Tel 087-7914517

**Cura**
Cura Centre, 20A Liberty Square,
Thurles, Co Tipperary
Tel 0504-26226

**Communications**
*Diocesan Counsellor*
Rev Nicholas J. Irwin
Borrisoleigh, Thurles
Tel 0504-51230

**Council of Priests**
*Chairman*
Rt Rev Mgr Christy O'Dwyer PP, VG
Cashel, Co Tipperary
Tel 062-61127
*Secretary:* Rev Michael Mullaney
Ballycahill, Thurles, Co Tipperary
Tel 0504-26080

**Ecumenism**
Archbishop's House, Thurles,
Co Tipperary
Tel 0504-21512

**Emigrant Commission**
Rev Loughlin Brennan CC
Upperchurch, Thurles, Co Tipperary
Tel 0504-54492

**Marriage Tribunal**
(See Marriage Tribunals section.)

**Pilgrimages**
*Director:* Rev Thomas Hearne CC
Bohergar, Brittas, Co Limerick
Tel 061-352223

**Pioneer Total Abstinence Association**
*Diocesan Director*
Very Rev William Hennessy PP
Knocklong, Co Limerick
Tel 062-53114

**Social Services**
*Director:* Rev Gerard Hennessy CC
Cathedral Prestybery, Thurles,
Co Tipperary
Tel 0504-22229/22779

**Travellers**
*Chaplain*
Rev Daniel O'Gorman CC
Herbertstown, Hospital, Co Limerick
Tel 061-385104

**Vocations**
*Director:* Rev Patrick Coffey
Lisgaugh, Doon, Co Limerick
Tel 061-380247
Email piusix@eircom.net

**World Missions Ireland**
*Diocesan Director*
Very Rev Canon Eugene Everard PP
The Parochial House, Templemore,
Co Tipperary
Tel 0504-31684

## PARISHES

*Mensal parishes are listed first. Other parishes follow alphabetically. Church titulars are in italic.*

**THURLES, CATHEDRAL OF THE ASSUMPTION**
Very Rev Martin Hayes Adm
Rev Gerard Hennessy CC
Rev Tomás O'Connell CC
Cathedral Presbytery, Thurles,
Co Tipperary
Tel 0504-22229/22779

**THURLES, SS JOSEPH AND BRIGID**
Rev Thomas Lanigan-Ryan CC
Bóthar na Naomh Presbytery,
Thurles, Co Tipperary
Tel 0504-22042/22688

**ANACARTY**
*St Brigid's, Anacarty*
*Immaculate Conception, Donohill*
Very Rev John Beatty PP
Anacarty, Co Tipperary
Tel 062-71104

**BALLINA**
*Our Lady and St Lua, Ballina,*
*Mary, Mother of the Church, Boher*
Very Rev Edmond V. O'Rahelly PP
Tel 061-376178
Rev Enda Brady CC
Tel 061-376430
Ballina, Co Tipperary

**BALLINAHINCH**
*St Joseph's, Ballinahinch,*
*Sacred Heart, Killoscully*
Very Rev Robert Fletcher PP
Déalginis, Garraun Upper, Ballinahinch,
Birdhill, via Killaloe, Co Clare
Tel 086-1927455/061-379862

**BALLINGARRY**
*Assumption*
Very Rev Gerard Quirke PP
Ballingarry, Thurles, Co Tipperary
Tel 052-9154115

**BALLYBRICKEN**
*St Ailbe's, Ballybricken,*
*Immaculate Heart of Mary, Bohermore*
Very Rev Canon Liam McNamara PP
Ballybricken, Grange, Kilmallock,
Co Limerick
Tel 061-351158

**BALLYLANDERS**
*Assumption of BVM*
Very Rev Thomas O. Breen PP
Ballylanders, Kilmallock,
Co Limerick
Tel 062-46705

**BANSHA AND KILMOYLER**
*Annunciation, Our Lady of the Assumption, Kilmoyler*
Very Rev Michael Hickey PP
Bansha, Co Tipperary
Tel 062-54132

**BOHERLAHAN AND DUALLA**
*Immaculate Conception, Boherlahan*
*Our Lady of Fatima, Dualla*
Very Rev Joseph Egan PP
Boherlahan, Cashel, Co Tipperary
Tel 0504-41114
Rev Peter Brennan CC
Tel 0504-41215
Ballinree, Boherlahan,
Cashel, Co Tipperary

**BORRISOLEIGH**
*Sacred Heart, Borrisoleigh*
Very Rev Liam Everard PP
Tel 0504-51259
Rev Nicholas J. Irwin CC
Tel 0504-51230
Rev Michael Barry CC
Tel 0504-51275
Borrisoleigh, Thurles, Co Tipperary

**CAHERCONLISH**
*Our Lady, Mother of the Church*
*Arch. O'Hurley Mem., Caherline*
Very Rev Roy Donovan PP
Tel 061-450730
Very Rev Patrick Currivan AP
Tel 061-351248
Caherconlish, Co Limerick

**CAPPAMORE**
*St Michael's*
Very Rev Richard Browne PP
Cappamore, Co Limerick
Tel 061-381288

**CAPPAWHITE**
*Our Lady of Fatima*
Very Rev Tadgh Furlong PP
Cappawhite, Co Tipperary
Tel 062-75427

**CASHEL**
*St John the Baptist, Cashel*
*St Thomas the Apostle, Rosegreen*
Rt Rev Mgr Christy O'Dwyer PP, VG
Tel 062-61127
Rt Rev Mgr James Ryan AP
Tel 062-61353
Rev James O'Donnell CC
Bohermore, Cashel, Co Tipperary
Tel 062-61409
Rev James Purcell CC
Rosegreen, Cashel, Co Tipperary
Tel 062-61713
Rev Bernard Moloney
Cahir Road, Cashel, Co Tipperary
Tel 062-61443

**CLERIHAN**
*St Michael's*
Very Rev Ailbe O'Bric PP
Clerihan, Clonmel, Co Tipperary
Tel 052-6135118

**CLONOULTY**
*Church of St John the Baptist, Clonoulty*
*Church of Jesus Christ Our Saviour, Rossmore*
Very Rev Thomas F. Egan PP
Tel 0504-42494
Clonoulty, Cashel,
Co Tipperary

**DOON**
*St Patrick's*
Very Rev Anthony Ryan PP
Parochial House,
Doon, Co Limerick
Tel 061-380165
Rev Patrick Coffey
Lisgaugh, Doon, Co Limerick
Tel 061-380165

**DRANGAN**
*Immaculate Conception, Visitation, Cloneen*
Very Rev Anthony Lambe PP
Drangan, Thurles, Co Tipperary
Tel 052-52103

**DROM AND INCH**
*St Mary's, Drom,*
*St Laurence O'Toole, Inch*
Very Rev Martin Murphy PP
Drom, Thurles, Co Tipperary
Tel 0504-51196

**EMLY**
*St Ailbe's*
Very Rev Seamus Rochford PP
Tel 062-57103
Rev Sean Kennedy CC
Tel 062-57111
Emly, Co Tipperary

**FETHARD**
*Holy Trinity, Fethard*
*Sacred Heart, Killusty*
Very Rev Canon Thomas F. Breen PP
Tel 052-6131178
Rev Anthony McSweeney CC
Tel 052-6131187
Fethard, Co Tipperary

**GALBALLY**
*Christ the King, Galbally*
*Sacred Heart, Lisvernane*
Very Rev Canon John O'Neill PP, VF
Lisvernane, Aherlow, Co Tipperary
Tel 062-56155
Very Rev Canon Denis Talbot AP
Galbally, Co Limerick
Tel 062-37929

**GOLDEN**
*Blessed Sacrament, Golden*
*St Patrick's, Kilfeade*
Very Rev Patrick O'Gorman PP
Golden, Co Tipperary
Tel 062-72146

**GORTNAHOE**
*Sacred Heart, Gortnahoe*
*SS Patrick & Brigid, Glengoole*
Very Rev John O'Rourke PP
Tel 056-8834128
Rev Joseph Walsh CC
Tel 056-8834867
Gortnahoe, Thurles, Co Tipperary

**HOLY CROSS**
*Holy Cross Abbey, Holy Cross*
*St Cataldus, Ballycahill*
Very Rev Thomas J. Breen PP
Holy Cross, Thurles, Co Tipperary
Tel 0504-43124
Rev Celsus Tierney CC
Holy Cross Abbey, Thurles, Co Tipperary
Tel 0504-43118

**HOSPITAL**
*St John the Baptist, Hospital*
*Sacred Heart, Herbertstown*
Very Rev Canon Conor Ryan PP, VF
Castlefarm, Hospital, Co Limerick
Tel 061-383108
Rev Danny O'Gorman CC
Herbertstown, Hospital, Co Limerick
Tel 061-385104

**KILBEHENNY**
*St Joseph's, Kilbehenny,*
*St Patrick's, Anglesboro*
Very Rev Richard Kelly PP
Kilbehenny, Mitchelstown, Co Cork
Tel 025-24040

**KILCOMMON**
*St Patrick's, Kilcommon*
*St Joseph's, Hollyford*
*Our Lady of the Visitation, Rearcross*
Very Rev Daniel Woods PP
Kilcommon, Thurles, Co Limerick
Tel 062-78103
Rev James O'Donoghue CC
Hollyford, Co Tipperary
Tel 062-71104

**KILLENAULE**
*St Mary's, Killenaule*
*St Joseph the Worker, Moyglass*
Very Rev Canon Liam Ryan PP, VF
Tel 052-9156244
Rev Francis McCarthy CC
Holycross House, Moyglass,
Fethard, Co Tipperary
Tel 052-6131343

**KILTEELY**
*SS Patrick & Brigid, Kilteely*
*St Bridget's, Dromkeen*
Very Rev Conor Hayes PP
Parochial House, Killeely, Co Limerick
Tel 061-384213

**KNOCKAINEY**
*Our Lady, Knockainey*
*St Patrick's, Patrickswell*
Very Rev Liam Holmes PP
Knockainey, Hospital, Co Limerick
Tel 061-383127
Rev Sean Fennelly
Barrysfarm, Hospital, Co Limerick
Tel 061-383565

**KNOCKAVILLA**
*Assumption, Knockavilla*
*St Bridget's, Donaskeigh*
Very Rev James Egan PP
Knockavilla, Dundrum,
Co Tipperary
Tel 062-71168

**KNOCKLONG**
*St Joseph's, Knocklong*
*St Patrick's, Glenbrohane*
Very Rev William Hennessy PP
Knocklong, Co Limerick
Tel 062-53114
Very Rev John J. Ryan AP
Garryspillane, Kilmallock,
Co Limerick
Tel 062-53189

**LATTIN AND CULLEN**
*Assumption, Lattin*
*St Patrick's, Cullen*
Very Rev John Egan PP
Lattin, Co Tipperary
Tel 062-55240

**LOUGHMORE**
*Nativity of Our Lady, Loughmore*
*St John the Baptist, Castleiney*
Very Rev Padraig Corbett PP
Parochial House, Castleiney,
Templemore, Co Tipperary
Tel 0504-31392
Very Rev Mgr Maurice Dooley AP
Loughmore, Templemore, Co Tipperary
Tel 0504-31375

**MOYCARKEY**
*St Peter's, Moycarkey*
*St James's, Two-Mile-Borris*
*Our Lady & St Kevin, Littleton*
Very Rev George Bourke PP
Moycarkey, Thurles, Co Tipperary
Tel 0504-44227
Rev Joseph Tynan CC
Ballydavid, Littleton,
Thurles, Co Tipperary
Tel 0504-44317

**MULLINAHONE**
*St Michael's*
Very Rev John McGrath PP
Mullinahone, Co Tipperary
Tel 052-53152

**MURROE AND BOHER**
*Holy Rosary, Murroe*
*St Patrick's, Boher*
Very Rev Canon Thomas J. Ryan PP, VF
Liscreagh, Murroe, Co Limerick
Tel 061-386227
Rev Thomas Hearne CC
Bohergar, Brittas, Co Limerick
Tel 061-352223

**NEW INN**
*Our Lady Queen, New Inn,*
*St Bartholomew's, Knockgrafton*
Very Rev Michael Kennedy PP
New Inn, Cashel, Co Tipperary
Tel 052-7462395

**NEWPORT**
*Most Holy Redeemer, Newport*
*Our Lady of the Wayside, Birdhill*
*Our Lady of Lourdes, Toor*
Very Rev Joseph Delaney PP
Clonbealy, Newport, Co Tipperary
Tel 061-378126
Rev John O'Keeffe CC
Birdhill, Killaloe, Co Tipperary
Tel 061-379172

**PALLASGREEN**
*St John the Baptist, Pallasgreen*
*St Brigid's, Templebraden*
Very Rev Pat Burns PP
Parochial House,
Pallasgreen, Co Limerick
Tel 061-384114

**SOLOHEAD**
*Sacred Heart, Oola*
Very Rev John Morris PP
Solohead, Co Limerick
Tel 062-47614

**TEMPLEMORE**
*Sacred Heart, Templemore*
*St Anne's, Clonmore*
*St James's, Killea*
Very Rev Canon Eugene Everard PP
Parochial House, Templemore,
Co Tipperary
Tel 0504-31684
Rev Michael Ryan CC
Tel 0504-31492
Rev James Walton CC
Tel 0504-31225
Rev Thomas Dunne CC
Tel 0504-32890
Templemore, Co Tipperary

**TEMPLETUOHY**
*Sacred Heart, Templetuohy*
*St Mary's, Moyne*
Very Rev Patrick Murphy PP
Templetuohy, Thurles, Co Tipperary
Tel 0504-53114
Very Rev John O'Connell AP
Moyne, Thurles, Co Tipperary
Tel 0504-45129

**TIPPERARY**
*St Michael's*
Venerable Matthew McGrath PP, VG
St Michael's Street, Tipperary Town
Tel 062-51536
Rev James Kennedy CC
St Michael's Street, Tipperary Town
Tel 062-51114
Rev Edward Cleary CC
Knockinrawley, Tipperary
Tel 062-51242

**UPPERCHURCH**
*Sacred Heart, Upperchurch*
*St Mary's, Drombane*
Very Rev Donal Cunningham PP
Parochial House, Upperchurch, Thurles,
Co Tipperary
Tel 0504-54181
Rev Loughlin Brennan
Upperchurch, Thurles, Co Tipperary
Tel 0504-54492

## INSTITUTIONS AND THEIR CHAPLAINS

**Cashel Community School**
Tel 062-61167
Rev Bernard Moloney

**Hospital Community School**
Tel 061-383565
Rev Sean Fennelly

**Tipperary Institue, Thurles**
Tel 062-71252
Rev James O'Donnell

**Vocational School, Thurles**
Tel 0504-22042
Rev Thomas Lanigan-Ryan

**Vocational School, Tipperary Town**
Tel 062-51242
Rev James Kennedy

## PRIESTS OF THE DIOCESE ELSEWHERE

Rev James Donnelly *(Sabbatical Leave)*
c/o Bothar na Naomh Presbytery,
Thurles, Co Tipperary
Rev John Littleton
The Priory Institute,
Tallaght Village, Dublin 24
Rev Joseph Ryan CC
St Matthew's,
11 Palmerstown Court, Dublin 20
Tel 01-6268772
Very Rev Seamus Ryan PP
No 1 Presbytery,
Blackditch Road, Dublin 10
Tel 01-6265695

## RETIRED PRIESTS

Very Rev James Feehan
1 Castle Court, Thurles, Co Tipperary
Tel 0504-24935
Very Rev James Holloway
Moymore, Pallasgreen, Co Limerick
Tel 061-384111
Very Rev Canon Denis O'Meara
Beechwood House Nursing Home,
Newcastlewest, Co Tipperary
Rev Daniel J. Ryan
c/o Archbishop's House,
Thurles, Co Tipperary
Very Rev Liam Ryan DD
Cappamore, Co Tipperary

## RELIGIOUS ORDERS AND CONGREGATIONS

## PRIESTS

**AUGUSTINIANS**
The Abbey, Fethard,
Co Tipperary
Tel 052-631273
*Prior:* Rev Martin Crean (OSA)

**BENEDICTINES**
Glenstal Abbey,
Murroe, Co Limerick
Tel 061-8386103 Fax 061-8386328
Email monks@glenstal.org
*Abbot*
Rt Rev Dom Mark Patrick Hederman (OSB)

**HOLY SPIRIT CONGREGATION**
Rockwell College,
Cashel, Co Tipperary
Tel 062-61444 Fax 062-61661
www.rockwell-college.ie
*Community Leader*
Rev Michael J. Knight (CSSp)
Secondary Residential and Day Boys School; Agricultural College

**PALLOTTINES**
Pallottine College, Thurles, Co Tipperary
Tel 0504-21202
*Rector:* Very Rev Emmet O'Hara (SCA)

## BROTHERS

**CHRISTIAN BROTHERS**
Christian Brothers Cowper Care,
Monastery Close, Templemore Road,
Thurles, Co Tipperary
Tel 0504-91152
*Community Leader:* Br Seamus Eill (CFC)
Community: 6

## SISTERS

**CONGREGATION OF THE SISTERS OF MERCY**
*The Sisters of Mercy minister throughout the diocese in pastoral and social work, community development, counselling, spirituality, education and health care, answering current needs.*

Sisters of Mercy, 28 Spafield Crescent,
Cashel, Co Tipperary
Tel 062-61402
Community: 1

Convent of Mercy, New Inn, Cashel,
Co Tipperary
Tel 052-7462205 Fax 052-7462315
Community: 4

Convent of Mercy, Newport,
Co Tipperary
Tel 061-378145 Fax 061-378809
Community: 6

Convent of Mercy, Templemore,
Co Tipperary
Tel 0504-31427 Fax 0504-56078
Community: 12

1 Church Street,
Templemore, Co Tipperary
Tel 0504-32019
Community: 2

Sisters of Mercy, 1 Parkview Drive,
Thurles, Co Tipperary
Tel/Fax 0504-21137
Community: 2

Sisters of Mercy, Stanwix House,
Dublin Road, Thurles, Co Tipperary
Tel/Fax 0504-22320
Community: 3

Convent of Mercy, Tipperary Town
Tel 062-51218 Fax 062-52277
Community: 17

Convent of Mercy,
Knockinrawley, Tipperary Town
Tel/Fax 062-51120
Community: 4

Convent of Mercy, Cappamore,
Co Limerick
Tel/Fax 061-381268
Community: 3

Sisters of Mercy, Clonbealy,
Newport, Co Tipperary
Tel/Fax 061-378072
Community: 2

Convent of Mercy,
Doon, Co Limerick
Tel 061-380660 Fax 061-380263
Community: 13

**PRESENTATION SISTERS**
Presentation Convent, Thurles,
Co Tipperary
Tel 0504-21250
*Local leader:* Sr Monica McGrath
Community: 26
Scoil Mhuire Primary School
Tel 0504-22331
Sacred Heart Secondary School
Tel 0504-21783

Presentation Sisters,
The Commons, Thurles, Co Tipperary
Tel 052-9154781
Contact: Sr Miriam O'Byrne
Community: 2

Presentation Convent, Hospital,
Co Limerick
Tel 061-383141
*Local Leader:* Sr Claude Meagher
Community: 8
Secondary School
St John The Baptist Community School
Tel 061-383283

Presentation Sisters,
14 Assumption Terrace, Ballingarry,
Thurles, Co Tipperary
Tel 052-9154118
*Contact:* Sr Patricia Wall
Community: 1
Secondary Co-educational School
Tel 052-54104

Presentation Convent, Fethard,
Co Tipperary
Tel 052-6131225
*Local Leader:* Sr Winnie Kirwan
Community: 11

Child care at St Bernard's group homes,
Rocklow Road, Fethard,
Co Tipperary
*Director:* Roisin Stewart
Tel 052-31141/31305/31392

16/17 Greenane Drive, Tipperary
Tel 062-31797
*Contact:* Sr Rosarii Treacy
Community: 3

**URSULINES**
Ursuline Convent, Thurles, Co Tipperary
Tel 0504-21561
Email ursulinethurles@eircom.net
*Local Leader:* Sr Cecelia O'Dwyer
Community: 12
Scoil Aingeal Naofa Primary School
Tel 0504-22561 Fax 0504-20763
Email scoilangela@unison.ie
Secondary School
Tel 0504-22147 Fax 0504-22737
Email sec.uct@oceanfree.net
Website www.uct.ie

## EDUCATIONAL INSTITUTIONS

**St Patrick's College**
Thurles, Co Tipperary
Tel 0504-21201 Fax 0504-23735
Email office@stpats.ie
*President:* Very Rev Thomas Fogarty
*Registrar:* Ms Paula Hourigan

**EDMUND RICE SCHOOLS TRUST**
Scoil Na Mbraithre Primary School,
Doon, Co Limerick
Tel 061-380239 Fax 061-380060
Email doonasns@eircom.net
*Principal:* Br J. Dormer

St Fintan's Secondary School,
Doon, Co Limerick
Tel 061-380388 Fax 061-380060
Email stfintandoon@eircom.net
*Principal:* Mr Eddie Bourke

Scoil Ailbhe Primary School,
Parnell Street, Thurles, Co Tipperary
Tel 0504-21448 Fax 0504-26094
Email scoilailbhecbs@eircom.net
*Principal:* Ms Miriam Anne Butler

Christian Brothers Secondary School,
Thurles, Co Tipperary
Tel 0504-22054/22171 Fax 0504-23645
Email reception@cbsthurles.ie
*Principal:* Mr Tiernan O'Donnell

The Abbey Secondary School,
Tipperary Town
Tel 062-52299/51624 Fax 062-52511
Email abbeyoffice@eircom.net
*Principal:* Mr J. Heffernan

## CHARITABLE AND OTHER SOCIETIES

**Apostolic Work Society**
Thurles Parish Centre, Cathedral Street,
Thurles, Co Tipperary
Tel 0504-22229 Fax 0504-22415
Email parishcentre@thurlesparish.ie
*President:* Mrs Anne Minihan
*Secretary:* Mrs Anna Maher

**Community Social Services Centres**
Rossa Street, Thurles, Co Tipperary
Tel 0504-22169

St Michael's Street,Tipperary Town
Tel 062-51622

Templemore, Co Tipperary
Tel 0504-31244
Sr Catherine Gannon

Cashel, Co Tipperary
Tel 062-61395

Art Glass
ARTISTS IN GLASS
028 71 357 555
www.artglassireland.com
SKEOGE BUSINESS PARK, DERRY BT48 8SE
www.artglassireland.com
philip@artglass2.fsnet.co.uk
sincoyle@hotmail.com

# C.B.C. DISTRIBUTORS

## CHURCH FURNISHINGS AND SUPPLIES

CHURCH CANDLES - ALTAR WINE - INCENSE & CHARCOAL - MASS KITS - PRIEST'S SICK CALL SETS
INDOOR & OUTDOOR STATUARY - VESTMENTS - STATIONS OF THE CROSS - LECTERNS - PRIEDIEUX
TABERNACLES - PAPAL BLESSINGS - CHALICES - CIBORIA

Greenbank - Newry - Co. Down BT34 2JP
Tel: (028) 3026 5216 Fax: (028) 3026 3927

If ringing from Irish Republic dial 048

E.Mail: sales@cbcdistributors.co.uk Website: www.cbcdistributors.co.uk

# R.P.D. LIMITED

## *(Incorporating Rosario Press)*

SPECIALISTS IN
CHURCH OFFERING ENVELOPES AND GENERAL PRINTING

- Calendars
- Christmas Cards
- Stationery
- Special Collection Envelopes
- 'Lotto' Envelopes

*Let RPD Ltd provide you with everything you need to run a successful Fundraising Campaign from sets of collection envelopes to receipt books and 'thank you' cards*

**Unit 25/26 Tolka Valley Business Park,**
**Ballyboggan Road, Glasnevin, Dublin 11**
**Telephone (01) 860 3088/860 3089 • Fax (01) 860 3092**
**Email tom@rpd.ie**

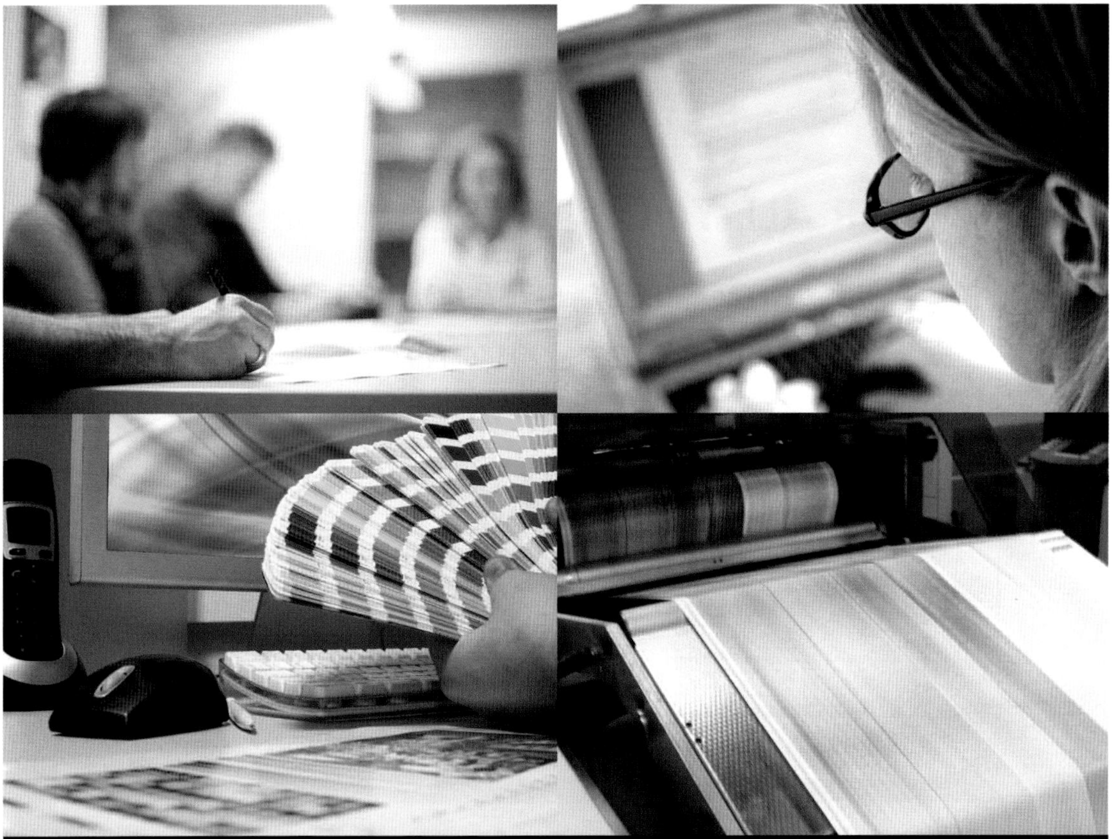



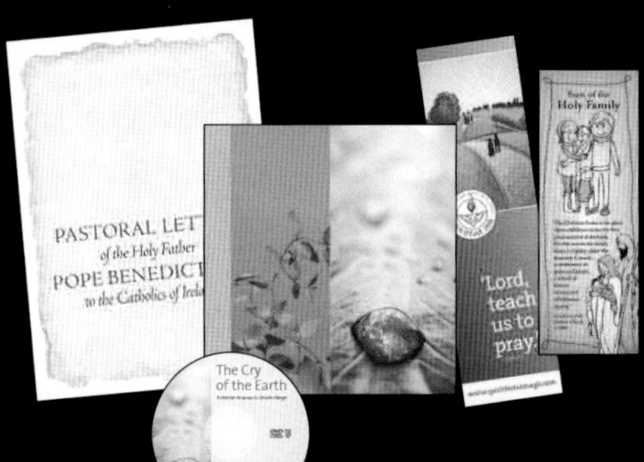
The Cry of the Earth
'Lord, teach us to pray.'

# ARCHDIOCESE OF TUAM

PATRON OF THE ARCHDIOCESE
ST JARLATH, 6 JUNE

SUFFRAGEN SEES: ACHONRY, CLONFERT, ELPHIN, KILLALA,
UNITED DIOCESES OF GALWAY AND KILMACDUAGH

INCLUDES HALF OF COUNTY MAYO, HALF OF COUNTY GALWAY
AND PART OF COUNTY ROSCOMMON

**Most Rev Michael Neary DD**
Archbishop of Tuam;
born 15 April 1946;
ordained priest 20 June 1971;
ordained bishop 13 September 1992; installed Archbishop of Tuam 5 March 1995.

Residence: Archbishop's House,
Tuam, Co Galway
Tel 093-24166 Fax 093-28070
Email
archdiocesetuam@gmail.com
Web www.tuamarchdiocese.org
www.onelifeonecalloneresponse.com
Twitter Tuamarchdiocese
Facebook Tuam Archdiocese

## CATHEDRAL OF THE ASSUMPTION, TUAM

The Cathedral of the Assumption is the metropolitan cathedral of the Western Province.

Archbishop Oliver Kelly (1815–34) laid the foundation stone on 30 April 1827 – before Catholic Emancipation. The cathedral was dedicated on 18 August 1836 by Archbishop John MacHale (1834–81). It cost £14,204.

The cathedral is English-decorated Gothic in style, is cruciform in shape and has a three-stage West Tower. It was designed by architect Dominick Madden. Nineteen windows light the cathedral. It has seating capacity for 1,100 people.

Among the cathedral's notable features are its superbly cut Galway and Mayo limestone, its plaster-vaulted ceiling with heads and bosses, and its cantilevered oak organ loft. Its huge Oriel window has eighty-two compartments, is forty-two feet high and eighteen feet wide; it is the work of Michael O'Connor and was made in Dublin in 1832. Four large windows from the Harry Clarke studio also grace the cathedral. It has a very fine Compton organ with 1,200 pipes, a unique set of early nineteenth-century Stations of the Cross, recently restored, and a seventeenth-century painting of the Assumption by Carlo Maratta.

The sanctuary, as shown above, was completely redesigned in 1991 under the direction of the late Ray Carroll. The altar is Wicklow granite, and all the timberwork is by local craftsman Tom Dowd.

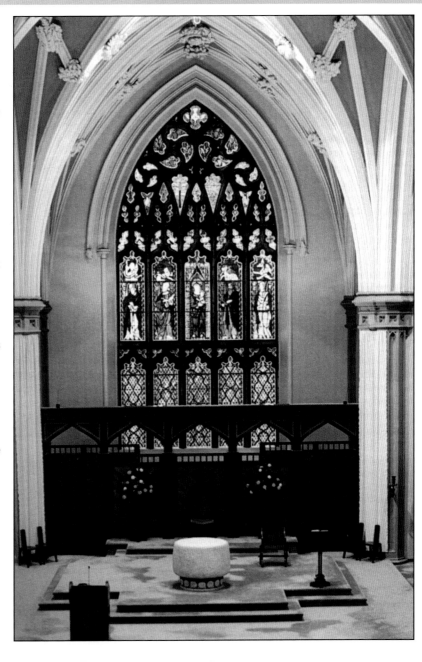

**Most Rev Joseph Cassidy DD, PP**
Retired Archbishop of Tuam; born 1933; ordained priest 1959; ordained Coadjutor Bishop of Clonfert 23 September 1979; succeeded 1 May 1982; translated to Tuam September 1987; resigned 28 June 1994; Apostolic Administrator until 5 March 1995; PP Moore 13 July 1995.
Residence: 1 Kilgarve Court, Creagh, Ballinasloe, Co Galway

## CHAPTER

*Dean:* Rt Rev Mgr Dermot Moloney VG
*Prebendaries*
Very Rev John Cosgrove PP
Castlebar
Very Rev Conal Eustace PP
The Parochial House, Ballinrobe, Co Mayo
Very Rev Austie Fergus PP
Mayo Abbey
Very Rev Anthony King PP, VF
Athenry
Rt Rev Mgr John O'Boyle
Diocesan Resource Office, Tuam
Very Rev Padraig O'Connor PP, VF
Mountbellew
Very Rev James Ronayne PP, VF
Clifden
Very Rev Brendan Kilcoyne
President, St Jarlath's College
Rev James Quinn CC
Taugheen, Claremorris
Very Rev Peter Waldron PP
Keelogues, Ballyvary, Castlebar
Very Rev James Walsh PP
Kilmeena, Westport

**Honorary Canons**
Very Rev Eamon Concannon PE, Knock
Very Rev Joseph Cooney PE, Knock
Very Rev John D. Flannery PE, Milltown
Very Rev Michael Flannery PE, Milltown
Very Rev Colm Kilcoyne PE, Castlebar
Very Rev Patrick Costello, Mountbellew
Very Rev Seamus Cunnane
Grove House, Tuam
Very Rev Arthur Devine PE, Castlebar
Very Rev Martin Gleeson AP, Belclare
Very Rev Des Grogan PE
Partry, Claremorris
Very Rev Michael Goaley PE
Glenamaddy
Very Rev James Kelly AP, Tooreen
Very Rev Liam Kitt
Cleveland, Ohio
Very Rev Joseph Moloney PE, Tuam
Very Rev Joseph Moran
Abbeybreaffy Nursing Home, Castlebar
Very Rev Martin Newell AP, Claran
Very Rev Colm Ó Ceannahbáin PE
An Tulach, Baile na hAbhann
Very Rev Tadhg Ó Móráin PE
Cornamona
Very Rev Kieran Waldron PE
Ballyhaunis
Venerable Patrick Williams PE
Tulla, Co Clare

## ADMINISTRATION

**Vicar General**
Rt Rev Mgr Dermot Moloney PP, VG
Crossboyne, Claremorris, Co Mayo
Tel 094-9371824

**Episcopal Vicar for Knock**
Rt Rev Mgr Joseph Quinn PP
Knock

**Chancellor**
Sr Mary Lyons RSM, JCD
Archbishop's House, Tuam
Tel 093-24166
Email chancellortuam@gmail.com

**Vicars Forane**
Very Rev Anthony King
Very Rev Conal Eustace
Very Rev Thomas Mannion
Very Rev James Ronayne
Very Rev Padraic O'Connor
Very Rev Charles McDonnell
Very Rev John Cosgrove
Very Rev Fergal Cunnane

**Judicial Collegium for Non-Matrimonial Cases**
Rev Michael Carragher (OP) JCD
Angelicum University, Rome
Rt Rev Mgr Michael Quinlan JCD, VG
Diocese of Salford, England
Rev Kevin Cahill JCD
Diocese of Ferns
Rev Paul Churchhill JCD
Archdiocese of Dublin
Rev Patrick Connolly JCD
Diocese of Clogher, University of Limerick

**Diocesan Secretary**
Rev Fintan Monahan
Archbishop's House, Tuam, Co Galway
Tel 093-24166
Email archdiocesetuam@gmail.com

**Council of Priests**
*Chairperson:* Rev Ray Flaherty, Tuam
Tel 093-24250
*Secretary:* Rev Pat Farragher, Castlebar
Tel 094-9035748

## CATECHETICS EDUCATION

**Director of Adult Religious Education**
Rev Tod Nolan
Diocesan Resource Centre,
Bishop Street, Tuam, Co Galway
Tel 093-52284
Email todnolan@gmail.com

**Post-Primary Education**
*Director:* Rt Rev Mgr John O'Boyle
Diocesan Resource Centre,
Bishop Street, Tuam, Co Galway
Tel 093-52284
*Assistant Director:* Sr Margaret Buckley
Email margaretbuckley10@gmail.com
Sisters of the Christian Retreat and
Sr Mary McDonagh, Presentation Sister
Email marymcdonagh10@gmail.com
Diocesan Resource Centre,
Bishop Street, Tuam, Co Galway
Tel 093-52284

**Advisory Council on Catholic Second-level Education**
*Chairperson:* Ms Bríd Kitching
*Secretary:* Mr Martin Hession

**Post-Primary School Retreats and Promotion of Universal Catechism**
*Director:* Rev Benny McHale CC
The Presbytery,
Athenry, Co Galway
Tel 091-844227

**Primary Catechetics**
*Director:* Sr Nancy Clarke
Diocesan Resource Centre,
Bishop Street, Tuam, Co Galway
Tel 093-52284

**Primary Education**
*Director:* Rt Rev Mgr John O'Boyle
Diocesan Resource Centre,
Bishop Street, Tuam, Co Galway
Tel 093-52284

**CPSMA – Diocesan Committee**
*Chairperson:* Mr Frank Burns
Dunmore

**Child Protection Office**
*Director:* Rt Rev Mgr John O'Boyle
Diocesan Resource Centre,
Bishop Street, Tuam, Co Galway
Tel 093-52284
*Assistant Delegate:* Mrs Mary Trench
Robeen, Hollymount, Co Mayo

**Safeguarding Children Committee**
*Chairperson:* Ms Maureen Walsh
*Co-ordinator of Training:* Fr Tod Nolan
*Designated Person:* Mgr John O'Boyle
*Designated Person:* Ms Mary Trench

## LITURGY

**Liturgical Commission, Sacred Art and Sacred Music**
*Chairman:* Vacant
*Secretary:* Very Rev Michael Molloy PP
The Presbytery, Moor, Ballydangan,
Athlone, Co Westmeath
Tel 090-9673539

**Diocesan Liturgical Resource Person**
Ms Mary Connolly
Diocesan Resource Centre,
Bishop Street, Tuam, Co Galway
Tel 093-52284
Email tuamliturgy@gmail.com

## PASTORAL

**Accord**
*Diocesan Directors*
Rev Conal Eustace PP
Ballinrobe, Co Mayo Tel 093-24342
Rev James Ronayne PP
Clifden, Co Galway Tel 095-21251
Rev Francis Mitchell Adm
Tuam, Co Galway Tel 093-24250

**Archives**
*Archivist/Historian*
Very Rev Kieran Canon Waldron PE
Ballyhaunis
Tel 094-9630246
Email pkwaldron@eircom.net

**Diocesan Pastoral Council**
*Chairperson:* Seán Staunton, Westport
Email seansknockfin@gmail.com
*Secretary:* Mary Connell, Castlebar
Tel 086-6038483
Email marygc@ireland.com

**Diocesan Youth Choir**
Rev Tod Nolan
Diocesan Resource Centre, Tuam
Tel 093-52284
Email todnolan@gmail.com

**Ecumenism**
*Contact:* Rev Francis Mitchell
The Presbytery, Tuam, Co Galway
Tel 093-24250
Email fmitchell@eircom.net

**Emigrants**
*Director:* Very Rev Gerard Burns PP
The Presbytery, Letterfrack, Co Galway
Tel 095-41053
Email ppachill@hotmail.com

**Eucharistic Congress**
Rev Patrick Farragher
The Monastery, Chapel Street, Castlebar, Co Mayo
Tel 094-9035748
Email patfarragher@oceanfree.net

**Family Ministry**
www.thefamilycentre.com
*Director:* Mr Cathal Kearney
The Family Centre, Castle Street, Castlebar, Co Mayo
Tel 094-9025900

**Family Prayer Apostolate**
*Director:* Mr Cathal Kearney
The Family Centre, Chapel Street, Castlebar, Co Mayo
Tel 094-9025900

**GMIT, Castlebar**
*Chaplains:* Rev Pat Farragher
Castlebar, Co Mayo
Tel 094-9035748
Email patfarragher@oceanfree.net
Mr Daniel Caldwell
Tel 094-9043150

**Grandparents Pilgrimage**
*Contact:* Ms Catherine Wiley
Tel 01-6625931
Email catherinewiley1@aol.com
www.nationalgrandparentspilgrimage.com

**Immigrants**
Very Rev Stephen Farragher PP
Ballyhaunis, Co Mayo
Tel 094-9630006
Email stephenfarragher@gmail.com

**John Paul II Awards**
Rev Tod Nolan
Diocesan Resource Centre, Tuam
Tel 093-52284
Email todnolan@gmail.com

**Knock Marriage Bureau**
Canon Joe Cooney
Tel 094-9375933

**L'Arche**
*National Chaplain:* Rev Fergal Cunnane PP
Dunmore, Co Galway
Tel 093-38124
Email fergcunnane@eircom.net

**Laity Commission**
*Diocesan Representative*
*Secretary:* Ms Eileen Gildea
Riverview, Dunmore, Co Galway
*Chairperson:* Ms Teresa Carey, Castlebar

**Marriage Tribunal**
(See Marriage Tribunals section.)

**Pastoral Councils Resource Person**
*Director:* Rev Patrick Farragher
The Monastery, Chapel Street, Castlebar, Co Mayo
Tel 094-9035748
Email patfarragher@oceanfree.net

**Pilgrimage Director**
Mr John McLoughlin
3 Trinity Court, Tuam, Co Galway
Tel 087-7627910
Email johnb46@eircom.net

**Pioneer Total Abstinence Association**
*Director:* Rev Seán Cunningham
The Presbytery, Tuam, Co Galway
Tel 093-24250
Rev John O'Gorman PP
Menlough, Ballinasloe, Co Galway
Tel 090-9684818

**Polish Chaplain**
Rev Krzysztof Sikora (SVD)
Knock Shrine, Co Mayo
Tel 094-9388100/087-3230382

**Pontificial Mission Societies**
*Diocesan Director*
Very Rev Patrick Mooney PP
The Parochial House, Glenamaddy
Tel 094-9659017

**Travellers**
*Chaplain*
Very Rev Francis Mitchell Adm
Tuam, Co Galway
Tel 093-24250
Email fmitchell@eircom.net

**Trócaire**
Fr Michael Molloy PP
Moore, Ballydangan,
Athlone, Co Roscommon
Tel 090-9673539

**World Youth Day**
*Contact:* Rev Tod Nolan, Tuam
Tel 093-52284
Email todnolan@gmail.com

**Vocations Committee**
*Contact:* Rev Fintan Monahan
Archbishop's House, Tuam, Co Galway
Tel 093-24166
Email archdiocesetuam@gmail.com
vocations@onelifeonecalloneresponse.com
www.onelifeonecalloneresponse.com

**Youth – Diocesan Youth Council**
*Chairperson:* Cliona Feerick
St Jarlath's College, Tuam
Tel 093-24342
*Secretary:* Stephen Bushell
Corofin, Tuam
www.dyctuam.ie
www.facebook.com/dyctuam

## PARISHES

*Mensal parishes are listed first. Other parishes follow alphabetically. Historical names are in parentheses.*

**TUAM (CATHEDRAL OF THE ASSUMPTION)**
www.tuamparish.com
Rev Francis Mitchell Adm
Rev Seán Cunningham CC
Rev Kazimierz Szalaj CC
Tuam, Co Galway
Tel 093-24250

**WESTPORT (AUGHAVAL)**
www.westportparish.ie
Rev Charlie McDonnell Adm
Email frchaz@gmail.com
Rev Karl Burns CC
Westport, Co Mayo
Tel 098-28871 Fax 098-26900
Email karlburns07@gmail.com
Very Rev Patrick Gill AP
Lecanvey, Westport, Co Mayo
Tel 098-64808

**ABBEYKNOCKMOY**
Very Rev Joseph O'Brien PP
Abbey, Tuam, Co Galway
Tel 093-43510
Email joeobrienabbey@eircom.net
Rev Enda Howley CC
Parochial House, Ryehill,
Monivea, Co Galway
Tel 091-849019
Email eannahowley@eircom.net

**ACHILL**
Very Rev Michael Gormally PP
Achill Sound, Achill, Co Mayo
Tel 098-45288
Rev Ronnie Boyle CC
Achill Sound, Achill, Co Mayo
Tel 098-45109
Email ronnieb@eircom.net
Rev Thomas Kearney, SMA, CC
Keel, Achill, Co Mayo
Tel 098-43123

**AGHAMORE**
Very Rev John Walsh PP
Aghamore, Ballyhaunis, Co Mayo
Tel 094-9367024
Email johnwalsh05@eircom.net
Rev James Canon Kelly AP
Tooreen, Ballyhaunis, Co Mayo
Tel 094-9649002
Email frjameskelly@eircom.net

**ARAN ISLANDS**
Very Rev Michéal Mannion PP
Kilronan, Aran Islands, Co Galway
Tel 099-61221
Email michealmannion@gmail.com
Rev Joseph Jennings (SM) CC
Inishere, Aran Islands, Co Galway
Tel 099-75003
Email antathairjoe@eircom.net

**ATHENRY**
www.athenryparish.ie
Very Rev Anthony Canon King PP, VF
Tel 091-844076
Email frtonyking@gmail.com
Rev Benny McHale CC
Tel 091-844169

**AUGHAGOWER**
Very Rev Jackie Conroy PP
Aughagower, Westport, Co Mayo
Tel 098-25057

**BALLA AND MANULLA**
Very Rev Denis Carney PP
Balla, Co Mayo
Tel 094-9365025
Email stcronansballa@eircom.net

**BALLINDINE (KILVINE)**
Very Rev Martin O'Connor PP
Ballindine, Co Mayo
Tel 094-9364423
Email kilvine@eircom.net

**BALLINLOUGH (KILTULLAGH)**
Very Rev Joseph Feeney PP
Ballinlough, Co Roscommon
Tel 094-9640155
Email frjoefeeney@eircom.net

**BALLINROBE**
Very Rev Conal Canon Eustace PP, VF
Ballinrobe, Co Mayo
Tel 094-9541085/9541784
Email eustaceconal@gmail.com

**BALLYHAUNIS (ANNAGH)**
Very Rev Stephen Farragher PP
Ballyhaunis, Co Mayo
Tel 094-9630006
Email stephenfarragher@gmail.com

**BEKAN**
www.bekan-parish.ie
Very Rev Brendan McGuinness PP
Bekan, Claremorris, Co Mayo
Tel 094-9380203
Email brendanmcguinness@eircom.net

**BURRISCARRA AND BALLINTUBBER**
www.ballintubberabbey.ie
Very Rev John Garvey PP
Carnacon, Claremorris, Co Mayo
Tel 094-9360205
Rev Francis Fahey CC
Ballintubber Abbey,
Claremorris, Co Mayo
Tel 094-9030934
Email btubabbey1@eircom.net

**CAHERLISTRANE (DONAGHPATRICK AND KILCOONA)**
Very Rev Pat O'Brien PP
Caherlistrane, Co Galway
Tel 093-55428
Email frpobrien@eircom.net

**CARNA (MOYRUS)**
Very Rev Padraic Standún PP
Carna, Co Galway
Tel 095-32232
Email pstandun@eircom.net
Rev Séamus Ó Dúill (SDS) CC
Cill Chiarain
Tel 095-33403
Email seamusoduill@eircom.net

**CARRAROE (KILEEN)**
Very Rev Ciarán Blake PP
Carraroe, Co Galway
Tel 091-595452
Email blake.ciaran@gmail.com
Rev Eamon Ó Conghaile CC
Tiernea, Lettermore, Co Galway
Tel 091-551133

**CASTLEBAR (AGLISH, BALLYHEANE AND BREAGHWY)**
Very Rev John Canon Cosgrove PP, VF
Tel 094-9021274
Email cbarpres@eircom.net
Rev Michael Farragher CC
Rev John Murray CC
Tel 094-9021253/21844
Castlebar, Co Mayo
Rev Patrick Burke, hospital chaplain
Email scoruiocht@yahoo.com
Rev John McCormack (SMA) CC
Breaffy, Castlebar, Co Mayo
Tel 094-9022799
Email jmcsma@eircom.net
*Parish Coordinator:* Mrs Mary Connell
The Monastery, Castlebar, Co Mayo
Tel 094-9028473
Email marygc@ireland.com

**CLARE ISLAND/INISHTURK**
Pastoral Care
Rev Karl Burns and priests of Westport Deanery
Tel 098-28871

**CLAREMORRIS (KILCOLMAN)**
Rev Peter Gannon PP
The Presbytery, Claremorris, Co Mayo
Tel 094-9362477
Email ganpete@eircom.net

**CLIFDEN (OMEY AND BALLINDOON)**
Very Rev James Canon Ronayne PP
Clifden, Co Galway
Tel 095-21251
Email clifdenparish@eircom.net
Rev Anthony Neville CC
Claddaghduff, Co Galway
Tel 095-44668

**CLONBUR (ROSS)**
Very Rev Peter Connolly PP
Clonbur, via Claremorris, Co Galway
Tel 094-9546304

**CONG AND NEALE**
Very Rev Patrick Gilligan PP
Cong, Co Mayo
Tel 094-9546030
Email patrickgilligan05@eircom.net

**CORRANDULLA (ANNAGHDOWN)**
Very Rev Hughie Loftus PP
Corrandulla, Co Galway
Tel 091-791125
Email newsletter@carrandullachurch.com
Rev Oliver McNamara CC
Annaghdown, Co Galway
Tel 091-791142

**CROSSBOYNE AND TAUGHEEN**
Rt Rev Msgr Dermot Moloney PP, VG
Crossboyne, Claremorris, Co Mayo
Tel 094-9371824
Email dermotmol@eircom.net
Rev James Canon Quinn CC
Taugheen, Claremorris, Co Mayo
Tel 094-9362500
Email frjquinn@eircom.net

**CUMMER (KILMOYLAN AND CUMMER)**
Very Rev Patrick Mullins PP
Cummer, Tuam, Co Galway
Tel 093-41427
Email frpatrickmullins@eircom.net
Very Rev Martin Gleeson AP
Belclare, Tuam, Co Galway
Tel 093-55429
Email belclarechurch@eircom.net

**DUNMORE**
Very Rev Fergal Cunnane PP, VF
Dunmore, Co Galway
Tel 093-38124
Email fergcunnane@eircom.net

**GLENAMADDY (BOYOUNAGH)**
www.glenamaddychurch.ie
Very Rev Patrick Mooney PP
Glenamaddy, Co Galway
Tel 094-9659017
Email paddymooney@eircom.net
Email glenamaddynewsletter@hotmail.com

**HEADFORD (KILLURSA AND KILLOWER)**
Rev Ray Flaherty Adm *(pro-tem)*
Headford, Co Galway
Tel 093-35448
Email rayflaherty@eircom.net
Very Rev Martin Canon Newell AP
Claran
Tel 093-35436
Email mnewell@eircom.net

**INISHBOFIN**
Rev Anthony Neville CC
Claddaghduff, Co Galway
Tel 095-44668

**ISLANDEADY**
www.islandeady.ie
Very Rev Patrick Donnellan PP
Islandeady, Castlebar, Co Mayo
Tel 094-9024125
Email patd@anu.ie
Rev Martin O'Keefe CC
Glenisland, Castlebar, Co Mayo
Tel 094-9024161
Email glenislandcc@eircom.net

**KEELOGUES**
Very Rev Peter Canon Waldron PP
Keelogues, Ballyvary, Co Mayo
Tel 094-9031009
Email epwal@eircom.net

**KILCONLY AND KILBANNON**
Very Rev Michael Kenny PP
Kilconly, Tuam, Co Galway
Tel 093-47613
Email frmichael@eircom.net

**KILKERRIN AND CLONBERNE**
Very Rev Thomas Commins PP
Kilkerrin, Ballinasloe, Co Galway
Tel 094-9659212

**KILLERERIN**
Very Rev Tod Nolan PP
Killererin, Barnderg, Tuam, Co Galway
Tel 093-49222
Email todnolan@gmail.com

**KILMAINE**
Very Rev John Fallon PP
Kilmaine, Co Galway
Tel 093-33378

**KILMEEN**
Rev Declan Kelly Adm
Killoran, Ballinasloe, Co Galway
Tel 090-9627120

**KILMEENA**
Very Rev James Walsh PP
Kilmeena, Westport, Co Mayo
Tel 098-41270

**KNOCK**
PP Vacant
Tel 094-9388100
Rev Richard Gibbons CC
Tel 094-9388100
Email gibbonsrj@eircom.net

**LACKAGH**
Very Rev Des Walsh PP
Turloughmore, Co Galway
Tel 091-797114
Email himselfdes@hotmail.com
Rev Bernard Shaughnessy CC
Coolarne, Turloughmore, Co Galway
Tel 091-797626
Email bjshaughnessy@eircom.net

**LEENANE (KILBRIDE)**
Very Rev Kieran Burke PP
Leenane, Co Galway
Tel 095-42251
Email rathfran@gmail.com

**LETTERFRACK (BALLINAKILL)**
Very Rev Gerry Burns PP
The Parochial House, Letterfrack,
Connemara, Co Galway
Tel 095-41053/087-2408171
Email ppachill@hotmail.com
ballinakillparish@eircom.net

**LOUISBURGH (KILGEEVER)**
Very Rev Martin Long PP
Louisburgh, Co Mayo
Tel 098-66198
Email louisburghparish@eircom.net

**MAYO ABBEY (MAYO AND ROSSLEA)**
Very Rev Austin Canon Fergus PP
Mayo Abbey, Claremorris, Co Mayo
Tel 094-9365086

**MENLOUGH (KILLASCOBE)**
Very Rev John O'Gorman PP
Menlough, Ballinasloe, Co Galway
Tel 090-9684818
email johncullmona@eircom.net

**MILLTOWN (ADDERGOLE AND LISKEEVEY)**
Very Rev J. J. Cribben PP
Milltown, Co Galway
Tel 093-51609

**MOORE**
Very Rev Michael Molloy PP
Ballydangan, Athlone, Co Roscommon
Tel 090-9673539
Email michaelmolloy471@gmail.com

**MOYLOUGH AND MOUNTBELLEW**
Very Rev Padraig Canon O'Connor PP, VF
Mountbellew, Ballinasloe, Co Galway
Tel 090-9679235
Email patrickjaoc@eircom.net

**NEWPORT (BURRISHOOLE)**
Very Rev Declan Carroll CC
Newport, Co Mayo
Tel 098-41123
Email frdeclan@eircom.net

**PARKE (TURLOUGH)**
Very Rev Michael Nohilly Adm
Parke, Castlebar, Co Mayo
Tel 094-9031314

**PARTRY (BALLYOVEY)**
Very Rev John Kenny PP
Partry, Claremorris, Co Mayo
Tel 094-9543013
Email frjohnkenny@yahoo.ie

**ROBEEN**
Very Rev Michael Murphy PP
Robeen, Hollymount, Co Mayo
Tel 094-9540026
Email mike.murphy@gmit.ie

**ROUNDFORT (KILCOMMON)**
Very Rev Michael Murphy PP
Roundfort, Hollymount, Co Mayo
Tel 094-9540934
Email mike.murphy@gmit.ie

**ROUNDSTONE**
Very Rev Jarlath Heraty PP *Protem*
Roundstone, Co Galway
Tel 095-35846

**SPIDDAL/KNOCK**
Very Rev Billy Reilly PP
Knock, Inverin, Co Galway
Tel 091-593122
Email wreilly@eircom.net

**WILLIAMSTOWN (TEMPLETOHER)**
Rev Francis McGrath Adm
Williamstown, Co Galway
Tel 094-9643007

## PRIESTS OF THE DIOCESE ELSEWHERE

Rev Eamon Conway
Mary Immaculate College,
University of Limerick,
South Circular Road, Limerick
Tel 061-204353
Email eamonn.conway@gmail.com
Very Rev Seamus Cunnane
Grove House, Tuam, Co Galway
Rev Denis Gallagher
'Shraheens', Achill South, Achill, Co Mayo
Rev Thomas Gallagher
Cloughmore, Achill, Co Mayo
Rev John Gavin
c/o Archbishop's House, Tuam
Very Rev Gerard Needham
Louisburgh, Co Mayo
Very Rev James O'Grady
Headford, Co Galway
Rev Michael O'Malley
c/o Archbishop's House, Tuam
Rev Michael Whelan
c/o Archbishop's House, Tuam

## RETIRED PRIESTS

Very Rev Padraic Audley PE
An Cheathrú Rua, Co na Gallimhe
Very Rev Seamus Carter
Abbeybreaffey Nursing Home,
Dublin Road, Castlebar, Co Mayo
Most Rev Dr Joseph Cassidy
1 Kilgarve Court, Creagh,
Ballinasloe, Co Galway
Very Rev Eamon Canon Concannon
Ballyhowley, Knock, Co Mayo
Very Rev Joe Cooney PE
25 Carrowmore Meadows,
Knock, Co Mayo
Tel 094-9375933
Very Rev Patrick Costello
51 Ashgrove, Mountbellew, Co Galway
Very Rev Arthur Devine PE
Rathbawn Road, Castlebar, Co Mayo
Rev John Fennelly
Our Lady's Manor, Dalkey
Very Rev John D. Canon Flannery
Cartron, Milltown, Co Galway
Very Rev Michael Canon Flannery PE
Cartron, Milltown, Co Galway
Very Rev Michael Canon Goaley
Glenamaddy, Co Galway
Very Rev Des Grogan PE
Partry, Co Mayo
Rev Paul Keane
Ballycrodick, Dunhill, Co Waterford
Very Rev Sean Kilbane PE
Clonfad, Oldtown, Athlone,
Co Roscommon
Tel 090-9673527
Very Rev Colm Canon Kilcoyne
20 Rathbawn Drive, Castlebar, Co Mayo
Rev Christopher Kilkelly
c/o Archbishop's House, Tuam, Co Galway
Rev Dr Enda Lyons
Bermingham Road, Tuam, Co Galway
Rev Enda McDonagh
St Patrick's College,
Maynooth, Co Kildare
Tel 01-6285222

Very Rev John McCarthy
76 Carrowmore Meadows, Knock, Co Mayo
Very Rev Joseph Moloney
Grove House, Vicar Street,
Tuam, Co Galway
Very Rev Joseph Canon Moran
Abbeybreaffey Nursing Home,
Dublin Road, Castlebar, Co Mayo
Very Rev Máirtín Ó Lainn
Carraroe, Co Galway
Very Rev Tadhg Ó Morain PE
Cornamona, Claremorris, Co Galway
Tel 094-9548003
Very Rev Kieran Waldron PE
Devlis, Ballyhaunis
Tel 094-9630246
Venerable Archdeacon Patrick Williams
Caherlohan, Tulla, Co Clare

## PERSONAL PRELATURE

**OPUS DEI**
Ballyglunin Park Conference Centre,
Tuam, Co Galway
Tel 093-41423
Rev Walter Macken, Chaplain

## RELIGIOUS ORDERS AND CONGREGATIONS

## PRIESTS

**OBLATES OF MARY IMMACULATE**
The Presbytery, Glenisland,
Castlebar, Co Mayo
Tel 085-1086639
Email glenislandcc@eircom.net

**ST PATRICK'S MISSIONARY SOCIETY (KILTEGAN FATHERS)**
Main Street, Knock,
Co Mayo
Tel 094-9388661
*House Leader*
Rev Donald McDonagh (SPS)

## BROTHERS

**ALEXIAN BOTHERS**
Regional Residence
Churchfield, Knock, Co Mayo
Tel 094-9376996
Email alexianbros@eircom.net
*Regional Leader:* Br Barry Butler (CFA)
Community: 3

**DE LA SALLE BROTHERS**
St Gerald's College
Tel 094-9021383 Fax 094-9026157
*Headmaster:* Mr Sean Burke

**FRANCISCAN BROTHERS**
Franciscan Brothers Generalate
Newtown, Mountbellew, Co Galway
Tel 090-9679295 Fax 090-9679687
Email franciscanbrs@eircom.net
*Minister General:* Br Peter Roddy (OSF)

Corrandulla, Co Galway
Tel 091-791127
*Local Minister:* Br Conal Thomas (OSF)
Community: 2

Clifden, Co Galway
Tel 095-21195
*Local Minister:* Br James Mungovan (OSF)
Community: 5

Franciscan Brothers, Newtown,
Mountbellew, Co Galway
Tel 090-9679906
*Local Minister:* Br Michael Burke (OSF)
Community: 9

Franciscan Brothers Agricultural College,
Mountbellew, Co Galway
Tel 090-9679205 Fax 090-9679276
Commmunity: 2

## SISTERS

**BENEDICTINE NUNS**
Kylemore Abbey,
Kylemore, Connemara, Co Galway
Tel 095-52000
Email info@kylemoreabbey.ie
*Abbess Administrator*
Sr Máire Hickey (OSB)
Community: 12
Abbey, Gothic Church, Craft Shop, Restaurant, Pottery Studio and 6-acre Victorian Walled Garden open to visitors. Soap and chocolate manufacturing by the Benedictine Community.
Website www.kylemoreabbey.com

**BON SECOURS SISTERS (PARIS)**
Sisters of Bon Secours, Drum,
Ballyhaunis Road, Knock, Co Mayo
Tel 094-9388439
*Contact:* Sr Felicitas O'Mahony
Community: 2
Prayer Ministry

99 Kilane View, Edenderry, Co Offaly
Tel 0405-33382
Community: 1
Health Ministry

**CARMELITES**
Carmelite Monastery,
Tranquilla, Knock, Co Mayo
Email tranquillacarmel@eircom.net
*Prioress:* Sr Catherine
Community: 18
Hidden life of prayer in the service of the Church

**CHRISTIAN RETREAT SISTERS**
'The Demense',
Mountbellew, Ballinasloe, Co Galway
Tel 090-9679311/9679939
*Contact:* Sr Margaret Buckley
Community: 5

Holy Rosary College Coeducational Secondary School
Tel 090-9679222
Pupils: 547
Catechetical and pastoral ministry

**CONGREGATION OF THE SISTERS OF MERCY**
Sisters of Mercy, The Glebe,
Tuam, Co Galway
Tel 093-25045
Community: 3

Convent of Mercy, Knock Road,
Ballyhaunis, Co Mayo
Tel 094-9630108
Community: 3

Cuan Chaitríona,
The Lawn, Castlebar, Co Mayo
Tel 094-9021171 Fax 094-9022031
Community: 20
Nursing Home: 15

Teach Mhuire,
The Lawn, Castlebar, Co Mayo
Tel 094-9022141 Fax 094-9025266
Community: 6

Ard Bhride,
The Lawn, Castlebar, Co Mayo
Tel 094-9286410 Fax 094-9286404
Community: 32

Pontoon Road, Castlebar, Co Mayo
Tel 094-9025463 Fax 094-9026695
Community: 5

7 Chapel Street, Castlebar, Co Mayo
Tel 094-9021734
Community: 2

6 Riverdale Court, Castlebar, Co Mayo
Tel/Fax 094-9023622
Community: 2

Manor Court, Westport Road,
Castlebar, Co Mayo
Community: 4

1a Lawn Park, Castlebar, Co Mayo
Tel 094-9027764
Community: 1

53 Spencer Manor, Spencer Street,
Castlebar, Co Mayo
Tel 094-9020075
Community: 1

1 Clareville, Claremorris, Co Mayo
Tel 094-9372654
Community: 2

Bethany, Dalton Street,
Claremorris, Co Mayo
Tel 094-9362198
Community: 3

Convent of Mercy, Dunmore, Co Galway
Tel 093-38141 Fax 093-38567
Community: 3

Sisters of Mercy,
37, 38, 39, 40 St Jarlath's Court,
The Glebe, Tuam, Co Galway
Community: 4

Sisters of Mercy,
18 The Beeches, Louisburgh, Co Mayo
Tel 098-66325
Community: 2

Apartment 4, St Dominic's Estate,
Barrack Hill, Newport, Co Mayo
Tel 098-41157
Community: 1

Convent of Mercy, Tuam, Co Galway
Tel 093-24363 Fax 093-25242
Community: 21

Sisters of Mercy, Ruah, Cappanraheen,
Craughwell, Co Galway
Tel 091-876646
Community: 3

37 Michael Davitt Park,
Westport, Co Mayo
Tel 098-27137
Community: 2

16 St Joseph's Court, Station Road,
Clifden, Co Galway
Tel 095-21550
Community: 1

19 St Joseph's Court, Galway Road,
Clifden, Co Galway
Tel 095-30838
Community: 1

Knock South, Cong, Co Mayo
Tel 094-9545833
Community: 1

7 Spencer Manor, Castlebar, Co Mayo
Tel 094-9035240
Community: 1

7 Liosdubh Court, Newport Road,
Castlebar, Co Mayo
Tel 094-9035240
Community: 1

50 An Sruthán, Turlough Road, Castlebar,
Co Mayo
Community: 1

13 Elm Park, Claremorris, Co Mayo
Tel 094-9377812
Community: 1

1 The Square, Claremorris, Co Mayo
Tel 094-9362963
Community: 1

26 Gratton Manor, Claremorris, Co Mayo
Tel 094-9373179

**DAUGHTERS OF CHARITY OF ST VINCENT DE PAUL**
St Mary's Hostel, Knock, Co Mayo
Tel 094-9388119
*Superior:* Sr Caitriona MacSweeney
Community: 7
Hostel for pilgrims

**FRANCISCAN SISTERS OF LITTLEHAMPTON**
Eden, Knock, Co Mayo
Tel 094-9388302
*Leader:* Sr Stanislaus Geraghty
*Bursar:* Sr Ignatius Foley
Sr Benignus
Community: 3

**MISSIONARY SISTERS OF OUR LADY OF APOSTLES**
52 Elm Park, Claremorris, Co Mayo
Tel 094-9373569
Community: 8

**POOR SERVANTS OF THE MOTHER OF GOD**
Cuan Mhuire, Coolarne, Turloughmore,
Athenry, Co Galway
Tel 091-737561
Community: 1
Counselling Ministry

**PRESENTATION SISTERS**
Presentation Convent, St Joseph's, Tuam,
Co Galway
Tel 093-24111 Fax 093-25584
Email presjos@eircom.net
*Community Leader:* Sr Mary Gannon
Community: 37
Care of sick and elderly sisters, school
and pastoral ministry
Presentation Primary School
Tel 093-28324
Email clochard.ias@eircom.net

Presentation Convent, Athenry, Co Galway
Tel 091-844077
*Community Leader:* Sr Marie Ward
Community: 11
School and pastoral ministry
Scoil Chroí Naofa Primary School
Tel 091-844510
Presentation College
Tel 091-844144 Fax 091-850862
Email pcathenry@hotmail.com

**ST JOSEPH OF THE SACRED HEART SISTERS**
Sisters have moved to new address
*(pending)*

**ST MARY MADELEINE POSTEL SISTERS**
'Fatima House', Kilkelly Road,
Knock, Co Mayo
*Apply:* Sister-in-charge
Tel 094-9388719
Community: 3

**URSULINES**
Ard Chiaráin Prayer Centre,
Shannonbridge, Co Roscommon
Tel 090-9674305/9674194
Email usac@eircom.net
Community: 3

## EDUCATIONAL INSTITUTIONS

**St Colman's College**
Claremorris, Co Mayo
Tel 094-9371442
*Principal:* Jimmy Finn
*Chaplain:* Rev Peter Gannon CC
Claremorris

**St Jarlath's College**
Tuam, Co Galway
Tel 093-24342
www.jarlaths.ie
*President*
Very Rev Brendan Canon Kilcoyne
Tel 093-24248
*Chaplain:* Rev Fintan Monahan
Tel 093-24166

**EDMUND RICE SCHOOLS TRUST**
St Patrick's Primary School,
Newport Road, Westport, Co Mayo
Tel 098-26450
*Principal:* Mr Stiofán Ó Moráin

Rice College, Castlebar Road,
Westport, Co Mayo
Tel 098-25698 Fax 098-26154
*Principal:* Ms Patricia Atkins

## CHARITABLE AND OTHER SOCIETIES

**Accord**
Shrine House, No 6 Bishop Street,
Tuam, Co Galway
Tel 093-24900/24776
*Contacts:* Rev Conal Eustace
Ms Anne Maguire
Mr Christopher Kelly
Castle Street, Castlebar
Tel 094-9022214

**Apostolic Work Society**
Branches at:
Abbeyknockmoy, Athenry, Achill, Ballinrobe, Ballyhaunis, Barnaderg, Balla, Belcarra, Brickens, Bekan, Castlebar, Claremorris, Carnacon, Claran, Clifden, Clonberne, Cortoon, Corofin, Caherlistrane, Dunmore, Glenamaddy, Headford, Kilkerrin, Knock, Kilconly, Lavally, Leenane, Louisburgh, Monivea, Mountbellew, Moylough, Newport, Tooreen, Westport, Robeen, Roundfort, Tuam, Tiernaul

**Cenacolo Community**
Our Lady of Knock,
Aughaboy, Knock, Co Mayo
*Contact:* Frank Walsh
Tel 087-9096007
Jean Ward
Tel 087-2687040
Email
cenacolocommunityireland@yahoo.ie

**Flats for Newly Weds**
Tuam Community Council

**Homes for the Elderly**
Conference of St Vincent de Paul,
Castlebar

**Information Centres**
Tuam, Ballinrobe, Claremorris,
Glenamaddy, Castlebar, Westport

**Social Services Centres**
Dublin Road, Tuam
Tel 093-24577
*Contact:* Sr Loreto

Community Centre, Westport, Co Mayo
Tel 098-25669
*Contact:* Sr Agnes

Castle Street, Castlebar, Co Mayo
Tel 094-9021880
*Contact:* Sr Dolores

**Society of St Vincent de Paul**
Conferences at: Castlebar, Tuam, Athenry, Westport, Dunmore, Claremorris, Ballyhaunis, Ballinrobe, Ballinlough, Headford, Monivea.

# DIOCESE OF ACHONRY

PATRONS OF THE DIOCESE
ST NATHY, 9 AUGUST; AT ATTRACTA, 11 AUGUST

INCLUDES PARTS OF COUNTIES MAYO, ROSCOMMON AND SLIGO

**Most Rev Brendan Kelly DD**
Bishop of Achonry;
born 20 May 1946;
ordained priest 20 June 1971;
ordained Bishop of Achonry
27 January 2008

Residence: Bishop's House,
Edmondstown,
Ballaghaderreen,
Co Roscommon
Tel 094-9860021
Fax 094-9860921
Email
bishop@achonrydiocese.org
Website www.achonrydiocese.org

## CATHEDRAL OF THE ANNUNCIATION AND ST NATHY, BALLAGHADERREEN

The building of the cathedral was begun in 1855 by Bishop Durcan. The architects were Messrs Hadfield & Goldie of Sheffield, while the Clerk of Works was Mr Charles Barker. It was completed in 1860.

The style is simple Gothic, known as Early English, of the Gothic Revival. The original intention was to have the roof fan-vaulted in wood and plaster, but it was abandoned owing to cost, and was finished in open timbers. The plan for a spire also had to be abandoned. This, however, was built in 1905 by Bishop Lyster, and a carillon of bells was installed.

The organ was built with continental pipes by Chestnutt of Waterford in 1925. The sanctuary was reconstructed to conform to the liturgical reforms of Vatican II in 1972. The baptistry in the left-hand Side Chapel was donated by Lydia Viscountess Dillon in memory of Charles Henry Viscount Dillon who died on 18 November 1865. The Apostles' Creed is carved on the baptistry lid.

There are commemorative plaques to former bishops of Achonry in the left-hand side Chapel: Bishops McNicholas, Durcan, Lyster and Morrisroe.

The window in the Lady Chapel has the inscription: 'This window to the Glory of God and Honour of the Blessed Virgin Mary was erected by united subscription of the Bishop, Clergy and 19 inhabitants of the Parish and neighbourhood to commemorate their respect and esteem for Charles Strickland and his wife Maria of Loughglynn and their zealous assistance in the erection of the Cathedral Church in 1860.' Charles Strickland was agent for Lord Dillon and was associated with the building of the neighbouring town of Charlestown and its church.
**Most Rev Thomas Flynn DD**

Bishop Emeritus of Achonry;
born 8 July 1931;
ordained priest 17 June 1956; ordained Bishop of Achonry 20 February 1977;
retired 20 November 2007

Residence: St Michael's,
Cathedral Grounds,
Ballaghaderreen, Co Roscommon
Tel 094-9877808
Email bishopflynn@achonrydiocese.org

## CHAPTER

*Dean*
Very Rev Michael Canon Joyce PP, Bohola
*Archdeacon*
Very Rev Patrick Canon Kilcoyne PP, Kiltimagh
Rt Rev Mgr Thomas Johnston PP, Charlestown
Very Rev James Canon Finan PP, Keash
Very Rev Patrick Canon Peyton PP, Collooney

## ADMINISTRATION

**Vicar General**
Rt Rev Mgr Thomas Johnston PP
Charlestown, Co Mayo
Tel 094-9254315

**College of Consultors**
Rt Rev Mgr Thomas Johnston
Very Rev Padraig Costello
Very Rev Thomas Towey
Very Rev Dermot Meehan
Rev James McDonagh

**Finance Committee**
*Chairman:* Mr Pat O'Connor
*Secretary:* Very Rev Martin Convey

**Vicars Forane**
Very Rev Michael Canon Joyce PP
Very Rev Gregory Hannan PP
Very Rev Patrick Lynch PP

**Church Property Advisory Commission**
Very Rev Michael Canon Joyce
Bohola, Claremorris, Co Mayo
Tel 094-9384115

**Church Building Advisory Commission**
Rt Rev Mgr Thomas Johnston PP
Charlestown, Co Mayo
Very Rev Joseph Caulfield PP
Gurteen, Co Sligo
Mr John Halligan
Charlestown, Co Mayo

**Historic Churches Advisory Committee**
*Chair*
Very Rev Patrick Canon Peyton PP
Tel 071-9167235
Very Rev Dermot Meehan
Tel 094-9252952

**Diocesan Communications Officer**
Very Rev Vincent Sherlock
Kilmovee, Ballaghaderreen, Co Mayo
Tel 094-9649137
Email vsherlock@achonrydiocese.org

## CATECHETICS EDUCATION

**Post-Primary Education**
*Secretary*
Very Rev Tomás Surlis DD
St Nathy's College, Ballaghaderreen, Co Roscommon
Tel 094-9260010

**Primary Education**
*Secretary*
Very Rev Patrick Canon Peyton PP
Collooney, Co Sligo
Tel 071-9167235

**Advisory Committee for Catholic Education**
*Contact*
Very Rev Martin Convey BSc, MLitt, PhD
St Nathy's College, Ballaghaderreen, Co Roscommon
Tel 094-9860010

**Religious Education in Schools**
*Diocesan Religious Adviser*
*Primary:* Sr Regina Lydon
Tel 071-9183350
Rev John Maloney
Kikelly, Co Mayo
Tel 094-9367031
*Post-Primary:* Rev Gerry Davey CC
Foxford, Co Mayo
Tel 094-9256401

## LITURGY

*Chairman*
Very Rev Patrick Lynch PP
Tubbercurry, Co Sligo
Tel 071-9185049
*Secretary*
Very Rev Thomas Towey PP
Ballisodare, Co Sligo
Tel 071-9167467

## PASTORAL

**Accord**
*Director*
Very Rev Joseph Caulfield PP
Gurteen, Co Sligo
Tel 071-9182551

**Council of Priests**
*Chairman*
Very Rev Dermot Meehan PP
Swinford, Co Mayo
Tel 094-9252952
*Secretary*
Very Rev Martin Henry CC
Ballaghaderreen, Co Roscommon
Tel 094-9860011

**Ecumenism**
*Director:* Vacant

**Emigrants**
*Director*
Very Rev Vincent Sherlock PP
Kilmovee, Ballaghaderreen, Co Mayo
Tel 094-9649137

**Marriage Tribunal**
(See Marriage Tribunals section)

**Pastoral Centre**
Rt Rev Mgr Thomas Johnston
St Nathy's Pastoral Centre,
Charlestown, Co Mayo
Tel 094-9254173

**Pioneer Total Abstinence Association**
*Spiritual Director*
Very Rev Joseph Gavigan PP
Ballaghaderreen, Co Roscommon
Tel 094-9860011

**Pontifical Mission Society**
*Diocesan Director*
Very Rev Peter Gallagher PP
Lavagh, Ballymote, Co Sligo
Tel 071-9184002

**Travellers**
*Chaplain*
Very Rev Patrick Canon Peyton PP
Collooney, Co Sligo
Tel 071-9167235

**Vocations**
*Director:* Rev Gabriel Murphy CC
Kiltimagh, Co Mayo
Tel 094-9381492

**Youth**
Rev Derek Gormley CC
Swinford, Co Mayo
Tel 094-9251143

## PARISHES

*The mensal parish is listed first. Other parishes follow alphabetically. Historical names are in parentheses. Church titulars are in italics.*

**BALLAGHADERREEN (CASTLEMORE AND KILCOLMAN)**
*Cathedral of The Annunciation & St Nathy*
*St Aidan, Monasteraden*
*SS John the Baptist & Colman, Derrinacartha*
*Sacred Heart, Brusna*
Very Rev Joseph Gavigan PP
Rev Martin Henry CC
The Presbytery, Ballaghaderreen, Co Roscommon
Tel 094-9860011 Fax 094-9860350

**ACHONRY**
*SS Nathy and Brigid, Achonry, Ballymote*
*Sacred Heart, Mullinabreena, Ballymote*
Very Rev Peter Gallagher PP
Lavagh, Ballymote, Co Sligo
Tel 071-9184002

**ATTYMASS**
*St Joseph's*
Very Rev Thomas Mulligan PP
Attymass, Ballina, Co Mayo
Tel 096-45095 Fax 096-45375

**BALLISODARE**
*St Brigid*
Very Rev Thomas Towey PP
Ballisodare, Co Sligo
Tel 071-9167467

**BALLYMOTE (EMLEFAD AND KILMORGAN)**
*Immaculate Conception, Ballymote*
*St Joseph's, Doo*
Very Rev Greg Hannan PP
Tel 071-9183361
Rev James McDonagh CC
Tel 071-9189778
Ballymote, Co Sligo

**BOHOLA**
*Immaculate Conception & St Joseph*
Very Rev Michael Joyce PP
Bohola, Claremorris, Co Mayo
Tel 094-9384115

**BONNICONLON (KILGARVAN)**
*Immaculate Heart of Mary*
Very Rev John Geelan PP
Parochial House, Bonniconlon,
Ballina, Co Mayo
Tel 096-45016

**BUNNINADDEN (KILSHALVEY, KILTURRA AND CLOONOGHILL)**
*Sacred Heart, Bunninadden*
*Immaculate Heart of Mary, Killavil*
Very Rev Michael Reilly PP
Bunninadden,
Ballymote, Co Sligo
Tel 071-9183232
Fax 071-9189167

**CARRACASTLE**
*St James', Carracastle*
*St Joseph's, Rooskey*
Very Rev Michael Quinn PP
Carracastle, Ballaghaderreen,
Co Mayo
Tel 094-9254301

**CHARLESTOWN (KILBEAGH)**
*St James', Charlestown*
*St Patrick's, Bushfield*
Rt Rev Mgr Thomas Johnston PP
Charlestown, Co Mayo
Tel 094-9254173

**COLLOONEY (KILVARNET)**
*Assumption, Collooney*
*SS Fechin & Lassara, Ballinacarrow*
Very Rev Patrick Peyton PP
Collooney, Co Sligo
Tel 071-9167235

**COOLANEY (KILLORAN)**
*Church of the Sacred Heart & St Joseph, Coolaney*
Very Rev Patrick Holleran PP
Coolaney, Co Sligo
Tel 071-9167235

**CURRY**
*Immaculate Conception, Curry*
*St Patrick's, Moylough*
Very Rev Martin Jennings PP
Curry, Ballymote, Co Sligo
Tel 094-9254508
Rev Seamus Collery
Curry, Ballymote, Co Sligo
Chaplain, St Attracta's Secondary School,
Tubbercurry, Co Sligo

**FOXFORD (TOOMORE)**
*St Michael's*
Very Rev Padraig Costello PP
Tel 094-9256131
Rev Gerard Davey CC
Tel 094-9256401
Foxford, Co Mayo

**GURTEEN (KILFREE AND KILLARAGHT)**
*St Patrick's, Gurteen*
*St Joseph's, Cloonloo*
*St Attracta's, Killaraght*
Very Rev Joseph Caulfield PP
Gurteen, Ballymote, Co Sligo
Tel 071-9182551
Fax 071-9182762

**KEASH (DRUMRAT)**
*St Kevin*
Our Lady of the Rosary, Culfadda
Very Rev James Canon Finan PP
Keash, Ballymote, Co Sligo
Tel 071-9183334

**KILLASSER**
*All Saints, Killasser*
*St Thomas', Callow*
Very Rev John Durkan PP
Killasser, Swinford, Co Mayo
Tel 094-9251431

**KILMOVEE**
*Immaculate Conception, Kilmovee*
*St Joseph's, Urlaur*
Very Rev Vincent Sherlock PP
Kilmovee, Ballaghaderreen, Co Mayo
Tel 094-9649137
*St Celsus, Kilkelly*
*St Patrick's, Glann*
Rev John Maloney CC
Kilkelly, Co Mayo
Tel 094-9367031

**KILTIMAGH (KILLEDAN)**
*Holy Family, Souls in Purgatory & St Aidan*
Very Rev Patrick Canon Kilcoyne PP
Tel 094-9381198
Rev Gabriel Murphy CC
Tel 094-9381492
Rev Stephen O'Mahony
Chaplain to school
Tel 094-9381261
Kiltimagh, Co Mayo

**STRAIDE (TEMPLEMORE)**
*SS Peter & Paul*
Very Rev Martin Convey PhD, PP
Straide, Foxford, Co Mayo
Tel 094-9031029

**SWINFORD (KILCONDUFF AND MEELICK)**
*Our Lady Help of Christians, Swinford*
*St Luke's, Meelick*
*St Joseph's, Midfield*
Very Rev Dermot Meehan PP
Tel 094-9252952
Rev Derek Gormley CC
Tel 094-9253338
Swinford, Co Mayo

**TOURLESTRANE (KILMACTIGUE)**
*St Attracta's, Tourlestrane*
*Our Lady of the Rosary, Kilmactigue*
*Sacred Heart, Loch Talt*
Very Rev John Glynn PP
Tourlestrane, Ballymote, Co Sligo
Tel 071-9181105

**TUBBERCURRY (CLOONACOOL)**
*St John the Evangelist, Tubbercurry*
Very Rev Patrick Lynch PP
Tubbercurry, Co Sligo
Tel 071-9185049
*St Michael's, Cloonacool*
Rev Dan O'Mahony CC
Cloonacool, Tubbercurry, Co Sligo
Tel 071-9185156

## PRIESTS OF THE DIOCESE ELSEWHERE

Rev Eugene Duffy DD
Mary Immaculate College,
South Circular Road, Limerick
Tel 061-204968
Rev Michael Maloney
c/o Parochial House,
Charlestown, Co Mayo
Rev Adrian McHugh
St Agnes Cathedral, 29 Queally Place,
Rockville Centre, NY11570 USA
Tel 001-516-7660205
Rev Ronan Murtagh
Ballymote Road, Tubbercurry, Co Sligo

## RETIRED PRIESTS

Very Rev Dermot Burns
Straide, Foxford, Co Mayo
Very Rev Farrell Cawley
Ballinacarrow, Co Sligo
Tel 086-0864347

Rt Rev Mgr John Doherty
*(Priest in residence)*
Charlestown, Co Mayo
Tel 094-9255793
Very Rev Dean Robert Flynn
Ballymote, Co Sligo
Tel 071-9183312
Very Rev Andrew Canon Johnston
c/o Innis Ree Lodge, Ballyleague,
Lanesborough, Co Roscommon
Tel 043-3327300
Very Rev Christopher Canon McLoughlin
Kilmactigue, Aclare, Co Sligo
Tel 071-9181007
*(Priest in residence, Tourlestrane Parish)*
Rt Rev Mgr Joseph Spelman
Collooney, Co Sligo
Tel 071-9167109
*(Priest in residence, Collooney Parish)*
Rev Paul Surlis
1684 Albermarle Drive, Crofton,
Maryland 21114, USA
Tel 001-410-4511459

## RELIGIOUS ORDERS AND CONGREGATIONS

## SISTERS

**CONGREGATION OF THE SISTERS OF MERCY**
Convent of Mercy,
Collooney, Co Sligo
Tel/Fax 071-9167153
Community: 6

Tabor
Swinford, Co Mayo
Tel 094-9252197
Community: 3

Convent of Mercy,
Ballymote, Co Sligo
Tel 071-9183350 Fax 071-9189177
Community: 5

Convent of Mercy,
Ballisodare, Co Sligo
Tel 071-9167279 Fax 071-9130538
Community: 5

Mercyville,
Ballaghaderren, Co Roscommon
Tel 094-9861193
Community: 4

Belgarrow, Sisters of Mercy,
Foxford, Co Mayo
Tel 094-9256573
Community: 2

Apt 4, Cormullen,
Foxford, Co Mayo
Community: 1

**MARIST SISTERS**
Marist Convent,
Tubbercurry, Co Sligo
Tel 071-9185018
Email ms3tub@eircom.net
Superior: Sr Angela Durkin
Community: 14
Primary school, parish visiting,
Marist laity
Day care centre (For HSE – Western Region)

Marist Convent,
Charlestown, Co Mayo
Tel 094-9254133
Email maristch@eircom.net
St Joseph's Secondary School
Tel 094-9254133
Community: 4
Teaching in secondary school, parish
ministry, Marist laity

**ST JOHN OF GOD SISTERS**
Dun Bhríd,
Ballymote, Co Sligo
Tel 071-9183196/9183973
Leader: Sr Vitalis Kilroy
Community: 9

**ST JOSEPH OF THE SACRED HEART SISTERS**
Sisters of St Joseph of Sacred Heart,
Killasser, Swinford, Co Mayo
Tel 094-9251265

**ST LOUIS SISTERS**
'Louisville', Cordarragh,
Kiltimagh, Co Mayo
Tel 094-9381205
Community: 6
Varied apostolates

St Louis Community School
Tel 094-9381228
Pupils: 570

Brooklodge,
Ballyhaunis Road, Knock, Co Mayo
Tel 094-9388020
Community: 1
Prayer ministry

## EDUCATIONAL INSTITUTIONS

**St Nathy's College**
Ballaghaderreen,
Co Roscommon
Tel 094-9860010 Fax 094-9860891
*President*
Very Rev Tomás Surlis DD
*Priests on Staff*
Rev Andrew Finan BA, HDE
Rev Leo Henry BA, HDE

## CHARITABLE AND OTHER SOCIETIES

**Hope House**
Foxford, Co Mayo
Tel 094-9256888 Fax 094-9256865
*Counsellors:* Sr Attracta Canny,
Sr Dolores Duggan
Treatment centre for addiction problems

**Fr Patrick Peyton Centre**
Attymass, Co Mayo
Tel 096-45374 Fax 096-45376
*Chaplain:* Fr Steve Gibson CSC

**Society of St Vincent de Paul**
*Contact:* Mr Liam McKibben
Swinford, Co Mayo
Tel 087-2522616

# DIOCESE OF ARDAGH AND CLONMACNOIS

Patron of the Diocese
St Mel, 7 February

INCLUDES NEARLY ALL OF COUNTY LONGFORD,
THE GREATER PART OF COUNTY LEITRIM
AND PARTS OF COUNTIES CAVAN, OFFALY, ROSCOMMON,
SLIGO AND WESTMEATH

**Most Rev Colm O'Reilly DD**
Bishop of Ardagh and Clonmacnois;
born 11 January 1935;
ordained priest 19 June 1960;
ordained Bishop of Ardagh and Clonmacnois 10 April 1983

Residence: St Michael's,
Longford,Co Longford
Tel 043-3346432
Fax 043-3346833
Email ardaghdi@iol.ie

## ST MEL'S CATHEDRAL, LONGFORD

On 19 May 1840, Bishop William O'Higgins laid the foundation stone of a new cathedral for the Diocese of Ardagh and Clonmacnois. The foundation stone was taken from the original Cathedral of St Mel at Ardagh. The preacher at that ceremony was the Archbishop of Tuam, Archbishop John MacHale. Four other bishops, one hundred and twenty priests and an estimated forty thousand people were present.

The architect of the cathedral was Mr John Benjamin Keane. The magnificent portico was not included in the original design. This was the work of another architect, Mr George Ashlin, and was not erected until 1883. Without any doubt Bishop O'Higgins influenced the original design, which reflected some of his own life experience, having been educated in Paris, Rome and having lived for a time in Vienna. The cathedral owes something in its design to the Madeleine in Paris, and the Pantheon and the Basilica of St John Lateran in Rome. Certainly something of the Lateran is to be seen in the attempt that was made to incorporate the bishop's house at the rear of the sanctuary.

Raising the money necessary to build the cathedral was an enormous challenge in poverty-stricken Ireland in the 1840s. Bishop O'Higgins travelled the length and breadth of the diocese and his appeals for help went well beyond the diocesan boundaries. He received great help, especially from the Dioceses of Elphin, Tuam and Meath, and contributions came from as far away as Belfast. A priest of the diocese toured North America and Canada to raise funds there.

By 1846 the walls, pillars and entire masonry were completed and the roof was the next stage in the building programme. Then the potato blight came and the Great Hunger. Work had to be suspended. Bishop O'Higgins would never see the great cathedral completed. He died in 1853.

Bishop John Kilduff, successor of Bishop O'Higgins, resumed work on the cathedral. It was opened for worship in September 1856. Though the work was not complete, it was a time of great rejoicing. Present on that special day were Archbishop Dixon of Armagh and Archbishop Cullen of Dublin, and fourteen other bishops.

It was Bishop Bartholomew Woodlock who commissioned the erection of the impressive portico, with its huge Ionic columns. He was still bishop of the diocese in 1893 when the cathedral was consecrated on 19 May.

Since 1893 much additional work has been done. Bishop Hoare, successor of Bishop Woodlock, added a pipe organ and bell chimes. Later still, two beautiful stained-glass windows, the work of the Harry Clarke Studios in Dublin, were installed in the transepts. In the 1970s a major restyling of the sanctuary was undertaken.

On Christmas Morning 2009 St Mel's Cathedral was badly damaged by fire. A restoration project has commenced.

## CHAPTER

*Trustee of St Mel's Diocesan Trust*
Very Reverend Jeremiah Macaulay
*Archdeacon*
Right Rev Mgr Patrick Earley
Very Rev Brian Brennan
Very Rev Padraig McGowan
Very Rev George Balfe
Very Rev Francis Gray
Very Rev Owen Devaney
Very Rev Peter Brady
Very Rev Aidan Ryan
Very Rev Bernard Hogan
Rt Rev Mgr Bernard Noonan
Very Rev Peter Burke
Very Rev Liam Murray

## ADMINISTRATION

**Vicars General**
Rt Rev Mgr Patrick Earley PP, VG
Rt Rev Mgr Bernard Noonan PP, VG

**Diocesan Chancellor**
Very Rev Michael Bannon PP, VF
Edgeworthstown, Co Longford
Tel 043-6671046

**College of Consultors**
Rt Rev Mgr Patrick Earley PP, VG
Rt Rev Mgr Bernard Noonan PP, VG
Rev Eamonn Corkery
Rev Francis Garvey
Rev Bernard Hogan
Rev Pat Murphy
Rev Tom Murray

**Vicars Forane**
Rt Rev Mgr Bernard Noonan PP, VG
Very Rev Francis Garvey PP
Very Rev Michael Bannon PP
Very Rev Simon Cadam PP

**Financial Administrator**
Rev Tom Murray
Diocesan Office, St Michael's, Longford
Tel 043-3346432 Fax 043-3346833

**Finance Committee**
*Chairman:* Very Rev Brian Brennan PP
Ballinalee, Co Longford
Tel 043-3323110
*Members*
Mr Frank Gearty, Solicitor
Mr Des Mooney, Accountant
Mr Brian Loughran
Mr Eddie Cowan
Mr Michael Glennon
Rev Michael Bannon
Rev Tom Murray

**Diocesan Archivist**
Rev Tom Murray
Diocesan Office, St Michael's, Longford
Tel 043-3346432 Fax 043-3346833

**Diocesan Secretary**
Rev Tom Murray
Diocesan Office, St Michael's, Longford
Tel 043-3346432 Fax 043-3346833
Email ardaghdi@iol.ie

## CATECHETICS EDUCATION

**Pastoral Renewal and Faith Development**
Rev James MacKiernan CC
Boher, Ballycumber, Co Offaly
Tel 057-9336119
Sr Anna Burke
31 Templemichael Glebe, Longford
Tel 043-3345255/3348240 (office)

**Religious Education in Schools**
*Diocesan Advisers*
*Primary:* Rev Michael McGrath CC
Carrick-on-Shannon, Co Leitrim
Tel 071-9620347
Sr Rose Moron
26 Castlepark, Newtownforbes, Co Longford
Tel 043-3348021
*Post-Primary:* Rev Tom Murray
Diocesan Office, St Michael's, Longford
Tel 043-3346432

**Diocesan Council of Catholic Primary School Managers' Association**
*Secretary:* Mrs Eileen Ward
Diocesan Office, St Michael's, Longford
Tel 043-3346432

## LITURGY

**Church Music**
*Director:* Rev Turlough Baxter CC
St Mary's, Athlone, Co Westmeath
Tel 090-6472088

**Liturgy Commission**
*Secretary:* Rev Turlough Baxter CC
St Mary's, Athlone, Co Westmeath
Tel 090-6472088

**Sacred Art and Architecture Commission**
*Secretary:* Rev Sean Casey PP
Killoe, Co Longford
Tel 043-3323119

## PASTORAL

**Accord**
*Director:* Very Rev Patrick Murphy PP
Parochial House, Mohill, Co Leitrim
Tel 071-9631024

**Committee for Special Marriage Preparation Procedures**
Rev Cathal Faughnan PP
Keadue, Boyle, Co Roscommon
Tel 071-9647212
Rev Thomas Healy Adm
The Presbytery, Longford
Tel 043-3346465
Very Rev Michael Bannon PP
St Mary's, Edgeworthstown, Co Longford
Tel 043-6671046

**Communications**
*Diocesan Counsellor*
Very Rev Patrick Murphy PP
Parochial House, Mohill, Co Leitrim
Tel 071-9631024

**Council of Priests**
*Chairman:* Very Rev Patrick Murphy PP
Parochial House, Mohill, Co Leitrim
Tel 071-9631024
*Secretary:* Rev Tom Murray
Diocesan Office, St Michael's, Longford
Tel 043-3346432

**CURA**
Tel 0902-74272 (Centre)/1850-626260

**Ecumenism**
Rev Padraig Kelliher CC
The Presbytery, Longford
Tel 043-3346465

**Family Ministry**
Very Rev Patrick Murphy PP
Parochial House, Mohill, Co Leitrim
Tel 071-9631024
Sr Angela Clarkson
Teallach Iosa, St Mel's Road, Longford
Tel 043-3346827

**Marriage Tribunal**
(See Marriage Tribunals section.)

**Pilgrimage (Lourdes)**
*Director*
Rt Rev Mgr Bernard Noonan PP, VG
Moate, Co Westmeath
Tel 090-6481180

**Pioneer Total Abstinence Association**
*Diocesan Director*
Very Rev Michael Campbell PP
Abbeylara, Co Longford
Tel 043-6686270

**Pontifical Mission Societies**
*Diocesan Director*
Very Rev Aidan Ryan PP
Ballinahown, Athlone, Co Westmeath
Tel 090-6430124

**Safeguarding Children Diocesan Committee**
Mr Sean Leydon, Mrs Trisha Nugent, Mrs Roisin O'Doherty, Mr Liam Faughnan, Mrs Mary Daly, Mrs Evelyn Breen, Sr Una Purcell, Rev Liam Murray, Rev Michael Bannon

**Spirituality Committee**
Very Rev Jeremiah Macaulay AP
Edgeworthstown, Co Longford
Tel 043-6671159

**Travellers**
*Chaplain:* Rev Nigel Charles CC
The Presbytery, Killashee, Co Longford
Tel 043-3345546

**Trócaire**
*Diocesan Director*
Very Rev Bernard Hogan PP
Drumlish, Co Longford
Tel 043-3324132

**Vocations**
*Director:* Very Rev Simon Cadam PP, VF
St Mary's, Granard, Co Longford
Tel 043-6686550

**Youth Commission**
*Diocesan Director:* Ms Anita Allen
St Mary's Youth Ministry Centre,
First Floor, St Mary's Hall,
Northgate Street, Athlone
Tel 090-6473358
Email info@aym.ie

## PARISHES

Mensal parishes are listed first. Other parishes follow alphabetically. Historical names are given in parentheses. Church titulars are in italics.

**LONGFORD (TEMPLEMICHAEL, BALLYMACORMACK)**
*St Mel's Cathedral; St Anne's, Curry, St Michael's, Shroid*
Rev Thomas Healy Adm
Rev Tom Murray CC
Rev Brendan O'Sullivan CC
Rev Padraig Kelliher CC
The Presbytery, Longford
Tel 043-3346465

**ATHLONE**
*St Mary's, Athlone*
*Our Lady Queen of Peace, Coosan*
Rev Liam Murray Adm
Rev Declan Shannon CC
Rev Turlough Baxter CC
Rev Charles Healy CC
Rev Mark Bennett CC
Rev Krzysztof Przanowski CC *(Polish Chaplaincy)*
St Mary's, Athlone, Co Westmeath
Tel 090-6472088

**ABBEYLARA**
*St Bernard's, Abbeylara*
*St Mary's, Carra*
Very Rev Michael Campbell PP
Carra, Granard, Co Longford
Tel 043-6686270

**ANNADUFF**
*Immaculate Conception, Annaduff*
*Immaculate Conception, Drumsna*
Very Rev John Wall PP
Annaduff, Carrick-on-Shannon, Co Leitrim
Tel 071-9624093

**ARDAGH AND MOYDOW**
*St Brigid's, Ardagh; Our Lady's, Moydow*
Very Rev George Balfe PP (on sick leave)
Rev Pat Lennon, Parish Administrator
Ardagh, Co Longford
Tel 043-6675006

**AUGHAVAS AND CLOONE**
*St Joseph's, Aughavas*
*St Stephen's, Rossan*
*St Mary's, Cloone*
Very Rev Samuel Holmes PP
Cloone, Co Leitrim
Tel 071-9636016

**BALLINAHOWN, BOHER AND POLLOUGH (LEMANAGHAN)**
*St Colmcille's, Ballinahown*
*St Manchain's, Ballycumber*
*St Mary's, Pollough*
Very Rev Aidan Ryan PP
Ballinahown, Athlone, Co Westmeath
Tel 090-6430124
Rev James MacKiernan CC
Boher, Ballycumber, Co Offaly
Tel 057-9336119

**BALLYMAHON (SHRULE)**
*St Matthew's, Ballymahon*
Very Rev Padraig MacGowan PP
Ballymahon, Co Longford
Tel 090-6432253

**BORNACOOLA**
*St Michael's, Bornacoola*
*St Joseph's, Clonturk*
Very Rev Gerard O'Brien PP
Bornacoola, Carrick-on-Shannon, Co Leitrim
Tel 071-9638229

**CARRICKEDMOND AND ABBEYSHRULE**
*(Taghshiney, Taghshinod & Abbeyshrule)*
*Sacred Heart, Carrickedmond*
*Our Lady of Lourdes, Abbeyshrule*
Very Rev Peter Tiernan PP
Carrickedmond, Colehill, Co Longford
Tel 044-9357442

**CARRICK-FINEA (DRUMLUMMAN SOUTH AND BALLYMACHUGH)**
*St Mary's, Carrick*
*St Mary's, Ballynarry*
Very Rev Francis Gray PP
Carrick, Finea, Mullingar, Co Westmeath
Tel 043-6681129

**CARRICK-ON-SHANNON (KILTOGHERT)**
*St Mary of the Assumption Carrick-on-Shannon*
*Sacred Heart, Jamestown*
*St Patrick's, Gowel*
*St Joseph's, Leitrim*
Very Rev Francis Garvey PP, VF
Carrick-on-Shannon, Co Leitrim
Tel 071-9620118
Rev Merlyn Kenny CC
Tel 071-9620054
Rev Michael McGrath CC
Tel 071-9620347
St Mary's, Carrick-on-Shannon, Co Leitrim

**CLOGHAN AND BANAGHER (GALLEN AND REYNAGH)**
*St Mary's, Cloghan*
*St Rynagh's Banagher*
Very Rev Michael Scanlon PP
Cloghan, Birr, Co Offaly
Tel 090-6457122
Rev Pierre Pepper CC
Banagher, Co Offaly
Tel 057-9151338

**CLONBRONEY**
*St James, Clonbroney*
*Holy Trinity, Ballinalee*
Very Rev Brian Brennan PP
Ballinalee, Co Longford
Tel 043-3323110

**CLOONE (CLOONE-CONMAICNE)**
*St Mary's, Cloone*
See Aughavas & Cloone

**COLMCILLE**
*St Colmcille's, Aughnacliffe*
*St Joseph's, Purth*
Very Rev Seamus McKeon PP
Aughnacliffe, Co Longford
Tel 043-6684118

**DROMARD**
*St Mary's, Legga; St Mary's, Moyne*
Very Rev Eamonn Corkery PP
Dromard, Moyne, Co Longford
Tel 049-4335248

**DRUMLISH**
*St Mary's, Drumlish*
*St Patrick's, Ballinamuck*
Very Rev Bernard Hogan PP
Drumlish, Co Longford
Tel 043-3324132
Rev Jim Sorahan CC
Ballinamuck, Co Longford
Tel 043-3324110

**DRUMSHANBO (MURHAUN)**
*St Patrick's, Drumshanbo*
Very Rev Peter Burke PP
Drumshanbo, Co Leitrim
Tel 071-9641010

**EDGEWORTHSTOWN (MOSTRIM)**
*St Mary of the Immaculate Conception*
Very Rev Michael Bannon PP, VF
St Mary's, Edgeworthstown, Co Longford
Tel 043-6671046
Very Rev Canon Jeremiah Macaulay AP
Edgeworthstown, Co Longford
Tel 043-6671159

**FENAGH**
*St Mary's, Foxfield*
See Mohill Parish

**FERBANE HIGH STREET AND BOORA (TISARAN AND FUITHRE)**
*Immaculate Conception, Ferbane*
*SS Patrick and Saran, Belmont*
*St Oliver Plunkett, Boora*
Very Rev Francis Murray PP
Tel 090-6454380
Rev Tom Cox CC
Tel 090-6454309
Ferbane, Co Offaly

**GORTLETTERAGH**
*St Mary's, Gortletteragh*
*St Thomas', Fairglass*
*St Joseph's, Cornageetha*
Very Rev John Quinn PP
Gortletteragh,
Carrick-on-Shannon, Co Leitrim
Tel 071-9631074

**GRANARD**
*St Mary's*
Very Rev Simon Cadam PP
St Mary's, Granard, Co Longford
Tel 043-6686550
Rev Thomas Flynn CC
Granard, Co Longford
Tel 043-6686591

**KEADUE, ARIGNA AND BALLYFARNON (KILRONAN)**
*Nativity of the Blessed Virgin, Keadue*
*Immaculate Conception, Arigna*
*St Patrick's, Ballyfarnon*
Very Rev Cathal Faughnan PP
Keadue, Boyle, Co Roscommon
Tel 071-9647212

**KILCOMMOC (KENAGH)**
*St Dominic's*
Rev Thomas Barden PIC
Kenagh, Co Longford
Tel 043-3322127

**KILLASHEE**
*St Patrick's, Killashee*
*St Brendan's, Clondra*
Rev Nigel Charles CC
Parochial House, Killashee, Co Longford
Tel 043-3345546

**KILLENUMMERY AND BALLINTOGHER (KILLENUMMERY AND KILLERY)**
*St Mary's, Killenummery*
*St Michael's, Killavoggy*
*St Teresa's, Ballintogher*
Very Rev Vincent Connaughton PP
Killenummery, Dramahair,
via Sligo, Co Leitrim
Tel 071-9164125

**KILLOE**
*St Mary's, Ennybegs*
*St Oliver Plunkett's, Cullyfad*
Very Rev Sean Casey PP
Ennybegs, Longford
Tel 043-3323119

**KILTUBRID**
*St Brigid's, Drumcong*
*St Joseph's, Rantogue*
Very Rev Tomás Flynn PP
Drumcong, Carrick-on-Shannon
Co Leitrim
Tel 071-9642021

**LANESBORO (RATHCLINE)**
*St Mary's, Lanesboro*
Very Rev Michael Reilly PP
Lanesboro, Co Longford
Tel 043-3321166

**LEGAN AND BALLYCLOGHAN (KILGLASS AND RATHREAGH)**
*Nativity of the Blessed Virgin Mary, Lenamore*
*St Ann's, Ballycloghan*
Very Rev Peter Brady PP
Lenamore, Co Longford
Tel 044-9357404

**LOUGH GOWNA AND MULLINALAGHTA (SCRABBY AND COLMCILLE EAST)**
*Holy Family, Lough Gowna*
*St Columba's, Mullinalaghta*
Very Rev PJ Fitzpatrick PP
Gowna, Co Cavan
Tel 043-6683120

**MOATE AND MOUNT TEMPLE (KILCLEAGH AND BALLYLOUGHLOE)**
*St Patrick's, Moate; St Ciaran's, Castledaly*
*Corpus Christi, Mount Temple*
Rt Rev Mgr Bernard Noonan PP, VG
Tel 090-6481180
Rev Liam Farrell CC
Tel 090-6481189
Moate, Co Westmeath
Rev Patrick Kiernan CC
Mount Temple, Moate,
Co Westmeath
Tel 090-6481239

**MOHILL (MOHILL-MANACHAIN)**
*St Patrick's, Mohill*
*St Joseph's, Gorvagh*
*St Mary's, Eslin Bridge*
*St Mary's, Foxfield*
Very Rev Patrick Murphy PP
Tel 071-9631024
Rev Sean Burke CC
Tel 071-9631097
Mohill, Co Leitrim

**MULLAHORAN AND LOUGHDUFF (DRUMLUMMAN NORTH)**
*Our Lady of Lourdes, Mullahoran*
*St Joseph's, Loughduff*
Very Rev Owen Devaney PP
Mullahoran, Kilcogy via Longford,
Co Cavan
Tel 043-6683141

**NEWTOWNCASHEL (CASHEL)**
*The Blessed Virgin*
Very Rev Gerard Brady PP
Newtowncashel, Co Longford
Tel 043-3325112

**NEWTOWNFORBES (CLONGUISH)**
*St Mary's*
Very Rev Ciaran McGovern PP
Newtownforbes, Co Longford
Tel 043-3346805

**RATHOWEN (RATHASPIC, RUSSAGH & STREETE)**
*St Mary's, Rathowen*
Rt Rev Mgr Patrick Earley VG
Rathowen, Mullingar,
Co Westmeath
Tel 043-6676044

**SHANNONBRIDGE (CLONMACNOIS)**
*St Ciaran's, Shannonbridge*
*St Ciaran's, Clonfanlough*
Very Rev Francis O'Hanlon PP
Shannonbridge,
Athlone, Co Westmeath
Tel 090-9674125

**STREETE**
*St Mary's*
*See Rathown (Rathaspic and Rossagh)*
Rev Joseph McGrath
Chaplain, Parochial House,
Boherquill, Lismacaffney,
Mullingar, Co Westmeath

## HOSPITALS AND THEIR CHAPLAINS

**St Joseph's and Mount Carmel Hospitals, Longford**
Rev James Regan (SPS)
Chaplain's Residence,
Dublin Road, Longford
Tel 043-3346211

**St Vincent's Hospital**
Athlone, Co Westmeath
Very Rev Liam Murray Adm
Tel 090-6472323; 6478318 (H)

## PRIESTS OF THE DIOCESE ELSEWHERE

Rev Colman Carrigy
Clonee, Killoe, Co Longford
Rev Gerard Carroll
Ballinalee Road, Longford
Rev Liam Cuffe
Chaplaincy, St Vincent's Hospital,
Dublin 4
Rev Christy Stapleton
Rev Hugh Turbitt
c/o Diocesan Office, St Michael's,
Longford
Rev P. J. Hughes
On mission to Equador
Rev Patsy McDermott
*(Sabbatical leave)*

## RETIRED PRIESTS

Very Rev Peter Beglan PE
12 Pairc na-hAbhainn,
Edgeworthstown, Co Longford
Rev Michael Killian
Mulross Nursing Home,
Carrick-on-Shannon, Co Leitrim
Rev Dominic Lynch
Gallen Nursing Home,
Ferbane, Co Offaly
Very Rev James O'Beirne
Moate, Co Westmeath
Very Rev Sean Tynan
Laurel Lodge Nursing Home,
Longford

## RELIGIOUS ORDERS AND CONGREGATIONS

### PRIESTS

**FRANCISCANS**
Franciscan Friary,
Athlone, Co Westmeath
Tel 090-6472095 Fax 090-6424713
Email athlonefriary@eircom.net
*Guardian*
Very Rev Michael Nicholas (OFM)

**MARIST FATHERS (SOCIETY OF MARY)**
Rev Tim Kenny (SM)
Fermoyle, Lanesboro, Co Longord

### BROTHERS

**MARIST BROTHERS**
Champagnat House, Athlone,
Co Westmeath
Tel 090-6472336
*Superior:* Br Gerard Cahill
Community: 4

Marist College, Athlone, Co Westmeath
Tel 090-6474491
Secondary pupils: 510

### SISTERS

**CONGREGATION OF THE SISTERS OF MERCY**
Villa Maria, Ardagh, Co Longford
Tel 043-6675080
Community: 1

Convent of Mercy, St Joseph's, Longford
Tel 043-3346435 Fax 043-3348392
Community: 20

Bracklin
Edgeworthstown, Co Longford
Tel/Fax 043-71015
Community: 3

Sisters of Mercy,
Shalom, Edgeworthstown, Co Longford
Tel 043-71852 Fax 043-72989
Community: 7

Sisters of Mercy,
Manor Lodge, Dublin Road,
Edgeworthstown, Co Longford
Tel 043-6671102
Community: 2

Upper Main Street, Ballymahon,
Co Longford
Tel 090-6432532
Community: 4

Convent of Mercy,
Lanesboro, Co Longford
Tel 043-3321105 Fax 043-3321436
Community: 5

14 Rathbeag, Abbeylara, Co Longford
Community: 1

7 Mill Street, Drumlish, Co Longford
Tel 043-29585
Community: 1

Sisters of Mercy, 2 Cnoc na Greine
Granard, Co Longford
Tel/Fax 043-6686633
Community: 1

Sisters of Mercy, 61 Cnoc na Greine,
Granard, Co Longford
Tel 043-6686563
Community: 2

Mount Carmel, Station Road,
Moate, Co Westmeath
Tel 090-6481912 Fax 090-6482803
Community: 5

Gort Mhuire, Knockdomney,
Moate, Co Westmeath
Tel/Fax 090-6482265
Community: 2

Shannagh Grove, Mohill, Co Leitrim
Tel 071-9631064
Community: 3

St Michele, Curryline,
Newtownforbes, Co Longford
Tel 043-46326
Community: 2

20 Annaly Gardens, Longford
Tel 043-3341407
Community: 2

19 Midara Gardens, Longford
Tel/Fax 043-3346702
Community: 1

6 Curryline, Newtownforbes,
Co Longford
Tel 043-41826
Community: 2

Sisters of Mercy,
31 Templemichael Glebe, Longford
Tel 043-3345255
Community: 1

Sisters of Mercy, The Lodge,
Drumshanbo, Co Leitrim
Tel 071-9641308
Community: 3

7 Ard Michael Park,
Ballinalee Road, Longford
Tel 043-3334248
Community: 3

19 Cara Court,
Carrick-on-Shannon, Co Leitrim
Tel 071-9622582
Community: 1

Parnell Row, Granard, Co Longford
Tel 043-6687624
Community: 1

107 Mostrim Oaks,
Edgeworthstown, Co Longford
Community: 1

**LA SAINTE UNION DES SACRES COEURS**
Our Lady's Bower, Athlone,
Co Westmeath
Tel 090-6472061/6472092
Fax 090-6474853
*Co-ordinator:* Sr Christopher Mary Callan
Community: 17

Secondary School (Boarding and day)
Pupils: 650
*Principal:* Sr Denise O'Brien
Tel 090-6474777/6475524
Fax 090-6476356
Email bower@iol.ie &
srdenise@eircom.net
Web www.ourladysbower.com
St Mary's National School (Parish)
*Headmistress:* Mrs Margaret Naughton
Tel 090-6472321

Mont Vista, House of the Sick,
Retreat Road, Athlone
Tel 090-6472887
*Sister in Charge*
Sr Mary Thecla Garvey
Sick and frail elderly, province ministry,
healthcare
Community: 12

Banagher, Co Offaly
Tel 0509-51319
Email lsu1@eircom.net
Community: 13
Teaching, Parish care of the Sick and Frail
Secondary School (Day pupils)
Tel 0509-51406 Fax 0509 51439
*Principal:* Mr Tom McGlacken
Pupils: 450

**MARIST SISTERS**
Marist Convent
Carrick-on-Shannon, Co Leitrim
Tel 071-9620010
Email maristconventcarrick@eircom.net
*Superior:* Sr Eva Horkin
Community: 12

6/7 Summerhill Grove,
Carrick-on- Shannon, Co Leitrim
Tel 071-9621396
Email maristgrove7@gmail.com
Community: 3
Health care ministry in St Patrick's
Hospital, pastoral ministry in St Patrick's
Hospital, Marist laity

**MISSIONARY SISTERS OF THE HOLY ROSARY**
Pullagh, Tullamore, Co Offaly
Tel 0506-36050
Community: 1

**POOR CLARES**
Poor Clare Monastery of Perpetual
Adoration, Drumshanbo, Co Leitrim
*Abbess:* Mother M. Angela McCabe
Community: 10
Contemplatives
Perpetual adoration of the Blessed
Sacrament
Small self-catering private retreat house
attached
Tel 071-9641308 Fax 071-9640789

**PRESENTATION SISTERS**
Presentation Sisters Provincialate,
Garden Vale, Athlone, Co Westmeath
Tel 090-6472186 Fax 090-6477617
Email presnpro@iol.ie
Administration of Northern Province of Presentation Sisters
*Provincial Leader:* Sr Elizabeth Maxwell
Community: 6

**ST JOSEPH OF CLUNY SISTERS**
St Joseph's Convent,
Main Street, Ferbane, Co Offaly
Tel 090-6454324
Email stjf@eircom.net
*Superior:* Sr Helena Egan
Community: 6
Pastoral Ministry

Gallen Priory,
Ferbane, Co Offaly
Tel 090-6454416
*Superior:* Sr Brigid Moore
Community: 12

## EDUCATIONAL INSTITUTIONS

**St Mel's College, Longford**
Tel 043-3346469
*Principal:* Mr Damian Cunningham
*Priests on Teaching Staff:*
Rev Joe McGrath
*Chaplain:* Rev Joe McGrath

**Athlone Institute of Technology**
Athlone, Co Westmeath
*Chaplain:* Rev Seamus Casey
Tel 090-6424400
*Res:* 11 Auburn Heights, Athlone, Co Westmeath
Tel 090-6478318

## CHARITABLE AND OTHER SOCIETIES

**Apostolic Work Society**
Mrs Nuala Claffey
Ferbane, Co Offaly

**Knights of St Columbanus**
St Mary's Square,
Athlone, Co Westmeath

**Legion of Mary**
Centres at Longford, Athlone, Carrick-on-Shannon, Granard, Mohill

**Our Lady's Nursing Home**
Edgeworthstown, Co Longford
Tel 043-6671007

St Christopher's
Battery Road, Longford
School for mentally handicapped

**St Hilda's**
Grace Park Road,
Athlone, Co Westmeath
School for mentally handicapped

**Social Service Council, Longford**
Tel 043-3346452
Mr Padraig Gearty

**Society of St Vincent de Paul**
*Longford:*
Mrs Anne Kane
*Athlone:*
Mr Eugene Lee
*Carrick-on-Shannon:*
Mr Patrick Keaney
*Mohill:*
Mr Sean McGuinness
*Drumshanbo:*
Mrs Bea Cullen
*Ferbane:*
Mrs Breda Connolly

# DIOCESE OF CLOGHER

PATRON OF THE DIOCESE
ST MACARTAN, 24 MARCH

INCLUDES COUNTY MONAGHAN, MOST OF COUNTY FERMANAGH
AND PORTIONS OF COUNTIES TYRONE, DONEGAL, LOUTH AND CAVAN

**Most Rev Liam S. MacDaid DD**
Bishop of Clogher;
born 19 July 1945;
ordained priest 15 June 1969;
ordained Bishop of Clogher
25 July 2010

Residence: Bishop's House,
Monaghan
Tel 047-81019 Fax 047-84773
Email diocesanoffice
@clogherdiocese.ie
Website www.clogherdiocese.ie

## ST MACARTAN'S CATHEDRAL, MONAGHAN

On Sunday, 3 January 1858, at a meeting of the Catholic inhabitants of the parish and vicinity of Monaghan, with the Bishop of Clogher, Dr Charles MacNally, presiding, it was formally resolved that a new Catholic church at Monaghan was urgently required. An eight-acre site was purchased by the bishop from Humphrey Jones of Clontibret for £800, and an architect, James Joseph McCarthy of Dublin, was employed to draw a design.

The style is French Gothic of the fourteenth century. In June 1861 the foundation stone was laid, and the work got underway the following year. Dr MacNally died in 1864, and work resumed under his successor, Dr James Donnelly, in 1865. The architect died in 1882 and was succeeded by William Hague, a Cavan man, who was responsible for the design of the spire and the gate-lodge. The work was completed in 1892, and the cathedral was solemnly dedicated on 21 August of that year.

Under the direction of Bishop Joseph Duffy, a radical rearrangement and refurbishing of the interior of the cathedral was begun in 1982 to meet the requirements of the revised liturgy. The artist responsible for the general scheme was Michael Biggs of Dublin, in consultation with local architect Gerald MacCann. The altar is carved from a single piece of granite from south County Dublin. The sanctuary steps are in solid Travertine marble. The sanctuary crucifix is by Richard Enda King; the cross is of Irish oak and the figure of Christ is cast in bronze. The Lady Chapel has a bronze Pietà by Nell Murphy, and the lettering of the Magnificat is by Michael Biggs. The tabernacle, made of silver-plated sheet bronze and mounted on a granite pillar, has the form of a tent and was designed and made by Richard Enda King. In the chapel of the Holy Oils the aumbry was designed by Michael Biggs, while the miniature bronze gates were executed by Martin Leonard. The five great tapestries on the east walls of the cathedral are a striking feature of the renovation; they were designed by Frances Biggs and woven by Terry Dunne, both of Dublin.

**Most Rev Joseph Duffy DD**
Bishop Emeritus
born 3 February 1934; ordained priest 22 June 1958; ordained Bishop of Clogher 2 September 1979
*Residence:* Doire na gCraobh, Monaghan
Tel 047-62725
Email doirenagcraobh@gmail.com

## CHAPTER

*Dean:* Rt Rev Mgr Seán Cahill
*Archdeacon:* Rt Rev Mgr Vincent Connolly
*Members*
Very Rev Macartan McQuaid
Very Rev Joseph Mullin
Very Rev John McKenna
Very Rev Laurence Dawson
Very Rev John Finnegan
Rt Rev Mgr Joseph McGuinness
Very Rev John McCabe
Very Rev Larry Duffy
Very Rev Ramon Munster
Very Rev Peter O'Reilly

## ADMINISTRATION

**Vicars General**
Rt Rev Mgr Seán Cahill VG
6 Boyhill Road, Maguiresbridge,
Enniskillen, Co Fermanagh BT94 4LN
Tel 028-67721258
Rt Rev Mgr Vincent Connolly PP, VG
St Joseph's, Carrickmacross,
Co Monaghan
Tel 042-9663200

**Chancellor**
Rt Rev Mgr Joseph McGuinness, Adm
Tyholland, Monaghan
Tel 047-85385 Fax 047-85051
Email diocesanoffice@clogherdiocese.ie

**Vicars Forane**
Very Rev Canon Larry Duffy
Very Rev Canon Joseph Mullin
Very Rev Patrick McHugh

**Council of Administration**
Rt Rev Mgr Seán Cahill
Rt Rev Mgr Vincent Connolly
Rt Rev Mgr Joseph McGuinness

**Finance Committee**
*Chairman:* Most Rev Liam S. MacDaid
*Members*
Rt Rev Mgr Sean Cahill
Rt Rev Mgr Vincent Connolly
Rt Rev Mgr Joseph McGuinness
Mr Desmond McKenna
*Financial Administrator*
Mr Joseph Berwick
Bishop's House, Monaghan
Tel 047-81019 Fax 047-84773
Email diocesanoffice@clogherdiocese.ie

**Diocesan Secretary**
Rt Rev Mgr Joseph McGuinness, Adm
Tyholland, Monaghan
Tel 047-85385 Fax 047-85051
Email diocesanoffice@clogherdiocese.ie

**Communications Officer & Co-ordinator of Diocesan Website**
Rev Noel McConnell CC
Shantonagh, Castleblayney, Co Monaghan
Tel 042-9745015
Email ntmcconnell@yahoo.co.uk

## CATECHETICS EDUCATION

**Adult Faith Development**
*Diocesan Adviser*
Very Rev Canon Macartan McQuaid
St Michael's College, Enniskillen,
Co Fermanagh BT74 6DE
Tel 028-66322935 Fax 028-66325128
Email mmcquaid@saintmichaels.org.uk

**Catholic Primary School Managers' Association (RI)**
*Diocesan Council Secretary*
Very Rev Michael Daly PP
Broomfield, Castleblayney, Co Monaghan
Tel 042-9743617
Email dalyml@eircom.net

**Diocesan Education (NI)**
*Administrator:* Ms Suzette Bracken
Clogher Diocesan Education Office,
8 Darling Street, Enniskillen,
Co Fermanagh BT74 7DP
Tel 028-66322709 Fax 028-66327939

**Religious Education**
*Diocesan Advisers*
*Primary:* Rev John Flanagan CC
Roslea, Enniskillen,
Co Fermanagh BT92 7LA
Tel 028-67751393
Mrs Eileen Gallagher
St Michael's College,
Enniskillen, Co Fermanagh
(NI Schools) (Friday 9.00am-5.00pm)
Tel 028-66328210
Email egallagher@stmichaels.org.uk
*Post-Primary:* Ms Claudine Marron
St Macartan's College, Monaghan
Tel 047-72795 Fax 047-83341
Email claudinesh@eircom.net

## LITURGY

**Church Music**
*Director*
Rt Rev Mgr Joseph McGuinness Adm
Parochial House, Tyholland, Monaghan
Tel 047-85385 Fax 047-85051

**Diocesan Liturgy Commission**
*Chairman*
Rt Rev Mgr Joseph McGuinness Adm
Parochial House, Tyholland, Monaghan
Tel 047-85385 Fax 047-85051
*Secretary*
Very Rev Owen J. McEneaney Adm
The Presbytery, Park Street, Monaghan
Tel 047-81220 Fax 047-84004
Email
parishoffice@stjosephspresbytery.com

## PASTORAL

**Accord**
*Diocesan Directors:* Rev John Chester
St Joseph's Presbytery,
Park Street, Monaghan
Tel 047-81220 Fax 047-84004
Email
parishoffice@stjosephspresbytery.com
Rev John Skinnader (CSSp) CC
4 Darling Street, Enniskillen,
Co Fermanagh BT74 7DP
Tel 028-66322075
Fax 028-66322248

**Asylum Network Liaison Group**
*Chairperson:* Very Rev Brian Early PP
Scotstown, Co Monaghan
Tel 047-89204 Fax 047-79772
Email bearly@eircom.net

**Council of Priests**
*Chairman*
Very Rev Canon Larry Duffy PP, VF
Clones, Co Monaghan
Tel 047-51048
Email clonesparish@eircom.net
*Secretary:* Rev Ian Fee CC
Lisnaskea, Co Fermanagh BT92 0JE
Tel 028-67721324
Email ianfee@aol.com

**Ecumenism**
*Director*
Rt Rev Mgr Vincent Connolly PP, VG
St Joseph's, Carrickmacross,
Co Monaghan
Tel 042-9663200
Email stjosephscarrickmacross@eircom.net

**Emigrants**
*Director:* Very Rev Lorcan Lynch PP
Derrygonnelly, Enniskillen,
Co Fermanagh BT93 6HW
Tel 028-68641207

**Lourdes Pilgrimage**
*Director*
Very Rev Canon Joseph Mullin PP, VF
Lisoneill, Lisnaskea,
Co Fermanagh BT92 0JE
Tel 028-67721342

**Marriage Tribunal**
*Clogher Office of Armagh Regional Marriage Tribunal*
Sr Elizabeth Fee
St Michael's Parish Centre,
28 Church Street, Enniskillen,
Co Fermanagh BT74 7EJ
Tel 028-66347860

**Pioneer Total Abstinence Association**
*Directors:* Rev James McPhillips CC
Killanny, Carrickmacross, Co Monaghan
Tel 042-9661452
Email jimmymcp@eircom.net
Rev Ian Fee CC
Lisnaskea, Enniskillen,
Co Fermanagh BT92 0JE
Tel 028-67721324
Email ianfee@aol.com

**Pontifical Mission Societies**
*Diocesan Director*
Very Rev Canon John McCabe PP
Parochial House, Roslea,
Co Fermanagh BT92 7LA
Tel/Fax 028-67751227

**Travellers**
*Chaplain:* Rev Michael Jordan CC
Parochial House, Donaghmoyne,
Co Monaghan
Tel 042-9661586
Email michaeljordan@eircom.net

**Vocations**
*Director and Chairman of Vocations Committee:* Rt Rev Mgr Seán Cahill VG
6 Boyhill Road, Maguiresbridge,
Enniskillen, Co Fermanagh BT94 4LN
Tel 028-67721258

**Youth Ministry Co-ordinator**
Mr Matthew McFadden
Clogher don Óige,
St Macartan's College, Monaghan
Tel 047-72784
Email info@clogherdonoige.com
Website www.clogherdonoige.com

## PARISHES

*The mensal parish is listed first. Other parishes follow alphabetically. In each case the postal name is given first, except where inappropriate, and the official name in parentheses. Church titulars are in italics.*

**MONAGHAN**
*St Macartan's Cathedral, St Joseph's, St Michael's*
Email parishoffice@stjosephspresbytery.com
Very Rev Owen J. McEneaney Adm
Rev Patrick McGinn CC
Rev John Chester CC
Email jchester@stjosephspresbytery.com
St Joseph's Presbytery, Park Street,
Monaghan
Tel 047-81220 Fax 047-84004

**ARNEY (CLEENISH)**
*St Mary's, Arney*
*St Patrick's, Holywell*
*St Joseph's, Mullaghdun*
Very Rev Canon John Finnegan PP
Arney, Enniskillen,
Co Fermanagh BT92 2AB
Tel 028-66348217
Email cleenish@btinternet.com
Rev Seamus Quinn CC
Belcoo, Enniskillen,
Co Fermanagh BT93 5FJ
Tel/Fax 028-66386225
Email ocoinne@gmail.com

**AUGHNAMULLEN EAST**
*Sacred Heart, Lough Egish*
*St Mary's, Carrickatee*
Very Rev Thomas Quigley PP
Latton, Castleblayney, Co Monaghan
Tel 042-9742212
Rev Noel McConnell CC
Shantonagh, Castleblayney, Co Monaghan
Tel 042-9745015
Email ntmcconnell@yahoo.co.uk

**BALLYBAY (TULLYCORBET)**
*St Patrick's, Ballybay*
*Holy Rosary, Tullycorbet*
*Our Lady of Knock, Ballintra*
Very Rev Laurence Flynn PP
Tel/Fax 042-9741032
Email contact@tullycorbetparish.com
Rt Rev Mgr Gerard McSorley PE
Tel/Fax 042-9741031
Ballybay, Co Monaghan

**BELLEEK-GARRISON (INIS MUIGHE SAMH)**
*Our Lady, Queen of Peace, Garrison*
*St John the Baptist, Toura*
*St Joseph's, Cashelnadrea*
*St Patrick's, Belleek*
*St Michael's, Mulleek*
Very Rev Tiernach Beggan PP
Belleek, Enniskillen,
Co Fermanagh BT93 3FJ
Tel 028-68658229
Email belleekgarrison@btinternet.com
Rev Joseph McVeigh CC
Loughside Road, Garrison, Enniskillen,
Co Fermanagh BT93 4AE
Tel 028-68659747
Very Rev Canon Patrick Lonergan PE
Garrison, Enniskillen,
Co Fermanagh BT93 4AE
Tel 028-68658234

**BROOKEBORO (AGHAVEA-AGHINTAINE)**
*St Mary's, Brookeboro*
*St Joseph's, Coonian*
*St Mary's, Fivemiletown*
Very Rev Denis Dolan PP
Fivemiletown,
Co Tyrone, BT75 OQP
Tel 028-89521291

**BUNDORAN (MAGH ENE)**
*Our Lady, Star of the Sea, Bundoran*
*St Joseph's, The Rock, Ballyshannon*
Very Rev Canon Ramon Munster PP
Bundoran, Co Donegal
Tel 071-9841290 Fax 071-9841596
Email ppbundoran@eircom.net
Rev Frank McManus CC
The Rock, Ballyshannon, Co Donegal
Tel 071-9851221
Email stjrock@eircom.net

**CARRICKMACROSS (MACHAIRE ROIS)**
*St Joseph's, Carrickmacross*
*St Michael's, Corduff*
*St John the Evangelist, Raferagh*
Rt Rev Mgr Vincent Connolly PP, VG
Tel 042-9663200
Email stjosephscarrickmacross@eircom.net
Rev Padraig McKenna CC
Tel 042-9661231
St Joseph's, Carrickmacross,
Co Monaghan
Rev Brendan McCague CC
Corduff, Carrickmacross, Co Monaghan
Tel 042-9669456

**CASTLEBLAYNEY (MUCKNO)**
*St Mary's, Castleblayney*
*St Patrick's, Oram*
Very Rev Patrick McHugh PP, VF
Tel 042-9740051
Rev Kevin Duffy CC
Rev Adrian Walshe CC
Email mucknoparish@eircom.net
Tel 042-9740027
Castleblayney, Co Monaghan

**CLOGHER**
*St Patrick's, St Macartan's*
Very Rev Canon Laurence Dawson PP
Clogher, Co Tyrone BT76 0TQ
Tel 028-85548600
Email dawson829@btinternet.com
Rev John F. McKenna CC
19 Ballagh Road, Clogher,
Co Tyrone BT76 0TQ
Tel 028-85548525
Email jmckenna420@live.ie

**CLONES**
*Sacred Heart, Clones*
*St Macartan's, Aghadrumsee*
*St Alphonsus, Connons*
Very Rev Canon Larry Duffy PP, VF
Clones, Co Monaghan
Tel 047-51048
Email clonesparish@eircom.net
Rev John Kearns CC
Priests' House, Clones, Co Monaghan
Tel/Fax 047-51064
Email jkearnzie@hotmail.com
Rev Owen Gorman (OCDS) CC
Aghadrumsee, Roslea, Enniskillen,
Co Fermanagh BT92 7NQ
Tel 028-67751231

**CLONTIBRET**
*St Michael's, Annyalla*
*St Mary's, Clontibret*
*All Saints, Doohamlet*
Very Rev Paudge McDonnell PP
Annyalla, Castleblayney, Co Monaghan
Tel 042-9740121
Email ppclontibretparish@eircom.net
Rev Keneth McCabe (SSCC) CC
Clontibret, Co Monaghan
Tel 047-80631
Very Rev Canon Philip Connolly PE
Doohamlet Castleblayney, Co Monaghan
Tel 042-9741239

**CORCAGHAN (KILMORE AND DRUMSNAT)**
*St Michael's, Corcaghan*
*St Mary's, Threemilehouse*
Very Rev Joseph McCluskey PP
Threemilehouse, Monaghan
Tel 047-81501
Email frmccluskey@gmail.com
Very Rev Thomas Coffey PE
Corcaghan, Monaghan
Tel 042-9744806

**DERRYGONNELLY (BOTHA)**
*St Patrick's, Derrygonnelly*
*Sacred Heart, Boho*
*Immaculate Conception, Monea*
Very Rev Lorcan Lynch PP
Derrygonnelly, Enniskillen,
Co Fermanagh BT93 6HW
Tel 028-68641207
Email frlynch@parishofbotha.com
Rev Seamus Quinn CC
Belcoo, Enniskillen,
Co Fermanagh BT93 5FJ
Tel/Fax 028-66386225
Email ocoinne@gmail.com

**DONAGH**
*St Mary's, Glennan*
*St Patrick's, Corracrin*
Very Rev Hubert Martin PP
Glaslough, Monaghan
Tel 047-88120
Email donaghparish@emyvale.eu
Very Rev Canon Macartan McQuaid
*(Weekends only)*
Emyvale, Co Monaghan
Tel 047-87221

**DONAGHMOYNE**
*St Lastra's, Donaghmoyne*
*St Patrick's, Broomfield*
*St Mary's, Lisdoonan*
Very Rev Michael Daly PP
Broomfield, Castleblayney, Co Monaghan
Tel 042-9743617
Email dalyml@eircom.net
Rev Michael Jordan CC
Parochial House, Donaghmoyne,
Co Monaghan
Tel 042-9661586
Email michaeljordan@eircom.net

**DROMORE**
*St Davog's*
Very Rev Patrick MacEntee PP
Shanmullagh, Dromore, Omagh,
Co Tyrone BT78 3DZ
Tel 028-82898641
Email pmacentee@tiscali.co.uk
Very Rev Canon Thomas Breen PE
37 Esker Road, Dromore, Omagh,
Co Tyrone BT78 3LE
Tel 028-82898216

**EDERNEY (CÚL MÁINE)**
*St Joseph's, Ederney*
*St Patrick's, Montiagh*
Very Rev Brendan Gallagher PP
Ederney, Enniskillen,
Co Fermanagh BT93 0DG
Tel 028-68631315
Email admin@culmaine.co.uk

**ENNISKILLEN**
*St Michael's, Enniskillen*
*St Mary's, Lisbellaw*
Very Rev Canon Peter O'Reilly PP
1 Darling Street, Enniskillen,
Co Fermanagh BT74 7DP
Tel 028-66322627
Email pp@st-michaels.net
Rev Noel McGahan CC
Rev John Skinnader (CSSp) CC
Rev Martin O'Reilly CC
4 Darling Street, Enniskillen,
Co Fermanagh BT74 7DP
Tel 028-66322075 Fax 028-66322248
Email parishcentre@st-michaels.net

**ERRIGAL TRUAGH**
*Holy Family, Ballyoisin*
*St Patrick's, Clara*
*Sacred Heart, Carrickroe*
Very Rev Seán Nolan PP
St Joseph's, Emyvale, Monaghan
Tel/Fax 047-87152
Email tru@tinet.ie
Very Rev Canon Macartan McQuaid
*(Weekends only)*
Emyvale, Monaghan
Tel 047-87221

**ESKRA**
*St Patrick's*
Very Rev Terence Connolly PP
178 Newtownsaville Road,
Omagh, Co Tyrone BT78 2RJ
Tel 028-82841306
Email terence.connolly1@btinternet.com

**FINTONA (DONACAVEY)**
*St Laurence's*
Very Rev James Moore PP
Tel 028-82841907
Email frjlm@hotmail.com
Very Rev Canon Patrick Marron PE
Tel 028-82841239 Fax 028-82840302
Email fintonaparish@hotmail.com
Fintona, Omagh, Co Tyrone BT78 2NS

**INNISKEEN**
*Mary, Mother of Mercy*
Very Rev Martin Treanor PP
Inniskeen, Dundalk, Co Louth
Tel 042-9378105
Email martintreanor@eircom.net
Rev Noel Conlon CC
Inniskeen, Dundalk, Co Louth
Tel 042-9378678

**IRVINESTOWN (DEVENISH)**
*Sacred Heart, Irvinestown*
*St Molaise, Whitehill*
Very Rev Michael McGourty PP
Irvinestown, Enniskillen,
Co Fermanagh BT94 1EY
Tel 028-68628600
Email mmcgourty210@live.co.uk
Very Rev Canon Gerald Timoney PE
Irvinestown, Enniskillen,
Co Fermanagh BT94 1GD
Tel 028-68621329

**KILLANNY**
*St Enda's*
Very Rev Martin Treanor PP
Inniskeen, Dundalk, Co Louth
Tel 042-9378105
Email martintreanor@eircom.net
Rev James McPhillips CC
Killanny, Carrickmacross, Co Monaghan
Tel 042-9661452
Email jimmymcp@eircom.net

**KILLEEVAN (CURRIN, KILLEEVAN AND AGHABOG)**
*St Livinus', Killeevan, St Mary's, Ture*
*Immaculate Conception, Scotshouse*
*St Mary's, Latnamard*
Very Rev Peter Corrigan PP
Shanco, Newbliss, Co Monaghan
Tel 047-54011
Email killeevanparish@eircom.net
Rev Cathal Deery CC
Scotshouse, Clones, Co Monaghan
Tel 047-56016
Email cdeery1966@gmail.com

**LATTON (AUGHNAMULLEN WEST)**
*St Mary's, Latton, St Patrick's, Bawn*
Very Rev Thomas Quigley PP
Latton, Castleblayney, Co Monaghan
Tel 042-9742212
Email tomquigleylatton@gmail.com

**LISNASKEA (AGHALURCHER)**
*Holy Cross, Lisnaskea*
*St Mary's, Maguiresbridge*
Very Rev Canon Joseph Mullin PP, VF
Tel 028-67721342
Rev Ian Fee CC
Tel 028-67721324
Email ianfee@aol.com
Lisnaskea, Enniskillen,
Co Fermanagh BT92 0JE
Rt Rev Mgr Seán Cahill VG
6 Boyhill Road, Maguiresbridge,
Enniskillen, Co Fermanagh BT94 4LN
Tel 028-67721258

**MAGHERACLOONE**
*St Patrick's (The Rock Chapel), Carrickasedge*
*SS Peter and Paul, Drumgossatt*
Very Rev Thomas Finnegan PP
Liscarnan, Magheracloone,
Carrickmacross, Co Monaghan
Tel 042-9663500
Email magheraclooneparish@eircom.net
Rev Philip Crowe (CSSp) CC
Drumgossatt, Carrickmacross,
Co Monaghan
Tel 042-9661388

**NEWTOWNBUTLER (GALLOON)**
*St Mary's, Newtownbutler*
*St Patrick's, Donagh, Lisnaskea*
Very Rev Michael King PP
Tel 028-67738229
Very Rev Canon Edward Murphy PE
Tel 028-67738640
Newtownbutler, Enniskillen,
Co Fermanagh BT92 8JJ

**PETTIGO**
*St Mary's, Pettigo*
*St Joseph's, Lettercran*
Rt Rev Mgr Richard Mohan Adm
Pettigo, Co Donegal
Tel 071-9861666
Lough Derg (See Charitable Societies)
Tel/Fax 071-9861518
Email pettigoparish@loughderg.org

**ROCKCORRY (EMATRIS)**
*Holy Trinity, St Mary's, Corrawacan*
Very Rev Thomas Quigley PP
Latton, Castleblayney, Co Monaghan
Tel 042-9742212
Very Rev Canon Gerard Ferguson PE
Rockcorry, Monaghan
Tel 042-9742243

**ROSLEA**
*St Tierney's, Roslea*
*St Mary's, Magherarney*
Very Rev Canon John McCabe PP
Parochial House, Roslea,
Co Fermanagh BT92 7LA
Tel/Fax 028-67751227
Email rosleaparish@btinternet.com
Rev John Flanagan CC
Roslea, Enniskillen,
Co Fermanagh BT92 7LA
Tel 028-67751393

**TEMPO (POBAL)**
*Immaculate Conception, Tempo*
*St Joseph's, Cradien*
Very Rev John Halton PP
Tempo, Enniskillen,
Co Fermanagh BT94 3LY
Tel 028-89541344
Email johnhalton19@btinternet.com

**TRILLICK (KILSKEERY)**
*St Macartan's, Trillick*
*St Mary's, Coa*
Very Rev Canon John McKenna PP
Trillick, Omagh, Co Tyrone BT78 3RD
Tel 028-89561350
Email john.mckenna35@btinternet.com
Very Rev Canon Thomas Marron PE
Trillick, Omagh, Co Tyrone BT78 3RD
Tel 028-89561217

**TYDAVNET**
*St Dympna's, Tydavnet*
*St Mary's, Urbleshanny*
*St Joseph's, Knockatallon*
Very Rev Brian Early PP
Scotstown, Co Monaghan
Tel 047-89204 Fax 047-79772
Email bearly@eircom.net
Very Rev Canon Sean Clerkin PE
Tydavnet, Co Monaghan
Tel/Fax 047-89402
Email sclerkin@utvinternet.com

**TYHOLLAND**
*St Patrick's*
Rt Rev Mgr Joseph McGuinness Adm
Tyholland, Monaghan
Tel 047-85385 Fax 047-85051
Email diocesanoffice@clogherdiocese.ie

## INSTITUTIONS AND THEIR CHAPLAINS

**Daughters of Our Lady of the Sacred Heart Convent**
Ballybay, Co Monaghan
Rev Gerard Jennings
Tel 042-9741524

**Erne Hospital, Enniskillen**
Curates of Enniskillen Parish
Tel 028-66322075 Fax 028-66322248

**Finner Army Camp**
Ballyshannon, Co Donegal
Rev Alan Ward CF
Tel 071-9842294

**Monaghan General Hospital**
Curates of Monaghan parish
Tel 047-81220 Fax 047-84004

**St Davnet's Hospital, Monaghan**
Curates of Monaghan parish
Tel 047-81220 Fax 047-84004

**St Mary's Hospital**
Castleblayney, Co Monaghan
Curates of Castleblayney parish
Tel 042-9740027

## PRIESTS OF THE DIOCESE ELSEWHERE

Rev Dr Patrick Connolly
Theology Department,
Mary Immaculate College,
South Circular Road, Limerick
Tel 061-204575 Fax 061-313632
Email patrick.connolly@mic.ul.ie
Rev Jeremiah Carroll
Archdiocese of Dublin/Defence Forces

*Study Leave/contact addresses*
Rev Benedict Hughes
Kellystown, Coolderry Road,
Carrickmacross, Co Monaghan
Tel 086-3864907
Rev Terence McElvaney
Church Square, Monaghan
Tel 047-82255

## RETIRED PRIESTS

Most Rev Joseph Duffy DD
Bishop Emeritus
Doire na gCraobh, Monaghan
Tel 047-62725
Email doirenagcraobh@gmail.com
Very Rev Liam Hughes PE
Inniskeen, Dundalk, Co Louth
Tel 042-9378338 Fax 042-9378988
Very Rev Canon Brian McCluskey PE
Apt 2, 2 Danesfort Park North,
Stranmillis Road, Belfast BT9 5RB
Tel 028-90683544
Very Rev Edmond Maguire PE
Newtownbutler Road, Clones,
Co Monaghan
Tel 047-51160
Rev Joseph McKenna
(Birmingham Diocese)
1 St Joseph's Villas, Church Road,
Bundoran, Co Donegal
Tel 071-9841756
Very Rev Canon Gerard McGreevy PE
Magherarney, Smithboro,
Co Monaghan
Tel 047-57011
Very Rev Canon Peter McGuinness PE
3 Castleross Retirement Village,
Carrickmacross, Co Monaghan
Tel 042-9690013

## RELIGIOUS ORDERS AND CONGREGATIONS

### PRIESTS

**PASSIONISTS**
St Gabriel's Retreat,
The Graan, Enniskillen, Co Fermanagh
Tel 028-66322272 Fax 028-66325201
*Superior:* Rev Brian D'Arcy (CP)
Email crccp@aol.com

**SACRED HEARTS COMMUNITY**
Cootehill, Co Cavan
Tel 049-5552188
Rev Jerry White (SSCC)
Email jerrysscc@eircom.net
Br Harry O'Gara (SSCC)

St Mary's,
Clontibret, Co Monaghan
Tel 047-80631
Rev Kenneth McCabe

### SISTERS

**CONGREGATION OF THE SISTERS OF MERCY**
Northern Province, Provincial House,
74 Main Street, Clogher,
Co Tyrone BT76 0AA
Tel 028-85548127 Fax 028-85549459
*Provincial Leader:* Sr Nellie McLaughlin

11 Castlehill Gardens, Augher,
Co Tyrone BT77 0HA
Tel 028-85548157

Castleblayney, Co Monaghan
Tel 042-9740069
*Contact:* Sr Margaret McQuaid
Community: 11

St Brigid's, 2 Ballagh Road, Clogher,
Co Tyrone BT76 0HE
Tel 028-85548015

Convent of Mercy, 6 Belmore Street,
Enniskillen, Co Fermanagh
Tel 028-66322561
*Shared Leaders:* Srs Monica Gallagher & Carmel McNally
Community: 20

55 Carrowshee Park, Lisnaskea,
Co Fermanagh BT92 0FR
Tel 028-67721955

Gate House, 72 Main Street, Clogher,
Co Tyrone BT76 0AA
Tel 028-85549545

Sisters of Mercy, 6 Gorminish Park,
Garrison, Co Fermanagh BT93 4GP
Tel 028-68659742

No. 16 The Grange,
Presentation Walk, Monaghan
Tel 047-84569

Buíochas, 29 The Commons, Bellanaleck,
Enniskillen, Co Fermanagh BT92 2BD
Tel 028-66349722

6 Ferndale,
Clogher, Co Tyrone BT76 0AS
Tel 028-85548163

St Faber's, 8 Castlecourt, Monea,
Co Fermanagh BT93 7AR
Tel 028-66341197

73 Scaffog Avenue, Sligo Road,
Enniskillen, Co Fermanagh BT74 7JJ
Tel 028-66327474

2 Erne Marina, Bellanaleck,
Enniskillen, Co Fermanagh BT92 2BA

The Graan Farmhouse,
Derrygonnelly Road, Enniskillen,
Co Fermanagh BT74 5PB
Tel 028-66346817

30 Silver Hill Manor, Enniskillen,
Co Fermanagh BT74 5JE
Tel 028-66320792

11 Coolcrannel Square, Maguiresbridge,
Co Fermanagh BT94 4RE
Tel 028-67723570

**DAUGHTERS OF OUR LADY OF THE SACRED HEART**
Ballybay, Co Monaghan
Tel 042-9741068
*Superior:* Sr Aloysius O'Rourke
Community: 6
St Joseph's Nursing Home
*Superior:* Sr Kathleen McQuillan
Tel 042-9741141. Beds: 26
Community: 17

**ST LOUIS SISTERS**
St Louis Convent, Louisville, Monaghan
Tel 047-81411
Community: 20
Varied apostolates
Post-Primary School. Tel 047-81422
Pupils: 820
Primary School. Tel 047-81305
Pupils: 237
Infant School. Tel 047-82913
Pupils: 278

Our Lady's Community,
Louisville, Monaghan
Tel 047-82006
Community: 5
Varied apostolates

5 Lakeview, Monaghan
Tel 047-84122
Community: 2
Varied apostolates

St Raphael, 3 Lakeview, Monaghan
Tel 047-84719
Community: 2
Varied apostolates

173 Mullaghmatt, Monaghan
Tel 047-84110
Community: 2
Varied apostolates

Rowan Tree Court,
24 Mullach Glas Close, Monaghan
Tel 047-38685
Community: 1

Carrickmacross, Co Monaghan
Tel 042-9661247
Community: 18
Varied apostolates
Secondary. Tel 042-9661587/9661467
Pupils: 600

Iona House, Farney Street
Carrickmacross, Co Monaghan
Tel 042-9663326
Community: 3
Varied apostolates

15 Plás Fionnbara, Taillte an Chlochair,
Carrickmacross, Co Monaghan
Tel 042-9670126
Community: 2
Varied Apostolates

Clondergole, Clones, Co Monaghan
Tel 047-51136
Community: 1
Parish work

4 White Maple Drive,
Bundoran, Co Donegal
Tel 071-9829505
Community: 3
Varied apostolates

5 White Maple Drive,
Bundoran, Co Donegal
Tel 071-9841330
Community: 1
Varied apostolates

## EDUCATIONAL INSTITUTIONS

**St Macartan's College**
Monaghan, Co Monaghan
Tel 047-81642/83365/83367
Fax 047-83341
Email admin@stmacartanscollege.ie
*Manager*
Very Rev Shane McCaughey BD
*Principal*
Mr Raymond McHugh BA, HDipEd, MSc
*Chaplain*
Rev Stephen Joyce
Email joyces@eircom.net

**St Michael's College**
Enniskillen, Co Fermanagh BT74 6DE
Tel 028-66322935
Fax 028-66325128
Email office@saintmichaels.org.uk
*Principal:* Mr Eugene McCullough
*Chaplain*
Very Rev Canon Macartan McQuaid
Email mmcquaid@stmichaels.org.uk

## CHARITABLE AND OTHER SOCIETIES

**ACCORD**
St Macartan's College, Monaghan
Tel 047-83359
(10am-1pm Mon-Fri)

Ros Erne House,
8 Darling Street, Enniskillen,
Co Fermanagh BT74 7EW
Tel 028-66325696
(9am-5pm Mon-Fri)

**CURA**
7 The Grange, Plantation Walk,
Monaghan
Tel 047-83600
*Contact person:* Sr Brenda McCrudden

**Lough Derg, St Patrick's Purgatory**
Pettigo, Co Donegal
Tel/Fax 071-9861518
Email info@loughderg.org
*Prior:* Rt Rev Mgr Richard Mohan
*Manager:* Ms Deborah Maxwell
Email manager@loughderg.org
Pilgrimage season, 1 June-15 August.
No advance booking or notice required.
Pilgrims arrive daily before 3 pm, having fasted from midnight, and remain on the island for two complete days of prayer and penance.
One-day retreats before and after main pilgrimage season.
School retreats also offered.
Tel for details and reservations.

**Veritas Bookshop & Christian Art Gallery**
Park Street, Monaghan
*Manager:* Ms Mary Flynn
Tel 047-84077

# DIOCESE OF CLONFERT

PATRON OF THE DIOCESE
ST BRENDAN, 16 MAY

INCLUDES PORTIONS OF COUNTIES GALWAY, OFFALY AND ROSCOMMON

**Most Rev John Kirby DD**
Bishop of Clonfert;
born October 1938;
ordained priest 23 June 1963;
ordained Bishop of Clonfert
9 April 1988

Residence: Coorheen,
Loughrea, Co Galway
Tel 091-841560
Fax 091-841818
Email clonfert@iol.ie

## ST BRENDAN'S CATHEDRAL, LOUGHREA

St Brendan's Cathedral stands at the western extremity of the Diocese of Clonfert on the main highway from Dublin to Galway. The foundation stone of the cathedral was laid on 10 October 1897, and the fabric was completed in 1902. Plans were drawn by the Dublin architect William Byrne for a building in the neo-Gothic style, having a nave and an aspidal sanctuary, lean-to aisles and shallow transepts, with a graceful spire at the western end. Its dimensions were determined by the needs of the parish of Loughrea. While not impressive, its proportions are good, and despite a departure from the original plan by curtailment of the sanctuary, the overall effect is pleasing. The simplicity of the exterior, however, hardly prepares the visitor for the riches within.

It was due to two fortuitous circumstances that St Brendan's became a veritable treasure house of the Celtic Revival in sculpture, stained glass, woodcarving, metalwork and textiles.

The first circumstance was that the building of a Catholic cathedral was delayed for various reasons until close to the turn of the last century. The Irish Literary Renaissance was by then well advanced. When the building was completed in 1902, the Arts and Crafts movement was having effect.

The second circumstance was that of Edward Martyn's birth at the home of his maternal grandfather, James Smyth, in the parish of Loughrea. Martyn was an ascetic man and devoted his time and fortune to the development of every phase of the Irish revival, the Gaelic League, Sinn Féin, the Irish Literary Theatre, Irish music, church music and church art. With innate business acumen, he insured by personal donation and the financial support of the Smyth family that the new cathedral would reflect his views. The bishop, Dr John Healy, who was sensitive to the prevailing trend, accepted the challenge and assigned the project to the supervision of a young curate in the parish, Fr Jeremiah O'Donovan, who was himself actively engaged in propaganda for Revival.

John Hughes was the foremost sculptor in the country at the time, and Bishop Healy commissioned him to do the modelling and carving. His work is found in the bronze figure of Christ on the reredos of the high altar and in the magnificent marble statue of the Virgin and Child. Michael Shortall, a student of Hughes in the Metropolitan School of Art, did the carvings on the corbels and executed the statue of St Brendan on the wall of the tower. His connection with the cathedral continued over twenty years, and he was responsible for carvings of incidents from the life and voyage of St Brendan carved on the capitals of the pillars.

The Yeats sisters, Lily and Elizabeth, along with their friend Evelyn Gleeson, set up the Dun Emer guild. They embroidered twenty-four banners of Irish saints for use in the cathedral. Jack B. Yeats and his wife Mary designed these banners. With an economy of detail and richness of colour, they almost achieve the effect of stained glass. Mass vestments, embroidered with silk on poplin, also came from the same studio.

More than anything else, St Brendan's is famous for its stained glass. Martyn was particularly concerned about the quality of stained glass then available in Ireland. He was eager to set up an Irish stained-glass industry. He succeeded in having Alfred E. Childe appointed to the Metropolitan School of Art, and he later persuaded Sarah Purser to open a co-operative studio, where young artists could be trained in the technique of stained glass. This new studio, An Túr Gloinne, opened in January 1903, with Childe as manager, and so began the work of the Loughrea stained-glass windows. Over the next forty years, Childe, Purser and Michael Healy executed almost all the stained-glass windows in the cathedral, and it is these windows that have given St Brendan's its place in the Irish Artistic Revival.

## ADMINISTRATION

**Vicar General**
Rt Rev Mgr Cathal Geraghty VG
St Brendan's Cathedral, Barrack Street,
Loughrea, Co Galway
Tel 091-841212

**Vicars Forane**
Very Rev Michael Finneran PP
Very Rev Ciaran Kitching PP
Very Rev Martin McNamara PP

**Bishop's Secretary**
Ms Marcella Fallon
Coorheen, Loughrea, Co Galway
Tel 091-841560
Email clonfert@iol.ie

**Diocesan Secretary**
Vacant

**Chancellor**
Rt Rev Mgr Cathal Geraghty VG
St Brendan's Cathedral, Barrack Street,
Loughrea, Co Galway
Tel 091-841212

**College of Consultors**
Very Rev Michael Finneran PP, VF
Very Rev Ciaran Kitching PP
Very Rev John Garvey Adm
Very Rev Cathal Geraghty Adm
Very Rev Martin McNamara PP

**Diocesan Finance Committe**
Most Rev John Kirby DD
Very Rev Cathal Geraghty VG
Very Rev Martin McNamara PP
Mr Gerard McInerney
Mr Terry Doyle
Mr Patrick McDonagh
Mr Sean O'Dwyer
Mrs Nancy O'Gorman

**Diocesan Council of Priests**
*Chairman*
Very Rev Seamus Bohan PP
Tynagh, Loughrea, Co Galway
Tel 090-9745113
*Secretary:* Very Rev P. J. Bracken PP
Fahy, Eyrecourt, Ballinasloe, Co Galway
Tel 090-9675116
*Members*
Most Rev John Kirby DD
Right Rev Mgr Ned Stankard PP
Very Rev Michael Finneran PP, VF
Very Rev Ciaran Kitching PP
Very Rev John Garvey Adm
Rt Rev Cathal Geraghty Adm
Rev Bernard Costello
Rev Iomar Daniels
Rev Declan Kelly
Rev Thomas Shanahan (ODC)

**Diocesan Archivist**
Very Rev Declan Kelly PP
St Andrew's Church, Leitrim,
Loughrea, Co Galway
Tel 091-841758

## CATECHETICS EDUCATION

**Adult Education**
Very Rev Ciaran Kitching PP
Killimor, Ballinasloe, Co Galway
Tel 090-9676151

**Catholic Primary School Managers' Association**
*Secretary:* Mr Eamon Lally
Gortnahorna, Clontuskert,
Ballinasloe, Co Galway
Tel 096-9643250

**Primary Schools**
*Diocesan Adviser*
Rev Declan McInerney
Our Lady of Lourdes, Creagh,
Ballinasloe, Co Galway
Tel 090-9645080

## PASTORAL

**Accord**
*Director:* Rev John Garvey Adm
St Michael's,
Ballinasloe, Co Galway
Tel 090-9643916

**Legion of Mary**
*Diocesan Director*
Very Rev Patrick Conroy PP
Ballinakill, Loughrea, Co Galway
Tel 090-9745021

**Marriage Tribunal**
(See Marriage Tribunals section)

**Mixed Marriages**
*Counsellor*
Rt Rev Mgr Edward Stankard PP
Cappatagle, Ballinasloe, Co Galway
Tel 091-843017

**Pilgrimages**
*Diocesan Director:* Rev Pat Conroy PP
Ballinakill, Loughrea, Co Galway
Tel 090-9745021

**Pioneer Total Abstinence Association**
*Diocesan Director*
Very Rev John Naughton PP
Eyrecourt, Ballinasloe, Co Galway
Tel 090-9675148

**Pontificial Mission Societies**
*Diocesan Director*
Very Rev Brendan Lawless PP
Dunkellin Terrace,
Portumna, Co Galway
Tel 090-9741092

**Travellers**
*Chaplain:* Very Rev John Naughton PP
Eyrecourt, Ballinasloe, Co Galway
Tel 090-9675148

**Trócaire**
Very Rev Brendan Lawless PP
Dunkellin Terrace, Portumna, Co Galway
Tel 090-9741092

**Vocations**
*Director:* Rev Iomar Daniels
Gate Lodge, St Joseph College,
Garbally Park, Ballinasloe, Co Galway
Tel 090-9642504

## PARISHES

*Mensal parishes are listed first. Other parishes follow alphabetically. Historical names are given in parentheses. Church titulars are in italics.*

**LOUGHREA, ST BRENDAN'S CATHEDRAL**
Very Rev Cathal Geraghty Adm, VG
Rev Sean Egan CC
Rev Aidan Costello CC
Rev Raymond Sweeney CC
The Presbytery, Loughrea, Co Galway
Tel 091-841212

**BALLINASLOE, CREAGH AND KILCLOONEY**
*St Michael's, Ballinasloe*
Very Rev John Garvey Adm
Rev Dan O'Donovan
Tel 090-9643916
*Our Lady of Lourdes, Creagh*
Rev Declan McInerney CC
Creagh, Ballinasloe, Co Galway
Tel 090-9645080

**AUGHRIM AND KILCONNELL**
*St Catherine's, Aughrim*
*Sacred Heart, Kilconnell*
Very Rev Gerard Geraghty PP
Aughrim, Ballinasloe, Co Galway
Tel 090-9673724/090-9686614

**BALLINAKILL**
*St Joseph's, Ballinakill*
*St Patrick's, Derrybrien*
Very Rev Pat Conroy PP
Ballinakill, Loughrea, Co Galway
Tel 090-9745021

**BALLYMACWARD AND GURTEEN (BALLYMACWARD AND CLONKEENKERRIL)**
*SS Peter and Paul*
*St Michael's*
Very Rev Sean Slattery PP
Ballymacward, Ballinasloe, Co Galway
Tel 090-9687614
Rev Joe Long (SPS) CC
Gorteen, Ballinasloe, Co Galway
Tel 090-9677085

**CAPPATAGLE AND KILRICKLE (KILLALAGHTAN AND KILRICKLE)**
*St Michael's, Cappatagle*
*Our Lady of Lourdes, Kilrickle*
Rt Rev Mgr Edward Stankard PP
Cappatagle, Ballinasloe, Co Galway
Tel 091-843017
Rev Michael Kennedy CC
Kilrickle, Ballinasloe, Co Galway
Tel 091-843015

**CLONTUSKERT**
*St Augustine's*
Very Rev Michael Finneran PP, VF
Clontuskert, Ballinasloe, Co Galway
Tel 090-9642256

**CLOSTOKEN AND KILCONIERAN (KILCONICKNY, KILCONIERAN AND LICKERRIG)**
*Holy Family, Immaculate Conception*
Very Rev Benny Flanagan PP
Carrabane, Athenry, Co Galway
Tel 091-841103

**DUNIRY AND ABBEY (DUNIRY AND KILNELEHAN)**
*Holy Family*
Very Rev Seán Lyons PP
Duniry, Loughrea, Co Galway
Tel 090-9745125
*Assumption*
Rev John Hickey CC
Abbey, Loughrea, Co Galway
Tel 090-9745217

**EYRECOURT, CLONFERT AND MEELICK (CLONFERT, DONANAGHTA AND MEELICK)**
*St Brendan's, St Francis*
Very Rev John Naughton PP
Eyrecourt, Ballinasloe, Co Galway
Tel 090-9675148

**FAHY AND QUANSBORO (FAHY AND KILQUAIN)**
*Consoler of the Afficted, Christ the King*
Very Rev P. J. Bracken PP
Fahy, Eyrecourt, Ballinasloe, Co Galway
Tel 090-9675116

**FOHENAGH AND KILLURE (FOHENAGH AND KILGERRILL)**
*St Patrick's*
*St Teresa's*
Very Rev Christy McCormack PP
Fohenagh, Ahascragh, Ballinasloe, Co Galway
Tel 090-9688623

**KILLIMOR AND TIRANASCRAGH (KILLIMORBOLOGUE AND TIRANASCRAGH)**
*St Joseph's*
Very Rev Ciaran Kitching PP
Killimor, Ballinasloe, Co Galway
Tel 090-9676151

**KILNADEEMA AND AILLE (KILNADEEMA AND KILTESKILL)**
*St Dympna's, St Mary's, Aille, Loughrea*
Very Rev Joseph Clarke PP
Kilnadeema, Loughrea, Co Galway
Tel 091-841201

**KILTULLA AND ATTYMON (KILLIMORDALY AND KILLTULAGH)**
*SS Peter & Paul, Kiltulla,*
*St Mary's, Cloncagh,*
*St Iomar's, Killimordaly*
Very Rev Martin McNamara PP
Kiltulla, Athenry, Co Galway
Tel 091-848021
Rev Richard McMahon (CSsR) CC
Tel 091-848208

**LAWRENCETOWN AND KILTORMER (KILTORMER AND OGHILL)**
*St Mary's, St Patrick's*
Very Rev Christopher O'Byrne PP
Lawrencetown, Ballinasloe, Co Galway
Tel 090-9685613

**LEITRIM AND BALLYDUGGAN (KILCOOLEY AND LEITRIM)**
*St Andrew's, St Jarlath's, Ballyduggan*
Very Rev Declan Kelly PP
Rev Máirlín O'Conaire (ODC) Adm
St Andrew's Church, Leitrim, Loughrea, Co Galway
Tel 091-841758

**LUSMAGH**
*St Cronan's*
Very Rev Phil Hearty (CSsR) Adm
Lusmagh, Banagher, Co Offaly
Tel 0509-51358

**MULLAGH AND KILLORAN (ABBEYGORMICAN AND KILLORAN)**
*St Brendan's*
*Our Lady of the Assumption*
Very Rev Niall Foley PP
Mullagh, Loughrea, Co Galway
Tel 091-843119

**NEW INN AND BULLAUN (BULLAUN, GRANGE AND KILLAAN)**
*St Killian's, New Inn*
*St Patrick's, Bullaun*
Very Rev Pat Kenny PP
St Killian Church, New Inn, Ballinasloe, Co Galway
Tel 090-9675819

**PORTUMNA (KILMALINOGUE AND LICKMOLASSEY)**
*St Brigid's, SS Peter & Paul, Ascension*
Very Rev Brendan Lawless PP
Dunkellin Terrace, Portumna, Co Galway
Tel 090-9741092

**TAGHMACONNELL**
*St Ronan's*
Very Rev Sean Neylon PP
Taghmaconnell, Ballinasloe, Co Galway
Tel 090-9683929

**TYNAGH**
*St Lawrence's, Sacred Heart*
Very Rev Seamus Bohan PP
Tynagh, Loughrea, Co Galway
Tel 090-9745113

**WOODFORD**
*St John the Baptist, St Brendan's*
Very Rev Kieran O'Rourke PP
Looscaun, Woodford, Co Galway
Tel 090-9749100

## INSTITUTIONS AND THEIR CHAPLAINS

**Emmanuel House of Providence**
Clonfert, Ballinasloe, Co Galway
*Director:* Mr Eddie Stones
*Chaplain:* Fr Michael Kennedy
Tel 057-9151552

**Portiuncula Hospital**
Ballinasloe, Co Galway
Tel 090-9648200
Rev Bernard Costello

**St Brendan's Home**
Loughrea, Co Galway
Tel 091-871200
Rt Rev Mgr Cathal Geraghty Adm
Tel 091-841212

**St Brigid's Hospital**
Ballinasloe, Co Galway
Tel 090-9642117
Rev Bernard Costello

**Vocational School**
Loughrea, Co Galway
Tel 091-841919
Rev Raymond Sweeney CC
Tel 091-841212

**Vocational School**
New Inn, Co Galway
Tel 090-9675811
Very Rev Pat Kenny PP
Tel 090-9675819

## PRIESTS OF THE DIOCESE ELSEWHERE

Rev Martin Hough, England

## PRIESTS WORKING OUTSIDE THE DIOCESE

Rev Michael Byrnes
Galway Marriage Tribunal
Rev T. J. O'Connell
Kent, England

## RETIRED PRIESTS

Rev Patrick Naughten
Woodford, Co Galway
Tel 090-9749010
Rev Cathal Stanley
Retirement Village, Portumna, Co Galway
Tel 090-9759182
Rev Vivian Twohig
Millrace Nursing Home, River Street, Ballinasloe, Co Galway
Tel 086-8116978

## RELIGIOUS ORDERS AND CONGREGATIONS

### PRIESTS

**CARMELITES (OCD)**
The Abbey,
Loughrea, Co Galway
Tel 091-841209
Fax 091-842343
*Prior:* Rev Willie Moran (OCD)

**REDEMPTORISTS**
St Patrick's, Esker,
Athenry, Co Galway
Tel 091-844549
Fax 091-845698
*Superior*
Rev Brendan O'Rourke (CSsR)
*Vicar Superior*
Rev Patrick O'Keeffe (CSsR)

### SISTERS

**CARMELITES**
St Joseph's Monastery,
Mount Carmel, Loughrea, Co Galway
*Prioress:* Sr Mary Magdalen Dineen
Community: 9
Contemplative order, primitive observance

**CONGREGATION OF THE SISTERS OF MERCY**
Convent of Mercy, Loughrea, Co Galway
Tel 091-841354 Fax 091-847271
Community: 19

St Laurence's Fields,
Loughrea, Co Galway
Tel 091-842989
Community: 3

Sisters of Mercy,
Lake Road, Loughrea, Co Galway
Tel/Fax 091-847715
Community: 6

Beech Haven, Church Street,
Ballinasloe, Co Galway
Tel 090-9642191
Community: 4

Mount Pleasant,
Ballinasloe, Co Galway
Tel 090-9631695
Community: 4

'Cana', Garbally Drive,
Ballinasloe, Co Galway
Tel 090-9644570 Fax 090-9644834
Community: 4

7 Woodview, The Pines,
Ballinasloe, Co Galway
Tel 090-9644055
Community: 1

20 Hymany Park,
Ballinasloe, Co Galway
Tel 090-9643716
Community: 2

17 Hawthorn Crescent,
Ballinasloe, Co Galway
Tel 090-9644171
Community: 2

An Gairdín, Portumna, Co Galway
Tel 090-9741689
Community: 2

Shannon Road,
Portumna, Co Galway
Tel 090-9741035
Community: 1

St Brendan's Convent of Mercy,
Eyrecourt, Co Galway
Tel 090-9675123
Community: 2

**FRANCISCAN MISSIONARIES OF THE DIVINE MOTHERHOOD**
Regional House,
Assisi, Harbour Road,
Ballinasloe, Co Galway
Tel 090-9648952
Community: 4

Franciscan Convent, Garbally Drive,
Ballinasloe, Co Galway
Tel 090-9642314/9648548
*Local Leader:* Sr Madeleine de Cruz
Community: 26

La Verna, Brackernagh,
Ballinasloe, Co Galway
Tel 090-9643679
Community: 3

St Clare's, Brackernagh,
Ballinasloe, Co Galway
Tel 090-9643986 Fax 090-9631757
Community: 3

Bethany, Brackernagh,
Ballinasloe, Co Galway
Tel 090-9643499
Community: 2

San Damiano, Ard Mhuire, Ballinasloe,
Co Galway
Community: 5

## EDUCATIONAL INSTITUTIONS

**Portumna Community School**
Portumna, Co Galway
*Chairman, BOM*
Very Rev P. J. Bracken BSc, HDE
Tel 090-9675116
*Chaplain:* Rev Abe Kennedy
St Molaise's, Portumna, Co Galway
Tel 090-9741188 (H)
Tel 090-9741053 (S)

**St Joseph's College**
Garbally Park, Ballinasloe, Co Galway
Tel 090-9642504 / 9642254
*President*
Very Rev Colm Allman BA, HDE
*Staff*
Rev Iomar Daniels

# DIOCESE OF CLOYNE

PATRON OF THE DIOCESE
ST COLMAN, 24 NOVEMBER

COVERS MOST OF COUNTY CORK

**Most Rev Dermot Clifford PhD, DD**
Archbishop of Cashel and Emly; born 25 January 1939; ordained priest 22 February 1964; ordained Coadjutor Archbishop 9 March 1986; installed Archbishop of Cashel and Emly 12 September 1988; appointed Apostolic Administrator of Cloyne 7 March 2009

Residence: Cloyne Diocesan Centre, Cobh, Co Cork
Tel 021-4811430
Fax 021-4811026
Email cloyne@indigo.ie

## ST COLMAN'S CATHEDRAL, COBH

St Colman's Cathedral, overlooking Cobh, enshrines within its walls the traditions of thirteen centuries of the Diocese of Cloyne.

Built in the form of a Latin cross, its exterior is of Dalkey granite, with dressings of Mallow limestone. The style of architecture is French Gothic. The architects were Pugin (the Younger), Ashlin and Coleman.

The cathedral took forty-seven years to build (1868–1915). The total cost was £235,000. Of this, £90,000 was raised by the people of Cobh, with the remainder coming from the diocese and from collections in America and Australia.

The spire was completed in 1915 and the famous carillon and the clock were installed in 1916. The carillon – the largest in Britain and Ireland – has forty-nine bells and is tuned to the accuracy of a single vibration. This unusual instrument covers a range of four octaves and is played from a console located in the belfry, consisting of a keyboard and pedalboard. Inside, the cathedral has all the hallmarks of Gothic grandeur: the massive marble pillars, the beautiful arches, the capitals with their delicate carving of foliage, the shamrock design on the Bath Stone, and mellow, delicate lighting.

The carved panels over the nave arches give a history of the Church in Ireland from the time of St Patrick. The stained-glass windows in the northern aisle depict the parables of Christ, while those in the southern aisle depict the miracles of Christ. Overhead, in the clerestory, are forty-six windows, each having the patron of one of the forty-six parishes of the diocese. The high altar and its surround was designed by Ashlin. The pulpit is of Austrian oak. Towards the rear of the cathedral is the magnificent rose window, which depicts St John's vision of the throne of God. The organ was built by Telford and Telford, and has a total of 2,468 pipes.

**Most Rev John Magee DD**
Retired Bishop of Cloyne;
born 24 September 1936;
ordained priest 17 March 1962;
ordained Bishop of Cloyne 17 March 1987;
retired 24 March 2010
*Residence:* 'Carnmeen', Convent Hill, Mitchelstown, Co Cork
Tel 025-41887

## CHAPTER

*Dean:* Rt Rev Mgr Eamonn Goold PP
Midleton
*Archdeacon:* Vacant
*Chancellor:* Very Rev Seán Cotter PP
Charleville
*Prebendaries*
*Aghulter:* Very Rev Timothy O'Leary CC, Mitchelstown
*Ballyhea:* Rt Rev Mgr Denis O'Callaghan PE, Mallow
*Buttevant:* Vacant
*Cahirulton:* Very Rev Michael Harrington PE, Buttevant
*Coole:* Very Rev Finbar Kelleher CC *(pro tem)*
Glanworth and Ballindangan
*Cooline:* Very Rev Patrick Twomey PP
Kildorrery
*Glanworth:* Very Rev Gerard Casey PP
Mallow
*Inniscarra:* Vacant
*Kilmaclenine:* Rt Rev Mgr James O'Donnell AP, Macroom
*Killenemer:* Vacant
*Subulter:* Very Rev John Terry PE
Kanturk
*Brigown:* Very Rev Mgr Denis Reidy PE, Carrigtwohill
*Kilmacdonogh*
Very Rev Vincent O'Donohue PE
Blarney
*Donoughmore*
Very Rev Michael O'Connell PE, Doneraile
*Laken*
Very Rev Patrick T. McSweeney PE, Glantane
*Honorary Canons*
Very Rev Colman O'Donovan PE
Inniscarra
Very Rev Tom Browne PP
Youghal
Very Rev Donal O'Mahony PP
Cloyne
Very Rev Jackie Corkery PP, Kanturk

## ADMINISTRATION

**College of Consultors**
*Secretary*
Very Rev Canon Gerard Casey PP
Mallow, Co Cork
Tel 022-21149

**Vicar General**
Office vacant due to vacancy of the See

**Finance Council**
*Financial Administrator*
Rt Rev Mgr Eamonn Goold PP
Midleton
Tel 021-4631750
*Accountants:* Messrs Deloitte & Touche
6 Lapp's Quay, Cork

**Diocesan Administration**
*Diocesan Secretary for Primary Education*
Very Rev Donal O'Brien PP
Tel 026-45042
*Diocesan Secretary for Second-level Education*
Vacant
*Diocesan Secretary for Canonical Affairs*
Very Rev William O'Donovan PP
Tel 058-59138

**Religious Education**
*Education Commission Secretary:*
Vacant
*Adult Religious Education*
Sr Emmanuel Leonard
5 Ashgrove, Cluain Ard, Cobh, Co Cork
Tel 021-4815305
*Diocesan Advisers*
Rev Gerard Condon CC
Shanballymore, Doneraile, Co Cork
Tel 022-25197
Sr Claire Fox
Darchno, Castleredmond,
Midleton, Co Cork
Tel 021-4631912

**Pastoral Coordinator**
Rev Jim Killeen
Cloyne Diocesan Centre, Cobh, Co Cork
Tel 021-4811430

**Administrative Secretary**
Mrs Eileen Greaney
Cloyne Diocesan Centre, Cobh, Co Cork
Tel 021-4811430
Email cloyne@indigo.ie

**Diocesan Archivist**
Vacant

## LITURGY

**Diocesan Director of Liturgy**
Rev Daniel Murphy
Castlelyons, Co Cork
Tel 025-36196

**Cathedral Master of Ceremonies**
Rev Robin Morrissey CC
1 Cathedral Terrace,
Cobh, Co Cork
Tel 021-4813951

**Liturgical Commission**
*Secretary:* Miss Anne Cox
Castletownroche

**Church Music**
*Director:* Very Rev Gerard Coleman PP
Castlelyons, Co Cork
Tel 025-36372

## PASTORAL

**Accord**
*Diocesan Director*
Very Rev Stephen O'Mahony PP
Liscarroll
Tel 022-48128
*Assistant Director:* Rev James Moore CC
Mallow, Co Cork
Tel 022-50626

**Communications**
*Diocesan Director:* Rev James Killeen
Cloyne Diocesan Centre, Cobh, Co Cork
Tel 021-4811430

**Cura**
*Diocesan Director*
Very Rev Francis O'Neill PP
Ballyclough, Mallow, Co Cork
Tel 022-27650

**Diocesan Youth Services**
*Chairman:* Mr Noel O'Connor
*Director:* Mr Brian Williams
Mallow Community Youth Centre,
New Road, Mallow, Co Cork
Tel 022-53526

**Ecumenism**
*Secretary*
Very Rev Canon Tom Browne PP
South Abbey, Youghal, Co Cork
Tel 024-93199

**Emigrant Apostolate**
*Diocesan Director*
Very Rev William O'Donovan PP
Conna, Co Cork
Tel 058-59138

**Diocesan Chaplaincy to the Deaf**
Very Rev Joseph McGuane
St Mary's, Church Street,
Youghal, Co Cork
Tel 024-93392

**Immigrant Apostolate**
*Diocesan Director:* Rev Andrew Carvill CC
Ballynoe, Mallow, Co Cork
Tel 058-59269

**Marriage Tribunal**
(See also Marriage Tribunals section)
*Cork Regional Marriage Tribunal:*
*Officialis:*
Very Rev Gerard Garrett VJ

**Perpetual Eucharistic Adoration**
*Diocesan Director:* Rev Patrick Winkle CC
Youghal, Co Cork
Tel 024-92270

**Pilgrimage Director**
Very Rev Tobias Bluitt PP
Doneraile, Co Cork
Tel 022-24156

**Pioneer Total Abstinence Association**
*Dicoesan Director*
Rev Eamonn McCarthy CC
Freemount, Charleville, Co Cork
Tel 022-28788

**Pontifical Mission Societies**
*Diocesan Director*
Very Rev Donal Coakley PP
Inniscarra, Co Cork
Tel 021-4385311

**Prayer and Retreat Ministries**
*Facilitator:* Rev Eamonn Barry
St Colman's College, Fermoy, Co Cork
Tel 025-31622 Fax 025-31634

**Prayer Groups**
*Co-ordinator*
Very Rev Michael Fitzgerald PP
Mitchelstown, Co Cork
Tel 025-84090

**Travellers**
*Chaplain:* Very Rev Padraig Keogh PP
Milford, Co Cork
Tel 063-80038

**Trócaire**
Rev Tom McDermott CC
Churchtown, Mallow, Co Cork
Tel 022-23385

**Vicar for Religious**
Very Rev Canon Sean Cotter PP
Charleville, Co Cork
Tel 063-81319

**Vocations**
*Director:* Rev Patrick Relihan CC
Youghal, Co Cork
Tel 024-92456
Assistant Director: Rev Jim Moore CC
Mallow, Co Cork
Tel 022-50626

**Ongoing Formation of the Clergy**
*Director:* Very Rev Patrick Buckley PP
Dromahane, Mallow, Co Cork
Tel 022-21244

## PARISHES

*Mensal parishes are listed first. Other parishes follow alphabetically. Historical names are given in parentheses.*

**COBH, ST COLMAN'S CATHEDRAL**
*Sacred Heart, Rushbrooke*
*Sacred Heart, Ballymore*
Very Rev Michael Leamy Adm
Rushbrooke, Cobh, Co Cork
Tel 021-4813144
Rev Robin Morrissey CC
Tel 021-4813951
Rev John McCarthy CC
Tel 021-4815619
Rev James Killeen CC
Tel 021-4813601
Rev Peter O'Farrell CC
Tel 021-4855983
Cobh, Co Cork

**FERMOY**
*St Patrick's*
Very Rev Aquin Casey Adm
The Presbytery, Ravenswood,
Fermoy, Co Cork
Tel 025-31414
Rev Eugene Baker CC
Greenhill, Fermoy, Co Cork
Tel 025-33507
Rev P. J. O'Driscoll CC
Monument Hill, Fermoy, Co Cork
Tel 087-6490381

**AGHABULLOGUE**
*St John's, Aghabullogue*
*St Patrick's, Coachford*
*St Olan's, Rylane*
Very Rev Peadar Murphy PP
Aghabullogue, Co Cork
Tel 021-7334035
Rev Brendan Mallon CC
Coachford, Co Cork
Tel 021-7334059

**AGHADA**
*St Erasmus, Aghada*
*St Mary's, Saleen*
*St Mary's, Ballinrostig*
Very Rev Denis Kelleher PP
Church Road, Aghada, Co Cork
Tel 021-4661298
Rev Eamonn Kelleher CC
Jamesbrook, Midleton, Co Cork
Tel 021-4652456

**AGHINAGH**
*St John the Baptist, Bealnamorrive, Rusheen, Ballinagree*
Very Rev John Ryan PP
Aghinagh, Coachford, Co Cork
Tel 026-48037

**BALLYCLOUGH**
*St John the Baptist, Ballyclough, Kilbrin*
Very Rev Francis O'Neill PP
Ballyclough, Mallow, Co Cork
Tel 022-27650
Rev Michael Campbell CC
Kilbrin, Kanturk, Co Cork
Tel 022-48169

**BALLYHEA**
*St Mary's*
Very Rev Mortimer Downing PP
Tel 063-81470

**BALLYMACODA AND LADYSBRIDGE**
*St Mary's, Ladysbridge*
*St Peter in Chains, Ballymacoda*
Very Rev David O'Riordan PP
Ladysbridge, Co Cork
Tel 021-4667173
Rev Kevin Mulcahy CC
Ballymacoda, Co Cork
Tel 024-98110

**BALLYVOURNEY**
*St Gobnait, Ballyvourney*
*Séipéal Ghobnatan, Cúil Aodha*
Very Rev Donal O'Brien PP
Tel 026-45042

**BANTEER (CLONMEEN)**
*St Fursey's, Banteer*
*St Nicholas', Kilcorney*
*St Joseph's, Lyre*
Very Rev William Winter PP
Banteer, Co Cork
Tel 029-56010

**BLARNEY**
*Immaculate Conception, Blarney*
*St Patrick's, Whitechurch*
*St Mary's, Waterloo*
Very Rev William Bermingham PP
Tel 021-4385105
Rev Timothy Hazelwood CC
Tel 021-4385229
Blarney, Co Cork

**BUTTEVANT**
*St Mary's, Buttevant*
*St Mary's, Lisgriffin*
Very Rev Michael Fitzgerald PP
Buttevant, Co Cork
Tel 022-23195

**CARRIGTWOHILL**
*St Mary's*
Very Rev Anthony O'Brien PP
Tel 021-4883236
Rev Gabriel Burke CC
Tel 021-4883867
Carrigtwohill, Co Cork

**CASTLELYONS**
*St Nicholas', Castlelyons*
*St Mary's, Coolagown*
Very Rev Gerard Coleman PP
Castlelyons, Fermoy, Co Cork
Tel/Fax 025-36372

**CASTLEMAGNER**
*St Mary's*
Very Rev Michael Dorgan PP
Castlemagner, Mallow, Co Cork
Tel 022-27600

**CASTLETOWNROCHE**
*Immaculate Conception, Castletownroche*
*Nativity of Our Lady, Ballyhooly*
Very Rev Patrick Scanlan PP
Castletownroche, Co Cork
Tel 022-26188
Very Rev Donal Broderick PE *(in residence)*
Ballyhooly, Co Cork
Tel 025-39148

**CHARLEVILLE**
*Holy Cross*
Very Rev Canon Seán Cotter PP
Tel/Fax 063-81319
Rev Brian Boyle CC
Tel 063-81437
Charleville, Co Cork

**CHURCHTOWN (LISCARROLL)**
*St Nicholas', Churchtown*
*St Joseph's, Liscarroll*
Very Rev Stephen O'Mahony PP
Liscarroll, Mallow, Co Cork
Tel 022-48128
Rev Thomas McDermott CC
Churchtown, Mallow, Co Cork
Tel 022-23385

**CLONDROHID**
*St Abina's, Clondrohid*
*St John the Baptist, Carriganimma*
Very Rev Anthony Wickham PP
Clondrohid, Macroom, Co Cork
Tel 026-41014
Rev Bartholomew Desmond CC
Carriganimma, Macroom, Co Cork
Tel 026-44027

**CLOYNE**
*St Colman's, Cloyne*
*Star of the Sea, Ballycotton*
*Immaculate Conception, Shanagarry*
*St Colmcille's, Churchtown South*
Very Rev Canon Donal O'Mahony PP
Cloyne, Midleton, Co Cork
Tel 021-4652597
Rev Joseph Rohan CC
Ballycotton, Midleton, Co Cork
Tel 021-4646726

**CONNA**
*St Catherine's, Conna*
*St Catherine's, Ballynoe*
*St Mary's, Glengoura*
Very Rev William O'Donovan PP
Conna, Mallow, Co Cork
Tel 058-59138
Rev Andrew Carvill CC
Ballynoe, Mallow, Co Cork
Tel 058-59269

**DONERAILE**
*The Nativity of the Blessed Virgin Mary, Doneraile*
*Christ the King, Shanballymore*
*St Joseph the Worker, Hazelwood*
Very Rev Tobias Bluitt PP
Tel 022-24156
Rev Anthony Sheehan CC
Tel 022-24120
Doneraile, Co Cork
Rev Gerard Condon CC
Shanballymore, Mallow, Co Cork
Tel 022-25197

**DONOUGHMORE**
*St Lachteen's, Stuake*
*St Joseph's, Fornaught*
Very Rev Jeremiah O'Riordan PP
Donoughmore, Co Cork
Tel 021-7337023

**GLANTANE**
*St Peter the Apostle, Dromahane*
*St John the Evangelist, Glantane*
*St Columba, Bweeng*
Very Rev Patrick Buckley PP
Dromahane, Mallow, Co Cork
Tel 022-21244
Very Rev Micheál Cogan PE,CC
Glantane, Mallow, Co Cork
Tel 022-47158
Rev Chris Donlon CC
Dromore, Mallow, Co Cork
Tel 022-21198

**GLANWORTH AND BALLINDANGAN**
*Holy Cross, Glanworth*
*Immaculate Conception, Ballindangan*
*Holy Family, Curraghagulla*
Very Rev Michael Corkery PP
Glanworth, Co Cork
Tel 025-38123
Very Rev Canon Finbar Kelleher CC *(Pro tem)*
Ballindangan, Mitchelstown, Co Cork
Tel 025-85563

**GRENAGH**
*St Lachteen's, Grenagh*
*St Joseph's, Courtbrack*
Very Rev Liam Kelleher PP
Grenagh, Co Cork
Tel 021-4886128

**IMOGEELA (CASTLEMARTYR)**
*Sacred Heart, Mogeely*
*St Joseph's, Castlemartyr*
*St Peter's, Dungourney*
*St Lawrence's, Clonmult*
Very Rev John Cogan PP
Castlemartyr, Co Cork
Tel 021-4667133
Rev Finbarr O'Flynn CC
Dungourney, Co Cork
Tel 021-4668406

**INNISCARRA**
*St Senan's, Cloghroe*
*St Mary's, Berrings*
*St Joseph's, Matehy*
Very Rev Donal Coakley PP
4 Upper Woodlands, Cloghroe, Co Cork
Tel 021-4385311
Rev Michael Lomasney CC
Cloghroe, Blarney, Co Cork
Tel 021-4385163
Rev Gerard Coleman CC
Berrings, Co Cork
Tel 021-7332155

**KANTURK**
*Immaculate Conception, Kanturk*
*St Joseph's, Lismire*
Very Rev Canon Jackie Corkery PP
Tel 029-50192
Rev Patrick Linehan CC
Tel 029-50061
Kanturk, Co Cork

**KILDORRERY**
*St Bartholomew's, Kildorrery*
*St Molaga's, Sraharla*
Very Rev Martin Heffernan PP
Kildorrery, Co Cork
Tel 022-25174

**KILLAVULLEN**
*St Nicholas', Kilavullen*
*St Crannacht's, Anakissa*
Very Rev Daniel Gould PP
Ballygriffin, Mallow, Co Cork
Tel 022-26153
Very Rev Richard Hegarty PE, CC
Killavullen, Co Cork
Tel 022-26125

**KILLEAGH**
*St John the Baptist, Killeagh*
*St Patrick's, Inch*
Very Rev John Broderick PP
Killeagh, Co Cork
Tel 024-95133
Rev Patrick Corkery CC
Inch, Killeagh, Co Cork
Tel 024-95148

**KILNAMARTYRA**
*St Lachtaín's, Kinamartyra, Renaniree*
Very Rev Richard Browne PP
Kilnamartyra, Macroom, Co Cork
Tel 026-40013

**KILWORTH**
*St Martin's, Kilworth*
*Immaculate Conception, Araglin*
Very Rev Donal Leahy PP
Kilworth, Co Cork
Tel 025-27186

**LISGOOLD**
*St John the Baptist, Lisgoold*
*Sacred Heart, Leamlara*
Very Rev Denis O'Hanlon PP
Tel 021-4642363

**MACROOM**
*St Colman's, Macroom*
*St John the Baptist, Caum*
Very Rev Donal Roberts PP
Rt Rev Mgr James O'Donnell AP
Tel 026-41042
Rev Francis Manning CC
Tel 026-41092
Rev Joseph O'Mahony CC
Tel 026-61049
Macroom, Co Cork

**MALLOW**
*St Mary's, Mallow*
*Resurrection, Mallow*
Very Rev Canon Gerard Casey PP
Tel 022-21149
Rev Micheál Leader CC
Tel 022-21382
Rev Jim Moore CC
Tel 022-50626
Rev Patrick McCarthy CC
Tel 086-3831621
Rev Tadhg O'Donovan *(Priest in residence)*
Mallow, Co Cork

**MIDLETON**
*Holy Rosary, Midleton*
*St Colman's, Ballintotas*
Rt Rev Mgr Eamonn Goold PP
Tel 021-4631750
Rev Micheál Ó Loingsigh CC
Tel 021-4631354
Rev Tom Naughton CC
Tel 021-4636704
Rev Gerard Cremin CC
Tel 021-4631094
Rev Marek Pecak CC *(in residence)*
Tel 021-4634027
Midleton, Co Cork

**MILFORD**
*Assumption of BVM, Milford*
*St Michael's, Freemount*
*St Berchert's, Tullylease*
Very Rev Pádraig Keogh PP
Milford, Charleville, Co Cork
Tel 063-80038
Rev Eamonn McCarthy CC
Freemount, Charleville, Co Cork
Tel 022-28788

**MITCHELSTOWN**
*Our Lady Conceived Without Sin, Mitchelstown*
*Holy Family, Ballygiblin, Killacluig*
Very Rev Michael Fitzgerald PP
Tel 025-84090
Very Rev Canon Timothy O'Leary CC
Tel 025-84088
Rev James Greene CC
Tel 025-84077
Mitchelstown, Co Cork

**MOURNE ABBEY**
*St Michael the Archangel, Analeentha*
*St John the Baptist, Burnfort*
Very Rev Joseph O'Keeffe PP
Burnfort, Mallow, Co Cork
Tel 022-29920

**NEWMARKET**
*Immaculate Conception, Newmarket*
*Holy Spirit, Taur*
Very Rev David Herlihy PP
Newmarket, Co Cork
Tel 029-60999

**RATHCORMAC**
*Immaculate Conception, Rathcormac*
*St Bartholomew's, Bartlemy*
Very Rev Cornelius O'Donnell PP
Rathcormac, Fermoy, Co Cork
Tel 025-36286
Rev Danny Murphy CC
Castlelyons, Co Cork
Tel 025-36196

**ROCKCHAPEL AND MEELIN**
*St Joseph's, Meelin*
*St Peter's, Rockchapel*
Very Rev Denis Stritch PP
Meelin, Newmarket, Co Cork
Tel 029-68007

**SHANDRUM**
*St Joseph's, Shandrum*
*St Peter & Paul's, Dromina*
Very Rev Patrick Lawton PP
Shandrum, Charleville, Co Cork
Tel 063-70016
Very Rev David Buckley PE, CC
Very Rev Canon Seán Cotter Adm *protem*
Dromina, Charleville, Co Cork
Tel 063-70207

**YOUGHAL**
*St Mary's, Our Lady of Lourdes, Holy Family, Youghal; St Ita's, Gortroe*
Very Rev Canon Thomas Browne PP
Tel 024-93199
Rev Patrick Winkle CC
Tel 024-92270
Rev Michael Murphy CC
Tel 024-92336
Rev Patrick Relihan CC
Tel 024-92456
Youghal, Co Cork

## PRIESTS OF THE DIOCESE ELSEWHERE

Rev Paul Bennett
Pontificio Collegio Irlandese,
Via dei Santi Quattro 1, 00184 Roma
Tel 0039-06-772631
Rev Sean Corkery
St Patrick's College, Maynooth,
Co Kildare
Rev Mgr Michael F. Crotty BA, JCL, D.Ecc.Hist
Section for Relations with States,
Secretariat of State,
00120 Vatican City
Tel 0039-06-69883546
Rev Mark Hehir
1 The Presbytery, Ballyphehane, Cork
Rev John Keane
c/o Cloyne Diocesan Centre,
Cobh, Co Cork
Tel 021-4811430
Rev Thomas Lane
Mount Saint Mary's Seminary,
16300 Old Emmitsburg Road,
Emmitsburg,
Maryland 21727-7797, USA
Rev Daniel McCarthy CF
Office of the Chaplain,
James Stephen's Barracks, Kilkenny City
Very Rev Mgr Joseph Murphy
Secretariat of State, (Section for Relations with States),
00120 Vatican City
Tel 0039-0669883193
Very Rev Declan O'Brien PP
St Mary's Parish, 160 Foster Street,
PO Box 22, DANDENONG,
VIC 3175, Australia
Tel 03-97914611 Fax 03-97917119
Rt Rev Mgr James O'Brien
Congregation for Divine Worship and the Discipline of the Sacraments,
Vatican City 00120, Italy
Tel 003906-69884551
Fax 003906-69883499
Rev Donal O'Callaghan
Muintir Mhuire, Ballybutler,
Ladysbridge, Co Cork
Tel 024-98852

## RETIRED PRIESTS

Very Rev Anthony Cronin PE
Newmarket, Co Cork
Tel 029-60605
Very Rev Robert Forde PE
Fermoy, Co Cork
Tel 025-34022
Rev James Hannon
Sandhill Road, Ballybunion, Co Kerry
Dr Patrick Hannon
Emeritus Professor of Theology,
St Patrick's College, Maynooth,
Co Kildare
Tel 01-6285222
Very Rev Canon Michael Harrington PE
Charleville, Co Cork
Tel 063-21833
Very Rev Michael Madden PE
Ballycrennane, Ballymacoda, Co Cork
Tel 024-98840
Very Rev Canon P. T. McSweeney PE
Nazareth House, Mallow, Co Cork
Tel 022-21561
Rt Rev Mgr Denis O'Callaghan PE
Mallow, Co Cork
Tel 022-21112
Very Rev Peadar O'Callaghan PE
Suaimhneas, Charleville, Co Cork
Tel 086-8054040
Very Rev Canon Michael O'Connell PE
Buttevant, Co Cork
Very Rev Canon Vincent O'Donohue PE
18 Kilcrea Park, Magazine Road, Cork
Tel 021-4856881

Very Rev Canon Colman O'Donovan PE
1 Youghal Road, Midleton, Co Cork
Tel 021-4621617
Very Rev Con O'Donovan PE
16 Deer Park Avenue,
St Joseph's Road, Mallow, Co Cork
Tel 022-51948
Very Rev Philip O'Keeffe PE
Kiliphilbeen, Ballynoe, Mallow, Co Cork
Tel 058-59526
Rev Martin O'Riordan
Lisgoold, Co Cork
Tel 021-4642543
Very Rev Mgr Denis Reidy PE
Teach an tSagairt, Main Street,
Carrigtwohill, Co Cork
Tel 021-4533776
Very Rev Liam Ryan PE
Mondaniel, Fermoy, Co Cork
Very Rev Canon John Terry PE
Terriville, Ballylanders, Cloyne, Co Cork
Tel 021-4646779
Very Rev Canon Patrick Twomey PE
Bellevue, Mallow, Co Cork
Rev Denis Vaughan
45 The Oaks, Maryborough Ridge,
Douglas, Cork

## RELIGIOUS ORDERS AND CONGREGATIONS

### BROTHERS

**PRESENTATION BROTHERS**
Presentation Monastery,
Cobh, Co Cork
Tel 021-4811218
*Contact:* Br Walter Hurley (FPM)
Community: 3

### SISTERS

**ADORERS OF THE SACRED HEART OF JESUS OF MONTMARTRE, OSB**
St Benedict's Priory,
The Mount, Cobh, Co Cork
Tel 021-4811354
*Prioress:* Mother Mary Vianney
Community: 6
Contemplative Benedictines
Residential retreats
*Contact person:* Guest Mistress

**BON SECOURS SISTERS (PARIS)**
38 Norwood Park, Cobh, Co Cork
Tel 021-4815350
*Co-ordinator:* Sr Paschal Barry
Community: 5
Parish Ministry, Care of Elderly

Sisters of Bon Secours,
Bon Secours Convent, Cobh, Co Cork
Tel 021-4811346
Community: 2
Day Care Centre/Care of Elderly

**CONGREGATION OF THE SISTERS OF MERCY**
'Trócaire', 6 Castleowen,
Blarney, Co Cork
Tel 021-4381745

Buttevant, Co Cork
Tel 022-23113 Fax 022-23634

Charleville, Co Cork
Tel 063-81276 Fax 063-81830

Kanturk, Co Cork
Tel 029-50068 Fax 029-50332

Dan Corkery Place,
Macroom, Co Cork
Tel 026-42673

Macroom, Co Cork
Tel 026-41068 Fax 026-42535

Fairy Hill, Kennell Hill,
Mallow, Co Cork
Tel 022-21395 Fax 022-43168

Holy Spirit Convent,
Bank Place, Mallow, Co Cork
Tel 022-21780

16 Meadow Grove, Summerhill,
Mallow, Co Cork
Tel 022-43624

3 Beechwood Grove, Cluain Ard, Cobh,
Co Cork
Tel 021-4815062

5 Ashgrove, Cluain Ard,
Cobh, Co Cork
Tel 021-4815305

Sirona, 57 Rockbrook Lawn,
Mallow, Co Cork
Tel 022-20769

41 Ivy Gardens, Mallow, Co Cork
Tel 022-58036

Convent Bungalow,
Bathview, Mallow, Co Cork
Tel 022-31905

Billkit, Hume's Terrace,
Mallow, Co Cork
Tel 022-21414

Island Road, Longacre,
Newmarket, Co Cork

17 Bromley Court,
Midleton, Co Cork
Tel 021-4632732

21 Whitepoint Avenue,
Rushbrooke, Co Cork
Tel 021-4811453

**INFANT JESUS SISTERS**
Bellevue, Mallow, Co Cork
Tel 022-43085
Community: 10
Retired sisters

**LITTLE COMPANY OF MARY**
Convent of the Maternal Heart,
Monument Hill, Fermoy, Co Cork
Tel 025-31679
Community: 3
Pastoral ministry, with special emphasis on bereavement counselling

Little Company of Mary, 'Lima',
College Road, Fermoy, Co Cork
Community: 1

**LORETO (IBVM)**
Loreto Community,
Fermoy, Co Cork
Tel 025-31207
*Community Leader*
Sr Veronica O'Donoghue
Community: 11
Secondary School
Tel 025-32124

Loreto Sisters, Copperton,
Corrin View Estate, Fermoy, Co Cork
Tel 025-33693
Community: 3
Secondary school, pastoral work

Greenlawn, Summerfield,
Youghal, Co Cork
Community: 6

8 Dún na Mara, Youghal, Co Cork
*Community Leader:* Sr Breda Rice
Community: 3

**MISSIONARIES OF CHARITY**
St Helen's Convent, Blarney, Co Cork
Tel 021-4382041
*Superior:* Sr M. Subrata (MC)
Community: 4
Residential Treatment Centre

**POOR SERVANTS OF THE MOTHER OF GOD**
St Aloysius' Convent,
Carrigtwohill, Co Cork
Tel 021-4883237 Fax 021-4883955
Community: 4
St Aloysius' Secondary School
Pastoral

**CONGREGATION OF THE SISTERS OF NAZARETH**
Nazareth House,
Mallow, Co Cork
Tel 022-21561 Fax 022-21147
Email nazarethmallow@eircom.net
*Superior:* Sr Victoire Mulligan
Community: 12
Home for elderly. Beds: 84

**PRESENTATION SISTERS**
Presentation Convent, Midleton, Co Cork
Tel 021-4631892
*Team Leadership*
Community: 12
Primary School Tel 021-4631593
St Mary's Secondary School
Tel 021-4631973

Presentation Primary School,
Doneraile, Co Cork
Tel 022-24512

Nagle Rice Secondary School,
Doneraile, Co Cork
Tel 022-24500

Presentation Convent,
Fermoy, Co Cork
Tel 025-31248
*Leader:* Sr Rosarii Shinnick
Community: 12
Primary School. Tel 025-31550

Presentation Lodge, College Road,
Fermoy, Co Cork
Tel 025-49928
Community: 1

Presentation Convent,
Front Strand, Youghal, Co Cork
Tel 024-93039
*Non-resident Leader*
Sr Mary John Staunton
Community: 5
Primary School. Tel 024-92700

Presentation Sisters, 'Darchno',
Castleredmond, Midleton, Co Cork
Tel 021-4631912
Community: 1

Presentation Primary School,
Mitchelstown, Co Cork
Tel 025-24264
Presentation Secondary School
Mitchelstown, Co Cork
Tel 025-24394

Nano Nagle Centre,
Presentation Sisters,
Ballygriffin, Mallow, Co Cork
Tel 022-26411 Fax 022-26953
Email nanonaglecentre@eircom.net
Community: 4
Website www.nanonaglebirthplace.ie

**ST JOSEPH OF THE SACRED HEART SISTERS**
Sisters of St Joseph of Sacred Heart,
Penola, 25B Harrison Place,
Charleville, Co Cork

## EDUCATIONAL INSTITUTIONS

**St Colman's College (Diocesan College)**
Fermoy, Co Cork
Tel 025-31622 Fax 025-31634
Email stcolmansfermoy@eircom.net
*Priests on Staff*
Rev Eamonn Barry, Facilitator for Prayer and Retreat Ministries (in residence)
Tel 025-31622/086-8157952

**EDMUND RICE SCHOOLS TRUST**
Midleton, Co Cork Secondary School
Tel 021-4631555 Fax 021-4631917
Email office@midletoncbs.ie
*Principal:* Mr Pat Hurley

Primary School, Baker's Road,
Charleville, Co Cork
Tel 063-89544
*Principal:* Mr. Jerry Murray

Secondary School, Baker's Road,
Charleville, Co Cork
Tel/Fax 063-81789 Staff 063-81669
Email charlevillecbs@gmail.com
*Principal:* Mr Maurice Keohane

Christian Brothers Secondary School,
Mitchelstown, Co Cork
Tel 025-24104 Fax 025-85153
Email donnchac@eircom.net
*Principal:* Mr Donncha Crowley

Nagle Rice Secondary School,
Doneraile, Co Cork
Tel 022-24500 Fax 022-24586
Email info@nrss.ie
*Principal:* Ms Bríd Lysaght

## CHARITABLE AND OTHER SOCIETIES

**St Mary's District Hospital**
Youghal, Co Cork

**County Hospital**
Mallow, Co Cork

**Society of St Vincent de Paul**
Conferences at: Ballyvourney, Castlemartyr, Cobh, Fermoy, Doneraile, Kanturk, Macroom, Mallow, Midleton, Mitchelstown, Youghal, Carrigtwohill, Lisgoold, Aghada, Charleville

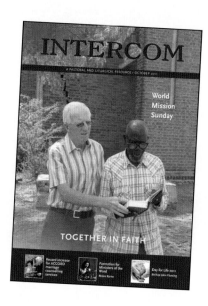

Wood carved
Fiberglass
7 Skerrif Road - Cullyhanna - Co Armagh
N Ireland - BT35 OJG
Tel: (028) 30861522 - Fax: (028) 30868352
From: ROI (048) 30861522 - Mobile: 077 861 369 85
KEVIN KEARNEY
RELIGIOUS ARTICLES
Email: info@kevinkearney.net - Web : www.kevinkearney.net

K N  C K

## OUR LADY'S SHRINE, KNOCK, CO. MAYO

Phone: (094) 9388100 Fax: (094) 9388295
www.knock-shrine.ie Email: info@knock-shrine.ie

***Programme of Ceremonies and Devotions 2012***

### SUNDAYS AND HOLYDAYS

29 April to 14 October (inclusive)
**Masses:** 8, 9.00, 10.30 am, 12 noon, 3 & 7 pm
(Eve of Sundays and Holydays: 7.30 pm)

**Confessions:** Continuously from 11 am to 5 pm

**Public Ceremonies:**
2.30 pm Anointing of the Sick
3.00 pm Concelebrated Mass followed by the Solemn Blessing of the Sick. Benediction of the Blessed Sacrament, Rosary Procession to the Shrine and the blessing of Pious objects.

### ALL WEEKDAYS

30 April to 13 October (inclusive)
**Masses:** 9, 11 am, 12 noon, 3 & 7.30 pm
**Confessions:** Continuously from 11 am to 5 pm
**Public Ceremonies:**
2.00 pm Stations of the Cross and Rosary Procession
3.00 pm Concelebrated Mass with Anointing of the Sick.

### NATIONAL PUBLIC NOVENA

August 14 to 22 (inclusive) Ceremonies Twice daily:
3.00 pm Mass in the Basilica. Eucharistic Blessing of the Sick and Rosary Procession.
8.30 pm Mass in the Basilica. Eucharistic Blessing of the Sick and Candlelight Rosary Procession

### YOUTH MINISTRY PROGRAMME FOR SCHOOLS

- Retreats
- Faith Development Programmes
- Youth Liturgies
- Use of Audio Visual Facilities

Further details: Phone: (094) 9388100

### KNOCK COUNSELLING SERVICE

Individual Counselling, Couple Counselling
Group Therapy, Clinical Supervision
Drop In Service Also Available
Tel: (094) 9375032
Email: counselling@knock-shrine.ie

**Pilgrims Guides, Knock Posters and details of main pilgrimage dates on request. For assistance in organising your pilgrimage, please contact the main office or:**

**Knock Shrine Office**, Veritas House,
7/8 Lower Abbey Street, Dublin 1
Tel/Fax: (01) 8733356
Email: dublinoffice@knock-shrine.ie

**Knock Shrine Office & Bookshop,**
76/77 Little Catherine Street, Limerick
Tel: (061) 419458 Fax: (061) 405178
Email: limerickoffice@knock-shrine.ie

**Knock Shrine Pilgrimages**, PO Box 210,
Newtownabbey, Co. Antrim, BT36 9DE
Tel/Fax: (028) 9077 4353
Email: knockshrinebelfast@gmail.com

**Knock Shrine Office & Bookshop,**
101, Deansgate, Manchester, M3 2BQ, England
Tel: (0161) 8192558 Fax: (0161) 8340744
Email: knockshrineoffice@btconnect.com

### KNOCK SHRINE BOOKSCENTRE

Knock Shrine, Knock, Co. Mayo
Tel: (094) 9375030 Fax: (094) 9375031
Email: bookshop@knock-shrine.ie

FOR A WIDE RANGE OF RELIGIOUS BOOKS & SOUVENIRS YOU CAN NOW SHOP ONLINE AT,
www.knock-shrine.ie/shop

### CAFÉ LE CHÉILE

At Knock Museum
*"Food for Thought"*
Groups Welcome
Tel: (094) 9375350
Email: cafelecheile@knock-shrine.ie
Web: www.cafelecheile.ie

Café le Chéile

### KNOCK MUSEUM

Captures the compelling story of the Knock Apparition of 1879
Opening Hours: May - October 10 - 6 pm daily
November - April 10 - 4 pm daily
Email: museum@knock-shrine.ie
Tel: (094) 9375034

# DIOCESE OF CORK AND ROSS

PATRON OF THE DIOCESE OF CORK
ST FINBARR, 25 SEPTEMBER

PATRON OF THE DIOCESE OF ROSS
ST FACHTNA, 14 AUGUST

INCLUDES CORK CITY AND PART OF COUNTY CORK

**Most Rev John Buckley DD**
Bishop of Cork and Ross;
born 1939;
ordained priest 1965;
ordained Titular Bishop of Leptis Magna 29 April 1984 and installed 6 February 1998

Residence:
Cork and Ross Offices,
Redemption Road, Cork
Tel 021-4301717
Fax 021-4301557

## CATHEDRAL OF ST MARY AND ST ANNE, CORK

The first cathedral on the site of the present Cathedral of St Mary and St Anne was the vision of Bishop Francis Moylan, who was Bishop of Cork from 1786 to 1815. The foundation stone was laid in 1799 and the cathedral was opened in 1808 as the parish church of the single parish then on the northside of the city – hence its local, popular name: the North Chapel. But in June 1820, the heat of the political climate struck the North Chapel when it was maliciously burned during the night.

Bishop John Murphy, one of the famous brewing family, wasted no time in calling a meeting to help restore the cathedral. The people of Cork generously rallied to the call.

The task of rebuilding was given to architect George Pain, who later designed Blackrock Castle, the court house and St Patrick's Church. The interior of the present-day cathedral, including the ornate ceiling, owes much to his creative gifts.

The next major alteration to the cathedral was undertaken in the 1870s when Canon Foley set about building the tower and the great Western Door – now the main door of the cathedral. The tower is higher than that of its more famous neighbour: St Anne's Church, Shandon, home of the much-played bells.

Almost a hundred years later, after the Second Vatican Council, Cornelius Lucey, then Bishop of Cork and Ross, added a further major extension at the other end of the cathedral. This included a completely new sanctuary and a smaller tower, and added capacity to the church, which served an area with a rapidly increasing population.

In 1994, major problems were discovered in the roof and other fabric of the building, which led to the closing of the cathedral for major refurbishment. The bishop, Michael Murphy, decided it was time to renovate the interior of the cathedral too. The task was entrusted to architect Richard Hurley, whose plan for the new interior saw a greater unity being achieved between the sanctuary and the rest of the floor area, and the new altar occupying the central place of prominence. The reordering and renovation was completed in 1996 at a cost of £2.5m and Bishop Murphy presided over its rededication – his last public function before he died a week later.

## CHAPTER

*Dean:* Very Rev Denis O'Connor
*Archdeacon:*
Venerable Kerry Murphy O'Connor
*Precentor:* Canon Jim O'Donovan
*Treasurer:* Canon Ted O'Sullivan
*Prebendaries*
*Kilbritain:* Very Rev Micheál O Dálaigh
*Desertmore:* Very Rev Tadhg Ó Mathúna
*Kilnaglory:* Very Rev Dan Crowley
*Holy Trinity:* Very Rev Thomas Kelleher
*Kilbrogan:* Very Rev Kevin O'Callaghan
*Caherlag:* Very Rev Donal Linehan
*Kilanully:* Very Rev John K. O'Mahony
*Killaspugmullane:* Rev Michael Murphy
*Liscleary:* Very Rev Liam O'Regan
*St Michael:* Very Rev Michael Riordan
*Inniskenny:* Canon Vincent Hodnett
*Drimoleague:* Very Rev Liam O'Driscoll

**Honorary Canons**
Very Rev Diarmuid Linehan
Very Rev Liam Leader
Very Rev Denis Forde
Very Rev Michael Crowley
Very Rev Michael G. O'Brien
Very Rev Michael Crowley

## ADMINISTRATION

**Vicars General**
Rt Rev Mgr Kevin O'Callaghan PP, VG
No. 2 Presbytery, Curnaheen, Cork
Tel 021-4346818
Rt Rev Mgr Leonard O'Brien PP, VG
Clonakilty, Co Cork
Tel 023-8833165

**Vicars Forane**
Rt Rev Mgr Kevin O'Callaghan
Fr Denis O'Leary

**Diocesan Secretary**
Rev Thomas Deenihan
Cork & Ross Offices,
Redemption Road, Cork
Tel 021-4301717
Email secretary@corkandross.org

## PASTORAL

**Catechetics**
*Primary:* Sr Geraldine Howard
North Presentation Convent, Cork
Tel 087-6115672
*Second-level:* Rev Mark Hehir
Cork and Ross Offices,
Redemption Road, Cork
Tel 021-4301717
Email catechetics@corkandross.org

**Child Protection**
*Diocesan Director:* Canon Liam O'Driscoll
Diocesan Offices, Redemption Road, Cork
Tel 021-4301717
Email liam.odriscoll@corkandross.org

**CMCC Marriage Counselling**
*Director:* Dr Colm O'Connor
34 Paul Street, Cork
Tel 021-4275678 Fax 021-4270932
ACCORD, 5 Main Street, Bantry, Co Cork
Tel 027-50272

**CURA**
*Adm. Secretary:* Mrs Anne Murphy
Tel 021-4277544

**Diocesan Education Office**
Cork and Ross Offices,
Redemption Road, Cork
Tel 021-4301717 Fax 021-4301557
*Secretary for Education*
Rev Dr Tom Deenihan
*Secretary:* Ms Clare O'Leary
Email clare.oleary@corkandross.org

**Immigrants**
Cois Tine, St Mary's, Pope's Quay, Cork
Tel 021-4557760
Email coistine@sma.ie
*Diocesan Chaplain to Polish Community*
Rev Piotr Galus
c/o St Augustine's,
Washington Street, Cork
Tel 021-4275390

**Marriage Tribunal**
(See Marriage Tribunals section)

**Parish Pastoral Development**
1 The Presbytery, Friar's Walk,
Ballyphehane, Cork
Tel 021-4537472
Email ppo@corkandross.org
*Director:* Rev Seán O'Sullivan
Email sean.osullivan@corkandross.org
*Co-ordinator:* Sr Karen Kent
Email karen.kent@corkandross.org
*Co-ordinator of Liturgy:*
Rev Christopher Fitzgerald
Email liturgy@corkandross.org
*Co-ordinator of Adult Religious Education:* Dr Anne Francis
Email are@corkandross.org

**Pilgrimages**
*Director*
Rt Rev Mgr Kevin O'Callaghan PP, VG
The Presbytery, Curraheen Road, Cork
Tel 021-4346463

**Pontifical Mission Society**
Rev Pat Fogarty PP
The Presbytery, Knocknaheeg, Cork
Tel 021-4392459

## PARISHES

*The mensal parishes are listed first. Other names follow alphabetically. Historical names are given in parentheses.*

**CATHEDRAL OF ST MARY & ST ANNE**
Very Rev Crislóir MacDonald Adm
Rev Tomás Walsh (SMA) AP
Cathedral Presbytery, Cork
Tel 021-4304325 Fax 021-4304204

**ST PATRICK'S CATHEDRAL, SKIBBEREEN**
Very Rev Martin O'Driscoll Adm
Rev Michael Anthony Buckley
The Presbytery, Skibbereen, Co Cork
Tel 028-22878

**ARDFIELD AND RATHBARRY**
Very Rev Patrick J. McCarthy Adm
Ardfield, Clonakilty, Co Cork
Tel 023-8840649

**AUGHADOWN**
Very Rev Donal Cahill Adm
Lisheen, Skibbereen, Co Cork
Tel 028-38111

**BALLINCOLLIG**
Very Rev George O'Mahony PP
Tel 021-4871206
Ballincollig, Co Cork
Rev James MacSweeney CC
64 Westcourt, Ballincollig, Co Cork
Tel 021-4870434
Rev Michael O'Mahony CC
8 The Meadows, Classis Lake,
Ballincollig, Co Cork
Tel 021-4877161
*Also in residence:* Rev Billy O'Sullivan
c/o Parochial House, Ballincollig, Co Cork
Tel 021-4371206

**BALLINEASPAIG**
Rev Kieran Twomey PP
Tel/Fax 021-4346818
Very Rev Dean Denis O'Connor PE
Tel 021-4542972
Very Rev Tom Clancy AP
Tel 021-4348588
Woodlawn, Model Farm Road,
Ballineaspaig, Cork

**BALLINHASSIG**
Very Rev Kieron O'Driscoll PP
Barrett's Hill, Ballinhassig, Co Cork
Tel 021-4885104
Rev Pearse Timoney
The Presbytery,
Ballygarvan, Co Cork
Tel 021-4888971

**BALLINLOUGH**
Very Rev Canon James O'Donovan PP
Tel 021-4292296
Very Rev Canon Michael Crowley PE
Tel 021-4292684
Very Rev Canon Vincent O'Donoghue AP
Ballinlough, Cork

**BALLINORA**
Very Rev Canon Donal Linehan PP
Ballinora, Waterfall, near Cork
Tel 021-4873448

**BALLYPHEHANE**
Very Rev Canon Michael Murphy PP
Tel 021-4965560
Rev Paul O'Donoghue AP
Tel 021-4310835

**BANDON**
Very Rev Denis J. O'Leary PP
Tel 023-8841278
Rev Myles McSweeney CC
Tel 023-8865067
Rev David O'Connell CC
The Presbytery, Bandon, Co Cork

**BANTRY**
Very Rev Donal Cotter PP
The Presbytery, Bantry, Co Cork
Tel 027-50096
Most Rev Patrick O'Donoghue AP
The Presbytery, Bantry, Co Cork
Tel 027-50082
Rev Anthony O'Mahony CC
The Presbytery, Bantry, Co Cork
Tel 027-50193

**BARRYROE**
Very Rev Eoin Whooley PP
Lislevane, Bandon, Co Cork
Tel 023-8846171 Fax 023-8846914

**BLACKPOOL/THE GLEN**
Very Rev John O'Donovan PP
Hattons Alley, Blackpool, Cork
Tel 021-4501022
Rev Damien O'Mahony CC
1 Kilmorna Heights,
Ballyvolane, Cork
Tel 021-4550425

**BLACKROCK**
Canon Tadhg Ó Mathúna SP
2 Parochial House, Blackrock, Cork
Tel 021-4358025
Rev J.P. O'Riordan (CSsR) CC
1 Parochial House, Blackrock, Cork
Tel 021-4358381

**CAHERAGH**
Rev Daniel Pyburn PP
The Presbytery, Dromore,
Bantry, Co Cork
Very Rev Michael O'Donovan AP
The Presbytery, Caheragh, Co Cork
Tel 028-31126

**CARRAIG NA BHFEAR**
Very Rev Michael Regan PP
Carraig na bhFear, Co Cork
Tel 021-4884119

**CARRIGALINE**
Very Rev Bartholomew O'Mahony PP
Tel 021-4371684
Rev Aidan Cremin CC
Tel 021-4372229
Rev Charles Nyhan CC
Cork Road, Carrigaline, Co Cork
Tel 021-4371860

**CASTLEHAVEN**
Very Rev Christopher Coleman (MSC) PP
Parish House, Union Hall,
Skibbereen, Co Cork
Tel 028-34940

**CLOGHEEN (KERRY PIKE)**
Canon Liam O'Driscoll Adm
Rev Paul Payyapilly AP
Church of the Most Precious Blood,
Clogheen, Co Cork
Tel 021-4392122

**CLONAKILTY AND DARRARA**
Right Rev Mgr Leonard O'Brien PP, VG
Tel 023-33165
Rev Edward J. Collins CC
Tel 023-33100
The Presbytery, Clonakilty, Co Cork

**CLONTEAD**
An tAth Tomás Ó Murchú Adm
Riverstick, Kinsale, Co Cork
Tel 021-4771332
Rev Daniel Burns PE
Belgooly, Co Cork

**COURCEYS**
Very Rev Canon Thomas Kelleher PP
Ballinspittle, Co Cork
Tel 021-4778055

**CROSSHAVEN**
Rev Patrick Stevenson PP
The Presbytery
Most Rev Patrick Coveney AP
Crosshaven, Co Cork
Tel 021-4831218

**CURRAHEEN ROAD**
Very Rev Canon Micheál Ó Dálaigh PP
Rt Rev Mgr Kevin O'Callaghan AP
The Presbytery, Curraheen Road, Cork
Tel 021-4343535

**DOUGLAS**
Very Rev Canon Teddy O'Sullivan PP
Parochial House, Douglas, Cork
Tel 021-4891265
Very Rev Canon Liam O'Regan AP
'Carraigin', Moneygourney,
Douglas, Cork
Tel 021-4363998
*St Patrick's, Rochestown:*
Rev Michael Keohane PIC
St Patrick's Presbytery,
Rochestown Road, Cork
Tel 021-4892363

**DRIMOLEAGUE**
Very Rev John O'Callaghan PP
Drimoleague, Co Cork
Tel 028-31133

**DUNMANWAY**
Very Rev Timothy Collins PP
Rev John O'Donovan CC
The Presbytery, Dunmanway, Co Cork
Tel 023-8845000

**ENNISKEANE AND DESERTSERGES**
Rev Tom Hayes PP
Parochial House, Enniskeane, Co Cork
Tel 023-8847769

**FARRANREE**
Rev Seán O'Driscoll PP
The Presbytery, Farranree, Cork
Tel 021-4393815/4210111

**FRANKFIELD-GRANGE**
Rev John Walsh PP
Tel 021-4361711
Rev Colin Doocey CC
Tel 021-4362377
The Presbytery, Frankfield, Cork

**GLANMIRE**
Very Rev Dr Noel O'Sullivan PP
Glanmire, Co Cork
Tel 021-4866307
Rev Ted Sheehan
Springhill, Glanmire, Co Cork
Tel 021-4866306

**GLOUNTHAUNE**
Very Rev John Paul Hegarty PP
Tel 021-4232881
Rev Gregory Howard (OSA) CC
Tel 021-4353078
Glounthaune, Co Cork

**GOLEEN**
Rev Alan O'Leary
The Presbytery, Schull, Co Cork

**GURRANABRAHER**
Rev Kevin O'Regan PP
Rev Owen O'Sullivan (OFMCap) CC
Rev Kevin Kiernan (OFMCap) CC
Ascension Presbytery,
Gurranabraher, Cork
Tel 021-4303655

**INNISHANNON**
Very Rev John Kingston PP
Innishannon, Co Cork
Tel 021-4775348

**KILBRITTAIN**
Very Rev John Heinhold Adm
Kilbrittain, Co Cork
Tel 023-8849637

**KILMACABEA**
Very Rev Patrick O'Sullivan (MSC) Adm
Leap, Co Cork
Tel 028-33177

**KILMEEN AND CASTLEVENTRY**
Very Rev Martin Keohane PP
Rossmore, Clonakilty, Co Cork
Tel 023-8838630

**KILMICHAEL**
Very Rev Jeremiah Cremin PP
Parochial House, Tirelton,
Macroom, Co Cork
Tel 026-46012/086-2578065

**KILMURRY**
Very Rev Bernard Donovan PP
Cloughdubh, Crookstown, Co Cork
Tel 021-7336054
Rev Seán O'Sullivan AP
Lissarda, Crookstown, Co Cork
Tel 021-7336053

**KINSALE**
Very Rev Robert Young PP
Tel 021-4774019
Very Rev Canon John K. O'Mahony AP
Tel 021-4773700 Fax 021-4773821
The Presbytery, Kinsale, Co Cork

**KNOCKNAHEENY/HOLLYHILL**
Very Rev Pat Fogarty PP
The Presbytery, Knocknaheeny, Cork
Tel 021-4392459
Tel 021-4392459 *(Parish Office)*

**THE LOUGH**
Very Rev Canon Vincent Hodnett PP
Tel 021-4273821
Very Rev Canon Michael Crowley AP
Tel 021-4322633
Rev Paul O'Donoghue CC
Tel 021-4322633
The Lough Presbytery,
St Finbarr's West, Cork

**MAHON**
Very Rev John Collins PP
1 The Presbytery,
Holy Cross Church, Mahon, Cork
Tel 021-4357394
Rev Kaz Nawalaniec
2 The Presbytery, Mahon, Cork
Tel 021-4515460
*Parish Office:* 021-4357040

**MONKSTOWN**
Very Rev John Newman PP
Rev Pat O'Donovan CC
Monkstown, Co Cork
Tel 021-4863267
Rev John Galvin AP
Passage West, Co Cork

**MUINTIR BHÁIRE**
Very Rev Gerard Galvin PP
Durrus, Co Cork
Tel 027-61013

**MURRAGH AND TEMPLEMARTIN**
Fr Finbarr Crowley Adm
Farnivane, Bandon, Co Cork
Tel 023-8820861

**OVENS**
Rev Liam Ó hÍcí PP
Ovens, Co Cork
Tel 021-4871180

**PASSAGE WEST**
Very Rev John Newman Adm
Tel 021-4863267
Rev John Galvin AP
Tel 021-4841267
Rev Pat O'Donovan CC
Passage West, Co Cork

**RATH AND THE ISLANDS**
Very Rev Martin O'Driscoll PP
North Street, Skibbereen
Tel 028-22878
Rev Peter Queally AP
Oiléan Cléire, Baltimore, Co Cork
Tel 028-39103
Rev Michael Anthony O'Mahony CC
The Presbytery, Skibbereen, Co Cork

**ROSSCARBERY AND LISSAVAIRD**
Very Rev John McCarthy PP
Rosscarbery, Co Cork
Tel 023-8848168
Rev Chris O'Donovan AP
Lissavaird, Rosscarbery, Co Cork
Tel 023-8834334

**SACRED HEART**
Very Rev John Fitzgerald (MSC) PP
Sacred Heart Parish, Western Road, Cork
Tel 021-4804120 Fax 021-4543823

**ST FINBARR'S SOUTH**
Very Rev Richard Hurley PP
South Presbytery, Dunbar Street, Cork
Tel 021-4272989

**ST JOSEPH'S (MAYFIELD)**
Very Rev Christopher Harrington PP
St Joseph's Presbytery, Mayfield, Cork
Tel 021-4501861

**ST JOSEPH'S (BLACKROCK ROAD)**
Very Rev Thomas Wade (SMA) PP
Rev Eugene McLoughlin (SMA) CC
St Joseph's, Blackrock Road, Cork
Tel 021-4292871

**ST PATRICK'S**
Very Rev Canon Dan Crowley PP
The Presbytery, Lower Road, Cork
Tel 021-4502696
Very Rev John Cotter PE
Tel 021-4551503
Very Rev Canon Liam Leader AP
Tel 021-4500282
The Presbytery, Lower Road, Cork

**ST VINCENT'S, SUNDAY'S WELL**
Very Rev Jack Harris (CM) PP
122 Sunday's Well Road, Cork
Tel 021-4304070 Fax 021-4300103
Email parishoffice@corkvinc.com

**SS PETER'S AND PAUL'S**
Very Rev Patrick A. McCarthy PP
35 Paul Street, Cork
Tel 021-4276573

**SCHULL**
Very Rev Alan O'Leary PP
The Presbytery, Schull
Tel 028-28171
Rev Joseph Spillane (SPS) CC
Ballydehob, Co Cork
Tel 028-3711

**TIMOLEAGUE AND CLOGAGH**
Very Rev Patrick Hickey Adm
The Presbytery, Clogagh,
Timoleague, Co Cork
Tel 023-8839114

**TOGHER**
Very Rev Robert Brophy PP
Tel 021-4316700
Very Rev Michael Riordan AP
Tel 021-4316800
The Presbytery, Togher, Cork
*Parish Office:* 021-4318899

**TRACTON ABBEY**
Very Rev George Murphy PP
Tel 021-4887105
Minane Bridge, Co Cork

**TURNER'S CROSS**
Ven Archdeacon Kerry Murphy O'Connor PP
Tel 021-4312466
Rev Charles Kiely CC
Tel 021-4313103
The Presbytery, Turner's Cross, Cork

**UIBH LAOIRE**
Very Rev Bernard Cotter PP
Parochial House,
Inchigeela, Macroom, Co Cork
Tel 026-49838/087-2691432

**UPPER MAYFIELD**
Very Rev Aidan O'Driscoll PP
Tel 021-4503116
Rev Pat O'Mahony (SMA) CC
Tel 021-4500828
The Presbytery, Upper Mayfield, Cork

**WATERGRASSHILL**
Very Rev Denis Cashman PP
Parochial House, Watergrasshill, Co Cork
Tel 021-4889103

**WILTON, ST JOSEPH'S**
Ver Rev Cormac Breathnach (SMA) PP
Rev Denis Collins (SMA) CC
St Joseph's, Wilton, Cork
Tel 021-4341362 Fax 021-4343940

## INSTITUTIONS AND THEIR CHAPLAINS

### THIRD LEVEL COLLEGES

**Cork Institute of Technology**
*Chaplaincy Office:* 021-4326225
*Chaplaincy Base:* 3 Elton Lawn,
Rossa Avenue, Bishopstown, Cork
Tel 021-4326256
*Chaplain*
Rev Dr David McAuliffe
Tel 021-4346244
*Co-ordinator of Pastoral Care*
Ms Edel Dullea
Tel 021-4326778

**University College, Cork**
*Chaplaincy Office:* Iona,
College Road, Cork
Tel 021-4902459
*Chaplains:* Rev Richard Hendrick (OFMCap)
Tel 021-4902704
Rev David Barrins (OP)
Sr Patricia O'Donovan

### HOSPITALS

**Bandon District Hospital**
Bandon, Co Cork
Tel 023-8841403
*Chaplain:* Parish clergy, Bandon

**Bantry Hospital**
Bantry, Co Cork
Tel 027-50133
*Chaplain:* Parish clergy, Bantry

**Bon Secours Hospital**
College Road, Cork
Tel 021-4542807
*Chaplain:* Rev Aidan Vaughan (OFMCap)
Tel 021-4546682
Mrs Pat Healy
Sr Claire O'Driscoll
Ms Anne Bermingham
Ms Catherine O'Regan

**Cork South Infirmary Victoria Hospital Ltd**
Old Blackrock Road, Cork
Tel 021-4926100
*Chaplains*
Sr Catherine Quane
Tel 021-4926100
Rev Francis Kelleher
Tel 021-4966555

**Cork University Hospital**
Wilton, Cork
Tel 021-4546400
*Chaplains*
Fr Ray Riordan (CSsR)
Tel 021-4546400
Rev Thomas Lyons
Tel 021-4546400/4922391
Rev Michael Forde
Tel 021-4546400

**District Hospital**
Skibbereen, Co Cork
Tel 028-21677
*Chaplain:* Parish Clergy

**Marymount Hospice**
Wellington Road, Cork
*Chaplain:* Rev Mark Hehir

**Mercy University Hospital**
Grenville Place, Cork
Tel 021-4271971
*Chaplains*
Rev Michael Burgess (OFMCap)
Rev Pierce Cormac

**Mount Carmel Hospital**
Clonakilty, Co Cork
Tel 023-8833205
*Chaplain:* Parish Clergy

**Sacred Heart Hospital**
Kinsale, Co Cork
Tel 021-4772202
*Chaplain:* Parish clergy, Kinsale

**St Anne's Hospital**
Shanakiel, Cork
Tel 021-4541901
*Chaplain:* Rev Paul Payyapilly

**St Anthony's Hospital**
Dunmanway, Co Cork
Tel 023-8845102
*Chaplain:* Parish clergy, Dunmanway

**St Finbarr's Hospital**
Douglas Road, Cork
Tel 021-4966555
*Chaplains:* Rev Francis Kelleher
Tel 021-4966555
Sr Eleanor Redican
Tel 021-4966553

**St Gabriel's Hospital**
Schull, Co Cork
Tel 028-28120
*Chaplain:* Parish clergy, Schull

**St Joseph's Hospital**
Mount Desert, Lee Road, Cork
Tel 021-4541765

**St Mary's Orthopaedic Hospital**
Baker's Road, Cork
Tel 021-4303264
*Chaplains:* Parish clergy, Gurranabraher
Tel 021-4303655

**St Patrick's Hospital**
Wellington Road, Cork
Tel 021-4501201
*Chaplains:* Rev Robert Talty (OP)
Rev Martin McCarthy (OP)
Sr Nan O'Mahony

**St Stephen's Hospital**
Glanmire, Co Cork
Tel 021-4821411
*Chaplain:* Rev Liam O'Callaghan (MSC)

**Shanakiel Hospital**
Shanakiel, Cork
Tel 021-4396955
*Chaplain:* Parish clergy, Clogheen
Tel 021-4392122

## Port

**Port Chaplaincy**
Rev Desmond Campion (SDB)
Tel 021-4378046

## PRISONS

**Cork Prison**
*Chaplain:* Fr Michael Kidney (SMA)
Tel 021-4518820/087-6836567

## PRIESTS OF THE DIOCESE ELSEWHERE

Rev Dr Pádraig Corkery
St Patrick's College,
Maynooth, Co Kildare
Tel 01-7083639
Rev Dr Gearóid Dullea
St Patrick's College, Maynooth,
Co Kildare
Rev Joseph O'Leary
1-38-16 Ekoda, Nakanoku, Tokyo,
16J0022 Japan

## RETIRED PRIESTS

Rev James Good
Park View, Church Street,
Douglas, Cork
Tel 021-4363913
Rev Edmund Keohan
The Bungalow, Turners Cross, Cork
Tel 021-4320592
Ven Archdeacon Michael O'Brien
Nazareth House, Mallow, Co Cork
Rev Michael O'Driscoll
Bushmount, Clonakilty, Co Cork
Tel 023-33991
Very Rev Canon Diarmuid Linehan
2 Maglin View, Ballincollig, Co Cork
Tel 021-4875857
Very Rev Cornelius White
Nazareth Home, Dromahane,
Mallow, Co Cork
Tel 022-50486
Very Rev Dan Burns
St Paul's, Bushmount,
Clonakilty, Co Cork
Tel 023-33991
Very Rev Jeremiah Hyde
The Presbytery, Kinsale, Co Cork
Very Rev Denis O'Connor
2 Woodlawn, Model Farm Road, Cork
Rev Pat Walsh
Priests House, Aliohill,
Enniskeane, Co Cork
Rev Patrick Keating
Drumoleague, Co Cork

## RELIGIOUS ORDERS AND CONGREGATIONS

### PRIESTS

**AUGUSTINIANS**
St Augustine's Priory,
Washington Street, Cork
Tel 021-4275398/4270410
Fax 021-4275381
*Prior:* Rev Pat Moran (OSA)

**CAPUCHINS**
Holy Trinity,
Father Mathew Quay, Cork
Tel 021-4270827 Fax 021-4270829
*Guardian:* Rev Sean Donohoe (OFMCap)
*Vicar:* Rev Richard Hendrick (OFMCap)

Capuchin Community,
Monastery Road, Rochestown, Co Cork
Tel 021-4896244 Fax 021-4895915
*Guardian:* Rev Paul O'Donovan (OFMCap)
*Vicar:* Rev Dermot Lynch (OFMCap)

St Francis Capuchin Franciscan College,
Rochestown, Co Cork
Tel 021-4891417 Fax 021-4361254

**CARMELITES (OCARM)**
Carmelite Friary, Kinsale, Co Cork
Tel 021-4772138
Email kinsale@irishcarmelites.com
*Prior:* Very Rev Frank McAleese (OCarm)

**DOMINICANS**
St Mary's, Pope Quay, Cork
Tel 021-4502267 Fax 021-4502307
*Prior:* Very Rev Joseph Kavanagh (OP)

St Dominic's Retreat House,
Montenotte, Cork
Tel 021-4502520 Fax 021-4502712
*Prior:* Very Rev Benedict Hegarty (OP)

**FRANCISCANS**
Franciscan Friary, Liberty Street, Cork
Tel 021-4270302 Fax 021-4271841
*Guardian:* Rev Eugene Barrett (OFM)

**MISSIONARIES OF THE SACRED HEART**
MSC Mission Support Centre,
PO Box 23, Western Road, Cork
Tel 021-4545704 Fax 021-4343587
*Director:* Rev Michael O'Connell (MSC)
www.mscireland.com

Western Road, Cork
Tel 021-4804120 Fax 021-4543823
*Leader & Parish Priest*
*Very* Rev John Fitzgerald (MSC) PP

Carrignavor, Co Cork
Tel 021-4884104
*Leader:* Rev Dan O'Connor (MSC)

Myross Wood Retreat House,
Leap, Skibbereen, Co Cork
Tel 028-33118 Fax 028-33793
*Director & Leader*
Rev Michael Curran (MSC)

**REDEMPTORISTS**
Scala, Castle Mahon House, Blackrock,
Cork
Tel 021-4358800 Fax 021-4359696
*Superior:* Rev Noel Kehoe (CSsR)

**ROSMINIANS**
Upton, Innishannon, Cork
Tel 021-4776268/4776923 Fax 021-4776268
Residential services for adults with
learning disabilities

**ST COLUMBAN'S MISSIONARY SOCIETY**
No. 2 Presbytery,
Our Lady Crowned Church,
Mayfield Upper, Cork
Tel 021-4508610
Rev Patrick O'Herlihy (SSC)

**ST PATRICK'S MISSIONARY SOCIETY**
Kiltegan House, 11 Douglas Road, Cork
Tel 021-4969371
*House Leader:* Rev Jim Barry (SPS)

**SOCIETY OF AFRICAN MISSIONS**
St Joseph's Provincial House, Feltrim,
Blackrock Road, Cork
Tel 021-4292871 Fax 021-4292873
Email provincial@sma.ie
*Provincial:* Rev Fachtna O'Driscoll (SMA)
*Superior:* Rev Colum P. O'Shea (SMA)

Wilton College, Cork
Tel/Fax 021-4541069
*Superior:* Rev John O'Keeffe (SMA)
*Bursar:* Rev Jarlath Walsh (SMA)

**VINCENTIANS**
St Vincent's,
122 Sunday's Well Road, Cork
Tel 021-4304070/4304529 Fax 021-4300103
*Superior:* Very Rev Jack Harris (CM) PP

## BROTHERS

**BROTHERS OF CHARITY**
Our Lady of Good Counsel, Lota,
Glanmire, Co Cork
Tel 021-4821012 Fax 021-4821711
*Chaplain:* Fr Paul Thettayil (IC)

**CHRISTIAN BROTHERS**
Christian Brothers House,
Ard Mhuire, Fair Hill, Cork
Tel 021-4300879
*Community Leader:* Br Gary O'Shea
Community: 6

Christian Brothers, 36 Beechwood Grove,
Onslow Gardens, Commons Road, Cork
Tel 021-2393119
Community: 2

Churchfield Community Trust,
109 Knockfree Avenue, Cork
Tel 021-4210348
Email cctrust@eircom.net
*Director:* Eileen O'Brien

Sunday's Well Life Centre,
6 Winter's Hill, Sunday's Well, Cork
Tel 021-4304391
Email thelifecentrecork@eircom.net
*Director:* Don O'Leary

**PRESENTATION BROTHERS**
2/3 Heatherton Park,
South Douglas Road, Cork
Tel 021-4364288
*Contact:* Br De Paul Hennessy (FPM)
Community: 3

4 Lynbrook, Glasheen Road, Cork
Tel 021-4346765 Fax 021-4346770
*Contact:* Br Donatus Brazil (FPM)

Mardyke House, Cork
Tel 021-4272239
Community: 4
*Contact:* Br Stephen O'Gorman (FPM)

Maiville, Turner's Cross, Cork
Tel 021-4272649
Community: 14
*Contact:* Br Hugh Sweeney (FPM)
Email presbrosmaiville@eircom.net

Mount St Joseph, Blarney Street, Cork
Tel 021-4392160
Community: 7
*Contact:* Br Bede Minehane (FPM)

## SISTERS

**BON SECOURS SISTERS (PARIS)**
Bon Secours Convent, College Road, Cork
Tel 021-4542416 Fax 021-4542533
*Country Leader:* Sr Marie Ryan
*Co-ordinator:* Sr Martha Leamy
Email marthaleamy@gmail.com
Community: 15
Parish and hospital ministry

Soilse Community
Mount Finbarr, Glasheen Road, Cork
Tel 021-4964804
*Contact:* Sr Columbanus Byrne
Community: 3

Cnoc Mhuire, Fernhurst,
College Road, Cork
Tel 021-4345410 Fax 021-4345491
*Co-ordinator:* Sr Maureen Condon
Community: 36
Pastoral, community, nursing and
hospital ministry, care of sick and poor in
their own homes

Casa Maria, Fernhurst, College Road, Cork
Tel 021-4345411
Community: 1
Pastoral and hospital ministry

3 Brookfield Villas, College Road, Cork
Tel 021-4545018
Community: 1

1 Aylsbury Lawn, Ballincollig, Co Cork
Tel 021-4872978
Community: 3

St Enda's, College Road, Cork
Tel 021-4542750
Community: 1

**CONGREGATION OF THE SISTERS OF MERCY**
Provincial Offices, Bishop Street, Cork
Tel 021-4975380 Fax 021-4915220
Email provincialoffice@mercysouth.ie
*Provincial:* Sr Liz Murphy

13 Kempton Park, Ballyvolane, Cork
Tel 021-4551375

14 Kempton Park, Ballyvolane, Cork
Tel 021-4551371

49 Hollymount, Blarney Road, Cork
Tel 021-4302123

13 Ronayn's Court,
Rochestown Road, Cork

2 Rowan Hill, Mount Oval Village,
Rochestown, Cork
Tel 021-4366611

19 Sheraton Court, Glasheen Road, Cork
Tel 021-4318092

144 Dun Eoin, Ballinrea Road,
Carrigaline, Co Cork
Tel 021-4919748
*Contact:* Sr Liz Murphy

2 Woodbrook Grove,
Bishopstown, Cork
Tel 021-4342286

St Columba's, Convent,
Bishopstown Avenue West, Cork
Tel 021-4545549

St Marie's of the Isle,
Sharman Crawford Street, Cork
Tel 021-4316029

38 Sheares Street, Cork
Tel 021-4272982

St Catherine's Convent,
Bishopstown Avenue, Cork
Tel 021-4541376

9 Sharman Crawford Street, Cork

1 Kinloch Court, Bishopstown Avenue,
Model Farm Road, Cork
Tel 021-4345332

15 Sheraton Court, Old Sheen Road, Cork
Tel 021-4315973

St Maries Bungalow, Convent Place,
Crosses Green, Cork
Tel 021-4318628

The Convent, Mercy Hospital,
Grenville Place, Cork
Tel 021-4271971

Convent of Our Lady Crowned,
Boherboy Road, Mayfield, Cork
Tel 021-4500080 Fax 021-4552267

'Lorg Dé', 27 St Joseph's Park,
Boherboy Road, Mayfield, Cork
Tel 021-4508519

56 Glenamoy Lawn, Mayfield, Cork
Tel 021-4509410

1 Sandymount Drive, Glasheen Road,
Cork
Tel 021-4541613

Cuan na Trócaire, 23 Benvoirlich Estate,
Bishopstown, Cork
Tel 021-4343371

Convent of Mercy, Winter's Hill, Kinsale,
Co Cork
Tel 021-4772165

Avila, Ard na Gaoithe Mór,
Bantry, Co Cork
Tel 027-50035

The Bungalow, Balindeasig,
Belgooly, Co Cork
Tel 021-4887954

Casa Maria Seskin, Bantry, Co Cork
Tel 027-51198

Schull, Co Cork
Tel 028-28189

'Tigh Amos', South Terrace,
Schull, Co Cork
Tel 028-28036

1 Park View, Church Hill,
Passage West, Co Cork
Tel 021-4863121

Arus Muire, McCurtain Hill, Scartagh,
Clonakilty, Co Cork
Tel 023-8833391

Mount Carmel Convent,
Clonakilty, Co Cork
Tel 023-8833072

Pairc-a-Tobair, Rosscarbery, Co Cork
Tel 023-8848963

Apt 1, Arus Muire, McCurtain Hill,
Scartagh, Clonakilty, Co Cork

Apt 2, Arus Muire, McCurtain Hill,
Scartagh, Clonakilty, Co Cork

Apt 3, Arus Muire, McCurtain Hill,
Scartagh, Clonakilty, Co Cork

Apt 4, Arus Muire, McCurtain Hill,
Scartagh, Clonakilty, Co Cork

Studio 26, Arus Muire, McCurtain Hill,
Scartagh, Clonakilty, Co Cork

2 The Drive, Priory Court,
Watergrasshill, Co Cork
Tel 021-4513949

**DAUGHTERS OF CHARITY OF ST VINCENT DE PAUL**
St Louise's, Hollyhill House,
Harbour View Road, Knocknaheeny, Cork
Tel 021-4392762
*Superior:* Sr Mary Connaire
Community: 7
Teaching, parish and social work
*AND*
Labouré House,
Mount Nebo, Blarney Street, Cork
Tel 021-4304207
Sister's residence, Pastoral work

**FRANCISCAN MISSIONARIES OF ST JOSEPH**
Convent of St Francis,
Blackrock Road, Cork
Tel 021-4317059
*Superior:* Sr Margaret Quinn
Community: 11

**GOOD SHEPHERD SISTERS**
Baile an Aoire, Leycester Lane,
Montenotte, Cork
Tel 021-4551200 Fax 021-4551202
Email rgsbaile@eircom.net
*Leader:* Sr Alexandra Eisenkratzer
Community: 13

Edel House, Residential Centre,
Grattan Street, Cork
Tel 021-4274240 Fax 021-4274160
Email gsscork@eircom.net

Bruac, Henry Street, Cork
Tel 021-4273890 Fax 021-4222977
Email gsscork@eircom.net

Riverview, 3 North Mall, Cork
Tel/Fax 021-4304205
Email gsscork@eircom.net

'The Well', Sunday's Well, Cork
Tel 021-4303216 Fax 021-4305250
Email rgsthewell@eircom.net
*Leader:* Sr Jennifer McAleer
Community: 2

17 Killiney Heights, Knockaheeny, Cork
Tel 021-4302660
Email janebmurphy@eircom.net
*Leader:* Sr Jane Murphy
Community: 2

**INFANT JESUS SISTERS**
10 Willow Drive, Muskerry Estate,
Ballincollig, Co Cork
Tel 021-4870625
Community: 3
Pastoral work

19 Cherry Walk, Muskerry Estate,
Ballincollig, Co Cork
Tel 021-4873599
Community: 3

St Joseph's, Model Farm Road, Cork
Tel 021-4342348
Community: 14
House for elderly sisters

**LA RETRAITE SISTERS**
22 Salmon Weir,
Hanover Street, Cork
Tel 021-4251100/4276789
*Contact:* Sr Bridget Dunne
Email bridgetdunne@eircom.net

**LITTLE SISTERS OF THE ASSUMPTION**
32 St Francis Gardens,
Thomas Davis Street, Blackpool, Cork
Tel 021-4391407

1 Ballinure Crescent, Mahon,
Blackrock, Cork
Tel 021-4358372
*Contact:* Sr Thérèse Farrell
Email lsamahck@eircom.net
Professional services to the family

2-3 College View,
Old Youghal Road, Cork
Tel 021-4500023

**MARIE REPARATRICE SISTERS**
7 Knockrea Lawn, Ballinlough Road, Cork
Tel 021-4313429
Email smrknock@eircom.net
*Superior:* Sr Catherine Corry
Community: 6
Parish ministry

**MISSIONARY SISTERS OF THE HOLY ROSARY**
7 The Circle, Broadale, Douglas, Cork
Tel 021-4362424
Healthcare, work with refugees
Community: 3

**MISSIONARY SISTERS OF OUR LADY OF APOSTLES**
Ardfoyle Convent, Ballintemple, Cork
Tel 021-4291851 Fax 021-4291105
Email prov@eircom.net
*Provincial:* Sr Mary Crowley
*Sister-in-Charge:* Sr Mary Barron
Community: 60

**OUR LADY OF THE CENACLE**
16 Mervue Lawn, Ballyvolane, Cork
Tel 021-4508059
Email cenacle@iol.ie
*Contact:* Cenacle Sisters
Community: 2

**POOR CLARES**
Poor Clare Colettine Monastery,
College Road, Cork
*Abbess:* Sr Colette-Marie O'Reilly
Community: 8
Contemplatives
Eucharistic Adoration: Daily 7am-6pm
Mass Times: Daily 10.00 am
Rosary: Monday-Saturday 5.30 pm
Sunday Rosary, Evening Prayer and Benediction: 5.00 pm

**PRESENTATION SISTERS**
Presentation Provincial Office,
Evergreen Street, Cork
Tel 021-4975190 Fax 021-4975192
Email swpres@iol.ie
*Provincial Leader:* Sr Mary Hoare

South Presentation Convent,
Douglas Street, Cork
Tel 021-4975042
*Leader:* Sr Callie Manley
Community: 11

115 Cathedral Road, Cork
Tel 021-4393086
Community: 1

Christ King Convent,
Turner's Cross, Cork
Tel 021-4966552
*Non-resident Leader:* Sr Antonia Murphy
Community: 8
Primary School. Tel 021-4963695
Christ King Girls' Secondary School
Tel 021-4961448

Presentation Convent,
Ballyphehane, Cork
*Non-resident Leader*
Sr Mary Jane Donaldson
Tel 021-4321606
Community: 7
Primary School (Junior). Tel 021-4315857
Primary School (Senior). Tel 021-4315724
Secondary School. Tel 021-4961765

18 The Orchards,
Montenotte, Cork
Tel 021-4501456
Community: 2

North Presentation Convent,
Gerald Griffin Street, Cork
Tel 021-4302878
Team Leadership
Community: 18
Primary School Tel 021-4307132
An Gleann Primary School
Tel 021-4504877

Regina Coeli Convent,
Farranree, Cork
Tel 021-4302770
*Non-resident Leader:* Sr Jo McCarthy
Community: 10
Aiséirí Chríost Primary School
Tel 021-4301383
Secondary School
Tel 021-4303330

25 Rosbarra, Deerpark,
Friar's Walk, Cork
Tel 021-4323321
Community: 2

Presentation Convent,
Bandon, Co Cork
Tel 023-8841476
*Non-resident Leader:* Sr Marie Wall
Community: 15
Primary School Tel. 023-8841809
Secondary School. Tel 023-8841814

Presentation Convent,
Crosshaven, Co Cork
Tel 021-4831189
*Non-resident Leader*
Sr Helen Dobbyn
Community: 9
Primary School. Tel 021-4831646
Coláiste Mhuire Secondary School
Tel 021-4831604

Ardán Mhuire, Togher Road, Cork
Tel 021-4961471
Community: 2

7 Churchfield Terrace West,
Gurranabraher, Cork
Tel 021-4306640
Community: 3

7 Old Waterpark, Carrigaline, Co Cork
Tel 021-4372718
Community: 2

20 Fairhill Drive, Fairhill, Cork
Tel 021-4399760
Community: 2

7 Avoca Crescent, The Glen, Cork
Tel 021-4504025
Community: 1

Dóchas, 21 Ashdene,
South Douglas Road, Cork
Tel 021-4897597
Community: 3

Presentation Centre,
Evergreen Street, Cork
Tel 021-4314255
Community: 4

44 Castlemeadows,
Mahon, Cork
Tel 021-4515944
Community: 2

44 Ashbrook Heights, Lehenaghmore,
Togher, Cork
Tel 021-4320006
Community: 2

78 Grange Way, Douglas, Cork
Tel 021-4899704
Community: 1

5 Abbey View, Nano Nagle Walk,
Douglas Street, Cork
Tel 021-4322097
Community: 1

18 Convent View, Nano Nagle Walk,
Douglas Street, Cork
Tel 021-4915380
Community: 1

Apt 37, Ard na Rí, Closes Green,
Farranree, Cork
Tel 021-4309262
Community: 1

Apt 39, Ard na Rí, Closes Green,
Farranree, Cork
Community: 1

'Fallsway', Boreenmanna Road,
Ballinlough, Cork
Community: 2

**RELIGIOUS SISTERS OF CHARITY**
St Vincent's Convent,
St Mary's Road, Cork
Tel 021-4211176/4211238
Various apostolic ministries

St Anthony's Convent, Vincent's Avenue,
St Mary's Road, Cork
Tel 021-4308162

**SACRED HEARTS OF JESUS AND MARY**
Blackrock, Cork
Tel 021-4357841
*Community Leader:* Sr Alexander

**URSULINES**
Ursuline Convent, Blackrock, Cork
Tel 021-4358663 Fax 021-4356077
Email corckucb@eircom.net
Community: 12
*Local Leader:* Sr Elizabeth Bradley
Primary School
Tel 021-4358476 Fax 021-4359073
Secondary School
Tel 021-4358012 Fax 021-4358012

58 Meadowgrove,
Blackrock, Cork
Tel 021-4357249
Community: 2

## EDUCATIONAL INSTITUTIONS

**Christ the King Secondary School**
South Douglas Road, Cork
Tel 021-4961448 Fax 021-4314563

**Christian Brothers College, Cork**
Tel 021-4501653 Fax 021-4504113

**Coláiste Chríost Rí, Cork**
Tel 021-4274904 Fax 021-4964784

**Coláiste an Spioraid Naoimh**
Bishopstown, Cork
Tel 021-4543790 Fax 021-4543625

**Deerpark CBS**
St Patrick's Road, Cork
Tel 021-4962025 Fax 021-4311792

**EDMUND RICE SCHOOLS TRUST**
Scoil Mhuire Fatima
North Monastery, Cork
Tel 021-4305340 Fax 01-4305011
*Principal:* Mr C. Higgins

Christian Brothers Secondary School,
North Monastery, Cork
Tel 021-4301318 Fax 021-4307994
Staff Tel 021-4301247
Careers Tel 021-4309330
Email northmonastery.ias@eircom.net
*Principal:* Mr Mick Evans

Gael Choláiste Mhuire,
An Mhainistir Thuaidh, Corcaigh
Tel 021-4307579 Fax 021-4288011
Email gaelcholaistemhuireag@eircom.net
*Principal:* Dónal O'Buachala

Scoil Cholmcille, Blarney Street, Cork
Tel/Fax 021-4397000
Email colmcillecbs.ias@eircom.net
*Principal:* Mr Billy Lynch

Coláiste Iognáid Rís,
St Patrick's Road, Cork
Tel 021-4963265 Fax 021-4311792
Email deerparkcbs@eircom.net
*Principal:* Mr Aidan McNally

Christian Brothers Junior School,
Sidney Hill, Wellington Road, Cork
Tel 021-4501653 Fax 021-4504113
Email christianscork@eircom.net
education@cbccork.ie

Christian Brothers College,
Sidney Hill, Wellington Road, Cork
Tel 021-4501653 Fax 021-4504113
Email christianscork@eircom.net
*Principal:* Dr L. Jordan

**Mercy Heights Secondary School**
Skibbereen, Co Cork
Tel 028-21550 Fax 028-21451

**Mercy Sisters Secondary School**
Roscarbery, Co Cork
Tel 023-8848114 Fax 023-8848520

**Mount Mercy College**
Model Farm Road, Cork
Tel 021-4542366 Fax 021-4542709

**North Monastery,**
Our Lady's Mount, Cork
Tel 021-4301318 Fax 021-4309891

**Presentation College, Cork**
Tel 021-4272743 Fax 021-4273147

**Presentation Convent**
Bandon, Co Cork
Tel 023-8841814 Fax 023-8841385

**Presentation Convent Secondary School**
Crosshaven, Co Cork
Tel/Fax 021-4831604

**Presentation Secondary School**
Ballyphehane, Cork
Tel 021-4961765/4961767
Fax 021-4312864

**Regina Coeli Convent Secondary School**
Farranree, Cork
Tel 021-4303330 Fax 021-4303411

**Sacred Heart College**
Carrig na bhFear, Co Cork
Tel 021-4884104 Fax 021-4884442

**Sacred Heart Secondary School**
Clonakilty, Co Cork
Tel 023-8833737 Fax 023-8833908

**St Aloysius School, Cork**
Tel 021-4316017 Fax 021-4316007

**St Angela's College, Cork**
Tel 021-4500059 Fax 021-4504515

**St Fachtna's Secondary School**
Skibbereen, Co Cork
Tel 028-21454 Fax 028-21256

**St Francis Capuchin College,**
Rochestown, Co Cork
Tel 021-4891417 Fax 021-4361254

**St Vincent's Secondary School, Cork**
Tel 021-4307730 Fax 021-4307252

**Ursuline Convent Secondary School**
Blackrock, Cork
Tel/Fax 021-435801

# DIOCESE OF DERRY

Patrons of the Diocese
St Eugene, 23 August; St Columba, 9 June

INCLUDES ALMOST ALL OF COUNTY DERRY,
PARTS OF COUNTIES DONEGAL AND TYRONE
AND A VERY SMALL AREA ACROSS THE RIVER BANN IN COUNTY ANTRIM

**Rt Rev Mgr Eamon Martin**
Diocesan Administrator,
Diocese of Derry;
born 1961;
ordained priest 1987;
elected Diocesan Administrator
November 2011

Office Address: PO Box 227,
Bishop's House, Derry BT48 9YG
Tel 028-71262302
Fax 028-71371960
Email
eamon.martin@derrydiocese.org

## ST EUGENE'S CATHEDRAL, DERRY

In the 1830s, following the Catholic Emancipation Act of 1829, the Catholic community of Derry was able to contemplate building a cathedral. In the summer of 1838, a number of Catholics of the city met with the then Bishop of Derry, Peter McLaughlin, to consider such a project. Over the next thirteen years a weekly collection was made in the city and eventually, on 26 July 1851, the foundation stone was laid by Bishop Francis Kelly.

The construction of the cathedral was sporadic as the funds became available over twenty-five years, and owing to the difficulty in raising money, it was agreed to postpone the building of the tower, belfry and spire until a later date. Due to the lack of funds in the diocese, the windows were initially all of plain glass, and it was only in later years that the stained glass was installed.

J. J. McCarthy (1817–1882) was the architect commissioned to design St Eugene's Cathedral. He was one of the most outstanding church architects in Ireland in his time and he designed many churches and convents all over the country, including St Patrick's Cathedral, Armagh, St Macartan's Cathedral, Monaghan and the Cathedral of the Assumption, Thurles.

The actual construction work took twenty-two years to complete, at a cost of £40,000. It was not until 1873 that the building was brought to a stage where it could be dedicated and used for liturgical celebrations. The cathedral was dedicated by Bishop Francis Kelly on 4 May 1873.

In 1899 it was decided to add a spire to the tower, which was estimated to cost £15,000. The spire was completed on 19 June 1903, and on 27 June the eight-foot-high granite cross was put in position by Fathers John Doherty and Lawrence Hegarty. The full complement of stained-glass windows was achieved in the Spring and Autumn of 1896 at a cost of £2,270. The ten bells of the cathedral first rang out on Christmas Eve, 1902.

St Eugene's was solemnly consecrated on 21 April 1936, the seventh cathedral in Ireland to be consecrated, and the event is celebrated annually on 21 April.

**Most Rev Seamus Hegarty DD**
Retired Bishop of Derry;
born 1940;
ordained priest 19 June 1966;
ordained Bishop of Raphoe
28 March 1982;
appointed Bishop of Derry
1 October 1994;
installed 6 November 1994; retired as
Bishop of Derry 23 November 2011
Residence: Ardstraw House, 21A
Buncrana Road, Derry BT48 8LA

**Most Rev Francis Lagan DD**
Retired Bishop of Sidnacestre and Auxiliary Bishop of Derry; born 1934; ordained priest 19 June 1960; ordained Bishop 20 March 1988; Retired as Auxiliary Bishop of Derry 6 May 2010
Residence: 9 Glen Road, Strabane,
Co Tyrone BT82 8BX
Tel 028-71884533 Fax 028-71884551
Email fblagan@gotadsl.co.uk

**Most Rev Edward Daly DD**
Retired Bishop of Derry: born 1933; ordained priest 16 March 1957; ordained Bishop of Derry 31 March 1974; retired as Bishop of Derry 26 October 1993
Residence: 9 Steelstown Road,
Derry BT48 8EU
Tel 028-71359809 Fax 028-71357098
Email Edward.Daly@btinternet.com

## ADMINISTRATION

**College of Consultors**
Rt Rev Mgr Joseph Donnelly PP, VF
Rt Rev Mgr Bryan McCanny PP
Rt Rev Mgr Eamon Martin
Very Rev Frank Bradley
Very Rev John Farren PP
Very Rev Michael Canny PP
Very Rev John Cargen PP
Very Rev Patrick McGoldrick CC

**Vicars Forane**
*Derry City Deanery*
Very Rev Colum Clerkin PP, VF
*Co Derry Deanery*
Very Rev Kieran O'Doherty PP, VF
*Co Tyrone Deanery*
Rt Rev Mgr Joseph Donnelly PP, VF
*Inishowen Deanery*
Very Rev James McGonagle PP, VF

**Diocesan Archives**
*Archivists:* Most Rev Edward Daly DD
Rev Kieran Devlin PEm
9 Steelstown Road,
Derry BT48 8EU
Tel 028-71359809
Email edward.daly@btinternet.com

**Derry Diocesan Trust**
(St Columb's Diocesan Trust is Trustee of the Derry Diocesan Trust)
*Directors:* Rt Rev Mgr B. Mc Canny PP
Rt Rev Mgr E. Martin
Very Rev James McGonagle PP, VF
Rev Aidan Mullan PP
Very Rev John Cargan PP
Very Rev Michael Canny PP
Ms Caroline McGonagle
Ms Kate Brolly
Ms Carmel McGilloway
Mr Gerry Murray
Mr Tony Jackson
*Secretary:* Teresa McMenamin

**Diocesan Office**
*Diocesan Administrator*
Rt Rev Mgr Eamon Martin
*Chancellor:* Rev Paul McCafferty
*Administrative & Financial Secretary*
Ms Teresa McMenamin
PO Box 227, Bishop's House,
Derry BT48 9YG
Tel 028-71262302 Fax 028-71371960
Email office@derrydiocese.org

**Diocesan Notaries**
Rev Kevin McElhennon Adm
Rev Francis Bradley
Very Rev Colum Clerkin PP, VF
Rev Eamonn Graham PP

**Priest Penitentiary**
Very Rev Kieran O'Doherty PP, VF
34 Moneysharvin Road, Swatragh
Co Derry BT46 5PY
Tel 028-79401236

## CATECHETICS EDUCATION

**Catholic Primary School Managers' Association**
*Contact:* Rev Peter Devlin PP
Parochial House, Malin, Co Donegal
Tel 074-9142022

**Catechetical Centre**
Derry Diocesan Catechetical Centre,
The Gate Lodge, 2 Francis Street,
Derry BT48 9DS
Tel 028-71264087 Fax 028-71269090
Email ddcc@derrydiocese.org
*Acting Director:* Rev Paul Farren
*Adviser:* Miss Thérèse Ferry
*Youth Co-ordinator:* Dominic O'Reilly
*Secretary:* Anne Marie Hickey

## LITURGY

**Diocesan Master of Ceremonies**
Rev Francis Bradley
Diocesan Pastoral Centre,
164 Bishop Street, Derry BT48 6UJ
Tel 028-71362475

## PASTORAL

**Accord**
***Derry Centre:*** Diocesan Pastoral Centre,
164 Bishop Street, Derry BT48 6UJ
Tel 028-71362475 Fax 028-71260970
***Omagh Centre:*** Mount St Columba
Pastoral Centre, 48 Brook Street, Omagh,
Co Tyrone BT78 5HD
Tel 028-82242439
***Maghera Centre:*** Pastoral Centre,
159 Glen Road, Maghera
Tel 028-79642983
***Inishowen Centre:*** Pastoral Centre
Church Road, Carndonagh, Co Donegal
Tel 074-9374103

**Chaplain to the Deaf**
Rev Eamon Graham PP
42 Glenedra Road, Feeny,
Dungiven, Co Derry BT47 4TW
Tel 028-77781223

**Charismatic Renewal**
*Director:* Rev Seamus Kelly PP
40 Derrynoid Road, Draperstown,
Co Derry BT45 7DN
Tel 028-79628376

**Columba Community**
*Chaplain:* Rev Neal Carlin
St Anthony's, Dundrean,
Burnfoot, Co Donegal
Tel 074-9368370
Email sarced@eircom.net
Columba House, 11 Queen Street,
Derry BT48 7E6
Tel 028-71262407

**Communications**
*Media Liaison Person:*
Rev Michael Canny PP
32 Chapel Road, Derry BT47 2BB
Tel 028-71342303
Email michaelcanny1958@gmail.com

**Ecumenism**
*Director:* Rev Eamon McDevitt PP
78 Lisnaragh Road, Dunamanagh,
Strabane, Co Tyrone BT82 0QN
Tel 028-71398212

**Family Care Society (NI)**
Colmcille House, 1A Millar Street,
Derry BT48 6SU
Tel 028-71368592

**Library/Museum**
*Curators:* Rev John R. Walsh PP
Buncrana
Rev Brian McGoldrick PP
Doneyloop
Very Rev Kieran Devlin PP, Gortin

**Marriage Tribunal**
(See Marriage Tribunals section)

**Migrants and Asylum Seekers**
Rev Pat O'Hagan PP
Parochial House, Moville,
Co Donegal
Tel 074-9382057

**NEST – New Existence for Survivors of Trauma**
*Ministry to adult victims of abuse of all kinds.*
*Centre:* Pastoral Centre,
Maghera BT46 5JN
Tel 028-79642983
Email nest.int@btconnect.com

**Pastoral Centres**
***Diocesan Pastoral Centre***
164 Bishop Street,
Derry BT48 6UJ
Tel 028-71362475 Fax 028-71260970
*Director:* Rev Francis Bradley

***Inishowen Pastoral Centre***
Carndonagh, Co Donegal
Tel 074-9374103
*Director:* Rev Con McLaughlin PP

***Maghera Pastoral Centre***
159 Glen Road, Maghera, Co Derry
Tel 028-79642983
*Director*
Very Rev Patrick Doherty PP, EV

***Omagh Pastoral Centre***
Mount St Columba Pastoral Centre,
48 Brooke Street, Omagh,
Co Tyrone BT78 5HD
Tel 028-82242439
*Director:* Rev John McDevitt CC

**Pilgrimages**
*Lourdes and Marian:*
Sr Perpetua McNulty
Thornhill Centre, Culmore Road,
Derry BT48 5JA
Tel 028-71351233

**Pioneer Total Abstinence Association**
*Director:* Rev John Downey CC
36 Moneyneena Road, Draperstown,
Magherafelt, Co Derry BT45 7DZ
Tel 028-79628375

**Travellers**
*Chaplain*
Very Rev Brian Donnelly PP, EV
20 Derbrough Road, Plumbridge,
Co Tyrone BT79 8EF

**Trócaire**
*Diocesan Representative:*
Rev Colm O'Doherty PP
16 Castlefin Road, Castlederg,
Co Tyrone BT81 7EB
Tel 028-81671393

**Vocations**
*Directors:* Rev Colm O'Doherty PP
16 Castlefin Road, Castlederg,
Co Tyrone BT81 7EB
Tel 028-81671393
Rev Paul Farren Adm
St Eugene's Cathedral,
Derry BT48 9AP
Tel 028-71262894

## PARISHES

*Mensal parishes are listed first, followed by other Derry city parishes. Other parishes follow alphabetically. Historical names are in parentheses. Church titulars are in italics.*

**DERRY CITY**
*Templemore (St Eugene's & St Columbas)*
Rev Paul Farren Adm
Rev Daniel McFaul CC
Parochial House, St Eugene's Cathedral,
Derry BT48 9AP
Tel 028-71262894/71365712
Fax 028-71377494
Email steugenes@btconnect.com
Rev Gerard Mongan CC
Rev Joseph Varghese *(priest in residence)*
St Columba's Presbytery,
18 Pump Street, Derry BT48 6JG
Tel 028-71262301
Fax 028-71372973
Email longtowerparish@aol.com

**THE THREE PATRONS**
Rev Michael M. Caughey PP
St Patrick's, Buncrana Road, Pennyburn,
Derry BT48 7QL
Tel 028-71262360
Rev Dermott Harkin CC
St Brigid's, Carnhill, Derry BT48 8HJ
Tel 028-71351261
Rev Dermot McGirr CC
St Joseph's, Fairview Road, Galliagh,
Derry BT48 8NJ
Tel 028-71352351

**ST MARY'S, CREGGAN**
Rev Thomas Canning Adm
Rev Gerald Hasson CC
Parochial House, St Mary's, Creggan,
Derry BT48 9QE
Tel 028-71263152 Fax 028-71264390
Email cregganchapel@aol.com

**OUR LADY OF LOURDES, STEELSTOWN**
Very Rev John Cargan PP
Rev Francis Bradley *(priest in residence)*
The Presbytery, 11 Steelstown Road,
Derry BT48 8EU
Tel 028-71351718 Fax 028-71357810
Email steelstown@aol.com

**HOLY FAMILY, BALLYMAGROARTY**
Rev Patrick O'Kane PP
1 Aileach Road, Ballymagroarty,
Derry BT48 0AZ
Tel 028-71267070 Fax 028-71308687

**AGHYARAN (TERMONAMONGAN)**
*St Patrick's*
Rev John Gilmore PP
11 Church Road, Aghyaran,
Castlederg, Co Tyrone BT81 7XZ
Tel 028-81670728
Email moregilj@enterprise.net

**ARDMORE**
*St Mary's*
Rev Neil Farren PP
Parochial House, 49 Ardmore Road,
Derry BT47 3QP
Tel 028-71349490

**BALLINASCREEN (DRAPERSTOWN)**
*St Columba's*
Rev Seamus Kelly PP
40 Derrynoid Road, Draperstown,
Magherafelt, Co Derry BT45 7DN
Tel 028-79628376
Rev John Downey CC
36 Moneyneena Road,
Draperstown, Magherafelt,
Co Derry BT45 7DZ
Tel 028-79628375

**BANAGHER**
*St Joseph's, Fincairn*
Rev Eamon Graham PP
42 Glenedra Road, Feeny,
Co Derry BT47 4TW
Tel 028-77781223
Rev Arthur P. O'Reilly CC
285 Foreglan Road, Dungiven,
Co Derry BT47 4PJ
Tel 028-71338261

**BELLAGHY (BALLYSCULLION)**
*St Mary's*
Rev Andrew Dolan PP
25 Ballynease Road, Bellaghy,
Magherafelt, Co Derry BT45 8JS
Tel 028-79386259
Email frdolan@bellaghyparish.com

**BUNCRANA (DESERTEGNEY AND LOWER FAHAN)**
*St Mary's, Cockhill*
Rev John Walsh PP
Parochial House, Buncrana,
Co Donegal
Tel 074-9361393 Fax 074-9361637
Rev George Doherty CC
Glebe, Linsfort, Buncrana,
Co Donegal
Tel 074-9361126
Rev Rafal Januszewski
2 Gortaugher, Lisnakelly,
Buncrana, Co Donegal
Tal 074-9363455
*Parish Office:* Tel 074-9361253
Fax 074-9361637
Email buncranaparish@eircom.net

**CARNDONAGH (DONAGH)**
*Sacred Heart*
Rev Con McLaughlin PP
Barrack Hill, Carndonagh,
Lifford, Co Donegal
Tel 074-9374104

**CASTLEDERG (ARDSTRAW WEST AND CASTLEDERG)**
*St Eugene's*
Rev Colm O'Doherty PP
16 Castlefin Road, Castlederg,
Co Tyrone BT81 7EB
Tel 028-81671393
Email c.odoherty@btinternet.com

**CLAUDY (CUMBER UPPER AND LEARMOUNT)**
*St Patrick's*
Rev David O'Kane PP
9 Church Street, Claudy,
Co Derry BT47 4AA
Tel 028-71337727
Fax 028-71338236

**CLONMANY**
*St Mary's*
Rev Fintan Diggin PP
Parochial House, Cleagh,
Clonmany, Co Donegal
Tel 074-9376264

**COLERAINE (DUNBOE, MACOSQUIN AND AGHADOWEY)**
*St John's*
Rev Charles Keaney PP
Chapelfield, 59 Laurel Hill,
Coleraine, Co Derry BT51 3AY
Tel 028-70343130

**CULDAFF**
*St Mary's, Bocan*
Very Rev James McGonagle PP, VF
Parochial House,
Culdaff, Co Donegal
Tel 074-9379107
Email caz_derg_1@compuserve.com

**CULMORE**
*Assumption*
Very Rev Colum Clerkin PP, VF
23 Thornhill Park, Culmore,
Derry BT48 4PB
Tel 028-71358519 Fax 028-71353161
Email info@culmore.com
Website www.culmore.com

**DESERTMARTIN (DESERTMARTIN AND KILCRONAGHAN)**
*St Mary's, Coolcalm*
Rev Peter Madden PP
50 Tobermore Road, Desertmartin,
Magherafelt, Co Derry BT45 5LE
Tel 028-79632196 Fax 028-79300051
Email desertmartin@aol.com

**DONEYLOOP (URNEY AND CASTLEFINN)**
*St Columba's*
Rev Brian McGoldrick PP
Doneyloop, Castlefin, Lifford, Co Donegal
Tel 074-9146183
Email bfmcfgoldrick@eircom.net
Rev Desmond Polke *(priest in residence)*
Parochial House, Castlefin,
Lifford, Co Donegal
Tel 074-9146251

**DRUMQUIN (LANGFIELD)**
*St Patrick's*
Fr Kevin Mullan PP
257 Dooish Road, Drumquin,
Omagh, Co Tyrone BT78 4RA
Tel 028-82831225

**DUNAMANAGH (DONAGHEADY)**
*St Patrick's*
Rev Eamon McDevitt PP
78 Lisnaragh Road, Dunamanagh,
Strabane, Co Tyrone BT82 0QN
Tel 028-71398212

**DUNGIVEN**
*St Patrick's*
Rev Aidan Mullan PP
19 Chapel Road, Dungiven,
Co Derry BT47 4RT
Tel 028-77741219 Fax 028-77742633
Email dungivenparish@aol.com
Rev Francis Lynch (OP) CC
2 Station Road, Dungiven,
Co Derry BT47 4LN
Tel 028-77741256 Fax 028-77742953
Rev Michael Mullan CC
300 Drumsurn Road, Limavady,
Co Derry BT49 0PX
Tel 028-77762165

**FAHAN (BURT, INCH AND FAHAN)**
*St Mura's*
Rev Neil McGoldrick PP
Parochial House, Fahan,
Lifford, Co Donegal
Tel 074-9360151
Rev Gerard Sweeney CC
Parochial House, Burt, Lifford, Co Donegal
Tel 074-9368155

**FAUGHANVALE (FAUGHANVALE AND LOWER CUMBER)**
*Star of the Sea*
Rev Patrick Mullan PP
Stella Maris House, Eglinton,
Co Derry BT47 3EA
Tel 028-71810240
Rev Noel McDermott CC
91 Ervey Road, Eglinton,
Co Derry BT47 3AU
Tel 028-71810235

**GARVAGH (ERRIGAL)**
*St Mary's, Ballerin*
Rev Brian Brady PP
78 Ballerin Road, Garvagh,
Co Derry BT51 5EQ
Tel 028-29558251
Rev Karl Haan CC
33 Glen Road, Garvagh, Co Derry BT51 5DB
Tel 028-29558342

**GORTIN (BADONEY LOWER)**
*St Patrick's*
Very Rev John Forbes PP
Parochial House, Gortin, Omagh,
Co Tyrone BT79 8PU
Tel 028-81648203

**GREENCASTLE**
*St Patrick's*
Rev Eugene Hasson PP
164 Greencastle Road, Omagh,
Co Tyrone BT79 7RU
Tel 028-81648474 Fax 028-81647829
Email smacridire@hotmail.com

**GREENLOUGH (TAMLAGHT O'CRILLY)**
*St Mary's*
Rev Oliver Crilly PP
230b Mayogall Road,
Clady, Portglenone,
Co Derry BT44 8NN
Tel 028-25821190

**ISKAHEEN (ISKAHEEN AND UPPER MOVILLE)**
*St Mary's*
Very Rev John Farren PP
Muff, Co Donegal
Tel 074-9384037 Fax 074-9384029
Rev Anthony Mailey CC
Parochial House
Quigley's Point, Co Donegal
Tel 074-9383008

**KILLYCLOGHER (CAPPAGH)**
*St Mary's*
Rev Eugene Boland PP
14 Killyclogher Road, Omagh,
Co Tyrone BT79 0AX
Rev Kevin McElhennon Adm *Protem*
5 Strathroy Road, Omagh,
Co Tyrone BT79 7DW
Tel 028-82251055
Rev Francis Murray CC
46 Knockmoyle Road, Omagh,
Co Tyrone BT79 7TB
Tel 028-82242793

**KILLYGORDON (DONAGHMORE)**
*St Patrick's*
Rev Patrick Arkinson PP
Sessiaghoneill, Ballybofey, Co Donegal
Tel 074-9131149
Rev Robert Devine *(priest in residence)*
Crossroads, Killygordon, Co Donegal
Tel 074-9149194

**KILREA (KILREA AND DESERTOGHILL)**
*St Mary's, Drumagarner*
Rev Brendan Doherty PP
4 Garvagh Road, Kilrea,
Co Derry BT51 5QP
Tel 028-29540343
Rev Charles Logue CC
91 Drumgarner Road, Kilrea,
Co Derry BT51 5TE
Tel 028-29540528

**LAVEY (TERMONEENY AND PART OF MAGHERA)**
*St Mary's*
Rev Patrick Baker PP
65 Mayogall Road, Knockloughrim,
Magherafelt, Co Derry BT45 8PG
Tel 028-79642458

**LECKPATRICK (LECKPATRICK AND PART OF DONAGHEADY)**
*St Mary's, Cloughcor*
Rev Michael Porter PP
Parochial House, 447 Victoria Road,
Ballymagorry, Strabane,
Co Tyrone BT82 0AT
Tel 028-718802274 Fax 028-71884353

**LIFFORD (CLONLEIGH)**
*St Patrick's, Murlog*
Rev Edward Kilpatrick PP
Murlog, Lifford, Co Donegal
Tel 074-9142022
Parish Office: St Patrick's Church,
Murlog, Lifford,
Co Donegal
Tel/Fax 074-9142001

**LIMAVADY (DRUMACHOSE, TAMLAGHT, FINLAGAN AND PART OF AGHANLOO)**
*St Mary's, Irish Green Street*
Rt Rev Mgr Bryan McCanny PP
119 Irish Green Street, Limavady,
Co Derry BT49 9AB
Tel 028-77765649 Fax 028-77765290
Rev Edward Gallagher CC
4 Scroggy Road, Limavady,
Co Derry BT49 0NA
Tel 028-77763944
Rev Liam Donnelly CC
20 Loughermore Road, Ogill, Ballykelly,
Co Derry BT49 9PD
Tel 028-77762721

**MAGHERA**
*St Patrick's, Glen*
Very Rev Patrick Doherty PP
159 Glen Road, Maghera,
Co Derry BT46 5JN
Tel 028-79642496
Fax 028-79644593
Rev Brian O'Donnell CC
157 Glen Road, Maghera,
Co Derry BT46 5JN
Tel 028-79642359
*Parish Office:* 159A Glen Road,
Maghera, Co Derry BT46 5JN
Tel 028-79642983

**MAGILLIGAN**
*St Aidan's*
Rev Francis O'Hagan PP
71 Duncrun Road, Bellarena,
Limavady, Co Derry BT49 0JD
Tel 028-77750226

**MALIN (CLONCA)**
*St Patrick's, Aghaclay*
Rev Peter Devlin PP
Malin, Co Donegal
Tel 074-9370615
Rev Brendan Crowley CC
Malin Head, Co Donegal
Tel 074-9370134

**MELMOUNT (MOURNE)**
*St Mary's, Melmount, Strabane*
Rev Michael Doherty PP
39 Melmount Road, Strabane,
Co Tyrone BT82 9EF
Tel 028-71882648
*Parish Office:*
Melmount Parish Centre,
Melmount Road, Strabane,
Co Tyrone BT82 9EF
Tel 028-71383777
Fax 028-71886469
Email melparish@aol.com

**MOVILLE (MOVILLE LOWER)**
*St Mary's, Ballybrack*
Rev Patrick O'Hagan PP
Tel 074-9382057
Rev Patrick McGoldrick CC
Tel 074-9382102
Parochial House,
Moville, Co Donegal

**NEWTOWNSTEWART (ARDSTRAW EAST)**
*St Eugene's, Glenock*
Rev Stephen Kearney PP
41 Moyle Road, Newtownstewart,
Co Tyrone BT78 4AP
Tel 028-81661445 Fax 028-81662462
Email ardstraw@btinternet.com

**OMAGH (DRUMRAGH)**
*St Mary's, Drumragh*
Rt Rev Mgr Joseph Donnelly PP, VF
52 Brook Street, Omagh,
Co Tyrone BT78 5HE
Tel 028-82243011
Fax 028-82252149
Email jopd@drumraghparish.com
Rev John McDevitt CC
50 Brook Street, Omagh,
Co Tyrone BT78 5HE
Tel 028-82242092
*Parish Office:* 48 Brook Street,
Omagh, Co Tyrone BT78 5HE
Tel 028-82442092
Fax 028-82252149

**PLUMBRIDGE (BADONEY UPPER)**
*Sacred Heart*
Very Rev Brian Donnelly PP
Parochial House, Plumbridge,
Omagh, Co Tyrone BT79 8EF
Tel 028-81648283

**SION MILLS**
*St Theresa's*
Rev Peter McLaughlin PP
143 Melmount Road, Sion Mills,
Strabane, Co Tyrone BT82 9EX
Tel 028-81658264

**STRABANE (CAMUS)**
*Immaculate Conception*
Rev Declan Boland PP
44 Barrack Street, Strabane,
Co Tyrone BT82 8HD
Tel 028-71883293
Fax 028-71882615
Email declan@strabaneparish.com

**STRATHFOYLE (STRATHFOYLE, ENAGH LOUGH)**
*St Oliver Plunkett*
Served by the Parish of Glendermot
Parochial House, Parkmore Drive,
Strathfoyle, Co Derry BT47 1XA
Tel 028-71342303

**SWATRAGH**
*St John the Baptist*
Very Rev Kieran O'Doherty PP, VF
34 Moneysharvin Road, Swatragh,
Maghera, Co Derry BT46 5PY
Tel 028-79401236

**WATERSIDE (GLENDERMOTT)**
*St Columb's*
Rev Michael Canny PP
Rev Roland Colhoun CC
Rev Chris Ferguson CC
Parochial House, 32 Chapel Road,
Waterside, Derry BT47 2BB
Tel 028-71342303 Fax 028-71345495
Website www.watersideparish.org

## INSTITUTIONS AND THEIR CHAPLAINS

**Altnagelvin Hospital, Derry**
**Waterside General Hospital**
Rev Neil Farren PP
Rev Chris Ferguson CC
Parochial House, 32 Chapel Road,
Waterside, Derry BT47 2BB
Tel 028-71342303

**Community Hospital, Lifford**
Rev Edward Kilpatrick PP
Townparks, Lifford, Co Donegal
Tel 074-9142001

**District Hospital, Carndonagh**
Rev Con McLaughlin PP
Parochial House, Carndonagh
Tel 074-9174104

**Foyle Hospice**
Most Rev Edward Daly DD
9 Steelstown Road, Derry BT48 8EU
Tel 028-71359809

**Gransha Hospital, Derry**
Rev Neil Farren PP
Rev Chris Ferguson CC
Parochial House, 32 Chapel Road,
Waterside, Derry BT47 2BB
Tel 028-71342303

**Magilligan Prison**
Point Road, Magilligan,
Limavady BT49 OLR, Co Derry
Rev Francis O'Hagan PP
Tel 028-77763311

**Nazareth House**
Bishop Street, Derry BT48 6UN
Rev John Irwin
Tel 028-71261425/71262180

**Nazareth House**
Fahan, Co Donegal
Rev Neil McGoldrick PP
Tel 074-9360151

**Tyrone County Hospital, Omagh**
Rev Kevin McElhennon Adm

**Tyrone and Fermanagh Hospital, Omagh**
Rev Kevin McElhennon Adm

**University of Ulster**
Magee College, Derry
Rev Paul Mc Cafferty
Derry Diocesan Office, Bishop's House,
Derry BT48 9AP
Tel 028-71262302

## PRIESTS OF THE DIOCESE ELSEWHERE

Rev Manus Bradley
St Ignatius of Loyola,
4455 West Broadway, Montreal,
Quebec H4B 2A7
Rt Rev Mgr Brendan Devlin MA, DD
St Patrick's College, Maynooth, Co Kildare
Tel 01-6285222
Rev Paul Fraser
c/o Our Lady Queen of Heaven,
111 Portsmouth Road, Frimley,
Camberley, Surrey GU16 7AA
Tel 01276-504876
Rev James McGrory
Armagh Regional Marriage Tribunal,
15 College Street, Armagh BT61 9BT
Tel 028-37524537
Rev Peter O'Kane
Pontificio Collegio Irlandese,
Via Dei SS Auattro 1, 00184 Roma
Rev Seamus O'Kane
12 Gortinure Road, Maghera,
Co Derry BT46 5RB
Tel 07989-946344
Email sokane@maghera.fsnet.co.uk

## RETIRED PRIESTS

Rev Bernard Bryson PEm
Rev Kieran Devlin PEm
Rev Joseph Doherty PEm
Rev T. Phil Donnelly PEm
Rev John Farrell PEm
Rev Kevin McKenna PEm
Rev George McLaughlin
Rev Colm Morris PEm
Rev John Ryder PEm
Rev John McCullagh PEm
Rev Michael Keaveny PEm
Rev Michael Collins PEm
Rev John Doherty PEm
Rev Patrick Crilly PEm
Rev Joseph O'Conor PEm
Rev Francis Murray PEm
Rt Rev Mgr Ignatius McQuillan PEm

## RELIGIOUS ORDERS AND CONGREGATIONS

### PRIESTS

**CARMELITES (OCD)**
St Joseph's Retreat House,
Termonbacca, Derry BT48 9XE
Tel 028-71262512 Fax 028-71373589
*Prior:* Rev Sean Conlon (OCD)
Community: 5

**FRANCISCAN FRIARS OF THE RENEWAL (CFR)**
St Columba Friary,
6 Victoria Place, Derry BT48 6TJ
Tel 028-71260390 Fax 028-71369274
*Local Servant (Superior)*
Rev Columba Jordan

### BROTHERS

**CHRISTIAN BROTHERS**
20 Kevlin Road, Omagh,
Co Tyrone BT78 2LD
Tel 028-82242103
*Community Leader:* Br Tom Gough
Community: 4

### SISTERS

**CONGREGATION OF THE SISTERS OF MERCY**
Thornhill Centre,
121 Culmore Road, Derry BT48 8JF
Tel 028-71351233
Sisters involved in prayer and retreat ministry

St Catherine's, Thornhill,
123 Culmore Road, Derry BT48 8JF
Tel 028-71354082
Community: 5
Nursing care unit for sick and aged sisters

3 Steelstown Road, Derry BT48 8EU
Tel 028-71351432
Community: 4

4 School House Mews,
Eglinton, Co Derry BT47 3WA
Tel 028-71811464

22 Newtownkennedy Street,
Strabane, Co Tyrone BT82 8HT
Tel 028-71882269
Community: 6

Buncrana, Co Donegal
Tel 074-9361054
Community: 5

8A Sheelin Park, Ballymagroarty,
Derry BT48 0PD
Tel 028-71260398
Community: 5

6 Ballycolman Road, Melmount,
Strabane, Co Tyrone BT82 9PH
Tel 028-71885913
Community: 3

60 Steelstown, Derry BT48 8JA
Tel 028-71352300

North Gate Lodge,
125 Culmore Road, Derry BT48 8JF
Tel 028-71350014

1 Lawrence Hill, Derry BT48 7NJ
Tel 028-71269854
Community: 5

103 Elmvale,
Culmore, Derry BT48 8SL
Tel 028-71358507
*Contact:* Sr Frances O'Kane
Investing in excellence

3 Milestone Way,
Fintona Road, Tattyreagh,
Omagh, Co Tyrone BT78 2LY
Sr Mary Daly RSM
Sr Maura Twohig PBVM

32 Berkeley Heights, Killyclogher,
Omagh, Co Tyrone BT79 7PR
Tel 028-82243329

44 Ballynagard Crescent,
Culmore, Derry BT48 8JR
Tel 028-71355776

17 Garvaghy Mews, Rarogan Road,
Dungannon, Co Tyrone BT70 2DP

31 Belmont Crescent,
Derry BT48 7RR
Tel 028-71358758

16 Papworth Avenue, Derry BT48 8PT
Tel 028-71358827
Community: 3

**CONGREGATION OF ST JOHN**
Sisters of St John
10 Belvoir Park, Culmore, Derry
Tel 028-71353414
*Prioress:* Sr Mary Magdalen

**GOOD SHEPHERD SISTERS**
Dungiven Road, Waterside,
Derry BT47 2AL
Tel 028-71342429 Fax 028-71341711
Email rgsderry@hotmail.com
*Leader:* Sr Breda O'Connell
Community: 9

45 Virginia Court,
Gobnascale, Waterside,
Derry BT47 2DX
Tel 028-71345127 Fax 028-71312621
Email vircourt@yahoo.com
Community: 2
Social work apostolate

**HOLY FAMILY OF BORDEAUX SISTERS**
Holy Family Convent,
2a The High Street, Draperstown,
Co Derry BT45 7AA
Tel 028-79628030
*Contact:* Sr Rose Devlin
Community: 1
Pastoral work, urban and rural community development, community relations work, religious education of both able-bodied and disabled adults.

**CONGREGATION OF THE SISTERS OF NAZARETH**
Nazareth House, Bishop Street,
Derry BT48 6UN
Tel 028-71262180 Fax 028-71263254
*Superior:* Sr Anastasia Marie Lenihan
Community: 8
Residential home for elderly
Primary School
*Principal:* Mr Paul O'Hea
Tel 028-71280212
Pupils: 400

Nazareth House, Fahan,
Lifford, Co Donegal
Tel 074-9360113 Fax 074-9360561
*Superior:* Sr Alice Kirwan
Community: 8
Home for aged. Residents: 48

**LORETO (IBVM)**
Convent Grammar, Omagh BT78 1DL
Tel 028-82243633
Primary School,
Brookmount Road, Omagh
Tel 028-82243551

Loreto Community, Coleraine,
Co Derry BT51 3JZ
Tel 028-70344426
*Superior:* Sr Máire Lagan
Community: 10
Loreto College, Coleraine BT51 3JZ
Tel 028-70343611

Loreto Sisters, 30 Buskin Way, Coleraine,
Co Derry BT51 3BD
Tel 028-70358065
Community: 2
Educational and pastoral work

Loreto Community,
Linsfort, Buncrana, Co Donegal
Tel 074-9362204
*Superior:* Sr Eveleen Hallahan
Retreat and pastoral work

**SACRED HEART OF JESUS SISTERS**
119 Irish Green Street,
Limavady, Co Derry BT49 9AB
Tel 015047-68357
*Superior:* Sr Eileen McElhone
Community: 2
Pastoral ministry

## EDUCATIONAL INSTITUTIONS

**EDMUND RICE SCHOOLS TRUST NORTHERN IRELAND**
Christian Brothers Grammar School,
Kevlin Road, Omagh BT78 1LD
Tel 028-82243567 Fax 028-82240656
*Principal:* Mr Paul Brannigan

## CHARITABLE SOCIETIES

**St Vincent de Paul Diocesan Centre**
Ozanam House,
22 Bridge Street, Derry
Tel 028-71265489

Parish. Protected by Allianz.
Wherever you go. Whatever you do. With over 100 years of specialised experience, Allianz continues to serve the insurance needs of parishes, religious orders and schools.
Allianz
Allianz, Allianz House, Elmpark, Merrion Road, Dublin 4, Ireland.
Tel: + 353 1 613 3966. Fax: + 353 1 613 3630.
Email: education@allianz.ie Web: www.allianz.ie/schools
Allianz p.l.c. is regulated by the Financial Regulator. Terms and conditions apply.
Calls may be recorded or monitored for regulatory, training and quality purposes.

***Parish Services to Housebound Parishioners via WPAS Radio Link***
***Live Streaming Video of Chruch Services on the Internet***

## BELLS & CLOCKS

- Bells – Automation, Restoration & Re-hanging
- Survey, Maintenance and Replacement of Bell Support Structures
- Digital Electronic Bells & Carillons via speakers – (1000 hymns/peals)
- Tower Clocks – Hour Ringing – Westminster Chime
- Liturgical Calendar Event Programming

## COMMUNICATIONS

- The Parish Radio Link System
- Live Streaming Video of Church Serives on the Internet
- Sound & PA Amplification, Radio Microphones etc
- Audio Induction Loops for the Deaf
- Church Music Systems & Radio Remote Control

## ENGINEERING & BUILDING MAINTENANCE

- Bell Support Structure installation and restoration
- Water ingress protection. Guttering & drains – cleaning – repair
- Pointing and sealing of stone. Roofing slates, tiles & flashing repairs
- Stone surface cleaning & restoration
- Lightning Protection: Dynasphere 3000 & Traditional systems
- Automation – Control of Heating, Lighting, Door opening etc
- Height Access for Surveys & Engineering reports
- Hoist Access to 75 mtrs – competitively priced

Installations by our Experienced, Highly Qualified and
Fully Insured Technical Team
Full Guarantees & After Sales Support
Contact Jim Doyle or Leo Brophy

Head Office: Dunleary House
83 Dublin Road, Sutton, Dublin 13
Tel/Fax 01-8392220 • Mobile 087-2538916
Email belltron@infatron.com • Website www.belltron.ie

# DIOCESE OF DOWN AND CONNOR

PATRONS OF THE DIOCESE
ST MALACHY, 3 NOVEMBER; ST MACNISSI, 4 SEPTEMBER

INCLUDES COUNTY ANTRIM, THE GREATER PART OF COUNTY DOWN AND PART OF COUNTY DERRY

**Most Rev Noel Treanor DD**
Bishop of Down and Connor; ordained priest 13 June 1976; ordained Bishop of Down and Connor 29 June 2008

Residence: Lisbreen,
73 Somerton Road,
Belfast, Co Antrim BT15 4DE
Tel 028-90776185
Fax 028-90779377
Email
dccuria@downandconnor.org

## HISTORY OF THE DIOCESE

St Patrick does not provide many geographical details in his Confession about his sojourn in Ireland, yet a later tradition associated his work as a slave with Slemish in Co Antrim, his return as a missionary with Saul in Co Down and his burial place with Downpatrick.

In the course of his evangelisation of Ireland St Patrick ordained bishops to minister to local communities. Among those bishops was Mac Nissi, who, following his baptism by St Patrick, founded the church of Connor. However, by the sixth century, after Christianity had been well established, the monastic system was becoming the dominant form of ecclesiastical life. About 555 St Comgall founded a monastery at Bangor that was destined to become one of the most famous in Ireland. Monasteries were also founded in France, Switzerland and Italy, and these became influential centres for the conversion of many peoples. Other monasteries founded in the early centuries of Christianity in Down and Connor include those at Moville, Nendrum, Inch, Drumbo, Antrim and Comber. Some of these later adopted the Benedictine or Augustinian Rule.

The Norsemen cast greedy eyes on Irish monasteries, especially those near the coast, which could be easily attacked and plundered for silver and gold. Bangor fell victim to one such raid in 823, when many monks were killed and the shrine of St Comgall was destroyed. The loss of life and damage to buildings helped weaken the discipline and commitment of the monks. When St Malachy, the great reformer, became Abbot of Bangor in 1123, he found much of the abbey in ruins and the Rule being poorly observed.

In 1111, at the Synod of Rathbreasail, Ireland was at last given the diocesan territorial system that had been common in the western Church. Among the dioceses created were Connor for the Kingdom of Dalriada and Down for the Kingdom of Uladh. Though separate, these dioceses were united under St Malachy in 1124. He continued to reside at Bangor and pursue his reforms, but was driven from the monastery and forced to take refuge at Lismore. In 1129 he was appointed Archbishop of Armagh but because of local opposition, was not able to take control of the See until five years later. In 1137 he resigned and returned to the Diocese of Down, which was again separate from Connor. Invited by his fellow bishops to travel to Rome to obtain the pallia for the archbishops of Armagh and Cashel, Malachy set off in 1139 and visited St Bernard at Clairvaux. Though unsuccessful in his quest, he was appointed papal legate for Ireland. He left some monks at Clairvaux to be trained in the Cistercian way of life and they established the first Cistercian monastery at Mellifont in 1142. A second journey to Rome in 1148 to seek the pallia was cut short by his death on 2 November in the arms of St Bernard. The great Cistercian abbot later wrote Malachy's life story, which ensured that his fame spread widely on the Continent. Malachy was canonised in 1190.

In 1177 the Anglo-Norman adventurer, John de Courcy, carved out the Lordship of Ulster for himself and set up his base at Dunlethglaisse which he renamed Downpatrick. He took a keen interest in ecclesiastical affairs and brought Anglo-Norman Benedictine monks to the cathedral at Downpatrick. His wife founded the Cistercian Monastery at Greyabbey in the Ards Peninsula and he brought other Orders, such as the Premonstratensian and the Augustinian Canons to his territories.

In 1192 the Diocese of Dromore was cut off from Down to make provision for the native Irish, as the part that retained the name Down was by then regarded as Anglo-Norman. The Dioceses of Down and Connor continued to be administered separately until the fifteenth century. In 1439 Pope Eugene IV decided that, after the death of John Sely, the Bishop of Down, the two Sees should be united, and, although Sely was deprived of office three years later for misbehaviour, the Archbishop of Armagh resisted the union of the two dioceses for several years and it did not take place until 1453. In the 1220s the newly founded mendicant Orders, the Dominicans and Franciscans, established houses in the diocese. By the sixteenth century the Third Order of Franciscans had numerous friaries.

Robert Blyth, an English Benedictine, was Bishop of Down and Connor when Henry VIII demanded recognition as supreme Head of the Church. Blyth surrendered in 1539 and received a substantial pension. The Pope then deprived him of office and appointed in his place Eugene Magennis. Magennis also accepted the royal supremacy but later retracted his submission and was able to retain his See under Mary Tudor. The Franciscan pluralist, Miler McGrath, who succeeded in 1565 and accepted the royal supremacy in 1567, was deposed by Pope Gregory XIII in 1580 but had already been appointed Archbishop of Cashel by Queen Elizabeth. Two years later the Donegal Franciscan, Conor O'Devany, became bishop and after a lengthy episcopate of nearly thirty years was cruelly martyred in Dublin in 1612. (In 1992 he was one of the seventeen Irish martyrs beatified by Pope John Paul II)

During the upheavals of the seventeenth century and the harsh penal legislation of the early eighteenth century, the diocese was left vacant for long periods. After the death of Bishop Daniel Mackey in 1673 no appointment was made until Terence O'Donnelly became vicar apostolic in 1711. When O'Donnelly's successor, James O'Sheil, died in 1724 the See remained vacant until 1727. After the death of Bishop John Armstrong in 1739 all subsequent vacancies never lasted more than a year.

In 1825 William Crolly, who had been parish priest of Belfast for thirteen years, became bishop. Several of his predecessors had lived in or near Downpatrick but he chose to remain in the growing town which he rightly foresaw would become the largest in the diocese. Not only was Belfast geographically more central and convenient but its Catholic population soon dwarfed that of Downpatrick and of all other parishes in the diocese. By 1900 Catholics numbered 85,000 and represented just under a quarter of the city's population. The number of priests serving in it had greatly increased and religious orders of men and women had been brought in to care for the spiritual, educational and social needs of the people.

The continued increase in the number of Catholics in and around Belfast accounts for the position Down and Connor holds as the second largest diocese in Ireland, with a population of approximately 300,000.

**Most Rev Anthony Farquhar DD**
Titular Bishop of Ermiana and Auxiliary Bishop of Down and Connor; ordained priest 13 March 1965; ordained Bishop 15 May 1983
Office: 73 Somerton Road, Belfast BT15 4DE Tel 028-90776185
Residence: 24 Fruithill Park, Belfast BT11 8GE Tel 028-90624252

**Most Rev Donal McKeown DD**
Titular Bishop of Killossy and Auxiliary Bishop of Down and Connor; ordained priest 3 July 1977; ordained Bishop 29 April 2001
Office: 73 Somerton Road, Belfast BT15 4DE Tel 028-90776185
Residence: 96 Downview Park West, Belfast BT15 5HZ Tel 028-90781642

**Most Rev Patrick J. Walsh DD**
Bishop Emeritus of Down and Connor; ordained priest 25 February 1956; ordained Titular Bishop of Ros Cré 15 May 1983; installed Bishop of Down and Connor 28 April 1991
Residence: 6 Waterloo Park North, Belfast BT15 5HW
Tel 028-90778182

## CHAPTER

*Dean:* Rt Rev Brendan McGee
*Archdeacon:* Venerable Kevin Donnelly
*Members*
Very Rev Dominic McHugh
Very Rev Bernard Magee
Very Rev Noel Conway
Very Rev Hugh Starkey
Very Rev Robert Fullerton
Very Rev Malachy Murphy
Very Rev Brendan Murray
Very Rev George O'Hanlon
Very Rev Alex McMullan
Very Rev Sean Rogan

*Honorary Canons*
Very Rev Joseph Cunningham
Rt Rev Mgr Sean Connolly

## ADMINISTRATION

**Chancellor**
Very Rev Eugene O'Hagan *(Ad Interim)*
Lisbreen, 73 Somerton Road, Belfast BT15 4DE
Tel 028-90776185 Fax 028-90779377

**Vicar General**
Rt Rev Mgr Sean Connolly VG
7 Tullyview, Loughguile, Co Antrim BT44 9JY
Tel 077-39223280

**Vicar for Religious**
Vacant
*Assistants:* Sr Majella, Dominican Sister
Sr Francis, Mercy Sister
Br Christopher, De La Salle Brother

**Consultors**
Most Rev Anthony J. Farquhar
Most Rev Donal McKeown
Rt Rev Mgr Sean Connolly
Very Rev Brian Daly
Very Rev Sean Emerson
Very Rev John Forsythe
Very Rev Canon Sean Rogan
Very Rev Patrick Delargy
Very Rev Michael Spence
Rt Rev Mgr Colm McCaughan

**Episcopal Vicar for Sick & Retired Priests**
Very Rev Canon Alex McMullan

**Council of Priests**
*Chairman:* Very Rev John Forsythe PP
165 Antrim Road, Newtownabbey, Co Antrim BT36 7QR
Tel 028-90832979
*Secretary:* Very Rev Joseph Rooney
45 Ballyholme Esplanade, Bangor, Co Down BT20 5NJ
Tel 028-91465425

**Judicial Vicar for Diocese of Down and Connor**
Very Rev Eugene O'Hagan JCL
The Good Shepherd Centre,
511 Ormeau Road, Belfast BT7 3GS
Tel 028-90491990 Fax 028-90491440

**Finance Committee**
*Chairman:* Most Rev Noel Treanor
*Secretary:* Ms Maria Morgan
*Members:* Most Rev Anthony Farquhar
Most Rev Donal McKeown
Very Rev Eugene O'Hagan
Rev Joseph M. Glover
Mr Kevin Delaney
Mr Anthony Harbinson
Mr Charles Jenkins
Mr John B. McGuckian
Ms Alice Quinn
*Diocesan Financial Controller*
Rev Joseph M. Glover
Lisbreen, 73 Somerton Road, Belfast BT15 4DE
Tel 028-90776185 Fax 028-90779377
*Diocesan Financial Administrator*
Ms Maria Morgan
Lisbreen, 73 Somerton Road, Belfast BT15 4DE
Tel 028-90776185 Fax 028-90779377

**Diocesan Property Administrator**
Mr David Gantley RICS
73 Somerton Road, Belfast BT15 4DE
Tel 028-90776185 Fax 028-90779377
Email david@downandconnor.org

**Seminary Fund Committee**
*Chairman:* Most Rev Noel Treanor
*Secretary:* Very Rev Michael Spence
St Malachy's College,
36 Antrim Road, Belfast BT15 2AE
Tel 028-90748285

**Media Liaison Officer**
Rev Edward McGee
St Malachy's College, 36 Antrim Road, Belfast BT15 2AE
Tel 078-11144268

**Diocesan Archivist**
Very Rev Canon George O'Hanlon
62 Coolkeeran Road, Armoy, Ballymoney, Co Antrim BT53 8XN
Tel 028-20751121
*Assistant:* Rev Thomas McGlynn
The Cathedral Presbytery, St Peter's Square, Belfast BT12 4BU
Tel 028-90327573

**Diocesan Secretary**
Rev Joseph M. Glover
Lisbreen, 73 Somerton Road, Belfast BT15 4DE
Tel 028-90776185 Fax 028-90779377

## CATECHETICS AND EDUCATION

**Trustees Support Service**
*Director:* Mr Gerard Lundy
c/o Ara Coeli, Armagh BT61 7QY
Tel 028-37522045

**Diocesan Education Office**
*Senior Management Officer*
Ms Susan Sullivan
160 High Street, Holywood, Co Down BT18 9HT
Tel 028-90426972 Fax 028-90424255

**Diocesan Advisers in Religious Education**
Mr Frank Donnelly *(post-primary sector)*
Mrs Kathleen Hagan *(primary sector)*
Miss Catherine McGinnity *(primary sector)*
Miss Breda McKay *(primary sector)*
511 Ormeau Road, Belfast BT7 3GS
Tel 028-90491886 Fax 028-90491440
Email readvisers@btconnect.com

## LITURGY

**Diocesan Commission on Liturgy**
*Chairman*
Very Rev Canon Robert Fullerton
501 Ormeau Road, Belfast BT7 3GR
Tel 028-90641064
*Secretary:* Rev Aidan McCaughan
2-4 Broughshane Road, Ballymena, Co Antrim
Tel 028-25641515

## PASTORAL

**Accord**
***Regional Office***
*Administration Officer:* Mrs Sandra Hamilton
Cana House, 56 Lisburn Road, Belfast BT9 6AF
Tel 028-90233002 Fax 028-90328113
Email info@accordni.com
www.accordni.com
***Belfast***
Curran House, Twin Spires, Northumberland Street, Belfast BT13 2JF
Tel 028-90339944
***Ballymena***
All Saints Parish Centre, 9 Cushendall Road, Ballymena, Co Antrim
Tel 028-38334781
***Downpatrick***
*Priest Director:* Very Rev Colm McGrady
*Appointments Secretary*
Mrs Sheila McPoland
99 Irish Street, Downpatrick, Co Down BT30 6BS
Tel 028-44613435

**Office of the Armagh Regional Marriage Tribunal**
511 Ormeau Road, Belfast BT7 3GS
Tel 028-90491990 Fax 028-90491440
*Administrator*
Very Rev Eugene O'Hagan JCL
*Notary:* Rev Joseph Rooney JCL

**Ecumenism (Diocesan Committee)**
*Secretary:* Rev Colin Grant
St Malachy's College, Antrim Road, Belfast BT15 2AE
Tel 028-90748285

**Pioneer Total Abstinence Association**
*Diocesan Director*
Rev Raymond McCullagh
1 Seafield Park South, Portstewart BT55 7LH
Tel 028-70832066

**Pontifical Mission Societies**
*Diocesan Director*
Very Rev Colm McGrady PP
Parochial House, 8 Shore Road, Strangford, Co Down BT30 7NL
Tel 028-44881206

**Vocations**
*Director:* Very Rev John Murray PP
200 Finaghy Road North, Belfast BT11 9EG
Tel 028-90913761
*Assistant Director:* Rev Kevin McGuckien
St Patrick's Presbytery,
199 Donegall Street, Belfast BT1 2FL
Tel 028-90324597

**Diocesan Family Ministry Commission**
*Secretary:* Rev Michael McGinnity
Family Ministry Office,
Good Shepherd Centre,
511 Ormeau Road, Belfast BT7 3GS
Tel 028-90492777 Fax 028-90491779

**Diocesan Social Affairs Commission**
*Secretary:* Rev Timothy Bartlett
Irish Bishops' Conference, Columba Centre, St Patrick's College, Maynooth, Co Kildare
Tel 01-5053102

**Diocesan Care Home**
Our Lady's Home,
68 Ard Na Va Road, Belfast BT12 6FF
*Director:* Very Rev John C. O'Connor
Tel 028-90325731/90242429
Fax 028-90249596

**Children's Home**
Glenmona Resource Centre
Glen Road, Belfast BT11 8BX
Tel 028-90301100
Director: Mr Liam Dumigan

**Diocesan Youth Commission**
68 Berry Street, Belfast BT1 1FJ
Tel 028-90232432 Fax 028-90239598
*Chairperson:* Ms Pauline Dowd
*Director:* Vacant

**Youth Link Training Offices**
143 University Street, Belfast BT7 1HP
Tel 028-90323217 Fax 028-90323247
*Training and Development Officer*
Rev Patrick White

## PARISHES

*Mensal parishes are listed first. Other parishes follow alphabetically, city parishes first. Historical names are in parentheses.*

**THE CATHEDRAL (ST PETER'S)**
Rev Thomas McGlynn Adm *(Ad Interim)*
St Peter's Cathedral Presbytery,
St Peter's Square, Belfast BT12 4BU
Tel 028-90327573
Rev Paul Turley (CSsR)
Rev Alphonsus Doran (CSsR)
Clonard Monastery,
1 Clonard Gardens, Belfast BT13 2RL
Tel 028-90445950

**ST MARY'S**
Very Rev James A. Boyle (MHM) Adm
Rev James O'Donoghue (MHM) CC
Rev John Nevin (MHM)
St Mary's, Marquis Street, Belfast BT1 1JJ
Tel 028-90320482

**ST PATRICK'S**
Very Rev Michael Sheehan Adm
Dean Brendan McGee
Rev Kevin McGuckien CC
St Patrick's Presbytery,
199 Donegall Street, Belfast BT1 2FL
Tel 028-90324597

**HOLY FAMILY**
Very Rev Gerard McCloskey Adm
Holy Family Presbytery,
Newington Avenue, Belfast BT15 2HP
Tel 028-90743119
Rev Colin Crossey CC
120 Cavehill Road, Belfast BT15 5BU
Tel 028-90714892
Very Rev Canon Brendan Murray
*(Priest in residence)*
Apt 13 Downview Manor, Belfast BT15 4JL

**ST COLMCILLE'S**
Very Rev Ciaran Feeney Adm
Rev Krzysztof Olejnik (SCHR) CC and providing pastoral care for the Polish community
191 Upper Newtownards Road, Belfast BT4 3JB
Tel 028-90654157

## CITY PARISHES

**CHRIST THE REDEEMER, LAGMORE**
Very Rev Martin Graham PP
81 Lagmore Grove, Dunmurry, Belfast BT17 0TD
Tel 028-90309011

**CORPUS CHRISTI**
Very Rev Darach Mac Giolla Catháin PP
Corpus Christi Presbytery,
4-6 Springhill Grove, Belfast BT12 7SL
Tel 028-90246857
Very Rev Aidan Denny
10 New Barnsley Green, New Barnsley, Belfast BT12 7HS
Tel 028-90328877

**DERRIAGHY**
Very Rev Paul Byrne PP
111 Queensway, Lambeg, Lisburn BT27 4QS
Tel 028-92662896

**GREENCASTLE**
Very Rev Anthony Alexander PP
824 Shore Road, Newtownabbey, Co Antrim BT36 7DG
Tel 028-90370845

**HOLY CROSS**
Very Rev Gary Donegan (CP) PP
Rev Casimir Haran (CP) CC
Rev John Craven (CP) CC
Holy Cross Retreat, 432 Crumlin Road, Ardoyne, Belfast BT14 7GE
Tel 028-90748231/2

**HOLY ROSARY**
Very Rev Patrick McKenna PP, VF
503 Ormeau Road, Belfast BT7 3GR
Tel 028-90642446
Very Rev Canon Robert Fullerton CC
Holy Rosary Presbytery,
501 Ormeau Road, Belfast BT7 3GR
Tel 028-90641064

**HOLY TRINITY**
Very Rev Matthew Wallace PP
Holy Trinity Presbytery,
26 Norglen Gardens, Belfast BT11 8EL
Tel 028-90590985/6

**THE NATIVITY**
Very Rev Patrick Sheehan PP
Rev Vincent Cushnahan CC
The Presbytery, Bell Steel Road, Poleglass, Belfast BT17 0PB
Tel 028-90625739

**OUR LADY QUEEN OF PEACE, KILWEE**
Very Rev Colm McBride PP
Netherley Lodge, 130 Upper Dunmurry Lane, Belfast BT17 0EW
Tel 028-90616300

**SACRED HEART**
Very Rev Ciaran Dallat PP
Sacred Heart Presbytery,
1 Glenview Street, Belfast BT14 7DP
Tel 028-90351851

**ST AGNES'**
Very Rev Peter Owens PP
143 Andersonstown Road, Belfast BT11 9BW
Tel 028-90615702/90603951
Rev Robert Markuszewski CC
139 Andersonstown Road, Belfast BT11 9 BW
Tel 028-90613724

**ST ANNE'S**
Very Rev Feargal McGrady PP
St Anne's Parochial House,
Kingsway, Finaghy, Belfast BT10 0NE
Tel 028-90610112

**ST ANTHONY'S**
Very Rev Stephen McBrearty PP
St Anthony's Presbytery, 4 Willowfield Crescent, Belfast BT6 8HP
Tel 028-90458158

**ST BERNADETTE'S**
Very Rev Paul Armstrong PP
28 Willowbank Park, Belfast BT6 0LL
Tel 028-90793023

**ST BRIGID'S**
Very Rev Edward O'Donnell PP
42 Derryvolgie Avenue, Belfast BT9 6FP
Tel 028-90665409

**ST GERARD'S**
Redemptorist Fathers
Very Rev Gerard Cassidy (CSsR) PP and Rector
Rev Patrick McLoughlin (CSsR) CC
722 Antrim Road, Newtownabbey,
Co Antrim BT36 7PG
Tel 028-90774833/4

**ST JOHN'S**
Very Rev Paul Strain PP
470 Falls Road, Belfast BT12 6EN
Tel 028-90321511
Rev Mariusz Dabrowski CC
Very Rev Anthony McLaverty *(priest in residence)*
470 Falls Road, Belfast BT12 6EN
Tel 028-90321102

**ST LUKE'S**
Very Rev Brian McCann PP
St Luke's Presbytery, Twinbrook Road,
Dunmurry, Co Antrim BT17 0RP
Tel 028-90619459

**ST MALACHY'S**
Very Rev Michael McGinnity PP
St Malachy's Presbytery,
24 Alfred Street, Belfast BT2 8EN
Tel 028-90321713

**ST MARY'S ON THE HILL**
Very Rev John Forsythe PP
Elmfield, 165 Antrim Road, Glengormley,
Newtownabbey, Co Antrim BT36 7QR
Tel 028-90832979
Rev Eugene O'Neill CC
142 Carnmoney Road, Newtownabbey,
Co Antrim BT36 6JU
Tel 028-90832488
Very Rev Brendan Beagon CC
1 Christine Road, Newtownabbey,
Co Antrim BT36 6TG
Tel 028-90841507

**ST MATTHEW'S**
Very Rev Aidan Keenan PP
St Matthew's Presbytery, Bryson Street,
Newtownards Road, Belfast BT5 4ES
Tel 028-90457626

**ST MICHAEL'S**
Very Rev John Murray PP
Rev Eamon McCreave (OSM)
St Michael's Presbytery,
206 Finaghy Road North, Belfast BT11 9EG
Tel 028-90913761

**ST OLIVER PLUNKETT**
Very Rev Martin Magill PP
27 Glenveagh Drive, Belfast BT11 9HX
Tel 028-90618180

**ST PAUL'S**
Very Rev Anthony Devlin PP
Rev Antony Perumayan CC and Guardian of the Syro-Malabar Catholics
St Paul's Presbytery, 125 Falls Road,
Belfast BT12 6AB
Tel 028-90325034
*Assistant Priest*
Rev Patrick Horgan (CSsR)
Clonard Monastery, Clonard Gardens,
Belfast BT13 2RL

**ST TERESA'S**
Very Rev Brendan Hickland PP
St Teresa's Presbytery, Glen Road,
Belfast BT11 8BL
Tel 028-90612855
Rt Rev Mgr Thomas Toner
43b Glen Road, Belfast BT11 8BB
Tel 028-90613949

**ST VINCENT DE PAUL**
Very Rev Patrick Devlin PP
St Vincent de Paul Presbytery,
169 Ligoniel Road, Belfast BT14 8DP
Tel 028-90713401

**WHITEABBEY (ST JAMES'S)**
Very Rev Anthony Alexander PP
824 Shore Road,
Newtownabbey BT36 7DG
Very Rev Samuel Kerr *(priest in residence)*
463 Shore Road, Whiteabbey,
Newtownabbey, Co Antrim BT37 0AE
Tel 028-90365773

**WHITEHOUSE**
Very Rev Anthony Alexander PP
824 Shore Road,
Newtownabbey BT36 7DG
Rev Joseph Glover *(priest in residence)*
Star of the Sea Presbytery,
305 Shore Road, Whitehouse,
Newtownabbey, Co Antrim BT37 9RY

## COUNTRY PARISHES

**AGHAGALLON AND BALLINDERRY**
Very Rev Laurence McElhill PP
Parochial House, 5 Aghalee Road,
Aghagallon, Craigavon,
Co Armagh BT67 0AR
Tel 028-92651214

**AHOGHILL**
Very Rev Hugh J O'Hagan PP
Parochial House, 31 Ballynafie Road,
Ahoghill BT42 1LF
Tel 028-25871351

**ANTRIM**
Very Rev Sean Emerson PP
Parochial House, 3 Oriel Road,
Antrim BT41 4HP
Tel 028-94428016
Very Rev Felix McGuckin
5 Oriel Road, Antrim BT41 4HP
Tel 028-94428086
Rev Michael McConville *(Assistant Priest)*
65 Moyle Road, Ballycastle,
Co Antrim BT54 6LG
Tel 078-81490543

**ARMOY**
Very Rev Christopher Nellis PP
Parochial House, Armoy,
Ballymoney, Co Antrim BT53 8RL
Tel 028-20751205

**BALLINTOY**
Very Rev Brian Daly Adm
Rev Hugh O'Kane (SMA) CC *(priest in residence)*
53 Ballinlea Road, Ballycastle,
Co Antrim BT54 6JL
Tel 028-20762498

**BALLYCASTLE (RAMOAN)**
Very Rev Brian Daly PP
Parochial House, 15 Moyle Road,
Ballycastle, Co Antrim BT54 6LB
Tel 028-20762223
Rev Hugh O'Kane (SMA) CC
53 Ballinlea Road,
Ballycastle, Co Antrim BT54 6JL
Tel 028-20762498
Rev Barney McCahery (CSsR) CC
6 Market Street,
Ballycastle, Co Antrim BT54 6DP
Tel 028-20762202

**BALLYCLARE AND BALLYGOWAN**
Very Rev Eugene O'Hagan Adm
Parochial House, 69 Doagh Road,
Ballyclare, Co Antrim BT39 9BG
Tel 028-93342226

**BALLYGALGET**
Very Rev Patrick Mulholland PP
Very Rev John McManus
Parochial House, 9 Ballygalget Road,
Portaferry, Co Down BT22 1NE
Tel 028-42771212

**BALLYMENA (KIRKINRIOLA)**
Very Rev Patrick Delargy PP, VF
Venerable Archdeacon Kevin Donnelly
Rev Paul Symonds *(on leave)*
Rev Aidan McCaughan *(priest in residence)*
Parochial House, 4 Broughshane Road,
Ballymena, Co Antrim BT43 7DX
Tel 028-25641515 Fax 028-25631493
Rev Liam Toland CC
Parochial House, 189 Carnlough Road,
Broughshane BT43 7DX
Tel 028-25684211
Rev Mariusz Urbanowski (SCHR)
4 Broughshane Road, Ballymena,
Co Antrim BT43 7DX
Tel 028-25641515

**BALLYMONEY AND DERRYKEIGHAN**
Very Rev Francis O'Brien PP
81 Castle Street, Ballymoney,
Co Antrim BT53 6JT
Tel 028-27662003
Very Rev Canon Dominic McHugh
79 Castle Street, Ballymoney,
Co Antrim BT53 6JT
Tel 028-27662259

**BANGOR**
Very Rev Joseph Gunn PP, VF
St Comgall's Presbytery,
27 Brunswick Road, Bangor,
Co Down BT20 3DS
Tel 028-91465522
Rev Joseph Rooney *(priest in residence)*
45 Ballyholme Esplanade, Bangor,
Co Down BT20 5NJ
Tel 028-91465425

**BRAID**
Very Rev Patrick Delargy Adm
Rev Liam Toland CC
189 Carnlough Road,
Broughshane, Co Antrim BT43 7JW
Tel 028-25684211

**CARNLOUGH**
Very Rev Peter Forde PP, VF
51 Bay Road, Carnlough,
Ballymena, Co Antrim BT44 0HJ
Tel 028-28885220

**CARRICKFERGUS**
Very Rev Anthony Curran PP
Parochial House, 8 Minorca Place,
Carrickfergus, Co Antrim BT38 8AU
Tel 028-93363269

**CASTLEWELLAN (KILMEGAN)**
Very Rev Denis McKinlay PP
Parochial House, 91 Main Street,
Castlewellan, Co Down BT31 9DH
Tel 028-43778259
Very Rev Canon Bernard Magee
41 Lower Square,
Castlewellan BT31 9DN
Tel 028-43770377

**COLERAINE**
Very Rev Gregory Cormican PP
72 Nursery Avenue, Coleraine,
Co Derry BT52 1LR
Tel 028-70343156

**CROSSGAR (KILMORE)**
Very Rev Maurice Henry PP
Parochial House, Crossgar,
Downpatrick, Co Down BT30 9EA
Tel 028-44830229
Rev Patrick McKenna CC
Teconnaught, 2 Drumnaconagher Road,
Crossgar BT30 9AN
Tel 028-44830342

**CULFEIGHTRIN**
Very Rev Raymond Fulton PP
87 Cushendall Road, Ballyvoy,
Ballycastle, Co Antrim BT54 6QY
Tel 028-20762248

**CUSHENDALL**
Very Rev Luke McWilliams PP
Parochial House,
28 Chapel Road, Cushendall,
Ballymena BT44 0RS
Tel 028-21771240

**CUSHENDUN**
Very Rev Luke McWilliams PP
Parochial House, 28 Chapel Road,
Cushendall, Ballymena,
Co Antrim BT44 0RS
Tel 028-21771240
Very Rev Canon Alex McMullan *(priest in residence)*
21 Knocknacarry Avenue,
Cushenden, Co Antrim BT44 0NX
Tel 028-21761269

**DOWNPATRICK**
Very Rev Canon Sean Rogan PP, VF
Parochial House,
54 St Patrick's Avenue,
Tel 028-44612443
Downpatrick, Co Down BT30 6DN
Rev Brendan Mulhall (CSsR) CC
Priest's House, 29 Killough Road,
Downpatrick, Co Down BT30 6PX
Tel 028-44613430
Very Rev Finbar Glavin
Parochial House, 16 Ballykilbeg Road,
Downpatrick, Co Down BT30 8HJ
Tel 028-44613203
Very Rev Canon Noel Conway *(Priest in residence)*
23 Rathkeltair Road, Downpatrick,
Co Down BT30 6NL
Tel 028-44614777

**DRUMAROAD AND CLANVARAGHAN**
Very Rev Peter Donnelly PP, VF *(on leave)*
Parochial House,
15 Drumaroad Hill,
Castlewellan, Co Down BT31 9PD
Tel 028-44811474

**DRUMBO**
Very Rev Martin Kelly PP
Parochial House,
546 Saintfield Road, Carryduff,
Belfast BT8 8EU
Tel 028-90812238
Rev Brian Watters CC
79 Ivanhoe Avenue, Carryduff,
Belfast BT8 8BW
Tel 028-90817410

**DUNDRUM AND TYRELLA**
Very Rev Gerard Patton PP
Parochial House, Dundrum,
Newcastle, Co Down BT33 0LU
Tel 028-43751212
Very Rev Canon Hugh Starkey *(Priest in residence)*
Parochial House,
26 Tyrella Road,
Ballykinlar, Downpatrick BT30 8DF
Tel 028-44851221

**DUNEANE**
Very Rev Patrick McWilliams PP
103 Roguery Road, Moneyglass,
Toomebridge, Co Antrim BT41 3PT
Tel 028-79650225

**DUNLOY AND CLOUGHMILLS**
Very Rev Aidan Brankin PP
7 Culcrum Road, Cloughmills BT44 9NH
Tel 028-27638267

**DUNSFORD AND ARDGLASS**
Very Rev Robert Fleck PP
Parochial House, Ardglass,
Co Down BT30 7TU
Tel 028-44841208

**GLENARIFFE**
Very Rev David White PP
Parochial House, 182 Garron Road,
Glenariffe, Co Antrim BT44 0RA
Tel 028-21771249

**GLENARM (TICKMACREEVAN)**
Very Rev Aidan Kerr PP
Parochial House, 1 The Cloney, Glenarm,
Co Antrim BT44 0AB
Tel 028-28841246

**GLENAVY AND KILLEAD**
Very Rev Sean Dillon PP
Parochial House, 59 Chapel Road,
Glenavy, Crumlin, Co Antrim BT29 4LY
Tel 028-94422262
Rev Brendan Smyth CC
Parochial House, Glenavy Road,
Crumlin, Co Antrim BT29 4LA
Tel 028-94422278

**GLENRAVEL (SKERRY)**
Very Rev Gabriel Lyons PP
119 Glenravel Road, Martinstown,
Ballymena, Co Antrim BT43 6QL
Tel 028-21758217

**HANNAHSTOWN**
Very Rev David Delargy PP
Parochial House, 23 Hannahstown Hill,
Belfast BT17 0LT
Tel 028-90614567
Rt Rev Mgr John Murphy *(priest in residence)*
18 Rock Road, Lisburn,
Co Antrim BT28 3SU
Tel 028-92648244

**HOLYWOOD**
Very Rev Peter O'Kane PP
2A My Lady's Mile, Holywood,
Co Down BT18 9EW
Tel 028-90422167

**KILCLIEF AND STRANGFORD**
Very Rev Colm McGrady PP
Parochial House, Strangford,
Co Down BT30 7NL
Tel 028-44881206

**KILCOO**
Very Rev Denis McKinlay Adm
Very Rev James O'Kane *(priest in residence)*
Parochial House, 121 Dublin Road,
Kilcoo, Co Down BT34 5HP
Tel 028-40630314

**KILKEEL (UPPER MOURNE)**
Very Rev Michael Murray PP
Parochial House, Greencastle Road,
Kilkeel, Co Down BT34 4DE
Tel 028-41762242
Rev Anthony Fitzsimons CC
Curates' Residence, Massforth,
152 Newry Road, Kilkeel,
Co Down BT34 4FT
Tel 028-41762257

**KILLOUGH (BRIGHT)**
Very Rev Peter O'Hare PP
16 Rossglass Road, Killough,
Co Down BT30 7QQ
Tel 028-44841221

**KILLYLEAGH**
Very Rev Colum Curran PP
4 Irish Street, Killyleagh,
Co Down BT30 9QS
Tel 028-44828211

**KIRCUBBIN (ARDKEEN)**
Very Rev Patrick Neeson PP
46 Blackstaff Road, Ballycranbeg,
Kircubbin, Newtownards,
Co Down BT22 1AG
Tel 028-42738294

**LARNE**
Very Rev Dermot McKay PP
Parochial House, 51 Victoria Road, Larne,
Co Antrim BT40 1LY
Tel 028-28273230/28273053
Rev John Burns CC
Parochial House, Ballycraigy Road,
Craigyhill, Larne, Co Antrim BT40 2LE
Tel 028-28260130

**LISBURN (BLARIS)**
Very Rev Dermot McCaughan PP
St Patrick's Presbytery, 29 Chapel Hill,
Lisburn, Co Antrim BT28 1EP
Tel 028-92662341
Rev Eamon Magorrian CC
Tel 028-92660206
Parochial House, 27 Chapel Hill, Lisburn,
Co Antrim BT28 1EP

**LOUGHGUILE**
Very Rev Robert Butler PP
Parochial House, 44 Lough Road,
Loughguile, Ballymena,
Co Antrim BT44 9JN
Tel 028-27641206
Very Rev Canon George O'Hanlon *(Priest in residence)*
62 Coolkeeran Road, Armoy,
Ballymoney, Co Antrim BT53 8XN
Tel 028-20751121

**LOUGHINISLAND**
Very Rev Kieran Whiteford PP
Parochial House, Loughinisland,
Downpatrick, Co Down BT30 8QH
Tel 028-44811661

**LOWER MOURNE**
Very Rev Sean Gilmore PP
Parochial House, 284 Glassdrumman Road,
Annalong, Newry, Co Down BT34 4QN
Tel 028-43768208

**NEWCASTLE (MAGHERA)**
Very Rev James Crudden PP
Rev Declan Mulligan CC
24 Downs Road, Newcastle,
Co Down BT33 0AG
Tel 028-43722401

**NEWTOWNARDS**
Very Rev Martin O'Hagan PP
71 North Street, Newtownards,
Co Down BT23 4JD
Tel 028-91812137

**PORTAFERRY (BALLYPHILIP)**
Very Rev Patrick Mulholland PP
Parochial House, Portaferry,
Co Down BT22 1RH
Tel 028-42728234

**PORTGLENONE**
Very Rev Henry McCann PP
St Mary's Presbytery, 12 Ballymena Road,
Portglenone, Co Antrim BT44 8BL
Tel 028-25821218

**PORTRUSH**
Very Rev Rory Sheehan PP
Parochial House,
111 Causeway Street,
Portrush, Co Antrim BT56 8JE
Tel 028-70823388

**PORTSTEWART**
Very Rev Austin McGirr PP, VF
Parochial House, 4 The Crescent,
Portstewart, Co Derry BT55 7AB
Tel 028-70832534
Rev Raymond McCullagh *(priest in residence)*
1 Seafield Park South,
Portstewart BT55 7LH
Tel 028-70832066

**RANDALSTOWN**
Very Rev Con Boyle PP
Parochial House, 1 Craigstown Road,
Randalstown, Co Antrim BT41 2AF
Tel 028-94472640

**RASHARKIN**
Very Rev John Murray PP
Parochial House, 9 Gortahor Road,
Rasharkin, Ballymena,
Co Antrim BT44 8SB
Tel 028-29571212

**SAINTFIELD AND CARRICKMANNON**
Very Rev Anthony McHugh PP
Parochial House, 33 Crossgar Road,
Saintfield, Ballynahinch,
Co Down BT24 7JE
Tel 028-97510237

**SAUL AND BALLEE**
Very Rev Paul Alexander PP
10 St Patrick's Road, Saul, Downpatrick,
Co Down BT30 7JG
Tel 028-44612525
Rev Anthony Meaney CC
Parochial House, Ballycruttle Road,
Downpatrick, Co Down BT30 7EL
Tel 028-44841213

## INSTITUTIONS AND THEIR CHAPLAINS

### HOSPITALS

**City Group of Hospitals, Belfast**
Tel 028-90329241
Rev Gerard Fox
201 Donegall Street, Belfast BT1 2FL
Tel 028-90263473 *(chaplain's office)*

**Mater Hospital, Belfast**
Tel 028-90741211
Rev Kevin McGuckien
St Patrick's Presbytery,
199 Donegall Street, Belfast BT1 2FL
Tel 028-90324597

**Musgrave Park Hospital, Belfast**
Tel 028-90902000
Rev Adrian Eastwood (CM)
99 Cliftonville Road, Belfast BT14 6JQ
Tel 028-90751771

**Royal Victoria Hospital, Belfast**
Tel 028-90240503
Rev Thomas McGlynn
The Cathedral Presbytery,
St Peter's Square, Belfast BT12 4BU

### PENAL INSTITUTIONS

**Maghaberry Prison**
Old Road, Ballinderry Upper, Lisburn,
Co Antrim BT28 2TP
*Pastoral Team:* Rev Frank Brady (SJ)
Br Brian Monaghan
Rev Gabriel Bannon
Sr Rosaleen McMahon
Tel 028-92614825
Prison General Office: 028-92611888

**Young Offenders' Detention Centre**
Hydebank Wood, Hospital Road,
Belfast BT8 8NA
*Co-ordinating Lead Chaplain of Catholic Pastoral Team*
Very Rev Stephen McBrearty
Tel 028-90253666
Sr Oona, Sisters of Nazareth (Women Prisoners)

### UNIVERSITIES

**Queen's University, Belfast**
Rev Gary Toman
The Chaplaincy, 28 Elmwood Avenue,
Belfast BT9 6AY
Tel 028-90669737

**University of Ulster, Coleraine**
Rev Raymond McCullagh
1 Seafield Park South, Portstewart,
Co Derry BT55 7LH
Tel 028-70832066

**University of Ulster, Jordanstown**
Rev Terence Howard (SJ)
Peter Faber House, 28 Brookvale Avenue,
Belfast BT14 6BW
Tel 028-90757615

## PRIESTS OF THE DIOCESE ELSEWHERE

Rev Peter Carlin
Padres de San Columbano
Apartado 073174, Lima 39, Peru
Rev Martin Henry
Rev Oliver Treanor
St Patrick's College, Maynooth, Co Kildare
Tel 01-6285222 Fax 01-6289063
Rev Gerard McFlynn
18 Maresfield Gardens,
London NW3 5SX
Rev Patrick McCafferty
52 Lower Rathmines Road, Dublin 6
Rev Timothy Bartlett
Columba Centre, St Patrick's College,
Maynooth, Co Kildare
Tel 01-5053000
Rev Stephen Quinn
Carmelite Priory, Boars Hill, Oxford OX1 5HB

## RETIRED PRIESTS

Rev Conleth Byrne
c/o 73 Somerton Road, Belfast BT15 4DE
Very Rev Sean Cahill
c/o 73 Somerton Road, Belfast BT15 4DE
Rev Colm Campbell
Holy Trinity Rectory, 213 West 82nd Street,
New York NY10024, USA
Tel 001-7185443304
Very Rev Harry Carlin
5 Fortwilliam Court, Belfast BT15 4DS
Tel 028-90772376
Rt Rev Mgr Sean Connolly VG
7 Tullyview, Loughguile,
Co Antrim BT44 9JY
Very Rev Canon Joseph Cunningham
Our Lady's Home, 68 Ardnava Road,
Belfast BT12 6FF
Very Rev John Fitzpatrick
116 Strangford Road, Ardglass, BT30 7SS
Very Rev Gerald Forrester
62 Rathgannon, Warrenpoint BT34 3TU
Very Rev Padraic Gallinagh
'Polperro', 8 Beverley Close,
Newtownards BT23 7FN
Very Rev Frank Harper
32 Bryansford Avenue,
Newcastle BT33 OEQ
Very Rev John Hutton
Apt 2, Ceara Court, Windsor Avenue,
Belfast BT9 6EJ
Tel 028-90683002
Very Rev Donal Kelly
7 Knocksinna Park, Bray Road,
Foxrock, Dublin 18
Tel 01-2894170
Rev Oliver P. Kennedy
68 Shore Road, Toomebridge,
Co Antrim BT41 3NW
Tel 028-79650213/79650618
Very Rev Sean McCartney
25 Alt-Min Avenue, Belfast BT8 6NJ
Rt Rev Mgr Colm McCaughan
3 Fortwilliam Demesne, Belfast BT15 4FD
Tel 028-90778111
Very Rev Francis McCorry
Our Lady's Home, 68 Ardnava Road,
Belfast BT12 6FF
Very Rev Joseph MacGurnaghan
14 Presbytery Lane, Dunloy, Ballymena,
Co Antrim BT44 9DZ
Tel 028-27657223
Rt Rev Mgr Ambrose Macaulay
89a Maryville Park, Belfast BT9 6LQ
Very Rev Gerard McConville
68 Main Street, Portglenone BT44 8HS
Rev Hugh McIldowney
7 Riverdale Close, Belfast BT11 9DH
Tel 028-90603042
Rev Gordon McKinstry
12 The Meadows, Randalstown,
Co Antrim BT41 2JB
Very Rev Brendan McMullan
26 Willowbank Park, Belfast BT6 0LL
Tel 028-90794440
Very Rev George McLaverty
518 Donegall Road, Belfast BT12 6DY
Very Rev Kevin McMullan
418 Oldpark Road, Belfast BT14 6QF
Tel 028-90748148
Very Rev Albert McNally
6 Hillside Avenue, Dunloy BT44 9DQ
Very Rev Patrick McVeigh
3 Broughshane Road, Ballymena,
Co Antrim BT43 7DX
Very Rev Vincent Maguire
26 Rodney Street, Portrush,
Co Antrim BT56 8LB
Very Rev John Moley
24 Mallard Road, Downpatrick,
Co Down BT30 6DY
Very Rev Canon Malachy Murphy
c/o 73 Somerton Road, Belfast BT15 4DE
Very Rev Eamon O'Brien
No. 5 Hopecroft, Main Street,
Glenavy BT29 4LN
Very Rev Prof Martin O'Callaghan
c/o 73 Somerton Road, Belfast BT15 4DE
Very Rev John O'Sullivan
6 Ferngrove Avenue, Aghagallon,
Craigavon BT67 0HA
Very Rev Jim Sheppard
189 Carrigenagh Road, Ballymartin,
Kilkeel, Co Down BT34 4GA
Very Rev Canon Hugh Starkey
26 Tyrella Road, Ballykinlar,
Downpatrick, Co Down BT30 8DF
Very Rev John Stewart
27F Windsor Avenue, Belfast BT9 6EE
Very Rev Daniel Whyte
53 Marlo Park, Bangor, Co Down BT19 6NL
Tel 078-12184624
Rev Desmond Wilson
6 Springhill Close, Belfast BT12 7SE
Tel 028-90326722

## RELIGIOUS ORDERS AND CONGREGATIONS

### PRIESTS

**CISTERCIANS**
Our Lady of Bethlehem Abbey,
11 Ballymena Road, Portglenone,
Ballymena, Co Antrim BT44 8BL
Tel 028-25821211 Fax 028-25822795
Email celsus@bethabbey.com
Website www.bethlehemabbey.com
*Abbot:* Rt Rev Dom Celsus Kelly (OCSO)

**JESUITS**
Peter Faber House, 28 Brookvale Avenue,
Belfast BT14 6BW
Tel/Fax 028-90747615
Email peter_faber@lineone.net
*Superior:* Rev Alan McGuckian (SJ)

**MILL HILL MISSIONARIES**
St Mary's Parish, 25 Marquis Street,
Belfast BT1 1JJ
Tel 028-90320482
Rev James A. Boyle (MHM) Adm
Rev Jim O'Donoghue (MHM) CC
Rev John Nevin (MHM)

**PASSIONISTS**
Holy Cross Retreat, Ardoyne,
Crumlin Road, Belfast BT14 7GE
Tel 028-90748231 Fax 028-90740340
*Superior:* Rev Gary Donegan (CP) PP

Passionist Retreat Centre, Tobar Mhuire,
Crossgar, Downpatrick,
Co Down BT30 9EA
Tel 028-44830242 Fax 028-44831382
*Superior:* Rev John Friel (CP)

**REDEMPTORISTS**
Clonard Monastery, 1 Clonard Gardens,
Belfast BT13 2RL
Tel 028-90445950 Fax 028-90445988
*Superior:* Rev Michael Murtagh (CSsR)

St Gerard's Parish,
722 Antrim Road, Newtownabbey,
Co Antrim BT36 7PG
Tel 028-90774833
Fax 028-90770923
*Superior & PP:* Rev Gerry Cassidy (CSsR)

**ST PATRICK'S MISSIONARY SOCIETY (KILTEGAN FATHERS)**
St Patricks, 21 Old Cavehill Road,
Belfast BT15 5GT
Tel 028-90778696

**VINCENTIANS**
99 Cliftonville Road,
Belfast BT14 6JQ
Tel 028-90751771 Fax 028-90740547
Email cmbelfast@ntlworld.co.uk
*Superior:* Very Rev Peter Gildea (CM)

### BROTHERS

**CHRISTIAN BROTHERS**
An Dúnán, 210 Glen Road,
Belfast BT11 8BW
Tel 028-90611343
*Community Leader:* Br Brendan Prior
Community: 7

The Open Doors Learning Centre
Barrack Street, Belfast BT12 4AH
Tel 028-90325867 Fax 028-90241013

Westcourt Centre
Barrack Street, Belfast BT12 4AH
Tel 028-90323009

681 Crumlin Road, Belfast BT14 7GD
Community: 4
Tel 028-90717694

**DE LA SALLE BROTHERS**
La Salle Secondary School,
Edenmore Drive, Belfast BT11 8LT
Tel 028-90508800
*Headmaster:* Mr Paul Barry

De La Salle Brothers, Glanaulin,
141 Glen Road, Belfast BT11 8BP
Tel 028-90614848
Superior: Br Ailbe Mangan
*Community:* 5

La Salle Pastoral Retreat Centre,
Glanaulin, 141 Glen Road,
Belfast BT11 8BP
Tel 028-90501932 Tax 028-90501932

La Salle House, 4 Stream Street,
Downpatrick, Co Down BT30 6DD
Tel 028-44612996
*Superior:* Br Mark Jordan
Community: 6

Miguel Pastoral Centre, 4 Stream Street,
Downpatrick, Co Down BT30 6DD
Tel 028-44615877

St Patrick's Grammar School,
Downpatrick, Co Down BT30 6NJ
Tel 028-44619722
*Headmaster:* Mr Sean Sloan

Secondary School, Struell Road,
Downpatrick, Co Down BT30 6JR
Tel 028-44612520
*Headmaster:* Mr Barry Sharvin

Primary School, St Dillon's Avenue,
Downpatrick, Co Down BT30 6HZ
Tel 028-44612787
*Headmaster:* Mr Hugh Kelly

**SAINT JOHN OF GOD ASSOCIATION**
Colcha Suite, 129 Ormeau Road,
Belfast BT7 1SH
Tel 028-90320909 Fax 028-90320907
Email association@sjoga.org
*Director:* Br Fintan Brennan-Whitmore (OH)
Residential service for people with intellectual disabilities and older people and domiciliary care.

'Iona', 7 Firmount, Fortwilliam, Belfast,
Co Antrim BT15 4HZ
Tel 028-90779808 Fax 028-90775925
*Superior:* Br Fintan Brennan-Whitmore (OH)
Community: 2

## SISTERS

**BON SECOURS SISTERS (PARIS)**
52A Tullymore Gardens,
Belfast BT11 8ND
Tel 028-90625757
Community: 1
Pastoral ministry

**CONGREGATION OF THE SISTERS OF MERCY**
Convent of Mercy, 2A Fruithill Park,
Belfast BT11 8GD
Tel 028-90616399

Convent of Mercy, Beechmount,
Ard Na Va Road, Belfast BT12 6FF
Tel 028-90319496
*Leader:* Sr Annie Jo Heduan
Community: 10

21 Ardlass Road,
Downpatrick, Co Down BT30 6JQ
Tel 028-44615645
Community: 2

27a Glenveagh Drive,
Belfast BT11 9HX
Tel 028-90602175
Community: 3

Mercy Convent, Whiteabbey,
453 Shore Road, Newtownabbey,
Co Antrim BT37 9SE
Tel 028-90863128
*Leader:* Sr Claire Loughran
Community: 4

Convent of Mercy,
252 Limestone Road, Belfast BT15 3AR
Tel 028-90748830

Sisters of Mercy
616 Crumlin Road, Belfast BT14 7GL
Tel 028-90717112
Community: 2

23 Fortwilliam Fold,
30 Fortwilliam Park,
Belfast BT15 4AN
Tel 028-90371268

21 Camberwell Court,
Limestone Road, Belfast BT15 3BH
Tel 028-90286584

Sisters of Mercy, 24 Floral Park,
Glengormley, Co Antrim BT36 7RU
Tel 028-90878384

Sisters of Mercy, 2 Lever Street,
Ligoniel, Belfast BT14 8EF
Tel 028-90710529

Sisters of Mercy, Ballysillan House,
614 Crumlin Road, Belfast BT14 7GL
Tel 028-90715758
Community: 4

27 Wheatfield Gardens,
Belfast BT14 7HU
Tel 028-90715478

Apt 8, Luxembourg Court,
Antrim Road, Belfast BT15 5AR
Tel 028-90582742

25 Camberwell Court,
Limestone Road, Belfast BT15 3BH
Tel 028-90290213

**CONGREGATION OF THE SISTERS OF NAZARETH**
Nazareth House Care Village,
514 Ravenhill Road,
Belfast BT6 0BX
Tel 028-90690600 Fax 028-90690601
*Superior:* Sr Teresa Walsh
Community: 12
Home for the elderly. Beds: 70

Bethlehem Nursery School,
514 Ravenhill Road, Belfast BT6 0BW
Tel 028-90640406
Pupils: 50
St Michael's Primary,
516 Ravenhill Road, Belfast BT6 0BW
Tel 028-90491529. Pupils: 400

**CONGREGATION OF THE SISTERS OF SION**
547 Ormeau Road, Belfast BT7 3JA
Tel 028-90643208
Email sionbelfast@hotmail.co.uk
Community: 3
Education, spirituality, counselling

**CROSS AND PASSION CONGREGATION**
6 Lisbon Street, Belfast BT5 4DA
Tel 028-90597914
Community: 2
Parish visitation and pastoral centre, SPRED

4 Innisfayle Road, Belfast BT15 4ER
Tel 028-90774238
Community: 3
Adult education, ecumenical work, healing ministries

St Teresa's Convent, 78 Glen Road,
Belfast BT11 8BH
Tel 028-90613955
Community: 4
Hospital chaplaincy and pastoral care, ecumenical work, bereavement counselling

Villa Pacis, 78A Glen Road,
Belfast BT11 8BH
Tel 028-90621766
*Superior:* Sr Mary Sloan
Community: 13
Care of sick and elderly

Cross and Passion Convent, Drumalis,
Glenarm Road, Larne, Co Antrim BT40 1DT
Tel 028-28272196
Community: 3
Retreat work

Drumalis Retreat Centre,
Larne, Co Antrim
Tel 028-28276455/28272196
Fax 028-28277999
Email drumalis@btconnect.com

Cross and Passion Convent
120 B Drains Bay, Larne, Co Antrim
Tel 028-28279428
Community: 3
Prayer and Retreat work

Cross and Passion Convent,
3 Gort an Chlochair, Ballycastle,
Co Antrim BT54 6NU
Tel 028-20762228
Community: 2
Parish ministry, education

5c Easton Avenue, Cliftonville road,
Belfast BT14 6LL
Tel 028-90749507
Community: 2
Retreat work, Bosnia project, counselling and facilitation

**DAUGHTERS OF CHARITY OF ST VINCENT DE PAUL**
23 Glen Road, Belfast BT11 8BA
Tel 028-9023052
Community: 2
Pastoral work and education

St Louise's Comprehensive College,
468 Falls Road, Belfast BT 6EN
Tel 028-90325631

Moyard House,
Moyard Park,Belfast BT12 7FR
Tel 028-90331562
Temporary accommodation for people who are homeless and parish work
*Superior:* Sr Mary Hayden
Community: 5

1c Grainne House
(for families in transition)
Newlodge, Belfast BT 2LA

**DOMINICAN SISTERS**
St Catherine's, 133 Falls Road,
Belfast BT12 6AD
Tel 028-90327056
Email opfalls@dominicansisters.com
*Prioress:* Sr Catherine Campbell
Community: 14
Grammar School. Tel 028-90320081
St Rose's High School. Tel 028-90240937

St Martin's Dominican Convent,
22 Gransha Rise, Belfast BT11 8ES
Tel 028-90619395
Community: 3

Dominican Convent,
Fortwilliam Park, Belfast BT15 4AP
Tel 028-90370008
Email ionahouse@btinternet.com
*Prioress:* Sr Aine Killen
Community: 10
Grammar School
Tel 028-90370298

**FAMILY OF ADORATION**
63 Falls Road, Belfast BT12 4PD
Tel 01232-325668
Email adorationsisters@utv.net
*Superior:* Sr Molly Caldwell
Community: 4
A contemplative community with mission of adoration, making of altar breads

**GOOD SHEPHERD SISTERS**
25 Rossmore Drive,
Belfast BT7 3LA
Tel 028-90641346 Fax 028-90646360
Email 25rossmoredrive@gmail.com
*Leader:* Sr Anne O'Byrne
Community: 16

Good Shepherd Contemplative Sisters,
Lysmarie, 19 Rossmore Drive,
Belfast BT7 3LA
Tel 028-90491820
Fax 028-90493565
Email lysmariesisters@yahoo.com
*Leader:* Sr Esther Boyle
Community: 11

Summerhill Road, Twinbrook,
Dunmurry, Belfast BT17 0RL
Tel 028-90618987
Fax 028-90302863
Community: 3
Sisters engaged in community services

Good Shepherd Sisters,
80 Glenholm Park, Four Winds,
Belfast BT8 6LR
Tel 028-90582391
Email gsglenholm@yahoo.co.uk
Community: 1
Counselling, spiritual direction and youth work

Good Shepherd Sisters,
49 Knockbreda Park, Rosetta,
Belfast BT6 0HD
Tel 028-90224236
Email peggetty@yahoo.com
Community: 1
Parish work

**MARIST SISTERS**
22 St Peter's Place, Belfast BT12 4SB
Tel 028-90246238
Email marist22belfast@yahoo.co.uk
Community: 2
Parish ministry

Grosvenor House,
259 Grosvenor Road, Belfast BT12 4LL
Tel 028-90310383
Email marbelfast@yahoo.co.uk
Community: 2
Hostel for the Homeless and hospital chaplaincy

**MISSIONARY SISTERS OF THE HOLY CROSS**
86 Glen Road, Belfast BT11 8BH
Tel 028-90614631 Fax 028-90614631
Email holycross3@sky.com
*Superior:* Sr Patricia Kelly
Email patkelly5@sky.com
Community: 5

**NOTRE DAME DES MISSIONS (OUR LADY OF THE MISSIONS SISTERS)**
125 Maghera Lane Road,
Randalstown, Co Antrim BT41 2PD
Tel 028-94478594
Community: 2
Parish ministry

442 Falls Road, Belfast BT12 6EN
Tel 01232-329776
Community: 3
Pastoral ministry

**POOR CLARES**
120 Cliftonville Road, Belfast BT14 6LA
Superior: Sr Immaculata Enderez OSC
Community: 6
Contemplatives
St Clare's Prayer Centre
Tel 028-90744064
Email poor.clare@btconnect.com
Private retreats, or quiet days.
Accommodation for four retreatants, self-catering

**POOR SERVANTS OF THE MOTHER OF GOD**
The Convent, 15 Martin's Lane, Carnagat,
Newry, Co Down BT35 8PJ
Community: 2
Pastoral

**RELIGIOUS OF SACRED HEART OF MARY**
100 Hillsborough Road, Lisburn,
Co Antrim BT28 1JU
Tel 01846-678501
Community: 4
Ministry in local area

28 Upper Green, Dunmurry,
Belfast BT17 0EL
Tel 01232-600792
Community 5
Ministry in local area and education

Sacred Heart of Mary Grammar School for Boys and Girls,
Rathmore, Finaghy, Belfast BT10 0LF
Pupils: 1,350
Tel 01232-610115
Email
userid.rathmore@schools.class-ni.org.uk.

**ROSMINIANS (SISTERS OF PROVIDENCE)**
6 Churchview Court, Belfast BT14 7RE
Tel 01232-756664
*Contact Person:* Sr Carmel Martin
Email sistercarmel1@utvinternet.com
Community: 2
Pastoral work

**SACRED HEARTS OF JESUS AND MARY**
The Curragh Community,
2 Workman Avenue, Belfast BT13 3SB
Tel 028-90312658

**ST CLARE SISTERS**
St Clare's Convent, Belfast BT6 0DL
Tel 028-90694108
Community: 3

**ST LOUIS SISTERS**
St Louis Grammar School, Kilkeel
Tel 016937-62747
Pupils: 573

St Louis Grammar School
Cullybackey Road, Ballymena,
Co Antrim BT43 5DW
Tel 01266-49534
Pupils: 989

14 Carndale Meadows, Carniny Road,
Ballymena BT43 5NX
Tel 028-25651683
Community: 2

21 Glenbawn Square, Poleglass,
Dunmurry, Belfast BT17 0TT
Tel 028-90225236
Community: 1

7 Riverdale Park Avenue, Belfast BT11 9BP
Tel 028-90209074
Community: 1

22 Riverdale Park North, Belfast BT11 9DL
Tel 028-90619375
Community: 1

Apartment 2 Hollycroft,
1-3 Inver Avenue, Belfast BT15 5DG
Tel 028-90721037
Community: 1

91 Hillhead Crescent,
Stewartstown Road, Belfast BT11 9FW
Tel 028-90621900
Community: 5
Varied Apostolates

49 Bracken Avenue, Castlewellan Road,
Newcastle, Co Down BT33 0HG
Tel 028-43726282
Community: 2

## EDUCATIONAL INSTITUTIONS

**Aquinas College**
518 Ravenhill Road, Belfast BT6 0BY
Tel 028-90643939
*Principal:* Mr Barry Kelly
Priest on staff
Rev Colin Grant MA, STL, PGCE

**Our Lady and St Patrick's College**
Knock, Belfast BT5 7DQ
Tel 028-90401184
*Principal:* Mr Dermot G. Mullan MA, PGCE

**St Killian's College**
25 Tower Road, Carnlough,
Co Antrim BT44 0JS
Tel 028-2885202
*Principal:* Mr Jonathan Brady

**St Malachy's College**
Antrim Road, Belfast BT15 2AE
Tel 028-90748285
*Principal*
Mr David Lambon
Priest on Staff
Very Rev Michael Spence BA, STL
*Resident Priests*
Rev Edward McGee (St Mary's University College)
Rev Colin Grant (Aquinas College)

**St Mary's University College**
A College of Queen's University Belfast
191 Falls Road,
Belfast 12 6FE
Tel 028-90327678
*Principal*
Professor Peter Finn BA MSSc
*Priest Lecturers*
Rev Feidhlimidh Magennis MA, BD, LSS (Dromore)
Rev Edward McGee BA, BD
Rev Paul Fleming BA, BD, STL
Rev Niall Coll BA, BD (Raphoe)

**EDMUND RICE SCHOOLS TRUST NORTHERN IRELAND**
St Mary's Grammar School,
Glen Road, Belfast BT11 8NR
Tel 028-90294000 Fax 028-90294009
*Principal:* Mr Jim Sheerin

Christian Brothers' Secondary School,
Glen Road, Belfast BT11 8BW
Tel 028-90808050 Fax 028-90808055
*Principal:* Mr Tommy Armstrong

Edmund Rice College,
96-100 Hightown Road, Glengormley,
Newtownabbey, Belfast BT36 7AU
Tel 028-90848433/90840566
Fax 028-90844924
*Principal:* Mr Kevin Gough

Edmund Rice Primary School,
Pim Street, Belfast BT15 2BN
Tel 028-90351206 Fax 028-90747192
*Principal:* Mr John Devine

St Aidan's Primary School,
Whiterock Road, Belfast BT12 7FW
Tel/Fax 028-90320565
*Principal:* Mr Raymond Hunter

## CHARITABLE AND OTHER SOCIETIES

**Apostolic Work Society**
Xavier House,
156 Cliftonpark Avenue,
Belfast BT14 6DT
Tel 028-90351912
Email apostolic.work@btinternet.com
Office hours:
Monday-Wednesday 9.00 am-2.30 pm
Society for lay women
*President:* Mrs Anne Donaghy

**Legion of Mary**
14 Cliftonville Road,
Belfast BT14 6JX
Tel 028-90746626
*President:* Mr Joe Drew

**Morning Star House**
2-12 Divis Street, Belfast
Tel 028-90333500

**Regina Coeli Hostel**
8-10 Lake Glen Avenue,
Belfast BT11 8FE
Tel 028-90612473
Night shelter for destitute and homeless women. Under the care of the Legion of Mary

**Society of St Vincent de Paul**
196-200 Antrim Road,
Belfast BT15 2AJ
Tel 028-90351561
*Regional Administrator*
Ms Aileen Coney

**St Joseph's Centre for the Deaf**
321 Grosvenor Road,
Belfast BT12 4LP
Tel 028-90448211
The Centre provides a wide range of facilities for the deaf.
*Co-ordinator:* Rev Paul Strain
*Northern Diocesan Lay Chaplain:*
Ms Denise Flack
Tel 078-77643961

# DIOCESE OF DROMORE

PATRONS OF THE DIOCESE
ST PATRICK, 17 MARCH; ST COLMAN, 7 JUNE

INCLUDES PORTIONS OF COUNTIES ANTRIM, ARMAGH AND DOWN

**Most Rev John McAreavey DD**
Bishop of Dromore; born 1949; ordained priest 10 June 1973; ordained Bishop of Dromore 19 September 1999

Residence:
Bishop's House,
44 Armagh Road,
Newry, Co Down BT35 6PN
Tel 028-30262444
Fax 028-30260496
Email
bishopofdromore@btinternet.com
Website dromorediocese.org

## ST PATRICK AND ST COLMAN'S CATHEDRAL, NEWRY

Newry cathedral was founded in 1825, at the centre of a growing and prosperous town. It symbolised, in many ways, the increasing confidence of the local Catholic population of the day, especially the newly emerging Catholic middle class.

The cathedral was designed by Thomas J. Duff, a prominent architect in the northern part of Ireland at the turn of the century. The building was dedicated in May 1829 by the then Irish Primate, Dr Curtis. It was believed to be the first major dedication ceremony in Ireland following the granting of Catholic Emancipation.

Originally, the cathedral was sparsely furnished, and it received its first significant interior decoration in 1851. The building was developed considerably between 1888 and 1891. During these years, its two transepts were added and a handsome bell tower erected. From 1904 to 1909, Bishop Henry O'Neill oversaw a further major phase of building. The main body of the church was extended in length by some forty feet and a new sanctuary was added. Much of the internal fabric of the cathedral, as we know it today, belongs to this period. Rich interior mosaic decoration was undertaken, side chapels were constructed and the cathedral's tubular organ was installed. The cathedral was solemnly consecrated in July 1925 – a century after its foundation! It enjoys the joint patronage of Ss Patrick and Colman.

Interior renovation was necessary in the wake of the Second Vatican Council. This work of extending and refurbishing the sanctuary area was undertaken by Bishop Francis Gerard Brooks from 1989 to 1990. It included the construction of the present marble altar, the rebuilding of the reredos of the former high altar, now in three parts, and the relocation of the bishop's chair to the front of the sanctuary. This work of renovation has earned widespread praise in the field of contemporary ecclesiastical architecture.

## CHAPTER

*Dean:* Vacant
*Archdeacon:* Vacant
*Prebendaries*
Saint Colman and Lann
Very Rev Canon Cathal Jordon PP
Seagoe
*Drumeragh*
Very Rev Canon Francis Boyle, Saval
*Lanronan*
Rt Rev Mgr Aidan Hamill PP, VG
Shankill, St Peter's
*Aghaderg*
Very Rev Canon Liam Stevenson PP, VF
Seapatrick
*Clondallon*
Very Rev Canon Michael Hackett PP
Kilbroney (Rostrevor)
*Kilmycon*
Very Rev Canon John Kearney Adm, VF
Warrenpoint
*Canon Penitentiary*
Very Rev Canon Francis Brown Adm, Newry
*Downaclone*
Very Rev Canon Gerard McCrory PP
Magheradroll, Canon Theologian
*Retired Members, Honorary Canons:*
Very Rev Liam Boyle
Very Rev Arthur Byrne
Very Rev Anthony Davies
Very Rev Desmond Knowles
Very Rev Patrick McAnuff
Very Rev Joseph O'Hagan

## ADMINISTRATION

**Vicar General**
Rt Rev Mgr Aidan Hamill PP, VG
Parochial House, 70 North Street,
Lurgan, Co Armagh
Tel 028-38323161

**Chancellor/Diocesan Secretary**
Very Rev Gerald Powell PP
Parochial House, 4 Holymount Road
Laurencetown, Craigavon BT63 6AT
Co Armagh
Tel 028-40624236 Fax 028-40625440
Email gpowellpp@aol.com

**Council of Priests**
*Chairman*
Very Rev Canon John Kearney Adm, VF
Riverfields, Warrenpoint,
Co Down BT34 3PU
Tel 028-41754684 Fax 028-41754685
*Secretary:* Very Rev Martin McAlinden PP
The Presbytery, 11 Tullygally Road,
Legahory, Craigavon BT65 5B
Tel 028-38341901
Email martinmcalinden@hotmail.com

**Finance Council**
*Administrator and Secretary*
Rev Feidlimidh Magennis
St Mary's University College, Belfast

**Bishop's Secretary**
Miss Agatha Larkin
Bishop's House, Newry, Co Down
Tel 028-30262444

## CATECHETICS EDUCATION

**Diocesan Advisers for Religious Education**
*Primary Schools:* Sr Attracta Devlin
*Post-Primary Schools:*
Mrs Elizabeth McNeice
Lismore Comprehensive School,
Craigavon

**Diocesan Education Committee**
*Chairman:* Rt Rev Mgr Aidan Hamill
70 North Street, Lurgan,
Co Armagh BT67 9AH
Tel 028-38326949
*Senior Management Officer*
Mr Martin Cromie
CCMS Office, 56 Armagh Road,
Newry, Co Down BT35 6DN
Tel 028-30262423

## LITURGY

**Music**
*Director:* Vacant

## PASTORAL

**Accord**
*Director:* Rev Niall Sheehan
Cathedral Presbytery, Newry
Tel 028-30262586

**Adult Faith Development**
Very Rev Martin McAlinden PP, VF
The Presbytery, 11 Tullygally Road,
Craigavon
Tel 028-38341901
Email martinmcalinden@hotmail.com

**Chaplaincy to Deaf People**
*Contact:* Fr Colum Wright
10 Oaklands, Loughbrickland, Co Down
Email colum.wright@btinternet.com

**Communications**
*Press Officer:* John O'Hagan
c/o Bishop's House,
Newry, Co Down

**Dromore Clerical Provident Society**
*Contact:* Very Rev Brian Brown
26 Bottier Road, Moira, Craigavon,
Co Armgh BT67 0PE
Tel 028-92611347

**Ecumenism**
*Director:* Rev Andrew McMahon CC
St Paul's Presbytery, Old Portadown Road,
Lurgan, Co Armagh BT66 8RG

**Emigrant Services**
*Director:* Very Rev Patrick J. Murray PP
Maypole Hill, Dromore,
Co Down BT25 1BQ
Tel 028-40623264

**Immigrant Services**
Rev Stanislaw Hajkowski
Cathedral Presbytery, Newry
Tel 028-30262586
Email frstanislaw@yahoo.com

**Knock Diocesan Pilgrimage**
*Director:* Very Rev Jarlath Cushenan PP
17 Castlewellan Road, Hilltown,
Newry BT34 5UY
Tel 028-4063026

**Lourdes Diocesan Pilgrimage**
*Director:* Very Rev Jarlath Cushenan PP
17 Castlewellan Road, Hilltown, Newry,
Co Down BT34 5UY
Tel 028-40630206

**Marriage Tribunal**
Rev Peter C. McNeill
Diocesan Office, 44 Armagh Road,
Newry, Co Down BT35 6PN
Tel 028-30269836

**Pastoral Planning**
*Director:* Vacant

**Permanent Diaconate**
Rev John Byrne CC
Cathedral Presbytery, 38 Hill Street,
Newry BT34 1AT
Tel 028-30262586

**Pioneer Total Abstinence Association**
*Diocesan Director:* Rt Rev Dean A. Davies
42 Old Killowen Road, Rostrevor,
Co Down BT34 3AD

**Pontifical Mission Societies and Dromore/Lodwar Mission Project**
*Diocesan Director:* Rev Desmond Mooney
13 Tullygally Road, Legahory, Craigavon
Tel 028-38343297
Email mooneydesmond@googlemail.com

**Safeguarding Children**
Diocesan Offices, 44 Armagh Road,
Newry, Co Down BT35 6PN
*Designated person and Director*
Ms Patricia Carville
*Chair, Advisory Panel:* Mrs Aileen Oates
*Chair, Safeguarding Committee*
Mr Paul Carlin

**Special Needs Committee – Reachout**
Mrs Anne Loughlin
22 Dallan Hill, Warrenpoint
Tel 077-34330336

**Travellers**
*Chaplain:* Rev Niall Sheehan CC
Cathedral Presbytery, Hill Street, Newry,
Co Down BT34 1AT
Tel 028-30262586

**Vocations**
*Director:* Very Rev Patrick J. Murray PP
Maypole Hill, Dromore
Tel 028-92692218

**Youth**
*Chair Youth Commission*
Very Rev Canon Francis Brown
38 Hill Street, Newry
Tel 028-30262586

**Youth Ministry**
Ms Anita Ryan
Pastoral Centre, The Mall, Newry
Tel 028-30833898
Email dromoreyd@btconnect.com

## PARISHES

*Mensal parishes are listed first. Other parishes follow alphabetically. Historical names are given in parentheses.*

**NEWRY**
Very Rev Canon Francis Brown Adm
Rev John Byrne CC
Rev Niall Sheehan CC
Rev Conor McConville CC
Rev Stanislaw Hajkowski (SC) CC
Cathedral Presbytery, 38 Hill Street, Newry BT34 1AT
Tel 028-30262586 Fax 028-30267505
Email newryparish@googlemail.com

**CLONALLON, ST PETER'S (WARRENPOINT)**
Very Rev Canon John Kearney Adm, VF
Riverfields, Warrenpoint, Co Down, BT34 3PU
Tel 028-41754684 Fax 028-41754685
Rev Brendan Kearns CC
14 Great George's Street, Warrenpoint, Co Down BT34 3PU
Tel 028-41772201
Email stpetersclonallon@hotmail.com
*Parish Office:* Tel 028-41759981
Fax 028-41759980

**AGHADERG**
Very Rev Colum Wright PP
10 Oaklands, Loughbrickland, Co Down BT32 3NH
Tel 028-40623264 Fax 028-41759980
Email colum.wright@btinternet.com

**ANNACLONE**
Very Rev Francis Kearney PP
17 Monteith Road, Annaclone, Banbridge, Co Down BT32 5AQ
Tel 028-40671201
Email annacloneparish@fsmail.net

**CLONALLON, ST MARY'S (BURREN)**
Very Rev Charles Byrne
84 Milltown Street, Burren, Warrenpoint, Co Down BT34 3PU
Tel 028-41772200
Email stmarysburren@btinternet.com
Rev Tom McAteer
15 Chapel Hill, Mayobridge, Newry, Co Down BT34 2EX
Tel 028-30851225 Fax 028-30851607

**CLONALLON, ST PATRICK'S (MAYOBRIDGE)**
Very Rev Charles Byrne
84 Milltown Street, Burren, Warrenpoint, Co Down BT34 3PU
Tel 028-41772200
Rev Tom McAteer
15 Chapel Hill, Mayobridge, Newry, Co Down BT34 2EX
Tel 028-30851225 Fax 028-30851607

**CLONDUFF (HILLTOWN)**
Very Rev Jarlath Cushenan PP
17 Castlewellan Road, Hilltown, Newry, Co Down BT34 5UY
Tel/Fax 028-40630206

**DONAGHMORE**
Very Rev Terence Rafferty PP
10 Barr Hill, Newry, Co Down BT34 1SY
Tel 028-30821252
Email terryrafferty@hotmail.com

**DROMORE**
Very Rev P. J. Murray PP
Maypole Hill, Dromore, Co Down BT25 1BQ
Tel 028-92692218

**DRUMGATH (RATHFRILAND)**
Very Rev Stephen Ferris PP
91 Newry Road, Barnmeen, Rathfriland, Co Down BT34 5AP
Tel 028-40630306 Fax 028-40631205

**DRUMGOOLAND**
Rev Peter C. McNeill Adm
58 Ballydrumman Road, Castlewellan, Co Down BT31 9UG
Tel 028-40650207 Fax 028-40650205
Email dromaradgooland@aol.co.uk

**DROMARA**
Rev Peter C. McNeill Adm
58 Ballydrumman Road, Castlewellan, Co Down BT31 9UG
Tel 028-40650207 Fax 028-40650205

**KILBRONEY (ROSTREVOR)**
Rev Brendan Kearns Adm
44 Church Street, Rostrevor, Co Down BT34 3BB
Tel 028-41738277 Fax 028-41738315
*Office:* Tel 028-41739495
Email kilbroneyparish@hotmail.com

**MAGHERADROLL (BALLYNAHINCH)**
Very Rev Canon Gerard McCrory PP
Church Street, Ballynahinch, Co Down BT24 8LP
Tel/Fax 028-97562410
Email magheradrollrc.parish@nireland.com
Rev Desmond Loughran CC
Drumaness, Ballynahinch, Co Down BT24 8NG
Tel 028-97561432
*Parish Office:* 028-97565429

**MAGHERALIN**
Very Rev Brian Brown PP
25 Bottier Road, Moira, Craigavon, Co Armagh BT67 0PE
Tel 028-92611347
*Parish Office:* 028-92617435

**MOYRAVERTY (CRAIGAVON)**
Very Rev Martin McAlinden PP, VF
The Presbytery, 11 Tullygally Road, Legahory, Craigavon BT65 5BL
Tel 028-38341901
Email martinmcalinden@hotmail.com
Rev Desmond Mooney CC
The Presbytery, 13 Tullygally Road, Legahory, Craigavon BT65 5BY
Tel 028-38343297
Email mooneydesmond@googlemail.com
*Parish Office:* Moyraverty, 10 Tullygally Road
Tel 028-38343013

**SAVAL**
Very Rev Canon Francis Boyle PP
4 Shinn School Road, Newry, Co Down BT34 1PA
Tel/Fax 028-40630276

**SEAGOE (DERRYMACASH)**
Very Rev Canon Cathal Jordan PP
6 Derrymacash Road, Lurgan, Co Armagh BT66 6LG
Tel 028-38341356

**SEAPATRICK (BANBRIDGE)**
Very Rev Canon Liam Stevenson PP, VF
6 Scarva Road, Banbridge, Co Down BT32 3AR
Tel 028-40662136
Rev Anthony Corr CC
100 Dromore Street, Banbridge, Co Down BT32 4DW
Tel 028-40622274 Fax 028-40622847
*Parish Office*
Tel 028-40624950 Fax 028-40626547
Email parishseapatrick@btconnect.com

**SHANKILL, ST PAUL'S (LURGAN)**
Very Rev Michael Maginn PP
Lisadell, 54 Francis Street, Lurgan, Co Armagh BT66 6DL
Tel 028-38327173 Fax 028-38317974
Rev Andrew McMahon CC
St Paul's Presbytery, Old Portadown Road, Lurgan, Co Armagh BT66 8RG
Tel 028-38326883 Fax 028-38321289
*St Paul's Parish Office:* Tel 028-38321289
Email parishsecretary@btinternet.com

**SHANKILL, ST PETER'S (LURGAN)**
Rt Rev Mgr Aidan Hamill PP, VG
70 North Street, Lurgan, Co Armagh BT67 9AH
Tel 028-38323161
Rev Marian Jachym (SC) CC
68 North Street, Lurgan, Co Armagh BT67 9AH
Tel 028-38323161 Fax 028-38347927
Email office@stpetersparishlurgan.org

**TULLYLISH**
Very Rev Gerald Powell PP
4 Holymount Road, Gilford, Craigavon, Co Armagh BT63 6AT
Tel 028-40624236 Fax 028-40625440
Email gpowellpp@aol.com
Rev Stephen Crossan CC
Hunter's Hill, Gilford, Co Armagh BT63 6AJ
Tel 028-38831256
Email stephen_crossan@yahoo.co.uk
*Parish Office:* Tel 028-40624236
Email tullylish.dromore@btinternet.com
Website www.tullylish.com

## HOSPITALS AND THEIR CHAPLAINS

**Craigavon Area Hospital**
Co Armagh
*Chaplains:* Rev Stephen Crossan
Sr Fiona Galligan

**District Hospital**
Lurgan and Portadown, Co Armagh
*Chaplain:* Very Rev Michael Maginn PP

**Hospice**
Southern Area Hospice Services,
St John's House, Courtenay Hill, Newry,
Co Down BT34 2EB
Tel 028-30267711 Fax 028-30268492
*Chaplain:* Sr Fiona Galligan

## PRIESTS OF THE DIOCESE ELSEWHERE

Rt Rev Mgr Hugh Connolly BA, DD
President, St Patrick's College,
Maynooth, Co Kildare
Rev Matthew McConville
c/o Bishop's House
Rev Feidlimidh Magennis LSS
St Mary's University College, Belfast

## RETIRED PRIESTS

Very Rev Liam Boyle
9 Gargory road, Ballyward, Castlewellan,
Co Down BT31 9RN
Very Rev Arthur Byrne
Castor's Bay Road, Lurgan
Very Rev P. G. Conway
Warrenpoint Road, Newry, Co Down
Very Rev John Joe Cunningham
Newcastle, Co Down
Very Rev Canon Anthony Davies
Killowen, Rostrevor
Rev Gerard Green
c/o Bishop's House
Very Rev Canon Desmond Knowles
Newry, Co Down
Very Rev Brendan McAteer
Warrenpoint, Co Down
Very Rev Arthur MacNeill
14 Ballyholland Road, Newry, Co Down
Very Rev Canon Patrick McAnuff
58 Armagh Road, Newry, Co Down
Rev T. J. McGuinness
South Africa
Very Rev Francis Molloy
Lurgan, Co Armagh
Very Rev Oliver Mooney
Newry, Co Down
Rev John Murtagh, Warrenpoint
Very Rev Canon Joseph O'Hagan
Cabra, Hilltown
Very Rev James Poland
Rostrevor, Co Down

## RELIGIOUS ORDERS AND CONGREGATIONS

## PRIESTS

**BENEDICTINES**
Holy Cross Monastery, 119 Kilbroney Road,
Rostrevor, Co Down BT34 3BN
Tel 028-41739979 Fax 028-41739978
*Superior:* Very Rev Dom Mark-Ephrem M. Nolan OSB
Email benedictinemonks@btinternet.com
Website www.benedictinemonks.co.uk

**DOMINICANS**
St Catherine's, Newry,
Co Down BT35 8BN
Tel 028-30262178 Fax 028-30252188
*Prior:* Very Rev Joseph Ralph (OP)

**SOCIETY OF AFRICAN MISSIONS**
Dromantine, Newry,
Co Down BT34 1RH
Tel 028-30821224 Fax 028-30821704
*Superior:* Rev Patrick O'Rourke (SMA)

Dromantine Retreat and Conference Centre
Newry, Co Down BT34 1RH
Tel 028-30821219 Fax 028-30821963
Email
d.conferencecentre@btopenworld.com
Website www.dromantineconference.com
*Director:* Vacant

## SISTERS

**CARMELITES**
Carmelite Monastery of Mary
Immaculate and St Therese,
42 Glenvale Road, Newry,
Co Down BT34 2RD
Fax 028/048-30252778
Email nuns@carmelitesglenvale.org
*Prioress:* Sr M. Carmel Clarke
Community: 4

**CONGREGATION OF THE SISTERS OF MERCY**
Convent of Mercy, Catherine Street,
Newry, Co Down BT34 6JG
Tel 028-30262065/30264964
*Contact:* Sr Perpetua McArdle
Community: 11

1 Home Avenue,
Newry, Co Down BT34 2DL
Community: 4
Tel 028-30267141

Sisters of Mercy, Arbour House,
16 Great George's Street South,
Warrenpoint, Co Down BT34 3HR
Tel 028-41774181
Services to people with learning difficulties

Convent of Mercy, 3 Glenashley,
Rostrevor, Co Down BT34 3FW
Tel 028-41738356
Community: 2

14 Victoria Place, Lurgan,
Co Armagh BT67 9DL
Tel 028-38348602

89 North Street, Lurgan,
Co Armagh BT67 9AH
Tel 028-38347858

Convent of Mercy, 9 Queen Street,
Warrenpoint, Co Down BT34 3HZ
Tel 028-41752221
Community: 2

12 Cloghogue Heights, Newry,
Co Down BT35 8BA
Tel 028-30261628

Sisters of Mercy, Edward Street,
Lurgan, Co Armagh BT66 6DB
Tel 028-38322635
Community: 6

No 4 Ummericam Road, Silverbridge,
Newry, Co Down BT35 9PB
Tel 028-30860441

8 The Woodlands,
Lower Dromore Road,
Warrenpoint, Co Down BT34 6WL
Tel 028-41752383

17 Oakleigh Grove, Lurgan,
Co Armagh BT67 9AY
Tel 028-38347984

Convent of Mercy,
42 Antrim Road,
Lurgan, Co Armagh BT67 9BW
Tel 028-38347415

Sisters of Mercy, 6 Portadown Road,
Lurgan, Co Armagh BT66 8QW
Tel 028-38327956

204 Drumglass, Craigavon,
Co Armagh BT65 5BB
Tel 028-38343266

8 Parkhead Crescent, Newry,
Co Down BT35 8PE
Tel 028-30264615

5B Catherine Street, Newry,
Co Down BT35 6JG
Tel 028-30263697

16 Oakleigh Fold, North Street,
Lurgan, Co Armagh BT67 9BS
Tel 028-38348852

Sisters of Mercy, 49 Ardfreelan,
Rathfriland Road, Newry,
Co Down BT34 1CD
Tel 028-30250951

Sisters of Mercy, 2 Carrickree,
Bridle Loanan, Co Down BT34 3FA
Tel 028-41752347

27 Catherine Street, Newry,
Co Down, BT35 6JG
Tel 028-30833641

Rose Cottage,
14 Drumbanagher Wall Road,
Drumbanagher, Newry,
Co Down BT35 6LR
Tel 028-30821425

78 Chapel Street,
Newry, Co Down BT34 2DN
Tel 028-30265342

76 Chapel Street,
Newry, Co Down BT34 2DN
Tel 028-30266309

1 Dominican Court,
Newry, Co Down
Tel 028-30265184

15 Bracken Grove, Armagh Road,
Newry, Co Down BT35 4PG
Tel 028-30250630

Apt 4, Carlinn's Cove, Warrenpoint Road,
Rostrevor, Co Down BT34 3GJ

Apt 12, Carlinn's Cove,
Warrenpoint Road, Rostrevor,
Co Down BT34 3GJ
Tel 028-41737843

24 Rossmara Park, Warrenpoint,
Co Down BT34 3NX
Tel 028-41773230

**MISSIONARY FRANCISCAN SISTERS OF THE IMMACLATE CONCEPTION**
28 Hawtorn Avenue,
Lurgan, Co Armagh BT66 6DU
Tel 028-38316958
Email elisegorman@btinternet.com

**MISSIONARY SISTERS OF THE ASSUMPTION**
Assumption Convent,
34 Crossgar Road, Ballynahinch,
Co Down BT24 8EN
Tel 028-97561765 Fax 028-97565754
Email mail@assumption.org
*Superior:* Sr Ursula Hinchion
Email srursula@msassumption.org
Community: 9
Assumption Grammar School
Tel 028-97562250
Pupils: 870

**MISSIONARY SISTERS OF OUR LADY OF APOSTLES**
Rostrevor, Newry, Co Down
Tel 028-41737653 Fax 028-417377656
Community: 4
Email olagreendale@hotmail.com
1 Greendale Crescent, Greenpark Road,
Rostrevor, Newry, Co Down BT34 3HF

**SISTERS OF ST CLARE**
St Clare's Convent,
12 Ashgrove Avenue, Newry,
Co Down BT34 1PR
Tel 028-30252179
*Contact:* Sr Sheila Ryan
Community: 33
St Clare's Primary School, High Street,
Newry, Co Down BT34 1HD
Tel 028-30264909. Pupils: 665

St Clare's Convent,
75 Upper Damolly Road,
Newry, Co Down BT34 1QW
Tel 028-30268471. Community: 4
Sacred Heart Grammar School,
10 Ashgrove Avenue,
Newry, Co Down BT34 1PR
Tel 028-30264632. Pupils: 875

**ST JOHN OF GOD SISTERS**
Southern Area Hospice Services,
St John's House, Courtenay Hill,
Newry, Co Down
Tel 028-30267711

## EDUCATIONAL INSTITUTIONS

**St Colman's College (Diocesan College)**
Violet Hill,
Newry, Co Down
Tel 028-30262451
*Principal:* Mr Cormac McKinney
*Vice Principals:* Mr Aidan Henry,
Mr Michael Doyle
*Chaplain:* Fr Niall Sheehan

**EDMUND RICE SCHOOLS TRUST NORTHERN IRELAND**
St Colman's Abbey Primary School,
Courtenay Hill, Newry, Co Down BT34 2ED
Tel 028-30262175
Fax 028-30250648
Principal: Mr Eddie Sweeney

Abbey Christian Brothers' Grammar
School, 77a Ashgrove Road,
Newry, Co Down BT34 1QN
Tel 028-30263142 Fax 028-30262514
Principal: Mr D. McGovern

## CHARITABLE AND OTHER SOCIETIES

**Accord**
Cana House,
Newry Parish Pastoral Centre, The Mall,
Newry, Co Down
Tel 028-30263577

**Society of St Vincent de Paul**
Conferences at:
Ballynahinch (St Patrick's)
Banbridge (St Patrick's)
Craigavon (St Anthony's)
Dromore (St Colman's)
Gilford (St John's)
Hilltown (St John's)
Laurencetown (St Patrick's)
Lurgan (St Peter's)
Newry (Cathedral)
Newry (St Brigid's)
Rathfriland (St Marys)
Rostrevor (St Bronach's)
Warrenpoint (St Patrick's)

# DIOCESE OF ELPHIN

Patrons of the Diocese
St Asicus, 27 April; Immaculate Conception, 8 December

INCLUDES PORTIONS OF COUNTIES ROSCOMMON, SLIGO, WESTMEATH AND GALWAY

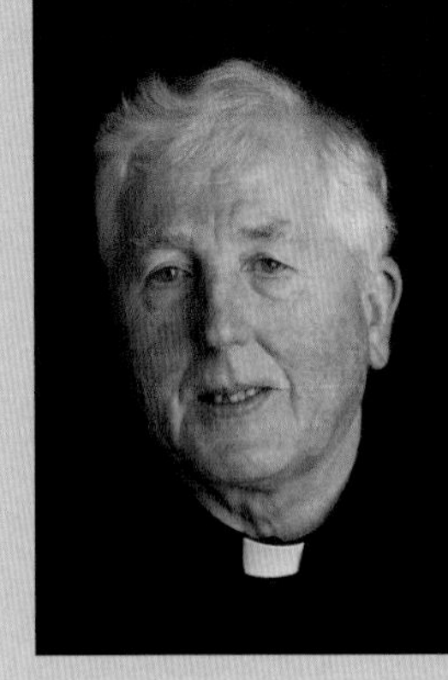

**Most Rev Christopher Jones DD**
Bishop of Elphin;
born 1936;
ordained priest 21 June 1962;
ordained Bishop of Elphin
15 August 1994

Residence: St Mary's,
Temple Street, Sligo
Tel 071-9162670/9162769
Fax 071-9162414
Email elphindo@eircom.net

## CATHEDRAL OF THE IMMACULATE CONCEPTION, SLIGO

The 125-year-old cathedral church dominates the skyline of Sligo town. It was erected during the episcopate of Bishop Laurence Gillooly (1858–1895), whose knowledge of ecclesiastical architecture is imprinted on every stone.

The foundation stone was laid on 6 October 1868. It was designed by a renowned English architect, George Goldie, and was modelled on Normano-Romano-Byzantine style. It was acclaimed by an eminent architect as a 'poem in stone'. It is 275 feet long, with transepts and nave, and can accommodate 4,000 people. A square tower incorporating the main entrance to the cathedral is surmounted by a four-sided pyramidal spire which reaches a height of 210 feet. The stained-glass windows and the original high altar are magnificent works of art.

Although the cathedral was open for public worship in 1874, it wasn't until 1882 that all construction work was completed. The cathedral was finally consecrated on 1 July 1897 and dedicated in honour of the Immaculate Conception of the Blessed Virgin Mary.

The cathedral has undergone extensive renovations on two occasions since it was erected, including the remodelling of the sanctuary to comply with liturgical norms in 1970.

## CHAPTER

*Castlerea:* Very Rev Joseph Fitzgerald
*Athlone:* Very Rev Liam Devine
*Roscommon*
Very Rev Eugene McLoughlin
*Boyle:* Very Rev Gerard Hanly
*Strandhill:* Very Rev Niall Ahern
*Frenchpark:* Very Rev Kevin Early
*Strokestown:* Very Rev Ciaran Whitney
*Sligo:* Very Rev Thomas Hever

## ADMINISTRATION

**Vicar General**
Right Rev Mgr Gerard Dolan PP, VG
Rosses Point, Co Sligo
Tel 071-9177133

**Vicars Forane**
Very Rev Canon Eugene McLoughlin
Very Rev Canon Thomas Hever
Very Rev Canon Joseph Fitzgerald
Very Rev Canon Ciaran Whitney
Very Rev Canon Gerard Hanly
Very Rev Canon Liam Devine

**Finance Committee**
*Secretary*
Rev Michael Duignan SThD
St Mary's, Temple Street, Sligo
Tel 071-9162670/9162679

**Building Committee**
*Chairman*
Very Rev Raymond Milton PP
Knockcroghery, Co Roscommon

**Diocesan Secretary**
Rt Rev Mgr Gerard Dolan VG
St Mary's, Temple Street, Sligo
Tel 071-9162670/9162769
Email elphindo@eircom.net

**Assistant Diocesan Secretary**
Rev Michael Duignan SThD
St Mary's, Temple Street, Sligo
Tel 071-9162670/9162679

## CATECHETICS EDUCATION

**Education (Post-Primary)**
*Secretary*
Rev Michael Duignan SThD
St Mary's, Temple Street, Sligo
Tel 071-9162670/9162679

**Education (Primary)**
*Secretary*
Rt Rev Mgr Austin McKeon PP
Tulsk, Castlerea, Co Roscommon
Tel 071-9639005

**Religious Instruction (Primary Schools)**
*Diocesan Director*
Sr Annette Duignan
Sisters of Mercy,
No. 1 St Patrick's Avenue, Sligo
Tel 071-9142731

## LITURGY

**Liturgical Music**
*Adviser Church Organ Music:*
Mr Charles O'Connor
Maugheraboy, Sligo
Tel 071-9145722

**Diocesan Liturgical Commission**
Very Rev Ian Kennedy PC
The Parochial House, Ballinafad,
Boyle, Co Roscommon
Tel 071-9666006

**Diocesan Magazine**
*The Angelus,* St Mary's, Sligo
Tel 071-9162670
*Editor:* Very Rev A. B. O'Shea PP
Sooey, via Boyle, Co Sligo
Tel 071-9165144
Email aboshea@eircom.net

## PASTORAL

**Accord**
*Director:* Rev James Murray CC
Carraroe, Sligo
Tel 071-9162136

**Adoption Society**
*Director:* Very Rev Thomas Hever VF
Sligo Social Services,
Charles Street, Sligo
Tel 071-9145682

**Council of Priests**
*Chairman:* Very Rev John Cullen PP
Kiltoom, Athlone, Co Roscommon
Tel 090-6489105
*Secretary:* Very Rev Donal Morris
c/o Diocesan Office,
St Mary's, Sligo
(on study break)

**CURA**
*Co-ordinator:* Ms Geraldine Doherty
Sligo Social Services,
Charles Street, Sligo
Tel 071-9145682

**Diocesan Pastoral Council**
*Secretary:* Ms Joan Geraghty
Elphin Diocesan Office,
St Mary's, Temple Street, Sligo
Tel 071-9162670/9162679

**Ecumenism**
Rev Pat Lombard CC
St Mary's, Sligo
Tel 071-9162670

**Family Ministry**
*Director:* Very Rev Brian Conlon
Family Life Centre, Boyle, Co Roscommon
Tel 071-9633000

**Marriage Tribunal**
(See Marriage Tribunals section)

**Pastoral Development**
*Diocesan Director:* Dr Justin Harkin
Pastoral Development Office,
Church Grounds, Elphin Street,
Strokestown, Co Roscommon
Tel 071-9634960

**Pilgrimage Directors (Lourdes)**
Rev Hugh McGonagle CC
7 Elm Park, Ballinode, Sligo
Tel 071-9143430
Very Rev Raymond Milton PP
Knockcroghery, Co Roscommon
Tel 090-6661127

**Pioneer Total Abstinence Association**
*Diocesan Director*
Very Rev Canon Liam Devine PP, VF
SS Peter and Paul, Athlone
Tel 090-6492171

**Pontifical Mission Societies**
*Diocesan Director*
Very Rev Ciaran Whitney PP, VF
Strokestown, Co Roscommon
Tel 071-9633027

**Social Services**
*Director:* Ms Christine McTaggart
Sligo Social Services, Charles Street, Sligo
Tel 071-9145682

**Travellers**
*Chaplain:* Rev John Carroll (SPS)
Cregg House, Rosses Point, Co Sligo
Tel 071-9177241

**Vocations to the Permanent Diaconate**
*Director:* Rev Michael Duignan
St Mary's, Sligo, Co Sligo
Tel 071-9162670

**Vocations to the Priesthood**
*Directors:* Rev James Murray
Carraroe, Sligo, Co Sligo
Tel 071-9162136
Rev John Coughlan CC
The Presbytery, Abbey Street,
Roscommon
Tel 090-6626189

**Youth Ministry and Safeguarding Children**
*Diocesan Director:* Mr Frank McGuinness
St Mary's, Sligo, Co Sligo
Tel 087-9880690

## PARISHES

*Mensal parishes are listed first. Other parishes follow alphabetically. Historical names are given in parentheses.*

**SLIGO, ST MARY'S**
Very Rev Canon Thomas Hever Adm, VF
Rev Patrick Lombard CC
*In Residence:* Rev Gerard Cryan
*In Residence:* Rev Andrzej Szulczynski
St Mary's, Temple Street, Sligo
Tel 071-9162670/9162769

**SLIGO, CALRY ST JOSEPH'S**
Very Rev Noel Rooney PP
279 Sunset Drive, Cartron Point, Sligo
Tel 071-9142422
Rev Hugh McGonagle CC
7 Elm Park, Ballinode, Sligo
Tel 071-9143430

**SLIGO, ST ANNE'S**
Very Rev Dominick Gillooly PP
Tel 071-9145028
Rev Stephen Walshe (CSSp) CC
Tel 071-9145028
St Anne's, Sligo
Rev James Murray CC
Carraroe, Co Sligo
Tel 071-9162136

**AHASCRAGH (AHASCRAGH AND CALTRA)**
Very Rev Kevin Reynolds (MHM) Adm
Ahascragh, Ballinasloe, Co Galway
Tel 090-9688617
Rev Vincent McDevitt (CSSp) CC
Caltra, Ballinasloe, Co Galway
Tel 090-9678125

**ATHLEAGUE (ATHLEAGUE AND FUERTY)**
Very Rev John Leogue PP
Athleague, Co Roscommon
Tel 090-6663338

**ATHLONE, SS PETER AND PAUL'S**
Very Rev Canon Liam Devine PP, VF
SS Peter and Paul's, Athlone
Tel 090-6492171
Rev John McManus (SPS) CC
10 Ashford, Monksland,
Athlone, Co Westmeath
Tel 090-6493262
Rev Seán O'Dowd (SSP) CC
Deerpark Road, Athlone,
Co Westmeath
Tel 090-6490575
Rev Michael McManus CC
Drum, Athlone, Co Westmeath
Tel 090-6437125

**AUGHRIM (AUGHRIM AND KILMORE)**
Rev Tomasz Grezegorzewski (SDB)
Aughrim, Hillstreet,
Carrick-on-Shannon, Co Roscommon
Tel 071-9637010

**BALLAGH (CLOONTUSKERT, KILGEFIN AND CURRAGHROE)**
Very Rev Raymond A. Browne PP
Kilrooskey, Roscommon
Tel 090-6626273
Rev Larry Shine (CSSp) CC
Ballyleague, Lanesboro, Co Longford
Tel 043-21171

**BALLINAFAD (AGHANAGH)**
Very Rev Ian Kennedy PC
Ballinafad, Boyle, Co Roscommon
Tel 071-9666006

**BALLINAMEEN (KILNAMANAGH AND ESTERSNOW)**
Very Rev Eamonn Conaty (SSC) PP
Ballinameen, Boyle, Co Roscommon
Tel 071-9668104

**BALLINTUBBER (BALLINTOBER AND BALLYMOE)**
Rev Joseph Poole (CSSp) PC
Ballintubber, Castlerea, Co Roscommon
Tel 094-9655226

**BALLYFORAN (DYSART AND TISRARA)**
Very Rev Francis Beirne PP
Four Roads, Roscommon
Tel 090-6623313

**BALLYGAR (KILLIAN AND KILLERORAN)**
Very Rev Michael Breslin PP
Ballygar, Co Galway
Tel 090-6624637
Very Rev Thomas Beirne CC
Newbridge, Ballinasloe, Co Galway
Tel 090-6660018

**BOYLE**
Very Rev Canon Gerard Hanly PP, VF
Tel 071-9662218
Rev Alan Conway CC
Tel 071-9662012
Boyle, Co Roscommon

**CASTLEREA (KILKEEVAN)**
Very Rev Canon Joseph Fitzgerald PP, VF
Tel 094-9620040
Rev Michéal Donnelly CC
Tel 094-9620039
Castlerea, Co Roscommon

**CLIFFONEY (AHAMLISH)**
Very Rev Christopher McHugh PP
Grange, Co Sligo
Tel 071-9163100
Rev Ireneuz Kuzmicki CC
Cliffoney, Co Sligo
Tel 071-9166133

**CLOVERHILL (ORAN)**
Very Rev Francis Glennon PP
Cams, Roscommon
Tel 090-6626275
Rev Thomas Leahy (SPS) CC
Ballinaheglish, Co Roscommon
Tel 090-6662229

**COOTEHALL (ARDCARNE)**
Very Rev Brian Conlon PC
Cootehall, Boyle,
Co Roscommon
Tel 071-9667004

**CREGGS (GLINSK AND KILBEGNET)**
Very Rev Phelim Jordan (SVD)
Donamon Castle, Co Roscommon
Tel 090-6662222

**CROGHAN (KILLUKIN AND KILLUMMOD)**
Very Rev Martin Mulvaney PP
Drumlion, Carrick-on-Shannon,
Co Roscommon
Tel 071-9620415

**DRUMCLIFF/MAUGHEROW**
Very Rev Michael Donnelly PP
Drumcliff, Sligo
Tel 071-9142779

**ELPHIN (ELPHIN AND CREEVE)**
Very Rev John J Gannon PP
Elphin, Co Roscommon
Tel 071-9635058
Very Rev James Tighe CC
Elphin, Co Roscommon
Tel 071-9635131

**FAIRYMOUNT (TIBOHINE)**
Very Rev James Creaton PC
Fairymount, Castlerea,
Co Roscommon
Tel 094-9870243

**FOURMILEHOUSE (KILBRIDE)**
Very Rev Raymond Browne PP
Fourmilehouse, Roscommon
Tel 090-6629518

**FRENCHPARK (KILCORKEY AND FRENCHPARK)**
Very Rev Canon Kevin Early PP
Frenchpark, Castlerea, Co Roscommon
Tel 094-9870105

**GEEVAGH**
Very Rev Laurence Cullen PP
Geevagh, Boyle,
Co Roscommon
Tel 071-9647107

**KILGLASS (KILGLASS AND ROOSKEY)**
Very Rev Kevin Fallon PP
Kilglass, Co Roscommon
Tel 071-9638162

**KILTOOM (KILTOOM AND CAM)**
Very Rev John Cullen PP
Kiltoom, Athlone, Co Roscommon
Tel 090-6489105
Rev Hugh Lee (MHM) CC
Curraghboy, Athlone, Co Roscommon
Tel 090-6488143

**KNOCKCROGHERY (ST JOHN'S)**
Very Rev Raymond Milton PP
Knockcroghery, Roscommon
Tel 090-6661127

**LOUGHGLYNN (LOUGHGLYNN AND LISACUL)**
Very Rev John O'Rourke PP
Loughglynn, Castlerea, Co Roscommon
Tel 094-9880007
Rev Brendan McDonagh (SPS) CC
Lisacul, Castlerea, Co Roscommon
Tel 094-9880068

**RIVERSTOWN**
Very Rev A.B. O'Shea PP
Sooey, Coola,
via Boyle, Co Sligo
Tel 071-9165144
Email aboshea@eircom.net

**ROSCOMMON**
Very Rev Canon Eugene McLoughlin PP, VF
Parochial House, Roscommon
Tel 090-6626298
Rt Rev Mgr Charles Travers CC
1 Convent Court, Roscommon
Tel 090-6628917
Rev John Coughlan CC
Curate's Residence, Abbey Street,
Roscommon
Tel 090-6626189
Rev Sean Beirne CC
Kilteevan, Roscommon
Tel 090-6626374
Rev James Heneghan (CSSp)
*(Chaplain to Brazilian Community)*
12 Abbeyville, Roscommon
Tel 090-6627978

**ROSSES POINT**
Rt Rev Mgr Gerard Dolan PP, VG
St Columba's,
Rosses Point, Co Sligo
Tel 071-9177133

**STRANDHILL/RANSBORO**
Very Rev Canon Niall Ahern PP
Strandhill, Co Sligo
Tel 071-9168147
Rev Christopher McCrann (LC) CC
Knocknahur, Sligo
Tel 071-9128470

**STROKESTOWN (KILTRUSTAN, LISSONUFFY AND CLOONFINLOUGH)**
Very Rev Ciaran Whitney PP, VF
Rev Ciaran O'Flynn (SPS) CC
Strokestown, Co Roscommon
Tel 071-9633027

**TARMONBARRY**
Very Rev Eamonn O'Connor PP
Tarmonbarry, Longford
Tel 043-26020

**TULSK (OGULLA AND BASLIC)**
Rt Rev Mgr Austin McKeon PP
Tulsk, Castlerea,
Co Roscommon
Tel 071-9639005
Rev Peter Gillooly (SPS) CC
Kilmurray,
Castlerea, Co Roscommon
Tel 094-9651018

## INSTITUTIONS AND THEIR CHAPLAINS

**Ballinode Vocational School**
Sligo
Tel 071-9147111
Very Rev Noel Rooney PP

**Castlerea Prison**
Tel 094-9625278
Email chaplaincastlereaprison@eircom.net
*Prison General Office:* 094-9625213

**Christian Brothers School,**
Roscommon
Tel 090-6626189
Rev John Coughlan CC

**Coola Vocational School**
Riverstown, Boyle, Co Roscommon
Tel 071-9165144
Very Rev A. B. O'Shea PP

**Cregg House, Sligo**
Tel 071-9177241
Rev John Carroll (SPS)

**Custume Barracks**
Athlone, Co Westmeath
Tel 090-6421277
Rev Gerard Dowd CF

**Grange Vocational School, Sligo**
Tel 071-9163100
Very Rev Christopher McHugh PP

**Nazareth House, Sligo**
Tel 071-9162278
Chaplain: Vacant

**Plunkett Home**
Boyle, Co Roscommon
Tel 071-9662012
Rev Alan Conway CC

**Post-Primary School, Elphin,**
Co Roscommon
Tel 071-9635058
Very Rev John J Gannon PP

**Post-Primary School, Strokestown**
Co Roscommon
Tel 071-9633041
Very Rev Ciaran Whitney PP

**Roscommon Hospital**
Tel 090-6620039
Rev Seán Beirne CC

**St Angela's College**
Lough Gill, Co Sligo
Tel 071-9143580
Rev Michael Duignan SThD

**St Cuan's College**
Castleblakeney, Ballinasloe, Co Galway
Tel 090-9678127
Rev Vincent McDevitt (CSSp) CC

**St Mary's Post-Primary School**
Ballygar, Co Galway
Tel 090-664637
Very Rev Michael Breslin PP

**Sligo General Hospital**
St Columba's, St John's
Tel 071-9171111
*Chaplains:* Rev J. Carroll,
Rev B. Conway

**Vocational School, Roscommon**
Rev John Coughlan CC
Roscommon
Tel 090-6626189

## PRIESTS OF THE DIOCESE ELSEWHERE

Rev Declan Brady
St Mary's College, Galway
Rev Anthony Conry, Brazil
Rev Michael Drumm STL
Columba Centre, Maynooth, Co Kildare
Very Rev Brian Hanley
Ballyhard, Glenamaddy, Co Galway

## RETIRED PRIESTS

Very Rev Seamus Cox
Ballyleague, Co Roscommon
Rev Thomas Garvey
Cloverhill, Co Roscommon
Very Rev Cyril Haran, Grange, Co Sligo
Rev Colm Hayes
15 St Patrick's Terrace, Sligo
Very Rev Canon Gerald Donnelly
Ballygar, Co Galway
Very Rev Patrick McHugh
22 Rosehill, Sligo
Rev Liam Sharkey
Ballyweelin, Rosses Point, Co Sligo
Rev Michael Glynn
Mullaghmore, Co Sligo
Very Rev Peadar Lavin
3 Slinagee, Golf Links Road, Roscommon
Very Rev Francis McGauran
Cuilmore, Strokestown, Co Roscommon

## RELIGIOUS ORDERS AND CONGREGATIONS

### PRIESTS

**DIVINE WORD MISSIONARIES**
Donamon Castle,
Roscommon
Tel 090-6662222
Fax 090-6662511
*Rector:* Very Rev Patrick Hogan (SVD)

**DOMINICANS**
Holy Cross, Sligo
Tel 071-9142700
Fax 071-9146533
*Prior:* Very Rev Timothy Mulcahy (OP)

**HOLY SPIRIT CONGREGATION**
Spiritan Community
Ballintubber, Castlerea, Co Roscommon
Tel 094-9655226

## SISTERS

**CONGREGATION OF THE SISTERS OF MERCY**
43 Battery Heights, Athlone,
Co Westmeath
Tel 090-6494748
Community: 3

Sisters of Mercy, 3 Newtown Terrace,
Athlone, Co Westmeath
Tel 090-6473944
Community: 4

Sisters of Mercy, Dún Mhuire,
Lyster Street, Athlone, Co Westmeath
Tel 090-6494166 Fax 090-6440079
Community: 22

Sisters of Mercy, Cois Abhann,
Lyster Street, Athlone, Co Westmeath
Community: 21

Tearmonn, Eirde, The Docks,
Athlone, Co Westmeath
Tel 090-6493941
Community: 1

St Cecilias, Coosan Road West,
Athlone, Co Westmeath
Tel 090-6472987
Community: 1

Sisters of Mercy, Bethany,
Chapel Hill, Sligo
Tel 071-9138498
Community: 6

Our Lady of Mercy,
3 St Patrick's Avenue, Sligo
Tel 071-9142731 Fax 071-9147090
Community: 12

Sisters of Mercy,
No 1 St Patrick's Avenue, Sligo
Tel 071-9142393
Community: 3

Sisters of Mercy,
No 2 St Patrick's Avenue, Sligo
Tel 071-9145755
Community: 2

Sisters of Mercy, 8 Cleveragh Road, Sligo
Tel 071-9162074
Community: 2

Sisters of Mercy,
1 Racecourt Manor, Tonaphubble, Sligo
Tel 071-9154656
Community: 3

Sisters of Mercy, Star of the Sea,
Mullaghmore, Co Sligo
Tel 071-9176722 Fax 071-9176710
Community: 3
Retreat house

McAuley House, Roscommon
Tel 090-6627904 Fax 090-6627581
Community: 7

Sisters of Mercy, Knockaire,
Galway Road, Roscommon
Tel 090-6625897
Community: 3

Sisters of Mercy, Crubyhill, Roscommon
Tel 090-6625725
Community: 3

Convent of Mercy,
St Catherine's, Roscommon
Tel 090-6626767
Community: 4

Convent of Mercy, Boyle, Co Roscommon
Tel 071-9662144
Community: 7

Galilee Community,
Sisters of Mercy, Tintagh,
Boyle, Co Roscommon
Tel 071-9664101 Fax 071-9664684
Community: 2

Lisroyne,
Strokestown, Co Roscommon
Tel 071-9633056
Community: 2

Breedogue, Co Roscommon
Tel 094-9870020
Community: 1

**CONGREGATION OF THE SISTERS OF NAZARETH**
Nazareth House, Sligo
Tel 071-9162278 Public
Tel 071-9160664 Fax 071-9160344
Tel Convent 071-9154446
*Superior:* Sr Bernardine Hannon
Email bhannan@hotmail.co.uk
Community: 10
Home for the elderly. Beds 50
Nursing Home now managed by
Nazareth House Management
Committee Ltd, Sligo
*Director of Service:* Suzanne Keenan
Tel 071-9180900

**DAUGHTERS OF WISDOM**
35 The Park,
Strandhill Road, Sligo
Tel 071-9154019
Community:1

12 The Greenlands, Rosses Point, Sligo
Tel 071-91977607
Community: 2

Weatherly, Ballincar, Sligo
Tel 071-9194299
*Co-ordinator:* Sr Maureen Seddon DW
Community: 3

**DISCIPLES OF THE DIVINE MASTER**
8 Castle Street, Athlone, Co Westmeath
Tel 090-6498755 *(Community)*
090-6492278 *(Liturgical Centre)*
Fax 090-6492649
Email pddmathlone@gmail.com
liturgicalcentre@gmail.com
*Sister-in-Charge:* Sr M. Brid Geraghty
Community: 5
Contemplative-apostolic, perpetual adoration, Liturgical apostolate, distributors and producers of high-quality Liturgical art, vestments, church goods. Private retreats, prayer groups.

**MISSIONARIES OF CHARITY**
Temple Street, Sligo
Tel 071-9154843
*Superior:* Sr M. Clare Anne (MC)
Community: 6
Contemplative

**PRESENTATION OF MARY SISTERS**
4 Lower John Street, Sligo
Tel 071-9160740
*Superior:* Sr Elenita Baguio (PM)
Email elenitapm2008@hotmail.com
Community: 5

**SISTERS OF ST JOSEPH OF THE APPARITION**
St Joseph's Convent, Garden Hill, Sligo
Tel 071-9162330 (Convent)
Fax 071-9152500
Email stjsligo@eircom.net
*Contact:* Sr Magdalen Ennis
Community: 10

**URSULINES**
Ursuline Convent, Temple Street, Sligo
Tel 071-9161538
*Local Leader:* Sr Dorothy Gallagher
Community: 12
Primary School
Tel 071-9154573 Fax 071-9154573
Secondary School
Tel 071-9161653 Fax 071-9146141

St Angela's College of Education
Lough Gill, Sligo
Tel 071-9143580 Fax 071-9144585
Email ursulines@stacs.edu.ie
Website www.stacs.edu.ie
*President:* Anne Taheny
St Ursula's Community House
Tel 071-9147218/47238
*Local Leader:* Sr Moya Hegarty
Community: 4

Ursuline Sisters,
'Brescia', Ballytivnan, Sligo
Community: 3
Pastoral Ministry

## EDUCATIONAL INSTITUTIONS

**College of the Immaculate Conception**
Summerhill, Sligo
Tel 071-9160311
*Principal:* Mr Tommy McManus
*Clerical Staff*
Rev Gerard Cryan BA, HDE, STB, L Eccl Hist

**St Aloysius College**
Athlone, Co Westmeath
Tel 090-6494153
*Principal:* Mr Gearoid O'Conamha

**St Joseph's College**
Summerhill, Athlone, Co Roscommon
Tel 090-6492383
*Principal:* Mr Liam Lally

**St Cuan's College**
Castleblakeney,
Ballinasloe, Co Galway
Tel 090-9678127
*Principal:* Mr Martin Giblin

**EDMUND RICE SCHOOLS TRUST**
Meán Mhuire na mBráithre,
Roscommon Town
Tel 090-6626496/6626279
*Principal:* Mr Pat Hanlon

## CHARITABLE AND OTHER SOCIETIES

**Family Life Centres**
***St Michael's Family Life Centre***
Church Hill, Sligo
Tel 071-9170329
*Director:* Ms Eileen Sheridan

***Boyle Family Life Centre***
Knocknashee, Boyle, Co Roscommon
Tel 071-9663000
*Director:* Very Rev Brian Conlon

***Vita House***
Roscommon
Tel 090-6625898
*Director:* Sr Mary Lee

***Cuan Aire Family Centre***
Castlerea, Co Roscommon
Tel 094-9620057

**Legion of Mary**
Assumpta House, John Street, Sligo

**Social Services Centre**
Charles Street, Sligo
Tel 071-9145682

**Society of St Vincent de Paul**
Conferences at Athlone, Boyle, Castlerea, Roscommon, Sligo

# DIOCESE OF FERNS

Patron of the Diocese
St Aidan, 30 January

INCLUDES ALMOST ALL OF COUNTY WEXFORD
AND PART OF COUNTY WICKLOW

**Most Rev Denis Brennan DD**
Bishop of Ferns
Ordained Bishop 23 April 2006

Residence: Bishop's House,
Summerhill, Wexford
Tel 053-9122177
Fax 053-9123436

## ST AIDAN'S CATHEDRAL, ENNISCORTHY

The foundation stone for St Aidan's Cathedral, Enniscorthy, was laid in 1843. The cathedral was designed by the architect Augustus Welby Northmore Pugin and is the largest church Pugin built in Ireland. The recent renovations of 1996 have restored to a great extent the original beautiful building as visualised by Pugin. The external stonework was executed by Irish stonemasons who were praised by Pugin. The restored stencilling of the interior gives some idea of what Pugin visualised for his churches.

Pugin, a Londoner, was as important an influence on the history of nineteenth-century English architecture as Frank Lloyd Wright was to be on American architecture. He was an extraordinarily gifted artist and designed ceramics, stained glass, wallpapers, textiles, memorial brasses, church plate, etc. His connection with the Diocese of Ferns came through the patronage of John, 16th Earl of Shrewsbury, Waterford and Wexford. Shrewsbury's wife was a native of Blackwater, Co Wexford. Her uncle, John Hyacinth Talbot, was the first Catholic MP for Co Wexford after Catholic Emancipation in 1829. A rich man through his marriage into the Redmond family, John Hyacinth Talbot introduced Pugin to Wexford, where through the patronage of the Talbot and Redmond family connections, he was to gain most of his Irish commissions.

Pugin was to die through overwork at the age of forty in 1852, but he has left a unique diocesan heritage to Ferns in his churches. His son and son-in-law, E.W. Pugin and George Ashlin, were to continue the building of Gothic Revival churches and monuments in Ireland.

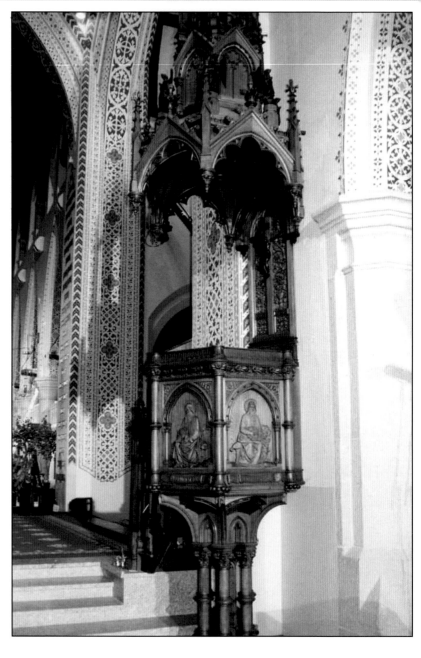

**Most Rev Brendan Comiskey DD**
Retired Bishop of Ferns
PO Box 40, Summerhill, Wexford

## CHAPTER

Rt Rev Mgr Patrick Corish
Very Rev James B. Curtis
Rt Rev Mgr Joseph L. Kehoe PA
Very Rev Seán McCarthy
Very Rev Nicholas Power
Very Rev Brendan Kirby
Very Rev Seamus De Val
Very Rev Thomas Curtis
Very Rev Felix Byrne
Very Rev Noel Hartley
Very Rev Lorenzo Cleary

## ADMINISTRATION

**College of Consultors**
Rt Rev Mgr Joseph L. Kehoe PA
Rt Rev Mgr Denis Lennon
Rt Rev Mgr Joseph McGrath VG
Very Rev Patrick Cushen
Very Rev James Hammel
Very Rev Noel Canon Hartley
Very Rev Anthony O'Connell
Very Rev James Byrne
Very Rev Richard Hayes
Very Rev Brian Broaders
Very Rev John Jordan

**Vicar General**
Rt Rev Mgr Joseph McGrath VF, VG
New Ross, Co Wexford
Tel 051-421348

**Vicar for Clergy**
Rt Rev Mgr Denis Lennon PP, VF
39 Beechlawn, Clonard, Wexford
Tel 053-9124417

**Vicars Forane**
Very Rev Patrick Cushen
Rt Rev Mgr Joseph McGrath
Rt Rev Mgr Denis Lennon

**Diocesan Finance Council**
Rt Rev Mgr Joseph McGrath VG, VF
Very Rev Patrick Cushen VF
Very Rev James Fegan Adm
Very Rev William Howell PP
Mr Pat Kent
Mrs Catherine O'Gara
Mr Liam Gaynor
Mr John Murphy
Mr Patrick F. Dore
Ms Eleanor Furlong
*Finance Officer and Chairman*
Mr Eugene Doyle

**Diocesan Archivist**
Very Rev Seamus Canon De Val
1 Irish Street, Bunclody, Co Wexford
Tel 053-9376140

**Bishop's Secretary**
Miss Theresa Gleeson
Bishop's Office, Summerhill, Wexford
Tel 053-9122177
Email adm@ferns.ie

**Diocesan Secretary & Chancellery**
Rev John Carroll
PO Box 40, Bishop's House,
Summerhill, Wexford
Tel 053-9124368
Email jc@ferns.ie

## CATECHETICS EDUCATION

**Catholic Primary School Management Association (CPSMA)**
Very Rev Francis Murphy PP
Bree, Enniscorthy, Co Wexford
Tel 053-9247843
Email fernsed@gmail.com

**Diocesan Adviser for Primary School Catechetics**
Rev John-Paul Sheridan CC
Blackwater, Enniscorthy, Co Wexford
Tel 053-9129288

**Director of Religious Education**
Sr Anna McDonagh
Ferns Diocesan Centre,
St Peter's College, Wexford
Tel 053-9145511

## PASTORAL

**Apostolic Work Society**
*Diocesan Director*
Very Rev Joseph Power PP
Kilrush, Bunclody, Co Wexford
Tel 053-9377262

**Chaplain to Special Needs Groups**
Very Rev Tom Dalton PP
Rathangan, Co Wexford
Tel 051-563104

**CORI (Ferns Branch)**
*Secretary:* Sr Teresa Walsh
Terrerath, New Ross, Co Wexford
Tel 051-428313
Email mshrterrerath@gmail.com

**Diocesan Mission Commission**
*Chairman:* Rt Rev Mgr Denis Lennon PP, VF
39 Beechlawn, Wexford
Tel 053-9124417

**Ecumenism**
*Director:* Very Rev Aidan G. Jones PP
Bunclody, Enniscorthy, Co Wexford
Tel 053-9377319

**FDYS Youth Work Ireland**
*Director*
Mr Kieran Donohoe,
Francis Street, Wexford
Tel 053-9123262

**Fatima Pilgrimage**
*Director*
Very Rev Thomas Doyle PP
Craanford, Gorey, Co Wexford
Tel 053-9428163

**House of Mission**
Rev Thaddeus Doyle
Shillelagh, Arklow, Co Wicklow
Tel 053-9429926

**Knock Pilgrimage**
*Director:* Very Rev Oliver Sweeney PP
Poulfur, Fethard-on-Sea, New Ross,
Co Wexford
Tel 051-397048

**Legion of Mary**
(Northern Curia)
Very Rev Seamus Canon De Val
1 Irish Street, Bunclody,
Co Wexford
Tel 053-9376140 (Southern Curia)
Very Rev Brendan Nolan PP
Our Lady's Island, Co Wexford
Tel 053-9131167

**Lourdes Pilgrimage**
*Director:* Rev Matthew Boggan CC
Galbally, Ballyhogue,
Enniscorthy, Co Wexford
Tel 053-9247814

**Marriage Tribunal**
(See also Marriage Tribunals section)
*Ferns Diocesan Auditor for Dublin Regional Marriage Tribunal*
Rev Kevin Cahill (DCL) CC
Ballymitty, Wexford
Tel 051-561128

**Our Lady's Island Pilgrimage**
*Director:* Very Rev Brendan Nolan PP
Our Lady's Island, Broadway,
Co Wexford
Tel 053-9131167

**Pioneer Total Abstinence Association**
*Diocesan Director*
Rev Michael Byrne CC
Boolavogue, Ferns,
Co Wexford
Tel 053-9233530

**Pontifical Mission Societies**
*Diocesan Director*
Very Rev Hugh O'Byrne PP
Blackwater, Co Wexford
Tel 053-9127118

**St Aidan Retirement Fund**
*Chairman*
Very Rev Joseph Power PP
Kilrush, Bunclody, Co Wexford
Tel 053-9377262

**St Joseph's Young Priests' Society**
*Diocesan Chaplain*
Right Rev Mgr Joseph McGrath PP, VF, VG
New Ross, Co Wexford
Tel 051-421348

**Travellers**
*Diocesan Co-ordinator*
Rev Ken Quinn
Traveller Resource Centre,
Mary Street, New Ross,
Co Wexford
Tel 051-422272

**Vocations**
*Director*
Very Rev James Finn PP
Crossabeg, Co Wexford
Tel 053-9159015

## PARISHES

*Mensal parishes are listed first. Other parishes follow alphabetically.*

**ENNISCORTHY, CATHEDRAL OF ST AIDAN**
Very Rev Denis Kelly Adm
Rev Patrick Sinnott CC
Rev Richard Lawless CC
St Aidan's, Enniscorthy, Co Wexford
Tel 053-9235777
Fax 053-9237700

**WEXFORD**
Very Rev James Fegan Adm
Rev Michael O'Shea CC
Rev Aodhan Marken CC
Rev Brian Whelan CC
The Presbytery,
12 School Street, Wexford
Tel 053-9122055 Fax 053-9121724

**ADAMSTOWN**
Very Rev Robert Nolan PP
Adamstown, Enniscorthy,
Co Wexford
Tel 053-9240512

**ANNACURRA**
Very Rev James Hammel PP
Annacurra, Aughrim, Co Wicklow
Tel 0402-36119

**BALLINDAGGIN**
Very Rev John Sinnott PP
Ballindaggin, Enniscorthy,
Co Wexford
Tel 053-9388559
Rev Fintan Morris CC
Kiltealy, Enniscorthy, Co Wexford
Tel 053-9255124

**BALLYCULLANE**
Very Rev Laurence O'Connor PP
Ballycullane, New Ross, Co Wexford
Tel 051-562123
Rev Patrick Banville CC
St Leonard's, Saltmills, New Ross,
Co Wexford
Tel 051-562135
Very Rev Sean Laffan CC
Gusserane, Co Wexford
Tel 051-562111

**BALLYGARRETT**
Very Rev James Butler PP
Ballygarrett, Gorey, Co Wexford
Tel 053-9427330

**BALLYMORE AND MAYGLASS**
Very Rev Martin Byrne PP
Ballymore, Killinick, Co Wexford
Tel 053-9158966

**BANNOW**
Very Rev James Kehoe PP
Carrig-on-Bannow,
Wellington Bridge, Co Wexford
Tel 051-561192
Rev Kevin Cahill (DCL) CC
Ballymitty, Co Wexford
Tel 051-561128

**BLACKWATER**
Very Rev Hugh O'Byrne PP
Tel 053-9127118
Rev John-Paul Sheridan CC
Tel 053-9129288
Blackwater, Enniscorthy,
Co Wexford

**BREE**
Very Rev Francis Murphy PP
Bree, Enniscorthy, Co Wexford
Tel 053-9247843
Rev Matthew Boggan CC
Galbally, Ballyhogue, Enniscorthy,
Co Wexford
Tel 053-9247814

**BUNCLODY**
(*Parish Office:* Tel/Fax 054-76190)
Very Rev Aidan G. Jones PP
Bunclody, Enniscorthy, Co Wexford
Tel 053-9377319
Rev Ignacio Mikalonis (IVE), CC
Rev Marco Mikalonis (IVE)
Kilmyshall, Enniscorthy, Co Wexford
Tel 053-9377188

**CAMOLIN**
Very Rev Joseph Kavanagh PP
Camolin, Co Wexford
Tel 053-9383136
Rev Thomas Orr CC
Ballycanew, Gorey, Co Wexford
Tel 053-9427184

**CARNEW**
Very Rev Martin Casey PP
Woolgreen, Carnew, Co Wicklow
Tel 053-9426888
Rev William Byrne CC
Coolfancy, Tinahely, Co Wicklow
Tel 0402-34725

**CASTLEBRIDGE**
Very Rev Walter Forde PP
Castlebridge, Co Wexford
Tel 053-9159769 Fax 053-9159158
Rev James Fitzpatrick CC
Ballymore, Screen,
Enniscorthy, Co Wexford
Tel 053-9137140

**CLONARD**
(*Parish Office:* Tel 053-9123672
Fax 053-9146699)
Rt Rev Mgr Denis Lennon PP, VF
39 Beechlawn, Wexford
Tel 053-9124417
Rev Seán Devereux CC
6 Meadowvale, Coolcotts, Wexford
Tel 053-9143932
Rev Martin Doyle CC
1 Clonard Park, Wexford
Tel 053-9147686

**CLONGEEN**
Very Rev Colm Murphy PP
Clongeen, Foulksmills, Co Wexford
Tel 051-565610

**CLOUGHBAWN**
Very Rev Richard Hayes PP
Clonroche, Enniscorthy, Co Wexford
Tel 053-9244115
Rev Robert McGuire CC
Poulpeasty, Clonroche,
Enniscorthy, Co Wexford
Tel 053-9244116

**CRAANFORD**
Very Rev Thomas Doyle PP
Craanford, Gorey, Co Wexford
Tel 053-9228163
Very Rev Felix Canon Byrne CC
Monaseed, Gorey, Co Wexford
Tel 053-9428207

**CROSSABEG AND BALLYMURN**
Very Rev James Finn PP
Crossabeg, Co Wexford
Tel 053-9159015

**CUSHINSTOWN**
Very Rev Michael Byrne PP
Cushinstown, Foulksmills, Co Wexford
Tel 051-428347
Rev Odhrán Furlong CC
Rathgarogue, New Ross, Co Wexford
Tel 051-424521

**DAVIDSTOWN AND COURTNACUDDY**
Very Rev James Nolan PP
Davidstown, Enniscorthy,
Co Wexford
Tel 053-9233382

**DUNCANNON**
Very Rev John P. Nolan PP
Duncannon, New Ross,
Co Wexford
Tel 051-389118

**FERNS**
Very Rev Patrick Cushen PP, VF
Ferns, Enniscorthy, Co Wexford
Tel 053-9366152
Rev Richard Redmond CC
(Ballyduff) The Square, Ferns,
Enniscorthy, Co Wexford
Tel 053-9366162

**GLYNN**
Very Rev Patrick Stafford PP
Glynn, Enniscorthy, Co Wexford
Tel 053-9128115
Rev John Carroll CC
(Diocesan Secretary)
Barntown, Co Wexford
Tel 053-9120853

**GOREY**
Very Rev William Howell PP
St Michael's, Gorey, Co Wexford
Tel 053-9421112
Rt Rev Mgr Donald Kenny CC
Rev William Flynn CC
Tel 053-9421117
St Patrick's, Gorey, Co Wexford

**HORESWOOD AND BALLYKELLY**
Very Rev Gerald O'Leary PP
Horeswood, Campile, Co Wexford
Tel 051-388129

**KILANERIN**
Very Rev Patrick O'Brien PP
Kilanerin, Gorey, Co Wexford
Tel/Fax 0402-37120
Rev Michael Doyle CC (Tyler, Texas)
Ballyfad, Gorey, Co Wexford
Tel 0402-37124

**KILLAVENEY**
Very Rev Raymond Gahan PP
Killaveney, Tinahely, Co Wicklow
Tel 0402-38188
Rev Donal Berney CC
St Kevin's, Tinahely, Co Wicklow
Tel 0402-38138

**KILMORE AND KILMORE QUAY**
Very Rev Denis Doyle PP
Kilmore, Co Wexford
Tel 053-9135181
Rev Patrick O'Conor (SSC) CC
Mulrankin, Co Wexford
Tel 053-9135166

**KILMUCKRIDGE (LITTER)**
Very Rev Seamus Larkin PP
Kilmuckridge, Gorey, Co Wexford
Tel 053-9130116
Rev James Doyle CC
Monamolin, Gorey, Co Wexford
Tel 053-9389223

**KILRANE AND ST PATRICK'S**
Very Rev Diarmuid Desmond PP
Kilrane, Co Wexford
Tel 053-9133128

**KILRUSH AND ASKAMORE**
Very Rev Joseph Power PP
Kilrush, Bunclody, Co Wexford
Tel 053-9377262

**MARSHALLSTOWN AND CASTLEDOCKRELL**
Very Rev Daniel McDonald PP
Marshallstown, Enniscorthy,
Co Wexford
Tel 053-9388521

**MONAGEER**
Very Rev William Cosgrave PP
Monageer, Ferns, Enniscorthy,
Co Wexford
Tel 053-9233530
Rev Michael Byrne CC
Boolavogue, Ferns, Wexford
Tel 053-9366282

**NEWBAWN AND RAHEEN**
Very Rev James Furlong PP
Newbawn, Co Wexford
Tel 051-428227

**NEW ROSS**
Rt Rev Mgr Joseph McGrath PP, VF, VG
New Ross, Co Wexford
Tel 051-447080
Rev Tomás Kehoe CC
Tel 051-447086
Rev Roger O'Neill CC
Tel 051-447081
New Ross, Co Wexford

**OULART**
Very Rev Patrick Browne PP
Oulart, Gorey, Co Wexford
Tel 053-9136139
Rev Dermot Gahan CC
The Ballagh, Wexford
Tel 053-9136200

**OUR LADY'S ISLAND AND TACUMSHANE**
Very Rev Brendan Nolan PP
Our Lady's Island, Broadway,
Co Wexford
Tel 053-9131167

**OYLEGATE AND GLENBRIEN**
Very Rev James Cogley PP
Oylegate, Co Wexford
Tel 053-9138163

**PIERCESTOWN**
Very Rev John O'Reilly PP
Piercestown, Co Wexford
Tel 053-9158851
Rev James Moynihan CC
Murrintown, Wexford
Tel 053-9139136

**RAMSGRANGE**
Very Rev Bernard Cushen PP
Ramsgrange, New Ross,
Co Wexford
Tel 051-389148

**RATHANGAN AND CLEARIESTOWN**
Very Rev Thomas Dalton PP
Rathangan, Duncormick, Co Wexford
Tel 051-563104
Very Rev James Ryan *(priest in residence)*
Cleariestown, Co Wexford
Tel 053-9139110

**RATHNURE AND TEMPLEUDIGAN**
Very Rev Anthony O'Connell PP
Rathnure, Co Wexford
Tel 054-55122

**THE RIVERCHAPEL, COURTOWN HARBOUR**
Very Rev James Butler Adm
The Riverchapel, Courtown Harbour,
Gorey, Co Wexford
Tel 053-9425241

**ST SENAN'S, ENNISCORTHY**
*Parish Office:* Tel 053-9237611
Very Rev Brian Broaders Adm
Rev John Byrne CC
The Presbytery, Templeshannon,
Enniscorthy, Co Wexford
Tel 053-9237611

**TAGHMON**
Very Rev Seán Gorman PP
Taghmon, Co Wexford
Tel 053-9134123
Rev David Murphy CC
Caroreigh, Taghmon, Co Wexford
Tel 053-9134113

**TAGOAT**
Very Rev Matthias Glynn PP
Tagoat, Co Wexford
Tel 053-9131139
Rev James Murphy CC
St Brigid's, Rosslare, Co Wexford
Tel 053-9132118

**TEMPLETOWN AND POULFUR**
Very Rev Oliver Sweeney PP
Poulfur, Fethard-on-Sea,
New Ross, Co Wexford
Tel 051-397113

## INSTITUTIONS AND THEIR CHAPLAINS

**Community School**
Gorey, Co Wexford
Tel 053-9421000

**Vocational College Wexford**
Rev David Murphy CC
Caroreigh, Taghmon, Co Wexford
Tel 053-9134113

**Wexford General Hospital**
Tel 053-9142233
*Chaplain:* Rev Ken Quinn
General Hospital, Wexford
Tel 053-9142233

**Community School**
Ramsgrange
Tel 051-389211
Ms Maria McCabe

**St John of God Convent**
Newtown Road, Wexford
Rt Rev Mgr J. L. Kehoe PA
13 Priory Court, Spawell Road, Wexford

## PRIESTS OF THE DIOCESE ELSEWHERE IN IRELAND

Right Rev Mgr Patrick Corish DD
Mill Lane Manor, Naas, Co Kildare
Tel 01-6285222
Rev Patrick Mernagh CF
McKee Barracks,
Blackhorse Avenue, Dublin 7
Rev Peter O'Connor
10 Cranfield Place, Dublin 4

## PRIESTS OF THE DIOCESE ABROAD

Rev Thomas Brennan, USA
Rev Denis Browne
c/o Bishop's House, Wexford
Rev Oliver Doyle
Diocese of Great Falls, Billings, Montana, USA
Rev Chris Hayden
Pontifical Irish College,
Via de SS Quattro 1, Roma 00184, Italy
Rev Willam Swan
Pontifical Irish College,
Via de SS Quattro 1, Roma 00184, Italy

## RETIRED PRIESTS

Very Rev James Byrne
Ballylannon, Wellingtonbridge,
Co Wexford
Rev James Cashman
11 Pinewood, Wexford
Very Rev Matthew L. Cleary
The Stables, Bridgetown, Co Wexford
Most Rev Brendan Comiskey (SSCC) DD
PO Box 40, Wexford
ery Rev James Curtis
3 Oldtown Court, Clongreen, Foulksmills,
New Ross, Co Wexford
Very Rev James B. Canon Curtis
Rathjarney, Drinagh, Co Wexford
Rev Thomas Canon Curtis
2 The Hollows, Lugduff, Tinahely,
Co Wicklow
Very Rev Seamus Canon De Val
1 Irish Streeet, Bunclody, Co Wexford
Very Rev Thomas Eustace
The Cools, Barntown, Wexford
Very Rev John French
Horeswood, New Ross, Co Wexford
Tel 051-593196
Very Rev Noel Canon Hartley
10 Donovan's Wharf, Crescent Quay,
Wexford
Very Rev John Jordan
Kyle, Oulart, Gorey, Co Wexford
Very Rev Liam Jordan
Coolamain, Oylegate, Co Wexford
Rt Rev Mgr J.L. Kehoe VG, PA
13 Priory Court, Spawell Road, Wexford
Very Rev Tobias Kinsella
Bloomfield Care Centre, Stocking Lane,
Rathfarnham, Dublin 16
Very Rev Brendan Canon Kirby
9 Kilmartin Hill, Wicklow, Co Wicklow
Very Rev Sean Canon McCarthy
Loma, Newtown Road, Wexford
Very Rev Thomas McGrath
Cois Tra, Chapel Road,
Duncannon, Co Wexford
Rev John O'Brien
Elmfield Mews, Spawell Road, Wexford
Very Rev Nicholas Canon Power
Moorfield, Rathaspeck, Co Wexford
Very Rev James Ryan
Cleariestown, Co Wexford

## RELIGIOUS ORDERS AND CONGREGATIONS

### PRIESTS

**AUGUSTINIANS**
St Augustine's Priory, New Ross,
Co Wexford
Tel 051-421237
*Prior:* Rev Michael Collender (OSA)
Community: 9

Good Counsel College,
New Ross, Co Wexford
Tel 051-421663/421909 Fax 051-421909

St Augustine's Priory,
Grantstown, New Ross, Co Wexford
Tel 051-561119
*Superior:* Rev Aidan O'Leary (OSA)
Community: 1

**CONVENTUAL FRANCISCANS**
The Friary, Wexford
Tel 053-9122758 Fax 053-9121499
*Guardian:* Rev Aidan Walsh (OFMConv)

### BROTHERS

**CHRISTIAN BROTHERS**
Christian Brothers' House,
Joseph Street, Wexford
Tel 053-45659
*Community Leader:* Br E. Kinsella
Community: 6

### SISTERS

**CARMELITES**
Mount Carmel Monastery,
New Ross, Co Wexford
Tel 051-421076
Email carmelites@eircom.net
*Prioress:* Sr Brenda Donovan
Community: 12
Contemplatives
Altar breads

**CONGREGATION OF THE SISTERS OF MERCY**
Convent of Mercy,
Clonard Road, Wexford
Tel 053-23024

Sisters of Mercy,
52 Westlands, Wexford
Tel 053-42917

Convent of Mercy, St Brigid's,
Rosslare Strand, Co Wexford
Tel 053-32104

Sisters of Mercy, Lower South Knock,
New Ross, Co Wexford
Tel 051-425340

'Misericordia', 1 Tower Grove,
New Ross, Co Wexford
Tel 051-422027

The Lodge, 38 Irishtown, New Ross,
Co Wexford

**DAUGHTERS OF CHARITY OF ST VINCENT DE PAUL**
Cluain Mhuire, Gorey Road, Carnew,
Arklow, Co Wicklow
Tel 053-9426371
*Superior:* Sr Mary Crosbie
Community: 4
Residential housing for elderly, day care centre, parish work

**FAMILY OF ADORATION**
St Aidan's Monastery of Adoration,
Ferns, Co Wexford
Tel 053-9366634
Email staidansferns@eircom.net
*Superior:* Sr Dolores O'Brien
Community: 3
Contemplative life with adoration of the Eucharist. 8 hermitages for private retreats. Icon reproduction workshop.
The Centre for Contemplative Outreach Ireland – Facilitating Centering Prayer Retreats
Email contemplativeoutreachireland@gmail.com

**MISSIONARY SISTERS OF THE HOLY ROSARY**
Parish House, Terrerath,
New Ross, Co Wexford
Tel 051-428313
Community: 3
Pastoral

**LORETO (IBVM)**
Loreto Community, Railway Road,
Gorey, Co Wexford
Tel 055-21257
*Superior:* Sr Helen O'Riordan
Community: 8
Primary School

Conabury,
11 Newtown Court, Wexford
Tel 053-43470
*Superior:* Sr Helen O'Riordan
Community: 1
Secondary School

**NOTRE DAME DES MISSIONS (OUR LADY OF THE MISSIONS SISTERS)**
60 Pineridge,
Summerhill, Wexford
Tel 053-9143170
*Contact:* Sr Anna McDonagh
Community: 1
RE Adviser

**PERPETUAL ADORATION SISTERS**
Perpetual Adoration Convent,
Bride Street, Wexford Town,
Co Wexford
Tel 053-9124134
Email adoration44@eircom.net
*Superior:* Sr Pius Flannery
Community: 10
Perpetual adoration of the Blessed Sacrament
Altar breads, vestments, altar linen

**PRESENTATION SISTERS**
Presentation Convent, Wexford
Tel 053-9122504
*Superior:* Sr Grace Redmond
Community: 10
Secondary School
Tel 053-24133/24138 Fax 053-24048

**ST JOHN OF GOD SISTERS**
St John of God Congregational Centre,
1 Summerhill Heights, Wexford
Tel 053-9142396 Fax 053-9141500
Email stjohnogoffice@eircom.net
*Congregational Leader*
Sr Bríd Ryan

St John of God Convent,
Newtown Road, Wexford
Tel 053-9142276
*Resident Leader:* Sr Anne Kenny
Community: 24
Primary School, The Faythe, Wexford
Tel 053-9123105

St John of God Sisters,
Kilpatrick, Kyle,
Crossabeg, Wexford
Tel 053-9128481
Community: 2
(Sisters of Ely Hospital)

St John of God Convent, Ballyvaloo,
Blackwater, Co Wexford
Tel 053-9137160
Community: 6
Holiday and retreat house

St John of God Sisters,
26 The Orchard, Bellefield,
Enniscorthy, Co Wexford
Tel 053-9233079
Community: 2

St John of God Sisters,
Moorefield House, Loreto Village,
Enniscorthy, Co Wexford
Community: 3
Sheltered home for the elderly

St John of God Sisters,
6 Parkside, Stoneybatter,
Wexford
Tel 053-9146058
Community: 3

St John of God Sisters,
Ard Coilm, 15 Millpark,
Castlebridge, Co Wexford
Tel 053-9159862
Community: 2

St John of God Sisters,
1 Beechville, Clonard, Wexford
Tel 053-9142601
Community: 2

St John of God Sisters,
26 Mansfield Drive,
Coolcots, Wexford
Tel 053-9144427
Community: 1

St John of God Sisters,
2 Farnogue Drive,
Newlands, Wexford
Tel 053-9146149
Community: 2

St John of God Sisters,
Caritas, Glenbrook,
Newtown Road, Wexford
Tel 053-9143752
Community: 3

St John of God Sisters,
9 Farnogue Drive,
Newlands, Wexford
Tel 053-9140537
Community: 2

**ST LOUIS SISTERS**
Convent of St Louis,
Ramsgrange,
Co Wexford
Tel 051-389119
Community: 6
Varied apostolates

## EDUCATIONAL INSTITUTIONS

**St Peter's Diocesan College**
Tel 053-9142071
*Principal:* Mr Robert O'Callaghan
*Chaplain/Counsellor*
Rev Aodhan Marken

**EDMUND RICE SCHOOLS TRUST**
New Ross, Co Wexford
Secondary School
Tel 051-21384/22976
Fax 051-425961
*Principal:* Mr Pat Rossiter

Scoil na mBráithre (Primary School),
Green Street, Wexford
Tel 053-41324/22186
Email edmundusc.ias@eircom.net
*Principal:* Mr Jos Furlong

Coláiste Eamonn Rís,
Thomas Street, Wexford
Tel 053-41391/24067
Fax 053-46803
Email admin@wexfordcbs.org
Website www.wexfordcbs.org
*Principal:* Mr Michael McMahon

Christian Brothers Secondary School
Enniscorthy,
Co Wexford
Tel 054-34330/35308
Fax 054-36424
Email cbsenniscorthy@eircom.net
*Principal:* Mr John Ryan

## CHARITABLE AND OTHER SOCIETIES

**Aiseiri**
Roxborough House,
Wexford
Tel 053-9141818

**Christian Media Trust**
Tel 053-9145176

**CURA**
Tel 053-9122255

**FDYS Youth Work Ireland**
Wexford
Tel 053-9123262/9123358

**Society of St Vincent de Paul**
17 Conferences in the Diocese of Ferns
*South Ferns President*
Ms Mary Dempsey
Ballinellard, Blackwater, Co Wexford
Tel 087-8313736
*North Ferns President*
Mr Edmund Roche
Woodbrook House, Ballinapierce,
Davidstown, Co Wexford
Tel 087-1413153

**Traveller Resource Centre**
Tel 051-422272

**Special Schools**
Our Lady of Fatima, Wexford
Tel 053-9123376
St John of God, Enniscorthy
Tel 053-9233419
St Patrick's, Enniscorthy
Tel 053-9233657
Dawn House, Wexford
Tel 053-9145351
Community Workshop
Enniscorthy Ltd
Tel 053-9233069
Community Workshop
New Ross Ltd
Tel 051-421956

# DIOCESE OF GALWAY, KILMACDUAGH AND KILFENORA

PATRONS OF THE DIOCESE
GALWAY – OUR LADY ASSUMED INTO HEAVEN, 15 AUGUST
KILMACDUAGH – ST COLMAN, 29 OCTOBER
KILFENORA – ST FACHANAN, 20 DECEMBER

INCLUDES PORTIONS OF COUNTIES GALWAY, MAYO AND CLARE
KILFENORA IS IN THE PROVINCE OF CASHEL BUT THE BISHOP OF GALWAY AND KILMACDUAGH IS ITS APOSTOLIC ADMINISTRATOR

**Most Rev Martin Drennan DD**
Bishop of Galway;
born 2 January 1944;
ordained priest 16 June 1968;
ordained Auxiliary Bishop of Dublin 21 September 1997;
installed Bishop of Galway 3 July 2005

Residence: Mount Saint Mary's, Taylor's Hill, Galway
Tel 091-563566
Fax 091-568333
Email galwaydiocese@eircom.net
Website www.galwaydiocese.ie

## CATHEDRAL OF OUR LADY ASSUMED INTO HEAVEN AND ST NICHOLAS, GALWAY

In 1484, the Church of St Nicholas in Galway became a collegiate church, with a warden and vicars. However, with the Reformation, after 1570, the Catholic people of Galway lost the right to practise their religion publicly. Mass was celebrated in private houses until the rigour of persecution moderated and a parish chapel was built in Middle Street about 1750. The Diocese of Galway was established in 1831, and the parish chapel became its pro-cathedral. A fund for the building of a more fitting cathedral was inaugurated in 1876 and was built up by successive bishops. In 1883 the Diocese of Kilmacduagh was joined with Galway, and the Bishop of Galway was made Apostolic Administrator of Kilfenora.

In 1941, Galway County Council handed over Galway Jail to Bishop Michael Browne as a site for the proposed new cathedral. The jail was demolished, and in 1949 John J. Robinson of Dublin was appointed architect for the new cathedral. Planning continued until 1957, when Pope Pius XII approved the plans submitted to him by Dr Browne. Cardinal D'Alton, the Archbishop of Armagh, blessed the site and the foundation stone on 27 October 1957. The construction, which began in February 1958, was undertaken by Messrs John Sisk Ltd of Dublin. The people of the diocese contributed to a weekly collection, and donations were received from home and abroad. The total cost, including furnishing, was almost one million pounds.

Pope Paul VI appointed Cardinal Richard Cushing, Archbishop of Boston, Pontifical Legate to dedicate the cathedral. The cathedral was dedicated on the Feast of the Assumption, 15 August 1965.

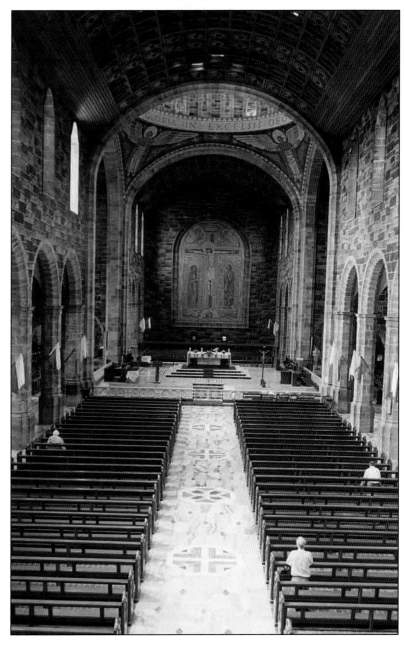

**Most Rev Eamonn Casey DD**
Born 1927; ordained priest June 1951; ordained Bishop of Kerry 9 November 1969; translated to Galway 19 September 1976; resigned 6 May 1992.
*Residence:* Shanaglish, Gort, Co Galway

## CHAPTER

Rt Rev Mgr Malachy Hallinan VG
Sacred Heart Church, Galway
*Members*
Very Rev Canon Michael Kelly, Craughwell
Very Rev Canon William Cummins
Mervue, Galway
Very Rev Michael Reilly
Castlegar, Galway
Very Rev Canon Richard Tarpey, Ennistymon
Very Rev Dean John O'Dwyer, Oranmore
Very Rev Canon Seán Manning
St Mary's College
Very Rev Canon Patrick Callanan, Kilbeacanty
Very Rev Canon Francis Larkin, Kinvara
Very Rev Canon Martin Moran
Killanin
Very Rev Canon Peter Rabbitte
The Cathedral

## ADMINISTRATION

**Vicar General**
Rt Rev Mgr Malachy Hallinan PP, VG
Church of the Sacred Heart,
Seamus Quirke Road, Galway
Tel 091-522713

**Vicars Forane**
Rt Rev Mgr Malachy Hallinan PP, VG
Very Rev Canon Michael Kelly PP
Very Rev Canon Peter Rabbitte PP
Very Rev Conor Cunningham PP
Very Rev Canon Martin Moran PP

**Chancellor**
Very Rev Ian O'Neill PP
Claregalway, Co Galway
Tel 091-798104

**Consultors**
Rt Rev Mgr Malachy Hallinan PP, VG
Very Rev Canon Peter Rabbitte PP, VF
Very Rev Martin Glynn PP
Very Rev Ian O'Neill
Rev Barry Horan

**Finance Committee**
Most Rev Martin Drennan, Chairman
Rt Rev Mgr Malachy Hallinan PP, VG
Mr John Rafferty
Miss Una Fleming
Rev Martin Whelan
Mr Thomas Kilgarriff, Secretary

**Financial Administrator**
Mr Thomas Kilgarriff
Diocesan Office, The Cathedral, Galway
Tel 091-563566

**Diocesan Development (Meitheal)**
*Director:* Mr Thomas Kilgarriff,
Diocesan Office, The Cathedral, Galway
Tel 091-563566
*Chairperson:* Most Rev Martin Drennan
*Members*
Rt Rev Mgr Malachy Hallinan PP, VG
Mr Frank Canavan
Mr Prionsias Ó Máille
Mrs Breda Ryan
Mrs Dairin Coen
Mr Pat McCambridge

**Diocesan Secretary**
Rev Martin Whelan CC
Diocesan Office, The Cathedral, Galway
Tel 091-563566
Email galwaydiocesemw@eircom.net

## CATECHETICS EDUCATION

**Primary Education**
*Diocesan Adviser:* Sr Breda Coyne (RJM)
Diocesan Pastoral Centre, Árus De Brún,
Newtownsmith, Galway
Tel 091-575050
Mr Tom O'Doherty (Irish schools)
Tel 091-565066

## LITURGY

**Liturgical Committee**
*Chairperson:* Rev Alan Burke
Pontifical Irish College,
Via dei SS Quattro 1, 00184 Roma
Tel 0039-06-772631
*Members*
Sr Breda Coyne,
Very Rev James Walsh PP
Mr Ray O'Donnell

**Sacred Music**
*Diocesan Director*
Mr Raymond O'Donnell MA, HDE, LTCL
Tel 091-563577/087-2241365
Fax 091-534881
Email music@galwaycathedral.ie

## PASTORAL

**Accord**
Árus de Brún, Newtownsmith, Galway
Tel 091-562331
*Diocesan Director*
Very Rev Fergal MacEoinin (OP) PP
St Mary's Priory, The Claddagh, Galway
Tel 091-582884
Email accordgalway@eircom.net

**Apostolic Work Society**
*President:* Mrs Marie Dempsey
Cregboy, Claregalway, Co Galway
Tel 091-798125
Secretary: Mrs Eileen Flannery
102 Hazel Park, Newcastle, Galway
Tel 091-523845

**Brazilian Community**
*Chaplain:* Rev Kevin Keenan (SVD)
26 Cloonarkin Drive,
Oranmore, Co Galway
Tel 091-788823

**Catholic Primary School Managers' Association**
Diocesan Education Office
Pastoral Centre, Árus de Brún,
Newtownsmith, Galway
Tel 091-565066
Co-ordinator: Mr P. J. Callanan

**Child Protection Office**
Ms Ita O'Mahony
Diocesan Pastoral Centre,
Arús de Brún, Newtownsmith, Galway
Tel 091-575051

**Communications Committee**
*Secretary:* Rev Seán McHugh PP
Spiddal, Co Galway
Tel 091-533155
Email cilleinde@eircom.net

**CURA**
Pastoral Centre, Árus de Brún,
Newtownsmith, Galway
Tel 091-562558
Email curagalway@eircom.net

**Diocesan Archivist**
Mr Tom Kilgarriff
Tel 091-563566
Email galwaydiocesetk@eircom.net

**Diocesan Pastoral Centre**
Árus de Brún,
Newtownsmith, Galway
Tel 091-565066
*Acting Director:* Mrs Eileen Kelly

**Diocesan Pilgrimage Committee**
*Chaplain to the Sick*
Rev David Murphy Adm
The Bungalow, Main Street,
Clarinbridge, Co Galway
Tel 091-485777
*Pilgrimage Director*
Very Rev Canon Martin Moran PP
Rosscahill, Co Galway
Tel 091-550106

**Diocesan Youth Faith Development**
Diocesan Pastoral Centre,
Árus de Brún, Newtownsmith, Galway
Tel 091-565066

**Diocesan Youth Ministry**
*Co-ordinator:* Ms Siobhan Bradley

**Drug Misuse Prevention**
*Contact Person*
Rev David Cribbin, Chaplain
University Hospital, Galway
Tel 091-524222

**Ecumenism**
Rev Diarmuid Hogan
Chaplain, NUI, Galway
Tel 091-495055/524853

**Emigrants Committee**
*Director*
Very Rev Gearóid Ó Griofa PP
Gort, Co Galway
Tel 091-631055
*Secretary*
Very Rev Canon Michael Reilly PP
Castlegar, Galway
Tel 091-751548

**Legion of Mary**
Annunciata House,
15 Fr Griffin Road, Galway
Tel 091-521871
*Contact:* Mr Bernard Finan
*Chaplain:* Rev Martin Keane
Tel 091-796106

**Marriage Tribunal**
*Officials:* Rev Michael Byrnes
Rev Barry Horan
(see also Marriage Tribunals section)

**Missions Committee**
*Chairman*
Very Rev Martin Downey PP
24 Presentation Road, Galway
Tel 091-562276

**Diocesan Council of Priests**
Most Rev Martin Drennan
Rt Rev Mgr Malachy Hallinan PP, VG
Vry Rev Canon Michael Kelly PP, VF
Very Rev Canon Peter Rabbitte PP, VF

*Members*
Very Rev Gerard Jennings
Rev Conor Cunningham *(Chairman)*
Very Rev Seán McHugh
Very Rev Joseph Roche
Very Rev Derek Feeney
Very Rev Barry Hogg
Very Rev Canon Edward Kelly PE
Rev Michael Screene (MSC)
Rev Hugh Clifford *(Secretary)*
Rev Barry Horan
Very Rev Michael McLoughlin
Very Rev Martin Downey

**Pioneer Total Abstinence Association**
*Diocesan Director*
Very Rev Canon Patrick Callanan PP
Kilbeacanty, Gort, Co Galway
Tel 091-631691

**Polish Community**
*Chaplain:* Rev Marek Cul (OP)
St Mary's Priory, Claddagh, Galway
Tel 091-582884

**Pontifical Mission Societies**
*Diocesan Director*
Rev Patrick O'Donohue
Chaplain, NUI, Galway
Tel 091-495055/582179

**St Joseph's Young Priests' Society**
*Diocesan Chaplain*
Rev Sean Kilcoyne
Chaplain, Bon Secours Hospital,
Renmore, Galway
Tel 091-757711

**Trócaire**
*Diocesan Director*
Rev Thomas Brady CF
Chaplain, Dun Ui Mhaoiliosa,
Renmore, Galway
Tel 091-701055

**Vocations Team**
*Director:* Rev Diarmuid Hogan
Chaplain, NUI, Galway
Tel 091-495055
Email diarmuid.hogan@nuigalway.ie

## PARISHES

*Church titulars, if different from parish name, are in italics.*

**CATHEDRAL**
*Our Lady Assumed into Heaven and St Nicholas*
Very Rev Canon Peter Rabbitte PP, VF
Tel 091-563577
Rev Martin Whelan CC
18 University Road, Galway
Tel 091-524875/563577
Email info@galwaycathedral.ie

*City Parishes*

**BALLYBANE**
*St Brigid*
Very Rev John D. Keane
St Brigid's, Ballybane, Galway
Tel 091-755381
Email stbrigidsballybane@gmail.com

**GOOD SHEPHERD**
Very Rev Martin Glynn PP
129 Túr Uisce, Doughiska, Galway
Tel 091-756823
Email goodshepherdgalway@gmail.com
Website www.goodshepherdgalway.com

**MERVUE**
*Holy Family*
Very Rev Canon William Cummins PP
Mervue, Galway
Tel 091-751721
Rev Michael Connolly CC
Curate's House, Walter Macken Road,
Mervue, Galway
Tel 091-771662

**RENMORE**
*St Oliver Plunkett*
Very Rev Canon Michael Mulkerrins PP
Tel 091-751707
Rev Robert McNamara (CSsR) CC
Tel 091-757859
Renmore Avenue, Renmore, Galway
email opcrenmore@gmail.com

**SACRED HEART CHURCH**
Rt Rev Mgr Malachy Hallinan PP, VG
Tel 091-522713
Rev Hugh Clifford CC
Tel 091-524751
Church of the Sacred Heart
Seamus Quirke Road, Galway
Email sacredheartgalway@eircom.net

**ST AUGUSTINE'S**
Very Rev Richard Lyng (OSA) PP
St Augustine's Priory,
St Augustine's Street, Galway
Tel 091-562524
Email rlyng@indigo.ie

**ST FRANCIS**
Very Rev Francis McGrath (OFM) PP
Rev Declan Timmons (OFM) CC
The Abbey,
St Francis Street, Galway
Tel 091-562518

**ST JOHN THE APOSTLE**
Very Rev Tadhg Quinn PP
St John the Apostle,
Knocknacarra, Galway
Tel 091-590059
Rev Kevin Keenan (SVD) AP
26 Cloonarkin Drive,
Oranmore, Co Galway
Tel 087-9905755

**ST JOSEPH'S**
Very Rev Martin Downey PP
24 Presentation Road, Galway
Tel 091-562276
Rev Martin Reilly (SPS) CC
7 Presentation Road, Galway
Tel 091-449727
Email saintjosephs@eircom.net

**ST MARY'S**
Very Rev Fergal MacEoinín (OP) PP
Rev John O'Reilly (OP) CC
Rev Denis Murphy (OP) CC
St Mary's Priory,
The Claddagh, Galway
Tel 091-582884

**ST PATRICK'S**
Very Rev Patrick Whelan PP
St Patrick's Presbytery,
Forster Street, Galway
Tel 091-567994

**SALTHILL**
*Christ the King*
Very Rev Gerard Jennings PP
Tel 091-523413
Rev Michael Baily (OFM) CC
Tel 091-526006
Curate's House, Monksfield,
Salthill, Galway
Email salthillparish@eircom.net

**TIRELLAN**
*Resurrection*
Very Rev Kevin Blade (MSC) PP
Rev Thomas Plower (MSC) CC
Church of the Resurrection,
Headford Road, Galway
Tel 091-762883
Email ballinfoyleparish@eircom.net

*Country Parishes*

**ARDRAHAN**
*St Teresa's*
Very Rev Joseph Roche PP
Ardrahan, Co Galway
Tel 091-635164
Email parishofardrahan@gmail.com

**BALLINDEREEN**
*St Colman's*
Very Rev Anthony Minniter PP
Ballindereen, Kilcolgan, Co Galway
Tel 091-796118
Email ballinderreenparish@eircom.net

**BALLYVAUGHAN**
*St John the Baptist*
Very Rev Desmond Forde PP
Ballyvaughan, Co Clare
Tel 065-7077045

**BARNA**
*Mary Immaculate Queen*
Very Rev Francis Lee PP
Barna, Galway
Tel 091-590956
Very Rev Dean Thomas Kyne AP
Réalt na Mara, Furbo, Co Galway
Tel 091-592457
Email bearnaparish@eircom.net

**CARRON AND NEW QUAY**
*St Columba's, Carron,*
*St Patrick's, New Quay*
Very Rev Enda Glynn PP
Rev Colm Clinton (SPS) *(Adm protem)*
New Quay, Co Clare
Tel 065-7078026

**CASTLEGAR**
*St Columba's*
Very Rev Canon Michael Reilly PP
Castlegar, Co Galway
Tel 091-751548
Email castlegaroffice@eircom.net

**CLAREGALWAY**
*Assumption and St James*
Very Rev Ian O'Neill PP
Claregalway, Co Galway
Tel 091-798104
Email claregalwayparish@eircom.net

**CLARINBRIDGE**
*Annunciation of the BVM*
Rev David Murphy Adm
The Bungalow, Main Street,
Clarinbridge, Co Galway
Tel 091-485777
Email thebridgeparish@gmail.com

**CRAUGHWELL**
*St Colman's*
Very Rev Canon Michael Kelly PP, VF
Craughwell, Co Galway
Tel 091-846057

**ENNISTYMON**
*Our Lady and St Michael*
Very Rev Derek Feeney PP
Tel 065-7071063
Very Rev Canon Richard Tarpey AP
Tel 065-7071346
Ennistymon, Co Clare

**GORT/BEAGH**
*St Colman's and St Ann*
Very Rev Thomas Marrinan PP
Tel 091-631220
Rev Gearóid Ó Griofa CC
Tel 091-631055
Gort, Co Galway
Email gortparish@eircom.net

**KILBEACANTY/PETERSWELL**
*St Columba and St Thomas Apostle*
Very Rev Canon Patrick Callanan PP
Kilbeacanty, Gort, Co Galway
Tel 091-631691

**KILCHREEST/CASTLEDALY**
*Nativity and Church of St Teresa*
Very Rev Joseph Roche (Priest in Charge)
Parochial House, Kilchreest,
Loughrea, Co Galway
Tel 091-840859

**KILFENORA**
*St Fachanan's*
Very Rev Edward Crosby PP
Kilfenora, Co Clare
Tel 065-7088006
Email kilfenoraparish@gmail.com

**KINVARA**
*St Colman's*
Very Rev Canon Francis Larkin PP
Kinvara, Co Galway
Tel 091-637154

**LETTERMORE**
*Naomh Colmcille*
Very Rev Michael Brennan PP
Lettermore, Co Galway
Tel 091-551169

**LISCANNOR**
*St Brigid's*
Very Rev Denis Crosby PP
Liscannor, Co Clare
Tel 065-7081248

**LISDOONVARNA AND KILSHANNY**
*Corpus Christi*
Very Rev Conor Cunningham PP, VF
The Rectory,
Lisdoonvarna, Co Clare
Tel 065-7074142
Email parishoffice@lisdoon.ie

**MOYCULLEN**
*Immaculate Conception*
Very Rev Michael McLoughlin PP
Moycullen, Co Galway
Tel 091-555106
Email moycullenparish@eircom.net
Website www.moycullenparish.com

**ORANMORE**
*Immaculate Conception*
Very Rev Canon John O'Dwyer PP
Oranmore, Co Galway
Tel 091-794634
*St Joseph's*
Very Rev Canon Richard Higgins AP
Maree, Oranmore, Co Galway
Tel 091-794113

**OUGHTERARD**
*Immaculate Conception*
Very Rev James Walsh PP
Oughterard, Co Galway
Tel 091-552290

**ROSMUC**
*Séipéal an Ioncolnaithe*
Very Rev Michael Brennan PP
*(Priest in charge)*
Rosmuc, Co Galway
Tel 091-551169

**ROSSCAHILL (KILLANIN)**
*Immaculate Heart of Mary*
Very Rev Canon Martin Moran PP
Rosscahill, Co Galway
Tel 091-550106

**SHRULE**
*St Joseph's*
Very Rev Michael Crosby PP
Shrule, Galway
Tel 093-31262

**AN SPIDÉAL**
*Cill Éinne*
An tAthair Seán MacAodh PP
Teach an Sagairt, An Spidéal,
Co na Gaillimhe
Tel 091-553155

## INSTITUTIONS AND THEIR CHAPLAINS

**Brothers of Charity**
Kilcornan, Clarinbridge, Co Galway
Rev Martin Keane
Tel 091-796106

**Dún Uí Mhaoilíosa**
Renmore, Galway
Rev Thomas Brady CF
Tel 091-701055
Email bradt56@hotmail.com

**Bon Secours Hospital**
Renmore, Galway
Rev Seán Kilcoyne
Tel 091-751534/757711

**Galway/Mayo Insititute of Technology**
Dublin Road, Galway
To be appointed
Tel 091-753161/757298

**Galway Clinic**
Doughiska, Galway
Chaplain's Office
Rev Joe Delaney
Sr Goretti Bohan
Tel 091-785000

**Gort Community School**
Chaplain's Office
Tel 091-632163
Ms Orla Duggan

**Merlin Park University Hospital**
Chaplains Office
Tel 091-757631
Rev Robert McNamara (CSsR)
Rev Michael Connolly
Mr Ray Gately

**Moneenageisha Community College**
Rev Martin Whelan
Tel 091-563577

**NUI, Galway**
Rev Diarmuid Hogan
Tel 091-524853/495055
Email diarmuid.hogan@nuigalway.ie
Rev Patrick O'Donohue
Tel 091-582719/495055
Email patrick.odonohue@nuigalway.ie

**St Enda's College**
Threadneedle Road,
Salthill, Galway
Sr Pauline Uhlemann (RJM)
Tel 091-522458

**St Joseph's Secondary College**
Nun's Island, Galway
Chaplain to be appointed
Tel 091-565980

**University Hospital**
Chaplain's Office
Tel 091-524222
Rev David Cribbin
Email david.cribbin@mailn.hse.ie
Rev Peter Joyce
Email peter.joyce@mailn.hse.ie

## PRIESTS OF THE DIOCESE ELSEWHERE

Rev Alan Burke
Pontifical Irish College,
Via dei SS Quattro 1, 00184 Roma
Tel 0039-06-772631
Rev Patrick Connaughton
St Columban's, Dalgan Park,
Navan, Co Meath
Tel 046-21525
Rev Michael Conway
St Patrick's College,
Maynooth, Co Kildare
Tel 01-6285222
Rev Vivian Loughrey
St Gregory the Great Parish,
200 Nr University Drive,
Plantation, FL 33324, USA
Rev Thomas Lyons
Cork University Hospital, Wilton, Cork
Tel 021-4546109
Rev Gregory Raftery
An Der Tiefenriede 11, 3000,
Hanover 1, Germany

## RETIRED PRIESTS

Rev Michael Carney PE
c/o Diocesan Office, The Cathedral,
Galway
Tel 091-563566
Very Rev Dean Patrick Considine PE
c/o The Diocesan Office,
The Cathedral, Galway
Tel 091-563566
Very Rev Canon Eamonn Dermody PE
Clarinbridge, Co Galway
Tel 091-796208
Very Rev Bernard Duffy PE
St Mary's Nursing Home,
Shantalla Road, Galway
Rev Stephen Keane PE
7 Garrai Sheann, Roscam, Galway
Tel 091-767528
Very Rev Canon Edward Kelly PE
No. 1 St Mary's College House,
Shantalla Road, Galway
Tel 091-586663
Very Rev Canon Joseph Keogh PE
No. 4 St Mary's College House,
Shantalla Road, Galway
Tel 091-587773
Rev Dr James Mitchell
11 St Mary's Terrace, Galway
Tel 091-524411
Very Rev Leo Morahan PE
2 The Beeches, Louisburg, Co Mayo
Tel 098-66869
Very Rev Dean Christopher O'Connor PE
Craughwell, Co Galway
Tel 091-846124
Rt Rev Mgr Seán O'Flaherty PE
Parkmore, Castlegar,
Galway
Tel 091-764764
Very Rev Canon J.A. O'Halloran PE
An Teaglach Uilinn, Moycullen,
Co Galway
Tel 091-555444

## PERSONAL PRELATURE

**Opus Dei**
Gort Ard University Residence,
Rockbarton North, Salthill, Galway
Tel 091-523846
Rev Walter Macken
Email watermacken@gmail.com
Rev Oliver Powell

## RELIGIOUS ORDERS AND CONGREGATIONS

## PRIESTS

**AUGUSTINIANS**
St Augustine's Priory, Galway
Tel 091-562524 Fax 091-564378
*Prior:* Rev Desmond Foley (OSA)

**DOMINICANS**
St Mary's, The Claddagh, Co Galway
Tel 091-582884 Fax 091-581252
*Prior and Parish Priest*
Very Rev Fergal MacEoinín (OP)

**FRANCISCANS**
The Abbey, 8 Francis Street, Galway
Tel 091-562581 Fax 091-565663
*Guardian:* Rev Patrick Younge (OFM)

**JESUITS**
St Ignatius Community & Church
27 Raleigh row, Salthill, Galway
Tel 091-523707
Email galway@jesuit.ie
*Rector:* Rev John Humphreys (SJ)

Coláiste Iognáid, 24 Sea Road, Galway
Tel 091-501500 Fax 091-501551
Email colaisteiognaid@eircom.net
*Headmaster:* Mr Bernard O'Connell

**MISSIONARIES OF THE SACRED HEART**
Croí Nua, Rosary Lane,
Taylor's Hill, Galway
Tel 091-520960 Fax 091-521168
*Leader:* Rev Michael Screene (MSC)

**SOCIETY OF AFRICAN MISSIONS**
Claregalway, Co Galway
Tel 091-798880 Fax 091-798879
Email smafathers@eircom.net
*Superior:* Rev Seamus Nohilly (SMA)

## BROTHERS

**BROTHERS OF CHARITY**
Regional Office, Kilcornan Centre,
Clarinbridge, Co Galway
Tel 091-796389/796413
*Regional Leader:* Br Noel Corcoran
*Chaplain:* Rev Martin Keane
Community: 3

**CHRISTIAN BROTHERS**
Christian Brothers' House,
Mount St Joseph, Ennistymon, Co Clare
Tel 065-7071130

12 Oldfield, Kingston, Galway
Tel 091-526705
*Community Leader:* Br Christy O'Carroll
Community: 4

**PATRICIAN BROTHERS**
Manor Drive, Kingston, Galway
Tel 091-523267
*Superior:* Br Niall Coll (FSP)
Community: 6

St Patrick's Primary School,
Market Street, Galway
Tel 091-568707. Pupils: 616
*Principal:* Mr Noel Cunningham
Email sfoc@eircom.net

St Joseph's Patrician College,
Nun's Island, Galway
Tel 091-565980
Pupils: 775
*Principal:* Mr Ciarán Doyle

## SISTERS

**BON SECOURS SISTERS (PARIS)**
Sisters of Bon Secours,
5 Glenina Heights, Mervue, Galway
Tel 091-755979
Community: 3
Hospital Ministry

Sisters of Bon Secours,
Apartment 9, Pointe Boise,
107-109 Upper Salthill, Galway
Community: 1
Parish Ministry

**BRIGIDINE SISTERS**
27 Cuimín Mór,
Cappagh Road, Bearna, Co Galway
Tel 091-592234
*Contact:* Sr Margaret Coyle
Education

**CONGREGATION OF THE SISTERS OF MERCY**
Convent of Mercy,
St Vincent's, Newtownsmith, Galway
Tel 091-565519 Fax 091-564739
Community: 16

Convent of Mercy,
47 Forster Street, Galway
Tel 091-562356 Fax 091-561304
Community: 9

61 The Green,
College Road, Galway
Tel 091-564148
Community: 2

Convent of Mercy, St Joseph's,
Oughterard, Co Galway
Tel 091-552154
Community: 2

Convent of Mercy, Clochar Éinde,
An Spidéal, Gaillimh
Guthán 091-553288
Community: 4

Convent of Mercy,
Gort, Co Galway
Tel 091-631069 Fax 091-631482
Community: 11

9 Forster Place, Galway
Tel 091-446828
Community: 1

46a Forster Street, Galway
Tel 091-532876
Community: 1

Sisters of Mercy, Station Road,
Lahinch, Co Clare
Tel 065-7081906 Fax 065-7082069
Community: 3

30/31 Gleann Bhreandáin,
St Brendan's Road,
Lisdoonvarna, Co Clare
Tel 065-7074319
Community: 3

Aisling Court, Ballyloughaun Road,
Renmore, Galway
Community: 4

Sisters of Mercy 3 Greenview Heights,
Inishannagh Park, Newcastle, Galway
Tel 091-526126
Community: 1

Sisters of Mercy,
49 Monalee Heights, Knocknacarra,
Galway
Tel 091-590735
Community: 2

146 Seacrest Road,
Knocknacarra, Galway
Tel 091-591685
Community: 1

Sisters of Mercy, 13 Beech Park,
Oranmore, Galway
Tel 091-794635
Community: 1

Sisters of Mercy, McAuley House,
7A Francis Street, Galway
Community: 3

17 Newtownsmith, Galway
Apt 1 Tel 091-563297
Apt 2 Tel 091-563698
Community: 2

Sisters of Mercy, Teaghlach Mhuire,
Ballyloughane Road, Renmore, Galway
Community: 41

22 Renmore road, Galway
Tel 091-755578
Community: 1

13 Seaview Court, College Road, Galway
Community: 1

St Anne's Lodge, Taylor's Hill Road,
Taylor's Hill, Galway
Tel 091-527710
Community: 1

**DAUGHTERS OF CHARITY OF ST VINCENT DE PAUL**
65 Shantalla Road, Galway
Tel 091-584410
*Superior:* Sr Patricia McLaughlin
Community: 4
SVP Hostel, pastoral work

**DOMINICAN SISTERS**
Dominican Convent, Taylor's Hill, Galway
Tel 091-522124/523975
Email dominicancg@eircom.net
*Prioress:* Sr Caitríona Gorman
Community: 14
Primary School. Tel 091-521517
Pupils: 715
Secondary School. Tel 091-523171

**FRANCISCAN MISSIONARIES OF MARY**
16 Tirellan Heights, Headford Road,
Galway
Tel 091-768272
*Superior:* Sr Doreen O'Connor
Email fmmgalway@irishbroadband.net
Community: 5
Sisters involved in pastoral and social work in parish

**GOOD SHEPHERD SISTERS**
93 Sandyvale Lawns, Headford Road,
Galway
Tel 091-759792
Community: 1

**JESUS AND MARY, CONGREGATION OF**
Convent of Jesus and Mary,
23 Lenaboy Gardens,
Salthill, Galway
Tel 091-524277
*Superior:* Sr Maria O'Toole
Community: 7
Sisters on staff of primary and post-primary schools

Scoil Íde Primary School
Tel 091-522716. Pupils: 279
Salerno Post-Primary School
Tel 091-529500. Pupils: 544

Convent of Jesus and Mary,
229 Castlepark, Ballybane, Galway
Tel 091-764320
*Superior:* Sr Mary Xavier McNamara
Community: 4

**LA RETRAITE SISTERS**
2 Distillery Road, Galway
Tel 091-524548
*Contact:* Sr Aileen Murphy
Email aileenlr@hotmail.com
Community: 3

**LITTLE SISTERS OF THE ASSUMPTION**
25 Sea Road, Galway
Tel 091-583979
Email lsagalway@eircom.net
Community: 8
Pastoral service to the family and social work

50 St Finbarr's Terrace,
Bohermore, Galway
Tel 091-568870
Community: 2
Professional services in the family, social work

**POOR CLARES**
St Clare's Monastery,
Nuns' Island, Galway
www.poorclares.ie
www.clairinibochta.ie
*Abbess:* Sr. M. Colette Hayden
Community: 12
Contemplatives. Adoration of the Blessed Sacrament. Altar breads

**PRESENTATION SISTERS**
Presentation Convent,
Presentation Road, Galway
Tel 091-561067 Fax 091-562384
Email presroad@eircom.net
*Community Leader:* Sr Helen Hyland
Community: 20
School and pastoral ministry
Scoil Chroí Íosa, Primary School
Tel 091-525904
Pupils: 142
Presentation Secondary School
Tel 091-563495
Fax 091-561875
Email presgalpdp@eircom.net

Shantalla Road, Galway
Tel 091-522598
Email presshantalla@eircom.net
Community: 6
School and pastoral ministry
Scoil Bhride Primary School
Tel/Fax 091-525052
Email sns.ias@eircom.net

160 Corrib Park, Newcastle, Galway
Tel 091-522678
Community: 2
Counselling ministry

34/35 Coill Tíre, Doughiska, Galway
Tel 091-449027
Community: 5

**RELIGIOUS SISTERS OF CHARITY**
Our Lady's Priory,
Clarinbridge, Co Galway
Tel 091-796254
Various apostolic ministries

## ASSOCIATION OF THE FAITHFUL

**FRATERNITY OF MARY IMMACULATE QUEEN**
'Síiol Dóchas', Ballard, Barna, Galway
Tel/Fax 091-592196
Email miq@eircom.net

## EDUCATIONAL INSTITUTIONS

**Coláiste Einde, Gaillimh**
Tel 091-522458/524904
*Principal:* Mrs Siobháin Quinn
*Chaplain's Office:* Tel 091-522458/524904
Sr Pauline Uhlemann (RJM)

**St Mary's College, Galway**
Tel 091-522369/521984
*President:* Very Rev Barry Hogg BA, HDE
*Principal:* Mr Bartley Fannin
*Chaplain:* Canon Seán Manning
Email smcollege@eircom.net

**EDMUND RICE SCHOOLS TRUST**
Primary School,
Ennistymon, Co Clare
Tel 065-7071909
Email etyn.ias@eircom.net
*Principal:* Ms Helen Sheridan

Meanscoil na mBráithre,
Ennistymon, Co Clare
Tel 065-7072005
Email cbsennistymon.ias@tinet.ie
*Principal:* Ms Ann Tuohy

## CHARITABLE AND OTHER SOCIETIES

**COPE Galway**
(Crisis Housing, Caring Support) Ltd
3-5 Calbro House,
Tuam Road, Galway
Tel 091-778750
*Director:* Jacquie Horan
Cope provides emergency accommodation for homeless persons and families and women and children experiencing domestic violence. It also provides a community catering service in Galway City and runs a day centre for older people in Mervue.

**Society of St Vincent de Paul**
Ozanam House,
St Augustine Street, Galway
Tel 091-563233/562254
*Director:* Mr Colm Noonan

# DIOCESE OF KERRY

PATRON OF THE DIOCESE
ST BRENDAN, 16 MAY

INCLUDES COUNTY KERRY, EXCEPT KILMURRILY, AND PART OF COUNTY CORK

**Most Rev William Murphy DD**
Bishop of Kerry;
born 6 June 1936;
ordained priest 18 June 1961;
ordained Bishop of Kerry
10 September 1995

Residence:
Bishop's House, Killarney,
Co Kerry
Tel 064-6631168
Fax 064-6631364
Email admin@dioceseofkerry.ie

## ST MARY'S CATHEDRAL, KERRY

The Cathedral of Our Lady of the Assumption, better known as St Mary's, was designed by Augustus Welby Pugin. The main part of the cathedral was built between 1842 and 1855. Work was suspended between 1848 and 1853 because of the Famine and the building was used as a shelter for victims of the Famine.

Between 1908 and 1912 the nave and side aisles were extended and the spire, sacristy and mortuary chapel were added.

In 1972/3 the cathedral was extensively renovated. The interior was reordered to meet the demands of the liturgical renewal that followed the Second Vatican Council.

## CHAPTER

Dean Sean Hanafin PP
Tralee
Rt Rev Mgr Daniel O'Riordan PP, VG
Castleisland
Very Rev Declan Canon O'Connor PP, VF
Listowel
*Archdeacon:* Venerable Thomas Crean
Kenmare
Very Rev William Canon Crean
Cahirciveen
Very Rev Thomas Canon Looney
Dingle
Very Rev Gearóid Canon Walsh
Castletownbere
Very Rev Michael Canon Fleming
Killorglin

*Honorary Canons*
Very Rev Larry Kelly, Rathmore
Very Rev Eoin Mangan, Knocknagoshel

*Retired Members*
Rt Rev Mgr Pádraig Ó Fiannachta
Very Rev Matthew Keane
Very Rev John McKenna
Very Rev Michael O'Doherty
Venerable Michael J. Murphy
Very Rev Denis O'Mahony
Very Rev Patrick Sheehan
Rev Rev James Linnane

*Retired Honorary Members*
Very Rev Patrick J. Horgan

## ADMINISTRATION

**College of Consultors**
Rt Rev Mgr Daniel O'Riordan PP, VG, VF
Very Rev Declan Canon O'Connor PP, VF
Dean Sean Hanafin PP, VF
Very Rev Gearóid Godley
Very Rev Nicholas Flynn Adm, VF
Rev Niall Howard CC
Very Rev Donal O'Neill

**Vicar General**
Rt Rev Mgr Daniel O'Riordan PP, VG, VF
The Presbytery, Castleisland, Co Kerry
Tel 066-7141241 Fax 066-7141273

**Vicars Forane**
Dean Sean Hanafin
Rt Rev Mgr Daniel O'Riordan
Venerable Thomas Crean
Very Rev William Canon Crean
Very Rev Gearóid Canon Walsh
Very Rev Michael Canon Fleming
Very Rev Declan Canon O'Connor
Very Rev Thomas Canon Looney
Very Rev Liam Comer
Very Rev John Lawlor
Very Rev Nicholas Flynn
Very Rev Tadhg Fitzgerald
Very Rev Jack Fitzgerald

**Finance Council**
Rt Rev Mgr Daniel O'Riordan PP, VG, VF
Very Rev Donal O'Neill, Mr Liam Chute,
Ms Mary Harty, Mr Dan Hourigan,
Mr Brian Durran, Rev Gearóid Godley,
Rev Bernard Healy, Mr Patrick McElligott,
Ms Noeleen O'Sullivan, Ms Bridget
McGuire, Mr John Collins, Mr John
O'Connor, Mr Pádraig O'Sullivan

**Foreign Missions Committee**
*Chairman:* Rev Gearóid Godley
John Paul II Pastoral Centre,
Rock Road, Killarney, Co Kerry
Tel 064-6630535 Fax 064-6631170

**Diocesan Archivist**
Ms Margaret de Brún
Diocesan Centre, Cathedral Walk,
Killarney, Co Kerry
Tel 064-6631168 Fax 064-6631364

**Diocesan Secretary**
Very Rev Donal O'Neill
Bishop's House, Killarney, Co Kerry
Tel 064-6631168 Fax 064-6631364
Email
diocesansecretary@dioceseofkerry.ie

**Diocesan Communications Officer**
Ms Mary Fagan
Tel 087-1301555/066-7123787
Email maryfagan@dioceseofkerry.ie

**Property Management Committee**
*Chairman:* Very Rev M. Canon Fleming
Killorglin, Co Kerry
Tel 066-9761172
*Secretary:* Mr Willie Wixted
Diocesan Centre, Cathedral Walk,
Killarney, Co Kerry
Tel 064-6631168

## CATECHETICS EDUCATION

**Post-Primary Religious Education**
*Director:* Ms Edwina Gottstein
John Paul II Pastoral Centre,
Rock Road, Killarney, Co Kerry
Tel 064-6632644 Fax 064-6631170

**Primary Religious Education**
*Director:* Sr Noreen Quilter
*Assistant Directors:* Mr Joe Linnane
Mrs Jean McGearailt
c/o John Paul II Pastoral Centre,
Rock Road, Killarney, Co Kerry
Tel 064-6632644

**Primary School Management**
*Secretary:* Very Rev John Lawlor PP, VF
The Presbytery, Ballydonoghue,
Co Kerry
Tel 068-47103 Fax 068-47230

## LITURGY

**Building Committee/Sacred Art and Architecture Commission**
*Chairman:* Very Rev Canon Michael Fleming
The Presbytery, Killorglin, Co Kerry
Tel 066-9761172 Fax 066-9762302
*Secretary:* Very Rev Donal O'Neill
Bishop's House, Killarney, Co Kerry
Tel 064-6631168 Fax 064-6631364

**Liturgical Committee**
*Chairman:*
Very Rev Canon Eoin Mangan PP
The Presbytery, Knocknagoshel, Co Kerry
Tel 068-46107 Fax 068-46494
*Secretary:* Ms Eileen Burke

## PASTORAL

**Accord**
*Killarney Centre:* John Paul II Pastoral Centre, Killarney, Co Kerry
Tel 064-6632644 Fax 064-6631170
Email jp2centre@eircom.net
*Director:* Very Rev Joseph Begley
*Tralee Centre:* St John's Pastoral Centre, Castle Street, Tralee, Co Kerry
Tel 066-7122280
*Director:* Rev Michael Moynihan

**Council of Priests**
*Chairman:* Dean Sean Hanafin
*Secretary:* Rev Niall Howard

**CURA**
Tel 066-7127355

**Diocesan Pastoral Centre**
*Director:* Rev Gearóid Godley
John Paul II Pastoral Centre,
Rock Road, Killarney, Co Kerry
Tel 064-6632644 Fax 064-6631170

**Diocesan Pastoral Council**
*Chairman:* Mr Tony Darmody
Kerry Parents & Friends Association, The Old Monastery, Port Road, Killarney
Tel 064-6632742
*Secretary:* Ms Frances Rowland
John Paul II Pastoral Centre,
Rock Road, Killarney, Co Kerry
Tel 064-6630508

**Diocesan Pastoral Strategic Plan**
*Co-ordinator:* Rev Gearoid Godley
John Paul II Pastoral Centre,
Killarney, Co Kerry
Tel 064-6630535

**Diocesan Safeguarding Children Committee**
*Chairman:* Very Rev G. Canon Walsh
Castletownbere, Co Cork
Tel 027-70849
*Secretary:* Very Rev Donal O'Neill
Bishop's House, Killarney, Co Kerry
Tel 064-6685313
*Designated Officer:*
Very Rev Pádraig Walsh
Our Lady & St Brendan's,
Upper Rock Street, Tralee, Co Kerry
Tel 066-7125932/087-6362780
*Deputy Designated Officer:*
Rev John Quinlan
c/o Diocesan Office, Killarney, Co Kerry

**Ecumenism**
*Secretary:* Very Rev Pat Crean-Lynch
The Presbytery, Ballymacelligott,
Tralee, Co Kerry
Tel 066-7137118 Fax 066-7137137

**Marriage Tribunal**
(See Marriage Tribunals Section)

**Pastoral Renewal Team**
Rev Gearóid Godley
Ms Frances Rowland
Ms Bernie McCaffrey
Pastoral Centre, Killarney, Co Kerry
Tel 064-6632644

**Pilgrimage Director**
Very Rev Nicholas Flynn Adm, VF
St Mary's Presbytery, Killarney, Co Kerry
Tel 064-6631014 Fax 064-6631148

**Pioneer Total Abstinence Association**
*Diocesan Director*
Very Rev Noel Spring PP
The Presbytery, Ballybunion, Co Kerry
Tel 068-27102 Fax 068-27153

**Pontifical Mission Societies**
*Diocesan Director:* Rev Gearóid Godley
John Paul II Pastoral Centre,
Killarney, Co Kerry
Tel 064-6630535 Fax 064-6631170

**Retreat Centre**
Ardfert, Co Kerry
*Director:* Very Rev Tadhg Fitzgerald
Tel 066-7134276 Fax 066-7133169

**Travellers**
*Chaplain:* Very Rev Luke Roche PP
Castlemaine, Co Kerry
Tel 066-9767322 Fax 066-9767467

**Vocations**
*Director:* Rev Liam Lovell
The Presbytery, Kenmare, Co Kerry
Tel 064-6642047
*Assistant Director:* Rev Michael Moynihan
The Presbytery, Castleisland, Co Kerry
Tel 066-7141241

**Youth Director**
Mr Tim O'Donoghue
Diocesan Youth Office, The Friary,
Killarney, Co Kerry
Tel 064-6631748 Fax 064-6636770

## PARISHES

*The mensal parish is listed first. Other parishes follow alphabetically Historical names are given in parentheses. Church titulars are in italics.*

**KILLARNEY**
*St Mary's Cathedral, Killarney*
*Holy Spirit, Muckross*
*Resurrection, Park Road*
Very Rev Nicholas Flynn Adm, VF
Rev Kevin McNamara (MSC) CC *(pro-tem)*
Very Rev Patrick Horgan *(Priest in residence)*
Killarney, Co Kerry
Tel 064-6631014 Fax 064-6631148
Rev Moses Muraya Muchunu *(pro-tem)*

**ABBEYDORNEY**
*St Bernard's, Abbeydorney*
Very Rev Denis O'Mahony PP
Abbeydorney, Co Kerry
Tel 066-7135146 Fax 066-7135204
*St Mary's, Kilflynn*
Rev Kevin Sullivan
Tel 066-7145639

**ADRIGOLE**
*St Fachtna's*
Very Rev Kieran O'Sullivan PP
Adrigole, Bantry, Co Cork
Tel 027-60006 Fax 027-60137

**ALLIHIES**
*St Michael's, Allihies,*
*St Michael's, Cahermore*
Allihies, Bantry, Co Cork
Tel 027-73012 Fax 027-73024

**ANNASCAUL**
*Sacred Heart, Annascaul*
*St Mary's, Camp*
*St Joseph's, Inch*
Very Rev John Buckley PP
Annascaul, Co Kerry
Tel 066-9157103 Fax 066-9157221

**ARDFERT**
*St Brendan's, Ardfert*
*Sacred Heart, Kilmoyley*
Very Rev Tadhg Fitzgerald PP
Ardfert, Co Kerry
Tel 066-7134131 Fax 066-7134148

**BALLINSKELLIGS (PRIOR)**
*St Michael the Archangel, Ballinskelligs,*
*St Patrick's, Portmagee,*
*Sacred Heart and St Finan, The Glen*
Very Rev David Gunn PP
St Michael's, Ballinskelligs, Co Kerry
Tel 066-9479108 Fax 066-9479193

**BALLYBUNION**
*St John's*
Very Rev Noel Spring PP
Ballybunion, Co Kerry
Tel 068-27102 Fax 068-27153

**BALLYDESMOND**
*St Patrick's*
Very Rev Pádraig MacCarthaigh PP
Ballydesmond, Mallow, Co Cork
Tel 064-7751104 Fax 064-7751154

**BALLYDONOGHUE**
*St Teresa's*
Very Rev John Lawlor PP
Ballydonoghue, Lisselton, Co Kerry
Tel 068-47103 Fax 068-47230

**BALLYFERRITER**
*Uinseann Naofa, Baile an Fheitearaigh*
*Naomh Gobnait, Dún Chaoin*
*Séipéal na Carraige*
Very Rev Eugene Kiely PP
Tel 066-9156131 Fax 066-9156440
Very Rev Tomás Ó hIceadha AP
Tel 066-9156499
Ballyferriter West, Tralee, Co Kerry

**BALLYHEIGUE**
*St Mary's*
Very Rev Thomas Leane PP
Ballyheigue, Tralee, Co Kerry
Tel 066-7133110 Fax 066-7133114

**BALLYLONGFORD**
*St Michael the Archangel*
Very Rev Philip O'Connell PP
Ballylongford, Co Kerry
Tel 068-43110 Fax 068-43187
*St Mary's*
Rev Joseph Tarrant CC
Asdee, Co Kerry
Tel 068-41152 Fax 068-41205

**BALLYMACELLIGOTT**
*Immaculate Conception, Ballymacelligott*
*St Brendan's, Clogher*
Very Rev Pat Crean-Lynch PP
Ballymacelligott, Co Kerry
Tel 066-7137118 Fax 066-7137137

**BEAUFORT (TUOGH)**
*St Mary's, Beaufort*
*Our Lady of the Valley, The Valley*
Very Rev Donal O'Connor PP
The Presbytery, Beaufort, Co Kerry
Tel 064-6644128 Fax 064-6644130

**BOHERBUE/KISKEAM**
*Immaculate Conception, Boherbue*
*Sacred Heart, Kiskeam*
Very Rev Séamus Kennelly PP
Boherbue, Mallow, Co Cork
Tel 029-76151 Fax 029-76178

**BROSNA**
*St Carthage, Brosna*
*Our Lady of the Assumption, Knockaclarig*
Very Rev Anthony O'Sullivan PP
Brosna, Co Kerry
Tel 068-44112 Fax 068-44176

**CAHIRCIVEEN**
*Holy Cross, O'Connell Memorial,*
*Immaculate Conception, Filemore;*
*St Joseph's, Aghatubrid*
Very Rev William Canon Crean PP, VF
Rev Niall Howard CC
Cahirciveen, Co Kerry
Tel 066-9472210
Fax 066-9473130

**CAHIRDANIEL**
*St Crohan's, Mary Immaculate, Lohar*
*Most Precious Blood, Castlecove*
Very Rev Fergal Ryan PP
Cahirdaniel, Co Kerry
Tel 066-9475111 Fax 066-9475001

**CASTLEGREGORY**
*St Mary's, Castlegregory*
*St Brendan's, Cloghane*
Very Rev Michael Hussey PP
*Assistant priest pro tem:* Rev Seán Sheehy
Castlegregory, Co Kerry
Tel 066-7139145 Fax 066-7139136

**CASTLEISLAND**
*SS Stephen and John*
Rt Rev Mgr Dan O'Riordan PP, VG, VF
Rev Michael Moynihan CC
Castleisland, Co Kerry
Tel 066-7141241 Fax 066-7141273
*Our Lady of Lourdes*
*Immaculate Conception, Cordal*

**CASTLEMAINE**
*St Gobnait, Keel*
*St Carthage, Kiltallagh*
Very Rev Luke Roche PP
Castlemaine, Co Kerry
Tel 066-9767322 Fax 066-9767467

**CASTLETOWNBERE AND BERE ISLAND**
*Sacred Heart, Castletownbere*
*St Bartholomew, Rossmacowen*
*St Michael's, Bere Island*
Very Rev Gearóid Walsh
Castletownbere, Co Cork
Tel 027-70849 Fax 027-70047

**CAUSEWAY**
*St John the Baptist*
*SS Peter and Paul*
Very Rev Brendan Walsh PP
Causeway, Co Kerry
Tel 066-7131148 Fax 066-7131355

**DINGLE**
*St Mary's, Dingle*
*St John the Baptist, Lispole*
*Naomh Caitlin, Ceann Trá*
Very Rev Thomas Canon Looney SP, VF
Tel 066-9151208
Rev Bernard Healy CC
Dingle, Co Kerry
Tel 066-9151208 Fax 066-9151173

**DROMTARIFFE**
*St John's, Dromagh*
*Presentation of the BVM, Derrinagree*
Very Rev Liam Comer PP, VF
Dromagh, Mallow, Co Cork
Tel 029-78096 Fax 029-78107

**DUAGH**
*St Brigid's, Duagh*
*Sacred Heart, Lyreacrompane*
Very Rev Patrick Moore PP
Duagh, Listowel, Co Kerry
Tel 068-45102 Fax 068-45149

**EYERIES**
*St Kentigern, Eyeries*
*Resurrection, Ardgroom*
Very Rev Jim Lenihan Adm
Eyeries, Co Cork
Tel 027-74008 Fax 027-74090

**FIRIES**
*St Gertrude, Firies*
*Sacred Heart, Ballyhar*
Very Rev Tadhg O'Dochartaigh PP
Firies, Killarney, Co Kerry
Tel 066-9764122 Fax 066-9764046

**FOSSA**
*Christ, Prince of Peace*
Very Rev Brendan Harrington PP
Fossa, Killarney, Co Kerry
Tel 064-6631996 Fax 064-6631906

**GLENBEIGH**
*St James's, Glenbeigh*
*St Stephen's, Glencar*
Very Rev Jerry Keane PP
Glenbeigh, Co Kerry
Tel 066-9768209 Fax 066-9768225

**GLENFLESK**
*St Agatha, Glenflesk*
*Sacred Heart, Barraduff*
*Our Lady of the Wayside, Clonkeen*
Very Rev William Radley PP
St Agatha's Parish Centre, Headford,
Killarney, Co Kerry
Tel 064-7754008 Fax 064-7754458

**GLENGARRIFF (BONANE)**
*Sacred Heart, Glengarriff*
*St Fachtna's, Bonane*
Very Rev Pádraig Kennelly PP
Glengarriff, Co Cork
Tel 027-63045 Fax 027-63615

**KENMARE**
*Holy Cross, Kenmare*
*Our Lady of Perpetual Help, Derreenderagh*
*Our Lady of the Assumption, Templemore*
Venerable Thomas Crean PP, VF
Tel 064-6641352 Fax 064-6641925
Rev Jerry Keane CC
Tel 064-6642047
Kenmare, Co Kerry

**KILCUMMIN**
*Our Lady of Lourdes*
Very Rev Joseph Begley PP
Kilcummin, Killarney, Co Kerry
Tel 064-6643176 Fax 064-6643220

**KILGARVAN**
*St Patrick's*
Very Rev Donal O'Neill Adm
Kilgarvan, Co Kerry
Tel 064-6685313 Fax 064-6685336

**KILLEENTIERNA**
*Immaculate Conception, Currow*
*SS Thérèse & Colmcille, Currans*
Very Rev Patrick Sugrue PP
Killeentierna, Killarney, Co Kerry
Tel 066-9764141 Fax 066-9764862

**KILLORGLIN**
*St James, Killorglin*
*Our Lady, Star of the Sea, Cromane*
Very Rev Canon Michael Fleming PP, VF
Tel 066-9761172 Fax 066-9761840
Rev Liam O'Brien AP
Tel 066-9761160 Fax 066-9796738
Killorglin, Co Kerry

**KNOCKNAGOSHEL**
*St Mary's*
Very Rev Eoin Mangan PP
Knocknagoshel, Co Kerry
Tel 068-46107 Fax 068-46494

**LISTOWEL**
*St Mary's*
Very Rev Declan Canon O'Connor PP, VF
Listowel, Co Kerry
Tel 068-21188 Fax 068-23655

**LIXNAW**
*St Michael's, Lixnaw*
*Our Lady of the Assumption, Rathea*
*Our Lady of Fatima and St Senan, Irremore*
Very Rev Maurice Brick PP
Tel 066-7132111 Fax 066-7132171
Rev Gerard O'Connell CC
Irremore, Listowel, Co Kerry
Tel 068-40244 Fax 068-40244

**MILLSTREET**
*St Patrick's, Millstreet*
*Our Lady of Lourdes, Ballydaly*
*Blessed Virgin Mary, Cullen*
Very Rev Jack Fitzgerald PP
Millstreet, Co Cork
Tel 029-70043 Fax 029-70919

**MILLTOWN**
*Sacred Heart, Milltown*
*Immaculate Conception, Listry*
Very Rev Pat O'Donnell PP
Milltown, Co Kerry
Tel 066-9767312 Fax 066-9767988

**MOYVANE**
*Assumption of the BVM, Moyvane*
*Corpus Christi, Knockanure*
Very Rev John Lucid PP
Moyvane, Listowel, Co Kerry
Tel 068-49308 Fax 068-49418

**RATHMORE**
*Christ the King, Knocknagree*
*St Joseph's, Rathmore*
*Our Lady of Perpetual Succour, Shrone*
*Holy Rosary, Gneeveguilla*
Very Rev Larry Canon Kelly PP
Rathmore, Co Kerry
Tel 064-7758026 Fax 064-7758110
Rev Con Buckley CC
Knocknagree, Mallow, Co Cork
Tel 064-7756029 Fax 064-7756018
Rev James Browne (WF) CC
Gneeveguilla, Rathmore, Co Kerry
Tel 064-7756188 Fax 064-7756332

**SNEEM**
*St Michael, Sneem; St Brendan, Glenlough; St Patrick, Tahilla*
Very Rev Patrick Murphy PP
Sneem, Co Kerry
Tel 064-6645141 Fax 064-6645941

**SPA**
*Church of the Purification, Churchill*
*St Joseph's, Fenit*
Very Rev Eamon Mulvihill PP
Fenit, Tralee, Co Kerry
Tel 066-7136145
Fax 066-7136327

**TARBERT**
*St Mary's*
Very Rev Daniel Broderick PP
Tel 068-36111 Fax 068-36572

**TRALEE, ST BRENDAN'S**
*Our Lady and St Brendan, Rock Street*
Very Rev Pádraig Walsh PP
Rev Patsy Lynch CC
St Brendan's, Tralee, Co Kerry
Tel 066-7125932
Fax 066-7127049

**TRALEE, ST JOHN'S**
*St John the Baptist, Castle Street, Tralee*
*Immaculate Conception, Rathass*
*St Brendan's, Curaheen*
Dean Sean Hanafin PP, VF
Rev Kieran O'Brien CC
Rev Gerard Finucane
Rev Francis Nolan
Rev Seámus Linnane AP
St John's Presbytery, Tralee, Co Kerry
Tel 066-7122522 Fax 066-7122760
Email stjohnscastlestreet@eircom.net

**TUOSIST**
*St Kilian's, Lauragh*
*Dawros, Dawros*
Very Rev Martin Sheehan Adm
St Joseph's, Lauragh, Killarney, Co Kerry
Tel 064-6683107 Fax 064-6683577

**VALENTIA**
*Immaculate Conception, Knightstown*
*SS Derarca and Teresa, Chapeltown*
Very Rev John Shanahan PP
Valentia Island, Co Kerry
Tel 066-9476104 Fax 066-9476408

**WATERVILLE (DROMOD)**
*St Finian's, Dromod*
Our Lady of the Valley, Cillin Liath
Very Rev John Kerin PP
Tel 066-9474495 Fax 066-9474703

## INSTITUTIONS AND THEIR CHAPLAINS

**Boherbue Comprehensive School**
Mallow, Co Cork
Mrs Rose Murphy
Tel 029-76032

**Castletownbere Community School,**
Co Cork
Ms Fiona Barry
Tel 027-70177/70026

**Causeway Comprehensive School**
Mr Paul Montgomery
Tel 066-7131197/7132513

**Coláiste na Sceilge**
Cahirciveen
Tel 066-9473335
Ms Philomena O'Neill

**Kenmare Pobalscoil Inbhear Scéine**
Sr Helen Lane
Tel 064-6640846

**Killarney Community College**
Rev Kevin McNamara (MSC)
Tel 064-6632764

**Killarney St Columbanus Home**
Sr Mary Boyle
Tel 064-6631038

**Killorglin Post-Primary Schools**
Parish Clergy
Tel 066-9761172

**Millstreet Community School**
Co Cork
Mr John Magee
Tel 029-70087/79028

**Listowel Presentation Convent**
Sr Eilis Daly
Tel 068-21452

**Our Lady of Fatima Home**
Oakpark, Tralee, Co Kerry
Tel 066-7125900
St John's Parish Clergy

**Pobalscoil Chorca Dhuibhne**
Dingle
Ms Agnes Gleeson
Tel 064-6640846

**Rathmore Community School**
Ms Yvonne O'Connor
Parish Clergy
Tel 064-6658027

**St Brendan's College**
Killarney, Co Kerry
Very Rev Joseph Begley
Rev Kevin McNamara (MSC)
Tel 064-6631021

**St Finian's Hospital**
Killarney, Co Kerry
Parish Clergy
Tel 064-6631022/6631014

**St Michael's College**
Listowel, Co Kerry
Parish Clergy
Tel 068-21049/21188

**Tarbert, Comprehensive School**
Listowel, Co Kerry
Sr Frances Day
Tel 068-36105/36177

**Tralee General Hospital**
Rev Teddy Linehan
Rev Martin Spillane
Mrs Mary Quinlan
Tel 066-7126222

**Tralee Institute of Technology**
Tralee, Co Kerry
Rev Kevin Sullivan
Tel 066-7145639/7135236

**Tralee Mercy Secondary Mounthawk**
Sr Nora Flynn
Tel 066-7102550

## PRIESTS OF THE DIOCESE ELSEWHERE

Rev George Hayes
c/o Diocesan Offices, Killarney, Co Kerry
Rev Seamus McKenna BA, HDE
Cork Regional Marriage Tribunal,
The Lough, Cork
Tel 021-4963653
Rev Gerard O'Leary
Institute of St Anselm, 51-59 Norfolk Road,
Cliftonville, Kent CT9 2EU, UK
Rev Seamus O'Connell
St Patrick's College,
Maynooth, Co Kildare
Tel 01-6285222
Rev Richard O'Connor
c/o Diocesan Offices, Killarney, Co Kerry
Rev Anthony O'Reilly
Newry, Co Armagh

## RETIRED PRIESTS

Rev P. Ahern
St John's Parish Centre, Castle Street,
Tralee, Co Kerry
Very Rev Denis Costello
Fatima Home, Oakpark, Tralee, Co Kerry
Rev Edward Corridan
Killarney Nursing Home, Rock Road,
Killarney, Co Kerry
Rev Jim Downey
Fatima Home, Oak Park, Tralee, Co Kerry
Very Rev Martin Hegarty
32 Knockmoyle Est, Tralee, Co Kerry
Very Rev Canon Matthew Keane
Ashborough Lodge, Lyre,
Milltown, Co Kerry
Very Rev Roger Kelleher
9 St Emmet's Terrace, Killarney, Co Kerry
Very Rev Lawrence Kelly
'Sunville', Kilgarvan, Co Kerry
Very Rev John Kennelly
24 Ferndene, Greenville, Listowel, Co Kerry
Very Rev Denis Leahy
34 Knockmoyle Estate, Tralee, Co Kerry
Very Rev Michael Maher
11 Woodlawn, Listowel, Co Kerry
Rt Rev Michael Manning
Fatima Home, Oak Park, Tralee, Co Kerry
Very Rev Canon John McKenna
Baile na Buaile, Daingean Uí Chúis,
Co Chiarraí
Very Rev Noel Moran
Lahard, Milltown, Co Kerry
Archdeacon Michael J. Murphy
No 1 Cathedral Place, Killarney, Co Kerry
Very Rev J. Nolan
36 Ashfield, Greenville, Listowel, Co Kerry
Very Rev Michael O'Dochartaigh
Ard an Aonaigh, Killarney, Co Kerry
Very Rev Canon Michael O'Doherty
No 1 Lynch Heights, Sun Hill,
Killorglin, Co Kerry
Rev Gearoid Ó Donnchadha
'An tSaoirse', Fenit, Tralee, Co Kerry
Rt Rev Mgr Pádraig Ó Fiannachta
An Diseart, Green Street, Dingle, Co Kerry
Very Rev Canon Denis O'Mahony
Killeagh, Farranfore, Co Kerry
Very Rev Thomas Pierse
32 Knockmoyle Estate, Tralee, Co Kerry
Rev John Quinlan
36 Clogher Lí, Tralee, Co Kerry
Tel 066-7181367
Very Rev Denis Quirke
St Nicholas Place, Bridge Street,
Milltown, Co Kerry
Very Rev Canon P. Sheehan
'Shalom', Rossbeigh, Glenbeigh, Co Kerry

## RELIGIOUS ORDERS AND CONGREGATIONS

### PRIESTS

**DOMINICANS**
Holy Cross, Tralee, Co Kerry
Tel 066-7121135 Fax 066-7180026
*Prior:* Very Rev Joseph Bulman (OP)

**FRANCISCANS**
Franciscan Friary, Killarney, Co Kerry
Tel 064-6631334/6631066
Fax 064-6637510
Email friary@eircom.net
*Guardian:* Rev Pádraig Breheny (OFM)

**OBLATES OF MARY IMMACULATE**
Department of Chaplaincy,
Tralee General Hospital, Co Kerry
Rev Edward Barrett
Tel 066-7126222

## BROTHERS

**CHRISTIAN BROTHERS**
Christian Brothers, 14 The Orchard,
Ballyrickard, Tralee, Co Kerry
Tel 066-71-3910
Community: 2

**PRESENTATION BROTHERS**
Presentation Novitiate, Killarney,
Co Kerry
Tel 064-6631267
*Contact:* Br Barry Noel (FPM)
Community: 6

**SAINT JOHN OF GOD KERRY SERVICES**
Cloonanorig, Monavalley,
Tralee, Co Kerry
Tel 066-7124333 Fax 066-7126197
Email kerry@sjog.ie
*Acting Director:* Ms Ann Ellard
Training and supported employment service with back-up residential service.

*Community Superior*
Br Michael Francis (OH)
Community: 1

Teach Eoin, 2 Bóthar an Mhuillean,
Ballyard, Tralee, Co Kerry
Tel 066-7194786 Fax 066-7194474

## SISTERS

**BON SECOURS SISTERS (PARIS)**
Bon Secours Hospital, Strand Street,
Tralee, Co Kerry
Tel 066-7149800 Fax 066-7129068
*Co-ordinator:* Sr Anne McCarthy
Community: 8
General hospital. Beds: 78
Pastoral ministry

1 Cahermoneen, Tralee, Co Kerry
Tel 066-7127600
*Contact:* Sr Katherine Therese Tierney
Community: 2
Pastoral parish ministry

5 Strand View Terrace, Tralee, Co Kerry
Tel 066-7181279
Community: 1
Hospital Ministry

6 Strand Street, Tralee, Co Kerry
Tel 066-7194647
Community: 2
Hospital Ministry

**CONGREGATION OF THE SISTERS OF MERCY**
Mercy Lodge, Balloonagh,
Tralee, Co Kerry
Tel 066-7126336 Fax 066-7125901

St John's, Balloonagh, Tralee, Co Kerry
Tel 066-7121199/7122370
Apartment, Catherine McAuley Home
Tel 066-7127517

Mercy Convent, Rock Road,
Killarney, Co Kerry
Tel 064-6631040/6631916

Suaineas, Woodlawn Road,
Killarney, Co Kerry
Tel 064-6633660

7 Arbutus Drive, Killarney, Co Kerry
Tel 064-6637484

11 Holy Cross Gardens,
Killarney, Co Kerry
Tel 064-6620554

21 The Grove, Mounthawk,
Tralee, Co Kerry
Tel 066-7189029

St Brigid's Convent, Greenville, Listowel,
Co Kerry
Tel 068-21557

Divine Providence, Castletownbere,
Co Cork
Tel 027-70061

'Mount St Michael', Rosscarbery,
Co Cork
Tel 023-8848116

Pairc a Tobair, Rosscarbery, Co Cork
Tel 023-8848963

14 Brandon Place, Basin Road,
Tralee, Co Kerry
Tel 066-7144997

9-10 Carraig Lí, Killerisk,
Tralee, Co Kerry
Tel 066-7121281

Goodwin House, The Mall,
Dingle, Co Kerry
Tel 066-9151943

Mercy Sisters, Aoibhneas,
103 Gort na Sidhe, Mounthawk,
Tralee, Co Kerry
Tel 066-7128056

2 Knocknacuig Place, Tralee, Co Kerry
Tel 066-7129196

7 Woodview, Moyderwell,
Tralee, Co Kerry
Tel 066-7118027

2 Carrigeendaniel Court, Caherslee,
Tralee, Co Kerry
Tel 066-7127517

Apartment, McAuley Home, Balloonagh,
Tralee, Co Kerry

**DAUGHTERS OF MARY AND JOSEPH**
Fairways, Killowen, Kenmare, Co Kerry
Tel 064-6640755
*Contact Person:* Sr Helen Lane (DMJ)
Community: 1
Chaplaincy

**DOMINICAN SISTERS (KING WILLIAM'S TOWN)**
Oak Park, Tralee, Co Kerry
Tel 066-71256641
Community: 4
Our Lady of Fatima Retirement Home
Tel 066-7125900 Fax 066-7180834
Email info@fatimahome.com
Beds: 66
Siena Court for Active Retired:
Bungalows: 10
*Contact Person:* Sr Teresa McEvoy OP
Email teresamcevoy@fatimahome.com

Muire na nGael, 22 Manor Avenue,
Tralee, Co Kerry
Tel 066-7128083
Sr Audrey McNamee OP
Community: 1

**FRANCISCAN MISSIONARIES OF THE DIVINE MOTHERHOOD**
Sancta Chiara, 5 St Margaret's Road,
Killarney, Co Kerry
Tel 064-6626866 Fax 064-6626414
Community: 4

**INFANT JESUS SISTERS**
Killarney Road, Millstreet, Co Cork
Tel 029-70143
Community: 6
Retired sisters

20 Blackrock, St Brendan's Road,
Tralee, Co Kerry
Tel 066-7127974
Community: 3
Teaching and pastoral ministry

**LITTLE COMPANY OF MARY**
Park Road, Killarney, Co Kerry
Tel 064-6671220 Fax 064-6671240
Community: 8

**LORETO (IBVM)**
Gortahoonig, Muckross,
Killarney, Co Kerry
Tel 064-6631077
Sr Pauline Boyle

**PRESENTATION SISTERS**
Teach na Toirbhirte,
Miltown, Co Kerry
Tel 066-9767387
*Non-resident Leader:* Sr Maureen Guerin
Community: 5
Primary School. Tel 066-9767626
Post-Primary School. Tel 066-9767168

Presentation Convent,
Killarney, Co Kerry
Tel 064-6631172
*Non-resident Leader:* Sr Kathleen Quinlan
Community: 10
Secondary School. Tel 064-6632209

Presentation Sisters,
25 Ballyspillane, Killarney, Co Kerry
Tel 064-6636389
Community: 2

Presentation Convent, Castle Street,
Tralee, Co Kerry
Tel 066-7122128
Team Leadership
Community: 15
Primary School. Tel 066-7123314
Secondary School. Tel 066-7122737

Presentation Convent, Dingle, Co Kerry
Tel 066-9151194
Community: 1
Primary School. Tel 066-9151154

Presentation Convent,
Cahirciveen, Co Kerry
Tel 066-9472005
*Non-resident Leader*
Sr Columbanus Quirke
Community: 3

Presentation Convent,
Castleisland, Co Kerry
Tel 066-7141256
*Non-resident Leader*
Sr Elizabeth McMahon
Community: 11
Primary School. Tel 066-7141147
Secondary School. Tel 066-7141178

Presentation Convent, Lixnaw, Co Kerry
Tel 066-7132138
*Non-resident Leader:* Sr Maureen Kane
Community: 6
Primary School. Tel 066-7132600

Presentation Convent,
Rathmore, Co Kerry
Tel 064-7758027
*Non-resident Leader:* Sr Margaret O'Brien
Community: 8
Primary School. Tel 064-7758499

Presentation Convent,
Millstreet, Co Cork
Tel 029-70067
*Non-resident Leader:* Sr Eileen McCarthy
Community: 4
Primary School. Tel 029-70957

48 Hawley Park, Tralee, Co Kerry
Tel 066-7122111
Community: 2

'Tigh na Féile', Ballygologue Road,
Listowel, Co Kerry
Tel 068-21156
Community: 2
Primary School. Tel 068-22294
Secondary School. Tel 068-21452
Nano Nagle Special School. Tel 068-21942

9 Beech Grove, Cahirdown,
Listowel, Co Kerry
Tel 068-53951
Community: 1

Mail Road, Cahirdown,Listowel, Co Kerry
Tel 068-22500
Community: 1

Presentation Sisters, 1 Glenard,
Mona Valley, Tralee, Co Kerry
Tel 066-7181318
Community: 3

7 Tamhnach Lí,
Monavalley, Tralee, Co Kerry
Tel 066-7180800
Community: 1

8 Tamhnach Lí,
Monavalley, Tralee, Co Kerry
Tel 066-7194174
Community: 1

9 Tamhnach Lí,
Monavalley, Tralee, Co Kerry
Tel 066-7195312
Community: 2

9 Woodbrooke Manor,
Monavalley, Tralee, Co Kerry
Tel 066-7185454
Community: 2

15 St Joseph's Gardens,
Millstreet, Co Cork
Tel 029-71655
Community: 1

31 St Joseph's Gardens,
Millstreet, Co Cork
Tel 029-71627
Community: 1

6 Meadowlands, Artigallivan, Headford,
Killarney, Co Kerry
Tel 064-7754030
Community: 1

20 Spring Well Gardens, Ballyard, Tralee,
Co Kerry
Tel 066-7102862
Community: 1

**SISTERS OF ST CLARE**
St Clare's Convent, Kenmare, Co Kerry
Tel 064-6641385
Community: 4
St Clare's Primary. Pupils: 151
Kenmare Community School
Tel 064-6640846/7

**ST JOSEPH OF ANNECY SISTERS**
St Joseph's Convent, Killorglin, Co Kerry
Tel 066-9761809 Fax 066-9761127
*Superior:* Sr Helena Lyne
Email margaret.lyne@talk21.com
Community: 4

St Joseph's Home for the Aged,
Killorglin, Co Kerry
Tel 066-9761124 (H)
Tel 066-9761808 (Patients)
Beds: 40

**ST JOSEPH OF THE SACRED HEART SISTERS**
Sisters of St Joseph of Sacred Heart,
St Joseph's, Brosna Road,
Castleisland, Co Kerry
Tel 066-7141472

Sisters of St Joseph of Sacred Heart,
St Joseph's, 5 Allman's Terrace,
Killarney, Co Kerry
Tel 064-6623528

## DIOCESAN SECONDARY SCHOOLS

**St Brendan's College (Diocesan College)**
Killarney, Co Kerry
Tel 064-6631021
*Principal:* Mr Sean Coffey

**St Michael's College**
Listowel, Co Kerry
Tel 068-21049
*Principal:* Mr John Mulvihill

## EDUCATIONAL INSTITUTIONS

**EDMUND RICE SCHOOLS TRUST**
Christian Brothers Primary School,
An Daingean, Co Kerry
Tel 066-9152157
Email iognaidris@eircom.net
*Principal:* Máire Bean Ní Fhlaighimh

Pobalscoil Chorca Dhuíbhne,
An Daingean, Co Kerry
*Principal:* An tUas Pádraig Feirtéar

Coláiste Scoil Mhuire na mBráithre
Críostaí Primary School, Clounalour,
Tralee, Co Kerry
Tel 066-7124029 Fax 066-7120522
*Principal:* Mr Denis Coleman

Christian Brothers Secondary School,
The Green, Tralee, Co Kerry
Tel 066-7145841/7145824
Fax 066-7129807
*Principal:* Mr Tony O'Keeffe
Email thegreen@eircom.net

## CHARITABLE AND OTHER SOCIETIES

**Legion of Mary**
Ardfert, Ballyheigue, Ballymacelligott, Castleisland, Castletownbere, Dingle, Eyeries, Firies, Fossa, Glenflesk, Kilcummin, Killarney, Killeentierna, Knocknagree, Listowel, Millstreet, Milltown, Rathmore, Sneem, Spa, Tuogh, Tralee

**St Vincent de Paul**
Conferences at: Annascaul, Ardfert, Ballybunion, Ballyduff, Ballyferiter, Ballyheigue, Ballylongford, Cahirciveen, Castlemaine, Castlegregory, Castleisland, Castletownbere, Dingle, Kenmare, Killarney (four conferences), Killorglin, Knocknagoshel, Listowel, Lixnaw, Millstreet, Milltown, Moyvane, Rathmore, Tralee (five conferences)

# DIOCESE OF KILDARE AND LEIGHLIN

Patrons of the Diocese
St Brigid, 1 February; St Conleth (Kildare), 4 May;
St Lazerian (Leighlin) 18 April

includes county carlow and parts of counties kildare, laois, offaly, kilkenny, wicklow and wexford

**Rt Rev Mgr Brendan Byrne PP**
Diocesan Administrator
Diocese of Kildare and Leighlin
Born 1935;
ordained priest 1961;
appointed Diocesan Administrator 2010

Residence:
c/o Bishop's House, Carlow
Tel 059-9176725
Fax 059-9176850
Email brendan.byrne@kandle.ie

## CATHEDRAL OF THE ASSUMPTION, CARLOW

The ancient cathedrals of the Diocese of Kildare and Leighlin passed into Protestant usage in the period of the Reformation. Thus the cathedrals of Kildare and Old Leighlin stand on the sites of the ancient monasteries of St Brigid and St Laserian. Even before the Catholic Emancipation Act passed through the Westminster Parliament (1829), Bishop James Doyle OSA was working on the building of the Cathedral of the Assumption, Carlow. It is built on the site of and incorporates parts of the previous parish church of Carlow, which had been built in the 1780s by Dean Henry Staunton.

Carlow cathedral is not particularly large, having more the dimensions of a big parish church. The architectural work was begun by Joseph Lynch, but the final building is stamped with the design of Thomas Cobden, who replaced Lynch in 1829. Cobden gave the cathedral quite an elaborate exterior, with the obvious influence of the Bruges Town Hall tower. The cost of the building work was about £9,000. At its opening in November 1833, the interior decoration was incomplete. In fact, many elements were integrated over the following hundred years, sometimes adding to the mixture of styles.

The cathedral was consecrated on the occasion of its centenary, on 29 November 1933. A thorough reordering of the interior was completed in 1997, giving a very bright, welcoming, prayerful location for both diocesan and parish liturgical celebrations. The most notable elements are: the baptistry, the aumbry, the bishop's and president's chairs, and the Hogan statue of James Doyle, former Bishop of Kildare and Leighlin popularly known as JKL.

**Most Rev James Moriarty DD**
Retired Bishop of Kildare and Leighlin, born 1936; ordained priest 1961; ordained Bishop 22 September 1991; installed as Bishop of Kildare & Leighlin on 31 August 2002; retired April 2010
Residence: 68 Clontarf Road, Dublin 3
Tel 01-8054738

## ADMINISTRATION

**Diocesan Website**
www.kandle.ie

**Vicars Forane**
Rt Rev Mgr Brendan Byrne PP
Tullow, Co Carlow
Tel 059-9152159
Rt Rev Mgr John Byrne PP
Dublin Road, Portlaoise, Co Laois
Tel 057-8621142
Very Rev Adrian Carbery PP
26 Beech Grove, Kildare
Tel 045-521900
Very Rev John Dunphy PP
Graiguecullen, Co Carlow
Tel 059-9141833
Very Rev Francis MacNamara PP
Mountmellick, Co Laois
Tel 057-8624198
Very Rev Declan Foley PP
Bagenalstown, Co Carlow
Tel 059-9721154
Very Rev William O'Byrne PP
Kill, Co Kildare
Tel 045-878008

**Consultors**
Rt Rev Mgr Brendan Byrne PP
Rt Rev Mgr John Byrne PP, VF
Rt Rev Mgr Thomas Coonan CC
Rev Bill Kemmy
Very Rev Francis MacNamara PP, VF
Rev Mícheál Murphy
Very Rev Pierce Murphy

**Chancellor/Diocesan Secretary**
Rev Bill Kemmy
Bishop's House, Carlow
Tel 059-9176725 Fax 059-9176850
Email chancellor@kandle.ie

**Diocesan Communications Liaison**
Ms Brenda Drumm
Tel 087-2337797
Email media@kandle.ie

**Finance Committee**
*Chairperson:* Mrs Anna-May McHugh
Fallaghmore, Ballylinan, Athy, Co Kildare
*Secretary:* Rev Bill Kemmy
Bishop's House, Carlow
Tel 059-9176725 Fax 059-9176850
Email chancellor@kandle.ie

**Churches and Buildings Committee**
*Chairman:* Very Rev Francis MacNamara PP
Mountmellick, Co Laois
Tel 057-8624198
*Secretary:* Very Rev Thomas McDonnell
Parochial House, Naas, Co Kildare
Tel 045-897703

**Child Protection – Delegate**
Rt Rev Mgr John McDonald
Curragh Camp, Co Kildare
Tel 045-441369
Email cpi@kandle.ie

**Archivist**
Very Rev Thomas McDonnell
Bishop's House, Carlow
Tel 059-9176725 Fax 059-9176850

## FAITH DEVELOPMENT SERVICES

**Faith Development Services**
Cathedral Parish Centre, College Street, Carlow Town
Tel 059-9164084 Fax 059-9164020
Email fds@kandle.ie
*Primary Diocesan Advisor*
Ms Maeve Mahon
Email maeve.mahon@kandle.ie
*Post-Primary Diocesan Advisor*
Sr Anne Holton
Email anne.holton@kandle.ie
*Youth Ministry/Meitheal Co-ordinator*
Mr Robert Norton
Email robert.norton@kandle.ie
Ms Yvonne Rooney
Email yvonne.rooney@kandle.ie
*Pastoral Resource Person*
Ms Julie Kavanagh
Email julie.kavanagh@kandle.ie

**Church Music**
Rev Liam Lawton
Crossneen, Carlow Tel 059-9134548
Email liam.lawton@ireland.com

**Catholic Primary School Managers Association**
*Chairman:* Very Rev Francis MacNamara PP
Mountmellick, Co Laois
Tel 057-8624198
*Secretary:* Br Camillus Regan
10 Hawthorne Drive, Tullow, Co Carlow
Tel 087-2244175
Email patbros@iol.ie

## PASTORAL

**Accord**
*Centre Directors*
*Carlow:* Rev John Cummins Adm
The Presbytery, Dublin Road, Carlow
Tel 059-9131227
*Portlaoise:* Ms Carmel Kelly
Tel 045-431394
Accord, Parish Office, Portlaoise, Co Laois
*Newbridge:* Very Rev Joseph McDermott PP
St Conleth's, Newbridge, Co Kildare
Tel 045-431741

**ALPHA**
Very Rev James O'Connell PP
Stradbally, Co Laois
Tel 057-8625132

**Conciliators**
Rt Rev Mgr John McDonald PP
Curragh Camp, Co Kildare
Tel 045-441369
Very Rev William O'Byrne PP
Kill, Co Kildare
Tel 045-878008
Ms Breda Parker
9 Moorepark, Newbridge, Co Kildare
Tel 045-431462
Mr Brian O'Sullivan
Drumcooley, Edenderry, Co Offaly
Tel 046-9731522 (W) 046-31435 (H)

**Ecumenism**
*Director:* Very Rev Tom Lalor PP
Leighlinbridge, Co Carlow
Tel 059-9721463
Rev Liam Morgan CC
Tinryland, Co Carlow
Tel 059-9131212
Very Rev Liam Merrigan PP
Drogheda Street, Monasterevin, Co Kildare
Tel 045-525346

**Pioneer Total Abstinence Association**
*Diocesan Director:* Rev Mark Townsend PP
Daingean, Co Offaly
Tel 057-9362006

**Pontifical Mission Societies**
*Diocesan Director:* Rev Eddie Kavanagh
Mountmellick, Co Laois
Tel 057-8679302

**Polish Chaplaincy**
Fr Tadeusz Durrajczyk
60 College Orchard, Newbridge, Co Kildare
Tel 086-2354320

**Prisons**
*Contact Priest:* Rev Eugene Drumm (SPS)
Portlaoise Prison, Portlaoise, Co Laois
Tel 057-8622549

**Travellers**
*Chaplains*
Very Rev Thomas Dooley PP
Portarlington, Co Laois
Tel 057-8643004
Rev John Brickley CC
Sallins Road, Naas, Co Kildare
Tel 045-897260

**Vocations Committee**
*Chairman:* Rev Ruairí Ó Domhnaill
Newbridge, Co Kildare
Tel 045-434069
Email vocations@kandle.ie

**Youth Ministry**
*Chairman:* Rev Liam Morgan
Tinryland, Co Carlow
Tel 059-9131212
*Meitheal Co-ordinator:* Mr Robert Norton
Email robert.norton@kandle.ie
Ms Yvonne Rooney
Faith Development Services,
Cathedral Parish Centre,
College Street, Carlow
Tel 059-9164084 Fax 059-9164020

## PARISHES

*Mensal parishes are listed first. Other parishes follow alphabetically. Historical names are given in parentheses. Church titulars are in italics.*

**CATHEDRAL, CARLOW**
*Cathedral of the Assumption*
Email info@carlowcathedral.ie
Website www.carlowcathedral.ie
Rev John Cummins Adm
The Presbytery, Carlow
Tel 059-9131227 Fax 059-9130805
Email johncummins@kandle.ie
Rev Rory Nolan CC
The Presbytery, Carlow
Tel 059-9131227
Cathedral/Parish Shop & Office
Tel 059-9164087

**ASKEA**
*Holy Family*
Email askeaparishcc@eircom.net
Very Rev Thomas Little Adm
Browneshill Avenue, Carlow
Tel 059-9131559
Email tomlittle@eircom.net
Rev Liam Morgan CC
Tinryland, Co Carlow
Tel 059-9131212

**ABBEYLEIX**
*Holy Rosary, Abbeyleix*
*St Patrick, Ballyroan*
Very Rev Gerard Ahern PP
Abbeyleix, Co Laois
Tel 057-8731135
Email aherngerard@eircom.net

**ALLEN**
*Holy Trinity, Allen*
*St Brigid's, Milltown*
*Immaculate Conception, Allenwood*
Very Rev Edward Moore PP
Allen, Kilmeague, Naas, Co Kildare
Tel 045-860135
Rev Brian Kavanagh CC
15 Lowtown Manor,
Robertstown, Naas, Co Kildare
Tel 045-890559
Email rbkav@gmail.com

**ARLES**
*Sacred Heart, Arles, St Anne's, Ballylinan*
*St Abban's, Maganey*
Very Rev John Dunphy Adm
Rev P.J. Madden CC
Graiguecullen, Carlow
Tel 059-9141833
Very Rev Thomas O'Shea CC
Ballylinan, Athy, Co Kildare
Tel 059-8625261
Email tommieoshea1@eircom.net
Rev Bill Kemmy
Arles, Ballickmoyler, Carlow
Tel 059-9147637
Email chancellor@kandle.ie

**BALLINAKILL**
*St Brigid's, Ballinakill*
*St Lazarian's, Knock*
Very Rev Seán Conlon PP
Ballinakill, Co Laois
Tel 057-8733336

**BALLON**
*SS Peter and Paul, Ballon*
*St Patrick's, Rathoe*
Very Rev Brendan Howard PP
Clonegal, Enniscorthy, Co Wexford
Tel 053-9377291
Rev Edward Whelan PE, CC
Ballon, Co Carlow
Tel 059-9159329

**BALLYADAMS**
*St Joseph's, Ballyadams*
*St Mary's, Wolfhill*
*Holy Rosary, Luggacurren*
Very Rev Daniel Dunne PP
Tullamoy, Stradbally, Co Laois
Tel 059-8627123

**BALLYFIN**
*St Fintan's*
Very Rev Pat Hennessy PP
Ballyfin, Portlaoise, Co Laois
Tel 057-8755227

**BALTINGLASS**
*St Joseph's, Baltinglass*
*St Oliver's, Grange Con*
*St Mary's, Stratford*
Very Rev Thomas Dillon PP
Baltinglass, Co Wicklow
Tel 059-6482768
Email tfdb@eircom.net

**BALYNA**
*St Mary's, Broadford,*
*St Patrick's Johnstownbridge,*
*St Brigid's, Clogherinchoe*
Email balynaparish@eircom.net
Website www.balynaparish.ie
Very Rev Gerard Breen PP
Broadford, Co Kildare
Tel 046-9551203

**BENNEKERRY**
*St Mary's*
Very Rev Thomas Little PP
St Mary's, Browneshill Avenue, Carlow
Tel 059-9131559
Email tomlittle@eircom.net

**BORRIS**
*Sacred Heart, Borris*
*St Patrick's, Ballymurphy*
*St Forchan's, Rathanna*
Rev John O'Brien PP
Tel 059-9773128
Email john51@eircom.net
Very Rev Pierce Murphy
Borris, Co Carlow via Kilkenny
Tel 059-9773128

**CARAGH**
*Our Lady and St Joseph, Caragh,*
Email parishoffice@caragh.net
Very Rev Joseph McDermott Adm
Chapel Lane, Newbridge, Co Kildare
Tel 045-431741

**CARBURY**
*Holy Trinity, Carbury*
*Holy Family, Derrinturn*
Email carburyparish@eircom.net
Very Rev John Fitzpatrick PP
Carbury, Co Kildare
Tel 046-9553355

**CLANE**
*SS Patrick and Brigid, Clane*
*Sacred Heart, Rathcoffey*
Email claneparish@eircom.net
Website www.claneparish.com
Very Rev Paul O'Boyle PP
Clane, Naas, Co Kildare
Tel 045-868249
Email oboylepaul@eircom.net

**CLONASLEE**
*St Manman's*
Very Rev Thomas O'Reilly PP
Clonaslee, Co Laois
Tel 057-8648030

**CLONBULLOGUE**
*Sacred Heart, Clonbullogue*
*St Brochan's, Bracknagh,*
*Immaculate Conception, Walsh Island*
Very Rev Patrick Gaynor PP
Walsh Island, Geashill, Co Offaly
Tel 057-8649510

**CLONEGAL**
*St Brigid's, Clonegal*
*St Lasarian's, Kildavin*
Very Rev Joseph Fleming Adm
Clonegal, Enniscorthy, Co Wexford
Tel 053-9377298

**CLONMORE**
*St Mary's, Ballyconnell*
*St Finian's, Kilquiggan*
*Our Lady of the Wayside, Clonmore*
*St Finian's Oratory, Killinure*
Very Rev James Gahan PP
Killinure, Tullow, Co Carlow
Tel 059-9156111
Email jkgahan@eircom.net

**COOLERAGH AND STAPLESTOWN**
*Christ the King, Cooleragh,*
*St Benignus, Staplestown*
Email standco@eircom.net
Very Rev Patrick Daly PP
Cooleragh, Coill Dubh, Naas, Co Kildare
Tel 045-860281

**CURRAGH CAMP**
*St Brigid's*
Very Rev Mgr John McDonald PP
Tel 045-441369
Rev P. J. Somers
Tel 045-441277
Email spj40@hotmail.com
Curragh Camp, Co Kildare

**DAINGEAN**
*Mary Mother of God, Daingean*
*SS Peter and Paul, Kilclonfert*
*St Francis of Assisi and St Brigid, Ballycommon; Oratory of the Immaculate Conception, Cappincur*
Rev Mark Townsend PP
Tel 057-9362006
Rev Patrick O'Byrne PE, CC
Tel 057-9344161
Daingean, Co Offaly

**DOONANE**
*St Abban's, Doonane*
Blessed Virgin Mary, Mayo
Very Rev Denis Murphy PP
Tolerton, Ballickmoyler, Carlow
Tel 056-4442126

**DROICHEAD NUA/NEWBRIDGE**
*St Conleth's, Newbridge*
*Cill Mhuire, Ballymany*
*St Eustace's, Dominican Church*
*Parish Office:* 045-431394
Email parishoffice@newbridgeparish.ie
Website www.newbridgeparish.ie
Very Rev Joseph McDermott PP
Tel 045-431741
Email jmcder@eircom.net
Rev Willie Byrne CC
Tel 045-433979
Email wmby@eircom.net
Rev Pat Hughes CC
Tel 045-438036
St Conleth's, Chapel Lane,
Droichead Nua, Co Kildare
Rev Rúairí Ó Dómhnaill CC
The Presbytery, Ballymany,
Droichead Nua, Co Kildare
Tel 045-434069
Rev Brian Reynolds (OP) CC
Droichead Nua, Co Kildare
Tel 045-431394

**EDENDERRY**
*St Mary's*
Very Rev P.J. McEvoy PP
Francis Street, Edenderry, Co Offaly
Tel 046-9731296
Rev Gregory Corcoran CC
Rhode, Co Offaly
Tel 046-9737010

**EMO**
*St Paul's, Emo; Sacred Heart, Rath*
Very Rev Tom Dooley PP
Portarlington, Co Laois
Tel 057-8643004
Email frtomdooley@eircom.net
Rev Thomas O'Byrne CC
Priest's House, Emo, Portlaoise, Co Laois
Tel 057-8646517
Email obyrneta@eircom.net

**GRAIGNAMANAGH**
*Duiske Abbey, Graignamanagh*
*Our Lady of Lourdes,*
*Skeoughvosteen, Co Kilkenny*
Very Rev Gerald Byrne PP
Parochial House,
Graignamanagh, Co Kilkenny
Tel 059-9724238
*Abbey Centre:* 059-9724238

**GRAIGUECULLEN**
*St Clare's, Graiguecullen*
*Holy Cross, Killeshin*
Very Rev John Dunphy PP
Tel 059-9141833
Email dunphyj@iol.ie
Rev PJ Madden
Tel 059-9141833
Graiguecullen, Carlow

**HACKETSTOWN**
*St Brigid's, Hacketstown*
*Our Lady, Killamoate*
*Church of the Immaculate Conception, Knockanna*
*Church of Our Lady, Askinagap*
Rev James McCormack (MSC) Adm
Hacketstown, Co Carlow
Tel 059-6471257

**KILCOCK**
*St Coca, Kilcock*
*Nativity of the BVM, Newtown*
Email stcocasparish@eircom.net
Website www.kilcockparish.net
Very Rev P. J. Byrne PP
Kilcock, Co Kildare
Tel 01-6287448
Rev Des Reid (CSSp)
Curate's House, Kilcock, Co Kildare
Tel 01-6287277

**KILDARE**
*St Brigid's*
*Our Lady of Victories, Kildangan*
*Sacred Heart, Nurney*
*Parish Office:* 045-521352
Email arasbride@eircom.net
Website www.kildareparish.ie
Very Rev Adrian Carbery PP, VF
26 Beech Grove, Kildare
Tel 045-521900
Rev Gaspar Habara CC
St Brigid's, Kildare
Tel 045-520347

**KILL**
*St Brigid's, Kill*
*St Anne's, Ardclough*
Email killparish@eircom.net
Website www.killparish.ie
Very Rev William O'Byrne PP
Kill, Co Kildare
Tel 045-878008
Very Rev Matthew Kelly PE, CC
60 Hartwell Green, Kill, Naas, Co Kildare
Tel 045-877880

**KILLEIGH**
*St Patrick's, Killeigh*
*St Joseph's, Ballinagar*
*St Mary's, Geashill*
Email killeighparish@eircom.net
Website www.killeigh.com
Very Rev John Stapleton PP
Killeigh, Co Offaly
Tel 057-9344161
Email johnstapleton@eircom.net
Rt Rev Mgr Thomas Coonan CC
Geashill, Co Offaly
Tel 057-9343517

**LEIGHLIN**
*St Laserian's, Leighlin*
*St Fintan's, Ballinabranna*
Very Rev Thomas Lalor PP
Leighlinbridge, Co Carlow
Tel 059-9721463

**MONASTEREVAN**
*SS Peter and Paul, Monasterevan*
Very Rev Liam Merrigan PP
Tougher Road, Monasterevan, Co Kildare
Tel 045-525346

**MOUNTMELLICK**
*St Joseph's, Mountmellick*
*St Mary's, Clonaghadoo*
Very Rev Francis MacNamara PP, VF
Tel 057-8624198
Rev Edward Kavanagh CC
Tel 057-8679302
Very Rev Noel Dunphy PE, CC
Tel 057-8624141
Mountmellick, Co Laois

**MOUNTRATH**
*St Fintan, Mountrath*
*Sacred Heart, Hollow*
Rev Patrick Hennessy PP
Ballyfin, Portlaoise, Co Laois
Tel 057-8755227
Rev Joe Brophy CC
Mountrath, Co Laois
Tel 057-8732234

**MUINEBHEAG/BAGENALSTOWN**
*St Andrew's, Bagenalstown*
*St Patrick's Newtown*
*St Laserian's, Ballinkillen*
Email info@bagenalstownparish.ie
Website www.bagenalstownparish.ie
Very Rev Declan Foley PP
Tel 059-9721154
Email pdlfoley@gmail.com
Rev Patrick Byrne CC
Tel 059-9723886
Email pmlb@eircom.net
Rev Thomas Bambrick (SM)
Tel 059-9721154
Muinebheag, Co Carlow

**MYSHALL**
*Exaltation of the Cross, Myshall*
*St Laserian's, Drumphea*
Very Rev Philip O'Shea PP
Myshall, Co Carlow
Tel 059-9157635
Rev Brendan Howard CC
Curate's House, Clonegal,
Enniscorthy, Co Wexford
Tel 053-9377291

**NAAS**
*Our Lady and St David, Naas*
*Irish Martyrs, Ballycane*
Very Rev Thomas McDonnell PP
Tel 045-897703
Rev John Brickley CC
Tel 045-897260
Rev Declan Thompson (SPS) CC
Tel 045-897150
Parochial House, Sallins, Co Kildare
Rev Paul Dempsey CC
Two-Mile-House, Naas, Co Kildare
Tel 045-876160

**PAULSTOWN**
*The Assumption, Paulstown*
*Holy Trinity, Goresbridge*
Very Rev John McEvoy PP
Goresbridge, Co Kilkenny
Tel 059-9775180

**PORTARLINGTON**
*St Michael's, Portarlington*
*St John the Evangelist, Killenard*
Very Rev Thomas Dooley PP
Portarlington, Co Laois
Tel 057-8643004
Email frtomdooley@eircom.net
Rev Thomas O'Byrne CC
Emo, Portlaoise, Co Laois
Tel 057-8646517

**PORTLAOISE**
*SS Peter and Paul, Portlaoise*
*The Assumption, The Heath*
*The Holy Cross, Ratheniska*
Email info@portlaoiseparish.ie
Website www.portlaoiseparish.ie
Rt Rev Mgr John Byrne PP, VF
Parochial House, Portlaoise, Co Laois
Tel 057-8692153
Email jmbyrne@eircom.net
Rev Jimmy O'Reilly (SPS) CC
St Mary's, Tower Hill,
Portlaoise, Co Laois
Tel 057-8621671
Rev Kevin Walsh CC
Dublin Road, Portlaoise, Co Laois
Tel 057-8622301
Email walshkev@hotmail.com

**PROSPEROUS**
*Our Lady and St Joseph, Prosperous*
Rev Pat O'Brien (SPS) CC
Curate's House, Prosperous, Co Kildare
Tel 045-868187

**RAHEEN**
*St Fintan's, Raheen*
*St Brigid's, Shanahoe*
Very Rev Jimmy Kelly PP
Raheen, Abbeyleix, Co Laois
Tel 057-8731182
Email jameskelly1@eircom.net

**RATHANGAN**
*Assumption and St Patrick*
Very Rev Gerard O'Byrne PP
Rathangan, Co Kildare
Tel 045-524316
Email gerobyrne@eircom.net

**RATHVILLY**
*St Patrick's, Rathvilly*
*St Brigid's, Talbotstown*
*Blessed Virgin Mary, Tynock*
Very Rev Michael Kelly Adm
Rathvilly, Co Carlow
Tel 059-9161114
Rev Michael Moloney CC
Kiltegan, Co Wicklow
Tel 059-6473211

**RHODE**
*St Peter's, Rhode*
*St Anne's, Croghan*
Website www.rhodeparish.ie
Very Rev P.J. McEvoy Adm
Francis Street, Edenderry, Co Offaly
Rev Gregory Corcoran CC
Rhode, Co Offaly
Tel 046-9737010

**ROSENALLIS**
*St Brigid's*
Email rosenallisparish@eircom.net
Website www.rosenallis.com
Very Rev Thomas Walshe PP
Rosenallis, Portlaoise, Co Laois
Tel 057-8628513

**ST MULLINS**
*St Moling's, Glynn*
*St Brendan's, Drummond*
Very Rev Edward Aughney PP
Glynn, St Mullins via Kilkenny
Tel 051-424563

**SALLINS**
*Our Lady of the Rosary & Guardian Angels*
Email sallinsparish@eircom.net
Very Rev Thomas McDonnell PP
Parochial House, Naas, Co Kildare
Tel 045-897703
Rev Declan Thompson (SPS) CC
Parochial House, Sallins, Co Kildare
Tel 045-897150

**STRADBALLY**
*Sacred Heart, Stradbally*
*Assumption, Vicarstown*
*St Michael, Timahoe*
Very Rev James O'Connell PP
Very Rev Seán Kelly PE, CC
Stradbally, Co Laois
Tel 057-8625132/057-8625831

**SUNCROFT**
*St Brigid's*
Email suncroftparish@eircom.net
Very Rev Barry Larkin PP
Suncroft, Curragh, Co Kildare
Tel 045-441586

**TINRYLAND**
*St Joseph's*
Website www.tinryland.ie
Very Rev Thomas Little Adm
Browneshill Avenue, Carlow
Tel 059-9131559
Email tomlittle@eircom.net
Rev Liam Morgan CC
Tinryland, Carlow
Tel 059-9131212

**TULLOW**
*Most Holy Rosary, Tullow*
*Immaculate Conception, Ardattin*
*St John the Baptist, Grange*
Email tullowparish@eircom.net
Website www.tullowparish.com
Rt Rev Mgr Brendan Byrne PP
Tullow, Co Carlow
Tel 059-9152159
Email frbrenby@eircom.net
Rev Andy Leahy CC
Tullow, Co Carlow
Tel 059-9180641
Email andyolaoithe@eircom.net

**TWO-MILE-HOUSE**
Very Rev Thomas McDonnell PP
Parochial House, Naas, Co Kildare
Tel 045-897150
Rev Paul Dempsey CC
Two-Mile-House, Naas, Co Kildare
Tel 045-876160

## INSTITUTIONS AND THEIR CHAPLAINS

**Abbeyleix District Hospital**
Very Rev Gerard Ahern PP
Tel 057-8731135

**Baltinglass District Hospital**
Very Rev Thomas Dillon PP
Tel 059-6482768

**County Hospital, Portlaoise**
Rt Rev Mgr John Byrne PP
Portlaoise, Co Laois
Tel 057-8621142

**Curragh Camp**
Rt Rev Mgr John McDonald
Tel 045-441369

**Edenderry Hospital**
Very Rev P. J. McEvoy
Tel 046-9731296

**Institute of Technology, Carlow**
Rev Martin Smith (SPS)
Tel 059-9142632

**Midlands Prison**
Rev Tom Sinnott
Tel 057-8672222
Ms Vera McHugh
Tel 057-8672221

**Portlaoise Prison**
Rev Eugene Drumm (SPS)
Tel 057-8622549

**Sacred Heart Hospital, Carlow**
Very Rev John Cummins Adm
Tel 059-9131227

**St Brigid's Hospital**
Shaen, Portlaoise, Co Laois
Rt Rev Mgr John Byrne PP
Tel 057-8621142

**St Dympna's Hospital, Carlow**
Very Rev John Cummins Adm
Tel 059-9131227

**St Fintan's Hospital, Portlaoise**
Rt Rev Mgr John Byrne PP
Dublin Road, Portlaoise, Co Laois
Tel 057-8621142

**St Vincent's Hospital, Mountmellick**
Very Rev Francis MacNamara PP, VF
Mountmellick, Co Laois
Tel 057-8624198

## PRIESTS OF THE DIOCESE ELSEWHERE

Very Rev Peter Cribbin
c/o Bishop's House, Dublin Road, Carlow
Very Rev Patrick Dunny
Wood Road, Graignamanagh, Co Kilkenny
Tel 059-9724518
Rev Paul McNamee
c/o Bishop's House, Dublin Road, Carlow
Rev Sean Maher
Irish College, Paris
Rev Mícheál Murphy
c/o Bishop's House, Dublin Road, Carlow
Rev Joe O'Neill
c/o Bishop's House, Dublin Road, Carlow
Rev Padraig Shelley
c/o Bishop's House, Dublin Road, Carlow

## RETIRED PRIESTS

Very Rev Patrick Breen PE
Timahoe, Portlaoise, Co Laois
Tel 057-8627023
Very Rev Charles Byrne
Holy Family Convent,
Newbridge, Co Kildare
Rev Denis Doyle PE, CC
77 Lakelands, Naas, Co Kildare
Tel 045-897470
Very Rev John Fingleton PE
Graiguecullen, Carlow
Tel 059-9142132
Very Rev Denis Harrington PE
Clane, Co Kildare
Tel 045-868224
Very Rev Edward Kelly PE
Rhode, Co Offaly
Tel 046-9737013
Very Rev Moling Lennon PE
364 Sundays Well, Naas, Co Kildare
Tel 045-888667
Very Rev Larry Malone PE
c/o Bishop's House, Dublin Road, Carlow
Very Rev Alphonsus Murphy PE
Carbury, Co Kildare
Tel 046-9553020
Very Rev Michael Noonan PE
Portarlington, Co Laois
Tel 057-8623431
Very Rev J. O'Connell PE
Caragh, Co Kildare
Tel 045-875602
Very Rev Sean O'Laoghaire PE
Paulstown, Gowran, Co Kilkenny
Tel 059-9726104
Very Rev Denis O'Sullivan PE
Monasterevin, Co Kildare
Tel 045-525351
Very Rev Pat Ramsbottom PE
Gorman's Cottage, Cooleragh, Co Kildare
Tel 045-890744
Very Rev Colum Swan PE
32 Cherrygrove, Naas, Co Kildare
Tel 045-856274
Very Rev John Walsh PE
Rath, Portlaoise, Co Laois
Tel 057-8626401

## RELIGIOUS ORDERS AND CONGREGATIONS

## PRIESTS

**CAPUCHINS**
Capuchin Friary, 43 Dublin Street, Carlow
Tel 0503-42543/41221 Fax 0503-42030
*Guardian:* Rev John Manley (OFMCap)
*Vicar:* Rev Michael Duffy (OFMCap)

**CARMELITES (OCARM)**
Carmelite Priory, White Abbey, Co Kildare
Tel 045-521391 Fax 045-522318
Email whiteabbey@eircom.net
*Prior:* Rev Anthony McDonald (OCarm)
*Bursar:* Rev Frederick Lally (OCarm)

**DOMINICANS**
Newbridge College,
Droichead Nua, Co Kildare
Tel 045-487200
*Prior:* Very Rev Stephen Hutchinson (OP)
Secondary School for Boys

**JESUITS**
Clongowes Wood College,
Naas, Co Kildare
Tel 045-868663/868202 Fax 045-861042
Email *(College)* reception@clongowes.ie
*(Community)* reception@clongowes.ie
*Rector:* Rev Michael Sheil (SJ)
*Headmaster:* Rev Leonard Moloney (SJ)
Boarding School for Secondary Pupils

**ST PATRICK'S MISSIONARY SOCIETY**
St Patrick's, Kiltegan, Co Wicklow
Tel 059-6473600 Fax 059-6473622
Email spsoff@iol.ie (office)
*Society Leader:* Rev Seamus O'Neill (SPS)
*Assistant Society Leader*
Rev David Walsh (SPS)
Fax *(Society Leader & Council)*
059-6473644

## BROTHERS

**CHRISTIAN BROTHERS**
Christian Brothers' House,
Friary's Road, Naas, Co Kildare
Tel 045-897884
*Commuity Leader:* Br P.J. McMahon
Community: 6

Christian Brothers' House,
Railway Street, Portlaoise, Co Laois
Tel 057-8621129
Community: 5

**DE LA SALLE BROTHERS**
St Joseph's Academy, Kildare Town
Tel 045-521788
*Headmaster:* Mr David Smyth

De La Salle Primary School, Kildare
Tel 045-521852
Headmaster: Mr Shay Nolan

**PATRICIAN BROTHERS**
Delany House, Castledermot Road,
Tullow, Co Carlow
Tel 059-9151244 Fax 059-9152063
Email patbros@iol.ie
*Superior:* Br Bosco Mulhare (FSP)
Community: 3

10 Hawthorn Drive, Tullow, Co Carlow
Tel 059-9181727 Fax 059-9181728
*Superior:* Br Camillus Regan (FSP)
Community: 2

Newbridge, Co Kildare
Tel 045-431475 Fax 045-431505
*Superior:* Br James O'Rourke (FSP)
Community: 6
Monastery National School
Tel 045-432174
Principal: Br Cormac Commins (FSP)
Patrician Secondary School
Tel 045-432410
*Principal:* Mr Patrick O'Leary

Rathmoyle, Abbeyleix, Co Laois
Tel 057-8731229
Community: 3
Scoil Mhuire Primary School
*Superior:* Br James Moran (FSP)

Patrician Brothers, Cavansheath,
Mountrath, Co Laois
Tel 057-8755964
*Superior:* Br Gerard Reburn (FSP)
Community: 2

Patrician Brothers
Shannon Road, Mountrath, Co Laois
Tel 057-8732260
*Superior:* Br Justin Madden (FSP)
Community: 2

The Irish Province has seven houses
in Kenya
*Regional Superior:* Br Peter Odvor (FSP)
Patrician Formation House,
PO Box 5064, via Eldoret, Kenya
Tel/Fax 0321-61134
Email pbroskam@africaonline.co.ke
Community: 9

## SISTERS

**BRIGIDINE SISTERS**
Brigidine Provincialate,
42 The Downs, Portlaoise, Co Laois
Tel/Fax 057-8680280
*Provincial Leader:* Sr Eileen Deegan
Community: 1

16 Mount Clare, Graguecullen, Co Carlow
Tel 059-9135869
*Contact:* Sr Maureen O'Leary
Community: 1
Education

Brigidine Convent, Tullow, Co Carlow
Tel 059-9151308
*Community Co-ordinator*
Sr Agnes Graham
Community: 10
Education, Parish Work, Pastoral Care

Brigidine Sisters, Delany Court, New
Chapel Lane, Tullow, Co Carlow
*Contact:* Sr Elizabeth Mary McDonald
Parish Work

Teach Bhríde, Tullow, Co Carlow
Tel/Fax 059-9152465
Email teachbhride@eircom.net
*Contact:* Sr Carmel McEvoy
Community: 1
Holistic education centre

11 The Rise,
Ballymurphy Road, Tullow, Co Carlow
Tel 059-9152498
*Contact:* Sr Betty McDonald
Community: 1
Education

1 Salem House,
Chantiere Gate, Portlaoise, Co Laois
Tel 057-8665516
*Contact:* Sr Kathleen Campion
Community: 1

1 Melrose, Chantiere Gate,
Portlaoise, Co Laois
Tel 057-8682743
*Contact:* Sr Angela Phelan
Adult Education

Carlow Road, Abbeyleix, Co Laois
Tel 057-8731467
Community: 2
*Contact:* Sr Mary Hiney
Parish, Adult education

Brigidine Convent, Castletown Road,
Mountrath, Co Laois
Tel 057-8732799
*Local Leader:* Sr Mary Sheedy
Community: 6
Parish and Pastoral Work

Kiln Lane, Mountrath, Co Laois
Tel 057-8732946
*Contact:* Sr Breda O'Neill
Community: 1
Community Work

Brigidine Convent,
Paulstown, Co Kilkenny
Tel 059-9726156
*Contact:* Sr Margaret Walsh
Community: 5

Solas Bhríde, 18 Dara Park, Kildare
Tel 045-522890 Fax 045-522212
*Contact:* Sr Mary Minehan
Community: 2
Education, spirituality centre

**CHARITY OF JESUS AND MARY, SISTERS OF**
Moore Abbey,
Monasterevan, Co Kildare
Tel 045-525327
*Superior:* Sr Mary-Anna Lonergan
Email maryannal@eircom.net
Community: 10
Residential centre for people with learning disability and community houses and day services

**CONGREGATION OF THE SISTERS OF MERCY**
*The Sisters of Mercy minister throughout the diocese in pastoral and social work, community development, counselling, spirituality, education and health care, answering current needs.*

St Leo's Convent of Mercy, Carlow
Tel 059-9131158 Fax 059-9142226
Community: 16

4 Pinewood Avenue,
Rathnapish, Carlow
Tel/Fax 059-9140408
Community: 4

Convent of Mercy,
Monasterevan, Co Kildare
Tel/Fax 045-525372
Community: 5

St Helen's Convent of Mercy,
Naas, Co Kildare
Tel/Fax 045-897673
Community: 4

Convent of Mercy, Rathangan, Co Kildare
Tel/Fax 045-524391
Community: 4

Convent of Mercy,
Leighlinbridge, Co Carlow
Tel 059-9721350 Fax 059-9721350
Community: 2

4 Lacken View, Naas, Co Kildare
Tel/Fax 045-874168
Community: 2

Parkmore, Baltinglass, Co Wicklow
Tel 059-6481561 Fax 059-6481561
Community: 2

59 Fr Byrne Park, Graiguecullen, Carlow
Tel/Fax 059-9141479
Community: 2

37 Lakelands, Naas, Co Kildare
Tel 045-875494 Tel 045-875496
Community: 3

9 Spring Gardens, Naas, Co Kildare
Tel 045-876013
Community: 3

**DAUGHTERS OF MARY AND JOSEPH**
3/4 Sycamore Road, Connell Drive,
Newbridge, Co Kildare
Tel 045-431842
Community: 3
Pastoral, development

**HOLY FAMILY OF BORDEAUX SISTERS**
Holy Family Convent,
Droichead Nua, Co Kildare
Tel 045-431268
*Contact:* Sr Catherine Moran
Community: 22
Retired sisters, parish work, teaching English to non-nationals, chaplaincy to secondary school

'Sonas Chríost', Moorfield Park,
Droichead Nua, Co Kildare
Tel 045-431939
*Contact:* Sr Eileen Murphy
Community: 2
Sisters involved in community and parish work

5 Glen Barrow, Ballyfin Road,
Portlaoise, Co Laois
Tel 057-8620365
*Contact Person:* The Superior
Community: 3
Pastoral care of the sick, nursing, pastoral work and counselling

**POOR CLARES**
Poor Clare Colettine Monastery,
Graiguecullen, Carlow
Email poorclarescarlow@gmail.com
*Abbess:* Sr M. Francis O'Brien
Community: 9
Perpetual adoration, contemplatives

**PRESENTATION SISTERS**
Generalate,
Monasterevin, Co Kildare
Tel 045-525335/525503 Fax 045-525209
Email adminpresevin@eircom.net
www.presentationsistersunion.org
*Congregational Leader*
Sr Terry Abraham

Presentation Sisters,
Nagle Community (Inter Provincial)
55 Kirwan Park, Mountmellick, Co Laois
Tel 057-8644005 Fax 057-8644372
Email presnagle@jmin.iol.ie
Community: 2
Justice ministry

Mount St Anne's
Retreat and Conference Centre,
Killenard, Portarlington, Co Laois
Tel 057-8626153 Fax 057-8626700
*Director:* Sr Roisin Gannon
Email msannes@iol.ie
Community: 5
Facilities available for seminars, conferences and meetings on request

Presentation Convent,
Ashbrook Gardens, Mountrath Road,
Portlaoise, Co Laois
Tel 057-8670877
*Community Leader:* Sr Maureen O'Rourke
School and counselling
Community: 10

Scoil Chroí Ró-Naofa Primary School
Tel/Fax 057-8621904
Scoil Mhuire Primary School
Tel 057-8621476
Scoil Chríost Rí Secondary School
Tel 057-8621441 Fax 057-8661437
Email scrport@eircom.net

17 Parnell Crescent, Knockmay,
Portlaoise, Co Laois
Tel 057-8620358
Community: 3
School and pastoral ministry

O'Moore Place, Portlaoise, Co Laois
Tel 057-8622919
Community: 2
School and pastoral ministry

Presentation Convent, Kildare Town
Tel 045-521481
Community: 15
*Community Leader:* Sr Cecilia Molloy
School and pastoral ministry
Scoil Bhride Naofa Primary School
Tel 045-521799 Fax 045-530653
Email sbpp@eircom.net
Presentation Secondary School
Tel 045-521654 Fax 045-521090
Email psskprincipal@eircom.net

56 Oakley Park, Tullow Road, Carlow
Tel 059-9143103
Community: 3
School ministry
Scoil Mhuire gan Smal Primary School
Tel 059-9142705 Fax 059-9140645
Email officesmns@eircom.net
Presentation College, Askea, Carlow
Tel 059-9143927 Fax 059-9140645
Email presentationcollege@eircom.net

Presentation Convent,
Bagenalstown, Co Carlow
Tel 059-9721263
Email presbagenalstown@eircom.net
*Community Leader:* Sr Kathleen Ryan
School and pastoral ministry
Community: 9
Queen of the Universe Primary School
Tel 059-9721075
Presentation/De La Salle Secondary School
Tel 059-9721860 Fax 059-9722558
Email pdlsbc@eircom.net

Presentation Convent, Bridge Street,
Mountmellick, Co Laois
Tel 057-8624129
Community: 14
*Community Leader:* Sr Elizabeth Starken
School and pastoral ministry
St Joseph's Primary School
Tel/Fax 057-8624540
Email stjosephsgns.ias@eircom.net
St Mary's Community School
Tel 057-8624220 Fax 057-8644126
Email mountmellick@eircom.net

Shalom, Kilcock, Co Kildare
Tel 01-6287018 Fax 01-6287316
Email culnacille@eircom.net
*Community Leader*
Sr Marie Ryan
Community: 34
Care of sick and elderly sisters
Scoil Choca Naofa Primary School
Tel 01-6287967
Email scoilchoca.ias@eircomm.net
Scoil Dara Secondary School
Tel 01-6287258 Fax 01-6284075
Email scoildara@eircom.net

Presentation Convent,
27 Abbeyfield, Kilcock, Co Kildare
Tel 01-6284579
Community: 4
*Community Leader:* Sr Anne Codd
Faith development, counselling and pastoral ministry

2 Wolfe Tone Court,
Mountmellick, Co Laois
Tel 057-8679481
Community: 2

**ST JOHN OF GOD SISTERS**
49 Blundell Wood, Edenderry, Co Offaly
Tel 046-9731582
Community: 1
St Mary's Primary School
Tel 0405-31424. Pupils: 606

St John of God Sisters,
1 Churchview Heights,
Edenderry, Co Offaly
Tel 046-9772717
Community: 3

St John of God Sisters,
88 Lakelands, Naas, Co Kildare
Tel 045-897056
Community: 2

## EDUCATIONAL INSTITUTIONS

**Carlow College (founded 1782)**
College Street, Carlow
Tel 059-9153200 Fax 059-9140258
Email infocc@carlowcollege.ie
Website www.carlowcollege.ie
*President*
Rt Rev Mgr Kevin O'Neill BA, MSc Ed
*Vice-President and Bursar*
Rev John McEvoy BA, STL
*Chaplain*
Rev Conn Ó Maoldhomhnaigh MA
Sr Mary Murphy (RSM) MA
*Priests on Staff*
Rev Fergus Ó Fearghaill DSS
Rev Liam Power STL
Rev Sean Maher LSS
Rev Terence Crotty (OP) PhD
Rev Fintan Morris Lic.Eccl.Hist
Rev Dermot Ryan DD

**St Mary's, Knockbeg College**
Knockbeg, Carlow
Tel 059-9142127 Fax 059-9134437
Email knockbegcollege@eircom.net
*Headmaster*
Mr Cyril Hughes
www.knockbegcollege.ie

**EDMUND RICE SCHOOLS TRUST**
St Mary's Academy, Station Road, Carlow
Tel 0503-42419 Fax 0503-30922
Email principal@cbscarlow.net
*Principal:* Mr Leo Hogan

Meanscoil Iognáid Rís, Naas, Co Kildare
Tel 045-886402/045-879587
Fax 045-881580
Email admin@naascbs.ie
Website www.naascbs.ie
*Principal:* Mr N. Merrick

St Mary's Secondary School,
Tower Hill, Portlaoise, Co Laois
Tel 0502-22849/66749
Fax 0502-61292
Email omar2@eircom.net
Website www.portlaoisecbs.20m.com
*Principal:* Mr Tony Brady

## CHARITABLE AND OTHER SOCIETIES

**Apostolic Work Society**
*President:* Mrs Carmel Shortt
Glendara, Dublin Road, Clane,
Co Kildare
Tel 045-8688420

**Community Services**
St Catherine's
Community Services Centre,
St Joseph's Road, Carlow
Tel 059-9131354

# DIOCESE OF KILLALA

PATRON OF THE DIOCESE
ST MUREDACH, 12 AUGUST

INCLUDES PORTIONS OF COUNTIES MAYO AND SLIGO

**Most Rev John Fleming DD, DCL**
Bishop of Killala;
born 16 February 1948;
ordained priest 18 June 1972;
ordained Bishop of Killala
7 April 2002

Residence: Bishop's House,
Ballina, Co Mayo
Tel 096-21518
Fax 096-70344
Email deocilala@eircom.net

## ST MUREDACH'S CATHEDRAL, BALLINA

In the lead-up to Catholic Emancipation and the erasing of restrictive laws on the building of Catholic places of worship, Killala diocese, one of the poorest in terms of resources and population, embarked on the massive project of building a new cathedral to replace the stone and thatch structure in Chapel Lane, which had served since 1740.

The project was first envisaged by the elderly Bishop Peter Waldron (1814–1835), but taken vigorously in hand by his coadjutor, Bishop John MacHale, who succeeded him for a short time before becoming Archbishop of Tuam.

In 1831 the first Mass was celebrated within the rough-hewn shell of the new cathedral. The architect was Dominick Madden, who designed Tuam cathedral. Because of financial restraints and the disruption caused by the Famine, several modifications of the design had to be made. It was not until 1853, some twenty-three years after the roofing of the main building, that work on the spire resumed. The entire work on the cathedral was completed in 1892.

The glory of the edifice is in the interior ceiling and overall design, modelled on the vaulting and ribbing of the Church of Santa Maria Sopra Minerva in Rome. The contract for the groining, plastering and stucco work was awarded to Arthur Canning, who undertook to have the bosses at the intersection of the rib mouldings, the centre over the intersections of the nave and transepts, the busts at the intersections of the groins of the naves and side aisles, and the crochets over the eastern windows 'executed by the first artists in the Kingdom'. How well he succeeded can be seen in the much-admired plasterwork of the cathedral ceiling, enhanced by the colour schemes and mosaics. The windows in the cathedral are the artistic treasuries of the building, all being the work of the Meyer studios of Munich, whose premises were destroyed by the Allied bombings in World War II.

The cathedral was completely renovated and refurbished in 2000, as part of a diocesan millennium project.

Photo: David Farrell, *The Western People*, Ballina

## CHAPTER

*Dean:* Vacant
*Chancellor:* Rt Rev Mgr Seán Killeen
*Archdeacon:* Very Rev Seán Durkan
*Members*
Very Rev Patrick Hegarty
Very Rev John McHale
Rt Rev Mgr Kevin Loftus
Rt Rev Mgr Seamus Heverin

**Honorary Canons**
Very Rev Thomas Finan
Very Rev John Flynn
Very Rev Mark Diamond
Very Rev Patrick Gallagher
Most Rev Thomas Finnegan DD, Bishop Emeritus

## ADMINISTRATION

**Vicars General**
Rt Rev Mgr Sean Killeen PP
Cloghans, Ballina, Co Mayo
Rt Rev Mgr Kevin Loftus PP
Easkey, Co Sligo
Tel 096-49011

**Vicars Forane**
Very Rev Michael Reilly PP
Very Rev Michael Harrison PP
Very Rev Gerard O'Hora
Very Rev Canon John George MacHale

**College of Consultors**
Most Rev John Fleming
Rt Rev Mgr Kevin Loftus
Rt Rev Mgr Sean Killeen
Very Rev Canon J. G. McHale
Very Rev Paddy Hoban
Very Rev Brendan Hoban
Very Rev Gerard O'Hora
Very Rev Kevin Hegarty
Rev Liam Reilly
Rev M. Gilroy

**Finance Secretary**
Right Rev Mgr Seamus Heverin
Enniscrone, Co Sligo
Tel 096-37802

**Diocesan Secretary**
Mrs Anne Forbes
Bishop's House, Ballina, Co Mayo
Tel 096-21518 Fax 096-70344
Email secretary@killaladiocese.org

## CATECHETICS EDUCATION

**Diocesan Advisers for Religious Education**
*Primary:* Sr Patricia Lynott
Convent of Jesus & Mary,
Gortnor Abbey, Crossmolina, Co Mayo
Tel 096-31395
*Post-Primary:* Vacant

**Diocesan Education Council**
*Chairman:* Mr John Cummins

## LITURGY

**Church Music**
*Director:* Ms Regina Deacy
c/o The Pastoral Centre, Ballina, Co Mayo
Tel 096-70555

**Diocesan Liturgy and Music Commission**
*Chairman:* Very Rev Michael Flynn PP
Parochial House, Knockmore,
Ballina, Co Mayo
Tel 094-58108

## PASTORAL

**Accord**
*Director:* Rev Gerard O'Hora
The Pastoral Centre, Ballina, Co Mayo
Tel 096-70555

**Building Committee**
*Chairperson:* Mgr S. Killeen

**Child Protection Committee**
*Chairperson:* Mrs Anne Fleming

**Communications**
*Directors:* Rev Gerard O'Hora,
Rev Muredach Tuffy

**Council of the Laity**
*Chairperson:* Peter McLoughlin

**Council of Priests**
*Chairperson:* Very Rev Michael Flynn PP
Knockmore, Co Mayo
Tel 094-9258108
*Secretary:* Rev Aidan O'Boyle CC
Crossmolina, Co Mayo
Tel 096-31344

**Diocesan Finance Committee**
*Chairman:* Bishop Fleming
*Secretary:* Ms Anne Forbes

**Ecumenism**
*Director:* Very Rev Anthony Gillespie PP
Templeboy, Co Sligo
Tel 096-47103

**Emigrants**
*Advisors*
Very Rev Michael Harrison PP
Ballycastle, Co Mayo
Tel 096-43010

**Immigrants**
*Diocesan Representative*
Vacant

**Legion of Mary**
Rev Kieran Holmes
Tel 096-36164

**Marriage Tribunal**
(See Marriage Tribunals section)

**Pilgrimages**
*Directors:* Rev Kieran Holmes CC
Enniscrone, Co Sligo
Tel 096-36164

**Pioneer Total Abstinence Association**
*Diocesan Director*
Very Rev Patrick Munnelly PP
Ardagh, Ballina, Co Mayo
Tel 096-31144

**Pontifical Mission Societies**
*Diocesan Director:* Rev Edward Rogan
Inver, Ballina, Co Mayo
Tel 097-84598

**Travellers**
*Chaplain:* Very Rev Michael Reilly PP
Belmullet, Co Mayo
Tel 097-81426

**Trócaire**
*Secretary:* Rev Michael Nallen
Aughoose, Ballina, Co Mayo
Tel 097-87990

**Vocations**
*Director:* Rev Muredach Tuffy
Newman Institute, Ballina, Co Mayo
Tel 096-72066

**Youth Ministry**
*Co-ordinators:* Rev Francis Judge,
Rev Muredach Tuffy

## PARISHES

**BALLINA (KILMOREMOY)**
*St Muredach's Cathedral, St Patrick's*
Very Rev Gerard O'Hora PP, VF
Cathedral Presbytery, Ballina, Co Mayo
Tel 096-71365
Rev Gabriel Rosbotham CC
Cathedral Close, Ballina, Co Mayo
Tel 096-71355
Rev Dr Michael Gilroy CC *(pro-tem)*
Cathedral Close, Ballina, Co Mayo
Tel 096-21764
Rev Martin O'Hare (SMA) CC
St Patrick's Presbytery, Ballina, Co Mayo
Tel 096-71360
*Parish Sister:* Sr Maureen McDonnell
Tel 096-23066

**BACKS**
*Christ the King*
Very Rev Michael Flynn PP
Knockmore, Ballina, Co Mayo
Tel 094-58108
*St Teresa's*
Rev Des Smith
Rathduff, Ballina, Co Mayo
Tel 096-21596

**ARDAGH**
Very Rev Patrick Munnelly PP
Ardagh, Ballina, Co Mayo
Tel 096-31144

**BALLYCASTLE (KILBRIDE AND DOONFEENY)**
*St Bridget's, St Teresa's*
Very Rev Michael Harrison PP
Ballycastle, Co Mayo
Tel 096-43010

**BALLYCROY**
*Holy Family*
Very Rev Christopher Ginnelly PP
Parochial House, Ballycroy,
Westport, Co Mayo
Tel 098-49134

**BALLYSOKEARY**
Very Rev James Corcoran PP
Cooneal, Ballina, Co Mayo
Tel 096-32242

**BELMULLET**
*Sacred Heart, Our Lady of Lourdes*
Very Rev Michael Reilly PP
Belmullet, Co Mayo
Tel 097-81426

**CASTLECONNOR**
*St Brendan's*
Very Rev Desmond Kelly PP
Corballa, Ballina, Co Mayo
Tel 096-36266

**CROSSMOLINA**
*St Tiernan's, Holy Souls,*
*Our Lady of Mercy, St Mary's*
Very Rev Francis Judge PP
Tel 096-31677
Rev Aidan O'Boyle
Tel 096-31344
Crossmolina, Ballina, Co Mayo
Rev Albert Slater CC
Keenagh, Ballina, Co Mayo
Tel 096-53018

**DROMORE-WEST (KILMACSHALGAN)**
Very Rev Gerard Gillespie PP
Dromore West, Co Sligo
Tel 096-47012

**EASKEY**
*St James's*
Rt Rev Mgr Kevin Loftus PP
Easkey, Co Sligo
Tel 096-49011

**KILCOMMON-ERRIS**
Very Rev Michael Nallen, Co-Pastor
Aughoose, Ballina, Co Mayo
Tel 097-87990
Very Rev Edward Rogan, Co-Pastor
Inver, Barnatra, Ballina
Tel 097-84598

**KILFIAN**
*Sacred Heart*
Very Rev James Corcoran Adm
Very Rev Peter O'Brien
Kilfian, Killala, Co Mayo
Tel 096-32420

**KILGLASS**
*Holy Family, Christ the King*
Very Rev Canon John George MacHale PP
Kilglass, Enniscrone, Ballina, Co Mayo
Tel 096-36191
Rev Kieran Holmes CC
Enniscrone, Ballina, Co Mayo
Tel 096-36164

**KILLALA**
*St Patrick's*
Very Rev Patrick Hoban PP
Killala, Co Mayo
Tel 096-32176

**KILMORE-ERRIS**
*St Joseph's, Holy Family, Seven Dolours*
Very Rev John Loftus, Co-Pastor
Binghamstown,
Belmullet, Co Mayo
Tel 097-82350
Rev Kevin Hegarty, Co-Pastor
Carne, Belmullet, Co Mayo
Tel 097-81011

**KILTANE**
*Sacred Heart*
*St Pius X*
Very Rev John Judge, Co-Pastor
Bangor Erris, Ballina, Co Mayo
Tel 097-83466
Very Rev James Cribben, Co-Pastor
Geesala, Bangor, Ballina, Co Mayo
Tel 097-86740

**LACKEN**
*St Patrick's*
Very Rev Brian Conlon PP
Carrowmore, Ballina, Co Mayo
Tel 096-34014

**LAHARDANE (ADDERGOOLE)**
*St Patrick's*
Very Rev John Reilly PP
Lahardane, Ballina, Co Mayo
Tel 096-51007
*St Mary's*
Rev Alan Munnelly CC
Glenhest, Newport, Co Mayo
Tel 098-41170

**MOYGOWNAGH**
*St Cormac's*
Very Rev Brendan Hoban PP
Moygownagh,
Ballina, Co Mayo
Tel 096-31288

**SKREEN AND DROMARD**
*St Adamnan's*
Very Rev Michael O'Horo PP
Skreen, Co Sligo
Tel 071-9166629

**TEMPLEBOY**
Very Rev Anthony Gillespie PP
Templeboy, Co Sligo
Tel 096-47103

## INSTITUTIONS AND THEIR CHAPLAINS

**An Coláiste**
Rossport, Ballina, Co Mayo
Tel 097-88940

**Convent of Mercy**
Belmullet, Co Mayo
Tel 097-81044
Rev Kevin Hegarty

**Convent of Jesus and Mary**
Enniscrone, Ballina, Co Mayo
Tel 096-36151
Rev Kieran Holmes CC

**Convent of Jesus and Mary**
Crossmolina, Co Mayo
Tel 096-30876/30877
Very Rev Francis Judge PP

**Distrist Hospital**
Ballina, Co Mayo
Tel 096-21166
Very Rev Brendan Hoban

**District Hospital**
Belmullet, Co Mayo
Tel 097-81301
Very Rev John Loftus

**St Mary's Secondary School**
Ballina, Co Mayo
Tel 096-70333
Rev Gerard O'Hora CC

**Vocational School**
Easkey, Co Sligo
Tel 096-49021
Rt Rev Mgr Kevin Loftus

**Vocational School**
Ballina, Co Mayo
Tel 096-21472
Rev Gabriel Rosbotham

**Vocational School**
Crossmolina, Co Mayo
Tel 096-31236
Rev Michael Reilly CC

**Vocational School**
Belmullet, Co Mayo
Tel 097-81437
Rev Michael Nallen

**Vocational School**
Lacken Cross, Co Mayo
Tel 096-32177
Very Rev Brian Conlon PP

## PRIESTS OF THE DIOCESE ELSEWHERE

Rev Martin Barrett
Saint Paul University, 223 Main Street,
Ottawa, Ontario, Canada KIS 1CU
Rev Thomas Finan
St Patrick's College,
Maynooth, Co Kildare
Tel 01-6285222
Rev Michael Gilroy *(on sabbatical leave)*
Very Rev Martin Keveny
Paroquia Sao Sebastiao,
Caixa Postal 94, CEP 77760-000
Colinas Do Tocantins, Brazil
Tel 63-8311427
Rev G. O'Donnell *(on sabbatical leave)*
Rev William Reilly
Casilla 09-01-5825, Guayaquil, Ecuador

## RETIRED PRIESTS

Very Rev Michael Cawley
Newman Institute, Ballina, Co Mayo
Very Rev Michael Conway
Barr Trá, Enniscrone, Co Sligo
Very Rev Canon Mark Diamond
Cathedral Close, Ballina, Co Mayo
Very Rev Sean Durkan
79 The Glebe, Ballina, Co Mayo
Very Rev Canon J. Flynn
Mount Falcon, Knockmore,
Ballina, Co Mayo
Most Rev Thomas Finnegan DD
Carrowmore Lacken,
Ballina, Co Mayo
Rt Rev Mgr Patrick Gallagher
Cathedral Close, Ballina
Very Rev Canon Patrick Hegarty
St Jude's Avenue, Crossmolina, Co Mayo
Rt Rev Mgr Seamus Heverin
Enniscrone, Co Sligo
Rt Rev Mgr Sean Killeen
Cloghans, Ballina, Co Mayo
Rev Sean McHugh
Bohernasup, Ballina, Co Mayo

*Retired Priests (Other Dioceses)*
Very Rev Joseph Cahill
Bohernasup, Ballina, Co Mayo
Rt Rev Mgr Patrick Fox
14 Amana Estate, Ballina, Co Mayo
Very Rev Tony Hannick
Ardnaree, Ballina, Co Mayo

## RELIGIOUS ORDERS AND CONGREGATIONS

## PRIESTS

**SPIRITUAL LIFE INSTITUTE**
Holy Hill Hermitage, Skreen, Co Sligo
Tel 071-66021
*Superior:* Rev Eric Haarer
Community: 8

## BROTHERS

**MARIST BROTHERS**
Convent Hill, Ballina, Co Mayo
Tel 096-22342
*Superior:* Br Sebastian Davis
Community: 4

## SISTERS

**CONGREGATION OF THE SISTERS OF MERCY**
Sisters of Mercy,
35 Amana Estate, Ballina, Co Mayo
Tel 096-76674 Fax 096-76675
Community: 2

Sisters of Mercy, 'Bethany',
8/9 Rockwell Estate, Killala Road,
Ballina, Co Mayo
Tel 096-23066
Community: 7

Sisters of Mercy, 11 Drom Ard,
Church Road, Belmullet, Co Mayo
Tel 097-81044 Fax 097-20737
Community: 3

Sisters of Mercy,
12 Weir Court, Ballina, Co Mayo
Tel 096-78748
Community: 1

Sisters of Mercy,
Larsyn, Bothar na Sop, Ballina, Co Mayo
Community: 2

**JESUS AND MARY, CONGREGATION OF**
Convent of Jesus and Mary,
Mullinmore Road,
Crossmolina, Co Mayo
Tel 096-30876/30877
*Contact person:* Sr Dolores McGee
*Headmistress:* Tel 096-31194/096-31597
Community: 4
Post-Primary Coeducational Day School
Tel 096-31131
Pupils: 421

Convent of Jesus and Mary,
Church Road, Enniscrone, Co Sligo
Tel 096-36151
*Superior:* Sr Goretti McGowan
Community: 6
Post-Primary, Coeducational School
Tel 096-36496
Pupils: 409

## EDUCATIONAL INSTITUTIONS

**St Muredach's College**
Ballina, Co Mayo
Tel 096-21298
*Principal:* Mr Leo Golden
Post-Primary Pupils: 400

**Newman Institute Ireland**
Centre for Pastoral Care,
Salmon Weir, Ballina, Co Mayo
Tel 096-72066
*Chancellor*
Most Rev John Fleming, DD, DCL
*Director:* Rev Muredach Tuffy

## CHARITABLE AND OTHER SOCIETIES

**Council for the West**
(Parish Renewal and Development)
Asahi Business Park, Killala, Co Mayo
Tel 096-32014

**Society of St Vincent de Paul**
Ozanam House, Teeling Street,
Ballina, Co Mayo
Tel 096-72905

**St Joseph's Young Priests Society**
c/o Pastoral Centre, Ballina, Co Mayo
Tel 096-70555

**Legion of Mary**
c/o Pastoral Centre, Ballina, Co Mayo
Tel 096-70555
Rev Kieran Holmes
Tel 096-36164

**Accord**
CMAC Centre
c/o Pastoral Centre, Ballina, Co Mayo
Tel 096-70555

# DIOCESE OF KILLALOE

PATRON OF THE DIOCESE
ST FLANNAN, 18 DECEMBER

INCLUDES PORTIONS OF COUNTIES CLARE, LAOIS, LIMERICK, OFFALY AND TIPPERARY

**Most Rev Kieran O'Reilly (SMA) DD**
Bishop of Killaloe;
born 1952;
ordained priest 17 June 1978;
ordained Bishop of Killaloe
29 August 2010

Residence:
Westbourne, Ennis, Co Clare
Tel 065-6828638
Fax 065-6842538
Email office@killaloediocese.ie
Website www.killaloediocese.ie

## CATHEDRAL OF SS PETER AND PAUL, ENNIS

The church that now serves as the cathedral of the Diocese of Killaloe was originally built to serve as the parish church of Ennis. The diocese had not had a permanent cathedral since the Reformation. In 1828, Francis Gore, a Protestant landowner, donated the site for the new Catholic church. Dominick Madden, who also designed the cathedrals in Ballina and Tuam, was chosen as the architect.

The construction of the new church was a protracted affair. Shortly after the work began, the project ran into financial difficulties and was suspended for three years. Aided by generous donations from local Protestants, including Sir Edward O'Brien of Dromoland and Vesey Fitzgerald, the work began again in 1831. Progress was slow throughout the 1830s and there were many problems. In September 1837 there was a serious accident on the site when the scaffolding collapsed, killing two and seriously injuring two more. Finally, in 1842, the roof was on and the parish priest, Dean O'Shaughnessy, was able to say the first Mass inside the still-unfinished building.

On 26 February 1843, the new church was blessed and placed under the patronage of Saints Peter and Paul, by Bishop Patrick Kennedy. Fr Matthew, 'The Apostle of Temperance', preached the sermon.

Much still remained to be done on the project, but the Great Famine brought the work to a halt. After the Famine, the work recommenced. J. J. McCarthy, one of the leading church architects in nineteenth-century Ireland, was commissioned to oversee the interior decoration of the building. Much of this is still visible, including the internal pillars and arches and the organ gallery.

A local committee decided in 1871 to complete the tower and spire, but owing to financial difficulties, it was not until 23 October 1874 that the final stone was put in place.

In 1889 Dr Thomas McRedmond was appointed coadjutor bishop and he was consecrated in 1890. He had full charge of the diocese, owing to the illness of Bishop Flannery. Though he was already Parish Priest of Killaloe, the new bishop chose to make Ennis his home, remaining there after he succeeded to the office of diocesan bishop, on the death of Dr Flannery. The Parish Church of Ss Peter and Paul was thus designated the pro-cathedral of the diocese.

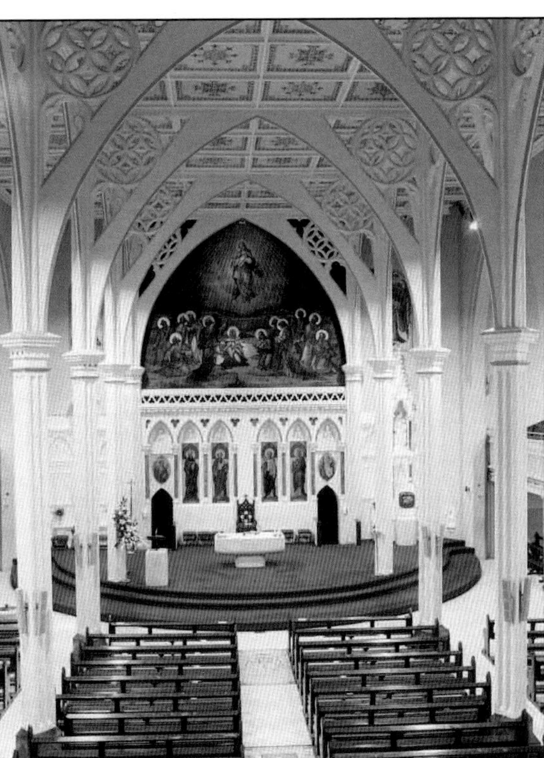

Major renovations were carried out in 1894. The present main entrance under the tower was constructed, a task that necessitated breaking through a six-foot-thick wall. The building was also redecorated. The improvements were under the direction of Joshua Clarke, father of the stained-glass artist Harry Clarke. The large painting of the Ascension, which dominates the sanctuary, the work of the firm Nagle and Potts, was also installed at this time. The building remained largely unchanged for the next eighty years. A new sacristy and chapter room were added in the 1930s, as were the pipe organ and chapter stalls for the canons.

Another major renovation was carried out in 1973 to bring the building into line with the requirements of the Second Vatican Council. The architect for the work was Andrew Devane and the main contractors were Ryan Brothers, Ennis. The artistic adviser was Enda King. The building was reopened after six months in December 1973. The Clare Champion reported: 'The main features of the renovation included new altar, ambo, new tabernacle on granite pillar, baptismal font located near sanctuary, new flooring. New heating system, new amplification system and complete reconstruction of the sanctuary.'

In 1990, 163 years after work on the building began, Bishop Harty named it his cathedral. The solemn dedication of the cathedral and the altar took place on 18 November 1990. A fire at a shrine in the cathedral in October 1995 caused serious internal damage. The sanctuary had to be rebuilt and the building redecorated. The restoration was celebrated with Solemn Evening Prayer in November 1996.

In 2006 major repair and refurbishment was completed on the Cathedral spire.

**Most Rev William Walsh DD**
Retired Bishop of Killaloe;
born 1935; ordained priest 21 February 1959; ordained Bishop of Killaloe 2 October 1994
*Residence:* Westbourne, Ennis, Co Clare
Tel 065-6828638 Fax 065-6842538

## CHAPTER

*Dean:* Vacant
*Archdeacon:* Venerable John F. Hogan AP
Ballycommon, Nenagh, Co Tipperary
*Chancellor:* Very Rev Brendan O'Donoghue, Shannon
*Precentor:* Very Rev Patrick O'Brien
Tuamgraney, Co Clare
*Treasurer:* Very Rev Patrick Taaffe, Ennis
*Members*
Very Rev Reuben Butler, Newmarket-on-Fergus
Very Rev Caimin O'Carroll, Barefield
Very Rev Seamus Mullin, Miltown Malbay

## COLLEGE OF CONSULTORS

Very Rev Seamus Gardiner
Rev Michael Sheedy
Rev Sean Sexton
Rev Tom Ryan
Rev David Carroll
Rev Brendan Quinlivan
Rev Ger Nash

## ADMINISTRATION

**Killaloe Diocesan Office**
*Diocesan Secretary (part-time)*
Rev Ger Nash
*Diocesan Financial Administrator*
Mr John Lillis
Email jlillis@killaloediocese.ie
*Diocesan Office Administrator*
Ms Margaret Flynn
*Secretarial:* Ms Mary Brohan
Westbourne, Ennis, Co Clare
Tel 065-6828638 Fax 065-6842538
Email office@killaloediocese.ie
*Education Secretary:* Rev Gerry Kenny
Westbourne, Ennis, Co Clare
Tel 085-7858344
Sr Marie McNamara
Parish Pastoral Office,
c/o Westbourne, Ennis, Co Clare
Tel 065-6842235
Email kpastoral5@eircom.net

**Vicars General**
Very Rev Seamus Gardiner PP
Portroe, Nenagh, Co Tipperary
Tel 067-23105
Rev Michael Sheedy PP
Kilrush, Co Clare
Tel 065-9051093

**Vicars Forane & Moderators of Clusters**
*Inis Cathaigh:* Rev John Kelly PP
Labasheeda, Co Clare
Tel 065-6830126
*South-East Clare:* Rev Pat Greed PP
Clonlara, Co Clare
Tel 061-354594
*Mid Clare:* Very Rev Pat Larkin
Mullagh, Co Clare
Tel 065-7087012
*Abbey:* Rev Tom Hogan
Cathedral, Ennis, Co Clare
Tel 065-6824043
*Imeall Boirne:* Rev Ger Nash
Crusheen, Co Clare
Tel 065-6827113
*Tradaree:* Rev Arnold Rosney
5 Drumgeely Avenue, Shannon, Co Clare
*East Clare:* Very Rev John Jones PP
Mountshannon, Co Clare
Tel 061-927213
*Odhrán:* Rev Brendan Moloney
Silvermines, Co Tipperary
Tel 067-25864
*Cronan:* Rev Michael Harding
Templemore Road, Roscrea
Tel 0505-21218
*Cois Deirge:* Rev Michael Cooney
Terryglass, Co Tipperary
Tel 067-22017

**Finance Committee**
*Chairman:* Mr Aidan Spooner
*Recording Secretary:* Mr John Lillis
Bishop Kieran O'Reilly (SMA)
Mr David Williams
Rev Gerard Kenny
Ms Teresa Felle
Canon Caimin O'Carroll
Mr Owen Smyth
Mr Des Leahy

**Killaloe Priests' Benevolent Fund**
*Secretary:* Mr John Lillis
c/o Westbourne, Ennis, Co Clare
Tel 065-6828638

**Killaloe Priests' Subsidy Fund**
*Secretary:* Mr John Lillis
c/o Westbourne, Ennis, Co Clare
Tel 065-6828638

**Killaloe Priests' Hospital Fund**
*Secretary:* Mr John Lillis
c/o Westbourne, Ennis, Co Clare
Tel 065-6828638 Fax 065-6842538

**Diocesan Archivist**
c/o Diocesan Secretary
Westbourne, Ennis, Co Clare
Tel 065-6828638

**Diocesan Secretary (part-time)**
Rev Ger Nash
c/o Westbourne, Ennis, Co Clare
Tel 065-6828638

**Episcopal Vicars for Retired Priests**
Very Rev Tim O'Brien PP
Carrigatoher, Nenagh, Co Tipperary
Tel 067-31231
Very Rev Joe Hourigan PP
Lissycasey, Co Clare
Tel 065-6834145

## CATECHETICS EDUCATION

**Boards of Management**
*Primary Schools:* St Senan's Education Office, Limerick Diocesan Office, Social Service Centre, Henry Street, Limerick
Tel 061-317743
*Director:* Fiona Shanley

**Religious Education in Primary Schools**
*Directors:* Sr Essie Hayes
Ashe Road, Nenagh, Co Tipperary
Tel 067-33835
Mr Joe Searson
Mullagh, Co Clare
Tel 065-7087875/087-6762023
Rev Anthony McMahon CC
Parochial House, Nenagh, Co Tipperary
Tel 067-37134

**Religious Education in Post-Primary Schools**
*Directors:* Rev Tom Hogan Adm
The Cathedral Presbytery,
Ennis, Co Clare
Tel 065-6824043
Sr Marie McNamara
Pastoral Office, Westbourne,
Ennis, Co Clare
Tel 065-6842235/086-8373922

## PASTORAL

**Parish Pastoral Office**
c/o Westbourne, Ennis, Co Clare
Tel 065-6842235
*Diocesan/Parish Resource Person*
Sr Mary Nash
Feighroe, Connolly, Ennis, Co Clare
Tel 065-6839339

**Pastoral Office and Biblical Ministry**
Sr Marie McNamara
c/o Killaloe Diocesan Office,
Westbourne, Ennis, Co Clare
Tel 065-6842235
Email kpastoral5@eirccom.net
*Pastoral Worker – West Clare Parishes*
Ms Maureen Kelly

**Diocesan Pastoral Council**
*Chairperson:* Mr Leonard Cleary
Ballyportry, Corofin, Co Clare
*Secretary:* Ms Margaret Flynn
Westbourne, Ennis, Co Clare

**Accord**
*Director:* Rev Tom Fitzpatrick
Ennis Accord Centre, c/o Clarecare,
Harmony Row, Ennis, Co Clare
Tel 1850-585000
*Director:* Very Rev W. Teehan
Nenagh Centre, Loretto House,
Kenyon Street,
Nenagh, Co Tipperary
Tel 067-31272

**CURA**
Barrack Street, Ennis, Co Clare
Tel 065-6829905/1850-58-5000

**Communications**
*Director:* Rev Brendan Quinlivan
c/o Bishop's House, Westbourne,
Ennis, Co Clare
Tel 065-6828638/061-924035

**Child Protection Committee**
*Chairperson:* Rev Pat Malone
Killaloe, Co Clare
*Delegates:* Rev Pat Malone
Tel 086-8096074
Mrs Christina Lemass
Tel 086-8096027

**Council of Priests**
*Chairperson:* Very Rev Michael Sheedy PP
Kilrush, Co Clare
Tel 065-9051093
*Secretary:* Rev David Carroll
Birr, Co Offaly
Tel 057-9120097

**Ecumenism**
*Director:* Very Rev Tom Corbett
Roscrea, Co Tipperary

**Lourdes Pilgrimage**
*Director:* Very Rev Tom Ryan PP
Shannon, Co Clare
Tel 061-361257

**Marriage Tribunal**
(See Marriage Tribunals section)

**Pastoral Care of Immigrants**
Sr Maureen Haugh
c/o Bishop's House, Westbourne, Ennis, Co Clare
Tel 065-6828638

**Pioneer Total Abstinence Association**
Diocesan Director
Very Rev Michael McInerney AP
Quin, Co Clare
Tel 065-6825649

**Polish Chaplain**
Rev Tomasz Daukszewicz
Cathedral Presbytery, Ennis, Co Clare
Tel 087-0515788

**Pontifical Mission Societies**
*Diocesan Director*
Very Rev Tom O'Halloran
Borrisokane, Co Tipperary
Tel 067-27105

**Ceifin, Centre for Values Led Change**
*Founder/Director*
Rev Harry Bohan BA, MScEcon
Westgate Business Park, Ennis, Co Clare
Tel 065-6824094

**Social Services**
North Tipperary Community Services
Kenyon Street, Nenagh, Co Tipperary
Tel 067-31800
Clarecare
Harmony Row, Ennis, Co Clare
Tel 065-6828178

**Travellers**
*Chaplain*
c/o Bishops House, Westbourne, Ennis, Co Clare
Tel 065-6828638

**Vocations**
*Director:* Rev Ignatius McCormack
St Flannan's College, Ennis, Co Clare
Tel 065-6828019/086-2777139

## PARISHES

*Parishes follow in cluster order. Historical names are given in parentheses. Church titulars are in italics.*

**ABBEY CLUSTER**
***Ennis***
*Cathedral: SS Peter & Paul*
Very Rev Tom Hogan Adm
Tel 065-6869097/087-6446410
Rev Ger Fitzgerald CC
Tel 065-6824043/086-1697595
Rev Tomasz Daukszewicz
Tel 065-6824043/087-0515788
Cathedral Presbytery, Ennis, Co Clare
Tel 065-6824043 Fax 065-6842541
Rev Fergal O'Neill CC
10 Beechwood, Lissane, Clarecastle, Co Clare
Tel 087-6615975
*St Joseph's, Lifford*
Very Rev John McGovern Adm
Tel 065-6822166/086-3221210
St Joseph's Presbytery, 52 Kincora Park, Lifford, Ennis, Co Clare
*Christ the King, Cloughleigh*
Rev Tom O'Gorman CC
Tel 065-6840715/087-2285355
Cloughleigh Presbytery, 1 Shallee Drive, Cloughleigh, Ennis, Co Clare
Tel 065-6840715/087-2285355
Rev Pat Taaffe AP
3 Cottage Gardens, Ennis, Co Clare
Tel 065-6891983/086-1731070
Rev Paddy Conway AP
Wesbourne, Ennis, Co Clare
Tel 065-6849818/087-6831992
*Parish Sisters:* Sr Ann Boland
Tel 065-6844742/087-1369517
Sr de Montfort
Tel 065-6828024/086-1993838

***Clarecastle (Clare Abbey)***
*SS Peter & Paul, Clarecastle*
*St John the Baptist, Ballyea*
Very Rev Harry Brady PP
Church Drive, Clarecastle, Co Clare
Tel 065-6823011/086-2349798

***Quin***
*St Mary, Quin*
*St Stephen, Maghera*
*Pope John XXIII Memorial Church, Clooney*
Very Rev Michael Collins PP
Parish House, Quin, Co Clare
Tel 065-6825612/086-3475085
Very Rev Michael McInerney AP
Quin, Co Clare
Tel 065-6825649

***Doora and Kilraghtis***
*St Brecan, Doora*
*The Immaculate Conception, Barefield*
Rev Jerry Carey
Tig an tSagairt, 3 The Woods, Cappahard, Tulla Road, Ennis, Co Clare
Tel 065-6822225/086-2508444
Very Rev Caimin Canon O'Carroll AP
Barefield, Ennis, Co Clare
Tel 065-6821190/087-2521388

**INIS CHATHAIGH CLUSTER**
***Carrigaholt & Cross (Kilballyowen)***
*Blessed Virgin Mary, Carrigaholt*
*The Holy Spirit, Doonaha*
*Our Lady of Lourdes, Cross*
*St John the Baptist, Kilbaha*
Very Rev Michael Casey PP
Cross, Co Clare
Tel 065-9058008/086-0842216
Very Rev Patrick Culligan AP
Carrigaholt, Co Clare
Tel/Fax 065-9058043 Tel 087-9863865

***Doonbeg (Killard) & Kilkee***
*Our Lady Assumed into Heaven, Doonbeg*
*St Senan, Bealaha*
*The Immaculate Conception & St Senan, Kilkee*
*St Flannan, Lisdeen*
Very Rev Gerry Kenny PP
Circular Road, Kilkee, Co Clare
Tel 065-9056580
Very Rev Joe Haugh AP
Bealaha, Doonbeg, Co Clare
Tel 065-9055022/087-2865434
Kilkee Parish Office, Circular Road, Kilkee, Co Clare
Email office@kilkeeparish.com
www.kilkeeparish.com

***Killimer & Kilrush***
*St Senan, Kilrush*
*St Senan, Knockerra*
*St Imy, Killimer*
*Little Senan Church, Monmore*
Very Rev Michael Sheedy PP
Toler Street, Kilrush, Co Clare
Tel 065-9051093/086-26203314
Rev Martin Blake CC
O'Gorman Street, Kilrush, Co Clare
Tel 065-9051016/087-9033682

***Cooraclare (Kilmacduane) & Kilmurry McMahon***
*St Senan, Cooraclare*
*St Mary, Cree*
*St Mary, Kilmurry McMahon*
*St Kerin, Labasheeda*
Very Rev John Kelly PP
Labasheeda, Co Clare
Tel 065-6830126/087-2439273
Very Rev Patrick Carmody AP
Cooraclare, Co Clare
Tel 065-9059010/086-3017371
Very Rev Peter O'Loughlin AP
Kilmihil, Co Clare

***Kilmihil***
*St Michael*
Very Rev Peter O'Loughlin PP
Kilmihil, Co Clare
Tel 065-9050016/086-8250016

***Pastoral Assistant, Inis Chathaigh Parishes***
Ms Maureen Kelly
Pastoral Office, Youth Centre, Kilrush, Co Clare
Tel 065-9062565/087-2890942

**IMEALL BÓIRNE CLUSTER**
***Corofin***
*St Brigid, Corofin*
*St Joseph, Kilnaboy*
*St Mary, Rath*
Rev Damien Nolan
1a Laghtagoona, Corofin, Co Clare
Tel 065-6837178/086-8396636

***Crusheen (Inchicronan)***
*St Cronan, Crusheen*
*The Immaculate Conception, Ballinruan*
Rev Ger Nash
Parochial House, Crusheen, Co Clare
Tel 065-6827113/086-8576153

***Dysart & Ruan***
*St Mary's, Ruan*
*St Tola, Dysart*
Rev Pat O'Neill
Ruan, Co Clare
Tel 065-6827799/086-2612124

***Tubber (Kilkeedy)***
*St Michael, Tubber*
*All Saints, Boston*
Rev Brian Geoghegan
Tubber, Co Clare
Tel 091-633124/087-2387067

### BRENDAN CLUSTER

***Birr***
*St Brendan, Birr*
*Our Lady of the Annunciation, Carrig*
Very Rev David Carroll PP
Tel 086-3467909
Rev Patrick Gilbert (Chaplain)
Tel 087-2431956
The Presbytery, John's Mall,
Birr, Co Offaly
Very Rev Tony Cahir AP
5 Woodlands Park, Birr, Co Offaly
Tel 057-9120097/086-2612121
Rev Michael Reddan (SVD)
The Presbytery, John's Mall,
Birr, Co Offaly
Tel 057-9121757/087-7599789

***Kilcolman***
*St Colman, Kilcolman*
*St Ita, Coolderry*
*St John, Ballybritt*
Very Rev Kieran Blake PP
Kilcolman, Sharavogue, Birr, Co Offaly
Tel/Fax 057-9120812/087-9302214

***Kinnitty***
*St Flannan, Kinnitty*
*St Luna, Cadamstown*
*St Finan Cam, Longford*
*St Molua, Roscomroe*
Very Rev Michael O'Meara PP
Kinnitty, Birr, Co Offaly
Tel 057-9137021/087-7735977

***Shinrone***
*St Mary, Shinrone*
*St Patrick, The Pike*
Very Rev Frank Meehan PP
Tel 0505-47167/087-2302413
Very Rev Francis Bergin AP
Tel 0505-47133
Shinrone, Co Offaly

### CRONAN CLUSTER

***Roscrea***
*St Cronan, Roscrea*
*St John the Baptist, Camblin*
Very Rev Tom Corbett PP
Convent Hill, Roscrea, Co Tipperary
Tel 0505-21108/086-8418570
Rev Pat Treacy CC
0505-21370/087-9798643
Rev Lorcan Kenny
Tel 0505-23637/087-6553402
Curate's House, Convent Hill,
Roscrea, Co Tipperary
Rev Michael Harding CC
Templemore Road, Roscrea, Co Tipperary
Tel 0505-21218/086-2491941

***Kyle and Knock***
*St Molua, Ballaghmore*
*St Patrick, Knock*
Service provided by priests of Roscrea Parish

***Dunkerrin***
*SS Mary & Joseph, Dunkerrin*
*St Joseph, Moneygall*
*Sacred Heart, Barna*
Very Rev Joe Kennedy PP
Monegall, Virr, Co Offaly
Tel 0505-45982/086-4072488
Rev Pat Deely
Dunkerrin, Birr, Co Offaly
Tel 0505-45982/086-8330225

***Bournea (Couraganeen)***
*St Patrick, Bournea*
*St Brigid, Clonakenny*
Service provided by priests of Roscrea Parish
Very Rev Noel Kennedy AP
Bournea, Roscrea, Co Tipperary
Tel 0505-43211/086-3576775

### COIS DEIRIGE CLUSTER

***Borrisokane***
*SS Peter & Paul, Borrisokane*
*St Michael the Archangel, Aglish*
Very Rev Tom O'Halloran PP
Borrisokane, Co Tipperary
Tel 067-27105
Rev J. J. Rodgers CC
Borrisokane, Co Tipperary
Tel 067-27140

***Cloughjordan***
*St Michael & St John, Cloughjordan*
*St Flannan, Ardcroney*
*St Ruadhán, Kilruane*
Rev Tom Whelan PP
Templemore Road, Cloughjordan,
Co Tipperary
Tel 0505-42266/087-2730299
Very Rev Enda Burke AP
Cloughjordan, Co Tipperary
Tel 0505-42120

***Lorrha and Dorrha***
*St Ruadhan, Lorrha*
*Our Lady Queen of Ireland, Rathcabbin*
*Redwood Church*
Very Rev Pat Mulcahy PP
Lorrha, Nenagh, Co Tipperary
Tel 090-9747009/087-6329913
Very Rev John Donnelly AP
Rathcabbin, Roscrea, Co Tipperary
Tel 057-9139072

***Portroe (Castletown Arrha)***
*Blessed Virgin Mary*
Very Rev Seamus Gardiner AP
Portroe, Nenagh, Co Tipperary
Tel 067-23105/086-8392741

***Puckane (Cloughprior and Monsea)***
*Our Lady & St Patrick, Puckane*
*St Mary's Church, Carrig*
Very Rev John Slattery PP
Puckane, Nenagh, Co Tipperary
Tel 067-24105/087-2794577
Archdeacon John F. Hogan AP
Ballycommon, Nenagh, Co Tipperary
Tel 067-24153/087-7536526

***Kilbarron and Terryglass***
*Immaculate Conception, Terryglass*
*St Barron, Kilbarron*
Very Rev Michael Cooney PP
Terryglass, Co Tipperary
Tel 067-22017/087-6548331
Email terryglasskilbarron@gmail.com

***Youghalarra (Burgess and Youghal)***
*Holy Spirit, Youghalarra*
*The Immaculate Conception, Ballywilliam*
Very Rev Timothy O'Brien PP
Carrigatoher, Nenagh, Co Tipperary
Tel 067-31231/087-2623922
Very Rev Edmund Kennedy AP
Newtown, Nenagh, Co Tipperary
Tel 067-23103

### TRADAREE CLUSTER

***Shannon***
*The Immaculate Mother of God, Shannon*
*SS John & Paul, Shannon*
Very Rev Tom Ryan PP
SS John & Paul Presbytery,
4 Dun na Rí, Shannon, Co Clare
Tel 061-364133/087-2349816
Rev Arnold Rosney CC
5 Drumgeely Avenue, Shannon, Co Clare
Tel 061-471513/087-8598710
Very Rev Canon Brendan O'Donoghue AP
12 Tullyglass Square, Shannon, Co Clare
Tel 061-361257/086-8308153
Email office@shannonparish.ie
www.shannonparish.ie

***Sixmilebridge***
*St Finaghta, Sixmilebridge*
*St Mary's, Kilmurry*
Very Rev Harry Bohan PP
172 Drumgeely Hill, Shannon, Co Clare
Tel 061-713682/086-8223362
*Parish Office:* The Green,
Sixmilebridge, Co Clare
Tel 061-713682

***Newmarket-on-Fergus***
*BVM of the Rosary, Newmarket-on-Fergus*
*Our Lady of the Wells*
*St Conaire, Carrygarry*
Very Rev Tom Fitzpatrick PP
Tel 061-700883/087-2720187
Very Rev Reuben Canon Butler AP
Tel 061-368433/087-2425390
Newmarket-on-Fergus, Co Clare

### ODHRÁN CLUSTER

***Nenagh***
*St Mary of the Rosary, Nenagh*
*St John the Baptist, Tyone*
Very Rev Pat Malone PP
'Maryville', Church Street,
Nenagh, Co Tipperary
Tel 067-37130

Rev Gerard Jones CC
Tel 067-37131/087-2137238
Rev Dan Fitzgerald (SSC)
Tel 067-37132
Rev Anthony McMahon CC
Tel 067-37134/086-8243801
The Presbytery, Nenagh,
Co Tipperary
Tel 067-31272
Very Rev Tom Seymour AP
Church Road, Nenagh,
Co Tipperary
Tel 067-31831/087-2889055
Sr Clare Slattery, Parish Sister
Tel 067-31357/086-8349120
*Parish Office:* 067-37136

***Silvermines***
*Our Lady of Lourdes, Silvermines*
*Our Lady of the Wayside, Ballinaclough*
Very Rev Brendan Moloney PP
Silvermines, Nenagh, Co Tipperary
Tel 067-25864/087-2907705

***Killanave and Templederry***
*Immaculate Conception, Templederry*
*Our Lady of the Wayside, Killeen*
*Our Lady of the Wayside, Curreeney*
Very Rev Willie Teehan PP
Templederry, Co Tipperary
Tel 0504-52988/087-2347927
Very Rev Leo Long AP
Killeen, Ballinaclough,
Nenagh, Co Tipperary
Tel 067-25870/086-8353388

***Toomevara***
*St Joseph, Toomevara*
*St Joseph, Ballinree*
*St Joseph, Gortagarry*
*St Joseph, Grennanstown*
Rev William McCormack PP
Toomevara, Co Tipperary
Tel 067-26023/087-4168855

**EAST CLARE CLUSTER**

***Ogonnelloe & Bodyke (Kilnoe and Tuamgraney)***
*St Molua, Ogonnelloe*
*St Mary, Ballybrohan*
*Our Lady Assumed into Heaven, Bodyke*
*St Joseph, Tuamgraney*
Very Rev Donagh O'Meara PP
Ballyheafey, Killaloe, Co Clare
Tel 061-376766/087-2322140
Very Rev Canon Patrick O'Brien AP
Tuamgraney, Co Clare
Tel 061-921056/087-4189208

***Feakle & Killanena-Flagmount***
*St Mary, Feakle*
*St Joseph, Kilclarin*
*St Mary, Killanena*
*St Mary, Flagmount*
Very Rev Brendan Quinlivan PP
Scariff, Co Clare
Very Rev James O'Brien
Feakle, Co Clare
Tel 061-924035/087-2665793

***Mountshannon (Clonrush)***
*St Caimin, Mountshannon*
*St Flannan, Whitegate*
Very Rev John Jones PP
St Caimin's, Mountshannon, Co Clare
Tel 061-927213/086-1933479

***Scariff (Moynoe)***
*Sacred Heart, Scariff*
*St Mary, Clonusker*
Very Rev Brendan Quinlivan PP
Scariff, Co Clare
Tel 061-921013/087-2736310

***Tulla***
*SS Peter & Paul, Tulla*
*The Immaculate Conception, Drumcharley*
*St James, Knockjames*
Very Rev Martin O'Brien PP
Newline, Tulla, Co Clare
Tel 065-6835117/087-2504075
Rev Brendan Lawlor CC
2 Powerscourt, Tulla, Co Clare
Tel 065-6835284/087-9845417

**MID-CLARE CLUSTER**

***Ballynacally (Clondegad)***
*Our Lady of the Wayside, Lissycasey*
*Christ the King, Ballynacally*
Very Rev Joseph Hourigan PP
Lissycasey, Ennis, Co Clare
Tel 065-6834145/086-8170700
Very Rev Tom O'Dea AP
Ballynacally, Co Clare
Tel 065-6838135/086-8107475

***Kilnamona (Inagh)***
*Immaculate Conception, Inagh*
*The Blessed Virgin Mary, Cloonanaha*
*St Joseph, Kilnamona*
Very Rev Sean Sexton PP
Kilnamona, Ennis, Co Clare
Tel 065-6829507/087-2621884

***Kildysart & Coolmeen (Kilfidane)***
*St Benedict, Coolmeen*
*St Mary, Cranny*
*St Michael, Kildysart*
Very Rev Colm Hogan PP
Kildysart, Co Clare
Tel 065-6832155/086-3011530

***Inch and Kilmaley***
*St John the Baptist, Kilmaley*
*Our Lady of the Wayside, Inch*
*St Michael the Archangel, Connolly*
Very Rev Michael McLaughlin PP
Airfield, Inch, Ennis, Co Clare
Tel 065-6839332/086-2213025
Rev Ignatius McCormack *(Assistant Priest)*
Tel 065-6839039/086-2777139

***Miltown Malbay (Kilfarboy)***
*St Joseph, Miltown Malbay*
*St Mary, Moy*
Very Rev Seán Murphy PP
Tel 065-7084129
Very Rev Canon Seamus Mullin AP
Tel 065-7084003
Miltown Malbay, Co Clare

***Mullagh (Kilmurray-Ibickane)***
*Our Lady, Star of the Sea, Quilty*
*St Mary, Mullagh*
*The Most Holy Redeemer, Coore*
Very Rev Pat Larkin PP
Carhuligane, Mullagh, Ennis, Co Clare
Tel 065-7087012/087-2300627
Email office@kibparish.ie
www.kibparish.ie

**SCÁTH NA SIONNAINE CLUSTER**

***Broadford***
*St Peter, Broadford*
*St Mary, Kilbane*
*St Joseph, Kilmore*
Very Rev John Bane PP
Parochial House, Broadford, Co Clare
Tel 061-473123/086-8246555

***Castleconnell***
*St Joseph, Castleconnell*
*St Patrick, Ahane*
Very Rev Brendan Kyne PP
The Spa, Castleconnell, Co Limerick
Tel 061-377170/087-2025038
Very Rev James Minogue AP
Castleconnell, Co Limerick
Tel 061-377166/087-6228674

***Clonlara (Doonas and Truagh)***
*St Senan, Clonlara*
*Mary, the Mother of God, Truagh*
Very Rev Pat Greed PP
18 Churchfield, Clonlara, Co Clare
Tel 061-354594/086-6067003
Very Rev Brendan Cleary AP
17 Churchfield, Clonlara, Co Clare
Tel 061-354028/086-8484550

***Killaloe***
*St Flannan, Killaloe*
*St Thomas, Bridgetown*
*Sacred Heart & St Lua, Garraunboy*
Very Rev James Grace PP
Killaloe, Co Clare
Tel 061-376137/087-6843315
Rev Noel Hayes (SPS) CC
Bridgetown, Co Clare
Tel 061-377158

***O'Callaghan's Mills***
*St Patrick's, O'Callaghan's Mills*
*St Senan, Kilkishen*
*St Vincent de Paul, Oatfield*
Very Rev Donal Dwyer
O'Callaghan's Mills, Co Clare
Tel 065-6835148/086-1050090

## INSTITUTIONS AND THEIR CHAPLAINS

**Carrigoran House**
Newmarket-on-Fergus, Co Clare
Tel 061-368100
Very Rev Tom Fitzpatrick
Tel 061-471406

**Community Hospital**
Kilrush, Co Clare
Tel 065-9051966
Very Rev Michael Sheedy PP, VG

**General Hospital, Ennis**
Acute Psychiatric Unit
Tel 065-6863218
Very Rev Tom Hogan Adm
Tel 065-6824043

**Cahercalla Community Hospital and Hospice**
Cahercalla, Ennis, Co Clare
Rev Tom Hogan
Tel 065-6824388

**Community Nursing Unit, Birr**
Co Offaly
Tel 057-9123200
Very Rev Anthony Cahir PP

**County Hospital, Nenagh**
Co Tipperary
Tel 067-31491
Very Rev Pat Malone PP

**District Hospital, Raheen**
Tuamgraney, Co Clare
Tel 061-923007
Rev Donagh O'Meara

**St Joseph's Hospital**
Ennis, Co Clare
Tel 065-6840666
Very Rev John McGovern Adm

**Welfare Home, Nenagh**
Co Tipperary
Tel 067-31893
Very Rev Pat Malone PP

**Welfare Home, Roscrea**
Co Tipperary
Tel 0505-21389
Very Rev Tom Corbett PP

**Regina House**
Kilrush, Co Clare
Tel 065-9051209
Very Rev Michael Sheedy PP, VG

**Community School, Roscrea**
Co Tipperary
Tel 0505-21454
Rev Lorcan Kenny

**St Anne's Community College**
Killaloe, Co Clare
Tel 061-376257
Veronica Molloy

**St Brendan's Community School**
Birr, Co Offaly
Tel 0509-20510
Rev Patrick Gilbert

**St Caimin's Community School**
Shannon, Co Clare
Tel 061-364211
Cora Guinnane

**Kilrush Community School**
Tel 065-9051359
Sr Margaret Pepper

**St Joseph's Community College**
Kilkee, Co Clare
Tel 065-9056138
Mrs Ann Healy

**St Patrick's Comprehensive School**
Shannon, Co Clare
Tel 061-361428
Nuala Murray

**Kiladysart Community College**
Co Clare
Tel 065-6832300
Joanne O'Brien

## PRIESTS OF THE DIOCESE ELSEWHERE

Rev Tony Casey
Padres de San Columbano,
Apartado 39-073/074, Lima 39, Peru
Rev Michael Collins
St Patrick's College, Maynooth,
Co Kildare
Tel 01-7084700/087-6389847
Rev Pat Cotter
c/o Killaloe Diocesan Office
Rev Neil Dargan
Presbytery No. 4, Dunmanus Road,Cabra West, Dublin 7
Tel 01-8380181
Rev Tom Hannon
Institute of St Anselm, Norfolk Road,
Cliftonville, Kent CT9 2EU, UK
Tel 0044-1843234704
Rev Pascal Hanrahan CF (RC)
20 Portal Road, Javelin Barracks, 41372
Niederkuruchten, Germany
Tel 0049-1722189793
Rev Maurice Harmon
Faculty of Education,
Mary Immaculate College,
South Circular Road, Limerick
Tel 061-774720
Rev Des Hillery
Padres de San Columbano,
Apartado 39-073/074, Lima 39, Peru
Rev Michael Hogan
c/o Killaloe Diocesan Office
Rev Seamus Horgan
Apostolic Nunciature, En Suisse,
Thunstrasse 60, Case Postale 259,
3000 Berne 6, Switzerland
Rev Michael Leonard
6020 West Ardmore Avenue,
Chicago, IL 60646, USA
Tel 001-7736775341
Rev Albert McDonnell
Vice Rector, Irish College,
Via dei SS Quattro 1, 00184 Roma, Italy
Tel 00-3906-772631
Rev John Molloy
Casilla 09-01-5825, Guayaquil,
Ecuador, South America
Tel 00593-87504590
Archbishop Eugene M. Nugent
Apostolic Nunciature, Villa Roma,
Ivandry BP 650, 101 Antananarivo,
Madagascar
Rev John O'Donovan
PO Box 897, Oldsmar, Florida 34677 USA
Rev Paul Ryan
c/o Killaloe Diocesan Office

## RETIRED PRIESTS

Rev Con Desmond
c/o Westbourne, Ennis, Co Clare
Very Rev Gerard Fitzpatrick
Cahercalla Community Hospital,
Ennis, Co Clare
Tel 065-6824388/086-2311923
Very Rev Paschal Flannery
Ballinderry, Nenagh, Co Tipperary
Tel 067-22916/086-2225099
Very Rev Charles Navin
Tubber, Gort, Co Galway
Tel 091-63323
Very Rev Oliver O'Doherty
The Presbytery, Church Road,
Nenagh, Co Tipperary
Very Rev Jack O'Keeffe
The Village Nursing Home, Craughwell,
Co Galway
Tel 091-777700
Very Rev Pat Sexton
5 Cottage Gardens, Station Road,
Ennis, Co Clare
Tel 065-6840828/087-2477814
Very Rev Tim Tuohy
Carrigoran Nursing Home,
Newmarket on Fergus, Co Clare

## RELIGIOUS ORDERS AND CONGREGATIONS

### PRIESTS

**CISTERCIANS**
Mount Saint Joseph Abbey
Roscrea, Co Tipperary
Tel 0505-25600 Fax 0505-25610
Email info@msjroscrea.ie
*Abbot*
Rt Rev Dom Richard Purcell (OCSO)

**FRANCISCANS**
Franciscan Friary, Ennis, Co Clare
Tel 065-6828751 Fax 065-6822008
Email friars.ennis@eircom.net
*Guardian:* Rev Liam Kelly (OFM)

### BROTHERS

**CHRISTIAN BROTHERS**
Christian Brothers' House,
New Road, Ennis, Co Clare
Tel 065-6821471/6828469 (office)
*Community Leader:* Br Liam Roche
Community: 6

Christian Brothers' House,
Nenagh, Co Tipperary
Tel 067-31557
*Community Leader:* Br John Dooley
Community: 7

**PRESENTATION BROTHERS**
Presentation Brothers,
Birr, Co Offaly
Tel 0509-20247
*Contact:* Br Ultan Rohan (FPM)
Community: 3

## SISTERS

**SISTERS OF CHARITY OF THE INCARNATE WORD**
St Michael Convent, Carrigoran,
Newmarket-on-Fergus, Co Clare
Tel 061-368381
Community: 3
Carrigoran House, Retirement and Convalescent Centre
Tel 061-368100 Fax 061-368170
Email info@carrigoranhouse.ie

**CONGREGATION OF THE SISTERS OF MERCY**
*The Sisters of Mercy minister throughout the diocese in pastoral and social work, community development, counselling, spirituality, education and health care, answering current needs.*

Mercy Sisters,
Garinis Clonroadmore, Ennis, Co Clare
Tel 065-6820768
Community: 2

St Xavier's, Ennis, Co Clare
Tel 065-6828024 Fax 065-6828776
Community: 22

1 Corovorrin Crescent, Ennis, Co Clare
Tel 065-6841375
Community: 5

7 Shalee Drive,
Cloughleigh, Ennis, Co Clare
Tel 065-6828894 Fax 065-6828892
Community: 4

8/9 Greendale, Clonroad, Ennis, Co Clare
Tel 065-6840385 Fax 065-6823869
Community: 6

5 & 6 Rosanore, Gort Road,
Ennis, Co Clare
Tel 065-6821554
Community: 4

Mercy Sisters, Killaloe, Co Clare
Tel 061-376138
Community: 6

Milltown Road, Kilkee, Co Clare
Tel 065-9056116
Community: 4

Convent of Mercy,
Kilkee Road, Kilrush, Co Clare
Tel 065-9051068
Community: 11

20 Sycamore Drive, Kilrush, Co Clare
Tel/Fax 065-9051957
Community: 2

31 Shannon Heights, Kilrush, Co Clare
Tel 065-9052354
Community: 2

64 Shannon Heights, Kilrush, Co Clare
Tel 065-9052789
Community: 2

Ashe Road, Nenagh, Co Tipperary
Tel 067-33835 Fax 067-34266
Community: 7

5 Dromin Court, Nenagh, Co Tipperary
Tel/Fax 067-31591
Community: 2

Spanish Point, Miltown Malbay, Co Clare
Tel 065-7084005 Fax 065-7084865
Community: 5

Tulla, Co Clare
Tel 065-6835118
Community: 4

1/2 Fergus Drive, Shannon, Co Clare
Tel 061-471637
Community: 5

St Mary's, Nenagh, Co Tipperary
Tel 067-31357 Fax 067-43586
Community: 18

33 Yewston Estate, Nenagh, Co Tipperary
Tel/Fax 067-32830
Community: 3

St John's, Riverside, Birr, Co Offaly
Tel 057-9120891
Community: 7

McAuley Drive, Birr, Co Offaly
Tel 057-9121023 Fax 057-9121303
Community: 3

84 Aughanteeroe, Gort Road,
Ennis, Co Clare
Tel/Fax 065-6844533
Community: 3

10/11 Ardlea Close,
Clare Road, Ennis, Co Clare
Tel 065-6842399
Community: 5

**DAUGHTERS OF CHARITY OF ST VINCENT DE PAUL**
St Vincent's, Woodstown House,
Lisnagry, Co Limerick
Tel 061-501490/332577
*Superior:* Sr Sheila Ryan
Community: 8
St Vincent's Special School, day and residential centre for people with intellectual disability.

**POOR CLARES**
Poor Clare Monastery,
Francis Street, Ennis, Co Clare
*Abbess:* Sr Bernardine Meskell
Email bernardinemeskell@eircom.net
Community: 13
Contemplative

**SACRED HEARTS OF JESUS AND MARY**
St Anne's, Sean Ross Abbey, Roscrea,
Co Tipperary
Tel 0505-21629 Fax 0505-22525
*School Principal:* Mr James McMahon
Tel 0505-21002
Special school for children with intellectual disabilities

St Mary's,
Corville Road, Roscrea, Co Tipperary
Tel 0505-31599

**ST JOHN OF GOD SISTERS**
St John of God Sisters,
19 Water Park View, Ennis Co Clare
Tel 065-6843579
Community: 1

**ST JOSEPH OF THE SACRED HEART SISTERS**
7 Woodlands, Kilrush Road,
Ennis, Co Clare
Tel 065-6844742
*Regional Leader:* Sr Anne Boland

57 Woodlands, Kilrush Road,
Ennis, Co Clare
Tel 065-6891178

Sisters of St Joseph,
24 Dun-an-Oir, Kilkee Housing Estate,
Kilkee, Co Clare

**ST MARY MADELEINE POSTEL SISTERS**
Park More Convent, Abbey Street,
Roscrea, Co Tipperary
Tel 0505-21038
*Local Superior:* Sr Marie Keegan
Community: 14

Mount Carmel Nursing Home,
Abbey Street, Roscrea, Co Tipperary
Tel 0505-21146/21084
*Apply:* Matron

## EDUCATIONAL INSTITUTIONS

**St Flannan's College (Diocesan College)**
Ennis, Co Clare
Tel 065-6828019 Fax 065-6840644
*President*
Rev Joseph McMahon BA, BD, HDE
Rev Ignatius McCormack

**EDMUND RICE SCHOOLS TRUST**
Bunscoil na mBráithre,
New Road, Ennis, Co Clare
Tel 065-6822150 Fax 065-6823865
Email cbsennis@eircom.net
*Principal:* Br Liam de Roiste

Rice College, New Road, Ennis, Co Clare
Tel 065-6822105 Fax 065-6824755
Email ricecollegecbs@eircom.net
Website www.ricecollege.ennis.ie
*Principal:* Mr Louis Mulqueen

CBS Primary School, Summer Hill,
Nenagh, Co Tipperary
Tel 067-32748
Email cbsnenagh@eircom.net
*Principal:* Mr Gerry Ryan

St Joseph's CBS Secondary School,
Summer Hill, Nenagh, Co Tipperary
Tel 067-34789 Fax 067-34967
Email cbsnen.ias@eircom.net
*Principal:* Mr Ray Cowan

## CHARITABLE AND OTHER SOCIETIES

**Apostolic Work Society**
Diocesan Headquarters at Maria Assumpta Hall, Station Road, Ennis, Co Clare

**Birr Social Service Council**
c/o 47 New Road, Birr, Co Offaly

**Clarecare**
Clarecare, Harmony Row,
Ennis, Co Clare
Tel 065-6828178

**Clare Youth Advisory Service**
Carmody Street, Ennis, Co Clare
Tel 065-684350

**Geriatric Centre**
Carrigoran House,
Newmarket-on-Fergus, Co Clare
Tel 061-368100

**Legion of Mary**
Headquarters at Maria Assumpta Hall,
Station Road, Ennis, Co Clare

**Mount Carmel Nursing home**
Parkmore, Abbey Street, Roscrea,
Co Tipperary
Tel 0505-21146

**North Tipperary Community Services**
Loreto House, Kenyon Street,
Nenagh, Co Tipperary
Tel 067-31800

**North Tipperary Youth Advisory Service**
c/o The Institute, Nenagh, Co Tipperary
Tel 067-32000

**Roscrea Community Service Centre**
Rosemary Street, Roscrea, Co Tipperary
Tel 0505-21498

**Schools for children with Special Needs**
***St Vincent's, Woodstown House,***
Lisnagry, Co Limerick
(Daughters of Charity)
Tel 061-501400

***St Anne's, residential and day school,***
Sean Ross Abbey,
Roscrea, Co Tipperary
Tel 0505-21187

***St Clare's, day school,***
Gort Road, Ennis, Co Clare
Tel 065-21899

***St Anne's, day school,***
Ennis, Co Clare
Tel 065-29072

**Society of St Vincent de Paul**
Conferences at: Birr, Castleconnell, Clarecastle, Cloughjordan, Ennis, Kilrush, Kilkee, Nenagh, Newmarket-on-Fergus, Roscrea, Scariff/Tuamgraney and Shannon

# DIOCESE OF KILMORE

PATRONS OF THE DIOCESE
ST PATRICK, 17 MARCH; ST FELIM, 9 AUGUST

INCLUDES ALMOST ALL OF COUNTY CAVAN,
AND A PORTION OF COUNTIES LEITRIM, FERMANAGH, MEATH AND SLIGO

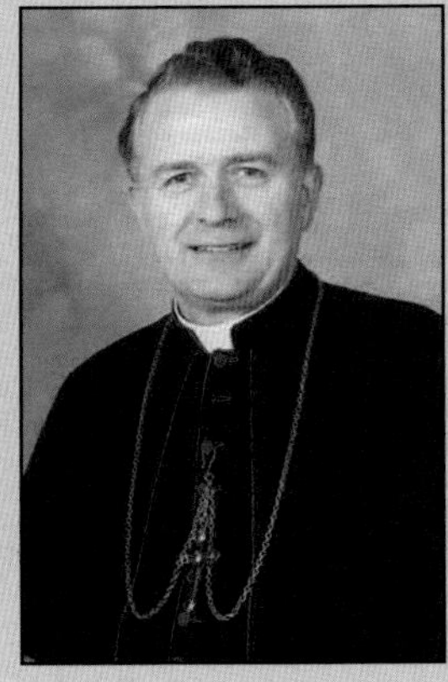

**Most Rev Leo O'Reilly DD**
Bishop of Kilmore;
born 1944;
ordained priest 15 June 1969;
ordained bishop 2 February 1997; installed as Bishop of Kilmore 15 November 1998

Residence:
Bishop's House,
Cullies, Co Cavan
Tel 049-4331496
Fax 049-4361796
Email bishop@kilmorediocese.ie
Website www.kilmorediocese.ie

## CATHEDRAL OF ST PATRICK AND ST FELIM, CAVAN

The original cathedral of the diocese was situated about four miles south of Cavan in the present parish of Kilmore. Some time in the sixth century, St Felim had established a church there. Bishop Andrew MacBrady (1445–1455) rebuilt the ancient church of St Felim and received permission from Pope Nicholas V to raise it to the status of a cathedral. After the confiscation of the Cathedral of St Felim at Kilmore, the diocese had no cathedral for three hundred years. Bishop James Browne extended Cavan parish church and erected it into a cathedral in 1862. It was replaced by the new Cathedral of St Patrick and St Felim, built by Bishop Patrick Lyons in the years 1938–1942. The architects were W. H. Byrne & Son and the contractors John Sisk & Son. The cathedral cost £209,000 and was opened and dedicated in 1942. It was consecrated in 1947.

The cathedral is neo-classical in style with a single spire rising to 230 feet. The portico consists of a tympanum supported by four massive columns of Portland stone with Corinthian caps. The tympanum figures of Christ, St Patrick and St Felim were executed by a Dublin sculptor, George Smith. The twenty-eight columns in the cathedral, the pulpit on the south side and all the statues are of Pavinazetto marble and came from the firm of Dinelli Figli of Pietrasanta in Italy.

The fine work of George Collie can be seen in the Stations of the Cross and in the mural of the Risen Christ on the wall of the apse. Directly above the mural are twelve small windows, showing the heads of the twelve apostles. The High Altar is of green Connemara marble and pink Middleton marble, while the altar rails are of white Carrara marble. The apse has two side-chapels on the north and two on the south. The Blessed Sacrament is now reserved in the south chapel closest to the altar. The six splendid stained-glass windows in the nave and one in the south transept came from the studios of Harry Clarke.

## ADMINISTRATION

**College of Consultors**
Rt Rev Mgr Michael Cooke
Very Rev Canon John Murphy
Very Rev Charles Heerey
Very Rev Raymond Brady
Very Rev Eamonn Lynch
Very Rev John Gilhooly
Rev Michael Router
Rev Ultan McGoohan
Rev Francis Duffy
Very Rev Oliver Kelly

**Vicar General**
Right Rev Mgr Michael Cooke
Manorhamilton, Co Leitrim
Tel 049-9522109

**Council of Priests**
*Chairman:* Very Rev Gerard Alwill PP
Drunkeerin, Co Leitrim
Tel 071-9648025
*Secretary:* Rev Francis Duffy

**Vicars Forane**
Very Rev Oliver Kelly
Very Rev Charles Heerey
Very Rev John Murphy
Rt Rev Mgr Michael Cooke

**Finance Committee**
Rt Rev Mgr Michael Cooke VG
Very Rev Anthony Fagan PP
Very Rev Fintan McKiernan PP
Mrs Joan Quinn
Ms Carmel Denning
Mr John Boyle
Mr Kevin O'Connor
Mr Paul Kelly

**Financial Administrator**
Rev Francis Duffy

**Chancellor/Diocesan Secretary**
Rev Francis Duffy
Bishop's House, Cullies, Co Cavan
Tel 049-4331496 Fax 049-4361796
Email bishop@kilmorediocese.ie

**Bishop's Secretary**
Kathleen Conaty
Bishop's House, Cullies, Co Cavan
Tel 049-4331496 Fax 049-4361796
Email bishop@kilmorediocese.ie

**Diocesan Archivist**
Rev Francis Duffy
Bishop's House, Cullies, Co Cavan
Tel 049-4331496 Fax 049-4361796

## CATECHETICS EDUCATION

**Catholic Primary School Managers' Association**
*Secretary:* Mrs Nancy Shiels
Kilmore Diocesan Pastoral Centre,
Cullies, Cavan
Tel 049-4375004 (ext 4) Fax 049-4327497
Email edsec@kilmorediocese.ie

**Diocesan Catechetical Advisers**
*Primary:* Sr Anna Smith
Sisters of Mercy, 2 Dún na Bó,
Willowfield Road, Ballinamore, Co Leitrim
Tel 071-9645973
Mr Terence Leddy
Drumsilla, Butlersbridge, Co Cavan
*Second level:* Mrs Patricia Sheridan
Kells Road, Bailieborough, Co Cavan

## LITURGY

*Pastoral Team:* Kilmore Diocesan Pastoral Centre, Cullies, Cavan
Tel 049-4375004
*Advisor:* Very Rev Daniel Sheridan
Killeshandra, Co Cavan
Tel 049-4334179
Email dannie88@eircom.net

**Church Music**
Kilmore Diocesan Pastoral Centre,
Cullies, Cavan
Tel 049-4375004

**Art, Architecture and Buildings**
*Chairman:* Very Rev Michéal Quinn

## PASTORAL

**Kilmore Diocesan Pastoral Centre**
Cullies, Cavan
*Director:* Rev Michael Router
Tel 049-4375004 Fax 049-3227497
Email pastoralcentre@kilmorediocese.ie

**Accord**
Kilmore Diocesan Pastoral Centre
Tel 049-4375004
*Diocesan Director:* Fr Kevin Donohoe
The Presbytery, Cavan
Tel 049-4331404

**Apostolic Society**
*Diocesan President:* Mrs Anne Fitzpatrick
Killygarry, Co Cavan
Tel 049-4332297
*Spiritual Director:* Rev John McMahon CC
Tel 071-9856987

**Communications**
*Diocesan Director:* Rev Francis Duffy
Bishop's House, Cullies, Co Cavan
Tel 049-4331496 Fax 049-4361796

**Diocesan Pastoral Council**
*Chairperson:* Sr Suzie Duffy (IBVM)
*Secretary:* Mr Sean Coll
Tel 049-4375004

**Ecumenism**
*Director:* Rev Andrew Tully CC
The Presbytery, Cavan
Tel 049-4331404

**Eucharistic Adoration**
*Chairperson:* Mr Andy Brady
Tel 049-8545160
*Chapain:* Rev John Cooney
Tel 046-9052129

**Family Ministry**
Rev Andrew Tully CC
The Presbytery, Cavan
Tel 049-4331404

**Knock Pilgrimage**
*Director:* Very Rev Anthony Fagan
Killinkere, Virginia, Co Cavan
Tel 049-8547307

**Legion of Mary**
*Spiritual Director:* Rev Pat Farrelly CC
Tel 049-9526252

**Lourdes Pilgrimage**
*Director:* Rev Kevin Fay
Lavey, Ballyjamesduff, Co Cavan
Tel 049-4330018

**Marriage Tribunal**
*Kilmore Office of Armagh Regional Marriage Tribunal*
Sr Elizabeth Fee
Kilmore Diocesan Pastoral Centre,
Cullies, Cavan
Tel 049-4375004
Email tribunal@kilmorediocese.ie
St Michael's Parish Centre,
28 Church Street, Enniskillen BT74 7EJ
Tel 028-66347860

**Adult Faith Formation**
*Director:* Rev Michael Router
Kilmore Diocesan Pastoral Centre,
Cullies, Cavan
Tel 049-4375004

**Safeguarding Children Diocesan Committee**
*Chairperson:* Ms Teresa Carroll
*Director:* Sr Suzie Duffy
Kilmore Diocesan Pastoral Centre
Tel 049-4375004
*Designated Persons*
Sr Suzie Duffy
Kilmore Diocesan Pastoral Centre
Tel 049-4375004
Rev Sean Mawn
Ballinaglera, Carrick-on-Shannon,
Co Leitrim
Tel 071-9643014

**Permanent Diaconate**
*Director:* Rev Gabriel Kelly
Kinawley, Enniskillen, Co Fermanagh
Tel 028-66348250

**Pioneer Total Abstinence Association**
*Diocesan Director:* Rev John Cusack
Virginia, Co Cavan
Tel 049-8547063

**Pontifical Mission Societies**
*Diocesan Director:* Rev John McMahon CC
Bridge Street, Manorhamilton, Co Leitrim
Tel 071-9856987

**St Joseph's Young Priests Society**
*Chaplain:* Very Rev Philip Brady PP
Laragh, Co Cavan
Tel 049-4330142
*Diocesan President:* Mr Pat Denning
Drumcave, Cavan
Tel 049-4331362

**Travellers**
*Chaplain:* Very Rev Tom McKiernan PP
Bawnboy, Co Cavan
Tel 049-9523103

**Vocations**
*Director:* Rev Noel Boylan
Kill, Cootehill, Co Cavan
Tel 049-5553218

**Youth Ministry Team**
*Youth Worker:* Ms Clare Coyle
Kilmore Diocesan Pastoral Centre,
Cullies, Co Cavan
Tel 049-4375004
Email youthministry@kilmorediocese.ie

## PARISHES

*Mensal parishes are listed first. Other parishes follow alphabetically. Historical names are given in parentheses. Church titulars appear in italics*

**CAVAN (URNEY AND ANNAGELLIFF)**
*Cathedral of SS Patrick and Felim, Cavan*
*St Clare's, Cavan*
*St Brigid's, Killygarry*
*St Aidan's, Butlersbridge*
Rev Kevin Donohoe Adm
Rev Ultan McGoohan CC
Rev Rafal Siwek CC
The Presbytery, Cavan
Tel 049-4331404/4332269 Fax 049-4332000
Information line 049-4371787
Email cavan@kilmorediocese.ie
Rev Tom Mannion CC
Butlersbridge, Co Cavan
Tel 049-4365266
Rev Darragh Connolly *(priest in residence)*
Tullacmongan, Cavan

**BAILIEBORO (KILLANN)**
*St Anne's, Bailieboro; St Anne's, Killann*
*St Patrick's, Shercock*
Very Rev Canon John Murphy PP, VF
Bailieboro, Co Cavan
Tel 042-9665117
Email bailieboro@kilmorediocese.ie
Rev Oliver O'Reilly CC
Parochial House, Shercock, Co Cavan
Tel 042-9669127
Email shercockparish@gmail.com

**BALLAGHAMEEHAN**
*St Aidan's, Ballaghameehan*
*St Mary's, Rossinver*
*St Aidan's, Glenaniff*
*St Patrick's, Kiltyclogher*
Very Rev John Phair PP
Rossinver, Co Leitrim
Tel 071-9854022
Email rossinver@kilmorediocese.ie

**BALLINAGLERA**
*St Hugh's, Ballinaglera*
*St Columcill, Newbridge*
*Immaculate Conception, Doobally*
Very Rev Sean Mawn PP
Ballinaglera, Carrick-on-Shannon,
Co Leitrim
Tel 071-9643014
Email ballinaglera@kilmorediocese.ie

**BALLINAMORE (OUGHTERAGH)**
*St Patrick's Ballinamore,*
*St Mary's Aughnasheelin*
Very Rev Charles Heerey PP, VF
Tel 071-9644039
Email ballinamore@kilmorediocese.ie
Very Rev James Duffy
Tel 071-9644050
Ballinamore, Co Leitrim

**BALLINTEMPLE**
*St Michael's, Potahee*
*St Mary's, Bruskey*
*St Patrick's, Aghaloora*
Very Rev Peter McPartlan PP
Ballintemple, Ballinagh, Co Cavan
Tel 049-4337106
Email potahee@kilmorediocese.ie
Rev Jason Murphy *(priest in residence)*
Carrigans, Ballinagh, Co Cavan

**BELTURBET (ANNAGH)**
*Immaculate Conception, Belturbet*
*St Patrick's, Drumalee*
*St Brigid's, Redhills*
Very Rev Michael Cooke PP, VG
Bridge Street, Belturbet, Co Cavan
Tel 049-9522109
Email belturbet2@kilmorediocese.ie
Rev Canon Patrick J. Corrigan
Fairgreen, Belturbet, Co Cavan
Tel 049-9522151
Email belturbet@kilmorediocese.ie

**CARRIGALLEN**
*St Mary's, Carrigallen*
*St Mary's, Drumeela*
*St Mary's, Drumreilly*
Very Rev Denis Murray PP
Carrigallen, Co Leitrim, via Cavan
Tel 049-4339610
Email carrigallen@kilmorediocese.ie

**CASTLERAHAN AND MUNTERCONNAUGHT**
*St Bartholomew's, Munterconnaught*
*St Mary's, Castlerahan*
*St Joseph's, Ballyjamesduff*
Very Rev Francis Kelleher PP
Knocktemple, Virginia, Co Cavan
Tel 049-8547435
Email frfkelleher@eircom.net
Very Rev Felim Kelly CC
Castlerahan, Ballyjamesduff, Co Cavan
Tel 049-8544150
Email castlerahan@kilmorediocese.ie
Rev Donal Kilduff CC
Ballyjamesduff, Co Cavan
Tel 049-8544410
Email
ballyjamesduff@kilmorediocese.ie

**CASTLETARA**
*St Mary's Ballyhaise,*
*St Patrick's, Castletara*
Very Rev Gerard Cassidy PP
Ballyhaise, Co Cavan
Tel 049-4338121
Email ballyhaise@kilmorediocese.ie

**COOTEHILL (DRUMGOON)**
*St Michael's, Cootehill*
*St Mary's, Middle Chapel*
*St Patrick's, Maudabawn*
Very Rev Owen Collins PP
Tel 049-5552120
Email cootehill@kilmorediocese.ie
Rev Paul Casey CC
Tel 049-5552163
Cootehill, Co Cavan

**CORLOUGH AND DRUMREILLY**
*St Patrick's, Corlough,*
*St Brigid's, Corraleehan,*
*St Patrick's, Aughawillan*
Very Rev Thomas McManus PP
Corlough, Belturbet, Co Cavan
Tel 049-9523122
Email corlough@kilmorediocese.ie

**CROSSERLOUGH**
*St Patrick's, Kilnaleck*
*St Mary's, Crosserlough*
*St Joseph's, Drumkilly*
Very Rev Michael Quinn PP
Crosserlough, Co Cavan
Tel 049-4336122
Email crosserlough@kilmorediocese.ie
Rev Patrick V. Brady CC
Drumkilly, Co Cavan
Tel 049-4336120

**DENN**
*St Matthew's, Crosskeys*
*St Matthew's, Drumavaddy*
Email crosskeys@kilmorediocese.ie
Very Rev Liam Kelly PP
Crosskeys, Co Cavan
Tel 049-4336102

**DERRYLIN (KNOCKNINNY)**
*St Ninnidh's, Derrylin*
*St Mary's, Teemore*
Very Rev Fintan McKiernan PP
56 Mary Street, Derrylin,
Co Fermanagh BT92 9LA
Tel 028-67748315
Email derrylin@kilmorediocese.ie

**DRUMAHAIRE AND KILLARGUE**
*St Patrick's, Drumahaire*
*St Mary's, Newtownmanor*
*St Brigid's, Killargue*
Very Rev John McTiernan PP
Drumahaire, Co Leitrim
Tel 071-9164143
Email drumahaire@kilmorediocese.ie
Rev John Sexton *(Priest in residence)*
Killargue, Drumahaire,
Co Leitrim
Tel 07-9164131

**DRUMKEERIN (INISHMAGRATH)**
*St Brigid's, Drumkeerin*
*St Patrick's, Termon*
*St Brigid's, Creevalea*
Very Rev Gerard Alwill PP
Drumkeerin, Co Leitrim
Tel 071-9648025
Email drumkeerin@kilmorediocese.ie

**DRUMLANE**
*St Mary's, Staghall*
*St Patrick's, Milltown*
Very Rev Gerard Comiskey PP
Staghall, Belturbet, Co Cavan
Tel 049-9522140
Email drumlaneparish@gmail.com

**GLENFARNE**
*St Michael's, Glenfarne*
*St Mary's, Brockagh*
Very Rev John Quinn PP
West Barrs, Glenfarne, Co Leitrim
Tel 071-9855134
Email glenfarne@kilmorediocese.ie

**KILDALLAN AND TOMREGAN**
*Our Lady of Lourdes, Ballyconnell*
*St Dallan's, Kildallan*
Very Rev Eamonn Lynch PP
Ballyconnell, Co Cavan
Tel 049-9526291
Email ballyconnell@kilmorediocese.ie
Rev Pat Farrelly CC
Kildallan, Ballyconnell, Co Cavan
Tel 049-9526252

**KILLESHANDRA**
*St Brigid's, Killeshandra*
*Sacred Heart, Arva*
*Immaculate Conception, Coronea*
Very Rev Daniel Sheridan PP
Killeshandra, Co Cavan
Tel 049-4334179
Email dannie88@eircom.net
Rev Eamonn Bredin *(priest in residence)*
Arva, Co Cavan
Tel 049-4335246
Email arva@kilmorediocese.ie

**KILLESHER**
*St Patrick's, Killesher*
*St Lasir's, Wheathill*
Very Rev Canon Brian McNamara Adm
Derrylester, Enniskillen,
Co Fermanagh
Tel 028-66348224
Email killesher@kilmorediocese.ie

**KILLINAGH AND GLANGEVLIN**
*St Patrick's, Killinagh*
*St Patrick's, Glangevlin*
*St Felim's, Gowlan*
Very Rev Charles O'Gorman PP
Blacklion, Co Cavan
Tel 071-9853012
Email blacklion@kilmorediocese.ie

**KILLINKERE**
*St Ultan's, Killinkere*
*St Mary's, Clanaphilip*
Very Rev Anthony Fagan PP
Killinkere, Virginia, Co Cavan
Tel 049-8547307
Email killinkere@kilmorediocese.ie

**KILMAINHAMWOOD AND MOYBOLOGUE**
*Sacred Heart*
Very Rev John Cooney PP
Kilmainhamwood, Kells,
Co Meath
Tel 046-9052129
Email
kilmainhamwood@kilmorediocese.ie
*St Patrick's*
Rev Brian Flynn *(priest in residence)*
Tierworker, via Kells,
Co Meath
Tel 042-9665374
Email tierworker@kilmorediocese.ie

**KILMORE**
*St Felim's, Ballinagh*
*St Patrick's, Drumcor*
Very Rev Peter Casey PP
Ballinagh, Co Cavan
Tel 049-4337232

**KILSHERDANY AND DRUNG**
*Immaculate Conception, Drung*
*St Patrick's, Corick*
*St Mary's, Bunnoe*
*St Brigid's, Kill*
Email drung@kilmorediocese.ie
Rev Noel Boylan CC
Kill, Cootehill, Co Cavan
Tel 049-5553218
Email kill@kilmorediocese.ie

**KINLOUGH AND GLENADE**
*St Aidan's, Kinlough*
*St Patrick's, Tullaghan*
*St Michael's, Glenade*
*St Brigid's, Ballintrillick*
Very Rev Thomas M. Keogan PP
Kinlough, Co Leitrim
Tel 071-9841428
Email kinlough@kilmorediocese.ie
Rev Maurice McMorrow CC
Glenade, Kinlough, Co Leitrim
Tel 071-9841461
Email glenade@kilmorediocese.ie

**KNOCKBRIDE**
*St Brigid's, Tunnyduff*
*St Brigid's, East Knockbride*
Very Rev Peter McKiernan PP
Knockbride, Bailieboro,
Co Cavan
Tel 042-9660112
Email frpetermckiernan@gmail.com

**LARAGH**
*St Brigid's, Laragh*
*St Brigid's, Carrickallen*
*St Michael's, Clifferna*
Very Rev Philip Brady
Laragh, Stradone, Co Cavan
Tel 049-4330142
Email laraghparish1@gmail.com
Rev Francis Duffy *(priest in residence)*
Clifferna, Stradone, Co Cavan
Tel 049-4330119

**LAVEY**
*St Dympna's, Upper Lavey*
*St Dympna's, Lower Lavey*
Very Rev Brian McElhinney PP
Lavey, Stradone, Co Cavan
Tel 049-4330125
Email lavey@kilmorediocese.ie
Rev Kevin Fay *(priest in residence)*
Lavey, Ballyjamesduff, Co Cavan
Tel 049-4330018
Email lavey1@kilmorediocese.ie

**MANORHAMILTON (KILLASNETT)**
*St Clare's, Manorhamilton*
*Annunciation, Mullies*
*St Osnat's, Glencar*
Very Rev Oliver Kelly PP, VF
Manorhamilton, Co Leitrim
Tel 071-9855042
Email manorhamilton@kilmorediocese.ie
Rev Patrick Sullivan CC
Glencar, Manorhamilton, Co Leitrim
Tel 071-9855433
Email glencar@kilmorediocese.ie
Rev John McMahon CC
Bridge Street, Manorhamilton, Co Leitrim
Tel 071-9856987
Email jmcmahon59@eircom.net

**MULLAGH**
*St Kilian's, Mullagh*
*St Mary's, Cross*
Very Rev John Gilhooly PP
Mullagh, via Kells, Co Meath
Tel 046-42208
Email mullagh@kilmorediocese.ie
Rev Loughlain Carolan CC
Cross, Mullagh, Kells, Co Meath
Tel 049-8547024

**SWANLINBAR (KINAWLEY)**
*St Mary's, Swanlinbar*
*St Naile's, Kinawley*
Very Rev Donald Hannon PP
Swanlinbar, Co Cavan
Tel 049-9521221/087-2830145
Email swanlinbar@kilmorediocese.ie
Rev Gabriel Kelly CC
Kinawley, Enniskillen, Co Fermanagh
Tel 028-66348250
Email kinawley@kilmorediocese.ie

**TEMPLEPORT**
*St Patrick's, Kilnavart,*
*St Mogue's, Bawnboy*
Very Rev Thomas McKiernan PP
Bawnboy, Co Cavan
Tel 049-9523103
Email bawnboy@kilmorediocese.ie

**VIRGINIA (LURGAN)**
*Mary Immaculate, Virginia*
*St Patrick's, Lurgan*
*St Matthew's, Maghera*
Very Rev John Cusack PP
Virginia, Co Cavan
Tel 049-8547063
Email virginia@kilmorediocese.ie
Rev Dermot Prior
Virginia, Co Cavan
Tel 049-8547015
Email priordermot@eircom.net

## INSTITUTIONS AND THEIR CHAPLAINS

**Bailieboro Community School**
*Chaplain:* Ms Mary Grimes
Tel 042-9665295

**Breifne College**
Cootehill Road, Cavan
*Catechist:* Rev Jason Murphy
Tel 049-4331735

**Carrigallen Vocational School**
*Visiting Chaplain:* Rev Denis Murray
Tel 049-4339640

**Cavan General Hospital**
Tel 049-4361399
Rev Martin Gilcreest

**Cavan Institute**
Cathedral Road, Cavan
*Chaplaincy and Pastoral Care*
Rev Ultan McGoohan and Clare Coyle
Tel 049-4332334

**Cavan and Monaghan Defence Forces**
*Chaplain:* Rev Sean McDermott
Dun Ui Neill, Cavan
Tel 049-4361631/087-8292333
Email jlmcdermott@eircom.net

**Fatima & Felim's Secondary School**
Ballinamore, Co Leitrim
*Visiting Chaplain:* Rev Tom McManus
Tel 071-9644049

**Loreto College, Cavan**
Tel 049-4331354
*Visiting Chaplain:* Rev Kevin Fay

**Lough Allen College**
Drumkeerin, Co Leitrim
*Visiting Chaplain:* Rev Gerard Alwill
Tel 071-9648017

**Loughan House**
Blacklion, Co Cavan
Rev John McMahon
*General Office:* 071-9853059

**St Aidan's Comprehensive School**
Cootehill, Co Cavan
Tel 049-5552161
*Chaplain:* Mr Gabriel McQuillan

**St Aidan's High School**
Derrylin, Co Fermanagh
*Visiting Chaplain:* Rev Fintan McKiernan
Tel 028-67748337

**St Bricin's Vocational School**
Belturbet, Co Cavan
Tel 049-9522170

**St Clare's College**
Ballyjamesduff, Co Cavan
*Visiting Chaplain:* Rev Donal Kilduff
Tel 049-854451

**St Clare's Comprehensive School, Manorhamilton**
*Chaplain:* Rev John Sexton
Tel 071-9855060

**St Mogue's College**
Bawnboy, Co Cavan
*Visiting Chaplain:* Rev Tom McKiernan
Tel 049-9523112

**St Patrick's College, Cavan**
*Chaplain:* Rev Kevin Fay
Tel 049-4361888

**Virginia College**
Virginia, Co Cavan
*Visiting Chaplain:* Rev John Cusack
Tel 049-8547050

## PRIESTS OF THE DIOCESE ELSEWHERE

Rev Bernard Fitzpatrick
Lagos, Nigeria
Rev Paul Prior
Director of Formation,
St Patrick's College, Maynooth, Co Kildare
Rev Brian Flynn
Administrator of the National Marriage Appeal Tribunal, St Patrick's College, Maynooth, Co Kildare
Rev Enda Murphy
Pontificio Collegio Irlandese, Rome, Italy
Rev Andrew Tully
Studies

## RETIRED PRIESTS

Rev Raymond Brady
8 Earlsvale Road, Cavan
Tel 049-4380369
Rev Edward Burns
Swellan Lower, Cavan
Rev Eugene Clarke
5 Brookside, Farnham Road, Cavan
Tel 049-4331755
Rev Eugene Dowd
51 Drumnavanagh, Farnham Road, Cavan
Tel 049-4326821
Rev Bernard Doyle
Kiltyclogher, Co Leitrim
Tel 071-9854302
Rev Colm Hurley
Killeshandra, Co Cavan
Tel 049-4334155
Rev Laurence Kearney (SPS)
Derrada, Ballinamore, Co Leitrim
Tel 071-9644067
Rev Felim McGovern
The Presbytery, Cavan
Tel 049-4331404
Rt Rev Mgr Patrick J. McManus
Kilnaleck, Co Cavan
Tel 049-4336118
Rev John O'Donnell
9 Rockview, Blacklion, Co Cavan
Rev Thomas Woods
Edenville, Kinlough, Co Leitrim
Very Rev Patrick Young
Billis, Cavan
Tel 049-4372386

## RELIGIOUS ORDERS AND CONGREGATIONS

### PRIESTS

**NORBERTINE CANONS**
Abbey of the Most Holy Trinity and St Norbert, Kilnacrott Abbey, Ballyjamesduff, Co Cavan
Tel 049-8544416
Fax 049-8544909
Email kilnacrottabbeytrust@eircom.net
*Prior:* Rt Rev Gerard Cusack (OPraem)

### SISTERS

**CONGREGATION OF THE SISTERS OF MERCY**
Church Street,
Belturbet, Co Cavan
Tel 049-9522110

No. 4 Oriel Lodge, Church Sreet,
Belturbet, Co Cavan
Tel 049-9524657

17 Castlemanor, Billis, Cavan, Co Cavan
Tel 049-4379267

Sisters of Mercy, Convent of Mercy,
Cootehill, Co Cavan
Tel 049-5552151
Community: 4

Sisters of Mercy,
2 Castle View, Manorhamilton,
Co Leitrim
Tel 071-9855401

No 2 Dun na Bo, Willowfield Road,
Ballinamore, Co Leitrim
Tel 071-9645973
Community: 4

No 16 Dun na Bo, Willowfield Road,
Ballinamore, Co Leitrim
Tel 071-9644006
Community: 4

25 Castlemanor, Billis, Cavan
Tel 049-4378155

**LORETO (IBVM)**
Loreto Post-Primary School
Tel 049-4331354

**MISSIONARY SISTERS OF THE HOLY ROSARY**
Cavan Town
Tel 049-4332735/4332733
Fax 049-4362077
Centre for mission education co-ordination
Pastoral, care of the elderly
Community: 28

27 Cherrymount, Keadue, Cavan Town
Tel 049-4372936
Pastoral, healthcare
Community: 2

**SISTERS OF ST CLARE**
St Clare's Convent, Cavan
Tel 049-4331134
Community: 3
Primary School. Pupils: 550
Tel 049-4332671

## EDUCATIONAL INSTITUTIONS

**St Clare's College**
Ballyjamesduff, Co Cavan
Tel 049-8544551
Fax 049-8544081
*Principal:* Mr Séan Fegan

**Fatima & Felim's Secondary School**
Ballinamore, Co Leitrim
Tel 071-9644049
Email felims.ias@eircom.net
Website www.ballinamorepps.ie
*Principal:* Mr Padraig Leyden
*Visiting Chaplain:* Rev Tom McManus
Tel 071-9644049

**St Patrick's College**
Cullies, Co Cavan
Tel 049-4361888
Email stpats@kilmorediocese.ie
*Principal*
Dr Liam McNiffe BA, HDip in ED, MA, MSc in ED Mngt, PhD
*Chaplain:* Rev Kevin Fay

# DIOCESE OF LIMERICK

PATRONS OF THE DIOCESE
ST MUNCHIN, 3 JANUARY; ST ITA, 15 JANUARY

INCLUDES THE GREATER PART OF COUNTY LIMERICK, PART OF COUNTY CLARE AND ONE TOWNLAND IN COUNTY KERRY

**Very Rev Anthony Mullins PP**
Diocesan Administrator
Email tonym@ldo.ie

Diocesan Office: Social Service Centre, Henry Street, Limerick
Tel 061-315856 Fax 061-310186
Email office@ldo.ie
Diocese of Limerick website
www.limerickdiocese.org

## ST JOHN'S CATHEDRAL, LIMERICK

Since the twelfth century, a church dedicated to St John has stood in the area of Limerick city known as Garryowen. The earliest reference to the first church comes from the year 1205 when the Cathedral Chapter of the Diocese of Limerick was founded by Bishop Donatus O'Brien, Bishop of Limerick from 1195 to 1207. In the document of foundation, the revenues from the Church of St John were given to the Archdeacon of Limerick. This medieval church was replaced by a penal church, which in turn was supplanted by the parish church of St John in the middle of the eighteenth century. With an increase in population in the area around Garryowen, it was decided to build a new church to accommodate the estimated 15,000 parishioners of St John's. An appeal for funds was so well received that the decision was made to abandon the plans for a parish church and build a cathedral for the diocese instead.

Designed by Philip Charles Hardwick, a contemporary and associate of Pugin, St John's Cathedral is revival Gothic in the early English style. It was opened for worship in 1861 and consecrated in 1894 by Cardinal Logue. The spire, standing at 308 feet, 3 inches, is the tallest in Ireland and was built between 1878 and 1883.

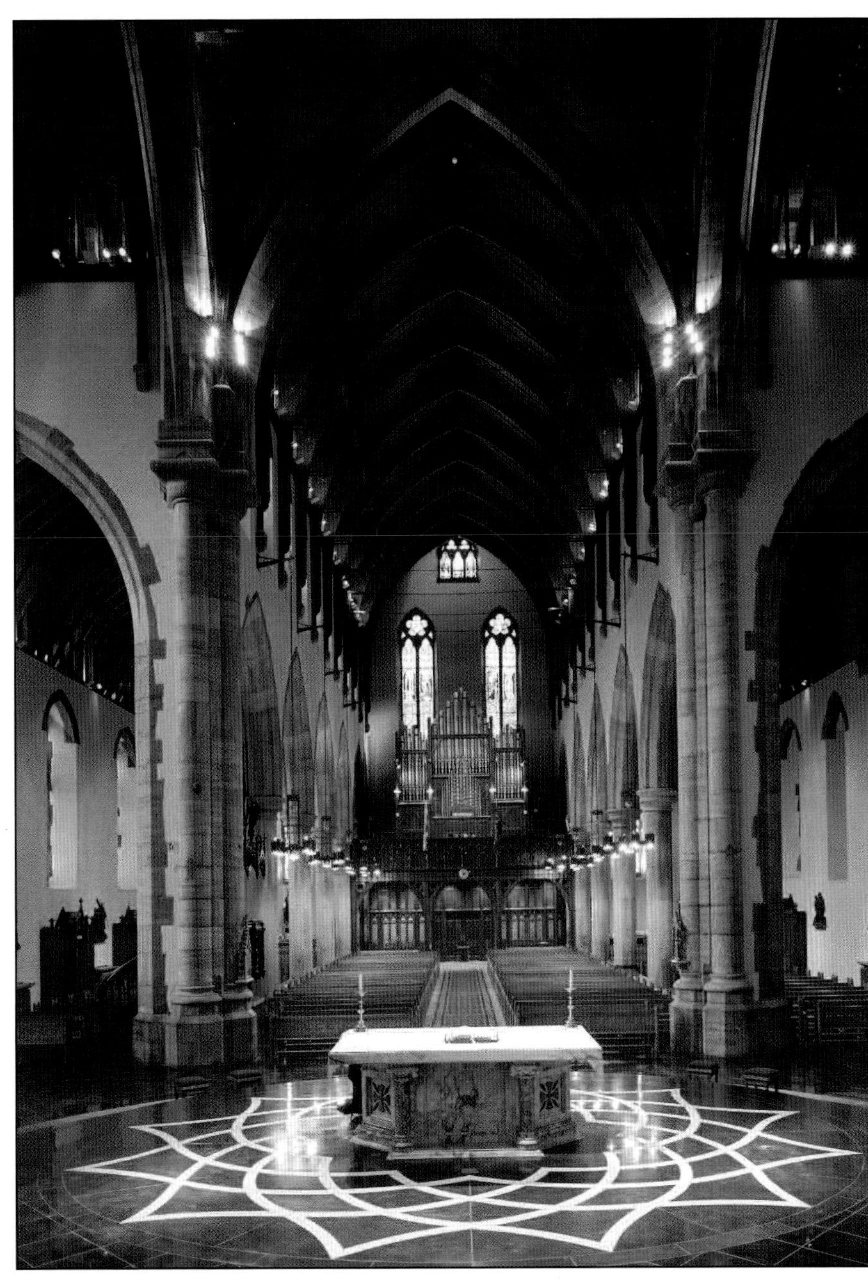

**Most Rev Donal Murray DD**
Bishop Emeritus
born 29 May 1940; ordained priest 22 May 1966; ordained bishop 18 April 1982; installed as Bishop of Limerick 24 March 1996; retired December 2009

## CHAPTER

*Dean:* Vacant
*Archdeacon:* Vacant
*Theologian*
Very Rev Donough Canon O'Malley
*Penitentiary*
Very Rev Garry Canon Bluett
*Chancellor*
Very Rev Frank Canon Duhig PP, VF
*Precentor*
Very Rev James Canon Ambrose PP
*Prebendaries and Canons*
*Dysart*
Very Rev John Canon O'Shea PP, VF
*Croagh:* Very Rev James Canon Neville
*Effin*
Very Rev James Canon Costello PP
*Killeedy*
Very Rev Donal Canon McNamara PP, VF
*Athnitt:* Very Rev Denis Canon Browne
*Tullybrackey*
Very Rev Anthony Canon O'Keeffe PP, VF
*Ardcanny:* Very Rev Patrick Canon Kelly PE
*St Munchin's*
Rt Rev Mgr Michael Lane
*Kilpeacon*
Very Rev Joseph Canon Dempsey
*Donaghmore*
Rt Rev Mgr Daniel Neenan PP
*Ballycahane*
Very Rev William Canon Fitzmaurice PP

## COLLEGE OF CONSULTORS

Rt Rev Mgr Michael Lane
Rt Rev Mgr Daniel Neenan PP
Very Rev David Gibson PP
Rev Chris O'Donnell
Very Rev Patrick O'Sullivan PP
Very Rev Thomas Crawford PP
Rev Richard Keane CC
Rev Richard Davern CC
Rev Paul Finnerty

## ADMINISTRATION

**Vicars General**
*Suspended due to vacancy of See*

**Vicars Forane/Pastoral Area Leaders/ Assistant Leaders**
Very Rev Thomas Carroll
Very Rev Thomas Crawford
Very Rev Michael Cussen
Very Rev Frank Canon Duhig
Very Rev Noel Kirwan
Very Rev Donal Canon McNamara
Very Rev Denis Mullane
Very Rev Muiris O'Connor
Very Rev Frank O'Dea
Very Rev Anthony Canon O'Keeffe
Very Rev Gerard O'Leary
Very Rev John Canon O'Shea

**Diocesan Secretary**
Rev Paul Finnerty
Diocesan Office, Social Service Centre, Henry Street, Limerick
Tel 061-315856 Fax 061-310186
Email paul@ldo.ie
Website www.limerickdiocese.org
*Finance Manager:* Mr Tony Sadlier
*Secretarial Staff:* Margaret Dalton
*Diocesan Spokesperson:* Rev Paul Finnerty

**Diocesan Archivist**
David Bracken
Diocesan Office, Social Service Centre, Henry Street, Limerick
Tel 061-315856

## DIOCESAN PASTORAL COUNCIL

*Suspended due to Vacancy of See*

## CATECHETICS EDUCATION

**Primary Level Religious Education**
*Director:* Rev Liam Enright
Church Road, Croom, Co Limerick
Tel 061-315856
Email liam@ldo.ie
Ms Nora Collins Email nora@ldo.ie
Ms Fiona Dineen Email fionad@ldo.ie
Tel 061-315856

**Second Level Religious Education**
*Adviser:* Rev Frank O'Connor
c/o Limerick Diocesan Pastoral Centre, St Michael's Courtyard, Denmark Street, Limerick
Tel 061-400133
Email foconnor@ldpc.ie

**Primary Education Secretary**
Ms Fiona Shanley
St Senan's Education Office, Social Service Centre, Henry Street, Limerick
Tel 061-317742 Fax 061-310186
Email fiona@ldo.ie
*Secretarial Staff*
Ciara Crowley Email sseo@ldo.ie
Linda Fleming Email linda@ldo.ie
Gwen O'Sullivan Email gwen@ldo.ie

## LITURGY

**Liturgical Music**
*Adviser:* Rev Terence Loughran
Parochial House, Cappagh, Askeaton, Co Limerick
Tel 086-8103482

## PASTORAL

**Accord**
Limerick City Centre:
St Munchin's College, Corbally, Limerick
Email accordlimerick@eircom.net
www.accord.ie
*Director:* Rev Joseph Shire PP
Ballyagran, Kilmallock, Co Limerick
Tel 063-82028
Enquiries: Tel 061-343000 Fax 061-350000
*Administrator:* Ms Katrina Quilligan
Newcastle West Centre:
Parish Centre, Newcastle West, Co Limerick
*Contact:* Helen Ahern
Tel 069-61000 (Mon-Fri 10.00am-1.00pm)
*Spiritual Director*
Very Rev Frank Duhig PP, VF
St Ita's Presbytery, Newcastle West, Co Limerick
Tel 069-62141/087-6380299

**Apostleship of the Sea, Foynes**
*Director and Port Chaplain*
Very Rev Anthony Canon O'Keeffe PP, VF
Shanagolden, Co Limerick
Tel 069-60112

**Charismatic Renewal Groups**
*Liaison Priest:* Rev Damian Ryan PP
Lourdes House, Childers Road, Limerick
Tel 061-301047/087-2274412

**Communications**
*Director:* Rev Paul Finnerty
Diocesan Office, Social Services Centre, Henry Street, Limerick
Tel 061-315856

**Council of Priests**
*Suspended due to Vacancy of See*

**CURA**
*Helpline:* Tel 061-318207
*Administrator:* Sr Anne McCarthy

**Limerick Diocesan Pastoral Centre**
St Michael's Courtyard, Denmark Street, Limerick
Tel 061-400133 Fax 061-400601
Email ldpc@eircom.net
http://www.limerickdiocese.org/ldpc/
*Director:* Very Rev Noel Kirwan PP

**Ecumenism**
*Director:* Rev Frank O'Connor
c/o Limerick Diocesan Pastoral Centre, Denmark Street, Limerick
Tel 061-400133

**Emigrant Apostolate**
*Director*
Very Rev William O'Gorman PP
Tournafulla, Co Limerick
Tel 069-81010/087-2580020

**Apostolate of the Laity**
*Adviser:* Very Rev Noel Kirwan PP
Limerick Diocesan Pastoral Centre, St Michael's Courtyard, Denmark Street, Limerick
Tel 061-400133 Fax 061-400601
Email ldpc@eircom.net

**Diocesan Representative on the National Council for the Laity**
*Diocesan Representative*
Ms Mary Sadlier
Rockfield, Crecora, Co Limerick
Tel 061-301044

**Marriage Encounter Movement**
Very Rev Liam Enright PP
Cratloe, Co Clare
Tel 061-357196/087-2546335
Email leppcrat@iol.ie

**Marriage Tribunal**
*Contact:* Mrs Jean Ryan
Diocesan Offices, Social Service Centre, Henry Street, Limerick
*Office hours:* Tuesday 2.00-5.00 pm
Thursday 9.00-5.00 pm
Tel 061-315856 Fax 061-310186
Email office@ldo.ie

**Military Chaplain**
Rev Seamus Madigan
Sarsfield Barracks, Limerick
Tel 061-316817

**Pioneer Total Abstinence Association**
*Spiritual Director:* Vacant

**Pilgrimage**
*(Lourdes) Director*
Very Rev Donal Canon McNamara PP
St Munchin's, Clancy Strand, Limerick
Tel 061-455635/087-2402518
Email donal@donalmcnamara.com

**Pre-Marriage Courses**
*Contact:* ACCORD
Limerick City Centre
Tel 061-343000 Fax 061-350000
Newcastle West Parish Centre
Tel 069-61000

**Pontifical Mission Societies**
*Diocesan Director*
Very Rev Thomas Crawford PP
Glin, Co Limerick
Tel 068-23897/087-2218078
Email tdec@eircom.net

**Safeguarding Children**
*Director of Safeguarding/Designated Person:* Ger Crowley
Email ger@ldo.ie
*Assistant Designated Person:* Liam Lawlor
*Safeguarding Children Co-ordinator:*
Margaret Dalton
Email margaret@ldo.ie
*Safeguarding Children Training Co-ordinator:* Aoife Walsh
Email awalsh@ldpc.ie

**Social Service Council**
*General Manager:* Mr Brian Ryan
Henry Street, Limerick
Tel 061-314111/314213

**Travelling Community**
*Diocesan Chaplain*
Very Rev Joseph Shire
Ballyagran, Kilmallock, Co Limerick
Tel 063-82028/087-6924563
Email taylor@eircom.net

**Trócaire**
*Director:* Very Rev Thomas Carroll PP
Parteen, Co Clare
Tel 061-345613
Email carrollgtom@gmail.com

**Vocations**
*Director:* Very Rev Noel Kirwan
Limerick Diocesan Pastoral Centre,
St Michael's Courtyard, Denmark Street, Limerick
Tel 061-400133/087-2616843
Email nkirwan@ldpc.ie

**Youth Apostolate**
*Director:* Rev Chris O'Donnell
Limerick Diocesan Pastoral Centre,
St Michael's Courtyard,
Denmark Street, Limerick
Tel 061-400133 Fax 061-400601
Email codonnell@ldpc.ie

## PARISHES

*Mensal and city parishes are listed first. Other parishes follow alphabetically. Church titulars are in italics.*

**ST JOHN'S**
*St John's Cathedral*
Very Rev Austin McNamara Adm
Rev Seán Harmon CC
Rev Leo McDonnell CC
Cathedral House,
Cathedral Place, Limerick
Tel 061-414624/087-2589279
Fax 061-316570
Email stjohnsparishlk@eircom.net

**ST JOSEPH'S**
*St Joseph's*
*Sacristy:* 061-313401 (10.00 am-1.00 pm)
Very Rev Thomas Mangan Adm
'Naomh Joseph', Lifford Avenue, Limerick
Tel 061-303777/087-2376032

**ST MICHAEL'S**
*St Michael's*
Very Rev Noel Kirwan PP
St Michael's Church,
Denmark Street, Limerick
Tel 061-400133 (work)
061-413315 (church)/087-2616843
Email nkirwan@ldpc.ie

**ST MARY'S**
*St Mary's*
Sacristy: 061-416300
Very Rev Donough Canon O'Malley PP
Rev John O'Byrne AP
St Mary's, Athlunkard Street, Limerick
Tel 061-414092

**ST MUNCHIN'S AND ST LELIA'S**
*St Munchin's and St Lelia's*
Sacristy: 061-455133
Email stmunchinspresbytery@eircom.net
St Lelia's, Ballynanty
Tel 061-328577
Very Rev Donal Canon McNamara PP
Clancy Strand, Limerick
Tel/Fax 061-455635
Email donal@donalmcnamara.com
Rev Richard Crowe CC
10 Mayorstone Park, Limerick
Tel 061-452952
Rev Patrick Seaver CC
4 Glenview Terrace, Farranshone, Limerick
Tel 061-328838
Email patseaver@hotmail.com

**ST PATRICK'S**
*St Patrick's & St Brigid's*
Very Rev David Gibson PP
St Patrick's, Dublin Road, Limerick
Tel 061-415397/087-2547707
Fax 061-417152
Rev Eamon Purcell CC
112 Hilltop, St Patrick's Road, Limerick
Tel 061-413734

**ST PAUL'S**
*St Paul's*
Very Rev John Leonard PP, VF
The Presbytery, 10 St Nessan's Park, Dooradoyle, Limerick
Tel 061-302729
Rev Eugene Boyce CC
14 Springfield Drive, Dooradoyle
Tel 061-304508/086-2542517

**ST SAVIOUR'S**
*St Saviour's*
Very Rev Jordan O'Brien (OP) PP
St Saviour's, Glentworth Street, Limerick
Tel 061-412333 Fax 061-311728
Email oplimerick@eircom.net

**OUR LADY QUEEN OF PEACE**
*Our Lady Queen of Peace*
*Sacristy:* 061-467676
Very Rev Patrick O'Sullivan PP
'Elm View', Roxboro Road, Limerick
Tel 061-410846/087-2237501

**OUR LADY OF LOURDES**
*Our Lady of Lourdes*
Very Rev Damian Ryan PP
Lourdes House, Childers Road, Limerick
Tel 061-467676
Email 4dlord@eircom.net

**OUR LADY OF THE ROSARY**
*Holy Rosary*
Very Rev William Walsh PP
8 Merval Crescent, Clareview, Limerick
Tel/Fax 061-453026
Very Rev Thomas Ryan CC
Gleneden, North Circular Road, Limerick
Tel 061-329448
Parish mobile 087-2997733

**HOLY FAMILY**
*Holy Family*
Very Rev Patrick Hogan PP
334 O'Malley Park, Southill, Limerick
Tel 061-414248
Email pkfhogan@yahoo.co.uk

**CHRIST THE KING**
*Christ the King*
Very Rev Thomas Ryan PP
5 Derravaragh Road,
Caherdavin Park, Limerick
Tel 061-452790
Rev Richard Davern CC
17 Alderwood Avenue,
Caherdavin Heights, Limerick
Tel 061-453226

**CORPUS CHRISTI**
*Corpus Christi*
Rev Tony O'Riordan (SJ) PP
134 Cosgrave Park,
Moyross, Limerick
Tel 061-451783/087-9286945
Email tony@jcfj.ie

**OUR LADY HELP OF CHRISTIANS**
*Our Lady, Help of Christians*
Very Rev Koenraad Van Gucht (SDB) PP
Email johncampion00@eircom.net
Rev Robbie Swinburne (SDB) CC
Email robei2iq@eircom.net
Salesian House, Milford,
Castletroy, Limerick
Tel 061-330268

**ST NICHOLAS**
*St Nicholas, St Munchin's College Chapel*
Very Rev John Daly PP
Rev Patrick Costelloe AP
St Nicholas' Presbytery, Westbury,
Limerick
Tel 061-340614/087-8180815
Email jgdalystnicholas@eircom.net

**ABBEYFEALE**
*Our Lady of the Assumption*
Very Rev John Canon O'Shea PP
Tel 068-31157/087-9708282
Very Rev Micheál Canon Liston,
Assistant Priest
Tel 087-2314804
Convent Street,
Abbeyfeale, Co Limerick
Email fealechurch@eircom.net

**ADARE**
*Holy Trinity Abbey*
Very Rev Joseph Noonan PP
Adare, Co Limerick
Tel 061-396172/087-2400700

**ARDAGH AND CARRICKERRY**
*St Molua, Ardagh*
*St Mary, Carrickerry*
Very Rev Laurence Madden PP
Ardagh, Co Limerick
Tel 069-76121/087-2286450

**ARDPATRICK**
*St Patrick*
Very Rev Michael Hanley Adm
Kilfinane, Co Limerick
Tel 063-91016/086-8595733

**ASKEATON AND BALLYSTEEN**
*St Mary, Askeaton*
*St Patrick, Ballysteen*
Very Rev Seán Ó Longaigh PP
Tel/Fax 061-392249
Email seanolongaigh@eircom.net
Rev Senan Murray (CSSp) CC
Askeaton, Co Limerick
Tel 061-392131

**ATHEA**
*St Bartholomew*
Very Rev Patrick Bowen PP
Tel 068-42116/087-6532842
Email pbowen@eircom.net
Very Rev Patrick Canon Kelly PE
Tel 068-42107
Athea, Co Limerick

**BALLINGARRY AND GRANAGH**
*Our Lady of the Immaculate Conception*
*St Joseph*
Very Rev Daniel Lane PP
Ballingarry, Co Limerick
Tel/Fax 069-68141/087-2533030
Email danfl@eircom.net

**BALLYAGRAN AND COLMANSWELL**
*St Michael/St Colman*
Very Rev Joseph Shire PP
Ballyagran, Kilmallock, Co Limerick
Tel 063-82028/087-6924563
Email taylor@eircom.net

**BANOGUE**
Very Rev Joseph Kennedy Adm *(Pro-tem)*
Croom, Co Limerick
Tel 061-397231/087-9217622
Email jkcrm@eircom.net
Rev Eamonn O'Brien
Church Road, Croom, Co Limerick
Tel 061-397213
Email eamonofsanjose@aol.com

**BRUFF/MEANUS/GRANGE**
*SS Peter & Paul (Bruff); St Mary (Meanus)*
*SS Patrick and Brigid (Grange)*
*SS Peter & Paul*
Very Rev James Canon Costello PP, VF
Tel 061-382555
Very Rev Joseph Foley CC
Tel 061-382290/087-2618412
Bruff, Kilmallock, Co Limerick

**BULGADEN/MARTINSTOWN**
*Our Lady of the Assumption*
Very Rev Gerard McNamara PP
Bulgaden, Kilmallock, Co Limerick
Tel/Fax 063-88005/087-2408998
Email gmcn@iol.ie
*Our Lady of the Assumption*
Martinstown, Kilmallock, Co Limerick

**CAPPAGH**
*St James*
Very Rev Terry Loughran
Parochial House, Cappagh,
Askeaton, Co Limerick
Tel 069-63432/086-8103482
Email terry.loughran44@hotmail.com

**COOLCAPPA**
*St Colman, Kilcolman*
St Kieran, Coolcappa
Very Rev Denis Mullane PP
Kilcolman, Ardagh, Co Limerick
Tel 069-60126
Email denisgermullane@gmail.com

**CRATLOE**
*St John, Cratloe*
*St John, Sixmilebridge*
Very Rev Liam Enright PP
Cratloe, Co Clare
Tel 061-357196/087-2546335
Fax 061-357230
Email leppcrat@iol.ie
www.cratloe.org

**CROAGH AND KILFINNY**
*St John the Baptist, Croagh*
*St Kieran, Kilfinny*
Very Rev Anthony Mulvihill PP
Croagh, Rathkeale, Co Limerick
Tel 069-64185/087-9059348

**CROOM**
*St Mary*
Very Rev Joseph Kennedy PP
Croom, Co Limerick
Tel 061-397231/087-9217622
Email jkcrm@eircom.net
Rev Eamonn O'Brien
Church Road, Croom, Co Limerick
Tel 061-397213/087-0767521
Email eamonnofsanjose@aol.com

**DONAGHMORE/KNOCKEA**
*St Patrick, Donaghmore*
*St Patrick, Knockea*
Very Rev Oliver Plunkett PP
Email dkrchurches@eircom.net
Donaghmore, Co Limerick
Tel 061-313898/087-6593176
Email dkrchurches@eircom.net

**DROMCOLLOGHER/BROADFORD**
*St Bartholomew*
*Our Lady of the Snows*
Very Rev Francis O'Dea PP
Dromcollogher, Charleville, Co Limerick
Tel 087-2443106
Email frankodea@eircom.net

**DROMIN & ATHLACCA**
*St John the Baptist*
Very Rev Anthony Mullins PP
Dromin, Kilmallock, Co Limerick
Tel 063-31962
Email tonym@ldo.ie
Rev Patrick Howard
Athlacca, Kilmallock, Co Limerick
Tel 063-90540

**EFFIN/GARRIENDERK**
*Our Lady, Queen of Peace (Effin)*
*St Patrick (Garrienderk)*
Very Rev Thomas Coughlan PP
Effin, Kilmallock, Co Limerick
Tel 063-71314

**FEDAMORE**
*St John the Baptist*
Very Rev Michael Cussen PP
Fedamore, Kilmallock, Co Limerick
Tel 061-390112/087-1279015
Email mcuss@eircom.net

**FEENAGH AND KILMEEDY**
*St Ita*
Very Rev Brendan Murphy PP
Feenagh, Kilmallock, Co Limerick
Tel 063-85013/086-8094490

**GLENROE AND BALLYORGAN**
*Our Lady of Ransom, Glenroe*
*St Joseph, Ballyorgan*
Very Rev Timothy O'Leary PP
Glenroe, Kilmallock, Co Limerick
Tel 063-86040

**GLIN**
*Immaculate Conception*
Very Rev Thomas Crawford PP
Glin, Co Limerick
Tel 068-26897

**KILCORNAN**
*St John the Baptist*
Very Rev Terry Loughran Adm
Cappagh, Askeaton, Co Limerick
Tel 069-63432
Rev Michael Irwin (SSC) *(Priest in residence)*
Kilcornan, Co Limerick
Tel 061-393113
Email mlmirwin@gmail.com

**KILDIMO AND PALLASKENRY**
*St Joseph, Kildimo*
*St Mary, Pallaskenry*
Very Rev John Donworth PP
Kildimo, Co Limerick
Tel 061-394134/087-2237501
Fax 061-394280
Email johndonworth@hotmail.com

**KILFINANE**
*St Andrew*
Very Rev Michael Hanley PP
Kilfinane, Co Limerick
Tel 063-91016/086-8595733

**KILLEEDY**
*St Ita's, Ashford; St Ita's, Killeedy*
Very Rev John Keating PP
Raheenagh, Ballagh, Co Limerick
Tel 069-85014

**KILMALLOCK**
*SS Peter & Paul, Kilmallock*
*St Mary, Ballingaddy*
Very Rev William Canon Fitzmaurice PP, VF
Killmallock, Co Limerick
Tel 063-98287/086-2423728
Email kilmallockchurch@eircom.net
Rev Joseph Cussen CC
Glenfield Road, Killmallock,
Co Limerick
Tel 063-98061

**KNOCKADERRY & CLONCAGH**
*St Mary, Cloncagh*
*St Munchin, Knockaderry*
Very Rev Edwin Irwin PP
Cloncagh, Ballingarry, Co Limerick
Tel 069-83006

**LOUGHILL/BALLYHAHILL**
*Our Lady of the Visitation (Ballyhahill)*
*Our Lady of the Wayside (Loughill)*
Very Rev Gerard O'Leary Adm
Parochial House, Ballyhahill, Co Limerick
Tel 069-82103/087-9378685
Email olearyg22@eircom.net

**MAHOONAGH**
*St John the Baptist, Castlemahon*
*St Mary, Feohanagh*
Very Rev John Duggan PP
Castlemahon, Co Limerick
Tel 069-72108/086-2600464

**MANISTER**
*St Michael*
Very Rev Garrett Canon Bluett PP
Manister, Croom, Co Limerick
Tel 061-397335

**MONAGEA**
*Church of Visitation of BVM*
Very Rev Frank Canon Duhig
St Ita's Presbytery, Newcastle West,
Co Limerick
Tel 069-62141
Email frank@tripswitch.com

**MONALEEN**
*St Mary Magdalene*
Right Rev Mgr Daniel Neenan PP, VG
1 Trinity Court, Monaleen Road,
Monaleen, Limerick
Tel 061-330974/087-2208547
Email danneenan@eircom.net
Rev Michael O'Shea CC
9 Castletroy Heights, Monaleen,
Limerick
Tel 061-335764/087-9791432

**MUNGRET/CRECORA**
*St Nessan, Raheen*
*St Oliver Plunkett, Mungret*
*SS Peter & Paul, Crecora*
Very Rev Michael Noonan PP
The Presbytery, Raheen, Limerick
Tel 061-301112/087-6796217
Email mnmcraheen@oceanfree.net
Rev Eamonn Fitzgibbon
Ballyduane, Clarina, Co Limerick

**NEWCASTLE WEST**
*Immaculate Conception of BVM*
Very Rev Frank Canon Duhig PP
St Ita's Presbytery,
Newcastle West, Co Limerick
Tel 069-62141/087-6380299
Rev Patrick Bluett CC
Gortboy, Newcastle West, Co Limerick
Tel 069-61881
Rev Richard Keane CC
Gortboy, Newcastle West, Co Limerick
Tel 069-77090/087-9552729
Email newparish@yahoo.co.uk

**PARTEEN/MEELICK**
*St Patrick, Parteen*
*St John the Baptist, Meelick*
Very Rev Thomas Carroll PP
Parteen, Co Clare
Tel 061-345613
Email carrollgtom@gmail.com
Rev Fred McDonnell CC
The Presbytery, Meelick, Co Clare
Tel 061-325556/087-7706023
Email frfred@gmail.com

**PATRICKSWELL/BALLYBROWN**
*Blessed Virgin Mary, Patrickswell*
*St Joseph, Ballybrown*
Very Rev Muiris O'Connor PP
Ballybrown, Clarina,
Co Limerick
Tel 061-353711/086-6075628
Email muirisoc@eircom.net

**RATHKEALE**
*St Mary*
Very Rev Alphonsus Cullinan PP
Lower Main Street, Rathkeale,
Co Limerick
Tel 069-63133
Rev William Russell CC
Enniscouch, Rathkeale, Co Limerick
Tel 069-63490/087-2272825

**ROCKHILL/BRUREE**
*St Munchin, Rockhill*
*Immaculate Conception, Bruree*
Very Rev Desmond McAuliffe Adm
Rockhill, Bruree, Co Limerick
Tel 063-90515/087-2336476
Email desmcauliffe@yahoo.co.uk

**SHANAGOLDEN & FOYNES**
*St Senan, Shanagolden*
*St Senan, Foynes*
*St Senan, Robertstown*
Very Rev Anthony Canon O'Keeffe PP, VF
Shanagolden, Co Limerick
Tel 069-60112/087-4163401
Rev James Noonan (SPS) CC
Foynes, Co Limerick
Tel 069-65165

**TEMPLEGLANTINE**
*Most Holy Trinity*
Very Rev Micheál Liston Adm
21 Sullane Crescent, Raheen Heights,
Limerick
Tel 087-2314804
Very Rev Thomas Hurley
Templeglantine, Co Limerick
Tel 069-84021
Email thurley@eircom.net

**TOURNAFULLA/MOUNTCOLLINS**
*St Patrick, Tournafulla*
*Our Lady of the Assumption, Mountcollins*
Very Rev William O'Gorman PP
Tournafulla, Co Limerick
Tel 069-81010/087-2580020

## INSTITUTIONS AND THEIR CHAPLAINS

**Askeaton Community College**
Coláiste Mhuire, Askeaton, Co Limerick
Ms Diane Brown
Tel 061-392368

**Brothers of Charity Services**
Bawnmore, Clonlong Road, Limerick
Rev Joseph Young
21 Marian Avenue, Janesboro, Limerick
Tel 061-405835

**Castletroy Community College**
Castletroy, Limerick
Tel 061-330785
Ms Brenda Cribben

**Coláiste Iosaf, Kilmallock**
Vacant
Tel 063-98275

**Coláiste Na Trócaire**
Rathkeale, Co Limerick
Rev Tim Curtin
Tel 069-63432

**County Prison, Limerick**
Mulgrave Street, Limerick
*Prison General Office:* Tel 061-415111
Rev John Walsh
Mountdavid House,
North Circular Road, Limerick
Tel 061-452063/087-2433488

**Croom County Hospital**
Croom, Co Limerick
Very Rev Garrett Canon Bluett
Tel 061-397335

**Regional Hospital**
Dooradoyle, Limerick
Tel 061-301111
Rev Michael McGuckian
'Della Strada',
Dooradoyle Road, Limerick
Tal 061-30111
Rev Robert Coffey
37 Gouldavoher Estate,
Dooradoyle, Limerick
Tel 061-482437/087-6540908

**Regional Maternity Hospital**
Ennis Road, Limerick
Parish clergy, Our Lady of the Rosary
087-2997733

**St Camillus's Hospital**
Shelbourne Road, Limerick
Rev Richard Crowe
Tel 061-452952

**St Enda's Community School, Limerick**
Old Cork Road, Limerick
Ms Deirdre Moore
Tel 061-419222

**St Ita's Hospital**
Newcastle West, Co Limerick
Tel 069-62311
Very Rev Frank Duhig PP
Tel 069-62141

**St John's Hospital, Limerick**
Pastoral Care Department
Tel 061-462111
Very Rev Austin McNamara Adm
Tel 087-2589279/061-414624
Ms Lourda O'Sullivan CHC
Ms Joyce O'Sullivan CHC

**St Joseph's Hospital, Limerick**
Tel 061-414624
Rev Sean Harmon

**St Nessan's Community College**
Moylish, Limerick
Tel 061-452422
Chaplaincy vacant

**St Paul's Home**
Dooradoyle, Limerick
Tel 061-228209
Clergy of St Paul's Parish
Tel 061-302729/307508

**Sarsfield Barracks, Limerick**
Tel 061-316817
Rev Seamus Madigan

## PRIESTS OF THE DIOCESE ELSEWHERE

Rev David Costello
c/o The Missionary Society of St James the Apostle, 24 Clark Street,
Boston, MA 02109, USA
Email davidmpc@oceanfree.net
Rev Brendan Fitzgerald
c/o Diocesan Office, Social Service Centre,
Henry Street, Limerick
Rev Gerard Garrett
Cork Regional Marriage Tribunal,
The Lough, Cork
Tel 021-4963653
Email ggarrett.tribunal@eircom.net
Rev Derek Leonard
c/o The Missionary Society of St James the Apostle, 24 Clark Street,
Boston, MA 02109, USA
Email derekleonard@eircom.net
Rev John McCarthy
Irish Pastoral Centre, 953 Hancock Street,
Quincy, Massachusetts CO2170, USA
Tel 001-617479740
Rev Leslie McNamara
Columban Missionary Society, Dalgan Park,
Dublin Road, Navan, Co Meath
Rev Terry O'Connell
c/o Diocesan Office, Social Service Centre,
Henry Street, Limerick

## PRIESTS ON STUDY LEAVE

Rev David Bracken
c/o Diocesan Office, Social Service Centre,
Henry Street, Limerick
Rev John Mockler
c/o Diocesan Office, Social Service Centre,
Henry Street, Limerick
Rev Gerard Slattery
c/o Diocesan Office, Social Service Centre,
Henry Street, Limerick

## RETIRED PRIESTS

Very Rev James Canon Ambrose
Dromcollogher, Charleville, Co Limerick
Tel 087-7740753
Rev Jeremiah Brouder
49 Halcyon Place, Park Village,
Castletroy, Limerick
Rt Rev Liam Boyle
Knockaderry, Co Limerick
Very Rev Denis Canon Browne
Kilmallock, Co Limerick
Rev Cornelius Collins
Patrickswell, Co Limerick
Rev Sean Condon
Cathedral House, Cathedral Place,
Limerick
Tel 061-414624
Rev Maurice Costello
Main Street, Rathkeale, Co Limerick
Tel 069-63452
Very Rev Peadar de Burca
Kilmeedy, Co Limerick
Tel 063-87008
Very Rev Patrick Howard
Athlacca, Kilmallock, Co Limerick
Very Rev Thomas Hurley
Templeglantine, Co Limerick
Tel 068-84021
Right Rev Michael Dean Kelly
St Catherine's Nursing Home,
Newcastle West, Co Limerick
Very Rev David Kennedy
Clonlusk Doon, Co Limerick
Rt Rev Mgr Michael Lane PE, VG
2 Meadowvale, Raheen, Limerick
Tel 061-228761
Email mwlane@esatclear.ie
Very Rev Michael Lane
Shravokee, Clonlara, near Limerick
Very Rev Micheál Canon Liston
21 Sullane Crescent,
Raheen Heights, Limerick
Very Rev Martin Madigan
Hamilton's Terrace, Glin, Co Limerick
Tel 087-9418568
Very Rev Frank Moriarty
Adare, Co Limerick
Tel 061-396177
Very Rev James Canon Neville
Cedarville, Abbeyfeale, Co Limerick
Tel 068-32884
Rev P. J. O'Donnell
c/o Diocesan Office, Social Service Centre,
Henry Street, Limerick
Rev Charles O'Neill
Colmanswell, Charleville, Co Limerick
Tel 063-89459
Rev Antóin Ó Tuathaigh
c/o Diocesan Office, Social Service Centre,
Henry Street, Limerick
Very Rev Seamus Power PE
'Sheen Lodge', Ennis Road, Limerick
Tel 061-454841

## PERSONAL PRELATURE

**OPUS DEI**
Rev Brian McCarthy
Castleville Study Centre,
Golf Links Road, Castletroy, Limerick
Tel 061-331223 Fax 061-331204
Email castleville@eircom.net

## RELIGIOUS ORDERS AND CONGREGATIONS

### PRIESTS

**AUGUSTINIANS**
St Augustine's Priory,
O'Connell Street, Limerick
Tel 061-415374
*Prior:* Rev Frank Sexton (OSA)

**DOMINICANS**
St Saviour's, Glentworth Street,
Limerick
Tel 061-412333 Fax 061-311728
*Prior:* Very Rev Jordan O'Brien (OP)

**FRANCISCAN FRIARS OF THE RENEWAL (CFR)**
St Patrick Friary
64 Delmege Park, Moyross Limerick
Tel 061-458071 Fax 061-457626
*Local Servant (Superior)*
Br Shawn Conrad O'Connor

**JESUITS**
Crescent College Comprehensive,
Dooradoyle, Limerick
Tel 061-480920 Fax 061-480928
Email dooradoyle@jesuit.ie
*Superior:* Rev Liam O'Connell (SJ)
*Headmaster:* Mr Nicholas Cuddihy
Tel 061-229655 Fax 061-229013
Email ccadmin.ias@eircom.net

**REDEMPTORISTS**
Mount St Alphonsus Mission House,
Limerick
Tel 061-315099 Fax 061-315303
*Superior*
Rev Adrian Egan (CSsR)

St Clement's College, Limerick
Tel 061-315878 Fax 061-316640
Email cssrlimerick@eircom.net
Secondary school for boys

**SALESIANS**
Salesian College, Pallaskenry, Co Limerick
Tel 061-393313 Fax 061-393021
*Rector:* Very Rev Martin Loftus (SDB)
Email salesian@indigo.ie
Secondary and agricultural schools

Salesian House, Milford,
Castletroy, Limerick
Tel 061-330268/330194
*Rector & Parish Priest*
Rev Koenraad Van Gucht (SDB) PP
*Vice-Rector:* Rev John Campion (SDB)
Student hostel and parish

### BROTHERS

**BROTHERS OF CHARITY**
Bawnmore, Clonlong Road, Limerick
Tel 061-412288 Fax 061-412389
*Chaplain:* Rev Joe Young

**CHRISTIAN BROTHERS**
Christian Brothers, St Teresa's,
North Circular Road, Limerick
Tel 061-451811
Community Leader: Br M. S. Hynes
Community: 4

### SISTERS

**SISTERS OF CHARITY OF OUR LADY MOTHER OF MERCY**
St Andrew's, 3 Avonmore Road,
Raheen, Limerick
Tel 061-229935 Fax 061-229984
*Superior:* Sr Nora Hayes
Community: 3

**CHARITY OF ST PAUL THE APOSTLE SISTERS**
St Paul's Convent,
Kilfinane, Co Limerick
Tel 063-91025 Fax 063-91639
Email stpaulstin@eircom.net
*Contact:* Sr Eileen Kelly
Community: 4
Secondary school day pupils, Parish work

St Paul's, Glenfield Road,
Kilmallock, Co Limerick
Tel 063-98086
Email sisterskilm@eircom.net
*Contact:* Sr Teresa Murphy
Community: 4
Primary school, parish and social work

**CONGREGATION OF THE SISTERS OF MERCY**
*The Sisters of Mercy minister throughout the diocese in pastoral and social work, community development, counselling, spirituality, education and health care, answering current needs.*

Convent of Mercy, Westbourne,
Ashbourne Avenue, Limerick
Tel 061-229388/229605 Fax 061-304088
Community: 11

Mountmahon,
Abbeyfeale, Co Limerick
Tel 068-31203
Community: 2

Mount St Vincent,
O'Connell Avenue, Limerick
Tel 061-314965 Fax 061-404175
Community: 19

Sisters of Mercy, St Mary's Convent,
Bishop Street, Limerick
Tel 061-317356 Fax 061-317361
Community: 9

St Anne's Convent,
Thomas Street, Rathkeale, Co Limerick
Tel 069-64175 Fax 069-63155
Community: 5

7 Sullane Crescent,
Raheen, Limerick
Tel/Fax 061-227436
Community: 3

16 Portland Estate, St Clare's, Newcastle
Tel/Fax 069-62373
Community: 3

33 Danesfort, Corbally, Limerick
Tel 061-341214
Community: 3

34 Danesfort, Corbally, Limerick
Tel/Fax 061-349411
Community: 2

7 Fitzhaven Square,
Ashbourne Avenue, Limerick
Tel/Fax 061-304614
Community: 2

Corpus Christi, 129 Cosgrave Park,
Moyross, Limerick
Tel/Fax 061-452511
Community: 4

1 Greenfields, Rosbrien, Limerick
Tel/Fax 061-229773
Community: 3

Catherine McAuley House
Old Dominic Street, Limerick
Tel 061-315313/315384 Fax 061-315455
Community: 31

136 Fortview Drive,
Ballinacurra Gardens, Limerick
Tel 061-304798
Community: 2

1 Mount Vincent Place,
O'Connell Avenue, Limerick
Tel 061-468448
Community: 4

Emmanuel, 2 Nessan Court,
Church Road, Raheen, Limerick
Tel/Fax 061-301363
Community: 2

22 Galtee Drive,
O'Malley Park, Southill, Limerick
Tel/Fax 061-416706
Community: 2

Cuan Mhuire, Bruree, Limerick
Tel 063-90555
Community: 1

Ballygrennan, Bruff, Co Limerick
Tel 061-382106
*Leader:* Sr Catherine Toomey
Community: 3
Secondary coeducational school
Chaplaincy, Parish
*Principal:* Mr Michael Clifford
Tel 061-382349 Fax 061-382511

**FRANCISCAN MISSIONARIES OF MARY**
Castle View Gardens,
Clancy Strand, Limerick
Tel 061-455320
Email annfmmcondon@hotmail.com
*Superior:* Sr Ann Condon
Community: 10
Pastoral work

**GOOD SHEPHERD SISTERS**
Good Shepherd Avenue,
12 Pennywell Road, Limerick
Tel 061-415178 Fax 061-415147
Email rgslim@eircom.net
*Leader:* Sr Geraldine Browne
Community: 22

Omega B, Roxboro Road,
Janesboro, Limerick
Tel 061-416676 Fax 061-418207
Email rgsroxboro@hotmail.com
Community: 4

Good Shepherd Sisters, 33 Salvia Court,
Keyes Park, Southill, Limerick
Tel 061-414990
Email rgsanna02@eircom.net
Community: 1
Assistance to people in difficulty and alcoholics

**LITTLE COMPANY OF MARY**
Milford House, Castletroy, Limerick
Tel 061-485800 Fax 061-330351
Community: 14
Milford Care Centre
Tel 061-485800 Fax 061-331181
Email milford@milfordcarecentre.ie
Hospice & nursing home and convalescent beds
*Manager of Nursing Services*
Ms Marian Moriarty
Tel 061-485856 Fax 061-330142
Email m.moriarty@milfordcarecentre.ie

St Joseph's Convent, Plassey Park Road,
Castletroy, Limerick
Tel 061-331144 Fax 061-331188
Apostolic Community: 4

'Genazzano', 1 Shrewsbury Lawn,
Westbury, Corbally, Limerick
Tel 061-345656
Apostolic community: 2

1 Mary Potter Court, Plassey Park Road,
Castletroy, Limerick
Tel/Fax 061-332798
Community: 1

2 Mary Potter Court,
Plassey Park Road, Castletroy, Limerick
Tel 061-332777
Community: 1

3 Mary Potter Court,
Plassey Park Road, Castletroy, Limerick
Tel 061-332755
Community: 1

**MARIE REPARATRICE SISTERS**
Laurel Hill Avenue,
South Circular Road, Limerick
Tel 061-315045 Fax 061-312561
Email smrlim@eircom.net
*Superior:* Sr Bernadette O'Driscoll
Community: 11
Spiritual direction/retreats

**POOR SERVANTS OF THE MOTHER OF GOD**
43 Liosan, Sheehan Road,
Newcastle West, Co Limerick
Community: 2
Daycare Centre

Dún Íosa, Main Street,
Drumcollogher, Co Limeick
Community: 2
Pastoral

Embury Close,
Adare, Co Limerick
Community: 1
Ministry to Elderly

**PRESENTATION SISTERS**
Presentation Sisters,
9-10 Butterfield Avenue,
Old Cork Road, Limerick
Tel 061-414812
Shared Leadership
Community: 4

Presentation Sisters,
8-9 Oakvale Drive, Dooradoyle, Limerick
Tel 061-302011
*Non-resident Leader*
Sr Colette Hourigan
Community: 4
Sexton Street Primary School
Tel 061-412494
Secondary School. Tel 061-410390

Roxboro Road, Limerick
Tel 061-417204
*Non-resident Leader*
Sr Jennie Clifford
Community: 13
Janesboro Primary. Tel 061-311285
Galvone National School. Tel 061-311286

34 McDonagh Avenue,
Janesboro, Limerick
Tel 061-594777
Community: 1

Apartment A,
6 Sexton Street, Limerick
Tel 061-467866
Community: 1

Apartment B,
6 Sexton Street, Limerick
Tel 061-467867
Community: 1

**SALESIAN SISTERS OF ST JOHN BOSCO**
Salesian Convent, Fernbank,
North Circular Road, Limerick
Tel 061-455322
*Superior:* Sr Sarah O'Rourke
Community: 11
Kindergarten and primary schools and related activities

34 Bracken Crescent,
North Circular Road, Limerick
Tel 061-455132
*Superior:* Sr Brigid Beggan
Community: 4
Teaching, related activities

Salesian Convent, Dun Ide,
Lower Shelbourne Road, Limerick
Tel 061-454511
*Superior:* Sr Bridget O'Connell
Community: 9
Secondary School. Tel 061-454699
Principal: Sr Bridget O'Connell

Salesian Convent, Ard Mhuire,
Caherdavin Heights, Limerick
Tel 061-451322
*Superior:* Sr Patricia Prenderville
Community: 11
Ministry to the elderly

Salesian Sisters, Cill Leala, New Road,
Thomondgate, Limerick
Tel 061-453099 Fax 061-455413
*Superior:* Sr Noelle Costello
Community: 4
Involvement in Ballynanty Resource Centre

Salesian Sisters, 14 Clonile,
Old Cratloe Road, Limerick
Tel 061-329673
*Superior:* Sr Maureen Mullen
Community: 3
Teaching and related activities; social work

Salesian Sisters, 3 Oakton Road,
Westbury, Corbally, Limerick
*Superior:* Sr Kathleen Barry
Community: 3
Social work

**ST JOSEPH OF THE SACRED HEART SISTERS**
Granagh, Kilmallock, Co Limerick
Tel 061-399027
*Regional Leader:* Sr Margaret O'Sullivan
Email lmargaretosullivan@eircom.net

Sisters of St Joseph of Sacred Heart,
7 Plassey Grove, Castletroy, Limerick
Tel 061-335794

Sisters of St Joseph of Sacred Heart,
Mackillop House, Dromcollogher,
Co Limerick
Tel 063-83911

Sisters of St Joseph of Sacred Heart,
No. 2 St Ita's Centre, Convent Street,
Abbeyfeale, Co Limerick
Tel 068-51984

Sisters of St Joseph of Sacred Heart,
4 Clover Field, Glin, Co Limerick
Tel 068-26015

Sisters of St Joseph of Sacred Heart,
14 Court Villas, Rathkeale, Co Limerick
Tel 069-63682

Sisters of St Joseph, St Catherine's,
Bungalow 2, Bothar Buí, Newcastle West,
Co Limerick
Tel 069-62584

Sisters of St Joseph, Apt 15, Liosan Court,
Gort Boy, Newcastle West, Co Limerick
Tel 069-69603

Sisters of St Joseph, St Joseph's,
Banogue Cross, Croom, Co Limerick
Tel 061-600932

## EDUCATIONAL INSTITUTIONS

**Limerick Institute of Technology**
Tel 061-327688
*Chaplain:* Rev Declan Murray (SJ)
142 Mayorstone Park, Limerick
Tel 061-327836/208302
Email declan.murray@lit.ie

**Mary Immaculate College of Education**
Tel 061-204300
*Chaplain:* Rev Michael Wall
Tel 061-204331
Email michael.wall@mic.ul.ie
*Head of Department of Theology & Religious Studies:* Rev Eamonn Conway
Tel 061-204353
Email eamonn.conway@mic.ul.ie

**St Munchin's College (Diocesan College)**
Corbally, Limerick
Tel 061-348922 Fax 061-340465
Email stmunchins@eircom.net
*President:* Very Rev Charles Irwin BD, HDE
*Chaplain:* T. Conneely

**University of Limerick**
*Chaplain:* Rev John Campion
Salesian House, Milford,
Castletroy, Limerick
Tel 061-330268/202180
Email johncampion00@eircom.net

**EDMUND RICE SCHOOLS TRUST**
Scoil Iosagáin Primary School,
Sexton Street, Limerick
Tel 061-413950 Fax 061-416011
Email cbslk@eircom.net
Website www.cbslk.com
*Principal:* Mr. P. Hanley

Coláiste Mhichil Secondary School,
Sexton Street, Limerick
Tel 061-416628/419261 Fax 061-416011
Email rice@iol.ie
*Principal:* Mr Noel Earlie

St Munchin's Primary School,
Shelbourne Road, Limerick
Tel 061-455180 Fax 061-455108
Email primarymun@eircom.net
*Principal:* Mr Michael Condon

Ardscoil Rís Secondary School,
North Circular Road, Limerick
Tel 061-453828/455251
Fax 061-325035
Email asroffice@eircom.net
Website www.ardscoil.com
*Principal:* Bríd de Brún

## CHARITABLE AND OTHER SOCIETIES

**Adapt**
Adapt House, Rosbrien, Limerick
Tel 061-412354
Contact: Ms Monica McElvaney

**Alcoholics Anonymous**
(Also Al/Anon and Alateen)
Social Service Centre,
Henry Street, Limerick
Tel 061-314111
24 hour service Tel 061-311222

**Apostolic Work Society**
*Contact:* Mrs Brid Shine
Glenbrohane, Garryspillane,
Kilmallock, Co Limerick
Tel 062-46612
Email dirb@iol.ie

**Catholic Housing Aid Society**
*Contact:* Very Rev Donal McNamara PP
Tel 061-455635

**Catholic Institute Athletic Club**
Rosbrien, Limerick
*President:* Tel 061-455635
*Secretary:* Tel 061-452023

**Doras Luimní**
**(Development organisation for Refugees and Asylum Seekers)**
Mount St Vincent, O'Connell Street,
Limerick
Tel 061-609960
Email dorasluimni@eircom.net

**Knights of St Columbanus**
*Contact:* Mr William Ryan
Tel 061-414173 (work)/061-227530 (home)

**Legion of Mary**
Assumpta House, Windmill Street,
Limerick
Tel 061-314071

**Limerick Youth Service**
5 Lower Glentworth Street, Limerick
Tel 061-412444/412545 Fax 061-412795
*Director:* Catherine Kelly
Email lys@limerickyouthservice.net

**Order of Malta**
7A Davis Street, Limerick
Tel/Fax 061-314250

**Samaritans**
20 Barrington Street, Limerick
Tel 061-412111/1850-609090

**St John's Hospital**
Limerick
Tel 061-415822

**St Joseph's Young Priests' Society**
*Contact:* Ms Una Nunan
10 Garravogue Road, Raheen, Limerick
Tel 061-227852

**St Vincent de Paul Society**
Ozanam House, Hartstonge Street,
Limerick
Tel 061-317327 Fax 061-310320
Email info@svpmw.com
*Administrator:* Ms Mary Leahy
*Drop-In Centre*
The Lane, Hartstonge Street, Limerick
*Manager:* Mr Tom Flynn
Tel 061-313557

# DIOCESE OF MEATH

PATRON OF THE DIOCESE
ST FINIAN, 12 DECEMBER

INCLUDES THE GREATER PART OF COUNTIES MEATH, WESTMEATH AND OFFALY, AND A PORTION OF COUNTIES LONGFORD, LOUTH, DUBLIN AND CAVAN

**Most Rev Michael Smith DCL, DD**
Bishop of Meath;
born 1940;
ordained priest 1963;
consecrated Bishop 29 January 1984; Co-adjutor Bishop of Meath 10 October 1988;
succeeded 16 May 1990

Residence: Bishop's House,
Dublin Road,
Mullingar, Co Westmeath
Tel 044-9348841 Fax 044-9343020
Email bishop@dioceseofmeath.ie
Website www.dioceseofmeath.ie

## CATHEDRAL OF CHRIST THE KING, MULLINGAR

As the Penal Laws began to be relaxed, Bishop Patrick Plunkett was appointed Bishop of Meath in 1778. He was to spend the next forty-nine years of his life restoring and rebuilding the diocese. He had no cathedral, but providing one was not his immediate priority. Towards the end of his time as bishop, work began on the magnificent new Church of St Mary in Navan. This was opened in 1830 and was considered the Cathedral Church of the Diocese. In 1870 Bishop Thomas Nulty decided to locate the bishop's residence in Mullingar, and the parish church there was designated Cathedral Church of the Diocese. It had been built in 1828 but was quite small.

On his appointment as bishop in 1900, Matthew Gaffney called a public meeting to discuss the building of a cathedral for the Diocese of Meath. This meeting adopted the following resolution: 'The Diocese of Meath not having a cathedral nor the parish of Mullingar a suitable church, be it resolved that a church be built in Mullingar which will fulfil this double purpose.' A building fund was established, and £15,000 was subscribed at this first meeting – a very sizeable sum at that time. It was not until the day of his consecration as bishop in 1929 that Thomas Mulvany was able to announce the decision to proceed with the project. Ralph A. Byrne, chief architect with William H. Byrne & Son, Dublin, prepared plans, which were accepted. Work began in 1932, and the Cathedral of Christ the King was opened for worship in September 1936. It was consecrated on 30 August 1939, the debt having been cleared. In recent years, a major renovation, including the replacement of the roof, has been completed.

## ADMINISTRATION

Diocesan website
www.dioceseofmeath.ie

**Vicars General**
Rt Rev Mgr Dermot Farrell PP, VG
Parochial House, Dunboyne, Co Meath
Tel 01-8255342 Fax 01-8252321
Rt Rev Mgr Seán Heaney PP, VG
Parochial House, Tullamore, Co Offaly
Tel 057-9321587 Fax 057-9351510

**Vicars Forane**
Very Rev John Byrne PP, VF
Parochial House, Kells, Co Meath
Tel 046-9240213 Fax 046-9293475
Very Rev Joseph Clavin PP, VF
Parochial House,
Dunshaughlin, Co Meath
Tel 01-8259114 Fax 01-8011614
Very Rev Richard Matthews PP, VF
Parochial House, Killucan, Co Westmeath
Tel 044-9374127
Very Rev Patrick Keary PP, VF
Parochial House, Clara, Co Offaly
Tel 057-9331170 Fax 057-9330100
Very Rev Patrick Moore PP, VF
Parochial House,
Castlepollard, Co Westmeath
Tel 044-9661126 Fax 044-9661881
Very Rev Andrew Doyle PP, VF
Parochial House, Durhamstown,
Bohermeen, Navan, Co Meath
Tel 046-9073805
Very Rev Denis Nulty PP, VF
St Mary's, Drogheda, Co Louth
Tel 041-9834958 Fax 041-9845144
Very Rev Patrick O'Connor PP, VF
Parochial House, Athboy, Co Meath
Tel 046-9432184 Fax 046-9430021

**College of Consultors**
Most Rev Michael Smith DD, DCL
Rt Rev Mgr Seán Heaney PP, VG
Rt Rev Mgr Dermot Farrell PP, VG
Very Rev John Byrne PP, VF
Very Rev Joseph Clavin PP, VF
Very Rev Richard Matthews, PP, VF
Very Rev Patrick Keary PP, VF
Very Rev Patrick Moore PP, VF
Very Rev Andrew Doyle PP, VF
Very Rev Denis Nulty PP, VF
Very Rev Patrick O'Connor PP, VF
Rev Paul Crosbie CC

**Diocesan Secretary**
Rev Paul Crosbie
Bishop's House, Dublin Road, Mullingar,
Co Westmeath
Tel 044-9348841 Fax 044-9343020
Email paul@dioceseofmeath.ie

**Secretary**
Mrs Irene Connaughton
Bishop's House, Dublin Road, Mullingar,
Co Westmeath
Tel 044-9348841 Fax 044-9343020
Email secretary@dioceseofmeath.ie

## CATECHETICS EDUCATION

**Education**
*Diocesan Secretary*
Rev Brendan Ludlow PC
St Mary's, Navan, Co Meath
Tel 087-1739700
Email cpsma@dioceseofmeath.ie

**Post-Primary Catechetics**
*Diocesan Director:* Mr Seán Wright
The Whinnies, Tierworker,
Kells, Co Meath
Tel 042-9665547 Fax 042-9666969
Email ppdd@eircom.net

**Primary Religious Education**
*Diocesan Advisers*
Rev Barry Condron CC
Tyrrellspass, Co Westmeath
Tel 044-9223115
Email tyrrellspass1@eircom.net
Very Rev Tony Gavin Adm
Parochial House,
Rosemount, Co Westmeath
Tel 090-6436110
Mrs Nuala Cosgrave, David Gavin,
Mrs Caitriona Flaherty,
Sr Annette O'Brien
Bishop's House, Dublin Road, Mullingar,
Co Westmeath
Tel 044-9348841

## LITURGY

**Liturgical Commission**
*Chairman:* Very Rev Joseph McEvoy PP
Parochial House, Moynalty, Co Meath
Tel 046-9244305
Email josephus@indigo.ie
*Secretary:* Mr James Walsh
18 Beechgrove, Laytown, Co Meath

## PASTORAL

**Accord**
*Spiritual Director, Mullingar Centre*
Very Rev Richard Matthews PP
Parochial House, Killucan,
Co Westmeath
*Chairperson, Navan Centre*
Mr D. Cordial
St Anne's Resource Centre,
Navan, Co Meath
*Director, Tullamore Centre*
Very Rev Gerry Boyle PP
Multyfarnham, Co Westmeath
Tel 057-9321587
www.dioceseofmeath.ie/marriage

**Apostolic Work Society**
*Mullingar Branch*
*Chaplain:* Rev Padraig Corcoran CC
Cathedral House, Mullingar,
Co Westmeath
Tel 044-9348338
*Navan Branch*
*Chaplain:* Rev Stephen Kelly CC
St Mary's, Navan, Co Meath
Tel 046-9027518

**CPSMA**
Rev Brendan Ludlow PC
St Mary's Presbytery, Navan, Co Meath
Tel 087-1739700

**Chaplain to Polish Community**
Rev Janusz Lugowski
Mount Rivers, Kells Road,
Navan, Co Meath
Tel 087-9538786

**Council of Priests**
*Chairman:* Very Rev Denis Nulty PP, VF
St Mary's Drogheda, Co Louth
Tel 041-9834958
*Secretary:* Rev Brendan Ludlow PC
St Mary's, Navan, Co Meath
Tel 046-9027518

**Dowdstown House (Blowick Conference Centre)**
Dowdstown House,
Navan, Co Meath
Tel 046-9021407 Fax 046-9073091
*Director:* Sr Elma Peppard
*Family Ministry Co-ordinators*
Sr Rose King, Sr Rose Sloan

**Ecumenism**
*Secretary:* Very Rev William Coleman PP
Parochial House, Rochfortbridge,
Co Westmeath
Tel 044-9222107

**Fr Matthew Union**
*Secretary:* Very Rev Seamus Houlihan PP
Parochial House,
Nobber, Co Meath
Tel 046-9052197

**Knock Pilgrimage**
*Director:* Very Rev Martin Halpin PP
Parochial House, Ballinabrackey,
Kinnegad, Co Westmeath
Tel 046-9739015

**Laity Commission**
*Diocesan Representative*
Mrs Molly Buckley
Moylena, Clara Road,
Tullamore, Co Offaly
Tel 0506-41357

**Lourdes Pilgrimage**
*Director*
Very Rev Joseph Gallagher PP
Parochial House, Kilcormac, Co Offaly
Tel 057-9135989

**Marriage Tribunal**
(See Marriage Tribunals section)

**Pioneer Total Abstinence Association**
Very Rev Seamus Houlihan PP
Parochial House, Nobber,
Co Meath
Tel 046-9052197

**Pontifical Mission Societies**
*Diocesan Director*
Very Rev Gerard Stuart PP
Parochial House, Ratoath, Co Meath
Tel 01-8256207

**Safeguarding Resource Team**
Mrs Sandra Neville
Email neville.sandra@gmail.com
Mrs Joan Walshe
Email joan.walshe@yahoo.co.uk

**Travellers**
*Chaplain:* Very Rev Patrick O'Connor PP, VF
Parochial House Athboy, Co Meath
Tel 046-9432184

**Vocations and Youth**
*Director:* Rev Mark English CC
Parochial House,
Dunboyne, Co Meath
Tel 01-8255342
Email mjpenglish@eircom.net

## PARISHES

*Mensal parishes are listed first. Other parishes follow alphabetically.*

**MULLINGAR,**
*Cathedral of Christ the King*
*St Paul's, Mullingar*
*Assumption, Walshestown*
*Immaculate Conception, Gainstown*
*Little Flower and Our Lady of Good Counsel, Brotenstown*
Very Rev Padraig McMahon Adm
Rev Padraig Corcoran CC
Rev Paul Crosbie CC
Rev Michael Kilmartin CC
Cathedral House, Mullingar, Co Westmeath
Tel 044-9348338/9340126
Fax 044-9340780
Email cathedral@dioceseofmeath.ie
Website www.mullingarparish.ie

**NAVAN**
*St Mary's; St Oliver's*
Very Rev Declan Hurley Adm
Rev Dwayne Gavin CC
Rev Brendan Ludlow PC
Rev Stephen Kelly CC
Rev Kevin Heery CC
St Mary's, Navan, Co Meath
Tel 046-9027518/9027414
Fax 046-9071774
Email stmarysnavan@eircom.net
Website www.navanparish.ie

**ARDCATH**
*St Mary's, Ardcath*
*St John the Baptist, Clonalvy*
Very Rev Philip Gaffney PP
Parochial House, Curraha, Co Meath
Tel 01-8350136
Email philgaffney@hotmail.com

**ASHBOURNE-DONAGHMORE**
*Immaculate Conception, Ashbourne*
*St Patrick, Donaghmore*
*Parish Office:* Tel/Fax 01-8353149
Email ashdon@indigo.ie
Website www.ashbourneparish.ie
Very Rev James Lynch PP
Parochial House, Ashbourne, Co Meath
Tel 01-8350406
Rev Derek Darby CC
54 Brookville, Ashbourne, Co Meath
Tel 01-8350547

**ATHBOY**
*St James', Athboy*
*St Lawrence, Rathmore*
*Naomh Pádraig, Rathcairn*
Very Rev Patrick O'Connor PP, VF
Parochial House, Athboy, Co Meath
Tel 046-9432184 Fax 046-9430021
Website www.athboyparish.ie

**BALLINABRACKEY**
*Assumption, Ballinabrackey*
*Trinity, Castlejordan*
Very Rev Martin Halpin PP
Parochial House, Ballinabrackey,
Kinnegad, Co Westmeath
Tel/Fax 046-9739015
Email mhalpin@eircom.net

**BALLYNACARGY**
*The Nativity, Ballynacargy*
*St Michael, Sonna*
Very Rev John Nally PP
Parochial House, Ballynacargy,
Co Westmeath
Tel 044-9373923

**BALLIVOR**
*St Columbanus*
Very Rev Oliver Devine PP
Parochial House, Ballivor, Co Meath
Tel/Fax 046-9546488
Email ballivorkildalkeyparish@eircom.net
Website www.ballivorkildalkey.ie

**BALLYMORE**
*The Holy Redeemer, Ballymore*
*St Brigid's, Boher*
Very Rev Philip Smith PP
Parochial House, Ballymore, Mullingar,
Co Westmeath
Tel 044-9356212
Email ballymoreparish@hotmail.com

**BEAUPARC**
*The Assumption, Beauparc*
*The Assumption, Kentstown*
Very Rev Peter Farrelly PP
Parochial House, Beauparc,
Navan, Co Meath
Tel 046-9024114
Email peterfarrelly@eircom.net
Very Rev P.J. Coyne PE
Kentstown, Navan, Co Meath
Tel 041-9825276 Fax 041-9825252
Email kentstownchurch@gmail.com
Website www.beauparcparish.ie

**BOHERMEEN**
*St Ultan's, Bohermeen*
*St Cuthbert's, Boyerstown*
*Christ the King, Cortown*
Very Rev Andrew Doyle PP, VF
Durhamstown, Bohermeen,
Navan, Co Meath
Tel 046-9073805
Email bohermeenparish1@eircom.net

**CARNAROSS**
*St Ciaran, Carnaross*
*Sacred Heart, Mullaghea*
Rt Rev Mgr John Hanly PP
Parochial House, Carnaross,
Kells, Co Meath
Tel 046-9245904

**CASTLEPOLLARD**
*St Michael's, Castlepollard*
*St Michael's, Castletown*
*St Mary's, Finea*
Very Rev Patrick A. Moore PP, VF
Parochial House, Castlepollard,
Co Westmeath
Tel 044-9661126 Fax 044-9661881
Email moorep@castlepollardparish.com
Rev Sean Connaughton (SSC)
Castletown-Finea, Co Westmeath
Tel 043-6681141

**CASTLETOWN-GEOGHEGAN**
*St Michael, Castletown-Geoghegan*
*St Stephen, Tyrrellspass*
*St Peter, Raheenmore*
Very Rev Seamus Giles PP
Parochial House,
Castletown-Geoghegan, Co Westmeath
Tel 044-9226118
Email castletown8@eircom.net
Rev Barry Condron CC
Tyrrellspass, Co Westmeath
Tel 044-9223115
Email tyrrellspass1@eircom.net

**CASTLETOWN-KILPATRICK**
*St Patrick's, Castletown-Kilpatrick*
*St Colmcille's, Fletcherstown*
Very Rev Martin McErlean PP
Parochial House, Castletown-Kilpatrick,
Navan, Co Meath
Tel 046-9055789
*Office:* Tel 046-9054142

**CLARA**
*St Brigid's, Clara*
*Sts Peter & Paul, Horseleap*
Very Rev Patrick Keary PP, VF
Parochial House, Clara, Co Offaly
Tel 057-9331170 Fax 057-9330100
Email claraparish@eircom.net

**CLONMELLON**
*Sts Peter & Paul, Clonmellon*
*St Bartholomew, Killallon*
Very Rev Sean Garland PP
Parochial House, Clonmellon
Navan, Co Meath
Tel 046-9433124
Email clonmellonparish@eircom.net

**COLLINSTOWN**
*St Mary's, Collinstown*
*St Feichin's, Fore*
Very Rev Michael Walsh PP
Parochial House, Collinstown,
Co Westmeath
Tel 044-9666326

**COOLE (MAYNE)**
*Immaculate Conception, Coole*
*St John the Baptist, Whitehall*
Very Rev Oliver Skelly PP
Parochial House, Coole, Co Westmeath
Tel 044-9661191
Email odgskelly@gmail.com

**CURRAHA**
*St Andrew's*
Very Rev Philip Gaffney PP
Parochial House, Curraha, Co Meath
Tel 01-8350136
Email philgaffney@hotmail.com

**DELVIN**
*Assumption, Delvin*
*St Livinius, Killulagh*
Very Rev Seamus Heaney PP
Parochial House, Delvin, Co Westmeath
Tel 044-9664127 Fax 044-9664534
Email info@delvinparish.ie
Website www.delvinparish.ie

**DONORE**
*Nativity, Donore*
*Nativity, Rosnaree*
Very Rev Michael Meade PP
Parochial House, Donore,
Drogheda, Co Louth
Tel 041-9823137

**DROGHEDA, HOLY FAMILY**
Very Rev David Bradley PP
The Presbytery, Ballsgrove,
Drogheda, Co Louth
Tel 041-9831991
Email holyfamilyballsgrove@eircom.net
Rev Anthony Gonoude CC
The Presbytery, Ballsgrove,
Drogheda, Co Louth
Tel 041-9836287 Fax 041-9836287

**DROGHEDA, ST MARY'S**
Very Rev Denis Nulty PP, VF
Email frdnulty@eircom.net
Rev Joseph Campbell CC
Email frjoecampbell@gmail.com
St Mary's, Drogheda, Co Louth
Tel 041-9834958 Fax 041-9845144
*Parish Office:* Tel 041-9834587
Email stmarysparishdheda@eircom.net
Website www.stmarysdrogheda.ie

**DRUMCONRATH**
*Sts Peter & Paul, Drumconrath*
*Sts Brigid & Patrick, Meath Hill*
Very Rev Finian Connaughton PP
Parochial House, Drumconrath,
Navan, Co Meath
Tel 041-6854146

**DRUMRANEY**
*Immaculate Conception, Drumraney*
*Immaculate Conception, Tang*
*Immaculate Conception, Forgney*
Very Rev Joseph Brilley PP
Drumraney, Athlone, Co Westmeath
Tel 044-9356207
Rev Jerry Murphy (SSC) CC
St Mary's, Tang,
Ballymahon, Co Longford
Tel 0906-432214

**DULEEK**
*St Cianan, Duleek*
*St Thérèse, Bellewstown*
Very Rev John Conlon PP
Parochial House, Duleek, Co Meath
Tel 041-9823205
Website www.duleek.net

**DUNBOYNE**
*SS Peter & Paul, Dunboyne*
*St Brigid & Sacred Heart, Kilbride*
Rt Rev Mgr Dermot Farrell PP, VG
Parochial House, Dunboyne, Co Meath
Tel 01-8255342 Fax 01-8252321
Email dunboynekilbride.parish@gmail.com
Website www.dunboynekilbrideparish.org
Rev Mark English CC
2 Orchard Court, Dunboyne, Co Meath
Rev Gabriel Flynn DD, PC
1 Orchard Court, Dunboyne, Co Meath
Tel 01-8255342
Email gabriel.flynn@materdei.dcu.ie

**DUNDERRY**
*Assumption, Dunderry*
*Assumption, Robinstown*
*Assumption, Kilbride*
Very Rev Noel Horneck PP
Parochial House, Dunderry,
Navan, Co Meath
Tel 046-9431433 Fax 046-9431474

**DUNSHAUGHLIN**
*Sts Patrick & Seachnall, Dunshaughlin*
*St Martin, Culmullen*
Very Rev Joseph Clavin PP, VF
Parochial House, Dunshaughlin, Co Meath
Tel 01-8259114 Fax 01-8011614
Email dunshaughlinparish@eircom.net
Rev Colm Browne CC
12 Supple Park, Dunshaughlin, Co Meath
Tel 01-8024592
Very Rev John Kerrane AP
'St Martin's', Culmullen, Drumree, Co Meath
Tel 01-8241976
Website
www.dunshaughlin-culmullenparish.ie

**DYSART**
*St Patrick's, Dysart*
*Assumption, Loughanavalley*
Very Rev Philip O'Connor PP
Parochial House, Dysart, Mullingar,
Co Westmeath
Tel 044-9226122
Email philocon@eircom.net

**EGLISH**
*St James, Eglish*
*St John the Baptist, Rath*
Very Rev John Moorhead PP
Parochial House, Eglish, Birr, Co Offaly
Tel 057-9133010
Website www.eglishdrumcullen.com

**ENFIELD**
*St Michael, Rathmolyon*
*Assumption, Jordanstown*
Very Rev Michael Whittaker PP
The Presbytery, Enfield, Co Meath
Tel 046-9541282
Very Rev Sean Fay AP
Parochial House, Rathmolyon, Co Meath
Tel 046-9555212
Email frfay@eircom.net

**GLASSON–TUBBERCLAIRE**
*Immaculate Conception, Tubberclaire*
Very Rev Seamus Mulvany PP
Parochial House, Tubberclaire-Glasson,
Athlone, Co Westmeath
Tel 090-6485103
Email tubberclairechurch@eircom.net
Website www.tubberclairchurch.com

**JOHNSTOWN**
*Nativity, Johnstown*
*Assumption, Walterstown*
Very Rev Martin Mulvaney PP
Parochial House, Johnstown,
Navan, Co Meath
Tel 046-9021731
Email mjmul@eircom.net

**KELLS**
*Columcille, Kells*
*Immaculate Conception, Girley*
Very Rev John Byrne PP, VF
Email frjohnbyrne@eircom.net
Rev Liam Malone CC
Parochial House, Kells, Co Meath
Tel 046-9240213 Fax 046-9293475
Email info@kellsparish.ie
Website www.kellsparish.ie

**KILBEG**
*Nativity of Our Lady, Kilbeg*
*St Michael, Staholmog*
Very Rev Michael Cahill PP
Parochial House, Kilbeg, Kells, Co Meath
Tel 046-9246604

**KILBEGGAN**
*St James, Kilbeggan*
*St Hugh, Rahugh*
Very Rev Brendan Corrigan PP
3 The Gallops, Kilbeggan, Co Westmeath
Tel 057-9332155
Email info@kilbegganparish.ie
Website www.kilbegganparish.ie

**KILCLOON**
*St Oliver Plunkett, Kilcloon*
*The Assumption, Batterstown*
*Little Chapel of the Assumption, Kilcock*
Very Rev Stan Deegan PP
Parochial House, Batterstown,
Dunboyne, Co Meath
Tel 01-8259267
Very Rev Gerard Rice PE
Kilcloon, Co Meath
Tel 01-6286252 Fax 01-6106404
Email johngmrice@eircom.net

**KILCORMAC**
*Nativity, Kilcormac*
*St Brigid, Mountbolus*
Very Rev Joseph Gallagher PP
Parochial House, Kilcormac, Co Offaly
Tel 057-9135989
Very Rev Edmond Daly AP
Mount Bolus, Tullamore, Co Offaly
Tel 057-9154035
Website
www.kilcormackillougheyparish.com

**KILDALKEY**
*St Dympna's*
Very Rev Oliver Devine Adm
Parochial House, Ballivor, Co Meath
Tel 046-9546488
Email ballivorkildalkeyparish@eircom.net
Website www.ballivorkildalkey.ie

**KILLUCAN**
*St Joseph's, Rathwire*
*St Brigid's, Raharney*
Very Rev Richard Matthews PP, VF
Parochial House, Killucan, Co Westmeath
Tel 044-9374127
Email killucanparish@eircom.net

**KILMESSAN**
*Nativity, Kilmessan*
*Assumption, Dunsany*
Very Rev Terence Toner PP
Parochial House, Kilmessan, Co Meath
Tel 046-9025172

**KILSKYRE**
*St Alphonsus Liguori, Kilskyre*
*Assumption, Ballinlough*
Very Rev John Brogan PP
Parochial House, Kilskyre, Kells, Co Meath
Tel 046-9243623
Email kilskyreparish1@eircom.net
Website www.kilskyreballinlough.ie

**KINGSCOURT**
*Immaculate Conception, Kingscourt*
*St Joseph's, Corlea*
*Our Lady of Mount Carmel, Muff*
Very Rev Gerard MacCormack PP
Parochial House, Kingscourt, Co Cavan
Tel 042-9667314 Fax 042-9668141
Email info@kingscourtparish.ie
Website www.kingscourtparish.ie

**KINNEGAD**
*Assumption, Kinnegad*
*St Agnes, Coralstown*
*St Finian, Clonard*
Very Rev Thomas Gilroy PP
Parochial House, Kinnegad, Co Meath
Tel 044-9375117
Rt Rev Mgr Eamonn Marron PE
Parochial House, Raharney, Co Westmeath
Tel 044-9374271
Email kinnegadparish@eircom.net
Website www.kinnegadparish.ie
*Parish Office:* 044-9391030
Fridays 10.00 am-4.00 pm

**LAYTOWN-MORNINGTON**
*Sacred Heart, Laytown*
*Star of the Sea, Mornington*
Very Rev Denis McNelis PP
Parochial House, Laytown, Co Meath
Tel 041-9827258
Rt Rev Mgr William Cleary AP
Star of the Sea, Mornington, Co Meath
Tel 041-9827384 Fax041-9827324
Email mgtparish@eircom.net

**LOBINSTOWN**
*Holy Cross*
Very Rev Michael Sheerin PP
Parochial House, Lobinstown,
Navan, Co Meath
Tel 046-9053155
Email frmlsheerin@eircom.net

**LONGWOOD**
*Assumption, Longwood*
*Assumption, Killyon*
Very Rev Patrick Kearney PP
Parochial House, Longwood, Co Meath
Tel 046-9555009

**MILLTOWN**
*St Matthew, Milltown*
*St Matthew, Empor*
*St Patrick, Moyvore*
Very Rev William Fitzsimons PP
Parochial House, Milltown,
Rathconrath, Co Westmeath
Tel 044-9355106

**MOUNTNUGENT**
*St Brigid, Mountnugent*
*Sts Brigid & Fiach, Ballinacree*
Very Rev Oliver J. Devine PP
Parochial House, Mountnugent, Co Cavan
Tel 049-8540123
Email froliverdevine@eircom.net

**MOYNALTY**
*Assumption, Moynalty*
*Assumption, Newcastle*
Very Rev Joseph McEvoy PP
Parochial House, Moynalty,
Kells, Co Meath
Tel 046-9244305
Email moynaltyparish@eircom.net
Website www.moynaltyparish.ie

**MOYNALVEY**
*Nativity, Moynalvey*
*Assumption, Kiltale*
Very Rev David Brennan Adm
Parochial House, Moynalvey,
Summerhill, Co Meath
Tel 046-9557031
Email fdbrennan@gmail.com

**MULTYFARNHAM**
*St Nicholas, Multyfarnham*
*St Patrick's, Leney*
Very Rev Gerry Boyle PP
Parochial House, Multyfarnham,
Co Westmeath
Tel 044-9371124

**NOBBER**
*St John the Baptist*
Very Rev Séamus Houlihan PP
Parochial House, Nobber, Co Meath
Tel 046-9052197
Email nobberparish@eircom.net

**OLDCASTLE**
*St Brigid, Oldcastle*
*St Mary, Moylough*
Very Rev Ray Kelly PP
Parochial House, Oldcastle, Co Meath
Tel 049-8541142 Fax 049-8542865
Website www.oldcastleparish.ie

**ORISTOWN**
*St Catherine, Oristown*
*St John the Baptist, Kilberry*
Very Rev John O'Brien PP
Parochial House, Oristown, Kells, Co Meath
Tel 046-9054124

**RAHAN**
*St Carthage, Killina*
*St Patrick, The Island*
*St Colman, Mucklagh*
Very Rev Martin Carley PP
Parochial House, Killina, Rahan,
Tullamore, Co Offaly
Tel/Fax 057-9355917
Rev John McEvoy (SSC) CC
Mucklagh, Tullamore, Co Offaly
Tel 057-9321892
Website www.rahanparish.ie

**RATHKENNY**
*Sts Louis & Mary, Rathkenny*
*St Patrick, Rushwee*
*St Brigid, Grangegeeth*
Very Rev John Hogan Adm
Parochial House, Rathkenny, Co Meath
Tel 046-9054138
Website www.rathkennyparish.ie

**RATOATH**
*Holy Trinity*
Very Rev Gerard Stuart PP
Parochial House, Ratoath, Co Meath
Tel 01-8256207 Fax 01-8256662
Email ratoathparish@eircom.net
Website www.ratoathparish.ie
Rev Brendan Ferris CC
35a Moatlands, Ratoath, Co Meath
Tel 01-8256207

**ROCHFORTBRIDGE**
*Immaculate Conception, Rochfortbridge*
*Sacred Heart, Meedin*
*St Joseph, Milltownpass*
Very Rev William Coleman PP
Parochial House, Rochfortbridge,
Co Westmeath
Tel 044-9222107
Email rochfortbridgeparish@eircom.net

**SKRYNE**
*St Colmcille, Skryne*
*Immaculate Conception, Rathfeigh*
Very Rev Thomas O'Mahony PP
Parochial House, Skryne, Tara, Co Meath
Tel 046-9025152
Very Rev Joseph Gleeson PE
Rathfeigh, Tara, Co Meath
Tel/Fax 041-9825159

**SLANE**
*St Patrick, Slane*
*Assumption, Monknewtown*
Very Rev Joseph Deegan PP
Parochial House, Slane, Co Meath
Tel 041-9824249

**STAMULLEN**
*St Patrick, Stamullen*
*St Mary's, Julianstown*
Very Rev Declan Kelly PP
Preston Hill, Stamullen, Co Meath
Tel/Fax 01-8412647
Email prestonhill@eircom.net
Parish email secsj@eircom.net
www.stamullenparish.ie
Rev Robert McCabe CF
Gormanston Military Camp, Gormanston,
Co Meath
Tel 01-8413990
Email robertmccabe@dioceseofmeath.ie
www.militarychaplaincy.ie

**SUMMERHILL**
*Our Lady of Lourdes, Dangan*
*Assumption, Coole*
Very Rev Thomas P. Gavin PP
Parochial House, Summerhill, Co Meath
Tel 046-9557021
Email tgavin48@gmail.com
Website www.summerhillparish.ie

**TAGHMON**
*Assumption, Taghmon*
*St Joseph, Turin*
Very Rev Declan Smith PP
Parochial House, Taghmon,
Mullingar, Co Westmeath
Tel 044-9372140

**TRIM**
*St Patrick, Trim*
*St Brigid, Boardsmill*
Very Rev Sean Henry PP
Rev Mark Mohan CC
Email trimcurate@gmail.com
Parochial House, Trim, Co Meath
Tel 046-9431251
Parish email spcctrim@eircom.net

**TUBBER**
*Holy Family, Tubber*
*St Thomas the Apostle, Rosemount*
Very Rev Tony Gavin Adm
Rosemount, Moate, Co Westmeath
Tel 090-6436110
Very Rev Michael Walsh PE
Springlawn, Tubber, Moate,
Co Westmeath
Tel 090-6481141

**TULLAMORE**
*Assumption, Tullamore*
*St Colmcille, Durrow*
Rt Rev Mgr Seán Heaney PP, VG
Email heaneysean@eircom.net
Rev Shane Crombie CC
Email frshane@gmail.com
Rev Patrick Donnelly CC
Parochial House, Tullamore, Co Offaly
Tel 057-9321587 Fax 057-9351510
Email tullamore@iol.ie
Website www.tullamoreparish.ie

## INSTITUTIONS AND THEIR CHAPLAINS

**St Francis Private Hospital**
Ballinderry, Mullingar, Co Westmeath
Tel 044-9341605

**St Loman's Hospital**
Mullingar, Co Westmeath
Tel 044-9340191

**Longford & Westmeath General Hospital**
Mullingar, Co Westmeath
Tel 044-9340221
Priests of the parish

**Our Lady's Hospital**
Navan, Co Meath
Tel 046-9021210
Priests of the parish

**Tullamore General Hospital**
Tullamore, Co Offaly
Tel 057-9321501
Priests of the parish

## PRIESTS OF THE DIOCESE ELSEWHERE

Rev James Crofton
L'Eremo Madonna della Croce,
06046 Campi, P.G., Italy
Rev Anthony Draper DD
All Hallows College,
Drumcondra, Dublin 9
Tel 01-373745
Email tdraper@allhallows.ie
Rev Ronan Drury
St Patrick's College, Maynooth, Co Kildare
Tel 01-6285222
Rev David Hanratty
Tierhogar, Portarlington, Co Laois
Tel 057-8645719
Rev Thomas O'Connor DD
St Patrick's College, Maynooth, Co Kildare
Tel 01-6285222
Rev David O'Hanlon
Pontificio Colegio Portugues,
Via Nicolo V, 2-00165 Roma, Italy

## RETIRED PRIESTS

Very Rev Ray Brady
c/o Bishop's House, Mullingar
Very Rev Eamonn Butler PE
10 Lynn Heights, Mullingar,
Co Westmeath
Tel 044-9344008
Very Rev Patrick Casey PE
5 St Mary's Terrace, Bishopsgate Street,
Mullingar, Co Westmeath
Tel 044-9342746
Very Rev Michael V. Daly PE
35 Herbert Place, Navan, Co Meath
Tel 046-9093935
Very Rev Nicholas Dunican PE
Knightsbridge Nursing Home,
Trim, Co Meath
Rt Rev Mgr Edward Dunne PE
Ratoath, Co Meath
Very Rev Andrew Farrell PE
Knightsbridge Nursing Home,
Trim, Co Meath
Very Rev Edward Flynn PE
Multyfarnham Retirement Village,
Co Westmeath
Very Rev Joseph Garvey PE
Kilbrew Nursing Home, Curaha,
Ashbourne, Co Meath
Very Rev Lauri Halpin PE
Kilbeggan, Co Westmeath
Very Rev John Kiernan PE
Holy Trinity Abbey, Kilnacrot,
Ballyjamesduff, Co Cavan
Rev Barney Maxwell PE
Empor, Ballymacargy, Co Westmeath
Very Rev Patrick A. Mackin PE
Bohermeen, Navan, Co Meath
Tel 046-9021439
Email patmack@iolfree.ie
Very Rev Frank McNamara PE
Portiuncula Nursing Home,
Multyfarnham, Co Westmeath
Very Rev Matthew Mollin PE
4 St Finbar, Maryfield, Chapelizod,
Co Dublin
Tel 01-6268851
Very Rev Michael Murchan PE
Knightsbridge Nursing Home,
Trim, Co Meath
Very Rev Colm Murtagh PE
1 Greenville, Kildalkey, Co Meath
Tel 046-9435133
Very Rev Eamonn O'Brien
Newbrook Nursing Home,
Mullingar, Co Westmeath
Very Rev F. X. O'Reilly PE
Portiuncula Nursing Home,
Multyfarnham, Co Westmeath
Rt Rev Mgr Thomas Woods DD
Newbrook Nursing Home,
Mullingar, Co Westmeath

## PERSONAL PRELATURE

**OPUS DEI**
Lismullin Conference Centre
Navan, Co Meath
Tel 046-9026936
Rev James Gavigan, Chaplain

## RELIGIOUS ORDERS AND CONGREGATIONS

## PRIESTS

**CAMILLIANS**
St Camillus Community,
Killucan, Co Westmeath
Tel 044-74115
*Superior:* Rev Frank Monks (OSCam)
Nursing Centre
Tel 044-74196

**CARMELITES (OCARM)**
Carmelite Priory,
Moate, Co Westmeath
Tel 090-6481160/6481398
Fax 090-6481879
Email carmelitemoate@eircom.net
*Prior:* Rev Martin Ryan (OCarm)

**FRANCISCANS**
Franciscan College,
Gormanston, Co Meath
Tel 01-8412203 Fax 01-8412685
Email friary@gormanstoncollege.ie
*Guardian:* Rev Brendan Scully (OFM)

Franciscan Abbey,
Multyfarnham, Co Westmeath
Tel 044-9371114/9371137
Fax 044-9371387
*Guardian:* Rev Bernard Jones (OFM)

**HOLY SPIRIT CONGREGATION**
Spiritan Missionaries,
Ardbraccan, Navan, Co Meath
Tel 046-9021441
*Community Leader:* Br Conleth Tyrrell (CSSp)

**ST COLUMBAN'S MISSIONARY SOCIETY**
St Columban's, Dalgan Park,
Navan, Co Meath
Tel 046-9021525
*Regional Director:* Rev Donal Hogan (SSC)

St Columban's Retirement Home,
Dalgan Park, Navan, Co Meath
Tel 046-9021525
*Director*
Rev Bernard Mulkerins (SSC)

**SALESIANS**
Salesian House
Warrenstown, Drumree, Co Meath
Tel 01-8259761
Community 01-8259894
Fax 01-8240298
*Rector:* Rev P. J. Nyland (SDB)

**SOCIETY OF ST PAUL**
St Paul Book Centre
Castle Street, Athlone, Co Westmeath
Tel/Fax 090-6492882
Email saintpaul_books@yahoo.com

## BROTHERS

**CHRISTIAN BROTHERS**
St Joseph's, Kells, Co Meath
Tel 046-9240239
*Community Leader:* Br John Devaney
Community: 4

Edmund Rice Centre
Bective Street, Kells, Co Meath
Tel 046-9240239

**FRANCISCAN BROTHERS**
The Monastery, Clara, Co Offaly
Tel 057-9331130
*Local Minister:* Br Charles Conway (OSF)
Community: 5

## SISTERS

**BLESSED SACRAMENT SISTERS**
Marian Hostel, High Street,
Tullamore, Co Offaly
Tel 057-9321182
Tel 057-9351371 (Convent)
Community: 3
Hostel for women
Day centre for children with mental handicap. Tel 057-9323774
Activation and resource centre for people with mental handicap
Tel 057-9351629

**CHARITY OF JESUS AND MARY SISTERS**
St Mary's Convent, South Hill, Delvin,
Co Westmeath
Tel 044-64108/9 Fax 044-64488
*Contact:* Sr Kathleen O'Connor
Community: 6
Residential and day services for children and adults with a learning disability

Aisling, Mitchelstown,
Delvin, Co Westmeath
Tel 044-64379
*Contact:* Sr Kathleen O'Connor

**CONGREGATION OF THE SISTERS OF MERCY**
St Mary's Convent of Mercy, Athlumney,
Navan, Co Meath
Tel 046-9021271
*Facilitator:* Sr Consilio Rock
Community: 8

Sisters of Mercy,
6 Meadowlands, Athboy, Co Meath
Tel 046-9430085

Sisters of Mercy,
3 St Brigid's Court, Connaught Street,
Athboy, Co Meath
Tel 046-9430047

Convent of Mercy, Charlestown,
Clara, Co Offaly
Tel 057-9331184

St Mary's Convent of Mercy,
Drogheda, Co Louth
Tel 041-9838184
*Leader:* Sr Claire Nugent
Community: 3

202 Ballsgrove, Drogheda, Co Louth
Tel 041-9830160

38 Congress Avenue,
Drogheda, Co Louth
Tel 041-9837876

21 Beaubec, Dublin Road,
Drogheda, Co Louth
Tel 041-9830605

Convent of Mercy, Kells, Co Meath
Tel 046-9240159
Community: 13

Sisters of Mercy
1 Circular Road, Kells, Co Meath
Tel 046-9249381

Cill na Gréine, Convent of Mercy,
Kells, Co Meath
Tel 046-9252536

Sisters of Mercy,
13 Grand Priory, Kells, Co Meath
Tel 046-9249027

Convent of Mercy, Tullamore Road,
Kilbeggan, Co Westmeath
Tel 057-9332161
*Leader:* Sr Concepta Brennan
Community: 6

Convent of Mercy, Kilcormac, Co Offaly
Tel 057-9335007
Community: 5

Sisters of Mercy, Ard Aoibhinn
Mount Bolus, Co Offaly
Tel 057-9354867

Sisters of Mercy, Loughcrew,
Laytown, Co Meath
Tel 041-9827432
Community: 2

29 Green Road,
Mullingar, Co Westmeath
Tel 044-9341680

10 College Court, College Street,
Mullingar, Co Westmeath
Tel 044-9330768

St Joseph's,
Leighsbrook, Navan, Co Meath
Tel 046-9071760
Community: 6

Sisters of Mercy,
Mount Carmel, 15 Aylesbury Lodge,
Navan, Co Meath
Tel 046-9071757
Community: 5

Sisters of Mercy, 4 Ferndale,
Navan, Co Meath
Tel 046-9023844

Sisters of Mercy, Sacre Coeur,
The Commons, Navan, Co Meath
Tel 046-9021970

Convent of Mercy,
Rochfortbridge, Co Westmeath
Tel 044-9322130
*Leader:* Sr Bridge Commins
Community: 6

Convent of Mercy, Trim, Co Meath
Tel 046-9431264
Shared Leadership
Community: 13

Sisters of Mercy,
1 Mornington Way, Trim, Co Meath
Tel 046-9437025 Fax 046-9437025
Community: 4

Convent of Mercy,
St Joseph's, Tullamore, Co Offaly
Tel 057-9321221
Community: 31
*Facilitator:* Srs Mildred Lynam
and Cecilia Cadogan

Sisters of Mercy, 130 Arden Vale,
Tullamore, Co Offaly
Tel 057-9352733

Sisters of Mercy, 47 Tara Crescent,
Clonminch, Tullamore, Co Offaly
Tel 057-9322150

106 Ballin Ri, Collins Lane,
Tullamore, Co Offaly
Tel 057-9329740

69 Carne Hill, Johnstown,
Navan, Co Meath
Tel 046-9091772

42 Blackcastle Estate, Navan, Co Meath
Tel 046-9073325

Sisters of Mercy,
Blackfriary, Trim, Co Meath
Tel 046-9437759

Sisters of Mercy,
5 Headfort Road, Kells, Co Meath
Tel 046-9249775
Community: 3

6 Friars Park, Trim, Co Meath
Tel 046-9437037
Community: 3

Sisters of Mercy, 133 College Hill,
Irishtown, Mullingar, Co Westmeath
Tel 044-9335303

Mission House,
St Colmcille's, Laytown, Co Meath
Tel 041-9887904
Community: 5

20 The Crescent, Athlumney,
Navan, Co Meath
Tel 046-9088940

135 Droim Liath, Collins Lane,
Tullamore, Co Offaly
Tel 057-9361133

No. 2 Bishopsgate Street,
Mullingar, Co Westmeath
Tel 044-9396721

Apartment 6, Knightsbridge Village,
Longwood Road, Trim, Co Meath
Tel 046-9486028

29 Cill Bán, Collins Lane,
Tullamore, Co Offaly
Tel 057-9361422

1 Oakfield, Church Road,
Tullamore, Co Offaly

52 Ushnagh Court,
Mullingar, Co Westmeath

20 The Crescent, Athlunney,
Navan, Co Meath
Tel 046-9088940

Harbour Road, Kilbeggan, Co Westmeath
Tel 057-9332147

No. 6 The Carmelite Centre,
Moate, Co Westmeath
Tel 090-6466525

**FRANCISCAN MISSIONARIES OF OUR LADY**
Franciscan Convent, Ballinderry,
Mullingar, Co Westmeath
Tel 044-9352000
*Superior:* Sr Cecilia Cody
Email ceciliacody1@gmail.com
Commmunity: 4

**HOLY FAMILY OF ST EMILIE DE RODAT**
Arden Road,
Tullamore, Co Offaly
Tel 057-9321577
*Superior:* Sr Mary-Paul English
Email mpe1809@eircom.net
Community: 7

**LORETO (IBVM)**
Loreto Community,
St Michael's, Navan, Co Meath
Tel 046-9021740
Email loretonavan@eircom.net
*Superior:* Sr Maria Barry
Community: 12
Loreto Secondary School
Tel 046-9023830
Day Care Centre

Loreto Sisters, Athlumney Road,
Navan, Co Meath
Tel 046-9073423
Community: 2
Education

Loreto Community,
Mullingar, Co Westmeath
Tel 044-48976
*Superior:* Sr Maria Barry
Community: 7
Loreto Secondary School
Tel 044-40184

Anam Aras, Laytown, Co Meath
Tel 041-9828952
Superior: Sr Julie Clinton
Retreat centre

**MEDICAL MISSIONARIES OF MARY**
Bruach na Mara,
Bettystown, Co Meath
Tel 041-9827207
Email mmmeuro@iol.ie

**MISSIONARY SISTERS OF THE HOLY ROSARY**
Holy Rosary Convent,
Coast Road, Bettystown, Co Meath
Tel 041-9827362
Community: 4
Pastoral

**PRESENTATION SISTERS**
15 Central Park, Mullingar,
Co Westmeath
Tel 044-9348402
Community: 6
School and pastoral ministry
Presentation Junior Primary School
Tel 044-9342166
Scoil na Maighdine Muire Primary School
Tel 044-9340933
Email pressnt.ias@eircom.net

Killina, Rahan,
Tullamore, Co Offaly
Tel 057-9355920
*Community Leader:* Sr Marie Walsh
Community: 5
School and pastoral ministry
Scoil Naomh Seosamh Primary School
Tel 056-9355790
Presentation Secondary School
Tel 057-9355706

**VISITATION SISTERS**
Visitandines, Monastery of the Visitation,
Stamullen, Co Meath
Tel 01-8417142 Fax 01-8412768
*Superior*
Sr Paul Mary Supple
Email visitationstamullen@gmail.com
Community: 6

## EDUCATIONAL INSTITUTIONS

**Diocesan Office for Post-Primary Schools**
*Director:* Mr Liam Murphy BA, HDE
Moatlands, Navan, Co Meath
Tel 046-9021847

**St Finian's College**
Mullingar, Co Westmeath
Tel 044-9348313 Fax 044-9345275
*President:* Rev Paul Connell PhD
Tel 044-9348672
*Chaplain:* Very Rev Gerry Boyle PP

**St Mary's Diocesan School**
Beamore Road,
Drogheda, Co Louth
Tel Office: 041-9837581
Staff: 041-9838001 Fax 041-9841151
*Headmaster*
Mr Jim Brady
*Chaplain:* Rev Joseph Campbell CC

**St Patrick's Classical School**
Mount Rivers, Moatlands,
Navan, Co Meath
Tel 046-9021847
*Principal:* Mr Colm O'Rourke
*Chaplain:* Rev Dwayne Gavin CC

**St Columba's College**
Tullamore, Co Offaly
Tel 057-9351756
*Headmaster:* Mr Colin Roddy
*Chaplain:* Rev Patrick Donnelly CC

**Boyne Community School**
Trim, Co Meath
Tel 046-9431358
*Headmaster:* Ms Elizabeth Cahill
*Chaplain:* Ms Aoife Daly

**Ashbourne Community School**
Ashbourne, Co Meath
Tel 01-8353066
*Headmaster:* Ms Aine O'Sullivan
*Chaplain:* Mr Ken Hogan

**St Peter's College**
Dunboyne, Co Meath
Tel 01-8252552
*Headmaster:* Mr Eamonn Gaffney
*Chaplain:* Mr John Tighe

**EDMUND RICE SCHOOLS TRUST**
Pobalscoil Chiaráin, Kells, Co Meath
Tel 046-9241551
*Principal:* Mr Francis Lafferty

Scoil Mhuire Primary School, Mullingar, Co Westmeath
Tel 044-9341517
*Principal:* Mrs Bernie McVeigh

Coláiste Mhuire Secondary School, Mullingar
Tel 044-9344743
*Principal:* Mr J. O'Meara

## CHARITABLE AND OTHER SOCIETIES

**Cathedral Social Services Centre**
Mullingar, Co Westmeath
The Secretary, Bishopsgate Street, Mullingar, Co Westmeath
Tel 044-9348707

**Society of St Vincent de Paul**
Ozanam Holiday Home, Mornington, Co Meath
Tel 041-9827924

# DIOCESE OF OSSORY

PATRON OF THE DIOCESE
ST KIERAN, 5 MARCH

INCLUDES MOST OF COUNTY KILKENNY
AND PORTIONS OF COUNTIES LAOIS AND OFFALY

**Most Rev Seamus Freeman (SAC) DD**
Bishop of Ossory;
born 23 February 1944;
ordained priest 12 June 1971;
Consecrated Bishop of Ossory
2 December 2007

Residence: Blessed Felix House, Tilbury Place, James's Street, Kilkenny
Tel 056-7762448
Fax 056-7763753
Email bishop@ossory.ie

## ST MARY'S CATHEDRAL, KILKENNY

It was only in the last decade of the twelfth century, during the episcopate of Felix O'Dulany, that Kilkenny became the seat of the Bishop of Ossory. The new cathedral, dedicated to St Canice, was begun early in the thirteenth century by Bishop Hugh de Rous and took over half a century to complete. During the period of the Confederation, it was David Rothe's cathedral church, and it was here that the aged bishop formally received the Papal Nuncio, Archbishop Rinuccini, in November 1645. With the coming of Cromwell, St Canice's reverted to Protestant hands and the Catholics had no cathedral. A small chapel in St Mary's parish – St James's Chapel, built in 1700 just outside St James's Gate – functioned as a cathedral and was in use up to 1857.

It was William Kinsella, appointed Bishop of Ossory in 1829, who initiated the building of St Mary's. William Deane Butler, the architect for St Kieran's College and the parochial church of Ballyragget, was chosen to be the architect of St Mary's. His neo-Gothic style marked a new and ambitious phase in church architecture and reflected the newfound confidence of the Catholic community.

The site chosen was Burrell's Hall, which housed the first Catholic college founded in Ireland after the repeal of the law against Catholic schoolmasters in 1782. Subscribers from St Mary's parish pledged over £1,500, including £100 from Bishop Kinsella and £20 from Fr Theobald Matthew. Money was also raised from door and street collections, from the sale of site materials and from bank loans. Work was begun in April 1843. On 18 August the foundation stone was laid by Bishop Kinsella, assisted by the administrator, Fr Robert O'Shea, and others. When Bishop Kinsella died in December 1845, the walls were only seven feet high.

The new bishop, Edmond Walsh, aided by Robert O'Shea and a very active lay committee, continued the project. They kept it going right through the famine years, providing much-needed work locally. Collections were taken up in all the parishes of the diocese and bank loans were obtained on the securities of local merchants. The much-publicised sermon of Dr Patrick Murray of Maynooth also helped to raise funds. The cost of the original building is estimated at £25,000. The grand opening took place on 4 October 1857.

The cathedral was described as 'of pure Gothic design, built entirely of chiselled limestone and cruciform in shape'. The tower, originally designed for St Kieran's College, rises to a height of 186 feet. The high altar of Italian marble was purchased in Italy. The relics of Ss Cosmos and Damian and St Clement were brought from Rome. Those of St Victoria came later. A statue of Our Lady by Benzoni was commissioned by Bishop Walsh and stands in the remodelled sanctuary. The railings around the cathedral were added in 1862.
During Bishop Brownrigg's time, a new sacristy and chapter room were added and many other improvements were made. The centre porch and organ gallery were remodelled, heating was installed and new statues purchased. James Pearse, the father of Patrick and Willie, completed the marble altar rails and erected the altar to the Sacred Heart. About £8,000 was expended and the refurbished cathedral was reopened on 9 April 1899 in the presence of Cardinal Logue, Archbishop Walsh of Dublin and many other dignitaries.

Less than thirty years later, Bishop Collier found it necessary to do further work on St Mary's. Turrets had to be repaired and a leaking roof overhauled. Mosaic work and painting were done on the sanctuary and side chapels, pitch pine seats were put in the aisles and transepts, an altar was erected to the Little Flower, the organ was remodelled at a cost of £2,500, and choir stalls introduced. The cost came to £28,000 and was raised by collections throughout the diocese.

During Bishop Birch's time, the cathedral was modernised to bring it into line with the requirements of Vatican II. Under the great tower was placed a new high altar of polished limestone surrounded by copper reliefs depicting scenes of Church life in Ossory. Many other changes were made, including a new tabernacle to facilitate exposition of the Blessed Sacrament and a new organ, constructed by a distinguished German organ-builder.

St Mary's Cathedral still dominates the landscape of Kilkenny. It stands as a reminder of the faith and growing confidence of a far-off generation.

**Most Rev Laurence Forristal DD**
Retired Bishop of Ossory
Born 5 June 1931; ordained priest 21 December 1955; ordained Titular Bishop of Rotdon and Auxiliary Bishop of Dublin 20 January 1980; installed Bishop of Ossory 13 September 1981; Retired 14 September 2007
*Residence*
Molassy, Freshford Road, Kilkenny
Tel/Fax 056-7777928/087-2330369
Email laurenceforristal@ossory.ie

## CHAPTER

*Dean:* Very Rev Seamus McEvoy
*Archdeacon*
Venerable Archdeacon Patrick Grace
*Members*
Very Rev Patrick Dalton
Very Rev Patrick Duggan
Very Rev Laurence Dunphy
Very Rev Brian Flynn
Very Rev Peter Grant
Very Rev Seamus Henry
Very Rev Thomas Murphy
Very Rev Sean O'Doherty
Very Rev Richard Phelan
Rt Rev Mgr Michael Ryan
*Honorary Members*
Very Rev Patrick Brennan
Very Rev James Carrigan
Rt Rev Mgr Thomas Maher
Very Rev Robert Raftice

## ADMINISTRATION

**Chancellor**
Very Rev William Dalton
c/o Diocesan Office, James's Street, Kilkenny
Tel/Fax 056-7725287

**College of Consultors**
Rt Rev Mgr Michael Ryan PP, VG
Very Rev Dean Seamus McEvoy
Rt Rev Mgr Kieron Kennedy
Very Rev Joseph Delaney
Very Rev Daniel Carroll
Very Rev Oliver Maher
Very Rv Patrick Canon Dalton
Vey Very Anthony O'Connor

**Vicars General**
Rt Rev Mgr Michael Ryan PP, VG

**Vicars Forane**
Very Rev Thomas Canon Murphy PP
Very Rev Daniel Cavanagh PP
Very Rev Patrick Canon Dalton PP

**Episcopal Vicars**
*Primary Education*
Very Rev Patrick Canon Dalton
*Family and Social Affairs*
Rt Rev Mgr Kieron Kennedy
*Retired Priests*
Rev Thomas O'Toole

**Diocesan Pastoral Co-Ordinator**
Very Rev Daniel Bollard PP
Thomastown, Co Kilkenny
Tel 056-7724279/087-6644858
Email dbollard@eircom.net

**Finance Committee**
*Chairman:* Mr Geoffrey Meagher
Slievanon, Granges Road, Kilkenny
Tel 056-7762092
*Secretary:* Mrs Joan Mahon
Diocesan Office, James's Street, Kilkenny
Tel 056-7762448

**Buildings and Properties Committee**
*Chairman:* Mr John Norris
Rathpatrick, Slieverue, Co Kilkenny
Tel 051-832495
*Secretary:* Mrs Frances Lennon
Diocesan Office, James's Street, Kilkenny
Tel 056-7762448

**Diocesan Secretary**
Mrs Frances Lennon
Diocesan Office, James's Street, Kilkenny
Tel 056-7762448 Fax 056-7763753
Email admin@ossory.ie

**Diocesan Finance**
Mrs Sheila Walshe
Diocesan Office, James's Street, Kilkenny

## CATECHETICS EDUCATION

**Diocesan Advisers for Religious Education**
*Primary Education:* Rev Kieran O'Shea CC
Ballycallan, Co Kilkenny
Tel 056-7769564/086-8272828
Email kieranoshea@ossory.ie
*Post Primary:* Rev Sean O'Connor
St John's Presbytery, Kilkenny
Tel 086-3895911

**Catholic Primary School Managers Association**
*Chairperson:* Mrs Maureen Daly
Granges Road, Kilkenny
*Secretary*
Very Rev Patrick Canon Dalton PP
Gowran, Co Kilkenny
Tel 056-7726128/086-8283478
Fax 056-7726134
Email pdalton@iolfree.ie

## LITURGY

**Liturgy Chairman**
Very Rev Richard Scriven PP
The Rower, Thomastown, Co Kilkenny
Tel 087-2420033
Email rscriven@eircom.net

## PASTORAL

**Accord**
Seville Lodge, Callan Road, Kilkenny
Tel 056-7722674
*Chaplain:* Rev Kieran O'Shea
Tel 086-8272828

**Adult Faith Formation**
*Director:* Rev Dermot Ryan
St Kieran's College, Kilkenny
Tel 056-7721086/086-6097483

**Advisory Committee on Housing Elderly People**
*Chairman:* Very Rev Liam Cassin PP
Hugginstown, Co Kilkenny
Tel 087-2312354/056-7768678

**Chaplain to the Deaf**
Very Rev Daniel Carroll
St Fiacre's Gardens, Bohernatonish Road, Loughboy, Kilkenny
Tel 056-7764400/087-9077769
Fax 056-7770173
Email dancarroll@ossory.ie

**Chaplain to the Travelling Community**
Rev Sean O'Connor
St John's Presbytery, Kilkenny
Tel 056-7756889/086-3895911
Email seanoconnor@ossory.ie

**Clerical Fund Society**
*Secretary:* Very Rev Kieran Cantwell PP
Danesfort, Co Kilkenny
Tel 056-7727137/087-2661228

**Communications**
*Director:* Very Rev Daniel Carroll
St Fiacre's Gardens, Bohernatonish Road, Loughboy, Kilkenny
Tel 056-7764400 Fax 056-7770173
Email dancarroll@ossory.ie

**Council of Priests**
*Chairman:* Very Rev Daniel Carroll
Tel 056-7764400/087-9077769
*Ossory Diocesan Pastoral Council*
*Chairperson:* Mr Diarmuid Healy
Tel 086-2619986
*Middle Deanery Pastoral Council*
*Chairperson:* Ms Olivia Maher
Tel 087-1273273
*Southern Deanery Pastoral Council*
*Chairperson:* Mr Jimmy Walsh
Tel 086-8229960
*Northern Deanery Pastoral Council*
*Chairperson:* Ms Eilis Costello
Tel 086-1273273

**CURA**
Tel 056-7722739 Fax 056-7770240
*Co Ordinator:* Mrs Ann Coyne
*Chaplain:* Rev Sean O'Connor
Tel 086-3895911

**Ecumenism**
Very Rev James Murphy PP
St Canice's Presbytery, Dean Street, Kilkenny
Tel 056-7752991/087-2609545
Email jimmurphy@ossory.ie

**Emigrant Commission**
Very Rev Laurence Wallace PP
Muckalee, Ballyfoyle, Co Kilkenny
Tel 056-4441271/087-2326807
Fax 056-4440007
Email muckalee@ossory.ie

**Lourdes Pilgrimage**
*Director:* Very Rev M. A. O'Connor PP
Glenmore, via New Ross, Co Kilkenny
Tel 051-880213/087-2517766

**Marriage Tribunal**
(See Marriage Tribunals section)

**Ossory Adoption and Referral Services**
Information and Guidance in all matters in relation to adoption Tel 056-7721685
Ms Mary Curtin, Social Service Centre, Waterford Road, Kilkenny
Tel 056-7721685

**Ossory Priests' Society**
*Secretary:* Rev Thomas O'Toole
Kilmacow, via Waterford, Co Kilkenny
Tel/Fax 051-88529/087-2240787

**Ossory Youth**
Desart Hall, New Street, Kilkenny
Tel 056-7761200 Fax 056-7752385
*Chairman:* Padraig Fleming
*CEO:* Ms Mary Mescal

**Pioneer Total Abstinence Association**
*Diocesan Director*
Very Rev Thomas Murphy PP
Ballyragget, Co Kilkenny
Tel 056-8833123/086-8130694

**Pontifical Mission Societies**
*Diocesan Director*
Very Rev John Lalor PP
Camross, Co Laois
Tel 057-8735122

**Vocations**
*Director:* Rev William Purcell CC
St Kieran's College, Kilkenny
Tel 056-7721086/087-6286858

## PARISHES

*Kilkenny city parishes are listed first. Other parishes follow alphabetically. Church titulars are in italics.*

**ST MARY'S**
*St Mary's Cathedral*
Rt Rev Mgr Kieron Kennedy Adm
Tel 056-7771253/087-2523521
Email kieronkennedy@ossory.ie
Rev Mark Condon CC
Tel 056-7721253/086-6005402
Email markcondon@ossory.ie
St Mary's Cathedral, Kilkenny

**ST JOHN'S**
*St John the Evangelist, Holy Trinity, St John the Baptist*
Email stjohns@ossory.ie
Website www.stjohnskilkenny.com
Very Rev Francis Purcell
Tel 056-7721072/086-6010001
Fax 056-7722209
Email jfpurcell@eircom.net
Rev Sean O'Connor
Tel 056-7756889/086-3895911
Fax 056-7722209
Email seanoconnor@ossory.ie
St John's Presbytery, Kilkenny

**ST CANICE'S**
*St Canice's*
Very Rev James Murphy PP
St Canice's Presbytery, Dean Street, Kilkenny
Tel 056-7752991/087-2609545
Fax 056-7721533
Email jimmurphy@ossory.ie

**ST PATRICK'S**
*St Patrick's, St Fiacre's, St Joseph's*
Very Rev Daniel Carroll PP
Tel 087-9077769/056-7764400
Email dancarroll@ossory.ie
Rev Liam Taylor
Tel 056-7764400/086-8180954
Email liamtaylor@ossory.ie
Rev Roderick Whearty
Tel 056-7764400/086-8133661
St Fiacre's Gardens, Bohernatownish Road, Loughboy, Kilkenny
Tel 056-7764400 Fax 056-7770173
Email stpatricksparish@ossory.ie
Website www.patricksparish.com

**AGHABOE**
*Immaculate Conception, St Canice*
Very Rev Noel Maher PP
Clough, Ballacolla, Portlaoise, Co Laois
Tel 057-878513 Fax 057-8738909
Email nmaher@eircom.net

**AGHAVILLER**
*St Brendan's, Stoneyford, St Brendan's, Newmarket Holy Trinity*
Very Rev Liam Cassin PP
Hugginstown, Co Kilkenny
Tel/Fax 056-7768693/087-2312354
Email liamcassin@ossory.ie
Very Rev Peter Hoyne PE
Newmarket, Hugginstown, Co Kilkenny
Tel/Fax 056-7768678

**BALLYCALLAN**
*Queen of Peace, St Molua, St Brigid*
Very Rev Richard Canon Phelan PP
Kilmanagh, Co Kilkenny
Tel 056-7769116/087-2843461
Fax 056-7769597
Email dickphelan@ossory.ie
Rev Kieran O'Shea CC
Ballycallan, Co Kilkenny
Tel 056-7769564/086-8272828
Email kieranoshea@ossory.ie
Parish email ballycallan@ossory.ie

**BALLYHALE**
*St Martin of Tours, Our Lady of the Assumption, All Saints*
Very Rev Peter Kehoe (OCarm) PP
Ballyhale, Co Kilkenny
Tel/Fax 056-7768686/7768675/ 086-8252093
Email knockcar@indigo.ie

**BALLYRAGGET**
*St Patrick's, Assumption of BVM*
Very Rev Thomas Murphy PP
Ballyragget, Co Kilkenny
Tel 056-8833123/086-8130694
Email tommurphy@ossory.ie

**BORRIS-IN-OSSORY**
*St Canice, Assumption, St Kieran*
Very Rev John Robinson PP
Borris-in-Ossory, Portlaoise, Co Laois
Tel/Fax 0505-41148/087-2431412
Email robjon@eircom.net

**CALLAN**
*Assumption, All Saints, Nativity of BVM*
Very Rev William Dalton PP
Callan, Co Kilkenny
Tel 056-7725287/086-8506215
Fax 056-7725287
Email williamdalton@ossory.ie
Website www.callanparish@irishchurch.net

**CAMROSS**
*St Fergal*
Very Rev John Lalor PP
Camross, Portlaoise, Co Laois
Tel/Fax 0502-35122/087-6888711
Email johnflalor@eircom.net

**CASTLECOMER**
*Immaculate Conception*
Rt Rev Mgr Michael Ryan PP
Tel 056-4441262/086-3693863
Fax 056-4441969
Rev Joseph Campion (SAC) CC
Tel 056-4441263/086-1775172
Email josecampion@yahoo.co.uk
Castlecomer, Co Kilkenny
Parish email castlecomer@ossory.ie

**CASTLETOWN**
*St Edmund*
Very Rev William Hennessy PP
Castletown, Portlaoise, Co Laois
Tel/Fax 0502-32622/087-8736155

**CLARA**
*St Coleman*
Very Rev Laurence O'Keeffe PP
Clifden Villa, Clifden, Co Kilkenny
Tel 056-7726560/087-2258443
Fax 056-7726558
Email larryokeeffe@ossory.ie
Parish email clara@ossory.ie

**CLOGH**
*St Patrick's, Sacred Heart*
Very Rev Martin Tobin PP
Clogh, Castlecomer, Co Kilkenny
Tel 056-4442135/086-2401278
Fax 056-4442135
Email martintobin@ossory.ie

**CONAHY**
*St Coleman, Our Lady of Perpetual Help*
Very Rev James Dollard PP
Conahy, Jenkinstown, Co Kilkenny
Tel 056-7767657 Fax 056-7767666
Email conahyparish@eircom.net

**DANESFORT**
*St Michael the Archangel, Holy Cross, Kells Holy Cross, Cuffesgrange*
Very Rev Kieran Cantwell PP
Danesfort, Co Kilkenny
Tel/Fax 056-7727137/087-2661228
Email kierancantwell@eircom.net
Rev Denis Purcell CC
Cuffesgrange, Co Kilkenny
Tel 056-7729299/087-1356687

**DUNAMAGGAN**
*St Leonard, St Eoghan*
Very Rev Nicholas Flavin PP
Dunamaggan, Co Kilkenny
Tel/Fax 056-7728173/087-2257498
Email naflavin@eircom.net

**DURROW**
*Holy Trinity, St Tighearnach*
Very Rev Seán Canon O'Doherty PP
Durrow, Portlaoise, Co Laois
Tel 057-8736156
Rev Thomas McGree CC
Durrow, Portlaoise, Co Laois
Tel 057-8736155/087-7619235
Fax 057-8736226

**FERRYBANK**
*Sacred Heart*
Very Rev James Crotty PP
Tel/Fax 051-832787
Email jimcrotty@ossory.ie
Rev Raymond Dempsey CC
Tel/Fax 051-832577/087-2859682
Email raydempsey@ossory.ie
Ferrybank, Waterford
Website www.ferrybankparish.com

**FRESHFORD**
*St Lachtain, St Nicholas*
Very Rev Patrick Comerford PP
Freshford, Co Kilkenny
Tel 056-8832461/086-1038430
Email patcomerford@ossory.ie

**GALMOY**
*Immaculate Conception*
Very Rev Thomas Coyle PP
Galmoy, Crosspatrick, via Thurles,
Co Kilkenny
Tel/Fax 056-8831227/087-7668969
Email tjcoyle@eircom.net

**GLENMORE**
*St James*
Very Rev Anthony O'Connor PP
Glenmore, via New Ross, Co Kilkenny
Tel/Fax 051-880213/087-2517766
Email maoc1@eircom.net

**GOWRAN**
*Assumption*
Very Rev Patrick Canon Dalton PP
Gowran, Co Kilkenny
Tel 056-7726128/086-8283478
Fax 056-7726134
Email pdalton@iolfree.ie

**INISTIOGE**
*St Columcille, Assumption, St Brendan*
Very Rev Richard Scriven PP
The Rower, Inistioge, Co Kilkenny
Tel/Fax 051-423619/087-2420033

**JOHNSTOWN**
*St Kieran, St Michael*
Very Rev Francis Maher PP
Johnstown via Thurles, Co Kilkenny
Tel/Fax 056-8831219/087-2402487
Email frankmaher@ossory.ie

**KILMACOW**
*St Senan*
Very Rev Brian Flynn PP
Tel 051-885122/087-2828391
Email brianflynn@ossory.ie
Email kilmacowparish@ossory.ie
Rev Thomas O'Toole CC
Tel/Fax 051-885269/087-2240787
Kilmacow, via Waterford, Co Kilkenny

**LISDOWNEY**
*St Brigid, St Munchin, St Fiacre*
Very Rev Patrick O'Farrell PP
Lisdowney, Ballyragget, Co Kilkenny
Tel 056-8833138/087-2353520
Fax 056-8833701
Email patofarrell@ossory.ie
Parish email lisdowney@ossory.ie

**MOONCOIN**
*Assumption, St Kevin, St Kilgoue*
Very Rev Martin Delaney Adm
Mooncoin, Co Kilkenny
Tel/Fax 051-895123/086-2444594
Email delaneymartin@eircom.net
Website www.mooncoinparish.com

**MUCKALEE**
*St Brendan, St Brigid, St Joseph*
Very Rev Laurence Wallace PP
Muckalee, Ballyfoyle, Co Kilkenny
Tel 056-4441271/087-2326807
Fax 056-4440007
Email wallace@eircom.net
Rev John Delaney CC
Coon, Carlow
Tel 056-4443116/086-8596321
Fax 056-4443283
Email jondel@eircom.net
Parish email muckalee@ossory.ie

**MULLINAVAT**
*St Beacon, St Paul*
Very Rev Liam Barron PP
Tel/Fax 051-898108/087-2722824
Mullinavat, via Waterford, Co Kilkenny
Email liambarron@ossory.ie

**RATHDOWNEY**
*Holy Trinity, Our Lady, Queen of the Universe*
Very Rev Eamon Foley PP
Rathdowney, Portlaoise, Co Laois
Tel 0505-46282 Fax 0505-46213
Email rathdowney@ossory.ie
Very Rev Dean Seamus McEvoy PE
Errill, Portlaoise, Co Laois
Tel 0505-44973/086-2634093

**ROSBERCON**
*Assumption, St David, St Aidan*
Very Rev Daniel Cavanagh PP
Rosbercon, New Ross, Co Wexford
Tel 051-421515/087-2335432
Fax 051-425093
Email danieljcavanagh@eircom.net
Very Rev Michael Norton PE
Rosbercon, New Ross, Co Wexford
Tel/Fax 051-420333/087-2580496

**SEIR KIERAN**
*St Kieran*
Very Rev Eamonn O'Gorman PP
Seir Kieran, Clareen,
Birr, Co Offaly
Tel/Fax 0509-31080/087-2236145
Email 1eamonnogorman@eircom.net

**SLIEVERUE**
*Assumption*
Very Rev Thomas Corcoran PP
Slieverue, Co Kilkenny
Tel/Fax 051-832773/087-6886678
Email tomjcorcoran1@gmail.com
Parish email slieverue@ossory.ie
Website www.slieverue.com

**TEMPLEORUM**
*Assumption*
Very Rev Paschal Moore PP
Piltown, Co Kilkenny
Tel 051-643112/087-2408078
Fax 051-644911
Email paschalmoore@eircom.net
Assumption
Rev John Condon CC
Templeorum, Piltown, Co Kilkenny
Tel/Fax 051-643124/086-8394615

**THOMASTOWN**
*Assumption*
Very Rev Daniel Bollard PP
Tel/Fax 056-7724279/087-6644858
Email dbollard@eircom.net
Rev Lorcan Moran CC
Tel 056-7793191/086-8550521
Thomastown, Co Kilkenny
Parish email thomastown@ossory.ie

**TULLAHERIN**
*St Bennet, St Kieran*
Very Rev Patrick Canon Duggan PP
Bennetsbridge, Co Kilkenny
Tel 056-7727140/087-6644858
Fax 056-7727755
Email patduggan@ossory.ie

**TULLAROAN**
*Assumption*
Very Rev Patrick Guilfoyle PP
Tullaroan, Co Kilkenny
Tel/Fax 056-7769141/087-6644858
Email guilfoylepat@eircom.net

**URLINGFORD**
*Assumption, St Patrick*
Very Rev Oliver Maher PP
Urlingford, Co Kilkenny
Tel 056-8831121/086-8323010
Email olivermaher@ossory.ie

**WINDGAP**
*St Nicholas, Windgap*
*St Nicholas, Tullahought*
Very Rev Martin Cleere PP
Windgap, Co Kilkenny
Tel/Fax 051-648111/087-2954010
Email mfcleere@eircom.net

## INSTITUTIONS AND THEIR CHAPLAINS

**Aut Even Hospital**
Aut Even, Kilkenny
Priests of St Canice's Parish
Tel 056-7721523/087-9335663

**City Vocational School, Kilkenny**
Rev Mark Condon CC
Tel 056-7721086 Ext 135/7722984/
7765058/087-2420033

**Community School**
Castlecomer, Co Kilkenny
Ms Edel O'Connor
Tel 056-4441447

**Abbey Community College**
Ferrybank, Waterford
Ms Claire Bolger
Tel 051-832930

**District Hospital**
Castlecomer, Co Kilkenny
Rt Rev Mgr Michael Ryan
Tel 056-4441262/086-3034155

**Orthopaedic Hospital**
Kilcreene, Kilkenny
Priests of St Mary's Parish
Tel 056-7721253 Ext 180/181

**St Canice's Hospital, Kilkenny**
Priests of St John's Parish
Tel 056-7721072

**St Columba's Hospital**
Thomastown, Co Kilkenny
Very Rev Daniel Bollard
Tel 056-7724279/087-6644858

**St Luke's Hospital, Kilkenny**
Rev Patrick Carey
Tel 056-7785000/7771815/087-2599087
Email paddycarey@ossory.ie

**Stephen Barracks, Kilkenny**
Rev Daniel McCarthy
Tel 056-7761852

## PRIESTS OF THE DIOCESE ELSEWHERE

*In Ireland*
Rt Rev Mgr James Cassin
St Patrick's College, Maynooth, Co Kildare
Tel 01-6285222/086-2380984
Email jamescassin@ossory.ie
Rev Fergus Farrell
Mater Dei Institute of Education,
Clonliffe Road, Dublin 3
Tel 01-8376027/086-0782066
Email fearghusof@materdei.ie/
sfofearghail@eircom.net
Most Rev Thomas White
6 Osborne Court, Seapoint Avenue,
Blackrock, Co Dublin
Tel 01-2806609

*Abroad*
Rt Rev Mgr Liam Bergin
Apt 1705, 2000 Commonwealth Avenue,
Brighton, MA 02135, USA
Email lbergin@ossory.ie
Rev John Duggan
St John and Paul Church,
341 South Main Street,
Coventary RI R102816-5987, USA
Te 001-401-8275022
Rev Thomas Norris
4109 Ocean Drive, Corpus Christi,
Texas 78411, USA

## RETIRED PRIESTS

Very Rev Patrick Canon Brennan
Gathabawn, Via Thurles, Co Kilkenny
Tel 056-8832110
Very Rev James Canon Carrigan
Ballacolla, Portlaoise, Co Laois
Tel 0502-34016
Very Rev Joseph Delaney
St Kieran's College, Kilkenny
Tel 056-7721086/086-8206730
Very Rev Liam Dunne
The Forge, Martin's Lane,
Upper Main Street, Arklow, Co Wicklow
Tel 0402-32779
Very Rev Laurence Canon Dunphy
Urlingford, Co Kilkenny
Tel 087-2300849
Venerable Archdeacon Patrick Grace
Inistioge, Co Kilkenny
Tel 056-7758429/086-8817628
Very Rev Patrick Canon Grant
Ballyragget, Co Kilkenny
Tel 056-8833120
Very Rev Seamus Canon Henry
Freshford, Co Kilkenny
Tel 056-8832146/086-0879296
Right Rev Mgr Thomas Maher
Archersrath Nursing Home, Kilkenny
Tel 056-7790137
Rev John O'Brien
'The Knock', Danville,
Bennettsbridge Road, Kilkenny
Tel 087-6430620
Very Rev Robert Canon Raftice
Mount Carmel, Callan, Co Kilkenny
Tel 056-7725301/7725553/086-0614682
Very Rev Donal Walsh
Tinnahinch, Graiguenamanagh,
Co Kilkenny
Tel 059-9725550

## RELIGIOUS ORDERS AND CONGREGATIONS

## PRIESTS

**CAPUCHINS**
Capuchin Friary, Friary Street,
Kilkenny
Tel 056-7721439 Fax 056-7722025
*Guardian:* Rev Benignus Buckley (OFMCap)
*Vicar:* Rev Donal Sweeney (OFMCap)

**CARMELITES (OCARM)**
Carmelite Priory, Knocktopher,
Co Kilkenny
Tel 056-7768675
Email knockcar@indigo.ie
*Prior:* Rev Peter Kehoe (OCarm) PP

**DOMINICANS**
Black Abbey, Kilkenny, Co Kilkenny
Tel 056-7721279 Fax 056-7721297
*Prior:* Very Rev Louis Hughes (OP)

**MILL HILL MISSIONARIES**
St Joseph's, Mill Hill Missionaries,
Waterford Road, Kilkenny
Tel 056-7721482 Fax 056-7751490
*Rector:* Rev Jim O'Connell (MHM)
Email jimocmhm@eircom.net

## BROTHERS

**BROTHERS OF CHARITY**
St Vincent's Brothers' Community,
Ferrybank, Waterford
Tel 051-832180 Fax 051-833490
*Community Leader:* Br Joseph Killoran
Email
jkilloran@waterford.brothersofcharity.ie
Community: 7

**CHRISTIAN BROTHERS**
Christian Brothers, Edmund Rice House,
Westcourt, Callan, Co Kilkenny
Tel 056-7725141
*Community Leader:* Br M. J. Keane
Community: 6

Edmund Rice Centre,
Callan, Co Kilkenny
Tel 056-7725993

Christian Brothers, 48 Clonkil,
Callan, Co Kilkenny
Tal 056-7706939
Community: 2

**DE LA SALLE BROTHERS**
De La Salle Monastery,
Castletown, Portlaoise, Co Laois
Tel 057-8732359 (residence)
Fax 057-8732925
*Superior:* Br Martin Curran
Community: 10

Miguel House, Castletown,
Portlaoise, Co Laois
Tel 057-8732136 Fax 057-8756648
*Superior:* Br David O'Riordan
Community: 19
House for retired brothers

La Salle Pastoral Centre, Castletown,
Portlaoise, Co Laois
Tel 057-8732442 Fax 057-872925
*Director:* Mr Derek Doherty
Retreat centre

## SISTERS

**CONGREGATION OF THE SISTERS OF MERCY**
Convent of Mercy, Ballyragget,
Co Kilkenny
Tel 056-8833114

Convent of Mercy, Aras Muire,
Thomastown, Co Kilkenny
Tel 056-7724226

Convent of Mercy,
Callan, Co Kilkenny
Tel 056-7725223

1 Mountain View, Borris-in-Ossory,
Portlaoise, Co Laois
Tel/Fax 0505-41964

Villa Maria, Talbot's Inch, Kilkenny
Tel 056 7765774

20 Archer's Court, Loughboy,
Kilkenny
Tel 056-7708789

**DAUGHTERS OF MARY AND JOSEPH**
Peace in Christ, Sion Road, Kilkenny
Tel 056-7721054 Fax 056-7770755
*Director of Retreat House*
Sr Margaret Moloney
Community: 4
Retreat work

**FRANCISCAN MISSIONARIES OF ST JOSEPH**
Prague House, Freshford, Co Kilkenny
Tel 056-8832281
*Regional Superior:* Sr Bridget Ann Lonergan
Community: 4
Residential care for elderly, general social work

**HOLY FAMILY OF BORDEAUX SISTERS**
Holy Family Convent, Moneenroe,
Castlecomer, Co Kilkenny
Tel 056-4442147
*Contact:* The Superior
Community: 3
Sisters involved in community, retreats and social work

**LITTLE COMPANY OF MARY**
Troy's Court, Kilkenny
Tel 056-7763117
Community: 3
Sheltered accommodation for older people

**LITTLE SISTERS OF THE POOR**
St Joseph's, Abbey Road, Ferrybank,
Waterford
Tel 051-833006
*Superior:* Sr Roseline
Community: 18
Care for the elderly

**LORETO (IBVM)**
Loreto Community, Freshford Road,
Kilkenny
Tel 056-7721187
*Superior:* Sr Brigid Tunney
Community: 10
Loreto Secondary School
Tel 056-7765131
Education and pastoral work

**MEDICAL MISSIONARIES OF MARY**
The Mews, Rosedale,
Kilmacow, via Waterford, Co Kilkenny
Tel 051-885931
Email mmmkilmacow@eircom.net

**PRESENTATION SISTERS**
Presentation Convent, Kilkenny
Tel 056-7721351
*Local Leader:* Srs Maura Murphy and Mary Martin
Community: 16
Primary School. Tel 056-7765598
Secondary School. Tel 056-7765684

Presentation Convent, Mooncoin,
Co Kilkenny
Tel 051-895114
*Local Leader:* Sr Mary Lenehan
Community: 11
Primary Girls' School
Tel 051-895503

Presentation Sisters, 8 Rosemount,
Newpark Drive, Kilkenny
Tel 056-7721693
*Contact:* Sr Nora McCarthy
Community: 4
Pastoral work

**RELIGIOUS OF SACRED HEART OF MARY**
Ferrybank, Waterford
Tel 051-832592
*Superior:* Sr Philippa O'Sullivan
Community: 12
Primary School. Pupils: 200+
Secondary School. Pupils: 630

22 Castle Oaks, Rockshire Road,
Ferrybank, Waterford
Tel 051-851606
Community: 3
Education, pastoral work

37 Castle Oaks, Rockshire Road,
Ferrybank, Waterford
Tel 051-833996
Community: 2
Education, pastoral work

**RELIGIOUS SISTERS OF CHARITY**
St Patrick's Convent,
Kells Road, Kilkenny
Tel 056-7770580
Various apostolic ministries

**ST JOHN OF GOD SISTERS**
Provincialate,
College Road, Kilkenny
Tel 056-7722870
Fax 056-7751411
Email sjgprovincialate@eircom.net
*Province Leader:* Sr Teresa Byrne
Secretary: Sr Maeve Cregan
Convent. Tel 056-7721914

St John of God Sisters
College Road, Kilkenny
*Resident Leader:* Sr Anne Harpur
Community: 28
Primary School. Tel 056-7721290
Pupils: 424
Altar breads department
Tel 056-7762278

St John of God Sisters,
Galtrim, Waterford Road, Kilkenny
Tel 056-7775510
Community: 3

St John of God Sisters, Moorville,
Rathdowney, Co Laois
Tel 0505-46258
Community: 3
Primary School. Pupils: 166
Tel 0505-46183

St John of God Sisters, 'Villa Marie',
Mooreville, Rathdowney, Co Laois
Tel 0505-46940
Community: 2

St John of God Sisters (Social Services)
Cuan Bhríde, Rathdowney, Co Laois
Tel 0505-46521
Community: 2

St Columba's Hospital, 7 Maudlin Court,
Thomastown, Co Kilkenny
Tel 056-7724046
Community: 2
Hospital Tel 056-7724178

Lady Sue Ryder House, Owning,
Co Kilkenny
Tel 051-643136
Community: 2

St John of God Sisters,
11 Dean's Court,
Waterford Road, Kilkenny
Tel 056-7764576
Community: 1

St John of God House, College Road,
Kilkenny
Leader: Sr Brenda Gardiner
Tel 056-7756788
Community: 8

St John of God Sisters, 'Fermoyle',
Greenshill, Kilkenny
Tel 056-7751259
Community: 3

St John of God Sisters
Aut Even Convent, Kilkenny
Tel 056-7761451
Community: 5

## EDUCATIONAL INSTITUTIONS

**St Kieran's College**
Kilkenny
Tel 056-7721086 Fax 056-7770001
Email skc1782@iol.ie
*Administrator*
Rt Rev Mgr Kieron Kennedy Ext 118
*Principal:* Mr John Curtis
Tel 056-7721086 Ext 223/7761707
*Chaplain:* Rev Sean O'Connor Ext 134

**Adult Educational Institute**
Seville Lodge, Callan Road, Kilkenny
Tel/Fax 056-7721453
*Business Manager:* Mr Richard Curtin

**EDMUND RICE SCHOOLS TRUST**
Scoil McAuley Rice Primary School,
West Street, Callan, Co Kilkenny
Tel 056-7725572 Fax 056-7725572
Email cbsnscallan.ias@eircom.net
*Principal:* Mr John Moloney

Coláiste Eamonn Rís Secondary School,
Callan, Co Kilkenny
*Principal:* Mr Frank McKenna
Tel 056-7725340
Tel 056-7725355 (staff) Fax 056-7725721
Email coleamannris@eircom.net

Scoil Iognáid de Rís,
CBS Primary School, Kilkenny
Tel 056-7761739 Fax 056-7771982
Email cbskilkenny.ias@eircom.net
*Principal:* Mr D. O'Reilly

Secondary School, James's Street,
Kilkenny
Tel 056-7761225 Fax 056-7763652
Email cbskk@indigo.ie
*Principal:* Mr Tom Clarke

## CHARITABLE AND OTHER SOCIETIES

**Good Shepherd Centre**
*Administrator:* Mr Seamus Roche
Hostel for transient homeless men
Tel 056-7722566

**Homes for Elderly People**
*Kilkenny:* Troy's Court
Tel 056-7763117
*St Patrick's Parish:* Tel 056-7764400
*St Johns' Parish:* Tel 056-7721072
*Ballyragget:* O'Gorman House
Tel 056-8833377
*St Mary's:* Tel 056-7721253
*Callan:* Mount Carmel
Tel 056-7725301
*Freshford:* Prague House
Tel 056-8832281
*Kilmacow:* Rosedale
Tel 051-885125
*Kilmoganny:* St Joseph's
Tel 051-648091
*Owning, Piltown:* Lady Sue Ryder Home
Tel 051-643136
*Rathdowney:* Cuan Bhríde
Tel 0505-46521
*Slieverue Parish:* Tel 051-832773

**L'Arche, Workshops and Accommodation for People with Learning Difficulties**
Moorefield House, Kilmoganny,
Co Kilkenny
Tel 051-64809
An Siol: 42 West Street, Callan,
Co Kilkenny
Tel 056-7725230
*Cluain Aoibhin:* Fairgreen, Callan,
Co Kilkenny
Tel 056-7725628

**Ossory Social Services**
Social Service Centre,
Waterford Road, Kilkenny
Tel 056-7721685 Fax 056-7763636
Email kilkenss@iol.ie
*Director:* Rt Rev Mgr Kieron Kennedy

*Local Social Services Centres:*
*Callan:* Sr Cecilia Dowley
Tel 056-7725223
*Castlecomer:* Ms Bridget McLean
Tel 056-4441679
*Ferrybank:* Sr Constance O'Sullivan
Tel 051-832592
*Freshford:* Sr Brigid Lonergan
Tel 056-8832281
*Moneenroe:* Sr Anne Kearney
Tel 056-4442147
*Rathdowney Cuan Bhride*
Sr Catherine O'Brien
Tel 0505-46521

**SOS (Kilkenny) Ltd, Sheltered Workshop and Accommodation for People with Learning Difficulties**
SOS (Kilkenny) Ltd,
Callan Road, Kilkenny
Tel 056-7764000 Fax 056-7761212

**Apostolic Work Society**
*Secretary:* Mrs Nora Ryan
Ross, Rathdowney, Co Laois
Tel 0505-46524

**St Joseph's Young Priests Society**
*Chairperson:* Mrs Marie Hogan
Freshford, Co Kilkenny
Tel 056-8832125
*Chaplain:* Rev William Purcell
St Kieran's College, Kilkenny
Tel 056-7721086/087-6286858
Email wpurcell@eircom.net

# DIOCESE OF RAPHOE

PATRON OF THE DIOCESE
ST EUNAN, 23 SEPTEMBER

INCLUDES THE GREATER PART OF COUNTY DONEGAL

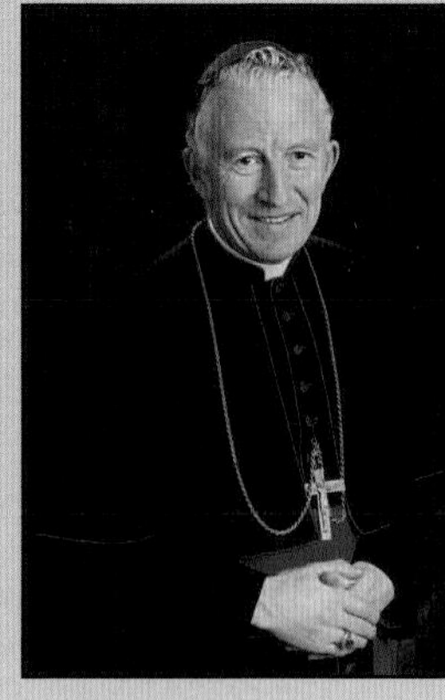

**Most Rev Philip Boyce (OCD) DD**
Bishop of Raphoe;
born 25 January 1940;
ordained priest 17 April 1966;
ordained Bishop of Raphoe
1 October 1995

Residence: Ard Adhamhnáin,
Letterkenny, Co Donegal
Tel 074-9121208
Fax 074-9124872
Email
raphoediocese@eircom.net
Website www.raphoediocese.ie

## ST EUNAN'S CATHEDRAL, LETTERKENNY

The old cathedral of Raphoe passed into Protestant hands at the Reformation. In the eighteenth century the Catholic bishops came to live in Letterkenny. A church was built circa 1820 and, having been extended by Bishop Patrick McGettigan, was used as a pro-cathedral. Bishop McDevitt (1871–1879) thought of building a new cathedral, and Lord Southwell promised a site, but it was not until 1891, when Bishop O'Donnell was in office, that actual building began. The cathedral was completed in 1901. Besides overseeing the cathedral project, Bishop O'Donnell had the task of providing a house for the bishop and priests of the cathedral parish.

The main benefactors were Fr J.D. McGarvey PP, Killygarvan, and Mr Neil Gillen of Airdrie. Various priests of the diocese spent considerable time fund-raising in Britain, the US and Canada.
The style is Gothic, with some Hiberno-Romanesque features, and the building is of white Mountcharles sandstone. The cathedral dominates the Letterkenny skyline. Among the artistic features to be noted are the 'Drumceat' window, by Michael Healy (North Transept); the pulpit, by Messrs Pearse (Patrick Pearse's family); the Great Arch, with its St Columba and St Eunan columns; and, outside, the fine statue of Bishop O'Donnell, by Doyle of Chelsea.

Remodelling of the cathedral took place in 1985, with the addition of an altar table and chairs; great care was taken to preserve the style and materials of the original altar. Bishop Hegarty promoted this tasteful restoration work, which left intact the architectural character of the building.

## CHAPTER

*Dean:* Very Rev Dean John Silke PE
Portnablagh
*Archdeacon*
Ven Archdeacon Patrick McShane PE
Donegal Town
*Members*
Very Rev Canon Denis McGettigan PP
Raphoe
Very Rev Canon John Gallagher
Hospital Chaplain, Letterkenny
Very Rev Canon Austin Laverty PP
Ardara
Very Rev Canon William McMenamin PE
Raphoe
Very Rev Canon John Silke PE
Portnablagh

## ADMINISTRATION

**Vicar General**
Rt Rev Mgr Daniel Carr PP, VG
St Johnston, Lifford, Co Donegal
Tel 074-9148203

**Diocesan Chancellor/Diocesan Secretary**
Rev Michael McKeever
Diocesan Office, Ard Adhamhnáin,
Letterkenny, Co Donegal
Tel 074-9121208 Fax 074-9124872
Email raphoediocese@eircom.net

**College of Consultors**
Rt Rev Mgr Daniel Carr PP, VG
St Johnston
Very Rev Kieran McAteer PP
Stranorlar
Very Rev Eamonn Kelly Adm
Letterkenny
Very Rev Francis McLoone PP
Killymard
Very Rev Cathal O'Fearraí PP, VF
Ballyshannon
Rev Donnchadh O'Baoill CC
Cnoc Fola

**Vicars Forane**
Rt Rev Mgr Daniel Carr PP, VG
St Johnston
Very Rev Canon Austin Laverty PP
Ardara
Very Rev Cathal O'Fearraí PP
Ballyshannon
Very Rev Eamonn Kelly Adm
Letterkenny
Very Rev Martin Collum PP
Rathmullan
Very Rev Michael Herrity PP
Annagry

**Financial Administrators**
Rt Rev Mgr Daniel Carr PP, VG
Mrs Carmel Doherty
Ard Adhamhnáin,
Letterkenny, Co Donegal

**Finance Committee**
Bishop Philip Boyce, Mgr Dan Carr,
Mr Noel O'Connell, Mrs Mary Foley,
Mr John McCreadie, Mr Peadar Murphy,
Mrs Carmel Doherty *(Secretary)*,
Ms Siobhan Logue, Mr Conal Boyle

**Building Committee**
Very Rev Canon Austin Laverty PP
Very Rev Canon John Gallagher

**Diocesan Archives**
Faíche Ó Dónaill Building
Ard Adhamhnáin, Letterkenny,
Co Donegal
Tel 074-9161109
Email raphoearchives@eircom.net

## CATECHETICS EDUCATION

**Religious Education in Primary Schools**
*Co-ordinator:* Rev Aodhan Cannon
Ardara, Co Donegal
Tel 074-9541930

**Religious Education in Secondary Schools**
Resource Centre, 13a Lower Main Street,
Letterkenny, Co Donegal
Tel 074-9177388
Sr Susan Evangelist Taegue
Drumkeen, Co Donegal
Rev Philip Kemmy CC
Convoy
Tel 074-9147238

## LITURGY

**Perpetual Eucharistic Adoration**
*Diocesan Director:* Rev Patrick Dunne
Parochial House, Kilmacrennan,
Letterkenny
Tel 074-9139018

## PASTORAL

**Accord**
*Letterkenny area:* Pastoral Centre,
Monastery Ave, Letterkenny
Tel 074-9122218
*Chairperson:* Mrs Marie Ferry
*Treasurer:* Mrs Sheila Leeper
*Secretary:* Mrs Sheila Leeper
*Chaplain:* Rev Eamonn Kelly
Open Monday-Friday 10.00 am-1.00 pm
*Donegal Town area:*
*Chairman:* Mr Tom Lynch
*Secretary:* Ms Brenda Burke
Tel 073-9723944
*Chaplain:* Very Rev John McLoone PP
Frosses
LoCall 1850-201878

**Child Safeguarding Office**
Pastoral Centre, Monastery Avenue,
Letterkenny, Co Donegal
Tel 074-9125669
Email cporaphoediocese@eircom.net

**Diocesan Resource Worker**
Bairbre Cahill
Pastoral Centre, Letterkenny, Co Donegal
Tel 074-9121853/086-0230157
bairbre.raphoepastoralrenewal@gmail.com

**Diocesan Social Worker**
Mr Seamus Gallagher
*Secretary:* Kathleen Kelly
The Pastoral Centre, Monastery Avenue,
Letterkenny, Co Donegal
Tel 074-9122047 Fax 074-9128433

**Ecumenism**
*Diocesan Director*
Very Rev Francis McAteer PP
Carrick, Co Donegal
Tel 074-9739008

**Family Ministry Centre**
The Pastoral Centre,
Letterkenny, Co Donegal
Tel 074-9121853 Fax 074-9128433

**Fatima Pilgrimage**
*Director:* Rev James Sweeney CC
Ardaghey, Co Donegal
Tel 074-9736007

**Knock Pilgrimage**
*Director:* Rev Michael McKeever
Churchill, Co Donegal
Tel 074-9137057

**Lourdes Pilgrimage**
*Director:* Very Rev Patrick McHugh PP
Parochial House, Termon, Co Donegal
Tel 074-9139016/074-9125090 *(Lourdes office)*

**Marriage Tribunal**
*(See also Marriage Tribunals section)*
*Secretary:* Kathleen Kelly
*Officialis:* Vacant
*Assistants:* Rev Joseph Briody
Rev Eamonn McLaughlin
The Pastoral Centre, Letterkenny,
Co Donegal
Tel 074-9121853

**Pioneer Total Abstinence Association**
*Diocesan Director*
Very Rev James Friel PE
Rathmullan, Co Donegal
Rev James Sweeney CC
Ardaghey, Co Donegal
Tel 074-9736007

**Raphoe Diocesan Directory**
Rev Michael McKeever
Ard Adhamhnáin, Letterkenny,
Co Donegal
Tel 074-9121208
Fax 074-9124872
Email raphoediocese@eircom.net

**Religious Broadcasting**
*Diocesan Director:* Rev Patrick Dunne
Parochial House, Kilmacrennan,
Letterkenny
Tel 074-9139018

**Vocations**
*Directors:* Rev Joseph O'Donnell CC
Church of the Irish Martyrs, Letterkenny
Tel 074-9122608
Rev Gerard Cunningham CC
Parochial House, Fintown
Tel 074-9546107
Rev Rory Brady
1 Cathedral Place,
Letterkenny, Co Donegal
Tel 074-9125182

**World Missions Ireland**
*Diocesan Director*
Very Rev Francis McAteer PP
Parochial House, Carrick, Co Donegal
Tel 074-9739008

## PARISHES

*The mensal parish is listed first. Other parishes follow alphabetically. Historical names are given in parentheses.*

**LETTERKENNY (CONWAL AND LECK)**
*Cathedral of St Eunan and St Columba*
Very Rev Eamonn Kelly Adm
Rev Damien McGroarty CC
Rev Francis Ferry CC
Parochial House, Letterkenny, Co Donegal
Tel 074-9121021 Fax 074-9122707
Email steunanscathedral@eircom.net
Letterkenny General Hospital
Rev Martin Chambers
2 Chaplain's House, Knocknamona, Letterkenny, Co Donegal
Tel 074-9125090
Canon John Gallagher
1 Chaplain's House, Knocknamona, Letterkenny, Co Donegal
Tel (Hospital) 074-9125888

**ANNAGRY**
Very Rev Michael Herrity PP
Annagry, Co Donegal
Tel 074-9548111

**ARDARA**
Very Rev Canon Austin Laverty PP, VF
Ardara, Co Donegal
Tel 074-9541135
Rev Aodhan Cannon CC
Ardara, Co Donegal
Tel 074-9541930
Rev Philip Daly CC
Kilclooney, Co Donegal
Tel 074-9545114

**AUGHANINSHIN**
Very Rev Brian Quinn PP
Ballyraine, Letterkenny, Co Donegal
Tel 074-9127600
Rev Joe O'Donnell CC
Carnamuggagh Lower, Letterkenny, Co Donegal
Tel 074-9122608

**BALLINTRA (DRUMHOLM)**
Very Rev Seamus Dagens PP
Ballintra, Co Donegal
Tel 074-9734016

**BALLYSHANNON (KILBARRON)**
Very Rev Cathal Ó Fearraí PP, VF
Tel 071-9851295
Rev Declan Boyce (SPS)
Tel 071-9851090

**BRUCKLESS (KILLAGHTEE)**
Very Rev Dermot McShane PP
Bruckless, Co Donegal
Tel 074-9737015

**BURTONPORT (KINCASSLAGH)**
Very Rev Pat Ward PP
Burtonport, Co Donegal
Tel 074-9542006
Rev John Joe Duffy CC
Arranmore Island, Co Donegal
Tel 074-9520504

**CARRICK (GLENCOLMCILLE)**
Very Rev Francis McAteer PP
Carrick, Co Donegal
Tel 074-9739008
Rev Bill McGeady CC
Cashel, Glencolmcille, Co Donegal
Tel 074-9730025

**CARRIGART (MEEVAGH)**
Very Rev Charles Byrne PP
Carrigart, Co Donegal
Tel 074-9155154

**CLOGHAN (KILTEEVOGUE)**
Very Rev Lorcan Sharkey PP
Cloghan, Lifford, Co Donegal
Tel 074-9133007

**DONEGAL TOWN (TAWNAWILLY)**
Very Rev William Peoples PP
Tel 074-9721026
Donegal Town, Co Donegal
Rev Danny McBrearty CC
Parochial House, Clar
Tel 074-9721093

**DRUMOGHILL (RAYMOCHY)**
Served from Cathedral Parish
Contact 074-9121021

**DUNFANAGHY (CLONDAHORKEY)**
Very Rev Martin Doohan PP
Dunfanaghy, Co Donegal
Tel 074-9136163
Rev Joseph Briody CC
Cleeslough, Co Donegal
Tel 074-9138011

**DUNGLOE (TEMPLECRONE AND LETTERMACAWARD)**
Very Rev Séamus Meehan PP
Tel 074-9521008
Rev Nigel Ó Galláchóir CC
Tel 074-9522194
Dungloe, Co Donegal
Rev Eamonn McLaughlin CC
Leitirmacaward, Co Donegal
Tel 074-9544102

**FALCARRAGH**
Very Rev Denis Quinn PP
Falcarragh, Co Donegal
Tel 074-9135196

**GLENSWILLY (GLENSWILLY AND TEMPLEDOUGLAS)**
Very Rev Hugh Sweeney PP
Glenswilly, New Mills, Letterkenny, Co Donegal
Tel 074-9137020

**GLENTIES (INISKEEL)**
Very Rev Patrick Prendergast PP
Tel 074-9551117
Rev Shane Gallagher CC
Tel 074-9551136
Glenties, Co Donegal
Rev Gerard Cunningham CC
Fintown, Donegal Town, Co Donegal
Tel 074-9546107

**GORTAHORK (TORY ISLAND)**
Very Rev Seán Ó Gallchóir PP
Tel 074-9135214
Rev Paul Gallagher CC (Tory Island)
Falcarragh, Co Donegal
Tel 074-9165356

**GWEEDORE**
Very Rev Pádraig Ó Baoighill PP
Tel 074-9531310
Rev Brian O'Fearraigh CC
Tel 074-9531947
Derrybeg, Letterkenny
Rev Donnchadh Ó Baoill CC
Bun-a-leaca, Letterkenny, Co Donegal
Tel 074-9531155

**INVER**
Very Rev John McLoone PP
Frosses, Co Donegal
Tel 074-9736006
Rev James Sweeney CC
Ardaghey, Co Donegal
Tel 074-9736007
Rev Adrian Gavigan CC
Mountcharles, Co Donegal
Tel 074-9735009

**KILCAR**
Very Rev Edward Gallagher PP
Kilcar, Co Donegal
Tel 074-9738007

**KILLYBEGS**
Very Rev Colm O'Gallchoir PP
Killybegs, Co Donegal
Tel 074-9731030

**KILLYMARD**
Very Rev Francis McLoone PP
Killymard, Co Donegal
Tel 074-9721929

**KILMACRENNAN**
Very Rev Patrick Dunne PP
Kilmacrennan, Co Donegal
Tel 074-9139018

**NEWTOWNCUNNINGHAM & KILLEA**
Very Rev Seamus Gallagher PP
Parochial House, Newtowncunningham, Lifford, Co Donegal
Tel 074-9156138

**RAMELTON (AUGHNISH)**
Very Rev Michael Carney PP
Ramelton, Co Donegal
Tel 074-9151304

**RAPHOE**
Very Rev Denis McGettigan PP
Raphoe, Lifford, Co Donegal
Tel 074-9145647
Rev Philip Kemmy CC
Convoy, Lifford, Co Donegal
Tel 074-9147238
Rev John Boyce
Drumkeen, Ballybofey,
Co Donegal
Tel 074-9134005

**RATHMULLAN (KILLYGARVAN AND TULLYFERN)**
Very Rev Martin Collum PP
Rathmullan, Co Donegal
Tel 074-9158156
Rev James Gillespie CC
Milford, Co Donegal
Tel 074-9153236
Very Rev Michael Sweeney AP
Glenvar
Tel 074-9150014

**ST JOHNSTON (TAUGHBOYNE)**
Rt Rev Mgr Daniel Carr PP, VG
St Johnston, Lifford, Co Donegal
Tel 074-9148203

**STRANORLAR**
Very Rev Kieran McAteer PP
Parochial House, Ballybofey,
Co Donegal
Tel 074-9131135
Rev Ciaran Harkin CC
Parochial House, Stranorlar,
Co Donegal
Tel 074-9131157

**TAMNEY (CLONDAVADDOG)**
Very Rev Patrick McGarvey PP
Fanavolty, Kindrum,
Letterkenny, Co Donegal
Tel 074-9159007
Rev Paul McGeehan
*(Priest in residence)*
Tamney, Letterkenny,
Co Donegal
Tel 074-9159015

**TERMON (GARTAN AND TERMON)**
Very Rev Patrick McHugh PP
Termon, Letterkenny,
Co Donegal
Tel 074-9139016
Rev Michael McKeever CC
Church Hill, Letterkenny,
Co Donegal
Tel 074-9137057
www.gartantermon.net

## INSTITUTIONS AND THEIR CHAPLAINS

**General Hospital**
Letterkenny, Co Donegal
Tel 074-9125888
Rev Martin Chambers
c/o General Hospital, Letterkenny
or 2 Chaplain's House,
Knocknamona, Letterkenny
Canon John Gallagher
1 Chaplain's House,
Knocknamona, Letterkenny

**Letterkenny Institute of Technology**
Letterkenny, Co Donegal
Tel 074-9124888
Rev John Boyce

**St Conal's Hospital**
Letterkenny, Co Donegal
Tel 074-9121022
Canon John Gallagher
Rev Martin Chambers

**St Joseph's Hospital**
Stranorlar, Co Donegal
Tel 074-9131038
Parochial clergy Stranorlar

## PRIESTS OF THE DIOCESE ELSEWHERE

Rev Patrick Bonner
140 Willowood Drive, Wantagh,
New York, USA
Rev Niall Coll
St Mary's College, Belfast
Rev Martin Cunningham
c/o Diocesan Office, Letterkenny,
Co Donegal
Rev Kevin Gillespie
Congregation for the Clergy, Rome
Rev Brendan McBride
St Philip's Church, 725 Diamond Street,
San Francisco, California, 94114
Rev Declan McCarron
c/o Diocesan Office, Letterkenny,
Co Donegal
Rev Martin Timoney
c/o Diocesan Office, Letterkenny,
Co Donegal

## RETIRED PRIESTS

Very Rev Canon Patrick McShane PE
Tully, Donegal Town, Co Donegal
Tel 074-9740150
Very Rev Connell Cunningham PE
Carrick, Co Donegal
Rev Thomas Curran
Glenview House, College Road,
Letterkenny, Co Donegal
Tel 074-9127617
Rev Anthony Griffith
Rushbrook, Laghey, Co Donegal
Tel 074-9734021
Very Rev Daniel O'Doherty PE
Ballyheerin, Fanad, Co Donegal
Very Rev John J. Silke PhD
'Stella Maris', Portnablagh, Co Donegal
Tel 074-9136122
Very Rev Seamus L. Gallagher PE
Glenlee, Killybegs, Co Donegal
Tel 074-9732729
Very Rev Kevin O'Doherty PE
Falcarragh, Co Donegal
Tel 074-9165356
Very Rev Desmond Sweeney PE
17 Meadowvale, Ramelton
Tel 074-9151085
Very Rev Michael Connaghan PE
6 Fields Court, Kilmacrennan, Co Donegal
Tel 074-9119871
Rev James Friel PE
Massreagh, Rathmullen, Co Donegal
Canon William McMenamin PE
'St Columba's', Meeting House Street,
Raphoe, Co Donegal
Tel 074-9144834

## RELIGIOUS ORDERS AND CONGREGATIONS

### PRIESTS

**CAPUCHINS (OFMCAP)**
Capuchin Friary, Ard Mhuire,
Creeslough, Letterkenny, Co Donegal
Tel 074-9138005 Fax 074-9138371
*Guardian*
Rev Silvester O'Flynn (OFMCap)
*Vicar*
Rev Kieran Shorten (OFMCap)

**FRANCISCANS (OFM)**
Franciscan Friary, Rossnowlagh,
Co Donegal
Tel 072-9851342 Fax 072-9852206
Email franciscanfriary@eircom.net
*Guardian*
Rev Paschal McDonnell (OFM)

### SISTERS

**CONGREGATION OF THE SISTERS OF MERCY**
Convent of Mercy, Donegal Town,
Co Donegal
Tel 074-9721175
Shared leadership
Community: 5

Convent of Mercy, 15 Blackrock Drive,
Ballybofey, Co Donegal
Tel 074-9132721
*Leader:* Sr Nuala Mullin
Community: 5

St Catherine's,
Ballyshannon, Co Donegal
Tel 071-9851268
*Shared leadership:* Sr Ursula Fox
Community: 6

Bethany, 23 Ernedale Heights,
Ballyshannon, Co Donegal
Tel 071-9852186

Dia Linn, Gortnamucklagh,
Glenties, Co Donegal
Tel 074-9551125

Convent of Mercy,
Carnmore Road, Dungloe,
Co Donegal
Tel 074-9521209

Sisters of Mercy,
Ceoil na Coille, Stranorlar,
Lifford, Co Donegal
Tel 074-9131245
Family Enrichment Centre
Dromboe Avenue, Stranorlar
Tel 074-9131245

Convent of Mercy, Windy Hall,
Letterkenny, Co Donegal
Tel 074-9122729
Community: 4

Sisters of Mercy,
St Anne's Convent,
Ballyshannon, Co Donegal
Tel 071-9852737
Community: 3

Sisters of Mercy,
No. 1 McCloskey Close,
Glenties, Co Donegal
Tel 074-9551713

Sisters of Mercy,
15 Taobh na Cille,
Moville, Co Donegal
Tel 074-9385454

Sisters of Mercy,
Glór na Mara, West End,
Bundoran, Co Donegal
Tel 071-9833899

18 Beinn Aoibhin,
Letterkenny, Co Donegal
Tel 074-9177837

2 Marina View, Dinglei Coush,
Bundoran, Co Donegal
Tel 071-9829832

**LORETO (IBVM)**
Loreto Community, Letterkenny,
Co Donegal
Tel 074-9122896
*Superior:* Sr Rosaleen O'Kane
Community: 10
Loreto Primary School
Tel 074-9122896
Loreto Secondary School
Tel 074-9124237

## NEW FORMS OF CONSECRATED LIFE

**THE SPIRITUAL FAMILY THE WORK OF CHRIST (FSO)**
Bishop's House, Ard Adhamhnáin,
Letterkenny, Co Donegal
Tel 074-9124898
Fax 074-9128142
Email thework@catholic.org
Website www.thework-fso.org
*Superior:* Sr Annie Dueringer FSO
Community: 2

## EDUCATIONAL INSTITUTIONS

**Coláiste Ailigh**
High Road, Letterkenny,
Co Donegal
Tel 074-9125943
*Príomh-Óid*
Mr Michael Gibbons
*Séiplineadh*
Mr Séan Ó Gallchóir

**Coláiste Cholmcille**
Ballyshannon, Co Donegal
Tel 071-9858288/9851369/9852459
*Principal:* Mr Jimmy Keogh
*Chaplain:* Ms Pauline Kilfeather

**Rosses Community School**
Dungloe, Co Donegal
Tel 074-9521122
*Principal:* Mr John Gorman
*Chaplain:* Rev Nigel Ó Gallchóir CC

**Comprehensive School**
Glenties, Lifford, Co Donegal
Tel 074-9551172
Fax 074-9551664
*Principal:* Mrs Frances Bonner
*Chaplain:* Rev Shane Gallagher CC

**Institute of Technology, Letterkenny**
*Director:* Mr Paul Hannigan
Tel 074-9124888
*Chaplain:* Rev John Boyce

**Loreto Convent Secondary School**
Letterkenny, Co Donegal
Tel 074-9121850
*Principal:* Mrs Susan Kenny
*Chaplain:* Parish Clergy

**Loreto Community School**
Milford, Co Donegal
Tel 074-9153253
Fax 074-9153518
*Principal:* Mr Andrew Kelly
Tel 074-9153399
*Chaplain:* Mr John Lynch

**Pobalscoil Chloich Cheannfhaola**
Falcarragh, Letterkenny, Co Donegal
Tel 074-9135424/9135231
Fax 074-9135019
*Príomh-Oide:* Ms Maeve Sweeney
*Séiplineach:* Rev Paul Gallagher CC

**Pobalscoil Ghaoth Dobhair**
Derrybeg, Letterkenny, Co Donegal
Tel 074-9531040
*Príomh-Oide:* Mr Noel Ó Gallchóir
*Séiplineach:* Rev Brian O'Fearraigh CC

**St Columba's College**
Stranorlar, Co Donegal
Tel 074-9131246
*Principal:* Mr Gerry Bennett
*Chaplain:* Parish Clergy

**St Eunan's College**
Letterkenny, Co Donegal
Tel 074-9121143
*Principal:* Mr Chris Darby
*Chaplain:* Rev Rory Brady

**Vocational Schools**
*Arranmore Island, Co Donegal*
Tel 074-9521747
*Principal:* Mrs Mary Doherty
*Chaplain:* Rev John Joe Duffy CC

*Ballinamore, Co Donegal*
Tel 074-9546133 Fax 074-9546256
*Principal:* Ms Fiona Bonner
*Chaplain:* Rev Gerard Cunningham CC
Fintown, Donegal Town, Co Donegal

*Carrick, Co Donegal*
Tel 074-9739017 Fax 074-9739265
*Principal:* Mr Tony Bonner
*Chaplain:* Very Rev Eddie Gallagher PP
Kilcar, Co Donegal

*Abbey Vocational School,*
Donegal Town, Co Donegal
Tel 074-9721105 Fax 074-9722851
*Principal:* Mr Emmanuel McCormick
*Chaplain:* Rev Adrian Gavigan CC

*Gairm Scoil Catríona,*
Killybegs, Co Donegal
Tel/Fax 074-9731491
*Principal:* Ms Mary Anne Looby

*Errigal College,*
Letterkenny, Co Donegal
Tel 074-9121047/9121861
Fax 074-9121861
*Principal:* Ms Anne McHugh
*Chaplain:* Rev Eamonn Kelly Adm

*Mulroy College,*
Milford, Co Donegal
Tel 074-9153346
*Principal:* Ms Rita Gleeson
*Chaplain:* Rev James Gillespie CC
Milford, Co Donegal

*Deele College,*
Raphoe, Co Donegal
Tel 074-9145277
*Principal:* Mr P. J. McGowan
*Chaplain:* Very Rev Denis McGettigan PP

*Finn Valley College,*
Stranorlar, Co Donegal
Tel 074-9131355
*Principal:* Mr Frank Dooley

## CHARITABLE AND OTHER SOCIETIES

**Ards Friary Retreat and Conference Centre**
*Manager:* Mr Benito Conangelo
Tel 074-9138909
Email info@ardsfriary.ie
Website www.ardsfriary.ie

**Society of St Vincent de Paul**
North West Region Council,
Meeting House Street,
Raphoe, Co Donegal
Tel/Fax 074-9173933
Email svpnorthwest@eircom.net

**St Mura's Adoption Society**
The Pastoral Centre, Monastery Avenue,
Letterkenny, Co Donegal
tel 074-9122047

**Trócaire**
Rev Aodhan Cannon CC
Parochial House, Ardara,
Co Donegal
Tel 074-9541930

# DIOCESE OF WATERFORD AND LISMORE

PATRONS OF THE DIOCESE
ST OTTERAN, 27 OCTOBER; ST CARTHAGE, 15 MAY;
ST DECLAN, 24 JULY

INCLUDES COUNTY WATERFORD
AND PART OF COUNTIES TIPPERARY AND CORK

**Most Rev William Lee DD**
Bishop of Waterford and Lismore; born 1941; ordained priest 19 June 1966; ordained Bishop of Waterford and Lismore 25 July 1993

Residence: Bishop's House, John's Hill, Waterford
Tel 051-874463
Fax 051-852703
Email
waterfordlismore@eircom.net

## CATHEDRAL OF THE MOST HOLY TRINITY, WATERFORD

The Cathedral of the Most Holy Trinity, Barronstrand Street, Waterford is the oldest Roman Catholic cathedral in Ireland. The work began in 1793 with the Protestant Waterford man, John Roberts, as architect. Roberts also designed the Church of Ireland cathedral.

Over the years, additions and alterations have been made. Most of the present sanctuary was added in the 1830s; the apse and a main altar in 1854. The beautiful baldachin, which is supported by five Corinthian columns, was erected in 1881.

The carved oak Baroque pulpit, the chapter stalls and bishop's chair, designed by Goldie and Sons of London and carved by Buisine and Sons of Lille, were installed in 1883.
The stained-glass windows, mainly by Meyer of Munich, were installed between 1883 and 1888.

The Stations of the Cross, which are attached to the columns in the cathedral, are nineteenth-century paintings by Alcan of Paris. The cut-stone front was built in 1892–1893 for the centenary of the cathedral.

In 1977, a new wooden altar was placed in the redesigned sanctuary. The Belgian walnut panels of the base of the altar were originally part of the altar rails at St Carthage's Church, Lismore.

There are many plaques in the cathedral. One of them commemorates fourteen famous Waterford men: Luke Wadding OFM; Peter Lombard; Patrick Comerford OSA; James White; Michael Wadding SJ: Peter Wadding SJ; Thomas White; Paul Sherlock SJ; Ambrose Wadding SJ; Geoffrey Keating; Luke Wadding SJ; Stephen White SJ; Thomas White SJ and Bonaventure Barron OFM.

Ten Waterford Crystal chandeliers were presented by Waterford Crystal in 1979.

In 1993 the Bicentenary of the Cathedral was celebrated.

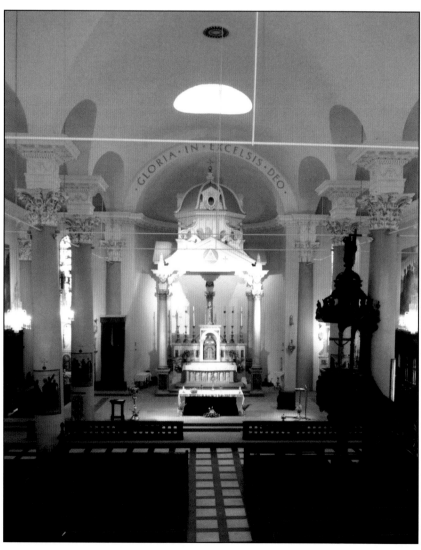

## CHAPTER

Right Rev Mgr Dean John Shine AP
Tramore
Right Rev Mgr Nicholas O'Mahony PP, VG
Tramore
Very Rev Gregory Power PE
St Mary's, Clonmel
Right Rev Mgr Michael Olden PE
Waterford
Very Rev Francis Hopkins AP
Ballybricken, Waterford
Very Rev Martin Slattery AP
Cathedral, Waterford
Very Rev Daniel O'Connor PE
Dungarvan
Very Rev William Ryan PP
Dungarvan
Very Rev Paul Beecher PE, Cahir
Very Rev Brendan Crowley PP
SS Peter & Paul's, Clonmel

**College of Consultors**
Right Rev Mgr Nicholas O'Mahony PP, VG
Very Rev Raymond Liddane AP
Very Rev Patrick Cooney PP
Very Rev Patrick Fitzgerald PP
Right Rev Mgr Michael Olden PE
Very Rev Liam Power Adm

## ADMINISTRATION

**Vicar General**
Right Rev Mgr Nicholas O'Mahony PP, VG
Parochial House, Tramore,
Co Waterford
Tel 051-381525

**Chancellor**
Rev Gerard Chestnutt CC
Sacred Heart Presbytery, The Folly,
Waterford
Tel 051-878429

**Diocesan Development Committee**
Right Rev Mgr Nicholas O'Mahony PP, VG
Very Rev Brendan Crowley PP, VF
Very Rev Patrick Fitzgerald PP
Very Rev Michael Hegarty (IC), PP
Very Rev Conor Kelly PP
Very Rev Liam Power Adm

**Diocesan Finance Committee**
Right Rev Mgr Nicholas O'Mahony PP, VG
Very Rev Peter Ahearne PP
Mr Anthony Brophy
Rev Gerard Chestnutt CC
Very Rev Canon Brendan Crowley PP, VF
Mr Michael Holland
Very Rev Gerard Langford Adm
Mrs Alice Pollard
Mr Sean Ryan
Very Rev William Ryan PP
Mr Tim Walsh

**Diocesan Financial Administrator**
Rev Gerard Chestnutt CC
Sacred Heart Presbytery, The Folly,
Waterford
Tel 051-878429

**Diocesan Building Projects Committee**
Right Rev Mgr Nicholas O'Mahony PP, VG
Very Rev Richard Doherty AP
Very Rev Patrick Fitzgerald PP
Very Rev Thomas Flynn PP
Mr Michael J. Maguire BE, CEng, MIEI
Very Rev Michael F. Walsh PE

**Diocesan Common Fund Committee**
Very Rev Raymond Liddane AP
Very Rev Garret Desmond PP
Very Rev Joseph Flynn PP
Very Rev Martin Keogh PP
Very Rev Canon William Ryan PP, VF

**Diocesan Retirement Fund Committee**
Right Rev Mgr Nicholas O'Mahony PP, VG
Rev Gerard Chestnutt CC
Very Rev Richard Doherty AP
Very Rev Patrick Cooney PP
Very Rev Martin Keogh PP
Very Rev Canon Brendan Crowley PP, VF
Rev Paul Waldron CC

**Diocesan Secretary**
Rev Gerard Chestnutt CC
Sacred Heart Presbytery, The Folly,
Waterford
Tel 051-878429

**Episcopal Vicar for Retired Priests**
Very Rev John Kiely PP
Cappoquin, Co Waterford
Tel 058-54216

## CATECHETICS EDUCATION

**Catechetics**
*Primary Schools Religious Education:*
Sr Antoinette Dilworth
Mercy Convent, Military Road, Waterford
Tel 051-874199
Sr De Lourdes Breen
Presentation Sisters, 158 Larchville,
Waterford
Tel 051-355496
Rev Edmond Hassett CC
Portlaw, Co Waterford
Tel 051-387227
Rev Richard O'Halloran CC
41 Lismore Park, Waterford
Tel 051-354034
Rev Paul Waldron CC
The Presbytery, Dungarvan, Co Waterford
Tel 058-42384
*Director Post-Primary Schools Religious Education:* Ms Roseanne Sinnott
St John's Pastoral Centre, John's Hill,
Waterford
Tel 051-874199

**Catholic Primary School Managers' Association**
*Secretary:* Very Rev Patrick Cooney PP
30 Viewmount Park, Waterford
Tel 051-873073
*Chairman:* Mr Michael O'Shea
West Street, Lismore, Co Waterford

## LITURGY

**Assistant to Parishes**
Ms Mary Dee
St John's Pastoral Centre,
John's Hill, Waterford
Tel 051-874199

**Diocesan Liturgy Committee**
Very Rev Canon William Ryan PP
Very Rev William Meehan PP
Rev Paul Waldron CC
Mr Noel Casey
Br Steve Hale
Ms Deirdre Moore
Ms Mary Dunphy
Ms Anna Fennessey

## PASTORAL

**Accord**
*Director:* Very Rev Liam Power Adm
St John's Pastoral Centre, John's Hill
Waterford
Tel 051-874199
Rev Raymond Reidy CC
Church of the Resurrection,
Fethard Road, Clonmel, Co Tipperary
Tel 052-6123239

**Charismatic Groups**
Very Rev Patrick Gear PP
Ballyneale, Carrick-on-Suir,
Co Tipperary
Tel 051-647011

**CURA**
St John's Pastoral Centre, John's Hill,
Waterford
Tel 051-876452

**Diocesan Archivist**
Sr Rita Fennell
St John's Pastoral Centre,
John's Hill, Waterford
Tel 051-874199

**Ecumenism**
*Director:* Very Rev Edmond Cullinan PP, VF
Parochial House, Chapel Street,
Carrick-on-Suir, Co Tipperary
Tel 051-640168

**Emigrant Bureau**
*Director:* Very Rev Michael Enright PE
Priest's Road, Tramore, Co Waterford
Tel 087-2371546

**Family Ministry**
*Director:* Ms Ann O'Farrell
Family Ministry Office,
St John's Pastoral Centre,
John's Hill, Waterford
Tel 051-874199/858772

**Historic Churches Advisory Committee**
Mr Eamonn McEneaney
Very Rev Canon William Ryan PP, VF
Very Rev Michael Walsh PE
Tel 051-874463

**Marriage Tribunal**
*Diocesan Official:* Rt Rev Mgr John Shine AP
Tramore, Co Waterford
Tel 051-381531
(See also Marriage Tribunals section)

**Media Spokesperson**
Very Rev Liam Power Adm
St John's Pastoral Centre, John's Hill
Waterford
Tel 051-874199

**Ministry to Polish Community**
Rev Emil Adler
St Anne's Presbytery, Convent Hill,
Waterford
Tel 087-4182223

**Pastoral Development**
Very Rev Liam Power Adm
St John's Pastoral Centre, John's Hill
Waterford
Tel 051-874199

**Pilgrimage**
*Director:* Very Rev Conor Kelly PP
Ring, Dungarvan, Co Waterford
Tel 058-46125

**Pioneer Total Abstinence Association**
*Diocesan Director:* Br Philip Ryan (CFC)
Mount Sion, Barrack Street, Waterford
Tel 051-874390

**Pontifical Mission Societies**
*Diocesan Director*
Very Rev Sean O'Dwyer PP
Parochial House, Cahir, Co Tipperary
Tel 052-7441404

**Senate of Priests**
*Chairperson*
Very Rev Patrick Fitzgerald PP
Parochial House, Lisduggan, Waterford
Tel 051-372257
*Secretary:* Rev John Treacy CC
14 Heathervue Road, Riverview,
Knockboy, Waterford
Tel 051-843207

**Travellers**
*Chaplain:* Very Rev Paul Murphy PP
Butlerstown, Co Waterford
Tel 051-384192

**Trócaire**
*Diocesan Director*
Very Rev Conor Kelly PP
Ring, Dungarvan, Co Waterford
Tel 058-46125

**Vocations**
*Director:* Very Rev William Meehan PP
St Mary's, Irishtown, Clonmel, Co Tipperary
Tel 052-6122954

**Youth Ministry**
Edmund Rice Youth & Community
Centre, Manor Street,
Waterford
Tel 051-872710

## PARISHES

*City parishes are listed first. Other parishes follow alphabetically. Italics denote church titulars where they differ from parish names.*

**TRINITY WITHIN AND ST PATRICK'S**
*Holy Trinity Cathedral*
Very Rev Gerard Langford Adm
Cathedral of the Most Holy Trinity,
Barronstrand Street, Waterford
Tel 051-392666
Very Rev Martin Slattery AP
Apt 5, Luke Wadding Suites,
Adelphi Wharf, Waterford
Tel 051-311561
*Sacristy:* Tel 051-875166

**ST JOHN'S**
Very Rev Liam Power Adm
Rev Thomas Burns
Rev Robert Grant CC
St John's Presbytery, New Street,
Waterford
Tel 051-874271
*Sacristy:* Tel 051-875849

**SS JOSEPH AND BENILDUS**
*SS Joseph & Benildus, Newtown*
*St Mary, Ballygunner*
Very Rev Patrick Cooney PP
30 Viewmount Park, Waterford
Tel 051-873073
Very Rev Raymond Liddane AP
Newtown, Waterford
Tel 051-874284
Rev John Treacy CC
14 Heathervue Road, Knockboy,
Waterford
Tel 051-843207
*Sacristy:* Tel 051-878977
*Parish Pastoral Worker:*
Ms Aoife McGrath
Tel 051-854690

**BALLYBRICKEN**
*Holy Trinity Without*
Very Rev Michael Mullins PP
Very Rev Canon Francis Hopkins AP
Rev Michael O'Brien
Rev Emil Adler
St Anne's Presbytery, Convent Hill,
Waterford
Tel 051-855819
*Sacristy:* Tel 051-874519

**HOLY FAMILY**
Very Rev Thomas Rogers PP
Holy Family Presbytery,
Luke Wadding Street, Waterford
Tel 051-375274

**ST PAUL'S**
Very Rev Patrick Fitzgerald PP
Parochial House, Lisduggan, Waterford
Tel 051-372257
Rev Richard O'Halloran CC
41 Lismore Park, Waterford
Tel 051-353938
*Sacristy:* Tel 051-378073

**SACRED HEART**
Very Rev Sean Melody PP
Sacred Heart Presbytery,
21 The Folly, Waterford
Tel 051-873759
Rev Gerard Chestnutt CC
The Presbytery, The Folly, Waterford
Tel 051-878429
Sacristy: Tel 051-873792

**ST SAVIOUR'S**
Very Rev Declan Corish (OP) PP
Rev Martin Crowe (OP) CC
Rev Richard Walsh (OP) CC
St Saviour's Priory, Kilbarry,
Waterford
Tel 051-376032 Fax 051-376581

**ABBEYSIDE**
*St Augustine, Abbeyside*
*St Laurence, Ballinroad*
*St Vincent de Paul, Garranbane*
Very Rev Timothy O'Riordan PP
Abbeyside, Dungarvan, Co Waterford
Tel 058-42036
Very Rev Richard Doherty AP
Abbeyside, Dungarvan, Co Waterford
Tel 058-42379

**AGLISH**
*Our Lady of the Assumption, Aglish*
*St James, Ballinameela*
*St Patrick, Mount Stuart*
Very Rev Gerard O'Connor PP
Aglish, Cappoquin, Co Waterford
Tel 024-96287

**ARDFINNAN**
*Holy Family, Ardfinnan*
*St Nicholas, Grange, Ballybacon Church*
Very Rev Robert Power Adm
Ardfinnan, Clonmel, Co Tipperary
Tel 052-7466216

**ARDMORE**
*St Declan, Ardmore*
Our Lady of the Assumption, Grange
Very Rev Michael Guiry PP
Ardmore, Youghal, Co Waterford
Tel 024-94275

**BALLYDUFF**
*St Michael*
Very Rev Gerard McNamara PP
Ballyduff, Co Waterford
Tel 058-60227

**BALLYLOOBY**
*Our Lady & St Kieran, Ballylooby*
*St John the Baptist, Duhill*
Very Rev James Denmead PP
Ballylooby, Cahir, Co Tipperary
Tel 052-7441489

**BALLYNEALE AND GRANGEMOCKLER**
*St Mary*
Very Rev Patrick Gear PP
Ballyneale, Carrick-on-Suir, Co Tipperary
Tel 051-640148
*St Mary*
Very Rev Matthew Cunningham AP
Grangemockler, Carrick-on-Suir,
Co Tipperary
Tel 051-647011

**BALLYPOREEN**
*Our Lady of the Assumption*
Very Rev Joseph Flynn PP
Ballyporeen, Cahir, Co Tipperary
Tel 052-7467105

**BUTLERSTOWN**
*St Mary*
Very Rev Paul Murphy PP
Parochial House, Butlerstown,
Co Waterford
Tel 051-384192

**CAHIR**
*St Mary*
Very Rev Sean O'Dwyer PP
Parochial House, Cahir, Co Tipperary
Tel 052-7441404

**CAPPOQUIN**
*St Mary's*
Very Rev John Kiely PP
Tel 058-54216
Very Rev Robert Arthure AP
Tel 058-54221
Cappoquin, Co Waterford

**CARRICKBEG**
*St Molleran, Carrickbeg*
*St Bartholomew, Windgap*
Very Rev Thomas Flynn PP
Carrickbeg, Carrick-on-Suir, Co Tipperary
Tel 051-640340

**CARRICK-ON-SUIR**
*St Nicholas, Carrick-on-Suir*
*St Patrick, Faugheen*
Very Rev Edmond Cullinan PP, VF
Parochial House, Carrick-on-Suir,
Co Tipperary
Tel 051-640168
Rev Richard Geoghegan CC
The Presbytery, Carrick-on-Suir,
Co Tipperary
Tel 051-640080

**CLASHMORE**
*St Cronan, Clashmore*
*St Bartholomew, Piltown*
Very Rev Maurice O'Gorman PP
Clashmore, Co Waterford
Tel 024-96110

**CLOGHEEN**
*St Mary, Clogheen*
*Our Lady of the Assumption, Burnecourt*
Very Rev Patrick Butler PP
Parochial House, Clogheen, Cahir,
Co Tipperary
Tel 052-7465268

**CLONMEL, ST MARY'S**
*St Mary*
Very Rev William Meehan PP
Tel 052-6122954
Rev Patrick Hayes CC
Tel 052-6121952
St Mary's, Clonmel, Co Tipperary

**CLONMEL, ST OLIVER PLUNKETT**
*St Oliver Plunkett*
Very Rev Michael Hegarty (IC) PP
Rev Vinod Kurian Thennatil
Cooleens, Glenconnor, Clonmel,
Co Tipperary
Tel 052-6125679

**CLONMEL, SS PETER AND PAUL'S**
*SS Peter and Paul's,*
*Church of the Resurrection*
Very Rev Canon Brendan Crowley PP, VF
SS Peter and Paul's, Clonmel,
Co Tipperary
Tel 052-6122138
Rev Raymond Reidy (SPS) CC
Church of the Resurrection,
Fethard Road, Clonmel, Co Tipperary
Tel 052-6122138

**DUNGARVAN**
*St Mary*
Very Rev Canon William Ryan PP, VF
Parochial House, Dungarvan,
Co Waterford
Tel 058-42374
Rev Paul Waldron CC
Tel 058-42384
Rev Matthew Cooney (OSA)
The Presbytery, Dungarvan,
Co Waterford

**DUNHILL**
*Sacred Heart, Dunhill*
*Immaculate Conception, Fenor*
Very Rev Michael Kennedy PP
Dunhill, Co Waterford
Tel 051-396109
Very Rev Paul F. Murphy Adm
Ballynageeragh, Dunhill, Co Waterford
Tel 051-396616

**KILGOBINET**
*St Gobnait, Kilgobinet*
*St Anne, Colligan*
*St Patrick, Kilbrian*
Very Rev Michael Kennedy PP
Parochial House, Colligan, Dungarvan,
Co Waterford
Tel 058-41629

**KILLEA (DUNMORE EAST)**
*Holy Cross, Killea*
*St John the Baptist, Crooke*
*St Nicholas, Faithlegg*
Very Rev Brian Power PP
Dunmore East, Co Waterford
Tel 051-383127

**KILROSSANTY**
*St Brigid, Kilrossanty*
*St Anne, Fews*
Very Rev John Delaney PP
Parochial House, Kilrossanty,
Kilmacthomas, Co Waterford
Tel 051-291985

**KILSHEELAN**
*St Mary, Gambonsfield*
*St John the Baptist, Kilcash*
Very Rev William Carey PP
Tel 052-6133118
Rev James O'Donoghue CC
Tel 052-6133292
Kilsheelan, Clonmel, Co Tipperary

**KNOCKANORE**
Very Rev Patrick T. Condon PP
Knockanore, Tallow, Co Waterford
Tel 024-97140

**LISMORE**
*St Carthage*
Very Rev Michael Cullinan PP, VF
Parochial House,
Lismore, Co Waterford
Tel 058-54246

**MODELIGO**
*Our Lady of the Assumption, Modeligo*
*St John the Baptist, Affane*
Priest in charge:
Very Rev John Kiely
Cappoquin, Co Waterford
Tel 058-54216

**NEWCASTLE AND FOURMILEWATER**
*Our Lady of the Assumption, Newcastle*
*Our Lady & St Laurence, Fourmilewater*
Very Rev Garrett Desmond PP
Newcastle, Clonmel, Co Tipperary
Tel 052-6136387

**NEWTOWN**
*All Saints, Newtown*
*St Mary, Saleen, Kill Church*
Very Rev Martin Keogh PP
Parochial House, Newtown,
Kilmacthomas, Co Waterford
Tel 051-294261
Very Rev William Callanan AP
Kill, Co Waterford
Tel 051-292212

**PORTLAW**
*St Patrick, Portlaw*
*St Nicholas, Ballyduff*
Very Rev Michael O'Byrne PP
Kilmeaden, Co Waterford
Tel 051-384117
Rev Edmond Hassett CC
Portlaw, Co Waterford
Tel 051-387227

**POWERSTOWN**
*St John the Baptist, Powerstown*
*St John the Baptist, Lisronagh*
Very Rev Peter Ahearne PP
Rathronan, Clonmel, Co Tipperary
Tel 052-6121891

**RATHGORMACK**
*SS Quan & Broghan, Clonea*
*Sacred Heart, Rathgormack*
No resident priest. Pastoral care provided by the priests of the pastoral area

**RING AND OLD PARISH**
*Nativity of the BVM*
*St Nicholas*
Very Rev Conor Kelly PP
Ring, Dungarvan, Co Waterford
Tel 058-46125

**STRADBALLY**
*Exaltation of the Holy Cross, Stradbally*
*St Anne, Ballylaneen, Faha Church*
Very Rev Jeremiah Condon PP
Stradbally, Kilmacthomas,
Co Waterford
Tel 051-293133

**TALLOW**
*Immaculate Conception*
*Priest in Charge*
Very Rev Gerard McNamara PP
Ballyduff Upper, Co Waterford
Tel 058-60227
Very Rev Michael Farrell AP
Parochial House, Tallow,
Co Waterford
Tel 058-56117

**TOURANEENA**
*St Mary, Touranleena, Nire Church*
Very Rev Cornelius Kelleher PP
Tournaneena, Ballinamult,
Clonmel, Co Tipperary
Tel 058-47138

**TRAMORE**
*Holy Cross, Tramore*
*Our Lady, Corbally*
Right Rev Mgr Nicholas O'Mahony PP, VG
Parochial House, Tramore,
Co Waterford
Tel 051-381525
Rt Rev Mgr John Shine AP
Priest's Road, Tramore,
Co Waterford
Tel 051-381531
Rev Michael Toomey CC
Priest's Road, Tramore,
Co Waterford
Tel 051-386642

## INSTITUTIONS AND THEIR CHAPLAINS

**Bon Sauveur Services**
Carriglea, Dungarvan, Co Waterford
Tel 058-41322 Fax 058-41432
Email bonsav@eircom.net

**Regional Hospital, Waterford**
Tel 051-873321
*Chaplians:* Rev Art McCoy OFM
Rev Baptist O'Toole OFM
Rev Br Isidore Cronin OFM

**South Tipperary General Hospital**
*Chaplain:* Very Rev Thomas Coffey (IC)
Tel 052-6177000

**Waterford Institute of Technology**
*Chaplain:* Rev David Keating
10 Claremont, Cork Road, Waterford
Tel 051-378878

## PRIESTS OF THE DIOCESE ELSEWHERE

Very Rev Michael O'Connor
c/o St John's Pastoral Centre,
John's Hill, Waterford
Email mnoc@iol.ie
Rev Charles Scanlan
Ballinwillin, Lismore, Co Waterford
Tel 058-54282

## RETIRED PRIESTS

Very Rev Canon Paul Beecher PE
Cahir, Co Tipperary
Tel 052-7443193
Very Rev John Callanan PE
Cairn Hill Nursing Home,
Westminister Road, Foxrock, Dublin
Very Rev Eanna Condon PE
St Mary's, Clonmel, Co Tipperary
Tel 052-6127870
Rev James Curran
61 Tournane Court, Dungarvan,
Co Waterford
Tel 058-45177
Very Rev Michael Enright PE
Priest's Road, Tramore, Co Waterford
Tel 087-2371546
Very Rev Patrick Fitzgerald PE
Priest's House, Ballinameela,
Cappagh, Co Waterford
Tel 058-68021
Very Rev James Griffin PE
10 Woodbrook Manor, Tralee, Co Kerry
Very Rev Francis Lloyd PE
The Presbytery, Dungarvan,
Co Waterford
Very Rev Finbarr Lucey PE
Ardmore, Youghal, Co Cork
Tel 024-94177
Very Rev James Mulcahy PE
St John's Pastoral Centre,
John's Hill, Waterford
Tel 051-858306
Very Rev Sean Nugent PE
6 James Street, Clonmel, Co Tipperary
Tel 052-6128815
Rt Rev Mgr Michael Olden PE
'Woodleigh', Summerville Avenue,
Waterford
Tel 051-874132
Rev John P. O'Callaghan
Mount Carmel, Carriglea,
Halfway House, Waterford
Tel 051-382919
Very Rev Canon Daniel O'Connor PE
The Presbytery, Dungarvan,
Co Waterford
Tel 058-42381
Very Rev Gregory Power PE
St Mary's, Clonmel, Co Tipperary
Tel 052-6182690
Very Rev Patrick Canon Quealy PE
Care Choice Dungarvan, The Burgery,
Dungarvan, Co Waterford
Tel 058-40200
Very Rev Michael J. Ryan PE
Clonmel Road, Cahir,
Co Tipperary
Tel 052-7443004
Very Rev Edmond Tobin PE
Munroe, Rehill, Ballylooby,
Cahir, Co Tipperary
Tel 052-7441975
Very Rev Michael F. Walsh PE
Ballinarrid, Bonmahon, Co Waterford
Tel 051-292992

## RELIGIOUS ORDERS AND CONGREGATIONS

### PRIESTS

**AUGUSTINIANS**
St Augustine's Priory, Dungarvan,
Co Waterford
Tel 058-41136 Fax 058-44534
*Prior:* Rev Seamus Humphries (OSA)

St Augustine's College,
Dungarvan, Co Waterford
Tel 058-41140/41152 Fax 058-41152

Duckspool House (Retirement Community)
Abbeyside, Dungarvan,
Co Waterford
Tel 058-23784
*Prior:* Rev Columba O'Donnell (OSA)

**CISTERCIANS**
Mount Melleray Abbey,
Cappoquin, Co Waterford
Tel 058-54404 Fax 058-52140
Email mountmellerayabbey@eircom.net
*Abbot*
Rt Rev Dom Augustine McGregor (OCSO)
*Prior:* Br Boniface McGinley (OCSO)
*Sub-Prior:* Br John Dineen (OCSO)

**DOMINICANS**
Bridge Street, Waterford
Tel 051-875061 Fax 051-858093
*Prior:* Very Rev James Harris (OP)

Ballybeg, Waterford
Tel 051-376032 Fax 051-376581
*Prior and Parish Priest*
Very Rev Declan Corish (OP) PP

**FRANCISCANS**
Franciscan Friary, Clonmel,
Co Tipperary
Tel 052-6121378 Fax 052-6125806
Email clonmel@eircom.net
*Vicar:* Br Isoidore Cronin (OFM)

Franciscan Friary,
Lady Lane, Waterford
Tel 051-874262 Fax 051-843062
Email waterfordfriary@eircom.net
*Guardian:* Rev Eamonn O'Driscoll (OFM)

**ROSMINIANS**
Rosminian House of Prayer,
Glencomeragh, Kilsheelan,
Co Tipperary
Tel 052-33181
*Rector:* Rev Michael Melican (IC)

St Joseph's Doire na hAbhann
Tickincor, Clonmel, Co Tipperary
Tel 052-26914Fax 052-26915
Residential centre for children in care

(See also under parishes – St Oliver Plunkett)

## BROTHERS

**CHRISTIAN BROTHERS**
Christian Brothers' House,
Brú na Cruinne, Carrick-on-Suir,
Co Tipperary
Tel 051-640335 Fax 051-642605
Email brunacruinne@eircom.net
Community: 5

Mount Sion, Waterford
Tel 051-879580 Fax 051-841578
Community: 5

International Heritage Centre & Chapel
Mount Sion, Barrack Street,
Waterford
Tel 051-874390 Fax 051-841578
*CEO:* Br Pat Madigan

**DE LA SALLE BROTHERS**
De La Salle College, Newtown,
Waterford
Tel 051-875294 Fax 051-841321
Email delasall@iol.ie
*Superior:* Br Amedy Hayes
Community: 6
Secondary School
*Headmaster:* Mr Gearoid O'Brien

De La Salle Brothers
25 Patrick Street, Waterford
Tel 051-874623
Community: 3
*Superior:* Mr Paudge Morris
St Stephen's Primary School
*Principal:* Br Martin Curran
Tel 051-871716

**PRESENTATION BROTHERS**
Glór na hAbhann, Ballinamona Lower,
Old Parish, Dungarvan,
Co Waterford
Tel 058-46904
*Contact:* Br John Hunt (FPM)

## SISTERS

**BON SAUVEUR SISTERS**
Carriglea, Dungarvan, Co Waterford
Tel 058-45884 Fax 058-45891
Email lbscarriglea@eircom.net
*Superior:* Sr Mary Fitzgerald
Community: 5
Pastoral Ministry to Carriglea Cairde Service – Residential and day care services for persons with an intellectual disability

**CARMELITES**
St Joseph's Carmelite Monastery, Tallow,
Co Waterford
Tel 058-56205
Email carmeltallow@eircom.net
*Superior:* Sr Teresa Gibbons
Community: 10
Contemplatives

**CISTERCIANS**
St Mary's Abbey, Glencairn, Lismore,
Co Waterford
Tel 058-56168 Fax 058-56616
Email glencairnabbey@eircom.net
*Abbess:* Sr Marie Fahy
Tel 058-56197
Email mbfahy@eircom.net
Community: 34
Monastic

**CONGREGATION OF THE SISTERS OF MERCY**
Convent of Mercy, Cahir,
Co Tipperary
Tel 052-7441294

Teach Bride, Convent Road,
Townspark, Cahir, Co Tipperary
Tel 052-7443809

St Mary's Mount Anglesby,
Clogheen, Co Tipperary
Tel 052-7465255

Greenhill, Carrick-on-Suir,
Co Tipperary
Tel 051-640059

Springwell, Pill Road,
Carrick-on-Suir, Co Tipperary
Tel 051-642870

12 Comeragh View,
Carrick-on-Suir, Co Tipperary
Tel 051-645012

10 Ash Park, Carrick-on-Suir,
Co Tipperary
Tel 051-640814

Apartment 1, William Street,
Carrick-on-Suir, Co Tipperary
Tel 051-642576

21 Heywood Heights,
Clonmel, Co Tipperary
Tel 052-6125235

31 Willow Park,
Clonmel, Co Tipperary
Tel 052-6128903

32 Willow Park,
Clonmel, Co Tipperary
Tel 052-6125809

Convent of Mercy, Church Street,
Dungarvan, Co Waterford
Tel 058-41293/41337

1 Park Lane Drive, Abbeyside,
Dungarvan, Co Waterford
Tel 058-48795

22 Blackrock Court, Youghal Road,
Dungarvan, Co Waterford
Tel 058-48286

16 Blackrock Court, Youghal Road,
Dungarvan, Co Waterford
Tel 058-45713

17 Blackrock Court, Youghal Road,
Dungarvan, Co Waterford
Tel 058-44865

11 Blackrock Court, Youghal Road,
Dungarvan, Co Waterford
Tel 058-24656

3 Marine View, Youghal Road,
Dungarvan, Co Waterford

Convent of Mercy,
Military Road, Waterford
Tel 051-74161/77909

Coolock House,
Grange Park Road, Waterford
Tel 051-878710

17/18 Bromley Close,
Ardkeen Village, Waterford
Tel 051-857684

2 Chestnut Grove,
Waterford
Tel 051-373542

93 Clonard Park,
Ballybeg, Waterford
Tel 051-379110

7 Aisling Court,
Hennessy's Road, Waterford
Tel 051-874592

5 Cul Rua, Portlaw,
Co Waterford
Tel 051-387125

**GOOD SHEPHERD SISTERS**
Virginia Crescent, Hennessy's Road,
Waterford
Tel 051-874294 Fax 051-855940
Email rgswat@eircom.net
*Leader:* Sr Bríd Mullins
Community: 19

**LITTLE COMPANY OF MARY**
36 Willowbrook,
Tallow, Co Waterford
Tel 058-55962
Apostolic community: 1

**LORETO (IBVM)**
Loreto Secondary School,
Clonmel, Co Tipperary
Tel 052-21402
Community: 2

**PRESENTATION SISTERS**
Presentation Sisters, Chapel Street,
Carrick-on-Suir, Co Tipperary
Tel 051-640069
*Contact:* Sr Immaculata Buckley

Presentation Convent,
Clonmel, Co Tipperary
Tel 052-6121538
*Local Leader:* Sr Marie Stella Mangan
Community: 19
Primary school, secondary school,
Maryville Home for sick and elderly
sisters

Presentation Convent, Youghal Road,
Dungarvan, Co Waterford
Tel 058-41359
*Local Leader:* Sr Assumpta O'Neill
Community: 9
Primary School

Presentation Sisters, 158 Larchville,
Waterford
Tel 051-355496
*Contact:* Sr de Lourdes Breen
Community: 3

Presentation Sisters, 81 Treacy Park,
Carrick-on-Suir, Co Tipperary
Tel 051-641733
*Contact:* Sr Veronica Casey
Community: 2
Primary School

Presentation Sisters,
50 Cathal Brugha Place,
Dungarvan, Co Waterford
Tel 058-45582
Community: 3

11 Convent Lodge, Mitchell Street,
Dungarvan, Co Waterford
*Contact:* Sr Martina O'Callaghan

Apartment 3, The Cloisters,
John's Hill, Waterford
*Contact:* Sr Catherine Mooney

**RELIGIOUS SISTERS OF CHARITY**
Star of the Sea,
Tramore, Co Waterford
Tel 051-381308
Various apostolic ministries

Comeragh Lodge,
St Patrick's Road,
Silver Springs, Clonmel,
Co Tipperary
Tel 052-6121092
Various apostolic ministries

**ROSMINIANS (SISTERS OF PROVIDENCE)**
Rosminian Convent,
Killea, Dunmore East, Co Waterford
*Contact person:* Sr Rosita Boylan
Email rositaboylan@yahoo.com
Tel 051-383491

**ST JOHN OF GOD SISTERS**
8 The Cloisters, John's Hill,
Waterford
Tel 051-874370
*Resident Leader:* Sr Una Guing
Community: 6
Primary School. Pupils: 344

St John of God Sisters,
41 Grange Cove, Waterford
Tel 051-374397
Community: 4

**ST JOSEPH OF CLUNY SISTERS**
Woodlock, Portlaw,
Waterford
Tel 051-387216
*Superior:* Sr Josephine Glynn
Community: 10

**URSULINES**
Ursuline Convent, Waterford
Tel 051-874068
Email ursuline94@eircom.net
*Local Leader:* Sr Margaret Breen
Community: 14
Primary School
Tel 051-873788/852855
Fax 051-852855
Secondary School
Tel 051-876121 Fax 051-879022

18 Shannon Drive,
Avondale, Waterford
Tel 051-854680
Email ursulinesisterswd@eircom.net
Community: 2

1 St Anne's,
Ursuline Court, Waterford
Tel 051-857015
Email onestannes@eircom.net
Community: 2

## EDUCATIONAL INSTITUTIONS

**EDMUND RICE SCHOOLS TRUST**
Christian Brothers School,
Carrick-on-Suir, Co Tipperary
Primary School
Tel 051-641333
*Principal:* Mr Pat Mansell
Secondary School
Tel 051-640512 Fax 051-640522
Email cbscus@eircom.net

Christian Brothers High School,
Kickham Street, Clonmel, Co Tipperary
Tel 052-24459 Fax 052-25320
Email ardscoilnamb@eircom.net
*Principal:* Mr S. Bannon

Dungarvan, Co Waterford
Secondary School
*Principal:* Mr John Murphy
Tel 058-41185/41955 Fax 058-48512

Blackwater Community School
Tel 055-53620/54349 Fax 058-53813
*Principal:* Vacant

Christian Brothers Secondary School,
Tramore, Co Waterford
*Principal:* Ms Mary Meade
Tel 051-386766/386560
Fax 051-3811492
Email office@cbstramore.com
Website www.cbstramore.com

Cnoc Síon Primary School,
Barrack Street, Waterford
Tel 051-377947 Fax 051-358304
Email cnocsion.ias@eircom.net
*Principal:* Mr Michael Walsh

Cnoc Síon Secondary School,
Barrack Street, Waterford
Tel 051-377378/376309 Fax 051-376468
Staff Tel 051-877456
Email mtsion.ias@eircom.net
*Principal:* Mr John McArdle

Waterpark College Secondary School
Park Road, Waterford
Tel 051-874445/893101 Fax 051-874040
Staff Tel 051-877456
Email waterparkcollege@eircom.net
Website www.waterparkcollege.com
*Principal:* Mr T. Beecher

## ST JOHN'S PASTORAL CENTRE

**St John's Pastoral Centre**
John's Hill, Waterford
Tel 051-874199 Fax 051-843107
Email stjohnspastoralcentre@eircom.net
*Administrator:* Ms Mary Dee

## CHARITABLE AND OTHER SOCIETIES

**Apostolic Work Society**
*President of Diocesan Council*
Mrs Nancy Kenny
10 Powerstown Road, Clonmel,
Co Tipperary
Centres at Dungarvan, Cappoquin, Carrick-on-Suir, Kilmacthomas, Dunmore East, Clogheen, Clonmel

**Hostels**
Men's Hostel, Ozanam House,
Lady Lane, Waterford
(St Vincent de Paul)

# PERSONAL PRELATURES

## Prelature of the Holy Cross and Opus Dei

Founded by Saint Josemaría Escrivá in 1928, it was erected as a Personal Prelature (cf CIC 294-297) in 1982, and is constituted by the Prelate (Bishop Javier Echevarría), incardinated clergy, and lay people. Members try to promote a deep consciousness of the universal call to holiness and apostolate in all sectors of society and, more specifically, an awareness of the sanctifying value of ordinary work.

*Information Office:*
10 Hume Street, Dublin 2
Tel 01-6614949

Website www.opusdei.ie
Email info@opusdei.ie

**Vicar for Ireland**
Rev Justin Gillespie DD
Harvieston,
Cunningham Road, Dalkey,
Co Dublin
Tel 01-2859877
Fax 01-2305059

**Archdiocese of Dublin**
Harvieston, Cunningham Road,
Dalkey, Co Dublin
Tel 01-2859877
Rt Rev Robert Bucciarelli
Rev Justin Gillespie
Rev Patrick Gorevan
Rev Brendan O'Connor
Rev Francis Planell

30 Knapton Road,
Dun Laoghaire, Co Dublin
Tel 01-2804353
Rev Daniel Cummings
Rev Thomas McGovern

Cleraun Study Centre, 90 Foster Avenue,
Mount Merrion, Co Dublin
Tel 01-2881734
Rev James Gavigan
Rev Martin Hannon

Nullamore, Richmond Avenue South,
Dublin 6
Tel 01-4971239
Rev Thomas Dowd
Rev Philip Griffin
Rev Donncha Ó hAodha

Ely University Centre
10 Hume Street, Dublin 2
Tel 01-6767420
Rev James Hurley
Rev Gavan Jennings

**Archdiocese of Tuam**
Ballyglunin Park Conference Centre,
Tuam, Co Galway
Tel 093-41423
Rev Walter Macken, Chaplain

**Diocese of Galway**
Gort Ard University Residence,
Rockbarton North, Galway
Tel 091-523846
Rev Walter Macken
Rev Oliver Powell

**Diocese of Limerick**
Castleville Study Centre,
Golf Links Road, Castletroy, Limerick
Tel 061-331223
Rev Brian McCarthy

**Diocese of Meath**
Lismullin Conference Centre
Navan, Co Meath
Tel 046-9026936
Rev James Gavigan, Chaplain

# RELIGIOUS ORDERS AND CONGREGATIONS

## MALE RELIGIOUS

### AUGUSTINIANS (OSA)

Irish Province
www.augustinians.ie

*Archdiocese of Dublin*

**St Augustine's**
Taylor's Lane,
Ballyboden, Dublin 16
Tel 01-4241000
Fax 01-4939915

*Provincial:* Rev Gerry Horan
Tel 01-4241030
Fax 01-4932457
Email osaprov@eircom.net
*Secretary:* Tel 01-4241040
Email
hibprovsec@irishbroadband.net
*Prior:* Rev John Lyng
*Bursar:* Rev Michael Brennock
*(Provincial Secretary)*

Rev John Bresnan
Rev Andrew Caples
Rev Matthew Curran
Rev Gabriel Daly
Rev Pádraig Daly
(PP Ballyboden)
Rev John Doran
Rev Patrick Farrell
Rev David Kelly
Rev John O'Sullivan
Rev John Williams

**St John's Priory**
Thomas Street, Dublin 8
Tel 01-6770393/0415/0601
Fax 01-6713102 (Mission Office)
Fax 01-6770423 (House)

*Prior:* Rev Tony Egan
*Bursar:* Rev Michael O'Sullivan
*Sub-Prior:* Rev Giles O'Halloran

Rev Niall Coghlan (PP Meath St)
Rev Thomas Cooney
Rev Finbarr Fortune
Rev Pat Gayer
Rev Richard Goode
Rev Peter Haughey
Rev John Hughes
Rev Nicholas Kearny
Rev Joseph Kirwan
Rev Kevin McManus
Rev Michael Mernagh
Rev Martin Nolan
Rev Louis O'Donnell
Rev Bernard Twomey

**Meath Street Parish**
Dublin 8
Tel 01-4543356
Fax 01-4738303

No Resident Community

**Augustinian Retreat Centre**
Orlagh Retreat Centre,
Old Court Road, Dublin 16
Tel 01-4930932/4933315/
4931163 Fax 01-4930987
Email orlagh@augustinians.ie
www.augustinians.ie/orlagh

*Prior:* Rev John Byrne

Rev Jude King
Rev Kieran O'Mahony

**Rivermount Parish**
Parochial House,
5 St Helena's Drive, Dublin 11
Tel 01-8343444/8343722
Fax 01-8642192

*Superior:* Rev Noel Hession
Very Rev Seamus Ahearne PP
*Bursar:* Rev Paddy O'Reilly

*Archdiocese of Armagh*

**St Augustine's Priory**
Shop Street,
Drogheda, Co Louth
Tel 041-9838409
Fax 041-9831847

*Sub-Prior:*
Rev Malachy Loughran

Rev Ignatius O'Donovan
*Bursar:* Rev David Crean

*Archdiocese of Cashel and Diocese of Emly*

**The Abbey**
Fethard, Co Tipperary
Tel 052-31273

*Prior:* Rev Martin Crean
*Sub-Prior:* Rev John Meagher

Rev Gerard Horan *(Provincial)*

*Diocese of Cork & Ross*

**St Augustine's Priory**
Washington Street, Cork
Tel 021-4275398/4270410
Fax 021-4275381

*Prior:* Rev Pat Moran
*Bursar:* Rev Francis Aherne

Rev Michael Boyle
Rev Sean Dowling
Rev James Furlong
Rev Michael Leahy
Rev James Maguire
Rev Michael O'Regan

*Diocese of Ferns*

**St Augustine's Priory**
Grantstown, New Ross,
Co Wexford
Tel 051-561119

Rev Aidan O'Leary
*Priest-in-residence*

**St Augustine's Priory (Residence)**
New Ross, Co Wexford
Tel 051-421237

*Prior:* Rev Michael Collender
*Sub-Prior*
Rev Vincent McCarthy
*Bursar:* Rev Philip Kelly
*School Principal*
Rev John Hennebry

Rev Michael Collender
Rev Seán Mac Gearailt
Rev Henry MacNamara
Rev Vincent McCarthy
Rev Ben O'Brien
Rev Aidan O'Leary
Rev John Power

**Good Counsel College**
New Ross, Co Wexford
Tel 051-421663/421909
Fax 051-421909

No Resident Community

*Diocese of Galway*

**St Augustine's Priory**
Galway
Tel 091-562524
Fax 091-564378

*Prior:* Rev Desmond Foley
*Sub-Prior:* Rev Richard Lyng PP

Rev John Whelan

*Diocese of Limerick*

**St Augustine's Priory**
O'Connell Street, Limerick
Tel 061-415374

*Prior:* Rev Frank Sexton
*Bursar:* Rev Jeremiah Hickey

Rev Michael Danaher
Rev Leo O'Sullivan
Rev William Prendiville
Rev Brendan Quirke
Rev Liam Ryan

*Diocese of Waterford & Lismore*

**St Augustine's College**
Dungarvan, Co Waterford
Tel 058-41140/41152
Fax 058-41152

No Resident Community

**Duckspool House**
*(Retirement Community)*
Abbeyside, Dungarvan,
Co Waterford
Tel 058-23784

*Prior:* Rev Columba O'Donnell
*Bursar:* Rev Joseph Crean

Rev Patrick Lennon
Rev Kieran O'Brien
Rev Columba O'Connor
Rev John Walsh

**St Augustine's Priory**
Dungarvan, Co Waterford
Tel 058-41136 Fax 058-44534

*Prior:* Rev Seamus Humphries
*Sub-Prior:* Rev Finbar Spring
*Bursar:* Rev David Slater

Rev Matthew Cooney
Rev Flor O'Callaghan

*Rome*

**St Patrick's College and Church**
Via Piemonte 60,
00187 Rome, Italy
Tel 00396-4203121
Fax 00396-4231236
Email st.patricks@rm.nettuno.it

*Prior:* Rev James Downey
*Bursar & Church Rector*
Rev Tony Finn

Rev Brian O'Sullivan

The Irish Province also has missions in Ecuador, Kenya and Nigeria.

*Irish Augustinian Personnel on Other Assignments*

Rev Ailbe Brennan (San Bernardino, CA)
Rev Paul Flynn (Orange, CA)
Rev Declan Fogarty (San Bernardino, CA)
Rev John Grace (Orange, CA)
Rev Paul O'Brien (Canada)

## BENEDICTINES (OSB)

*Archdiocese of Cashel and Diocese of Emly*

Attached to the Benedictine Congregation of the Annunciation, Belgium.

**Glenstal Abbey**
Murroe, Co Limerick
Tel 061-8386103
Fax 061-8386328
Email monks@glenstal.org

*Abbot:* Right Rev Dom Mark Patrick Hederman
*Prior & Novice Master*
Very Rev Brendan Coffey
*Sub-Prior*
Very Rev Senan Furlong
*Abbot 1992-2008*
Right Rev Dom Christopher Dillon
*Abbot 1980-92*
Right Rev Dom Celestine Cullen
*Headmaster*
Br Martin Browne
*Guestmaster*
Rev Christopher Dillon

*Directors of Associates and Oblates*
Rev David Conlon
Rev Columba McCann

Rev Anselm Barry
Rev Cuthbert Brennan
Br Matthew Corkery
Rev Alan Crawford
Rev Bonaventure Dunne
Rev William Fennelly
Br Ciarán Forbes
Rev Basil Forde
Br Denis Hooper
Br Anselm Hurt
Br Anthony Keane
Br Cyprian Love
Rev Fintan Lyons
Rev Joseph McGilloway
Br Timothy McGrath
Br Pádraig McIntyre
Rev Francis McHenry
Rev James McMahon
Rev Luke Macnamara
Rev Brian Murphy
Rev Placid Murray
Rev Paul Nash
Rev Andrew Nugent
Rev John O'Calliaghan
Br Colmán Ó Clabaigh
Br Michael O'Connor
Br Emmaus O'Herlihy
Br Cillian Ó Sé
Rev Henry O'Shea
Rev Simon Sleeman
Rev Mark Tierney
Rev Philip Tierney
Rev Ambrose Tinsley

*Diocese of Dromore*

Attached to the Benedictine congregation of St Mary of Monte Oliveto.

**Benedictine Monks**
Holy Cross Monastery,
119 Kilbroney Road,
Rostrevor, Co Down BT34 3BN
Tel 028-41739979
Fax 028-41739978
Email benedictinemonks@btinternet.com
Website www.benedictinemonks.co.uk

*Superior*
Very Rev Dom Mark-Ephrem M. Nolan

Rev D. Eric M. Loisel
Rev D. Thierry M. Marteaux
D. Benoît M. Charlet
D. Pascal M. Jouy
D. Joshua M. Domenzain Canul

## BLESSED SACRAMENT CONGREGATION (SSS)

*Provincial*
Rev Patrick Costello
Blessed Sacrament Chapel
20 Bachelors Walk, Dublin 1
Tel 01-8724597
Fax 01-8724724
Email pjcostello@aol.com

*Archdiocese of Dublin*

**Blessed Sacrament Chapel**
20 Bachelors Walk, Dublin 1
Tel 01-8724597
Fax 01-8724724
Email sssdublin@eircom.net

*Superior*
Rev James Campbell

Rev Patrick Costello
Br Joseph Donegan
Rev Renato Esoy
Rev James Hegarty
Br Timothy McLoughlin
Br Andrew McTeigue
Rev Maurice Rouleau

## CAMILLIANS (OSCam) Order of St Camillus

Anglo-Irish Province

*Archdiocese of Dublin*

**St Camillus**
South Hill Avenue,
Blackrock, Co Dublin
Tel 01-2882873/2833380

*Superior:* Rev Denis Sandham *(Chaplain to Beaumont Hospital)*

Br Gabriel Brady
Rev Jayan Joseph *(Chaplain to St Luke's Hospital)*
Rev Pat O'Brien *(Chaplain to St James' Hospital)*
Rev Tom O'Connor

**St Camillus**
11 St Vincent Street North,
Dublin 7
Tel 01-8300365 (residence)
Tel 01-8301122 (Mater Hospital)

*Superior & Provincial*
Rev Stephen Forster
Tel 01-8304635

Rev John Philip *(Chaplain to Mater Hospital)*
Rev Vincent Xavier *(Chaplain to Mater Hospital)*
4 St Vincent Street North

*Diocese of Meath*

**St Camillus**
Killucan, Co Westmeath
Tel 044-74196 (nursing centre)
Tel 044-74115 (community)
Fax 044-74309

*Superior:* Rev Frank Monks
Email fmonks@libero.it

Rev Noel Carrigg
Rev Andrew Carroll
Rev Martin Geraghty *(Chaplain to Connolly Memorial Hospital, Blanchardstown)*
Rev Nik Houlihan
Br Augustine McCormack
Rev P. McKenna
Br John O'Brien
Rev Tom Smith

## CAPUCHINS (OFM Cap)

Province of Ireland

Includes nine friaries in Ireland, three friaries in South Korea and New Zealand and Vice-Provinces in South Africa and Zambia.

*Archdiocese of Dublin*

**Provincial Office**
12 Halston Street, Dublin 7
Tel 01-8733205 Fax 01-8730294
Email capcurirl@eircom.net

*Provincial Minister*
Very Rev Desmond McNaboe

Rev Adrian Curran
Rev Patrick Cleary
Rev Christopher Twomey

**Capuchin Friary**
Church Street, Dublin 7
Tel 01-8730599
Fax 01-8730250

*Guardian:* Rev Bryan Shortall (PP, Halston Street Parish)
*Vicar:* Rev Kevin Crowley

Rev Martin Bennett
Rev Terence Harrington
Rev Paul Murphy
Rev Piaras Ó Dúill
Rev Angelus O'Neill
Rev Bruno McKnight
Rev Alphonsus Ryan

**Capuchin Friary**
Station Road,
Raheny, Dublin 5
Tel 01-8313886
Fax 01-8511498

*Guardian:* Rev John Wright
*Vicar:* Rev Eustace McSweeney

Rev Anthony Boran
Rev Oliver Brady
Rev Simeon Breen
Rev Tom Forde
Rev Michael Murphy
Rev Pádraig Ó Cuill
Rev Dan Joe O'Mahony

**Capuchin Friary**
Clonshaugh Drive,
Priorswood, Dublin 17
Tel 01-8474469
Fax 01-8487296

*Guardian*
Rev Patrick Flynn (PP, St Francis of Assissi Parish)

Rev Sean Kelly (Curate, St Francis of Assissi Parish)
Rev Ignatius Galvin
Rev Kevin Kiernan
Rev Bill Ryan

*Diocese of Cork & Ross*

**Holy Trinity**
Fr Mathew Quay, Cork
Tel 021-4270827
Fax 021-4270829

*Guardian:* Rev Sean Donohoe
*Vicar:* Rev Richard Hendrick

Rev Albert Cooney
Rev Edwin Flynn
Rev Jeremy Heneghan
Rev Ronan Herlihy
Rev John Hickey
Rev Joe Nagle
Rev Edward Neville
Rev Brendan O'Mahony
Rev Kenneth Reynolds
Rev Aidan Vaughan

**St Francis Capuchin Friary**
Rochestown, Co Cork
Tel 021-4896244
Fax 021-4895915

*Guardian*
Rev Paul O'Donovan
*Vicar*
Rev Dermot Lynch

Rev Paul Barrett
Rev Michael Burgess
Br Felix Carroll
Rev Hugh Davis
Rev Sylvius McCarthy
Rev Anthony O'Keeffe
Rev Owen O'Sullivan
Rev Jack Twomey

**St Francis Capuchin Franciscan College**
Rochestown, Co Cork
Tel 021-4891417
Fax 021-4361254

*Principal*
Mr Diarmaid Ó Mathúna

*Diocese of Kildare & Leighlin*

**St Anthony's Capuchin Friary**
43 Dublin Street, Carlow
Tel 059-9142543
Fax 059-9142030

*Guardian:* Br John Manley
*Vicar:* Rev Michael Duffy

Rev Joe Gallagher
Rev Alexius Healy
Rev Leo McAuliffe

*Diocese of Ossory*

**Capuchin Friary**
Friary Street, Kilkenny
Tel 056-7721439
Fax 056-7722025

*Guardian*
Rev Benignus Buckley
*Vicar:* Rev Donal Sweeney

Rev Philip Connor
Rev James Harrington
Rev Paul Tapley
Rev Philip Tobin

*Diocese of Raphoe*

**Capuchin Friary**
Ard Mhuire, Creeslough,
Letterkenny, Co Donegal
Tel 074-9138005
Fax 074-9138371

*Guardian*
Rev Silvester O'Flynn
*Vicar*
Rev Kieran Shorten

Rev Brian Browne
Rev Edward Dunne
Rev Vianney Holmes
Rev Flann Lynch
Rev Bernard McAllister
Rev James Ryan
Rev Charles Stewart

*New Zealand*

**Holy Cross Friary & Vice-Provincial Residence**
PO Box 21082, Henderson,
Auckland 8, New Zealand
Tel 0064-9-8388663
Fax 0064-9-8387114
Email capauck@ihug.co.nz

*Korea*

**Capuchin Friars Minor**
Hyochang-Dong 5-40,
Yong San-Gu, Seoul,
South Korea 140-120
Tel 0082-2-7015727
Fax 0082-2-7176128

*Vice-Province of Zambia*

**Vice-Provincialate**
PO Box 33705,
Lusaka, Zambia
Tel 00260-1250205
Fax 00260-1252828

*Vice-Province of South Africa*

**Vice-Provincialate**
PO Box 118, Howard Place 7450,
South Africa
Tel 00272-16370026
Fax 00272-16370014

For further details concerning the missions contact:
Capuchin Mission Office,
Church Street, Dublin 7
Tel 01-8731022
Fax 01-8740478

## CARMELITES (OCARM)

Irish Province

*Archdiocese of Dublin*

**Provincial Office and Carmelite Community**
Gort Muire, Ballinteer,
Dublin 16
Tel 01-2984014
Fax 01-2987221

*Provincial*
Very Rev Martin Kilmurray
Email mkilmurray@eircom.net
*Assistant Provincial*
Rev Patrick Staunton
Email
pstaunton@gortmuire.com

*Prior/Bursar:* Rev Martin Baxter
*Sub-Prior:* Rev Simon Nolan

Rev Albert Breen
Rev Michael Cremin
Rev PJ Cunningham
Rev Liam Fennell
Rev Patrick Gallagher
Rev Paul Hughes
Rev Dermot Kelly
Rev Brian Kiernan
Rev William Langan
Rev Anthony McKinney
Rev Joseph Mothersill
Rev Patrick Mullins
Rev Reuben Pinheiro

**Whitefriar Street Church**
56 Aungier Street, Dublin 2
Tel 01-4758821
Fax 01-4758825
Email whitefriars@eircom.net

*Prior:* Rev David Weakliam
*Sub-Prior:* Rev Bernard Murphy
*PP and Director of Whitefriar Street Community Centre*
Rev Charles Hoey

Rev Donal Byrne
Rev Daniel Callaghan
Rev Christopher Conroy
Rev Sean Coughlan
Rev Christopher Crowley
Rev Patrick (Alan) Fitzpatrick
Rev Patrick Graham
Rev Thomas Higgins
Rev Desmond Kelly CC
Rev Charles Keogh
Rev Brian McKay
Rev Robert Manik
Rev Jarlath O'Hea
Rev Fergus O'Loan

**Terenure College**
Terenure, Dublin 6W
Tel 01-4904621
Fax 01-4902403
Email admin@terenurecollege.ie

*Prior/Manager*
Rev Michael Troy
*Sub-Prior:* Rev Eoin Moore
*Principal Senior School*
Rev Eanna Ó hÓbáin
*Principal Junior School*
Rev Michael Troy

Rev P. J. Breen
Rev Richard Byrne
Rev James Eivers
Rev Desmond Flanagan
Rev John Madden
Rev Benedict O'Callaghan
Rev Christopher O'Donnell
Rev Francis O'Gara

**St Colmcille's**
The Presbytery,
Idrone Avenue,
Knocklyon, Dublin 16
Tel 01-4941204/4944986
Fax 01-4946842
Email presbytery@
knocklyonparish.com

*Parish Priest/Prior*
Rev James Murray

Rev Seán Ford CC
Rev Michael Morrissey CC
Rev Martin Parokkaran
Rev David Twohig

*Diocese of Cork & Ross*

**Carmelite Friary**
Kinsale, Co Cork
Tel 021-4772138
Email
kinsale@irishcarmelites.com

*Prior*
Rev Frank McAleese
*Bursar*
Rev Stan Hession

Rev Anthony Heaslip
Rev Mariusz Placek

*Diocese of Kildare & Leighlin*

**Carmelite Priory**
White Abbey,
Co Kildare
Tel 045-521391
Fax 045-522318
Email whiteabbey@eircom.net

*Prior*
Rev Anthony McDonald
*Bursar*
Rev Frederick Lally

Rev John Lawler
Rev Aloysius Ryan
Rev Patrick Smyth

*Diocese of Meath*

**Carmelite Priory**
Moate, Co Westmeath
Tel 090-6481160/6481398
Fax 090-6481879
Email
carmelitemoate@eircom.net

*Prior*
Rev Martin Ryan
*Sub-Prior*
Rev Jaison Kuthanapillil
*Bursar*
Rev Brendan O'Reilly

*Diocese of Ossory*

**Carmelite Priory (Knocktopher/Ballyhale)**
Knocktopher, Co Kilkenny
Tel 056-7768675
Fax 056-7768237
Email knockcar@indigo.ie

*Prior/Parish Priest*
Rev Peter Kehoe
*Bursar:* Rev Laurence Lynch

Rev Philip Brennan
Rev Fintan Burke

## CARMELITES (OCD)

Anglo-Irish Province

The Province has five communities in Ireland and thirteen overseas including five in Nigeria.

*Provincial:* Rev James Noonan
53 Marlborough Road,
Donnybrook, Dublin 4
Tel 01-6617163/6601832
Fax 01-6683752
Email jnoonan@ocd.ie
Website www.ocd.ie

*Archdiocese of Dublin*

**St Teresa's**
Clarendon Street, Dublin 2
Tel 01-6718466/6718127
Fax 01-6718462

*Prior:* Rev Christopher Clarke
Email stteresa@ocd.ie

Rev Michael Brown
Rev Michael Coen
Rev Joe Glynn
Rev Michéal MacLaifeartaigh
Rev Desmond McCaffrey
Rev Harry McGale
Rev Nicholas Madden
Rev Paul O'Sullivan
Rev Michael Spain
Br Patrick Walsh

**Avila**
Bloomfield Avenue,
Morehampton Road, Dublin 4
Tel 01-6430200 Fax 01-6430281
Email avila@ocd.ie

*Prior:* Rev Michael McGoldrick

Rev Joe Birmingham
Rev Stanislaus Callanan
Rev Eugene McCaffrey
Br Noel O'Connor
Rev Tom Stone

**Karmel**
53/55 Marlborough Road,
Dublin 4
Tel 01-6601832

*Prior:* Rev Edward Smyth

Rev Terence Carey
Rev Liam Ó Bréartúin
Rev Herman Doolan

**St Joseph's**
Berkeley Road, Dublin 7
Tel 01-8306356/8306336
Fax 01-8304681

*Prior*
Rev David Donnellan PP

Rev Pat Beecher
Rev Peter Cryan
Rev Patrick Keenan
Rev Richard Young

*Diocese of Clonfert*

**The Abbey**
Loughrea, Co Galway
Tel 091-841209
Fax 091-842343

*Prior:* Rev Willie Moran

Rev Bernard Cuffe
Rev Cronan Glynn
Rev Ambrose McNamee
Rev Mairtín Ó Conaire
Rev Tom Shanahan

*Diocese of Derry*

**St Joseph's Carmelite**
Retreat Centre
Termonbacca,
Derry BT48 9XE
Tel 028-71262512
Fax 028-71373589

*Prior:* Rev Sean Conlon

Rev Jeremiah Fitzpatrick
Rev Louis Gallagher
Rev Stephen McKeogh
Rev John McNamara

## CISTERCIAN ORDER (OCSO)

The mother house of the Cistercian Order is the Archabbey of Citeaux, Cóte d'Or, France.

*Archdiocese of Armagh*

**Mellifont Abbey**
Collon, Co Louth
Tel 041-9826103
Fax 041-9826713
Email
mellifontabbey@eircom.net

*Superior*
Rev Laurence McDermott
*Prior*
Br Joseph Ryan

Br Brian Berkeley
Rev Dom Bernard Boyle
Br Andrew Considine
Rev William Cullinan
Br Brendan Garry
Br Thomas Maher
Rev Alphonsus O'Connor
Br Cornelius Ogwu
Br Ifunanya Onwe
Rev Andrew Ward

*Archdiocese of Dublin*

**Bolton Abbey**
Moone, Co Kildare
Tel 059-8624102
Fax 059-8624309
Email info@boltonabbey.ie
Website www.boltonabbey.ie

*Abbot*
Rt Rev Dom Peter Garvey
*Guestmaster*
Rev Eoin de Bhaldraithe
*Novice Director*
Rev Ambrose Farrington

Rev Martin Garry
Br Alberic Turner
Br Anthony Jones
Br William Kinsella
Br Brian O'Dowd
Br Francis McLean
Rev Michael Ryan

*Diocese of Down & Connor*

**Our Lady of Bethlehem Abbey**
11 Ballymena Road,
Portglenone, Ballymena,
Co Antrim BT44 8BL
Tel 028-25821211
Fax 028-25822795
Email celsus@bethabbey.com
www.bethlehemabbey.com

*Abbot*
Rt Rev Dom Celsus Kelly

*Retired Abbot*
Rt Rev Dom Aengus Dunphy
*Prior*: Rev Martin Dowley
*Sub-Prior:* Rev Philip Scott

Rev Herman Hickey
Br Michael McCourt
Br Finbar McLoughlin
Rev Aelred Magee
Rev Francis Morgan
Br Brendan Murphy
Rev Chrysostom O'Connell
Br Vianney O'Donnell
Br Veder O'Kane
Br Columba O'Neill
Rev Finnian Owens
Br Joseph Skehan

*Diocese of Killaloe*

**Mount Saint Joseph Abbey**
Roscrea, Co Tipperary
Tel 0505-25600
Fax 0505-25610
Email info@msjroscrea.ie

*Abbot*
Rt Rev Dom Richard Purcell
*Prior*
Rev Dom Laurence Walsh
*Abbot Emeritus*
Rev Dom Colmcille O'Toole
*Abbot Emeritus*
Rev Dom Kevin Daly

Rev Eanna Henderson
Rev Flannan Hogan
Rev Robert Kelly
Br Niall Maguire
Rev Gabriel McCarthy
Br John McDonnell
Br Laurence Molloy
Rev Anthony O'Brien
Rev Liam O'Connor
Rev Ciaran Ó Sabhaois
Br Malachy Thompson
Br Dominic Tobin
Br Oliver Tyrrell

*Diocese of Waterford & Lismore*

**Mount Melleray Abbey**
Cappoquin, Co Waterford
Tel 058-54404 Fax 058-52140
Email mountmellerayabbey@
eircom.net

*Abbot:* Rt Rev Dom Augustine McGregor
*Prior:* Br Boniface McGinley
*Sub-Prior:* Br John Dineen

Rev Michael Ahern
Br Camillus Canning
Br Peter Cassidy
Rev Denis Collins
Br Seamus Corrigan
Br Edmund Costine
Rev Bonaventure Cumiskey
Br Donal Davis
Rev Kevin Fogarty
Rev Ignatius Hahessy
Rev Columban Heaney
Rev Cornelius Justice
Br Declan Murphy
Rev Alphonsus O'Connell
Rev Denis Luke O'Hanlon
Rev Celestine O'Leary
Rev Vincent O Maidin
Rev Declan O'Rourke
Rev Patrick Ryan
Br Malachy Sutton
Fr Francis Carton

## COMBONI MISSIONARIES (MCCJ)

Verona Fathers

*Provincial:* Rev Martin Devenish
Comboni Missionaries,
London Road, Sunningdale,
Berks SL5 OJY, UK

*Archdiocese of Dublin*

**8 Clontarf Road**
Clontarf, Dublin 3
Tel/Fax 01-8330051
Email
combonimission@eircom.net

*Superior:* Rev Antonio Benetti

## Congregation of the Sacred Hearts of Jesus and Mary (SSCC)

### Sacred Hearts Community

*Archdiocese of Dublin*

**Provincialate**
Coudrin House,
27 Northbrook Road,
Dublin 6
Tel 01-6604898 (Provincialate)
Email ssccdublin@eircom.net
Tel 01-6686584(Community)
Fax 01-6686590
Website www.sacredhearts.ie

*Provincial*
Very Rev Derek Laverty
Tel 01-6473750
Email
dereklaverty2005@yahoo.co.uk
*Provincial Secretary*
Sheila O'Dowd

Most Rev Brendan Comiskey DD
Rev George Foley
Tel 01-6473751
Rev Michael F. Foley
Tel 01-6473759
Email michaelffoley@eircom.net
Br Anthony McMorrow
Tel 01-6473754
Br Ultan Naughton, vt
Rev Andy Wafer
Tel 01-6473755
Email andywafer@eircom.net

**Sacred Heart Presbytery**
St John's Drive,
Clondalkin,
Dublin 22
Tel 01-4570032

Rev Michael Ruddy
Email mikeruddy@eircom.net
Rev Eamon Aylward
Email ssccmoz@eircom.net
Rev Pearse Mullen
Email
pearsepmullen@yahoo.com

*Diocese of Clogher*

**Cootehill**
Co Cavan
Tel 049-5552188

Rev Jerry White
Email jerrysscc@eircom.net
Br Harry O'Gara

St Mary's
Clontibret, Co Monaghan
Tel 047-80631

Rev Kenneth McCabe

## DIVINE WORD MISSIONARIES (SVD)

Irish & British Province

Each Province of the Society is independent. When members are assigned to work in the missions, they automatically become members of the territory to which they are assigned and are no longer members of the Irish British Province.

*Archdiocese of Dublin*

**3 Pembroke Road,**
Dublin 4
Tel 01-6680904
*Praeses:* Rev Albert Escoto
Email
albert_escoto2000@yahoo.com

Rev Pat Claffey
Rev Gaspar Habara

**133 North Circular Road,**
Dublin 7
Tel 01-8386743
*Praeses:* Rev John Feighery

*Provincial:* Rev Patrick Byrne
Email
provincial@svdireland.com

Rev Henry Barlage
Rev Patrick Lee
Rev Anthony O'Riordan
Rev Finbarr Tracey

**City Quay**
*Immaculate Heart of Mary*
City Quay, Dublin 2
Tel 01-6773073
Email stjohnsp@gofree.indigo.ie

Rev Paul St John
*(administrator)*
Rev John Owen

**Maynooth**
Co Kildare
Tel 01-6286391/2
Fax 01-6289184
Email dv.twomey@may.ie

*Rector*
Rev D. Vincent Twomey
*Provincial Treasurer*
Rev Jega Susai

Rev Brendan Casey
Rev Daniel Daly
Rev Liam Dunne
*(Mission Procurator)*
Rev Tadeusz Durajcyk
Rev Richard Kelly
Br Paul Hurley
Rev Francis Kom
Rev Binoy Mathew
Rev Gerard McCarthy
Rev George Millar
Rev Barthlomiej Parys
Rev Jim Perry

**Divine Word School of English**
Tel 01-6289512
Fax 01-6289748
Email dwse@eircom.net

*Director*
Rev Michael Fitzgerald

*Diocese of Elphin*

**Donamon Castle**
Roscommon
Tel 090-6662222
Fax 090-6662511

*Rector*
Very Rev Patrick Hogan

Rev Tony Coote
Rev Norman Davitt
Br Brendan Fahey
Rev Richard Flanagan
Rev Charles Guthrie
Rev Michael Joyce
Rev Kevin Keenan
Rev Gerry Lanigan
Rev Peter Maloney
Rev Michael Reddan
Rev Noel S. Ruane
Rev Krzysztof Sikora
Rev Kazimierz Szalaj

*British District*

**London**
8 Teignmouth Road,
London, NW2 4HN
Tel 020-84528430

*Praeses*
Fr Michael Egan

Rev Kieran Fitzharris
Rev Martin McPake
Rev Kevin O'Toole

**Liverpool**
10 Blackwood Avenue,
Liverpool L25 4RW
Tel 0151-2911197

*Praeses*
Rev Brian Gilmore

Rev Oliver O'Connor
Rev Thomas Morris

**Bristol**
St Mary-on-the-Quay
Presbytery,
20 Colston Street,
Bristol BS1 5AE
Tel 0117-9264702

*Parish Priest*
Rev Nicodemus Lobo Ratu

Rev John Bettison

## DOMINICAN ORDER (OP)

### Order of Preachers

Irish Province

*Archdiocese of Dublin*

**Provincial Office**
St Mary's, Tallaght, Dublin 24
Tel 01-4048118/4048112
Fax 01-4515584
Email provincialop@eircom.net

*Provincial:* Very Rev Pat Lucey
*Provincial Bursar and Provincial Secretary*
Rev Tom Monahan
*Children Protection Officer*
Rev Vincent Travers

**Dominican Community**
St Mary's Priory
Tallaght, Dublin 24
Tel 01-4048100
Parish 01-4048188
Fax 01-4596784
Email parish@stmarys-tallaght.ie
Retreat House
Tel 01-4048189/8123/8191
Fax 01-4596080
Email domretreat@eircom.net

*Prior*
Very Rev Donal Sweeney PP
Email dsyop@eircom.net

Rev Wilfrid Harrington
Rev Paschal Tiernan
Rev Gabriel Harty
Rev Thomas McInerney
Rev Luke Dempsey
Rev Hugh Fenning
Rev Philip Gleeson
Rev Leonard Perrem
Rev Donagh O'Shea
Rev Thomas O'Flynn
Rev Brian McKevitt
Br Martin Cogan
Rev Donal Roche
Br Eamonn Moran
Br Michael Neenan
Br James Ryan
Rev Gerard Norton
Rev Séamus Touhy
Rev Terence Crotty
Rev Robert Regula
Rev Rodrigo Rivero

**St Saviour's**
Upper Dorset Street,
Dublin 1
Tel 01-8897610
Fax 01-8734003
Email stsaviours@eircom.net

*Prior*
Very Rev Gregory Carroll PP
Email gregcop@eircom.net

Rev Clement Greenan
Rev Cyprian Candon
Rev Edward Foley
Rev Liam Walsh
Rev Diarmuid Clifford
Rev Martin Boyle
Rev Joseph Dineen
Rev John Harris
Rev Marcin Szymanski
Rev Bernard McCay-Morrissey
Rev Cezary Binkiewicz
Rev Maurice Colgan
Rev Brian Doyle
Rev David Walker
Br Colm Mannion
Br Luuk Jansen
Br Matthew Martinez
Rev Denis Murphy
Br David McGovern
Br Damian Polly
Br Ronan Connolly
Br James Cassidy
Br Patrick Desmond
Br Daragh McNally
Br Conor McDonough
Br Stephen Jones
Br Eoin Casey
Br Alan Hopkins
Br Paul Hughes

**Glasnevin**
40 Iona Road, Dublin 9
Tel 01-8305880/8602790

Rev Gerard Dunne
Rev Marek Grubka

**47 Leeson Park**
Dublin 6
Tel 01-6602427

*Superior*
Very Rev Bernard Treacy

Rev Ambrose O'Farrell
Rev Andrew Allen

**St Aengus's**
Tymon North, Balrothery,
Tallaght, Dublin 24
Tel 01-4513757
Fax 01-4624038

*Superior*
Very Rev Benedict Moran PP
Email benmoran@indigo.ie

Rev Albert Leonard CC

**St Dominic's**
St Dominic's Road,
Tallaght, Dublin 24
Tel 01-4510620 Fax 01-4623223

*Superior:*
Very Rev Laurence Collins Adm
Email collinsl@eircom.net

Rev Tom Jordan

**St Dominic's**
Athy, Co Kildare
Tel 059-8631573
Fax 059-8631649

*Prior:* Very Rev Joseph O'Brien

Rev Ignatius Candon
Rev Gerard O'Keeffe
Rev Andrew Kane
Rev John Heffernan
Rev Dominic O'Connor

*Archdiocese of Armagh*

**St Malachy's**
Dundalk, Co Louth
Tel 042-9334179/9333714
Fax 042-9329751

*Prior*
Very Rev Bede McGregor

Rev Conor O'Riordan
Rev Anthony McMullan
Rev Ronan Cusack

**St Magdalen's**
Drogheda, Co Louth
Tel 041-9838271
Fax 041-9832964

*Prior*
Very Rev Dermot Brennan

Rev Humbert O'Brien
Rev Joseph Heffernan

*Diocese of Cork & Ross*

**St Mary's**
Pope Quay, Cork
Tel 021-4502267
Fax 021-4502307

*Prior*
Very Rev Joseph Kavanagh
Email joe39@indigo.ie

Rev Robert Talty
Rev Finian Lynch
Rev Simon Roche
Rev Adrian Farrelly
Rev Martin MacCarthy
Rev Philip McShane
Rev David Barrins

**St Dominic's Retreat House**
Montenotte, Co Cork
Tel 021-4502520
Fax 021-4502712

*Prior*
Very Rev Benedict Hegarty

Br James Beausang
Br Thomas Casey
Rev Stephen Cummins
Rev Frank Downes
Rev Archie Byrne
Rev Denis Keating

*Diocese of Dromore*

**St Catherine's**
Newry, Co Down BT35 8BN
Tel 028-30262178
Tel 028-30252188

*Prior:* Very Rev Joseph Ralph

Br Mark McGreevy
Rev Stephen Tumilty
Rev Noel McKeown
Rev Maurice Fearon

*Diocese of Elphin*

**Holy Cross**
Sligo, Co Sligo
Tel 071-9142700
Fax 071-9146533

*Prior*
Very Rev Timothy Mulcahy

Rev Anthony Morris
Rev Sean Cunningham

*Diocese of Galway*

**St Mary's**
The Claddagh, Co Galway
Tel 091-582884 Fax 091-581252

*Prior*
Very Rev Fergal Mac Eoinín PP

Rev Peter Gaffney
Rev Terence McLoughlin
Rev John O'Reilly
Br Christopher O'Flaherty
Rev Walter Hegarty
Rev Denis Murphy
Rev Marek Cul

*Diocese of Kerry*

**Holy Cross**
Tralee, Co Kerry
Tel 066-7121135/7129185
Fax 066-7180026

*Prior:* Very Rev Joseph Bulman

Rev Placid Nolan
Rev James Duggan
Rev John O'Rourke
Rev Krzysztof Kupczakiewicz

*Diocese of Kildare & Leighlin*

**Newbridge College**
Droichead Nua, Co Kildare
Tel 045-487200 Fax 045-487234
Email
newbridgepriory@ireland.com
Secondary School for Boys

*Prior*
Very Rev Stephen Hutchinson

Rev Raymond O'Donovan
Rev Brian Reynolds
Rev Edmund Murphy
Rev Benedict MacKenna
Rev Thomas McCarthy
Rev Michael Commane
Rev Laurence Kelly

*Diocese of Limerick*

**St Saviour's**
Glentworth Street, Limerick
Tel 061-412333
Fax 061-311728
*Prior*
Very Rev Jordan O'Brien PP

Rev Vincent Kennedy
Rev Brendan Clifford
Rev Thomas Brodie
Rev James Donleavy
Rev Donal Mehigan

*Diocese of Ossory*

**Black Abbey**
Kilkenny, Co Kilkenny
Tel 056-7721279
Fax 056-7721297

*Prior:* Very Rev Louis Hughes

Rev Dominic Browne
Rev Finbar Kelly
Rev Stanislaus Foley
Rev Edward Conway
Rev Vincent Mercer

*Diocese of Waterford & Lismore*

**St Saviour's**
Bridge Street, Waterford
Tel 051-875061 Fax 051-858093

*Prior:* Very Rev James Harris

Rev Anselm Ryan
Rev Raymond Collins
Rev Canice Murphy

**St Saviour's**
Ballybeg, Waterford
Tel 051-376032 Fax 051-376581

*Superior*
Very Rev Declan Corish PP

Rev Martin Crowe CC
Rev Richard Walsh CC

*Rome*

**Convent of SS Xystus and Clement**
Collegio San Clemente,
Via Labicana 95, 00184 Roma
Tel 0039-06-7740021

*Prior*
Very Rev Michael Dunleavy

Rev Michael Carragher
Rev Carlyle Fortune
Rev Marcin Lisak
Rev John Walsh
Rev Fergus Ryan

*Lisbon*

**Convento dos Padres Dominicanos Irlandeses**
Praceta Infante D. Henrique,
lote5, l-Dto, Rua do Murtal
San Pedro do Estoril, 2765-531
Estoril, Portugal
Tel 351-21-4673771

*Superior and Parish Priest*
Very Rev Augustine Champion

## FRANCISCAN ORDER (OFM)

Province of Ireland

Provincial Office,
Franciscan Friary,
4 Merchant's Quay, Dublin 8
Tel 01-6742500 Fax 01-6742549
Email greccio@eircom.net

*Provincial*
Rev Hugh McKenna
Email hughmck@gmail.com

*Vicar Provincial*
Rev Kieran Cronin
Dún Mhuire, Seafield Road,
Killiney, Co Dublin
Tel 01-2826760
Email kierancronin@eircom.net
*Secretary of the Province*
Rev Joseph MacMahon
Email secprovofm@eircom.net

*Archdiocese of Dublin*

**Adam & Eve's**
4 Merchant's Quay, Dublin 8
Tel 01-6771128 Fax 01-6771000

*Guardian:* Br Niall O'Connell
*Vicar:* Rev Gabriel Kinahan

Br David Collins
Rev Patrick Hudson
Rev Richard Kelly
Br Philip Lane
Rev Angelus Lee
Rev Jude O'Riordan
Br Jack O'Riordan (Canterbury)
Rev Fintan O'Shea
(3 The Millhouse, Steelworks,
Foley Street, Dublin 1)
Br Sebastian Tighe
Rev Joseph Walsh

**Franciscan House of Studies**
Dún Mhuire, Seafield Road,
Killiney, Co Dublin
Tel 01-2826760 Fax 01-2826993
Email dmkilliney@eircom.net

*Guardian:* Rev Kieran Cronin
*Vicar:* Rev Patrick Conlan

Rev Ronald Bennett
Rev Pádraig Coleman
(Firhouse)
Rev Liam Costello (Dalkey)
Rev Francis Cotter
Rev John Dalton
(4 McSweeney House,
Berkeley Road, Dublin 7)
Rev Ignatius Fennessy
Rev Alexis King
Rev Simon O'Byrne
Rev Hugh O'Donnell
Rev Maelisa Ó Huallacháin
Rev Paschal Slevin

*Diocese of Ardagh & Clonmacnois*

**Franciscan Friary**
Friary Lane, Athlone,
Co Westmeath
Tel 090-6472095
Fax 090-6424713

*Guardian:* Rev Michael Nicholas
*Vicar:* Rev Brian Allen

Br Salvador Kenny
Rev Ralph Lawless
Rev Laurence Murphy
Rev John O'Brien

*Diocese of Cork & Ross*

**Franciscan Friary**
Liberty Street, Cork
Tel 021-4270302
Fax 021-4271841

*Guardian:* Rev Eugene Barrett
*Vicar:* Rev Brendan McGrath

Rev John Bosco O'Byrne
Rev Philip Deane
Rev Iain Duggan
Rev Oswald Gill
Rev Henry Houlihan
Rev Seraphin Kennedy
Rev Laurence Mulligan
Rev Oscar O'Leary
Rev Ambrose O'Mahony
Rev Christopher Regan

*Diocese of Galway*

**The Abbey**
8 Francis Street, Galway
Tel 091-562518 Fax 091-565663
Email
galwayabbeyofm@eircom.net

*Guardian:* Rev Patrick Younge
*Vicar, Parish Priest*
Rev Francis McGrath

Rev Michael Bailey *(Curate's Residence, Monksfield, Salthill, Galway)*
Rev Cathal Duddy
Rev Philip Forker
Rev Colin Garvey
Rev Patrick Lynch
Rev Peter O'Grady
Br Martin Thompson
Rev Declan Timmons

*Diocese of Kerry*

**Franciscan Friary**
Killarney, Co Kerry
Tel 064-6631334/6631066
Fax 064-6637510
Email friary@eircom.net

*Guardian*
Rev Pádraig Breheny
*Vicar:* Rev Joseph Condren

Rev Christopher Connelly
Br Seán Murphy
Rev Hilary Steblecki

*Diocese of Killaloe*

**Franciscan Friary**
Ennis, Co Clare
Tel 065-6828751
Fax 065-6822008
Email friars.ennis@eircom.net

*Guardian:* Rev Liam Kelly
*Vicar/Novice Master*
Rev Caoimhín Ó Laoide
*Pro-Vicar*
Rev Fergus McEveney

Rev Séamus Donohoe
Rev Cletus Noone
Br Elzear O'Brien
Rev Feidhlim Ó Seasnáin

*Diocese of Meath*

**Franciscan College**
Gormanston, Co Meath
Tel 01-8412203 Fax 01-8412685
Email
friary@gormanstoncollege.ie

*Guardian:* Rev Brendan Scully
*Vicar:* Rev Ailbe Ó Mhurchú

Rev Laurence Brady
Rev P. J. Brady
Rev Edward Burke
Rev Seán Cassin
Rev Augustine Hughes
Br Kevin McKenna
Rev Eamonn Newell
Br Gerard Phayer
Rev Malcom Timothy
Rev Ulic Troy

**Franciscan Abbey**
Multyfarnham, Co Westmeath
Tel 044-9371114/9371137
Fax 044-9371387

*Guardian:* Rev Bernard Jones
*Vicar:* Rev Lomán Mac Aodha

Rev John Kealy
Rev Michael Holland

*Diocese of Raphoe*

**Franciscan Friary**
Rossnowlagh, Co Donegal
Tel 072-9851342
Fax 072-9852206
Email
franciscanfriary@eircom.net

*Guardian*
Rev Paschal McDonnell
*Vicar:* Rev Thomas Russell

Rev Florian Farrelly
Rev Seán Gildea
Rev Pius McLaughlin

*Diocese of Waterford & Lismore*

**Franciscan Friary**
Clonmel, Co Tipperary
Tel 052-6121378
Fax 052-6125806
Email clonmel@eircom.net

***Filial House of Waterford***
*Vicar:* Br Isidore Cronin

Rev Richard Callanan
Rev John Harty
Rev Diarmaid Ó Riain

**Franciscan Friary**
Lady Lane, Waterford
Tel 051-874262 Fax 051-843062
Email
waterfordfriary@eircom.net
*Chaplaincy*
Tel 051-842244

*Guardian*
Rev Eamonn O'Driscoll
*Vicar*
Rev Edward O'Callaghan

Rev Patrick Cogan
*(15 Orchard Drive, Ursuline Court, Waterford/ Tel 087-236039/Respond! Office Tel 051-876865)*
Rev Ultan McCaffrey
Rev Art McCoy
Rev Rory O'Leary
Rev Peter Baptist O'Toole
Br Nicholas Shanahan
Rev Bonaventure Ward

*Other Individual Addresses*

Rev Pádraig B. Coleman
Presbytery 2, Ballycullen Ave,
Firhouse, Dublin 24
Rev Bernard Hall
PO Box 7026, Katutura,
Windlock, Republic of Namibia
Rev William Hoyne
Hermanos Franciscanos, Iglesia
Parroquial 'Dios con Nostros',
1a Av, 5a-6a Calles, Monzana
10, Elmezquital, Zana 12, 10102
Guatemala City, Guatemala
Rev Crispin Keating
5225 North Himes Avenue,
Tampa, Fl 33614-6623, USA
Rev Matthew McDonald
Lawson House, Knockrathkyle,
Glenbrien, Enniscorthy,
Co Wexford
Rev Aidan McGrath
Curia Generalizia dei Frati
Minori, Via S. Maria Mediatrice
25, 00165 Roma, Italy
Most Rev Fiachra Ó Ceallaigh
'St Cecilia's', 19 St Anthony
Road, Rialto, Dublin 8
Rev Adrian Peelo
Old Mission San Luis Rey,
4050 Mission Avenue,
Oceanside, CA 92057-6497, USA

*Franciscan Communities Abroad*

**St Anthony's Parish**
*(English-Speaking Chaplaincy)*
23/25 Oudtrijderslaan,
1950 Kraainem, Belgium
Tel +32-2-7201970
Fax +32-2-7255810

Rev Patrick Power *(Provincial Delegate/Parish Priest)*
Rev Vincent Gallogley
*(Associate Pastor)*

**Collegio S. Isidoro**
Via degli Artisti 41,
00187 Roma, Italy
Tel +39-06-4885359
Fax +39-06-4884459
Email collegio_s_isidoro@libero.it

*Guardian*
Rev Micheál Mac Craith

Rev Louis Brennan
Br Solanus Hughes
Br Stephen O'Kane

**Franciscan Missionaries in** Zimbabwe
*Custos:* Rev Emmanuel Musara

Rev Nicholas Banhwa
Br Tawanda Chirigo
Rev Walter Gallahue
Rev James Hasson
Rev Maxwell Jaya
Br Raymond Kondo
Br Francis Lembani
Rev Fanuel Magwidi
Rev Thomas Makamure
Br Naison Manjovha
Rev Liam McCarthy
Br Albert Mhari
Br Linous Mukumbuzi
Rev Xavier Mukupo
Br Salicio Mukuwe
Br Onward Murape
Br Juniper O'Brien
Br Stephen O'Kane *(Collegio S. Isidoro, Rome)*
Br Stephen Office
Br Ndabaningi Sithole
Br Patience Tigere
Rev Alfigio Tunha
Br Clemence Wiziki

## CONVENTUAL FRANCISCANS (OFMConv)

General Delegation Office
St Patrick's Friary
26 Cornwall Road, Waterloo, London SE1 8TW, England
Tel 020-79288897

*General Delegate*
Very Rev James McCurry

*Archdiocese of Dublin*

**Friary of the Visitation of the BVM**
Fairview Strand, Dublin 3
Tel 01-8376000 Fax 01-8376021

Rev Joseph Connick PP
Rev Ciprian Budu
Rev Patrick Griffin
Rev Antony Nallukunnel

*Diocese of Ferns*

**The Friary,** Wexford
Tel 053-9122758 Fax 053-9121499

Rev Aidan Walsh, Guardian
Rev Fritz O'Kelly
Rev Dariusz Dawidowski
Br Donald Thielsan

## FRANCISCAN FRIARS OF THE RENEWAL (CFR)

Community of the Franciscan Friars of Renewal
*Community Servant*
Rev Mauriusz Casimir Koch
Most Blessed Sacrament Friary,
375 13th Avenue, Newark,
NJ 07103-2124
Tel 001-973-6226622

*Diocese of Derry*

**St Columba Friary**
6 Victoria Place,
Derry BT48 6TJ
Tel 028-71260390
Fax 028-71369274
*Local Servant (Superior)*
Rev Columba Jordan

*Diocese of Limerick*

**St Patrick Friary**
64 Delmege Park, Moyross
Limerick
Tel 061-458071
Fax 061-457626
*Local Servant (Superior)*
Br Shawn Conrad O'Connor

## HOLY SPIRIT CONGREGATION (CSSp)

Province of Ireland

*Archdiocese of Dublin*

**Holy Spirit Provincialate**
Temple Park, Richmond Avenue South, Dublin 6
Tel 01-4975127/4977230
Fax 01-4975399
Email secretaryspiritan@irishspiritans.ie

*Provincial Leadership Team*
Rev Brian Starken
Rev Peter Conaty
Rev Seán O'Leary
*Provincial Bursar*
Rev Conor Courtney
*Provincial Secretary*
Rev Eddie O'Farrell

*Archivist:* Rev Peter Raftery
*Communications Manager*
Mr Peter O'Mahony
Email communications@irishspiritans.ie

**Holy Spirit Education Office,**
(Des Places Educational Association Ltd)
Kimmage Manor, Dublin 12
Tel 01-4997610
www.desplaces.ie
Awareness Education Office
Rev Tony Byrne
Tel/Fax 01-8388888
Email
info@awarenesseducation.org

**Holy Spirit Missionary College**
Kimmage Manor,
Whitehall Road, Dublin 12
Tel 01-4064300 Fax 01-4920062
Email
reception@kimmagemanor.ie

*Community Leader*
Rev Michael Kilkenny

Rev James Adjei-Buor
Rev Enzo Agnoli
Rev Savino Agnoli
Rev Desmond Arigho
Rev Michael Begley
Rev John Brown
Br Albert Buckley
Rev Christopher Burke
Rev James Byrnes
Rev Francis Caffrey
Rev John Cahill
Rev Brian Carey
Bishop Michael J. Cleary
Rev Patrick Cleary
Rev John J. Coleman
Rev Martin J. Collins
Rev Frank Comerford
Rev Timothy Connolly
Rev Kevin Corrigan
Rev James Corry
Rev Conor Courtney
Rev Noel Cox
Rev Patrick Cully
Rev James Daly
Rev Stephen Darcy
Rev Anthony Darragh
Rev Dermot Doran
Rev Frank Duffy
Rev Colm Duggan
Rev James F. Duggan
Rev Patrick Dundon
Rev Bartholomew Egan
Rev John Egan
Rev Francis Toochukwu Ekwomadu
Rev Richard Eneji
Rev Hugh Fagan
Rev Matthew Farrelly
Rev Thomas Farrelly
Rev John A. Finucane *(Concern)*
Rev Aloysius P. Flood
Rev Anthony Geoghegan
Rev Reginald Gillooly
Rev Cothraí Gogan
Rev Edward Grimes
Rev Brendan Heeran
Rev Anthony Heerey
Rev John Hogan
Rev Thomas Hogan
Rev Gregory Iwuozor
Rev William Jenkinson
Rev Michael Kane
Rev Patrick James Kelly
Rev Patrick Joseph Kelly
Rev Michael Kilkenny
Rev John Joe King
Rev John Laizer
Rev Jeremiah Lambe
Rev Owen Lambert
Rev Francis Laverty
Rev Francis Leahy
Rev Patrick Leddy
Rev Jude Lynch *(Bursar)*
Rev Liam Martin
Rev James McCaffrey
Rev Michael McCarthy
Rev Martin McDonagh
Rev Peter J. McEntire
Rev Leo McGarry
Rev Patrick McGlynn
Rev Laurence McHugh
Rev Brian McLaughlin
Rev Walter McNamara
Rev Linus Mbajo
Rev Thomas F. Meagher
Rev Henry Moloney
Rev John Moriarty
Rev James Morrow
Rev Michael Mulvihill
Rev James Murphy
Rev Jack Nugent
Rev William Nugent
Rev Brendan J. O'Brien
Rev Valentine O'Brien
Rev John (Seán) O'Connell
Rev Vincent O'Connell
Rev David O'Connor
Rev Sean O'Donoghue
Rev Timothy O'Driscoll
Rev Anthony O'Farrell
Rev Vincent O'Grady
Rev Noel O'Meara
Rev Hugh O'Reilly
Bishop John C. O'Riordan
Rev Sean O'Shaughnessy
Rev Desmond L. O'Sullivan
Rev John L. O'Sullivan
Rev Liam O'Sullivan
Rev Lorcan O'Toole
Rev Michael B. Reynolds
Rev Denis Robinson
Rev Gerard Ryan
Rev Patrick J. Ryan
Rev Ciaran Shanley
Rev Cyril Sheedy
Rev Joseph Sheehan
Rev Jim Stapleton
Rev Joseph M. Steele
Rev Paul Walsh
Rev William Walsh
Rev Enda Watters
Rev Marc Whelan
Rev Patrick A. Whelan
Rev Tom Whelan

**Kimmage Development Studies Centre**
Kimmage Manor, Dublin 12
Tel 01-4064386 Fax 01-4064388
www.kimmagedsc.ie

*Director:* Mr Patrick Reilly

**Church of the Holy Spirit**
Kimmage, Dublin 12
Tel 01-4558316
www.kimmagemanorparish.com

Very Rev Patrick Doody PP

**Blackrock College**
Blackrock, Co Dublin
Tel 01-2888681 Fax 01-2834267
www.blackrockcollege.com
Email
info@blackrockcollege.com

*Community Leader*
Rev Tom Nash
*Principal:* Alan MacGinty

Rev Kevin A. Browne
Rev Vincent Browne
Rev Seán Casey
Rev John (Seán) P. Farragher
Rev Thomas Farrelly
Rev Brendan Foley
Rev Norman Fitzgerald
Rev Denis J. Gavin
Rev Brian M. Gogan
Rev Joseph A. Gough
Rev Liam Kehoe
Rev Brian Kilbride
Rev Malachy Kilbride
Rev Thomas McDonald
Rev James McDonnell
Rev Hyacinth Nwnkuna
Rev Cormac Ó Brolcháin
Rev Richard J. Thornton

**Willow Park**
Tel 01-2881651 Fax 01-2783353
Email
admin@willowparkschool.ie

*Principal Senior School*
Mr Donal Brennan
*Principal Junior School*
Mr Jim Casey

**St Mary's College**
Rathmines, Dublin 6
Community Tel 01-4995760
Fax 01-4972621
www.stmarys.ie
Junior School Tel 01-4995721
Email junsec@stmarys.ie
Senior School Tel 01-4995700
Fax 01-4972574
Email sensec@stmarys.ie

*Community Leader*
Rev John B. Doyle
*Principal Secondary School*
Mr Denis Murphy
*Principal Junior School*
Ms Mary O'Donnell

Rev Michael J. Buckley
Br Ignatius Curry
Rev Michael Duggan
Rev John P. Flavin
Rev Leo Layden
Rev Anthony Little
Rev James J. McNulty
Rev Brian O'Toole

**St Michael's College**
Ailesbury Road, Dublin 4
Tel 01-2189400 Fax 01-2698862
www.stmichaelscollege.com
Email stmcoll@indigo.ie

*Principal:* Mr Tim Kelleher
*Principal Junior School*
Ms Lorna Heslin

**Spiritan House**
**Spiritan Asylum Services Initiative (SPIRASI)**
213 North Circular Road,
Dublin 7
Tel 01-8389664/8683504
Fax 01-8686500
www.spirasi.ie
Mr Greg Straton *(Director, SPIRASI)*

*Community Leader*
Rev Brendan Carr
Rev John Kilcrann
Rev Patrick McNamara
Br Liam Sheridan
Mr James Lynch

**Templeogue College**
Templeville Road, Dublin 6W
Tel 01-4903909 Fax 01-4920903
www.templeoguecollege.ie
Email
info@templeoguecollege.ie

*Community Leader*
Rev John Byrne
*Principal:* Ms Aoife O'Donnell

Rev Seamus Galvin
Rev Patrick Keegan
Rev Frank Mulloy
Rev Peter Raftery
Rev Thomas Raftery
Rev Noel Redmond
Rev Patrick Reedy

**Church of the Holy Spirit**
Greenhills, Dublin 12
Tel 01-4504040
www.holyspiritparish
greenshills.ie

Very Rev Myles Healy PP

Rev Roderick Curran
Rev Richard Eneji

**Church of the Transfiguration**
Presbytery, Bawnogue,
Clondalkin, Dublin 22
Tel 01-4592273/4519810
Fax 01-4670038

Very Rev Joseph Beere PP

Rev Marino Nguekam

**Newlands Institute for Counselling**
2 Monastery Road, Clondalkin,
Dublin 22
Tel 01-4594573

Rev Ronan Grimshaw
Rev Patrick Coughlan

**Parish of St Ronan's**
Deansrath, Clondalkin,
Dublin 22
Tel 01-4570380

Rev Daithi Kenneally PP

*Archdiocese of Cashel and Diocese of Emly*

**Rockwell College**
Cashel, Co Tipperary
Tel 062-61444 Fax 062-61661
www.rockwell-college.ie
Email info@rockwellcollege.ie

Secondary Residential and Day School

*Community Leader*
Rev Matthew J. Knight
*Principal:* Mr Patrick O'Sullivan

Br Gerard Cummins
Rev Colm Cunningham
Rev Tom Cunningham
Rev Patrick Downes
Rev Bernard M. Frawley
Rev Gerard Griffin
Rev Brendan Hally
Rev James Hurley
Rev William Kingston
Rev Jeremiah Kirwin
Rev John Meade
Rev Michael Moore
Rev Noel Murphy *(Promotions)*
Rev William Murphy
Rev Edmond Purcell
Rev Peter Queally

*Diocese of Elphin*

**Spiritan Community**
Ballintubber, Castlerea,
Co Roscommon
Rel 094-9655226

Rev Joseph Poole

*Diocese of Meath*

**Spiritan Missionaries**
Ardbraccan, Navan, Co Meath
Tel 046-9021441 Fax 046-9021178

*Community Leader*
Br Conleth Tyrrell

Rev Brian Murtagh
Rev Edward Nealon
Rev Patrick O'Toole

*Rome*

**Clivo di Cinna 195, 00136**
Roma, Italy
Tel +39-06-3540461
Fax +39-06-35450676

*Superior General*
Most Rev Jean-Paul Hoch

## JESUITS (SJ) SOCIETY OF JESUS

Irish Province

*Archdiocese of Dublin*

**Irish Jesuit Provincialate**
Milltown Park,
Sandford Road, Dublin 6
Tel 01-4987333 Fax 01-4987334
Email curia@jesuit.ie

*Provincial:* Rev Tom Layden
*Assistant Provincial*
Rev Noel Barber

**Jesuit Centre for Faith and Justice**
26 Upper Sherrard Street,
Dublin 1
Tel 01-8556814
Fax 01-8364377
Email info@jcfj.ie
www.jcfj.ie
*Acting Director:*
Rev John K. Guiney

**Jesuit Communication Centre**
Irish Jesuit Provincialate,
Milltown Park,
Sandford Road, Dublin 6
Tel 01-4987347/4987348
*Manager:* Ms Pat Coyle
Email coylep@jesuit.ie
geraldine@jesuit.ie
amdg@jesuit.ie
jcc@jesuit.ie
pwandrews@gmail.com
amdgexpress@gmail.com

**Jesuit Curia Community**
Loyola House, Milltown Park,
Sandford Road, Dublin 6
Tel 01-2180276
Email loyola@jesuit.ie

*Superior:* Rev Noel Barber
*Minister*
Rev Michael Drennan

Rev Peter Sexton

Applications for *retreats* to
Rev Finbarr Lynch SJ
Manresa House, Dollymount,
Dublin 3
Tel 01-8331352

Enquiries in respect of *foreign missions* to Rev Director, Jesuit Foreign Missions,
28 Upper Sherrard Street,
Dublin 1
Tel 01-8366509 Fax 01-8366510

**St Francis Xavier's**
Upper Gardiner Street, Dublin 1
Tel 01-8363411 Fax 01-8555624
Email sfxcommunity@jesuit.ie
Parish church and residence

*Superior*
Rev Bernard McGuckian
*Vice-Superior*
Rev William Reynolds
*Minister:* Br Tom Phelan
*Parish Priest*
Very Rev Donal Neary PP

Rev Derek Cassidy
Rev James Culliton
Br Eamonn Davis
Rev Paul Farquharson
Rev John K. Guiney
Rev Frank Keenan
Rev Mícheál Mac Gréil
Br Gerard Marks
Rev Dermot McKenna
Rev Liam McKenna
Rev John Moylan
Br Martin Murphy
Rev Lucas Mg'hwagi (AOR)
Rev John O'Holohan
Rev Kevin O'Rourke
Rev James Smyth
Rev Brendan Staunton

*Residing Elsewhere*
Rev Brian Lennon
Rev Peter McVerry
Rev Neil O'Driscoll

**Belvedere College**
Great Denmark Street, Dublin 1
*Community resides in SFX Gardiner Street*

Secondary day school
Tel 01-8586600 (College)
Fax 01-8744374
*Rector:* Rev Bruce Bradley
*Headmaster:* Mr Gerard Foley

**35 Lower Leeson Street**
Dublin 2
Tel 01-6761248 Fax 01-7758598
Residence

*Superior:* Rev Brian Grogan
*Vice-Superior*
Rev Edmond Grace

Rev Gerard Bourke (JPN)
Rev Philip Fogarty
Rev Michael O. Gallagher
Rev Brendan Kearney
Rev Kevin Laheen
Rev John Looby
Rev James Moran
Rev Fergus O'Donoghue

*Residing Elsewhere*
Rev Richard Cremins (Zam-Mal)
Rev John FitzGerald (Zam)
Rev Ronan Geary
Rev Brendan Kearney
Br Joseph Osborne
Rev Francis Sammon

*Sacred Heart Messenger* – a Jesuit Publication
37 Lower Leeson Street, Dublin 2
Tel 01-6767491
*Editor:* Rev John Looby
*Manager:* Ms Triona McKee
Email manager@messenger.ie

*Sacred Space*
*Acting Director*
Rev Brian Grogan
Website www.sacredspace.ie

**Campion House Residence**
28 Lower Hatch Street, Dublin 2
Tel 01-6383990
Fax 01-6762805
Email campion@jesuit.ie

*Superior:* Rev John O'Keeffe
*Provincial:* Rev Tom Layden

Rev Patrick Hume
Rev Michael O'Sullivan
Rev Joseph Palmisano (NEN)

**Manresa House**
Dollymount, Dublin 3
Tel 01-8331352
Fax 01-8331002
Email manresa@jesuit.ie
Retreat House

*Rector:* Rev Joseph Dargan
*Director of Retreat House/ Vice-Rector*
Rev Patrick Carberry
*Plant Manager*
Br Joseph Ward
Br Peter Doyle
Rev Patrick Greene
Rev Peter Hannan
Rev Finbarr Lynch
Rev Dermot Mansfield
Rev Thomas Morrissey
Rev Ciary Quirke
Rev Jan Van de Poll (NER)

*Residing Elsewhere*
Rev Kevin O'Higgins
217 Sillogue Road, Ballumun, Dublin 11

**Dominic Collins' House Residence**
129 Morehampton Road, Dublin 4
Tel 01-2693075 Fax 01-2698462
*Vice-Superior*
Rev David Coghlan

Rev Martin Curry
Rev David Tuohy

**Milltown Park**
Sandford Road, Dublin 6
Tel 01-2698411/2698113
Fax 01-2600371
Email milltown@jesuit.ie

*Rector:* Rev Conall O'Cuinn
*Vice-Rector:* Rev Paul Andrews
*Plant Manager:* Br John Adams

Rev John Brady
Rev Fergal Brennan
Rev Liam Browne
Rev William Callanan
Rev Finbarr Clancy
Rev Brendan Comerford
Rev Brendan Duddy
Br George Fallon
Rev David Gaffney
Rev Henry Grant
Rev John Guiney
Rev Conor Harper
Rev James Kelly
Rev Patrick Kelly
Rev Colm Lavelle
Br John Maguire
Rev William Mathews
Br James McCabe
Rev Raymond Moloney
Rev Brian O'Leary
Rev Hugh O'Neill
Rev Stephen Redmond
Rev Brendan Woods

*Residing Elsewhere*
Br Joseph Cleary
Rev John Dooley
Br James Dunne
Br Brendan Hyland
Rev John McAuley (Zam-Mal)
Rev Charles O'Connor
Rev Edmund O'Keefe
Rev John Redmond

**Lay Retreat Association of Saint Ignatius**
Milltown Park, Dublin 6
Tel 01-2698411/2180274
Lay apostolate for the promotion of retreats in different locations

*Spiritual Director*
Rev Fergus O'Keefe
Tel 01-2951856

**Milltown Institute of Theology and Philosophy**
Milltown Park,
Sandford Road, Dublin 6
Tel 01-2776300 Fax 01-2692528
Email info@milltown-institute.ie

*Acting President*
Rev Finbarr Clancy
*Rector of the Ecclesiastical Faculty*
Professor of Theology at Milltown

**Gonzaga College**
Sandford Road, Dublin 6
Tel 01-4972943 (community)
Fax 01-4960849 (community)
Tel 01-4972931 (college)
Fax 01-4967769
Email
*(Community)* gonzaga@jesuit.ie
*(College)* office@gonzaga.ie

*Rector:* Rev Myles O'Reilly
*Minister:* Rev Kennedy O'Brien
*Headmaster:* Mr Kevin Whirdy

Rev Joseph Brennan
Rev Colm Brophy
Rev John Callanan
Rev Tomasz Homa (PME)
Rev Alan Mowbray
Rev Edward O'Donnell
Rev Desmond O'Grady
Rev Colin Warrack

**John Sullivan House**
56/56A Mulvey Park, Dundrum, Dublin 14
Tel 01-2983978
Email sullivan@jesuit.ie
Residence for scholastics attending universities

*Superior:* Rev Gerard Clarke
Tel 01-2986424
*Minister:* Rev Fergus O'Keefe

Rev Irenus, David (MAS)

*Jesuit Scholastic*
Augustine Ekeno (AOR)

**Arrupe Community**
217 Sillogue Road, Ballymun, Dublin 11
Tel 01-8420886

Rev Peter McVerry
Rev Kevin O'Higgins

25 Croftwood Park
Cherry Orchard, Dublin 10
Tel 01-6267413

Rev Gerard O'Hanlon
Rev William Toner

**Jesuit Community**
27 Leinster Road, Rathmines, Dublin 6
Tel 01-4970250
Email leinster@jesuit.ie

*Vice-Superior*
Rev James Corkery
*Minister:* Rev Leon Ó Giolláin

Rev Yong-su P. Kim (KOR)
Rev Krzysztof Nowak (S.Pol)

*Jesuit Scholastics*
Bala Kumar Bollineni (Andhra)
Jakub Garcar (SVK)
Tomasz Stapor (PME)

*Archdiocese of Armagh*

**Iona**
211 Churchill Park
Portadown, BT62 1EU
Tel 028-38330366
Fax 028-38338334
Email iona@jesuit.ie

*Superior*
Rev Brendan MacPartlin
Rev Michael Bingham *(Prov Brit)*
Br David Byrne
Rev Proinsias Mac Brádaigh

*Diocese of Down & Connor*

**Peter Faber House**
28 Brookvale Avenue
Belfast BT14 6BW
Tel 028-90757615
Fax 028-90747615
Email
peter_faber@lineone.net

*Superior:* Rev Alan McGuckian

Rev Patrick Davis
Rev Terence Howard
Rev Senan Timoney

*Diocese of Galway*

**St Ignatius Community & Church**
27 Raleigh Row, Salthill, Galway
Tel 091-523707
Email galway@jesuit.ie

*Rector:* Rev John Humphreys
*Minister*
Rev Enda O'Callaghan

Rev Paul Brassil (ZAM)
Edward Cosgrove *(Scholastic)*
Shane Daly *(Scholastic)*
Rev Charles Davy
Rev Anthony Farren (CHN)
Ronan McCoy *(Scholastic)*
Rev Paul Tonna (MAL)

*Residing Elsewhere*
Rev Dermot Cassidy
Rev James Lynch
Rev Connla O Duláine

**Coláiste Iognáid**
24 Sea Road, Galway
College Tel 091-501550
Fax 091-501551
Email
colaisteiognaid@eircom.net

*Secondary School Headmaster*
Mr Bernard O'Connell
*Scoil Iognaid (National School)*
*Principal:* Maree Ui Chonaill
Tel 091-584491

*Diocese of Kildare & Leighlin*

**Clongowes Wood College**
Naas, Co Kildare
Tel 045-868663/868202
Fax 045-861042
Email *(College)*
reception@clongowes.net
*(Community)*
reception@clongowes.net
Secondary Boarding School

*Rector:* Rev Michael Sheil
*Headmaster*
Rev Leonard Moloney
Email hm@clongowes.net
*Minister:* Vacant

Rev Joseph Brereton
Mariusz Balcerak (SVK)
*(Scholastic)*
Br Charles Connor
Rev Vincent Murphy
Rev Laurence Murphy
Rev Dermot Murray

*Residing Elsewhere*
Rev Patrick Crowe
Rev Patrick Lavery

*Diocese of Limerick*

**Crescent College Comprehensive**
Dooradoyle, Limerick
*(Community)*
Tel 061-480920 Fax 061-480927
Email dooradoyle@jesuit.ie
*(College)*
Tel 061-229655 Fax 061-229013
Email ccadmin.ias@eircom.net
Comprehensive Day School for Boys and Girls

*Superior:* Rev Liam O'Connell
*Minister:* Rev James Maher
Rev Michael McGuckian
Rev Declan Murray
Rev Anthony O'Riordan
Kensy, Joseph *(Scholastic)*
*Headmaster*
Mr Nicholas Cuddihy

*Jesuits temporarily outside Ireland*

Correspondence to
Irish Jesuit Provincialate
Milltown Park,
Sandford Road, Dublin 6
Tel 01-4987333
Email curia@jesuit.ie

Rev Kiaran Barry-Ryan
Rev Brendan Carmody
Rev Thomas Casey
Rev Kevin Casey
Rev John Dardis
Rev Cathal Doherty
Rev Hugh Duffy
Rev Ashley Evans
Rev Michael P. Gallagher
Rev Donal Godfrey
Rev James Hayes
Rev Timothy Healy
Rev Patrick Heelan
Rev Bartholomew Kiely
Rev Niall Leahy
Rev Brian MacCuarta
Rev James Murphy
Rev Dermot O'Connor
Rev Richard O'Dwyer
Rev Patrick Riordan
Rev Patrick Sheary
Rev Patrick Tyrrell

*Jesuit Scholastic*
Niall S. Leahy

## LEGIONARIES OF CHRIST (LC)

*Archdiocese of Dublin*

**Community**
Leopardstown Road,
Foxrock, Dublin 18
Tel 01-2955902 Fax 01-2957773
Email ireland@legionaries.org

*Superior*
Rev Anthony Bannon
*Vocations Director*
Rev Fergal O'Dúill
Email foduill@legionaries.org
*Regnum Christi*
Rev Michael Mullan
Email
mmullan@legionaries.org

**Clonlost Retreat and Youth Centre**
Killiney Road,
Killiney, Co Dublin
Tel 01-2350064
Day school retreats,
pre-confirmation retreats,
Creidim Leadership
Programme

*Chaplain:* Rev Feargal O'Duill

**Dublin Oak Academy**
Kilcroney, Bray,
Co Wicklow
Tel 01-2863290 Fax 01-2865315
Email secretary@
dublinoakacademy.com

*Director:* Rev Francisco Cepeda
*Chaplain:* Rev Steven Kwon

**Woodlands Academy**
Wingfield House, Bray
Co Wicklow
Tel 01-2866323
Fax 01-2864918

*Chaplain:* Rev Steven Kwon

**Faith and Family Centre**
Dal Riada House,
Avoca Avenue, Blackrock,
Co Dublin
Tel 01-2889317
Email
faithandfamilycentre@arcol.org

Marriage Enrichment days, Spiritual retreats, Evenings of Reflection, Family days, Faith development programmes and personal spiritual direction

*Director:* Rev Michael Mullan

## MARIANISTS (SM) Society of Mary

**Provincial Headquarters**
4425 West Pine Boulevard,
St Louis, MO 63108-2301, USA
Tel 314-533-1207

*Provincial:* Rev Martin Solma

*Archdiocese of Dublin*

**St Columba's**
Church Avenue, Ballybrack,
Co Dublin
Tel 01-2858301
Residence for religious and candidates; religious centre

*Director:* Br James Contadino
Email
jimcontadino@yahoo.co.uk

Rev Michael Reaume
Br Fred Rech
Br Gerry McAuley

**St Laurence College**
Loughlinstown, Shankill PO,
Co Dublin
Tel 01-2826930 Fax 01-2821878
Coeducational Secondary Day School

*Principal:* Mr John Carr

## MARIST FATHERS (SM) Society of Mary

*Archdiocese of Dublin*

**Marist Regional Office**
Mount St Mary's,
Dundrum Road, Milltown,
Dublin 14
Tel 01-2698100/087-9573973
Email corrigan@dna.ie

*Regional Superior*
Rev David Corrigan

**Mount St Mary's, Milltown,**
Dublin 14
Tel 01-2697322

*Superior*
Rev Brendan Bradshaw

Rev P. J. Byrne
Rev Sean Fagan
Rev Liam Forde
Rev Denis Green
Rev Frank Hennigan
Rev Des Hunt
Rev Declan Marmion

**St Brendan's Parish**
Coolock Village, Dublin 5
Tel 01-8484799

*Moderator:* Rev John Hand
*Superior:* Rev John Harrington

Rev P. G. Byrne

**Catholic University School**
89 Lower Leeson Street,
Dublin 2
Tel 01-6762586

*Headmaster:* Rev Martin Daly

*CUS Community*
Tel 01-6760247

*Superior:* Rev Martin Daly

Rev David Corrigan
Rev Tony Malone

**Chanel College**
Coolock, Dublin 5
Tel 01-8480655/8480896

*Headmaster*
Mr Declan Mowlds

*Chanel Community*
Tel 01-8477133

*Superior*
Rev Kieran Butler AP
St Brendan's Parish

Rev Thomas Butler
Rev Patrick Corcorcan
Rev Ray Staunton

**St Teresa's**
Donore Avenue, Dublin 8
Tel 01-4542425/4531613

*Parish Priest*
Rev Edwin McCallion

Rev Tom Dalzell
Rev Bobby Kelly CC
Rev Sean McArdle CC

*Archdiocese of Armagh*

**Cerdon**
Marist Fathers, St Mary's Road,
Dundalk, Co Louth
Tel 042-9334019

*Superior:* Rev Kevin Cooney

Rev Jim Johnston
Rev James McElroy
Rev Joseph McKenna
Rev Michael Maher
Rev Patrick Meehan
Rev John Mulligan

**St Mary's College**
Dundalk, Co Louth
Tel 042-9339984

*Principal:* Mr Con McGinley

**Holy Family Parish**
Parochial House,
Dundalk, Co Louth
Tel 042-9336301

*Superior*
Rev Jimmy O'Connell Adm

Rev Frank Corry
Rev Paddy Stanley

*Marist Fathers elsewhere in Ireland*

*Armagh*
Rev Barney King CC
Glassdrummond, Crossmaglen, Newry, Co Down

*Dublin*
Rev Tom Dooley CC,
4 Greenmount Road, Terenure

*Replacement Army Chaplain*
Rev Tom Tuohy

*Parish in Kildare & Leighlin*
Rev Tom Bambrick CC,
Railway Road, Muinebheag, Co Carlow

*Tuam*
Rev Joseph Jennings CC,
Inisheer Island, Aran Islands, Co Galway

*Ardagh & Clonmacnois*
Rev Tim Kenny
Fermoyle, Lanesboro, Co Longord

*Marist Fathers outside Ireland*

Rev Aidan Carvill, Australia
Rev Eddie Duffy, London
Rev Larry Duffy, Rome
Rev John Hannan,Rome
Rev Laurence Hannan, Fiji
Rev Niall Kernan, Solomon Islands

Rev Patrick Muckian, Philippines
Rev Paddy O'Hare, Japan
Archbishop Adrian Smith, Honiara, Solomon Islands
Rev Paul Walsh, London
Rev Martin McAnaney, Paris
Rev Roger McCarrick, Fiji
Rev Seamus McMahon, Australia
Rev Cormac McNamara, Mexico
Rev Rory Mulligan, Norway
Rev Joe Rooney, England
Rev Jim Ross, Fiji
Rev Tom Stokes, USA

## MILL HILL MISSIONARIES (MHM)

*Archdiocese of Dublin*

**St Joseph's House**
50 Orwell Park,
Rathgar, Dublin 6
Tel 01-4127700
Email josephmhm@eircom.net

*Regional Superior*
Rev Michael Corcoran
Tel 01-4127773/4127735/ 086-2239051
Email millhillregional@eircom.net

*Rector:* Rev Patrick Molloy
*Vice Rector*
Rev Patrick O'Connell
*Bursar:* Rev Patrick Murray
Email millhill@iol.ie

Rev Patrick L. Bracken
Rev James Dolan
Rev Jeremiah Doona
Rev Matthew Dunne
Rev Lawrence English
Rev Christopher Fox
Rev Terence Gogarty
Rev Denis Hartnett
Rev Bartholomew Hayes
Rev Ray Hogan
Rev Joseph Jones
Rev Paddy Neville
Rev Sean O'Brien
Rev Christopher O'Connor
Rev Kevin Reynolds
Rev Patrick J. Ryan
Rev John Slater
Rev Joseph O. Whelan
Rev Joseph P. Whelan

*Diocese of Down & Connor*

**St Mary's Parish**
25 Marquis Street,
Belfast BT1 1JJ
Tel 028-90320482

Rev James A. Boyle Adm
Rev John Nevin
Rev Jim O'Donoghue

*Diocese of Ossory*

**St Joseph's**
Mill Hill Missionaries,
Waterford Road, Kilkenny
Tel 056-7721482
Fax 056-7751490

*Rector and Editor of Advocate:* Rev Jim O'Connell
Email jimocmhm@eircom.net
*Organising Secretary*
Rev Maurice Crean

Rev Donal Harney
Rev Maurice McGill
Rev Fachtna Staunton
Email mcreanmhm@eircom.net

*Elsewhere in Ireland*

Rev Noel Hanrahan
Rev Thomas Keogan
Rev Hugh Lee
Rev Roger McGorty
Rev Anthony Murphy
Rev Kevin O'Rourke
Rev Kevin Reynolds
Rev Thomas Sinnott

*Generalate*

**Mill Hill Missionaries**
1 Colby Gardens,
Cookham Road,
Maidenhead SL6 7GZ, England
Tel +44-1628-588401

*Superior General*
Very Rev Anthony Chantry

## MISSIONARIES OF AFRICA (White Fathers)

Province of Europe
Irish Sector

*Archdiocese of Dublin*

**Provincialate**
Cypress Grove Road,
Templeogue, Dublin 6W
Tel 01-4055263 (House)
Tel 01-4992346 (Delegate Superior)
Tel 01-4992344 (Treasurer)
Email provirl@indigo.ie

*Delegate Superior*
Rev P. J. Cassidy
*Provincial Treasurer*
Rev Neil Loughrey

**Cypress Grove**
Templeogue, Dublin 6W
Tel 01-4055263/4055264
Tel 01-4055526 (Promotion)
Email provirl@indigo.ie
House of promotion/retired priests and brothers/studies

*Superior:* Vacant
*Promotion Director:* Vacant
*Mite Boxes:* Br Tim Murphy

Rev Thomas Bradley
Rev James Fitzpatrick
Rev Eugene Lewis
Rev Pierre Simson

*Working in Provinces other than Africa*

Rev James Greene
Br Raymond Leggett
Rev Michael O'Sullivan
Rev Charles Timoney

*Working in Dioceses in Ireland*

Rev James Browne

## MISSIONARIES OF THE SACRED HEART (MSC)

The Missionaries of the Sacred Heart is a congregation of 16 provinces. Members of the Irish Province work in England, USA, South Africa, Venezuela and Russia.

*Archdiocese of Dublin*

**Provincialate**
65 Terenure Road West,
Dublin 6W
Tel 01-4906622
Fax 01-4920148

*Provincial Leader*
Rev Joseph McGee

**Woodview House**
Mount Merrion Avenue,
Blackrock, Co Dublin
Tel 01-2881644 (community)

*Leader:* Rev David Smith

Rev Daniel Cleary
Rev James Corbally
Rev Joseph Falloon
Rev Desmond Farren
Rev John McCarthy
Rev Kevin McNamara
Rev Martin McNamara
Rev Liam O'Brien
Rev Tadhg Ó Dálaigh
Rev John O'Mahony
Rev John O'Sullivan
Rev Patrick Sheehan
Rev Greard Thornton

**Sacred Heart Parish**
Killinarden, Tallaght,
Dublin 24
Tel 01-4522251

Rev Manus Ferry PP
Rev John Finn

*Diocese of Cork & Ross*

**MSC Mission Support Centre**
PO Box 23,
Western Road, Cork
Tel 021-4545704
Fax 021-4343587
www.mscireland.com

Rev Michael O'Connell

**Western Road**
Cork
Tel 021-4804120
Fax 021-4543823

*Leader:* Rev John Fitzgerald
*Parish Priest*
Rev John Fitzgerald

Rev Charles Conroy
Rev John Kevin Fleming
Rev Tim Gleeson
Br Donal Hallissey
Rev Donncha Mac Carthaigh
Rev Jim Mannix
Rev Donal McCarthy
Rev Michael O'Connell
Rev Patrick Walsh
Rev Michael Whelan

**Carrignavar,**
Co Cork
Tel 021-4884044

*Leader:* Rev Dan O'Connor

Rev Patrick Breen
Rev Christopher Coleman
Rev William Fleming
Rev Sean Horgan
Rev Terence O'Brien
Rev Liam O'Callaghan
Rev Daniel O'Neill

**Coláiste an Chroí Naofa**
Carraig na Bhfear,
Co Chorcaí
Tel 021-4884104
Secondary School

**Myross Wood Retreat House**
Leap, Skibbereen,
Co Cork
Tel 028-33118
Fax 028-33793

*Leader & Director*
Rev Michael Curran

Rev Michael Crowley
Rev Timothy Cullinane
Rev Dominic Duffy
Rev Brendan Hanley
Rev Thomas Mulcahy
Rev Daniel O'Brien

**Castlehaven Parish**
Parish House,
Union Hall, Skibbereen,
Co Cork
Tel 028-34940

*Parish Priest*
Rev Patrick Courtney PP

**Leap-Glandore Parish**
Parish House, Leap,
Skibbereen,
Co Cork
Tel 028-33177

*Parish Priest*
Áth Pádraig Ó Súilleabháin PP

*Diocese of Galway*

**'Croí Nua'**
Rosary Lane,
Taylor's Hill,
Galway
Tel 091-520960
Fax 091-521168

*Leader*
Rev Michael Screene

Rev Eamon Donohoe
Rev Patrick Kelly
Rev Michael Smyth
Rev Augustine O'Brien

**Parish of the Resurrection**
Ballinfoyle,
Headford Road,
Galway
Tel 091-762883

*Parish Priest*
Rev Kevin Blade PP

Rev Thomas Plower

## NORBERTINE CANONS (OPraem)

*Diocese of Kilmore*

**Abbey of the Most Holy Trinity and St Norbert**
Kilnacrott,
Ballyjamesduff, Co Cavan
Tel 049-8544416
Fax 049-8544909
Email kilnacrottabbeytrust@eircom.net

*Prior:* Rt Rev Gerard Cusack

Rev Paul Madden
Rev Oliver Martin
Rev Kilian Mitchell
Br Kevin O'Brien
Rt Rev Kevin Smith
Rev Terry Smyth

*Priests working elsewhere in Ireland*
Rev Joseph O'Donohoe
Rev Pat Reilly

## OBLATES OF MARY IMMACULATE (OMI)

*Archdiocese of Dublin*

**Provincial Residence**
Oblates of Mary Immaculate
House of Retreat,
Tyrconnell Road, Inchicore,
Dublin 8
Tel 01-4541160/4541161
Fax 01-4541138
Email omisec@eircom.net

*Provincial*
Very Rev William Fitzpatrick
*Provincial Treasurer*
Rev Anthony Clancy

**Oblate House of Retreat**
Inchicore, Dublin 8
Tel 01-4534408/4541805
Fax 01-4543466

*Superior:* Rev Anthony Clancy
*Moderator of Pastoral Area of Inchicore/Bluebell*
Very Rev Michael O'Connor

Rev Paul Byrne
Rev Edward Carolan
Rev Patrick Carolan
Rev Gerard Clenaghan
Rev Eugene Clerkin
Br John Delaney
Br Francis Flanagan
Br Patrick Flanagan
Rev Michael Guckian
Rev Richard Haslam
Rev Eoghan Haughey
Rev James Hyland
Rev Sean Hynes
Br William Kelly
Rev Gerard Kenny
Rev Peter McCluskey
Rev Sean McDermott
Rev Vincent Mulligan
Rev John Murphy
Rev Denis O'Connell
Rev Kevin O'Connor
Rev Desmond O'Donnell
Rev William O'Donovan
Rev Joseph O'Melia
Rev John Poole
Rev Eamon Reilly
Rev Thomas Scully

**170 Merrion Road,**
Ballsbridge, Dublin 4
Tel 01-2693658 Fax 01-2600597

Rev Charles O'Connor
Rev Conor Murphy

**Oblate Scholasticate**
St Anne's, Goldenbridge Walk,
Inchicore, Dublin 8
Tel 01-4540841/4542955
Fax 01-4731903

Rev Peter Clucas
Rev Michael Hughes
Rev Thomas McCabe
Rev Kevin McLaughlin

**Inchicore**
St Michael's Parish
52a Bulfin Road,
Inchicore, Dublin 8
Tel 01-4531660 Fax 01-4548191

Rev Bernard Halpin
Rev L. McDermott
Rev D. Mills
Br M. Moore

**Bluebell Parish**
Our Lady of the Wayside
118 Naas Road,
Bluebell, Dublin 12
Tel 01-4501040
olowbluebell@oceanfree.net

Very Rev Tomas Koscinski
Rev R. Warren

**Darndale Parish**
The Presbytery,
Darndale, Dublin 17
Tel 01-8474547
Fax 01-8479295
Email omiddale@eircom.net

*Superior & Parish Priest*
Very Rev Leo Philomin PP

Rev Peter Daly CC
Rev Edward Quinn CC

*Archdiocese of Tuam*

**The Presbytery,**
Glenisland, Castlebar,
Co Mayo
Tel 085-1086639
Email glenislandcc@eircom.net

Rev Martin O'Keeffe

*Diocese of Kerry*

**Department of Chaplaincy,**
Tralee General Hospital,
Tralee, Co Kerry
Tel 066-7126222

Rev Edward Barrett

## PALLOTTINES (SAC) Society of the Catholic Apostolate

The Pallottine houses in Ireland and Britain are united in the Irish Province, as are the houses in Kenya, Tanzania, Rome, Argentina and the USA.

*Archdiocese of Dublin*

**Provincial House**
'Homestead', Sandyford Road,
Dundrum, Dublin 16
Tel 01-2956180/2954170
Email
motherofdivinelove@gmail.com

*Provincial*
Very Rev Jeremiah Murphy
*Rector:* Rev Michael Irwin
Email mirwin99@eircom.net
*Provincial Bursar/Secretary for Missions/Vice Provincial*
Rev John Kelly
Email
pallbursar@oceanfree.net
*Director of Formation*
Rev Michael Irwin
*Provincial Secretary*
Rev John O'Connor

Rev John Coen
Rev John Howlett
Rev Michael Kiely
Rev Donal McCarthy *(Archivist)*
Rev Ned O'Brien
Rev Louis Sisti
Br Tony Doherty

*Attached to Provincial House*
Rev Patrick Murray,
Droum, Gleinbeigh,
Co Kerry

**St Anne's**
Shankill, Co Dublin
Rev John O'Connor PP
*(Provincial Secretary)*
St Benin's, Dublin Road,
Shankill, Co Dublin
Tel 01-2824425

Rev Michael O'Dwyer CC
Rev Eamonn Monson CC
St Benin's, Dublin Road,
Shankill, Co Dublin
Tel 01-2824381

**St Patrick's**
Corduff, Blanchardstown,
Dublin 15
Tel 01-8213596/8215930

Rev Liam McClarey PP
Rev Joseph McLoughlin CC

*Archdiocese of Cashel and Diocese of Emly*

**Pallottine College**
Thurles, Co Tipperary
Tel 0504-21202

*Rector:* Rev Emmet O'Hara

Rev Patrick Dwyer
Rev John Egan
Rev Roger Rafter
Rev John Bergin
Rev Matthew Shanka
Rev Phil Barry
Rev William Hanly
Rev Edmund Ryan

*Attached to Pallottine College*
Rev Vincent Kelly
18 Slivercourt,
Silversprings, Cork
Rev Joseph Campion
Castlecomer, Co Kilkenny

## PASSIONISTS (CP) Congregation of the Passion

Province of St Patrick: houses in Ireland, Scotland and Paris; missions in Africa.

*Archdiocese of Dublin*

**St Paul's Retreat**
Mount Argus, Dublin 6W
Tel 01-4992000 Fax 01-4992001
Email
passionistsmtargus@eircom.net
Provincial Office
Tel 01-4992050 Fax 01-4992055
passionistprov@eircom.net

*Provincial:* Rev Pat Duffy
*Superior:* Rev Bernard Lowe

Rev Kenneth Brady
Br Martin Denny
Rev Ralph Egan
Rev Ambrose Fay
Rev Frank Keevins
Rev Anselm Keleghan
Rev Joseph Kennedy
Rev Brian Mulcahy
Br Vincent McCaughey
Rev Brendan McDermott
Rev Sylvius McGaughey
Rev Brendan McKeever
Rev Denis McLoughlin
Rev Nicholas O'Grady
Rev Patrick Rogers
Rev James Sheridan
Rev Patrick Sheridan
Rev Ignatius Waters

Applications for missions and retreats to Rev Superior of any of our local Communities

*Diocese of Clogher*

**St Gabriel's Retreat**
The Graan, Enniskillen,
Co Fermanagh
Tel 028-66322272
Fax 028-66325201

*Superior:* Rev Brian D'Arcy
*Bursar:* Rev Anthony O'Leary

Fr Victor Donnelly
Rev Marius Donnelly
Br Mark O'Reilly

*Diocese of Down & Connor*

**Passionist Retreat Centre**
Tobar Mhuire, Crossgar,
Co Down BT30 9EA
Tel 028-44830242
Fax 028-44831382

*Superior:* Rev John Friel

Fr Ephrem Blake
Fr Mel Byrne
Fr Myles Kavanagh
Fr Tom Scanlon

**Holy Cross Retreat**
Ardoyne, Belfast BT14 7GE
Tel 028-90748231
Fax 028-90740340

*Superior:* Rev Gary Donegan
*Bursar:* Rev Casimir Haran

Rev John Craven
Rev Charles Cross
Rev Salvian Maguire

*Scotland*

**St Mungo's Retreat**
52 Parson Street,
Glasgow G4 ORX, Scotland
Tel 141-552-1823
Fax 141-553-1838

**St Gabriel's Presbytery**
Westloan, Prestonpans
EH32 9JX, Scotland
Tel 1875-810052
Fax 1875-814974

*France*

**St Joseph's Church**
50 Avenue Hoche, 75008 Paris
Tel 33-1-42272856
Fax 33-1-42278649

*Botswana*

**Passionist Community**
Forest Hill, PO Box 1216
Gaborone
Tel 267-3904382
Fax 267-3951693

*Republic of South Africa*

**Passionist Community**
PO Box 1395, Wingate 0153,
Republic of South Africa
Tel 27-11-3161852
Fax 27-11-3163763

## REDEMPTORISTS (CSSR) Congregation of the Most Holy Redeemer

The Irish Province of the Redemptorists is a complete province, with one dependent Vice-Province in Brazil, fifteen other members assigned to the Province of CEBU /Philippines and one member assigned to the Province of Bangalore, India.

*Archdiocese of Dublin*

**Liguori House**
75 Orwell Road, Dublin 6
Tel 01-4067100 Fax 01-4922654
provincial@redemptorists.ie
Provincial administration

*Provincial*
Rev Michael G. Kelleher
*Provincial Vicar*
Rev Brendan O'Rourke
*2nd Provincial Consultor*
Rev Peter Burns
*Provincial Treasurer*
Mr Michael Dangerfield

*Secretary to the Provincial*
Ms Brid Raleigh
*Designated Officer, Child Safeguarding:* Mr Phil Mortell
Tel 061-327184/087-2252415
*Delegate for the Proclamation of the Word*
Rev Ciarán O'Callaghan
*Youth/Young Adult Ministry contact person*
Rev Noel Kehoe
Tel 021-4358800

*Human Resources Delegate*
Mr Phil Mortell

**Marianella/Liguori House**
75 Orwell Road, Dublin 6
Tel 01-4067100 Fax 01-4929635
Mission house and seminary

*Superior:* Rev Con J. Casey
*Vicar-Superior & Formator*
Rev Ciarán O'Callaghan

Rev John Casey
Rev Michael Condon
Rev John F. Corbett
Rev Flannan Daffy
Rev Peter Flannery
Br Nicholas Healy
Rev Thomas Hogan
Rev John Keeling
Rev Michael Kelleher
Rev Patrick Kelly Jnr
Rv Patrick Horgan
Rev Patrick Howell
Rev Brendan McConvery
Br Anthony McCrave
Rev Robert McNamara
Rev Gerard Moloney
Rev Pat O'Connell
Rev Denis O'Connor
Br Jarlath O'Neill
Rev Alexander Reid
Rev Martin Ryan
Rev Paud Sheils
Rev James Stanley
Rev George Wadding

**Most Holy Sacrament Parish**
Cherry Orchard, Dublin 10
Tel 01-6267930

*Co-ordinator*
Rev Gerry O'Connor
Rev Patrick Reynolds PP
Rev Seán Duggan CC

**Redemptorist Communications**
75 Orwell Road,
Dublin 6
Tel 01-4922488

*Editor:* Rev Gerard Moloney

**Ballyfermot Assumption Parish**
197 Kylemore Road,
Ballyfermot, Dublin 10
Tel 01-6264789

Rev Richard Delahunty PP & Coordinator
Rev Cornelius Kenneally CC
Winifred Pauly CC

*Archdiocese of Armagh*

**St Joseph's**
Dundalk, Co Louth
Tel 042-9334042/9334762
Fax 042-9330893
Mission house and parish

*Superior & PP*
Rev Michael Cusack
*Vicar-Superior*
Rev Eamonn Hoey

Rev Seán Bennett
Rev Peter Burns
Rev Finbarr Connolly
Rev Cathal Cumiskey
Rev Michael Dempsey
Br Patrick Doherty
Rev Louis Eustace
Rev Laurence Gallagher
Rev Patrick Kelly Snr
Rev Denis Luddy
Rev Clement MacManuis
Rev John McAlinden
Br Dermot McDonagh
Rev Brian McGrath
Rev Anthony Mulvey
Rev Joseph Naughton
Rev Tony Rice
Rev Ned Rocks
Rev Patrick Sugrue
Rev Richard Tobin

*Diocese of Clonfert*

**St Patrick's**
Esker, Athenry, Co Galway
Tel 091-844549 Fax 091-845698
Mission house, retreat house and Youth Village

*Superior*
Rev Brendan O'Rourke
*Vicar Superior*
Rev Patrick O'Keeffe

Rev James Buckley
Rev Thomas Byrne
Br James Casey
Rev Séamus Devitt
Rev Patrick Egan
Rev Anthony Flannery
Rev Brian Foley
Br Augustine Forrie
Rev Michael Heagney
Rev Philip Hearty
Rev Vincent Kavanagh
Rev John Long
Rev Edward Lynch
Rev Richard McMahon
Rev Dermot O'Connor
Rev Michael O'Flynn

*Diocese of Cork & Ross*

**Scala**
Castle Mahon House,
Blackrock, Cork
Tel 021-4358800
Fax 021-4359696
*Co-ordinator:* Rev Noel Kehoe

Rev Michael Forde
Rev John Hanna
Rev John P. O'Riordan CC
Blackrock Parish

*Diocese of Down & Connor*

**Clonard Monastery**
1 Clonard Gardens,
Belfast, BT13 2RL
Tel 028-90445950
Fax 028-90445988
Mission house

*Superior:* Rev Michael Murtagh
*Vicar:* Rev William McGettrick

Rev Michael Browne
Rev Edmond Creamer
Rev Patrick Cunning
Rev Johnny Doherty
Rev Alphonsus Doran
Rev Philip Dunlea
Br Michael Gilleece
Rev Brendan Keane
Rev Sean Keeney
Rev Barney McCahery
Rev Sean Moore
Rev Brendan Mulhall
Rev Patrick O'Donnell
Rev Gerard Reynolds
Rev Derek Ryan
Rev Paul Turley
Br Thomas Walsh
Rev Peter Ward

**St Gerard's Parish**
722 Antrim Road,
Newtownabbey,
Co Antrim BT36 7PG
Tel 028-90774833
Fax 028-90770923

*Superior & PP*
Rev Gerry Cassidy

Rev Pat McLaughlin CC

*Diocese of Limerick*

**Mount Saint Alphonsus**
Limerick
Tel 061-315099
Fax 061-315303 (Church)
Mission house

*Superior:* Rev Adrian Egan
*Vicar Superior*
Rev Seamus Enright

Rev Patrick Breen
Rev Kevin Browne
Rev Peter Byrne
Br Seamus Campion
Br John Cashman
Rev John Goode
Rev Sean Lawlor
Rev John Lucey
Rev David McNamara
Rev Joseph McLoughlin
Rev Derek Meskell
Rev James Murphy
Rev Brian Nolan
Rev James O'Connor
Rev Michael G. O'Connor
Rev John J. O'Riordáin
Rev Denis O'Sullivan
Rev Patrick O'Sullivan
Rev William Power
Rev Patrick Walsh

**St Clement's College**
Limerick
Tel 061-315878/318749 (staff)
Tel 061-310294 (students)
Fax 061-316640
Secondary School for Boys

*Principal:* Mr Vincent Foley

*Province of Cebu (Philippines)*

**PO Box 280,**
6000 Cebu City,
Philippine Islands
Tel +63-32-2553954

*Provincial*
Rev Cruzito Manding

*Province of Bangalore (India)*

**RCM,**
Chenchupet, Tenali, A.P.,
India 522 202
Tel +91-8644-223382

Rev Martin Cushnan

*Vice-Province of Fortaleza (Brazil)*

**Missionarios Redentoristas**
Caixa Postal 85
60,001-970 Fortaleza
Est. do Ceara, Brazil
Tel +55-8532232016

*Vice-Provincial*
Rev Eridian Gonçalves de Lima

*Mission in Luxembourg*

**European Parish**
Communauté Des
Rédemptoristes,
32, Rue Des Capucins,
L-1313 Luxembourg
Tel +352-224880

Rev Eamonn Breslin

*Mission in Rome*

**Via Merulana 31**
CP 2458, 00185 Rome, Italy
Tel +39-06-494901
Rev Martin McKeever
*(President, Alphonsian Academy)*
Rev Seán Cannon
*(Alphonsian Academy)*
Rev Raphael Gallagher
*(Alphonsian Academy)*

*Mission in Siberia*

**Redemptorysci**
Box 878, 650099 Kemerovo,
Sibir, Russia
Tel +7-3846-699103

Rev Anthony Branagan

*Mission in Mozambique/ Malawi*

Rev Brian Holmes
Rev John Bermingham
c/o Provincial

## ROSMINIANS (IC) Institute of Charity

Irish Province

*Archdiocese of Dublin*

**Clonturk House**
Ormond Road,
Drumcondra, Dublin 9
Tel 01-6877014

*Provincial:* Rev David Myers
*Vocations Director*
Rev James Browne
*Rector:* Rev Matt Gaffney

Rev Gerald Cunningham
Br Eamon Fitzpatrick
Rev Tom Griffin
Rev Thomas Hubbart
Br Jim Kane
Rev John Mullen
Rev Terence O'Donnell
Rev Frank Quinn
Rev Edmund Spillane (Nursing Home)
Rev William Stuart
Rev Donal Sullivan
Rev Sean Walsh

*Archdiocese of Armagh*

**Faughart Parish**
St Brigid's, Kilcurry,
Dundalk, Co Louth
Tel 042-9334410

*Parish Priest*
Very Rev Christopher McElwee

Rev Bernard Hughes
Rev James Pollock

*Diocese of Cork & Ross*

**St Patrick's**
Upton, Innishannon, Co Cork
Residential centre for adults with learning disabilities
Tel 021-4776268/4776923
Fax 021-4776268

Rev Matthew Corcoran
Rev Seamus McKenna
Rev Polachan Thettayil

*Diocese of Waterford & Lismore*

**St Joseph's**
Doire na hAbhann, Tickincar,
Clonmel, Co Tipperary
Tel 052-26914 Fax 052-26915

Rev Tom Coffey
Rev P. J. Fegan
Rev Thomas Marley

**Rosminian House of Prayer**
Glencomeragh House,
Kilsheelan, Co Tipperary
Tel 052-33181

*Rector:* Rev Michael Melican

Rev Pat Pierce

**St Oliver Plunkett's Parish**
Cooleens, Clonmel,
Co Tipperary
Tel 052-61225679

Rev Michael Hegarty PP
Rev Vinod Kurian Thennatil CC

*Enquiries concerning the missions to:* Rev Frank Quinn
Clonturk House,
Ormond Road,
Drumcondra, Dublin 9

## SACRED HEART FATHERS (SCJ) Congregation of the Priests of the Sacred Heart of Jesus

British-Irish Province

*Archdiocese of Dublin*

**Sacred Heart Fathers**
Fairfield, 66 Inchicore Road, Dublin 8
Tel 01-4538655
Email scjdublin@eircom.net

*Superior & Formation Director*
Rev John Kelly
*Promotions Director*
Rev James Lawless

Rev Owen Wynne
Rev Anselmus Inharjanto
Br Francis Murphy

**Ardlea Parish**
St John Vianney
Ardlea Road, Dublin 5
Tel 01-8474123/8474173
Email jvianney@indigo.ie

Rev Robert Mann *(Moderator)*
Rev David Marsden
Rev Liam Rooney
Rev Marian Szalwa

## ST COLUMBAN'S MISSIONARY SOCIETY (SSC)

Maynooth Mission to China – Ireland

*Superior General*
Rev Thomas Muphy
Suite 504, Tower 1, Silvercord, 30 Canton Road Tst, Kowloon, Hong Kong SAR
Email sg@columbangeneralcouncil.com
*Vicar General:* Rev Trevor Trotter
Email trevor@columbangeneralcouncil.com
*Councillors:* Rev John Burger
Email John@columbangeneralcouncil.com
Rev Eamon Sheridan
Email eamon@columbangeneralcouncil.com
*Procurator General*
Padhraic O'Loughlin
Collegio San Colombano, Corso Trieste 57, 00198 Roma
Email procol.roma@gmail.com
*Bursar General:* Rev Otto Imholte
St Columban's Dalgan Park, Navan, Co Meath
Tel 046-9021525
Email bursargeneral@columban.com
*Columban Intercom Editor*
Rev John Colgan
St Columban's Dalgan Park, Navan, Co Meath
Tel 046-9021525
Email intercom@columban.com
*Research on JPIC Priorities*
Rev Sean McDonagh
St Columban's Dalgan Park, Navan, Co Meath
Tel 046-9021525
Email seanmcdonagh10@gmail.com
*Research on Mission and Culture:* Rev Sean Dwan
48 Princess Margaret Road, Homantin, Kowloon, Hong Kong SAR

*Archdiocese of Dublin*

**St Columban's**
Grange Road, Donaghmede, Dublin 13
Tel 01-8476647

Rev Patrick Crowley
Rev Aidan Larkin
Email info@columbancompanions.ie
*Columban Lay Missionary Co-ordinator:* Ms Serafina Ranadi
Email serafinarv@gmail.com

**St Columban's**
67-68 Castle Dawson, Rathcoffey Road, Maynooth, Co Kildare
Tel 01-6286036
Rev William Curry
*(Priest in charge)*

**St Joseph's**
Balcurris, Dublin 11
Tel 01-8423865
Rev Val Kyne PP
Rev John Chute
Rev Gerald French

*Diocese of Cork & Ross*

No. 2 Presbytery, Our Lady Crowned Church, Mayfield Upper, Cork
Tel 021-4568610
Rev Pat O'Herlihy

*Diocese of Meath*

**St Columban's**
Dalgan Park, Navan, Co Meath
Tel 046-9021525
Email regionaldirector@columban.ie

*Regional Director*
Rev Donal Hogan
*Regional Vice-Director*
Rev Patrick Raleigh
Email patraleigh@columban.com
*Regional Secretary*
Celine Tuite
Fax 046-9022799

***Regional Council***
Rev Frank Carr
Rev Noel Daly
Rev Padraig O'Donovan

***Regional Offices***
Fax 046-9071297
Email missionoffice@columban.com
*Regional Bursar*
Rev David Kenneally
Email regionalbursar@columban.ie
*Assistant Bursar*
Rev Desmond Quinn
*Mission Outreach Co-ordinator*
Ms Claire Carey
Email info@columbancompanions.ie
*Society Archivist*
Rev Michael Molloy
*Communications Co-ordinator*
Rev Malachy Smyth
*Justice & Peace/Ongoing Education:* Rev Patrick Raleigh
*Mission Education*
Michael O'Sullivan
*Lay Missionary Contact Person*
Angie Escarsa
*Vocations Contact Person*
Rev Padraig O'Donovan
*Regional Newsletter*
Rev Michael A. Duffy
*Office Manager:* Rev Noel Daly
*Far East Editor:* Rev Cyril Lovett
*Website Editor*
Rev Michael O'Sullivan
www.columban.com
*Personnel Counsellor*
Rev Patrick J. Smyth
*Board of Reconciliation*
Rev Gerald French
*Alcoholic Advisory Board*
Rev Michael A. Duffy,
Rev Valentine Kyne
*Apostolic Work Liaison*
Rev Peadar O'Loughlin
*Columban History*
Rev Neil Collins
*Librarian*
Rev Patrick McManus
*Staff*
Rev Cornelius K. Campion
Rev Sean A. Dunne
Rev Seamus Egan
Rev Brendan MacHale

**St Columban's**
Dalgan Park, Navan, Co Meath
Tel 046-9021525
Fax 046-9022799

*House Superior*
Rev Peter O'Neill
*Bursar:* Rev Frank Carr
Fax 046-9098214
*Residents*
Rev Sean Brazil
Rev Frank Carr
Rev Charles Coulter
Rev Noel Daly
Rev Joseph Dolan
Rev Noel Doyle
Rev Michael Duffy
Rev Seamus Egan
Rev Brendan Fahey
Rev Patrick Fahey
Rev Kevin Fleming
Rev John Gilmore
Rev Malachy Hanratty
Rev Donal Hogan
Rev David Kenneally
Rev Oliver Kennedy
Rev Cyril Lovett
Rev Charles Meagher
Rev Martin Murphy
Rev Brendan Murray
Rev Brendan MacHale
Rev Sean McDonagh
Rev Joseph McDonnell
Rev Sean McGrath
Rev Austin McGuinness
Rev Patrick McManus
Rev Padraig O'Donovan
Rev Francis O'Kelly
Rev Owen O'Leary
Rev Peadar O'Loughlin
Rev Desmond Quinn
Rev Patrick Raleigh
Rev Matthew Reilly
Rev Eugene Ryan
Rev Malachy Smyth
Rev Patrick J. Smyth
Rev Bernard Steed

**St Columban's Retirement Home**
Dalgan Park, Navan, Co Meath
Tel 046-9021525

*Director*
Rev Bernard Mulkerins

*Staff*
Rev Sean Brazil
Rev Brendan Fahey
Rev Brendan Murray

*Residents*
Rev Dan Baragry
Rev Eamonn Byrne
Rev Daniel Canniffe
Rev Leo Clarke
Rev Patrick Clarke
Rev Sean A. Dunne
Rev Brendan Fahey
Rev John Vincent Gallagher
Rev Joseph Gallagher
Rev James Gavigan
Rev Eugene Griffin
Rev Frederick Hanson
Rev Michael Healy
Rev Patrick Healy
Rev Sean Holloway
Rev Mark Kavanagh
Rev Sean McGrath
Rev Gerald McNicholas
Rev Francis Mannion
Rev Patrick Meehan
Rev John Molloy
Rev Francis Mullany
Rev Cyril Murphy
Rev Donal O'Farrell
Rev Thomas Parker
Rev Geoffrey Revatto
Rev Thomas Revatto
Rev Sean Ryle
Rev Sean Rainey
Rev Michael Scully
Rev Patrick Scully
Rev James Sheehy
Rev Joseph Shiels
Rev Patrick Smyth
Rev Terence Twohig
Rev David Wall
Rev Vincent Walsh

*Vocations & Promotion Work/Mission Awareness*
Rev Bredan Hoban
Rev Joseph McDonnell
Rev Padraig O'Donovan
Rev Pat O'Herlihy
Rev Bernard Steed
Angie Escarsa LM

*Priests on Special Work*
Rev Donal N. Bennett (Philippine Chaplaincy)
Rev Joseph Cahill (Designated Officer)
Rev P. Aloysius Connaughton (Myanmar/Burma)
Rev Patrick Donohoe (Columban Sisters, Magheramore, Co Wicklow)
Rev Patrick G. Dooher (Director, Mission Institute)
Rev Owen Doyle (Chaplain, St John of God, Louth)
Rev John Gilmore (Immigration Apostolate)
Rev E. Norman Jennings
Rev Sean McDonagh (Research JPIC)
Rev Austin McGuinness (Chaplain, St Joseph's, Trim)
Rev Neil Magill (Myanmar/Burma)
Rev Patrick J. Smyth (Retreat Work)

*Priests on diocesan work in Ireland*
Rev Eamon Conaty (Elphin)
Rev Sean Connaughton (Meath)
Rev Patrick Conway (Killaloe)
Rev Daniel Fitzgerald (Killaloe)
Rev Kevin Fleming (Meath)
Rev John Hickey (Clonfert)
Rev Michael Irwin (Limerick)
Rev John McEvoy (Meath)
Rev Jeremiah Murphy (Meath)
Rev Kevin O'Boyle (Killaloe)
Rev Patrick O'Conor (Ferns)
Rev Michael O'Loughlin (Killaloe)
Rev Seamus O'Neill (Derry)

*Columban Lay Missionaries working in Ireland*
Gracia Kibad
Angie Escarsa (Co-ordinator)
Lorelei Ocaya
Lenette Toledo
*All from the Philippines*

## ST PATRICK'S MISSIONARY SOCIETY (SPS)

*Diocese of Kildare & Leighlin*

**St Patrick's**
Kiltegan, Co Wicklow
Tel 059-6473600
Fax 059-6473622
*Society Leader*
Rev Seamus O'Neill
*Assistant Society Leader*
Rev David Walsh
*Councillors*
Rev Thomas McDonnell
Rev Tom O'Connor
Fax *(Society Leader & Council)* 059-6473644
Email spsgen@iol.ie
*Society Justice Co-ordinator*
Mr Joseph Murray
*House Leader – Rome*
Rev Paddy O'Reilly
*Bursar General*
Rev Denis O'Rourke
*Regional Leader for Ireland*
Rev Liam Blayney
*Assistant Regional Leader*
Rev Joseph Cantwell
Tel 059-6473680
Fax 059-6473623
Email spsireland@iol.ie
*Kiltegan Leader*
Rev Patrick Connolly
*Director of Promotion*
Rev William Fulton
Fax 059-6473622
Email spsoff@iol.ie
*Office Manager*
Ms Joanne Fortune
*Kiltegan House Manager*
Ms Marie Hyland
*Editor, Africa*
Rev Tim Redmond
Email africa@spms.org
*Slí an Chroí*
Rev Seamus Whitney
Tel 059-6473488
Rev Michael Kane

Rev Jim Birmingham
Rev Eugene Bree
Rev Alfie Byrne
Rev Tom Cafferty
Rev John P. Carroll
Rev Stan Connolly
Rev Michael Conroy
Rev Dermot Connolly
Rev Tony Cronin
Rev Con Cronin
Rev Sean Dillon
Rev Martin Dwan
Rev Jim English
Rev Padraig Flanagan
Rev Leonard Forristal
Rev Michael Golden
Rev Ned Grace
Rev John Jones
Rev Andy Keating
Rev Michael Kelly
Rev Thomas Kiggins
Rev James McAuliffe
Rev Henry McCarney
Rev Francis McElhatton
Rev Des McKeever
Rev Sean McTiernan
Rev P. J. Melican
Rev Patrick Moore
Rev Nicholas Motherway
Rev Joseph Mulcahy
Rev Ray Murtagh
Rev Joe O'Conor
Rev Martin O'Connell
Rev Kevin O'Doherty
Rev Bartie O'Doherty
Rev Pádraig Ó Fatharta
Rev Leo O'Sullivan
Rev Seamus Reihill
Rev Martin Reilly
Rev Noel Ryan
Rev Jack Rodgers
Rev Liam V. Scanlan
Rev Ted Smyth
Rev Donal Twomey
Rev T. T. Vaughan
Rev Nicky Walsh
Rev Seamus Whelan

*Priests on promotion work*

Rev Con Cronin
Rev Bartie O'Doherty

*Archdiocese of Dublin*

**St Patrick's**
21 Leeson Park, Dublin 6
Tel 01-4977897 Fax 01-4962812
*House Leader*
Rev Danny Gibbons

Rev Peter Coyle
Rev Donal Dorr
Rev Richard Filima
Rev Kieran Flynn
Rev Vincent MacNamara
Rev Padraig Ó Máille
Rev Denis O'Neill

*Archdiocese of Tuam*

**St Patricks**
Main Street, Knock, Co Mayo
Tel 094-9388661
*House Leader*
Rev Donald McDonagh

Rev Steve Donohoe
Rev Gerard O'Carroll

*Diocese of Cork & Ross*

**Kiltegan House**
11 Douglas Road, Cork
Tel 021-4969371
*House Leader:* Rev Jim Barry

*Diocese of Down & Connor*

**St Patrick's**
21 Old Cavehill Road, Belfast BT15 5GT
Tel 028-90778696

*Priests on special ministries*

Rev Michael Browne
Rev Joe Flynn
Rev Dermot Foley
Rev Thomas Grenham
Rev Gary Howley
Rev Patrick Kelly
Rev Michael Long
Rev Michael Rodgers
Tearmann Spirituality Centre, Brockagh, Glendalough, Co Wicklow
Tel 0404-45208
Rev Martin Smith

*Priests on temporary diocesan work*

Rev Declan Boyce
Rev John Carroll
Rev Colm Clinton
Rev Bernard Conway
Rev Eugene Drumm
Rev John Flanagan
Rev Peter Gillooly
Rev Noel Hayes
Rev Peter Hegarty
Rev John Heinhold
Rev Laurence Kearney
Rev John Kearns
Rev Michael Kelly
Rev Thomas Leahy
Rev Joseph Long
Rev Brendan McDonagh
Rev John McManus
Rev Kyran Murphy
Rev James Noonan
Rev Patrick O'Brien
Rev Thomas O'Connor
Rev Timothy O'Connor
Rev Sean O'Dowd
Rev Ciaran O'Flynn
Rev James O'Reilly
Rev James Regan
Rev Ray Reidy
Rev Martin Reilly
Rev Joseph Spillane
Rev Martin Spillane
Rev Declan Thompson

## SALESIANS (SDB)

The Irish Province includes Ireland, Malta and Tunisia.

*Archdiocese of Dublin*

**Provincialate**
Salesian House, 45 St Teresa's Road, Crumlin, Dublin 12
Tel 01-4555787 Fax 01-4558781
Email (Secretary) tdunnesdb@gmail.com

*Provincial*
Very Rev Michael Casey
Email ruanet@ireland.com
michael_casey@eircom.net

**Salesian House**
45 St Teresa's Road, Crumlin, Dublin 12
Tel 01-4555605
House of residence

*Rector:* Rev Michael Ross
*Vice-Rector*
Rev Peter Coffey CC
*Provincial Secretary*
Rev Thomas Dunne

Rev John Finnegan
Rev John Foster CC
Br Colum Maguire
Rev Florence McCarthy
Rev Michael Scott CC

**Rinaldi House**
72 Sean McDermott Street, Dublin 1
Tel 01-8363358 Fax 01-8552320
Post-Novitiate, house of formation

*Rector:* Rev Val Collier
*Vice-Rector:* Rev John Quinn

Rev Charles Cunningham
Rev Yohannes Deneke
Rev Amanuel Kidus
Rev James O'Halloran

**Don Bosco Houses**
12 Clontarf Road, Dublin 3
Tel 01-8336009/8337045

*Priest-in-Charge:* Rev Val Collier

**Our Lady of Lourdes Parish**
Seán McDermott Street, Dublin 1
Tel 01-8363554

Rev Timothy Wrenn Adm
Rev Hugh O'Donnell CC

**Salesian College**
Maynooth Road, Celbridge, Co Kildare
Tel 01-6275058/60
Fax 01-6272208
Secondary School
Tel 01-6272166/6272200

*Rector:* Rev Daniel Carroll
*Bursar:* Rev A. McEvoy

Rev Tesfay Asfaha
Br Dominic Binh
Br Paul Binh
Rev Michael Browne
Rev John Butler
Rev Daniel Colonel
Rev Pat Egan
Rev Patrick Hennessy *(Vice-Rector)*
Rev Eunan McDonnell
Br Virgaleh Weldeyhannes

*Diocese of Limerick*

**Salesian College**
Pallaskenry, Co Limerick
Tel 061-393313 Fax 061-393354
Secondary and agricultural schools
Salesian Mission Office
Tel 061-393223 Fax 061-393021

*Rector:* Very Rev Martin Loftus
*Vice-Rector & Bursar*
Rev Raymond McIntyre
*Mission Procurator*
Rev Dan Devitt

Br Patrick Coye
Rev Thomas Ingoldsby
Br Padraig McDonald
Br Thomas Sage

**Salesian House**
Milford, Castletroy, Limerick
Tel 061-330268/330914
Student hostel and parish

*Rector*
Rev Koenraad Van Gucht PP
*Vice-Rector, Bursar and Chaplain, University of Limerick:* Rev John Campion

Rev Vincent Diffley
Rev John Fagan
Rev Joseph Harrington *(Chaplain, Milford House)*
Rev John Horan *(In Charge of Spirituality Centre)*
Rev Bob Swinburne CC

*Diocese of Meath*

**Salesian House**
Warrenstown, Drumree, Co Meath
Tel 01-8259761
Community 01-8259894
Fax 01-8240298

*Rector:* Rev P. J. Nyland
*Vice-Rector:* Rev Thomas Kenny
*Bursar:* Br James O'Hare

Rev Patrick Brewster
Rev David Cahill
Br Colm Kennedy
Rev George McCaughey

*Elsewhere in Ireland*
Rev Desmond Campion *(Chaplain Naval Service, Haulbowline, Cobh, Cork)*
Rev G. Dowd *(Chaplain, Custume Barracks, Athlone)*
Rev P. J. Healy CC
162 Walkinstown Road, Dublin 12
Rev James Somers CC
Chapelizod
Rev Patrick J. Somers *(Chaplain, The Curragh, Co Kildare)*
Rev Joseph Whittle
Kilcullen Road, Dunlavin, Co Wicklow
Rev Gerard O'Neill (Chaplain, Collins Barracks, Cork)
Rev Tomasz Grzegorzewski CC
Aughrim, Carrick-on-Shannon, Co Roscommon

## SALVATORIANS (SDS)

*Archdiocese of Dublin*

**Our Lady of Victories**
Sallynoggin, Dun Laoghaire, Co Dublin
Tel 01-2854667 Fax 01-2847024
Email sallynogginparish@eircom.net

*Superior:* Rev Henry Nevins

Rev Eric Powell
Rev Liam Talbot

## SERVITES (OSM) Order of Friar Servants of Mary

*Provincial*
Rev Bernard Thorne
Servite Priory, Benburb, Co Tyrone BT71 7JZ
Northern Ireland
Tel 028-37548241

Province of the Isles

*Archdiocese of Dublin*

**Servite Priory**
St Peregrine, Kiltipper Road, Tallaght, Dublin 24
Tel 01-4517115

*Prior:* Rev Tim Flynn

Rev Jimmy Kelly *(Chaplain, Mountjoy Prison)*
Br Joe Whelan

**Servite Oratory**
Rathfarnham Shopping Centre, Dublin 14
Tel 01-4936300

*Director:* Rev Timothy M. Flynn

**Church of the Divine Word**
Marley Grange, 25-27 Hermitage Downs, Rathfarnham, Dublin 16
Tel 01-4944295/4941064
Fax 01-4941069

*Prior*
Very Rev Colm McGlynn PP

Rev Camillus McGrane CC
Rev Liam Tracey

*Archdiocese of Armagh*

**Servite Priory**
Benburb, Dungannon, Co Tyrone, BT71 7JZ
Tel 028-37548241
Tel 01861-548241/548533
Retreat, Conference Centre and youth centre

*Prior*
Very Rev Chris O'Brien

Rev Gabriel Bannon
Rev Sean Lennon
Rev Eamonn McCreave
Rev Colum McDonnell
Very Rev Raymond O'Connell
Rev Eoin O'Malley
Rev Bernard Thorne
Br Eugene Traynor

*Outside Ireland*

Br Patrick Gethins (OSM)
Curia Generalizia, Piazza S. Marcello, Al Corso 5, 00187 Roma, Italy
Tel 00396-699301

## SOCIETY OF AFRICAN MISSIONS (SMA) Societas Missionum Ad Afros

*Diocese of Cork & Ross*

**African Missions**
Provincial House
Feltrim, Blackrock Road, Cork
Tel 021-4292871
Fax 021-4292873
Email provincial@sma.ie

*Provincial*
Rev Fachtna O'Driscoll
*Vice Provincial*
Rev John Dunne
*Provincial Councillor*
Rev Damian Bresnahan

**African Missions**
Blackrock Road, Cork
Tel 021-4292871

*Superior*
Rev Colum P. O'Shea
*Vice-Superior*
Rev Edward O'Connor
*Bursar*
Rev Edward O'Connor
*Provincial Bursar*
Rev Malachy Flanagan
*Assistant Provincial Bursar*
Rev Oscar Welsh
*Provincial Archivist*
Rev Edmund M. Hogan
*Provincial Development Officer:* Rev Martin Kavanagh
*Director of Communications*
Rev Martin Kavanagh
*JPIC Director*
Rev Angelo Lafferty

Rev Liam Burke
Rev Anthony J. Butler
Rev Michael Cahill
Rev Tim Carroll
Rev John Casey
Rev John Clancy
Rev Denis Collins
Rev Bernard Cotter
Rev Michael Darcy
Br Patrick Dowd
Rev Thomas Faherty
Rev James Fegan
Br Thomas Fitzgerald
Rev Francis Furey
Rev William Ghent
Rev Hugh Harkin
Rev Jeremiah Healy
Rev James Higgins
Re Michael Igoe
Rev Patrick Jennings
Rev James Kirstein
Rev Sean Lynch
Rev Joseph Maguire
Rev Seán MacCarthy
Rev Michael McEgan
Rev Patrick McGovern
Rev H. McLoughlan
Rev Thomas Mullahy

Rev Gerard Murray
Rev Daniel Murphy
Rev Fionnbarra O'Cuilleanáin
Rev Con O'Leary
Rev Eugene O'Riordan
Rev Robert O'Regan
Rev William O'Sullivan
Rev John Quinlan
Rev Bernard J. Raymond
Rev Desmond Smith

**SMA House**
Wilton, Cork
Tel 021-4541069/4541884

*Superior:* Rev John O'Keeffe
*Bursar:* Rev Jarlath Walsh

Rev Daniel Cashman
Rev Francis Coltsmann
Rev James Conlon
Rev John Flynn
Rev William Foley
Rev Thomas Furlong
Rev Thomas Gorman
Rev Terence Gunn
Rev John Horgan
Rev William Kennedy
Rev Angelo Lafferty
Rev Liam O'Callaghan
Rev James O'Hea
Rev Denis O'Sullivan
Rev Leo Silke

**St Joseph's**
African Missions Parish
Blackrock Road, Cork
Tel 021-4293325
Email smapar@oceanfree.net

Rev Thomas Wade PP

**St Joseph's Parish**
Wilton, Cork
Tel 021-4341362
Fax 021-4343940

Rev Cormac Breathnach PP

**Coís Tíne Pastoral**
Outreach to Immigants
21 Victoria Avenue,
Cork
Tel 021-4316593
Email coistine@sma.ie

*Director:* Rev Angelo Lafferty

*Archdiocese of Dublin*

**SMA House**
82 Ranelagh Road,
Ranelagh, Dublin 6
Tel 01-4968162/3
Fax 01-4968164

*Superior:* Rev John O'Brien
*Bursar:* Rev Owen McKenna

Rev John Bowe
Rev Joseph Egan
Rev Seán Hayes
Rev Francis Meehan

**Parish of St Peter the Apostle**
Neilstown, Clondalkin,
Dublin 22
Tel 01-4573546

Very Rev Donal Toal PP
Rev Paul Monahan CC

*Also in Dublin*
Rev Sean Healy
Social Justice Ireland,
Arena House, Arena Road,
Sandyford, Dublin 18
Tel 01-2130724
www.socialjustice.ie
Rev Thomas McNamara
Religious Formation
Programme, Loretto House,
Dublin
Rev Kevin O'Gorman
St Patrick's College,
Maynooth, Co Kildare

*Diocese of Galway*

**SMA House**
Claregalway, Co Galway
Tel 091-798880
Fax 091-798879
Email smafathers@eircom.net

*Superior:* Rev Seamus Nohilly
*Bursar:* Rev Patrick Whelan

Rev Brendan Dunning
Rev Thomas Fenlon
Rev Daniel O'Neill
Rev Gerard Sweeney

*Diocese of Dromore*

**Dromatine College**
Dromantine, Newry,
Co Down BT34 1RH
Tel 028-30821224
Fax 028-30821704

*Superior:* Rev Patrick O'Rourke
*Bursar:* Rev Peter Thompson
*Leadership Team*
Rev Patrick O'Rourke and
Rev John Denvir

Rev Lee Cahill
Rev Edward Deeney
Rev Maurice Kelleher
Rev Hugh McKeown
Rev Kevin Mulhern
Rev Martin Nolan
Rev John Travers

**Dromantine Retreat and Conference Centre**
Dromatine College,
Newry, Co Down BT34 1RH
Tel 028-30821219
Fax 028-30821963
Email d.conferencecentre
@btopenworld.com
www.dromatineconference.com
*Accommodation:* 40 single en suite rooms, 30 double en suite rooms, 8 conference rooms

*Director:* Vacant

Temporary diocesan work in *Ireland*

Rev Thomas Kearney
Rev Michael Kidney
Rev Patrick Lynch
Rev John McCormack
Rev Kieran Morahan
Rev Michael Nohilly
Rev Martin O'Hare
Rev Hugh O'Kane
Rev Patrick O'Mahony
Rev Seán Ryan

*Retired in Ireland outside SMA houses*

Rev Michael Boyle
Rev Edward Casey
Rev Martin Costello
Rev Eamonn Kelly
Rev Sean Kilbane
Rev Vincent Lawless
Rev Patrick Mackle
Rev Donal O'Connor

**Church of Our Lady of the Rosary and St Patrick**
61 Blackhorse Road,
Walthamstow,
London E17 7AS, England
Tel 20-85203647

Very Rev John Brown PP

*Retired in Britain*

Rev Martin Walsh

*Rome*

**Generalate**
Via della Nocetta 111,
00164 Rome, Italy
Tel 06-6616841 Fax 06-66168490
Email smaroma@smainter.org

*Superior General*
Rev Jean-Marie Guillaume
*Anglophone Secretary*
Rev Derek Kearney
*Bursar General*
Rev Didier Eloi Lawson

*Seconded to US Province*

Rev Patrick Kelly

## SOCIETY OF ST PAUL (SSP)

The Society of St Paul in Ireland operates exclusively through the mass media.

*Archdiocese of Dublin*

**Society of St Paul**
Moyglare Road,
Maynooth, Co Kildare
Tel 01-6285933 Fax 01-6289330
Email book@stpauls.ie

*Superior:* Rev Pius Nechikattil

Rev Alex Anadam
Rev John Echavarria
Br Pio Rizzo

*Diocese of Meath*

**St Paul Book Centre**
Castle Street,
Athlone, Co Westmeath
Tel/Fax 090-6492882
Email
saintpaul_books@yahoo.com

## SONS OF DIVINE PROVIDENCE (FDP)

The Irish Foundation is part of the Missionary English-speaking Delegation of 'Mary Mother of the Church'.

*Regional Superior*
Rev Malcolm Dyer
c/o Don Orione 8, Rome, Italy
*Local Co-ordinator*
Rev Philip Kehoe
25 Lower Teddington Road,
Kingston-on-Thames, Surrey
Tel 208-9775130

*Archdiocese of Dublin*

**Sarsfield House**
Sarsfield Road,
Ballyfermot, Dublin 10
Tel 01-6266193/6266233
Fax 01-6260303
Email don-orion@clubi.ie

Rev Michael Moss
Rev John Perrotta
Email cperrotta@yahoo.com

## VINCENTIANS (CM)

Vincentian communities of the Irish Province are established in Ireland and England.

*Archdiocese of Dublin*

**Provincial Office**
St Paul's, Sybil Hill,
Raheny, Dublin 5
Tel 01-8510840/8510842
Fax 01-8510846
Email cmdublin@iol.ie
www.vincentians.ie

*Provincial:* Very Rev Brian Moore

**All Hallows Institute for Mission and Ministry**
Drumcondra, Dublin 9
Tel 01-8373745/6
Fax 01-8377642
Email info@allhallows.ie
*President*
Very Rev Patrick J. McDevitt
*Superior*
Very Rev Joseph McCann

Seminary/Pastoral Ministry/
Pastoral Leadership
Rev Desmond Beirne
Rev Eugene Curran
Rev Brian Nolan
Ministry to Priests, Missions
and Retreats
Tel 01-8373745/6

Rev Kevin Scallon

**11 Iona Drive**
Glasnevin, Dublin 9
Tel 01-8305238

*Superior*
Very Rev Stephen Monaghan

Rev Sean Farrell

**St Paul's College**
Raheny, Dublin 5
Tel 01-8314011/2 (college)
Tel 01-8318113 (community)
Fax 01-8316387
Secondary School

*Superior*
Very Rev Eamon Flanagan

Rev Simon Clyne
Rev Cornelius Curtin
Rev Michael Dunne
Rev Aidan Galvin
Rev Sean Johnston
Rev Richard McCullen
Rev James McCormack
Rev Bernard Meade
Rev Brian Mullan
Rev Brendan Steen
Rev Thomas Woods

**Phibsboro**
St Peter's, Dublin 7
Tel 01-8389708/8389841
Email vinphibs@iol.ie

*Superior*
Very Rev Paschal Scallon

Rev Joseph Cunningham
Rev Eamon Devlin
Rev Patrick Hughes
Rev John Concannon
Rev Lazarus Iwueke
Rev Mark Noonan
Rev Andrew Spelman

**St Joseph's**
44 Stillorgan Park,
Blackrock, Co Dublin
Tel 01-2886961

*Superior*
Very Rev Colm McAdam

Rev Denis Collins
Rev Patrick Collins
Rev Thomas Davitt
Rev Francis MacMorrow

**St Vincent's College**
Castleknock, Dublin 15
Tel 01-8213051
Secondary Day School for Boys

*President/Superior*
Very Rev Peter Slevin

Rev Stanislaus Brindley
Rev Roderic Crowley
Rev John Gallagher
Rev Michael McCullagh
Rev Cornelius Nwaogwugwu
Rev Eamon Raftery
Rev Henry Slowey

*Diocese of Cork & Ross*

**St Vincent's**
122 Sunday's Well Road, Cork
Tel 021-4304070/4304529
Fax 021-4300103
Email
parishoffice@corkvins.com

*Superior*
Very Rev Jack Harris PP

Rev Timothy Casey CC
Rev Aidan McGing

*Diocese of Down & Connor*

**99 Cliftonville Road**
Belfast BT14 6JQ
Tel 028-90751771
Fax 028-90740547
Email cmbelfast@ntlworld.co.uk

*Superior:* Very Rev Peter Gildea

Rev Adrian Eastwood
Rev James Rafferty

## COMMUNITIES OF RELIGIOUS BROTHERS

*In this section, details of each community's main house are given, followed by a list of the dioceses in which the community is present. For more information on houses in particular dioceses, please see the entry for the appropriate diocese.*

## ALEXIAN BROTHERS (CFA)

Anglo-Irish Province

**Regional Residence**
Churchfield, Knock, Co Mayo
Tel 094-9376996
Email alexianbros@eircom.net

*Regional Leader*
Br Barry Butler

Dublin, Tuam

## BROTHERS OF CHARITY

St Joseph's Region

**Regional Office**
Regional Administration
Kilcornan Centre,
Clarinbridge, Co Galway
Tel 091-796389/796413
Fax 091-796352
Email bronoelcorcoran@
galway.brothersofcharity.ie

*Regional Leader*
Br Noel Corcoran

Cork & Ross, Galway,
Limerick, Ossory

## CHRISTIAN BROTHERS (CFC)

European Province

**Province Centre**
Marino, Griffith Avenue,
Dublin 9

Leadership Team
*Province Leader:* Br J. K. Mullan
*Deputy Leader:* Br J. Burke

Br Edmund Garvey
Br M. O'Flaherty
Br E. Coupe
Br J. Donovan

Cashel & Emly, Dublin, Cork, Derry, Down & Connor, Ferns, Galway, Kerry, Kildare & Leighlin, Killaloe, Limerick, Meath, Ossory, Waterford & Lismore

As of the 1 September 2008, The Edmund Rice Schools Trust became Trustees of the 97 schools previously under the trusteeship of the Christian Brothers. The Company is established for the following charitable objects: to ensure and foster the advancement of education and to further the aims and purposes of Catholic Education in the Edmund Rice tradition in colleges, schools and other educational projects in Ireland owned or operated by the Company in accordance with the religion and education philosophy of the Company as stated in the Edmund Rice Schools Trust Charter, and so that they may continue to provide Catholic education in the spirit and tradition of Blessed Edmund Rice into the future for the people of Ireland.

## DE LA SALLE BROTHERS (FSC)

**Provincialate**
121 Howth Road,
Dublin 3
Tel 01-8331815
Fax 01-8339130
Email province@iol.ie

*Provincial*
Br Francis Manning

Armagh, Dublin, Tuam, Down & Connor, Kildare & Leighlin, Ossory, Waterford & Lismore

## FRANCISCAN BROTHERS (OSF)

Franciscan Brothers of the Third Order Regular

A branch of the Regular Third Order of Penance of St Francis of Asissi, with communities in East Africa and the USA as well as Ireland.

**Generalate**
Mountbellew, Co Galway
Tel 090-9679295
Fax 090-9679687
Email franciscanbrs@eircom.net

*Minister General*
Br Peter Roddy
*Assistant General*
Br Michael Burke
*Councillors*
Br Sean Conway
Br Boniface Kyalo
Br Conal Thomas
*Procurator General*
Br Conal Thomas
*Bursar General*
Br Gerald Smith
*Secretary General*
Br Conal Thomas

Dublin, Tuam, Meath

## MARIST BROTHERS (FMS)

The Marist Brothers in Ireland are part of the province of West Central Europe principally involved in education.

**Provincialate**
Sophiaweg 4
NL-6523 NJ Nijmegen
Netherlands
Email provincial@maristen.nl

*Provincial Superior*
Br Brendan Geary

Dublin, Ardagh & Clonmacnois, Killala

## PATRICIAN BROTHERS (FSP)

Brothers of St Patrick

**Delany Place**
18 Boomerang Road,
The Entrance, NSW 2261,
Australia

*Superior General*
Br Jerome Ellens
*Vicar:* Br Paul O'Keeffe

*Councillors*
Br Felim Ryan
Br George Mangara

Dublin, Kildare & Leighlin,
Galway

## PRESENTATION BROTHERS (FPM)

**Generalate**
Mount St Joseph,
Blarney Street, Cork
Tel 021-4392160
Fax 021-4398200
Email presgen@eircom.net

*Congregation Leader*
Br Martin Kenneally

**Provincial House**
Glasthule, Dun Laoghaire,
Co Dublin
Tel 01-2842228
Fax 01-2801711
Email fpmoffice@ireland.com

*Province Leader*
Br Andrew Hickey

Dublin, Cloyne, Cork & Ross, Kerry, Killaloe, Waterford & Lismore

## SAINT JOHN OF GOD BROTHERS (OH)

Hospitaller Order of Saint John of God

West European Province of Saint John of God (Ireland, UK, New Jersey, USA and Malawi, Africa)

**Provincial Curia**
Hospitaller Order of Saint John of God, Granada,
Stillorgan, Co Dublin
Tel 01-2771495
Fax 01-2831274
Email provincial@sjog.ie

*Provincial:* Br Laurence Kearns

**Provincial Administration**
Hospitaller Order of Saint John of God,
Hospitaller House,
Stillorgan, Co Dublin
Tel 01-2771500
Fax 01-2831257

Saint John of God Communty Services
*Chief Executive*
Andrew Heffernan
Email
andrew.heffernan@sjog.ie

*Regional Office*
St Bede's House, Morton Park,
Darlington CL1 4XZ,
Co Durham, England
Tel +44-1325-373700
Fax +44-1325-373707
*Chief Executive:* Bridget Doogan

Armagh, Dublin, Down & Connor, Kerry

## COMMUNITIES OF RELIGIOUS SISTERS

*In this section, details of each community's main house are given, followed by a list of the dioceses in which the community is present. For more information on houses in particular dioceses, please see the entry for the appropriate diocese.*

## ADORERS OF THE SACRED HEART OF JESUS OF MONTMARTRE (OSB)

**St Benedict's Priory**
The Mount, Cobh, Co Cork
Tel/Fax 021-4811354

*Prioress*
Mother Mary Vianney

Cloyne

## AUGUSTINIAN SISTERS

**'Villa Nova' Prayer House**
Grangecon, Co Wicklow
Tel 045-403874

*Contact:* Sr Mary Bernard

Kildare & Leighlin

## BENEDICTINE NUNS (OSB)

**Kylemore Abbey**
Kylemore, Connemara,
Co Galway
Tel 095-52000
Email info@kylemoreabbey.ie

*Abbess Administrator*
Sr Máire Hickey

Tuam

## BLESSED SACRAMENT SISTERS

**Blessed Sacrament Convent**
High Street,
Tullamore, Co Offaly
Tel 057-9351371
Email rsstlm@eircom.net

Dublin, Meath

## BON SAUVEUR SISTERS

**Carriglea**
Dungarvan, Co Waterford
Tel 058-45884 Fax 058-45891
Email lbscarriglea@eircom.net

*Superior:* Sr Mary Fitzgerald

Waterford & Lismore

## BON SECOURS SISTERS (Paris)

**Leadership Office**
College Road, Cork
Tel 021-4543310
Fax 021-4542533

*Country Leader:* Sr Marie Ryan
Email mryan@congregation.bonsecours.ie

Dublin, Tuam, Cloyne, Cork & Ross, Down & Connor, Galway, Kerry

Sisters are also working in Peru and Tanzania and South Africa

## BRIGIDINE SISTERS Sisters of St Brigid

**Brigidine Generalate**
Albert Park, 52 Beaconsfield Parade, Victoria 3206,
Australia

*Congregational Leader*
Sr Louise Cleary

Dublin, Galway, Kildare & Leighlin

## CARMELITE MONASTERIES

*Archdiocese of Dublin*

**Carmelite Monastery of the Immaculate Conception**
Roebuck, Dublin 14
Tel 01-2884732
Fax 01-2780145
Altar Breads Fax 01-2835037
Email
carmel@roebuckcarmel.com

*Prioress:* Sr Teresa Whelan

**Carmelite Monastery of the Assumption**
Firhouse, Dublin 24
Tel 01-4526474
Email firhousecarmel.firhouse@gmail.com

*Prioress*
Sr M. Veronica O'Connell

**Carmelite Monastery of the Immaculate Heart of Mary**
Delgany, Co Wicklow
Email contact@carmelitemonasterydelgany.ie

*Prioress:* Sr Monica Lawless

**Carmelite Monastery of St Joseph**
Seapark, Malahide,
Co Dublin
Email community@malahidecarmelites.ie

*Prioress:* Sr Rosalie Burke

**Carmelite Monastery of St Joseph**
Upper Kilmacud Road,
Stillorgan, Co Dublin
Email
contact@kilmacudcarmel.ie

*Prioress*
Sr Mary Brigeen Wilson

*Archdiocese of Tuam*

**Carmelite Monastery**
Tranquilla, Knock,
Co Mayo
Email
tranquillacarmel@eircom.net

*Prioress:* Sr Catherine

*Diocese of Clonfert*

**St Joseph's Monastery**
Mount Carmel, Loughrea,
Co Galway
Email theholychild1@eircom.net

*Prioress*
Sr Mary Magdalen Dineen

*Diocese of Dromore*

**Carmelite Monastery**
42 Glenvale Road, Newry,
Co Down BT34 2RD
Fax 028/048-30252778
Email
nuns@carmelitesglenvale.org

*Prioress:* Sr M. Carmel Clarke

*Diocese of Ferns*

**Mount Carmel Monastery**
New Ross, Co Wexford

*Prioress:* Sr Brenda Donovan

*Diocese of Waterford & Lismore*

**St Joseph's Carmelite Monastery**
Tallow, Co Waterford
Tel 058-56205
Email carmeltallow@eircom.net

*Prioress:* Sr Teresa Gibbons

## CARMELITE SISTERS FOR THE AGED AND INFIRM

**Our Lady's Manor**
Bullock Castle,
Dalkey, Co Dublin
Tel 01-2806993 Fax 01-2844802
Email
ourladysmanor1@eircom.net

*Superior*
Sr Therese Eileen Mulvaney
Email sistereileen@eircom.net
*Administrator*
Sr Bernadette Murphy

Dublin

## SISTERS OF CHARITY OF THE INCARNATE WORD

**Carrigoran House**
Newmarket-on-Fergus, Co Clare
Tel 061-368100 Fax 061-368170
Email
carrigoranhouse@eircom.net

*Administrator*
Sr Christina Murphy

Killaloe

## CHARITY OF JESUS AND MARY SISTERS

**Anglo-Irish Province**
Moore Abbey
Monasterevin, Co Kildare
Tel 045-525327

*Contact*
Sr Mary-Anna Lonergan
Email maryannal@eircom.net
*Provincial Superior*
Sr Elizabeth Roche
108 Spring Road, Letchworth,
Hertfordshire SG6 3B
Tel 0462-675694

While we have two residential centres, our services cover three geographical regions: Moore Abbey and South Kildare; Laois/Offaly; Westmeath, Meath and Longford.

Dublin, Kildare & Leighlin, Meath

## CHARITY OF NEVERS SISTERS

**76 Cherrywood,**
Loughlinstown Drive,
Dun Laoghaire, Co Dublin
Tel 01-2720453

Dublin

## SISTERS OF CHARITY OF OUR LADY MOTHER OF MERCY

**St Andrews**
3 Avonmore Road,
Raheen, Limerick
Tel 061-229935

*Superior:* Sr Nora Hayes

Limerick

## CHARITY OF ST PAUL THE APOSTLE SISTERS

**St Paul's Convent**
Greenhills, Dublin 12
Tel 01-4505358 Fax 01-4505132

*Superior:* Sr Mary Lyons
Email
marylyons2010@gmail.com

Dublin, Limerick

## CHRISTIAN RETREAT SISTERS

**'The Demense'**
Mountbellew, Ballinasloe,
Co Galway
Tel 090-9679311/9679939

Contact: Sr Margaret Buckley
Email
margaretmbuckley@eircom.net
*Regional Superior*
Sr Melanie Kingston

**House of Prayer**
35 Seymour Road, East Molesey,
Surrey KT8 0PB, England
Tel 0044-2089412313

Tuam

## CISTERCIANS

**St Mary's Abbey**
Glencairn, Lismore,
Co Waterford
Tel 058-56168 Fax 058-56616
Email
glencairnabbey@eircom.net

*Abbess:* Sr Marie Fahy

Waterford & Lismore

## CLARISSAN MISSIONARY SISTERS OF THE BLESSED SACRAMENT

**Our Lady of Guadalupe Residence for Students**
28 Waltersland Road,
Stillorgan, Co Dublin
Tel/Fax 01-2886600
Email misclaridub@hotmail.com
www.guadaluperesidence.com

*Superior:* Sr Gabriela Luna

Dublin

## CONGREGATION OF THE SISTERS OF MERCY

The Congregation of the Sisters of Mercy is an International Congregation. It has 2,332 members currently serving in Ireland, Britain, Brazil, Kenya, South Africa, Peru, Nigeria, Zambia and the US.

**Congregational Leadership Team**
Sr Coirle McCarthy
*(Congregational Leader)*
Sr Cáit O'Dwyer
Sr Susan DeGuide
Sr Kathy Rule
Sr Miriam Kerrisk

**Congregational Offices**
'Rachamim',
13/14 Moyle Park, Convent Road, Clondalkin, Dublin 22
Tel 01-4673737 Fax 01-4673749
Email mercy@csm.ie
Website www.sistersofmercy.ie

**The Northern Province**
comprising the dioceses of Raphoe, Derry, Down & Connor, Armagh, Dromore, Clogher, Kilmore, Meath and the regions of Nigeria and Zambia.

*Provincial:* Sr Nellie McLaughlin

Sr Joan Dunne
Sr Rose Marie Conlan
Sr Anne Lyng
Sr Winnie Lynott
Sr Eleanor Murphy

Provincial Office
74 Main Street, Clogher,
Co Tyrone BT76 0AA
Tel 028-85548127
Fax 028-85549459
Email mercy@mercynth.org

**The Western Province**
Comprising the dioceses of Killala, Achonry, Elphin, Galway, Tuam, Clonfert, Ardagh & Clonmacnois.

*Provincial*
Sr Elizabeth Manning

Sr Mary Walsh
Sr Martina Barrett
Sr Margaret Farrell
Sr Angela Forde

Provincial Office
Caoineas, Society Street,
Ballinasloe, Co Galway
Tel 090-9645202
Fax 090-9645203
Email caoineas@smwestprov.ie

**The South Central Province**
Comprising the dioceses of Dublin, Cashel & Emly, Kildare & Leighlin, Killaloe, Limerick.

*Provincial:* Sr Peggy Collins

Sr Thomasina Finn
Sr Therese Barry
Sr Breda Coman
Sr Anne Doyle
Sr Patricia O'Meara

Provincial Office, Oldtown,
Sallins Road, Naas, Co Kildare
Tel 045-876784 Fax 045-871509
Email provoffice@mercyscp.ie

**The Southern Province**
Comprising the dioceses of Cork & Ross, Cloyne, Kerry, Ferns, Ossory, Waterford & Lismore.

*Provincial:* Sr Liz Murphy

Sr Maria Goretti Comerford
Sr Veronica Mangan
Sr Monica Mohally
Sr Nuala O'Gorman

Provincial Office
Bishop Street, Cork
Tel 021-4975380
Fax 021-4915220
provincialoffice@mercysouth.ie

## CROSS AND PASSION CONGREGATION

**Provincial Office,**
299 Boarshaw Road, Middleton,
Manchester M24 2PF
Tel 0161-6553184
Fax 0161-6533666
*Provincial*
Sr Máire Ní Shúilleabháin

Dublin, Down & Connor

## DAUGHTERS OF CHARITY OF ST VINCENT DE PAUL

**St Catherine's Provincial House**
Dunardagh, Blackrock,
Co Dublin
Tel 01-2882669/2882896/
2882660 Fax 01-2834485

*Local Superior*
Sr Carmel McArdle
*Provincial Superior*
Sr Catherine Prendergast

Armagh, Dublin, Tuam, Cork & Ross, Down & Connor, Ferns, Galway and Killaloe

## DAUGHTERS OF THE CROSS OF LIÈGE

**Daughters of the Cross**
Beech Park Convent,
Beechwood Court, Stillorgan,
Co Dublin
Tel 01-2887401/2887315
Fax 01-2881499
Email beechpark@eircom.net

*Superior:* Sr Anne Kelly

Dublin

## DAUGHTERS OF THE HEART OF MARY

**St Joseph's**
Tivoli Road, Dun Laoghaire,
Co Dublin
Tel 01-2801204

Dublin

## DAUGHTERS OF THE HOLY SPIRIT

**88 Foxfield Road**
Raheny, Dublin 5
Tel 01-8312795

*Contact person*
Sr Teresa Buckley DHSp

*Provincial Superior*
Sr Dympna Connolly
Provincial House,
103 Harlestone Road,
Northhampton,
Norths NN5 7AQ, England

Dublin

## DAUGHTERS OF JESUS

*Provincial Superior*
55 Nightingale Road,
Rickmansworth,
Herts WD3 7BU, England
Tel 01923-897386

Dublin

## DAUGHTERS OF MARY AND JOSEPH

*Leadership Team*
Email dmjirishregion@eircom.net

Dublin, Kerry, Kildare & Leighlin, Ossory

## DAUGHTERS OF OUR LADY OF THE SACRED HEART

**Provincial House**
14 Rossmore Avenue,
Templeogue, Dublin 6W
Tel 01-4903200
Tel/Fax 01-4903113
Email olshprov@eircom.net

*Provincial:* Sr Vianney Murray

Dublin, Clogher

## DAUGHTERS OF WISDOM (LA SAGESSE)

**Wisdom Services**
Cregg House, Sligo
Tel 071-9177229
*Contact Person:* Grainne Hilton
Tel 01-8316508

Dublin, Elphin

## DISCIPLES OF THE DIVINE MASTER

**Newtownpark Avenue,**
Blackrock, Co Dublin
Tel 01-2114949/2886414
Fax 01-2836935

*Regional Superior*
Sr Kathryn Williams
Email
kathrynwilliams@pddm.org
www.pddm.org/ireland

Dublin, Elphin

## DOMINICAN CONTEMPLATIVES

**Monastery of St Catherine of Siena**
The Twenties, Drogheda,
Co Louth
Tel 041-9838524
Email siena@eircom.net

*Prioress:* Sr M. Breda Carroll OP

Armagh

## DOMINICAN SISTERS (King William's Town)

**Our Lady of Fatima Convent**
Oakpark, Tralee, Co Kerry
Tel 066-7125641/066-7125900
Fax 066-7180834
Email teresamcevoy@fatimahome.com

*Contact:* Sr Teresa McEvoy OP

Kerry

## DOMINICAN SISTERS

**Region Offices**
Mary Bellew House,
Dominican Campus, Cabra,
Dublin 7
Tel 01-8299700 Fax 01-8299799
Email regionop@gmail.com

*Region Prioress*
Sr Elisabeth Healy

Dublin, Down & Connor, Galway

## FAMILY OF ADORATION SISTERS

**St Aidan's Monastery**
Ferns, Co Wexford
Tel 053-9366634
Email staidansferns@eircom.net

*Superior:* Sr Dolores O'Brien

Ferns, Down & Connor

## FRANCISCAN MISSIONARIES OF THE DIVINE MOTHERHOOD

**Regional House**
Assisi, Harbour Road,
Ballinasloe, Co Galway
Tel 090-9642320
Fax 090-9642648

*Regional Leader*
Sr Anne O'Brien
Email anne4@gofree.indigo.ie

Dublin, Armagh, Clonfert, and Kerry

## FRANCISCAN MISSIONARIES OF MARY

**Provincial House**
5 Vaughan Avenue,
London W6 0XS
Tel 020-87484077

*Provincial Superior*
Sr Marie Thérèse Chambers
Email mariechambersfmm@gmail.com

Dublin, Galway, Limerick

## FRANCISCAN MISSIONARIES OF OUR LADY

**Ballinderry**
Mullingar, Co Westmeath
Tel 044-9352000

*Regional Superior*
Sr Cecilia Cody
Email ceciliacody1@gmail.com

Meath

## FRANCISCAN MISSIONARIES OF ST JOSEPH

**Prague House**
Freshford, Co Kilkenny
Tel 056-8832281

*Regional Superior*
Sr Bridget Anne Lonergan

Dublin, Cork & Ross, Ossory

## FRANCISCAN MISSIONARY SISTERS FOR AFRICA

**Generalate**
34a Gilford Road,
Sandymount, Dublin 4
Tel 01-2838376 Fax 01-2602049
Email fmsagen@iol.ie

*Congregational Leader*
Sr Miriam Duggan

Armagh, Dublin

## FRANCISCAN SISTERS

**3 St Andrew's Fairway**
Lucan,
Co Dublin
Tel 01-6108756
Email citaearls@yahoo.com

Dublin

## FRANCISCAN SISTERS OF THE IMMACULATE CONCEPTION

**Franciscan Sisters,**
97/99 Riverside Park,
Clonshaugh, Dublin 17
Tel 01-8474214

*Contact person*
Sr Louise McGlone
Tel 01292-475016
Email srlouise@tisali.co.uk
St Teresa's, 86 Saracen Street,
Glasgow G22 5AD,
Scotland
Tel 0044-141-3363027
Fax 0044-141-3364096

Dublin

## FRANCISCAN SISTERS OF LITTLEHAMPTON

**Eden**
Knock, Co Mayo
Tel 094-9388302

*Leader*
Sr Stanislaus Geraghty

Tuam

## FRANCISCAN SISTERS MINORESS

**St Anthony's Convent**
1 Cabra Grove,
Cabra, Dublin 7
Tel 01-8380185

*Superior*
Sr Barbara Flynn

*Mother General*
Sr Thomas More Roddy
Franciscan Convent,
Dalby Road,
Melton Mowbray,
Leicestershire LE13 0BP,
England
Tel 0044-1664-562422

Dublin

## GOOD SHEPHERD SISTERS

Good Shepherd Provincialate
245 Lower Kilmacud Road,
Goatstown, Dublin 14
Tel 01-2982699
Email rgsdublin@eircom.net
www.goodshepherdsireland.com

*Provincial Leader*
Sr Bernie McNally

Dublin, Cork & Ross, Derry, Down & Connor, Limerick, Galway, Waterford & Lismore

## HANDMAIDS OF THE SACRED HEART OF JESUS

**St Raphaela's**
Upper Kilmacud Road,
Stillorgan, Co Dublin
Tel 01-2889963
Fax 01-2889536

*Superior:* Sr Patricia Lynch
Email trishaci@yahoo.com

Dublin

## HOLY CHILD JESUS, SOCIETY OF THE

**Provincial**
Sr Monica Matthews
Victoria Charity Centre,
11 Belgrave Road,
London SW1V 1RB
Email europoff@shcj.co.uk

*Provincial Representative*
Sr Eileen Crowley
21 Grange Park Avenue,
Raheny, Dublin 5
Email ecrowley@shcj.org

Dublin

## HOLY FAITH SISTERS

**Generalate**
Aylward House,
Glasnevin, Dublin 11
Tel 01-8371426
Fax 01-8377474
Email aylward@eircom.net

*General Leader*
Sr Vivienne Keely

*Regional Leader*
Sr Rosaleen Cunniffe
68 Iona Road, Dublin 9
Tel 01-8301404
Fax 01-8303530
Email ionahfs@eircom.net

Dublin

## HOLY FAMILY OF BORDEAUX SISERS

**Holy Family Sisters**
11 Arran Road, Drumcondra,
Dublin 9

*Regional Superior*
Sr Bernadette Deegan

Armagh, Derry, Dublin, Kildare & Leighlin, Ossory

## HOLY FAMILY OF SAINT EMILIE DE RODAT

**Holy Family of St Emilie de Rodat**
Arden Road, Tullamore,
Co Offaly
Tel 057-9321577
Email mpe1809@eircom.net

*Superior:* Sr Mary-Paul English

Meath

## INFANT JESUS SISTERS

**Provincial House**
56 St Lawrence Road,
Clontarf, Dublin 3
Tel 01-8338930

*Provincial:* Sr Kitty Ellard
Email kittyijs@gmail.com

Dublin, Cloyne, Cork & Ross, Kerry

## JESUS AND MARY, CONGREGATION OF

The sisters from the Irish Province work in Haiti, Cameroon, Ekpoma, Lagos and Pakistan. The sisters are involved in education, working with the handicapped and in formation, including a house of formation in Nigeria.

**Provincialate, 'Errew House'**
110 Goatstown Road,
Dublin 14
Tel 01-2966059

*Provincial Superior*
Sr Mary Mulrooney
Tel 01-2993130/2969150
Email
mulrooney.mary@gmail.com
*Local Superior*
Sr Pauline Caffrey

Dublin, Galway, Killala

## SISTERS OF LA RETRAITE

**77 Grove Park**
Rathmines, Dublin 6
Tel 01-491171

*Contact:* Sr Barbara Stafford
Email
barbarastaffordlr@eircom.net

Dublin, Cork & Ross, Galway

## LA SAINTE UNION DES SACRES COEURS

**Provincial Office**
53 Croftdown Road,
London NW5 1EL
Tel 020-74827225
Fax 020-72844760

*Province leadership Team*
Sr Una Burke
Sr Mary Patricia Daly
Sr Helen Randles

Dublin, Ardagh & Clonmacnois

## LITTLE COMPANY OF MARY

**Provincialate**
Cnoc Mhuire, 29 Woodpark,
Ballinteer Avenue,
Dublin 16
Tel 01-2987040
Fax 01-2961936
Email lcom@irishbroadband.net

*Province Leader*
Sr Teresa Corby

Dublin, Cloyne, Kerry, Limerick, Ossory, Waterford & Lismore

## LITTLE SISTERS OF THE ASSUMPTION

**Provincial House**
42 Rathfarnham Road,
Terenure, Dublin 6W
Tel 01-4909850 Fax 01-4925740
Email pernet42@eircom.net

*Provincial:* Sr Mary Keenan

Dublin, Cork & Ross, Galway

## LITTLE SISTERS OF THE POOR

**Sacred Heart Residence**
Sybil Hill Road,
Raheny, Dublin 5
Tel 01-8332308
Email pcedublin@aol.com

*Provincial:* Sr Christine Devlin

Dublin, Ossory

## LORETO (IBVM)

**Provincialate**
Loreto House, Beaufort,
Dublin 14
Tel 01-4933827
Email
lorprovbeaufort@eircom.net

*Provincial*
Sr Noelle Corscadden

Dublin, Cloyne, Derry, Ferns, Kerry, Kilmore, Meath, Ossory, Raphoe, Waterford & Lismore

## MARIE AUXILIATRICE SISTERS

**7 Florence Street,**
Portobello, Dublin 8
Tel/Fax 01-4537622

Dublin

## MARIE REPARATRICE SISTERS

**Regional House,**
Laurel Hill Avenue,
South Circular Road, Limerick
Tel 061-464572 Fax 061-312561

*Regional Superior*
Sr Bernadette O'Driscoll

Dublin, Cork & Ross, Limerick

## MARIST SISTERS

**Provincialate**
51 Kenilworth Square, Dublin 6
Tel 01-4972196
Email secirl@eircom.net
*Leader – Ireland*
Sr Brigid M. McGuinness

Dublin, Achonry, Ardagh & Clonmacnois, Down & Connor

## MEDICAL MISSIONARIES OF MARY

**Rosemount,**
Rosemount Terrace,
Booterstown, Co Dublin
Tel 01-2882722 Fax 01-2834626
Email rcsmmm@eircom.net

Armagh, Dublin, Meath, Ossory

## MISSIONARIES OF CHARITY

**Gift of Love**
223 South Circular Road,
Dublin 8
Tel 01-4534141

*Regional Superior*
Sr M. Amada
177 Bravington Road
London W9 3AR
Tel 0208-9602644

Armagh, Dublin, Cloyne, Elphin

## MISSIONARY FRANCISCAN SISTERS OF THE IMMACULATE CONCEPTION

**Franciscan Convent**
Assisi House, Navan Road,
Dublin 7
Tel 01-8682216

Dublin

## MISSIONARY SISTERS OF THE ASSUMPTION

**Assumption Convent**
34 Crossgar Road, Ballynahinch,
Co Down BT24 8EN
Tel 028-97561765
Fax 028-97565754

*Superior:* Sr Ursula Hinchion

Dromore

## MISSIONARY SISTERS OF THE HOLY CROSS

**86 Glen Road,**
Belfast BT11 8BH
Tel 028-90614631
Fax 028-90614631
Email holycross3@sky.com

*Superior*
Sr Patricia Kelly

Down & Connor

## MISSIONARY SISTERS OF THE HOLY ROSARY

**Regional House**
Drumullac, 42 Westpark,
Artane, Dublin 5
Tel 01-8392070 Fax 01-8392025
Email mshrreg@eircom.net

*Regional Superior for Ireland and England*
Sr Conchita McDonnell

Dublin, Cork, Ferns, Kilmore, Meath, Ardagh & Clonmacnois

## MISSIONARY SISTERS OF OUR LADY OF APOSTLES

**Provincialate**
Ardfoyle Convent,
Ballintemple, Cork
Tel 021-4294076
Fax 021-4291105
Email prov@eircom.net

*Provincial:* Sr Mary Crowley

Dublin, Tuam, Cork & Ross, Dromore

## MISSIONARY SISTERS OF ST COLUMBAN

**St Columban's Convent**
Magheramore,
Wicklow
Tel 0404-67348
Fax 0404-67364

*Community Leader*
Sr Ita McElwain

Dublin

## MISSIONARY SISTERS OF ST PETER CLAVER

**Our Lady of the Angels**
81 Bushy Park Road,
PO Box 22881,
Terenure, Dublin 6
Tel 01-4909360
Fax 01-4920918

*Contact Person*
Sr Lucyna Wisniowska
Email claver4@hotmail.com

Dublin

## MISSIONARY SISTERS SERVANTS OF THE HOLY SPIRIT

**Regional House,**
143 Philipsburgh Avenue
Fairview, Dublin 3
Tel 01-8369383
Email sspsfairview@yahoo.com

*Community Leader*
Sr Carmen Lee

Dublin

## NOTRE DAME DES MISSIONS
## Our Lady of the Missions

**Upper Churchtown Road,**
Dublin 14
Tel 01-2983308/2989991

Armagh, Dublin, Down & Connor, Ferns

## OUR LADY OF THE CENACLE

**3 Churchview Drive,**
Killiney,
Co Dublin
Tel 01-2840175
Email cenacledublin@eircom.net

Dublin, Cork & Ross

## OUR LADY OF CHARITY SISTERS

**Regional Administration**
63 Lower Sean McDermott
Street, Dublin 1
Tel 01-8711109 Fax 01-8366526
Email regionaloffice@olc.ie

*Regional Leader*
Sr Sheila Murphy

Dublin

## OUR LADY OF SION SISTERS

*Provincial*
Sr Brenda McCole
49 St Peter's Road,
Harborne, Birmingham B17 0AU
Tel 0121-4266679
Email
brenda.mccole@btinternet.com

Dublin

## PERPETUAL ADORATION SISTERS

**Perpetual Adoration Convent**
Wexford
Tel 053-9124134
Email
adoration44@eircom.net

*Superior:* Sr Pius Flannery

Ferns

## POOR CLARES

*Archdiocese of Dublin*

**St Damian's**
Simmonscourt Road,
Ballsbridge, Dublin 4
Fax 01-6685464
Email pccdamians@mac.com

*Abbess/Contact:* Sr M. Brigid

*Diocese of Ardagh & Clonmacnois*

**Poor Clare Monastery of Perpetual Adoration**
Drumshanbo, Co Leitrim

*Abbess*
Mother M. Angela McCabe

*Diocese of Cork & Ross*

**Poor Clare Colettine Monastery**
College Road, Cork

*Abbess*
Sr Colette-Marie O'Reilly

*Diocese of Down & Connor*

**120 Cliftonville Road**
Belfast BT14 6LA

*Superior*
Sr Immaculata Enderez OSC

*Diocese of Galway*

**St Clare's Monastery**
Nuns' Island, Galway

*Abbess*
Sr M. Colette Hayden

*Diocese Kildare & Leighlin*

**Poor Clare Colettine Monastery**
Graiguecullen, Carlow

*Abbess*
Sr M. Francis O'Brien

*Diocese of Killaloe*

**Poor Clare Monastery**
Francis Street,
Ennis, Co Clare

*Abbess*
Sr Bernardine Meskell
Email
bernardinemeskell@eircom.net

## POOR SERVANTS OF THE MOTHER OF GOD

**Generalate**
Maryfield Convent,
Mount Angelus Road,
Roehampton SW15 4JA,
England
Tel 0208-7884351

*General:* Sr Mary Whelan

*Local Leader (Dublin region)*
Sr Margaret Cashman
Email margaretcashmansmg@
eircom.net
*Local Leader (outside Dublin)*
Sr Catherine Gleeson
Email
cgleesonsmg1@eircom.net

Dublin, Tuam, Cloyne, Down & Connor, Limerick

## CONGREGATION OF THE SISTERS OF NAZARETH

**Nazareth House**
Malahide Road, Dublin 3
Tel 01-8332024
Fax 01-8334988
Email
regional.ie@nazarethcare.com

*Regional Superior*
Sr Cataldus Courtney

Dublin, Cloyne, Derry, Down and Connor, Elphin

## PRESENTATION SISTERS

**Generalate**
Monasterevin, Co Kildare
Tel 045-525335/525503
Fax 045-525209
Email
adminpresevin@eircom.net
Website www.
presentationsistersunion.org

*Congregational Leader*
Sr Terry Abraham

Armagh, Dublin, Cashel, Tuam, Ardagh & Clonmacnois, Cloyne, Cork and Ross, Ferns, Galway, Kerry, Kildare and Leighlin, Limerick, Meath, Ossory, Waterford & Lismore

## PRESENTATION OF MARY SISTERS

**4 Lower John Street,**
Sligo
Tel 071-9160740

*Superior:* Sr Elenita Baguio
Email
elenitapm2008@hotmail.com

Elphin

## REDEMPTORISTINES

**Monastery of St Alphonsus**
St Alphonsus Road, Dublin 9

*Superior:* Sr Gabrielle
Email
gabrielle.fox@redemptorists.ie

Dublin

## RELIGIOUS OF CHRISTIAN EDUCATION

**Provincial Office**
3 Bushy Park House,
Templeogue Road, Dublin 6W
Tel 01-4901668 Fax 01-4901101
Email
redyalooney@yahoo.co.uk

*Provincial Superior*
Sr Rosemary O'Looney

Dublin

## RELIGIOUS OF SACRED HEART OF MARY

**13/14 Huntstown Wood,**
Mulhuddart, Dublin 15
Tel 01-8223566
*Contact person*
Sr Regina King

Dublin, Down & Connor, Ossory

## RELIGIOUS SISTERS OF CHARITY

**Generalate**
Caritas, 15 Gilford Road,
Sandymount, Dublin 4
Tel 01-2697833/2697935

Provincialate, Provincial House,
Our Lady's Mount,
Harold's Cross, Dublin 6W
Tel 01-4973177

Dublin, Cork & Ross, Galway, Ossory, Waterford & Lismore

## ROSMINIANS (SISTERS OF PROVIDENCE)

**104a Griffith Court**
Fairview, Dublin 3
Tel 01-8375021

Dublin, Down & Connor, Waterford & Lismore

## SACRED HEART SOCIETY

**Provincial Administration Office**
76 Home Farm Road,
Drumcondra, Dublin 9
Tel 01-8375412 Fax 01-8375542

*Provincial Secretary*
Email rscjirs@gmail.com
*Provincial Superior*
Sr Aideen Kinlen

Armagh, Dublin

## SACRED HEARTS OF JESUS AND MARY (PICPUS)

**Sector House**
11 Northbrook Road
Ranelagh, Dublin 6
Tel 01-4910173 (Co-ordinator)
Tel 01-4974831 (Community)
Fax 01-4965551

*Contact*
Sr Mary McCloskey SSCC

Dublin

## SACRED HEARTS OF JESUS AND MARY

**St Anne's**
Sean Ross Abbey,
Roscrea, Co Tipperary
Tel 0505-21629
Fax 0505-22525
Email mdobbin@eircom.net

*Community Leader*
Sr Margaret Dobbin

Cork & Ross, Down & Connor, Killaloe

## SALESIAN SISTERS OF ST JOHN BOSCO

**Provincialate**
203 Lower Kilmacud Road,
Stillorgan, Co Dublin
Tel 01-2985188
Email prov@salsisdb.iol.ie

*Provincial Superior*
Sr Mary Doran

Dublin, Limerick

## SISTERS OF ST CLARE

**St Clare's Generalate**
63 Harold's Cross Road,
Dublin 6W
Tel 01-4966880/4995135
Fax 01-4966388
Email annedkelly@yahoo.com

*Abbess General:* Sr Anne Kelly

Armagh, Dublin, Down & Connor, Dromore, Kerry, Kilmore

*Regional Superior*
Sr Mercedes Coen
St Clare's Convent,
Keady, Co Armagh BT60 3RW
Tel/Fax 028-37530554

## ST JOHN OF GOD SISTERS

**St John of God Congregational Centre**
1 Summerhill Heights, Wexford
Tel 053-9142396
Fax 053-9141500
Email stjohnogoffice@eircom.net

*Congregational Leader*
Sr Bríd Ryan

Dublin, Achonry, Dromore, Ferns, Kildare & Leighlin, Killaloe, Ossory, Waterford & Lismore

## ST JOSEPH OF ANNECY SISTERS

**St Joseph's Convent**
Killorglin, Co Kerry
Tel 066-9761809
Fax 066-9761127
Email
margaret.lyne@talk21.com

*Superior:* Sr Helena Lyne

Kerry

## ST JOSEPH OF THE APPARITION SISTERS

**St Joseph's Convent**
Garden Hill, Sligo
Tel 071-9162330 (Convent)
Fax 071-9152500
Email stjsligo@eircom.net

Elphin

## SISTERS OF ST JOSEPH OF CHAMBERY

**St Joseph's Convent**
Springdale Road, Raheny,
Dublin 5
Tel 01-8478351 (Convent)
Fax 01-8485764 (Convent)
Email mpraleigh@eircom.net
Tel 01-8478433/8478008
(Hospital)

*Superior:* Sr Mary Peter Raleigh
Email mpraleigh@eircom.net

Dublin

## ST JOSEPH OF CLUNY SISTERS

Mt Sackville Convent
Chapelizod, Dublin 20
Tel 01-8213134 Fax 01-8224002
Email clunyprov@sjc.ie
Website www.sjc.ie

*Provincial Superior*
Sr Rowena Galvin

Dublin, Ardagh & Clonmacnois, Waterford & Lismore

## ST JOSEPH OF LYON SISTERS

**3 St Margaret's Avenue,**
Raheny, Dublin 5
Tel 01-8325896

*Contact:* Sr Marie Kiernan

Dublin

## ST JOSEPH OF THE SACRED HEART SISTERS

**Granagh**
Kilmallock, Co Limerick
Tel 061-399027

*Regional Leader*
Sr Margaret O'Sullivan

Dublin, Tuam, Achonry, Cloyne, Killaloe, Limerick, Kerry

## ST LOUIS SISTERS

**St Louis Regional House**
60 Ard Easmuinn,
Dundalk, Co Louth
Tel 042-9334752/9334753
Fax 042-9334651
Email regionalate@stlouisirl.ie

*Regional Leader*
Sr Anne Kavanagh

Armagh, Dublin, Achonry, Clogher, Down & Connor, Ferns

## ST MARY MADELEINE POSTEL SISTERS

**Park More Convent**
Abbey Street, Roscrea,
Co Tipperary
Tel 0505-21038

*Local Superior*
Sr Marie Keegan

Dublin, Tuam, Killaloe

## ST PAUL DE CHARTRES SISTERS

**Queen of Peace Centre**
Garville Avenue,
Rathgar, Dublin 6
Tel 01-4975381/4972366
Fax 01-4964084
Email spcqueen@eircom.net

*Regional Superior*
Sr Rose Margaret Nuval

Dublin

## URSULINES

**Ursuline Generalate**
17 Trimleston Drive,
Booterstown, Co Dublin
Tel 01-2693503
Email angemer@eircom.net
Website www.ursulines.ie

*Congregational Leader*
Sr Mary McHugh
*Assistant:* Sr Anne Harte Barry

Dublin, Tuam, Cashel & Emly, Cork & Ross, Elphin, Waterford & Lismore

## URSULINES OF JESUS

**26 The Drive**
Seatown Park,
Swords, Co Dublin
Tel 01-8404323

*Delegated Councillor*
Sr Hazel Dalton
St Ursula's Convent,
11 Amhurst Park, Stamford Hill,
London N16 5DH, England
Tel 020-88020256
Email supgb@dircon.co.uk

Dublin

## VISITATION SISTERS

**Monastery of the Visitation**
Stamullen, Co Meath
Tel 01-8412533

*Superior:* Sr Paul Mary Supple
Email visitationstamulen
@gmail.com

Meath

# INSTITUTES

## LAY SECULAR INSTITUTES

Lay secular institutes come under the jurisdiction of the Sacred Congregation for Religious Secular Institutes as laid down by the Apostolic Constitution, *Provida Mater Ecclesia*.

**Caritas Christi**
Secular institute of pontifical right founded in 1937 for laywomen.

*Priest Assistant*
Rev Finian Lynch (OP)
St Mary's Priory,
Pope's Quay, Cork
Tel 021-4502267
Fax 021-4502307
Email simonrop@eircom.net

*Priest Assistant for Dublin*
Rev Gregory Carroll (OP)
St Saviour's Priory,
Upper Dorsett Street, Dublin 1
Email gregcop@eircom.net

*Contacts:* www.ccinfo.org
Brigid Tel 086-8445644
Kathleen Tel 087-9005767

**Columba Community**
Private association of the faithful involved in prayer, Christian teaching, counsel, reconciliation and healing and rehabilitation from drugs and alcohol.

Columba House,
11 Queen Street,
Derry BT48 7EG
Tel 028-71262407
Email columbacommunity@
hotmail.com
Website
www.columbacommunity.com

*Spiritual Director*
Rev Neal Carlin
*Treasurer:* Ms Kathleen Devlin
*Contact:* Tommy McCay

**Servitium Christi**
A Secular Institute of Pontifical right for women in the Eucharistic Family of St Peter Julian Eymard (also includes the Congregation of the Blessed Sacrament).

*Enquiries:* Mary Keane
58 Moyne Road,
Ranelagh, Dublin 6

**Society of Our Lady of the Way**
Founded in Austria in 1936 for single or widowed laywomen; membership worldwide.

*Enquiries:* Mary C. Peyton
18 Rock Road, Lisburn,
Co Antrim BT28 3SU
Tel Lisburn 92648244
Email
mary.peyton@talktalk.net
Miss Helen Spellman
22 Avondale Road,
Highfield Park, Galway
Tel 091-521872

## NEW FORMS OF CONSECRATED LIFE

Next to already existing institutes of consecrated life new forms of evangelical life spring up, 'through which God in his goodness enriches the Church, enabling her to follow her Lord in a constant outpouring of generosity and attentive to God's invitation revealed through the signs of the times' (John Paul II) (Annuario Pontificio p1646).

**The Spiritual Family**
**The Work of Christ Familia Spiritualis Opus (FSO)**
Family of consecrated life pontifical right. Founded in Belgium in 1938 by Julia Verhaeghe. It consists of a Priests' Community and of a Sisters' Community of Consecrated Women. The nucleus of The Work is made up of members in the strict sense who are consecrated to the Sacred Heart of Jesus in a 'Holy Covenant in the three evangelical counsels'. They strive to unite contemplation, the apostolic life and the sanctification of the world. They follow above all the example of St Paul, imitating his love for Christ and his body, the Church. They seek to help with the new evangelisation as spiritual fathers and mothers in a spirit of unity and respectful complementarity. They are joined by members in a wider sense, and by lay faithful who are spiritually associated with the Work of Christ.

*Enquiries*
Sr Annie Dueringer FSO
Bishop's House,
Ard Adhamhnáin,
Letterkenny, Co Donegal
Tel 074-9124898
Fax 074-9128142
Email thework@catholic.org
www.thework-fso.org

Raphoe

# SEMINARIES AND HOUSES OF STUDY

## SEMINARIES

**PONTIFICAL IRISH COLLEGE, ROME**
Founded in 1628 the Irish National College in Rome provides formation to seminarians and priests for the diocesan priesthood in Ireland and beyond.
Via dei SS Quattro 1, 00184 Roma, Italy
Tel 003906-772631 Fax 003906-77263323
Email ufficio@irishcollege.org
www.irishcollege.org
*Rector:* Rev Ciarán O'Carroll DEcclesHist
*Vice-Rector*
Rev Albert McDonnell STL, MA, JCL
*Spiritual Director*
Rev Chris Hayden STL, PhD
*Director of Formation*
Rev William Swan BSc, BTh, STL

**ST PATRICK'S COLLEGE, MAYNOOTH**
Founded in 1795, the National Seminary for Ireland and Pontifical University, Maynooth, Co Kildare
Tel 01-7084700 Fax 01-7083959
Email president@spcm.ie
*College Officers*
*President*
Rt Rev Mgr Hugh Connolly BA, DD
*Financial Officer*
Ms Fidelma Madden ACA, AITI
*Registrar and Supervisor of Examinations*
Rev Professor Michael Mullaney
*Directors of Formation*
Rev Paul Prior
Rev Michael Collins
*Dean of Faculty of Theology*
Rev Dr Padraig Corkery BSc, STD (CUA), LSS, HDE
*Dean of Faculty of Philosophy*
Vacant
*Librarian:* Cathal McCauley
*Archivist:* Rt Rev Mgr Patrick J. Corish MA, DD, MRIA
*Acting Director of Human Resources*
Rosaleen McCarthy

Pontifical University Courses:
*Professors/Department Heads*
*Canon Law*
Rev Professor Michael Mullaney
*Dogmatic Theology*
Rev Professor Brendan Leahy, BL, STD
*Ecclesiastical History*
Prof Salvador Ryan
*Liturgy:* Rev Professor Liam Tracey (OSM) STB, SLD, DipMar, DipPastoral Theology
*Moral Theology:* Rev Dr Padraig Corkery, BSc, STD (CUA)
*Sacred Scripture*
Rev Professor Seamus O'Connell BSc, LSS
*Faith and Culture*
Rev Professor Michael A. Conway

**MILLTOWN INSTITUTE OF THEOLOGY AND PHILOSOPHY**
Milltown Park, Sandford Road, Ranelagh, Dublin 6
Tel 01-2776300
Fax 01-2692528
Email info@milltown-institute.ie
www.milltown-institute.ie
Founded in 1968. A Pontifical Athenaeum and a designated institution of HETAC.
*Patron:* Dr Diarmuid Martin Archbishop of Dublin
*Chancellor:* Adolfo Nicólas SJ
*Vice-Chancellor:* John Dardis SJ
*Acting President:* Dr Cornelius Casey CSsR
*School of Undergraduate Studies*
*Dean of Theology*
Dr Thomas R. Whelan CSSp
*Dean of Philosophy*
Prof Santiago Sia
*School of Postgraduate Studies and Research*
*Head of School:* Dr Anthony White
*Head of Department: Scripture:*
Dr Kieran O'Mahoney OSA
*Head of Department: Systematic Theology and History*
Dr Declan Marmion SM
*Head of Department Spirituality*
Dr Denis Robinson CSSp
*Acting Head of Department Moral Theology and Canon Law*
Dr Thomas R. Whelan CSSp
*Head of Department: Pastoral Theology*
Dr Thomas Grenham SPS
*Head of Department Mission Theology & Cultures*
Dr Patrick Claffey SPS
*Editor, Milltown Studies*
Dr Joseph Egan SMA
*Assistant to the President*
Mr Philip FitzPatrick
*Registrar:* Dr Anthony White
*Acting Librarian:* Ms Mary Glennon
*Financial Advisor:* Mr Patrick Lally
*Head of Student Services:*
Mrs Dierdre Tallan
*Chaplain:* Mrs Bairbre De Burca
*Contact Person:* Registrar

**ALL HALLOWS COLLEGE DUBLIN**
Grace Park Road, Drumcondra, Dublin 9
Tel 01-8373745/8373746 Fax 01-8377642
Email info@allhallows.ie
www.allhallows.ie
Founded in 1842. Prepares students for priestly ministry and lay people for mission and ministry.
*President*
Dr Patrick J. McDevitt (CM) PhD
*Vice-President:* Rev John Joe Spring MA
*Vice-President of Development*
Rev Robert Whiteside, MA
*Financial Manager*
Mr Ian Baker, BBS, BA, FCA
*Dean of Studies and Acting Registrar*
Mr Ronan Tobin, BA, HDipEd, MA
*Senior Office Administrator, Registry Office:* Lisa Maye-Gregory MA
*Director of Vocations*
Rev John Joe Spring MA
Sr Dorothy Balfe (OP) MA
Ms Jean Cleary MA
Rev Eugene Curran CM, BA, BD, DMin
Rev Thomas Dalzell (SM) BA, STL, PhD
Rev Anthony Draper DD, BA, HDE
Kevin Egan STL, MS, DMin
Sr Mary Ann Maxwell SCIS, BA, BEd, MEd
Maureen Gainey (LSU) BA, HDipEd, Dip Couns & Psychotherapy, MIACT
Sr Bernadette Flanagan BA (Th), HDE, DipIT, MA, PhD
Rev Michael O'Sullivan (SJ) BSocSc, BacPhil, BD, MTh, STL, PhD
Ciarán Dalton MA, MSc, QMIGC
Dr Jean Berry EdD
Ms Kathleen Soden, MBCS, MSc
Ms Carolanne Henry, BA
Sr Patricia Holden (SHCJ) BMus, DipLit
Rev James McCormack (CM) PhD
Ms Jean Mullen MA
Rev James Murphy (CM) PhD
Rev Brian Nolan (CM) STD, LSS
Ms Helen Bradley BA, MPhil, MLIS
Rev Joseph McCann, CM, PhD
Mr Patrick Quinn, BA, BD, MA, PhD, HDE, DCG
Ms Anne Marie Lowry, MA
Ms Cora Lambert, MA
Ms Marjorie Fitzpatrick, MA
Ms Geraldine Holton
Ms Debra Snoddy BATh, MTh, MFSS, STL
Ms Mary Ivers PhD
Ms Cathríona Russell PhD

*Purcell House*
Retreat/Conference Centre
Tel 01-8373745 Fax 01-8571135
*Director*
Ms Mary McPhillips BA, HDip, Grad.Dip.Past
*Administrator*
Ms Mary Hayes, Ms Yvonne Graham
*Ministry to Priests*
Rev Kevin Scallon (CM) MA
*Co-ordinator of Ember Mission Team*
Ms Mary O'Broin, MA

## HOUSES OF STUDY

*For details see Religious Orders and Congregations Section*

**Augustinians (OSA)**
*Prior:* Rev John Lyng OSA
St Augustine's, Ballyboden, Dublin 16
Tel 01-4241000 Fax 01-4939915

**Camillians (OSCam)**
St Camillus, South Hill Avenue,
Blackrock, Co Dublin
Tel 01-2882873/2833380

**Carmelites (OCarm)**
*Prior:* Rev Martin Baxter
Gort Muire, Ballinteer, Dublin 16
Tel 01-2984014 Fax 01-2987221
Email gortmuire@gortmuire.com
Email mvjbaxter@eircom.net

**Divine Word Missionaries (SVD)**
Divine Word Missionaries,
Maynooth, Co Kildare
Tel 01-6286391/2
Fax 01-6289184
Email dv.twomey@may.ie

**Dominicans (OP)**
St Mary's Priory, Tallaght, Dublin 24
Tel 01-4048100 Fax 01-4596784
The Priory Institute
Tel 01-4048124 Fax 01-4626084
Email enquiries@prioryinstitute.com

St Saviour's Priory, Upper Dorset Street,
Dublin 1
Tel 01-8897610 Fax 01-8734003
Email stsaviours@eircom.net

Dominican Biblical Institute,
Upper Cecil Street, Limerick
Tel 061-490600 Fax 061-468604
Email info@dbclimerick.ie

**Franciscans (OFM)**
Dún Mhuire, Seafield Road,
Killiney, Co Dublin
Tel 01-2826760 Fax 01-2826993
Email dmkilliney@eircom.net

**Missionaries of Africa (White Fathers)**
Cypress Grove, Templeogue, Dublin 6W
Tel 01-4055263
*Contact Person:* Fr P. J. Cassidy
Email provirl@indigo.ie

**Oblates (OMI)**
St Anne's, Goldenbridge Walk, Inchicore,
Dublin 8
Tel 01-4540841

**Redemptorists (CSsR)**
Scala, Castlemahon House, Castle Road,
Blackrock, Cork
*Contact Person:* Dan Baragry CSsR
(Director of Formation)

**Salesians (SDB)**
St Catherine's Centre, North Campus,
Maynooth, Co Kildare
Tel 01-6286111 Fax 01-6286268
Email sdbmaynooth@iol.ie
Members part of Celbridge community

## SPECIAL INSTITUTES OF EDUCATION

**Dominican Biblical Institute**
Cecil Street Upper, Limerick
*Moderator:* Rev Thomas Brodie (OP)
Tel 061-490600
061-490603 (secretary)
Fax 061-468604
www.dbil.ie

**IMU Mission Institute**
St Columba's, Dalgan Park, Navan,
Co Meath
Tel 046-9021525 Fax 046-9022799
Email imuinst@eircom.net
*Director:* P. Dooher (SSC)

**Irish School of Ecumenics**
**Trinity College Dublin**
Bea House, Milltown Park, Dublin 6
*Contact:* Professor Geraldine Smyth,
Head of Department
Tel 01-2601144 Fax 01-2601158
Email isedir@tcd.ie
www.tcd.ie/ise

**Irish School of Ecumenics**
**Trinity College Dublin**
683 Antrim Road, Belfast BT15 4EG
Tel 028-90775010 Fax 028-90373986

**Mater Dei Institute of Education**
Clonliffe Road, Dublin 3
Tel 01-8086500 Fax 01-8370776
Email info@materdei.dcu.ie
www.materdei.ie
Director: Dr Andrew G. McGrady
Tel 01-8086504
Email andrew.mcgrady@materdei.dcu.ie

# RETREAT AND PASTORAL CENTRES

## RETREAT HOUSES

### ANTRIM

Drumalis, Glenarm Road,
Larne, Co Antrim BT40 1DT
Tel 028-28272196/28276455
Fax 028-28277999
Email drumalis@btconnect.com
www.drumalis.co.uk
*Retreat Team:* Sr Margaret Rose McSparran CP, Sr Anna Hainey CP
*Acc:* twin 37, doubles 13, singles 3, group 3
Cross & Passion Sisters
Parkview: self-catering cottage in grounds, sleeps 5
*Contact:* Katrina Hartin, Coordinator of Administration Services

### CORK

Myross Wood House, Leap, Co Cork
Tel 028-33118 Fax 028-33793
Email mscmyross@eircom.net
*Acc:* singles 32, doubles 6
Offering preached, directed and themed retreats throughout the year
*Director/Contact person*
Fr Michael Curran (MSC)
Missionaries of the Sacred Heart

St Benedict's Priory Retreat House
The Mount, Cobh, Co Cork
Tel/Fax 021-4811354
*Acc:* 6 single rooms, 2 double rooms available for private individual or group retreats, private day retreats, opportunity to share in the liturgical life of the Sisters – Holy Mass, Liturgy of the Hours and Eucharistic Adoration. Quiet peaceful setting, Bible Garden, all meals supplied.
*Contact for private retreats:* Guest Mistress

Ennismore Retreat & Conference Centre,
Ennismore, Montenotte, Cork
Tel 021-4502520 Fax 021-4502712
Email ennismore@eircom.net
www.ennismore.ie
*Contact person:* Mary Smith
*Acc:* singles 36, doubles 2
Dominicans

### DERRY

Carmelite Retreat Centre
Termonbacca, Derry BT48 9XE
Tel 028-71262512 Fax 028-71373589
Email ocdderry@hotmail.co.uk
www.ocd.ie
*Contact person:* Fr Sean Conlon (OCD)
*Acc:* singles 20, twin 20, ensuite rooms 5
Carmelites (OCD)

### DONEGAL

St Anthony's Retreat Centre
Dundrean, Burnfoot, Co Donegal
Tel/Fax 074-9368370
Email columbacommunity@hotmail.com or sarce@eircom.net
*Acc:* 5 hermitages, 1 double (3 en suite)
*Director:* Rev Neal Carlin
Spiritual direction available

### DOWN

Dromantine Retreat and Conference Centre, Newry, Co Down BT34 1RH
Tel 028-30821964 Fax 028-30821963
Email
admin@dromantineconference.com
www.dromatineconference.com
*Contact:* Rev Paddy O'Rourke SMA
*Accommodation:* 40 single en suite rooms, 30 double en suite rooms, 8 conference rooms

The Christian Renewal Centre –
A House of Prayer for Ireland
44 Shore Road, Rostrevor, Newry,
Co Down BT34 3ET Tel 028-41738492
Email crc-rostrevor@lineone.net
*Acc:* singles 3, double/family 1, twin 5, disabled 1
*Contact:* Harry Smith (Director)
www.crc-rostrevor.org

Passionist Retreat Centre,
Tobar Mhuire, Crossgar,
Downpatrick, Co Down BT30 9EA
Tel 028-44830242 Fax 028-44831382
Email
secretary@tobarmhuirecrossgar.com
*Acc:* twin 6, family 9 (1 double, 1 single)

### DUBLIN

Avila Carmelite Centre
Bloomfield Avenue
Morehampton Road, Dublin 4
Tel 01-6430200 Fax 01-6430281
Email avila@ocd.ie
*Prior:* Fr Michael McGoldrick (OCD)
Carmelites (OCD)

Dominican Retreat and Pastoral Centre
Tallaght Village, Dublin 24
Tel 01-4048189 Fax 01-4596080
Email retreathouse@eircom.net
www.goodnews.ie
*Secretary/Contact:* Anita Kenny
*Acc:* singles 30, 1 large, 3 medium conference rooms, oratory
Dominicans

Emmaus, Lissenhall, Swords, Co Dublin
Tel 01-8700050 Fax 01-8408248
Email admin@emmauscentre.ie
www.emmauscentre.ie
Residential accommodation
63 ensuite bedrooms, 3 prayer rooms, 13 meeting rooms
*Office Administrator:* Nora Meenaghan
Christian Brothers, Holy Faith Sisters

Tallaght Rehabilitation Project
Kiltalown House, Jobstown,
Tallaght, Dublin 24
Tel 01-4597705 Fax 01-4148123
Email info@tallaghtrehabproject.ie
*Co-ordinator:* Marie Hayden

Manresa House, Dollymount, Dublin 3
Tel 01-8331352 Fax 01-8331002
Email manresa@jesuit.ie
*Acc:* singles 41
*Director:* Rev Patrick Carberry SJ
*Contact:* Eileen Toomey. Jesuits

Orlagh Retreat Centre
Old Court Road, Dublin 16
Tel 01-4958190 Fax 01-4930987
Email info@orlagh.ie www.orlagh.ie
*Acc:* singles 24, doubles 1; 1 large, 1 medium and 2 small conference rooms
*Director:* John Byrne (OSA)
Email john@orlagh.ie
Augustinians

Purcell House, All Hallows College
Drumcondra, Dublin 9
Tel 01-8520754 Fax 01-8571135
Email purcell_house@allhallows.ie
*Acc:* singles ensuite 50
*Director:* Mary McPhillips
*Contact:* Mary or Alicia

Stella Maris Retreat Centre
Carrickbrack Road, Baily, Howth, Co Dublin
Est. 1893
Tel 01-8322228 Fax 01-8063469
Email stellamarisretreatcentre@gmail.com
Web www.stellamarisretreats.ie
Community: 6, Chaplains: Parish Clergy
Spirituality centre, centre for retreats, meetings, days of prayer for groups, self-catering hermitage. Ashram experience 2012.

### GALWAY

Emmanuel House of Providence
Clonfert, Ballinasloe, Co Galway
Tel 057-9151552/9151641
Email contact@emmanuelhouse.ie
www.emmanuelhouse.ie
*No Accommodation*
Eddie and Lucy Stones
Catholic centre for prayer and evangelisation. It is a new community of Christ's faithful, a spiritual hospital where people can experience the healing power of God in spirit, mind and body.

Esker Retreat House and Youth Village
Athenry, Co Galway
Tel 091-844549 Fax 091-845698
Email eskerret@indigo.ie
www.eskercommunity.net
*Acc:* singles 17, doubles 26 in retreat house, 70 in 2 dorms in youth village
*Retreat House Co-ordinator:* Fr Fonsie Doran CSsR
Email rev_dorancssr@yahoo.com
*Youth Village Co-ordinator*
Fr Michael Cusack CSsR
*Contact:* The Secretary

**KERRY**
Ardfert Retreat Centre
Ardfert, Co Kerry
Tel 066-7134276 Fax 066-7134867
Email ardfertretreat@eircom.net
*Acc:* 29 rooms
*Contact Person:* Sr Angela Kiely RSM
Kerry Diocese and Intercongregational *Team:* Mercy/Presentation and Ursuline Sisters

**KILKENNY**
Peace in Christ,
Sion Road, Kilkenny
Tel 056-7721054 Fax 056-7770755
Email peaceinchrist@eircom.net
*Acc:* singles 26
*Contact:* Sr Margaret Moloney
Daughters of Mary and Joseph

**LAOIS**
La Salle Pastoral Centre, Castletown, Portlaoise, Co Laois
Tel 057-8732442 Fax 057-8732925
*Contact:* Br Stephen Dignan
*Acc:* 40. De La Salle Brothers

Mount St Anne's Retreat and Conference Centre, Killenard, Portarlington, Co Laois
Tel 057-8626153 Fax 057-8626700
Email msannes@eircom.net
http://www.mountstannes.com
*Acc:* singles 22, doubles 6
*Director:* Sr Róisín Gannon (PBVM)
roisingannon@eircom.net
*Contact Person*
Christine or Catherine

**LIMERICK**
Diocesan Pastoral Centre
St Michael's Courtyard,
Denmark Street, Limerick
Tel 061-400133 Fax 061-400601
Email ldpc@eircom.net
www.limerickdiocese.pastoralcentre.com
*Director:* Rev Éamonn Fitgibbon
Diocese of Limerick

**LOUTH**
Dominican Nuns
Monastery of St Catherine of Siena, The Twenties, Drogheda, Co Louth
Tel 041-9838524
Email sienamonastery@eircom.net
www.dominicannuns.ie
http://dominicannunsireland.blogspot.com
In a quiet country setting – self-catering Retreat House
*Acc:* 4 en suite rooms (2 of which have individual kitchenettes). Oratory with reserved Blessed Sacrament; fully equipped kitchen; private garden. Conference room suitable for day groups. Opportunity to participate in sung Monastic Liturgy and Eucharistic Adoration with the community.
*Contact:* Sister in Charge (Retreat Rooms)

**TIPPERARY**
House of Prayer, Glencomeragh, Kilsheelan, Co Tipperary
Tel 052-33181 Fax 052-33636
Email info@glencomeragh.ie
www.glencomeragh.ie
*Contact:* Rev Patrick Pierce (IC)
*Acc:* singles 18, doubles 8, twin 2
Available for preached, directed or private retreats, groups or individuals, lay, religious or priests, conferences and seminars; 4 hermitages and self-catering also available.
Rosminians. A recent addition to grounds is the 'Glencomeragh Labyrinth'.

**TYRONE**
Servite Priory, Benburb, Dungannon, Co Tyrone BT71 7JZ
Tel 028-37548241/028-37548533
Fax 028-37548524
Email servitepriory@btinernet.com
www.servites-benburb.com
Open to all who wish to call
*Contact:* Programme Co-ordinator

**WEXFORD**
St John of God Sisters Retreat House
Ballyvaloo, Blackwater, Co Wexford
Tel 053-9137160
Email ballyvalooretreatcentre1@eircom.net
www.ballyvaloo.ie
*Director:* Sr Leonie Dobbyn
*Acc:* ensuite rooms 33

**WICKLOW**
Chrysalis
Tel/Fax 045-404713
Email peace@chrysalis.ie
www.chrysalis.ie
*Contact:* The Manager
Chrysalis is no longer a Retreat House but still organises retreats. They are on sabbatical at the moment and are aiming to relaunch with a new programme of events in spring 2012. Please visit their website for further details.

Catholic Youth Care
Teach Chaoimhín,
Glendasan, Glendalough, Co Wicklow
(Enquiries to CYC,
Arran Quay, Dublin 7)
Tel 01-8725055 Fax 01-8725010
Email info@cyc.ie
*Acc:* small dormitories,
22 bunk beds

Catholic Youth Care
Teach Lorcain, Glendasan,
Glendalough, Co Wicklow
(Enquiries to CYC,
Arran Quay, Dublin 7)
Tel 01-8725055 Fax 01-8725010
Email info@cyc.ie
*Acc:* small dormitories,
23 beds including bunks

## PASTORAL CENTRES

**CORK**
Dominican Pastoral Centre
Popes Quay, Cork
Tel 021-4502067/021-4502267
Fax 021-4502307
Email dompc@eircom.net
*Director:* Rev Simon Roche (OP)
*Acc:* 2 conference rooms, 1 hall
Non-residential

Nano Nagle Centre
Ballygriffin, Mallow,
Co Cork
Tel 022-26411
Email enquiries@nanonaglebirthplace.ie
www.nanonaglebirthplace.ie
Presentation Sisters
Ecology and spirituality centre with opportunities to work with the earth. Facilities for self-catering private/group retreats conferences, workshops.

**DONEGAL**
Whiteoaks Rehabilitation Centre
Derryvane, Muff, Co Donegal
Tel 07493-84400
Fax 07493-84883
Email whiteoaksrehabcentre@hotmail.com
www.whiteoaksrehabcentre.com
*Director:* Fr Neal Carlin
*Manager:* Sharon McMullan
The purpose of White Oaks is to aid the recovery of people suffering from addictions. We offer a 30-day residential treatment programme, for people addicted to drugs, alcohol and gambling, based on the 12-step model. There is a two year aftercare programme.
The Centre has full international accreditation for the quality of its services. It is approved by VHI, Aviva and Quinn Healthcare Insurances.

**KERRY**
John Paul II Centre
Rock Road, Killarney, Co Kerry
Tel 064-6632644 Fax 064-6631170
Email pastoralcentre@dioceseofkerry.ie
Non-residential
*Director:* Rev Gearóid Godley
Kerry Diocese

**KILKENNY**
Seville Lodge Trust, Callan Road, Kilkenny
Tel/Fax 056-7721453
Conferences, retreats, courses
*Acc:* 30 beds
*Contact:* Dick Curtin (Manager)
Diocese of Ossory

**LIMERICK**
Limerick Diocesan Pastoral Centre
St Michael's Courtyard,
Denmark Street, Limerick
Tel 061-400133 Fax 061-400601
Email ldpc@eircom.net
www.pastoralcentre.limerickdiocese.org
*Director:* Rev Noel Kirwan

**MEATH**
Dowdstown House, Blowick Centre,
Dalgan Park, Navan, Co Meath
Tel 046-9021407 Fax 046-9073091
Email dowdstownhouse@eircom.net
www.dowdstownhouse.com
*Acc:* single 23, shared rooms 50
*Director:* Elma Peppard (RSM)
Meath Diocese

**WATERFORD**
St John's Pastoral Centre
John's Hill, Waterford
Tel 051-874199 Fax 051-843107
*Administrator:* Ms Mary Dee
Email stjohnspastoralcentre@eircom.net

## PRIVATE RETREATS

**ANTRIM**
Adoration Sisters
63 Falls Road, Belfast BT12 4PD
Tel 02890 325668
www.adorationsisters.com
Altar Bread Suppliers
'Saint Joseph's House of Bread'
Tel 02890 247175
*Contact:* Sr Molly Caldwell

Our Lady of Bethlehem Abbey
11 Ballymena Road, Portglenone,
Co Antrim BT44 8BL
Tel 028-25821211 Fax 028-25822795
Email celsus@bethabbey.com
www.bethlehemabbey.com
*Contact:* Rev Guestmaster
9.30am-5.00 pm, Monday-Saturday
*Acc:* 10 rooms: 8 singles/doubles, 2 singles
Cistercians

**DERRY**
Columba Community
Columba House of Prayer and Reconciliation
11 Queen Street, Derry BT48 7EG
Tel 028-71262407
Email columbacommunity@hotmail.com
www.columbacommunity.com
*Director:* Rev Neal Carlin
*Contact:* Tommy McCay
Email columbacommunity@hotmail.com
A basic Christian community with 20 members offering opportunities for private reflection and group worship. Prayer and pastoral counselling available on a one-to-one and group basis.
Blessed Sacrament Chapel open daily 9.30am-5.00pm
Monday to Friday: all welcome
Thursday 7.30pm Mass and Prayer for Healing

**DOWN**
Holy Cross Monastery
119 Kilbroney Road, Rostrevor,
Co Down BT34 3BN
Tel 028-41739979 Fax 028-41739978
Email benedictinemonks@btinternet.com
www.benedictinemonks.co.uk
*Contact:* The Guestmaster
Accommodation: 8 singles/doubles
Benedictines

**GALWAY**
La Retraite Hermitage
2 Distillery Road, Newcastle, Galway
Tel 091-524548
*Contact:* The community
Self-catering, retreat direction available
La Retraite Sisters

**LEITRIM**
La Verna, Convent Avenue,
Drumshanbo, Co Leitrim
Tel 071-9641308
*Contact:* Sr Helen Keegan
Self-catering: 3 bedroom retreat house
Poor Clare Monastery of Perpetual Adoration

**LIMERICK**
Glenstal Abbey, Monastic Guest House,
Murroe, Co Limerick
Tel 061-386103 Ext 225
*Contact:* Fr Christopher Dillon OSB
Email guestmaster@glenstal.org
*Acc:* 12
Benedictines

**WEXFORD**
St Aidan's Monastery of Adoration
Ferns, Co Wexford
Tel 053-9366634
Email staidansferns@eircom.net
Web www.staidans-ferns.org
*Contact:* Sr M. Dolores O'Brien
*Acc:* 8 hermitages, 1 wheelchair-friendly, 3 for couples.
House: sleeps 2 – single rooms.
Centre for Contemplative Outreach, Ireland

# ORGANISATIONS, SOCIETIES AND RELIGIOUS PERIODICALS

## ORGANISATIONS AND SOCIETIES

**Accord Catholic Marriage Care Service**
*President:* Most Rev William Walsh
*Vice-President:* Most Rev Raymond Field
*National Director:* Ms Ruth Barror
*National Chaplain:* Rev Peter Murphy
*Central Office:* Columba Centre, Maynooth, Co Kildare
Tel 01-5053112 Fax 01-6016410
Email admin@accord.ie
www.accord.ie

*For details, see Departments of the Irish Episcopal Conference.*

**Aid to the Church in Need**
*National Director:* J.F. Declan Quinn
151 St Mobhi Road, Glasnevin, Dublin 9
Tel 01-8377516 Fax 01-8369189
Email info@acnirl.org
www.kirche-in-not.org
Registered Charity No 9492

An association of Pontifical Right. The principal goal of the association is to support the Church pastorally, especially where she is persecuted and threatened. It also supports refugees and appeals to the faithful to assist in this work by prayers and donations.

**Alpha Ireland**
*National Co-ordinator*
Paddy Monaghan
72 Hillcourt Road, Glenageary, Co Dublin
Tel 01-2369821 Fax 01-2369800
Email alphairel@eircom.net
www.alphacourse.ie
Facebook: www.facebook.com/alphaireland

The 10-week Alpha Course explores the basics of the creed – Who is Jesus? Why did Jesus die? This user-friendly course on Evangelisation is endorsed by Church leaders. Archbishop Diarmuid Martin said, 'We believe that our diocese, our cities and towns, indeed our culture and especially our young people neet to know Jesus Christ. I commend the *Alpha Course* as one pathway whereby people can come to a knowledge and understanding of Jesus Christ today.'

It is aimed at those outside the church but also helps churchgoers renew their faith. 300 Alpha courses were held in Ireland last year. A Youth Alpha Co-ordinator has been appointed along with CYC and Scripture Union; 14 Youth Alpha courses are happening in Transition Year. Alpha has just launched the Parenting course run over 5 weeks for children and teenagers.

**Apostolic Work Society**
*President:* Mrs Anne Minihan
Abbey Road, Thurles
*Secretary:* Mrs Anna Maher
5 Bohernamona, Thurles
*Contact:* Thurles Parish Centre, Cathedral Street, Thurles
Tel 0504-22229 Fax 0504-22414
Email parishcentre@thurlesparish.ie

**Apostleship of Prayer**
*National Secretary*
Rev Bernard J. McGuckian (SJ)
St Francis Xavier Residence, Gardiner Street, Dublin 1
Tel 01-8363411
Email sales@messenger.ie
www.messenger.ie

A world-wide union of the faithful who, by the making of a daily offering and by praying for the Pope's intentions for the Church and the world, unite themselves with Christ in the Mass and with the prayers of his heart. *The Sacred Heart Messenger*, published monthly, is the official magazine. Messenger publications is a Jesuit Apostolate and publishes a range of religious booklets and calendars, as well as the *Sacred Heart Messenger*.

**Apostleship of the Sea**
*Episcopal Promoter:* Vacant
*Correspondence to President:*
Ms Rose Kearney
Stella Maris Seafarers' Club, 3 Beresford Place, Dublin 1
Tel 01-8749061/8742428 (7pm to 10.30pm nightly)

**Apostolate of Perpetual Eucharistic Adoration**
*National Co-ordinator*
Mr Joe Connolly KCHS
23 Merrion Square, Dublin 2
Tel 01-6625899/087-2478519
Email info@eucharisticadoration.ie
www.eucharisticadoration.ie

An Association of the faithful dedicated to promoting and spreading Eucharistic Adoration. The mission of the Apostolate of Perpetual Eucharistic Adoration is to assist dioceses and parishes in establishing, developing and maintaining viable weekly Eucharistic adoration programmes in conformity with the teaching of the Church and in full obedience to the bishops and priests. Eucharistic adoration is a devotion whereby members of a parish unite in making continuous adoration before the Blessed Sacrament, for as many hours as may be possible, based on the number of people who pledge to do a weekly holy hour when the programme is presented at Masses over a weekend.

**Association for Church Archives Ireland**
*Chairperson:* Dominique Horgan (OP)
*Vice-Chairperson:* Noelle Dowling
*Treasurer:* Marie Feely (OSC)
*Editor of Newsletter*
Teresa Delaney (RSM)
*Committee members:* David Kelly (OSA)
*Secretary:* Sr Mary Dalton (CSB)
5 Delany Court, Tullow, Co Carlow
Tel 059-9180054
Email marycatherine@eircom.net

The Association for Church Archives Ireland is concerned with the records and archives of the Christian Churches in Ireland. These include the records and archives of dioceses and parishes, religious congregations and societies. Membership is open to all who are intersted in promoting the objectives of the Association.

**Association of Irish Liturgists**
*Contact:* Rev Hugh P. Kennedy
Cathedral Presbytery, St Peter's Square, Belfast BT12 4BU
Tel 028-90327573

An informal association of people engaged in the study and teaching of liturgy.

**Association of Papal Orders in Ireland**
*President*
Donal Downes KSG (Galway)
*Vice President*
Gearóid O'Broin, GCPO
*Secretary*
Peter F. Durnin KC*SG (Armagh)
'Rosaire', Crosslanes, Drogheda, Co Louth
Email peternora12281@eircom.net
*Chaplain:* Rev Fr Timothy Bartlett

The Association is open to all ladies and gentlemen resident in or native of Ireland who have recieved a Knighthood from the Holy Father. It meets twice yearly.

**Association of Primary Teaching Sisters**
7/8 Lower Abbey Street, Dublin 1
*President:* Sr Mary Collins
*Secretary/Treasurer:* Sr Margaret Ivers
Tel 01-8781986 Fax 01-8781986
Email srmarycollins@eircom.net

Aims to unite its members through their religious consecration to share in the mission of the Church by ensuring Catholic education in schools and fostering the Christian message; to facilitate communication and liaison to improve the educational opportunity of children in primary schools.

**Catholic Boy Scouts of Ireland (see Scouting Ireland)**

**Catholic Guides of Ireland (Banóglaigh Catoilicí na hÉireann)**
*Chief Commissioner:* Catherine Lenihan
*Assistant Chief Commissioner*
Dolores Farnan
*National Treasurer:* Cecilia Browne
*National Chaplain*
Rev Eamonn McCamley
*National Office Coordinator*
Laura Saunders
*National Secretary:* Martha McGrath
*National Office:* 12 Clanwilliam Terrace, Grand Canal Quay, Dublin 2
Tel 01-6619566 Fax 01-6765691
Email nat.office@girlguidesireland.ie
www.girlguidesireland.ie

The Catholic Guides of Ireland (CGI) is a voluntary nationwide association open to all girls and women. It is organised on a diocesan basis, providing challenging indoor and outdoor activities which encourage the overall development of the individual. CGI through the Council of Irish Guiding Associations (CIGA) is a member of the World Association of Girl Guides and Girl Scouts (WAGGGS). CGI's youth programmes are available for 5-18 year olds at local community level. There are also opportunities for volunteer adult leadership, who receive training and support for this role.

**Catholic Nurses Guild of Ireland**
*National President:* Ms Breda Murphy
Ballyshane, Inishtigue, Kilkenny
*National Vice-President*
Sr Brid Commins, 29 Green Road, Mullingar, Co Westmeath
*National Secretary and Contact*
Ms Therese McCormack White Hart House, Ballbriggan, Co Dublin
*National Treasurer:* Sr Margaret Vincent
Sisters of Charity, Ard Mhuire, Harold's Cross, Dublin 6
*Headquarters:* Central Catholic Library, 74 Merrion Square, Dublin 2
Tel 01-6761264

The Guild is a response to the Vatican's Decree on the Apostolate of the Laity. Its role is to promote the social, educational, professional and spiritual development of its members so as to help them to work effectively in the service of life. There are several branches of the Guild active throughout Ireland.

**Catholic Communications Office**
*(Incorporating the Catholic Press and Information Office)*
Irish Bishops' Conference,
St Patrick's College, Maynooth,
Co Kildare
*Director:* Mr Martin Long
*Communications Officer*
Ms Brenda Drumm
Tel 01-5053000 Fax 01-6016413
Email info@catholiccommunications.ie
www.catholiccommunications.ie

**CatholicIreland.net**
St Mary's, Bloomfield Avenue,
Donnybrook, Dublin 4
Tel 01-6680505 Fax 01-6319755
Email info@catholicireland.net
www.catholicireland.net;
www.getonline.ie; www.gettingmarried.ie
*Chairman:* Fr Alan McGuckian (SJ)
*Chief Executive:* Mr Tony Bolger
*Patron:* Cardinal Sean Brady

CatholicIreland.net is an organisation whose aim is to promote the Catholic faith using modern communications like the world wide web. The site is a dynamic and attractive internet portal, which gathers and disseminates a wealth of quality information and resources, including the times of all masses in Ireland and a daily news service, to support believers and to reach out to others, in Ireland and throughout the world. Catholic Ireland also designs and builds websites for dioceses, parishes, schools and other Church-related groups.

**Catholic Primary School Management Association (CPSMA)**
*Chairman:* Mrs Maria Spring
11 The Enclosure, Oldtown Demesne, Naas, Co Kildare
Tel 045-879235 Fax 045-879270
*General Secretary:* Ms Eileen Flynn
*Assistant General Secretary*
Ms Margaret Gorman
*Office Manager:* Ms Linda Gorman
New House, St Patrick's College, Maynooth, Co Kildare
Tel 01-6292462/1850-407200
Fax 01-6292654
Email info@cpsma.ie
Website www.cpsma.ie

**Catholic Historical Society of Ireland**
*Secretary:* Dáire Keogh
*Treasurer:* Colm Lennon
*Conference Secretary:* Mary Ann Lyons
*Editor (Contact):* Dr Thomas O'Connor
Tel 01-7083926 Fax 01-7083314
Email thomas.oconnor@nuim.ie
www.archivium-hibernicum.ie

Founded in 1911, its annual journal *Archivium Hibernicum* publishes documents and studies dealing with Irish ecclesiastical history and Irish history in general.

**Catholic Men and Women's Society of Ireland**
*Patron:* Most Rev Donal Murray, Bishop of Limerick
*President:* Mr Eamon Hennessy
Tel 045-525165
*Hon Secretary:* Mr Ken Butterworth
Tel 087-1257132
*Hon Treasurer:* Ms Esther Brady
Tel 045-522094
*National Chaplain:* Vacant
2A Irishtown Road, Dublin 4

The Society strives for the personal development of its members through spiritual, intellectual, social and physical activities. The basic unit is called the branch. The society is organised at national level by the governing body, the National Council.

**CEIST**
*Chairperson, Board of Directors*
Ms Miriam Barry (Acting)
*CEO:* Ms Anne Kelleher
*Director of Faith Development*
Mr Ned Prendergast
Email nprendergast@ceist.ie
*Director of School Support Services*
Mr Michael Lane (Acting)
*Director of Finance:* Mr Mike Higgins
*ICS Manager:* Mr John Woods
First Floor, Block A, Maynooth Business Campus, Maynooth, Co Kildare
Tel 01-6510350 Fax 01-6510180
Email info@ceist.ie
www.ceist.ie

CEIST: Catholic Education – An Irish Schools Trust is a collaborative trustee body for the voluntary secondary schools of the following congregations:
- Presentation Sisters
- Sisters of the Christian Retreat
- Congregation of the Sisters of Mercy
- Missionaries of the Sacred Heart
- Daughters of Charity

CEIST Ltd was incorporated in May 2007
*Vision:* A compassionate and just society inspired by the life and teachings of Jesus Christ.

*Mission Statement:* To provide a holistic education in the Catholic tradition
*Values:* Promoting spiritual and human development, achieving quality in teaching and learning, showing respect for every person, creating community and being just and responsible.

**Central Catholic Library**
*Chairman:* Rev Noel Barber (SJ)
*Correspondence to:*
*Librarian:* Ms Teresa Whitington
74 Merrion Square, Dublin 2
Tel 01-6761264
Email catholiclibrary@imagine.ie
www.catholiclibrary.ie

Nationally important collection (founded 1922 by Fr Stephen Brown) of over 90,000 books with reference, research and lending departments. Emphasis on theology, scripture, spirituality, Church history, etc., but also on Irish history and culture (including Gaelic); literature and foreign languages (including important Dante collection), biography, history, travel; an extensive collection on art and architecture; and the philosophy, religion and sociology books of the old Central Students Library (for loan). Some pre-1800 titles. Runs of 400 journals (from 1814) in these areas. Audio and audio-visual materials. A voluntary subscription library, with an annual fee for borrowing rights; the reference and research departments are open to the public. Managed by an elected council, the library relies on public support for its continued existence and welcomes new members. Open: Mon-Fri 11.00-18.00; Saturday 11.00-17.50.

**Charismatic Renewal Movement**
Emmanuel, 3 Pembroke Park,
Ballsbridge, Dublin 4

The Charismatic Renewal Movement seeks to foster spiritual renewal under the inspiration of the Holy Spirit and to promote Christian unity. There are over 450 prayer groups in Ireland which are open to all. The movement maintain an office at 'Emmanuel'. Tel 01-6670570 NSC, Box 2434, Dublin 4. All telephone messages will be returned. The office is manned on Tuesday and Thursday 10.30am to 12.30pm

*Office of the National Service Committee for Catholic Charismatic Renewal in Ireland*
*Chairperson:* Marie Beirne
Tel 071-9624404
*Liaison Bishop to Charismatic Renewal:*
Bishop Martin Drennan
Email nsc@iol.ie

**Christian Life Communities**
35/36 Lower Leeson Street, Dublin 2
Tel 01-6471096
Email clc@jesuit.ie
www.jesuit.ie/clc

CLC is a worldwide lay association which has special links with the Society of Jesus. Founded in 1563 as the 'Sodality of Our Lady', it has changed radically since the Second Vatican Council. Members of CLC are helped to integrate their faith and daily living through the carism of the Spiritual Exercises of St Ignatius of Loyola. They meet on a regular basis, in groups of between six and ten, thereby getting support from each other. This form of spirituality, supported by the Group, leads to a sense of mission, which is rooted in the whole quality of presence which we bring to the world in which we live.

At present there are more than twenty thousand members in over 50 countries in every continent.

*For more information, contact:*
Fr Michael Gallagher (SJ)
Tel 01-7758596
Email mgallagher@jesuit.ie

**Church Resources/Church Telecom/Staffroom.ie**
St Mary's, Bloomfield Avenue,
Donnybrook, Dublin 4
Tel 01-6680505 Fax 01-6319755
Email info@churchresources.ie
www.churchresources.ie
www.churchresources.co.uk
*Chairman:* Fr Alan McGuckian SJ
*Chief Executive:* Mr Tony Bolger

Church Resources exists to combine the purchasing power of church organisations, including parishes, schools, religious congregations, care facilities and all other ministries and Church-related groups, to achieve financial savings on their everyday essential purchases. The savings that each group makes can then be used to finance their ministry activity. In the process this activity attracts a small commission from each of Church Resources' suppliers, which is in turn used to finance the maintenance and expansion of Churchservices.tv

**ChurchServices.tv**
St Mary's, Bloomfield Avenue,
Donnybrook, Dublin 4
Tel 01-6680505 Fax 01-6319755
Email info@churchservices.iv
www.churchservices.tv

ChurchServices.tv provides live video streaming from Cathedrals, Churches, or any other location via the internet. The video streaming can come from a permanent installation or from a one-off broadcast from a conference or any other single event. Video documentaries or other video material can also be streamed from ChurchServices.tv.

**Communion and Liberation**
*Contact:* Margaret Biondi
Tel 01-2987564
Email cldublin@eci.iewww.clonline.org

An international movement founded by Mgr Luigi Giussani in Italy in 1954 and approved by the Church. It is present in over seventy countries throughout the world. The essence of its charism is the announcement of the Incarnation of Christ who is present in the here and now and can be encountered in the unity of his people which is the Church.

**Concern Worldwide**
*Office:* Camden Street, Dublin 2
Tel 01-4177700 Fax 01-4757362
Email info@concern.net
www.concern.net
*Chief Executive:* Mr Tom Arnold
*Chairperson:* Frances O'Keeffe
*Secretary:* Tom Shipsey

Concern Worldwide is an international humanitarian organisation dedicated to tackling poverty and suffering in the world's poorest countries. We work in partnership with the very poorest people in these countries, directly enabling them to improve their lives, as well as using our knowledge and experience to influence decisions made at a local, national and international level that can significantly reduce extreme poverty.

**Conference of Religious of Ireland**
Bloomfield Avenue,
off Morehampton Road, Dublin 4,
Tel 01-6677322 Fax 01-6689460
Email secretariat@cori.ie
www.cori.ie
*Director General*
Sr Marianne O'Connor (OSU)
*President:* Sr Conchita McDonnell (MSHR)
Rev Jim Noonan (OCD)
Education 01-6677346,
Healthcare 01-6677349,
Northern Ireland 028-90694443

The Conference is a voluntary coming together of religious. Among its objectives are: to promote the spiritual and religious welfare of the congregations of Irish religious; to foster an ever-increasing effectiveness in the apostolate of the congregations; to effect a closer co-operation between congregations and with all members of the Church; to provide appropriate and official representation with civil government and bishops.

**Council of Irish Adoption Agencies**
*Chairperson:* Ms Sheila Gallagher
St Attracta's Adoption Society,
St Mary's Sligo
Tel 071-9143058
Email ciadoptionagencies@gmail.com
*Vice Chairperson:* Ms Marian Bennett
Social Worker, Health Centre,
Coosan Road, Athlone, Co Westmeath
Tel 090-6483136
Email marian.bennett@hse.ie
*Secretary:* Margaret Comaskey
Adoption Service, St Mary's Hospital,
Dublin Road, Drogheda, Co Louth
Tel 041-9832963
Email margaret.comaskey@hse.ie
*Treasurer:* Laura O'Callaghan
St Catherine's Adoption Society,
Clarecare, Harmony Row, Ennis, Co Clare
Tel 065-6828178

The Council of Irish Adoption Agencies represents statutory and voluntary adoption agencies. The Council aims to standardise adoption policy and practice, highlight adoption issues, influence policy, campaign for changes in adoption leglisation, develop services for all those with concerns in relation to adoption.

**Council of Management of Catholic Secondary Schools**
*President:* Mr Noel Merrick
Secretariat of Secondary Schools
Emmet House, Dundrum Road, Dublin 14
Tel 01-2838255 Fax 01-2695461
Email info@secretariat.ie
www.jmb.ie
CMCSS and AMCSS

The Council of Management of Catholic Secondary Schools (CMCSS) was founded in the 'sixties' and since 1972 has become a national organisation which includes representatives of the Irish Catholic Hierarchy. The Council of Management of Catholic Secondary Schools is the governing body of the Secretariat of Secondary Schools which is the administrative centre of information, research and action on behalf of the schools. The Council of Management of Catholic Secondary Schools maintains contacts and interacts with other national and International groups interested in Catholic education.

**CPRSI (See Cúnamh)**

**Cumann na Sagart**
*Uachtarán:* An tAth Tadhg Ó Móráin
Corr na Móna, Co na Gaillimhe
Guthán 094-9548003
Email tomorain5@eircom.net
*Rúnaí:* An tAth Tadhg Furlong
Ceapach na bhFaoiteach,
Co Thiobraid Arann
Guthán 062-75427
*Cathaoirleach*
An tAth Seamus Ó hÉanaigh SP
Delvin, Co na hIarmhí
Guthán 044-9644127

Is é aidhm an Chumainn ná dúchas creidimh na tíre a chothú, agus tacaíocht a thabhairt do shagairt a bhfuil an Ghaeilge in úsáid acu. Tugtar faoin aidhm seo a chur i gcrích: (a) trí léachtaí ag tionól bliantúil ina bpléitear gné éigin den dúchas creidimh; (b) trí fhoilseacháin liotúirge, scrioptúir, diagachta agus cultúir dhúchais; (c) trí chomhoibrú le pobal gach deoise tré mhéan Ionadaí an Deoise, agus trí imeachtaí éagsúla fríd an tír; (d) trí chomhoibriú le heagrais eile chun traidisiún dúchasach an phobail logánta a chothú, go háirithe i gcomórtas *Ghlór na nGael*. Tá suíomh idirlín ag Cumann na Sagart www.cumannnasagart.ie

**Cúnamh (formerly Catholic Protection and Rescue Society of Ireland) (CPRSI)**
*Secretary/Senior Social Worker*
Julie Kerins, BSocSc, CQSW, MSocSC
30 South Anne Street, Dublin 2
Tel 01-6779664
Email info@cunamh.com
www.cunamh.com

Cúnamh is a registered adoption agency providing pre- and post-natal counselling for pregnant girls, their partners and families; short-term foster care and adoption. Cúnamh provides support and advice for adoptive parents and an information and trace service for adult adoptees and birthparents.

**CURA Pregnancy Counselling Service**
*President:* Most Rev Gerard Clifford D.D.
*National Co-ordinator:* Louise Graham
*National Office:* Columba Centre, Maynooth, Co Kildare
Tel 01-5053040/1 Fax 01-6292364
Email curacares@cura.ie
www.cura.ie
National Helpline: 1850-622626

CURA is an agency of the Catholic Church and was established in 1977 as a caring, counselling and support service for those whose pregnancy is or has become a crisis.

Cura services:
- Crisis or Unplanned Pregnancy Support and Counselling
- Pregnancy Testing
- Counselling and Support after an Abortion
- Support to Mothers of a new baby
- Cura Schools Awareness Programme.

All services also available to men and other family members.
Services are free, confidential and non-judgemental.

**Dialogue Ireland Trust**
7/8 Lower Abbey Street, Dublin 1
Tel 01-8309384/087-2396229
Fax 01-8744913
*Director:* Mike Garde
Email info@dialogueireland.org
www.dialogueireland.org

The Dialogue Ireland Trust was established to promote awareness and understanding of 'cultist' New Religious Movements (NRMs) and to assist with advice and documentation. Dialogue Ireland Trust is an independent organisation at the service of Irish Society. Our mission is to assist in the protection of Religious freedom and to alert the public to the challenge cults pose to our mental health and our democratic freedoms. A specific area addressed is our schools programme directed at 6th years at Secondary School as a preparation for third level.

**Eco-Congregation Ireland**
Eco-Congregation aims to encourage churches to celebrate the gift of Gods creation, to recognise the interdependence of all creation and to care for it in their life and mission and through the members personal lifestyles
*Communications Officer:* Fiona Murdoch
Email info@ecocongregationireland.org
Tel 01-4939387/086-1706923

**ERST – Edmund Rice School Trust**
*Chairperson, Board of Directors*
Mr Pat Diggins
*Chief Executive:* Mr Gerry Bennett
*Co-ordinator of Ethos:* Mr Tony McCann
*Co-ordinator of Governance*
Ms Helen O'Brien
*Finance/Property Officer*
Ms Louise Callaghan
Meadow Vale, Clonkeen Road
Blackrock, Co Dublin
Tel 01-2897511 Fax 01-2897540
Email reception@erst.ie
www.erst.ie

The Edmund Rice Schools Trust, an independent lay company based in Dublin, ensure that the schools in the former Christian Brother Network (currently 98) will continue to provide a Catholic education into the future, in the spirit and tradition of Blessed Edmund Rice, for the people of Ireland.
ERST was incorporated in May 2008.
*Vision:* Promoting full personal and social development in caring Christian communities of learning and teaching.
*Mission Statement:* To provide Catholic Education in the Edmund Rice tradition.

The five keys elements of an Edmund Rice Schools Trust School are:
- Nurturing faith, Christian spirituality and Gospel-based values;
- Promoting partnership in the school community;
- Excelling in teaching and learning;
- Creating a caring school community;
- Inspiring transformational leadership.

**Equestrian Order of the Holy Sepulchre of Jerusalem, Lieutenancy of Ireland**
*Lieutenant*
HE Nicholas McKenna KSG, KCHS
'ByeWays', 27 Old Galgorm Road,
Ballymena, Co Antrim BT42 1AL
Tel 048-25663401
Email
nicholas.mckenna@galgormgroup.com
*Grand Prior:* Cardinal Séan Brady
Archbishop of Armagh
*Secretary:* Peter F. Durnin KSG, GCHS
Rosarie, Moneymore, Drogheda, Co Louth

The Lieutenancy of All Ireland of the Equestrian Order of the Holy Sepulchre of Jerusalem was established in July 1986. The venue for investitures is St Patrick's College, Maynooth, Co Kildare.

**Equipes Notre-Dame (Teams of Our Lady)**
Carmel and Pat Cunneen
Tel 01-2882528
Rev Gerard Cassidy (CSsR)
Email ireland@teams-transatlantic.org
www.equipes-notre-dame.com

An international movement of spirituality for married couples which has received official recognition from the Pontifical Council for the Laity. A team consists of five or six couples and a priest, and meets once a month. United by the sacrament of marriage, the couples seek, by deepening their spirituality, to strengthen their faith and increase their love. Informal evenings are arranged for couples wishing to know more about the movement.

**Evangelical Catholic Initiative**
72 Hillcourt Road,
Glenageary, Co Dublin
Tel 01-2369821 Fax 01-2369800
Email evancat@eircom.net
*Secretary:* Paddy Monaghan
60 Shore Road, Rostrevor,
Co Down BT34 3AA
Tel 028-41738801
Email boylecb@aol.com
*Secretary:* Eugene Boyle

ECI is an initiative for a New Evangelisation, comprised of Catholic Christians who are evangelical by conviction and committed to a personal relationship with Jesus Christ. It seeks to promote the kingdom of God under the guidance and empowering of the Holy Spirit, through working for a Christ-centred, biblically based renewal in the Catholic Church, through fostering reconciliation and unity among Christians and through building up Jewish/Christian relationships.

Email for a new document 'What is the Kerygma?', which sets out the core of the Catholic faith.

**Family and Media Association**
*Chairman:* Dr Ivo O'Sullivan PhD
*Contact:* Donal O'Sullivan, Executive *Development Officer*
Alberione Media Centre, Newtownpark Avenue, Blackrock, Co Dublin
Tel 01-2789288 Fax 01-2103834
Email info@fma.ie
www.familyandmedia.ie

Aims: to promote respect by the media for Christian values, especially those relating to the family; to seek high standards of honesty, decency, fairness and truthfulness in the media; to promote effective dialogue between the media and the public; to promote public understanding of the functioning and power of the media, and to assess and enhance the value of the media to the individual, the family and the community.

**The Family of God**
The Oratory, Carroll Village, Dundalk, Co Louth
Tel 042-9335566
Email fogoratory@eircom.net
*Contact:* Mr Teddy Lambe

The community was founded in Ireland in 1979. The community is non-residential and it is essentially a lay organisation although priests, religious and sisters are welcome to become associate members. The community is committed to a lifestyle of prayer, service and evangelisation. It is a registered charity in Ireland and Northern Ireland. The community has been recognised as a Private Association of the Faithful since July 1995 and it is a council member of the Catholic Fraternity, an international association of Catholic communities formally recognised by the Pontifical Council for the Laity.

**Father Matthew Union**
*President:* Most Rev Thomas A. Finnegan
*Spiritual Director*
Most Rev Francis McKiernan
*Secretary:* Rev Seán Moore CC
Parochial House, Carnmore Drive, Newry, Co Down Tel 01693-68512

An organisation of priests interested in promotion of temperance. Its branches operate on a diocesan basis. The Union works in liaison with Catholic and interdenominational temperance groups, with Alcoholics Anonymous and with the Irish National Council on Alcoholism.

**Focolare Movement**
*National Centre:* Focolare Centre, Curryhills, Prosperous, Co Kildare
Tel 045-840410
Fax 045-840104
Email focolare@focolare.ie, czmdublin@eircom.net
*Contact:*
Ms Juanita Majury/Mr David Hickey
*Dublin Centres:* 20 Ramleh Close, Milltown, Dublin 6
Tel 01-2698081
Email ramleh@focolare.ie

*Contact:* Ms Paola Grazia
8 Clareville Road, Harold's Cross, Dublin 6 Tel 01-4922709
*Contact:* Mr Marco Rossetti
Email focmdublin@eircom.net
www.focolare.org

An international movement founded by Chiara Lubich in 1943, at Trent in Northern Italy. Subsequently approved by the Church, its principal aim is to help bring about the fulfilment of the prayer of Jesus 'That All may be One'.

**Glencree Centre for Peace and Reconciliation**
Glencree, Enniskerry, Co Wicklow
Tel 01-2829711
Fax 01-2766085
Email info@glencree.ie
www.glencree.ie
*Chief Executive:* John Flood
*Chairperson:* Peter Keenan
*Contact:* Sue Paterson

A non-profit, non-governmental organisation committed to peacebuilding and reconciliation within and between communities. The centre provides services expressly devoted to peacebuilding issues in Ireland, North and South, Britain and beyond.

**Irish Biblical Association**
*President:* Fr Gerard Deighan
Email gdeighan@eircom.net
*Vice President:* Dr Kieran O'Mahony
Email komahony@milltown-institute.ie
*Secretary:* Tom Gillen
Email iba@iolfree.ie
*Treasurer:* Ms Máire Byrne
Email mairebyrne@gmail.com
www.irish-biblical-association.com

The IBA was established in 1966. The aims of the association are to: (a) assist the Irish Church in its work of understanding and proclaiming the word of God; (b) promote the scientific study of the Bible and related branches of learning; (c) organise conferences, study groups and lectures on biblical subjects; (d) support the publication of scientific studies on the scripture; (e) contribute to articles on biblical matters which will be of assistance in promoting a general biblical apostolate.

The association publishes an annual periodical, the Proceedings of the Irish Biblical Association. The members of the Irish Biblical Association are engaged professionally with and/or take a personal interest in the Jewish and Christian Scriptures. The Irish Biblical Association welcomes new members. There are two kinds of membership, ordinary and associate. Associate members are those interested in supporting and taking part in the events arranged by the IBA. Ordinary membership is for people with a post-graduate qualification in biblical studies.

Membership is accepted at the annual AGM in the spring and in the meantime prospective members are, of course, welcome in our meetings and can be on our mailing list.

**The Irish Chaplaincy in Britain**
*(For details, see Episcopal Commissions and Advisory Bodies and Chaplains)*

**Irish Church Music Association (Cumann Ceol Eaglasta na hÉireann)**
National Centre for Liturgy,
St Patrick's College, Maynooth, Co Kildare
*Chairperson:* Fr Paul Kenny
St Nicholas of Myra, Francis Street, Dublin 8 Tel 01-4542172
*Secretary:* Mrs Grace Lyons
134 Rialto Cottages, Dublin 8
Tel 01-4538750

An association for the promotion of church music. Activities include the publication of music, the organisation of regional meetings of church musicians and an annual summer school. A newsletter is issued regularly.

**Irish College, Paris**
Founded in 1578
5 Rue des Irlandais, 75005-Paris
*Rector:* Rt Rev Mgr Brendan P. Devlin
*Communicating Secretary*
Dr Thomas O'Connor
Maynooth College, Co Kildare
Tel 01-6285222
Email history.department@nuim.ie

The college is now vested in the Fondation Irlandaise, a trust for the education of Irish people and their accommodation in Paris. The college also hosts a full scale cultural centre. Visitors' rooms are periodically available to Irish people on application to the administrator, Ms Sheila Pratschke.
Tel 00-331-58 52 10 30
*Resident Chaplain:* Rev David Bracken
Tel 00-331-58 52 10 89

**Irish Council of Churches**
Inter-Church Centre,
48 Elmwood Avenue, Belfast BT9 6AZ
Tel 028-90663145
Email info@churchesinireland.com
www.churchesinireland.com
*(For details, see General Information section)*

**Irish Episcopal Council for Emigrants**
Columba Centre, Maynooth, Co Kildare
Tel 01-5053155 Fax 01-6016401
*Chair:* Most Rev Seámus Hegarty
*Secretary:* Ms Caroline Navagh
Email emigrants@iecon.ie

**Irish Episcopal Commission for Liturgy**
*National Secretary:* Rev Patrick Jones
National Centre for Liturgy
St Patrick's College, Maynooth, Co Kildare
Tel 01-7083478 Fax 01-7083477
Email liturgy@may.ie

**IHCPT The Irish Pilgrimage Trust**
Kilcuan, Clarenbridge, Co Galway
Tel 091-796622 Fax 091 796916
Email info@irishpilgrimagetrust.com
*Chairman:* John O'Reilly
*Honorary Treasurer:* James White
*Contact:* National Co-ordinator
Bernadette Connolly (for further information and application forms)
Email bconnolly@irishpilgrimagetrust.com

IHCPT The Irish Pilgrimage Trust is a voluntary organisation which brings young people with special needs to Lourdes at Easter time. The helpers pay their own fares and raise the funds for the young people. The Irish Pilgrimage Trust has a holiday house, Kilcuan, in Clarenbridge, Co Galway, which caters for groups with special needs. The trust has also recently opened a holiday house in Kilrane, Rosslare Harbour, Co Wexford. *For further details contact*
Tel 091-796622

**Irish Hospitalité of Our Lady of Lourdes (Affiliated to Hospitalité Notre Dame de Lourdes)**
Ely House, 8 Ely Place, Dublin 2
*President:* Ms Rosita McHugh
*Secretary/Contact Person*
Ms Deirdre O'Sullivan
26 Vernon Street, Dublin 8
Tel 01-6570138
Email deirdreosullivan@gmail.com
*Treasurer:* Mr Gerard Bennett
*Spiritual Director:* Rev Vincent Mulligan

Founded in 1930, under the patronage of the Archbishop of Dublin. An organisation of people, from all walks of life, who are dedicated to working with the sick in Lourdes.

**Irish Inter-Church Meeting**
Inter-Church Centre, 48 Elmwood Avenue, Belfast BT9 6AZ
Tel 028-90663145
Email info@churchesinireland.com
www.churchesinireland.com
*Co-Presidents:* Cardinal S. Brady
Most Rev R.L. Clarke
*Joint Secretaries:* Very Rev K. McDermott, Mr M. McCullagh
*Executive Officer:* Mr M. McCullagh
*Administrator:* Ms K. Kelly
*Treasurer:* Mr E. Fleming KCSG

**Irish Inter-Church Meeting Church in Society Forum**
*Chairperson:* Ms E. Gallagher

**Irish Inter-Church Meeting Theologly Forum**
*Chairpersons:* Rev Prf B. Leahy and Ms G. Kingston

**Irish Missionary Union (IMU)**
*Headquarters:* 563 South Circular Road, Dublin 8
Tel 01 4923326/4923325/4923337
Fax 01-4923316
Email executive@imu.ie
*President, Executive Council*
Sr Maureen O'Malley (MSHR)
*Vice President:* Fr John Guiney (SJ)
*Executive Secretary*
Fr Eamon Aylward (SSCC)
*Contact Person:* Fr Eamon Aylward (SSCC)
Email executive@imu.ie

The Irish Missionary Union is a collaborative network of Missionary Groups that promotes the understanding, development and sharing of Mission and strives to be a prophetic voice in society. It promotes the call of all Christians to Mission, and supports those sent to witness to the gospel of Jesus Christ and the reign of God in other cultures. The IMU runs: The IMU Mission Institute; The IMU Religion Formation Ministry Programme.

**IMU Mission Institute**
*Director:* Rev Patrick Dooher (SSC)
St Columban's, Dalgan Park, Navan
Tel 046-9021525 Ext 332
Fax 046-9073726/9022799
Email imuinst@eircom.net
www.imudalganpark.com

General renewal programme for priests and sisters. Centre for Theology and Ecology

**Irish School of Ecumenics, Trinity College, Dublin**
Ireland's Centre for Reconciliation Studies
*Head of Department*
Professor Sr Geraldine Smyth (OP)
Bea House, Milltown Park, Dublin 6
Tel 01-2601144 Fax 01-2601158
683 Antrim Road, Belfast BT15 4EG
Tel 028-90775010 Fax 028-90373986
Email isedir@tcd.ie
www.tcd.ie/ise

The Irish School of Ecumenics, Trinity College Dublin, is located in Dublin and Belfast. It is committed to the study and promotion of dialogue, peace and reconciliation in Ireland and around the world. It is recognised for its interdisciplinary approach to taught programmes and research, drawing on the fields of politics, sociology, ethics, theology and religion. Applied research is at the heart of all work undertaken at ISE, where students engage with crucial issues currently facing governments, religions, NGOs and peace organisations. The M. Phil programmes in Intercultural theology and Interreligious Studies, International Peace Studies and the Postgraduate Diploma in Conflict and Dispute Resolutions Studies are based in Dublin, while the M. Phil programme in Conflict Resolution and Reconciliation is based in Belfast. Please use the website: www.tcd.ie/ise to find detailed information about our taught programmes, research, and up-to-date news and events. Please note that applications should be made online at www.pac.ie. A one term (twelve week) non-degree programme is also available and is ideal for those on sabbatical, or for those who prefer a shorter period of study. There is also the option of attending one course. Students taking research degrees CM Lit or PhD can choose to do their research within School context – Dublin or Belfast.

ISE also provides a broad-ranging Continuing Education programme on inter-church and cross-community topics, in Northern Ireland and the border counties.

**Irish School of Evangelisation – ISOE**
The ISOE is an Association of Christ's Faithful [Can 298] founded in 1994 to promote initiatives of the 'New Evangelisation' e.g. Life in the Spirit Seminars/Retreats. The ISOE is a member of the "Catholic Bible Federation" and is affiliated with 'TINE' in Ireland and 'Evangelisation 2000' in Rome.

*Contact:* Joe O'Callaghan, 9A Wyattville Park, Dunlaoghaire, Co. Dublin.
Tel 01 2827658
Email isoe@esatclear.ie
www.esatclear.ie/~isoe

**Irish Theological Association**
*Secretary:* Tony McNamara
66 Foxfield Avenue, Raheny, Dublin 5
Tel 087 2903493
Email mctony@eircom.net
Email russelc@tcd.ie
www.theology.ie

Founded in 1965, the object of the association is to promote theological studies, and for this purpose it organises conferences and meetings for discussion, lectures and the general exchange of ideas.

**Jesuit Communication Centre**
36 Lower Leeson Street, Dublin 2
Tel 01-6768408 Fax 01-6629292
*Communications Manager:* Ms Pat Coyle
Email jcc@jesuit.ie
www.jesuit.ie

**Jesus Caritas Fraternity of Priests**
*National Responsible*
Rev Joseph Deegan PP
Slane, Co Meath, Tel 041-9824249
Email jpdeegan@gmail.com

An international association of priests who, following the spirituality of Charles de Foucauld, try to help one another to live their priesthood through mutual

support, in their presence to Jesus in daily Eucharistic adoration, in the Gospel and in his people. The National Responsible along with the four Regional Responsibles and the National Treasurer constitute the Irish Fraternity Council. Occasional meetings of the Council are held during each year.

**Kairos Communications Ltd**
*Director:* Fr Finbarr Tracey (SVD)
Tel 01-6286007 Fax 01-6286511
Email info@kairoscomms.ie

Kairos Communications Ltd, is the media arm of Divine Word Missionaries, Ireland. Established in 1973, Kairos is now one of the biggest Christian communications facilities in Europe. Equipped with its own studios and outside broadcast facilities, it produces masses/services for RTÉ television from all parts of the country on a monthly basis. Other religious productions for RTE television include the daily 'iWitness' and Angelus. On the education front Kairos works closely with St Patrick's College, Maynooth (Pontifical University), and the National University of Ireland, Maynooth (NUIM). Courses running at the moment include: Postgraduate Diploma in Christian Communications and Development (St PCM); Diploma in Communications (St PCM); BA in Media Studies (NUIM); MA in Radio and Television Production (NUIM), BA in Multimedia (NUIM).

**Knights of St Columbanus**
*Supreme Secretary*
Ely House, 8 Ely Place, Dublin 2
Tel 01-6761835 Fax 01-6762839
Email koc@iol.ie
www.knightsofstcolumbanus.ie

Organised into twelve Provincial Areas throughout Ireland. A member of Unum Omnes (International Federation of Catholic Men), based in Rome, since 1966. Foundation member of the International Alliance of Catholic Knights, which has 2.6 million members in Europe, Africa, Australasia and America.

**Knock Shrine Pilgrimages**
Promoting Knock Shrine, Co Mayo, as a place of pilgrimage. For details and dates of ceremonies and/or assistance in organising a pilgrimage or school tour to Knock, please contact:

*Secretary:* Knock Shrine Office,
Knock, Co Mayo
Tel 094-9388100 Fax 094-9388295
Email info@knock-shrine.ie
www.knock-shrine.ie

*Secretary:* Knock Shrine Pilgrimages,
Veritas Bookshop 7-8 Lower Abbey
Street, Dublin 1 Tel/Fax 01-8733356
Email dublinoffice@knock-shrine.ie

*Secretary:* Knock Shrine Pilgrimages
76/77 Little Catherine Street, Limerick
Tel 061-419458 Fax 061-405178
Email limerickoffice@knock-shrine.ie

*Secretary:* Knock Shrine Pilgrimages
PO BOX 210, Newtown, Abbey, Co. Antrim,
BT 36 9 DE
Tel/Fax 02890 774353
Email knockshrinebelfast@gmail.com

**Lay Fraternity of Blessed Charles de Foucauld**
*Enquiries:* Seán Ryan
146 Norwood Park, Limerick
Tel 087-6157867

Composed of small groups of lay people, married or single, who, after the example of Charles de Foucauld, seek to follow the way of Jesus present to them in the Gospel, in the Eucharist, and in their fellow men and women.

**Legion of Mary**
*President:* Síle Ní Chochláin
*Secretary:* Mr Patrick Fay
Concilium Legionis Mariae,
International Centre of the Legion of Mary, De Montfort House, Morning Star Avenue, Brunswick Street, Dublin 7
Tel 01-8723153/8725093 Fax 01-8726386
Email concilium@legionofmary.ie
www.legionofmary.ie

Catholic lay organisation for men and women. Its members are engaged in charitable and apostolic work.

**Life in the Eucharist Team**
Blessed Sacrament Chapel
20 Bachelors Walk, Dublin 1
*Contact:* Rev Jim Campbell (SSS)
Mary Keane *(Secretary)*
Tel 01-8724597 Fax 01-8724724
Email sssdublin@eircom.net
www.blessedsacramentuki.org

A team of dedicated trained lay people under the direction of a priest who, through weekend or evening seminars, lead participants into a fuller awareness of the Eucharist as a living experience in daily life. It is a source of nourishment for new and existing ministers of the Eucharist and Adoration groups. Lay people interacting with lay people from personal experience.

**Lough Derg**
*(For details, see Diocese of Clogher)*

**Marriage Encounter**
*Ecclesial Leadership Team*
Philip and Patricia Friel, 12 Largy Road,
Portglenone, Ballymena,
Co Antrim BT44 8BX
Tel 028-25821109
Email pafriel@aol.com
Fr Otto Imholte
St Columban's, Navan, Co Meath
Email bursargeneral@columban.com
www.marriageencounter.ie

Worldwide Marriage Encounter is a movement dedicated to the renewal of Matrimony, Priesthood and Religious Life. It provides the opportunity for participants to reflect upon their vocation in a private and positive way. It is for those who are committed to living out their sacrament in a dedicated way. Weekends are held all over Ireland. The Marriage Encounter weekend is not a retreat or counselling workshop, rather it is an enriching experience based on deepening communication skills within the marriage relationship, within parishes and within religious communities.

**Micah Community**
*Micah Coordinator:* Stephanie Birk
St Peter's Church, Phibsboro, Dublin 7
Tel 01-8102573
Email hello@micah.ie
www.micah.ie

We are a parish-based ministry for young adults providing opportunity for friendship, faith information, and outreach to an international community of young people living in Ireland.

**National Association of Christian Brothers Past Pupils Unions**
*National Officers*
*President:* Sean O'Callaghan
56 Park Court, Ballyvolane, Cork
*Secretary/Contact Person:* John Cooley,
73 Lansdowne Road, Belfast BT15 44B
Tel 028-90777491
Email johncooley50@hotmail.com
*Treasurer:* Richard Cruise
44 Granitefield, Cabinteely, Dublin 18

Established in 1976. The Association meets quarterly, generally in Dublin. Its aims include: co-operating with regional, national and international bodies of Past Pupils' Unions of Christian Brothers and with other organisations whose objectives and aims are similar in purpose and intent with those of the Association; promoting the cause of Blessed Edmund Rice with a view to canonisation; assisting the Edmund Rice Schools in their efforts to ensure that the tradition of Christian education as maintained by the Edmund Rice Schools Trust will not be lost, materially diluted or obscured; preserving and fostering the national heritage.

**National Association Executive of Primary Diocesan Advisors**
*Chairperson:* Rev Pat Coffey
Lisgaugh, Doon, Co Limerick
Tel 061-380247
Email piusix@eircom.net
*Secretary:* Ms Therese Ferry
The Gate Lodge, 2 Francis Street,
Derry City BT48 9DS
Tel 028-71264087
Email tferry@derrydiocese.org

The National Association of Primary Diocesan Advisors in Religious Education is a national organisation whose members support, educate and resource the partners in religious education at a primary school level in Ireland.

Membership of the Association is open to all full-time or part-time primary Diocesan Advisers. Associate membership is open to others who work in the area of Religious Education in primary schools.

The association aims to:

- support individual members in their work.
- provide a forum for discussion and debate.
- offer further formation and education for the members.
- review nationally the work of religious education in the Primary School and to actively encourage continual evaluation of progress.
- liaise with other agencies involved in the field of Religious Education.
- articulate nationally the needs of Religious Education at primary level.
- foster co-operation between the three partners involved in Religious Education – home, school and parish.

The association holds an Annual Conference and a minimum of two other meetings during the year. It is represented and organised by an executive, which is elected by the membership and holds office for three years. Members of the Executive represent the Association at the Catholic Primary School Management Association, the Episcopal Commission on Catechetics, and the Consultation Group for the National Primary School Programme.

**National Association of Healthcare Chaplains**
*Members of The NAHC Executive Committee 2011/2012*
*Chairperson:* Ms Margaret Mulcaire
NAHC Office, PO Box 10858, Blackrock, Co Dublin
Tel 087-9980274
*Vice Chairperson:* Mr Jim Owens
Secretary: Marie Gribbon
*Treasurer:* Rev Brian Gough

***Republic of Ireland Members***
*HSE Dublin/Mid-Leinster*
Rev Brian Gough, Sr Margaret Mulcaire, Ms Renée Dilworth
*HSE Western:* Mr Raymond Gately, Rev Patrick Burke, Rev Michael McGuckian (SJ)
*HSE Dublin/North-Eastern*
Mr Jim Owens, Marie Gribbon, Ms Susan Dawson
*HSE Southern*
Rev Daniel Nuzum, Rev Pierce Cormac

***Northern Ireland Members***
*Southern H&SS Board:* Vacant
*Eastern H&SS Board:* Vacant
*Western H&SS Board:* Vacant

***Hierarchy Representative***
Most Rev Raymond Field DD
*Secretary to the Executive*
Danielle Browne
NAHC, PO Box 10858, Blackrock, Co Dublin
Tel/Fax 01-2782693
Email nahc@eircom.net
Website www.nahc.ie

National Association of Healthcare Chaplains is a support organisation for Chaplains working in hospitals and healthcare facilities. The Executive is composed of representatives from each of the HSE areas.

**National Centre for Liturgy**
St Patrick's College, Maynooth, Co Kildare
Tel 01-7083478 Fax 01-7083477
Email liturgy@may.ie
www.liturgy-ireland.ie
*(For details, see Episcopal Commissions and Advisory Bodies)*

**National Chaplaincy for Deaf People**
40 Lower Drumcondra Road, Dublin 9
Tel 01-8305744 Fax 01-8600284
Email office@ncdp.ie
www.ncdp.ie
Fr Gerard Tyrrell, Director of the National Chaplaincy for Deaf People
Email gerard@ncdp.ie
Ms Frankie Berry, National Chaplain
Email frankie@ncpd.ie
Ms Veronica White, Chaplain in Cork and Kerry
Email veronica@ncdp.ie
*Lay Chaplain*: Ms Denise Flack
Email denise@ncdp.ie
Northern Ireland Tel 0044 78 77643961

The Chaplaincy gives a sacramental and pastoral service to the deaf community, seeks to increase awareness among priests and the wider church community of the pastoral needs of the deaf community and to promote an interest in the apostolate at diocesan level.

**National Mission Council of Ireland**
IMU, St Paul's Retreat, Mount Argus, Lower Kimmage Road, Dublin 6W
Tel 01-4923326, 4923325 Fax 01-4923316
Email executive@imu.ie
*(For details, see Episcopal Commissions)*

**Order of Malta, Ireland**
Services provided include

***First Aid Training Services***
Courses in Occupational First Aid, Basic First Aid, Manual Handling, Defibrillation Training (AED) and Refresher courses can be provided at your premises, a local venue or at our Training Centre in Ballsbridge, Dublin 4

***Malta Services Drogheda***
Provision of education and training to people with physical and learning disabilities on a daily basis. The service is run in partnership with the Health Service Executive.

***Malta-Share, Lisnaskea, Co Fermanagh, N Ireland***
Holidays for older people, respite care facilities for people with disabilities.

***General Community Care activities include:***
Day care, supper clubs for the elderly. Pilgrimages to Knock and Lourdes and an International Camp for Young People with disabilities.

***International***
Many Order of Malta projects are supported particularly the Holy Family Maternity Hospital, Bethlehem, Palestine.

*President:* Adrian FitzGerald
*Chancellor:* John Graeme Igoe
St John's House, 32 Clyde Road, Ballsbridge, Dublin 4
Tel 01-6140031 Fax 01-6685288
Email chancellery@orderofmalta.ie
www.orderofmalta.ie

**Order of Malta Ambulance Corps**
Provides a range of first aid, ambulance and emergency care services at major national and local level events in most of the principal cities and towns throughout the island of Ireland. As part of the major emergency plans it provides assistance to the statutory services, drawing on its fleet of over 150 ambulances and vehicles, ranging from minibuses, 4WD support vehicles to full accident and emergency ambulances. It also provides youth development services through Order of Malta Cadets – a National Youth Organisation.

*National Director:* Comdr Winifred Maye
St John's House, 32 Clyde Road, Dublin 4
Tel 01-6140033/6 Fax 01-6685288
Email info@orderofmalta.ie
www.orderofmalta.ie

**Pax Christi – International Catholic Movement for Peace (Irish Section)**
*National President*
Most Rev Raymond Field
*Chairperson:* Mr Gearoid Duffy
*Vice-Chairperson:* Mr Peadar O'Neill
*Treasurer:* Mr Fintan Mullally
*Headquarters:* 52 Lower Rathmines Road, Dublin 6
Tel 01-4965293
Email info@paxchrist.ie
*Contact:* Mr Tony D'Costa, General Secretary

Pax Christi is an international Catholic peace movement, with national sections in four continents. Its international office is in Belgium. Its activities are mainly related to the issues of security and disarmament; human rights; East-West contacts; North-South relations; peace education; peace spirituality; non-violence; faith, dialogue and reconciliation. Pax Christi has consultative status at the United Nations, UNESCO and the Council of Europe.

**People's Eucharistic League**
Blessed Sacrament Chapel
20 Bachelors Walk, Dublin 1
*Contact:* Br Timothy McLoughlin

An association of men and women with special devotion to the Holy Eucharist. Founded by St Peter Julian Eymard, members are associated with the apostolate of the Congregation of the blessed Sacrament. Members undertake to spend one hour per month in prayer before the Blessed Sacrament.

**Pioneer Total Abstinence Association of the Sacred Heart**
*Chief Executive Officer* Mr Padraig Brady
*Information Officer:* Ms Róisín Fulham
*Central Spiritual Director*
Rev Bernard J. McGuckian (SJ)
27 Upper Sherrard Street, Dublin 1
Tel 01-8749464 Fax 01-8748485
Email pioneer@jesuit.ie
www.pioneerassociation.ie

The Association has as its chief aim the promotion of temperance and sobriety, and prayer and self-sacrifice as its principal means. The members use their independence of alcohol to engage in good work and the organisation of counter-attractions to drinking.
*(For details of spiritual directors see dioceses)*

**The Radharc Trust**
*Trustees:* Mr Peter Dunn, Phil Donnelly Miriam Dunn, Donna Doherty and Peter V. Kelly
*Director:* Mr Peter Dunn
18 Newbridge Ave, Sandymount, Dublin 4
Tel 01-2755909/087-2520158
Email mail@radharc.ie
peter@radharc.ie
www.radharc.ie
www.radharcfilms.com

Preserving the Radharc Archive of over 400 documentary films. The films were made in 75 countries by the Radharc team of Dublin priests and lay people for Irish television during the period 1962 to 1997. They were one of the most popular programmes on Irish television during that time.

Showing the films in Parish Halls and Community Centres, School etc. for educational and entertainment purposes.

Sponsoring events in the Media that reflect the ethos of Radharc and promote the Good News.

**Regnum Christi**
*Contact:* Rev Michael Mullan (LC)
The Faith and Family Centre,
Avoca Avenue, Blackrock, Co Dublin
Tel 01-2889317
Email faithandfamilycentre@arcol.org
www.regnunchristi.org

Regnum Christi is an apostolic movement whose specific charism is to know, live and preach Christ's commandment of love. Through the formation of its members it seeks to support the ministry of the local dioceses and parish life. The areas of apostolate include: youth and family work, missions, educational and catechetical works.

**Religious Press Association**
*Chairperson and Public Relations Consultant:* Garry O'Sullivan, Journalist, c/o 36 Lower Leeson Street, Dublin 2
Email garryos@yahoo.ie
*Treasurer:* Lillian Webb 66 Roseville, Naas, Co Kildare Tel 045-866160

Association of editors of religious papers and magazines in Ireland. Seeks to improve the quality of and develop the influence of the religious press.

**Retreats Ireland**
*President:* Sr Breda Ahearn (CP)
Tearmann Spirituality Centre, Brockagh, Glendalough, Co Wicklow
Tel 0404-45639
Email bredaahearn@eircom.net
*Secretary:* Sr Geraldine Collins
Glendalough Hermitage Retreat, Laragh, Glendalough, Co Wicklow
Te 0404-45791
Email gercollinsrsm@gmail.com
*Treasurer:* Sr Eileen Egan
St John of God Retreat Centre,
Ballyvaloo, Blackwater, Co Wexford
Te 053-9137160
Email eileen.ejog@gmail.com
Benito Colango
Ards Friary, Creeslough,
Letterkenny, Co Donegal
Email info@ardsfriary.ie
Des Corrigan
Dromantine Retreat and Conference Centre
Email dcorrigan@utvinternet.com
Roisin Gannon
Mount St Anne's, Killenard,
Portarlington, Co Laois
Email roisingannon@eircom.net
Martina Lehane Sheehan
Ennismore Retreat Centre (St Dominic's),
Montenotte, Cork
Email martinalehane@hotmail.com
Pius McLaughlin
La Verna, Franciscan Friary,
Rossnowlagh, Co Donegal
Email piusmcl@hotmail.com
Margaret Prendergast
Glendalough Hermitage Centre,
Glendalough, Co Wicklow
Email mqtmprendergast@eircom.net

The aim of Retreats Ireland is to promote retreat work, to provide an information service, to offer training programmes, to encourage mutual support and co-operation in the context of retreat and pastoral centres in Ireland.

**RNN (Religious News Network)**
36 Lower Leeson Street, Dublin 2
Tel 01-7758515 Fax 01-6767493
Email info@rnn.ie
*Director:* Eileen Good
Tel 01-7758516
Email eileengood@rnn.ie
*Production Administrator:* Jeanann Cox
Tel 01-7758515
Email jeanann@rnn.ie
*Editor:* Miriam Gormally
Email miriam@rnn.ie
www.rnn.ie

RNN is a new syndication service of religious and social affairs, supplying more than 30 local, community and hospital radio stations throughout Ireland with live and recorded news, reaction stories and features. The service is funded by the religious congregations (CoRI) and the Church of Ireland.

**Saint Joseph's Young Priests Society**
*President:* Mrs Marie Hogan
23 Merrion Square, Dublin 2
Tel 01-6762593 Fax 01-6762549
Email sjyps@eircom.net
www.sjyps.com

An Irish lay organisation founded in 1895 with branches in every diocese in Ireland. Its members promote vocations to the priesthood and religious life and assist students financially, at home and abroad.

**School Chaplains Association (Cumann na Seiplineach Scoile)**
*Chairperson:* Mr Sean Wright
Pobalscoil Chiarain, Kells, Co Meath
Tel 046-9241551
Email ppdd@eircom.net
*Vice-chairperson:* Rev Bernie Moloney
Cashel Community School,
Cashel, Co Tipperary
Tel 062-61026
Email cashelchaplain@eircom.net
www.schoolchaplains.ie

**Scouting Ireland**
*Chief Scout:* Michael John Shinnick
*National Secretary:* Mr Mick Devins
*National Treasurer:* Mr Niall Walsh
*Communications Commissioner*
Mr Joe Boland
*CEO:* Mr Eamonn Lynch
Administration and Resource Centre,
Larch Hill, Dublin 16
Tel 01-4956300 Fax 01-4956301
www.scouts.ie

The aim of Scouting Ireland is to encourage the physical, intellectual, character, emotional, social and spiritual development of young people so they may achieve their full potential and, as responsible citizens, to improve society.

Scouting Ireland has a 32-county membership of 40,000 including 60,000 adult volunteers. It provides young people with opportunities to take part and lead a progressive programme through fun, friendship and challenge.

**Secular Franciscan Order**
*National President:* John Murray, Cork
*National Headquarters*
c/o Mary Tiernan SFO
3 St Mary's Terrace, Chapelizod, Dublin 20
Tel 01-6262264
Email sfohq@eircom.net
*Contact:* Mary Tiernan

An Order of lay people who seek to follow Christ in their everyday life in the footsteps of St Francis of Assisi (going from gospel to life and life to gospel).

**Society of St Vincent de Paul – National Office**
*National President:* Ms Mairead Bushnell
*Contact:* Kieran Murphy
*Headquarters:* SVP House,
91-92 Sean MacDermott Street, Dublin 1
Tel 01-8386990
Email info@svp.ie
www.svp.ie

An international lay organisation, which endeavours to alleviate need and redress situations which cause it. Its principal work is visiting people in their homes, but it also provides holidays, hostels for the homeless, youth clubs, housing for the elderly, and good-as-new shops.

**The Teresian Association**
St Patrick's Cottage,
21 Beaufield Park, Stillorgan, Co Dublin
Tel 01-2056937
Email irelandta@eircom.net

The Teresian Association is an International Association of the Faithful for lay Christians, present today in 30 countries. It was started in 1911 by Saint Pedro Poveda, a Spanish diocesan priest, canonised by Pope John Paul II in Madrid on 4 May 2003. It aims to help transform society through education and culture in the light of the Gospel. Its members are women and men who, according to their specific calling, live out their vocation of Christian lay people in society, working in educational, cultural and professional areas. They witness to Gospel values in all they do and are involved in a wide variety of areas across society. Their particular focus, however, is education at all levels and in its broadest sense. Members do this through the way they live their professional, occupational and family lives. The Association supports and sustains a number of non-governmental organisations and collaborates with Church programmes and other institutions. It also runs a number of educational centres in different countries, including the Teresian School in Dublin.

The Teresian School, *(Pre-School, Kindergarten, Junior and Secondary School)*
12 Stillorgan Road, Dublin 4
Tel 01-2691376 Fax 01-2602878
Email school@teresian.ie

**Trócaire**
*Lenten Campaigns Organiser*
Claire Whelan
*Press & Communications*
Emer Mullins, Maynooth, Co Kildare
Tel 01-6293333 Fax 01-6290661
*Offices and Resource Centres*
12 Cathedral Street, Dublin 1
9 Cook Street, Cork
50 King Street, Belfast BT1 6AD
*(For details, see Episcopal Commissions)*

**Veritas Communications**
Veritas House,
7-8 Lower Abbey Street, Dublin 1
Tel 01-8788177 Fax 01-8786507
*(For details, see Episcopal Commissions)*

**Veritas Company Ltd**
Veritas House,
7-8 Lower Abbey Street, Dublin 1
Tel 01 8788177 Fax 01-8744913
*(For details, see Episcopal Commissions)*

**Veritas Publications**
Veritas House,
7-8 Lower Abbey Street, Dublin 1
Tel 01-8788177 Fax 01-8786507
*(For details, see Episcopal Commissions)*

**Viatores Christi**
8 New Cabra Road, Phibsboro, Dublin 7
Tel 01-8689986 Fax 01-8689891
Email info@viatoreschristi.com
www.viatoreschristi.com

A voluntary Catholic lay missionary association. Recruits, prepares and facilitates the placement of people who wish to work overseas, for one year or more, in areas of need such as Africa, South America, Asia and parts of Canada, USA and Europe. Viatores Christi offers a 6 month part-time preparation programme.

**Vocations Ireland**
St Mary's, Bloomfield Avenue,
Donnybrook, Dublin 4
*Director:* Sr Eileen Linehan, IBVM
Tel 01-6689954/086-7820149
Email info@vocationsireland.com
www.vocationsireland.com

Vocations Ireland presents Religious life as a creative opportunity to live the mission of Christ in today's world. It provides information about missionary and religious life as well as support, resources and in-service opportunities for those in vocation ministry. It also provides personal accompaniment and discernment programmes for prospective candidates.

**Volunteer Missionary Movement**
VMM, The Priory, John Street West,
Dublin 8
Tel 01-3664421
Email mission@vmm.ie
www.vmm.ie
*Contact:* Dr Vincent Kenny, Director
VMM (Europe)

The VMM is an international lay, missionary organisation, founded in 1969. VMM currently have 65 professional volunteers currently working in East Africa and Central America. Following completion of their overseas contract. They are enouraged to maintain their Christian commitment through working for change within their home community.

**World Missions, Ireland. The work of the Pontificial Mission Societies.**
*National Director*
Rev Gary Howley (SPS)
64 Lower Rathmines Road, Dublin 6
Tel 01-4972035/4972422 Fax 01-4960140
Email director@wmi.ie
www.wmi.ie
Registered Charity Number: CHY 2318

The Pontifical Mission Societies form one institution with four branches:

***Society for the Propagation of the Faith***
Purpose: supports as many as 1096 mission dioceses throughout the world. Each year the Society endeavours to increase clerical, religious and laity awareness of mission work. The Society is responsible for organising the Church's annual universal celebration of mission – Mission Sunday – encouraging spiritual and material support for Catholic missions worldwide.

***Society of St Peter Apostle***
Purpose: invites spiritual and finanancial support to assist young mission Churches in the training of their own priests, brothers and sisters.

***Society of Missionary Children***
Purpose: encourages Irish children to connect with children in mission lands through the sharing of prayer and material gifts. The Society's motto – 'Children Helping Children' – illustrates how Irish children of primary school age can make small gestures which will help to improve the lives of other children who experience war, famine, poverty and suffering.

***Missionary Union***
Purpose: unites clergy, religious, seminarians and catechists in helping the missionary activity of the Church by the sanctity of their lives and prayer. The Society promotes mission awareness among those involved in the pastoral ministry of the Church.

**Young Christian Workers (Saotharaithe Ógra Críostaí)**
*National Co-ordinator:* Ms Vicky Rattigan
Email vicky@ycw.ie
*Development Worker:* Gerry Keegan
*National Chaplain:* Rev Eoin McCrystal
YCW National Office, 11 Talbot Street,
Dublin 1
Tel 01-8780291
Email info@ycw.ie
www.ycw.ie

The Young Christian Workers is an international youth movement which values the dignity and worth of each young person. It enables its members to challenge social exclusion and take action to bring about change in their home, their workplace and their social life. Many useful skills are acquired through attendance at weekly meetings, socials, international exchanges and training weekends. YCW IMPACT! 'Change through Action' Programme is aimed at young people in the 16-18 age group. A starter pack for working with young people aged 18 plus and a media resource complete with accompanying DVD are also available at our national office. YCW handbook also available to assist in the formation of YCW groups and provide a practical experience of the See, Judge, Act Method. For further details on retreats and events check our website: www.ycw.ie.

## RELIGIOUS PERIODICALS

### PUBLICATION OF THE IRISH CATHOLIC BISHOPS' CONFERENCE

**Intercom**
*Editor:* Mr Francis Cousins
Email fcousins@catholicbishops.ie
Columba Centre, St Patrick's College Maynooth, Co Kildare
A pastoral and liturgical resource for people in ministry, published by the Veritas Group, an agency of the Irish Catholic Bishops' Conference.
Publiched ten times a year.
*Subscriptions:* Ross Delmar
7-8 Lower Abbey Street, Dublin 1
Tel 01-8788177 Fax 01-8786507
Email ross.delmar@veritas.ie

### OTHER RELIGIOUS PERIODICALS

**Africa**
*Editors:* Rev Tim Redmond (SPS)
Email africa@spms.org
*Circulation Manager*
Rev William Fulton (SPS)
Tel 059-6473600Fax 059-6473622
Email spsoff@iol.ie
International family mission magazine with topical articles on Christianity today; Bible reflections; youth and children's features. Nine issues per year.
Published by St Patrick's Missionary Society, Kiltegan, Co Wicklow

**African Missionary**
*Editor:* Rev Martin Kavanagh SMA
Newsletter Presentation of Missionary News and Profiles of the Lives and activities of SMA and OLA members in Africa and elsewhere,Three issues per year (including Calendar issue).
Published by the Society of African Missions, Blackrock Road, Cork
Tel 021-4616318 Fax 021-4616399
Email publications@sma.ie
www.sma.ie

**Alive!**
*Editor:* Rev Brian McKevitt (OP)
Free 16-page Catholic tabloid paper with news, features, interviews. Available free for distribution by parishes, churches, shops, praesidia, etc. nationwide.
Circulation: 385,000.
Published monthly from
St Mary's Priory, Tallaght, Dublin 24
*Contact:* Breda
Tel 01-4048187 Fax 01-4596784
Email alivepaper@gmail.com

**Being One**
*Editor:* Rev Brendan Leahy
Focolare Centre, Prosperous, Co Kildare
Tel 045-840430
Email beingone@eircom.net
Published three times a year.

**Bulletin of St Vincent de Paul**
*Editor:* Tom MacSweeney
Published quarterly by the Society of St Vincent de Paul in Ireland at National Office, SVP House,
91-92 Sean MacDermot Street, Dublin 1
Tel 01-8386990 Fax 018387355
Email editorbulletin@svp.ie
www.svp.ie

**Catholic Voice Newspaper**
*Editor:* Anthony Murphy
PO Box 11559, Dublin 1
Tel 059-8627268
Email editor@catholicvoice.ie
Tabloid 28 pages. Rrp €1/£1

**Church of Ireland Gazette**
*Editor:* Rev Canon Ian Ellis
Office: 3 Wallace Avenue, Lisburn, Co Antrim BT27 4AA
Tel Lisburn 9267 5743
Email gazette@ireland.anglican.org
The Church of Ireland Gazette is an editorially independent weekly newspaper.

**Daystar**
*Editor:* Sr Ann McColl
Email annca7349@yahoo.co.uk
*Contact:* Sr Nora Bergin
Published bi-annually by the Franciscan Missionary Sisters for Africa
Mount Oliver, Dundalk, Co Louth
Tel 042-9371123
Fax 042-9371159
Email fmsamto@gofree.indigo.ie
*Regional Leader*
Sr Jeanette Watters (FMSA)
Franciscan Missionary Sisters of Africa
142 Raheny Road, Raheny, Dublin 5
Tel (01) 8473140 Fax (01) 8481428
Email fmsanar@iol.ie
www.iol.ie/~fmsanar

**Doctrine and Life**
*Editor:* Rev Bernard Treacy (OP)
Published ten times a year by Dominican Publications,
42 Parnell Square, Dublin 1
Tel 01-8721611 Fax 01-8731760
Email
subscriptions@dominicanpublications.com

**Corpus Christi National Apostolate for Eucharistic Adoration.**
*Editor:* Joe Conroy
www.eucharisticadoration.ie

**Face Up**
*Editor:* Gerard Moloney (CSsR)
For teens who want something deeper, published eight times a year by Redemptorist Communications,
75 Orwell Road, Rathgar, Dublin 6
Tel 01-4922488
Fax 01-4927999
Email info@faceup.ie
www.faceup.ie

**The Far East**
*Editor:* Rev Cyril Lovett (SSC)
Full colour, emphasis on Christian mission and related topics.
Circulation: 100,000 in Ireland and Britain. Published eight times a year by the Missionary Society of St Columban, St Columban's, Navan, Co Meath
Tel 046-9098272 Fax 046-9071297
Email editorfareast@columban.com
www.columban.com
*Manager:* Rev Noel Daly

**Foundations**
*Editor:* Fr Sean Fennelly
Cashel and Emly diocesan magazine
Hospital, Co Limerick
Tel 061-383565
Email foundations@cashel-emly.com

**The Furrow**
*Editor:* Rev Ronan Drury
Published monthly by
The Furrow Trust, St Patrick's College, Maynooth, Co Kildare
Tel 01-7083741 Fax 01-7083908
Email furrow.office@may.ie
www.thefurrow.ie

**Irish Catholic**
*Managing Editor:* Mr Garry O'Sullivan
Published weekly by The Agricultural Trust, The Irish Catholic is Ireland's largest and best selling Catholic Newspaper since 1888
Irish Farm Centre, Blubell, Dublin 12
Tel 01-4276400 Fax 01-4276450
Email news@irishcatholic.ie, advertising@irishcatholic.ie

**Irish Theological Quarterly**
*Editor-in-Chief:* Rev Michael A. Conway
*Secretary:* Prof Salvador Ryan
*Review Editor:* Rev Liam Tracey
*Business Manager:* Ms Fidelma Madden
Published by members of the Faculty of Theology, St Patrick's College, Maynooth, Co Kildare
Tel 01-7083496 Fax 01-6289063
Email itq.editor@may.ie

**Maria Legionis**
(Journal published quarterly by the Legion of Mary)
Presentata House,
263 North Circular Road, Dublin 7
Tel 01-8387770
Email marialegionis@eircom.net

**Medical Missionaries of Mary**
*Editor:* Sr Carol Breslin (MMM)
*Healing & Development* Annual report plus supplementary newsletters in spring and autumn, available from MMM Communications, Rosemount Terrace, Booterstown, Co Dublin
Tel 01-2887180 Mobile 087-9701891
Fax 01-2834626
Email mmm@iol.ie
www.mmmworldwide.org

**Milltown Studies**
*Editor:* Dr Joseph Egan (SMA)
Milltown Institute of Theology and Philosophy, Milltown Park, Dublin 6
Tel 01-2776300 Fax 01-2692528
Email mseditor@milltown-institute.ie

**New Liturgy**
*Editor:* Rev Patrick Jones
Bulletin of the National Secretariat, Irish Episcopal Commission for Liturgy, published quarterly at the National Centre for Liturgy, St Patrick's College, Maynooth, Co Kildare
Tel 01-7083478 Fax 01-7083477
Email liturgy@may.ie
www.liturgy-ireland.ie

**Non-Subscribing Presbyterian Magazine**
*Editor:* Rev Dr A. D. G. Steers
223 Upper Lisburn Road,
Belfast BT10 0LL
Tel 028-90947850
Email nspresb@hotmail.com

**Pioneer**
*Editor:* Fr Bernard J. McGuckian (SJ)
*Sub-editor:* Ms Róisín Fulham
Published monthly by Pioneer Total Abstinence Association,
27 Upper Sherrard Street, Dublin 1
Tel 01-8749464 Fax 01-8748485
Email pioneer@jesuit.ie
www.pioneerassociation.ie

**Presbyterian Herald**
*Editor:* Stephen Lynas
Published monthly by Presbyterian Church in Ireland, Church House, Fisherwick Place, Belfast BT1 6DW
Tel 028-90322284 Fax 028-90417307
Email herald@presbyterianireland.org
www.presbyterianireland.org

**Proceedings of the Irish Biblical Association**
Published by IBA Publications
*Contact:* Noel Fitzpatrick
16 Granville Park, Blackrock, Co Dublin
Email njfitzpatrick712@gmail.com
iba@iolfree.ie

**Reality**
*Editor:* Rev Gerard R. Moloney (CSsR)
*Marketing:* Paul Copeland
Published monthly by Redemptorist Communications, 75 Orwell Road, Rathgar, Dublin 6
Tel 01-4922488
Fax 01-4927999
Email info@redcoms.org
www.redcoms.org

**Religious Life Review**
*Editor:* Rev Thomas McCarthy (OP)
Published six times a year by Dominican Publications,
42 Parnell Square, Dublin 1
Tel 01-8587103 Fax 01-8731760
Email dompubs@iol.ie

**Sacred Heart Messenger**
*Editor:* Rev John Looby (SJ)
Official publication of the Apostleship of Prayer, published monthly by Messenger Publications at
37 Lower Leeson Street, Dublin 2
Tel 01-6767491 Fax 01-6767493
Email sales@messenger.ie
www.messenger.ie

**An Sagart**
*Eagarthóir:*
An Mgr Pádraig Ó Fiannachta
Foilsítear ceithre uair sa bhliain ag An Sagart, An Díseart, An Daingean, Trá Lí, Co Chiarraí
Tel 066-915000
Ephost pof@diseart.ie
www.ansagart.ie
Síntiús Bliana €15

**The Salesian Bulletin**
*Editor:* Rev Pat Egan (SDB)
Salesian College, Celbridge, Co Kildare
Tel 01-6275060 Fax 01-6303601
Email frpegan@iol.ie
homepage.eircom.net/~sdbmedia
*Subscriptions*
Rev Dan Devitt (SDB)
Salesian Missions, PO Box 50, Pallaskenry, Co Limerick
Tel 061-393223 Fax 061-393354
Published quarterly for the Salesians of Don Bosco by Salesian Bulletin.

**Scripture in Church**
*Editor in Chief*
Rev Martin McNamara (MSC)
Published quarterly by Dominican Publications,
42 Parnell Square, Dublin 1
Tel 01-8721611 Fax 01-8731760
Email
subscriptions@dominicanpublications.com

**The Sheaf**
formerly *St Joseph's Sheaf*
*Editor:* Dominic Dowling FCII KCHS
St Joseph's Young Priests Society
23 Merrion Square, Dublin 2
Tel 01-6762593 Fax 01-6762549
Email sjyps@eircom.net
and jddowling@iname.com
Its purpose is twofold:
(a) to foster vocations to priesthood and religious life
(b) to promote the vocation of the laity.
www.thesheaf.vpweb.ie

**Spirituality**
*Editor:* Rev Tom Jordan (OP)
Published six times a year by Dominican Publications,
42 Parnell Square, Dublin 1
Tel 01-8721611 Fax 01-8731760
Email
tom.jordan@dominicanpublications.com
www.dominicanpublications.com

**The St Anthony Brief**
*Editor:* Bernard Jones (OFM)
Email bernardofm@eircom.net
Published every two months by the Franciscan Missionary Union,
8 Merchant's Quay, Dublin 8
Tel 01-6777651 Fax 01-6777293

**St Joseph's Advocate**
*Editor:* Fr Jim O'Connell (MHM)
Tel 056-7753631
Published quarterly by Mill Hill Missionaries,
St Joseph's, Waterford Road, Kilkenny
Tel 056-7721482 Fax 056-7751490
Email jimocmhm@eircom.net

**St Martin Magazine**
*Editor:* Rev Diarmuid Clifford (OP)
Published monthly by St Martin Apostolate,42 Parnell Square, Dublin 1
Tel 01-8745464/8730147 Fax 01-8731989
From UK 00-353-1-8745465
Email stmartin@iol.ie
Personal Email dcop@eircom.net

**Studies – An Irish Quarterly Review**
*Editor:* Rev Fergus O'Donoghue (SJ)
Published by the Irish Jesuits,
35 Lower Leeson Street, Dublin 2
Tel 01-6766785 Fax 01-6767493
Email studies@jesuit.ie
www.studiesirishreview.com

**Timire an Chroí Naofa**
Bunaíodh 1911
*Eagarthóir Feidhmitheach*
An tAth Alan MacEochagán (SJ)
*Eagarthóir:* Fionnuala Mac Aodha
37 Sr Líosáin Íocht, Baile Átha Cliath 2
Ephost timire@jesuit.ie
*Bainistíocht:* Coiste an Timire,
Teach Manresa SJ, Baile na gCorr,
Cluain Tarbh, Baile Áth Cliath 3
Fón 01-8325138

**Traces**
*Subscriptions:* Lee Sorensen
PO Box 7060, Dublin 6
Tel 01-4973361 Fax 01-4975008
Email cldublin@eci.ie
*Traces* is the monthly publication of Communion and Liberation, the international Catholic Movement founded by Luigi Giussani. It expresses the life and viewpoint of people in this movement which is now a living reality in the Church's social and ecclesial horizon.

**The Universe Catholic Weekly**
*Editor:* Joseph Kelly
The Universe Media Group Limited
4th Floor, Landmark House,
Station Road, Cheadle Hulme SK8 7JH,
Cheshire, UK

# MARRIAGE TRIBUNALS

By Decree dated 24 March 1975, the Irish Episcopal Conference decided to establish four Regional Marriage Tribunals of first instance to be located at Armagh, Dublin, Cork and Galway. This decree was formally approved by the Supreme Tribunal of the Apostolic Signatur on 6 May 1975. In accordance with the terms of the Roman rescript, the Episcopal Conference, in a decision of 30 September 1975, determined the Regional Tribunals would come into effect on 1 January 1976. From that date they replaced all previous diocesan marriage tribunals.

By the same process which established in Ireland Regional Marriage Tribunals of first instance, the Episcopal Conference set up a sole Appeal Tribunal, located in Dublin, to hear cases on appeal from each of the four Regional Tribunals. It also came into effect on 1 January 1976. Its personnel and administration are wholly distinct from the Dublin Regional Marriage Tribunal.

## NATIONAL MARRIAGE APPEAL TRIBUNAL

Columba Centre, Maynooth, Co Kildare
Tel 01 5053119 Fax 01-5053122
Email brian.flynn@iecon.ie
*Judicial Vicar*
Rev Michael Smyth (MSC), STL, JUD
*Administrator:* Mrs Stephanie Walpole
*Vice Officialis*
Rt Rev Mgr Joseph Donnelly PP, VF
*Associate Judges*
Very Rev Canon Eugene Mangan PP (Kerry), Very Rev Gerard McNamara PP (Limerick), Rt Rev Mgr John Shine BD, LCL, LPh, PP, (Waterford and Lismore), Very Rev Patrick Gill AP, Very Rev John Canon O'Boyle BA, Very Rev Patrick Williams AP, Very Rev S.J. Clyne PP, VF, Rev Patrick Connolly DCL, Rev Brendan Kilcoyne LCL, Rev Michael Mullaney DCL, Rev William Dalton, Sr Mairín McDonagh (SJM), Rev John Whelan (OSA), Mr Michael V. O'Mahony, Rev Seán O'Neill, Very Rev Francis Maher PP, Rev Lorcan Moran, Rt Rev Mgr Gerard Dolan, PP, LCL
*Defenders of the Bond*
Rev Brian Flynn, Rev Michael Bannon
Rev Gabriel Kelly, Rev Kevin O'Gorman
*Correspondence to:* Administrator

## REGIONAL MARRIAGE TRIBUNALS

### ARMAGH REGIONAL MARRIAGE TRIBUNAL

*Regional Office:* 15 College Street, Armagh BT61 9BT
Tel 028-37524537 Fax 028-37528763
Email armthq@btconnect.com
*Judicial Vicar:* Rev Eugene D. O'Hagan JCL
Email armt@btconnect.com
*Administrator:* Rev James McGrory JCD
*Presiding Judges:* Rev Francis Bradley JCL, Rev James McGrory JCD, Sr Carmel Maguire JCL, Rev Joseph Rooney JCL, Rev Michael Toner JCL
*Correspondance to*
Mrs Marie Kelly, Secretary

*Contact Person for Constituent Dioceses*
*Armagh:* Rev Michael Toner JCL, Rev John McKeever JCL
*Clogher:* Sr Elizabeth Fee
*Derry:* Rev Francis Bradley JCL
*Down & Connor*
Rev Eugene D. O'Hagan JCL
*Dromore:* Rev Peter C. McNeill
*Kilmore:* Sr Elizabeth Fee
*Raphoe:* Rev Eamonn McLaughlin, Rev Joseph Briody

### DUBLIN REGIONAL MARRIAGE TRIBUNAL

Diocesan Offices,
Archbishop's House, Dublin 9
Tel 01-8379253 Fax 01-8368309
Email dublinrmt@eircom.net
*Judicial Vicar:* Vacant
*Acting Judicial Vicar:* Rev Paul Churchill
*Judges*
Rev Kilian Byrne LCL (Kildare and Leighlin)
Rev Kevin Cahill DCL (Ferns)
Rev Paul Churchill DCL (Dublin)
Sr Mary Grennan LCL (PBVM)
Rev Brian Kavanagh LCL (Dublin)
Rev William Richardson PhD, JCD (Dublin)
Mgr Alex Stenson DCL (Dublin)
*Defenders of the Bond*
Very Rev Laurence Collins (OP)
*Tribunal Assistants*
Cathy Barry, Maeve Cotter, Mr Paul MacKay, Grace Murray, Collette Nugent, Jane O'Donoghue, Mary O'Kane, Carolyn O'Toole, Edna Powell, Pamela van de Poll
*Correspondence to:* The Rev Judicial Vicar
*Constituent Dioceses:* Dublin, Ferns, Kildare and Leighlin, Meath, Ossory

### CORK REGIONAL MARRIAGE TRIBUNAL

Tribunal Offices, The Lough, Cork
Tel 021-4963653 Fax 021-4314149
*Judicial Vicar*
Very Rev Gerard Garrett LCL, MCL, LLM
Email ggarrett.tribunal@eircom.net
*Associate Judicial Vicar*
Vacant
*Judge:* Very Rev Seamus McKenna BA, HDE, LCL
Email smckenna.tribunal@eircom.net
*Constituent Dioceses*
Cashel, Cloyne, Cork and Ross, Kerry, Limerick, Waterford and Lismore
*Correspondence to:* Mrs Marlies Ferriter, *(Administrator)*
Email mferriter.tribunal@eircom.net

### GALWAY REGIONAL MARRIAGE TRIBUNAL

7 Waterside, Woodquay, Galway
Tel 091-565179 Fax 091-563512
Email 7waterside@eircom.net
*Judicial Vicar:* Very Rev Michael Byrnes BA JCL
Rev Barry Horan JCL
Mairéad Uí Mhurchadha
*Correspondence to the Administrator:*
Nicola Burke
*Constituent Dioceses:* Tuam, Achonry, Ardagh and Clonmacnois, Clonfert, Elphin, Galway,Killala, Killaloe

# CHAPLAINS

## THE DEFENCE FORCES CHAPLAINCY SERVICE

*Head Chaplain*
Rt Rev Mgr Eoin Thynne HCF
Tel 01-8042637
Email eointhynne@eircom.net
*Administration Secretary*
Sgt. John Kellett
Defence Headquarters,
Infirmary Road, Dublin 7
Tel 01-8042638
Email john.kellett@defenceforces.ie

**Aiken Barracks**
Dundalk, Co Louth
Tel 042-9331759
Rev Bernard McCay-Morrissey CF
Email bernardmm@eircom.net

**Casement Aerodrome**
Baldonnel, Co Dublin
Tel 01-4037536
Rev Jeremiah Carroll CF
Email jerryzulu@eircom.net

**Cathal Brugha Barracks**
Rathmines, Dublin 6
Tel 01-8046484
Rev David Tyndall CF
Email davidtyndall@yahoo.ie

**Collins Barracks (Cork)**
Tel 021-4502734
Rev Gerard O'Neill CF
Email frgerryoneill@eircom.net

**Curragh Camp**
Co Kildare
Rt Rev Mgr John McDonald CF
Tel 045-441369
Email frjohnmcdonald@gmail.com
Rev P.J. Somers CF
Tel 045-441277
Email spj40@hotmail.com

**Custume Barracks**
Athlone, Co Westmeath
Tel 0902-21277
Rev Gerard Dowd CF
Email gerard.dowd@yahoo.co.uk

**Dún Uí Néill Barracks**
Cavan
Rev Sean McDermott CF
Tel 049-4361632
Email jlmcdermott@vodofone.ie

**Finner Camp**
Bundoran, Co Donegal
Tel 071-9842294
Email awcf@hotmail.com
Rev Alan Ward CF

**Gormanston Camp**
Co Meath
Tel 01-8413990
Rev Robert McCabe CF
Email robert@militarychaplaincy.ie

**McKee Barracks**
Dublin 7
Tel 01-8046268
Rev Patrick Mernagh CF
Email pat.mernagh@defenceforces.ie

**The Naval Base**
Haulbowline, Co Cork
Tel 021-4378046
Rev Desmond Campion (SDB) CF
Email campiond@eircom.net

**Renmore Barracks**
Galway
Rev Tom Brady CF
Tel 087-2904879
Email bradt56@hotmail.com

**Saint Bricin's Hospital**
Infirmary Road, Dublin 7
Tel 01-8042637
Rt Rev Mgr Eoin Thynne HCF

**Sarsfield Barracks**
Limerick
Tel 061-316817
Rev Seamus Madigan CF
Email seamusmadigan@hotmail.com
Tel 086-8441609

**James Stephens Barracks**
Kilkenny
Tel 056-7761852
Rev Dan McCarthy CF
Tel 086-8575155
Email danielmaccarthy@eircom.net

**International Military Pilgrimage to Lourdes (Pèlerinage Militaire International)**
*Director:* Rt Rev Mgr Eoin Thynne HCF
Dept. of Defence,
Defence Forces Headquarters,
Infirmary Road, Dublin 7
Tel 01-8042637

## PRISONS AND PLACES OF DETENTION IN IRELAND

***There are fourteen prisons or places of detention in the Republic of Ireland***

**Liason Bishop between Prison Chaplains and the Bishops' Conference**
Bishop Eamonn Walsh
'Naomh Brid,' Blessington Road
Tallaght, Dublin 24
Tel 01-4598032
Email elmham@eircom.net

**National Co-ordinator of Prison Chaplains in the Republic of Ireland**
Rev Ciaran Enright
Arbour Hill Prison, Dublin 7
Tel 01-4724030
Email ccenright@irishprisons.ie

**Arbour Hill Prison**
Ard na Gaoithe,
Arbour Hill, Dublin 7
Rev Ciaran Enright
Tel 01-4724030
Email ccenright@irishprisons.ie
Prison General Office Tel 01-4724019

**Castlerea Prison**
Castlerea, Co Roscommon
Margaret Connaughton
Tel 094-9625278
Email maconnaugh@irishprisons.ie
Prison General Office Tel 094-9625213

**Cloverhill Remand Prison**
Cloverhill Road,
Clondalkin, Dublin 22
Rev John O'Sullivan (MSC)
Tel 01-6304586
Email jjosullivan@irishprisons.ie
Sr Carmel Miley CP
Tel 01-6304585
Email cmmiley@irishprisons.ie
Sr Margaret O'Donovan DC
Tel 01-6304584
Email mmodonovan@irishprisons.ie
Prison General Office Tel 01-6304531/2

**Cork Prison**
Rathmore Road, Cork
Rev Fr Michael Kidney (SMA)
Tel 021-4518892
email mjkidney@irishprisons.ie
Sr Mary Jo Sheehy RSM
Tel 021-4518891 *(part-time)*
Email mjsheehy@irishprisons.ie
Prison General Office Tel 021-45188000

**Dóchas Centre Mountjoy Women's Prison**
North Circular Road, Dublin 7
Sr Mary Mullins
Tel 01-8858920
Email mtmullins@irishprisons.ie
Prison General Office Tel 01-8858987

**Limerick Prison**
Mulgrave Street, Limerick
Rev John Walsh
Tel 061-204714
Mount David House,
North Circular Road, Limerick
Email jwalsh@irishprisons.ie
Prison General Office Tel 061-204700

**Loughan House**
Blacklion, Co Cavan
Fr John McMahon PP
Main St, Manorhamilton, Co Leitrim
Tel 071-9853170 (w) Tel 071-9856987 (h)
General Office Tel 071-9836000
Email manorhamilton@kilmorediocese.ie

**Midlands Prison**
Dublin Road, Portlaoise, Co Laois
Michael Loughnane *(Part-time)*
Tel 057-8672110
Email mjloughnane@irishprisons.ie
Vera Mc Hugh
Tel 057-8672221
Email vamchugh@irishprisons.ie
Rev Tom Sinnott (MHM)
Tel 057-8672222
Email tgsinnott@irishprisons.ie
Prison General Office Tel 057-8672110

**Mountjoy Prison**
North Circular Road, Dublin 7
Ruth Breen *(Part-time)*
Tel 01-8062843
Email rabreen@irishprisons.ie
Mark Davis *(Part-time)*
Tel 01-8062843
Email mcdavis@irishprisons.ie
Sr Gráinne Haslam (RSM)
Tel 01-8062846
Email gphaslam@irishprisons.ie
Rev Jimmy Kelly OSM
Tel 01-8062843
Email jxkelly@irishprisons.ie
Prison General Office Tel 01-8062800

**Portlaoise Prison**
Dublin Road, Portlaoise, Co Laois
Rev Eugene Drumm
Tel 057-8621318
Email eadrum@irishprisons.ie
General Office Tel 057-8621318

**Saint Patrick's Institution**
North Circular Road, Dublin 7
Miss Ruth Comerford
Tel 01-8858945/8062894
Email rmcomerford@irishprisons.ie
General Office Tel 01-8062906

**Shelton Abbey**
Arklow, Co Wicklow
Sr Patricia Egan (RSCJ) *(Part-time)*
Tel 040-242321
Email pxegan@irishprisons.ie
General Office Tel 040-242300

**Training Unit**
Glengarrif Parade, Dublin 7
Sr Mairead Gahan LCM
Tel 01-8858964
Email mxgahan@irishprisons.ie
Prison General Office Tel 01-8062881

**Wheatfield Prison**
Cloverhill Road, Clondalkin, Dublin 22
Sr Joan Kane (OSU)
Tel 01-6209446
Email jakane@irishprisons.ie
Sr Esther Murphy (RSM)
Tel 01-6209447
Email esmurphy01@irishprisons.ie
Sr Kathleen Cunningham *(Part-time)*
Email ktcunningh@irishprisons.ie
Tel 01-6209446/7
Sr Imelda Wickham (PBVM) *(Part-time)*
Tel 01-6209466
Email imwickham@irishprisons.ie
Prison General Office Tel 01-6209400

***There are three Prisons and Places of Detention in Northern Ireland, administered by the Northern Ireland Office (Use prefix (048) from Republic)***

**HMP Maghaberry**
Old Road, Ballinderry Upper,
Lisburn, Co Antrim, BT28 2TP
Tel 028-92614825
*Pastoral Team*
Br Brian Monaghan
Email bmonaghan@btinternet.com
Rev Frank Brady (SJ)
Email frank.brady@dojni.x.gsi.gov.uk
Rev Gabriel Bannon
Email gabriel.bannon@dojni.x.gsi.gov.uk
Rev Brian Lennon
Email brian.lennon@dojni.x.gsi.gov.uk
Sr Rosaleen McMahon
Email macmahon2000@yahoo.co.uk
Fr John McCallion
Email revtrad@btinternet.com
Tel 02892 614825

**HMP Magilligan**
Point Road, Magilligan,
Limavaddy BT49 OLR, Co Derry
Rev Francis O'Hagan
Email www.frohagan@aol.com
Prison General Office Tel 028-77763311

**Hydebank Young Offenders' Centre**
Hydebank Wood, Hospital Road,
Belfast BT8 8NA, Co Antrim
Tel 028-90253666
*Pastoral Team*
Rev Stephen McBrearty
Email smc02@hotmail.com
Sr Oonah Hanrahan
Email oonahhanrahan2002@yahoo.co.uk

## BRITAIN

**The Irish Chaplaincy in Britain**
*Director:* Ms Philomena Cullen
50-52 Camden Square
London NW1 9XB
Tel 0044-2074825528 Fax 0044-2074824815
Direct Line: 020-74828964
Email philomena.cullen@irishchaplaincy.org.uk
*Board of Trustees:* Mr John Walsh (Chair), Mgr Canon Tom Egan (Hon. Treasurer), Sr Raymunda Jordan (OP), Mr John Higgins KSG, Ms Nicola O'Regan, Mr Stephen Hargrave, Ms Kathleen Walsh, Ms Vicky Cosstick
*PA/Administrator:* Declan Ganly
Email declan.ganly@irishchaplaincy.org.uk

## PARISH APOSTOLATES

Northampton Diocese

**Luton**
Rev John Daly
Holy Ghost, Beech Hill,
33 Westbourne Road, Luton,
Beds LU4 8JD
Tel 00-44-1582728849

## SPECIALISED APOSTOLATES

**Alcohol Recovery Project**
Br Barry Butler (CFA), Paula Bruce
28 Delancey Street
London NW1 7NH
Tel 0207-8370100

**Homeless**
Sr Eileen O'Mahony (DC)
Sr Antoinette McGrath (OSC)
Sr Maureen Coen (DC)
Luton Day Centre for the Homeless,
141 Park Street, London LU1 3HG
Tel 01582-728416/482029
Fax 01582-486757

**Irish Prisoners Project**
*Irish Council for Prisoners Overseas (ICPO)*
50-52 Camden Square, London NW1 9XB
Tel 0044-2074824148
Fax 0044-2074824815
Email prisoners@irishchaplaincy.org.uk

**Irish Travellers Project**
50-52 Camden Square
London NW1 9XB
Tel 0044-2074825525
Fax-0044-2074824815
Email joebrowne@irishchaplaincy.org.uk

**Older Persons Programme**
*Project Manager:* Paul Raymond
50-52 Camden Square
London NW1 9XB
Tel 0044-2074823274
Fax 0044-207482825
Email paul.raymond@irishchaplaincy.org.uk

For all news, events and details please see www.irishchaplaincy.org.uk

## HOSTELS

**St Louise's (Female)**
*Sister in Charge*
33 Medway Street
London SW1P 2BE
Tel 0171-2222071/2226588

## COMMUNITY CARE/ ADVICE CENTRES

**London Irish Centre**
50-52 Camden Square,
London NW19 XB
Tel 0044-2079162222
Fax 0044-2079162638
Email director@irishcentre.org

**Irish Welfare and Information Centre**
*Director:* Mrs Bridie Nugent
Plunkett Room, 14-20 High Street,
Deritend, Birmingham B12 OLN
Tel 0044-1216046111
Email bridie@iwic.org.uk

**Manchester Irish Centre**
89 Cheetham Hill Road,
Manchester, M8 OSN
Tel 0044-1612059105
Email iccmanchester.org.uk

## EUROPE

**Brussels**
Rev Vincent Gallogley (OFM)
23/25 Ave des Anciens Combattants,
1950 Kraainem, Belgium
Tel 0032-2-7201970
Fax 0032-2-7255810

**Copenhagen**
Rev Patrick Shiels (CSSR)
Skt Annae Kirke, Hans Bogbinders Alle 2,
2300 Copenhagen S, Denmark
Tel 0045-31-582102

**Lisbon**
Rev Gus Champion
St Mary's, Rua do Murtal 368
San Pedro do Estoril
2765 Estoril, Portugal
Tel 00-351-1-4673771 *(Residence)*
Tel 00-351-1-4681676 *(Parish)*

**Luxembourg**
Rev Eamonn Breslin
European Parish, 34 Rue des Capucins,
Luxembourg BP 175
Tel 00352-470039 Fax 00352-220859

**Munich**
Rev Chetus Cohace
Landsberger Strasse 39,
80399 Munich, Germany
Email englischsprachige-mission.muenchen@erzbistum-muenchen.de
Tel 0049-89-5003580
Fax 0049-89-50035826
www.englishspeking-mission-munic.de

**Paris**
Rev Tom Scanlon (CP)
Rev Anthony Behan (CP)
St Joseph's Church,
50 Avenue Hoche, 75008 Paris, France
Tel 0033-1-42272856
Fax 0033-1-42278649
Rev Declan Hurley
Irish College, Paris, 5 Rue des Irlandais,
75005 Paris, France
Tel 0033-1-58521030 *(College)*
Email dechurley@eircom.net

**Rome**
Rev Raphael Gallagher (CSSR)
Redentoristi, Via Merulana 31,
CP2458, Rome, Italy Tel 0039-6-494932
Email rgallagher@alfonsiana.edu

## AUSTRALIA

**Sydney**
Rev Tom Devereux OMI
Parish of St Patrick's,
2 Wellington St, Bondi, NSW 2026
Tel 0061-02-93651195
Fax 0061-02-93654002
Mobile 0061-04-07347301
Email stpatbon@bigpond.net.au

## UNITED STATES OF AMERICA

*Director:* Rev Brendan McBride
Irish Immigration Pastoral Centre
5340 Geary Boulevard #206,
San Francisco, CA 94121
Tel 001-4157526006
Fax 001-4157526910
Email nationaloffice@usairish.org
Cellphone 001-4157609818
*Administrator:* Ms Geri M. Garvey
Irish Apostolate USA
1005 Downs Drive,
Silver Spring, MD 20904
Tel/Fax 001-3013843375
Email administrator@usairish.org

**Boston**
*Irish Pastoral Centre*
*Executive Director:* Sr Marguerite Kelly
953 Hancock Street,
Quincy, MA 02170
Tel 001-617-4797404
Fax 001-617-4790541
Email ipcboston@yahoo.com
*Chaplain:* Rev John McCarthy
15 Rita Road, Dorchester, MA 02124
Tel 001-617-4797404
Fax 001-617-4790541
Cellphone 001-617-4121331
Email jmccarthyipc@yahoo.com

**Chicago**
*Chicago Irish Immigrant Support*
*Chaplain:* Rev Michael Leonard
3525 S. Lake Park Avenue,
Chicago, IL 60653
Tel 312-5348445
Fax 312-5348446
Email irishoverhere@sbcglobal.net
www.ci-is.com

**Ocean City, Maryland**
*(Open June–September)*
*Irish Student Outreach*
*Co-ordinator:* William Ferguson
13701 Sailing Rd, Ocean City, MD 21842
Tel 001-410-2500362
001-443-7837893
Email wfergus4@aol.com

**Milwaukee**
Irish Immigrant Service of Milwaukee
John Gleeson, 2133 Wisconsin Ave,
Milwaukee, WI 53233-1910
Tel 001-414-3458800
Email gleeson@uwm.edu
www.ichc.net

**New York**
*Project Irish Outreach*
*Co-ordinator:* Patricia O'Callaghan
1011 First Avenue, New York NY 10022
Tel 001-212-3171011
Fax 001-212-7551526
Email patricia.ocallaghan@archny.org

*Aisling Irish Community Centre*
990 McLean Avenue, Yonkers, NY 10704
*Chaplain:* Sr Christine Hennessey
Tel 001-914-2375121
Fax 001-914-2375172
Email Sr.Christine.Hennessy@archny.org,
aislingirishcc@mindspring.com
www.aislingirishcenter.org

**Philadelphia**
*Philadelphia Immigration Resource Centre*
*Executive Director:* Siobhan Lyons
7 South Cedar Lane
Upper Darby, PA 19082 2816
Tel 001-610-7896355 Fax 001-7896352
Email irishimmigration@aol.com
www.irishimmigrants.org

**San Diego**
*Irish Outreach San Diego Inc.*
Bernadette Cashmann
2725 Congress Street 2G,
San Diego, CA 92110
Tel 001-619-2911630
Email irishsd@sbcglobal.net
www.irishoutreachsd.org

**San Francisco**
*Irish Immigration Pastoral Centre*
Celine Kennelly
5340 Geary Boulevard #206,
San Francisco, CA 94121
Tel 001-415-7526006
Fax 001-415-7526910
Email iipc@pacbell.net
www.sfiipc.org
Cellphone 001-415-7605762

**Seattle**
*Seattle Immigration Support Group*
*Chairman:* James Cummins
5819 St Andrews Drive, Mukileto,
WA 98275
Tel 001-425-2445147
Email siisg@irishclub.org

# GENERAL INFORMATION

## OBITUARY LIST

*Beata mortui qui in Domino moriuntur*
Rv 14:13

### PRIESTS AND BROTHERS

Beere, Frank (CFC) 19 January 2011
Bradley, Patrick (SSCC) 21 January 2011
Bredin, Sean (OSCam) 14 August 2010
Breen, Daniel (Dublin) 14 March 2011
Brooks, Francis Gerard (Dromore) 4 September 2010
Burke, Thomas (Killaloe) 17 November 2011
Byrne, David (FSP) 26 May 2011
Cantillon, Eric (SJ) 2 April 2011
Carolan, Francis Walter (Derry) 2 January 2011
Carragher, Arthur (CSSp) 10 January 2011
Casey, Peter (Dublin) 10 July 2010
Clune, Patrick Anthony (CM) 25 July 2011
Coleman, John J. (CSSp) 15 May 2011
Colleton, Edward (CSSp) 26 April 2011
Colohan, Pat (CFC) 6 March 2011
Conlon, James (SMA) 3 April 2011
Connolly, Eugene (SMA) 28 April 2011
Connolly, Maurice (Dublin) 15 January 2011
Connors, Kevin (SSC) 13 July 2011
Conway, Brendan (OSCam) 22 August 2009
Coughlan, Leonard (OFMCap) 31 July 2011
Creaton, Patrick (SSC) 19 July 2011
Crotty, Gerald (CSSr) 12 June 2011
Cullen, Joseph (OP) 19 August 2011
Cummins, Norbert John (OCD) 19 July 2011
Curtin, Jerome (Dublin) 20 September 2010
Curran, Dermot (SPS) 20 May 2011
Donaghy, John (Armagh) 23 March 2011
Drumgoole, Joseph (Dublin) 21 July 2011
Duffy, Austin (Derry) 12 August 2011
Egan, David (OSCam) 27 February 2009
Fahey, Patrick (SSC) 10 July 2011
Farrell, Thomas (Virgilius) (CSsR) 2 November 2010
✠ Finnegan, Thomas Anthony (Killala) 25 December 2011
Fitzgerald, John (Tuam) 27 February 2011
Fitzgerald, Shane (SVD) 24 September 2011
Fleming, Laurence (Kildare & Leighlin) 2 July 2011
Fogarty, James (Cashel & Emly) 19 July 2011
Foley, James (Cashel & Emly) 25 May 2011
Foley, James C. (CSSp) 4 August 2011
Foley, Liam (Cloyne) 20 February 2011
Gaffney, Thomas W. (Kilmore) 12 October 2011
Gillespie, Liguori (CFC) 19 May 2011
Gilmartin, Joseph (Elphin) 4 June 2011
Goulding, John (CFC) 6 February 2011
Grealy, Thomas (SPS) 8 April 2011
Griffin, Gerald (SSC) 4 July 2010
Hackett, Gerard (SMA) 31 March 2011
Halliden, Donal (SSC) 1 October 2011
Hanahoe, Thomas (SSC) 2 September 2011
Hardy, Francis (Dublin) 28 July 2010
Harkin, Ken (CFC) 13 January 2011
Heffernan, Michael J. (OSA) 8 April 2011
Higgins, Columba (OSA) 10 May 2011
Horkan, Kevin (CFC) 13 December 2010
Hurley, John (Cork & Ross) 29 June 2011
Hurley, Michael (SJ) 15 April 2011
Kavanagh, Aidan (Ferns) 22 June 2011
Keogh, Henry (Galway) 10 August 2011
Kelly, Anthony (SSC) 12 April 2011
Kelly, Michael J. (Kilmore) 7 February 2011
Kennedy, Conor (CSSp) 9 July 2011
Kinsella, Nivard (OCSO) 2 November 2010
Lane, Thomas (CM) 28 August 2011
Leahy, Michael (Kerry) 9 October 2011
Lehane, Aidan P. (CSSp) 8 August 2011
Lynch, Florence (Dublin) 26 July 2010
Lynch, Noel (SSC) 24 June 2011
MacNicholas, Raymond (SPS) 6 May 2011
Madden, Noel (Dublin) 12 July 2011
Madden, Paul Mary (CP) 13 April 2011
Maguire, Aidan (SAC) 10 October 2010
Maguire, Bernard (Kilmore) 10 April 2011
Mannion, Thomas (Tuam) 11 September 2011
Masterson, James (CSSp) 31 December 2010
McCrory, James (Derry) 10 October 2010
McCauley, John (Dromore) 2 March 2011
McChrystal, Paul (OCarm) 21 May 2011
McDonnell, Martin (OCSO) 13 May 2011
McEvoy, James Joseph (Down & Connor) 2 October 2010
McGinnity, Paddy (CFC) 5 May 2011
McGovern, Gregory (SMA) 27 December 2010
McGrath, Patrick (OP) 19 April 2011
McKeogh, Columbanus (SMA) 2 June 2011
McLaughlin, Patrick (Derry) 17 April 2011
McLoughlin, Aidan (OCarm) 19 June 2011
McMullin, Ernan (Raphoe) 8 February 2011
McMyler, Francis (Tuam) 9 August 2011
McParland, Peter (Armagh) 6 May 2011
McTiernan, Michael (CSSp) 11 April 2011
Meade, John (CFC) 15 April 2011
Mellon, Malachy (OCSO) 7 July 2011
Melvin, Bonaventure (OCSO) 7 November 2010
Morrissey, Brendan (SM) 22 October 2010
Mullan, Brian (CM) 6 May 2011
Mullane, Finbarr (Dublin) 11 January 2011
Mullin, John P. (Seán) (CSsR) 19 January 2011
Murphy, John (Armagh) 8 June 2011
Murphy, Patrick (SVD) 31 May 2011
Murray, Kevin (CFC) 5 November 2010
Murray, Nicolas (SSC) 21 April 2011
Murray, Raymond (SM) 1 January 2011
Nugent, Thomas (Waterford & Lismore) 28 February 2011
O'Brien, Jeremiah (Dublin) 3 February, 2011
O'Brien, Michael (Cloyne) 22 July 2011
O'Brien, Nicholas (OSA) 26 June 2011
O'Byrne, John (OCSO) 3 March 2011
O'Byrne, Thomas Christopher (CSSp) 16 December 2010
Ó'Cearbhaill, Seán (CFC) 28 May 2011
O'Connell, Benjamin (OFMCap) 3 December 2010
O'Connell, William (CSsR) 16 June 2010
O'Donnell, Tony (SMA) 20 December 2010
O'Dowd, Hugh (Killaloe) 5 August 2011
O'Fathaigh, Máirtín (CFC) 13 February 2011
Ó'Fionnagáin, Proinsías (SJ) 7 March 2011
O'Leary, Michael (Kerry) 3 January 2011
O'Leary, Partolan (IC) 21 August 2010
O'Reilly, Andrew (OCarm) 23 July 2011
O'Reilly, Charles (OSA) 19 January 2011
O'Reilly, Eugene (SPS) 12 May 2011
O'Riordan, Diarmuid (MSC) 21 April 2011
O'Neill, Francis (SJ) 6 April 2011
O'Neill, Philip (Jarlath) (CSsR) 21 September 2011
Prendergast, Edmund (MHM) 29 March 2011
Purcell, Bernard (OCSO) 30 March 2011
Purcell, Gerard (Waterford & Lismore) 16 April 2011
Quinn, Francis (OCD) 22 August 2011
Quinn, Joseph (Tuam) 1 December 2011
Rodgers, Denis Gerard (CSSp) 6 October 2010
Rodgers, Manus (Killaloe) 30 August 2011
Ross, Cyril Nigel (OP) 21 August 2011
Ruth, Carthage (OFMCap) 26 December 2010
Scott, Patrick ( CSsR) 20 May 2011

Sheridan, Hugh (Down & Connor) 25 May 2011
Sheridan, Patrick (OMI) 9 September 2010
Sherry, Brendan (Elphin) 30 March 2011
Slevin, Osmund (CP) 23 October 2010
Sreenan, Peadar (CFC) 8 October 2010
Swords, Liam (Achonry) 19 February 2011
Tobin, Laserian (OCSO) 29 December 2009
Walsh, Joseph (MHM) 11 September 2010
Walsh, Timothy (OSA) 22 April 2011
Ward, Edward (OCarm) 26 July 2011
Ward, Seamus (SJ) 22 February 2011

## SISTERS

Begadon, Catherine (Presentation) 24 November 2010
Berkery, Liguori (Presentation) 3 April 2011
Boyle, Immaculata (Mercy) 10 July 2011
Brennan, Rita (Mercy SCP) 26 January 2011
Byrne, Eileen Mary (Mercy SCP) 23 May 2011
Byrne, Paul (Mercy SCP) 21 January 2011
Browne, Brigid (Dolsh) 17 November 2010
Buckley, Nora (Presentation) 31 July 2011
Burke, Margaret (OLC) 7 March 2011
Burke, Katherine (Presentation) 3 April 2011
Butterly, Elizabeth (Religious of Christian Education) 19 March 2011
Cahill, Kathleen (Religious of Christian Education) 26 November 2010
Campbell, Pauline (Society of the Sacred Heart) 18 May 2011
Cassidy, Imelda (Good Shepherd Sisters) 26 July 2011
Clarke, Mary Joseph (Discalced Carmelite Nuns) 8 Dec 2010
Coleman, Ethelbert (OLA) 7 June 2011
Collier, Angels (Mercy, Southern Provence) 8 May 2011
Connolly, Gemma (Little Sisters of the Assumption) 14 October 2010
Connolly, M. Hyacinth (Missionary Sisters of the Assumption) 20 August 2011
Connelly, Teresa Eucharia (Religious Sisters of Charity) 14 January 2011
Commins, Marie Clare (Sisters of St Louis) 3 March 2011
Cooney, Therese (Mercy, Southern Provence) 12 January 2011
Cotter, Lelia (Eileen) (Missionary Sisters of the Holy Rosary) 19 February 2011
Cowhey, Roberta (Sisters of St Louis) 17 June 2011
Creed, Therese (Mercy, Southern Provence) 20 October 2010
Crowley, M. Columba (Poor Clares) 17 January 2011
Cullen, Nessa (Mercy SCP) 8 August 2011
Cummins, Anna (Marie Reparatrice Sisters) 20 February 2011
Cummins, Redemptoris (Mercy, Southern Provence) 8 January 2011
Cunningham, Joseph (Mercy, Southern Provence) 2 December 2010
Cunningham, Theresa (Good Shepherd Sisters) 28 August 2010
Curran, Carmel (Little Sisters of the Assumption) 29 July 2011
Dempsey, Agnes (Daughters of Jesus) 20 August 2011
Devine, Gemma (Good Shepherd Sisters) 30 December 2010
Devitt, Mary Ailbe (Bon Secours) 10 August 2011
Doherty, Antoinette (OP) 20 August 2011
Dolan, Patricia (Little Sisters of the Assumption) 18 May 2011
Donnelly, Annunciata (OLA) 6 March 2011
Donnelly, Madeline (Sisters of St Clare) 9 December 2010
Donovan, Delia (Presentation) 17 May 2011
Dooley, Cornelia (OP) 3 December 2010
Doran, Teresa (Mercy SCP) 18 May 2011
Doyle, Mary Dominic (Little Sisters of the Poor) 10 May 2011
Dunne, Muriel (Mercy SCP) 26 February 2011
English, Joseph (Mercy, Southern Provence) 15 March 2011
Everard, Kathleen (Daughters of Charity) 29 September 2010
Faherty, Sarah (Daughters of Charity) 19 September 2010
Falvey, Helen (Infant Jesus Sisters) 9 April 2011
Farrell, Gabriel (Mercy) 5 August 2011
Fitzgerald, Marie (Mercy SCP) 11 October 2010
Flanagan, Breda (FMSA) 23 February 2011
Foley, Fanchea (OP) 12 November 2010
Forde, Mary (Poor Clares of Perpetual Adoration) 7 March 2011
Gallagher, Celine (Missionary Sisters of the Holy Rosary) 12 March 2011
Gallagher, Immaculata (Mercy SCP) 3 July 2011
Gallagher, Maureen (Missionary Sisters of the Holy Rosary) 24 September 2011
Galvin, Finian (Bon Secours) 4 July 2011
Goode, Catherine (Presentation) 10 August 2011
Gorman, Stephanie (Marist Sisters) 19 February 2011
Grealy, M. Josephine (MMM) 3 January 2011
Greaney, Agnes (Poor Clares of Perpetual Adoration) 22 March 2011
Greany, Brenda (Mercy, Southern Provence) 1 March 2011
Hallon, Mary (Missionary Sisters of the Holy Rosary) 13 July 2011
Halloran, Francis (Mercy SCP) 3 October 2010
Halpin, Cronan (OP) 14 January 2011
Hanbury, Perpetua (OLA) 3 November 2010
Hannan, Laurence (Mercy SCP) 15 November 2010
Haran, Mary Ann (FMM) 16 December 2010
Harney, Mathilde (Holy Family of Bordeaux) 6 November 2010
Haughey, Mary Bernadette (Carmelite ODC) 9 January 2011
Hennessy, Helen (FMSA) 15 July 2011
Hennessy, Helen (Infant Jesus Sisters) 6 July 2011
Herlihy, Agnes (Mercy, Southern Provence) 26 April 2011
Hetherton, Martha (OP) 6 May 2011
Heverin, Bridie (Presentation) 17 April 2011
Hickey, Bosco (Mercy SCP) 16 December 2010
Higgins, Eilish (Missionary Sisters of the Holy Rosary) 8 April 2011
Hogan, Brid (Mercy SCP) 7 July 2011
Horan, Clare (Society of the Sacred Heart) 14 January 2011
Houlihan, Evelyn (Infant Jesus Sisters) 2 April 2011
Hughes, Annunciata (Little Company of Mary) 4 June 2011
Humphries, Josephine (Presentation) 21 September 2011
Johnston, Catherine (OLC) 27 August 2011
Jones, Mairín (MMM) 26 April 2011
Jordan, Elizabeth Marie (Bon Secours) 25 July 2011
Judge, Rose Ellen (Marie Reparatrice Sisters) 19 June 2011
Kelleher, Raymond (Mercy, Southern Provence) 2 June 2011
Kelly, Benignus (Mercy) 22 November 2010
Kelly, Marie Anna (Dolsh) 29 October 2010
Kennedy, Laurentina (Holy Faith Sisters) 2 January 2011
Kennedy, Vianney (Mercy, Southern Provence) 31 March 2011
Keogan, Eileen Carmel (MMM) 1 June 2011
Keogan, Oliver (Presentation) 21 June 2011
Kevins, Anthony (Cistercians) 4 October 2010
Kinsella, Josephine (Mercy SCP) 27 June 2011
Laffan, Joan (Missionary Sisters of the Holy Rosary) 24 August 2011
Leahy, Gerard (OP) 2 February 2011
Leonard, Catherine (Presentation) 9 April 2011
Lillis, Mercy (Mercy SCP) 4 July 2011
Linehan, Martin (Mercy) 25 August 2011
Lohan, Dorothy (Little Sisters of the Poor) 24 June 2011
Lonergan, Perpetua (Presentation) 5 November 2010
Lynch, Aloysius (Presentation) 14 March 2010
Macken, Margaret (Holy Faith Sisters) 26 July 2011
Mackie, Jane Frances (FMSA) 4 May 2011

Magner, Cornelia (Mercy SCP) 10 July 2011
Maguire, Carmel Rita (Religious Sisters of Charity) 22 July 2011
Maher, Irene (Sisters of Nazareth) 25 March 2011
Mathews, Sheila (Daughters of Charity) 19 January 2011
Marley, Leontia (Good Shepherd Sisters) 24 July 2011
Marshall, Clare (Sisters of St Louis) 24 June 2011
McAuliffe, Basil (Presentation) 21 December 2010
McCann, Camillus (Holy Faith Sisters) 30 January 2011
McConville, Stanislaus (Mercy) 3 October 2010
McCullagh, M. Eugene (MMM) 25 January 2011
McDonnell, Maureen (Marist Sisters) 3 October 2010
McElligott, Máire (Presentation) 19 January 2011
McHugh, Bernadette (Mercy) 5 April 2011
McHugh, Kenneth (Bon Secours) 15 October 2010
McHugh, Ursula (Mercy) 20 December 2010
McKee, Madeleine Sophie (Society of the Sacred Heart) 29 January 2011
McKee, Margaret Mary (Society of the Sacred Heart) 19 August 2011
McLaughlin, Margaret (Daughters of Charity) 23 August 2011
McNulty, Therésè (Little Sisters of the Assumption) 21 March 2011
McSweeney, Fergal (Mercy SCP) 4 May 2011
Meany, Maria Assumpta (Presentation) 24 January 2011
Molloy, Phelim (Sisters of St Louis) 11 May 2011
Moran, Salome (Sisters of St Louis) 8 January 2011
Mulcahy, M. Helena (MMM) 13 June 2011
Mulhern, Clare (Sisters of St Louis) 28 October 2010
Murphy, Catherine (Daughters of Charity) 13 July 2011
Murphy, Canisius (Mercy, Southern Provence) 25 May 2011
Murphy, M. Leo (Missionary Sisters of the Holy Rosary) 2 March 2011
Murphy, Nora (Mercy, Southern Provence) 18 January 2011
Murphy, Perpetua (Mercy) 13 March 2011
Murray, Margaret Dolores (Religious Sisters of Charity) 3 June 2011
Nea, Teresa (Daughters of Charity) 29 July 2011
Nolan, Agnes Cecilia (Mercy SCP) 7 November 2010
Nolan, Eileen Teresa (FMM) 11 January 2011
O'Brien, Bernard (Sisters of St Clare) 1 November 2010
O'Brien, Margaret Mary (Society of the Sacred Heart) 7 March 2011
O'Brien, Paschal (Mercy SCP) 25 November 2010
O'Brien, Veronica (Mercy, Southern Provence) 5 October 2010
O'Connor, Loreto (Mercy SCP) 16 May 2011
O'Connor, Vincent (Presentation) 18 April 2011
O'Conor, Margaret (MMM) 9 June 2011
O'Donnell, Teresa (Columban Sisters) 26 January 2011
O'Driscoll, Mary (Sisters of St Louis) 27 May 2011
O'Farrell, Kevin (Cistercians) 28 November 2010
O'Gorman, Hannah (Sisters of St Louis) 30 December 2010
O'Halloran, Josephine (OLA) 31 May 2011
O'Hara, Josephine (Mercy SCP) 1 November 2010
O'Hare, De Sales (Sisters of St Clare) 11 June 2011
O'Keeffe, Terence (OP) 9 December 2010
O'Looney, Veronica (Mercy SCP) 9 November 2010
O'Mahony, Facthna (Mercy, Southern Provence) 15 May 2011
O'Mahony, Redempta (Mercy SCP) 29 December 2010
O'Neill, Austin (Mercy, Southern Provence) 20 March 2011
O'Neill, Mary (Holy Faith Sisters) 6 February 2011
O'Rourke, Assumpta (Presentation) 3 September 2010
O'Sullivan, Cathaldus (Bon Secours) 21 July 2011
Payne, Winifred (Little Sisters of the Poor) 18 December 2010
Penny, Alice (Little Sisters of the Poor) 11 July 2011
Phelan, Josepha (Mercy, Southern Provence) 15 October 2010
Phelan, Joseph Ignatius (Religious Sisters of Charity) 4 December 2010
Pierce, Clare (Mercy, Southern Provence) 25 March 2011
Power, Martha Magdalen (Religious Sisters of Charity) 19 August 2011
Reilly, Luke (Sisters of St Clare) 4 September 2010
Regan, Helen (Sisters of St Louis) 19 September 2011
Richardson, Eucharia (Mercy, Southern Provence) 8 February 2011
Roberts, Helen (Mercy, Southern Provence) 10 April 2011
Roche, Lucy (Little Sisters of the Assumption) 3 February 2011
Russell, Michael Damien (Bon Secours) 26 May 2011
Russell, Teresa (Good Shepherd Sisters) 18 February 2011
Ryan, Brenda (Holy Family of Bordeaux) 5 April 2011
Ryan, Catherine (Sisters of St Clare) 22 June 2011
Saunders, Sheila (Franciscan Missionaries of Our Lady) 10 December 2010
Scannell, Réidín (Infant Jesus Sisters) 17 June 2011
Slevin, Marie (MMM) 13 June 2011
Sliney, Mary (Holy Faith Sisters) 6 December 2010
Smith, Sadie (Society of the Sacred Heart) 5 December 2010
Stanley, M. Antonia (Maureen) (Missionary Sisters of the Holy Rosary) 30 January 2011
Stewart, Mary Teresita (Religious Sisters of Charity) 21 March 2011
Thornberry, Marcelle (Sisters of St Joseph of Lyon) 23 March 2011
Trant, Bríd (OP) 12 July 2011
Trant, Jane (Holy Faith Sisters) 29 October 2010
Traynor, Imelda (Mercy) 21 March 2011
Treacy, Breeda (Little Company of Mary) 22 May 2011
Webster, Perpetua (FMSA) 29 April 2011
Waldron, Margaret Imelda (Religious Sisters of Charity) 4 May 2011
Walsh, Cecelia (Coronata) (Missionary Sisters of the Holy Rosary) 21 November 2010
Walsh, Enda (Mercy, Southern Provence) 10 November 2010
Walsh, M. Annette (MMM) 12 July 2011
Walsh, Mary Xavier (Religious Sisters of Charity) 13 March 2011
Whelan, Vincent (OLC) 13 March 2011
Williams, Joseph Emmanuel (Visitation) 18 December 2010
Wynne, Helen (Infant Jesus Sisters) 19 May 2011

## 2011 ORDINATIONS

Barrins, David (OP) 21 November 2010
Brennan, Cuthbert (OSB) 11 July 2010
Buckley, Michael Anthony (Cork & Ross) 4 June 2011
Colgan, Maurice (OP) 18 September 2011
Conway, Kevin (SMA) 18 June 2011
Doyle, Brian (OP) 3 September 2011
Fitzgerald, Gerard (Killaloe) 19 June 2011
Heery, Kevin (Meath) 9 October 2011
Jones, Gerard (Killaloe) 21 August 2011
Meehan, Conleth (Dublin) 10 July 2010
Murphy, Denis (OP) 18 September 2011
Parys, Bartlomiej (SVD) 8 May 2011
Ryan, Derek Patrick (CSsR) Dec 2011
Sweeney, Raymond (Clonfert) 12 June 2011

# OBITUARY ADDENDA

Ahern, Patrick (SDB) 23 January 2009
Arthur, Francis (SDS) 15 May 2010
Bluett, Richard D.H. (SMA) 27 February 2010
Boyle, John (Waterford & Lismore) 31 January 2010
Brady, Bernard (OPraem) 10 December 2009
Browne, David (Limerick) 17 October 2011
Burns, Patrick (MCCJ) 17 December 2009
Byrne, P.J. (OMI) 4 August 2011
Byrne, Tom (OFM) 12 August 2009
Cafferty, Tom (SPS) 22 October 2011
Carroll, Noel (SVD) 3 October 2011
Clear, John B. (SJ) 21 September 2009
Clenaghan, Gerard (OMI) 20 September 2011
Cody, John Joseph (LC) 12 July 2009
Colleran, (Martin) Gabriel (Dublin) 8 September 2011
Connell, Roy (Dublin) 15 September 2011
Connon, Francis Warwick (CSsR) 9 March 2011
Cribbin, John (OMI) 10 September 2011
Culhane, Michael (Liverpool) 23 February 2010
Culleton, Edward (Ted) (CSSp) 26 April 2011
Cummins, Anthony (Clonfert) 20 January 2010
Donlon, Aidan A. (SCA) 24 January 2009
Doolan, Ailbe (Seamus) (OCD) 18 April 2010
Doolan, William (Limerick) 13 December 2009
Doyle, Frank (SJ) 17 March 2011
Drohan, Frank (SDB) 12 September 2010
Dunican, Seamus (Meath) 23 January 2010
Dunne, Fred (CSsR) 23 December 2009
Evans, Peter Robert (OP) 22 January 2009
Feeney, John (SMA) 2 November 2010
Fitzgerald, Michael (ODC) 9 July 2009
Ford, Eugene Christopher (OMI) 2 March 2009
Forristal, James (Ossory) 3 October 2010
Galvin, Micheál (Kerry) 23 August 2010
Houlihan, Tomás (Kerry) 4 February 2009
Hudson, Robert (CSSp) 5 March 2009
Hurley, Charles Edward (Hubert) (CP) 16 January 2009
Ievers, Brian (OMI) 28 September 2009
Johnston, William (SJ) 12 October 2010
Keane, Michael (Tuam) 27 August 2011
Kelliher, Anthony (OCD) 27 February 2009
Kelly, Evangelist (OFMCap) 16 March 2010
Kennelly, Michael F. (SJ) 3 January 2011
Kernan, Niall (SM) 30 October 2011
Kett, Joe (Dublin) 5 August 2010
Lynch, Tommy (SVD) 7 October 2011
Lysaght, Gerard (OFMCap) 22 August 2011
MacCabe, Robert (OCarm) 28 May 2011
MacMorrow, Desmond (CM) 26 August 2009
Manly, Greg (CP) 9 February 2010
Mansfield, Frank (SVD) 20 January 2010
Martin, Paddy (CSsR) 26 April 2010
McArdle, Jack (SSCC) 22 January 2009
McCarthy, Garry (CSSp) 3 January 2009
McCarthy, Fylvius (Timsie) (OFMCap) 20 October 2011
McCarthy, John Berchmans Mortimer (OFMCap) 8 July 2010
McElligott, David (Kerry) 18 December 2009
McFall, Henry (OMI) 12 February 2010
McGarry, Cecil (SJ) 24 November 2009
McGlinchey, James (Derry) 4 November 2011
McKeown, Hugh (SMA) 8 October 2011
McMahon, Paddy (OMI) 18 September 2009
Moloney, Patrick (Paddy) (SJ) 25 June 2011
Murray, Liam (Killaloe) 6 May 2010
Murray, Paddy (Elphin) 28 September 2011
Newman, Denis (SPS) 25 June 2009
Nolan, Daniel (Ferns) 12 September 2009
Nolan, John M. (Dublin) 14 December 2009
Noone, Sean (SCA) 31 October 2009
O'Byrne, Simon (OFM) 3 October 2011
O'Connell, Michael (Raphael) (OCD) 15 February 2009
O'Connor, Martin (Galway) 17 May 2010
O'Doherty, Dan J. (Kerry) 7 July 2010
O'Dwyer, Noel (OFM) 24 January 2010
O'Flatharta, Michael (CSsR) 16 November 2009
O'Keeffe, Edmund (SJ) 13 October 2011
O'Loughlin, Padhraic (SSC) 19 October 2011
O'Mahony, John (MSC) 26 October 2011
O'Neill, Peter (OFM) 6 February 2010
Orr, Peter (SJ) 17 April 2010
Peoples, Aloysius (John Joseph) (OSM) 24 May 2009
Quigley, Joe (MHM) 19 August 2010
Raymond, Bernard J. (Bennie) (SMA) 19 September 2011
Redmond, John (SJ) 29 September 2011
Reynolds, John M. (KCHS) 13 December 2009
Rhatigan, Edward (Ossory) 14 July 2010
Rouleau, Maurice (SSS) 28 August 2009
Ryan, Seamus (OMI) 14 January 2010
Scallan, Oliver (MHM) 26 April 2010
Sweeney, Denis (IC) 1 February 2009
Tohill, Bernard (SDB) 21 December 2010
Winters, Paul Desmond (OMI) 4 January 2011
Woods, Tom (CM) 21 October 2011

# IRISH COUNCIL OF CHURCHES

**Irish Council of Churches**
*President:* Most Rev R. L. Clarke
*Vice-President:* Rev Fr G. O'Donnell

**Inter-Church Centre**
48 Elmwood Avenue, Belfast BT9 6AZ
Tel 028-90663145
Email info@churchesinireland.com
Website www.churchesinireland.com
*Executive Officer:* Mr M. McCullagh

**Member Churches of Council**
Antiochian Orthodox Church in Ireland; Church of Ireland; Greek Orthodox Church in Ireland; Lutheran Church in Ireland; Methodist Church in Ireland; Moravian Church, Irish District; Non-Subscribing Presbyterian Church in Ireland; Presbyterian Church in Ireland; Religious Society of Friends; Cherubim and Seraphim Church; Romanian Orthodox Church in Ireland; Russian Orthodox Church in Ireland; Salvation Army (Ireland Division)

*Leaders of Member Churches*
**Antiochian Orthodox Church in Ireland**
Rev Fr Irenaeus Du Plessis
Antiochian Orthodox Church,
8 Wheatfield Gardens, Belfast BT14 7HU
Tel 028-90712523
Email irenaeus@btinternet.com

**Church of Ireland**
Most Rev A. E. T. Harper
Archbishop of Armagh, Primate of All Ireland, Diocesan Office, Church House,
46 Abbey Street, Armagh BT61 7DZ
Tel 028-37522851 (H), 028-37527144 (O)
Fax 028-37510596
Email archbishop@armagh.anglican.org

**Greek Orthodox Church**
Church of the Annunciation
46 Arbour Hill, Dublin 7
Rev Fr Tom Carroll PP
Moneygall, Roscrea, Co Tipperary
Tel 0505-45849
Email fr.tomcarroll@gmail.com
*Contact Person*
Mrs Toulla Efthimiou Conran
103 Walkinstown Avenue, Dublin 12
Tel 01-4566509

**Lutheran Church in Ireland**
Pastors C. & J. Diestelkamp, Luther House,
24 Adelaide Road, Dublin 2
Tel 01-6766548
Email info@lutheran-ireland.org
www.lutheran-ireland.org

**Methodist Church in Ireland**
*President:* Rev Ian D. Henderson
Methodist Manse, Glebe Crest,
Donegal, Co Donegal
Tel 074-9723588
*Secretary:* Rev Donald P. Ker
1 Fountainville Avenue, Belfast BT9 6AN
Tel 028-90324554 Fax 028-90239467
*President-Designate*
Rev R. Kenneth Lindsay
67 Main Street, Ballinamallard,
Co Fermanagh
Tel 028-66388200

**Moravian Church, Irish District**
Rev Paul M. Holdsworth, Chairman
Moravian Church, Irish District,
5 Locksley Park, Finaghy, Belfast BT10 0AR
Tel 028-90619755
Email paul.holdsworth@moravian.org.uk

**Non-Subscribing Presbyterian Church**
*Moderator:* Right Rev S. J. Peden
56 Milebush Road, Dromore,
Co Down BT25 1RV
Tel 028-92692094
*Contact Person:* Rev N. Hutton
*(Clerk of General Synod)*
25 Weavers Meadow, Banbridge,
Co Down BT32 4RL
Email norman.hutton3@btinternet.com
Tel 028-40626902
Rev Dr A.D.G. Steers *(Editor, Non-Subscribing Presbyterian Magazine)*
223 Upper Lisburn Road, Belfast BT10 0LL
Tel 028-90947850
Email nspresb@hotmail.com
*Clerk of the Presbytery of Antrim*
Rev Dr J. W. Nelson
102 Carrickfergus Road,
Larne, Co Antrim BT40 3JX
Tel 028-28272600
*Clerk of the Presbytery of Bangor*
Rev I. Gilpin
15 Windmill Hill, Comber,
Co Down BT23 5WH
Tel 028-91872265
*Clerk of the Synod of Munster*
Mr F. Spengeman
12 Knocknasuff, Waterloo,
Blarney, Co Cork
Tel 087-8101943

**Presbyterian Church in Ireland**
Right Rev Dr Ivan Patterson
Moderator, c/o Assembly Buildings,
Fisherwick Place, Belfast BT1 6DW
Tel 028-90322284 Fax 028-90417301
Email moderator@presbyterianireland.org
Rev Dr Donald Watts, Clerk
Assembly Buildings, Belfast BT1 6DW
Tel 028-90417208 Fax 028-90417301
Email clerk@presbyterianireland.org

**Religious Society of Friends**
Felicity A. McCartney
Clerk of Yearly Meeting
49 Vauxhall Park, Belfast BT9 5HB
For information contact
National Administrative Office,
Quaker House Dublin,
Stocking Lane, Dublin 16
Tel 01-4998003
Email office@quakers.ie

**Rock of Ages Cherubim & Seraphim Church in Ireland**
Rev Mother Agnes O. Aderanti
Rock of Ages Cherubim & Seraphim Church, 46 Priory Gate, Athboy, Co Meath
Tel 046-9487977/086-8134747
Email rockofagescs@hotmail.com
Website rockofagescs@hotmail.com

**Romanian Orthodox Church in Ireland**
Romanian Orthodox Parish of the Exaltation of the Holy Cross,
Christ Church, Leeson Park, Dublin 6
*Parish Priest:* Fr Calin Florea
18 Portersgate Green, Clonsilla, Dublin 15
Tel 087-6148140
Email revcalin.florea@gmail. com
*Assistant Priest:* Fr Godfrey O'Donnell
5 Cherry Park, Rathingle, Swords, Co Dublin
Tel 01-8404302/087-6780150
Email godo@eircom.net

**Russian Orthodox Church in Ireland**
Russian Orthodox Church St Peter-St Paul,
Moscow Patriarchate Representation,
Harold's Cross Road, Dublin 6W
Tel 01-4969038
*Dean:* Very Rev Fr Michael Gogoleff
Tel 0044-1225-858792 Fax 0044-1225-852211
*Deputy:* Fr Nikolai Evseev
Tel 086-1009531
Email priest.nikolay@stpeterstpaul.net
*Affiliated Parishes:* Cork, Galway, Waterford, Stradbally, Belfast
*Services*
Saturday Vespers – Matins: 6.00 pm
Sunday Liturgy: 10.00 am
Feast Days Liturgy: 10.00 am
Wednesday Pastoral Talks: 7.00 pm
Church Shop: religious books, candles, icons
Languages: Services in English and Slavonic

**Salvation Army**
Major Alan Watters
Divisional Commander,
Divisional Headquarters, 12 Station Mews,
Sydenham, Belfast BT4 1TL
Tel 028-90675000 Fax 028-90675011
Email alan.watters@salvationarmy.org.uk
Captain James Wadsorth
Dublin City Corps
Tel 01-8481690
Email
james.wadsworth@salvationarmy.org.uk
Captain Marcus Mylechreest
Dublin South
Tel 01-4126494
Email marcus.mylechreest@salvationarmy.ie

## CHURCH OF IRELAND ARCHBISHOPS AND BISHOPS

**Armagh**
Most Rev A. E. T. Harper, OBE, BA
Archbishop of Armagh, Primate of All Ireland and Metropolitan,
Diocesan Office, Church House,
46 Abbey Street, Armagh BT61 7DZ
Tel 028-37522851 (H), 028-37527144 (O)
Fax 028-37510596
Email archbishop@armagh.anglican.org
*Diocesan Secretary:* Mrs J. Leighton
Church House, 46 Abbey Street,
Armagh BT61 7DZ
Tel 028-37522858 Fax 028-37510596
Email secretary@armagh.anglican.org

**Dublin**
Most Rev M.G. St A. Jackson MA, PhD, DPhil
Archbishop of Dublin, Bishop of Glendalough, Primate of Ireland and Metropolitan, The See House,
17 Temple Road, Dartry, Dublin 6
Tel 01-4977849 Fax 01-4976355
Email archibishop@dublin.anglican.org
*Diocesan Secretary:* Mrs S. Heggie
Diocesan Office, Church of Ireland House,
Church Avenue, Rathmines, Dublin 6
Tel 01-4966981 Fax 01-4972865
Email secretary@dublin.anglican.org

**Meath and Kildare**
Most Rev R. L. Clarke MA, BD, PhD
Bishop of Meath and Kildare,
Bishop's House, Moyglare,
Maynooth, Co Kildare
Tel 01-6289354
Email bishop@meath.anglican.org
*Diocesan Secretary:* Mrs K. Seaman
Meath & Kildare Diocesan Centre
Moyglare, Maynooth, Co Kildare
Tel/Fax 01-6275352
Email office@meath.anglican.org

**Cashel and Ossory**
Right Rev M. A. J. Burrows MA, MLitt, Prof.Dip.Th
Bishop of Cashel, Waterford, Lismore, Ossory, Ferns and Leighlin,
Bishop's House, Troysgate, Kilkenny
Tel 056-7786633
Email cashelossorybishop@eircom.net
*Diocesan Secretary:* Mrs D. Hughes
Diocesan Office, St Canice's Library, Kilkenny
Tel 056-7761910/7727248
Fax 056-7751813
Mon-Wed 9.30 am-1.00 pm
Email office@cashel.anglican.org

**Ferns**
*Diocesan Secretary:* Mrs G. Rothwell
Ballyeaton, Glynn,
Enniscorthy, Co Wexford
Tel 053-9128114
Email office@ferns.anglican.org

**Down and Dromore**
Right Rev H. C. Miller MA, BA (Hons), DPS
Bishop of Down and Dromore,
The See House, 32 Knockdene Park South,
Belfast BT5 7AB
Tel 028-90237602 Fax 028-90231902
Email bishop@down.anglican.org
*Diocesan Secretary:* Mrs J. Butler
Diocesan Office, Church of Ireland House,
61-67 Donegall Street, Belfast BT1 2QH
Tel 028-90828850/90828830
Fax 028-90321635
Email office@diocoff-belfast.org

**Derry and Raphoe**
Rt Rev K. R. Good BA (Hons), MEd, HDipEd, DPS
Bishop of Derry and Raphoe,
The See House, 112 Culmore Road,
Londonderry BT48 8JF
Tel 028-71351206/028-71262440
Fax 028-71352554
Email bishop@derry.anglican.org
*Diocesan Secretary:* Mr G. Kelly
Diocesan Office, 24 London Street,
Londonderry BT48 6RQ
Tel 028-71262440 Fax 028-71372100
Email office.derry@btconnect.com

**Limerick and Killaloe**
Right Rev T. R. Williams BA, BA, DPs
Bishop of Limerick, Ardfert, Aghadoe, Killaloe, Kilfenora, Clonfert, Kilmacduagh and Emly,
Rien Roe, Adare, Co Limerick
Tel 061-396244
Email bishop@limerick.anglican.org
*Diocesan Secretary:* Ven. R. Warren
St John's Rectory, Tralee, Co Kerry
Tel 066-7124152 Fax 066-7129004
Email secretary@limerick.anglican.org

**Tuam**
Right Rev P. W. Rooke, CertTh, BA, MPhil
Bishop of Tuam, Killala and Achonry,
Bishop's House, 2 Summerfield,
Cahergowan, Claregalway, Co Galway
Tel 091-799359
Email bptuam@iol.ie
*Diocesan Secretary:* Mrs H. Sherlock
Stonehall House, Ballisodare, Co Sligo
Tel 071-9167280 Fax 071-9130264
Email hsherlock@iolfree.ie

**Clogher**
Right Rev F. J. McDowell, BAHons, BTh, DipBS
Bishop of Clogher, The See House,
Fivemilestown, Co Tyrone BT75 0QP
Tel 028-89522461
Email bishop@clogher.anglican.org
*Diocesan Secretary:* Mr G. M. T. Moore
Clogher Diocesan Office,
St Macartin's Cathedral Hall,
Hall's Lane, Enniskillen,
Co Fermanagh BT74 7DR
Tel 028-85549690
Email secretary@clogher.anglican.org

**Cork**
Right Rev W. P. Colton BCL, DipTh, MPhil, LL.M
Bishop of Cork, Cloyne and Ross,
St Nicholas' House, 14 Cove Street, Cork
Tel 021-4316114/5005080 Fax 021-4320960
Email bishop@ccrd.ie
*Diocesan Secretary:* Mr W. F. Baker
St Nicholas House, 14 Cove Street, Cork
Tel 021-5005080 Fax 021-4320960
Email secretary@cork.anglican.org

**Kilmore**
Right Rev K. H. Clarke BA
Bishop of Kilmore, Elphin and Ardagh,
48 Carrickfern, Cavan, Co Cavan
Tel 049-4372759
Email bishop@kilmore.anglican.org
*Diocesan Secretary:* Miss M. Cunningham
Kilmore Diocesan Office,
The Rectory, Cootehill, Co Cavan
Tel 049-5559954 Fax 049-5559954
Email secretary@kilmore.anglican.org

**Elphin and Ardagh**
*Diocesan Secretary:* Mrs B. Barrett
The Market House, Main Street,
Blacklion, Co Cavan
Tel 071-9853792
Email diosecea@eircom.net

**Connor**
Right Rev A. F. Abernethy
Bishop of Connor, 3 Upper Malone Road,
Belfast BT9 6TD
Tel 028-90828870 (office)
Email bishop@connor.anglican.org
*Diocesan Secretary:* Mrs J. Butler
The Diocesan Office,
Church of Ireland House,
61-67 Donegall Street, Belfast BT1 2QH
Tel 028-90322268 Fax 028-90321635
Email office@diocoff-belfast.org

## GREEK ORTHODOX CHURCH IN IRELAND

Greek Orthodox Church of the Annunciation, 46 Arbour Hill, Dublin 7
Rev Fr Tom Carroll PP
Monegall, Roscrea, Co Tipperary
Tel 0505-45849
Email fr.tomcarroll@gmail.com
*Contact Person*
Mrs Toulla Efthimiou Conran
103 Walkinstown Avenue, Dublin 12
Tel 01-4566509

## METHODIST CHURCH IN IRELAND

*District Superintendents*
*Dublin:* Rev William D. Mullally
233 Beech Park, Lucan, Co Dublin
Tel 01-6280666
*Midlands and Southern*
Rev Brian D. Griffin
The Manse, Roscrea, Co Tipperary
Tel 0505-21670
*Enniskillen and Sligo*
Rev Stephen R. Taylor
Ardaghowen, Co Sligo
Tel 071-9142346

*North West*
Rev John M. Sweeney
9 Dergmoney Place, Omagh,
Co Tyrone BT78 1HS
Tel 028-82243572
*North East:* Rev W. Brian Fletcher
30 Shelling Hill Road, Cullybrackey,
Ballymena, Co Antrim BT42 1NF
*Belfast:* Rev R. Ivan McElhinney
33 Dorchester Drive, Newtownabbey,
Co Antrim BT36 5WP
*Down:* Rev Robert Cooper
'Epworth', 16 Brooklands Road,
Newtownards, Co Down BT23 4TL
Tel 028-91815959
*Portadown:* Rev David G. Clements
28 Margretta Park, Portadown,
Co Armagh BT63 5DF
Tel 028-38332616

## PRESBYTERIES OF THE PRESBYTERIAN CHURCH

**Ards**
Rev Dr R.A. Russell
46 Dunover Road, Ballywalter, BT22 2LE
Tel 028-42758788
Email arussell@presbyterianireland.org

**Armagh**
Rev James Gordon
30 Crossmore Road, Keady BT60 3RH
Tel 028-37531512
Email jgordon@presbyterianireland.org

**Ballymena**
Rev J. J. Andrews
1 Forthill Park, Ballymena BT42 2HL
Tel 028-25645544
Email jandrews@presbyterianireland.org

**East Belfast**
Mr Douglas Cowan
16 Ferndene Gardens,
Dundonald BT16 2EP
Tel 028-90481292
Email dcowan@presbyterianireland.org

**North Belfast**
Rev T. C. Morrison
39 Old Cavehill Road, Belfast BT15 5FH
Tel 028 9077 0301
Email cmorrison@presbyterianireland.org

**South Belfast**
Mr Cecil Graham
97 Orby Drive, Belfast BT5 6AG
Tel 028-90289702
Email cgraham@presbyterianireland.org

**Carrickfergus**
Rev T. J. Stothers
168 Upper Road, Greenisland,
Carrickfergus BT38 8RW
Tel 028-90864657
Email jstothers@presbyterianireland.org

**Coleraine and Limavady**
Rev W. I. Hunter
8 Ballywatt Road, Coleraine BT52 2LT
Tel 028-20731310
Email ihunter@presbyterianireland.org

**Derry and Donegal**
Rev Stanley Stewart
35 Glencosh Road, Donemana,
Strabane BT82 0LY
Tel 028-71397186
Email sstewart@presbyterianireland.org

**Down**
Rev Dr Brian Black
Ballygowan Church Office,
Church Hill, Ballygowan BT23 6JA
Tel 028-97521096
Email bblack@presbyterianireland.org

**Dromore**
Rev J. I. Davey
2 Lisburn Road, Hillsborough BT26 6AA
Tel 028-92683696
Email jdavey@presbyterianireland.org

**Dublin and Munster**
Mr Stuart Ferguson
'Brianna', Ballyclough, Camolin,
Enniscorthy, Co Wexford
Tel 053-9383854
Email stuartfer@gmail.com

**Iveagh**
Rev Gordon Best (Acting)
28 Manse Road, Ballynagarrick,
Craigavon BT63 5NW
Tel 028-38831265
Email gbest@presbyterianireland.org

**Monaghan**
Rev Sam Anketell
Corglass Manse, Bailieborough
Tel 042-9665745
Email sanketell@presbyterianireland.org

**Newry**
Rev S. A. Finlay
156 Glassdrumman Road, Annalong,
Newry BT34 4QL
Tel 028-43768232
Email sfinlay@presbyterianireland.org

**Omagh**
Rev Robert Herron
10 Mullaghmenagh Avenue,
Omagh BT78 5QH
Tel 028-82243776
Email rherron@presbyterianireland.org

**Route**
Rev Noel McClean
Kilraughts Manse, 24 Topp Road,
Ballymoney BT53 8LT
Tel 028-27667618
Email nmcclean@presbyterianireland.org

**Templepatrick**
Rev John Murdock
50 Killead Road, Aldergrove,
Crumlin BT29 4EN
Tel 028-94422436
Email jmurdock@presbyterianireland.org

**Tyrone**
Rev T. J. Conway
74 Ballymacilcurr Road,
Upperlands BT46 5TT
Tel 028-79642278
Email tconway@presbyterianireland.org

# IRELAND'S CARDINALS

Since 1866, when Ireland received its first residential cardinal, to the present, nine Irish bishops have been elected to the Sacred College. By 'Irish bishops' is meant those who, while exercising actual pastoral government, were cardinals; not included are those Irish prelates who were made cardinals but whose ministry was spent overseas (e.g. Cardinal Glennon), or in the service of the Roman Curia (e.g. Cardinal Browne), or those who, having been territorial bishops in Ireland, were elevated to the Sacred College while exercising pastoral government in a diocese overseas (e.g. Cardinal Moran).

**Paul Cullen (1803-78)**
Ordained Archbishop of Armagh (1850); translated to Dublin (1852); created Cardinal (22 June 1866) by Pius IX.

**Edward McCabe (1816-85)**
Ordained Bishop of Gadara and appointed auxiliary to the Archbishop of Dublin, Cardinal Cullen (1877); appointed Archbishop of Dublin, following Cardinal Cullen's death (1879); created Cardinal (27 March 1882) by Leo XIII.

**Michael Logue (1840-1924)**
Ordained Bishop of Raphoe (1879); translated to be Co-adjutor to Archbishop Daniel McGettigan of Armagh (March 1887), whom he succeeded (December 1887); created Cardinal (16 January 1893) by Leo XIII.

**Patrick O'Donnell (1856-1927)**
Ordained Bishop of Raphoe (1888); translated to be Co-adjutor to Cardinal Logue (1922), whom he succeeded as Archbishop of Armagh (1924); created Cardinal (14 December 1925) by Pius XI.

**Joseph MacRory (1861-1945)**
Ordained Bishop of Down and Connor (1915); translated to Armagh as Archbishop in succession to Cardinal O'Donnell (1928); created Cardinal (12 December 1929) by Pius XI.

**John D'Alton (1882-1963)**
Ordained Bishop of Binda and appointed Co-adjutor to the Bishop of Meath (1942), whom he succeeded (1943); translated to Armagh in succession to Cardinal MacRory (1946); created Cardinal (12 January 1953) by Pius XII.

**William Conway (1913-77)**
Ordained Bishop of Neve and appointed auxiliary to the Archbishop of Armagh, Cardinal D'Alton (1958), whom he succeeded (1963); created Cardinal (22 February 1965) by Paul VI.

**Tomás Ó Fiaich (1923-90)**
Ordained Archbishop of Armagh (1977) and created Cardinal (30 June 1979) by John Paul II.

**Cahal Brendan Daly (1917-2009)**
ordained priest 22 June 1941; ordained Bishop of Ardagh and Clonmacnois 16 July 1967; installed Bishop of Down and Connor 17 October 1982; installed Archbishop of Armagh 16 December 1990; created Cardinal 28 June 1991 by John Paul II; retired 1 October 1996.

The tenth Irish Cardinal is the Archbishop of Dublin, H. E. **Cardinal Desmond Connell** *(see Diocese of Dublin)*

The eleventh Irish Cardinal is the Archbishop of Armagh, H. E. **Cardinal Seán Brady** *(see Diocese of Armagh)*

# STATISTICS

### TABLE 1: CATHOLIC CHURCH PERSONNEL 2006

| | Number |
|---|---|
| Diocesan | 3,078 |
| Clerical Religious Orders | 3,278 |
| Sisters' Orders | 8,891 |
| Brothers' Orders | 697 |
| TOTAL | 15,944 |

*Source:* Council for Research and Development 2007

### TABLE 2: VOCATIONS 2006

| | | Entrants |
|---|---|---|
| Diocesan | | 28 |
| Clerical Religious Orders | | 15 |
| Sisters' Orders | | 9 |
| Brothers' Orders | | 1 |
| TOTAL | | 53 |

*Source:* Council for Research and Development 2007

### TABLE 3: NULLITY OF MARRIAGE

| Year | Applications | Decrees of Nullity |
|---|---|---|
| 2001 | 421 | 489 |
| 2002 | 406 | 386 |
| 2003 | 402 | 295 |
| 2004 | 499 | 272 |
| 2005 | 434 | 395 |
| 2006 | 391 | 701 |
| 2007 | 332 | 517 |
| 2008 | 309 | 314 |
| 2009 | 268 | 298 |
| 2010 | 295 | 263 |

*EXPLANATORY NOTES:*

1. The above figures relate to the 32 counties.
2. Only a minority of applications persist beyond the preliminary stages. About 40% are found to have no *prima facie* case for nullity and do not reach the stage of formal investigation; a further third are withdrawn by the applicants.
3. In about 75–80% of cases ending with a nullity decree, a veto – technically called a *vetitum* – on marriage in the Church is imposed on one or both parties. This is because the defect which caused the nullity is judged to be still present, putting at risk the validity of a future marriage. The *vetitum* may be lifted by the local bishop only if he is satisfied, after investigation, of the person's fitness for marriage in all essential respects. The purpose of the *vetitum* is to prevent the sacrament of marriage being brought into disrepute and to protect the genuine interests of any future spouse.
4. Before a decree is granted a) a case must be judged independently by two tribunals – in Ireland, first, by a regional tribunal and then by the National Appeals Tribunal; b) it must be established with moral certainty – probability alone is not enough – that nullity exists in a particular case; that is, that, because of fundamental defect of capacity for, or consent to, that marriage, established to have been present at the time of marriage, there was in fact, no valid marriage. The tribunal starts with the presumption that the marriage is valid; the onus is on the applicants to provide convincing evidence that it is not.
5. COST OF THE PROCEDURE: The costs involved for the applicant are kept as low as possible and are, in fact, very modest. Applicants are expected to pay if they can afford it. However, each applicant is formally told that the progress of the case or its outcome does not in any way depend on the ability or willingness to pay any or all of these expenses. If they genuinely cannot pay, the Church will come to their aid. In practice, only a minority pay the full case fee. Over half pay nothing.

**TABLE 4: CATHOLICS 2011** | **TABLE 5: CATHOLIC SCHOOLS 2011**

| | Parishes | Catholic Population | Churches | Schools (no) | | School Population | |
|---|---|---|---|---|---|---|---|
| | | | | Primary | Secondary[1] | Primary | Secondary[1] |
| Armagh | 61 | 237,141 | 150 | 149 | 27 | 26,309 | 19,078 |
| Dublin | 199 | 1,199,000 | 247 | 473 | 186 | 129,122 | 88,478 |
| Cashel | 46 | 82,275 | 84 | 121 | 21 | 11,074 | 8,432 |
| Tuam | 56 | 122,134 | 131 | 195 | 18 | 15,421 | 8,482 |
| Achonry | 23 | 34,826 | 47 | 49 | 9 | 3,780 | 3,969 |
| Ardagh[2] | 41 | 71,806 | 80 | 86 | 20 | 11,256 | 7,857 |
| Clogher[2] | 37 | 86,047 | 85 | 96 | 18 | 11,862 | 9,376 |
| Clonfert[2] | 24 | 36,000 | 47 | 50 | 7 | 6,800 | 3,200 |
| Cloyne | 46 | 160,370 | 107 | 124 | 28 | 21,636 | 11,589 |
| Cork & Ross | 68 | 220,000 | 124 | 180 | 48 | n/a | n/a |
| Derry | 50 | 243,362 | 104 | 135 | 26 | 21,846 | 18,610 |
| Down & Connor | 87 | 338,059 | 150 | 163 | 38 | 30,144 | 26,335 |
| Dromore[2] | 23 | 63,400 | 48 | 51 | 14 | 10,270 | 11,524 |
| Elphin | 37 | 70,500 | 90 | 120 | 19 | 10,100 | 4,010 |
| Ferns | 49 | 99,796 | 101 | 96 | 20 | 16,492 | 10,802 |
| Galway | 39 | 112,253 | 71 | 85 | 20 | 13,781 | 6,688 |
| Kerry[2] | 53 | 127,850 | 110 | 168 | 33 | 17,200 | 12,400 |
| Kildare & Leighlin | 56 | 219,817 | 117 | 172 | 43 | 30,864 | 17,707 |
| Killala | 22 | 40,137 | 48 | 65 | 11 | 4,470 | 3,392 |
| Killaloe | 58 | 118,240 | 133 | 150 | 21 | 15,885 | 11,500 |
| Kilmore | 36 | 62,438 | 95 | 83 | 14 | 9,370 | 5,681 |
| Limerick | 60 | 184,340 | 94 | 107 | 22 | 22,000 | 20,000 |
| Meath[2] | 69 | 242,000 | 149 | 198 | 36 | 30,000 | 24,000 |
| Ossory | 42 | 89,394 | 89 | 86 | 16 | 11,397 | 6,497 |
| Raphoe | 33 | 81,300 | 71 | 101 | 20 | 10,662 | 13,151 |
| Waterford & Lismore | 45 | 148,267 | 85 | 98 | 24 | 16,892 | 12,380 |
| Totals[3] | 1,360 | 4,449,752 | 2,657 | 3,401 | 759 | 508,633 | 365,138 |

**Notes:**

1. Includes voluntary secondary schools and state schools.

*Source:* Diocesan returns

2. Data unchanged from 2011.
3. Total estimates only.

## TABLE 6: NUMBER OF PRIESTS AND RELIGIOUS

| | Active in Diocese[1] | Others[2] | RELIGIOUS ORDERS | | |
|---|---|---|---|---|---|
| | | | Clerical | Brothers | Sisters |
| Armagh | 99 | 28 | 52 | 22 | 315 |
| Dublin | 284 | 147 | 849 | 300 | 2,305 |
| Cashel | 83 | 9 | 48 | 12 | 139 |
| Tuam | 77 | 35 | 9 | 14 | 172 |
| Achonry | 36 | 9 | 1 | 0 | 48 |
| Ardagh[3] | 59 | 13 | 5 | 9 | 190 |
| Clogher[3] | 73 | 10 | 5 | 2 | 134 |
| Clonfert | 37 | 5 | 18 | 0 | 93 |
| Cloyne | 95 | 37 | 0 | 3 | 200 |
| Cork & Ross[3] | 119 | 30 | 141 | 36 | 580 |
| Derry | 82 | 31 | 7 | 6 | 96 |
| Down & Connor | 138 | 36 | 58 | 28 | 216 |
| Dromore | 32 | 19 | 7 | 3 | 134 |
| Elphin | 48 | 12 | 7 | 0 | 110 |
| Ferns | 84 | 29 | 17 | 6 | 150 |
| Galway | 50 | 22 | 38 | 16 | 235 |
| Kerry[3] | 78 | 25 | 10 | 5 | 292 |
| Kildare & Leighlin | 95 | 20 | 93 | 54 | 380 |
| Killala[3] | 47 | 18 | 4 | 3 | 54 |
| Killaloe | 93 | 26 | 16 | 21 | 191 |
| Kilmore | 64 | 16 | 7 | 1 | 50 |
| Limerick[3] | 89 | 31 | 52 | 15 | 305 |
| Meath[3] | 109 | 19 | 102 | 20 | 163 |
| Ossory | 59 | 18 | 20 | 36 | 210 |
| Raphoe | 64 | 20 | 10 | 3 | 46 |
| Waterford & Lismore | 66 | 22 | 52 | 36 | 305 |
| Totals[4] | 2,160 | 687 | 1,628 | 651 | 7,113 |

**Notes:**
1. Diocesan priests only.
2. Priests of the diocese retired, sick, on study leave or working in other dioceses in Ireland and abroad. Details are listed under the diocese.
3. Data unchanged from 2011.
4. Totals estimates only.

*Source:* Diocesan returns

# CATHOLIC ARCHBISHOPS AND BISHOPS OF BRITAIN

## APOSTOLIC NUNCIO

Most Rev Antonio Mennini
54 Parkside, London SW19 5NF
Tel 020-89447189
Fax 020-89472494

## ENGLAND AND WALES

### PROVINCE OF WESTMINSTER

Most Rev Vincent Nichols
*Archbishop of Westminister*

**Auxiliaries**
Rt Rev Bernard Longley
Rt Rev Alan Hopes
Rt Rev John Arnold
Rt Rev John Sherrington

**Suffragans**
Right Rev Thomas McMahon
*Bishop of Brentwood*
Right Rev Malcolm MacMahon
*Bishop of Nottingham*
Sede Vacante
*Bishop of East Anglia*
Right Rev Peter Doyle
*Bishop of Northhampton*

### PROVINCE OF BIRMINGHAM

Most Rev Bernard Longley
*Archbishop of Birmingham*

**Auxilary**
Rt Rev David McGough
Rt Rev William Kenney

**Suffragans**
Right Rev Mark Davies
*Bishop of Shrewsbury*
Right Rev Declan Lang
*Bishop of Clifton*

### PROVINCE OF LIVERPOOL

Most Rev Patrick Kelly
*Archbishop of Liverpool*

**Auxilary**
Right Rev Thomas Williams

**Suffragans**
Right Rev Terence Brain
*Bishop of Salford*
Right Rev Arthur Roche
*Bishop of Leeds*
Right Rev John Rawsthorne
*Bishop of Hallam*
Right Rev Terence Drainey
*Bishop of Middlesbrough*
Right Rev Seamus Cunningham
*Bishop of Hexham and Newcastle*
Right Rev Michael Campbell
*Bishop of Lancaster*

### PROVINCE OF CARDIFF

Most Rev George Stack
*Archbishop of Cardiff*

**Suffragans**
Right Rev Tom Burns
*Bishop of Menevia*
Right Rev Edwin Regan
*Bishop of Wrexham*

### PROVINCE OF SOUTHWARK

Most Rev Peter Smith
*Archbishop of Southwark*

**Auxiliaries**
Right Rev John Hine, Rt Rev Patrick Lynch, Rt Rev Paul Hendricks

**Suffragans**
Right Rev Christopher Budd
*Bishop of Plymouth*
Right Rev Kieran Conry
*Bishop of Arundel and Brighton*
Right Rev Crispian Hollis
*Bishop of Portsmouth*

**Bishop of the Forces**
Right Rev Richard Moth

## BISHOPS' CONFERENCE OF ENGLAND AND WALES

Bishop's Conference
39 Eccleston Square, London SW1V 1BX
Tel 020-76308220 Fax 020-79014821
Email secretariat@cbcew.org.uk

Most Rev Vincent Nichols
Archbishop's House, Ambrosden Avenue, London SW1P 1QJ
Tel 020-77989033 Fax 020-77989077

Right Rev Declan Lang
Bishop of Clifton, St Ambrose, North Road, Leigh Woods, Bristol BS8 3PW
Tel 0117-9733027 Fax 0117 9735913

Most Rev Peter Smith
Archbishop of Southwark,
Archbishop's House, St George's Road, Southwark, London SE1 6HX
Tel 020 79282495 Fax 020 79287833

Right Rev Michael Campbell
Bishop of Lancaster,
Bishop's Office, Balmoral Road,
Lancaster LA1 3BT
Tel 01524-596050

Right Rev Christopher Budd
Bishop of Plymouth,
31 Wyndham Street West, Plymouth,
Devon PL1 5RZ
Tel 01752-224414 Fax 01752-223750

Sede Vacante
The White House, 21 Upgate,
Poringland, Norwich, Norfolk NR14 7SH
Tel 01586-2202/3956 Fax 01586-5358

Most Rev Bernard Longley
Archbishop of Birmingham,
8 Shadwell Street, Birmingham B4 6EY
Tel 0121-2369090 Fax 0121-2120171

Right Rev Mark Davis
Bishop of Shrewsbury,
Curial Offices, 2 Park Road South,
Prenton, Wirral CH43 4UX
Tel 0151-6529855

Right Rev Edwin Regan
Bishop of Wrexham, Bishop's House,
Sontley Road, Wrexham,
Clwyd LL13 7EW
Tel 01978-262726 Fax 01978-354257

Right Rev Terence Drainey
Bishop of Middlesbrough,
Bishop's House, 16 Cambridge Road,
Middlesbrough, Cleveland TS5 5NN
Tel 01642-818253 Fax 01642-850548

Right Rev John Hine
Auxiliary in Southwark, The Hermitage,
More Park, West Malling,
Kent ME19 6NH
Tel 01732-845486 Fax 01732-845888

Right Rev Crispian Hollis
Bishop of Portsmouth, Bishop's House,
Edinburgh Road, Portsmouth PO1 3HG
Tel 01705-820894 Fax 01705-863086

Right Rev Terence Brain
Bishop of Salford, Wardley Hall, Worsley,
Manchester M28 5ND
Tel 0161-7942825 Fax 0161-7278592

Right Rev Arthur Roche
Bishop of Leeds, Bishop's House,
13 North Grange Road, Headingley,
Leeds LS6 2BR
Tel 01532-304533 Fax 01532-789890

Right Rev Seamus Cunningham
Bishop of Hexham and Newcastle,
Bishop's House,
East Denton Hall, 800 West Road,
Newcastle Upon Tyne NE5 2BJ
Tel 0191-2280003 Fax 0191-2740432

Right Rev Peter Doyle
Bishop of Northampton,
Bishop's House, Marriott Street,
Northhampton NN2 6AW
Tel 01604-715635 Fax 01604-792186

Right Rev Malcolm MacMahon
Bishop of Nottingham, Bishop's House,
27 Cavendish Road East, The Park,
Nottingham NG7 1BB
Tel 01602-474786 Fax 01602-475235

Right Rev Thomas McMahon
Bishop of Brentwood, Bishop's House,
Stock, Ingatestone, Essex CM4 9BU
Tel 01277-232266 Fax 01277-214060

Right Rev John Sherrington
Auxiliary Bishop of Westminster
Archbishop's House,
Ambrosden Avenue, London SWIP IQJ
Tel 020-7798 9033 Fax 020-7798 9077

Right Rev Alan Hopes
Auxiliary Bishop of Westminster
Archbishop's House,
Ambrosden Avenue, London SWIP IQJ
Tel 020-7798 9033 Fax 020-7798 9077

Right Rev John Rawsthorne
Bishop of Hallam, Bishop's House
75 Norfolk Road, Sheffield 52 2SZ
Tel 0114 278 7988 Fax 0114 278 7988

Right Rev Tom Burns
Bishop of Menevia,
79 Walter Road, Swansea SA1 4PS
Tel 01792-650534 Fax 01792-458641

Right Rev Kieran Conry
Bishop of Arundel and Brighton
Highoaks, Old Brighton Road North,
Pease Pottage, West Sussex RH11 9AJ
Tel 01293-526428 Fax 01293-385276

Right Rev Richard Moth
Bishop of the Forces, Bishop's Oak,
26 The Crescent, Farnborough Park,
Farnborough, Hants GU14 7AS
Tel 01252-543649 Fax 01252-373748

Most Rev George Stack
Archbishop of Cardiff,
Archbishop's House,
42-43 Cathedral Road, Cardiff CF1 9HD
Tel 01222-20411 Fax 01222-345950

Most Rev Patrick Kelly
Archbishop of Liverpool,
Archbishop's House, Lowood,
Carnatic Road, Liverpool L18 8BY
Tel 0151-7246398 Fax 0151-7246405

Right Rev Thomas Williams
14 Hope Place, Liverpool L1 9BG
Tel 0151-7030109 Fax 0151-7030267

Rt Rev John Arnold
Auxiliary Bishop of Westminster
Archbishop's House,
Ambrosden Avenue,
London SWIP IQJ
Tel 020-77989033 Fax 020-77989077

Rt Rev Paul Hendricks
Auxiliary Bishop of Southwark,
95 Carshalton Road, Sutton,
Surrey SMI 4LL
Tel 020-86438007

Rt Rev Patrick Lynch
Auxiliary Bishop of Southwark,
68 Crooms Hill, Greenwich SE10 8HG
Tel 020-82931238

Rt Rev David McGough
Auxiliary Bishop of Birmingham,
160 Draycott Road, Tean,
Stoke on Trent ST10 4JT
Tel 01538-722433 Fax 01538-722433

Rt Rev William Kenney
Auxiliary Bishop of Birmingham,
St Hugh's House, 27 Hensington Road,
Woodstock, Oxfordshire OX20 1JH
Tel/Fax 01993-812234

## UKRAINIAN APOSTOLIC EXARCH

Right Rev Hlib Lonchyna
Ex-Arch of the Ukrainians
90 Binney Street, London W1Y 1YN
Tel 0171-6291534

## RETIRED BISHOPS IN ENGLAND AND WALES

Right Rev Frederick Hall (MHM)
former Bishop of Kisumu,
Herbert House, 41 Victoria Road,
Freshfield, Liverpool L37 1LW

Right Rev Patrick Kalilombe (WF)
former Bishop of Lilongwe,
Malawi, 31 Westholme Croft,
Birmingham B30 1TR

Right Rev Leo McCartie
Emeritus Bishop of Northampton
Aston Hall, Aston by Stone
Staffordshire ST1S OBJ

Right Rev Daniel Joseph Mullins
Emeritus Bishop of Menevia
79 Walter Road, Swansea SA1 4PS

Right Rev John Jukes (OFMConv)
Former Auxiliary in Southwark
St Margaret's, 30 Chapel Street,
Huntly, Aberdeenshire AB54 5BS

Right Rev Francis Walmsley
Bishop of the Forces, Emeritus,
St John's Convent, Linden Hill Lane,
Reading RG10 9XP

Most Rev Michael Bowen
Emeritus Archbishop of Southwark
54 Parkside, Vanbrugh Park,
London SE3 7QF

Right Rev Howard Tripp
Former Auxiliary in Southwark
67 Haynt Walk, London SW20 9NY

Right Rev Patrick O'Donoghue
Emeritus Bishop of Lancaster,
c/o Cathedral House,
Balmoral Road, Lancaster LA1 3BT

Right Rev Philip Pargeter
Auxiliary in Birmingham, Grove House,
90 College Road, Sutton Coldfield,
West Midlands B73 5AH

Right Rev Mark Jabalé
Emeritus Bishop of Menevia,
Holy Trinity Presbytery,
London Road, Chipping Norton,
Oxon OX7 5AX

Most Rev Kevin McDonald
Emeritus Archbishop of Southwark,
c/o Archbishop's House,
St George's Road, Southwark,
London SE1 6HX

Right Rev Brian Noble
Emeritus Bishop of Shrewsbury,
Laburnum Cottage,
97 Barnston Road, Barnston,
Wirral CH61 1BW

## THE HIERARCHY OF SCOTLAND

### PROVINCE OF ST ANDREWS AND EDINBURGH

His Eminence Keith Patrick
Cardinal O'Brien
Archbishop of St Andrews and
Edinburgh, 42 Greenhill Gardens,
Edinburgh EH10 4BJ
Tel 0131-4473337
Fax 0131-4470816

**Suffragans**
Right Rev Hugh Gilbert
Bishop of Aberdeen,
Bishop's House, 3 Queen's Cross,
Aberdeen AB9 2NL
Tel 01224-319154
Fax 01224-325570

Right Rev Vincent Logan
Bishop of Dunkeld, Bishop's House,
29 Roseangle, Dundee DD1 4LX
Tel 01382-225453
Fax 01382-204585

Right Rev Joseph A. Toal
Bishop of Argyll and The Isles
Bishop's House, Esplanade, Oban,
Argyll PA34 5AB
Tel 01631-571395
Fax 01631-564930

Right Rev John Cunningham
Bishop of Galloway, Candida Casa,
8 Corsehill Road, Ayr KA7 2ST
Tel 01292-266750
Fax 01292-289888

### PROVINCE OF GLASGOW

Most Rev Mario Joseph Conti
Archbishop of Glasgow
40 Newlands Road, Glasgow G43 2JD
Tel 0141-2265898
Fax 0141-2252600

**Suffragans**

Right Rev Joseph Devine
Bishop of Motherwell,
27 Smithcroft, Hamilton ML3 7UL
Tel 01698-459129

Right Rev Philip Tartaglia
Bishop of Paisley, Bishop's House,
107 Corsebar Road, Paisley,
Renfrewshire PA2 9PY
Tel 0141-8897200 Fax 0141-8496053

## BISHOPS' CONFERENCE OF SCOTLAND

*General Secretary:* Mgr Paul M. Conroy
General Secretariat,
64 Aitken Street, Airdrie,
Lanarkshire ML6 6LT
Tel 01236-764061 Fax 01236-762489
Email gensec@bpsconfscot.com
www.bpsconfscot.com

## RETIRED BISHOPS IN SCOTLAND

Right Rev Maurice Taylor
Bishop Emeritus (Galloway Diocese)
41 Overmills Road,
Ayr KA7 3LH

Right Rev John A. Mone
Bishop Emeritus (Paisley Diocese)
Carnmore, 30 Esplande,
Greenock PA16 7RU

Right Rev Ian Murray
Bishop Emeritus (Argyll and The Isles)
St Columba's, 9 Upper Gray Street,
Edinburgh EH9 1SN

Right Rev Peter A. Moran
Bishop Emeritus of Aberdeen,
10 Cathedral Square, Fortrose IV10 8TB

# FORMS OF ECCLESIASTICAL ADDRESS

These notes should be understood as a guide to present-day practice in Ireland, rather than as 'prescriptive' rules. Forms of address – for example, whether someone is 'Very Rev', 'Right Rev', or 'Most Rev' – vary from country to country and language to lanquage. The aim here has been to reflect Irish usage. These conventions are not static but are subject to gradual change. Some of the more involved forms of address have disappeared, and a dual standard of formality has emerged. For instance, 'Canon John Nonnullus' has in recent years tended to replace 'John Canon Nonnullus'. Where the older form is still found, the norm of normal address is given with the older form in parentheses ( ) as the more formal form of address. Since the form used is often a matter of preference of the person addressed, or the customary usage of a particular diocese or religious order, where this is known it should be followed. This directory uses what is considered to be the normal Irish form.

## THE HIERARCHY

**The Apostolic Nuncio**
Written address: His Excellency Most Rev Dr John Nonnullus
Spoken address: same
In conversation: Your Excellency.
Reference to: 'The Nuncio said...'
('His Excellency said...')

**Cardinals**
Written address: His Eminence Cardinal John Nonnullus (H.E. John Cardinal Nonnullus)
Spoken address: Cardinal John Nunnullus (the more formal address is either of the written forms)
In conversation: Cardinal (Your Eminence)
Reference to: 'The Cardinal said...'
('His Eminence said...')

*Note:* The majority of cardinals are bishops, and they are divided into three groups, a small number known as the 'cardinal bishops', another small group who are the 'cardinal deacons', and the majority, who are called 'cardinal priests'. From this has arisen the form 'Cardinal-Archbishop of ...' or 'the cardinal-archbishop said', sometimes used in the media for emphasis. There is no category of 'cardinal-archbishops'; rather there are bishops and archbishops who are also cardinals. If one wishes to refer to a cardinal and also to draw attention to the see of which he is bishop, the following form should be used: 'Cardinal John Nunnullus, the Archbishop of Nusquam'.

**Archbishops**
Written address: The Most Rev John Nonnullus
Spoken address: Archbishop Nonnullus (His Grace the Archbishop of Nusquam)
In conversation: Your Grace
Reference to: 'The Archbishop said...'
('His Grace said...')

**Bishops**
Written address: The Most Rev John Nonnullus
Spoken address: Dr John Nonnullus, Bishop of Nusquam (His Lordship Dr...)
In conversation: Doctor (My Lord)
Reference to: 'The Bishop said...'

*Note:* The practice of using the word 'Bishop' in spoken address (e.g. Bishop John Nonnullus of Nusquam) and in conversation (e.g. 'Bishop, I am pleased to meet you') is becoming increasingly common.

## CLERGY

*Secular:*
**Monsignor**
Written: Right Rev Mgr
Spoken: Monsignor

*Capitular Dignitaries:*
**Archdeacon**
Written: The Venerable John Nonnullus, Archdeacon of Nusquam
Spoken: Archdeacon

**Dean**
Written: The Very Rev Dean Nonnullus
Spoken: Dean

**Canon**
Written: The Very Rev Canon John Nonnullus (John Canon Nonnullus)
Spoken: Canon

**Others**
Those holding other capitular offices (e.g. precentor) are addressed as canons.

**Parish Priest**
Written: The Very Rev John Nonnullus PP
Spoken: Father

**Curates**
Written: The Very Rev John Nonnullus CC
Spoken: Father

**Other Priests**
Secular priests not included above:
Written: Rev John Nonnullus
Spoken: Father
Priests using academic titles are referred to by these titles, and in writing these are prefixed by 'Rev', e.g. Rev Prof John Nonnullus

**Deacons**
Written: Rev John Nonnullus
Spoken: Mister (Rev Mister)

**Regular**
The conventional protocol varies with religious orders, many of whom preserve forms of address peculiar to themselves. A general rule is that priests are addressed as found under
Other priests above, and superiors (of houses or provinces) are addressed in writing as 'The Very Rev'.

**Abbots**
Written: 'The Right Rev' is placed before the conventional form of address of a member of that community.

## NON-CLERICAL RELIGIOUS

**Men**
Non-clerical religious orders of men and non-clerical members of clerical religious orders are referred to as 'Br John Nonnullus' on writing, and `Brother' in speech.

*Note 1.* The use of Christian name or surname (e.g. 'Br John' or 'Br Nonnullus') depends on the usage of the order.

*Note 2.* Some orders have traditional ways of referring to their non-clerical members other than 'Brother'.

**Women**
Members of religious orders of women are referred to as 'Sr' in writing and 'Sister' in speech, irrespective of the position they hold in their institute.
Note 1. The form 'Reverend Mother' is obsolete and its use does not arise.
Note 2. The use of Christian name, name in religion, or surname, or the prefixing of the forename with 'M' (Mary) depends on the usage of the order.
Note 3. Some orders, in particular monastic and enclosed orders, use titles derived from their own traditions (e.g. abbess and prioress). There is no consistent usage with regard to these titles (e.g. it may be `Mother Abbess' or 'Sr Mary, the Abbess') and the usage depends on the order or the house.

# THE ROMAN PONTIFFS

Information includes the name of the Pope, in many cases his name before becoming Pope, his birth-place or country of origin, the date of accession to the Papacy, and the date of the end of reign which, in all but a few cases, was the date of death. Double dates record the day of election and coronation.
Source: *Annuario Pontificio*

**St Peter** (Simon Bar-Jona) of Bethsaida, in Galilee, Prince of the Apostles, who received from Jesus Christ supreme pontifical power to be transmitted to his successors, resided first at Antioch, then at Rome, where he was martyred in the year 64 or 67, having governed the Church from that city for twenty-five years.
**St Linus**, Tuscany, 67-76
**St Anacletus** (Cletus), Rome 76-88
**St Clement**, Rome 88-97
**St Evaristus**, Greece, 97-105
**St Alexander I**, Rome, 105-25
**St Sixtus I**, Rome, 115-25
**St Telesphorus**, Greece, 125-36
**St Hyginus**, Greece, 136-40
**St Pius I**, Aquilea, 140-55
**St Anictus**, Syria, 155-66
**St Soter**, Campania, 166-75
**St Eleutheius**, Nicopolis in Epirus, 175-89

*Up to the time of St Eleutherius, the years indicated for the beginning and end of pontificates are not certain. Also, up to the middle of the eleventh century, there are some doubts about the exact days and months given in chronological tables.*

**St Victor I**, Africa, 189-99
**St Zephyrinus**, Rome, 199-217
**St Callistus I**, Rome, 217-22
**St Urban I**, Rome, 222-30
**St Pontian**, Rome, 21 July 230 to 28 Sept 235
**St Anterus**, Greece, 21 Nov 235 to 3 Jan 236
**St Fabian**, Rome, 10 Jan 236 to 20 Jan 250
**St Cornelius**, Rome, Mar 251 to June 253
**St Lucius I**, Rome, 12 May 254 to 2 Aug 254
**St Stephen I**, Rome, 12 May 254 to 2 Aug 257
**St Sixtus II**, Greece, 30 Aug 257 to 6 Aug 258
**St Dionysius**, birthplace unknown, 22 July 259 to 26 Dec 268
**St Felix I**, Rome, 5 Jan 269 to 30 Dec 274
**St Eutychian**, Luni, 4 Jan 275 to 7 Dec 283
**St Caius**, Dalmatia, 17 Dec 283 to 22 Apr 296
**St Marcellinus**, Rome, 30 June 296 to 25 Oct 304
**St Marcellus I**, Rome, 27 May 308 or 26 June 308 to 16 Jan 309
**St Eusebius**, Greece, 18 Apr 309 or 310 to 17 Aug 309 or 310
**St Melchiades** (Miltiades), Africa, 2 July 311 to 11 Jan 314
**St Sylvester I**, Rome, 31 Jan 314 to 31 Dec 335

*Most of the popes before St Sylvester I were martyrs.*

**St Marcus**, Rome, 18 Jan 336 to 7 Oct 336
**St Julius I**, Rome, 6 Feb 337 to 12 Apr 352
**Liberius**, Rome, 17 May 352 to 24 Sept 366
**St Damasus I**, Spain, 1 Oct 366 to 11 Dec 384
**St Siricius**, Rome, 15 or 22 or 29 Dec 384 to 26 Nov 399
**St Anastasius I**, Rome, 27 Nov 399 to 19 Dec 401
**St Innocent I**, Albano, 22 Dec 401 to 12 Mar 417
**St Zozimus**, Greece, 18 Mar 417 to 26 Dec 418
**St Bonifice I**, Rome, 28 or 29 Dec 418 to 4 Sept 422
**St Celestine I**, Campania, 10 Sept 422 to 27 July 432
**St Sixtus III**, Rome, 31 July 432 to 19 Aug 440
**St Leo I** (the Grant), Tuscany, 29 Sept 440 to 10 Nov 461
**St Hilary**, Sardinia, 19 Nov 461 to 29 Feb 468
**St Simplicius**, Tivoli, 3 Mar 468 to 10 Mar 483
**St Felix III (II)**, Rome, 13 Mar 483 to 1 Mar 492

*He should be called Felix II, and his successors of the same name should be numbered accordingly. The discrepancy in the numerical designation of popes named Felix was caused by the erroneous insertion in some lists of the name of St Felix of Rome, a martyr.*

**St Gelasius I**, Africa, 1 Mar 492 to 21 Nov 496
**Anastasius II**, Rome, 24 Nov 496 to 19 Nov 498
**St Symmachus**, Sardinia, 22 Nov 498 to 19 July 514
**St Hormisdas**, Frosinone, 20 July 514 to 6 Aug 523
**St John I**, Martyr, Tuscany, 13 Aug 523 to 18 May 526
**St Felix IV (III)**, Samnium, 12 July 526 to 22 Sept 530
**Boniface II**, Rome, 22 Sept 530 to 17 Oct 532
**John II**, Rome, 2 Jan 533 to 8 May 535

*John II was the first pope to change his name. His given name was Mercury.*

**St Agapitus I**, Rome, 13 May 535 to 22 Apr 536
**St Silverius**, Martyr, Campania, 1 or 8 June 536 to 11 Nov 537 (d. 2 Dec 537)

*St Silverius was violently deposed in March 537 and abdicated on 11 Nov 537. His successor, Vigilius, was not recognised as pope by all the Roman clergy until his abdication.*

**Vigilius**, Rome, 29 Mar 537 to 7 June 555
**Pelagius I**, Rome, 16 Apr 556 to 4 Mar 561
**John III**, Rome, 17 July 561 to 13 July 574
**Benedict I**, Rome, 2 June 575 to 30 July 579
**Pelagius II**, Rome, 26 Nov 579 to 7 Feb 590
**St Gregory I** (the Great), Rome, 3 Sept 590 to 12 Mar 604
**Sabinian**, Blera in Tuscany, 13 Sept 604 to 22 Feb 606
**Bonifcace III**, Rome, 19 Feb 607 to 12 Nov 607
**St Boniface IV**, Abruzzi, 25 Aug 608 to 8 May 615
**St Deusdedit** (Adeodatus I), Rome, 19 Oct 615 to 8 Nov 618
**Boniface V**, Naples, 23 Dec 619 to 25 Oct 625
**Honorius I**, Campania, 27 Oct 625 to 12 Oct 638
**Severinus**, Rome, 28 May 640 to 2 Aug 640
**John IV**, Dalmatia, 24 Dec 640 to 12 Oct 642
**Theodore I**, Greece, 24 Nov 642 to 14 May 649
**St Martin I**, Martyr, Todi, July 649 to 16 Sept 655 (in exile from 17 June 653)
**St Eugene I**, Rome, 10 Aug 654 to 2 June 657

*St Eugene I was elected during the exile of St Martin I, who is believed to have endorsed him as pope.*

**St Vitalian**, Segni, 30 July 657 to 27 Jan 672
**Adeodatus II**, Rome, 11 Apr 672 to 17 June 676
**Donus**, Rome, 2 Nov 676 to 11 Apr 678
**St Agatho**, Sicily, 27 June 678 to 10 Jan 681
**St Leo II**, Sicily, 17 Aug 682 to 3 July 683
**St Benedict II**, Rome, 26 June 684 to 8 May 685
**John V**, Syria, 23 July 685 to 2 Aug 686
**Conon**, birthplace unkown, 21 Oct 686 to 21 Sept 687
**St Sergius I**, Syria, 15 Dec 687 to 8 Sept 701
**John VI**, Greece, 30 Oct 701 to 11 Jan 705
**John VII**, Greece, 1 Mar 705 to 18 Oct 707
**Sisinnius**, Syria, 15 Jan 708 to 4 Feb 708
**Constantine**, Syria, 25 Mar 708 to 9 Apr 715
**St Gregory II**, Rome, 19 May 715 to 11 Feb 731
**St Gregory II**, Syria, 18 May 731 to Nov 741
**St Zachary**, Greece, 10 Dec 741 to 22 Mar 752

**Stephen II (III)**, Rome, 26 Mar 752 to 26 Apr 757

*After the death of St Zachary, a Roman priest named Stephen was elected but died (four days later) before his consecration as Bishop of Rome, which would have marked the beginning of his pontificate. Another Stephen was elected to succeed Zachary as Stephen II. (The first pope with this name was St Stephen 254-7). The ordinal III appears in parentheses after the name of Stephen II because the name of the earlier elected but deceased priest was included in some lists. Other Stephens have double numbers.*

**St Paul I**, Rome, Apr (29 May) 757 to 28 June 767
**Stephen III (IV)**, Sicily, 1 (7) Aug 768 to 24 Jan 772
**Adrian I**, Rome, 1 (9) Feb 772 to 25 Dec 795
**St Leo III**, Rome, 26 (27) Dec 795 to 12 June 816
**Stephen IV (V)**, Rome, 22 June 816 to 24 Jan 817
**St Paschal I**, Rome, 25 Jan 817 to 11 Feb 824
**Eugene II**, Rome, Feb (May) 824 to Aug 827
**Valentine**, Rome, Aug 827 to Sept 827
**Gregory IV**, Rome, 827 to Jan 844
**Sergius II**, Rome, Jan 844 to 27 Jan 847
**St Leo IV**, Rome, Jan (10 Apr) 847 to 17 Jan 855
**Benedict III**, Rome, July (29 Sept) 855 to 17 Apr 858
**St Nicholas I (the Great)**, Rome, 24 Apr 858 to 13 Nov 867
**Adrian II**, Rome, 14 Dec 867 to 14 Dec 872
**John VIII**, Rome, 14 Dec 872 to 16 Dec 882
**Marinus I**, Gallese, 16 Dec 882 to 15 May 884
**St Adrian III**, Rome, 17 May 884 to Sept 885
**Stephen V (VI)**, Rome, Sept 885 to 14 Sept 891
**Formosus**, Portus, 6 Oct 891 to 4 Apr 896
**Boniface VI**, Rome, Apr 896 to Apr 896
**Stephen VI (VII)**, Rome, May 896 to Aug 897
**Romanus**, Gallese, Aug 897 to Nov 897
**Theodore II**, Rome, Dec 897 to Dec 897
**John IX**, Tivoli, Jan 898 to Jan 900
**Benedict IV**, Rome, Jan (Feb) 900 to July 903
**Leo V**, Ardea, July 903 to Sept 903
**Sergius III**, Rome, 29 Jan 904 to 14 Apr 911
**Anastasius III**, Rome, Apr 911 to June 913
**Landus**, Sabina, July 913 to Feb 914
**John X**, Tossignano (Imola), Mar 914 to May 928
**Leo VI**, Rome, May 928 to Dec 928
**Stephen VII (VIII)**, Rome, Dec 928 to Feb 931
**John XI**, Rome, Feb (Mar) 931 to Dec 935
**Leo VII**, Rome, 3 Jan 936 to 13 July 939
**Stephen VIII (IX)**, Rome, 14 July 939 to Oct 942
**Marinus II**, Rome, 30 Oct 942 to May 946
**Agapitus II**, Rome, 10 May 946 to Dec 955
**John XII** (Octavius), Tusculum, 16 Dec 955 to 14 May 964 (date of his death)
**Leo VIII**, Rome, 4 (6) Dec 963 to 1 Mar 965
**Benedict V**, Rome, 22 May 964 to 4 July 966

*Confusion exists concerning the legitamcy of claims to the pontificate by Leo VII and Benedict V. John XII was deposed on 4 Dec 963 by a Roman council. If this deposition was invalid, Leo was an antipope. If the deposition of John was valid, Leo was the legitimate pope and Benedict was an antipope.*

**John XIII**, Rome, 1 Oct 965 to 6 Sept 972
**Benedict VI**, Rome, 19 Jan 973 to June 974
**Benedict VIII**, Rome, Oct 974 to 10 July 983
**John XIV** (Peter Campenora), Pavia, Dec 983 to 20 Aug 984
**John XV**, Rome, Aug 985 to Mar 996
**Gregory V** (Bruno of Carinthia), Saxony, 3 May 996 to 18 Feb 999
**Sylvester II** (Gerbert), Auvergne, 2 Apr 999 to 12 May 1003
**John XVII** (Siccone), Rome, June 1003 to Dec 1003
**John XVIII** (Phasianus), Rome, Jan 1004 to July 1009
**Sergius IV** (Peter), Rome, 31 July 1009 to 12 May 1012

*The custom of changing one's name on election to the papacy is generally considered to date from the time of Sergius IV. Before his time, several popes had changed their names. After his time, this became a regular practice, with few exceptions, e.g. Adrian VI and Marcellus II.*

**Benedict VIII** (Theophylactus), Tusculum, 18 May 1012 to 9 Apr 1024
**John XIX** (Rosmanus), Tusculum, Apr (May) 1024 to 1032
**Benedict IX** (Theophylactus), Tusculum, 1032-44
**Sylvester III** (John), Rome, 20 Jan 1045 to 10 Feb 1045

*Sylvester III was an antipope if the forcible removal of Benedict IX in 1044 was not legitimate.*

**Benedict IX** (second time), 10 Apr 1045 to 1 May 1045
**Gregory VI** (John Gratian), Rome, 5 May 1045 to 20 Dec 1046
**Clement II** (Suitger, Lord of Morsleben and Homburg), Saxony, 24 (25) Dec 1046 to 9 Oct 1047

*If the resignation of Benedict IX in 1045 and his removal at the December 1046 synod were not legitimate, Gregory VI and Clement II were antipopes.*

**Benedict IX** (third time), 8 Nov 1047 to 17 July 1028 (d. c.1055)
**Damasus II** (Poppo), Bavaria, 17 July 1028 to 9 Aug 1028
**St Leo IX** (Bruno), Alsace 12 Feb 1049 to 19 Apr 1054
**Victor II** (Gebhard), Swabia, 16 Apr 1055 to 28 July 1057
**Stephen IX (X)** (Frederick), Lorraine, 3 Aug 1057 to 29 Mar 1058
**Nicholas II** (Gerard), Burgundy, 24 Jan 1059 to 27 July 1061
**Alexander II** (Anselmo da Baggio), Milan, 1 Oct 1061 to 21 Apr 1073
**St Gregory VII** (Hildebrand), Tuscany, 22 Apr (30 June) 1073 to 25 May 1085
**Bl Victor III** (Dauferius; Desiderius), Benevento, 24 May 1086 to 15 Sept 1087
**Bl Urban II** (Otto di Lagery), France, 12 Mar 1088 to 29 July 1099
**Paschall II** (Raniero), Ravenna, 13 (14) Aug 1099 to 21 Jan 1118
**Gelasius II** (Giovanni Caetani), Gaeta, 24 Jan (10 Mar) 1118 to 28 Jan 1119
**Callistus II** (Guido of Burgundy), Burgundy, 2 (9) Feb 1119 to 13 Dec 1124
**Honorius II** (Lamberto), Fiagnano (Imola), 15 (21) Dec 1124 to 13 Feb 1130
**Innocent II** (Gregorio Paperschi), Rome, 14 (23) Feb 1130 to 24 Sept 1143
**Celestine II** (Guido), Cittá di Castello, 26 Sept (3 Oct) 1143 to 8 Mar 1144
**Lucius II** (Gerardo Caccianemici), Bologna, 12 Mar 1144 to 15 Feb 1145
**Bl Eugene III** (Bernardo Paganelli di Montemagno), Pisa, 15 (18) Feb 1145 to 8 July 1153
**Anastasius IV** (Corrado), Rome, 12 July 1153 to 3 Dec 1154
**Adrian IV** (Nicholas Breakspear), England, 4 (5) Dec 1154 to 1 Sept 1159
**Alexander III** (Rolando Bandinelli), Siena, 7 (20) Sept 1159 to 30 Aug 1181
**Lucius III** (Ubaldo Allucingoli), Lucca, 1 (6) Sept 1181 to 25 Sept 1185
**Urban III** (Uberto Crivelli), Millan, 25 Nov (1 Dec) 1185 to 20 Oct 1187
**Gregory VIII** (Alberto de Morra), Benevento, 21 (25) Oct 1187 to 17 Dec 1187
**Clement III** (Paolo Scolari), Rome, 19 (20) Dec 1187 to Mar 1191
**Celestine III** (Giacinto Bobone), Rome, 30 Mar (14 Apr) 1191 to 8 Jan 1198
**Innocent III** (Lotario dei Conti di Segni), Anagni, 8 Jan (22 Feb) 1198 to 16 July 1216
**Honorius III** (Cencio Savelli), Rome, 18 (24) July 1216 to 18 Mar 1227
**Gregory IX** (Ugolino, Count of Segni), Anagni, 19 (21) Mar 1227 to 22 Aug 1241
**Celestine IV** (Goffredo Castiglioni), Milan, 25 (28) Oct 1241 to 10 Nov 1241
**Innocent IV** (Sinibaldo Fieschi), Genoa, 25 (28) June 1243 to 7 Dec 1254
**Alexander IV** (Rinaldo, Count of Segni)
**Anagni**, 12 (20) Dec 1254 to 25 May 1261
**Urban IV** (Jacques Pantaléon), Troyes, 29 Aug (4 Sept) 1261 to 2 Oct 1264
**Clement IV** (Guy Foulques or Guido le Gros), France, 5 (15) Feb 1265 to 29 Nov 1268
**Bl Gregory X** (Teobaldo Visconti), Piacenza, 1 Sept 1271 (27 Mar 1272) to 10 Jan 1276
**Bl Innocent V** (Peter of Tarentaise), Savoy, 21 Jan (22 Feb) 1276 to 22 June 1276
**Adrian V** (Ottobono Fieschi), Genoa, 11 July 1276 to 18 Aug 1276

**John XXI** (Petrus Juliani or Petrus Hispanus), Portugal, 8 (20) Sept 1276 to 20 May 1277

*Elimination was made of the name of John XX in an effort to rectify the numerical designation of popes named John. The error dates back to the time of John XV.*

**Nicholas III** (Giovanni Gaetano Orsini), Rome, 25 Nov (26 Dec) 1277 to 22 Aug 1280
**Martin IV** (Simon de Brie), France, 22 Feb (23 Mar) 1281 to 28 Mar 1285

*The names of Marinus I (882-4) and Marinus II (942-6) were construed as Martin. In view of these two pontificates and the earlier reign of St Martin I (649-55), this pope was called Martin IV.*

**Honorius IV** (Giacomo Savelli), Rome, 2 Apr (20 May) 1285 to 3 Apr 1287
**Nicholas IV** (Girolamo Masci), Ascoli, 22 Feb 1288 to 4 Apr 1292
**St Celestine V** (Pietro del Murrone), Isernia, 5 July (29 Aug) 1294 to 13 Dec 1294; d. 1296. Canonised 5 May 1313
**Boniface VIII** (Benedetto Caetani), Anagni, 24 Dec 1294 (23 Jan 1295) to 11 Oct 1303
**Bl Benedict XI** (Niccolo Boccasini), Treviso, 22 (27) Oct 1303 to 7 July 1304
**Clement V** (Bertrand de Got), France, 5 June (14 Nov) 1305 to 20 Apr 1314 (first of Avignon popes)

*From 1309 to 1377 Avignon was the residence of a series of French popes during a period of power struggles between the rulers of France, Bavaria and England and the Church. Despite some positive achievments it was the prologue to the Western Schism which began in 1378.*

**John XXII** (Jacques d'Euse), Cahors, 7 Aug (5 Sept) 1316 to 4 Dec 1334
**Benedict XII** (Jacques Fournier), France, 20 Dec 1334 (8 Jan 1335) to 25 Apr 1342
**Clement VI** (Pierre Roger), France, 7 (19) May 1342 to 6 Dec 1352
**Innocent VI** (Etienne Aubert), France, 18 (30) Dec 1352 to 12 Sept 1362
**Bl Urban V** (Guillaume de Grimoard), France, 28 Sept (6 Nov) 1362 to 19 Dec 1370
**Gregory XI** (Pierre Roger de Beaufort), France, 30 Dec 1370 (5 Jan 1371) to 26 Mar 1378 (last of Avignon popes)
**Urban VI** (Bartolomeo Prignano), Naples, 8 (18) Apr 1378 to 15 Oct 1389
**Boniface IX** (Pietro Tomacelli), Naples, 2 (9) Nov 1389 to 1 Oct 1404
**Innocent VII** (Cosma Migliorati), Sulmona, 17 Oct (11 Nov) 1404 to 6 Nov 1406
**Gregory XII** (Angelo Correr), Venice, 30 Nov (19 Dec)1406 to 4 July 1415 when he voluntarily resigned from the papacy to permit the election of his successor.

*This brought to an end in the Council of Constance the Western Schism which had divided Christendom into two and then three papal obediences from 1370 to 1417. Gregory XII died on 18 Oct 1417.*

**Martin V** (Oddone Colonna), Rome, 11 (21) Nov 1417 to 20 Feb 1431
**Eugene IV** (Gabriel Condulmer), Venice, 3 (11) Mar 1431 to 23 Feb 1447
**Nicholas V** (Tommaso Parentucelli), Sarzana, 6 (19) Mar 1447 to 24 Mar 1455
**Callistus III** (Alfonso Borgia), Jativa (Valencia), 8 (20) Apr 1455 to 6 Aug 1458
**Pius II** (Enea Silvio Piccolomini), Siena, 19 Aug (3 Sept) 1458 to 14 Aug 1464
**Paul II** (Pietro Barbo), Venice, 30 Aug (16 Sept) 1464 to 26 July 1471
**Sixtus IV** (Francesco della Rovere), Savona, 9 (25) Aug 1471 to 12 Aug 1484
**Innocent VIII** (Giovanni Battista Cibo), Genoa, 29 Aug (12 Sept) 1484 to 25 July 1492
**Alexander VI** (Rodrigo Borgia), Jativa (Valencia), 11 (26) Aug 1492 to 18 Aug 1503
**Pius III** (Francesco Todeschini-Piccolomini), Siena, 22 Sept (1, 8 Oct) 1503 to 18 Oct 1503
**Julius II** (Guiliano della Rovere), Savona, 31 Oct (26 Nov) 1503 to 21 Feb 1513
**Leo X** (Giovanni de' Medici), Florence, 9 (19) Mar 1513 to 1 Dec 1521
**Adrian VI** (Adrian Florensz), Utrecht, 9 Jan (31 Aug) 1522 to 14 Sept 1523
**Clement VII** (Giulio de' Medici), Florence, 19 (26) Nov 1523 to 25 Sept 1534
**Paul III** (Alessandro Farnese), Rome, 13 Oct (3 Nov) 1534 to 10 Nov 1549
**Julius III** (Giovanni Maria Ciocchi del Monte), Rome, 7 (22) Feb 1550 to 23 Mar 1555
**Marcellus II** (Marcello Cervini), Montepulciano, 9 (10) Apr 1555 to 1 May 1555
**Paul IV** (Gian Pietro Carafa), Naples, 23 (26) May 1555 to 18 Aug 1559
**Pius IV** (Giovan Angelo de' Medici), Milan, 25 Dec 1559 (6 Jan 1560) to 9 Dec 1565
**St Pius V** (Antonio-Michele Ghislieri), Bosco (Alexandria), 7 (17) Jan 1566 to 1 May 1572. Canonised 22 May 1712
**Gregory XIII** (Ugo Buoncompagni), Bologna, 13 (25) May 1572 to 10 Apr 1585
**Sixtus V** (Felice Peretti), Grottammare (Ripatransone), 24 Apr (1 May) 1585 to 27 Aug 1590
**Urban VII** (Giovanni Battista Castagna) Rome, 15 Sept 1590 to 27 Sept 1590
**Gregoryy XIV** (Niccolo Sfondrati), Cremona, 5 (8) Dec 1590 to 16 Oct 1591
**Innocent IX** (Giovanni Antonio Facchinetti), Bologna, 19 Oct (3 Nov) 1591 to 30 Dec 1591
**Clement VIII** (Ippolito Aldobrandini), Florence, 30 Jan (9 Feb) 1592 to 3 Mar 1605
**Leo XI** (Alessandro de' Medici), Florence, 1 (10) Apr 1605 to 27 Apr 1605
**Paul V** (Camillo Borghese), Rome, 16 (29) May 1605 to 28 Jan 1621
**Gregory XV** (Alessandro Ludovisi), Bologna, 9 (14) Feb 1621 to 8 July 1623
**Urban VIII** (Maffeo Barberini), Florence, 6 Aug (29 Sept) 1623 to 29 July 1644
**Innocent X** (Giovanni Battista Pamfili), Rome, 15 Sept (4 Oct) 1644 to 7 Jan 1655
**Alexander VII** (Fabio Chigi), Siena, 7 (18) Apr 1655 to 22 May 1667
**Clement IX** (Giulio Rospigliosi), Pistoia, 20 (26) June 1667 to 9 Dec 1669
**Clement X** (Emilio Altieri), Rome, 29 Apr (11 May) 1670 to 22 July 1676
**Bl Innocent XI** (Benedetto Odescalchi), Como, 21 Sept (4 Oct) 1676 to 12 Aug 1689. Beatified 7 Oct 1956
**Alexander VIII** (Pietro Ottoboni), Venice, 6 (16) Oct 1689 to 1 Feb 1691
**Innocent XII** (Antonio Pignatelli), Spinazzola, 12 (15) July 1691 to 27 Sept 1700
**Clement XI** (Giovanni Francesco Albani), Urbino, 23, 30 Nov (8 Dec) 1700 to 19 Mar 1721
**Innocent XIII** (Michelangelo dei Conti), Rome, 8 (18) May 1721 to 7 Mar 1724
**Benedict XIII** (Pietro Francesco [in religion Vincenzo Maria] Orsini), Gravina (Bari), 29 May (4 June) 1724 to 21 Feb 1730
**Clement XII** (Lorenzo Corsini), Florence, 12 (16) July 1730 to 6 Feb 1740
**Benedict XIV** (Prospero Lambertini), Bologna, 17 (22) Aug 1740 to 3 May 1758
**Clement XIII** (Carlo Rezzonico), Venice, 6 (16) July 1758 to 2 Feb 1769
**Clement XIV** (Giovanni Vincenzo Antonio [in religion Lorenzo] Gaganelli), Rimini, 19, 28 May (4 June) 1769 to 22 Sept 1774
**Pius VI** (Giovanni Angelo Braschi), Cesena, 15 (22 Feb) 1775 to 29 Aug 1799
**Pius VII** (Barnabà [in religion Gregirio] Chiaramonti, Cesena, 14 (21) Mar 1800 to 20 Aug 1823
**Leo XII** (Annibale della Genga), Genga (Fabriano), 28 Sept (5 Oct) 1823 to 10 Feb 1829
**Pius VIII** (Francesco Saverio Castiglioni), Cingoli, 31 Mar (5 Apr) 1829 to 30 Nov 1830
**Gregory XVI** (Bartolomeo Alberto [in relgion Mauro] Cappellari), Belluno, 2 (6) Feb 1831 to 1 June 1846
**Pius IX** (Giovanni M. Mastai-Ferretti), Senigallia, 16 (21) June 1846 to Feb 1878
**Leo XIII** (Gioacchino Pecci), Carpineto (Anagni), 20 Feb (3 Mar) 1878 to 20 July 1903
**St Pius X** (Giuseppe Sarto), Riese (Treviso), 4 (9) Aug 1903 to 20 Aug 1914. Canonised 29 May 1954
**Benedict XV** (Giacomo della Chiesa), Genoa, 3 (6) Sept 1914 to 22 Jan 1922
**Pius XI** (Achille Ratti), Desio (Milan), 6 (12) Feb 1922 to 10 Feb 1939
**Pius XII** (Eugenio Pacelli), Rome, 2 (12) Mar 1939 to 9 Oct 1958
**John XXIII** (Angelo Giuseppe Roncalli), Sotto il Monte (Bergamo), 28 Oct (4 Nov) 1958 to 3 June 1963
**Paul VI** (Giovanni Battista Montini), **Concessio** (Brescia, 21 (30) June 1963 to 6 Aug 1978
**John Paul I** (Albino Luciani), Forno di Canale (Belluno), 26 Aug (3 Sept) 1978 to 28 Sept 1978
**John Paul II** (Karol Wojtyla), Wadowice, Poland, 16 (22) Oct 1978 to 2 April 2005
**Benedict XVI** (Joseph Ratzinger), Germany, April 2005A

# Index of Advertisers

# ALPHABETICAL LIST OF CLERGY IN IRELAND

**DIOCESAN, RELIGIOUS AND MISSIONARY**

Irish Diocesan clergy working or studying abroad are also listed.

Telephone numbers are included in this list.
For all other forms of telephonic or electrical communications, including mobiles, faxes, email addresses and websites, please refer to the main entries in this directory.

**All STD numbers in this Directory are listed with both the number and the local area code.**
**Callers from the Irish Republic to Northern Ireland simply need to dial 048 followed by the 8-digit local number.**

## A

AcAuliffe, James (SPS)
St Patrick's, Kiltegan,
Co Wicklow
Tel 059-6473600

Adjei-Buor, James (CSSp)
Holy Spirit Missionary
College, Kimmage Manor,
Dublin 12
Tel 01-4064300

Adler, Emil
Ministry to Polish
Community,
St Anne's Presbytery,
Convent Hill, Waterford
Tel 087-4182223/051-855819
(Waterford & L.)

Agnoli, Enzo (CSSp)
Holy Spirit Missionary
College, Kimmage Manor,
Dublin 12
Tel 01-4064300

Agnoli, Savino (CSSp)
Holy Spirit Missionary
College, Kimmage Manor,
Dublin 12
Tel 01-4064300

Aguilar-Díez, Juan José (SJ)
John Sullivan House,
56/56A Mulvey Park,
Dundrum, Dublin 14
Tel 01-2983978

Ahearne, Peter, Very Rev, PP
Rathronan, Clonmel,
Co Tipperary
Tel 052-6121891
(*Powerstown*, Waterford & L.)

Ahearne, Seamus (OSA), Very Rev, PP
The Presbytery,
60 Glenties Park,
Finglas South, Dublin 11
Tel 01-8343722/087-6782746
(*Rivermount*, Dublin)

Ahern, Dan (SSC)
c/o St John's Parish Centre,
Castle Street, Tralee,
Co Kerry
(Columban, Retired)

Ahern, Gerard, Very Rev, PP
Abbeyleix, Co Laois
Tel 057-8731135
(*Abbeyleix*, Kildare & L.)

Ahern, Michael (OCSO)
Mount Melleray Abbey,
Cappoquin, Co Waterford
Tel 058-54404

Ahern, Niall, Very Rev Canon, PP
Strandhill, Co Sligo
Tel 071-9168147
(*Strandhill/Ransboro*, Elphin)

Ahern, P.
St John's Parish Centre,
Castle Street, Tralee,
Co Kerry
(Kerry, retired)

Aherne, Francis (OSA)
St Augustine's Priory,
Washington Street, Cork
Tel 021-2753982

Aikoye, John, PC
c/o The Sacristy,
St Vincent de Paul Church,
Griffith Avenue, Dublin 9
Tel 01-8332772
(*Marino*, Dublin)

Akpan, Inimabasi Macjoe
(supply priest)
St Patrick's, Leeson Park,
Dublin 6
(Dublin)

Alexander, Anthony, Very Rev, PP
824 Shore Road,
Newtownabbey,
Co Antrim BT36 7DG
Tel 028-90370845
(*Greencastle*, Down & C.)

Alexander, Paul, Very Rev, PP
10 St Patrick's Road, Saul,
Downpatrick,
Co Down BT30 7JE
Tel 028-44612525

Allen, Andrew (OP)
47 Leeson Park, Dublin 6
Tel 01-6602427

Allen, Brian (OFM)
Vicar, Franciscan Friary,
Friary Lane, Athlone,
Co Westmeath
Tel 090-6472095

Allman, Colm, Very Rev, BA, HDE
President,
St Joseph's College,
Garbally Park, Ballinasloe,
Co Galway
Tel 090-9642504/9642254
(Clonfert)

Alwill, Gerard, Very Rev, PP
Drumkeerin, Co Leitrim
Tel 071-9648025
Visiting Chaplain,
Lough Allen College,
Drumkeerin, Co Leitrim
Tel 071-9648017
(*Drumkeerin*, Kilmore)

Ambrose, James, Very Rev Canon
Dromcollogher, Charleville,
Co Limerick
Tel 087-7740753
(Limerick, retired)

Anadam, Alex (SSP)
Society of St Paul,
Moyglare Road,
Maynooth, Co Kildare
Tel 01-6285933

Andrews, Paul (SJ)
Milltown Park,
Sandford Road, Dublin 6
Tel 01-2698411/2698113

An Nguyen, Dan, CC
The Presbytery,
Montrose Park,
Beaumont, Dublin 5
(*Beaumont*, Dublin)

Arackaparambil, Matthew, CC
The Presbytery,
St Martin de Porres Parish,
Aylesbury, Dublin 24
Tel 01-4510160
(*Tallaght, Oldbawn*, Dublin)

Arkinson, Patrick, PP
Sessiaghoneill, Ballybofey,
Co Donegal
Tel 074-9131149
(*Killygordon*, Derry)

Armstrong, Paul, Very Rev, PP
28 Willowbank Park,
Belfast BT6 0LL
Tel 028-90793023
(*St Bernadette's*, Down & C.)

Arnasius, Egidijus
48 Westland Row, Dublin 2
Tel 01-6761030/087-7477554
(*Westland Row*, Dublin)

Arockia Doss, Nayagiam, PC
Parochial House, Rathdrum,
Co Wicklow
Tel 0404-46517
(*Rathdrum*, Dublin)

Arthure, Robert, Very Rev, AP
Cappoquin, Co Waterford
Tel 058-54221
(*Cappoquin*, Waterford & L.)

Asare, Anthony
47 Westland Row, Dublin 2
Tel 085-2778177
(*Westland Row*, Dublin)

Asfaha, Tesfay (SDB)
Salesian College,
Maynooth Road,
Celbridge, Co Kildare
Tel 01-6275058/60

Audley, Padraic, Very Rev, PP
An Cheathru Rua,
Co Na Gallimhe
(Tuam, retired)

Aughney, Edward, Very Rev, PP
Glynn,
St Mullins via Kilkenny
Tel 051-424563
(*St Mullins*, Kildare & L.)

Aylward, Eamon (SSCC), Adm
Sacred Hearts Presbytery,
St Johns Drive, Sruleen,
Dublin 22
Tel 01-4570032
(*Sruleen*, Dublin)

Bailey, Michael (OFM), CC
Curate's Residence,
Monksfield, Salthill, Galway
Tel 091-526006
(*Salthill*, Galway)

Baker, Eugene, CC
Greenhill, Fermoy, Co Cork
Tel 025-33507
(*Fermoy*, Cloyne)

Baker, Patrick, PP
65 Mayogall Road,
Knockloughrim,
Magherafelt,
Co Derry BT45 8PG
(*Lavey (Termoneeny and Part of Maghera)*, Derry)

Balfe, George, Very Rev, PP
Ardagh, Co Longford
Tel 043-75006
(*Ardagh and Moydow*, Ardagh & Cl.)

Bambrick, Thomas (SM), CC
Railway Road, Muinebheag,
Co Carlow
Tel 059-9721154
(*Muinebheag/ Bagenalstown*, Kildare & L.)

Bane, John, Very Rev, PP
Parochial House, Broadford,
Co Clare
Tel 061-473123/086-8246555
(*Broadford*, Killaloe)

Bannon, Anthony (LC)
Superior, Novitiate,
Leopardstown Road,
Foxrock, Dublin 18
Tel 01-2955902

Bannon, Gabriel (OSM)
Servite Priory, Benburb,
Dungannon,
Co Tyrone BT71 7JZ

Bannon, Michael, Very Rev, PP, VF
St Mary's, Edgeworthstown,
Co Longford
Tel 043-6671046
(*Edgeworthstown*, Ardagh & Cl.)

Banville, Patrick, CC
St Leonard's, Saltmills,
New Ross, Co Wexford
Tel 051-562135
(*Ballycullane*, Ferns)

Baragry, Dan (CSsR)
Scala, Castlemahon House,
Castle Road, Cork
Tel 021-4358800

Baragry, Dan (SSC)
St Columban's Retirement Home, Dalgan Park,
Navan, Co Meath
Tel 046-9021525

Barber, Noel (SJ)
Superior, Jesuit Curia Community,
Loyola House,
Milltown Park,
Sandford Road, Dublin 6
Tel 01-2180276

Barden, Thomas, PIC
Kenagh, Co Longford
Tel 043-3322127
(*Kilcommoc*, Ardagh & Cl.)

Barlage, Henry (SVD)
133 North Circular Road,
Dublin 7
Tel 01-8386743

Barrett, Edward (OMI)
Department of Chaplaincy,
Tralee General Hospital,
Tralee, Co Kerry
Tel 066-7126222

Barrett, Eugene (OFM)
Guardian,
Franciscan Friary,
Liberty Street, Cork
Tel 021-4270302

Barrett, Martin
Saint Paul University,
223 Main Street,
Ottawa, Ontario,
Canada KIS 1CU
(Killala)

Barrett, Paul (OFMCap)
St Francis Capuchin Friary,
Rochestown, Co Cork
Tel 021-4896244

Barrins, David (OP)
St Mary's, Pope Quay,
Cork
Tel 021-4502267

Barron, Liam, Very Rev, PP
Mullinavat, via Waterford,
Co Kilkenny
Tel 051-898108/087-2722824
(*Mullinavat*, Ossory)

Barry-Ryan, Kieran (SJ)
Irish Jesuit Provincialate,
Milltown Park,
Sandford Road, Dublin 6
Tel 01-4987333

Barry, Anselm (OSB)
Glenstal Abbey, Murroe,
Co Limerick
Tel 061-386103

Barry, Eamonn,
Facilitator for Prayer and Retreat Ministries
(priest in residence)
St Colman's College,
Fermoy, Co Cork
Tel 025-31622
(Cloyne)

Barry, Edward, CC
The Presbytery,
Ashford, Co Wicklow
Tel 0404-40224
(*Aughrim*, Dublin)

Barry, Jim (SPS)
House Leader,
Kiltegan House,
11 Douglas Road, Cork
Tel 021-4969371

Barry, Maurice (OCarm)
Carmelite Friary, Kinsale,
Co Cork
Tel 021-772138

Barry, Michael, CC
Borrisoleigh, Thurles,
Co Tipperary
Tel 0504-51275
(*Borrisoleigh*, Cashel & E.)

Barry, Phil (SAC)
Pallottine College, Thurles,
Co Tipperary
Tel 0504-21202

Bartlett, Timothy
Irish Bishops' Conference,
Columba Centre,
St Patrick's College,
Maynooth, Co Kildare
Tel 01-5053102
(Down & C.)

Bartley, Kevin, Adm
14 Rosemount Crescent,
Roebuck Road, Clonskeagh,
Dublin 14
Tel 01-8322396/087-2755413
(*Clonskeagh*, Dublin)

Battelle, John, Very Rev Canon, PE
14 Pine Valley,
Grange Road,
Rathfarnham,
Dublin 16
(Dublin, retired)

Battelle, Patrick, Very Rev, PE
14 Pine Valley,
Grange Road,
Rathfarnham,
Dublin 16
Tel 01-4935962
(*Ballinteer*, Dublin)

Baxter, Martin (OCarm)
Prior, Gort Muire,
Ballinteer, Dublin 16
Tel 01-2984014

Baxter, Turlough, CC
St Mary's, Athlone,
Co Westmeath
Tel 090-6472088
(Ardagh & Cl.)

Beagon, Brendan, Very Rev, CC
1 Christine Road,
Newtownabbey,
Co Antrim BT36 6TG
Tel 028-90841507
(*St Mary's on the Hill*, Down & C.)

Beatty, John, Very Rev, PP
Anacarty, Co Tipperary
Tel 062-71104
(*Anacarty*, Cashel & E.)

Beecher, Patrick (OCD)
St Joseph's, Berkeley Road,
Dublin 7
Tel 01-8306356/8306336
(*Berkeley Road*, Dublin)

Beecher, Paul, Very Rev Canon, PE
Cahir, Co Tipperary
Tel 052-7443193
(Waterford & L., retired)

Beere, Joseph (CSSp), Very Rev, PP
The Presbytery,
Bawnogue,
Clondalkin, Dublin 22
Tel 01-4592273/087-6952153
(*Bawnogue*, Dublin)

Beggan, Nguekam Tiernach, Very Rev, PP
Belleek, Enniskillen,
Co Fermanagh BT93 3FJ
Tel 028-68658229
(*Belleek-Garrison*, Clogher)

Beglan, Peter, Very Rev, PE
12 Pairc na-hAbhainn,
Edgeworthstown,
Co Longford
(Ardagh & Cl., retired)

Begley, George P., Co-PP
257 Pace Road, Littlepace,
Dublin 15
Tel 01-2868412/2862955
(*Huntstown*, Dublin)

Begley, Joseph, Very Rev, PP
Kilcummin, Killarney,
Co Kerry
Tel 064-6643176
(*Kilcummin*, Kerry)

Behan, Laurence (Moderator), VF
The Presbytery, St Fergal's,
Killarney Road, Bray,
Co Wicklow
Tel 01-2768191
(*Ballywaltrim*, Dublin)

Behan, Richard M., Very Rev, VF
Presbytery No. 1,
Ballinteer Avenue,
Dublin 16
Tel 01-4944448
(*Ballinteer*, Dublin)

Beirne, Desmond (CM)
All Hallows Institute for Mission and Ministry,
Drumcondra, Dublin 9
Tel 01-8373745/6

Beirne, Francis, Very Rev, PP
Four Roads, Roscommon
Tel 090-6623313
(*Ballyforan*, Elphin)

Beirne, Seán, CC
Kilteevan, Roscommon
Tel 090-6626374
(*Roscommon*, Elphin)

Beirne, Thomas, Very Rev, CC
Newbridge,
Ballinasloe, Co Galway
Tel 090-6660018
(*Ballygar*, Elphin)

Belton, Liam, Very Rev, PP, VF
Parochial House,
La Touche Road,
Greystones, Co Wicklow
Tel 01-2819252
(*Greystones*, Dublin)

Benetti, Antonio (MCCJ)
8 Clontarf Road, Clontarf,
Dublin 3
Tel 01-8330051

Bennett, Donal N. (SSC)
Philippine Chaplaincy
27 Kylemore Gardens,
Omagh, Co Tyrone BT79 7LL

Bennett, John (MSC)
Grace Dieu Retreat House,
Tramore Road, Waterford
Tel 051-374417/373372

Bennett, Mark, CC
St Mary's, Athlone,
Co Westmeath
Tel 090-6472088
(*Athlone*, Ardagh & Cl.)

Bennett, Martin (OFMCap)
Capuchin Friary,
Church Street, Dublin 7
Tel 01-8730599

Bennett, Paul, CC
Pontificio Collegio Irlandese,
Via dei Santi Quattro 1,
00184, Rome
Tel 0039-06-772631
(Cloyne)

Bennett, Roch (OFMCap)
Capuchin Friary,
Ard Mhuire, Creeslough,
Letterkenny, Co Donegal
Tel 074-9138005

Bennett, Ronald (OFM)
Franciscan House of Studies,
Dun Mhuire, Seafield Road,
Killiney, Co Dublin
Tel 01-2826760

Bennett, Seán (CSsR)
St Joseph's, Dundalk,
Co Louth
Tel 042-9334042/9334762

Bennett, Terence (SSC)
St Columban's Retirement
Home, Dalgan Park,
Navan, Co Meath
Tel 046-9021525

Bergin, Denis T., Very Rev
76 Trintonville Road,
Sandymount, Dublin 4
(Dublin, retired)

Bergin, Francis, Very Rev, AP
Shinrone, Co Offaly
Tel 0505-47133
(*Shinrone*, Killaloe)

Bergin, John (SAC)
Pallottine College, Thurles,
Co Tipperary
Tel 0504-21202

Bergin, Liam, Rt Rev Mgr
Apt 1705, 2000
Commonwealth Ave,
Brighton, MA 02135, USA
(Ossory)

Bermingham, John (CSsR)
Mission in
Mozambique/Malawi
c/o Marianella,
75 Orwell Road, Rathgar,
Dublin 6
Tel 01-4067100

Bermingham, William, Very
Rev, PP
Parochial House, Blarney,
Co Cork
Tel 021-4385105
(*Blarney*, Cloyne)

Berney, Donal, CC
St Kevin's, Tinahely,
Co Wicklow
Tel 0402-38138
(*Killaveney*, Ferns)

Biamse, Pius, PC
80 St Mary's Road,
East Wall, Dublin 3
Tel 01-8745317
(*East Wall*, Dublin)

Bingham, Michael (SJ)
Iona, 211 Churchill Park,
Portadown BT62 1EU
Tel 028-38330366

Binkiewicz, Cezary (OP), CC
St Saviour's,
Upper Dorset Street,
Dublin 1
Tel 01-8897610
(*Dominick Street*, Dublin)

Birmingham, Jim (SPS)
St Patrick's, Kiltegan,
Co Wicklow
Tel 059-6473600

Birmingham, Joseph (OCD)
Avila, Bloomfield Avenue,
Morehampton Road,
Dublin 4
Tel 01-6430200

Blade, Kevin (MSC), PP
Church of the Resurrection,
Headford Road, Galway
Tel 091-762883
(*Tirellan*, Galway)

Blake, Ciarán, Very Rev, PP
Carraroe, Co Galway
Tel 099-61221
(*Aran Islands*, Tuam)

Blake, Declan, Adm
Parochial House,
49 Seville Place, Dublin 1
Tel 01-8740796
(*North Wall-Seville Place*,
Dublin)

Blake, Ephrem (CP)
Passionist Retreat Centre,
Tobar Mhuire, Crossgar,
Co Down BT30 9EA
Tel 028-44830242

Blake, Kieran, Very Rev, PP
Kilcolman, Sharavogue,
Birr, Co Offaly
Tel 057-9120812/
087-9302214
(*Kilcolman*, Killaloe)

Blake, Martin,
O'Gorman Street,
Kilrush, Co Clare
Tel 065-9051016/
087-9033682
(Killaloe)

Blayney, Liam (SPS)
Regional Leader,
St Patrick's, Kiltegan,
Co Wicklow
Tel 059-6473680

Bluett, Garrett, Very Rev
Canon, PP
Manister, Croom,
Co Limerick
Tel 061-397335
(*Manister*, Limerick)

Bluett, Patrick, CC
Gortboy, Newcastle West,
Co Limerick
Tel 069-61881
(*Newcastle West*, Limerick)

Bluitt, Tobias, Very Rev, PP
Doneraile, Co Cork
Tel 022-24156
(*Doneraile*, Cloyne)

Boggan, Matthew, CC
Galbally, Ballyhogue,
Enniscorthy, Co Wexford
Tel 053-9247814
(*Bree*, Ferns)

Bohan, Harry, Very Rev, PP
172 Drumgeely Hill,
Shannon, Co Clare
Tel 061-713682/086-8223362
(Killaloe)

Bohan, Seamus, Very Rev, PP
Tynagh, Loughrea,
Co Galway
Tel 090-9745113
(Clonfert)

Boland, Andrew P., Rt Rev
Mgr, Canon, PE
13 Griffith Avenue,
Dublin 9
(Dublin, retired)

Boland, Declan, PP
44 Barrack Street, Strabane,
Co Tyrone BT82 8HD
Tel 028-71883293
(*Strabane*, Derry)

Boland, Dominic S. (OFMCap)
St Anthony's Capuchin
Friary, 43 Dublin Street,
Carlow
Tel 059-9142543

Boland, Eugene, PP
14 Killyclogher Road,
Omagh,
Co Tyrone BT79 0AX
Tel 028-82243375
(*Killyclogher*, Derry)

Bollard, Daniel, Very Rev, PP
Chaplain,
St Columba's Hospital,
Thomastown, Co Kilkenny
Tel 056-7724279/
087-6644858
(Ossory)

Bonner, Patrick
140 Willowood Drive,
Wantagh, New York, USA
(Raphoe)

Boran, Anthony (OFMCap)
Capuchin Friary,
Station Road, Raheny,
Dublin 5
Tel 01-8313886

Bourke, Eamonn, PC
25 The Haven, Dublin 9
Tel 083-3318910
(*Glasnevin*, Dublin)

Bourke, George, Very Rev, PP
Moycarkey, Thurles,
Co Tipperary
Tel 0504-44227
(*Moycarkey*, Cashel & E.)

Bourke, Gerard (SJ)
35 Lower Leeson Street,
Dublin 2
Tel 01-6761248

Bowe, John (SMA)
SMA House,
82 Ranelagh Road,
Ranelagh, Dublin 6
Tel 01-4968162/3

Bowen, Patrick, Very Rev, PP
Athea, Co Limerick
Tel 068-42116/087-6532842
(*Athea*, Limerick)

Boyce, Declan, (SPS)
On temporary diocesan
work

Boyce, Eugene, CC
14 Springfield Drive,
Dooradoyle
Tel 061-304508/086-2542517
(*St Paul's*, Limerick)

Boyce, John
Drumkeen, Ballybofey,
Co Donegal
Tel 074-9134005
(*Raphoe*, Raphoe)

Boyce, Philip (OCD), Most Rev,
DD
Bishop of Raphoe,
Ard Adhamhnáin,
Letterkenny, Co Donegal
Tel 074-9121208
(Raphoe)

Boyers, John
16 'Wilfield',
Sandymount Avenue,
Ballsbridge, Dublin 4
Tel 01-2888149
(*Donnybrook*, Dublin)

Boylan, Noel, CC
Kill, Cootehill, Co Cavan
Tel 049-5553218
(Kilmore)

Boyle, Bernard Dom (OCSO),
Superior, Mellifont Abbey,
Collon, Co Louth
Tel 041-9826103

Boyle, Brian
Charleville, Co Cork
Tel 063-81437
(*Charleville*, Cloyne)

Boyle, Con, Very Rev, PP
Parochial House,
1 Craigstown Road,
Randalstown,
Co Antrim BT41 2AF
Tel 028-94472640
(*Randalstown*, Down & C.)

Boyle, Francis, Very Rev Canon, PP
4 Shinn School Road, Newry, Co Down BT34 1PA
Tel 028-40630276
(*Saval*, Dromore)

Boyle, Gerry, Very Rev, PP
Parochial House, Multyfarnham, Co Westmeath
Tel 044-9371124
(*Multyfarnham*, Meath)

Boyle, James A. (MHM), Adm
St Mary's Parish, 25 Marquis Street, Belfast BT1 1JJ
Tel 028-90320482
(*St Mary's*, Down & C.)

Boyle, Lawrence, Very Rev, PP
'Glenshee', Dublin Road, Newry, Co Down BT35 8DA
Tel 028-30262376
(*Middle Killeavy*, Armagh)

Boyle, Liam, Rt Rev
Knockaderry, Co Limerick
(Limerick, retired)

Boyle, Liam, Very Rev
9 Gargory Road, Ballyward, Castlewellan, Co Down BT31 9RN
Tel 028-40650234
(*Dromore*, retired)

Boyle, Martin (OP)
St Saviour's, Upper Dorset Street, Dublin 1
Tel 01-8897610

Boyle, Michael (OSA)
St Augustine's Priory, Washington Street, Cork
Tel 021-2753982

Boyle, Michael (SMA)
Retired in Ireland outside SMA houses

Boyle, Patrick, PC
29 Glenayle Road, Edenmore, Dublin 5
Tel 01-6765517
(*Edenmore*, Dublin)

Boyle, Ronnie, CC
Achill Sound, Achill, Co Mayo
Tel 098-45109
(*Achill*, Tuam)

Bracken, John, CC
83 The Rise, Mount Merrion, Dublin 4
Tel 01-2895780
(*Mount Merrion*, Dublin)

Bracken, P. J., Very Rev, PP
Fahy, Eyrecourt, Ballinasloe, Co Galway
Tel 090-9675116
(Clonfert)

Bracken, Patrick L. (MHM)
St Joseph's House, 50 Orwell Park, Rathgar, Dublin 6
Tel 01-4127700

Bradley, Bruce (SJ)
Rector, Belvedere College, Great Denmark Street, Dublin 1
Tel 01-858 6600

Bradley, David, Very Rev, PP
The Presbytery, Ballsgrove, Drogheda, Co Louth
Tel 041-9831991
(*Drogheda, Holy Family*, Meath)

Bradley, Francis
Director, Diocesan Pastoral Centre, 164 Bishop Street, Derry BT48 6UJ
Tel 028-71362475
The Presbytery, 11 Steelstown Road, Derry BT48 8EU
Tel 028-71351718
(*Our Lady of Lourdes*, Steelstown, Derry)

Bradley, John, Very Rev, PE
8 Killymeal Road, Dungannon, Co Tyrone BT71 6BE
Tel 028-87722183
(*Armagh*, retired)

Bradley, Manus
St Ignatius of Loyola, 4455 West Broadway, Montreal, Quebec H4B 2A7
(Derry)

Bradley, Philip, Adm
67 Ramleh Park, Milltown, Dublin 6
Tel 01-6280205
(*Milltown*, Dublin)

Bradley, Thomas (White Fathers)
Cypress Grove, Templeogue, Dublin 6W
Tel 01-4055263/4055264

Bradshaw, Brendan (SM)
Superior, Mount St Mary's, Milltown, Dublin 14
Tel 01-2697322

Brady, Bernard, Very Rev Canon
61 Glasnevin Hill, Dublin 9
Tel 01-8379506
(*Dublin*, retired)

Brady, Brian, PP
78 Ballerin Road, Garvagh, Co Derry BT51 5EQ
Tel 028-29558251
(*Garvagh*, Derry)

Brady, Declan
St Mary's College, Galway
(Elphin)

Brady, Enda, CC
Ballina, Co Tipperary
Tel 061-376430
(*Ballina*, Cashel & E.)

Brady, Frank, (SJ), PC
The Presbytery, Shangan Road, Ballymun, Dublin 9
Tel 01 8421551
(*Ballymun*, Dublin)

Brady, Gerard, Very Rev, PP
Newtowncashel, Co Longford
Tel 043-3325112
(*Newtowncashel*, Ardagh & Cl.)

Brady, Harry, Very Rev, PP
Church Drive, Clarecastle, Co Clare
Tel 065-682301/086-2349798
(*Clarecastle*, Killaloe)

Brady, John (SJ)
Milltown Park, Sandford Road, Dublin 6
Tel 01-2698411/2698113

Brady, Kenneth (CP), CC
St Paul's Retreat, Mount Argus, Dublin 6W
Tel 01-4992000
(*Mount Argus*, Dublin)

Brady, Lawrence
Franciscan College, Gormanston, Co Meath
Tel 01-8412203

Brady, Macarten, Venerable Archdeacon, PE
Sacred Heart Residence, Sybil Hill Road, Killester, Dublin 5
(Dublin, retired)

Brady, Oliver (OFMCap)
Capuchin Friary, Station Road, Raheny, Dublin 5
Tel 01-8313886

Brady, P. J. (OFM)
Franciscan College, Gormanston, Co Meath
Tel 01-8412203

Brady, Patrick V., Very Rev, VF
Drumkilly, Kilnaleck, Co Cavan
Tel 049-4336120
(Kilmore)

Brady, Peter, Very Rev, PP
Lenamore, Co Longford
Tel 044-9357404
(*Legan and Ballycloghan*, Ardagh & Cl.)

Brady, Philip, Very Rev
Laragh, Stradone, Co Cavan
Tel 049-4330142
(*Laragh*, Kilmore)

Brady, Ray, Very Rev
c/o Bishop's House, Mullingar
(Meath, retired)

Brady, Raymond, Very Rev, PP
8 Earlsvale Road, Cavan
Tel 049-4380369
(Kilmore)

Brady, Rory
1 Cathedral Place, Letterkenny
Tel 074-9125182
Chaplain, Letterkenny Institute of Technology, Letterkenny, Co Donegal
Tel 074-9124888
(Raphoe)

Brady, Seán, His Eminence Cardinal, DCL, DD
Archbishop of Armagh, Ara Coeli, Cathedral Road, Armagh BT61 7QY
Tel 028-37522045
(Armagh)

Brady, Thomas, CF
Chaplain, Dún Uí Mhaoilíosa, Renmore, Galway
Tel 091-701055
(Galway)

Branagan, Anthony (CSsR)
Mission in Siberia, Redemptorysci, Box 878, 650099 Kemerovo, Siberia, Russia

Brankin, Aidan, Very Rev, PP
7 Culcrum Road, Cloughmills BT44 9NH
Tel 028-27638267
(*Dunloy and Cloughmills*, Down & C.)

Brannigan, David, Co-PP
89 Sperrin Road, Drimnagh, Dublin 12
Tel 01-8412116
(*Mourne Road*, Dublin)

Brassil, Paul (SJ) (ZAM)
St Ignatius Community & Church, 27 Raleigh Row, Salthill, Galway
Tel 091-523707

Brazil, Sean (SSC)
St Columban's, Dalgan Park, Navan, Co Meath
Tel 046-9021525

Breathnach, Cormac, Very Rev (SMA), PP
St Joseph's, Wilton, Cork
Tel 021-4341362
(*Wilton, St Joseph's*, Cork & R.)

Bredin, Eamonn
(priest in residence)
Arva, Co Cavan
Tel 049-4335246
(*Killeshandra*, Kilmore)

Bree, Eugene (SPS)
St Patrick's, Kiltegan, Co Wicklow
Tel 059-6473600

Breen, Albert (OCarm)
Gort Muire, Ballinteer, Dublin 16
Tel 01-2984014

Breen, Gerard, Very Rev, PP
Broadford, Co Kildare
Tel 046-9551203
(*Balyna*, Kildare & L.)
Breen, P. J. (OCarm)
Terenure College, Terenure, Dublin 6W
Tel 01-4904621
Breen, Patrick (CSsR)
Mount Saint Alphonsus, Limerick
Tel 061-315099
Breen, Patrick (MSC)
Carrignavar, Co Cork
Tel 021-4884044
Breen, Patrick, Very Rev, PE
Timahoe, Portlaoise, Co Laois
Tel 057-8627023
(Kildare & L., retired)
Breen, Sean, Very Rev, PP
The Presbytery, Ballymore Eustace, Naas, Co Kildare
Tel 045-864114
(*Ballymore Eustace*, Dublin)
Breen, Simeon (OFMCap)
Capuchin Friary, Station Road, Raheny, Dublin 5
Tel 01-8313886
Breen, Thomas F., Very Rev Canon, PP, VF
Fethard, Co Tipperary
Tel 052-31178
(*Fethard*, Cashel & E.)
Breen, Thomas J., Very Rev, PP
Holy Cross Abbey, Thurles, Co Tipperary
Tel 0504-43124
(*Holy Cross*, Cashel & E.)
Breen, Thomas O., Very Rev, PP
Ballylanders, Kilmallock, Co Limerick
Tel 062-46705
(*Ballylanders*, Cashel & E.)
Breen, Thomas, Very Rev Canon, PE
37 Esker Road, Dromore, Omagh, Co Tyrone BT78 3LE
Tel 028-82898216
(*Dromore*, Clogher)
Breheny, Pádraig (OFM), Very Rev
Guardian, Franciscan Friary, Killarney, Co Kerry
Tel 064-6631334/6631066
Brennan, Brian, Very Rev, PP
Ballinalee, Co Longford
Tel 043-3323110
(Ardagh & Cl.)
Brennan, David, Very Rev, Adm
Parochial House, Moynalvey, Summerhill, Co Meath
Tel 046-9557031
(*Moynalvey*, Meath)

Brennan, Declan (OSA), CC
St Catherine's, Meath Street, Dublin 8
Tel 01-4543356
(*Meath Street*, Dublin)
Brennan, Denis, Most Rev, DD
Bishop of Ferns, Bishop's House, Summerhill, Wexford
Tel 053-9122177
(Ferns)
Brennan, Dermot (OP), Very Rev
St Magdalen's, Drogheda, Co Louth
Tel 041-9838271
Brennan, Dermot J. (OP), Adm
St Mary's Priory, Tallaght, Dublin 24
Tel 01-4048100
(*Tallaght, St Mary's*, Dublin)
Brennan, Fergal (SJ)
Milltown Park, Sandford Road, Dublin 6
Tel 01-2698411/2698113
Brennan, Joseph (SJ)
Gonzaga College, Sandford Road, Dublin 6
Tel 01-4972943
Brennan, Kilian, CC
Presbytery No. 1, Thormanby Road, Howth, Co Dublin
Tel 01-8451902
(*Howth*, Dublin)
Brennan, Loughlin, CC
Upperchurch, Thurles, Co Tipperary
Tel 0504-54492
(Cashel & E.)
Brennan, Louis (OFM)
Collegio S. Isidoro, Via degli Artisti 41, 00187 Roma, Italy
Tel +39-06-4885359
Brennan, Michael, Very Rev, PP
(priest in charge)
Rosmuc, Co Galway
Tel 091-551169
(*Rosmuc*, Galway)
Brennan, Oliver, Very Rev, PP
Parochial House, Grianán Mhuire, Main Street, Blackrock, Dundalk, Co Louth
Tel 042-9321621
(*Haggardstown and Blackrock*, Armagh)
Brennan, Patrick, Very Rev Canon
Gathabawn, Via Thurles, Co Kilkenny
Tel 056-8832110
(Ossory, retired)

Brennan, Peter, CC
Ballinree, Boherlahan, Cashel, Co Tipperary
Tel 0504-41215
(*Boherlahan and Dualla*, Cashel & E.)
Brennan, Philip (OCarm)
Carmelite Priory, Knocktopher, Co Kilkenny
Tel 056-7768675
(*Knocktopher/Ballyhale*, Ossory)
Brennan, Thomas
USA
(Ferns)
Brennock, Michael (OSA)
St Augustine's, Taylor's Lane, Ballyboden, Dublin 16
Tel 01-4944966
(*Ballyboden*, Dublin)
Brereton, Joseph (SJ)
Clongowes Wood College, Naas, Co Kildare
Tel 045-868663/868202
Breslan, Fergus, CC
Hospital Road, Newry, Co Down, BT35 8DL
(*Middle Killeavy*, Armagh)
Breslan, Oliver, Very Rev, PP
Parochial House, Hanover Square, Coagh, Cookstown, Co Tyrone BT80 0EF
Tel 028-86737212
(*Coagh*, Armagh)
Breslan, Patrick, Very Rev, PE, AP
Parochial House, 55 Dermanaught Road, Galbally, Dungannon, Co Tyrone BT70 2NR
Tel 028-87758277
(*Donaghmore*, Armagh)
Breslin, Eamonn (CSsR)
European Parish, Communauté Des Rédemptoristes, 32 Rue Des Capucins, L-1313 Luxembourg
Tel 00352-224880
Breslin, Michael, Very Rev, PP
Ballygar, Co Galway
Tel 090-6624637
(Elphin)
Bresnahan, Damian (SMA)
Provincial Councillor, African Missions, Provincial House, Feltrim, Blackrock Road, Cork
Tel 021-4292871
Bresnan, John (OSA)
St Augustine's, Taylor's Lane, Balyboden, Dublin 16
Tel 01-4241000

Brewster, Patrick (SDB)
Salesian House, Warrenstown, Drumree, Co Meath
Tel 01-8259894
Brick, Maurice, Very Rev, PP
Irremore, Listowel, Co Kerry
Tel 066-7132111
(*Lixnaw*, Kerry)
Brickley, John, CC
Chapel Lane, Sallins Road, Naas, Co Kildare
Tel 045-897260
(Kildare & L.)
Brilley, Joseph, Very Rev, PP
Drumraney, Athlone, Co Westmeath
Tel 044-9356207
(*Drumraney*, Meath)
Brindley, Stanislaus (CM)
St Vincent's College, Castleknock, Dublin 15
Tel 01-8213051
Briody, Joseph, CC
Cleeslough, Co Donegal
Tel 074-9138011
(*Dunfanaghy*, Raphoe)
Briscoe, Peter, Rt Rev Mgr, Adm, PP
12 The Warren, Malahide, Co Dublin
Tel 01-6684265
(*Yellow Walls, Malahide*, Dublin)
Broaders, Brian, Very Rev, Adm
The Presbytery, Templeshannon, Enniscorthy, Co Wexford
Tel 053-9237611
(*St Senan's, Enniscorthy*, Ferns)
Broderick, Daniel, Very Rev, PP
St Mary's, Tarbert, Co Kerry
Tel 068-36111
(*Tarbert*, Kerry)
Broderick, Donal, Very Rev, PE
Ballyhooly, Co Cork
Tel 025-39148
(Cloyne, retired)
Broderick, John, Very Rev, PP
Killeagh, Co Cork
Tel 024-95133
(*Killeagh*, Cloyne)
Brodie, Thomas (OP)
St Saviour's, Glentworth Street, Limerick
Tel 061-412333
Brogan, John, Very Rev, PP
Parochial House, Kilskyre, Kells, Co Meath
Tel 046-9243623
(*Kilskyre*, Meath)
Brophy, Colm (SJ)
Gonzaga College, Sandford Road, Dublin 6
Tel 01-4972943

Brophy, Joseph, CC
Mountrath, Co Laois
Tel 057-8732234
(*Mountrath*, Kildare & L.)

Brophy, Robert, Very Rev, PP
The Presbytery,
Togher, Cork
Tel 021-4316700
(*Togher*, Cork & R.)

Brouder, Jeremiah
49 Halcyon Place,
Park Village,
Castletroy, Limerick
(Limerick, retired)

Brough, David, Very Rev, PP, VF
85 Tymon Crescent,
Oldbawn, Dublin 24
Tel 01-7168543/2605582
(*Bohernabreena,* Dublin)

Brown, Brian, Very Rev, PP
26 Bottier Road,
Moira, Craigavon,
Co Armagh BT67 0PE
Tel 028-92611347
(*Magheralin*, Dromore)

Brown, Francis, Very Rev Canon, Adm
Cathedral Presbytery,
38 Hill Street,
Newry BT34 1AT
Tel 028-30262586
(*Newry*, Dromore)

Brown, John (CSSp)
Holy Spirit Missionary College, Kimmage Manor,
Whitehall Road
Dublin 12
Tel 01-4064300

Brown, John (SMA), Very Rev, PP
Church of Our Lady of the Rosary and St Patrick,
61 Blackhorse Road,
Walthamstow,
London E17 7AS, England
Tel 20-85203647

Brown, Michael (OCD)
St Teresa's,
Clarendon Street, Dublin 2
Tel 01-6718466/6718127

Browne, Brian (OFMCap)
Capuchin Friary,
Ard Mhuire, Creeslough,
Letterkenny, Co Donegal
Tel 074-9138005

Browne, Colm, CC
12 Supple Park,
Dunshaughlin, Co Meath
Tel 01-8024592
(*Dunshaughlin*, Meath)

Browne, Denis
c/o Bishop's House, Wexford
(Ferns)

Browne, Denis, Very Rev Canon
Kilmallock, Co Limerick
(Limerick, retired)

Browne, Dominic (OP)
Black Abbey, Kilkenny,
Co Kilkenny
Tel 056-7721279

Browne, James (IC)
Clonturk House,
Ormond Road, Drumcondra,
Dublin 9
Tel 01-6877014

Browne, James (WF), CC
Gneeveguilla, Rathmore,
Co Kerry
Tel 064-7756188
(*Rathmore*, Kerry)

Browne, James (White Fathers)
c/o Cypress Grove,
Templeogue, Dublin 6
Tel 01-6771128

Browne, Joseph
The Presbytery,
St Mellitus Church,
Tollington Park,
London N4 3AG
Tel 0171-2723415
(Cashel & E.)

Browne, Kevin (CSsR)
Mount Saint Alphonsus,
Limerick
Tel 061-315099

Browne, Kevin A. (CSSp)
Blackrock College,
Blackrock, Co Dublin
Tel 01-2888681

Browne, Liam (SJ)
Milltown Park,
Sandford Road, Dublin 6
Tel 01-2698411/2698113

Browne, Michael (CSsR)
Clonard Monastery,
1 Clonard Gardens,
Belfast, BT13 2RL
Tel 028-90445950

Browne, Michael (SDB)
Salesian College,
Maynooth Road, Celbridge,
Co Kildare
Tel 01-6275058/60

Browne, Michael (SPS)
Tearmann Spirituality Centre,
Brockagh, Glendalough,
Co Wicklow
Tel 0404-45208

Browne, Patrick, Very Rev, PP
Oulart, Gorey,
Co Wexford
Tel 053-9136139
(*Oulart*, Ferns)

Browne, Raymond A., Very Rev, PP
Ballagh, Kilrooskey,
Roscommon
Tel 090-6626273
(*Ballagh*, Elphin)

Browne, Raymond, Very Rev, PP
Fourmilehouse,
Roscommon
Tel 090-6629518
(*Fourmilehouse*, Elphin)

Browne, Richard, Very Rev, PP
Cappamore, Co Limerick
Tel 061-381288
(*Cappamore*, Cashel & E.)

Browne, Richard, Very Rev, PP
Kilnamartyra, Macroom,
Co Cork
Tel 026-40013
(*Kilnamartyra*, Cloyne)

Browne, Thomas, Very Rev Canon, PP
Youghal, Co Cork
Tel 024-93199
(*Youghal*, Cloyne)

Browne, Vincent (CSSp)
Blackrock College,
Blackrock, Co Dublin
Tel 01-2888681

Bryson, Bernard, PE
Anniscliff House,
141 Moneysharvin Road,
Maghera, Co Derry
(Derry, retired)

Bucciarelli, Robert, Rt Rev, DD
Vicar for Ireland,
Harvieston,
Cunningham Road, Dalkey,
Co Dublin
Tel 01-2859877
(Opus Dei)

Buckley, Benignus (OFMCap)
Guardian Capuchin Friary,
Kilkenny
Tel 056-7721439

Buckley, Con, CC
Knocknagree, Mallow,
Co Cork
Tel 064-7756029
(*Rathmore*, Kerry)

Buckley, David, Very Rev, PE, CC
Dromina, Charleville,
Co Cork
Tel 063-70207
(*Shandrum*, Cloyne)

Buckley, James (CSsR)
St Patrick's, Esker, Athenry,
Co Galway
Tel 091-844549

Buckley, John, Most Rev, DD
Bishop of Cork and Ross,
Cork and Ross Offices,
Redemption Road, Cork
Tel 021-4301717
(Cork & R.)

Buckley, John, Very Rev, PP
Annascaul, Co Kerry
Tel 066-9157103
(*Annascaul*, Kerry)

Buckley, Michael, A.
The Presbytery,
Skibbereen, Co Cork
(*St Patrick's Cathedral, Skibbereen*, Cork & R.)

Buckley, Michael J. (CSSp)
St Mary's College,
Rathmines, Dublin 6
Tel 01-4995760

Buckley, Patrick, Very Rev, PP
Dromahane, Mallow,
Co Cork
Tel 022-21244
(Cloyne)

Budau, Ciprian (OFMConv), CC
Friary of the Visitation,
Fairview Strand, Dublin 3
Tel 01-8376000
(*Fairview*, Dublin)

Bulman, Joseph (OP), Very Rev
Prior, Holy Cross,
Tralee, Co Kerry
Tel 066-7121135/29185

Burger, John (SSC)
General Council,
504 Tower 1 Silvercord,
30 Canton Road TST,
Kowloon, Hong Kong, SAR

Burger, John (SSC)
Knock, Mayo
(Retired)

Burgess, Michael (OFMCap)
St Francis Capuchin Friary,
Rochestown, Co Cork
Tel 021-4896244

Burke, Alan
Pontifical Irish College
Via Dei SS. Quattro 1,
00184 Rome, Italy
Tel 003906-7726331

Burke, Christopher (CSSp)
Holy Spirit Missionary College,
Kimmage Manor,
Dublin 12
Tel 01-4064300

Burke, Colm, Very Rev, AP
Barnacarroll, Claremorris,
Co Mayo
Tel 094-9388189
(Tuam, retired)

Burke, Dermot, PE
Ballyshannon, Raphoe
(Ballyshannon, Raphoe)

Burke, Edward (OFM)
Franciscan College,
Gormanston, Co Meath
Tel 01-8412203

Burke, Enda, Very Rev, AP
Cloughjordan, Co Tipperary
Tel 0505-42120
(*Cloughjordan*, Killaloe)

Burke, Fintan (OCarm)
Carmelite Priory,
Knocktopher,
Co Kilkenny
Tel 056-7768675

Burke, Gabriel, CC
Carrigtwohill, Co Cork
Tel 021-4883867
(*Carrigtwohill*, Cloyne)

Burke, Kieran, CC
Leenane, Co Galway
Tel 095-42251
(*Ballyhaunis (Annagh)*, Tuam)

Burke, Liam (SMA)
African Missions,
Blackrock Road, Cork
Tel 021-4292871

Burke, Patrick
Hospital Chaplain, Castlebar, Co Mayo
(*Castlebar*, Tuam)

Burke, Peter, Very Rev, PP
Drumshanbo, Co Leitrim
Tel 071-9641010
(*Drumshanbo*, Ardagh & Cl.)

Burke, Sean,
Mohill, Co Leitrim
Tel 071-9631097
(Ardagh & Cl.)

Burns, Daniel, PE
Parochial House, Belgooly,
Co Cork
(Cork & R., retired)

Burns, Dermot, Very Rev
Straide, Foxford,
Co Mayo
(Achonry, retired)

Burns, Edward, CC
Swellan Lower, Cavan
(Kilmore, retired)

Burns, Gerard, Very Rev, PP
The Parochial House,
Letterfrack, Connemara,
Co Galway
Tel 095-41053/087-2408171
(*Letterfrack (Ballinakill)*, Tuam)

Burns, John, CC
Parochial House,
Ballycraigy Road, Craigyhill,
Larne, Co Antrim BT40 2LE
Tel 028-28260130
(*Larne*, Down & C.)

Burns, Karl, Very Rev, CC
Westport, Co Mayo
Tel 098-28871
(*Parke (Turlough)*, Tuam)

Burns, Pat, PP
Parochial House,
Pallasgreen, Co Limerick
Tel 061-384114
(Cashel & E.)

Burns, Peter (CSsR)
St Joseph's, Dundalk,
Co Louth
Tel 042-9334042/9334762
2nd Provincial Consultor,
Liguori House,
75 Orwell Road, Dublin 6
Tel 01-4067100

Burns, Thomas
St John's Presbytery,
New Street, Waterford
Tel 051-874271
(*St John's*, Waterford & L.)

Butler, Anthony J. (SMA)
African Missions,
Blackrock Road, Cork
Tel 021-4292871

Butler, Eamonn, Very Rev, PE
10 Lynn Heights, Mullingar,
Co Westmeath
Tel 044-9344008
(Meath, retired)

Butler, James, Adm
The Riverchapel,
Courtown Harbour, Gorey
Co Wexford
Tel 053-9425241
(*The Riverchapel, Courtown Harbour*, Ferns)

Butler, John (SDB)
Salesian College,
Maynooth Road, Celbridge,
Co Kildare
Tel 01-6275058/60

Butler, Kieran (SM), PC
St Brendan's Presbytery,
Coolock Village, Dublin 5
Tel 01-8484799
(*Coolock, St Brendan's*, Dublin)

Butler, Patrick, Very Rev, PP
Parochial House,
Clogheen, Cahir,
Co Tipperary
Tel 052-7465268
(*Clogheen*, Waterford & L.)

Butler, Reuben, Very Rev Canon, AP
Newmarket-on-Fergus,
Co Clare
Tel 061-368433
(*Newmarket-on-Fergus*, Killaloe)

Butler, Robert, Very Rev, PP
Parochial House,
44 Lough Road,
Loughguile, Ballymena,
Co Antrim BT44 9JN
Tel 028-27641206
(*Loughguile*, Down & C.)

Butler, Thomas (SM)
Chanel Community,
Coolock, Dublin 5
Tel 01-8477133

Byrne, Alfie (SPS)
St Patrick's, Kiltegan,
Co Wicklow
Tel 059-6473600

Byrne, Archie (OP)
St Dominic's Retreat House,
Montenotte, Co Cork
Tel 021-4502520

Byrne, Arthur, Very Rev
Castor's Bay Road, Lurgan
(Dromore, retired)

Byrne, Brendan, Rt Rev Mgr, PP
Tullow, Co Carlow
Tel 059-9152159
(Kildare & L.)

Byrne, Charles, Very Rev
Holy Family Convent,
Newbridge, Co Kildare
(Kildare & L., retired)

Byrne, Charles, Very Rev, Adm
Administrator,
15 Chapel Hill,
Mayobridge, Newry,
Co Down BT34 2EX
Tel 028-30851225
Parish
84 Milltown Street,
Burren, Warrenpoint,
Co Down BT34 3PU
Tel 028-41772200
(*Clonallon, St Mary's (Burren)*, Dromore)

Byrne, Charles, Very Rev, PP
Carrigart, Co Donegal
Tel 074-9155154
(*Carrigart*, Raphoe)

Byrne, Conleth,
c/o 73 Somerton Road,
Belfast BT15 4DE
(Down & C., retired)

Byrne, Desmond (CSSp), CC
45 Woodford Drive,
Monastery Road,
Clondalkin, Dublin 22
Tel 01-4592323
(*Clondalkin*, Dublin)

Byrne, Diarmuid, Adm
18 St Anthony's Road,
Rialto, Dublin 8
Tel 01-4534469
(*Dolphin's Barn, Rialto*, Dublin)

Byrne, Donal (OCarm),
Whitefriar Street Church,
56 Aungier Street, Dublin 2
Tel 01-4758821

Byrne, Eamonn (SSC)
St Columban's Retirement Home, Dalgan Park,
Navan, Co Meath
Tel 046-9021525

Byrne, Felix, Very Rev Canon, CC
Monaseed, Gorey,
Co Wexford
Tel 053-9428207
(*Craanford*, Ferns)

Byrne, Gareth, PC
107 Mount Prospect Avenue,
Clontarf, Dublin 3
Tel 01-8339301
(*Dollymount*, Dublin)

Byrne, Gerald, Very Rev, PP
Parochial House,
Graignamanagh,
Co Kilkenny
Tel 059-9724238
(*Graignamanagh*, Kildare & L.)

Byrne, Gerard
Chaplain, Blackrock Clinic,
Dublin
Tel 01-2832222
(Dublin)

Byrne, James, Very Rev
Ballylannon,
Wellingtonbridge,
Co Wexford
(Ferns, retired)

Byrne, John (CSSp)
Community Leader,
Templeogue College,
Dublin 6W
Tel 01-4903909

Byrne, John (OSA)
Augustinian Retreat Centre,
Old Court Road,
Dublin 16
Tel 01-4930932

Byrne, John, CC
Cathedral Presbytery,
38 Hill Street,
Newry BT34 1AT
Tel 028-30262586
(Dromore)

Byrne, John, CC
The Presbytery,
Templeshannon,
Enniscorthy,
Co Wexford
Tel 053-9237611
(*St Senan's, Enniscorthy*, Ferns)

Byrne, John, Rt Rev Mgr, PP
Parochial House,
Dublin Road, Portlaoise,
Co Laois
Tel 057-8692153
(Kildare & L.)

Byrne, John, Very Rev, PP, VF
Parochial House, Kells,
Co Meath
Tel 046-9240213
(Meath)

Byrne, Martin, Very Rev, PP
Ballymore, Killinick,
Co Wexford
Tel 053-9158966
(*Ballymore and Mayglass*, Ferns)

Byrne, Mel (CP)
Passionist Retreat Centre,
Tobar Mhuire, Crossgar,
Co Down BT30 9EA
Tel 028-44830242

Byrne, Michael, CC
Boolavogue, Ferns,
Wexford
Tel 053-9366282
(*Monageer*, Ferns)

Byrne, Michael, Very Rev, PP
Cushinstown, Foulksmills,
Co Wexford
Tel 051-428347
(*Cushinstown*, Ferns)

Byrne, P. G. (SM)
St Brendan's Parish,
Coolock Village,
Dublin 5
Tel 01-8484799
(*Coolock, St Brendan's*, Dublin)

Byrne, P. J. (SM)
Mount St Mary's,
Milltown, Dublin 14
Tel 01-2697322
Byrne, P. J., Very Rev, PP
Kilcock, Co Kildare
Tel 01-6287448
(*Kilcock*, Kildare & L.)
Byrne, Patrick G., (SM), PC
The Presbytery, Coolock
Village, Dublin 5
Tel 01-8484799
(*Coolock*, Dublin)
Byrne, Pat (SVD)
133 North Circular Road,
Dublin 7
Tel 01-8386743
Byrne, Patrick, CC
Muinebheag, Co Carlow
Tel 059-9723886
(*Muinebheag/ Bagenalstown*, Kildare & L.)
Byrne, Paul (OMI)
Oblate House of Retreat,
Inchicore, Dublin 8
Tel 01-4534408/4541805
Byrne, Paul, PP
111 Queensway, Lambeg
Lisburn BT27 4QS
Tel 028-92662896
Byrne, Paul, Very Rev, PP
Parochial House,
31 Brackaville Road,
Coalisland,
Co Tyrone BT71 4NH
Tel 028-87740221
(*Coalisland*, Armagh)
Byrne, Peter (CSsR)
Mount Saint Alphonsus,
Limerick
Tel 061-315099
Byrne, Peter (LC)
(Team Assistant)
c/o Legionaries of Christ,
Leopardstown Road,
Foxrock, Dublin 18
Tel 01-2956414
(*Sandyford*, Dublin)
Byrne, Richard (OCarm)
Terenure College, Terenure,
Dublin 6W
Tel 01-4904621
Byrne, Thomas (CSsR)
St Patrick's, Esker,
Co Galway
Tel 091-844549
Byrne, Tony (CSSp)
Awareness Education Office,
3 Cabra Grove, Dublin 7
Tel 01-8388888
Byrne, William, CC
Coolfancy, Tinahely,
Co Wicklow
Tel 0402-34725
(*Carnew*, Ferns)
Byrne, William, CC
Newbridge, Co Kildare
Tel 045-433979
(Kildare & L.)
Byrne, Willie, CC
St Conleth's,
Chapel Lane,
Droichead Nua, Co Kildare
Tel 045-433979
(*Droichead Nua/Newbridge*, Kildare & L.)
Byrnes, James (CSSp)
Holy Spirit Missionary
College,
Kimmage Manor,
Dublin 12
Tel 01-4064300
Byrnes, Michael
Galway Marriage Tribunal
(Clonfert)
Byrnes, Michael
Marriage Tribunal,
7 Waterside, Woodquay,
Galway
(Galway)

## C

Cadam, Simon, Very Rev, PP, VF
St Mary's, Granard,
Co Longford
Tel 043-6686550
(Ardagh & Cl.)
Caffrey, Francis (CSSp)
Holy Spirit Missionary
College,
Kimmage Manor, Whitehall
Road, Dublin 12
Tel 01-4064300
Caffrey, James F., Very Rev, PP
'Marmion', 87 Iona Road,
Dublin 9
Tel 01-8305651/8725055
(*Iona Road*, Dublin)
Cahill, David (SDB)
Salesian House,
Warrenstown, Drumree,
Co Meath
Tel 01-8259894
Cahill, Donal, Very Rev, Adm
Lisheen, Skibbereen,
Co Cork
Tel 028-38111
(*Aughadown*, Cork & R.)
Cahill, Eamonn, Adm
Parish of the Annunciation,
7 Cardifcastle Road,
Finglas West, Dublin 7
Tel 01-2956317
(*Finglas West*, Dublin)
Cahill, John (CSSp)
Holy Spirit Missionary
College,
Kimmage Manor,
Dublin 12
Tel 01-4064300
Cahill, Joseph (SSC)
Bother na Sop, Ballina,
Co Mayo
Tel 096-22984
Cahill, Kevin (DCL) CC
Ballymitty, Co Wexford
Tel 051-561128/053-9165108
(Ferns)
Cahill, Lee (SMA)
Dromantine College,
Dromantine, Newry,
Co Down BT34 1RH
Tel 028-30821224
Cahill, Michael (SMA)
African Missions,
Blackrock Road, Cork
Tel 021-4292871
Cahill, Michael, Very Rev, PP
Parochial House, Kilbeg,
Kells, Co Meath
Tel 046-9246604
(*Kilbeggan*, Meath)
Cahill, Seán, Rt Rev Mgr, VG
6 Boyhill Road,
Maguriesbridge, Enniskillen
Co Fermanagh BT94 4LN
Tel 028-67721258
(Clogher)
Cahill, Sean, Very Rev
c/o 73 Someron Road,
Belfast BT15 4DE
(Down and C., retired)
Cahill, Thomas (SVD)
Donamon Castle,
Roscommon
Tel 090-6662222
Cahir, Anthony, Very Rev, PP
5 Woodlands Park,
Birr Co Offaly
Tel 057-9120097/
086-2612121
Chaplain, District Hospital,
Birr, Co Offaly
Tel 0509-20819
Chaplain, Welfare Home,
Birr, Co Offaly
Tel 0509-20248
Callaghan, Daniel (OCarm)
Whitefriar Street Church,
56 Aungier Street, Dublin 2
Tel 01-4758821
Callan, Paul, Very Rev Mgr
Archbishop's Secretary,
Archbishop's House,
Drumcondra, Dublin 9
Tel 01-8373732
(Dublin)
Callanan, John (SJ)
Gonzaga College,
Sandford Road, Dublin 6
Tel 01-4972943
Callanan, John, Very Rev, PE
Cairn Hill Nursing Home,
Westminster Road,
Foxrock, Dublin
(Waterford & L., retired)
Callanan, Patrick, Very Rev
Canon, PP
Kilbeacanty, Gort,
Co Galway
Tel 091-631691
(Galway)
Callanan, Richard (OFM)
Franciscan Friary, Clonmel,
Co Tipperary
Tel 052-6121378
Callanan, Stanislaus (OCD)
Avila, Bloomfield Avenue,
Morehampton Road,
Dublin 4
Tel 01-6430200
Callanan, William (SJ)
Milltown Park,
Sandford Road, Dublin 6
Tel 01-2698411/2698113
Callanan, William, Very Rev, AP
Kill, Co Waterford
Tel 051-292212
(*Newtown*, Waterford & L.)
Campbell, Colm
Holy Trinity Rectory
213 West 82nd Street
New York,
NY10024, USA
(Down & C., retired)
Campbell, Garrett, CC
St Patrick's Presbytery,
Roden Place, Dundalk,
Co Louth
Tel 042-9334648
(*Dundalk, St Patrick's*, Armagh)
Campbell, Gerard, Very Rev, PP, VF
Parochial House, Kilkerley,
Dundalk, Co Louth
Tel 042-9333482
(*Kilkerley*, Armagh)
Campbell, James (SSS)
Superior,
Blessed Sacrament Chapel,
20 Bachelors Walk, Dublin 1
Tel 01-8724597
Campbell, Joseph, CC
St Mary's, Drogheda,
Co Louth
Tel 041-9834958
(*Drogheda, St Mary's*, Meath)
Campbell, Michael, CC
Kilbrin, Kanturk, Co Cork
Tel 022-48169
(*Ballyclough*, Cloyne)
Campbell, Michael, Very Rev, PP
Carra, Granard,
Co Longford
Tel 043-6686270
(*Abbeylara*, Ardagh & Cl.)
Campbell, Noel
Ballysmutton, Manor
Kilbride, Blessington,
Co Wicklow
(Dublin, retired)
Campion, Cornelius K. (SSC)
St Columban's, Dalgan Park,
Navan, Co Meath
Tel 046-9021525
Campion, Desmond (SDB)
Chaplain Naval Service,
Haulbowline, Cobh, Cork

Campion, John (SDB), Very Rev
Salesian House, Milford, Castletroy, Limerick
Tel 061-330268

Campion, Joseph (SAC)
Castlecomer, Co Kilkenny
Tel 056-4441263/ 086-1775172
(*Castlecomer*, Ossory)

Canavan, Colm, Very Rev Canon, AP
Tully, Ballinahown, Co Galway
Tel 091-593142
(Tuam, retired)

Candon, Cyprian (OP)
St Saviour's, Upper Dorset Street, Dublin 1
Tel 01-8897610

Candon, Ignatius (OP)
St Dominic's, Athy, Co Kildare
Tel 059-8631573

Canniffe, Daniel (SSC)
St Columban's Retirement Home, Dalgan Park, Navan, Co Meath
Tel 046-9021525

Canning, Thomas, Adm
Parochial House, St Mary's, Creggan, Derry BT48 9QE
Tel 028-71263152
(*St Mary's, Creggan*, Derry)

Cannon, Aodhan, CC
Parochial House, Ardara, Co Donegal
Tel 074-9541930
(Raphoe)

Cannon, Seán (CSsR)
Alphonsian Academy, Via Merulana 31, CP 2458, 00100 Rome, Italy
Tel 49490-1

Canny, Bryan M., Rt Rev Mgr, PP
St Patrick's Presbytery, Buncrana Road, Derry BT48 7QL
Tel 028-71262360
(Derry)

Canny, Michael, Very Rev, PP
Parochial House, 32 Chapel Road, Derry BT47 2BB
Tel 028-71342303
(*Waterside (Glendermott)*, Derry)

Cantwell, Brendan, Very Rev, PP
Parochial House, Castledermot, Co Kildare
Tel 059-9144164/ 086-2528545
(*Castledermot*, Dublin)

Cantwell, Joe (SPS)
Assistant Regional Leader, St Patrick's, Kiltegan, Co Wicklow
Tel 059-6473600

Cantwell, Kieran, Very Rev, PP
Danesfort, Co Kilkenny
Tel 056-7727137/087-2661228
(*Danesfort*, Ossory)

Caples, Andrew (OSA)
St Augustine's, Taylor's Lane, Balyboden, Dublin 16
Tel 01-4241000

Caraher, Laurence, Very Rev, PE, AP
The Ravel, School Lane, Tullyallen, Drogheda, Co Louth
Tel 041-9834293
(*Mellifont*, Armagh)

Carberry, Fernardo (CP)
St Paul's Retreat, Mount Argus, Dublin 6W
Tel 01-4992000

Carberry, Patrick (SJ)
Director of Retreat House/ Vice-Rector, Manresa House, Dollymount, Dublin 3
Tel 01-8331352

Carbery, Aidrian, Very Rev, PP
26 Beech Grove, Kildare
Tel 045-521900
(Kildare & L.)

Carbery, Brendan F., Very Rev Canon
Elmhurst, Hampstead, Avenue, Glasnevin, Dublin 11
(Dublin, retired)

Carey, Brian (CSSp)
Holy Spirit Missionary College, Kimmage Manor, Dublin 12
Tel 01-4064300

Carey, Jerry, Very Rev, Adm
3 The Woods, Cappahard, Tulla Road, Ennis, Co Clare
Tel 065-6822225/ 086-2508444
(*Doora*, Killaloe)

Carey, John, Co-PP
The Presbytery, Oldtown, Co Dublin
Tel 01-8433133
(*Rolestown*, Dublin)

Carey, Michael, Very Rev, Adm
151 Swords Road, Whitehall, Dublin 9
Tel 01-8374887
(*Larkhill-Whitehall-Santry*, Dublin)

Carey, Patrick
Chaplain, St Luke's Hospital, Kilkenny
Tel 056-7785000
(Ossory)

Carey, Terence (OCD)
53/55 Marlborough Road, Dublin 4
Tel 01-6601832

Carey, William, Very Rev, PP
Kilsheelan, Clonmel, Co Tipperary
Tel 052-6133118
(*Kilsheelan*, Waterford & L.)

Cargan, John, Very Rev, PP
The Presbytery, 11 Steelstown Road, Derry BT48 8EU
Tel 028-71351718
(*Our Lady of Lourdes, Steelstown*, Derry)

Carley, Martin, CC
St Mary's, Drogheda, Co Louth
Tel 041-9834958
(*Drogheda, St Mary's*, Meath)

Carlin, Harry, Very Rev
5 Fortwilliam Court, Belfast BT15 4DS
Tel 028-90772376
(Down & C., retired)

Carlin, Neal
St Anthony's, Dundrean, Burnfoot, Co Donegal
Tel 074-9368370
(Derry)

Carlin, Peter, Very Rev, PP
Padres de San Columbano Apartado 073174, Lima 39, Peru
(Down & C.)

Carmody, Brendan (SJ)
Irish Jesuit Provincialate, Milltown Park, Sandford Road, Dublin 6
Tel 01-4987333

Carmody, Patrick, Very Rev, AP
Cooraclare, Co Clare
Tel 065-9059010
(*Cooraclare*, Killaloe)

Carmody, Patrick, Very Rev, PP
Parochial House, Main Street, Celbridge, Co Kildare
Tel 01-6288827
(*Celbridge*, Dublin)

Carney, Denis, Very Rev
Balla, Co Mayo
Tel 094-9365025
(*Balla and Manulla*, Tuam)

Carney, Michael, PE
c/o Diocesan Office, The Cathedral, Galway
Tel 091-563566
(Galway, retired)

Carney, Michael, Very Rev, PP
Ramelton, Co Donegal
Tel 074-9151304
(*Ramelton*, Raphoe)

Carolan, Edward (OMI)
Oblate House of Retreat, Inchicore, Dublin 8
Tel 01-4534408/4541805

Carolan, Loughlain
Cross, Mullagh, Kells, Co Meath
Tel 049-8547024
(Kilmore)

Carolan, Patrick (OMI), Very Rev, Co-PP
Oblate House of Retreat, Inchicore, Dublin 8
Tel 01-4534408/4541805/ 4541117

Carr, Brendan (CSSp)
Community Leader, SPIRASI, Spiritan House, 213 North Circular Road, Dublin 7
Tel 01-8389664/01-8683504

Carr, Daniel, Rt Rev Mgr, PP, VG
St Johnston, Lifford, Co Donegal
Tel 074-9148203
Ard Adhamhnáin, Letterkenny, Co Donegal
(Raphoe)

Carr, Frank (SSC)
St Columban's, Dalgan Park, Navan, Co Meath
Tel 046-9021525

Carragher, Michael (OP)
Convent of SS Xystus and Clement, Collegio San Clemente, Via Labicana 95, 00184 Roma
Tel (39-06) 7740021

Carrig, Noel (MI)
St Camillus, Killucan, Co Westmeath
Tel 044-74115

Carrigan, James, Very Rev Canon
Ballacolla, Portlaoise, Co Laois
Tel 0502-34016
(Ossory, retired)

Carrigan, William (SSC)
58 Aylesbury, Freshford Road, Kilkenny
(Retired)

Carrigy, Colman
Clonee, Killoe, Co Longford
(Ardagh & Cl.)

Carroll, Aidan, CC
'Carraig Donn', 23 Glenageary Woods, Dun Laoghaire, Co Dublin
Tel 01-4972816
(*Dun Laoghaire*, Dublin)

Carroll, Andrew (MI)
St Camillus, Killucan,
Co Westmeath
Tel 044-74115
Carroll, Daniel (SDB)
Rector, Salesian College,
Maynooth Road,
Celbridge, Co Kildare
Tel 01-6275058/60
Carroll, Daniel, Very Rev, PP
St Fiacre's Gardens,
Bohernatounish Road,
Loughboy, Kilkenny
Tel 056-7764400/
087-9077769
(Ossory)
Carroll, David, PP
The Presbytery, John's Mall,
Birr, Co Offaly
Tel 057-9120097/
086-3467909
(*Birr*, Killaloe)
Carroll, Declan, Very Rev, CC
Mulrany, Co Mayo
Tel 098-36107
(*Newport (Burrishoole)*,
Tuam)
Carroll, Denis
85 Hillcrest Drive,
Lucan, Co Dublin
Tel 01-6280948
(Dublin, retired)
Carroll, Felix (OFMCap)
St Francis Capuchin Friary,
Rochestown, Co Cork
Tel 021-4896244
Carroll, Gerard
Ballinalee Road,
Longford
(Ardagh & Cl.)
Carroll, Gregory (OP), Very
Rev, PP
Prior, St Saviour's,
Dominick Street, Dublin 1
Tel 01-8897610
(*Dominick Street*, Dublin)
Carroll, J.
Chaplain,
Sligo General Hospital
Tel 071-9171111
(Elphin)
Carroll, James, Rt Rev Mgr, PP,
VF
Parochial House,
9 Fair Street, Drogheda,
Co Louth
Tel 041-9838537
(*Drogheda*, Armagh)
Carroll, Jeremiah
(study leave)
Archdiocese of
Dublin/Defence Forces
(Clogher)
Carroll, Jerry
Casement Aerodrome,
Baldonnell, Co Dublin
Tel 01-4592497
(Dublin)
Carroll, John P. (SPS)
St Patrick's, Kiltegan,
Co Wicklow
Tel 059-6473600
Carroll, John, CC
Diocesan Secretary and
Chancellery,
PO Box 40, Bishop's House,
Summerhill, Wexford
Tel 053-9124368
Diocesan Secretary,
Barntown, Co Wexford
Tel 053-9120853
(*Glynn*, Ferns)
Carroll, Patrick F., Very Rev,
Co-PP, VF
124 New Cabra Road,
Dublin 7
Tel 01-8385244
(*Cabra*, Dublin)
Carroll, Thomas, Very Rev, PP,
VF
Parteen, Co Clare
Tel 061-345613
(*Parteen/Meelick*, Limerick)
Carroll, Timothy (SMA)
African Missions,
Blackrock Road, Cork
Tel 021-4292871
Carter, Seamus, Very Rev
Abbeybreaffey Nursing
Home,
Dublin Road,
Castlebar, Co Mayo
(Tuam, retired)
Carton, Francis (OCSO)
Mount Melleray Abbey,
Cappoquin, Co Waterford
Tel 058-54404
Carvill, Aidan (SM)
Australia
Carvill, Andrew, CC
Ballynoe, Mallow,
Co Cork
Tel 058-59269
(*Conna*, Cloyne)
Carvill, Gregory, CC
Parochial House,
17 Carnmore Drive, Newry,
Co Down BT35 8SB
Tel 028-30269047
(*Middle Killeavy*, Armagh)
Casey Thomas (SJ)
Irish Jesuit Provincialate,
Milltown Park,
Sandford Road, Dublin 6
Tel 01-4987333
Casey, Aquin, Very Rev, Adm
The Presbytery,
Ravenswood, Fermoy,
Co Cork
Tel 025-31414
(*Fermoy*, Cloyne)
Casey, Brendan
Maynooth, Co Kildare
Tel 01-6286391/2
Casey, Cornelius (CSsR)
Acting President,
School of Undergraduate
Studies
Milltown Institute of
Theology and Philosophy
Tel 01-2776300
Casey, Eamonn, Most Rev, DD
Shanaglish, Gort,
Co Galway
(Galway, retired)
Casey, Edward (SMA), CC
c/o Dromantine Retreat and
Conference Centre,
Dromatine College,
Newry, Co Down BT34 1RH
Tel 028-30821219
(Retired in Ireland outside
SMA houses)
Casey, Gerard, Very Rev
Canon, PP
Mallow, Co Cork
Tel 022-21149
(*Mallow*, Cloyne)
Casey, John (CSsR)
28 Broadway Road,
Blanchardstown,
Dublin 15
Tel 01-8213716
(*Blanchardstown*, Dublin)
Casey, John (CSsR)
Marianella, 75 Orwell Road,
Dublin 6
Tel 01-4067100
Casey, John (SMA)
African Missions,
Blackrock Road, Cork
Tel 021-4292871
Casey, Kevin (SJ)
Irish Jesuit Provincialate,
Milltown Park,
Sandford Road, Dublin 6
Tel 01-4987333
Casey, Martin, Very Rev, PP
Woolgreen, Carnew,
Co Wicklow
Tel 053-9426888
(*Carnew*, Ferns)
Casey, Michael (SDB), Very
Rev
Provincialate,
Salesian House,
45 St Teresa's Road,
Crumlin, Dublin 12
Tel 01-4555787
Casey, Michael, Very Rev, PP
Cross, Kilrush,
Co Clare
Tel 065-9058008/
086-0842216
(*Carrigaholt and Cross*,
Killaloe)
Casey, Patrick, Very Rev, PE
St Mary's Terrace,
Bishopsgate Street,
Mullingar, Co Westmeath
Tel 044-9342746
(Meath, retired)
Casey, Paul, CC
Cootehill, Co Cavan
Tel 049-5552163
(*Lavey*, Kilmore)
Casey, Peter, Very Rev, PP
Ballinagh, Co Cavan
Tel 049-4337232
(*Kilmore*, Kilmore)
Casey, Seamus
11 Auburn Heights,
Athlone, Co Westmeath
Tel 090-6478318
(Ardagh & Cl.)
Casey, Seán (CSSp)
Blackrock College,
Blackrock, Co Dublin
Tel 01-2888681
Casey, Sean, Very Rev, PP
Ennybegs, Longford
Tel 043-3323119
(*Killoe*, Ardagh & Cl.)
Casey, Thomas (SJ)
c/o Jesuit Provincial Curia,
IMI Centre, Sandyford Road,
Dublin 16
Tel 01-2932820
Casey, Timothy (CM), CC
122 Sunday's Well Road,
Cork
Tel 021-4304070
(*St Vincent's, Sunday's Well*,
Cork & R.)
Casey, Tony
Padres de San Columbano,
Apartado 39-073/074,
Lima 39, Peru
(Killaloe)
Cashman, Daniel (SMA)
SMA House, Wilton, Cork
Tel 021-4541069/4541884
Cashman, Denis, Very Rev, PP
Parochial House,
Watergrasshill, Co Cork
Tel 021-4889103
(*Watergrasshill*, Cork & R.)
Cashman, James
1 Pinewood, Wexford
(Ferns, retired)
Cassidy, Dermot (SJ)
St Ignatius Community &
Church,
27 Raleigh Row,
Salthill, Galway
Tel 091-523707
Cassidy, Eoin G., PC
The Presbytery,
Haddington Road, Dublin 4
Tel 01-6600075
(*Haddington Road*, Dublin)
Cassidy, Gerard, PP
Ballyhaise, Co Cavan
Tel 049-4338121
(Kilmore)
Cassidy, Gerard, Very Rev
(CSsR), PP
722 Antrim Road,
Newtownabbey,
Co Antrim BT36 7PG
Tel 028-90774833/4
(*St Gerard's*, Down & C.)

Cassidy, Joseph, Most Rev, DD, PP
Retired Archbishop of Tuam,
1 Kilgarve Court, Creagh, Ballinasloe, Co Galway
(Tuam, retired)

Cassidy, P.J. (White Fathers)
Superior, Provincialate, Cypress Grove Road, Templeogue, Dublin 6W
Tel 01-4055263

Cassidy, Seamus, Very Rev
Tavis, Kilmainham Wood, Kells, Co Meath
(Dublin, retired)

Cassin, James, Rt Rev Mgr
St Patrick's College, Maynooth, Co Kildare
Tel 01-6285222/086-2380984
(Ossory)

Cassin, Liam, Very Rev, PP
Hugginstown, Co Kilkenny
Tel 087-2312354/056-7768678
(Ossory)

Cassin, Seán (OFM)
Franciscan College, Gormanston, Co Meath
Tel 01-8412203

Cavanagh, Daniel, Very Rev, PP
Rosbercon, New Ross, Co Wexford
Tel 051-421515/087-2335432
(*Rosbercon*, Ossory)

Cawley, Farrell, Very Rev
Ballinacarrow, Co Sligo
Tel 086-0864347
(Achonry, retired)

Cawley, Michael, Very Rev
Newman Institute, Ballina, Co Mayo
(Killala, retired)

Cepeda, Francisco (LC)
Director, Dublin Oak Academy, Kilcroney, Bray, Co Wicklow
Tel 01-2863290

Chambers, Martin, PP
2 Chaplain's House, Knocknamona, Letterkenny, Co Donegal
Tel 074-9125090
(*Letterkenny*, Raphoe)

Champion, Augustine (OP), PP
Superior, Convento dos Padres Dominicanos Irlandesses, Praceta Infante D. Henrique, lote 5, 1-Dto, Rua do Murtal, San Pedro Do Estoril
2765-531 Estoril Portuagal
Tel (351-21) 4673771
(Lisbon)

Charles, Nigel, CC
Parochial House, Killashee, Co Longford
Tel 043-3345546
(*Killashee*, Ardagh & Cl.)

Chester, John, CC
St Joseph's Presbytery, Park Street, Monaghan
Tel 047-81220
(Clogher)

Chestnutt, Gerard, CC
Sacred Heart Presbytery, The Folly, Waterford
Tel 051-878429
(*Sacred Heart*, Waterford & L.)

Chisholm, John (CSSp)
135 The Stiles Road, Clontarf, Dublin 3
Tel 01-8339025

Christy, Myles
Elmhurst Nursing Home, Hampstead Avenue, Glasnevin, Dublin 9
(Dublin, retired)

Chute, John (SSC), Very Rev, CC
St Joseph's, Balcurris, Ballymun, Dublin 11
Tel 01-8423865
(*Balcurris*, Dublin)

Claffey, Pat (SVD), CC
The Presbytery, Haddington Road, Dublin 4
Tel 01-6600075
(*Haddington Road*, Dublin)

Clancy, Anthony (OMI)
Provincial Treasurer, Provincial Residence, Oblates of Mary Immaculate House of Retreat, Tyrconnell Road, Inchicore, Dublin 8
Tel 01-4541160/4541161
Superior, Oblate House of Retreat, Inchicore, Dublin 8
Tel 01-4534408/4541805

Clancy, Finbarr G. (SJ)
Rector of Ecclesiastical Faculty and Professor of Theology at Milltown, Milltown Institute of Theology and Philosophy, Milltown Park, Sandford Road, Dublin 6
Tel 01-2698411

Clancy, John (SMA)
African Missions, Blackrock Road, Cork
Tel 021-4292871

Clancy, Peter, CC
75 Newtown Park, Leixlip, Co Kildare
Tel 01-8386231
(*Confey*, Dublin)

Clancy, Tom, Very Rev, AP
Woodlawn, Model Farm Road, Ballineaspaig, Cork
Tel 021-4348588
(*Ballineaspaig*, Cork & R.)

Clarke, Christopher (OCD), Very Rev, PP
Prior, St Teresa's, Clarendon Street, Dublin 2
Tel 01-6718466

Clarke, Dermot, Very Rev Mgr, PP
Parochial House, 34 Aughrim Street, Dublin 7
Tel 01-8386571
(*Aughrim Street*, Dublin)

Clarke, Eamonn, CC
The Presbytery, Kilcoole, Co Wicklow
Tel 01-2876207
(*Kilquade*, Dublin)

Clarke, Eugene
5 Brookside, Farnham Road, Cavan
Tel 049-4331755
(Kilmore, retired)

Clarke, Gerard (SJ)
Superior, John Sullivan House, 56/56A Mulvey Park, Dundrum, Dublin 14
Tel 01-2986424

Clarke, Joseph, Very Rev, PP
Kilnadeema, Loughrea, Co Galway
Tel 091-841201
(*Kilnadeema and Aille*, Clonfert)

Clarke, Leo (SSC)
St Columban's Retirement Home, Dalgan Park, Navan, Co Meath
Tel 046-9021525

Clarke, Martin, Very Rev, PP
No. 1, The Presbytery, Stillorgan Road, Dublin 4
Tel 01-2802130
(*Donnybrook*, Dublin)

Clarke, Patrick (SSC)
St Columban's Retirement Home, Dalgan Park, Navan, Co Meath
Tel 046-9021525

Clarke, Peter, Very Rev, PP
Parochial House, Tallanstown, Dundalk, Co Louth
Tel 042-9374197
(*Tallanstown*, Armagh)

Clavin, Joseph, Very Rev, PP, VF
Parochial House, Dunshaughlin, Co Meath
Tel 01-8259114
(Meath)

Clayton-Lea, Paul, Very Rev, PP, VF
Parochial House, Clogherhead, Drogheda, Co Louth
Tel 041-9822438
(*Clogherhead*, Armagh)

Cleary, Brendan, Very Rev, AP
17 Churchfield, Clonlara, Co Clare
Tel 061-354028/086-8484550
(*Clonlara*, Killaloe)

Cleary, Daniel (MSC)
Woodview House, Mount Merrion Avenue, Blackrock, Co Dublin
Tel 01-2881644

Cleary, Edward, CC
Knockinrawley, Tipperary
Tel 062-51242
(*Tipperary*, Cashel & E.)

Cleary, Lorenzo, Very Rev
The Stables, Hayestown, Wexford
(Ferns)

Cleary, Matthew L., Very Rev
The Stables, Bridgetown, Co Wexford
(Ferns, retired)

Cleary, Michael J. (CSSp), Most Rev
Holy Spirit Missionary College, Kimmage Manor, Dublin 12
Tel 01-4064300

Cleary, Patrick (OFMCap)
Provincial Office, 12 Halston Street, Dublin 7
Tel 01-8733205

Cleary, Patrick B. (CSSp)
Holy Spirit Missionary College, Kimmage Manor, Whitehall Road, Dublin 12
Tel 01-4064300

Cleary, William, Rt Rev Mgr, AP
Star of the Sea, Mornington, Co Meath
Tel 041-9827384
(*Laytown-Mornington*, Meath)

Cleere, Martin, Very Rev, PP
Windgap, Co Kilkenny
Tel 051-648111/087-2954010
(*Windgap*, Ossory)

Clenaghan, Gerard (OMI)
Oblate House of Retreat, Inchicore, Dublin 8
Tel 01-4534408/4541805

Clerkin, Colum, Very Rev, PP, VF
23 Thornhill Park, Culmore, Derry BT48 4PB
Tel 028-71358519
(*Culmore*, Derry)

Clerkin, Eugene (OMI)
Oblate House of Retreat, Inchicore, Dublin 8
Tel 01-4534408/4541805

Clerkin, Sean, Very Rev Canon, PE
Tydavnet, Co Monaghan
Tel 047-89402
(*Tydavnet*, Clogher)

Clifford, Brendan (OP)
St Saviour's, Glentworth Street, Limerick
Tel 061-412333

Clifford, Dermot, Most Rev, PhD, DD
Archbishop of Cashel and Emly, Archbishop's House, Thurles, Co Tipperary
Tel 0504-21512
(Cashel & E.)

Clifford, Diarmuid (OP)
St Saviour's, Upper Dorset Street, Dublin 1
Tel 01-8897610

Clifford, Gerard, Most Rev, DD
Titular Bishop of Geron and Auxiliary Bishop to the Archbishop of Armagh, Annaskeagh, Ravensdale, Dundalk, Co Louth
Tel 042-9371012
(Armagh)

Clifford, Hugh
Church of the Sacred Heart, Seamus Quirke Road, Galway
Tel 091-524751
(*Sacred Heart Church*, Galway)

Clinton, Colm (SPS)
(*Adm protem*)
New Quay, Co Clare
Tel 065-7078026
(*Carron and New Quay*, Galway)

Clucas, Peter (OMI)
Oblate Scholasticate, St Anne's, Goldenbridge Walk, Inchicore, Dublin 8
Tel 01-4540841/4542955

Clyne, S. James, Very Rev Canon, PE, AP
24 Chapel Road, Killeavy, Newry, Co Down BT35 8JY
Tel 028-30848222
(*Cloghogue (Killeavy Upper)*, Armagh)

Clyne, Simon (CM)
St Paul's College, Raheny, Dublin 5
Tel 01-8318113

Coady, Michael, Very Rev, PP
Parochial House, Carrickbrennan Road, Monkstown, Co Dublin
Tel 01-6684192
(*Monkstown*, Dublin)

Coakley, Donal, Very Rev, PP
4 Upper Woodlands, Cloghroe, Co Cork
Tel 021-4385311
(*Inniscarra*, Cloyne)

Coen, John (SAC)
Provincial House, 'Homestead', Sandyford Road, Dundrum, Dublin16
Tel 01-2956180/2954170

Coen, Michael (OCD)
St Teresa's, Clarendon Street, Dublin 2
Tel 01-6718466/6718127

Coffey, Brendan (OSB), Very Rev
Glenstal Abbey, Murroe, Co Limerick
Tel 061-386103

Coffey, Patrick
Lisgaugh, Doon, Co Limerick
Tel 061-380247
(Cashel & E.)

Coffey, Peter (SDB), Co-PP
Salesian House, St Teresa's Road, Crumlin, Dublin 12
Tel 01-4555605
(*Crumlin*, Dublin)

Coffey, Robert
37 Gouldavoher Estate, Dooradoyle, Limerick
Tel 061-482437/087-6540908
(Limerick)

Coffey, Thomas, Very Rev, (IC)
Corcaghan, Monaghan
Tel 042-9744806
(*Corcaghan*, Clogher)

Coffey, Tom (IC)
St Joseph's, Doire na hAbhann, Tickincar, Clonmel, Co Tipperary
Tel 052-26914

Cogan, John, Very Rev, PP
Castlemartyr, Co Cork
Tel 021-4667133
(*Imogeela (Castlemartyr)*, Cloyne)

Cogan, Micheál, Very Rev, PE, CC
Glantane, Mallow, Co Cork
Tel 022-47158
(*Glantane*, Cloyne)

Cogan, Patrick (OFM)
15 Orchard Drive, Ursuline Court, Waterford
Tel 087-2360239
Respond! Office
Tel 051-876865

Coghlan, David (SJ)
Vice-Superior, Dominic Collins' House Residence, 129 Morehampton Road, Dublin 4
Tel 01-2693075

Coghlan, Kieran, Very Rev, PP
The Presbytery, Chapel Green, Rush, Co Dublin
Tel 01-8438024
(*Rush*, Dublin)

Coghlan, Niall (OSA), PP
St John's Priory, Thomas Street, Dublin 8
Tel 01-6770393/0451/0601/4944966

Cogley, James, Very Rev, CC
Oylegate, Co Wexford
Tel 053-9138163
(*Oylegate*, Ferns)

Colclough, Robert, CC
'Shirley', Sidmonton Road, Bray, Co Wicklow
Tel 01-2868413
(Dublin)

Coleman, Christopher, Very Rev (MSC)
Carrignavar, Co Cork
Tel 021-4884044

Coleman, Gerard, CC
Berrings, Co Cork
Tel 021-7332155
(*Inniscarra*, Cloyne)

Coleman, Gerard, Very Rev, PP
Castlelyons, Fermoy, Co Cork
Tel 025-36372
(*Castlelyons*, Cloyne)

Coleman, Padraig, (OFM)
Franciscan House of Studies, Dún Mhuire, Seafield Road, Killiney, Co Dublin
Tel 01-2826760

Coleman, William, Very Rev, PP
Parochial House, Rochfortbridge, Co Westmeath
Tel 046-9222107
(*Rochfortbridge*, Meath)

Colgan, John (SSC)
Columban Intercom, St Columban's, Dalgan Park, Navan, Co Meath
Tel 046-9021525

Colgan, Maurice (OP)
St Saviour's, Upper Dorset Street, Dublin 1
Tel 01-8897610

Colhoun, Roland, CC
Parochial House, 32 Chapel Road, Waterside, Derry BT47 2BB
Tel 028-71342303
(St Columba's, Long Tower (*Templemore*, Derry)

Coll, Francis, CC
Parochial House, 17 Carnmore Drive, Newry, Co Down, BT35 8SB
Tel 028 3026 9047
(Armagh)

Coll, Niall
St Mary's College, Belfast
(Raphoe)

Collender, Michael (OSA)
St Augustine's Priory (Residence), New Ross, Co Wexford
Tel 051-421237

Collery, Seamus
Curry, Ballymote, Co Sligo
(*Curry*, Achonry)

Collier, Bernard, CC
2 Knightswood, Coolock Lane, Santry, Dublin 9
Tel 01-4540811
(*Larkhill, Whitehall, Santry*, Dublin)

Collier, Val (SDB)
Rector, Rinaldi House, 72 Sean McDermott Street, Dublin 1
Tel 01-8363358

Collins, Cornelius
Patrickswell, Co Limerick
(Limerick, retired)

Collins, Denis (CM)
St Joseph's, 44 Stillorgan Park, Blackrock, Co Dublin
Tel 01-2886961

Collins, Denis (OCSO)
Mount Melleray Abbey, Cappoquin, Co Waterford
Tel 058-54404

Collins, Denis (SMA), CC
African Missions, Blackrock Road, Cork
Tel 021-4292871
(*Wilton, St Joseph's*, Cork & R.)

Collins, Edward J., CC
The Presbytery, Clonakilty, Co Cork
Tel 023-33100
(*Clonakilty and Darrara*, Cork & R.)

Collins, Gregory (OSB)
Dormition Abbey, Mount Sion, PO Box 22, IL-91000, Jerusalem, Israel

Collins, John, Very Rev (Moderator)
The Presbytery, James's Street, Dublin 8
Tel 01-4534921
(*James's Street*, Dublin)

Collins, John, Very Rev, PP
1 The Presbytery Holy Cross Church, Mahon, Cork
Tel 021-4357394
(*Mahon*, Cork & R.)

Collins, Laurence (OP), Adm
The Presbytery, St Dominic's, St Dominic's Road, Tallaght, Dublin 24
Tel 01-4510620
(*Tallaght, Dodder*, Dublin)

Collins, Martin J. (CSSp)
Holy Spirit Missionary College,
Kimmage Manor,
Dublin 12
Tel 01-4064300

Collins, Michael, CC
The Presbytery,
St Mary's Parish,
Haddington Road, Dublin 4
Tel 01-2983557
(*Haddington Road*, Dublin)

Collins, Michael E.,
St Patrick's College,
Maynooth, Co Kildare
Tel 01-7084700/0876389847
(Killaloe, retired)

Collins, Michael, PP
119 Irish Green Street,
Limavady,
Co Derry BT49 9AB
Tel 028-77765649
(Derry, retired)

Collins, Michael, Very Rev, PP
Parish House, Quinn,
Co Clare
Tel 065-6825612/
086-3475085
(*Quinn*, Killaloe)

Collins, Neil (SSC)
St Columban's, Dalgan Park,
Navan, Co Meath
Tel 046-9021525

Collins, Owen, Very Rev, PP
Cootehill, Co Cavan
Tel 049-5552120
(*Cootehill*, Kilmore)

Collins, P. Gerard, Very Rev
The Presbytery,
Passage West, Co Cork
(Cork & R., retired)

Collins, Patrick (CM)
St Joseph's,
44 Stillorgan Park,
Blackrock, Co Dublin
Tel 01-2886961

Collins, Raymond (OP)
St Saviour's, Bridge Street,
Waterford
Tel 051-875061

Collins, Timothy, Very Rev, PP
The Presbytery,
Dunmanway, Co Cork
Tel 023-8845000
(*Dunmanway*, Cork & R.)

Collum, Martin, Very Rev, PP, VF
Rathmullan, Co Donegal
Tel 074-9158156
(*Rathmullan*, Raphoe)

Colonel, Daniel (SDB)
Salesian College,
Maynooth Road, Celbridge,
Co Kildare
Tel 01-6275058/60

Colreavy, Tom, Very Rev, PP
28 Glentworth Park,
Ard-na-Gréine, Dublin 13
Tel 01-8484836
(*Ayrfield*, Dublin)

Coltsmann, Francis (SMA)
SMA House, Wilton, Cork
Tel 021-4541069/4541884

Comer, Liam, Very Rev, PP, VF
Dromagh, Mallow, Co Cork
Tel 029-78096
(*Dromtariffe*, Kerry)

Comer, Míceál, Very Rev, PP
The Presbytery, Eadestown,
Naas, Co Kildare
(*Eadestown*, Dublin)

Comerford, Brendan (SJ)
Milltown Park,
Sandford Road, Dublin 6
Tel 01-2698411

Comerford, Frank (CSSp)
Holy Spirit Missionary College,
Kimmage Manor, Dublin 12
Tel 01-4064300

Comerford, Patrick, Very Rev, PP
Freshford, Co Kilkenny
Tel 056-8832461/
086-1038430
(*Freshford*, Ossory)

Comiskey, Brendan (SSCC), Most Rev, DD
Coudrin House, 27
Northbrook Road, Dublin 6
Tel 01-6473751/01-6686590

Comiskey, Brendan, Most Rev, DD
Retired Bishop of Ferns,
PO Box 40, Summerhill,
Wexford
(Ferns, retired)

Comiskey, Gerard, Very Rev, PP
Staghall, Belturbet,
Co Cavan
Tel 049-9522140
(*Drumlane*, Kilmore)

Commane, Michael (OP)
Newbridge College,
Droichead Nua, Co Kildare
Tel 045-487200

Commins, Thomas, CC
Kilkerrin, Ballinasloe,
Co Galway
Tel 094-9659212
(*Kilkerren and Clonberne*, Tuam)

Conaghan, Michael, Very Rev, PE
6 Fields Court,
Kilmacrennan, Co Donegal
Tel 074-91198711
(Raphoe, retired)

Conaty, Eamonn (SSC), Very Rev, PP
Ballinameen, Boyle,
Co Roscommon
Tel 071-9668104
(*Ballinameen (Kilnamanagh and Estersnow)*, Elphin)

Conaty, Peter (CSSp)
Provincial Assistant,
Holy Spirit Provincialate,
Temple Park,
Richmond Avenue South,
Dublin 6
Tel 01-4975127/4977230

Concannon, Eamonn, Very Rev Canon, PE
Balleyhowley, Knock,
Co Mayo
(Tuam, retired)

Concannon, John (CM)
St Peter's, Phibsboro,
Dublin 7
Tel 01-8389708/8389841

Condon, Eanna, Very Rev, PE
St Mary's, Clonmel,
Co Tipperary
Tel 052-6127870
(Waterford & L., retired)

Condon, Gerard, CC
Shanballymore, Mallow,
Co Cork
Tel 022-25197
(*Doneraile*, Cloyne)

Condon, Jeremiah, Very Rev, PP
Stradbally, Kilmacthomas,
Co Waterford
Tel 051-293133
(*Stradbally*, Waterford & L.)

Condon, John, CC
Templeorum, Piltown,
Co Kilkenny
Tel 051-643124/086-8394615
(*Templeorum*, Ossory)

Condon, Joseph, Very Rev, PP
Ballymabin, Dunmore East,
Co Waterford
(Waterford & L.)

Condon, Mark, CC
St Mary's Cathedral,
Kilkenny
Tel 056-7721253
(*St Mary's*, Ossory)

Condon, Michael (CSsR)
The Marlay Nursing Home,
Kellystown Road,
Rathfarnham, Dublin 16
Tel 01-4994444

Condon, Patrick T., Very Rev, PP
Knockanore, Tallow,
Co Waterford
Tel 024-97140
(*Knockanore*, Waterford & L.)

Condon, Sean
Cathedral House,
Cathedral Place, Limerick
Tel 061-414624
(Limerick, retired)

Condren, Joseph (OFM)
Franciscan Friary, Killarney,
Co Kerry
Tel 064-6631334/6631066

Condron, Barry, CC
Parochial House,
Dunshaughlin,
Co Meath
Tel 01-8259114
(*Dunshaughlin*, Meath)

Conlan, Alex, Very Rev, PP
Parochial House, Ballybrack,
Co Dublin
Tel 01-2826404
(*Ballybrack-Killiney*, Dublin)

Conlan, Anthony
Chaplain,
St Vincent's University Hospital
Elm Park, Dublin 4
Tel 01-2694533
(Dublin)

Conlan, Patrick (OFM)
Franciscan House of Studies,
Dun Mhuire, Seafield Road,
Killiney, Co Dublin
Tel 01-2826760

Conlon, Brian, Very Rev, PC
Director,
Boyle Family Life Centre,
Knocknashee, Boyle,
Co Roscommon
Tel 071-9663000
Parish
Cootehall, Boyle,
Co Roscommon
Tel 071-9667004
(*Cootehall*, Elphin)

Conlon, Brian, Very Rev, PP
Carrowmore,
Ballina, Co Mayo
Tel 096-34014
(*Lacken*, Killala)

Conlon, David (OSB)
Glenstal Abbey, Murroe,
Co Limerick
Tel 061-386103

Conlon, John, Very Rev, PP
Parochial House, Duleek,
Co Meath
Tel 041-9823205
(*Duleek*, Meath)

Conlon, Malachy, Very Rev, PP, VF
Top Rath, Cooley,
Carlingford, Co Louth
Tel 042-9376105
(*Cooley*, Armagh)

Conlon, Noel, CC
Inniskeen, Dundalk,
Co Louth
Tel 042-9378678
(*Inniskeen*, Clogher)

Conlon, Sean (OCD)
Prior,
St Joseph's Carmelite
Retreat Centre,
Termonbacca,
Derry BT48 9XE
Tel 028-71262512

Conlon, Seán, Very Rev, PP
Ballinakill, Co Laois
Tel 057-8733336
(*Ballinakill*, Kildare & L.)

Connaughton, Finian, Very Rev, PP
Parochial House, Drumconrath, Navan, Co Meath
Tel 041-6854146
(*Drumconrath*, Meath)

Connaughton, P. Aloysius (SSC)
St Columban's, Dalgan Park, Navan, Co Meath
Tel 046-9021525

Connaughton, Patrick
St Columban's, Dalgan Park, Navan, Co Meath
Tel 046-21525
(Galway)

Connaughton, Sean (SSC)
Castletown Finea, Co Westmeath
Tel 043-6681141
(Meath)

Connaughton, Vincent, Very Rev, PP
Killenummery, Dromahair, via Sligo, Co Leitrim
Tel 071-9164125
(*Killenummery and Ballintogher*, Ardagh & Cl.)

Connell, Desmond, His Eminence, Cardinal Emeritus, Archbishop of Dublin,
Archbishop's House, Drumcondra, Dublin 9
Tel 01-8373732
(Dublin)

Connell, Paul, PhD
President, St Finian's College, Mullingar, Co Westmeath
Tel 044-9348672
(Meath)

Connell, Seamus (SSC)
Padres de San Columbano, Apartado 073/074, Lima 39, Peru

Connelly, Christopher (OFM)
Franciscan Friary, Killarney, Co Kerry
Tel 064-6631334/6631066

Connick, Joseph (OFMConv), Very Rev
Friary of the Visitation, Fairview Strand, Dublin 3
Tel 01-8376000
(*Fairview*, Dublin)

Connolly, Charles, (Opus Dei) CC
31 Herbert Avenue, Dublin 4
Tel 01-2691825
(*Merrion Road*, Dublin)

Connolly, Darragh
(priest in residence)
Tullacmongan, Cavan
(*Cavan (Urney and Annagelliff)*, Kilmore)

Connolly, Diarmuid
4 Summerfield Lawn, Blanchardstown, Dublin 15
(Dublin, retired)

Connolly, Dermot (SPS)
St Patrick's, Kiltegan, Co Wicklow
Tel 059-6473600

Connolly, Finbarr (CSsR)
St Joseph's, Dundalk, Co Louth
Tel 042-9334042/9334762

Connolly, Hugh, Rt Rev Mgr, BA, DD
President, St Patrick's College, Maynooth, Co Kildare
Tel 01-6285222
(Dromore)

Connolly, John, Very Rev, PP
75 Clonfeacle Road, Blackwatertown, Dungannon, Co Tyrone BT71 7HP
(*Moy (Clonfeacle)*, Armagh)

Connolly, Joseph, Very Rev, PP
Parochial House, Donabate, Co Dublin
Tel 01-8436011
(Dublin)

Connolly, Michael
54 Wyattville Park, Loughlinstown, Co Dublin
(Dublin, retired)

Connolly, Michael, CC
Curate's House, Walter Macken Road, Mervue, Galway
Tel 091-771662
NUI, Galway
Tel 091-582719
(Galway)

Connolly, Patrick (SPS)
Kiltegan Leader, St Patrick's, Kiltegan, Co Wicklow
Tel 059-6473600

Connolly, Patrick, Dr
Theology Department, Mary Immaculate College, South Circular Road, Limerick
Tel 061-204575
(Clogher)

Connolly, Peter, Very Rev, PP
Clonbur, via Claremorris, Co Galway
Tel 094-9546304
(*Clonbur (Ross)*, Tuam)

Connolly, Philip, Very Rev Canon, PE
Doohamlet, Castleblayney, Co Monaghan
Tel 042-9741239
(*Clontibret*, Clogher)

Connolly, Sean, Rt Rev Mgr, VG
7 Tullyview, Loughguile, Co Antrim BT44 9JY
(Down & C., retired)

Connolly, Stan (SPS)
St Patrick's, Kiltegan, Co Wicklow
Tel 059-6473600

Connolly, Terence, Very Rev, PP
178 Newtownsaville Road, Omagh, Co Tyrone BT78 2RJ
Tel 028-82841306
(*Eskra*, Clogher)

Connolly, Timothy (CSSp)
Holy Spirit Missionary College, Kimmage Manor, Dublin 12
Tel 01-4064300

Connolly, Vincent, Rt Rev Mgr, PP, VG
St Joseph's, Carrickmacross, Co Monaghan
Tel 042-9663200
(Clogher)

Connor, Philip (OFMCap)
Capuchin Friary, Friary Street, Kilkenny
Tel 056-7721439

Conroy, Charles (MSC)
Western Road, Cork
Tel 021-4804120

Conroy, Christopher (OCarm)
Whitefriar Street Church, 56 Aungier Street, Dublin 2
Tel 01-4758821

Conroy, Jackie, Very Rev, PP
Aughagower, Westport, Co Mayo
Tel 098-25057
(*Aughagower*, Tuam)

Conroy, Michael (SPS)
St Patrick's, Kiltegan, Co Wicklow
Tel 059-6473600

Conroy, Patrick, Very Rev, PP
Ballinakill, Loughrea, Co Galway
Tel 090-9745021
(Clonfert)

Conry, Anthony
Brazil
(Elphin)

Considine, Patrick, Very Rev Dean, PE
c/o The Diocesan Office, The Cathedral, Galway
Tel 091-563566
(Galway, retired)

Convey, Martin, Very Rev, BSc, MLitt, PhD, PP
Straide, Foxford, Co Mayo
Tel 094 9031029
(*Straide*, Achonry)

Conway, Alan, CC
Chaplain, Plunkett Home, Boyle, Co Roscommon
Tel 071-9662012
(Elphin)

Conway, B.
Chaplain, Sligo General Hospital
Tel 071-9171111
(Elphin)

Conway, Bernard (SPS)
On temporary diocesan work

Conway, Eamon (Tuam)
Head of Department of Theology & Religious Studies,
Mary Immaculate College, University of Limerick, South Circular Road, Limerick
Tel 061-204353
(Limerick)

Conway, Edward (OP), Very Rev
Black Abbey, Kilkenny, Co Kilkenny
Tel 056-7721279

Conway, Edward, Very Rev, PC
1 Maretimo Gardens West, Blackrock, Co Dublin
Tel 01-2882248
(*Blackrock*, Dublin)

Conway, Michael
St Patrick's College, Maynooth, Co Kildare
Tel 01-6285222
(Galway)

Conway, Michael, Very Rev
Barr Tra, Enniscrone, Co Sligo
(Killala, retired)

Conway, Noel, Very Rev
(priest in residence)
23 Rathkeltair Road, Downpatrick, Co Down BT30 6NL
Tel 024-4461477
(*Downpatrick*, Down & C.)

Conway, P.G., Very Rev
Warrenpoint Road, Newry, Co Down
(Dromore, retired)

Conway, Paddy, AP
c/o Westbourne, Ennis, Co Clare
Tel 065-6849818/087-6831992
(*Ennis*, Killaloe)

Conway, Patrick (SSC)
c/o Bishop's Residence, Westbourne, Ennis, Co Clare
Tel 065-6828638

Conway, Seamus, Rt Rev Mgr, PP
Parochial House, Booterstown Avenue, Co Dublin
Tel 01-2882889
(*Booterstown*, Dublin)

Cooke, Michael, Very Rev, PP, VG
Bridge Street, Belturbet, Co Cavan
Tel 049-9522109
(*Belturbet*, Kilmore)

Coonan, Thomas, Rt Rev Mgr, CC
Geashill, Co Offaly
Tel 057-9343517
(Kildare & L.)

Cooney, Albert (OFMCap)
Holy Trinity, Fr Mathew Quay, Cork
Tel 021-4270827

Cooney, John, Very Rev, PP
Kilmainhamwood, Kells, Co Meath
Tel 046-9052129
(*Kilmainhamwood and Moybologue*, Kilmore)

Cooney, Joseph, Very Rev, PE
25 Carrowmore Meadows, Knock, Co Mayo
Tel 094-9375933
(Tuam, retired)

Cooney, Kevin (SM)
Superior, Cerdon, Marist Fathers, St Mary's Road, Dundalk, Co Louth
Tel 042-9334019

Cooney, Matthew (OSA)
The Presbytery, Dungarvan, Co Waterford
(*Dungarvan*, Waterford & L.)

Cooney, Michael, CC
Presbytery No. 1, Thormanby Road, Howth, Co Dublin
Tel 01-8323193
(*Howth*, Dublin)

Cooney, Michael, Very Rev, PP
Terryglass, Nenagh, Co Tipperary
Tel 067-22017/087-6548331
(*Kilbarron and Terryglass*, Killaloe)

Cooney, Patrick, Very Rev, PP
30 Viewmount Park, Waterford
Tel 051-873073
(Waterford & L.)

Cooney, Thomas (OSA)
St John's Priory, Thomas Street, Dublin 8
Tel 01-6770393

Coote, Tony (SVD)
Donamon Castle, Roscommon
Tel 090-6662222

Coote, Tony, Adm
79 The Rise, Mount Merrion, Co Dublin
Tel 01-7162100/2839290
(*Kilmacud, Mount Merrion*, Dublin)

Corbally, James (MSC)
Woodview House, Mount Merrion Avenue, Blackrock, Co Dublin
Tel 01-2881644

Corbett, John F. (CSsR)
Marianella, 75 Orwell Road, Dublin 6
Tel 01-4067100

Corbett, Padraig, CC
The Parochial House, Castleiney, Templemore Co Tipperary
Tel 0504-31392
(Cashel & E.)

Corbett, Tom, Very Rev Dr, PP
Convent Hill, Roscrea, Co Tipperary
Tel 0505-21108/086-8418570
Chaplain, Welfare Home, Roscrea, Co Tipperary
Tel 0505-21389
(Killaloe)

Corcoran, Gerard, CC (*Moderator*)
The Presbytery, Shangan Road, Ballymun, Dublin 9
Tel 01-8421551/8421451
(*Ballymun*, Dublin)

Corcoran, Gregory, CC
Rhode, Co Offaly
Tel 046-9737010
(*Edenderry*, Kildare & L.)

Corcoran, James, Very Rev, Adm
Kilfian, Killala, Co Mayo
Tel 096-32420
(*Kilfian*, Killala)

Corcoran, Matthew (IC)
St Patrick's, Upton, Innishannon, Co Cork
Tel 021-4776268/4776923

Corcoran, Michael (MHM)
St Joseph's House, 50 Orwell Park, Rathgar, Dublin 6
Tel 01-4127773/0862239051

Corcoran, Pádraig, CC
Parochial House, Tullamore, Co Offaly
Tel 057-9321587
(Meath)

Corcoran, Philip, Very Rev, PP
73 Newtown Park, Leixlip, Co Kildare
Tel 01-6244637
(Dublin, retired)

Corcoran, Thomas, Very Rev, PP
Slieverue, Co Kilkenny
Tel 051-832773/087-6886678
(*Slieverue*, Ossory)

Corcorcan, Patrick (SM)
Chanel Community, Coolock, Dublin 5
Tel 01-8477133

Corish, Declan (OP), PP
St Saviour's Priory, Kilbarry, Waterford
Tel 051-370632
(*St Saviour's*, Waterford & L.)

Corish, Patrick, Rt Rev Mgr, DD
St Patrick's College, Maynooth, Co Kildare
Tel 01-6285222
(Ferns)

Corkery, Eamonn, Very Rev, PP
Dromard, Moyne, Co Longford
Tel 049-4335248
(*Dromard*, Ardagh & Cl.)

Corkery, Jackie, Very Rev Canon, PP
Kanturk, Co Cork
Tel 029-50192
(*Kanturk*, Cloyne)

Corkery, James (SJ)
Vice-Superior, Jesuit Community, 27 Leinster Road, Rathmines, Dublin 6
Tel 01-4970250

Corkery, Michael, Very Rev, PP
Glanworth, Co Cork
Tel 025-38123
(*Glanworth*, Cloyne)

Corkery, Pádraig, Dr
St Patrick's College, Maynooth, Co Kildare
Tel 01-7083639
(Cork & R.)

Corkery, Patrick, CC
Inch, Killeagh, Co Cork
Tel 024-95148
(*Killeagh*, Cloyne)

Corkery, Sean
St Patrick's College, Maynooth, Co Kildare
Tel 01-7084700
(Cloyne)

Cormac, Pierce
Chaplain, Mercy University Hospital, Cork
Tel 021-4271971
(Cork & R.)

Cormican, Gregory, Very Rev, PP
72 Nursery Avenue, Coleraine, Co Derry BT52 1LR
Tel 028-70343156
(*Coleraine*, Down & C.)

Corr, Anthony, CC
100 Dromore Street, Banbridge, Co Down BT32 4DW
Tel 028-40622274
(*Seapatrick (Banbridge)*, Dromore)

Corr, Sean (SSC)
38 Washingbay Road, Coalisland, Co Tyrone BT71 4PU

Corridan, Edward
Killareny Nursing Home, Rock Road, Co Kerry
(Kerry, retired)

Corrigan, Brendan, Very Rev, PP
5 The Gallops, Kilbeggan, Co Westmeath
Tel 057-9332155
(*Kilbeg*, Meath)

Corrigan, David (SM)
Catholic University School, 89 Lower Leeson Street, Dublin 2
Tel 01-6762586

Corrigan, Desmond
c/o Ara Coeli, Armagh BT61 7QY
(Armagh, retired)

Corrigan, Desmond (SMA)
Director, Dromantine Retreat and Conference Centre, Dromantine College, Newry, Co Down BT34 1RH
Tel 028-30821219

Corrigan, Kevin (CSSp)
Holy Spirit Missionary College, Kimmage Manor, Dublin 12
Tel 01-4064300

Corrigan, Patrick J., Rev Canon
Fairgreen, Belturbet, Co Cavan
Tel 049-9522151
(*Belturbet*, Kilmore)

Corrigan, Peter, Very Rev, PP
Shanco, Newbliss, Co Monaghan
Tel 047-54011
(*Killeevan*, Clogher)

Corry, Edward
Presbytery 2, Treepark Road, Kilnamanagh, Dublin 24
(Dublin, retired)

Corry, Francis (SM), CC
Holy Family Parish, Dundalk, Co Louth
Tel 042-9336301
(*Dundalk, Holy Family*, Armagh)

Corry, James (CSSp)
Holy Spirit Missionary College, Kimmage Manor, Dublin 12
Tel 01-4064300

Cosgrave, William, Very Rev, PP
Monageer, Ferns, Enniscorthy, Co Wexford
Tel 053-9233530
(*Monageer*, Ferns)

Cosgrove, Edward (SJ)
St Ignatius Community & Church,
27 Raleigh Row,
Salthill, Galway
Tel 091-523707

Cosgrove, John, Very Rev Canon, PP, VF
Castlebar, Co Mayo
Tel 094-9021274
(Tuam)

Cosgrove, Martin, Very Rev, PP
Parochial House, Arklow, Co Wicklow
Tel 0402-32294
(*Arklow*, Dublin)

Costello, Aidan, CC
The Presbytery, Loughrea, Co Galway
Tel 091-841212
(*Loughrea, St Brendan's Cathedral*, Clonfert)

Costello, Bernard
Creagh, Ballinasloe, Co Galway
(Clonfert)

Costello, David
c/o The Missionary Society of St James the Apostle,
24 Clark Street, Boston, MA 02109, USA
(Limerick)

Costello, Denis, Very Rev
Fatima Home, Oakpark, Tralee, Co Kerry
(Kerry, retired)

Costello, James, Very Rev Canon, PP, VF
Bruff, Kilmallock, Co Limerick
Tel 061-382555
(*Bruff/Meanus/Grange*, Limerick)

Costello, Liam (OFM)
Franciscan House of Studies,
Dún Mhuire, Seafield Road,
Killiney, Co Dublin
Tel 01-2826760

Costello, Martin (SMA)
Retired in Ireland outside SMA houses

Costello, Maurice
Main Street, Rathkeale, Co Limerick
Tel 069-63452
(Limerick, retired)

Costello, Pádraig, Very Rev, PP
Foxford, Co Mayo
Tel 094-9256131
(*Foxford*, Achonry)

Costello, Patrick (SSS)
Provincial,
Blessed Sacrament Chapel,
20 Bachelors Walk, Dublin 1
Tel 01-8724597

Costello, Patrick, Very Rev
51 Ashgrove, Mountbellew, Co Galway
(Tuam, retired)

Costelloe, Morgan
Our Lady's Manor,
Bullock Harbour,
Dalkey, Co Dublin
Tel 01-2718007
(Dublin, retired)

Costelloe, Patrick, AP
St Nicholas' Presbytery,
Westbury, Limerick
Tel 061-340614/087-8180815
(*St Nicholas*, Limerick)

Cotter, Bernard (SMA)
African Missions,
Blackrock Road, Cork
Tel 021-4292871

Cotter, Bernard, Very Rev, PP
Parochial House, Inchigeela,
Macroom, Co Cork
Tel 026-49838
(*Uibh Laoire*, Cork & R.)

Cotter, Donal, Very Rev, PP
The Presbytery, Bantry, Co Cork
Tel 027-50096
(*Bantry*, Cork & R.)

Cotter, Francis (OFM)
Franciscan House of Studies,
Dun Mhuire, Seafield Road,
Killiney, Co Dublin
Tel 01-2826760

Cotter, John, Very Rev, PE
The Presbytery,
Lower Road, Cork
Tel 021-4551503
(*St Patrick's*, Cork & R.)

Cotter, Pat
c/o Killaloe Diocesan Office
(Killaloe)

Cotter, Sean, Very Rev Canon, PP
Charleville, Co Cork
Tel 063-81319
(*Charleville*, Cloyne)

Coughlan, John, CC
Curate's Residence, Roscommon
Tel 090-6626189
(*Roscommon*, Elphin)

Coughlan, Patrick (CSSp)
Newlands Institute for Counselling,
2 Monastery Road,
Clondalkin, Dublin 22
Tel 01-4594573

Coughlan, Sean (OCarm)
Whitefriar Street Church,
56 Aungier Street, Dublin 2
Tel 01-4758821

Coughlan, Thomas, PC
The Presbytery,
Ss Mary and Patrick Parish,
Avoca, Co Wicklow
Tel 059-8624109
(*Avoca*, Dublin)

Coughlan, Thomas, Very Rev, PP
Effin, Kilmallock, Co Limerick
Tel 063-71314
(*Effin/Garrienderk*, Limerick)

Coulter, Charles (SSC)
St Columban's, Dalgan Park,
Navan, Co Meath
Tel 046-9021525

Courtney, Conor (CSSp)
Holy Spirit Missionary College,
Kimmage Manor, Dublin 12
Tel 01-4064300
Provincial Bursar,
Holy Spirit Provincialate,
Temple Park,
Richmond Avenue South, Dublin 6
Tel 01-4975127/4977230

Courtney, Patrick (MSC), PP
Castlehaven Parish,
Parish House, Union Hall,
Skibbereen, Co Cork
Tel 028-34940

Coveney, Patrick, Most Rev, AP
Crosshaven, Co Cork
Tel 021-4831218
(*Crosshaven*, Cork & R.)

Cox, Noel (CSSp)
Holy Spirit Missionary College,
Kimmage Manor,
Whitehall Road, Dublin 12
Tel 01-4064300

Cox, Seamus, Very Rev
Ballyleague, Co Roscommon
(Elphin, retired)

Cox, Tom, CC
Ferbane, Co Offaly
Tel 090-6454309
(Ardagh & Cl.)

Coyle, Harry
(priest in residence)
Lisieux, 99 Loup Road,
Ballynenagh, Moneymore,
Co Derry BT45 7ST
Tel 028-79418235
(Moneymore (Ardtrea), Armagh)

Coyle, Mark (OFMCap)
Capuchin Friary,
Ard Mhuire, Creeslough,
Letterkenny, Co Donegal
Tel 074-9138005

Coyle, Paul, CC
194 Navan Road, Dublin 7
Tel 01-6290553
(*Navan Road*, Dublin)

Coyle, Peter (SPS)
St Patrick's, 21 Leeson Park, Dublin 6
Tel 01-4977897

Coyle, Rory, CC
Parochial House,
42 Abbey Street,
Armagh BT61 7DZ
Tel 028-37522802
(*Armagh*, Armagh)

Coyle, Thomas, Very Rev, PP
Galmoy, Crosspatrick,
via Thurles, Co Kilkenny
Tel 056-8831227/ 087-7668969
(*Galmoy*, Ossory)

Coyne, Joseph (*Moderator*)
St Ciaran's,
36 Ashfield Lawn,
Huntstown, Dublin 15
Tel 01-8249695
(*Hartstown*, Dublin)

Coyne, P. J., PE
Kentstown, Navan, Co Meath
Tel 041-9825276
(*Beauparc*, Meath)

Craven, John (CP), CC
Holy Cross Retreat,
432 Crumlin Road, Ardoyne,
Belfast BT14 7GE
Tel 028-90748231/2
(*Holy Cross*, Down & C.)

Crawford, Alan (OSB)
Glenstal Abbey, Murroe, Co Limerick
Tel 061-386103

Crawford, Thomas, Very Rev, PP, VF
Glin, Co Limerick
Tel 068-26897
(*Glin*, Limerick)

Crawley, Michael, Very Rev Canon, PP, VF
Parochial House,
34 Madden Row, Keady,
Co Armagh BT60 3RW
Tel 028-37531242
(*Keady (Derrynoose)*, Armagh)

Creamer, Edmond (CSsR)
Clonard Monastery,
1 Clonard Gardens,
Belfast BT13 2RL
Tel 028-90445950

Crean-Lynch, Pat, Very Rev
The Presbytery,
Ballymacelligott, Tralee, Co Kerry
Tel 066-7137118
(Kerry)

Crean, Joseph (OSA)
Duckspool House
(Retirement Community),
Abbeyside, Dungarvan, Co Waterford
Tel 058-23784

Crean, Martin (OSA)
The Abbey, Fethard, Co Tipperary
Tel 052-6131273

Crean, Maurice (MHM)
Organising Secretary,
St Joseph's,
Freshford House, Kilkenny
Tel 056-7721482
Crean, Thomas, Venerable
Archdeacon PP, VF
Kenmare, Co Kerry
Tel 064-6641352
(*Kenmare*, Kerry)
Crean, William, Very Rev
Canon, PP, VF
Cahirciveen, Co Kerry
Tel 066-9472210
(*Cahirciveen*, Kerry)
Creaton, James, Very Rev, PC
Fairymount, Castlerea,
Co Roscommon
Tel 094-9870243
(*Fairymount*, Elphin)
Cremin, Aidan, CC
Cork Road, Carrigaline,
Co Cork
Tel 021-4372229
(*Carrigaline*, Cork & R.)
Cremin, Gerard, CC
Midleton, Co Cork
Tel 021-4631094
(*Midleton*, Cloyne)
Cremin, Jeremiah, Very Rev,
PP
Parochial House, Tirelton,
Macroom, Co Cork
Tel 026-46012/086-2578065
(*Kilmichael*, Cork & R.)
Cremin, Michael (OCarm)
Gort Muire, Ballinteer,
Dublin 16
Tel 01-2984014
Cremins, Richard (SJ)
35 Lower Leeson Street,
Dublin 2
Tel 01-6761248
(Zam-Mal)
Cribben, J. J., Very Rev, PP
Milltown, Co Galway
Tel 093-51609
(*Milltown (Addergole and
Liskeevey),* Tuam)
Cribbin, David
Chaplain,
University Hospital,
Galway
Tel 091-524222
(Galway)
Cribbin, James, Very Rev
Geesala, Bangor,
Ballina, Co Mayo
Tel 097-86740
(*Kiltane*, Killala)
Cribbin, Peter, Very Rev
c/o Bishop's House,
Dublin Road, Carlow
(Kildare & L.)
Crilly, Oliver, PP
230b Mayogall Road, Clady,
Portglenone,
Co Derry BT44 8NN
Tel 028-25821190
(*Greenlough*, Derry)

Crilly, Patrick
35 Rocktown Lane,
Knockloughrim,
Magerafelt,
Co Derry BT45 8QF
(Derry, retired)
Cristóbal, Jimenez A. (SJ)
Jesuit Community,
27 Leinster Road,
Rathmines, Dublin 6
Tel 01-4970250
Crofton, James
'Vinea Mea',
Via S. Francesco, 4,
Lappiano, 50064 Incisa (FI),
Italy
(Meath)
Crombie, Shane, CC
Parochial House, Tullamore,
Co Offaly
Tel 057-9321587
(Meath)
Cronin, Anthony, Very Rev, PE
Newmarket, Co Cork
Tel 029-60605
(Cloyne, retired)
Cronin, Con (SPS)
St Patrick's, Kiltegan,
Co Wicklow
Tel 059-6473600
Cronin, Isadore (OFM)
Vicar, Franciscan Friary,
Clonmel, Co Tipperary
Tel 052-6121378
Cronin, Kieran (OFM)
Guardian,
Franciscan House of Studies,
Dún Mhuire, Seafield Road,
Killiney, Co Dublin
Tel 01-2826760
Cronin, Tony (SPS)
St Patrick's, Kiltegan,
Co Wicklow
Tel 059-6473600
Crosbie, Paul, CC
Cathedral House, Mullingar,
Co Westmeath
Tel 044-9348338/9340126
(*Mullingar*, Meath)
Crosby, Denis, Very Rev, PP
Liscannor, Co Clare
Tel 065-7081248
(*Liscannor*, Galway)
Crosby, Edward, PP
Parochial House, Kilfenora,
Co Clare
Tel 065-7088006
(*Kilfenora*, Galway)
Crosby, Michael, Very Rev, PP
Shrule, Galway
Tel 093-31262
(*Shrule*, Galway)
Cross, Charles (CP)
Holy Cross Retreat,
432 Crumlin Road, Ardoyne,
Belfast BT14 7GE
Tel 028-90748231
(*Holy Cross*, Down & C.)

Crossan, Stephen, CC
Hunter's Hill, Gilford,
Co Armagh, BT63 6AJ
(*Tullylish*, Dromore)
Crossey, Colin, CC
120 Cavehill Road, Belfast
BT15 5BU
Tel 028-90714892
(*Holy Family*, Down & C.)
Crosson, Eamonn, Very Rev,
PP
Parochial House, Avoca,
Co Wicklow
Tel 0402-35156
(*Avoca*, Dublin)
Crotty, James, Very Rev, PP
Ferrybank, Waterford
Tel 051-832787/087-8317711
(Ossory)
Crotty, Michael F., Rev Mgr,
BA, JCL, D.ECC Hist.
Sections for Relations With
States,
Secretariat of State,
00120 Vatican City
Tel 0039-06 698 83546
(Cloyne)
Crotty, Oliver, Very Rev, Adm
Parochial House,
Glendalough, Co Wicklow
Tel 0404-46214
(*Glendalough*, Dublin)
Crotty, Terence (OP)
Dominican Community,
St Mary's Priory, Tallaght,
Dublin 24
Tel 01-4048100
Crowe, Martin (OP), CC
St Saviour's Priory, Kilbarry,
Waterford
Tel 051-376581
(*St Saviour's*, Waterford &
L.)
Crowe, Patrick (SJ)
Clongowes Wood College,
Naas, Co Kildare
Tel 045-868663/868202
Crowe, Philip (CSSp), CC
Drumgossatt,
Carrickmacross,
Co Monaghan
Tel 042-9661388
(*Magheracloone*, Clogher)
Crowe, Richard, CC
10 Mayorstone, Park,
Limerick
Tel 061-452952
(*St Munchin's and St Lelia's*,
Limerick)
Crowley, Adrian
Instituto de Idiomas
Maryknoll Padres,
Casilla 550, Cochabamba,
Bolivia
(Dublin)
Crowley, Brendan, CC
Malin Head, Co Donegal
Tel 074-9370134
(*Malin*, Derry)

Crowley, Brendan, Very Rev
Canon, PP, VF
SS Peter and Paul's,
Clonmel, Co Tipperary
Tel 052-6122138
(*Clonmel, SS Peter and
Paul's*, Waterford & L.)
Crowley, Christopher (OCarm)
Whitefriar Street Church,
56 Aungier Street, Dublin 2
Tel 01-4758821
Crowley, Dan, Very Rev
Canon, PP
The Presbytery,
Lower Road, Cork
Tel 021-4502696
(*St Patrick's*, Cork & R.)
Crowley, Finbarr, Adm
Farnivane, Bandon, Co Cork
Tel 023-8820861
(*Murragh and
Templemartin*, Cork & R.)
Crowley, James, Very Rev, PE
Parochial House,
60 Aughnagar Road,
Ballygawley, Dungannon,
Co Tyrone BT70 2HP
Tel 028-85568399
(Armagh, retired)
Crowley, Kevin (OFMCap)
Vicar, Capuchin Friary,
Church Street, Dublin 7
Tel 01-8730599
Crowley, Michael (MSC)
Myross Wood Retreat
House,
Leap, Skibbereen,
Co Cork
Tel 028-33118
Crowley, Michael, Very Rev
Canon, AP
Ballinlough, Cork
Tel 021-4292684
(*Ballinlough*, Cork & R.)
Crowley, Michael, Very Rev
Canon, PE
The Lough Presbytery,
St Finbarr's West, Cork
Tel 021-4322633
(*The Lough*, Cork & R.)
Crowley, Patrick (SSC)
St Columban's,
Grange Road,
Donaghmede, Dublin 13
Tel 01-8476647
Crowley, Roderic (CM)
St Vincent's College,
Castleknock, Dublin 15
Tel 01-8213051
Crudden, James, Very Rev, PP
24 Downs Road, Newcastle,
Co Down BT33 0AG
Tel 028-43722401
(*Newcastle (Maghera)*,
Down & C.)

Cryan, Gerard, BA, HDE, STB, L Eccl Hist
(priest in residence)
St Mary's, Sligo
Tel 071-9162670/9162769
College of the Immaculate Conception,
Summerhill, Sligo
Tel 071-9160311
(Elphin)
Cryan, Peter (OCD)
St Joseph's, Berkeley Road,
Dublin 7
Tel 01-8306356
Cuffe, Bernard (OCD)
The Abbey, Loughrea,
Co Galway
Tel 091-841209
Cuffe, Liam
Chaplain,
St Vincent's Hospital,
Elm Park, Dublin 4
Tel 01-2094325
(Ardagh & Cl.)
Cul, Marek (OP)
St Mary's, The Claddagh,
Co Galway
Tel 091-582884
Culhane, Patrick J., Very Rev
138 Lucan Road,
Chapelizod, Dublin 20
(Dublin, retired)
Cullen, Celestine (OSB), Rt Rev Dom
Glenstal Abbey, Murroe,
Co Limerick
Tel 061-386103
Cullen, John, Very Rev, PP
Kiltoom, Athlone,
Co Roscommon
Tel 090-6489105
(*Kiltoom*, Elphin)
Cullen, Kevin, Very Rev, PP, VF
Parochial House,
Tullinavall Road,
Cullyhanna, Newry,
Co Down BT35 OPZ
Tel 028-30861235
(*Cullyhanna (Creggan Lower)*, Armagh)
Cullen, Laurence, Very Rev, PP
Geevagh, Boyle,
Co Roscommon
Tel 071-9647107
(*Geevagh*, Elphin)
Cullen, Michael, Very Rev, PP
The Presbytery,
Church Grounds,
Castleknock, Dublin 15
Tel 01-8379253/8484800
(*Laurel Lodge-Carpenterstown*, Dublin)
Cullen, Seamus
2 Ceol Na Mara,
Lower Main Street,
Rush, Co Dublin
Tel 01-8438024
(Dublin, retired)

Culligan, Patrick, Very Rev
Carrigaholt, Co Clare
Tel 065-9058043/087-9863865
(*Carrigaholt and Cross*, Killaloe)
Cullinan, Alphonsus
Lower Main Street,
Rathkeale, Co Limerick
Tel 061-63133
(*Rathkeale*, Limerick)
Cullinan, Edmond, Very Rev, PP, VF
Parochial House,
Chapel Street,
Carrick-on-Suir,
Co Tipperary
Tel 051-640168
(Waterford & L.)
Cullinan, William (OCSO)
Mellifont Abbey,
Collon, Co Louth
Tel 041-9826103
Cullinane, Michael, Very Rev, PP, VF
Parochial House, Lismore,
Co Waterford
Tel 058-54246
(*Lismore*, Waterford & L.)
Cullinane, Timothy (MSC)
Myross Wood Retreat House,
Leap, Skibbereen,
Co Cork
Tel 028-33118
Culliton, James (SJ)
St Francis Xavier's,
Upper Gardiner Street,
Dublin 1
Tel 01-8363411
Cully, Patrick (CSSp)
Holy Spirit Missionary College,
Kimmage Manor,
Dublin 12
Tel 01-4064300
Cumiskey, Bonaventure (OCSO)
Mount Melleray Abbey,
Cappoquin, Co Waterford
Tel 058-54404
Cumiskey, Cathal (CSsR)
St Joseph's, Dundalk,
Co Louth
Tel 042-9334042/9334762
Cummings, Daniel
30 Knapton Road,
Dun Laoghaire, Co Dublin
Tel 01-2804353
(Opus Dei)
Cummins, John, Adm
The Presbytery,
Dublin Road, Carlow
Tel 059-9131227
(Kildare & L.)
Cummins, Stephen (OP)
St Dominic's Retreat House,
Montenotte, Co Cork
Tel 021-4502520

Cummins, William, Very Rev Canon, PP
Mervue, Galway
Tel 091-751721
(*Mervue*, Galway)
Cunnane, Fergal, PP, VF
Dunmore, Co Galway
Tel 093-38124
(*Dunmore*, Tuam)
Cunnane, Seamus, Very Rev
Grove House, Tuam,
Co Galway
(Tuam)
Cunning, Patrick (CSsR), CC
Clonard Monastery,
1 Clonard Gardens,
Belfast BT13 2RL
Tel 028-90445950
Cunningham, Charles (SDB)
Rinaldi House,
72 Sean McDermott Street,
Dublin 1
Tel 01-8363358
Cunningham, Colm (CSSp)
Rockwell College, Cashel,
Co Tipperary
Tel 062-61444
Cunningham, Connell, Very Rev, PE
Carrick, Co Donegal
(Raphoe, retired)
Cunningham, Conor, PP,VF
The Rectory, Lisdoonvarna,
Co Clare
Tel 065-7074142
(Galway)
Cunningham, Donal, Very Rev, PP
Parochial House,
Upperchurch, Thurles,
Co Tipperary
Tel 0504-54181
(*Upperchurch*, Cashel & E.)
Cunningham, Enda, Very Rev, PP
St Mary's Parochial House,
Saggart, Co Dublin
Tel 01-4589209
(*Saggart*, Dublin)
Cunningham, Gerald (IC)
Clonturk House,
Ormond Road,
Drumcondra, Dublin 9
Tel 01-6877014
Cunningham, Gerard, CC
Fintown, Donegal Town,
Co Donegal
Tel 074-9546107
(*Glenties*, Raphoe)
Cunningham, John Joe, Very Rev
Newcastle, Co Down
(Dromore, retired)
Cunningham, Joseph (CM), Very Rev
Phibsboro, St Peter's,
Dublin 7
Tel 01-8389708/8389841

Cunningham, Joseph, Very Rev Canon
Our Lady's Home,
68 Ardnava Road,
Belfast BT12 6FF
(Down & C., retired)
Cunningham, Martin
c/o Diocesan Office,
Letterkenny, Co Donegal
(Raphoe)
Cunningham, Matthew, Very Rev, AP
Grangemockler,
Carrick-on-Suir,
Co Tipperary
Tel 051-647011
(*Ballyneale and Grangemockler*, Waterford & L.)
Cunningham, PJ (OCarm)
Gort Muire, Ballinteer,
Dublin 16
Tel 01-2984014
Cunningham, Seán
The Presbytery, Tuam,
Co Galway
Tel 093-24250
(Tuam)
Cunningham, Sean (OP)
Holy Cross, Sligo, Co Sligo
Tel 071-9142700
Cunningham, Tom (CSSp)
Rockwell College,
Cashel, Co Tipperary
Tel 062-61444
Curran, Adrian (OFMCap)
Provincial Office,
12 Halston Street, Dublin 7
Tel 01-8733205
Curran, Anthony, Very Rev, PP, VF
Parochial House,
8 Minorca Place,
Carrickfergus,
Co Antrim BT38 8AU
Tel 028-93363269
(*Carrickfergus*, Down & C.)
Curran, Colum, Very Rev, PP
4 Irish Street, Killyleagh,
Co Down BT30 9QS
Tel 028-44828211
(*Killyleagh*, Down & C.)
Curran, Eugene (CM), Very Rev
All Hallows Institute for Mission and Ministry,
Drumcondra, Dublin 9
Tel 01-8373745/6
Curran, James
61 Tournane Court,
Dungarvan, Co Waterford
Tel 058-45177
(Waterford & L., retired)
Curran, Matthew (OSA)
St Augustine's,
Taylor's Lane,
Balyboden, Dublin 16
Tel 01-4241000

Curran, Michael (MSC)
Leader & Director,
Myross Wood Retreat House,
Leap, Skibbereen,
Co Cork
Tel 028-33118
Parish House, Union Hall,
Skibbereen, Co Cork
Tel 028-34940
(*Castlehaven*, Cork & R.)
Curran, Philip, Very Rev, PP
Presbytery No. 1,
Treepark Road,
Kilnamanagh, Tallaght,
Dublin 24
Tel 01-8378552/086-2408188
(*Kilnamanagh*, Dublin)
Curran, Roddy (CSSp), CC
104 St Joseph's Road,
Greenhills, Dublin 12
Tel 01-4509191
(*Greenhills*, Dublin)
Curran, Thomas
Glenview House,
College Road, Letterkenny,
Co Donegal
Tel 074-9127617
(Raphoe, retired)
Currivan, Patrick, Very Rev, AP
Caherconlish, Co Limerick
Tel 061-351248
(*Caherconlish*, Cashel & E.)
Curry, Colum, Rt Rev Dean, PP, VG
Parochial House,
4 Circular Road,
Dungannon,
Co Tyrone BT71 6BE
Tel 028-87722775
(Armagh)
Curry, Martin (SJ)
Dominic Collins' House Residence,
129 Morehampton Road,
Dublin 4
Tel 01-2693075
Curry, William (SSC)
(priest in charge)
St Columban's,
67-68 Castle Dawson,
Rathcoffey Road,
Maynooth, Co Kildare
Tel 01-6286036
Curtin, Cornelius (CM)
St Paul's College, Raheny,
Dublin 5
Tel 01-8314011/2
Curtin, Tim
Chaplain,
Coláiste Na Trócaire,
Rathkeale,
Co Limerick
Tel 069-63432
(Limerick)
Curtis, James B., Very Rev Canon
Rathjarney, Drinagh,
Co Wexford
(Ferns, retired)
Curtis, James, Very Rev
3 Oldtown Court,
Clongreen, Foulksmills,
New Ross, Co Wexford
(Ferns, retired)
Curtis, Thomas, Very Rev Canon
2 The Hollows, Lugduff,
Tinahely, Co Wicklow
(Ferns, retired)
Cusack, Gerard (OPraem), Rt Rev
Prior,
Abbey of the Most Holy Trinity and St Norbert,
Kilnacrott,
Ballyjamesduff, Co Cavan
Tel 049-8544416
Cusack, John, Very Rev, PP
Virginia, Co Cavan
Tel 049-8547063
(*Virginia*, Kilmore)
Cusack, Michael (CSsR) Adm
St Joseph's,
St Alphonsus Road,
Dundalk, Co Louth
Tel 042-9334042
(*Dundalk, St Joseph's*, Armagh)
Cusack, Ronan (OP), Very Rev
St Malachy's, Dundalk,
Co Louth
Tel 042-9334179
Cushen, Bernard, Very Rev, PP
Ramsgrange,
New Ross, Co Wexford
Tel 051-389148
(*Ramsgrange*, Ferns)
Cushen, Patrick, Very Rev, PP, VF
Ferns, Enniscorthy,
Co Wexford
Tel 053-9366152
(*Ferns*, Ferns)
Cushenan, Jarlath, Very Rev, PP
17 Castlewellan Road,
Hilltown, Newry BT34 5UY
Tel 028-40630206
(Dromore)
Cushnahan, Vincent, CC
The Presbytery,
Bell Steel Road, Poleglass,
Belfast BT17 0PB
Tel 028-90625739
(*The Nativity*, Down & C.)
Cushnan, Martin (CSsR)
R.C.M., Chenchupet, Tenali,
A.P., India 522 202
Tel +91-8644-223-382
Cussen, Joseph, CC
Glenfield Road, Killmallock,
Co Limerick
Tel 063-98061
(*Kilmallock*, Limerick)
Cussen, Michael, Very Rev, PP, VF
Fedamore, Kilmallock,
Co Limerick
Tel 061-390112/087-1279015
(*Fedamore*, Limerick)

## D

D'Arcy, Aidan, CC
2 Knightswood,
Coolock Lane, Santry,
Dublin 9
Tel 01-8428283
(*Larkhill-Whitehall-Santry*, Dublin)
D'Arcy, Brian (CP)
Superior,
St Gabriel's Retreat,
The Graan, Enniskillen,
Co Fermanagh
Tel 028-66322272
D'Arcy, Paul A. (SMA)
Provincial Secretary,
African Missions,
Blackrock Road, Cork
Tel 021-4292871
D'Souza, Darryl (SDB)
Salesian House,
45 St Teresa's Road,
Crumlin, Dublin 12
Tel 01-4555605
(India)
Dabrowski, Mariusz, CC
470 Falls Road,
Belfast BT12 6EN
Tel 028-90321102
(*St John's*, Down & C.)
Daffy, Denis Flannan (CSsR)
Marianella, 75 Orwell Road,
Rathgar, Dublin 6
Tel 01-4067100
Dagens, Seamus, Very Rev, PP
Ballintra, Co Donegal
Tel 074-9734016
(*Ballintra*, Raphoe)
Dallat, Ciaran, Very Rev, PP
Sacred Heart Presbytery,
1 Glenview Street,
Belfast BT14 7DP
Tel 028-90351851
(*Sacred Heart*, Down & C.)
Dalton, John (OFM)
Franciscan House of Studies,
Dún Mhuire, Seafield Road,
Killiney, Co Dublin
Tel 01-2826760
Dalton, Patrick, Very Rev Canon, PP
Gowran, Co Kilkenny
Tel 056-7726128/
086-8283478
(Ossory)
Dalton, Thomas, Very Rev, PP
Rathangan, Duncormick,
Co Wexford
Tel 051-563104
(*Rathangan and Cleariestown*, Ferns)
Dalton, William, Very Rev, PP
Callan, Co Kilkenny
Tel 056-7725287/
086-8506215
(*Callan*, Ossory)
Daly, Brian, Very Rev, PP, VF
Parochial House,
15 Moyle Road, Ballycastle,
Co Antrim BT54 6LB
Tel 028-20762223
(*Ballycastle (Ramoan),* Down & C.)
Daly, Daniel (SVD)
Maynooth, Co Kildare
Tel 01-6286391/2
Daly, Edmond, Very Rev, AP
Mount Bolus, Tullamore,
Co Offaly
Tel 057-9354035
(*Kilcormac*, Meath)
Daly, Edward, Most Rev, DD
Retired Bishop of Derry,
9 Steelstown Road,
Derry BT48 8EU
Tel 028-71359809
(Derry)
Daly, Gabriel (OSA)
St Augustine's,
Taylor's Lane,
Balyboden, Dublin 16
Tel 01-4241000
Daly, Hugh M., Very Rev, PE
50 Cremore Road,
Glasnevin, Dublin 11
Tel 01-8341598
(Dublin, retired)
Daly, James (CSSp)
Holy Spirit Missionary College,
Kimmage Manor,
Whitehall Road,
Dublin 12
Tel 01-4064300
Daly, John, Very Rev, PP
St Mochta's, Porterstown,
Dublin 15
Tel 01-8213218
(*Porterstown-Clonsilla*, Dublin)
Daly, John, Very Rev, PP
St Nicholas' Presbytery,
Westbury, Limerick
Tel 061-340614/087-8180815
(*St Nicholas*, Limerick)
Daly, Kevin (OCSO), Dom
Abbot Emeritus,
Mount Saint Joseph Abbey,
Roscrea, Co Tipperary
Tel 0505-25600

Daly, Martin (SM)
Superior,
Catholic University School,
89 Lower Leeson Street,
Dublin 2
Tel 01-6762586

Daly, Martin J., Very Rev, PP,
Parochial House,
Chapelizod, Dublin 20
Tel 01-2832302
(*Chapelizod*, Dublin)

Daly, Michael V., Very Rev, PE
35 Herbert Place, Navan,
Co Meath
Tel 046-9093935
(Meath, retired)

Daly, Michael, Very Rev, PP
Broomfield, Castleblayney,
Co Monaghan
Tel 042-9743617
(*Donaghmoyne*, Clogher)

Daly, Noel (SSC)
St Columban's, Dalgan Park,
Navan, Co Meath
Tel 046-9021525

Daly, Pádraig (OSA), Very Rev, PP
St Augustine's,
Taylor's Lane, Ballyboden,
Dublin 16
Tel 01-4944966
(*Ballyboden*, Dublin)

Daly, Patrick, Very Rev, PP
Cooleragh, Coill Dubh,
Naas, Co Kildare
Tel 045-860281
(*Cooleragh and Staplestown*, Kildare & L.)

Daly, Peter (OMI), CC
The Presbytery, Darndale,
Dublin 17
Tel 01-8474547
(*Darndale-Belcamp*, Dublin)

Daly, Philip, CC
Kilclooney, Co Donegal
Tel 074-9545114
(*Ardara*, Raphoe)

Daly, Thomas, Very Rev, PP
Parochial House,
Boicetown, Togher,
Drogheda, Co Louth
Tel 041-6852110
(*Togher*, Armagh)

Dalzell, Tony (SM)
St Teresa's, Donore Avenue,
Dublin 8
Tel 01-4542425/4531613
(*Donore Avenue, St Teresa's*, Dublin)

Danaher, Michael (OSA)
St Augustine's Priory,
O'Connell Street,
Limerick
Tel 061-415374

Daniels, Iomar
Chaplaincy Department,
NUIG, St Declan's,
Distillery Road, Galway
Tel 091-492168
(Clonfert)

Darby, Derek, CC
54 Brookville, Ashbourne,
Co Meath
Tel 01-8350547
(*Ashbourne-Donaghmore*, Meath)

Darby, Gary (OS Cam), CC
41 Grangemore Grove,
Donaghmede, Dublin 13
Tel 01-8301122/8032000/8032293/8032411
(*Donaghmede*, Dublin)

Darcy, Michael (SMA)
African Missions,
Blackrock Road, Cork
Tel 021-4292871

Darcy, Stephen (CSSp)
Holy Spirit Missionary College,
Kimmage Manor,
Dublin 12
Tel 01-4064300

Dardis, John (SJ)
c/o Irish Jesuit Provincialate,
Milltown Park,
Sandford Road, Dublin 6
Tel 01-4987333

Dargan, Joseph (SJ)
Rector, Manresa House,
Dollymount, Dublin 3
Tel 01-8331352

Dargan, Neil, Very Rev, PP
Presbytery No. 4,
Dunmanus Road,
Cabra West, Dublin 7
Tel 01-8380181
(*Cabra West*, Dublin)

Darragh, Anthony (CSSp)
Holy Spirit Missionary College,
Kimmage Manor,
Dublin 12
Tel 01-4064300

Darragh, Vincent, Very Rev, PE
81 Mullinahoe Road,
Ardboe, Dungannon,
Co Tyrone BT71 5AU
Tel 028-86735774
(Armagh)

Daukszewicz, Tomasz
Polish Chaplain,
Cathedral Presbytery,
O'Connell Street,
Ennis, Co Clare
Tel 065-6824043/087-0515788
(*Ennis*, Killaloe)

Davern, Richard, CC
17 Alderwood Avenue,
Caherdavin Heights,
Limerick
Tel 061-453226
(*Christ the King*, Limerick)

Davey, Gerard, CC
Foxford, Co Mayo
Tel 094-9256401
(*Foxford*, Achonry)

David, Irenus (SJ) (MAS)
John Sullivan House,
56/56A Mulvey Park,
Dundrum, Dublin 14
Tel 01-2983978

David, Kelly (OSA)
St Augustine's,
Taylor's Lane,
Balyboden, Dublin 16
Tel 01-4241000

Davies, Anthony, Very Rev Canon
Killowen, Rostrevor
(Dromore, retired)

Davies, Dean A.,
42 Old Killowen Road,
Rosstrevor,
Co Down BT34 3AD

Davis, Hugh (OFMCap)
St Francis Capuchin Friary,
Rochestown, Co Cork
Tel 021-4896244

Davis, Patrick (SJ)
Peter Faber House,
28 Brookvale Avenue,
Belfast BT14 6BW
Tel 028-90757615

Davitt, Norman (SVD)
Donamon Castle,
Roscommon
Tel 090-6662222

Davitt, Thomas (CM)
St Joseph's,
44 Stillorgan Park,
Blackrock, Co Dublin
Tel 01-2886961

Davy, Charles (SJ)
St Ignatius Community & Church,
27 Raleigh Row,
Salthill, Galway
Tel 091-523707

Dawson, Laurence, Very Rev Canon, PP
Clogher,
Co Tyrone BT76 0TQ
Tel 028-85548600
(*Clogher*, Clogher)

de Bhaldraithe, Eoin (OCSO)
Guestmaster, Bolton Abbey,
Moone, Co Kildare
Tel 059-8624102

de Burca, Peadar, Very Rev
Kilmeedy, Co Limerick
Tel 063-87008
(Limerick, retired)

De Lima, Eridian Goncalves (CSsR)
Missionaries Redentoristas,
Caixa Postal 85,
60,000-970 Fortaleza,
Est. do Ceara, Brazil
Tel +55-8532232016

De Val, Seamus, Very Rev Canon
1 Irish Street, Bunclody,
Co Wexford
Tel 053-9376140
(Ferns, retired)

Deane, Philip (OFM)
Franciscan Friary,
Liberty Street, Cork
Tel 021-4270302

Deasy, Declan (OSA)
St Patrick's College and Church,
Via Piemonte 60,
00187 Rome, Italy
Tel 00396-4203121

Deasy, John F., Very Rev Mgr,
(Team Assistant)
55 St Agnes' Road, Crumlin,
Dublin 12
Tel 01-4550955
(*Crumlin*, Dublin)

Deegan, Gerard PP
Presbytery, Montrose Park,
Beaumont, Dublin 5
Tel 01-8473209
(*Beaumont*, Dublin)

Deegan, Joseph, Very Rev, PP
Parochial House, Slane,
Co Meath
Tel 041-9824249
(*Slane*, Meath)

Deegan, Stan, Very Rev, PP
Parochial House,
Batterstown,
Dunboyne, Co Westmeath
Tel 01-8259267
(*Kilcloon*, Meath)

Deely, Pat
Dunkerrin, Birr, Co Offaly
Tel 0505-45982/087-6329913
(*Dunkerrin*, Killaloe)

Deeney, Edward (SMA)
Dromantine College,
Dromantine, Newry,
Co Down BT34 1RH
Tel 028-30821224

Deenihan, Thomas
Cork & Ross Offices,
Redemption Road, Cork
Tel 021-4301717
(Cork & R.)

Deery, Cathal, CC
Emyvale, Monaghan
Tel 047-87221
(*Donagh*, Clogher)

Deighan, Gerard, Very Rev, CC
The Presbytery,
Harrington Street,
Dublin 8
Tel 01-2107858
(*Harrington Street*, Dublin)

Delahunty, Richard (CSsR), Very Rev, PP
The Presbytery,
197 Kylemore Road,
Ballyfermot, Dublin 10
Tel 01-6264789

Delaney, Denis M., Very Rev
(*Moderator*)
Parochial House, The Naul,
Co Dublin
Tel 01-8401514
(*Naul*, Dublin)

Delaney, Joe
Chaplain's Office, Galway Clinic, Doughiska, Galway
Tel 091-785000
(Galway)

Delaney, John, CC
Coon, Carlow
Tel 056-4443116/ 086-8596321
(*Muckalee*, Ossory)

Delaney, John, Very Rev, PP
Parochial House, Kilrossanty, Kilmacthomas, Co Waterford
Tel 051-291985
(*Kilrossanty*, Waterford & L.)

Delaney, John, Very Rev, PP
137 Ballymun Road, Dublin 9
Tel 01-8376347
(Dublin)

Delaney, Joseph, Very Rev
St Kieran's College, Kilkenny
Tel 056-7721086/ 086-8206730
(Ossory, retired)

Delaney, Joseph, Very Rev, PP
Clonbealy, Newport, Co Tipperary
Tel 061-378126
(*Newport*, Cashel & E.)

Delaney, Martin, Very Rev, Adm
Mooncoin, Co Kilkenny
Tel 086-2444594
(*Mooncoin*, Ossory)

Delany, John, Very Rev, Adm
24 Barclay Court, Blackrock, Co Dublin
Tel 01-8375440
(*Blackrock*, Dublin)

Delargy, David, Very Rev, PP
Parochial House, 23 Hannahstown Hill, Belfast BT17 0LT
Tel 028-90614567
(*Hannahstown*, Down & C.)

Delargy, Patrick, Very Rev, PP, VF
Parochial House, 4 Broughshane Road, Ballymena, Co Antrim BT43 7DX
Tel 028-25641515
(*Ballymena (Kirkinriola)*, Down & C.)

Delimat, Piotr, CC
Our Lady of Lourdes Presbytery, Hardman's Gardens, Drogheda, Co Louth
Tel 041-9831899
(*Drogheda*, Armagh)

Dempsey, Luke (OP)
Dominican Community, St Mary's Priory, Tallaght, Dublin 24
Tel 01-4048100

Dempsey, Michael (CSsR)
St Joseph's, Dundalk, Co Louth
Tel 042-9334042/9334762

Dempsey, Michael Vincent, Very Rev, PP
The Presbytery, Barndarrig, Co Wicklow
Tel 0404-48130
(*Kilbride and Barndarrig*, Dublin)

Dempsey, Paul
Two-Mile-House, Naas, Co Kildare
Tel 045-876160
(*Naas*, Kildare & L.)

Dempsey, Raymond, CC
Ferrybank, Waterford
Tel 051-832577/087-2859682
(*Ferrybank*, Ossory)

Deneke, Yohannes (SDB)
Rinaldi House, 72 Sean McDermott Street, Dublin 1
Tel 01-8363358

Denmead, James, CC
Ballylooby, Cahir, Co Tipperary
Tel 052-7441489
(*Ballylooby*, Waterford & L.)

Dennehy, Philip, PE
4 Stanhope Place, Athy, Co Kildare
Tel 059-8631696
(Dublin, retired)

Denny, Aidan, Very Rev
10 New Barnsley Green, New Barnsley, Belfast BT12 7HS
Tel 028-90328877
(*Corpus Christi*, Down & C.)

Dermody, Eamonn, Very Rev Canon, PE
Clarinbridge, Co Galway
Tel 091-796208
(Galway, retired)

Derry, Cathal, CC
Scotshouse, Clones, Co Monaghan
Tel 047-56016
(Clogher)

Desmond, Bartholomew, CC
Carriganimma, Macroom, Co Cork
Tel 026-44027
(*Clondrohid*, Cloyne)

Desmond, Con
c/o Westbourne, Ennis, Co Clare
(Killaloe, retired)

Desmond, Diarmuid, Very Rev, PP
Kilrane, Co Wexford
Tel 053-9133128
(*Kilrane and St Patrick's*, Ferns)

Desmond, Garrett, Very Rev, PP
Newcastle, Clonmel, Co Tipperary
Tel 052-6136387
(*Newcastle and Fourmilewater*, Waterford & L.)

Desmond, Patrick
The Lodge, Mount Sackville, Chapelizod, Dublin 20
Tel 01-8214004
(Dublin)

Devaney, Owen, Very Rev, PP
Mullahoran, Kilcogy via Longford, Co Cavan
Tel 043-6683141
(*Mullahoran and Loughduff*, Ardagh & Cl.)

Deveney, Cathal, CC
Parochial House, 3 Convent Road, Cookstown, Co Tyrone BT80 8QA
Tel 028-86763293
(Armagh)

Devenish, Martin (MCCJ)
Provincial, Comboni Missionaries
London Road, Sunningdal, Berks Sl5 OJY, UK

Devereux, Sean
6 Meadowvale, Coolcotts, Wexford
Tel 053-9143932
(*Clonard*, Ferns)

Devine, Arthur, Very Rev, PE
Rathbawn Road, Castlebar, Co Mayo
(Tuam, retired)

Devine, Liam, Very Rev Canon, PP, VF
SS Peter and Paul, Athlone
Tel 090-6492171
(Elphin)

Devine, Oliver J., Very Rev, PP
Parochial House, Mountnugent, Co Cavan
Tel 049-8540123
(*Mountnugent*, Meath)

Devine, Oliver, Very Rev, PP
Parochial House, Ballivor, Co Meath
Tel 046-9546488
(*Ballivor*, Meath)

Devine, Robert
(priest in residence)
Crossroads, Killygordon, Co Donegal
Tel 074-9149194
(*Killygordon*, Derry)

Devitt, Dan (SDB)
Mission Procurator, Salesian College, Pallaskenry, Co Limerick
Tel 061-393313

Devitt, Patrick, Adm
No. 1 Prebytery, Castle Street, Dalkey, Co Dublin
Tel 01-8373869
(*Dalkey*, Dublin)

Devitt, Séamus (CSsR)
St Patrick's, Esker, Co Galway
Tel 091-844549

Devlin, Anthony, Very Rev, PP
St Paul's Presbytery, 125 Falls Road, Belfast BT12 6AB
Tel 028-90325034
(*St Paul's*, Down & C.)

Devlin, Brendan, Rt Rev Mgr, MA, DD
St Patrick's College, Maynooth, Co Kildare
Tel 01-6285222
(Derry)

Devlin, Eamon (CM), Co-PP
St Peter's, Phibsboro, Dublin 7
Tel 01-8389708
(*Phibsboro*, Dublin)

Devlin, Kieran, PE
Colon House, 21 Buncrana Road, Derry BY48 8LA
(Derry, retired)

Devlin, Patrick, PP
St Vincent de Paul Presbytery, 169 Ligoniel Road, Belfast BT14 8DP
Tel 028-90713401
(*St Vincent de Paul*, Down & C.)

Devlin, Peter, PP
Parochial House, Malin, Co Donegal
Tel 074-9142022
(Derry)

Diamond, Mark, Very Rev Canon
Cathedral Close, Ballina, Co Mayo
(Killala, retired)

Diffley, Vincent (SDB)
Salesian House, Milford, Castletroy, Limerick
Tel 061-330268/330914

Diggin, Fintan, PP
Parochial House, Cleagh, Clonmany, Co Donegal
Tel 074-9376264
(*Clonmany*, Derry)

Dillon, Christopher (OSB), Rt Rev Dom
Glenstal Abbey, Murroe, Co Limerick
Tel 061-386103

Dillon, Sean (SPS)
St Patrick's, Kiltegan, Co Wicklow
Tel 059-6473600

Dillon, Sean, Very Rev, PP
Parochial House,
59 Chapel Road,
Glenavy, Crumlin,
Co Antrim BT29 4LY
Tel 028-294422262
(*Glenavy and Killead*, Down and C.)

Dillon, Thomas, Very Rev, PP
Baltinglass, Co Wicklow
Tel 059-6482768
(*Baltinglass*, Kildare & L.)

Dineen, Joseph (OP)
St Saviour's,
Upper Dorset Street,
Dublin 1
Tel 01-8897610

Dobbin, Séamus, CC
St Patrick's Presbytery,
Roden Place, Dundalk,
Co Louth
Tel 042-9334648
(*Dundalk, St Patrick's*, Armagh)

Doherty, Brendan, PP
4 Garvagh Road, Kilrea,
Co Derry BT51 5QP
Tel 028-29540343
(*Kilrea*, Derry)

Doherty, Cathal (SJ)
Irish Jesuit Provincialate,
Milltown Park,
Sandford Road, Dublin 6
Tel 01-4987333

Doherty, George, CC
Glebe, Linsfort, Buncrana,
Co Donegal
Tel 074-9361126
(*Buncrana*, Derry)

Doherty, John (CSsR)
Clonard Monastery,
1 Clonard Gardens,
Belfast BT13 2RL
Tel 028-90445950

Doherty, John, PP
Parochial House,
447 Victoria Road,
Ballymagorry, Strabane,
Co Tyrone BT82 0AT
Tel 028-718802274
(Derry, retired)

Doherty, John, Rt Rev Mgr
(priest in residence),
Charlestown, Co Mayo
Tel 094-9255793
(Achonry, retired)

Doherty, Joseph, PEm
Clarcarricknagun,
Donegal Town,
Co Donegal
Tel 073-21259
(Derry, retired)

Doherty, Kevin, CC
Parochial House, Celbridge,
Co Kildare
Tel 01-6288827
(*Celbridge*, Dublin)

Doherty, Michael, PP
39 Melmount Road,
Strabane,
Co Tyrone, BT82 9EF
Tel 028-71882648
(*Melmount*, Derry)

Doherty, Patrick, Very Rev, PP
159 Glen Road,
Maghera, Co Derry BT46 5JN
Tel 028-79645496
(*Maghera*, Derry)

Doherty, Richard, Very Rev, AP
Abbeyside, Dungarvan,
Co Waterford
Tel 058-42379
(*Abbeyside*, Waterford & L.)

Doherty, Sean (SSC)
St Columban's, Dalgan Park,
Navan, Co Meath
Tel 046-9021525

Dolan, Andrew, PP
25 Ballynease Road,
Bellaghy, Magherafelt,
Co Derry BT45 8JS
Tel 028-79386259
(*Bellaghy (Ballyscullion)*, Derry)

Dolan, Denis, Very Rev, PP
Fivemiletown,
Co Tyrone BT75 OQP
Tel 028-89521291
(*Brookeboro*, Clogher)

Dolan, Gerard, Rt Rev Mgr, PP, VG
St Columba's, Rosses Point,
Co Sligo
Tel 071-9177133
Diocesan Secretary,
St Mary's, Sligo
Tel 071-9162670/9162769
(Elphin)

Dolan, James (MHM)
St Joseph's House,
50 Orwell Park, Rathgar,
Dublin 6
Tel 01-4127700

Dolan, John, Rt Rev Mgr, LCL
The Chancellery,
Archbishop's House,
Dublin 9
Tel 01-8379253
(Dublin)

Dolan, Joseph (SSC)
St Columban's, Dalgan Park,
Navan, Co Meath
Tel 046-9021525

Dolan, Martin, Adm
The Presbytery,
Francis Street, Dublin 8
Tel 01-4544861
(*Francis Street*, Dublin)

Dollard, James, Very Rev, PP
Conahy, Jenkinstown,
Co Kilkenny
Tel 056-7767657
(*Conahy*, Ossory)

Donaghy, Kevin
(priest in residence)
Parochial House,
86 Maydown Road,
Artasooley, Tullysaran,
Benburb,
Co Armagh BT71 7LN
Tel 028-37548210
Headmaster,
St Patrick's Grammar School,
Armagh
Tel 028-37522018
(Armagh)

Donegan, Gary, Very Rev (CP), PP
Holy Cross Retreat,
432 Crumlin Road,
Ardoyne,
Belfast BT14 7GE
Tel 028-90748231/2
(*Holy Cross*, Down & C.)

Donleavy, James (OP)
St Saviour's,
Glentworth Street,
Limerick
Tel 061-412333

Donlon, Chris, CC
Dromore, Mallow,
Co Cork
Tel 022-21198
(*Glantane*, Cloyne)

Donnellan, David (OCD), PP
St Joseph's, Berkeley Road,
Dublin 7
Tel 01-8306356/8306336
(*Berkeley Road*, Dublin)

Donnellan, Patrick, Very Rev, PP
Islandeady, Castlebar,
Co Mayo
Tel 094-9024125
(*Islandeady*, Tuam)

Donnelly, Brian, Very Rev, PP
Parochial House,
Plumbridge, Omagh,
Co Tyrone, BT79 8EF
Tel 028-81648283
(*Plumbridge (Badoney Upper)*, Derry)

Donnelly, Francis, Rt Rev Archdeacon, PE
64 Meadow Grove, Dundalk,
Co Louth
Tel 042-9353264
(Armagh, retired)

Donnelly, Gerald, Very Rev Canon
Ballygar, Co Galway
(Elphin, retired)

Donnelly, James
(sabbatical leave)
c/o Bother na Naomh
Presbytery,
Thurles, Co Tipperary
(Cashel & E.)

Donnelly, John, Very Rev, AP
Rathcabbin, Roscrea,
Co Tipperary
Tel 057-9139072
(*Lorrha and Dorrha*, Killaloe)

Donnelly, Joseph, Rt Rev Mgr, PP, VF
52 Brook Street, Omagh,
Co Tyrone BT78 5HE
Tel 028-82243011
(*Omagh*, Derry)

Donnelly, Kevin, Venerable Archdeacon
Parochial House,
4 Broughshane Road,
Ballymena,
Co Antrim BT43 7DX
Tel 028-25641515
(*Ballymena (Kirkinriola)*, Down & C.)

Donnelly, Liam, CC
20 Loughermore Road,
Ogill, Ballykelly,
Co Derry BT49 9PD
Tel 028-77762721
(*Limavady*, Derry)

Donnelly, Marius (CP)
St Gabriel's Retreat,
The Graan, Enniskillen,
Co Fermanagh
Tel 028-66322272

Donnelly, Michael, Very Rev, PP
The Presbytery, Castlerea,
Co Roscommon
Tel 094-9620039
(*Castlerea*, Elphin)

Donnelly, Michéal, CC
The Presbytery, Castlerea,
Co Roscommon
Tel 094-9620039
(*Castlerea*, Elphin)

Donnelly, Patrick, CC
Parochial House,
Tullamore, Co Offaly
Tel 057-9321587
(Tullamore, Meath)

Donnelly, Peter, Very Rev, PP, VF
Parochial House,
15 Drumaroad Hill,
Castlewellan,
Co Down BT31 9PD
Tel 028-44811474
(Down & C., on leave)

Donnelly, Peter, Very Rev, PP, VF
Parochial House,
130 Ballinderry Bridge Road,
Coagh, Cookstown,
Co Tyrone BT80 0AY
Tel 028-79418244
(*Ballinderry*, Armagh)

Donnelly, T. Phil, PEm
Nazareth House, Fahan,
Co Donegal
(Derry, retired)

Donnelly, Victor (CP)
St Gabriel's Retreat,
The Graan, Enniskillen,
Co Fermanagh
Tel 028-66322272

Donohoe, Eamon (MSC)
'Croí Nua', Rosary Lane,
Taylor's Hill, Galway
Tel 091-520960

Donohoe, Kevin, Adm
The Presbytery, Cavan
Tel 049-4331404
(Kilmore)

Donohoe, Patrick (SSC)
Columban Sisters,
Magheramore, Co Wicklow

Donohoe, Seamus (OFM)
Franciscan Friary, Ennis,
Co Clare
Tel 065-6828751

Donohoe, Sean (OFMCap)
Guardian, Holy Trinity,
Fr Mathew Quay, Cork
Tel 021-4270827

Donohoe, Steve (SPS)
St Patrick's, Main Street,
Knock, Co Mayo
Tel 094-9388661

Donovan, Bernard, Very Rev, PP
Cloughdubh, Crookstown,
Co Cork
Tel 021-7336054
(*Kilmurry*, Cork & R.)

Donovan, Roy, PP
Caherconlish, Co Limerick
Tel 061-450730
(Cashel & E.)

Donworth, John, Very Rev, PP
Kildimo, Co Limerick
Tel 061-394134/087-2237501
(*Kildimo and Pallaskenry*, Limerick)

Doocey, Colin, CC
The Presbytery,
Frankfield, Cork
Tel 021-4362377
(*Frankfield-Grange*, Cork & R.)

Doody, Patrick (CSSp), Very Rev, PP
66 Rockfield Avenue,
Dublin 12
Tel 01-4558316
(*Kimmage Manor*, Dublin)

Doohan, Martin, Very Rev, PP
Dunfanaghy, Co Donegal
Tel 074-9136163
(*Dunfanaghy*, Raphoe)

Dooher, Patrick G. (SSC)
St Columban's, Dalgan Park,
Navan, Co Meath
Tel 046-9021525

Doolan, Herman (OCD)
53/55 Marlborough Road,
Dublin 4
Tel 01-6601832

Dooley, Francis Desmond, Very Rev, PP
The Presbytery, Baldoyle,
Dublin 13
Tel 01-8322060
(*Baldoyle*, Dublin)

Dooley, John (SJ)
Milltown Park,
Sandford Road, Dublin 6
Tel 01-2698411/2698113

Dooley, Maurice, Rt Rev Mgr, AP
Loughmore, Templemore,
Co Tipperary
Tel 0504-31375
(*Loughmore*, Cashel & E.)

Dooley, Seán, PP
Parochial House, Tullyallen,
Co Louth
Tel 041-9838520
(Armagh)

Dooley, Tom (SM), CC
4 Greenmount Road,
Dublin 6
Tel 01-4904959
(*Terenure*, Dublin)

Doona, Jeremiah (MHM)
St Joseph's House,
50 Orwell Park, Rathgar,
Dublin 6
Tel 01-4127700

Doran, Dermot (CSSp)
Holy Spirit Missionary College,
Kimmage Manor,
Whitehall Road, Dublin 12
Tel 01-4064300

Doran, Fonsie (CSsR)
Clonard Monastery,
1 Clonard Gardens,
Belfast BT13 2RL
Tel 028-90445950

Doran, John (OSA)
St Augustine's,
Taylor's Lane,
Balyboden, Dublin 16
Tel 01-4241000

Doran, Joseph, CC
The Presbytery, Brittas Bay,
Co Wicklow
(*Kilbride and Barndarrig*, Dublin)

Doran, Kevin, PC
IEC General Secretary,
c/o International Eucharistic Congress 2012,
Sandymount, Co Dublin
Tel 0404-45140
(*Marino*, Dublin)

Dorgan, Michael, Very Rev, PP
Castlemagner, Mallow,
Co Cork
Tel 022-27600
(*Castlemagner*, Cloyne)

Dorr, Donal (SPS)
St Patrick's, 21 Leeson Park,
Dublin 6
Tel 01-4977897

Dougherty, Ciarán (OP)
(studying in USA)
St Malachy's, Dundalk,
Co Louth
Tel 042-9334179/9333714

Dowd, Eugene, Canon
51 Drumnavanagh,
Farnham Road, Cavan
Tel 049-4326821
(Kilmore, retired)

Dowd, G. (SDB)
Chaplain, Custume Barracks,
Athlone
Tel 0902-21277

Dowd, Gerard, CF
Chaplain, Custume Barracks,
Athlone, Co Westmeath
Tel 090-6421277
(Elphin)

Dowd, Thomas
Ely University Centre,
10 Hume Street, Dublin 2
Tel 01-6767420
(Opus Dei)

Dowley, Martin (OCSO)
Prior,
Our Lady of Bethlehem Abbey,
11 Ballymena Road,
Portglenone, Ballymena,
Co Antrim BT44 8BL
Tel 028-25821211

Dowling, Cornelius
St Anthony's,
13 Richmond Grove,
Monkstown, Co Dublin
Tel 01-2800789
(Dublin, retired)

Dowling, Patrick, Canon
Holy Family Residence,
Roebuck Road,
Dundrum, Dublin 14
(Dublin)

Dowling, Seán (OSA)
St Augustine's Priory,
Washington Street, Cork
Tel 021-275398
(Cork & R.)

Downes, Edward, CC
Parochial House,
St Joseph's Parish Cross,
Valleymount, Co Wicklow
Tel 01-2826895
(Dublin)

Downes, Frank (OP)
St Dominic's Retreat House,
Montenotte, Co Cork
Tel 021-4502520

Downes, Patrick (CSSp)
Rockwell College, Cashel,
Co Tipperary
Tel 062-61444

Downes, Teddy, CC,
Parochial House, Cross,
Valleymount,
Co Wicklow
Tel 045-867151
(*Valleymount*, Dublin)

Downey, James
Catherine McAuley Home,
Balloonagh, Tralee,
Co Kerry
Tel 066-7129700
(Kerry, retired)

Downey, James (OSA)
St Patrick's College and Church,
Via Piemonte 60,
00187 Rome, Italy
Tel 00396-4203121

Downey, Jim
Fatima Home, Oak Park
Tralee, Co Kerry
(Kerry, retired)

Downey, John, CC
36 Moneyneena Road,
Draperstown, Magherafelt,
Co Derry BT45 7DZ
Tel 028-79628375
(Derry)

Downey, Martin, Very Rev, PP
24 Presentation Road,
Galway
Tel 091-562276
(Galway)

Downing, Mortimer, Very Rev, PP
Ballyhea, Co Cork
Tel 063-81470
(*Ballyhea*, Cloyne)

Doyle, Andrew, Very Rev, PP
Durhamstown, Bohermeen,
Navan, Co Meath
Tel 046-9073805
(*Bohermeen*, Meath)

Doyle, Bernard
Kiltyclogher, Co Leitrim
Tel 071-9854302
(Kilmore, retired)

Doyle, Brian (OP)
St Saviour's,
Upper Dorset Street,
Dublin 1
Tel 01-8897610

Doyle, Declan, PC
56 Foxfield Saint John,
Dublin 5
Tel 01-8144340
(*Kilbarrack-Foxfield*, Dublin)

Doyle, Derek, Co-PP
The Presbytery,
St Thomas the Apostle Parish,
Jobtown, Tallaght,
Dublin 24
Tel 01-2819253
(*Jobstown*, Dublin)

Doyle, Denis, PE, CC
77 Lakelands, Naas,
Co Kildare
Tel 045-897470
(*Naas*, Kildare & L.)

Doyle, Denis, Very Rev, PP
Kilmore, Co Wexford
Tel 053-9135181
(*Kilmore*, Ferns)

Doyle, Desmond G., CC
Chaplain's Residence,
Dublin Airport, Co Dublin
Tel 01-8144340
(*Swords*, Dublin)

Doyle, Gerard, Co-PP
70 Maplewood Road,
Tallaght, Dublin 24
Tel 01-4628336
(*Springfield*, Dublin)

Doyle, James, CC
Monamolin, Gorey,
Co Wexford
Tel 053-9389223
(*Kilmuckridge (Litter)*, Ferns)

Doyle, James, CC
c/o Bishop's House, Carlow
(Kildare & L., retired)

Doyle, John B. (CSSp)
St Mary's College,
Rathmines, Dublin 6
Tel 01-499 5760

Doyle, Martin, CC
1 Clonard Park, Wexford
Tel 053-9147686
(*Clonard*, Ferns)

Doyle, Michael, CC (Tyler, Texas)
Ballyfad, Gorey, Co Wexford
Tel 0402-37124
(*Kilanerin*, Ferns)

Doyle, Noel (SSC)
St Columban's, Dalgan Park,
Navan, Co Meath
Tel 046-9021525

Doyle, Oliver
Diocese of Great Falls,
Billings, Montana, USA
(Ferns)

Doyle, Owen (SSC)
St John of God Brothers,
St Mary's Drumcar,
Dunleer, Co Louth

Doyle, Rossa, CC
Sandyhills,
South Shore Road,
Rush, Co Dublin
Tel 01-8430973
(*Rush*, Dublin)

Doyle, Thaddeus
Shillelagh, Arklow,
Co Wicklow
Tel 053-9429926
(Ferns)

Doyle, Thomas, Very Rev, PP
Craanford, Gorey,
Co Wexford
Tel 053-9428163
(Ferns)

Draper, Anthony, DD
All Hallows College,
Drumcondra, Dublin 9
Tel 01-373745
(Meath)

Drennan, Martin, Most Rev, DD
Bishop of Galway,
Mount Saint Mary's,
Taylor's Hill, Galway
Tel 091-563566
(Galway)

Drennan, Michael (SJ)
Jesuit Curia Community,
Loyola House,
Milltown Park,
Sandford Road, Dublin 6
Tel 01-2180276

Drumm, Eugene (SPS)
On temporary diocesan work

Drumm, Michael
(Team Assistant)
47 Westbury Drive, Lucan,
Co Dublin
Tel 01-8376027/8328396
(*Esker-Doddsboro-Adamstown*, Dublin)

Drumm, Michael, STL
Columba Centre, St Patrick's College, Maynooth
(Elphin)

Drury, Ronan
St Patrick's College,
Maynooth, Co Kildare
Tel 01-6285222
(Meath)

Duddy, Brendan (SJ)
Milltown Park,
Sandford Road, Dublin 6
Tel 01-2698411/2698113

Duddy, Cathal (OFM)
The Abbey, 8 Francis Street,
Galway
Tel 091-562518

Duffy, Aquinas T., Very Rev, PP
22 Wainsfort Park,
Terenure, Dublin 6W
Tel 01-8842592
(*Templeogue*, Dublin)

Duffy, Bernard, Very Rev, PE
St Mary's Nursing Home,
Shantalla Road, Galway
(Galway, retired)

Duffy, Dominic (MSC)
Myross Wood Retreat House,
Leap, Skibbereen,
Co Cork
Tel 028-33118

Duffy, Eddie (SM)
London

Duffy, Eugene, DD
Mary Immaculate College,
South Circular Road,
Limerick
Tel 061-204968
(Achonry)

Duffy, Francis
Bishop's House, Cullies,
Co Cavan
Tel 049-4331496
(Kilmore)

Duffy, Frank (CSSp)
Holy Spirit Missionary College,
Kimmage Manor,
Dublin 12
Tel 01-4064300

Duffy, Hugh (SJ)
Irish Jesuit Provincialate,
Milltown Park,
Sandford Road, Dublin 6
Tel 01-4987333

Duffy, James, Very Rev, VF
Ballinamore, Co Leitrim
Tel 071-9644050
(*Ballinamore*, Kilmore)

Duffy, John Joe, CC
Arranmore Island,
Co Donegal
Tel 074-9520504
Chaplain, Vocational School,
Arranmore Island,
Co Donegal
Tel 074-9521747
(Raphoe)

Duffy, Joseph, Most Rev, DD
Doire na gCraobh,
Monaghan
Tel 047-62725
(Clogher)

Duffy, Kevin, CC
Castleblayney,
Co Monaghan
Tel 042-9740027
(*Castleblayney*, Clogher)

Duffy, Larry (SM)
Rome

Duffy, Larry, Very Rev Canon, PP, VF
Clones, Co Monaghan
Tel 047-51048
(*Clones*, Clogher)

Duffy, Michael (OFMCap)
Vicar, St Anthony's
Capuchin Friary,
43 Dublin Street, Carlow
Tel 059-9142543

Duffy, Michael (SSC)
St Columban's, Dalgan Park,
Navan, Co Meath
Tel 046-9021525

Duffy, Pat (CP)
Provincial, St Paul's Retreat,
Mount Argus, Dublin 6W
Tel 01-4992050

Duffy, Stephen, Very Rev, PP
Parochial House, Fieldstown,
Monasterboice, Drogheda,
Co Louth
Tel 041-9822839
(*Monasterboice*, Armagh)

Duggan, Colm (CSSp)
Holy Spirit Missionary College,
Kimmage Manor, Dublin 12
Tel 01-4064300

Duggan, Frank
Parochial House No. 2,
Bonnybrook, Dublin 17
Tel 01-8485194
(*Bonnybrook*, Dublin)

Duggan, Iain (OFM)
Franciscan Friary,
Liberty Street, Cork
Tel 021-4270302

Duggan, James (OP)
Holy Cross, Tralee,
Co Kerry
Tel 066-7121135/29185

Duggan, James F. (CSSp)
Holy Spirit Missionary College,
Kimmage Manor,
Dublin 12
Tel 01-4064300

Duggan, John
St John and Paul Church,
341 South Main Street,
Coventary RI R102816-5987, USA
(Ossory)

Duggan, John, Very Rev, PP
Castlemahon, Co Limerick
Tel 069-72108/086-2600464
(*Mahoonagh*, Limerick)

Duggan, Michael (CSSp)
St Mary's College,
Rathmines, Dublin 6
Tel 01-499 5760

Duggan, Patrick, Very Rev Canon, PP
Bennetsbridge, Co Kilkenny
Tel 056-7727140/
087-6644858
(*Tullaherin*, Ossory)

Duggan, Seán (CSsR), CC
Most Holy Sacrament Parish,
Cherry Orchard, Dublin 10
Tel 01-6267930

Duhig, Frank, Very Rev Canon, PP, VF
St Ita's Presbytery,
Newcastle West, Co Limerick
Tel 069-62141
(Limerick)

Duignan, Michael, SThD
St Mary's, Sligo, Co Sligo
Tel 071-9162670
(Elphin)

Dullea, Gearóid, Dr
St Patrick's College,
Maynooth, Co Kildare
(Cork & R.)

Dundon, Patrick (CSSp)
Holy Spirit Missionary College,
Kimmage Manor,
Dublin 12
Tel 01-406 4300

Dunican, Nicholas, Very Rev, PE
Knightsbridge Nursing Home, Trim, Co Meath
(Meath, retired)

Dunlea, Philip (CSsR)
Clonard Monastery,
1 Clonard Gardens,
Belfast BT13 2RL
Tel 028-90445950

Dunleavy, John (SMA)
African Missions,
Claregalway, Co Galway
Tel 091-798880
Dunleavy, Michael, Very Rev (OP)
Prior, Convent of SS. Xystus and Clement,
Collegio San Clemente,
Via Labicana 95,
00184 Roma
Tel (39-06) 7740021
Dunne, Aidan, CC
Parochial House,
6 Circular Road,
Dungannon,
Co Tyrone BT71 6BE
Tel 028-87722631
(*Dungannon (Drumglass, Killyman and Tullyniskin)*, Armagh)
Dunne, Bonaventure (OSB)
Glenstal Abbey, Murroe,
Co Limerick
Tel 061-386103
Dunne, Daniel, Very Rev, PP
Tullamoy, Stradbally,
Co Laois
Tel 059-8627123
(*Ballyadams*, Kildare & L.)
Dunne, Edward (OFMCap)
Capuchin Friary,
Ard Mhuire, Creeslough,
Letterkenny, Co Donegal
Tel 074-9138005
Dunne, Edward, Rt Rev Mgr, PE
Ratoath, Co Meath
(Meath, retired)
Dunne, Gerard (OP)
40 Iona Road, Glasnevin,
Dublin 9
Tel 01-8305880/8602790
Dunne, John (SMA)
Vice Provincial,
African Missions,
Provincial House, Feltrim,
Blackrock Road, Cork
Tel 021-4292871
Dunne, Liam (SVD)
(Mission Procurator)
Maynooth, Co Kildare
Tel 01-6286391/2
Dunne, Liam, Very Rev
The Forge, Martin's Lane,
Upper Main Street, Arklow,
Co Wicklow
Tel 0402-32779
(Ossory, retired)
Dunne, Matthew (MHM)
St Joseph's House,
50 Orwell Park, Rathgar,
Dublin 6
Tel 01-4127700
Dunne, Michael (CM)
St Paul's College, Raheny,
Dublin 5
Tel 01-8318113
Dunne, Patrick, PP
Parochial House,
Kilmacrennan,
Co Donegal
Tel 074-9139018
(Raphoe)
Dunne, Paul, CC
60 Grange Park Grove,
Raheny, Dublin 5
Tel 01-4519416/087-6902246
(*Grange Park*, Dublin)
Dunne, Ronal, CC
91 Grange Road, Baldoyle,
Dublin 13
Tel 01-8323046
(*Baldoyle*, Dublin)
Dunne, Sean A. (SSC)
St Columban's Retirement Home,
Dalgan Park, Navan,
Co Meath
Tel 046-9021525
Dunne, Thomas (SDB)
Provincial Secretary,
Salesian House,
45 St Teresa's Road,
Crumlin, Dublin 12
Tel 01-4555605
Dunne, Thomas, CC
Templemore, Co Tipperary
Tel 0504-32890
(Cashel & E.)
Dunning, Brendan (SMA)
SMA House, Claregalway,
Co Galway
Tel 091-798880
Dunny, Patrick, Very Rev
Wood Road,
Graignamanagh,
Co Kilkenny
Tel 059-9724518
(Kildare & L.)
Dunphy, Aengus (OCSO), Rt Rev Dom
Retired Abbot,
Our Lady of Bethlehem Abbey,
11 Ballymena Road,
Portglenone, Ballymena,
Co Antrim BT44 8BL
Tel 028-25821211
Dunphy, John, Adm
30 Wheatfields Close,
Clondalkin, Dublin 22
Tel 01-6263920
(*Rowlagh and Quarryvale*, Dublin)
Dunphy, John, Very Rev, Adm
Graiguecullen, Co Carlow
Tel 059-9141833
(*Graiguecullen*, Kildare & L.)
Dunphy, Laurence, Very Rev Canon
Urlingford, Co Kilkenny
Tel 087-2300849
(Ossory, retired)
Dunphy, Noel, Very Rev, PE, CC
Mountmellick, Co Laois
Tel 057-8624141
(*Mountmellick*, Kildare & L.)
Dunphy, Paul
Two-Mile-House,
Naas, Co Kildare
Tel 045-876160
(*Naas*, Kildare & L.)
Durajcyk, Tadeusz (SVD)
Maynooth, Co Kildare
Tel 01-6286391/2
Durcan, Sean, Venerable Archdeacon
79 The Glebe, Ballina,
Co Mayo
(Killala, retired)
Durkan, John, Very Rev, PP
Killasser, Swinford, Co Mayo
Tel 094-9251431
(*Killasser*, Achonry)
Durrajczyk, Tadeusz
Polish Chaplaincy,
60 College Orchard,
Newbridge, Co Kildare
Tel 086-2354320
(Kildare & L.)
Dwan, Martin (SPS)
St Patrick's, Kiltegan,
Co Wicklow
Tel 059-6473600
Dwan, Sean (SSC)
48 Princess Margaret Road,
Homantin, Kowlon,
Hong Kong SAR
Dwyer, Donal, Very Rev
O'Callaghan's Mills, Co Clare
Tel 065-6835148/ 086-1050090
(Killaloe)
Dwyer, Patrick (SAC)
Pallottine College, Thurles,
Co Tipperary
Tel 0504-21202
Dyer, Malcolm (FDO)
Regional Superior,
c/o Don Orione 8, Rome,
Italy

## E

Earley, Patrick, Rt Rev Mgr, PP, VG
Rathowen, Co Westmeath
Tel 043-6676044
(Ardagh & Cl.)
Early, Brian, Very Rev, PP
Scotstown, Co Monaghan
Tel 047-89204
(Clogher)
Early, Kevin, Very Rev Canon, PP
Frenchpark, Castlerea,
Co Roscommon
Tel 094-9870105
(*Frenchpark*, Elphin)
Early, Thomas
23 Estuary Road, Malahide,
Co Dublin
(Dublin, retired)
Eastwood, Adrian (CM)
99 Cliftonville Road,
Belfast BT14 6JQ
Tel 028-90751771
Echavarria, John (SSP)
Society of St Paul,
Moyglare Road,
Maynooth, Co Kildare
Tel 01-6285933
Edwards, Brian, Co-PP
3 Sweetmount Drive,
Dundrum, Dublin 14
Tel 01-2952869
(*Dundrum*, Dublin)
Egan, Adrian (CSsR)
Superior,
Mount Saint Alphonsus,
Limerick
Tel 061-315099
Egan, Bartholomew (CSSp)
Holy Spirit Missionary College,
Kimmage Manor,
Dublin 12
Tel 01-4064300
Egan, James, Very Rev, PP
Knockavilla, Dundrum,
Co Tipperary
Tel 062-71168
(*Knockavilla*, Cashel & E.)
Egan, John (CSSp)
Holy Spirit Missionary College,
Kimmage Manor,
Dublin 12
Tel 01-4064300
Egan, John (SAC)
Pallotine College, Thurles,
Co Tipperary
Tel 0504-21202
Egan, John, Very Rev, PP
Lattin, Co Tipperary
Tel 062-55240
(*Lattin and Cullen*, Cashel & E.)
Egan, Joseph (SMA)
SMA House,
82 Ranelagh Road,
Ranelagh, Dublin 6
Tel 01-4968162/3
Egan, Joseph, Very Rev, PP
Boherlahan, Cashel,
Co Tipperary
Tel 0504-41114
(*Boherlahan and Dualla*, Cashel & E.)
Egan, Pat (SDB)
Salesian College,
Maynooth Road, Celbridge,
Co Kildare
Tel 01-6275058/60
Egan, Patrick (CSsR)
St Patrick's, Esker, Athenry,
Co Galway
Tel 091-844549

Egan, Ralph (CP), CC
St Paul's Retreat,
Mount Argus, Dublin 6W
Tel 01-4992000

Egan, Seamus (SSC)
St Columban's, Dalgan Park,
Navan, Co Meath
Tel 046-9021525

Egan, Sean, CC
The Presbytery, Loughrea,
Co Galway
Tel 091-841212
(*Loughrea, St Brendan's Cathedral*, Clonfert)

Egan, Thomas F., Very Rev, PP
Clonoulty, Cashel,
Co Tipperary
Tel 0504-42494
(*Clonoulty*, Cashel & E.)

Egan, Tony (OSA)
St John's Priory,
Thomas Street, Dublin 8
Tel 01-6770393

Ekeno, Augustine (SJ) (AOR)
John Sullivan House,
56/56A Mulvey Park,
Dundrum, Dublin 14
Tel 01-2986424

Ekwomadu, Francis Toochukwu (CSSp)
Holy Spirit Missionary College,
Kimmage Manor,
Dublin 12
Tel 01-4064300

Emechebe, Anselm (MSP) CC
Parochial House,
Hale Street, Ardee, Co Louth
Tel 041-6860080
(*Ardee & Collon*, Armagh)

Emerson, Sean, Very Rev, Adm, VF
Parochial House,
3 Oriel Road,
Antrim BT41 4HP
Tel 028-94428016
(*Antrim, St Comgall's and St Joseph's*, Down & C.)

Eneji, Richard (CSSp)
Church of the Holy Spirit,
Greenhills, Dublin 12
Tel 01-4509191
(*Greenhills*, Dublin)

English, Jim (SPS)
St Patrick's, Kiltegan,
Co Wicklow
Tel 059-6473600

English, Lawrence (MHM)
St Joseph's House,
50 Orwell Park, Rathgar,
Dublin 6
Tel 01-4127700

English, Mark, CC
2 Orchard Court, Dunboyne,
Co Meath
Tel 01-8255342
(*Dunboyne*, Meath)

Ennis, John, CC
1 Maypark Road, Dublin 5
Tel 01-459 9018
(*Donnycarney*, Dublin)

Enright, Ciarán
Chaplain, Arbour Hill Prison,
Ard na Gaoithe, Arbour Hill,
Dublin 7
Tel 01-6770901
(Dublin)

Enright, Liam
Church Road, Croom,
Co Limerick
Tel 061-315856
(Limerick)

Enright, Liam, Very Rev, PP
Cratloe, Co Clare
Tel 061-357196/087-2546335
(*Cratloe*, Limerick)

Enright, Michael, Very Rev, PE
Priest's Road, Tramore,
Co Waterford
Tel 087-2371546
(Waterford & L., retired)

Enright, Séamus (CSsR)
Mount Saint Alphonsus,
Limerick
Tel 061-315099

Escoto, Albert (SVD)
Praeses, 3 Pembroke Road,
Dublin 4
Tel 01-6680904

Esoy, Renato (SSS)
Blessed Sacrament Chapel,
20 Bachelors Walk,
Dublin 1
Tel 01-8724597

Eustace, Conal, Very Rev Canon, PP, VF
The Parochial House,
Ballinrobe, Co Mayo
Tel 094-9541784
(*Ballinrobe*, Tuam)

Eustace, Louis (CSsR)
St Joseph's, Dundalk,
Co Louth
Tel 042-9334042/9334762

Eustace, Thomas, Very Rev
The Cools, Barntown,
Wexford
(Ferns, retired)

Evans, Ashley (SJ)
Irish Jesuit Provincialate,
Milltown Park,
Sandford Road, Dublin 6
Tel 01-4987333

Evans, Ian
Deputy Assistant,
Chaplain General and Chancellor of the Diocese of the Forces,
England
(Dublin)

Everard, Eugene, Very Rev Canon, PP
Parochial House,
Templemore, Co Tipperary
Tel 0504-31684
(*Templemore*, Cashel & E.)

Everard, Liam, Very Rev, PP
Borrisoleigh, Thurles,
Co Tipperary
Tel 0504-51259
(*Borrisoleigh*, Cashel & E.)

Ezenwegbu, Stephen Ifeanyi, PC
23 Clare Road, Drumcondra,
Dublin 9
Tel 01-8378552
(*Drumcondra*, Dublin)

## F

Fagan, Anthony, Very Rev
Killinkere, Virginia,
Co Cavan
Tel 049-8547307
(Kilmore)

Fagan, Hugh (CSSp)
Holy Spirit Missionary College,
Kimmage Manor, Dublin 12
Tel 01-4064300

Fagan, John (SDB)
Salesian House, Milford,
Castletroy, Limerick
Tel 061-330268/330914

Fagan, Patrick, Very Rev Canon, PE
The Presbytery,
Ballyboughal, Co Dublin
(Dublin, retired)

Fagan, Sean (SM)
Mount St Mary's, Milltown,
Dublin 14
Tel 01-2697322

Faherty, Thomas (SMA)
African Missions,
Blackrock Road, Cork
Tel 021-4292871

Fahey, Brendan (SSC)
St Columban's, Dalgan Park,
Navan, Co Meath
Tel 046-9021525

Fahey, Francis, CC
Ballintubber Abbey,
Claremorris, Co Mayo
Tel 094-9030934
(Tuam)

Fallon, John, Very Rev, PP
Kilmaine, Co Galway
Tel 093-33378
(*Kilmaine*, Tuam)

Fallon, Kevin, Very Rev, PP
Kilglass, Co Roscommon
Tel 071-9638162
(Elphin)

Falloon, Joseph (MSC)
Woodview House,
Mount Merrion Avenue,
Blackrock, Co Dublin
Tel 01-2881644

Farnon, Damian, CC
St Cecilia's, New Road,
Clondalkin,
Dublin 22
Tel 01-4592665
(*Clondalkin*, Dublin)

Farquhar, Anthony, Most Rev, DD
Titular Bishop of Ermiana and Auxiliary Bishop of Down and Connor,
24 Fruithill Park,
Belfast BT11 8GE
Tel 028-90624252
(Down & C.)

Farquharson, Paul (SJ)
Vice-Superior,
St Francis Xavier's,
Upper Gardiner Street,
Dublin 1
Tel 01-8363411

Farragher, John (Seán) P. (CSSp)
Blackrock College,
Blackrock, Co Dublin
Tel 01-2888681

Farragher, Michael, CC
Castlebar, Co Mayo
Tel 094-901253/21844
(*Castlebar (Aglish, Ballyheane and Breaghwy)*, Tuam)

Farragher, Patrick
The Monastery,
Chapel Street,
Castlebar, Co Mayo
Tel 094-9035748
(Tuam)

Farragher, Stephen, Very Rev, PP
Ballyhaunis, Co Mayo
Tel 094-9630006
(Tuam)

Farrell, Andrew, Very Rev, PE
Parochial House, Trim,
Co Meath
Tel 046-9431251
(*Trim*, Meath)

Farrell, Derek, Very Rev, PP
Ministry to the Travelling People,
St Laurence House,
6 New Cabra Road,
Phibsboro, Dublin 7
Tel 01-4628441
(*Travelling People*, Dublin)

Farrell, Dermot, Rt Rev Mgr, PP, VG
Parochial House, Dunboyne,
Co Meath
Tel 01-8255342
(*Dunboyne*, Meath)

Farrell, Fergus
Mater Dei Institute of Education,
Clonliffe Road, Dublin 3
Tel 01-8376027/086-0782066
(Ossory)

Farrell, Fergus, PC
St Laurence O'Toole's Presbytery,
49 Seville Place, Dublin 1
Tel 01-8740796
(North Wall-Seville Place, Dublin)

Farrell, John, PEm
5 Ballyreagh Road, Portrush, Co Antrim
(Derry, retired)

Farrell, Liam, CC
Moate, Co Westmeath
Tel 090-6481189
(*Moate and Mount Temple*, Ardagh & Cl.)

Farrell, Michael, Very Rev, AP
Parochial House, Tallow, Co Waterford
Tel 058-56117
(*Tallow*, Waterford & L.)

Farrell, Patrick (OSA)
St Augustine's,
Taylor's Lane,
Ballyboden, Dublin 16
Tel 01-4241000

Farrell, Sean (CM)
11 Iona Drive, Glasnevin, Dublin 9
Tel 01-8305238

Farrell, William, Very Rev, CC
Parochial House, St Joseph's, Glasthule, Co Dublin
Tel 0404-40540
(*Glasthule*, Dublin)

Farrelly, Adrian (OP) Very Rev
St Mary's, Pope Quay, Cork
Tel 021-4502267

Farrelly, Florian (OFM)
Franciscan Friary,
Rossnowlagh, Co Donegal
Tel 072-9851342

Farrelly, Matthew (CSSp)
Holy Spirit Missionary College,
Kimmage Manor,
Dublin 12
Tel 01-4064300

Farrelly, Pat, CC
Kildallan, Ballyconnell, Co Cavan
Tel 049-9526252
(*Kildallan and Tomregan*, Kilmore)

Farrelly, Peter, Very Rev, PP
Parochial House, Beauparc, Navan, Co Meath
Tel 046-9024114
(*Beauparc*, Meath)

Farrelly, Thomas (CSSp)
Holy Spirit Missionary College,
Kimmage Manor,
Dublin 12
Tel 01-406 4300

Farren, Anthony (SJ) (CHN)
St Ignatius Community & Church,
27 Raleigh Row,
Salthill, Galway
Tel 091-523707

Farren, Desmond (MSC)
Woodview House,
Mount Merrion Avenue,
Blackrock, Co Dublin
Tel 01-2881644

Farren, John, Very Rev, PP
Muff, Co Donegal
Tel 074-9384037
(*Iskaheen*, Derry)

Farren, Neil, PP
Parochial House,
32 Chapel Road, Waterside,
Derry BT47 2BB
Tel 028-71342303
(Derry)

Farren, Paul, Adm
Parochial House,
St Eugene's Cathedral,
Derry BT48 9AP
Tel 028-71262894
(Derry)

Farrington, Ambrose (OCSO)
Novice Director,
Bolton Abbey, Moone, Co Kildare
Tel 059-8624102

Faughnan, Cathal, PP
Keadue, Boyle,
Co Roscommon
Tel 071-9647212
(Ardagh & Cl.)

Fay, Ambrose (CP)
St Paul's Retreat,
Mount Argus, Dublin 6W
Tel 01-4992000

Fay, Kevin, CC
Lavey, Ballyjamesduff, Co Cavan
Tel 049-4330018
(*Cavan*, Kilmore)

Fay, Sean, Very Rev, AP
Parochial House,
Rathmolyon, Co Meath
Tel 046-9555212
(*Enfield*, Meath)

Fearon, Maurice (OP), Very Rev
Prior, St Catherine's,
Newry, Co Down BT35 8BN
Tel 028-30262178

Fee, Benedict PP
Parochial House,
Magheralanfield,
140 Mountjoy Road,
Coalisland,
Co Tyrone BT71 5DY
Tel 028-87738381
(Armagh)

Fee, Ian, CC
Lisnaskea, Enniskillen,
Co Fermanagh BT92 0JE
Tel 028-67721324
(Clogher)

Feehan, James, Very Rev
1 Castle Court, Thurles, Co Tipperary
Tel 0504-24935
(Cashel & E., retired)

Feeney, Ciarán, CC
191 Upper Newtownards Road,
Belfast BT 3JB
Tel 028-9065417
(*St Colmcille's*, Down & C.)

Feeney, Derek, Very Rev, PP
Ennistymon, Co Clare
Tel 065-7071063
(*Ennistymon*, Galway)

Feeney, Joseph, Very Rev, PP
Ballinlough, Co Roscommon
Tel 094-9640155
(*Ballinlough (Kiltullagh)*, Tuam)

Fegan, James (SMA)
African Missions,
Blackrock Road, Cork
Tel 021-4292871

Fegan, James, Very Rev, Adm
The Presbytery,
12 School Street, Wexford
Tel 053-9122055
(*Wexford*, Ferns)

Fegan, P. J. (IC)
St Joseph's,
Doire na hAbhann,
Tickincar, Clonmel,
Co Tipperary
Tel 052-6126914

Fehily, G. Thomas, Rt Rev Mgr, PE
Hampstead Hospital,
Glasnevin, Dublin 11
(Dublin, retired)

Feighery, John (SVD)
Praeses,
133 North Circular Road, Dublin 7
Tel 01-8386743

Fenlon, Thomas (SMA)
SMA House, Claregalway, Co Galway
Tel 091-798880

Fennell, Liam (OCarm)
Gort Muire, Ballinteer, Dublin 16
Tel 01-2984014

Fennelly, John
Our Lady's Manor, Dalkey
(Tuam, retired)

Fennelly, Sean
Barrysfarm, Hospital, Co Limerick
Tel 061-383565
(*Knockainey*, Cashel & E.)

Fennelly, William (OSB)
Glenstal Abbey, Murroe, Co Limerick
Tel 061-386103

Fennessy, Ignatius (OFM)
Franciscan House of Studies,
Dún Mhuire, Seafield Road,
Killiney, Co Dublin
Tel 01-2826760

Fenning, Hugh (OP)
St Mary's Priory, Tallaght, Dublin 24
Tel 01-4048100

Fergus, Austin, Very Rev Canon, PP
Mayo Abbey, Claremorris, Co Mayo
Tel 094-9365086
(*Mayo Abbey (Mayo and Rosslea)*, Tuam)

Ferguson, Chris, CC
Parochial House,
32 Chapel Road, Waterside,
Derry BT47 2BB
Tel 028-71342303
(Derry)

Ferguson, Gerard, Very Rev Canon, PE
Rockcorry, Monaghan
Tel 042-9742243
(*Rockcorry*, Clogher)

Ferris, Brendan, CC
Tyrrellspass, Co Westmeath
Tel 044-9223115
(*Castletown-Geoghegan*, Meath)

Ferris, John, Co-PP
75 Ludford Drive,
Dundrum, Dublin 16
Tel 01-8405948
(*Meadowbrook*, Dublin)

Ferris, Stephen, Very Rev, PP
91 Newry Road,
Barnmeen, Rathfriland,
Co Down BT34 5AP
Tel 028-40630306
(*Drumgath (Rathfriland)*, Dromore)

Ferry, Francis, CC
Parochial House,
Letterkenny, Co Donegal
Tel 074-9121021
(*Letterkenny (Conwal and Leck)*, Raphoe)

Ferry, Manus (MSC), Very Rev, PP
The Presbytery,
Sacred Heart Parish,
Killinarden, Tallaght,
Dublin 24
Tel 01-4522251
(*Killinarden*, Dublin)

Field, Raymond, Most Rev, DD, VG
Titular Bishop of Ard Mor and Auxiliary Bishop of Dublin,
3 Castleknock Road,
Blanchardstown, Dublin 15
Tel 01-8209191
(Dublin)

Filima, Richard (SPS)
St Patrick's
21 Leeson Park, Dublin 6
Tel 01-4977897

Finan, Andrew, BA, HDE
St Nathy's College,
Ballaghaderreen,
Co Roscommon
Tel 094-9860010
(Achonry)

Finan, James, Very Rev Canon, PP
Keash, Ballymote, Co Sligo
Tel 071-9183334
(Keash (Drumrat), Achonry)

Finan, Thomas
St Patrick's College,
Maynooth, Co Kildare
Tel 01-6285222
(Killala)

Fingleton, James
279 Howth Road, Raheny,
Dublin 5
(Dublin, retired)

Fingleton, John, Very Rev, PE
Graiguecullen, Carlow
Tel 059-9142132
(Kildare & L., retired)

Finn, John, Very Rev, PE
Moorehall Lodge
Nursing Home,
Hale Street, Ardee,
Co Louth
Tel 041-6871942
(Armagh, retired)

Finn, John (MSC), CC
Sacred Heart Parish,
Killinarden, Tallaght,
Dublin 24
Tel 01-4522251
(*Killinarden*, Dublin)

Finn, Patrick, Very Rev Mgr, PP
St Mary's, Haddington Road,
Dublin 4
Tel 01-6643295/086-3848432
(*Haddington Road*, Dublin)

Finn, Tony (OSA)
St Patrick's College and
Church,
Via Piemonte 60,
00187 Rome, Italy
Tel 00396-4203121

Finn, William (OCD)
St Teresa's,
Clarendon Street, Dublin 2
Tel 01-6718466/6718127

Finnegan, John (SDB)
Salesian House,
45 St Teresa's Road,
Crumlin, Dublin 12
Tel 01-4555605

Finnegan, John, Very Rev Canon, PP
Arney, Enniskillen,
Co Fermanagh BT92 2AB
Tel 028-66348217
(*Arney (Cleenish)*, Clogher)

Finnegan, Thomas, Very Rev, PP
Liscarnan, Magheracloone,
Carrickmacross,
Co Monaghan
Tel 042-9663500
(*Magheracloone*, Clogher)

Finneran, Michael, Very Rev, PP, VF
Clontuskert, Ballinasloe,
Co Galway
Tel 090-9642256
(*Clontuskert*, Clonfert)

Finnerty, Liam (OCD)
Prior, The Abbey, Loughrea,
Co Galway
Tel 091-841209

Finnerty, Paul
Diocesan Secretary and
Spokesperson,
Diocesan Office,
Social Service Centre,
Henry Street, Limerick
Tel 061-315856
(Limerick)

Finnerty, Peter, Very Rev, PP, VF
2 Maypark, Malahide Road,
Dublin 5
Tel 01-8404162
(*Donneycarney*, Dublin)

Finucane, Gerard, Adm (pro-tem)
St John's Presbytery, Tralee,
Co Kerry
Tel 068-7122522
(*Tralee, St John's*, Kerry)

Finucane, John A. (CSSp)
Holy Spirit Missionary
College,
Kimmage Manor, Dublin 12
Tel 01-4064300

Fitzgerald, Brendan
c/o Diocesan Office,
Social Service Centre,
Henry Street, Limerick
(Limerick)

Fitzgerald, Christopher
1 The Presbytery,
Friar's Walk, Ballyphehane,
Cork
Tel 021-4537472
(Cork & R.)

Fitzgerald, Dan (SSC)
The Presbytery, Nenagh,
Co Tipperary
Tel 067-37132
(*Nenagh*, Killaloe)

Fitzgerald, Ger
Cathedral Presbytery,
Ennis, Co Clare
Tel 065-6824043/
086-1697595
(Killaloe)

Fitzgerald, Jack, Very Rev, PP, VF
Millstreet, Co Cork
Tel 029-70043
(*Millstreet*, Kerry)

FitzGerald, John (SJ) (ZAM)
(residing elsewhere)
35 Lower Leeson Street,
Dublin 2
Tel 01-6761248

Fitzgerald, John, Very Rev (MSC), PP
Sacred Heart Parish,
Western Road, Cork
Tel 021-4804120
(*Sacred Heart*, Cork & R.)

Fitzgerald, John, Very Rev, PP
Abbeydorney, Co Kerry
Tel 066-7135146
(*Abbeydorney*, Kerry)

Fitzgerald, John, Very Rev, PP
Parish Administrator
Rockhill, Bruree,
Co Limerick
087-6522746
(*Rockhill/Bruree*, Limerick)

Fitzgerald, Joseph, Very Rev Canon, PP, VF
Castlerea, Co Roscommon
Tel 094-9620040
(*Castlerea*, Elphin)

Fitzgerald, Michael (SVD)
Director,
Divine Word School of
English
Tel 01-6289512

Fitzgerald, Michael, PP
Buttevant, Co Cork
Tel 022-23195
(*Buttevant*, Cloyne)

Fitzgerald, Michael, Very Rev, PP
Mitchelstown, Co Cork
Tel 025-84090
(*Mitchelstown*, Cloyne)

Fitzgerald, Norman (CSSp)
Blackrock College,
Blackrock, Co Dublin
Tel 01-288 8681

Fitzgerald, Patrick, Very Rev, PE
Priest's House, Ballinameela,
Cappagh, Co Waterford
Tel 058-68021
(Waterford & L., retired)

Fitzgerald, Patrick, Very Rev, PP
Parochial House, Lisduggan,
Waterford
Tel 051-372257
(*St Paul's*, Waterford & L.)

Fitzgerald, Tadhg, Very Rev, PP
Ardfert, Co Kerry
Tel 066-7134131
Ardfert Retreat Centre
Tel 066-7134276
(*Ardfert*, Kerry)

Fitzgibbon, Eamonn, Rt Rev, VG
Ballyduane, Clarina,
Co Limerick
Tel 087-6921191
(Limerick)

Fitzgibbon, John, Very Rev Canon, PE
Parochial House,
Chapel Road, Lusk,
Co Dublin
Tel 01-8438023
(Dublin, retired)

Fitzmaurice, William, Very Rev Canon, PP
Killmallock, Co Limerick
Tel 063-98287/086-2423728
(*Kilmallock*, Limerick)

Fitzpatrick, Bernard
Lagos, Nigeria
(Kilmore)

Fitzpatrick, Gerard, Very Rev
Cahercalla Community
Hospital,
Ennis, Co Clare
Tel 065-6824388/
086-2311923
(Killaloe, retired)

Fitzpatrick, James (White Fathers)
Cypress Grove,
Templeogue, Dublin 6W
Tel 01-4055263/4055264

Fitzpatrick, James, CC
Ballymore, Screen,
Enniscorthy, Co Wexford
Tel 053-9137140
(*Castlebridge*, Ferns)

Fitzpatrick, Jeremiah (OCD)
St Joseph's Carmelite
Retreat Centre,
Termonbacca,
Derry BT48 9XE
Tel 028-71262512

Fitzpatrick, John V., Rt Rev Mgr, PP, EV
Episcopal Vicar,
3 Glencarraig, Church Road,
Sutton, Co Dublin
Tel 01-8323147
(*Sutton*, Dublin)

Fitzpatrick, John, Very Rev
116 Strangford Road,
Ardglass BT30 7SS
(Down & C., retired)

Fitzpatrick, John, Very Rev, PP
Carbury, Co Kildare
Tel 046-9553355
(*Carbury*, Kildare & L.)

Fitzpatrick, P.J., Very Rev, PP
Gowna, Co Cavan
Tel 043-6683120
(*Lough Gowna and Mullinalaghta*, Ardagh & Cl.)

Fitzpatrick, Patrick (Alan) (OCarm)
Whitefriar Street Church,
56 Aungier Street, Dublin 2
Tel 01-4758821

Fitzpatrick, Tom, Very Rev, PP
Newmarket-on-Fergus,
Co Clare
Tel 061-368127
(*Newmarket-on-Fergus*, Killaloe)

Fitzpatrick, William (OMI), Very Rev
Provincial,
Provincial Residence,
Oblates of Mary Immaculate
House of Retreat,
Tyrconnell Road, Inchicore,
Dublin 8
Tel 01-4541160/4541161

Fitzsimons, Anthony, CC
Curates' Residence,
Massforth, 152 Newry Road,
Kilkeel, Co Down BT34 4ET
Tel 028-41762257
(*Kilkeel (Upper Mourne),* Down & C.)

Fitzsimons, Patrick, Very Rev Canon
Holy Family Residence,
Roebuck, Dundrum,
Dublin 14
(Dublin, retired)

Fitzsimons, William, Very Rev, PP
Parochial House, Milltown,
Rathconrath, Co Westmeath
Tel 044-9355106
(*Milltown*, Meath)

Flaherty, John, Very Rev Canon, VF
(Team Moderator)
Parochial House,
Sperrin Road, Drimnagh,
Dublin 12
Tel 01-4556103
(*Mourne Road*, Dublin)

Flaherty, Raymond, Adm (pro-tem)
Headford, Co Galway
Tel 093-35448
(*Headford (Killursa and Killower),* Tuam)

Flanagan, Benny, Very Rev, PP
Carrabane, Athenry,
Co Galway
Tel 091-841103
(*Clostoken and Kilconieran,* Clonfert)

Flanagan, Desmond (OCarm)
Terenure College, Terenure,
Dublin 6W
Tel 01-4904621

Flanagan, Eamon (CM)
St Paul's College, Raheny,
Dublin 5
Tel 01-8318113

Flanagan, John (SPS), CC
Parochial House,
6 Tullydonnell Road,
Dungannon,
Co Tyrone BT70 3JE
Tel 028-87758224
(*Cookstown (Desertcreight and Derryloran),* Armagh)

Flanagan, John, CC
Roslea, Enniskillen,
Co Fermanagh BT92 7LA
Tel 028-67751393
(*Roslea*, Clogher)

Flanagan, Malachy (SMA)
Provincial Bursar,
African Missions,
Blackrock Road, Cork
Tel 021-4292871

Flanagan, Padraig, (SPS) St Patrick's, Kiltegan,
Co Wicklow
Tel 059-6473600
(*Kiltegan*, Kildare and L.)

Flanagan, Richard (SVD)
Donamon Castle,
Roscommon
Tel 090-6662222

Flannery, Anthony (CSsR)
St Patrick's, Esker, Athenry,
Co Galway
Tel 091-844549

Flannery, John D., Very Rev Canon, PE
Cartron, Milltown,
Co Galway
(Tuam, retired)

Flannery, Michael, Very Rev Canon, PE
Cartron, Milltown,
Co Galway
(Tuam, retired)

Flannery, Paschal, Very Rev
Ballinderry, Nenagh,
Co Tipperary
Tel 067-22916/086-2225099
(Killaloe, retired)

Flannery, Peter (CSsR)
Marianella/Liguori House,
75 Orwell Road, Dublin 6
Tel 01-4067100

Flavin, John P. (CSSp)
St Mary's College,
Rathmines, Dublin 6
Tel 01-4995760

Flavin, Nicholas, Very Rev, PP
Dunamaggan, Co Kilkenny
Tel 056-7728173/
087-2257498
(*Dunamaggan*, Ossory)

Fleck, Robert, Very Rev, PP
Parochial House, Ardglass,
Co Down BT30 7TU
Tel 028-44841208
(*Ardglass (Dunsford),* Down & C.)

Fleming, David, CC
The Presbytery,
Bohernabreena, Tallaght,
Dublin 24
Tel 01-4555794
(*Tallaght, Dodder*, Dublin)

Fleming, Gerard (SAC), Very Rev, CC
437 South Circular Road,
Rialto, Dublin 8
Tel 01-4533490
(*Rialto*, Dublin)

Fleming, John Kevin (MSC)
Western Road, Cork
Tel 021-4804120

Fleming, John, Most Rev, DD, DCL
Bishop of Killala,
Bishop's House, Ballina,
Co Mayo
Tel 096-21518
(Killala)

Fleming, Joseph, Very Rev, Adm
Clonegal, Enniscorthy,
Co Wexford
Tel 053-9377298
(*Clonegal*, Kildare & L.)

Fleming, Kevin (SSC)
St Columban's, Dalgan Park,
Navan, Co Meath
Tel 046-9021525
(Meath)

Fleming, Michael, Very Rev Canon, PP, VF
The Presbytery, Killorglin,
Co Kerry
Tel 066-9761172
(Kerry)

Fleming, Paul, BA, BD, STL
St Mary's University College,
191 Falls Road,
Belfast 12 6FE
Tel 028-90327678
(Down & C.)

Fleming, Seamus (CSSp)
Chaplain,
Cherry Orchard Hospital,
Ballyfermot, Dublin 10
Tel 01-6206000

Fleming, William (MSC)
Carrignavar, Co Cork
Tel 021-4884044

Fletcher, Robert, CC
Dealginis, Garraun Upper,
Ballinahinch, Birdhill,
via Killaloe, Co Clare
Tel 086-1927455/061-379862
(*Ballinahinch*, Cashel & E.)

Flood, Aloysius P. (CSSp)
Holy Spirit Missionary College,
Kimmage Manor,
Dublin 12
Tel 01-4064300

Flynn, Brian
Administrator of the
National Marriage Appeal Tribunal,
St Patrick's College,
Maynooth, Co Kildare
(Kilmore)

Flynn, Brian
Administrator of the
National Marriage Appeal Tribunal,
St Patrick's College,
Maynooth, Co Kildare
(Kilmore)

Flynn, Brian, Very Rev, PP
Kilmacow, via Waterford,
Co Kilkenny
Tel 051-885122/087-2828391
(*Kilmacow*, Ossory)

Flynn, Edward, Very Rev, PE
Multyfarnham Retirement Village,
Co Westmeath
(Meath, retired)

Flynn, Edwin (OFMCap)
Holy Trinity,
Fr Mathew Quay, Cork
Tel 021-4270827

Flynn, Gabriel, DD, PC
1 Orchard Court, Dunboyne,
Co Meath
Tel 01-8255342
(*Dunboyne*, Meath)

Flynn, Joe (SPS)
Tearmann Spirituality Centre,
Brockagh, Glendalough,
Co Wicklow
Tel 0404-45208

Flynn, John (SMA)
SMA House, Wilton, Cork
Tel 021-4541069/4541884

Flynn, John, Very Rev Canon
Mount Falcon, Knockmore,
Ballina, Co Mayo
(Killala, retired)

Flynn, Joseph, Very Rev, PP
Ballyporeen, Cahir,
Co Tipperary
Tel 052-7467105
(*Ballyporeen*, Waterford & L.)

Flynn, Kieran (SPS)
St Patrick's, 21 Leeson Park,
Dublin 6
Tel 01-4977897

Flynn, Laurence, Very Rev, PP
Ballybay, Co Monaghan
Tel 042-9741032
(*Ballybay*, Clogher)

Flynn, Michael, Very Rev, PP
Knockmore, Ballina,
Co Mayo
(Killala)

Flynn, Nicholas, Very Rev, Adm, VF
St Mary's Presbytery,
Killarney, Co Kerry
Tel 064-6631014
(*Killarney*, Kerry)

Flynn, Patrick (OFMCap), CC
Guardian, Capuchin
Parochial Friary,
Clonshaugh Drive,
Priorswood, Dublin 17
Tel 01-8474469/8474538
(*Priorswood*, Dublin)

Flynn, Robert, Very Rev Dean
Ballymote, Co Sligo
Tel 071-9183312
(Achonry, retired)

Flynn, Thomas, CC
Granard, Co Longford
Tel 043-6686591
(*Granard*, Ardagh & Cl.)

Flynn, Thomas, Most Rev, DD
Bishop Emeritus of Achonry,
St Michael's,
Cathedral Grounds,
Ballaghaderreen,
Co Roscommon
Tel 094-9877808
(Achonry)

Flynn, Thomas, Very Rev, PP
Carrickbeg, Carrick-on-Suir,
Co Tipperary
Tel 051-640340
(*Carrickbeg*, Waterford & L.)

Flynn, Tim (OSM)
Prior, Servite Priory,
St Peregrine, Kiltipper Road,
Tallaght, Dublin 24
Tel 01-4517115

Flynn, Timothy (OSM)
Director, Servite Oratory,
Rathfarnham Shopping
Centre,
Dublin 14
Tel 01-4936300

Flynn, Tomás, Very Rev, PP
Drumcong,
Carrick-on-Shannon,
Co Leitrim
Tel 071-9642021
(*Kiltubrid*, Ardagh & Cl.)

Flynn, William, CC
St Patrick's, Gorey,
Co Wexford
Tel 053-9421117
(*Gorey*, Ferns)

Fogarty, Kevin (OCSO)
Mount Melleray Abbey,
Cappoquin, Co Waterford
Tel 058-54404

Fogarty, Pat, Very Rev, PP
The Presbytery,
Knocknaheeny, Cork
Tel 021-4392459
(*Knocknaheeny/Hollyhill*,
Cork & R.)

Fogarty, Philip (SJ)
35 Lower Leeson Street,
Dublin 2
Tel 01-6761248

Fogarty, Thomas, Very Rev
President,
St Patrick's College, Thurles,
Co Tipperary
Tel 0504-21201
(Cashel & E.)

Foley, Brendan (CSSp)
Blackrock College,
Blackrock, Co Dublin
Tel 01-288 8681

Foley, Brian (CSsR)
St Patrick's, Esker, Athenry,
Co Galway
Tel 091-844549

Foley, Declan, Very Rev, PP
Bagenalstown, Co Carlow
Tel 059-9721154
(Kildare & L.)

Foley, Denis, Very Rev, PE
32 Walkinstown Road,
Dublin 12
Tel 01-4501350
(Dublin, retired)

Foley, Dermot (SPS)
Tearmann Spirituality
Centre,
Brockagh, Glendalough,
Co Wicklow
Tel 0404-45208

Foley, Desmond (OSA)
St Augustine's Priory,
Galway
Tel 091-562524

Foley, Eamon, Very Rev, PP
Rathdowney, Portlaoise,
Co Laois
Tel 0505-46282
(*Rathdowney*, Ossory)

Foley, Edward (OP)
St Saviour's,
Upper Dorset Street,
Dublin 1
Tel 01-8897610

Foley, George (SSCC)
Coudrin House,
27 Northbrook Road,
Dublin 6
Tel 01-6473759/01-6686590

Foley, Joseph, Very Rev, CC
Bruff, Kilmallock,
Co Limerick
Tel 061-382290/087-2618412
(*Bruff/Meanus/Grange*,
Limerick)

Foley, Michael F. (SSCC)
Coudrin House,
27 Northbrook Road,
Dublin 6
Tel 01-6686584/01-6686590

Foley, Niall, BSc, BD, HDE
Vice-President,
St Joseph's College,
Garbally Park, Ballinasloe,
Co Galway
Tel 090-9642504/9642254
(Clonfert)

Foley, Stanislaus (OP)
Black Abbey, Kilkenny,
Co Kilkenny
Tel 056-7721279

Foley, William (SMA)
SMA House, Wilton, Cork
Tel 021-4541069/4541884

Forbes, John, Very Rev, PP
Parochial House,
Gortin, Omagh,
Co Tyrone BT79 8PU
Tel 028-81648203
(*Gortin*, Derry)

Ford, Seán (OCarm), CC
The Presbytery,
Idrone Avenue, Knocklyon,
Dublin 16
Tel 01-4941204/4944986
(*Knocklyon*, Dublin)

Forde, Basil (OSB)
Glenstal Abbey, Murroe,
Co Limerick
Tel 061-386103

Forde, Denis, Very Rev
Tigh an tSagairt,
Clogheen, Cork
(Cork & R.)

Forde, Des, Very Rev, PP
Ballyvaughan, Co Clare
Tel 065-7077045
(Ballyvaughan, Galway)

Forde, Liam (SM)
Mount St Mary's, Milltown,
Dublin 14
Tel 01-2697322

Forde, Michael (CSsR)
Scala, Castlemahon House,
Castle Road, Cork
Tel 021-4358800

Forde, Peter, Very Rev, PP, VF
51 Bay Road, Carnlough,
Ballymena,
Co Antrim BT44 0HJ
Tel 028-28885220
(*Carnlough*, Down & C.)

Forde, Robert, Very Rev, PE
Fermoy, Co Cork
Tel 025-34022
(Cloyne, retired)

Forde, Tom (OFMCap)
Capuchin Friary,
Station Road, Raheny,
Dublin 5
Tel 01-8313886

Forde, Walter, Very Rev, PP
Castlebridge, Co Wexford
Tel 053-9159769
(*Castlebridge*, Ferns)

Forker, Philip (OFM)
The Abbey,
8 Francis Street, Galway
Tel 091-562518Forrester,
Gerald, Very Rev
62 Rathgannon,
Warrenpoinnt BT34 3TU
(Down & C., retired)

Forristal, Desmond, Very Rev
St Joseph's Centre,
Crinken Lane, Shankill,
Co Dublin
(Dublin, retired)

Forristal, Laurence, Most Rev,
DD
Retired Bishop of Ossory,
Molassy, Freshford Road,
Kilkenny
Tel 056-7777928/
087-2330369
(Ossory)

Forristal, Leonard (SPS)
St Patrick's, Kiltegan,
Co Wicklow
Tel 059-6473600

Forster, Stephen (MI)
Superior and Provincial,
St Camillus,
4 St Vincent Street North
Dublin 7
Tel 01-8300365

Forsythe, John, Very Rev, PP
Elmfield, 165 Antrim Road,
Glengormley,
Newtownabbey,
Co Antrim, BT36 7QR
Tel 028-90832979
(Down & C.)

Fortune, Carlyle (OP)
Prior, Convent of SS. Xystus
and Clement,
Collegio San Clemente,
Via Labicana 95,
00184 Roma
Tel (39-06) 7740021

Fortune, Finbarr (OSA)
St John's Priory,
Thomas Street,
Dublin 8
Tel 01-6770393

Fortune, Karl, CC
23 Wainsfort Grove,
Terenure, Dublin 6W
Tel 01-4905284/087-9672258
(*Templeogue*, Dublin)

Fortune, William, CC
32 Newtownpark Avenue,
Blackrock, Co Dublin
Tel 01-2100337
(*Newtownpark*, Dublin)

Foster, John (SDB)
(Team Assistant)
Salesian House,
St Teresa's Road,
Crumlin, Dublin 12
Tel 01-4555605
(*Crumlin*, Dublin)

Fox, Christopher (MHM)
St Joseph's House,
50 Orwell Park, Rathgar,
Dublin 6
Tel 01-4127700

Fox, Gerard
201 Donegall Street,
Belfast BT1 2FL
Tel 028-90263473
(Down & C.)

Fox, John, Very Rev, PP
Parochial House,
153 Aughrim Road,
Toomebridge,
Antrim BT41 3SH
Tel 028-79468277
(*Newbridge*, Armagh)

Fraser, Paul
c/o Our Lady Queen of
Heaven,
111 Portsmouth Road,
Frimley, Camberley,
Surrey GU16 7AA
Tel 01276-504876

Frawley, Bernard M. (CSSp)
Rockwell College, Cashel,
Co Tipperary
Tel 062-61444

Freeman, Seamus (SAC), Most Rev, DD
Bishop of Ossory,
Blessed Felix House,
Tilbury Place, James's Street, Kilkenny
Tel 056-7762448
(Ossory)

Freeney, Paul, Very Rev, PE
Parochial House,
43 Upper Beechwood Avenue,
Ranelagh, Dublin 6
Tel 01-4972687
(Dublin, retired)

French, Gerry (SSC)
St Joseph's, Balcurris,
Ballymun, Dublin 11
Tel 01-8423865
(*Balcurris*, Dublin)

French, John, Very Rev
Horeswood, New Ross,
Co Wexford
Tel 051-593196
(Ferns, retired)

Friel, James, Very Rev, PE
Massreagh, Rathmullan,
Co Donegal
(Raphoe, retired)

Friel, John (CP)
Superior,
Passionist Retreat Centre,
Tobar Mhuire, Crossgar,
Co Down BT30 9EA
Tel 028-44830242

Fullerton, Robert, Very Rev Canon
501 Ormeau Road,
Belfast BT7 3GR
Tel 028-90641064
(*Holy Rosary*, Down & C.)

Fulton, Raymond, Very Rev, PP
87 Cushendall Road,
Ballyvoy, Ballycastle,
Co Antrim BT54 6QY
Tel 028-20762248
(*Culfeightrin*, Down & C.)

Fulton, William (SSC)
St Patrick's, Kiltegan,
Co Wicklow
Tel 059-6473600

Furey, Francis (SMA)
African Missions,
Blackrock Road, Cork
Tel 021-4292871

Furlong, James (OSA)
St Augustine's Priory,
Washington Street, Cork
Tel 021-2753982

Furlong, James, Very Rev, PP
Newbawn, Co Wexford
(*Newbawn and Raheen,* Ferns)

Furlong, Odhrán, CC
Rathgarogue, New Ross,
Co Wexford
Tel 051-424521
(*Cushinstown*, Ferns)

Furlong, Senan (OSB), Very Rev
Glenstal Abbey, Murroe,
Co Limerick
Tel 061-386103

Furlong, Tadgh, Very Rev, PP
Cappawhite, Co Tipperary
Tel 062-75427
(*Cappawhite*, Cashel & E.)

Furlong, Thomas (SMA)
SMA House, Wilton, Cork
Tel 021-4541069/4541884

## G

Gaffney, David (SJ)
Milltown Park,
Sandford Road, Dublin 6
Tel 01-2698411/2698113

Gaffney, Matthew (IC)
Clonturk House,
Ormond Road,
Drumcondra, Dublin 9
Tel 01-6877014

Gaffney, Peter (OP)
St Mary's, The Claddagh,
Co Galway
Tel 091-582884

Gaffney, Philip, Very Rev, Adm
Parochial House, Curraha,
Ashbourne, Co Meath
Tel 01-8350136
(*Curraha*, Meath)

Gahan, Dermot, CC
The Ballagh, Wexford
Tel 053-9136200
(*Oulart*, Ferns)

Gahan, James, Very Rev, PP
Killinure, Tullow,
Co Carlow
Tel 059-9156111
(*Clonmore*, Kildare & L.)

Gahan, Raymond, Very Rev, PP
Killaveney, Tinahely,
Co Wicklow
Tel 0402-38188
(*Killaveney*, Ferns)

Gallagher, Brendan, Very Rev, PP
Ederney, Enniskillen,
Co Fermanagh BT93 0DG
Tel 028-68631315
(*Ederney*, Clogher)

Gallagher, Colm, PP
Historical Churches Advisory Commission,
Dublin
(Dublin)

Gallagher, Colm, Very Rev Mgr
594 Howth Road, Raheny,
Dublin 5
(Dublin, retired)

Gallagher, Declan, CC
No. 3 Prebytery,
Castle Street, Dalkey,
Co Dublin
Tel 01-2692052
(*Dalkey*, Dublin)

Gallagher, Denis
'Shraheens', Achill South,
Achill, Co Mayo
(Tuam)

Gallagher, Eddie, Very Rev, PP
Kilcar, Co Donegal
(Raphoe)

Gallagher, Edward, CC
4 Scroggy Road, Limavady,
Co Derry BT49 0NA
Tel 028-77763944
(*Limavady*, Derry)

Gallagher, Edward, Very Rev, PP
Kilcar, Co Donegal
Tel 074-9738007
(*Kilcar*, Raphoe)

Gallagher, Joe (OFMCap)
St Anthony's Capuchin Friary,
43 Dublin Street, Carlow
Tel 059-9142543

Gallagher, John (CM)
St Vincent's College,
Castleknock, Dublin 15
Tel 01-8213051

Gallagher, John Vincent (SSC)
St Columban's Retirement Home,
Dalgan Park, Navan,
Co Meath
Tel 046-9021525

Gallagher, John, Canon
1 Chaplain's House,
Knocknamona,
Letterkenny, Co Donegal
Tel 074-9125888 (Hospital)
(Raphoe)

Gallagher, Joseph (SSC)
St Columban's Retirement Home,
Dalgan Park, Navan,
Co Meath
Tel 046-9021525

Gallagher, Joseph, Very Rev, PP
Parochial House, Kilcormac,
Co Offaly
Tel 057-9335013
(*Kilcormac*, Meath)

Gallagher, Laurence (CSsR)
St Joseph's, Dundalk,
Co Louth
Tel 042-9334042/9334762

Gallagher, Louis (OCD)
St Joseph's Carmelite Retreat Centre,
Termonbacca,
Derry BT48 9XE
Tel 028-71262512

Gallagher, Michael O. (SJ)
35 Lower Leeson Street,
Dublin 2
Tel 01-6761248

Gallagher, Michael P. (SJ)
Irish Jesuit Provincialate,
Milltown Park,
Sandford Road, Dublin 6
Tel 01-4987333

Gallagher, Patrick (OCarm)
Gort Muire, Ballinteer,
Dublin 16
Tel 01-2984014

Gallagher, Patrick, Rt Rev Mgr
Cathedral Close, Ballina,
Co Mayo
(Killala, retired)

Gallagher, Paul, CC
Falcarragh, Co Donegal
Tel 074-9165356
(*Gortahork (Tory Island)*, Raphoe)

Gallagher, Peter, Very Rev, PP
Lavagh, Ballymote,
Co Sligo
Tel 071-9184002
(Achonry)

Gallagher, Raphael (CSsR)
(Alphonsian Academy)
Via Merulana 31, CP 2458,
00185 Rome, Italy
Tel 0039-06494901

Gallagher, Seamus L., Very Rev, PE
Glenlee, Killybegs,
Co Donegal
Tel 074-9732729
(Raphoe, retired)

Gallagher, Seamus, Very Rev, PP
Parochial House,
Newtowncunningham,
Lifford, Co Donegal
Tel 074-9156138
(*Newtowncunningham*, Raphoe)

Gallagher, Shane, CC
Glenties, Co Donegal
Tel 074-9551136
(*Glenties*, Raphoe)

Gallagher, Thomas
Cloughmore, Achill,
Co Mayo
(Tuam)

Gallinagh, Padraic, Very Rev
'Polperro', 8 Beverley Close,
Newtownards BT23 7FN
(Down & C., retired)

Gallogley, Vincent (OFM)
Associate Pastor,
St Anthony's Parish (English-Speaking Chaplaincy),
23/25 Oudstrijderslaan,
1950 Kraainem, Belgium
Tel +32-2-7201970

Galus, Piotr
Diocesan Chaplain to Polish Community,
c/o St Augustine's,
Washington Street, Cork
Tel 021-4275390
(Cork & R.)

Galvin, Aidan (CM)
St Paul's College, Raheny, Dublin 5
Tel 01-8318113

Galvin, Gerard, Very Rev, PP
Durrus, Co Cork
Tel 027-61013
(*Muintir Bhaire*, Cork & R.)

Galvin, Ignatius (OFMCap)
Capuchin Parochial Friary, Clonshaugh Drive, Priorswood, Dublin 17
Tel 01-8474469/01-8474358
(*Priorswood*, Dublin)

Galvin, John, AP
Passage West, Co Cork
Tel 021-4841267
(*Monkstown*, Cork & R.)

Galvin, John, CC
48 Lower Rathmines Road, Dublin 9
(*Rathmines*, Dublin)

Galvin, Séamus (CSSp)
Templeogue College, Templeville Raod, Dublin 6W
Tel 01-490 3909

Gannon, John J., Very Rev, PP
Elphin, Co Roscommon
Tel 071-9635058
(*Elphin*, Elphin)

Gannon, Peter, CC
The Presbytery, Claremorris, Co Mayo
Tel 094-9362477
(*Claremorris (Kilcolman)*, Tuam)

Gardiner, Seamus, Very Rev, AP
Portroe, Nenagh, Co Tipperary
Tel 067-23105/086-8392741
(*Portroe*, Killaloe)

Garland, Sean, Very Rev, PP
Parochial House, Clonmellon, Navan, Co Meath
Tel 046-9433124
(*Clonmellon*, Meath)

Garrett, Gerard, Very Rev, VJ
Cork Regional Marriage Tribunal, The Lough, Cork
Tel 021-4963653
(Limerick)

Garry, Martin (OCSO)
Bolton Abbey, Moone, Co Kildare
Tel 059-8624102

Garvey, Colin (OFM)
The Abbey, 8 Francis Street, Galway
Tel 091-562518

Garvey, Francis, Very Rev, PP, VF
Carrick-on-Shannon, Co Leitrim
Tel 071-9620118
(*Carrick-on-Shannon*, Ardagh & Cl.)

Garvey, John, Very Rev, Adm
St Michael's, Creagh, Ballinasloe, Co Galway
Tel 090-9643916
(Clonfert)

Garvey, John, Very Rev, PP
Carnacon, Claremorris, Co Mayo
Tel 094-9360205
(*Burriscarra and Ballintubber*, Tuam)

Garvey, Joseph, Very Rev, PE
Kilbrew Nursing Home, Curaha, Ashbourne, Co Meath
(Meath, retired)

Garvey, Peter (OCSO), Rt Rev Dom
Abbot, Bolton Abbey, Moone, Co Kildare
Tel 059-8624102

Garvey, Thomas
Cloverhill, Co Roscommon
(Elphin, retired)

Gates, John, Very Rev, PP, VF
Parochial House, 30 King Street, Magherafelt, Co Derry BT45 6AS
Tel 028-79632439
(*Magherafelt and Ardtrea North*, Armagh)

Gaughan, J. Anthony, Very Rev, PE
56 Newtownpark Avenue, Blackrock, Co Dublin
Tel 01-2833897
(Dublin, retired)

Gavigan, Adrian, CC
Mountcharles, Co Donegal
Tel 074-9735009
(*Inver*, Raphoe)

Gavigan, James
Cleraun Study Centre, 90 Foster Avenue, Mount Merrion, Co Dublin
Tel 01-2881734
Chaplain, Lismullin Conference Centre, Navan, Co Meath
Tel 046-9026936
(Opus Dei)

Gavigan, James (SSC)
St Columban's Retirement Home, Dalgan Park, Navan, Co Meath
Tel 046-9021525

Gavigan, Joseph, Very Rev, PP
The Presbytery, Ballaghaderreen, Co Roscommon
Tel 094-9860011
(Achonry)

Gavin, Denis J. (CSSp)
Blackrock College, Blackrock, Co Dublin
Tel 01-2888681

Gavin, Dwayne, CC
St Mary's, Navan, Co Meath
Tel 046-9027518/9027414
(*Navan*, Meath)

Gavin, Fintan, Rev PC
97 Ballymun Road, Dublin 9
Tel 01-6761322
(*Ballymun*, Dublin)

Gavin, John
c/o Archbishop's House, Tuam
(Tuam)

Gavin, Thomas P., Very Rev, PP
Parochial House, Summerhill, Co Meath
Tel 046-9557021
(*Summerhill*, Meath)

Gavin, Tony, Very Rev, Adm
Parochial House, Rosemount, Co Westmeath
Tel 090-6436110
(*Tubber*, Meath)

Gayer, Pat (OSA)
St John's Priory, Thomas Street, Dublin 8
Tel 01-6770393

Gaynor, Harry, CC
112 Ballygall Road East, Glasnevin, Dublin 11
(*Ballygall*, Dublin)

Gaynor, Patrick, Very Rev, PP
Walsh Island, Geashill, Co Offaly
Tel 057-8649510
(*Clonbullogue*, Kildare & L.)

Geaney, Michael
3 Hillview Cross, Douglas Road, Cork
(Dublin, retired)

Gear, Patrick, Very Rev, PP
Ballyneale, Carrick-on-Suir, Co Tipperary
Tel 051-640148
(*Ballyneale and Grangemockler*, Waterford & L.)

Geary, Ronan (SJ)
35 Lower Leeson Street, Dublin 2
Tel 01-6761248
(Zam-Mal)

Geelan, John, Very Rev, PP
Parochial House, Bonniconlon, Ballina, Co Mayo
Tel 096-45016
(*Bonniconlon*, Achonry)

Geoghegan, Anthony (CSSp)
Holy Ghost Missionary College, Kimmage Manor, Dublin 12
Tel 01-4064300

Geoghegan, Brian
Tubber, Co Clare
Tel 091-633124/087-2387067
(*Tubber*, Killaloe)

Geoghegan, Richard, CC
The Presbytery, Carrick-on-Suir, Co Tipperary
Tel 051-640080
(*Carrick-on-Suir*, Waterford & L.)

Geraghty, Cathal, Very Rev Mgr, VG
Chancellor, The Presbytery, Barrack Street, Loughrea, Co Galway
Tel 091-841212
(Clonfert)

Geraghty, Gerard, Very Rev, PP
Aughrim, Ballinasloe, Co Galway
Tel 090-9673724/090-9686614
(*Aughrim and Kilconnell*, Clonfert)

Geraghty, Martin (MI)
St Camillus, Killucan, Co Westmeath
Tel 044-74196/044-74115

Gesla, Marceli (OFM)
Chaplain to Polish Community
Franciscan Friary, Killarney, Co Kerry
Tel 064-6631334/6631066

Ghent, William (SMA)
African Missions, Blackrock Road, Cork
Tel 021-4292871

Gibbons, Danny (SPS)
House Leader, St Patrick's, 21 Leeson Park, Dublin 6
Tel 01-4977897

Gibbons, Richard, CC
Knock, Co Mayo
Tel 094-9388100
(*Knock*, Tuam)

Gibson, David, Very Rev, PP
St Patrick's, Dublin Road, Limerick
Tel 061-415397/087-2547707
(*St Patrick's*, Limerick)

Gibson, Steve (CSC)
Attymass, Co Mayo
Tel 096-45374
(Tuam)

Gilbert, Patrick
The Presbytery, John's Mall, Birr, Co Offaly
Tel 057-9120098/087-2431956
Chaplain, St Brendan's Community School, Birr, Co Offaly
Tel 0509-20510
(Killaloe)

Gilcreest, Martin
Chaplain, Cavan General Hospital
Tel 049-4361399
(Kilmore)

Gildea, Peter (CM), Very Rev
Superior,
99 Cliftonville Road,
Belfast BT14 6JQ
Tel 028-90751771

Gildea, Seán (OFM)
Franciscan Friary,
Rossnowlagh, Co Donegal
Tel 072-9851342

Giles, Seamus, Very Rev, PP
Parochial House,
Castletown-Geoghegan,
Co Westmeath
Tel 044-9226118
(*Castletown-Geoghegan*, Meath)

Gilhooly, John, Very Rev, PP
Mullagh, via Kells, Co Meath
Tel 046-42208
(*Mullagh*, Kilmore)

Gill, Oswald (OFM)
Franciscan Friary,
Liberty Street, Cork
Tel 021-4270302

Gill, Patrick, Very Rev, AP
Lecanvey, Westport,
Co Mayo
Tel 098-64808
(*Westport (Aughaval)*, Tuam)

Gillan, Hugh (OH)
St John of God Hospital,
Stillorgan, Co Dublin
(Dublin)

Gillespie, Anthony, Very Rev, PP
Templeboy, Co Sligo
Tel 096-47103
(Killala)

Gillespie, Gerard, Very Rev, PP
Templeboy, Co Sligo
Tel 096-47102
(*Dromore-West*, Killala)

Gillespie, James, CC
Milford, Co Donegal
Tel 074-9153236
(*Rathmullan*, Raphoe)

Gillespie, Kevin
Congregation for the Clergy,
Rome
(Raphoe)

Gilligan, John, Very Rev, VF
47 Westland Row, Dublin 2
Tel 01-6765517
Director,
Lourdes Pilgrimage Office,
Holy Cross College,
Clonliffe Road, Dublin 3
Tel 01-7005268/8368746
(*Westland Row*, Dublin)

Gilligan, Patrick, Very Rev, PP
Cong, Co Mayo
Tel 094-9546030
(*Cong and Neale*, Tuam)

Gillooly, Dominick, Very Rev, PP
St Anne's, Sligo
Tel 071-9145028
(*Sligo, St Anne's*, Elphin)

Gillooly, Peter, (SPS), CC
Kilmurray, Castlerea,
Co Roscommon
Tel 094-9651018
(*Tulsk*, Elphin)

Gillooly, Reginald (CSSp)
Holy Ghost Missionary
College, Kimmage Manor,
Dublin 12
Tel 01-4064300

Gilmore, John (SSC)
St Columban's, Dalgan Park,
Navan, Co Meath
Tel 046-9021525

Gilmore, John, PP
11 Church Road,
Aghyaran, Castlederg,
Co Tyrone BT81 7XZ
Tel 028-81670728
(*Aghyaran (Termonamongan)*, Derry)

Gilmore, Sean, Very Rev, PP
Parochial House,
284 Glassdrumman Road,
Annalong,
Newry, Co Down BT34 4QN
Tel 028-43768208
(*Lower Mourne*, Down & C.)

Gilroy, Michael, Dr
(on sabbatical leave)
Cathedral Close,
Ballina, Co Mayo
Tel 096-217464
(Killala)

Gilroy, Thomas, Very Rev, PP
Parochial House, Kinnegad,
Co Westmeath
Tel 044-9375117
(*Kinnegad*, Meath)

Gilsenan, Michael CC
St Mary's, Clontibert,
Co Monaghan
Tel 047-80631

Gilton, Michael, CC
48 Aughrim Street,
Dublin 7
Tel 01-8386176
(*Aughrim Street*, Dublin)

Ginnelly, Christopher, PP
Parochial House, Ballycroy,
Westport, Co Mayo
Tel 098-49134
(*Ballycroy*, Killala)

Glavin, Finbar, Very Rev
Parochial House,
16 Ballykilbeg Road,
Downpatrick,
Co Down BT30 8HJ
Tel 028-44613203
(*Downpatrick*, Down & C.)

Gleeson, Joseph, Very Rev, PE
Rathfeigh, Tara, Co Meath
Tel 041-9825159
(*Skryne*, Meath)

Gleeson, Martin, Very Rev, AP
Belclare, Tuam, Co Galway
Tel 093-55429
(*Cummer (Kilmoylan and Cummer)*, Tuam)

Gleeson, Padraig
3 Maypark, Malahide Road,
Dublin 5
Tel 086-8754424
Chaplain,
DIT, Bolton Street, Dublin
Tel 01-4023618
(Dublin)

Gleeson, Patrick, CC
The Presbytery,
St Paul's Parish,
8 Slademore Close,
Ard-na-Gréine, Dublin 13
Tel 01-6081260/6767316
(*Ayrfield*, Dublin)

Gleeson, Philip (OP)
St Mary's Priory, Tallaght,
Dublin 24
Tel 01-4048100

Gleeson, Tim (MSC)
Western Road, Cork
Tel 021-4804120

Glennon, Francis, Very Rev, PP
Cams, Roscommon
Tel 090-6626275
(*Cloverhill*, Elphin)

Glocko, Daniel (SChr) CC
Parochial House,
6 Circular Road,
Dungannon,
Co Tyrone BT71 6BE
Tel 028-87722631
(*Dungannon (Drumglass, Killyman and Tullyniskin)*, Armagh)

Glover, Joseph M.
Star of the Sea Presbytery,
305 Shore Road,
Whitehouse,
Newtownabbey, Co Antrim
BT37 9RY
Tel 028-90365142
(*Whitehouse*, Down & C.)

Glynn, Cronan (OCD)
The Abbey, Loughrea,
Co Galway
Tel 091-841209

Glynn, Enda, Very Rev, PP
New Quay, Co Clare
Tel 065-7078026
(*Carron and New Quay*, Galway)

Glynn, Joe (OCD)
St Teresa's,
Clarendon Street, Dublin 2
Tel 01-6718466/6718127

Glynn, John, Very Rev, PP
Parochial House,
Tourlestrane, Ballymote,
Co Sligo
Tel 071-9181105
(*Tourlestrane (Kilmactigue)*, Achonry)

Glynn, Martin, Very Rev, PP
129 Túr Uisce, Doughiska,
Galway
Tel 091-756823
(*Good Shepherd*, Galway)

Glynn, Matthias, Very Rev, PP
Tagoat, Co Wexford
Tel 053-9131139
(*Tagoat*, Ferns)

Glynn, Michael
Chaplain,
Convent of Mercy,
Mullaghmore, Co Sligo
Tel 071-9166345
(Elphin)

Gnoumou, Expedit, PC
The Presbytery,
Shangan Road, Ballymun,
Dublin 9
(*Ballymun*, Dublin)

Goaley, Michael, Very Rev Canon
Glenamaddy, Co Galway
(Tuam, retired)

Godfrey, Donal (SJ)
Irish Jesuit Provincialate,
Milltown Park,
Sandford Road, Dublin 6
Tel 01-4987333

Godley, Gearóid
John Paul II Pastoral Centre,
Rock Road, Killarney,
Co Kerry
Tel 064-6630535
(Kerry)

Gogan, Brian M. (CSSp)
Blackrock College,
Blackrock, Co Dublin
Tel 01-2888681

Gogan, Cothraí (CSSp)
Holy Spirit Missionary
College,
Kimmage Manor, Dublin 12
Tel 01-406 4300

Gogarty, Terence (MHM)
St Joseph's House,
50 Orwell Park, Rathgar,
Dublin 6
Tel 01-4127700

Golden, Michael (SPS)
St Patrick's, Kiltegan,
Co Wicklow
Tel 059-6473600

Gonoude, Anthony, CC
The Presbytery, Ballsgrove,
Drogheda, Co Louth
Tel 041-9836287
(*Drogheda, Holy Family*, Meath)

Good, James
Park View, Church Street,
Douglas, Cork
Tel 021-4363913
(Cork & R., retired)

Goode, John (CSsR)
Mount Saint Alphonsus,
Limerick
Tel 061-315099

Goode, Richard (OSA), CC
St John's Priory,
Thomas Street, Dublin 8
Tel 01-6770393/0415/0601

Goold, Eamonn, Rt Rev Mgr, PP
Midleton, Co Cork
Tel 021-4631750
(*Midleton*, Cloyne)

Gorevan, Patrick
Harvieston,
Cunningham Road, Dalkey, Co Dublin
Tel 01-2859877
(Opus Dei)

Gormally, Michael, Very Rev, PP
Achill Sound, Achill, Co Mayo
Tel 098-45288
(*Achill*, Tuam)

Gorman, Owen, (OCDS), CC
Aghadrumsee, Roslea, Enniskillen,
Co Fermanagh BT92 7NQ
Tel 028-67751231
(*Clones*, Clogher)

Gorman, Seán, Very Rev, PP
Taghmon, Co Wexford
Tel 053-9134123
(*Taghmon*, Ferns)

Gorman, Thomas (SMA)
SMA House, Wilton, Cork
Tel 021-4541069/4541884

Gormley, Derek, CC
Swinford, Co Mayo
Tel 094-9253338
(*Swinford (Kilconduff and Meelick)*, Achonry)

Gormley, Joseph, CC
2 Station Road, Dungiven, Derry BT47 4LN
Tel 028-77741256
(*Dungiven*, Derry)

Gough, Brian
Chaplain,
St James's Hospital,
James's Street, Dublin 8
Tel 01-4103659/4162023
(Dublin)

Gough, Joseph A. (CSSp)
Blackrock College,
Blackrock, Co Dublin
Tel 01-2888681

Gould, Daniel, Very Rev, PP
Ballygriffin, Mallow, Co Cork
Tel 022-26153
(*Killavullen*, Cloyne)

Grace, Edmond (SJ)
Vice-Superior,
35 Lower Leeson Street, Dublin 2
Tel 01-6761248

Grace, James, Very Rev, PP
Killaloe, Co Clare
Tel 061-376137/087-6843315
(*Killaloe*, Killaloe)

Grace, Ned (SPS)
St Patrick's, Kiltegan, Co Wicklow
Tel 059-6473600

Grace, Patrick, Venerable Archdeacon
Inistioge, Co Kilkenny
Tel 056-7758429/ 086-8817628
(Ossory, retired)

Graham, Eamon, PP
42 Glenedra Road,
Feeny, Dungiven,
Co Derry BT47 4TW
Tel 028-77781223
(Derry)

Graham, Martin, Very Rev, PP
81 Lagmore Grove,
Dunmurry, Belfast BT17 0TD
Tel 028-90309011
(*Christ the Redeemer, Lagmore*, Down & C.)

Graham, Patrick (OCarm)
Whitefriar Street Church,
56 Aungier Street, Dublin 2
Tel 01-4758821

Grant, Colin, MA, STL, PGCE
St Malachy's College,
Antrim Road,
Belfast BT15 2AE
Tel 028-90748285
Aquinas College,
518 Ravenhill Road,
Belfast BT6 0BY
Tel 028-90643939
(Down & C.)

Grant, Henry (SJ)
Milltown Park,
Sandford Road, Dublin 6
Tel 01-2698411/2698113

Grant, Patrick, Very Rev Canon, PE
Ballyragget, Co Kilkenny
Tel 056-8833120
(Ossory, retired)

Grant, Robert, CC
St John's Presbytery,
New Street, Waterford
Tel 051-874271
(*St John's*, Waterford & L.)

Gray, Francis, Very Rev, PP
Carrick, Finea,
Mullingar, Co Westmeath
Tel 043-6681129
(*Carrick-Finea*, Ardagh & Cl.)

Greed, Pat, Very Rev, PP
18 Churchfield,
Clonlara, Co Clare
Tel 061-354594/086-6067003
(*Clonlara*, Killaloe)

Green, Denis (SM)
Mount St Mary's, Milltown, Dublin 14
Tel 01-2697322

Green, Gerard
c/o Bishop's House
(Dromore, retired)

Greenan, Clement (OP)
St Saviour's,
Upper Dorset Street, Dublin 1
Tel 01-8897610

Greene, James (White Fathers)
c/o Cypress Grove Road,
Templeogue, Dublin 6W
Tel 01-4055263

Greene, James, CC
Mitchelstown, Co Cork
Tel 025-84077
(*Mitchelstown*, Cloyne)

Greene, John, Very Rev (Moderator)
No. 3 Presbytery,
Dunmanus Court,
Cabra West, Dublin 7
Tel 01-6275663
(*Cabra West*, Dublin)

Greene, Patrick (SJ)
Manresa House,
Dollymount, Dublin 3
Tel 01-8331352

Grenham, Thomas (SPS)
Tearmann Spirituality Centre,
Brockagh, Glendalough, Co Wicklow
Tel 0404-45208

Griffin, Edward, Very Rev, PP
10 The Oaks,
Loughlinstown Drive,
Dun Laoghaire, Co Dublin
Tel 086-2395706/01-8480917
(*Loughlinstown*, Dublin)

Griffin, Eugene (SSC)
St Columban's Retirement Home,
Dalgan Park, Navan, Co Meath
Tel 046-9021525

Griffin, Gerard (CSSp)
Rockwell College,
Cashel, Co Tipperary
Tel 062-61444

Griffin, James, Very Rev, PE
10 Woodbrook Manor,
Tralee, Co Kerry
(Waterford & L., retired)

Griffin, Pat
Ashborough Lodge, Lyre,
Milltown, Co Kerry
(Kerry, retired)

Griffin, Patrick (OFMConv), CC
Friary of the Visitation,
Fairview Strand, Dublin 3
Tel 01-8376000
(*Fairview*, Dublin)

Griffin, Philip
Nullamore, Richmond Avenue South, Dublin 6
Tel 01-4971239
(Opus Dei)

Griffin, Tom (IC)
Clonturk House,
Ormond Road,
Drumcondra, Dublin 9
Tel 01-6877014

Griffith, Anthony
Rushbrook, Laghey, Co Donegal
Tel 074-9734021
(Raphoe, retired)

Grimes, Edward (CSSp)
Holy Ghost Missionary College,
Kimmage Manor, Dublin 12
Tel 01-4064300

Grimes, James, Very Rev, PE
61 Castlecaulfield Road, Donaghmore,
Co Tyrone BT70 3HF
Tel 028-87767727
(Armagh, retired)

Grimshaw, Ronan (CSSp)
Newlands Institute for Counselling,
2 Monastery Road,
Clondalkin, Dublin 22
Tel 01-4594573

Grogan, Brian (SJ)
Superior,
35 Lower Leeson Street, Dublin 2
Tel 01-6761248

Grogan, Desmond, Very Rev Canon, PE
Partry, Claremorris, Co Mayo
Tel 094-9543013
(Tuam, retired)

Grubka, Marek (OP)
Glasnevin, 40 Iona Road, Dublin 9
Tel 01-8305880/8602790

Grzegorzewski, Tomasz (SDB), CC
Aughrim,
Carrick-on-Shannon
Co Roscommon

Guckian, Michael (OMI)
Oblate Fathers,
House of Retreat, Inchicore, Dublin 8
Tel 01-454111
(*Inchicore, Mary Immaculate*, Dublin)

Guckian, Patrick, CC
44 Woodview Grove,
Blanchardstown, Dublin 15
Tel 01-8341894
(*Blanchardstown*, Dublin)

Guilfoyle, Patrick, Very Rev, PP
Tullaroan, Co Kilkenny
Tel 056-7769141/ 087-6644858
(*Tullaroan*, Ossory)

Guiney, John (SJ)
Milltown Park,
Sandford Road, Dublin 6
Tel 01-2698411/2698113

Guiney, John K. (SJ)
St Francis Xavier's,
Upper Gardiner Street, Dublin 1
Tel 01-8363411

Guiry, Michael, Very Rev, PP
Ardmore, Youghal, Co Waterford
Tel 024-94275
(*Ardmore*, Waterford & L.)

Gunn, David, PP
St Michael's, Ballinskelligs
Co Kerry
Tel 066-9479108
(*Ballinskelligs*, Kerry)

Gunn, Joseph, Very Rev, PP, VF
St Comgall's Presbytery,
27 Brunswick Road, Bangor,
Co Down BT20 3DS
Tel 028-91465522
(*Bangor*, Down & C.)

Gunn, Terence (SMA)
SMA House, Wilton, Cork
Tel 021-4541069/4541884

Guthrie, Charles (SVD)
Donamon Castle,
Roscommon
Tel 090-6662222

## H

Haan, Karl, CC
33 Glen Road, Garvagh,
Co Derry BT51 5DB
Tel 028-29558342
(*Garvagh*, Derry)

Habara, Gaspar (SVD), CC
3 Pembroke Road, Dublin 4
Tel 01-6680904

Habara, Gaspard (SVD)
3 Pembroke Road, Dublin 4
Tel 01-6680904

Hackett, Brian, Very Rev, PE, AP
Parochial House,
31 Church Street,
Ballygawley,
Co Tyrone BT70 2HA
Tel 028-85568219
(*Ballygawley (Errigal Kieran)*, Armagh)

Hackett, Michael, Very Rev Canon, PP
44 Church Street, Rostrevor,
Co Down BT34 3BB
Tel 028-41738277
(Dromore, on leave)

Hahessy, Ignatius (OCSO)
Mount Melleray Abbey,
Cappoquin, Co Waterford
Tel 058-54404

Hajkowski, Stanislaw (SC), CC
Cathedral Presbytery,
38 Hill Street,
Newry BT34 1AT
Tel 028-30262586
(*Newry*, Dromore)

Hall, Bernard (OFM)
PO Box 7026, Katutura,
Windlock, Republic of Namibia

Hallinan, Malachy, Rt Rev Mgr, VG
The Presbytery, Seamus Quirke Road, Galway
Tel 091-522713
(*Sacred Heart Church*, Galway)

Hally, Brendan (CSSp)
Rockwell College, Cashel,
Co Tipperary
Tel 062-61444

Halpin, Bernard (OMI), Co-PP
52a Bulfin Road, Dublin 8
Tel 01-4531660
(*Inchicore, St Michael's*, Dublin)

Halpin, David, CC
The Presbytery,
18 Straffan Way,
Maynooth, Co Dublin
Tel 01-4415001
(*Maynooth*, Dublin)

Halpin, Lauri, Very Rev, PE
Parochial House, Kilbeggan,
Co Westmeath
Tel 057-9332155
(Meath, retired)

Halpin, Martin, Very Rev, PP
Parochial House,
Ballinabrackey, Kinnegad,
Co Westmeath
Tel 046-9739015
(*Ballinabrackey*, Meath)

Halpin, Rory (SJ)
Crescent College Comprehensive,
Dooradoyle, Limerick
Tel 061-480920

Halton, John, Very Rev, PP
Tempo, Enniskillen,
Co Fermanagh BT94 3LY
Tel 028-89541344
(*Tempo*, Clogher)

Hamill, Aidan, Rt Rev Mgr, PP, VG
Parochial House,
70 North Street, Lurgan,
Co Armagh BT67 9AH
Tel 028-38323161
(*Shankill St Peter's (Lurgan)*, Dromore)

Hamill, Thomas
'Shekinah',
25 Wynnes Terrace,
Dundalk, Co Louth
Tel 042-9331023
(Armagh)

Hammel, James, Very Rev, PP
Annacurra, Aughrim,
Co Wicklow
Tel 0402-36119
(*Annacurra*, Ferns)

Hampson, Paul, PC
Parochial House,
Chapel Road, Lusk, Co Dublin
Tel 087-2452161
(*Lusk*, Dublin)

Hanafin, Sean, Dean, PP
St John's Presbytery, Tralee,
Co Kerry
Tel 066-7122522
(*Tralee, St John's*, Kerry)

Hand, John (SM)
(*Moderator*)
The Presbytery,
Coolock Village, Dublin 5
Tel 01-8484799
(*Coolock*, Dublin)

Hanley, Brendan (MSC)
Myross Wood Retreat House,
Leap, Skibbereen, Co Cork
Tel 028-33118

Hanley, Brian, Very Rev
Ballyhard, Glenamaddy,
Co Galway
(Elphin)

Hanley, Michael, Very Rev, PP
Kilfinane Co Limerick
Tel 063-91016/086-8595733
(*Kilfinane*, Limerick)

Hanlon, Joseph, Very Rev (assistant priest)
St Mary's Presbytery,
Willbrook Road,
Rathfarnham, Dublin 14
Tel 01-4932390
(*Rathfarnham*, Dublin)

Hanly, Gerard, Very Rev Canon, PP, VF
Boyle, Co Roscommon
Tel 071-9662218
(*Boyle*, Elphin)

Hanly, John, Rt Rev Mgr, PP
Parochial House, Carnaross,
Kells, Co Meath
Tel 046-9245904
(*Carnaross*, Meath)

Hanly, Rory (SAC), CC
9 Seaview Lawn, Shankill,
Co Dublin
Tel 01-2822277
(*Shankill*, Dublin)

Hanly, William (SAC)
Pallottine College, Thurles,
Co Tipperary
Tel 0504-21202

Hanna, John (CSsR)
Scala, Castlemahon House,
Castle Road, Cork
Tel 021-4358800

Hannan, Greg, Very Rev, PP
Ballymote, Co Sligo
Tel 071-9183361
(*Ballymote (Emlefad and Kilmorgan)*, Achonry)

Hannan, John (SM)
Rome

Hannan, Laurence (SM)
Fiji

Hannan, Peter (SJ)
Manresa House,
Dollymount, Dublin 3
Tel 01-8331352

Hannigan, Patrick, Very Rev, PP, VF
Parochial House,
65 Tullyallen Road,
Dungannon,
Co Tyrone BT70 3AF
Tel 028-87761211
(*Killeeshil*, Armagh)

Hannon, Donald, Very Rev, PP
Swanlinbar, Co Cavan
Tel 049-9521221/087-2830145
(*Swanlinbar*, Kilmore)

Hannon, James
Chaplain, St Mary's Hospital,
Phoenix Park, Dublin 20
Tel 01-6778132
(Dublin)

Hannon, James
Sandhill Road, Ballybunion,
Co Kerry
(Cloyne, retired)

Hannon, Martin
Cleraun Study Centre,
90 Foster Avenue,
Mount Merrion, Co Dublin
Tel 01-2881734
(Opus Dei)

Hannon, Patrick, Dr
Emeritus Professor of Theology,
St Patrick's College,
Maynooth, Co Kildare
Tel 01-6285222
(Cloyne, retired)

Hannon, Patrick, PC,
St Mary's, Donabate,
Co Dublin
Tel 01-8434574
(*Donabate*, Dublin)

Hannon, Ray, CC
(Dublin, retired)

Hannon, Timothy, PP
The Abbey, Wicklow,
Co Wicklow
Tel 0404-46229
(*Wicklow*, Dublin)

Hannon, Tom, PP
Institute of St Anselm,
Norfolk Road, Cliftonville,
Kent CT9 2EU, UK
Tel 0044-1843234704
(Killaloe)

Hanrahan, Noel (MHM)
St Joseph's House
50 Orwell Park,
Rathgar, Dublin 6
Tel 01-4127700

Hanrahan, Paschal, CF, (RC)
20 Poratal Road, Javelin Barracks,
41372 Niederkuruchten
Germany
Tel +49 1722 189793
(Killaloe)

Hanratty, David
Tierhogar, Portarlington,
Co Laois
Tel 057-8645719
(Meath)

Hanratty, Malachy (SSC)
St Columban's, Dalgan Park,
Navan, Co Meath
Tel 046-9021525

Hanratty, Oliver
The Bungalow,
Crescent Road, Rogerstown,
Rush, Co Dublin
(Dublin, retired)

Hanson, Frederick (SSC)
St Columban's Retirement Home,
Dalgan Park, Navan,
Co Meath
Tel 046-9021525

Haran, Casimir (CP), CC
Holy Cross Retreat,
432 Crumlin Road, Ardoyne,
Belfast BT14 7GE
Tel 028-90748231/2
(*Holy Cross*, Down & C.)

Haran, Cyril, Very Rev
Grange, Co Sligo
(Elphin, retired)

Harding, Michael, CC
Templemore Road, Roscrea,
Co Tipperary
Tel 0505-21218
(*Roscrea*, Killaloe)

Harkin, Ciarán, CC
Parochial House, Stranorlar,
Co Donegal
Tel 074-9131157
(*Stranorlar*, Raphoe)

Harkin, Dermott, CC
St Brigid's, Carnhill,
Derry BT48 8HJ
Tel 028-71351261
(Derry)

Harkin, Hugh (SMA)
African Missions,
Blackrock Road, Cork
Tel 021-4292871

Harmon, Maurice
Faculty of Education,
Mary Immaculate College,
South Circular Road,
Limerick
(Killaloe)

Harmon, Sean
Chaplain,
St Joseph's Hospital, Limerick
Tel 061-414624
(Limerick)

Harmon, Seán, CC
Cathedral House,
Cathedral Place, Limerick
Tel 061-414624/087-2589279
(*St John's*, Limerick)

Harney, Donal (MHM)
St Joseph's,
Freshford House, Kilkenny
Tel 056-7721482

Harper, Conor (SJ), CC
Jesuit Community,
Sandford Road,
Ranelagh, Dublin 6
Tel 01-2180244
(*Donnybrook*, Dublin)

Harper, Frank, Very Rev
32 Bryansford Ave,
Newcastle BT33 OEQ
(Down & C., retired)

Harrington, Brendan, Very Rev, PP
Fossa, Killarney, Co Kerry
Tel 064-6631996
(*Fossa*, Kerry)

Harrington, Christopher, Very Rev, PP
St Joseph's Presbytery,
Mayfield, Cork
Tel 021-4501861
(*St Joseph's (Mayfield)*, Cork & R.)

Harrington, Denis, Very Rev, PE, CC
Clane, Naas, Co Kildare
Tel 045-868224
(Kildare & L., retired)

Harrington, James (OFMCap)
Vicar, Capuchin Friary,
Friary Street, Kilkenny
Tel 056-7721439

Harrington, John (SM), PC
Superior,
St Brendan's Parish,
Coolock Village, Dublin 5
Tel 01-8484799
(*Coolock*, Dublin)

Harrington, Joseph (SDB)
Chaplain,
Milford House,
Salesian House, Milford,
Castletroy, Limerick
Tel 061-330268/330914

Harrington, Michael, Very Rev Canon, PE
Charleville, Co Cork
Tel 063-21833
(Cloyne, retired)

Harrington, Terence (OFMCap), Very Rev
Capuchin Friary,
Church Street, Dublin 7
Tel 01-8730599

Harrington, Wilfred (OP)
St Mary's Priory, Tallaght,
Dublin 24
Tel 01-4048100

Harris, Derek (SSC)
44 Harbour View, Howth,
Co Dublin
Tel 01-8395161

Harris, Jack (CM), PP
122 Sunday's Well Road, Cork
Tel 021-4304070
(*St Vincent's, Sunday's Well*, Cork & R.)

Harris, James (OP), Very Rev
Prior, St Saviour's,
Bridge Street, Waterford
Tel 051-875061

Harris, John (OP)
St Saviour's,
Upper Dorset Street, Dublin 1
Tel 01-8897610

Harris, Walter, Very Rev Canon, PE
151 Clonsilla Road,
Blanchardstown, Dublin 15
Tel 01-8213716
(Dublin, retired)

Harrison, Michael, Very Rev, PP, VF
Ballycastle, Co Mayo
Tel 096-43010
(*Ballycastle (Kilbride and Doonfeeny)*, Killala)

Harrison, Michael (SSC)
St Columban's, Dalgan Park,
Navan, Co Meath
Tel 046-9021525

Harte, Martin, CC
Presbytery No. 2,
Church Grounds,
Lower Kilmacud Road,
Kilmacud, Co Dublin
Tel 01-2882257
(*Kilmacud-Stillorgan*, Dublin)

Hartley, Noel, Very Rev Canon
10 Donovan's Wharf,
Crescent Quay, Wexford
(Ferns, retired)

Hartnett, Denis (MHM)
St Joseph's House,
50 Orwell Park, Rathgar,
Dublin 6
Tel 01-4127700

Harty, Gabriel (OP)
St Mary's Priory, Tallaght,
Dublin 24
Tel 01-4048100

Harty, John (OFM)
Franciscan Friary, Clonmel,
Co Tipperary
Tel 052-6121378

Haslam, Richard (OMI)
Oblate House of Retreat,
Inchicore, Dublin 8
Tel 01-4534408/4541805

Hassett, Edmond, CC
Portlaw, Co Waterford
Tel 051-387227
(Waterford & L.)

Hassett, John, VF
(*Moderator*)
127 Castlegate Way,
Adamstown, Co Dublin
Tel 01-62812088
(*Esker-Doddsboro-Adamstown*, Dublin)

Hasson, Eugene, PP
164 Greencastle Road,
Omagh,
Co Tyrone BT79 7RU
Tel 028-81648474
(*Greencastle*, Derry)

Hasson, Gerald, CC
Parochial House, St Mary's,
Creggan, Derry BT48 9QE
Tel 028-71263152
(*St Mary's, Creggan*, Derry)

Hasson, James (OFM)
Franciscan Missionaries in Zimbabwe

Hastings, Michael, Very Rev, PP
103 Mount Prospect Drive,
Clontarf, Dublin 3
Tel 01-8335255
(Dublin, retired)

Haugh, Joseph, Very Rev
Bealaha, Doonbeg, Co Clare
Tel 065-9055022/
087-2603314
(*Doonbeg and Killard*, Killaloe)

Haughey, Eoghan (OMI)
Oblate House of Retreat,
Inchicore, Dublin 8
Tel 01-4534408/4541805

Haughey, Peter (OSA)
St John's Priory,
Thomas Street, Dublin 8
Tel 01-6770393

Hawis, Jack (CM), Very Rev, PP
St Vincent's,
122 Sunday Well Road,
Cork
Tel 021-4304070/4304529

Hayden, Chris
Pontifical Irish College,
Via de SS Quattro 1,
Roma 00184, Italy
(Ferns)

Hayden, Desmond
(assistant priest)
St Mary's Presbytery,
Willbrook Road,
Rathfarnham, Dublin 14
Tel 01-8338424
(*Rathfarnham*, Dublin)

Hayes, Bartholomew (MHM)
St Joseph's House,
50 Orwell Park, Rathgar,
Dublin 6
Tel 01-4127700

Hayes, Colm, Very Rev
15 St Patrick's Terrace, Sligo
(Elphin, retired)

Hayes, Conor, Very Rev, CC
The Parochial House,
Kilteely, Co Limerick
Tel 061-384213
(*Kilteely*, Cashel & E.)

Hayes, George, Very Rev
c/o Diocesan Offices,
Killarney, Co Kerry
(Kerry)

Hayes, James (SJ)
Irish Jesuit Provincialate,
Milltown Park, Sandford
Road, Dublin 6
Tel 01-4987333

Hayes, Martin, Very Rev, Adm
Cathedral Presbytery,
Thurles, Co Tipperary
Tel 0504-22229/22779
(*Thurles, Cathedral of the Assumption*, Cashel & E.)

Hayes, Noel (SPS)
Bridgetown, Co Clare
Tel 061-377158
(*Killaloe*, Killaloe)

Hayes, Patrick, CC
St Mary's, Clonmel,
Co Tipperary
Tel 052-6121952
(*Clonmel, St Mary's*, Waterford & L.)

Hayes, Richard, Very Rev, PP
Clonroche, Enniscorthy, Co Wexford
Tel 053-9244115
(*Cloughbawn*, Ferns)

Hayes, Seán (SMA)
SMA House, 82 Ranelagh Road, Ranelagh, Dublin 6
Tel 01-4968162/3

Hayes, Tom, PP
Parochial House, Enniskeane, Co Cork
Tel 023-8847769
(*Enniskeane and Desertserges*, Cork & R.)

Hazelwood, Timothy, CC
Blarney, Co Cork
Tel 021-4385229
(*Blarney*, Cloyne)

Heagney, John, Very Rev, PP
Parochial House, Mullaghbawn, Newry, Co Down BT35 9XN
Tel 028-30888286
(*Mullaghbawn (Forkhill)*, Armagh)

Heagney, Michael (CSsR)
St Patrick's, Esker, Athenry, Co Galway
Tel 091-844549

Healy, Alexius (OFMCap)
St Anthony's Capuchin Friary, 43 Dublin Street, Carlow
Tel 059-9142543

Healy, Bernard, CC
Dingle, Co Kerry
Tel 066-9151208
(*Dingle*, Kerry)

Healy, Charles, CC
St Mary's, Athlone, Co Westmeath
Tel 090-6472088
(*Athlone*, Ardagh & Cl.)

Healy, Jeremiah (SMA)
African Missions, Blackrock Road, Cork
Tel 021-4292871

Healy, Michael (SSC)
St Columban's Retirement Home, Dalgan Park, Navan, Co Meath
Tel 046-9021525

Healy, Myles (CSSp), Very Rev, PP
55 Fernhill Road, Greenhills, Dublin 12
Tel 01-4509191
(*Greenhills*, Dublin)

Healy, Patrick J. (SDB), CC
162 Walkinstown Road, Dublin 12
Tel 01-4501372
(*Walkinstown*, Dublin)

Healy, Peter, CC
16 Brookwood Grove, Artane, Dublin 5
Tel 01-8377337
(*Artane*, Dublin)

Healy, Sean (SMA)
Social Justice Ireland, Arena House
Arena Road, Sandyford, Dublin 18
Tel 01-2130724

Healy, Thomas, Adm
The Presbytery, Longford
Tel 043-3346465
(Ardagh & Cl.)

Healy, Timothy (SJ)
Irish Jesuit Provincialate, Milltown Park, Sandford Road, Dublin 6
Tel 01-4987333

Heaney, Columban (OCSO)
Mount Melleray Abbey, Cappoquin, Co Waterford
Tel 058-54404

Heaney, Seamus, Very Rev, PP
Parochial House, Delvin, Co Westmeath
Tel 044-9664127
(*Delvin*, Meath)

Heaney, Seán, Rt Rev Mgr, PP, VG
Parochial House, Tullamore, Co Offaly
Tel 057-9321587/057-9351510
(Meath)

Hearne, Thomas, CC
Bohergar, Brittas, Co Limerick
Tel 061-352223
(*Murroe and Boher*, Cashel & E.)

Hearty, Phil, Very Rev (CSsR), Adm
Lusmagh, Banagher, Co Offaly
Tel 0509-51358
(*Lusmagh*, Clonfert)

Heaslip, Anthony (OCarm)
Carmelite Friary, Kinsale, Co Cork
Tel 021-4772138

Hearty, Philip (CSsR)
St Patrick's, Esker, Athenry, Co Galway
Tel 091-844549

Hederman, Mark Patrick (OSB), Rt Rev Dom Abbot, Glenstal Abbey, Murroe, Co Limerick
Tel 061-386103

Heelan, Patrick (SJ)
Irish Jesuit Provincialate, Milltown Park, Sandford Road, Dublin 6
Tel 01-4987333

Heeran, Brendan (CSSp)
Holy Ghost Missionary College, Kimmage Manor, Dublin 12
Tel 01-4064300

Heerey, Anthony (CSSp)
Holy Spirit Missionary College, Kimmage Manor, Whitehall Road, Dublin 12
Tel 01-4064300

Heerey, Charles, Very Rev, PP
Ballinamore, Co Leitrim
Tel 071-9644039
(*Ballinamore*, Kilmore)

Heery, Kevin, CC
St Mary's, Navan, Co Meath
Tel 046-9027518/9027414
(*Navan*, Meath)

Heinhold, John, Very Rev, Adm
Kilbrittain, Co Cork
Tel 023-8849637
(*Kilbrittain*, Cork & R.)

Heffernan, John (OP)
St Dominic's, Athy, Co Kildare
Tel 059-8631573

Heffernan, Joseph (OP)
St Magdalen's, Drogheda, Co Louth
Tel 041-9838271

Heffernan, Martin, Very Rev, PP, Ph.D
Kildorrery, Mallow, Co Cork
Tel 022-25174
(*Kildorrery*, Cloyne)

Hegarty, Benedict (OP), CC
Presbytery, St Dominic's Road, Tallaght, Dublin 24
Tel 01-4510620
(*Tallaght, Dodder*, Dublin)

Hegarty, Benedict (OP), Very Rev, Prior,
St Dominic's Retreat House, Montenotte, Co Cork
Tel 021-4502520

Hegarty, Ciarán
The Presbytery, 30A Deanby Gardens, Belfast BT14 6NN
Tel 028-90745140
(Down & C., on study leave)

Hegarty, James (SSS)
Blessed Sacrament Chapel, 20 Bachelors Walk, Dublin 1
Tel 01-8724597

Hegarty, John Paul, Very Rev, PP
Glounthaune, Co Cork
Tel 021-4232881
(*Glounthaune*, Cork & R.)

Hegarty, Kevin, Very Rev
Carne, Belmullet, Co Mayo
Tel 097-81011
(*Kilmore-Erris*, Killala)

Hegarty, Martin, Very Rev, PP
32 Knockmoyle Est, Tralee, Co Kerry
(Kerry, retired)

Hegarty, Michael (IC), Very Rev, PP
Cooleens, Glenconnor, Clonmel, Co Tipperary
Tel 052-6125679
(*Clonmel, St Oliver Plunkett*, Waterford & L.)

Hegarty, Patrick, Very Rev Canon, PP
St Jude's Avenue, Crossmolina, Co Mayo
(Killala, retired)

Hegarty, Peter (SPS)
On temporary diocesan work

Hegarty, Richard, Very Rev, PE, CC
Killavullen, Co Cork
Tel 022-26125
(*Killavullen*, Cloyne)

Hegarty, Seamus, Most Rev, DD
Ardstraw House, 21A Buncrana Road, Derry BT48 8LA
(Derry, retired)

Hegarty, Seán, Very Rev, PE
1a Convent Road, Cookstown, Co Tyrone BT80 80A
Tel 028-86769629
(Armagh, retired)

Hegarty, Walter (OP)
St Mary's, The Claddagh, Co Galway
Tel 091-582884

Hehir, Mark, CC (Cloyne)
Cork and Ross Offices, Redemption Road, Cork
Tel 021-4301717
(Cork & R.)

Henderson, Eanna (OCSO)
Mount Saint Joseph Abbey, Roscrea, Co Tipperary
Tel 0505-25600

Hendrick, Richard (OFMCap)
Vicar, Holy Trinity, Fr Mathew Quay, Cork
Tel 021-4270827

Heneghan, James (CSSp)
(Chaplain to Brazilian Community)
12 Abbeyville, Roscommon
Tel 090-6627978
(*Roscommon*, Elphin)

Heneghan, Jeremy (OFMCap)
Holy Trinity, Fr Mathew Quay, Cork
Tel 021-4270827

Heneghan, Kieran (SSC)
Knock, Co Mayo

Hennessy, Gerard, CC
Cathedral Presbytery, Thurles, Co Tipperary
Tel 0504-22229/22779
(Cashel & E.)

Hennessy, Patrick (SDB)
Salesian College,
Maynooth Road, Celbridge,
Co Kildare
Tel 01-6275058/60

Hennessy, Patrick, Very Rev, PP
Ballyfin, Portlaoise, Co Laois
Tel 057-8755227
(*Mountrath*, Kildare & L.)

Hennessy, William, Very Rev, PP
Castletown, Portlaoise,
Co Laois
Tel 0502-32622/087-8736155
(*Castletown*, Ossory)

Hennessy, William, Very Rev, PP
Knocklong, Co Limerick
Tel 062-53114
(*Knocklong*, Cashel & E.)

Hennigan, Frank (SM)
Mount St Mary's, Milltown,
Dublin 14
Tel 01-2697322

Henry, Denis, Co-PP
1A Ballydowd Grove, Lucan,
Co Dublin
Tel 01-2955541
(*Lucan*, Dublin)

Henry, Leo, BA, HDE
St Nathy's College,
Ballaghaderreen,
Co Roscommon
Tel 094-9860010
(Achonry)

Henry, Martin
St Patrick's College,
Maynooth, Co Kildare
Tel 01-6285222
(Down & C.)

Henry, Martin, CC
The Presbytery,
Ballaghaderreen,
Co Roscommon
Tel 094-9860011
(Achonry)

Henry, Maurice, Very Rev, PP, Adm
Parochial House, Crossgar,
Downpatrick,
Co Down BT30 9EA
Tel 028-44830229
(*Crossgar (Kilmore)*, Down & C.)

Henry, Seamus, Very Rev Canon
Freshford, Co Kilkenny
Tel 056-8832146/
086-0879296
(Ossory, retired)

Henry, Seán, Very Rev, PP
Parochial House, Trim,
Co Meath
Tel 046-9431251
(*Trim*, Meath)

Heraty, Jarlath, PP (pro-tem)
Roundstone, Co Galway
Tel 095-35846
(*Roundstone*, Tuam)

Herlihy, David, Very Rev, PP
Newmarket, Co Cork
Tel 029-60999
(*Newmarket*, Cloyne)

Herlihy, Ronan (OFMCap)
Holy Trinity,
Fr Mathew Quay, Cork
Tel 021-4270827

Herrity, Michael, Very Rev, PP
Annagry, Co Donegal
Tel 074-9548111
(*Annagry*, Raphoe)

Herron, Frank, Very Rev, Adm
11 Foxrock Court, Foxrock,
Dublin 18
Tel 01-4513109
(*Foxrock*, Dublin)

Hession, Noel (OSA), CC
Parochial House,
St Helena's Drive, Dublin 11
Tel 01-8343444
(*Rivermount*, Dublin)

Hession, Stan (OCarm)
Carmelite Friary, Kinsale,
Co Cork
Tel 021-772138

Hever, Thomas, Very Rev Canon, Adm, VF
St Mary's, Sligo
Tel 071-9162670/9162769
Sligo Social Services,
Charles Street, Sligo
Tel 071-9145682
(*Sligo, St Mary's*, Elphin)

Heverin, Seamus, Rt Rev Mgr
Enniscrone, Co Sligo
Tel 096-37802
(Killala, retired)

Hickey, Herman (OCSO)
Our Lady of Bethlehem Abbey,
11 Ballymena Road,
Portglenone, Ballymena,
Co Antrim BT44 8BL
Tel 028-25821211

Hickey, Jeremiah (OSA)
St Augustine's Priory,
O'Connell Street, Limerick
Tel 061-415374

Hickey, John (OFMCap)
Holy Trinity,
Fr Mathew Quay, Cork
Tel 021-4270827

Hickey, John (SSC)
Catholic Rectory, Abbey,
Loughrea, Co Galway
Tel 0909-745217

Hickey, John, CC
Abbey, Loughrea,
Co Galway
Tel 090-9745217
(*Duniry and Abbey*, Clonfert)

Hickey, Liam, Very Rev
St Ciaran's,
1 Cherryfield Park,
Hartstown, Dublin 15
Tel 01-8214863
(Dublin, retired)

Hickey, Michael (CSSp), CC
Parochial House, Tenure,
Dunleer, Co Louth
Tel 041-6851281
(*Monasterboice*, Armagh)

Hickey, Michael, Very Rev, PP
Bansha, Co Tipperary
Tel 062-54132
(*Bansha and Kilmoyler*, Cashel & E.)

Hickland, Brendan, Very Rev, PP
St Teresa's Presbytery,
Glen Road,
Belfast BT11 8BL
Tel 028-90612855
(*St Teresa's*, Down & C.)

Higgins, James (SMA)
African Missions,
Blackrock Road, Cork
Tel 021-4292871

Higgins, Richard, Very Rev Canon, AP
Maree, Oranmore,
Co Galway
Tel 091-794113
(Galway, retired)

Higgins, Thomas (OCarm)
Whitefriar Street Church,
56 Aungier Street, Dublin 2
Tel 01-4758821

Hillery, Des
Padre de San Columbano,
Apartado 39-073/074,
Lima 39, Peru
(Killaloe)

Hilliard, Alan
Chaplain,
19 Springlawn Close,
Blanchardstown, Dublin 15
Tel 01-5053055
(*Blanchardstown*, Dublin)

Hoban, Brendan (SSC)
St Columban's, Dalgan Park,
Navan, Co Meath
Tel 046-9021525

Hoban, Brendan, Very Rev, PP
Moygownagh, Ballina,
Co Mayo
Tel 096-31288
(*Moygownagh*, Killala)

Hoban, Patrick, Very Rev, PP
Killala, Co Mayo
Tel 096-32176
(*Killala*, Killala)

Hodnett, Vincent, Very Rev Canon, PP
The Lough Presbytery,
St Finbarr's West, Cork
Tel 021-4273821
(*The Lough*, Cork & R.)

Hoey, Charles, (OCarm), Very Rev, PP
Carmelite Priory,
56 Aungier Street, Dublin 2
Tel 01-8062846
(*Whitefriar Street*, Dublin)

Hoey, Eamonn, (CSsR), CC
St Joseph's,
St Alphonsus Road,
Dundalk, Co Louth
Tel 042-9334042
(*Dundalk, St Joseph's*, Armagh)

Hogan, Bernard, Very Rev, PP
Drumlish, Co Longford
Tel 043-3324132
(*Drumlish*, Ardagh & Cl.)

Hogan, Colm PP
Kildysart, Co Clare
Tel 065-6832155/
086-3011530
(*Kildysart and Coolmeen*, Killaloe)

Hogan, Diarmuid
Chaplain, NUI, Galway
Tel 091-524853/495055
(Galway)

Hogan, Donal (SSC)
Regional Director,
St Columban's, Dalgan Park,
Navan, Co Meath
Tel 046-9021525

Hogan, Edmund M. (SMA)
African Missions,
Blackrock Road, Cork
Tel 021-4292871

Hogan, Flannan (OCSO)
Mount Saint Joseph Abbey,
Roscrea, Co Tipperary
Tel 0505-25600

Hogan, John (CSSp)
Holy Ghost Missionary College,
Kimmage Manor, Dublin 12
Tel 01-4064300

Hogan, John F., Venerable Archdeacon, AP
Ballycommon, Nenagh,
Co Tipperary
Tel 067-24153/087-7536526
(*Puckane*, Killaloe)

Hogan, John, CC
St Mary's, Drogheda,
Co Louth
Tel 041-9834958
(*Drogheda, St Mary's*, Meath)

Hogan, Martin, Co-PP
187 Clontarf Road, Clontarf,
Dublin 3
Tel 01-8338575/0879721213
(*Clontarf, St John's*, Dublin)

Hogan, Michael
c/o Killaloe Diocesan Office,
Westbourne, Ennis, Co Clare
(Killaloe)

Hogan Patrick (SVD)
Donamon Castle,
Roscommon
Tel 090-6662222

Hogan, Patrick, Very Rev, PP
334 O'Malley Park, Southill,
Limerick
Tel 061-414248
(*Holy Family*, Limerick)

Hogan, Ray (MHM)
St Joseph's House,
50 Orwell Park, Rathgar,
Dublin 6
Tel 01-4127700
Hogan, Thomas (CSSp)
Holy Spirit Missionary
College,
Kimmage Manor,
Whitehall Road,
Dublin 12
Tel 01-4064300
Hogan, Thomas (CSsR)
Marianella, 75 Orwell Road,
Dublin 6
Tel 01-4067100
Hogan, Tom, Very Rev
Cathedral Presbytery,
O'Connell Street,
Ennis, Co Clare
Tel 065-6869097
(Killaloe)
Hogg, Barry, Very Rev
President, St Mary's College,
Galway
Tel 091-522458/524904
(Galway)
Holahan, Ciarán, Very Rev, PP
11 Foxrock Court, Foxrock,
Dublin 18
Tel 01-2893229
(Dublin, retired)
Holland, Michael (OFM)
Franciscan Abbey,
Multyfarnham,
Co Westmeath
Tel 044-9371114/9371137
Holleran, Patrick, Very Rev, PP
Coolaney, Co Sligo
Tel 071-9167745
(*Coolaney (Killoran),*
Achonry)
Holloway, James, Very Rev, PP
Moymore, Pallasgreen,
Co Limerick
Tel 061-384111
(Cashel & E., retired)
Holloway, Sean (SSC)
St Columban's Retirement
Home,
Dalgan Park, Navan,
Co Meath
Tel 046-9021525
Holmes, Brian (CSsR)
Mission in
Mozambique/Malawi
c/o Marianella,
75 Orwell Road,
Rathgar, Dublin 6
Tel 01-4067100
Holmes, Kieran, CC
Enniscrone, Ballina,
Co Mayo
Tel 096-36164
(*Kilglass*, Killala)
Holmes, Liam, Very Rev, PP
Knockaney, Hospital,
Co Limerick
Tel 061-383127
(*Knockaney*, Cashel & E.)
Holmes, Samuel, PP
Cloone, Co Leitrim
Tel 071-9636016
(*Aughavas and Cloone*,
Ardagh & Cl.)
Holmes, Vianney (OFMCap)
Vicar, Capuchin Friary,
Ard Mhuire, Creeslough,
Letterkenny, Co Donegal
Tel 074-9138005
Homa, Tomasz (PME)
Gonzaga College,
Sandford Road, Dublin 6
Tel 01-4972943
Hopkins, Francis, Very Rev
Canon, AP
St Anne's Presbytery,
Convent Hill, Waterford
Tel 051-855819
(*Ballybricken*, Waterford &
L.)
Horan, Gerry (OSA)
St Augustine's,
Taylor's Lane,
Balyboden, Dublin 16
Tel 01-4241000
Horan, John (SDB), Very Rev
Salesian House, Milford,
Castletroy, Limerick
Tel 061-330268/330914
Horgan, John (SMA)
Salesian House, Milford,
Castletroy, Limerick
Tel 061-330268/330914
Horgan, Patrick (CSsR)
Clonard Monastery,
Clonard Gardens,
Belfast BT13 2RL
Tel 028-90445950
(*St Paul's*, Down & C.)
Horgan, Patrick, Very Rev
(priest in residence)
Killarney, Co Kerry
Tel 064-31014
(*Killarney*, Kerry)
Horgan, Seamus
Apostolic Nunciature,
En Suisse, Thunstrasse 60,
Case Pastale 259,
3000 Berne 6, Switzerland
(Killaloe)
Horgan, Sean (MSC)
Carrignavar, Co Cork
Tel 021-4884044
Horneck, Noel, Very Rev, PP
Parochial House, Dunderry,
Navan, Co Meath
Tel 046-9431433
(*Dunderry*, Meath)
Hough, Martin
England
(Clonfert)
Houlihan, Brendan, Rt Rev
Mgr, PP
Parochial House,
Mount Saint Mary's,
Thormanby Road, Howth,
Dublin 13
Tel 01-8322036
(*Howth*, Dublin)
Houlihan, Henry (OFM)
Franciscan Friary, Liberty
Street, Cork
Tel 021-4270302
Houlihan, Nik (MI)
St Camillus, Killucan,
Co Westmeath
Tel 044-74115
Houlihan, Seamus, Very Rev,
PP
Parochial House, Nobber,
Co Meath
Tel 046-9052197
(Meath)
Hourigan, Joseph, Very Rev,
PP
Lissycasey, Ennis,
Co Clare
Tel 065-6834145
(*Ballynacally*, Killaloe)
Howard, Brendan, CC
Curate's House, Clonegal,
Enniscorthy, Co Wexford
Tel 053-9377291
(*Myshall*, Kildare & L.)
Howard, Niall, CC
Cahirciveen, Co Kerry
Tel 066-9472210
(*Cahirciveen*, Kerry)
Howard, Patrick, Very Rev
Athlacca, Kilmallock,
Co Limerick
Tel 063-90540
(Limerick, retired)
Howard, Terence (SJ)
Peter Faber House,
28 Brookvale Avenue,
Belfast BT14 6BW
Tel 028-90757615
Howell, Patrick (CSsR)
Marianella, 75 Orwell Road,
Rathgar, Dublin 6
Tel 01-4067100
Howell, William, Very Rev, PP
St Michael's, Gorey,
Co Wexford
Tel 053-9421112
(*Gorey*, Ferns)
Howlett, John (SAC)
Provincial House,
'Homestead',
Sandyford Road, Dundrum,
Dublin 16
Tel 01-2956180/2954170
Howley, Enda, CC
Parochial House, Ryehill,
Monivea, Galway
Tel 091-849019
(*Abbeyknockmoy*, Tuam)
Howley, Gary (SPS)
Tearmann Spirituality
Centre,
Brockagh, Glendalough,
Co Wicklow
Tel 0404-45208
Hoyne, Peter, Very Rev, PE
Newmarket, Hugginstown,
Co Kilkenny
Tel 056-7768678
(*Aghaviller*, Ossory)
Hoyne, William (OFM)
Hermanos Franciscanos,
Iglesia Parroquial 'Dios con
Nostros',
1a Av, 5a-6a Calles,
Manzana 10,
Elmezquital, Zana 12,
10102 Guatemala City,
Guatemala
Hubbart, Thomas (IC)
Clonturk House,
Ormond Road,
Drumcondra, Dublin 9
Tel 01-6877014
Hudson, Patrick (OFM)
Adam and Eve's,
4 Merchant Quay, Dublin 8
Tel 01-6771128
Hughes, Augustine (OFM)
Franciscan College,
Gormanston, Co Meath
Tel 01-8412203
Hughes, Benedict
Kellystown, Coolderry Road,
Carrickmacross,
Co Monaghan
Tel 086-3864907
(Clogher)
Hughes, Bernard (IC), CC
St Brigid's, Kilcurry,
Dundalk, Co Louth
Tel 042-9334410
(*Faughart*, Armagh)
Hughes, Eoin
Chaplain,
Beaumont Hospital,
Beaumont Road, Dublin 9
Tel 01-8477573
(Dublin)
Hughes, John (OSA)
St John's Priory,
Thomas Street, Dublin 8
Tel 01-6770393
Hughes, John, Very Rev, PC
Archibishop's House,
Drumcondra, Dublin 9
Tel 01-8373732
(Dublin)
Hughes, John, Very Rev, PE,
CC
Parochial House,
Benburb Road,
Moy, Dungannon,
Co Tyrone BT71 7SQ
Tel 028-87784240
(*Moy (Clonfeacle),* Armagh)
Hughes, Liam, Very Rev, PE
Inniskeen, Dundalk,
Co Louth
Tel 042-9378338
(Clogher, retired)
Hughes, Louis (OP), Very Rev
Prior, Black Abbey,
Kilkenny, Co Kilkenny
Tel 056-7721279

Hughes, Martin (Team Assistant)
The Presbytery,
St Aidan's Parish,
Brookfield Road, Tallaght, Dublin 24
Tel 01-4624410
(*Brookfield*, Dublin)

Hughes, Michael (OMI)
Oblate Scholasticate,
St Anne's,
Goldenbridge Walk,
Inchicore, Dublin 8
Tel 01-4540841/4542955

Hughes, Pat, CC
St Conleth's, Chapel Lane,
Droichead Nua, Co Kildare
Tel 045-438036
(*Droichead Nua/Newbridge*, Kildare & L.)

Hughes, Patrick (CM)
St Peter's, Phibsboro,
Dublin 7
Tel 01-8389708

Hughes, Patrick, Very Rev, PP
Parochial House,
10 Cloughfin Road,
Kildress, Cookstown,
Co Tyrone BT80 9JB
Tel 028-86751206
(*Kildress*, Armagh)

Hughes, Paul (OCarm)
Gort Muire, Ballinteer,
Dublin 16
Tel 01-2984014

Hume, Patrick (SJ)
Campion House Residence,
28 Lower Hatch Street,
Dublin 2
Tel 01-6383990

Humphreys, John (SJ)
Rector,
St Ignatius Community & Church,
27 Raleigh Row, Salthill,
Galway
Tel 091-523707

Humphries, Seamus (OSA)
St Augustine's Priory,
Dungarvan,
Co Waterford
Tel 058-41136

Hunt, Anselm (OSB)
Abbot, Glenstal Abbey,
Murroe, Co Limerick
Tel 061-386103

Hunt, Des (SM)
Mount St Mary's, Milltown,
Dublin 14
Tel 01-2697322

Hurley, Colm, Very Rev Canon, PP
Killeshandra, Co Cavan
Tel 049-4334155
(Kilmore)

Hurley, Declan, Very Rev, Adm
St Mary's, Navan, Co Meath
Tel 046-9027518/9027414
(*Navan*, Meath)

Hurley, James (CSSp)
Rockwell College, Cashel,
Co Tipperary
Tel 062-61444

Hurley, Michael C., Very Rev Canon, PP, VF
Killeshandra, Co Cavan
Tel 049-4334155
(*Killeshandra*, Kilmore)

Hurley, Michael J., Very Rev, PP
(on sabbatical)
(Dublin)

Hurley, Richard, Very Rev, PP
South Presbytery,
Dunbar Street, Cork
Tel 021-4272989
(*St Finbarr's South*, Cork & R.)

Hurley, Thomas, Very Rev
Templeglantine,
Co Limerick
Tel 068-84021
(Limerick, retired)

Hussey, Michael, Very Rev, PP
Castlegregory, Co Kerry
Tel 066-7139145
(*Castlegregory*, Kerry)

Hutchinson, Stephen (OP), Very Rev
Prior,
Newbridge College,
Droichead Nua, Co Kildare
Tel 045-487200

Hutton, John, Very Rev
Apt 2, Ceara Court,
Windsor Avenue,
Belfast BT9 6EJ
Tel 028-90683002
(Down & C., retired)

Hyde, Jeremiah, Very Rev
The Presbytery, Kinsale,
Co Cork
(Cork & R., retired)

Hyland, James (OMI)
Oblate House of Retreat,
Inchicore, Dublin 8
Tel 01-4534408/4541805

Hyland, Richard, Very Rev, PP
42 Strand Street, Skerries,
Co Dublin
Tel 01-8106771
(*Skerries*, Dublin)

Hynes, James (OFM)
98 Bld de Montpernasse,
95014 Paris, France

Hynes, Sean (OMI)
Oblate House of Retreat,
Inchicore, Dublin 8
Tel 01-4534408/4541805

## I

Igoe, Michael (SMA)
African Missions,
Blackrock Road, Cork
Tel 021-4292871

Imholte, Otto (SSC)
St Columban's, Dalgan Park,
Navan, Co Meath
Tel 046-9021525

Ingoldsby, Thomas (SDB)
Salesian College,
Pallaskenry, Co Limerick
Tel 061-393313

Inharjanto, Anselmus (SCJ)
Sacred Heart Fathers,
Fairfield, 66 Inchicore Road,
Dublin 8
Tel 01-4538655

Irwin, Charles, Very Rev, BD, HDE
President,
St Munchin's College,
Corbally, Limerick
Tel 061-348922
(Limerick)

Irwin, Edwin, Very Rev, PP
Cloncagh, Ballingarry,
Co Limerick
Tel 069-83006
(*Knockaderry and Cloncagh*, Limerick)

Irwin, John
Chaplain, Nazareth House,
Bishop Street,
Derry BT48 6UN
Tel 028-71261425
(Derry)

Irwin, Michael (SAC)
Rector, Provincial House,
'Homestead',
Sandyford Road, Dundrum,
Dublin 16
Tel 01-2956180/2954170

Irwin, Michael (SSC)
(priest in residence)
Kilcornan, Co Limerick
Tel 061-393113
(*Kilcornan*, Limerick)

Irwin, Nicholas J., CC
Diocesan Secretary/
Chancellor,
Archbishop's House,
Thurles, Co Tipperary
Tel 0504-21512
Parish
Borrisoleigh, Thurles,
Co Tipperary
Tel 0504-51230
(Cashel & E.)

Issac, Sunil (SCJ)
Sacred Heart Fathers,
Fairfield, 66 Inchicore Road,
Dublin 8
Tel 01-4538655

Iwueke, Lazarus (CM)
St Peter's, Phibsboro,
Dublin 7
Tel 01-8389708

Iwuozor, Gregory (CSSp)
Holy Ghost Missionary College,
Kimmage Manor, Dublin 12
Tel 01-4064300

## J

Jachym, Marian (SC), CC
68 North Street, Lurgan,
Co Armagh BT67 9AH
Tel 028-38323161
(*Shankill, St Peter's (Lurgan)*, Dromore)

Jacob, John, Very Rev, Adm
12 Walkinstown Road,
Dublin 12
Tel 01-4501372
(*Walkinstown*, Dublin)

Januszewski, Rafal
2 Gortaugher, Lisnakelly,
Buncrana, Co Donegal
Tel 074-9363455
(Derry)

Jenkinson, William (CSSp)
Holy Spirit Missionary College,
Kimmage Manor,
Whitehall Road, Dublin 12
Tel 01-4064300

Jennings, E. Norman (SSC)
CPE, Mater Hospital,
Dublin

Jennings, Gavan
Harvieston,
Cunningham Road, Dalkey,
Co Dublin
Tel 01-2859877
(Opus Dei)

Jennings, Gerard
Chaplain,
Daughters of Our Lady of the Sacred Heart Convent,
Ballybay, Co Monaghan
Tel 042-9741524
(Clogher)

Jennings, Gerard, Very Rev, PP
Salthill, Galway
Tel 091-523413
(*Salthill*, Galway)

Jennings, Joseph (SM), CC
Inishere, Aran Islands,
Co Galway
Tel 099-75003
(*Aran Islands*, Tuam)

Jennings, Martin, Very Rev, PP
Curry, Ballymote, Co Sligo
Tel 094-9254508
(*Curry*, Achonry)

Jennings, Norman (SSC)
St Columban's, Dalgan Park,
Navan, Co Meath
Tel 046-9021525

Jennings, Patrick (SMA)
African Missions,
Blackrock Road, Cork
Tel 021-4292871

Johnston, Andrew, Very Rev Canon
c/o Innis Ree Lodge,
Ballyleague, Lanesborough,
Co Roscommon
Tel 043-3327300
(Achonry, retired)

Johnston, Anthony, CC
8 Corrig Park,
Dun Laoghaire, Co Dublin
Tel 01-2805594
(Dublin)

Johnston, Cecil
8 Corrig Park,
Dun Laoghaire, Co Dublin
Tel 01-2805594
(*Dun Laoghaire*, Dublin)

Johnston, Jim (SM)
Cerdon, Marist Fathers,
St Mary's Road, Dundalk,
Co Louth
Tel 042-9334019

Johnston, Sean (CM)
St Paul's College, Raheny,
Dublin 5
Tel 01-8318113

Johnston, Thomas, Very Rev
Mgr, PP
Pastoral Centre,
Charlestown, Co Mayo
Tel 094-9254315
(Achonry)

Jones, Aidan G., Very Rev, PP
Bunclody, Enniscorthy,
Co Wexford
Tel 053-9377319
(Ferns)

Jones, Bernard (OFM)
Guardian, Franciscan Abbey,
Multyfarnham,
Co Westmeath
Tel 044-9371114/9371137

Jones, Christopher, Most Rev,
DD
Bishop of Elphin,
St Mary's, Sligo
Tel 071-9162670/9162769
(Elphin)

Jones, Gerard, CC
The Presbytery, Nenagh,
Co Tipperary
Tel 067-37131/087-2137238
(Killaloe)

Jones, Joe
30 Willow Park Crescent,
Glasnevin, Dublin 11
(Dublin)

Jones, John, (SPS)
St Patrick's, Kiltegan,
Co Wicklow
Tel 059-6473600
(*Kiltegan*, Kildare and L.)

Jones, John, Very Rev, PP
Parochial House,
Blanchardstown, Dublin 15
Tel 01-8213660
(*Blanchardstown*, Dublin)

Jones, John, Very Rev, PP
St Caimin's, Mountshannon,
Co Clare
Tel 061-927213/086-1933479
(*Mountshannon*, Killaloe)

Jones, Joseph (MHM)
St Joseph's House,
50 Orwell Park, Rathgar,
Dublin 6
Tel 01-4127700

Jones, Patrick
Director,
National Centre for Liturgy,
St Patrick's College,
Maynooth, Co Kildare
Tel 01-7083478
(Dublin)

Jordan, Cathal, Very Rev
Canon, PP
6 Derrymacash Road,
Lurgan, Co Armagh BT66 6LG
Tel 028-38341356
(*Seagoe (Derrymacash)*,
Dromore)

Jordan, Columba (CFR)
St Columba Friary,
6 Victoria Place,
Derry BT48 6TJ
Tel 028-71260390

Jordan, John, Very Rev, PP
Kyle, Oulart,
Gorey, Co Wexford
(Ferns, retired)

Jordan, Liam, Very Rev
Coolamain, Oylegate,
Co Wexford
(Ferns, retired)

Jordan, Michael, CC
Parochial House,
Donaghmoyne,
Co Monaghan
Tel 042-9661586
(Clogher)

Jordan, Phelim (SVD), Very
Rev
Donamon Castle,
Co Roscommon,
Tel 090-6662222
(Elphin)

Jordan, Thomas (OP)
(priest in residence)
Presbytery,
St Dominic's Road, Tallaght,
Dublin 24
Tel 01-4510620
(*Tallaght, Dodder*, Dublin)

Joseph, Jayan (OSCam)
Chaplain,
St James's Hospital
St Camillus, South Hill Ave,
Blackrock, Co Dublin

Joyce, Michael (SVD)
Donamon Castle,
Roscommon
Tel 090-6662222

Joyce, Michael, Very Rev
Canon
Bohola, Claremorris, Co Mayo
Tel 094-9384115
(Achonry)

Joyce, Peter, CC
Chaplain, University
Hospital, Galway
Tel 091-794113
(Galway)

Joyce, Stephen
Kilnaclay, Threemilehouse,
Co Monaghan
Tel 047-57867
(Clogher)

Judge, Francis, Very Rev, PP
Crossmolina, Ballina
Co Mayo
(*Crossmolina*, Killala)

Judge, John, Very Rev, PP
Bangor, Erris, Ballina,
Co Mayo
Tel 097-83466
(*Kiltane*, Killala)

Justice, Cornelius (OCSO)
Mount Melleray Abbey,
Cappoquin,
Co Waterford
Tel 058-54404

## K

Kakkadampallil, Vincent
Xavier (OSCam)
Chaplain, Mater Hospital,
Eccles Street, Dublin 7
Tel 01-8301122
(Dublin)

Kalema, Godfrey (Team
Assistant)
Holy Redeemer Parish,
Herbert Road,
Bray, Co Dublin
Tel 01-2868413
(*Bray Holy Redeemer*,
Dublin)

Kane, Andrew (OP)
St Dominic's, Athy,
Co Kildare
Tel 059-8631573

Kane, Gerry, Very Rev, PP
213B Harold's Cross Road,
Dublin 6W
Tel 01-4947303
(*Harold's Cross*, Dublin)

Kane, Michael (CSSp)
Holy Ghost Missionary
College,
Kimmage Manor, Dublin 12
Tel 01-4064300

Kane, Michael (SPS)
St Patrick's, Kiltegan,
Co Wicklow
Tel 059-6473600

Kane, Michael,
Claremount Nursing Home,
Claremorris, Co Mayo
(Tuam, retired)

Kavanagh, Brian, CC
15 Lowtown Manor,
Robertstown, Naas,
Co Kildare
Tel 045-890559
(*Allen*, Kildare & L.)

Kavanagh, Dermot (CSSp)
Ballybeg, Rathnew,
Co Wicklow
Tel 0404-69774

Kavanagh, Edward, CC
Mountmellick, Co Laois
Tel 057-8679302
(*Mountmellick*, Kildare & L.)

Kavanagh, Hugh, Very Rev,
Co-PP
1 Brookfield Road, Tallaght,
Dublin 24
Tel 01-4624410
(*Brookfield*, Dublin)

Kavanagh, Joseph (OP)
St Mary's, Pope Quay, Cork
Tel 021-4502267

Kavanagh, Joseph, Very Rev,
PP
Camolin, Co Wexford
Tel 053-9383136
(*Camolin*, Ferns)

Kavanagh, Mark (SSC)
St Columban's Retirement
Home,
Dalgan Park, Navan,
Co Meath
Tel 046-9021525

Kavanagh, Martin (SMA)
African Missions,
Blackrock Road, Cork
Tel 021-4292871

Kavanagh, Myles (CP)
Passionist Retreat Centre,
Tobar Mhuire, Crossgar,
Co Down, BT30 9EA
Tel 028-44830242

Kavanagh, Vincent (CSsR)
St Patrick's, Esker, Athenry,
Co Galway
Tel 091-844549

Kealy, John (OFM)
Franciscan Abbey,
Multyfarnham,
Co Westmeath
Tel 044-9371114/9371137

Keane, Brendan (CSsR)
Clonard Monastery,
1 Clonard Gardens,
Belfast, BT13 2RL
Tel 028-90445950

Keane, Jerry, Very Rev, PP
Glenbeigh, Co Kerry
Tel 066-9768209
(*Glenbeigh*, Kerry)

Keane, John D., Very Rev
St Brigid's, Ballybane,
Galway
Tel 091-755381
(Ballybane, Galway)

Keane, John
c/o Cloyne Diocesan Centre,
Cobh, Co Cork
Tel 021-4811430
(Cloyne)

Keane, Martin
Chaplain,
Brothers of Charity,
Kilcornan, Clarinbridge,
Co Galway
Tel 091-796106
(Galway)

Keane, Matthew, Very Rev
Canon
Ashborough Lodge, Lyre,
Milltown, Co Kerry
(Kerry, retired)

Keane, Paul
Ballycrodick, Dunhill,
Co Waterford
(Tuam, retired)

Keane, Richard, CC
Gortboy, Newcastle West,
Co Limerick
Tel 069-77090/087-9552729
(*Newcastle West*, Limerick)

Keane, Stephen, PE
7 Garrai Sheann, Roscam,
Galway
Tel 091-767528
(Galway, retired)

Keaney, Charles, PP
Chapelfield,
59 Laurel Hill, Coleraine,
Co Derry BT51 3AY
Tel 028-70343130
(*Coleraine*, Derry)

Kearney, Brendan (SJ)
(residing elsewhere)
35 Lower Leeson Street,
Dublin 2
Tel 01-6761248

Kearney, Derek (SMA)
Anglophone Secretary,
Generalate,
Via della Nocetta 111,
00164 Rome, Italy
Tel 06-6616841

Kearney, Francis, Very Rev, PP
17 Monteith Road,
Annaclone, Banbridge,
Co Down BT32 5AQ
Tel 028-40671201
(*Annaclone*, Dromore)

Kearney, John, Very Rev
Canon, Adm, VF
Riverfields, Warrenpoint,
Co Down, BT34 3PU
Tel 028-41754684
(*Clonallon, St Peter's (Warrenpoint)*, Dromore)

Kearney, Laurence (SPS)
Derrada, Ballinamore,
Co Leitrim
Tel 071-9644067
(Kilmore, retired)

Kearney, Patrick, Very Rev, PP
Parochial House, Longwood,
Co Meath
Tel 046-9555009
(*Longwood*, Meath)

Kearney, Stephen, PP
41 Moyle Road,
Newtownstewart,
Co Tyrone BT78 4AP
Tel 028-81661445
(*Newtownstewart*, Derry)

Kearney, Thomas (SMA) CC
Keel, Achill, Co Mayo
Tel 098-43123
(*Achill*, Tuam)

Kearney, Thomas, CC
137 Shantalla Road,
Whitehall, Dublin 9
Tel 01-8313806
(*Larkhill-Whitehall-Santry*, Dublin)

Kearns, Brendan, CC
14 Great George's Street,
Warrenpoint,
Co Down BT34 3PU
Tel 028-4177220
(*Clonallon, St Peter's (Warrenpoint)*, Dromore)

Kearns, Gerard M.
Director, Kilmore Diocesan
Pastoral Centre, Cullies,
Cavan
Tel 049-4375004
(Kilmore)

Kearns, John (SPS)
On temporary diocesan
work

Kearns, John, CC
Priests' House, Clones,
Co Monaghan
Tel/Fax 047-51064
(*Clones*, Clogher)

Kearny, Nicholas (OSA)
St John's Priory,
Thomas Street, Dublin 8
Tel 01-6770393

Keary, Patrick, Very Rev, PP,
VF
Horseleap, Co Offaly
Tel 057-9335922
(Meath)

Keating, Andy (SPS)
St Patrick's, Kiltegan,
Co Wicklow
Tel 059-6473600

Keating, Crispin (OFM)
5225 North Himes Avenue,
Tampa, Fl 33614-6623, USA

Keating, David
Chaplain,
Waterford Institute of
Technology,
10 Claremont, Cork Road,
Waterford
Tel 051-378878
(Waterford & L.)

Keating, Denis (OP)
St Dominic's Retreat House,
Montenotte, Co Cork
Tel 021-4502520

Keating, John, Very Rev, PP
Raheenagh, Ballagh,
Co Limerick
Tel 069-85014
(*Killeedy*, Limerick)

Keating, Patrick, Very Rev, PP
Drimoleague
(Cork & R., retired)

Keaveny, Michael, CC
53 Brisland Road, Eglinton,
Co Derry BT47 3EA
Tel 028-71810234
(Derry, retired)

Keegan, John F., Very Rev, Co-PP
Parochial House, Rolestown,
Swords, Co Dublin
Tel 01-2826404
(*Rolestown-Oldtown*, Dublin)

Keegan, Patrick (CSSp)
Templeogue College,
Dublin 6W
Tel 01-4903909

Keeling, John (CSsR)
Marianella/Liguori House,
75 Orwell Road, Dublin 6
Tel 01-4067100

Keenan, Aidan, Very Rev, PP
St Matthew's Presbytery,
Bryson Street,
Newtownards Road,
Belfast BT5 4ES
Tel 028-90457626
(*Portglenone*, Down & C.)

Keenan, Brian (SM)
CUS Community,
89 Lower Leeson Street,
Dublin 2
Tel 01-6762586

Keenan, Frank (SJ)
St Francis Xavier's,
Upper Gardiner Street,
Dublin 1
Tel 01-8363411

Keenan, Kevin (SVD)
26 Cloonarkin Drive,
Oranmore, Co Galway
Tel 087-9905755
(*St John the Apostle*, Galway)

Keenan, Kevin (SVD)
Donamon Castle,
Roscommon
Tel 090-6662222

Keenan, Pádraig, Very Rev, PP
Parochial House,
Chapel Road, Haggardstown,
Dundalk, Co Louth
Tel 042-9321621
(*Haggardstown and Blackrock*, Armagh)

Keenan, Patrick (OCD), CC
The Presbytery,
Berkeley Road, Dublin 7
Tel 01-8306356/8306336
(*Berkeley Road*, Dublin)

Keeney, Sean (CSsR)
Clonard Monastery,
1 Clonard Gardens,
Belfast, BT13 2RL
Tel 028-90445950

Keevins, Frank (CP), Very Rev,
PP
St Paul's Retreat,
Mount Argus, Dublin 6W
Tel 01-4923165
(*Mount Argus*, Dublin)

Kehoe, James, Very Rev, PP
Carrig-on-Bannow,
Wellington Bridge,
Co Wexford
Tel 051-561192
(*Bannow*, Ferns)

Kehoe, Joseph L., Rt Rev Mgr,
PA
13 Priory CT, Spawell Road,
Wexford
Tel 053-9180599
(Ferns, retired)

Kehoe, Liam (CSSp)
Blackrock College,
Blackrock, Co Dublin
Tel 01-2888681

Kehoe, Noel (CSsR)
Co-ordinator,
Scala, Castlemahon House,
Castle Road, Cork
Tel 021-4358800

Kehoe, Patrick, Very Rev, CC
c/o Bishop's House,
Co Carlow
(Kildare & L., retired)

Kehoe, Peter, (OCarm), Very
Rev, PP
Ballyhale, Co Kilkenny
Tel 056-7768686/086-8252093
(*Ballyhale*, Ossory)

Kehoe, Philip (FDP)
25 Lower Teddington Road,
Kingston-on-Thames, Surrey
Tel 208-9775130

Kehoe, Tomás, CC
New Ross, Co Wexford
Tel 051-447086
(*New Ross*, Ferns)

Keleghan, Anselm (CP)
St Paul's Retreat,
Mount Argus, Dublin 6W
Tel 01-4992000

Kelleher, Cornelius, Very Rev,
PP
Tournaneena, Ballinamult,
Clonmel, Co Tipperary
Tel 058-47138
(*Tournaneena*, Waterford & L.)

Kelleher, Denis, Very Rev, PP
Church Road, Aghada,
Co Cork
Tel 021-4661298
(*Aghada*, Cloyne)

Kelleher, Eamonn, CC
Jamesbrook, Midleton,
Co Cork
Tel 021-4652456
(*Aghada*, Cloyne)

Kelleher, Finbar, Very Rev
Canon, CC (pro-tem)
Ballindangan, Mitchelstown,
Co Cork
Tel 025-85563
(*Glanworth and Ballindangan*, Cloyne)

Kelleher, Francis
Chaplain,
Cork South Infirmary,
Old Blackroad, Cork
Tel 021-4966555
(Cork & R.)

Kelleher, Francis, Very Rev, PP
Knocktemple, Virginia,
Co Cavan
Tel 049-8547435
(*Castlerahan and Munterconnaught*, Kilmore)

Kelleher, Liam, Very Rev, PP
Grenagh, Co Cork
Tel 021-4886128
(*Grenagh*, Cloyne)

Kelleher, Maurice (SMA)
Dromantine College,
Dromantine, Newry,
Co Down BT34 1RH
Tel 028-30821224

Kelleher, Michael G. (CSsR)
Marianella/Liguori House,
75 Orwell Road, Dublin 6
Tel 01-4067100

Kelleher, Roger, Very Rev
9 Emmet's Terrace,
Killarney, Co Kerry
(Kerry, retired)

Kelleher, Thomas, Very Rev Canon, PP
Ballinspittle, Co Cork
Tel 021-4778055
(*Courceys*, Cork & R.)

Kelliher, Padraig, CC
The Presbytery, Longford
Tel 043-3346465
(*Longford*, Ardagh & Cl.)

Kelly Jnr, Patrick (CSsR)
Marianella, 75 Orwell Road,
Dublin 6
Tel 01-4067100

Kelly Snr, Patrick (CSsR)
St Joseph's, Dundalk,
Co Louth
Tel 042-9334042/9334762

Kelly, Brendan, Most Rev, DD
Bishop of Achonry,
Bishop's House,
Edmondstown,
Ballaghaderreen,
Co Roscommon
Tel 094-9860021
(Achonry)

Kelly, Celsus (OCSO), Rt Rev Dom
Abbot, Our Lady of
Bethlehem Abbey,
11 Ballymena Road,
Portglenone, Ballymena,
Co Antrim BT44 8BL
Tel 028-25821211

Kelly, Conor, Very Rev, PP
Ring, Dungarvan,
Co Waterford
Tel 058-46125
(*Ring*, Waterford & L.)

Kelly, Declan, Adm
Killoran, Ballinasloe,
Co Galway
Tel 090-9627120
(*Kilmeen*, Tuam)

Kelly, Declan, Adm
St Andrew's Church, Leitrim,
Loughrea, Co Galway
Tel 091-841758
(Clonfert)

Kelly, Declan, Very Rev, PP
Preston Hill, Stamullen,
Co Meath
Tel 01-8418066
(*Stamullen*, Meath)

Kelly, Denis, Very Rev, Adm
St Aidan's, Enniscorthy,
Co Wexford
Tel 053-9235777
(*Enniscorthy, Cathedral of St Aidan*, Ferns)

Kelly, Dermot (OCarm)
Gort Muire, Ballinteer,
Dublin 16
Tel 01-2984014

Kelly, Desmond (OCarm), CC
Carmelite Priory,
56 Aungier Street,
Dublin 2
Tel 01-4758821
(*Whitefriar Street*, Dublin)

Kelly, Desmond, Very Rev, PP
Corballa, Ballina,
Co Mayo
Tel 096-36266
(*Castleconnor*, Killala)

Kelly, Donal, Very Rev
7 Knocksinna Park,
Bray Road, Foxrock,
Dublin 18
Tel 01-2894170
(Down & C., retired)

Kelly, Eamonn (SMA)
Retired in Ireland outside
SMA houses

Kelly, Eamonn, Very Rev, Adm
Parochial House,
Letterkenny, Co Donegal
Tel 074-9121021
Chaplain,
Errigal College, Letterkenny,
Co Donegal
Tel 074-9121047/9121861
(*Letterkenny*, Raphoe)

Kelly, Edward, Very Rev Canon, PE
No. 1 St Mary's College
House,
Shantalla Road, Galway
Tel 091-586663
(Galway, retired)

Kelly, Edward, Very Rev, PE
Rhode, Co Offaly
Tel 046-9737013
(Kildare & L., retired)

Kelly, Felim, Very Rev, CC
Castlerahan, Ballyjamesduff,
Co Cavan
Tel 049-8544150
(*Castlerahan and Munterconnaught*, Kilmore)

Kelly, Finbar (OP)
Black Abbey, Kilkenny,
Co Kilkenny
Tel 056-7721279

Kelly, Gabriel
Kinawley, Enniskillen,
Co Fermanagh
Tel 028-66348250
(Kilmore)

Kelly, Gilbert
Ballycarron House, Golden,
Co Tipperary
(Dublin, retired)

Kelly, James (SJ)
Milltown Park,
Sandford Road, Dublin 6
Tel 01-2698411/2698113

Kelly, James J., Very Rev, PE
Parochial House,
Clogher Road, Dublin 12
(Dublin, retired)

Kelly, James, Canon, AP
Tooreen, Ballyhaunis,
Co Mayo
Tel 094-9649002
(*Aghamore*, Tuam)

Kelly, Jimmy (OSM)
Chaplain, Mountjoy Prison,
Servite Priory, St Peregrine,
Kiltipper Road, Tallaght,
Dublin 24
Tel 01-4517115

Kelly, Jimmy, Very Rev, PP
Raheen, Abbeyleix,
Co Laois
Tel 057-8731182
(*Raheen*, Kildare & L.)

Kelly, Joe, CC
5 Bayside Square East,
Sutton, Dublin 13
Tel 01-8322305
(*Bayside*, Dublin)

Kelly, John
Chaplain,
Adelaide and Meath
Hospital,
Tallaght, Dublin 24
Tel 01-4142000/4142480
(Dublin)

Kelly, John (SAC)
Bursar/Secretary for Missions
and Vice Provincial,
Provincial House,
'Homestead',
Sandyford Road, Dundrum,
Dublin 16
Tel 01-2956180/2954170

Kelly, John (SCJ)
Superior & Formation
Director,
Sacred Heart Fathers,
Fairfield, 66 Inchicore Road,
Dublin 8
Tel 01-4538655

Kelly, John, Very Rev, PP
Labasheeda, Co Clare
Tel 065-6830126
(*Kilmurry McMahon*, Killaloe)

Kelly, Larry, Very Rev Canon, PP
Rathmore, Co Kerry
Tel 064-7758026
(*Rathmore*, Kerry)

Kelly, Laurence (OP)
Newbridge College,
Droichead Nua,
Co Kildare
Tel 045-487200

Kelly, Lawrence, Very Rev
'Sunville', Kilgarvan,
Co Kerry
(Kerry, retired)

Kelly, Liam (OFM)
Guardian, Franciscan Friary,
Ennis, Co Clare
Tel 065-6828751

Kelly, Liam, Very Rev, PP
Crosskeys, Co Cavan
Tel 049-4336102
(*Denn*, Kilmore)

Kelly, Martin, Very Rev, PP
Parochial House,
546 Saintfield Road,
Carryduff, Belfast BT8 8EU
Tel 028-90812238
(*Drumbo*, Down & C.)

Kelly, Matthew, Very Rev, PE, CC
60 Hartwell Green, Kill,
Naas, Co Kildare
Tel 045-877880
(*Kill*, Kildare & L.)

Kelly, Michael (SPS)
St Patrick's, Kiltegan,
Co Wicklow
Tel 059-6473600

Kelly, Michael, Adm
Rathvilly, Co Carlow
Tel 059-9161114
(*Rathvilly*, Kildare & L.)

Kelly, Michael, Co-PP
94 Old County Road,
Crumlin Dublin 12
Tel 01-4542308
(*Crumlin*, Dublin)

Kelly, Michael, Rt Rev Dean
St Catherine's Nursing
Home,
Newcastle West, Co Limerick
(Limerick, retired)

Kelly, Michael, Very Rev Canon, PP, VF
Craughwell, Co Galway
Tel 091-846057
(*Craughwell*, Galway)

Kelly, Oliver, Very Rev, PP, VF
Manorhamilton, Co Leitrim
Tel 071-9855042
(*Manorhamilton*, Kilmore)

Kelly, Patrick (MSC)
'Croí Nua', Rosary Lane,
Taylor's Hill, Galway
Tel 091-520960

Kelly, Patrick (SJ)
Milltown Park,
Sandford Road, Dublin 6
Tel 01-2698411/2698113

Kelly, Patrick (SMA)
Seconded to US Province

Kelly, Patrick (SPS)
Tearmann Spirituality
Centre,
Brockagh, Glendalough,
Co Wicklow
Tel 0404-45208

Kelly, Patrick James (CSSp)
Holy Spirit Missionary
College,
Kimmage Manor, Dublin 12
Tel 01-4064300

Kelly, Patrick Joseph (CSSp)
Holy Spirit Missionary College,
Kimmage Manor, Dublin 12
Tel 01-4064300

Kelly, Patrick, Very Rev Canon, PE
Athea, Co Limerick
Tel 068-42107
(*Athea*, Limerick)

Kelly, Paul, Very Rev, PP
The Presbytery, Roundwood, Co Wicklow
Tel 01-2818149
(*Roundwood*, Dublin)

Kelly, Ray, Very Rev, PP
Parochial House, Oldcastle, Co Meath
Tel 049-8541142
(*Oldcastle*, Meath)

Kelly, Richard (OFM)
Adam and Eve's,
4 Merchant Quay, Dublin 8
Tel 01-6771128

Kelly, Richard (SVD)
Maynooth, Co Kildare
Tel 01-6286391/2

Kelly, Richard, Very Rev, PP
Kilbehenny, Mitchelstown, Co Cork
Tel 025-24040
(*Kilbehenny*, Cashel & E.)

Kelly, Robert (OCSO)
Mount Saint Joseph Abbey,
Roscrea, Co Tipperary
Tel 0505-25600

Kelly, Robert (SM), CC
The Presbytery,
Donore Avenue, Dublin 8
Tel 01-4542425/4531613
(*Donore Avenue*, Dublin)

Kelly, Seamus, Rev, PP
40 Derrynoid Road,
Draperstown,
Co Derry BT45 7DN
Tel 028-79628376
(*Ballinascreen (Draperstown)* Derry)

Kelly, Sean (OFMCap), CC
Capuchin Parochial Friary,
Clonshaugh Drive,
Priorswood, Dublin 17
Tel 01-8474469/01-8474358
(*Priorswood*, Dublin)

Kelly, Seán, Very Rev, PE, CC
Stradbally, Co Laois
Tel 057-8625831
(*Stradbally*, Kildare & L.)

Kelly, Terence, Very Rev, PE
3 Cranagh, Ballinderry Bridge Road, Coagh,
Cookstown,
Co Tyrone BT80 0AS
(Armagh, retired)

Kelly, Thomas V., Very Rev
Castlebar Road, Westport, Co Mayo
(Dublin, retired)

Kelly, Vincent (SAC)
(Attached to Pallotine College)
18 Silvercourt,
Silversprings, Cork

Kemmy, Bill
(priest in residence)
Arles, Ballickmoyler, Carlow
Tel 059-9147637
(*Arles*, Kildare & L.)

Kemmy, Philip, CC
Parochial House, Convoy
Tel 074-9147238
(*Convoy*, Raphoe)

Kenneally, Cornelius (CSsR), CC
The Presbytery,
197 Kylemore Road,
Ballyfermot, Dublin 10
Tel 01-6264789

Kenneally, Daithi (CSSp), Very Rev, PP
St Ronan's Presbytery,
Deansrath, Clondalkin, Dublin 22
Tel 01-4125222
(*Deansrath*, Dublin)

Kenneally, David (SSC)
Regional Bursar,
St Columban's, Dalgan Park,
Navan, Co Meath
Tel 046-9021525

Kennedy, Abe
St Molaise's, Portumna, Co Galway
Tel 090-9741188
(Clonfert)

Kennedy, Bernard, MA, MSc, Adm
67 Edenvale Road, Dublin 6
Tel 01-4972165
(*Beechwood Avenue*, Dublin)

Kennedy, David, Very Rev
Clonlusk Doon, Co Limerick
(Limerick, retired)

Kennedy, Denis, (CSSp), CC
St Joseph's Presbytery,
Glasthule, Co Dublin
Tel 01-2800403
(*Glasthule*, Dublin)

Kennedy, Edmund, Very Rev, AP
Newtown, Nenagh,
Co Tipperary
Tel 067-23103
(*Youghalarra*, Killaloe)

Kennedy, Eugene
7 Riverwood Vale,
Carpenterstown,
Castleknock, Dublin 15
(Dublin, retired)

Kennedy, Hugh, Very Rev
Cathedral Presbytery,
St Peter's Square,
Belfast BT12 4BU
Tel 028-90327573
(*The Cathedral (St Peter's)*, Down & C.)

Kennedy, Ian, Very Rev, PC
The Parochial House,
Ballinafad, Boyle,
Co Roscommon
Tel 071-9666006
(*Ballinafad*, Elphin)

Kennedy, James, CC
St Michael Street,
Tipperary Town
Tel 062-51114
(*Tipperary*, Cashel & E.)

Kennedy, Joe, Very Rev, PP
Moneygall, Birr Co Offaly
Tel 0505-45982/ 086-4072488
(Killaloe)

Kennedy, John
(Congregation for the Doctrine of the Faith)
Via del Mascherino 12,
00193 Roma, Italy
(Dublin)

Kennedy, Joseph (CP)
St Paul's Retreat,
Mount Argus, Dublin 6W
Tel 01-4992000
(*Mount Argus*, Dublin)

Kennedy, Joseph, Very Rev, (pro-tem)
Croom, Co Limerick
Tel 061-397231/087-9217622
(*Croom*, Limerick)

Kennedy, Kieron, Rt Rev Mgr, Adm
St Mary's Cathedral,
Kilkenny
Tel 056-7771253/ 087-2523521
(*St Mary's*, Ossory)

Kennedy, Michael, CC
Kilrickle, Ballinasloe,
Co Galway
Tel 091-843015
(Clonfert)

Kennedy, Michael (CSSp)
Chaplain, NRH,
Rochestown Avenue,
Dun Laoghaire, Co Dublin
Tel 01-2355272

Kennedy, Michael, Very Rev, PP
Dunhill, Co Waterford
Tel 051-396109
(*Dunhill*, Waterford & L.)

Kennedy, Michael, Very Rev, PP
Parochial House, Colligan,
Dungarvan, Co Waterford
Tel 058-41629
(*Kilgobinet*, Waterford & L.)

Kennedy, Michael, Very Rev, PP
The Parochial House,
New Inn, Cashel,
Co Tipperary
Tel 052-7462395
(Cashel & E.)

Kennedy, Noel, Very Rev, PP
Bournea, Roscrea,
Co Tipperary
Tel 0505-43211/086-3576775
(*Bournea*, Killaloe)

Kennedy, Oliver (SSC)
St Columban's, Dalgan Park,
Navan, Co Meath
Tel 046-9021525

Kennedy, Oliver P.
68 Shore Road,
Toomebridge, Co Antrim
BT41 3NW
Tel 028-79650213/79650618
(Down & C., retired)

Kennedy, Sean, CC
Emly, Co Tipperary
Tel 062-57111
(*Emly*, Cashel & E.)

Kennedy, Seraphin (OFM)
Franciscan Friary, Liberty Street, Cork
Tel 021-4270302

Kennedy, Thomas, Very Rev, Co-PP
14 Roselawn, Lucan,
Co Dublin
Tel 01-6280205/01-2882162
(*Lucan*, Dublin)

Kennedy, Vincent (OP)
St Saviour's,
Glentworth Street, Limerick
Tel 061-412333

Kennedy, William (SMA)
SMA House, Wilton, Cork
Tel 021-4541069/4541884

Kennelly, John, Very Rev
24 Ferndene, Greenville,
Listowel, Co Kerry
(Kerry, retired)

Kennelly, Pádraig, PP
Glengarriff, Co Cork
Tel 027-63045
(*Glangarriff (Bonane)*, Kerry)

Kennelly, Séamus, Very Rev, PP
Boherbue, Mallow, Co Cork
Tel 029-76151
(*Boherbue/Kiskeam*, Kerry)

Kenny, Colm, Adm
137 Ballymun Road,
Dublin 11
Tel 01-8341051
(*Ballymun Road*, Dublin)

Kenny, Donald, Rt Rev Mgr, CC
St Patrick's, Gorey,
Co Wexford
Tel 051-9421117
(*Gorey*, Ferns)

Kenny, Gerard
Circular Road, Kilkee,
Co Clare
Tel 065-9056580
(Killaloe)

Kenny, Gerard (OMI)
Oblate House of Retreat,
Inchicore, Dublin 8
Tel 01-4534408/4541805

Kenny, Jim, CC
The Presbytery,
5 St Mary's Terrace,
Arklow, Co Wicklow
Tel 0402-32483
(*Arklow*, Dublin)

Kenny, John, Very Rev, PP
Dunmore, Co Galway
Tel 093-38124
(Tuam)

Kenny, Lorcan
Curates House, Convent Hill,
Roscrea, Co Tipperary
Tel 0505-21454
Chaplain, The Valley,
Roscrea, Co Tipperary
Tel 0505-23637/087-6553402
(*Roscrea*, Killaloe)

Kenny, Martin, Very Rev, PP
Our Lady of Lourdes
Presbytery,
Hardman's Gardens,
Drogheda, Co Louth
Tel 041-9831899

Kenny, Merlyn CC
St Mary's,
Carrick-on-Shannon,
Co Leitrim
Tel 071-9620054
(*Carrig-on-Shannon*, Ardagh & Cl.)

Kenny, Michael, Very Rev, PP
Kilconly, Tuam, Co Galway
Tel 093-47613
(*Kilconly and Kilbannon*, Tuam)

Kenny, Pat, Very Rev, PP
St Killian Church, Newinn,
Ballinasloe, Co Galway
Tel 090-9675819
(*New Inn and Bullaun*, Clonfert)

Kenny, Paul, Very Rev, Adm
Parochial House,
St Kevin's Parish,
Harrington Street, Dublin 8
Tel 01-4542172
(*Harrington Street*, Dublin)

Kenny, Thomas (SDB)
Vice-Rector,
Salesian House,
Warrenstown, Drumree,
Co Meath
Tel 01-8259894

Kenny, Tim (SM)
Fermoyle, Lanesboro,
Co Longford

Kensy, Joseph (SJ) (BRI)
Crescent College
Comprehensive,
Dooradoyle, Limerick
Tel 061-480920

Keogan, Thomas (MHM)
St Joseph's,
Mill Hill Missionaries,
Waterford Road, Kilkenny
Tel 056-7721482

Keogan, Thomas M., Very Rev, PP
Kinlough, Co Leitrim
Tel 071-9841428
(*Kinlough and Glenade*, Kilmore)

Keogh, Charles
Whitefriar Street Church,
56 Aungier Street, Dublin 2
Tel 01-4758821

Keogh, Joseph, Very Rev Canon, PE
No. 4 St Mary's College House,
Shantalla Road, Galway
Tel 091-587773
(Galway, retired)

Keogh, Martin, Very Rev, PP
Parochial House, Newtown,
Kilmacthomas,
Co Waterford
Tel 051-294261
(*Newtown*, Waterford & L.)

Keogh, Pádraig, Very Rev, PP
Milford, Charleville,
Co Cork
Tel 063-80038
(*Milford*, Cloyne)

Keohan, Edmund
The Bungalow,
Turners Cross, Cork
Tel 021-4320592
(Cork & R., retired)

Keohane, Martin, Very Rev, PP
Rossmore, Clonakilty,
Co Cork
Tel 023-8838630
(*Kilmeen and Castleventry*, Cork & R.)

Keohane, Michael, PIC
St Patrick's Presbytery,
Rochestown Road, Cork
Tel 021-4892363
(*Douglas*, Cork & R.)

Kerin, John, Very Rev, PP
Our Lady of the Valley,
Cillin Liath, Killarney,
Co Kerry
Tel 066-9474495
(*Waterville*, Kerry)

Kerketta, Athnas (MSFS)
(supply priest)
St Vincent de Paul Church,
Marino, Dublin 3
Tel 01-8332772/087-2506786
(*Marino*, Dublin)

Kerr, Aidan, Very Rev, PP
Parochial House,
1 The Cloney, Glenarm,
Co Antrim BT44 0AB
Tel 028-28841246
(*Glenavy and Killead*, Down & C.)

Kerr, Peter, Very Rev, PP
Parochial House,
194 Newtown Hamilton Road,
Ballymacnab,
Armagh BT60 2QS
Tel 028-37531641
(*Killcluney*, Armagh)

Kerr, Samuel, Very Rev
(priest in residence)
463 Shore Road,
Whiteabbey,
Newtownabbey,
Co Antrim BT37 0AE
Tel 028-90365773
(*Whiteabbey (St James's)*, Down & C.)

Kerrane, John, Very Rev, AP
'St Martin's', Culmullen,
Drumree, Co Meath
Tel 01-8241976
(*Dunshaughlin*, Meath)

Kett, Patrick J., Very Rev
27 Huntsgrove, Ashbourne,
Co Meath
(Dublin, retired)

Keveny, Martin, Very Rev
Paroquia Sao Sebastiao,
Caixa Postal 94,
CEP 77760-000,
Colinas Do Tocantins, Brazil
Tel 63-8311427
(Killala)

Kidney, Michael (SMA)
Temporary diocesan work in Ireland

Kidus, Amanuel (SDB)
Rinaldi House,
72 Sean McDermott Street,
Dublin 1
Tel 01-8363358

Kiely, Bartholomew (SJ)
Irish Jesuit Provincialate,
Milltown Park,
Sandford Road, Dublin 6
Tel 01-4987333

Kiely, Charles, CC
The Presbytery,
Turner's Cross, Cork
Tel 021-4313103
(*Turner's Cross*, Cork & R.)

Kiely, Eugene, Very Rev, PP
Ballyferriter West,
Tralee, Co Kerry
Tel 066-9156131
(*Ballyferriter*, Kerry)

Kiely, John, Very Rev, PP
Cappoquin, Co Waterford
Tel 058-54216
(*Cappoquin*, Waterford & L.)

Kiely, Michael (SAC)
Provincial House,
'Homestead',
Sandyford Road, Dundrum,
Dublin 16
Tel 01-2956180/2954170

Kieran, Aidan, CC
No. 1 the Glebe,
Peamount Road,
Newcastle Lyons, Co Dublin
Tel 01-2852509
(*Newcastle*, Dublin)

Kiernan, Brian (OCarm)
Gort Muire, Ballinteer,
Dublin 16
Tel 01-2984014

Kiernan, John, Very Rev, PE
Holy Trinity Abbey,
Kilnacrott, Ballyjamesduff,
Co Cavan
(Meath, retired)

Kiernan, Kevin (OFMCap), CC
Chaplain,
Beaumont Hospital,
Beaumont Road, Dublin 9
Tel 01-8377755/8092815
(Dublin)

Kiernan, Patrick, CC
Mount Temple, Moate,
Co Westmeath
Tel 090-6481239
(*Moate and Mount Temple*, Ardagh & Cl.)

Kiggins, Thomas (SPS)
St Patrick's, Kiltegan,
Co Wicklow
Tel 059-6473600

Kilbane, Seán (SMA), Very Rev, PE
Clonfad, Oldtown, Athlone,
Co Roscommon
Tel 090-9673527
(Tuam, retired)

Kilbride, Brian (CSSp)
Blackrock College,
Blackrock, Co Dublin
Tel 01-2888681

Kilbride, Malachy (CSSp)
Blackrock College,
Blackrock, Co Dublin
Tel 01-2888681

Kilcoyne, Brendan, Very Rev Canon
President,
St Jarlath's College, Tuam,
Co Galway
Tel 093-24248
(Tuam)

Kilcoyne, Colm, Very Rev Canon, PE
20 Rathbawn Drive,
Castlebar, Co Mayo
(Tuam, retired)

Kilcoyne, Patrick, Very Rev Canon, PP
Kiltimagh, Co Mayo
Tel 094-9381198
(*Kiltimagh (Killedan)*, Achonry)

Kilcoyne, Seán
Chaplain,
Bon Secours Hospital,
Renmore, Galway
Tel 091-751534/757711
(Galway)

Kilcrann, John (CSSp)
Spiritan House,
213 North Circular Road,
Dublin 7
Tel 01-838 9664/8683504

Kilduff, Donal, CC
Ballyjamesduff, Co Cavan
Tel 049-8544410
(*Castlerahan and Munterconnaught*, Kilmore)

Kilkelly, Christopher
c/o Archbishop's House,
Tuam, Co Galway
(Tuam, retired)

Kilkenny, Michael (CSSp)
Community leader,
Holy Spirit Missionary College,
Kimmage Manor, Dublin 12
Tel 01-4064300

Killeen, James, CC
Cobh, Co Cork
Tel 021-4813601
(*Cobh, St Colman's Cathedral*, Cloyne)

Killeen, John D., Very Rev, PP
20 Abbey Court,
Abbey Road, Blackrock,
Co Dublin
Tel 01-2982282
(*Kill-O'-The-Grange*, Dublin)

Killeen, Seán, Rt Rev Mgr,
Cloghans, Ballina, Co Mayo
(Killala, retired)

Killian, Michael
Mulross Nursing Home,
Carrick-on-Shannon,
Co Leitrim
(Ardagh & Cl., retired)

Kilmartin, Michael, CC
Cathedral House, Mullingar,
Co Westmeath
Tel 044-9348338/9340126
(*Mullingar*, Meath)

Kilmurray, Martin (OCarm)
Provincial, Provincial Office,
Gort Muire, Ballinteer,
Dublin 16
Tel 01-2984014

Kilpatrick, Edward, PP
Orchard Park, Murlog,
Lifford, Co Donegal
Tel 074-9142022
(Derry)

Kilroy, Peter, CC
74 Iona Road, Dublin 9
Tel 01-8308257
(*Iona Road*, Dublin)

Kim, Yong-su P. (SJ)
Jesuit Community,
27 Leinster Road,
Rathmines, Dublin 6
Tel 01-4970250

Kinahan, Gabriel (OFM)
Vicar, Adam and Eve's,
4 Merchant Quay,
Dublin 8
Tel 01-6771128

King, Alexis (OFM)
Franciscan House of Studies,
Dún Mhuire, Seafield Road,
Killiney, Co Dublin
Tel 01-2826760

King, Anthony, Very Rev Canon, PP, VF
Athenry, Co Galway
Tel 091-844076
(*Athenry*, Tuam)

King, Bernard (SM), CC
Parochial House,
Glassdrummond,
Crossmaglen, Newry,
Co Down BT35 9DY
Tel 028-30861270
(*Crossmaglen (Creggan Upper)*, Armagh)

King, John Joe (CSSp)
Holy Ghost Missionary College,
Kimmage Manor, Dublin 12
Tel 01-4064300

King, Jude (OSA)
Augustinian Retreat Centre,
Old Court Road,
Dublin 16
Tel 01-4930932

King, Michael, Very Rev, PP
Newtownbutler, Enniskillen,
Co Fermanagh BT92 8JJ
Tel 028-67738229
(*Newtownbutler*, Clogher)

King, William, PP
23 Clare Road, Drumcondra,
Dublin 9
Tel 01-8378552
(*Drumcondra*, Dublin)

Kingston, John, Very Rev, PP
Innishannon, Co Cork
Tel 021-4775348
(*Innishannon*, Cork & R.)

Kingston, William (CSSp)
Rockwell College, Cashel,
Co Tipperary
Tel 062-61444

Kinsella, Tobias, Very Rev, PP
Bloomfield Care Centre,
Stocking Lane,
Rathfarnham, Dublin 16
(Ferns, retired)

Kirby, Brendan, Very Rev Canon
9 Kilmartin Hill, Wicklow,
Co Wicklow
(Ferns, retired)

Kirby, John, Most Rev, DD
Bishop of Clonfert,
Coorheen, Loughrea,
Co Galway
Tel 091-841560
(Clonfert)

Kirstein, James (SMA)
African Missions,
Blackrock Road, Cork
Tel 021-4292871

Kirwan, Jeremiah M (CSSp)
Rockwell College, Cashel,
Co Tipperary
Tel 062-61444

Kirwan, Joseph (OSA)
St John's Priory,
Thomas Street, Dublin 8
Tel 01-6770393

Kirwan, Noel, Very Rev, PP, VF
St Michael's Church,
Denmark Street, Limerick
Tel 061-400133/061-413315/087-2616843
(*St Michael's*, Limerick)

Kitching, Ciarán, Very Rev, PP
Killimor, Ballinasloe,
Co Galway
Tel 090-9676151
(Clonfert)

Kitt, Liam, Very Rev
Cleveland, Ohio
(Tuam)

Knight, Matthew J. (CSSp)
Community Leader,
Rockwell College, Cashel,
Co Tipperary
Tel 062-61444

Knowles, Desmond, Very Rev Canon
Newry, Co Down
(Dromore, retired)

Kom, Francis (SVD)
Maynooth, Co Kildare
Tel 01-6286391/2

Kombanathottathil, Binoy Mathew (SVD) CC
Presbytery No. 2,
St Mary's Terrace,
Arklow, Co Wicklow
(*Arklow*, Dublin)

Kondowe, Raymond
Holy Trinity Parish,
12 Grangemore Road,
Donaghmede, Dublin 13
Tel 01-8470591
(*Donaghmede*, Dublin)

Koscinski, Tomas, Very Rev (OMI), Co-PP
Bluebell Parish,
Our Lady of the Wayside,
118 Naas Road, Bluebell,
Dublin 12
Tel 01-4501040
(*Inchicore, St Michael's*, Dublin)

Kowalski, Wojciech (SJ)
Jesuit Community,
27 Leinster Road,
Rathmines, Dublin 6
Tel 01-4970250

Krawiec, Jaroslaw (OP)
St Saviour's,
Upper Dorset Street,
Dublin 1
Tel 01-8897610

Kumar, Santosh (SAC)
(supply priest)
Pallottine Fathers,
Sandyford Road, Dublin 16
(*Balally*, Dublin)

Kupczakiewicz, Krzysztof (OP)
Holy Cross, Tralee, Co Kerry
Tel 066-7121135/29185

Kuthanapillil, Jaison (OCarm)
Carmelite Priory, Moate,
Co Westmeath
Tel 090-6481160/6481398

Kyne, Brendan, Very Rev, PP
The Spa, Castleconnell,
Co Limerick
Tel 061-377170/086-1050090
(*Castleconnell*, Killaloe)

Kyne, Thomas, Very Rev Dean, AP
Réalt na Mara, Furbo,
Co Galway
Tel 091-592457
(*Barna*, Galway)

Kyne, Val (SSC), PP
St Joseph's, Balcurris,
Ballymun, Dublin 11
Tel 01-8423865
(*Balcurris*, Dublin)

Kwon, Steven (LC)
Chaplain,
Dublin Oak Academy,
Kilcroney, Bray, Co Wicklow
Tel 01-2863290
Chaplain,
Woodlands Academy,
Wingfield House, Bray,
Co Wicklow
Tel 01-2866323

## L

Lacey, Liam, CC
8 Greenfield Road, Sutton,
Dublin 13
Tel 01-4627080
(*Sutton*, Dublin)

Laffan, Sean, Very Rev, CC
Gusserane, Co Wexford
Tel 051-562111
(*Ballycullane*, Ferns)

Lafferty, Angelo (SMA)
African Missions,
Blackrock Road, Cork
Tel 021-4292871

Lagan, Francis, Most Rev, DD
Titular Bishop of Sidnacestre and Auxiliary Bishop of Derry,
9 Glen Road, Strabane,
Co Tyrone BT82 8BX
Tel 028-71884533
(Derry, retired)

Lagan, Hugh (SMA)
Further studies, Maryland,
USA

Laheen, Kevin (SJ)
35 Lower Leeson Street,
Dublin 2
Tel 01-6761248

Laizer, John (CSSp)
Holy Ghost Missionary College,
Kimmage Manor, Dublin 12
Tel 01-4064300

Lally, Fredrick (OCarm)
Bursar, Carmelite Priory,
White Abbey, Co Kildare
Tel 045-521391
Lalor, John, Very Rev, PP
Camross, Portlaoise,
Co Laois
Tel 057-8735122
(*Camross*, Ossory)
Lalor, Tom, Very Rev, PP
Leighlinbridge, Co Carlow
Tel 059-9721463
(Kildare & L.)
Lambe, Jeremiah (CSSp)
Holy Ghost Missionary
College,
Kimmage Manor, Dublin 12
Tel 01-4064300
Lambe, Michael, Very Rev, PE
The Bungalow Presbytery,
St Mary's Church Grounds,
Lucan
Tel 01-6280954
(*Lucan*, Dublin)
Lambe, Tony, Very Rev, PP
Drangan, Thurles,
Co Tipperary
Tel 052-52103
Lambert, Owen (CSSp)
Holy Ghost Missionary
College,
Kimmage Manor, Dublin 12
Tel 01-4064300
Lane, Daniel, Very Rev, DD, PP
Ballingarry, Co Limerick
Tel 069-68141/087-2533030
(*Ballingarry and Granagh*,
Limerick)
Lane, Dermot A., Very Rev, PP
162 Sandyford Road,
Dublin 16
Tel 01-2956165
(*Balally*, Dublin)
Lane, Michael, Rt Rev Mgr
2 Meadowvale, Raheen,
Limerick
Tel 061-228761/087-2544450
(Limerick, retired)
Lane, Michael, Very Rev
Shrakovee, Clonlara,
near Limerick
(Limerick, retired)
Lane, Thomas
Mount Saint Mary's
Seminary,
16300 Old Emmitsburg Road,
Emmitsburg,
Maryland 21727-7797, USA
(Cloyne)
Langan, William (OCarm)
Gort Muire, Ballinteer,
Dublin 16
Tel 01-2984014
Langford, Gerard, Very Rev,
Adm
Cathedral of the Most Holy
Trinity,
Barronstrand Street,
Waterford
Tel 051-392666
(*Trinity Within and St
Patrick's*, Waterford & L.)
Lanigan-Ryan, Thomas, CC
Bóthar na Naomh
Presbytery,
Thurles, Co Tipperary
Tel 0504-22042/22688
(*Thurles, SS Joseph and
Brigid*, Cashel & E.)
Lanigan, Gerry (SVD)
Donamon Castle,
Roscommon
Tel 090-6662222
Larkin, Aidan (SSC)
St Columban's,
Grange Road,
Donaghmede, Dublin 13
Tel 01-8476647
Larkin, Barry, Very Rev, PP
Suncroft, Curragh,
Co Kildare
Tel 045-441586
(*Suncroft*, Kildare & L.)
Larkin, Francis, Very Rev
Canon, PP
Kinvara, Co Galway
Tel 091-637154
(*Kinvara*, Galway)
Larkin, James
(assistant priest)
The Presbytery,
72 Bird Avenue,
Clonskeagh, Dublin 14
Tel 01-2837948
(*Clonskeagh*, Dublin)
Larkin, Pat, Very Rev, PP
Carhuligane, Mullagh,
Co Clare
Tel 065-7087012/
087-2300627
(*Mullagh*, Killaloe)
Larkin, Patrick, Very Rev, PE,
AP
Parochial House,
Jenkinstown, Dundalk,
Co Louth
Tel 042-9371328
(*Lordship (and
Ballymascanlon)*, Armagh)
Larkin, Seamus, Very Rev, PP
Kilmuckridge, Gorey,
Co Wexford
Tel 053-9130116
(*Kilmuckridge*, Ferns)
Larkin, Seán, PP
Parochial House,
11 Chapel Road, Bessbrook,
Newry, Co Down BT35 7AU
Tel 028-30830206
(*Bessbrook (Killeavy Lower)*,
Armagh)
Lavelle, Colm (SJ)
Milltown Park,
Sandford Road, Dublin 6
Tel 01-2698411/2698113
Lavelle, Paul, Very Rev, PP
123 Foxfield Grove, Dublin 5
Tel 01- 8390433
(*KIlbarrack-Foxfield*, Dublin)
Lavery, Patrick (SJ)
Clongowes Wood College,
Naas, Co Kildare
Tel 045-868663/868202
Laverty, Austin, Very Rev
Canon, PP, VF
Ardara, Co Donegal
Tel 074-9541135
(*Ardara*, Raphoe)
Laverty, Denis, PC
Pro-Cathedral House,
83 Marlborough Street,
Dublin 1
Tel 01-8745441
(*Pro-Cathedral*, Dublin)
Laverty, Derek (SSCC)
Provincial,
Coudrin House,
27 Northbrook Road,
Dublin 6
Tel 01-6686584/01-6686590
Laverty, Francis (CSSp)
Holy Spirit Missionary
College,
Kimmage Manor, Dublin 12
Tel 01-406 4300
Lavin, Peadar, Very Rev
Canon, PP
3 Slinagee, Golf Links Road,
Roscommon
(Elphin, retired)
Lawler, John (OCarm)
Carmelite Priory,
White Abbey, Co Kildare
Tel 045-521391
Lawless, Brendan, Very Rev,
PP
Dunkellin Tce, Portumna,
Co Galway
Tel 090-9741092
(Clonfert)
Lawless, Brian, Very Rev, Adm
Presbytery,
St Agatha's Parish,
North William Street,
Dublin 1
Tel 01-6244568
(*North William Street*,
Dublin)
Lawless, James (SCI)
Promotions Director,
Sacred Heart Fathers,
Fairfield, 66 Inchicore Road,
Dublin 8
Tel 01-4538655
Lawless, Ralph (OFM)
Franciscan Friary,
Friary Lane, Athlone,
Co Westmeath
Tel 090-6472095
Lawless, Richard, CC
St Aidan's Cathedral,
Enniscorthy, Co Wexford
Tel 053-9235777
(Ferns)
Lawless, Vincent (SMA)
Dromantine Retreat and
Conference Centre
Dromatine College,
Newry, Co Down BT34 1RH
Tel 028-30821219
(Retired in Ireland outside
SMA houses)
Lawlor, Brendan, CC
2 Powerscourt, Tulla,
Co Clare
Tel 065-6835284/087-
9845417
(*Tulla*, Killaloe)
Lawlor, John, Very Rev, PP, VF
The Presbytery,
Ballydonoghue, Co Kerry
Tel 068-47103
(Kerry)
Lawlor, Sean (CSsR)
Mount Saint Alphonsus,
Limerick
Tel 061-315099
Lawton, Liam
Crossneen, Carlow
Tel 059-9134548
(Kildare & L.)
Lawton, Patrick, Very Rev, PP
Shandrum, Charleville,
Co Cork
Tel 063-70016
(*Shandrum*, Cloyne)
Layden, Leo (CSSp)
St Mary's College,
Rathmines, Dublin 6
Tel 01-4995760
Layden, Thomas (SJ)
Campion House Residence,
28 Lower Hatch Street,
Dublin 2
Tel 01-6383990
Leader, Liam, Very Rev Canon,
AP
The Presbytery,
Lower Road, Cork
Tel 021-4500282
(*St Patrick's*, Cork & R.)
Leader, Micheál, CC
Mallow, Co Cork
Tel 022-21382
(*Mallow*, Cloyne)
Leahy, Andy, CC
Tullow, Co Carlow
Tel 059-9180641
(*Tullow*, Kildare & L.)
Leahy, Brendan
St Patrick's College,
Maynooth, Co Kildare
(Dublin)
Leahy, Denis, Very Rev, PP
34 Knockmoyle Est,
Tralee, Co Kerry
(Kerry, retired)

Leahy, Donal, Very Rev, PP
Kilworth, Co Cork
Tel 025-27186
(*Kilworth*, Cloyne)
Leahy, Francis (CSSp)
Holy Spirit Missionary College,
Kimmage Manor, Dublin 12
Tel 01-406 4300
Leahy, Michael (OSA)
St Augustine's Priory,
Washington Street, Cork
Tel 021-2753982
Leahy, Niall (SJ)
c/o Irish Jesuit Provincialate,
Milltown Park,
Sandford Road, Dublin 6
Tel 01-4987333
Leahy, Thomas (SPS) CC
Ballinaheglish,
Co Roscommon
Tel 090-6662229
(*Cloverhill (Oran)*, Elphin)
Leamy, Michael, Very Rev, Adm
Rushbrook, Cobh,
Co Cork
Tel 021-4813144
(Cloyne)
Leane, Thomas, Very Rev, PP
Ballyheigue, Tralee,
Co Kerry
Tel 066-7133110
(*Ballyheigue*, Kerry)
Leddy, Patrick (CSSp)
Holy Ghost Missionary College,
Kimmage Manor, Dublin 12
Tel 01-4064300
Lee, Angelus (OFM)
Adam & Eve's,
4 Merchant's Quay, Dublin 8
Tel 01-6771128
Lee, Francis, PP
Barna, Co Galway
Tel 091-590956
(*Barna*, Galway)
Lee, Hugh (MHM), CC
Curraghboy, Athlone,
Co Roscommon
Tel 090-6488143
(*Kiltoom*, Elphin)
Lee, Patrick (SVD)
133 North Circular Road,
Dublin 7
Tel 01-8386743
Lee, William, Most Rev, DD
Bishop of Waterford and Lismore,
Bishop's House,
John's Hill, Waterford
Tel 051-874463
(Waterford & L.)
Lenihan, Jim, Adm
Eyeries, Co Cork
Tel 027-74008
(*Eyeries*, Kerry)
Lennon, Brian (SJ)
St Francis Xavier's,
Upper Gardiner Street,
Dublin 1
Tel 01-8363411
(Zam-Mal)
Lennon, Denis, Rt Rev Mgr, PP, VF
39 Beechlawn, Clonard,
Wexford
Tel 053-9124417
(*Clonard*, Ferns)
Lennon, James, CC
(Hexham & Newcastle)
Castledockrell, Ballycarney,
Enniscorthy, Co Wexford
Tel 053-9388569
(*Marshallstown*, Ferns)
Lennon, Moling, Very Rev, PE
364 Sundays Well, Naas,
Co Kildare
Tel 045-888667
(Kildare & L., retired)
Lennon, Pat,
Parish Administrator,
Ardagh, Co Longford
Tel 043-6675006
(*Ardagh and Moydow*, Ardagh & Cl.)
Lennon, Patrick (OSA)
Duckspool House,
(Retirement Community),
Abbeyside, Dungarvan,
Co Waterford
Tel 058-23784
Lennon, Sean (OSM)
Servite Priory, Benburb,
Dungannon,
Co Tyrone, BT71 7JZ
Tel 028-37548241
Leogue, John, Very Rev, PP
Athleague, Co Roscommon
Tel 090-6663338
(*Athleague*, Elphin)
Leonard, Albert (OP), CC
Presbytery, St Aengus's,
Balrothery, Tallaght,
Dublin 24
Tel 01-4513757
(*Tallaght, Tymon North*, Dublin)
Leonard, Derek
c/o The Missionary Society of St James the Apostle,
24 Clark Street, Boston,
MA 02109, USA
(Limerick)
Leonard, John, Very Rev, PP, VF
The Presbytery,
10 St Nessan's Park,
Dooradoyle, Limerick
Tel 061-302729
(*St Paul's*, Limerick)
Leonard, Michael
6020 West Ardmore Avenue,
Chicago, IL 60646, USA
Tel 001-7736775341
(Killaloe)
Lewis, Eugene (White Fathers)
Cypress Grove, Templeogue,
Dublin 6W
Tel 01-4055263/4055264
Leycock, Dermot, Very Rev, PP
64 Newtownpark Avenue,
Blackrock, Co Dublin
Tel 01-8333793
(*Newtownpark*, Dublin)
Liddane, Raymond, Very Rev, AP
Newtown, Waterford
Tel 051-874284
(*SS Joseph and Benildus*, Waterford & L.)
Linehan, Diarmuid, Very Rev Canon
2 Maglin View, Ballincollig,
Co Cork
Tel 021-4875857
(Cork & R., retired)
Linehan, Donal, Very Rev Canon, PP
Ballinora, Waterfall,
near Cork
Tel 021-4873448
(*Ballinora*, Cork & R.)
Linehan, Patrick, CC
Kanturk, Co Cork
Tel 029-50061
(*Kanturk*, Cloyne)
Linnane, James, Very Rev Canon, PP, VF
Listowel, Co Kerry
Tel 068-21188
(Kerry, retired)
Linnane, Seamus, Very Rev, AP
St John's Presbytery,
Tralee, Co Kerry
Tel 066-7122522
(*Tralee, St John's*, Kerry)
Lisak, Marcin (OP)
Convent of SS. Xystus and Clement,
Collegio San Clemente,
Via Labicana 95,
00184 Roma
Tel (39-06) 7740021
Liston, Micheál, Very Rev Canon, Adm
21 Sullane Crescent,
Raheen Heights, Limerick
Tel 087-2314804
(*Templeglantine*, Limerick)
Little, Anthony G. (CSSp)
St Mary's College,
Rathmines, Dublin 6
Tel 01-499 5760
Little, Thomas, Very Rev, Adm
Browneshill Avenue, Carlow
Tel 059-9131559
(*Tinryland*, Kildare & L.)
Littleton, John
The Priory Institute,
Tallaght Village, Dublin 24
(Cashel & E.)
Littleton, Patrick, Adm
St Luke's, Kilbarron Road,
Kilmore West, Dublin 5
Tel 01-8486806
(*Kilmore Road West*, Dublin)
Lloyd, Enda, Rt Rev Mgr, EV, Co-PP
Cluian Mhuire,
Killarney Road,
Bray, Co Wicklow
Tel 01-2868413
(*Bray Holy Redeemer*, Dublin)
Lloyd, Francis, Very Rev, PE
The Presbytery, Dungarvan,
Co Waterford
(Waterford & L.)
Loftus, Hughie, Very Rev, PP
Corrandulla, Co Galway
Tel 091-791125
(*Corrandulla (Annaghdown)*, Tuam)
Loftus, John, Very Rev
Binghamstown, Belmullet
Co Mayo
Tel 097-82350
(*Kilmore-Erris*, Killala)
Loftus, Kevin, Rt Rev Mgr, PP
Easkey, Co Sligo
Tel 096-49011
(Killala)
Loftus, Martin (SDB)
Rector,
Salesian College,
Pallaskenry, Co Limerick
Tel 061-393313
Logue, Charles, CC
91 Drumgarner Road, Kilrea,
Co Derry BT51 5TE
Tel 028-29540528
(*Kilrea*, Derry)
Loisel, D. Eric M. (OSB)
Benedictine Monks,
Holy Cross Monastery,
119 Kilbroney Road,
Rostrevor,
Co Down BT34 3BN
Tel 028-41739979
Lomasney, Michael, CC
Cloghroe, Blarney, Co Cork
Tel 021-4385163
(*Inniscarra*, Cloyne)
Lombard, Patrick, CC
St Mary's, Sligo
Tel 071-9162670/9162769
(*Sligo, St Mary's*, Elphin)
Lonergan, Patrick, Very Rev Canon, PE
Garrison, Enniskillen,
Co Fermanagh BT93 4AE
Tel 028-68658234
(*Belleek-Garrison*, Clogher)
Long, John (CSsR)
St Patrick's, Esker,
Co Galway
Tel 091-844549
Long, Joseph, (SPS)
On temporary diocesan work

Long, Leo
Killeen, Ballinaclough, Nenagh
Tel 067-25870/086-8353388
(*Killanave and Templederry*, Killaloe)

Long, Martin, Very Rev, PP
Louisburgh, Co Mayo
Tel 098-66198
(*Louisburgh (Kilgeever)*, Tuam)

Long, Michael (SPS)
Tearmann Spirituality Centre,
Brockagh, Glendalough, Co Wicklow
Tel 0404-45208

Looby, John (SJ)
35 Lower Leeson Street, Dublin 2
Tel 01-6761248
(Editor, Sacred Heart Messenger)
37 Lower Lesson Street, Dublin 2
Tel 01-6767491

Looney, Thomas, Very Rev Canon, SP, VF
Dingle, Co Kerry
Tel 066-9151208
(*Dingle*, Kerry)

Loughran, Desmond, CC
Drumaness, Ballynahinch, Co Down BT24 8NG
Tel 028-97561432
(*Magheradroll/Ballynahinch*), Dromore)

Loughran, James, Very Rev Canon, PE
Parochial House, Esker, Lucan, Co Dublin
(Dublin, retired)

Loughran, Malachy (OSA)
St Augustine's Priory, Shop Street,
Drogheda, Co Louth
Tel 041-9838409

Loughran, Terence, Adm
Cappagh, Askeaton, Co Limerick
Tel 069-63432
(*Kilcornan*, Limerick)

Loughrey, Neil (White Fathers)
Provincial Treasurer, Provincialate,
Cypress Grove Road, Templeogue, Dublin 6W
Tel 01-4992344

Loughrey, Vivian
St Gregory The Great Parish,
200 Nr. University Drive, Plantation,
FL 33324, USA
(Galway)

Lovell, Liam, CC
The Presbytery, Kenmare
Co Kerry
Tel 064-6642047

Lovett, Cyril (SSC)
(Editor, *Far East* Magazine),
St Columban's, Dalgan Park,
Navan, Co Meath
Tel 046-9021525

Lowe, Bernard (CP)
Superior, St Paul's Retreat,
Mount Argus, Dublin 6W
Tel 01-4992000

Lucey, Finbarr, Very Rev, PP
Ardmore, Youghal
Co Cork
Tel 024-94177
(Waterford & L.)

Lucey, John (CSsR)
Mount Saint Alphonsus, Limerick
Tel 061-315099

Lucey, Pat (OP), Very Rev
Provincial, Provincial Office,
St Mary's, Tallaght, Dublin 24
Tel 01-4048118/4048112

Lucid, John, Very Rev, PP
Moyvane, Listowel, Co Kerry
Tel 068-49308
(*Moyvane*, Kerry)

Luddy, Denis (CSsR)
St Joseph's, Dundalk, Co Louth
Tel 042-9334042/9334762

Ludlow, Brendan, PC
St Mary's, Navan, Co Meath
Tel 046-9027518/087-1739700
(*Navan*, Meath)

Lumsden, David, Very Rev, PP
83 Tonlegee Drive, Raheny, Dublin 5
Tel 01-4592665
(*Edenmore*, Dublin)

Lynch, Dermot (OFMCap)
Vicar,
St Francis Capuchin Friary,
Rochestown, Co Cork
Tel 021-4896244

Lynch, Dermot (SJ)
St Ignatius Community & Church,
27 Raleigh Row, Salthill, Galway
Tel 091-523707

Lynch, Dominic
Gallen Nursing Home,
Ferbane, Co Offaly
(Ardagh & Cl., retired)

Lynch, Eamonn, Very Rev, PP
Ballyconnell, Co Cavan
Tel 049-9526291
(*Kildallan and Tomregan*, Kilmore)

Lynch, Edward (CSsR)
St Patrick's, Esker, Athenry, Co Galway
Tel 091-844549

Lynch, Finbarr (SJ)
Manresa House, Dollymount, Dublin 3
Tel 01-8331352

Lynch, Finian (OP)
St Mary's, Pope Quay, Cork
Tel 021-4502267

Lynch, Flannan (OFMCap)
Capuchin Friary,
Ard Mhuire, Creeslough,
Letterkenny, Co Donegal
Tel 074-9138005

Lynch, Francis, PP
2 Station Road, Dungiven, Derry BT47 4LN
Tel 028-77741256
(*Dungiven*, Derry)

Lynch, James (SJ)
St Ignatius Community & Church,
27 Raleigh Row, Salthill, Galway
Tel 091-523707

Lynch, James, Very Rev, PP
Parochial House, Ashbourne, Co Meath
Tel 01-8350406
(*Ashbourne-Donaghmore*, Meath)

Lynch, John
2 Cooleen Avenue, Beaumont, Dublin 9
(Dublin, retired)

Lynch, Jude (CSSp)
Bursar,
Holy Spirit Missionary College,
Kimmage Manor, Dublin 12
Tel 01-4064300

Lynch, Laurence (OCarm)
Carmelite Priory,
Knocktopher, Co Kilkenny
Tel 056-7768675
(*Knocktopher/Ballyhale*, Ossory)

Lynch, Lorcan, Very Rev PP
Derrygonnelly, Enniskillen,
Co Fermanagh BT93 6HW
Tel 028-68641207
(*Derrygonnelly*, Clogher)

Lynch, Owen, CC
The Presbytery, Blacklion, Co Wicklow
Tel 01-2874025
(*Greystones*, Dublin)

Lynch, Patrick (OFM)
The Abbey,
8 Francis Street, Galway
Tel 091-562518

Lynch, Patrick (SMA)
Temporary diocesan work in Ireland

Lynch, Patrick, Very Rev, PP
Tubbercurry, Co Sligo
Tel 071-9185049
(Achonry)

Lynch, Patsy, CC
St Brendan's, Tralee, Co Kerry
Tel 066-7125932
(*Tralee, St Brendan's*, Kerry)

Lynch, Sean (SMA)
African Missions,
Blackrock Road, Cork
Tel 021-4292871

Lyng, John (OSA) CC
St Augustine's,
Taylor's Lane,
Ballyboden, Dublin 16
Tel 01-4543356
(*Ballyboden*, Dublin)

Lyng, Richard, Very Rev (OSA), PP
St Augustine's, Galway
Tel 091-562524
(*St Augustine's*, Galway)

Lyon, Kevin, CC
Archdeacon of Glendalough,
Parochial House,
Crosschapel, Blessington, Co Wicklow
Tel 045-865215
(*Blessington*, Dublin)

Lyons, Enda, Dr
Bermingham Road, Tuam, Co Galway
(Tuam, retired)

Lyons, Fintan (OSB)
Glenstal Abbey, Murroe, Co Limerick
Tel 061-386103

Lyons, Gabriel, Very Rev, PP
119 Glenravel Road,
Martinstown, Ballymena,
Co Antrim BT43 6QL
Tel 028-21758217
(*Glenravel (Skerry)*, Down & C.)

Lyon, Kevin, Rev Archdeacon, CC,
Parochial House,
Crosschapel,
Blessington, Co Wicklow
Tel 01-865215
(*Blessington*, Dublin)

Lyons, Seán, Very Rev, PP
Duniry, Loughrea, Co Galway
Tel 090-9745125
(*Duniry and Abbey*, Clonfert)

Lyons, Thomas
Chaplain,
Cork University Hospital,
Wilton, Cork
Tel 021-4546400/4922391/4546109
(Galway)

## M

MacAodh, Seán, PP
Teach an Sagairt,
An Spidéal, Co na Gaillimhe
Tel 091-553155
(*An Spidéal*, Galway)

MacAodha, Loman (OFM)
Vicar, Franciscan Abbey, Multyfarnham, Co Westmeath
Tel 044-9371114/9371137

Macaulay, Ambrose, Rt Rev Mgr
89a Maryvile Park, Belfast BT9 6LQ
(Down and C., retired)

Macaulay, Jeremiah, Very Rev Canon, AP
Edgeworthstown, Co Longford
Tel 043-6671159
(Ardagh & Cl.)

MacBradaigh, Proinsias (SJ)
Superior, Arrupe Community, 127 Shangan Road, Ballymun, Dublin 9
Tel/Fax 01-8625345

MacCarthaigh, Donncha (MSC)
Western Road, Cork
Tel 021-4804120

MacCarthaigh, Pádraig, Very Rev, PP
The Presbytery, Ballydesmond, Mallow, Co Cork
Tel 064-7751104
(*Ballydesmond*, Kerry)

MacCarthy, Martin (OP)
St Mary's, Pope Quay, Cork
Tel 021-4502267

MacCarthy, Seán (SMA)
African Missions, Blackrock Road, Cork
Tel 021-4292871

MacCormack, Gerard, Very Rev, PP
Parochial House, Kingscourt, Co Cavan
Tel 042-9667314
(*Kingscourt*, Meath)

MacCourt, Aloysius, CC
Parochial House, 55 West Street, Stewartstown, Dungannon, Co Tyrone BT71 5HT
Tel 028-87738252
(Armagh)

MacCraith, Micheál (OFM)
Guardian, Collegio S. Isidoro, Via degli Artisti 41, 00187 Roma, Italy
Tel +39-06-4885359

MacCuarta, Brian (SJ)
c/o Irish Jesuit Provincialate, Milltown Park, Sandford Road, Dublin 6
Tel 01-4987333

MacDaid, Liam S., Most Rev, DD
Bishop's House, Monaghan
Tel 047-81019
(Clogher)

MacDonagh, Fergal, CC
The Presbytery, 1A St Patrick's Parish, Irishtown Road, Dublin 4
Tel 01-6684724
(*Ringsend*, Dublin)

MacDonald, Criostóir, Very Rev, Adm
Cathedral Presbytery, Cork
Tel 021-4304325
(*Cathedral of St Mary & St Anne*, Cork & R.)

MacEntee, Patrick, Very Rev, PP
Shanmullagh, Dromore, Omagh, Co Tyrone BT78 3DZ
Tel 028-82898641
(*Dromore*, Clogher)

MacEoinín, Fergal (OP), Very Rev, PP
St Mary's Priory, The Claddagh, Galway
Tel 091-582884
(*St Mary's*, Galway)

MacGiolla Catháin, Darach, PP
Corpus Christi Presbytery, 4-6 Springhill Grove, Belfast BT12 7SL
Tel 028-90246857
(*St Luke's*, Down & C.)

MacGiollarnáth, Sean, (OCarm), CC
Carmelite Presbytery, Idrone Avenue, Knocklyon, Dublin 16
Tel 01-4941204
(*Knocklyon*, Dublin)

MacGowan, Padraig, Very Rev, PP
Ballymahon, Co Longford
Tel 090-6432253
(*Ballymahon*, Ardagh & Cl.)

MacGréil, Mícheál (SJ)
St Francis Xavier's, Upper Gardiner Street, Dublin 1
Tel 01-8363411

MacGurnaghan, Joseph, Very Rev
14 Presbytery Lane, Dunloy, Ballymena, Co Antrim BT44 9DZ
Tel 028-27657223
(Down & C., retired)

MacHale, Brendan (SSC)
St Columban's, Dalgan Park, Navan, Co Meath
Tel 046-9021525

MacHale, John George, Very Rev Canon, PP, VF
Kilglass, Enniscrone, Ballina, Co Mayo
Tel 096-36191
(*Kilglass*, Killala)

Macken, Walter
Gort Ard University Residence, Rockbarton North, Galway
Tel 091-523846
Chaplain, Ballyglunin Park Conference Centre, Tuam, Co Galway
Tel 093-41423
(Opus Dei)

MacKenna, Benedict (OP)
Newbridge College, Droichead Nua, Co Kildare
Tel 045-487200

MacKeone, Kieran, Very Rev, PE, AP
Parochial House, 132 Washing Bay Road, Coalisland, Dungannon, Co Tyrone BT71 4QZ
Tel 028-87740376
(*Clonoe*, Armagh)

Mackey, Niall, Very Rev, PP
Parochial House, 1 River Valley Heights, Swords, Co Dublin
Tel 01-8403400
(*River Valley*, Dublin)

MacKiernan, James, CC
Boher, Ballycumber, Co Offaly
Tel 057-9336119
(Ardagh & Cl.)

Mackin, Patrick A., Very Rev, PE
Bohermeen, Navan, Co Meath
Tel 046-9021439
(Meath, retired)

Mackle, Patrick (SMA)
Retired in Ireland outside SMA houses

MacLaifeartaigh, Michael (OCD)
St Teresa's, Clarendon Street, Dublin 2
Tel 01-6718466/6718127

MacLochlainn, Piaras, CC
10 Finglaswood Road, Finglas West, Dublin 11
Tel 01-8347041
(*Finglas West*, Dublin)

MacMahon, James Ardle, Rt Rev Mgr, Canon
Queen of Peace Centre, 6 Garville Avenue, Rathgar, Dublin 6
(Dublin, retired)

MacMahon, John, Very Rev Canon, PE
Holy Family Residence, Roebuck Road, Dundrum, Dublin 14
(Dublin, retired)

MacMahon, Joseph (OFM)
Secretary of Province and Guardian, Provincial Office, La Verna, Gormanston, Co Meath
Tel 01-8020951

MacManuis, Clement (CSsR)
St Joseph's, Dundalk, Co Louth
Tel 042-9334042/9334762

MacMorrow, Francis (CM)
St Joseph's, 44 Stillorgan Park, Blackrock, Co Dublin
Tel 01-2886961

MacNamara, Francis, Very Rev, PP, VF
Mountmellick, Co Laois
Tel 057-8624198
(Kildare & L.)

MacNamara, Luke (OSB)
Glenstal Abbey, Murroe, Co Limerick
Tel 061-386103

MacNamara, Vincent (SPS)
St Patrick's, 21 Leeson Park, Dublin 6
Tel 01-4977897

MacNamee, David, Very Rev Canon
St Bernadette's, 13 Osmington Terrace, Thomondgate, Limerick
(Limerick)

MacNeill, Arthur, Very Rev
14 Ballyholland Road, Newry, Co Down
(Dromore, retired)

MacOscar, Kieran, Very Rev, PE, AP
Parochial House, 10 Mullavilly Road, Tandragee, Co Armagh BT62 2LX
Tel 028-38840840
(Armagh, retired)

MacPartlin, Brendan (SJ)
Superior, Iona, 211 Churchill Park, Portadown BT62 1EU
Tel 028-38330366

MacRaois, Brian, Very Rev, PP
Parochial House, Chapel Hill, Carlingford, Co Louth
Tel 042-9373111
(*Carlingford and Clogherny*, Armagh)

MacSuibhne, Domhnall (OP), Very Rev, PP
Prior, St Mary's, The Claddagh, Co Galway
Tel 091-582884
(*The Claddagh*, Galway)

MacSweeney, James, CC
64 Westcourt, Ballincollig, Co Cork
Tel 021-4870434
(*Ballincollig*, Cork & R.)

Madden, Brendan, Very Rev, PP
67 Anne Devlin Park, Ballyroan, Dublin 14
Tel 01-4037536
(*Ballyroan*, Dublin)

Madden, Christopher J., Lisieux
196 Oakcourt Avenue, Palmerstown, Dublin 20
(Dublin, retired)

Madden, John (OCarm)
Terenure College, Terenure, Dublin 6W
Tel 01-4904621

Madden, Laurence, Very Rev, PP
Ardagh, Co Limerick
Tel 069-76121/087-2286450
(*Ardagh and Carrickerry*, Limerick)

Madden, Michael, Very Rev, PE
Ballycrennane, Ballymacoda, Co Cork
Tel 024-98840
(Cloyne, retired)

Madden, Nicholas (OCD)
St Teresa's, Clarendon Street, Dublin 2
Tel 01-6718466/6718127

Madden, P.J., CC
Graiguecullen, Carlow
Tel 059-9141833
(*Graiguecullen*, Kildare & L.)

Madden, Patrick, Very Rev, PP, VF
Presbytery 1, Ballycullen Avenue, Firhouse, Dublin 24
Tel 01-4599855
(*Firhouse*, Dublin)

Madden, Paul (OPraem)
Abbey of the Most Holy Trinity and St Norbert, Kilnacrott, Ballyjamesduff, Co Cavan
Tel 049-8544416

Madden, Peter, PP
50 Tobermore Road, Desertmartin, Magherafelt, Co Derry BT45 5LE
Tel 028-79632196
(*Desertmartin*, Derry)

Madigan, Martin, Very Rev
Hamilton's Terrace, Glin, Co Limerick
Tel 087-9418568
(Limerick, retired)

Madigan, Seamus
Chaplain, Sarsfield Barracks, Limerick
Tel 061-316817
(Limerick)

Magee, Aelred (OCSO)
Our Lady of Bethlehem Abbey, 11 Ballymena Road, Portglenone, Ballymena, Co Antrim BT44 8BL
Tel 028-25821211

Magee, Bernard, Very Rev Canon
41 Lower Square, Castlewellan BT31 9DN
Tel 028-43770377
(*Castlewellan (Kilmegan)*, Down & C.)

Magee, Gerard
Cistercian Monastery, Portglenone
(Down & C.)

Magee, John, Most Rev, DD
Bishop Emeritus of Cloyne, Mitchelstown, Co Cork
Tel 025-41887
(Cloyne)

Magennis, Feidlimidh, LSS
St Mary's University College, Belfast
(Dromore)

Magill, Martin, Very Rev, PP
St Oliver Plunkett Presbytery, 27 Glenveagh Drive, Belfast BT11 9HX
Tel 028-90618180
(Down & C.)

Magill, Neil (SSC)
St Columban's, Dalgan Park, Navan, Co Meath
Tel 046-9021525

Maginn, Michael, Very Rev, PP
Lisadell, 54 Francis Street, Lurgan, Co Armagh BT66 6DL
Tel 028-38327173
(*Shankill, St Paul's (Lurgan)*, Dromore)

Magorrian, Eamon, CC
Parochial House, 27 Chapel Hill, Lisburn, Co Antrim BT28 1EP
Tel 028-92660206
(*Lisburn (Blaris)*, Down & C.)

Maguire, Edmond, Very Rev, PE
Newtown Butler Road, Clones, Co Monaghan
Tel 047-51160
(Clogher, retired)

Maguire, James (OSA)
St Augustine's Priory, Washington Street, Cork
Tel 021-2753982

Maguire, Joseph (SMA)
African Missions, Blackrock Road, Cork
Tel 021-4292871

Maguire, Salvian (CP)
Holy Cross Retreat, Ardoyne, Belfast BT14 7GE
Tel 028-90748231

Maguire, Vincent, Very Rev
26 Rodney Street, Portrush, Co Antrim BT56 8LB
(Down and C., retired)

Maher, Francis, Very Rev, PP
Johnstown via Thurles, Co Kilkenny
Tel 056-8831219/087-2402487
(*Johnstown*, Ossory)

Maher, James (SJ) Minister, Crescent College Comprehensive, Dooradoyle, Limerick
Tel 061-480920

Maher, Michael (SM)
Cerdon, Marist Fathers, St Mary's Road, Dundalk, Co Louth
Tel 042-9334019

Maher, Michael, Very Rev
11 Woodlawn, Listowel, Co Kerry
(Kerry, retired)

Maher, Noel, Very Rev, PP
Clough, Ballacolla, Portlaoise, Co Laois
Tel 057-878513
(*Aghaboe*, Ossory)

Maher, Oliver, Very Rev, PP
Urlingford, Co Kilkenny
Tel 056-8831121/086-8323010
(*Urlingford*, Ossory)

Maher, Sean, CC
Irish College, Paris
(Kildare & L.)

Maher, Thomas, Rt Rev Mgr
Archersrath Nursing Home, Kilkenny
Tel 056-7790137
(Ossory, retired)

Mailey, Anthony, CC
Parochial House, Quigley's Point, Co Donegal
Tel 074-9383008
(*Iskaheen*, Derry)

Malik, Asif Imran, PC
32 Wheatfields Close, Clondalkin, Dublin 22
Tel 01-6261010
(*Rowlagh and Quarryvale*, Dublin)

Mallon, Brendan, CC
Coachford, Co Cork
Tel 021-7334059
(*Aghabullogue*, Cloyne)

Mallon, Dominic
13 Richview Heights, Keady, Co Armagh BT60 3SW
(Armagh)

Mallon, Thomas, Very Rev, PE, AP
Parochial House, 170 Loughmacrory Road, Omagh, Co Tyrone BT79 9LG
Tel 028-80761230
(*Termonmaguirc (Carrickmore, Loughmacrory & Creggan)*, Armagh)

Malone, Douglas, Adm,
The Presbytery, Dunlavin, Co Wicklow
Tel 045-401227
(*Dunlavin*, Dublin)

Malone, Laurence, Very Rev, PE
c/o Bishop's House, Carlow
(Kildare & L., retired)

Malone, Liam, CC
Parochial House, Kells, Co Meath
Tel 046-9240213
(*Kells*, Meath)

Malone, Pat, Very Rev, PP
'Maryville', Church Road, Nenagh, Co Tipperary
Tel 067-37130
Chaplain, County Hospital, Nenagh, Co Tipperary
Tel 067-31491
Chaplain, Welfare Home, Nenagh, Co Tipperary
Tel 067-31893
(Killaloe)

Malone, Tony (SM)
CUS Community, 89 Lower Leeson Street, Dublin 2
Tel 01-6762586

Maloney, Dermot, Very Rev, PP, VF
Parochial House, 40 The Village, Jonesboro, Newry, Co Down BT35 8HP
Tel 028-3084945
(Armagh)

Maloney, John
Curate's House, Kikelly, Co Mayo
Tel 094-9367031
(Achonry)

Maloney, Michael
c/o Parochial House, Charlestown, Co Mayo

Maloney, Peter (SVD)
Donamon Castle, Roscommon
Tel 090-6662222

Mandi, Josephat
Parish Chaplain, 287 South Circular Road, Dublin 8
Tel 01-4533490
(*Dolphin's Barn*, Dublin)

Manding, Cruzito (CSsR)
PO Box 280, 6000 Cebu City, Philippine Islands
Tel +63-32-2553954

Mangan, Cyril, Very Rev, PP
5 Lissenhall Park,
Seatown Road, Swords,
Co Dublin
Tel 01-8403378
(*Swords*, Dublin)
Mangan, Eoin, Very Rev Canon, PP
The Prebytery,
Knockagoshel, Co Kerry
Tel 068-46107
(*Knocknagoshel*, Kerry)
Mangan, Patrick J., Very Rev, PE
Dún Mhuire,
44 Beechwood Avenue Upper, Dublin 6
Tel 01-4975180
(Dublin, retired)
Mangan, Thomas, Very Rev, Adm
'Naomh Joseph',
Lifford Avenue, Limerick
Tel 061-303777/087-2376032
(*St Joseph's*, Limerick)
Manik, Robert (OCarm)
Whitefriar Street Church,
56 Aungier Street, Dublin 2
Tel 01-4758821
Manley, John (OFMCap), CC
Guardian, St Anthony's Capuchin Friary,
43 Dublin Street, Carlow
Tel 059-9142543
Mann, Robert (SCJ), Very Rev (*Moderator*)
Parochial House,
St John Vianney,
Ardlea Road, Dublin 5
Tel 01-8474173
(*Ardlea*, Dublin)
Manning, Francis, CC
Macroom, Co Cork
Tel 026-41092
(*Macroom*, Cloyne)
Manning, Michael, Rt Rev, AP
Fatima House, Oak Park
Tralee, Co Kerry
(Kerry, retired)
Manning, Seán, Very Rev Canon
St Mary's College, Galway
(Galway)
Mannion, Francis (SSC)
St Columban's Retirement Home,
Dalgan Park, Navan,
Co Meath
Tel 046-9021525
Mannion, John, CC
Killoran, Ballinasloe,
Co Galway
Tel 090-9627120
(*Mullagh and Killoran*, Clonfert)
Mannion, Michéal, PP
Kilronan, Aran Islands,
Co Galway
Tel 099-61221
Mannion, Tom, CC
Butlersbridge, Cavan
Tel 049-4365266
(*Cavan*, Kilmore)
Mannix, Jim (MSC)
Western Road, Cork
Tel 021-4804120
Mansfield, Dermot (SJ)
(Team Assistant)
Maressa House,
Clontarf Road, Dublin 3
Tel 01-8057209/087-6942844
(*Dollymount*, Dublin)
Marken, Aodhan, CC
Chaplain/Counsellor,
St Peter's Diocesan College,
Wexford
Tel 053-9142071
Parish
The Presbytery,
12 School Street, Wexford
Tel 053-9122055
(*Wexford*, Ferns)
Markuszewski, Robert, CC
139 Andersonstown Road,
Belfast BT11 9BW
Tel 028-90613724
(*St Agnes*', Down & C.)
Marley, Thomas (IC)
St Joseph's,
Doire na hAbhann,
Tickincar, Clonmel,
Co Tipperary
Tel 052-26914
Marmion, Declan (SM)
Mount St Mary's,
Milltown, Dublin 14
Tel 01-2697322
Marrinan, Thomas, Very Rev, PP
Gort, Co Galway
Tel 091-631220
(*Gort/Beagh*, Galway)
Marron, Eamonn, Rt Rev Mgr, PE
Parochial House, Raharney,
Co Westmeath
Tel 044-9374271
(*Kinnegad*, Meath)
Marron, Patrick, Very Rev Canon, PE
Fintona, Omagh,
Co Tyrone BT78 2NS
Tel 028-82841239
(*Fintona*, Clogher)
Marron, Thomas, Very Rev Canon, PE
Trillick, Omagh,
Co Tyrone BT78 3RD
Tel 028-89561217
(*Trillick*, Clogher)
Marsden, David (SCJ)
Parochial House,
St John Vianney,
Ardlea Road, Dublin 5
Tel 01-8474123
(*Ardlea*, Dublin)
Marteaux, D. Thierry (OSB)
Benedictine Monks,
Holy Cross Monastery,
119 Kilbroney Road,
Rostrevor,
Co Down BT34 3BN
Tel 028-41739979
Martin, Diarmuid, Most Rev, DD
Archbishop of Dublin and Primate of Ireland,
Archbishop's House,
Drumcondra, Dublin 9
Tel 01-8373732
(Dublin)
Martin, Eamon, Rt Rev Mgr
Diocesan Administrator,
Bishop's House, PO Box 227,
Derry, BT48 9YG
Tel 028-71262302
(Derry)
Martin, Hubert, Very Rev, PP
Glaslough, Monaghan
Tel 047-88120
(*Donagh*, Clogher)
Martin, Liam (CSSp)
Holy Spirit Missionary College,
Kimmage Manor, Dublin 12
Tel 01-4064300
Martin, Oliver (OPraem)
Abbey of the Most Holy Trinity and St Norbert,
Kilnacrott,
Ballyjamesduff, Co Cavan
Tel 049-8544416
Martin, Valentine, Very Rev, PP
The Presbytery, Jobstown,
Tallaght, Dublin 24
Tel 01-4523595
(Dublin, retired)
Mathew, Binoy (SVD)
Maynooth, Co Kildare
Tel 01-6286391/2
Mathews, Colm, CC
47 Old Court Manor,
Dublin 24
Tel 01-4525624
(*Bohernabreena*, Dublin)
Mathews, William (SJ)
Milltown Park,
Sandford Road, Dublin 6
Tel 01-2698411/2698113
Matthews, Richard, Very Rev, PP, VF
Parochial House, Killucan,
Co Westmeath
Tel 044-9374127
(*Killucan*, Meath)
Mawn, Sean
Ballinaglera,
Carrick-on-Shannon,
Co Leitrim
Tel 071-9643014
(Kilmore)
Maxwell, Barney
Empor, Ballymacargy,
Co Westmeath
(Meath, retired)
Mbajo, Linus (CSSp)
Holy Spirit Missionary College,
Kimmage Manor, Dublin 12
Tel 01-4064300
Mbombo Mukaya, Jean-Marie (CICM)
Presbytery, Putland Road,
Bray, Co Wicklow
Tel 01-2867303
(*Bray, Putland Road*, Dublin)
McAdam, Colm (CM), Very Rev
St Joseph's,
44 Stillorgan Park,
Blackrock, Co Dublin
Tel 01-2886961
McAleer, Brendan, Very Rev, PP
Parochial House,
Garristown, Co Dublin
Tel 01-8354138
(*Garristown*, Dublin)
McAleer, Gerard, Very Rev, PP
Parochial House,
63 Castlecaulfield Road,
Donaghmore, Dungannon,
Co Tyrone BT70 3HF
Tel 028-87761327
(*Donaghmore*, Armagh)
McAleese, Frank (OCarm)
Carmelite Friary,
Kinsale, Co Cork
Tel 021-772138
McAlinden, John (CSsR), CC
Parochial House, Slane Road, Mell, Drogheda,
Co Louth
Tel 041-983 8278
(*Drogheda*, Armagh)
McAlinden, Martin, Very Rev, PP, VF
The Presbytery,
11 Tullygally Road,
Legahory,
Craigavon BT65 5BL
Tel 028-38341901
(*Moyraverty (Craigavon)*, Dromore)
McAllister, Bernard (OFMCap)
Capuchin Friary,
Ard Mhuire, Creeslough,
Letterkenny, Co Donegal
Tel 074-9138005
McAnaney, Martin (SM)
Paris
McAnenly, Peter, PP
10 Killymeal Road,
Dungannon,
Co Tyrone BT71 6DP
Tel 028-87722906
(*Eglish*, Armagh)

McAnerney, Arthur, Very Rev, PE, AP
Parochial House,
10 Aughrim Road,
Magherafelt,
Co Derry BT45 6AY
Tel 028-79632351
(*Magherafelt and Ardtrea North*, Armagh)

McAnuff, Patrick, Very Rev Canon
58 Armagh Road,
Newry, Co Down
(Dromore, retired)

McArdle, Martin, Very Rev, PP
Parochial House,
10 Springhill Road,
Moneymore, Magherafelt,
Co Derry BT45 7NG
Tel 028-86748242
(*Moneymore (Ardtrea)*, Armagh)

McArdle, Sean (SM), CC
The Presbytery,
Donore Avenue, Dublin 8
Tel 01-4542425
(*Donore Avenue*, Dublin)

McAreavey, John, Very Rev, DD
Bishop of Dromore,
Bishop's House,
44 Armagh Road, Newry,
Co Down BT35 6PN
Tel 028-30262444
(Dromore)

McAteer, Brendan, Very Rev
Warrenpoint, Co Down
(*Dromore*, retired)

McAteer, Francis, Very Rev, PP
Parochial House, Carrick,
Co Donegal
Tel 074-9739008
(Raphoe)

McAteer, Kieran, Very Rev, PP
Parochial House, Ballybofey,
Co Donegal
Tel 074-9131135
(*Stranorlar*, Raphoe)

McAteer, Tom, CC
15 Chapel Hill, Mayobridge,
Newry, Co Down BT34 2EX
Tel 028-30851225
(*Clonallon, St Patrick's (Mayobridge)*, Dromore)

McAuley, John (SJ)
Milltown Park,
Sandford Road, Dublin 6
Tel 01-2698411/2698113

McAuliffe, David
Chaplain, University College,
Iona, College Road, Cork
Tel 021-4902704
(Cork & R.)

McAuliffe, Desmond, Very Rev, Adm
Rockhill, Bruree,
Co Limerick
Tel 063-90515/087-2336476
(*Rockhill/Bruree*, Limerick)

McAuliffe, Leo (OFMCap)
St Anthony's Capuchin Friary,
43 Dublin Street, Carlow
Tel 059-9142543

McBrearty, Danny, CC
Parochial House, Clar,
Co Donegal
Tel 074-9721093
(*Donegal Town (Tawnawilly)*, Raphoe)

McBrearty, Stephen, Very Rev, PP
St Anthony's Presbytery,
4 Willowfield Crescent,
Belfast BT6 8HP
Tel 028-90253666
(*St Anthony's*, Down & C.)

McBride, Brendan
St Philip's Church,
725 Diamond Street,
San Francisco,
California, 94114
(Raphoe)

McBride, Colm, Very Rev, PP
Netherley Lodge,
130 Upper Dunmurry Lane,
Belfast BT17 0EW
(*Our Lady Queen of Peace, Kilwee*, Down & C.)

McCabe, John, Very Rev Canon, PP
Parochial House, Roslea,
Co Fermanagh BT92 7LA
Tel 028- 67751227
(Clogher)

McCabe, Kenneth (SSCC) CC
St Mary's, Clontibret,
Co Monaghan
Tel 047-80631
(*Clontibret*, Clogher)

McCabe, Robert, CF
Gormanston Military Camp,
Gormanston, Co Meath
Tel 01-8413990
(*Stamullen*, Meath)

McCabe, Thomas (OMI)
Oblate Scholasticate,
St Anne's,
Goldenbridge Walk,
Inchicore, Dublin 8
Tel 01-4540841/4542955

McCafferty, Patrick, PC
48 Lower Rathmines Road,
Dublin 6
Tel 01-4976148
(*Rathmines*, Dublin)

McCafferty, Paul
Derry Diocesan Office,
Bishop's House,
Derry BT48 9AP
Tel 028-71262302
(Derry)

McCaffrey, Desmond (OCD)
St Teresa's,
Clarendon Street, Dublin 2
Tel 01-6718466/6718127

McCaffrey, Eugene
Avila, Bloomfield Avenue,
Morehampton Road,
Dublin 4
Tel 01-6430200

McCaffrey, James (CSSp) CC
Holy Spirit Missionary College,
Kimmage Manor, Dublin 12
Tel 01-406 4300/4526514

McCaffrey, Ultan (OFM)
Franciscan Friary, Lady Lane,
Waterford
Tel 051-874262

McCague, Brendan, CC
Corduff, Carrickmacross,
Co Monaghan
Tel 042-9669456
(*Carrickmacross*, Clogher)

McCahery, Barney (CSsR), CC
Clonard Monastery,
1 Clonard Gardens,
Belfast BT13 2RL
Tel 028-90445950

McCallion, Edwin (SM), Very Rev, PP
The Presbytery,
Donore Avenue, Dublin 8
Tel 01-4542425
(*Donore Avenue*, Dublin)

McCallion, John, CC
Parochial House,
18 Annaghmore Road,
Coalisland, Dungannon,
Co Tyrone BT71 4QZ
(*Clonoe*, Armagh)

McCamley, Eamonn, Very Rev, PP
Parochial House,
17 Eagralougher Road,
Loughgall,
Co Armagh BT61 8LA
Tel 028-38891231
(*Loughgall*, Armagh)

McCann, Brian, Very Rev, PP
St Luke's Presbytery,
Twinbrook Road, Dunmurry,
Co Antrim BT17 0RP
(*St Luke's*, Down & C.)

McCann, Charles, AP
Parochial House,
2 Tullynure Road
Cookstown,
Co Tyrone BT80 9XH
Tel 028-86763674
(*Lissan*, Armagh)

McCann, Columba (OSB)
Glenstal Abbey, Murroe,
Co Limerick
Tel 061-386103

McCann, Henry, PP
St Mary's Presbytery,
12 Ballymena Road,
Portglenone,
Co Antrim BT44 8BL
Tel 028-25821218
(*Portglenone*, Down & C.)

McCann, Joseph (CM)
All Hallows Institute for Mission and Ministry,
Drumcondra, Dublin 9
Tel 01-8373745/6

McCanny, Bryan, Rt Rev Mgr, PP
119 Irish Green Street,
Limavady,
Co Derry BT49 9AB
Tel 028-77729759
(Derry)

McCarney, Eugene, Very Rev, PE
Parochial House,
Castletown, Gorey,
Co Wexford
Tel 0402-37115
(Dublin, retired)

McCarney, Henry (SPS)
St Patrick's, Kiltegan,
Co Wicklow
Tel 059-6473600

McCarrick, Roger (SM)
Fiji

McCarron, Declan
c/o Diocesan Office,
Letterkenny, Co Donegal
(Raphoe)

McCarron, Peter, CC
The Presbytery,
2 River Valley Heights,
Swords, Co Dublin
Tel 01-8404162
(*River Valley*, Dublin)

McCartan, Sean, Adm
Parochial House
Moortown, Cookstown,
Co Tyrone BT80 0HT
Tel 028-86737236
(*Ardboe*, Armagh)

McCarthy, Berchmans (OFMCap)
St Francis Capuchin Friary,
Rochestown, Co Cork
Tel 021-4896244

McCarthy, Brian
Castleville Study Centre,
Golf Links Road, Castletroy,
Limerick
Tel 061-331223
(Opus Dei)

McCarthy, Daniel, CF (Cloyne)
Chaplain,
Stephen's Barracks, Kilkenny
Tel 056-7761852
(Ossory)

McCarthy, Dermod
RTÉ, Donnybrook, Dublin 4
Tel 01-2083237/087-2499719
(Dublin)

McCarthy, Donal (MSC)
Western Road, Cork
Tel 021-4804120

McCarthy, Donal (SAC)
Provincial House,
'Homestead',
Sandyford Road, Dundrum,
Dublin 16
Tel 01-2956180/2954170

McCarthy, Eamonn, CC
Freemount, Charleville
Tel 022-28788
(*Milford,* Cloyne)
McCarthy, Eamonn, CC
The Presbytery, Donard,
Co Wicklow
Tel 045-404614
(*Dunlavin*, Dublin)
McCarthy, Eugene (CP), Very Rev, PP
24 The Court,
Mulhuddart Wood,
Mulhuddart, Dublin 15
Tel 01-8128941
(*Mulhuddart*, Dublin)
McCarthy, Florence (SDB)
Salesian House,
45 St Teresa's Road,
Crumlin, Dublin 12
Tel 01-4555605
McCarthy, Francis, CC
Holycross House, Moyglass,
Fethard, Co Tipperary
Tel 052-6131343
(*Killeanaule*, Cashel & E.)
McCarthy, Gabriel (OCSO)
Mount Saint Joseph Abbey,
Roscrea, Co Tipperary
Tel 0505-25600
McCarthy, Gerard (SVD)
Donamin Castle,
Roscommon
Tel 090-6662222
McCarthy, John
Irish Pastoral Centre,
953 Hancock Street, Quincy,
Massachusetts CO2170, USA
Tel 001-617479740
(Limerick)
McCarthy, John (MSC)
Woodview House,
Mount Merrion Avenue,
Blackrock, Co Dublin
Tel 01-2881644
McCarthy, John, CC
Cobh, Co Cork
Tel 021-4815619
(*Cobh, St Colman's Cathedral,* Cloyne)
McCarthy, John, Very Rev
76 Carrowmore Meadows,
Knock, Co Mayo
(Tuam, retired)
McCarthy, John, Very Rev, PP
Rosscarbery, Co Cork
Tel 023-8848168
(*Rosscarbery and Lissavaird*, Cork & R.)
McCarthy, Liam (OFM)
Franciscan Missionaries in Zimbabwe
McCarthy, Michael (CSSp)
Holy Spirit Missionary College,
Kimmage Manor, Dublin 12
Tel 01-4064300
McCarthy, Patrick A., Very Rev, PP
35 Paul Street, Cork
Tel 021-4276573
(*Ss Peter's and Paul's*, Cork & R.)
McCarthy, Patrick J., Very Rev, Adm
Ardfield, Clonakilty,
Co Cork
Tel 023-8840649
(*Ardfield and Rathbarry*, Cork & R.)
McCarthy, Patrick, CC
Mallow, Co Cork
Tel 086-3831621
(*Mallow*, Cloyne)
McCarthy, Sean, Very Rev Canon
Loma, Newtown Road,
Wexford
(Ferns, retired)
McCarthy, Sylvius (OFMCap)
St Francis Capuchin Friary,
Rochestown, Co Cork
Tel 021-4896244
McCarthy, Thomas
119 The Stilesroad, Dublin 3
Tel 01- 8384325
(*Clontarf, St Anthony's*, Dublin)
McCarthy, Thomas (OP)
Newbridge College,
Droichead Nua, Co Kildare
Tel 045-487200
McCarthy, Vincent (OSA)
St Augustine's Priory (Residence),
New Ross, Co Wexford
Tel 051-421237
McCartney, Sean, Very Rev, PP
25 Alt-Min Avenue,
Belfast BT8 6NJ
(Down & C., retired)
McCathy, Anthony (OParem)
Abbey of the Most Holy Trinity and St Norbert,
Kilnacrott,
Ballyjamesduff, Co Cavan
Tel 049-8544416
McCaughan, Aidan (priest in residence)
Parochial House,
2-4 Broughshane Road,
Ballymena,
Co Antrim BT43 7DX
Tel 028-25641515
(*Ballymena (Kirkinriola),* Down & C.)
McCaughan, Colm, Rt Rev Mgr
3 Fortwilliam Demesne,
Belfast BT15 4FD
Tel 028-90778111
McCaughan, Dermot, Very Rev, PP
St Patrick's Presbytery,
29 Chapel Hill, Lisburn,
Co Antrim BT28 1EP
Tel 028-92662341
(*Lisburn (Blaris),* Down & C.)
McCaughey, George (SDB)
Salesian House,
Warrenstown, Drumree,
Co Meath
Tel 01-8240298
McCaughey, Michael, PP
St Patrick's, Buncrana road,
Pennyburn, Derry BT48 7QL
Tel 028-71262301
(Derry)
McCaughey, Shane, Very Rev, BD
Manager,
St Macartan's College,
Monaghan, Co Monaghan
Tel 047-81642/83365/83367
(Clogher)
McCay-Morrissey, Bernard (OP)
St Saviour's,
Upper Dorset Street,
Dublin 1
Tel 01-8897610
McClarey, Liam Very Rev, (SCA), PP, VF
Parochial House Corduff,
Blanchardstown, Dublin 15
(*Corduff*, Dublin)
McCloskey, Gerard, Very Rev, Adm
Holy Family Presbytery,
Newington Avenue,
Belfast BT15 2HP
Tel 028-90743119
(*Holy Family*, Down & C.)
McCluskey, Brian, Very Rev Canon, PE
Apt 2,
2 Danesfort Park North,
Stranmillis Road,
Belfast BT9 5RB
Tel 028-90683544
(Clogher, retired)
McCluskey, Joseph, Very Rev, PP
Threemilehouse, Monaghan
Tel 047-81501
(*Corcaghan*, Clogher)
McCluskey, Peter (OMI)
Oblate House of Retreat,
Inchicore, Dublin 8
Tel 01-4534408/4541805
McConnell, Noel, CC
Shantonagh, Castleblayney,
Co Monaghan
Tel 042-9745015
(*Aughnamullen East*, Clogher)
McConvery, Brendan (CSsR)
Liguori House,
75 Orwell Road, Dublin 6
Tel 01-4067100
McConville, Conor, CC
Cathedral Presbytery,
38 Hill Street,
Newry BT34 1AT
Tel 028-30262586
(*Newry*, Dromore)
McConville, Gerard, Very Rev
68 Main Street,
Portglenone BT44 8HS
(Down & C., retired)
McConville, Matthew
c/o Bishop's House
(Dromore)
McConville, Michael
65 Moyle Road, Ballycastle,
Co Antrim, BT54 6LG
Tel 078-81490543
(*Antrim*, Down & C.)
McCormack, Christy
Fohenagh, Ahascragh,
Ballinasloe, Co Galway
Tel 090-9688623
(*Fohenagh and Killure*, Clonfert)
McCormack, Ignatius
St Flannan's College, Ennis,
Co Clare
Tel 065-6839039/
086-2777139
(Killaloe)
McCormack, James (CM)
St Paul's College, Raheny,
Dublin 5
Tel 01-8314011/2
McCormack, James (MSC), Adm
Hacketstown, Co Carlow
Tel 059-6471257
(*Hacketstown*, Kildare & L.)
McCormack, John (SMA), CC
Breaffy, Castlebar,
Co Mayo
Tel 094-9022799
(*Castlebar (Aglish, Ballyheane and Breaghwy),* Tuam)
McCormack, Martin (SDB)
Salesian College,
Pallaskenry, Co Limerick
Tel 061-393313
McCormack, William, Very Rev, PP
Toomevara, Co Tipperary
Tel 067-26023/087-4168855
(*Toomevara*, Killaloe)
McCormick, Diarmuid, CC
Kilkishen, Co Clare
Tel 061-367193
(*O'Callaghan's Mills*, Killaloe)
McCorry, Francis, Very Rev
Our Lady's Home,
68 Ardnava Road,
Belfast BT12 6FF
(Down & C., retired)
McCoy, Art (OFM)
Franciscan Friary,
Lady Lane, Waterford
Tel 051-874262

McCoy, Ronan (SJ)
St Ignatius Community & Church,
27 Raleigh Row, Salthill, Galway
Tel 091-523707

McCrann, Christopher (LC), CC
Knocknahur, Sligo
Tel 071-9128470
(*Strandhill/Ransboro*, Elphin)

McCreave, Eamonn (OSM)
St Michael's Presbytery,
200 Finaghy Road North,
Belfast BT11 9EG
(*St Michael's*, Down & C.)

McCrory, Gerard, Very Rev Canon, PP
Church Street, Ballynahinch,
Co Down BT24 8LP
Tel 028-97562410
(*Magheradroll (Ballynahinch)*, Dromore)

McCrory, Patrick, J., Very Rev, PE
Parochial House,
Sixemilecross, Omagh,
Co Tyrone BT79 9NF
Tel 028-80758344
(Armagh, retired)

McCrossan, Oliver (SSC)
St Columban's, Dalgan Park,
Navan, Co Meath
Tel 046-9021525

McCrystal, Eoin, Very Rev, PP
12 Grangemore Grove,
Dublin 13
Tel 01-8476392
(*Donaghmede*, Dublin)

McCullagh, John
Parochial House,
46 Barrack Street, Strabane,
Co Tyrone BT82 8HD
Tel 028-71882215
(Derry, retired)

McCullagh, Michael (CM), Very Rev, PP
St Peter's, Phibsboro,
Dublin 7
Tel 01-8389708
(*Phibsboro*, Dublin)

McCullagh, Raymond
1 Seafield Park South,
Portstewart,
Co Derry BT55 7LH
Tel 028-70832066
(Down & C.)

McCullen, Richard (CM)
St Paul's College, Raheny,
Dublin 5
Tel 01-8318113

McCurry, James (OFMConv), Very Rev
General Delegate,
General Delegation Office,
St Patrick's Friary,
26 Cornwall Road,
Waterloo, London SE1 8TW,
England
Tel 020-79288897

McDermott, Brendan (CP)
St Paul's Retreat,
Mount Argus, Dublin 6W
Tel 01-4992000

McDermott, Joseph, Very Rev, Adm
Chapel Lane, Newbridge,
Co Kildare
Tel 045-431741
(Kildare & L.)

McDermott, Kieran, Very Rev, Co-PP
'Emmaus', Main Street,
Dundrum, Dublin 14
Tel 01-2984348
(*Dundrum*, Dublin)

McDermott, Laurence (OCSO)
Prior, Mellifont Abbey,
Collon, Co Louth
Tel 041-9826103

McDermott, Louis (OMI)
52a-52b Bulfin Road,
Dublin 8
Tel 01-4531660
(*Inchicore, St Michael's*, Dublin)

McDermott, Niall, CC
12 Blackberry Rise,
Portmarnock, Dublin
Tel 01-8461398
(*Portmarnock*, Dublin)

McDermott, Noel, CC
91 Ervey Road, Eglinton,
Co Derry BT47 3AU
Tel 028-71810235
(*Faughanvale*, Derry)

McDermott, Paraic, (CSSp), CC
The Presbytery,
Manor Kilbride, Blessington,
Co Wicklow
Tel 01-4582154
(*Blessington*, Dublin)

McDermott, Patrick, CC
(sabbatical leave)
Youth Chaplaincy House,
Moyne, Co Longford
Tel 090-473358
(Ardagh & Cl.)

McDermott, Sean
Chaplain,
Cavan and Monaghan
Defence Forces,
Dun Ui Neill, Cavan
Tel 049-4361631/
087-8292333
(Kilmore)

McDermott, Sean (OMI)
Oblate House of Retreat,
Inchicore, Dublin 8
Tel 01-4534408/4541805

McDermott, Thomas
Churchtown, Mallow,
Co Cork
Tel 022-23385
(*Churchtown (Liscarroll)*, Cloyne)

McDevitt, Eamon, PP
78 Lisnaragh Road,
Dunamanagh, Strabane,
Co Tyrone BT82 0QN
Tel 028-71398212
(Derry)

McDevitt, John, CC
50 Brook Street, Omagh,
Co Tyrone BT78 5HE
Tel 028-82242092
Director,
Omagh Pastoral Centre,
Mount St Columba Pastoral Centre,
48 Brooke Street, Omagh,
Co Tyrone BT78 5HD
Tel 028-82242439
(Derry)

McDevitt, Patrick (CM), Very Rev
President,
All Hallows Institute for
Mission and Ministry,
Drumcondra, Dublin 9
Tel 01-837373745/6

McDevitt, Vincent (CSSp), CC
Caltra, Ballinasloe
Co Galway
Tel 090-9678125
(*Ahascragh (Ahascragh and Caltra)*, Elphin)

McDonagh, Brendan (SPS)
On temporary diocesan work

McDonagh, Donald (SPS)
House Leader,
St Patricks, Main Street,
Knock, Co Mayo
Tel 094-9388661

McDonagh, Enda
St Patrick's College,
Maynooth, Co Kildare
Tel 01-6285222
(Tuam, retired)

McDonagh, James, CC
Ballymote, Co Sligo
Tel 071-9189778
(*Ballymote (Emlefad and Kilmorgan)*, Achonry)

McDonagh, John, Very Rev, PP
Stella Maris,
15 Oswald Road,
Sandymount, Dublin 4
Tel 01-2857773
(*Sandymount*, Dublin)

McDonagh, Martin, (CSSp)
Holy Spirit Missionary College,
Kimmage Manor, Dublin 12
Tel 01-406 4300

McDonagh, Sean (SSC)
(Research JPIC)
St Columban's, Dalgan Park,
Navan, Co Meath
Tel 046-9021525

McDonald, Anthony (OCarm)
Prior, Carmelite Priory,
White Abbey, Co Kildare
Tel 045-521391

McDonald, Daniel, Very Rev, PP
Marshallstown, Enniscorthy,
Co Wexford
Tel 053-9388521
(*Marshallstown*, Ferns)

McDonald, John, CC
3 Stanhope Place, Athy,
Co Kildare
Tel 059-8631698
(*Athy*, Dublin)

McDonald, John, Rt Rev Mgr, PP
Curragh Camp, Co Kildare
Tel 045-441369
(Kildare & L.)

McDonald, Joseph, CC
59 Auburn Road,
Dun Laoghaire, Co Dublin
Tel 01-2852509
(*Johnstown-Killiney*, Dublin)

McDonald, Matthew (OFM)
Lawson House,
Knockrathkyle, Glenbrien,
Enniscorthy, Co Wexford

McDonald, Thomas (CSSp)
Blackrock College,
Blackrock, Co Dublin
Tel 01-2888681

McDonnell, Albert
Vice Rector,
Irish College,
Via dei SS Quattro 1,
00184 Roma, Italy
Tel 00-3906-772631
(Killaloe)

McDonnell, Charles, Very Rev, VF, Adm
Westport, Co Mayo
(*Westport*, Tuam)

McDonnell, Colum (OSM)
Servite Priory, Benburb,
Dungannon,
Co Tyrone BT71 7JZ
Tel 028-37548241

McDonnell, Eunan (SDB)
Salesian College,
Maynooth Road, Celbridge,
Co Kildare
Tel 01-6275058/60

McDonnell, Francis, Very Rev, PP
Parochial House,
83 Terenure Road East,
Dublin 6
Tel 0404-67196
(*Terenure*, Dublin)

McDonnell, Fred, CC
The Presbytery, Meelick,
Co Clare
Tel 061-325556/087-7706023
(*Parteen/Meelick*, Limerick)

McDonnell, James (CSSp)
Blackrock College,
Blackrock, Co Dublin
Tel 01-2888681

McDonnell, Joseph (SSC)
St Columban's, Dalgan Park,
Navan, Co Meath
Tel 046-9021525

McDonnell, Leo, CC
Cathedral House,
Cathedral Place, Limerick
Tel 061-414624/087-2589279
(*St John's*, Limerick)

McDonnell, Paschal (OFM)
Guardian,
Franciscan Friary,
Rossnowlagh, Co Donegal
Tel 072-9851342

McDonnell, Patrick, Very Rev Canon, PE, AP
Our Lady of Lourdes Presbytery,
Hardman's Gardens,
Drogheda, Co Louth
Tel 041-9831899
(*Drogheda*, Armagh)

McDonnell, Paudge, Very Rev, PP
Annyalla, Castleblayney,
Co Monaghan
Tel 042-9740121
(*Clontibret*, Clogher)

McDonnell, Thomas (SPS)
St Patrick's, Kiltegan,
Co Wicklow
Tel 059-6473600

McDonnell, Thomas, Very Rev, PP
Parochial House, Naas,
Co Kildare
Tel 045-897703
(*Naas*, Kildare & L.)

McDunphy, Aodhán (OCSO)
Mount Melleray Abbey,
Cappoquin, Co Waterford
Tel 058-54404

McEgan, Michael (SMA)
African Missions,
Blackrock Road, Cork
Tel 021-4292871

McElhatton, Francis (SPS)
St Patrick's, Kiltegan,
Co Wicklow
Tel 059-6473600

McElhennon, Kevin, Adm
5 Strathroy Road, Omagh,
Co Tyrone BT79 7DW
Tel 028-82251055
Director of Adult Education,
The Gate Lodge,
2 Francis Street,
Derry BT48 9DS
Tel 028-71264087
(Derry)

McElhill, Laurence, Very Rev, PP
Parochial House,
5 Aghalee Road,
Aghagallon, Craigavon,
Co Armagh BT67 0AR
Tel 028-92651214
(*Aghagallon and Ballinderry*, Down & C.)

McElhinney, Brian, Very Rev, PP
Lavey, Stradone, Co Cavan
Tel 049-4330125
(*Lavey*, Kilmore)

McElroy, James (SM)
Cerdon, Marist Fathers,
St Mary's Road, Dundalk,
Co Louth
Tel 042-9334019

McElvaney, Terence
Church Square,
Co Monaghan
Tel 047-82255
(Clogher)

McElwee, Christopher (IC), Very Rev, PP
St Brigid's, Kilcurry,
Dundalk, Co Louth
Tel 042-9334410
(*Faughart*, Armagh)

McEneaney, Owen J., Very Rev, Adm
St Joseph's Presbytery,
Park Street, Monaghan
Tel 047-81220
(Clogher)

McEnroe, Patrick, Very Rev, PP, VF
Darver, Readypenny,
Dundalk, Co Louth
Tel 042-9379147
(*Darver and Dromiskin*, Armagh)

McEntire, Peter J. (CSSp)
Holy Spirit Missionary College,
Kimmage Manor, Dublin 12
Tel 01-4064300

McErlean, Martin, Very Rev, PP
Parochial House,
Castletown-Kilpatrick,
Navan, Co Meath
Tel 046-9055789
(*Castletown-Kilpatrick*, Meath)

McEveney, Feargus (OFM)
Franciscan Friary, Ennis,
Co Clare
Tel 065-6828751

McEvoy, A. (SDB)
Bursar, Salesian College,
Maynooth Road, Celbridge,
Co Kildare
Tel 01-6275058/60

McEvoy, Francis, Very Rev, PP, VF
Parochial House,
Crookstown, Athy,
Co Kildare
Tel 059-8624109
(*Moone*, Dublin)

McEvoy, John, (SSC), CC
Mucklagh, Tullamore,
Co Offaly
Tel 057-9321892
(*Rahan*, Meath)

McEvoy, John, Very Rev, PP
Goresbridge, Co Kilkenny
Tel 059-9775180
(*Paulstown*, Kildare & L.)

McEvoy, Joseph, Very Rev, PP
Parochial House, Moynalty,
Kells, Co Meath
Tel 046-9244305
(Meath)

McEvoy, P. J., Very Rev, PP
Francis Street, Edenderry,
Co Offaly
Tel 046-9737010
(*Rhode*, Kildare & L.)

McEvoy, Seamus, Very Rev Dean, PP
Erill, Portlaoise, Co Laois
Tel 0505-44973
(Ossory)

McEvoy, Seán, Very Rev, PP
Parochial House,
19 Caledon Road,
Aughnacloy,
Co Tyrone BT69 6HX
Tel 028-85557212
(*Aughnacloy (Aghaloo)*, Armagh)

McFaul, Daniel, CC
Parochial House,
St Eugene's Cathedral,
Derry BT48 9AP
Tel 028-71262894/71365712
(*Derry City*, Derry)

McFlynn, Gerard
18 Maresfield Gardens,
London NW3 5SX
(Down & C.)

McGahan, Noel, CC
4 Darling Street, Enniskillen,
Co Fermanagh BT74 7DP
Tel 028-66322075
(*Enniskillen*, Clogher)

McGale, Harry (OCD)
St Teresa's,
Clarendon Street, Dublin 2
Tel 01-6718466/6718127

McGarry, Leo J. (CSSp)
Holy Spirit Missionary College,
Kimmage Manor, Dublin 12
Tel 01-406 4300

McGarvey, Patrick, Very Rev, PP
Fanavolty, Kindrum,
Letterkenny, Co Donegal
Tel 074-9159007
(*Tamney (Clondavaddog)*, Raphoe)

McGaughey, Sylvius (CP)
St Paul's Retreat,
Mount Argus, Dublin 6W
Tel 01-4992000

McGauran, Francis, Very Rev, PP
Cuilmore, Strokestown,
Co Roscommon
(Elphin, retired)

McGeady, Bill, CC
Cashel, Glencomille,
Co Donegal
Tel 074-9730025
(Carrick (Glencolmcille), Raphoe)

McGee, Brendan, Dean
St Patrick's Presbytery,
199 Donegall Street,
Belfast BT1 2FL
Tel 028-90324597
(*St Patrick's*, Down & C.)

McGee, Edward
St Malachy's College,
36 Antrim Road,
Belfast BT15 2AE
Tel 078-11144268
(Down & C.)

McGee, Edward, BA, BD
St Mary's University College,
191 Falls Road,
Belfast 12 6FE
Tel 028-90327678
(Down & C.)

McGee, Joseph (MSC)
Provincial Leader,
65 Terenure Road West,
Dublin 6W
Tel 01-4906622

McGeehan, Paul
(priest in residence)
Parochial House, Tamney,
Letterkenny, Co Donegal
Tel 074-9159015
(*Tamney (Clondavaddog)*, Raphoe)

McGeough, Thomas, Very Rev, PE, AP
Parochial House,
Hale Street, Ardee, Co Louth
Tel 041-6850920
(*Ardee & Collon*, Armagh)

McGettigan, Denis, Very Rev, PP
Raphoe, Lifford,
Co Donegal
Tel 074-9145647
Chaplain, Deele College,
Raphoe, Co Donegal
Tel 074-9145277
(*Raphoe*, Raphoe)

McGettrick, William (CSsR)
Clonard Monastery,
1 Clonard Gardens,
Belfast BT13 2RL
Tel 028-90445950

McGill, Maurice (MHM)
St Joseph's,
Mill Hill Missionaries,
Waterford Road, Kilkenny
Tel 056-7721482

McGillicuddy, Cornelius
Sacred Heart Residence,
Sybil Hill Road, Killester,
Dublin 5
(Dublin, retired)

McGilloway, Joseph (OSB)
Glenstal Abbey, Murroe,
Co Limerick
Tel 061-386103

McGing, Aidan (CM)
122 Sunday's Well Road,
Cork
Tel 021-4304070

McGinley, Séamus, Very Rev, PP
Parochial House,
Beragh, Omagh
Co Tyrone BT79 OSY
Tel 028-80758206
(*Beragh*, Armagh)
McGinn, Emlyn
Parochial House, Barn Road,
Dunleer, Co Louth
Tel 041-6863822
Chaplain,
Dundalk Institute of Technology, Dublin Road,
Dundalk, Co Louth
Tel 042-9370224
(Armagh)
McGinn, Patrick, CC
St Joseph's Presbytery,
Park Street, Monaghan
Tel 047-81220
(*Monaghan*, Clogher)
McGinnity, Gerard, Very Rev, PP
Parochial House,
Knockbridge, Dundalk,
Co Louth
Tel 042-9374125
(*Knockbridge*, Armagh)
McGinnity, Michael, PP
St Malachy's Presbytery,
24 Alfred Street,
Belfast BT2 8EN
Tel 028-90321713
(*St Malachy's*, Down & C.)
McGirr, Austin, Very Rev, PP, VF
Parochial House,
4 The Crescent, Portstewart,
Co Derry BT55 7AB
Tel 028-70832534
(*Portstewart*, Down & C.)
McGirr, Dermot, CC
St Joseph's, Fairview Road,
Galliagh, Derry BT48 8NJ
Tel 028-71352351
(*The Three Patrons*, Derry)
McGlynn, Colm (OSM), Very Rev, PP
Prior,
25/27 Hermitage Downs,
Marley Grange,
Rathfarnham, Dublin 16
Tel 01-4944295/8210874
(*Marley Grange*, Dublin)
McGlynn, Fergus, Co-PP
10 Bearna Park, Sandyford,
Dublin 18
Tel 01-2956414
(*Sandyford*, Dublin)
McGlynn, Patrick (CSSp)
Holy Spirit Missionary College,
Kimmage Manor, Dublin 12
Tel 01-406 4300
McGlynn, Thomas, Adm
The Cathedral Presbytery,
St Peter's Square,
Belfast BT12 4BU
Tel 028-90327573
(*The Cathedral, St Peter's*, Down & C.)
McGoldrick, Brian, PP
Doneyloop, Castlefin,
Lifford, Co Donegal
Tel 074-9146183
(*Doneyloop*, Derry)
McGoldrick, John
(priest in residence)
Parochial House,
56 Minterburn Road,
Laireakean, Caledon,
Co Tyrone BT68 4XH
Tel 028-37568288
(*Aughnacloy (Aghaloo)*, Armagh)
McGoldrick, Neil, PP
Parochial House, Fahan,
Lifford, Co Donegal
Tel 074-9360151
McGoldrick, Michael (OCD)
Avila, Bloomfield Avenue,
Morehampton Road,
Dublin 4
Tel 01-6430200
McGoldrick, Patrick, CC
Parochial House, Moville,
Co Donegal
Tel 074-9382102
(*Moville*, Derry)
McGonagle, Hugh, CC
7 Elm Park, Ballinode, Sligo
Tel 071-9143430
(Elphin)
McGonagle, James, Very Rev, PP, VF
Parochial House, Culdaff,
Co Donegal
Tel 074-9379107
(*Culdaff*, Derry)
McGoohan, Ultan, CC
The Presbytery, Cavan
Tel 049-4331404/4332269
(*Cootehill*, Kilmore)
McGorty, Roger (MHM)
St Joseph's,
Mill Hill Missionaries,
Waterford Road, Kilkenny
Tel 056-7721482
McGourty, Michael, Very Rev, PP
Irvinestown, Enniskillen,
Co Fermanagh BT94 1EY
Tel 028-68628600
(*Irvinestown*, Clogher)
McGovern, Ciarán, Very Rev, PP
Newtownforbes,
Co Longford
Tel 043-3346805
(*Newtownforbes*, Ardagh & Cl.)
McGovern, Felim
The Presbytery, Cavan
Tel 049-4331404
(Kilmore, retired)
McGovern, John, Very Rev
St Joseph's Presbytery,
52 Kincora Park, Lifford,
Ennis, Co Clare
Tel 065-6822166/
086-3221210
(*Ennis*, Killaloe)
McGovern, Patrick (SMA)
African Missions,
Blackrock Road, Cork
Tel 021-4292871
McGovern, Thomas
30 Knapton Road,
Dun Laoghaire, Co Dublin
Tel 01-2804353
(Opus Dei)
McGowan, Michael, PC
7 St Patrick's Crescent,
Rathcoole, Co Dublin
Tel 01-4589210
(*Saggart*, Dublin)
McGowan, Padraig, Very Rev
Parochial House,
Ballymahon, Co Longford
(Ardagh & Cl.)
McGowan, Thomas, Co-PP
Parochial House,
Garristown,
Co Dublin
Tel 01-8412932
(*Garristown*, Dublin)
McGrady, Colm, Very Rev, PP
Parochial House,
8 Shore Road, Strangford,
Co Down BT30 7NL
Tel 028-44881206
(*Kilclief and Strangford*, Down & C.)
McGrady, Fergal, Very Rev, PP
St Anne's Parochial House,
Kingsway, Finaghy,
Belfast BT10 0NE
Tel 028-90610112
McGrane, Camillus (OSM), CC
25/27 Hermitage Downs,
Marley Grange,
Rathfarnham, Dublin 16
Tel 01-4944295
(*Marley Grange*, Dublin)
McGrath, Aidan (OFM)
Curia Generalizia dei Frati Minoti,
Via S. Maria Mediatrice 25,
00165 Roma, Italy
McGrath, Brendan (OFM)
Vicar,
Franciscan Friary,
Liberty Street, Cork
Tel 021-4270302
McGrath, Brian (CSsR)
St Joseph's, Dundalk,
Co Louth
Tel 042-9334042/9334762
McGrath, Francis
Williamstown, Co Galway
Tel 094-964300
(*Williamstown (Templetoher)*, Tuam)
McGrath, Francis (OFM), Very Rev, PP
The Abbey, St Francis Street,
Galway
Tel 091-562518
McGrath, John, Very Rev, PP
Mullinahone, Thurles,
Co Tipperary
Tel 052-53152
(*Mullinahone*, Cashel & E.)
McGrath, Joseph, Rt Rev Mgr, VG
Chaplain, Parochial House,
Boherquill, Lismacaffney,
Mullingar, Co Westmeath
(*Streete*, Ardagh & Cl.)
McGrath, Joseph, Rt Rev, PP, VF, VG
New Ross, Co Wexford
Tel 051-447080
(*New Ross*, Ferns)
McGrath, Matthew, Venerable, PP, VG
St Michael's Street,
Tipperary Town
Tel 062-51536
(*Tipperary*, Cashel & E.)
McGrath, Michael, CC
St Mary's,
Carrick-on-Shannon,
Co Leitrim
Tel 071-9620347
(*Carrick-on-Shannon*, Ardagh & Cl.)
McGrath, Sean (SSC)
St Columban's, Dalgan Park,
Navan, Co Meath
Tel 046-9021525
McGrath, Thomas, Very Rev
Cois Tra, Chapel Road,
Duncannon, Co Wexford
(Ferns, retired)
McGree, Thomas, CC
Durrow, Portlaoise,
Co Laois
Tel 057-8736155/
087-7619235
(*Durrow*, Ossory)
McGreevy, Gerard, Very Rev Canon, PE
Magherarney, Smithboro,
Co Monaghan
Tel 047-57011
(Clogher, retired)
McGregor, Augustine (OCSO), Rt Rev
Abbot,
Mount Melleray Abbey,
Cappoquin, Co Waterford
Tel 058-54404

McGregor, Bede (OP), Very Rev
Prior,
St Malachy's, Dundalk,
Co Louth
Tel 042-9334179/9333714

McGroarty, Liam
Chaplain,
Coláiste Mhuire, Marino,
Griffith Avenue, Dublin 9
(Dublin)

McGroarty, Wiliam, CC
Parochial House,
Letterkenny, Co Donegal
Tel 074-9121021

McGrory, James
Armagh Regional Marriage Tribunal,
15 College Street,
Armagh BT61 9BT
Tel 028-37524537
(Derry)

McGuane, Joseph, Very Rev
St Mary's, Church Street,
Youghal, Co Cork
Tel 024-93392
(Cloyne)

McGuckian, Alan, (SJ)
Superior,
Peter Faber House,
28 Brookvale Avenue,
Belfast BT14 6BW
Tel 028-90757615

McGuckian, Bernard (SJ)
Superior,
St Francis Xavier's,
Upper Gardiner Street,
Dublin 1
Tel 01-8363411

McGuckian, Michael, (SJ)
Crescent College Comprehensive,
Dooradoyle Road, Limerick,
Tel 061-30111

McGuckien, Kevin
St Patrick's Presbytery,
199 Donegall Street,
Belfast BT1 2FL
Tel 028-90324597
(Down & C.)

McGuckin, Felix, Very Rev
5 Oriel Road,
Antrim BT41 4HP
Tel 028-94428086
(*Antrim, St Comgall's*, Down & C.)

McGuckin, Patrick, Very Rev, PE
79 Reclain Road, Galbally,
Dungannon,
Co Tyrone BT70 2PG
Tel 028-87759692
(Armagh)

McGuinness, Austin (SSC)
Chaplain,
St Joseph's, Trim,
St Columban's, Dalgan Park,
Navan, Co Meath
Tel 046-9021525
(on special work)

McGuinness, Brendan, Very Rev, PP
Bekan, Claremorris, Co Mayo
Tel 094-9380203
(*Bekan*, Tuam)

McGuinness, David
St Joseph's Catholic Church,
134 Prince Avenue, Athens,
Georgia 30601, USA
(Waterford & L.)

McGuinness, Joseph, Rt Rev Mgr, Adm
Parochial House, Tyholland,
Monaghan
Tel 047-85385
(Clogher)

McGuinness, Peter, Very Rev Canon, PE
3 Castleross Retirement Village,
Carrickmacross,
Co Monaghan
Tel 042-9690013
(Clogher, retired)

McGuinness, T. J.
South Africa
(Dromore, retired)

McGuire, Robert, CC
Poulpeasty, Clonroche,
Enniscorthy, Co Wexford
Tel 053-9244116
(*Cloughbawn*, Ferns)

McHale, Benny, CC
Athenry, Co Galway
Tel 091-844227
(*Athenry*, Tuam)

McHenry, Francis (OSB)
Glenstal Abbey, Murroe,
Co Limerick
Tel 061-386103

McHugh, Adrian
St Agnes Cathedral,
29 Queally Place,
Rockville Centre, NY11570,
USA
Tel 001-516-7660205
(Achonry)

McHugh, Anthony, Very Rev, PP
Parochial House,
33 Crossgar Road, Saintfield,
Ballynahinch,
Co Down BT24 7JE
Tel 028-97510237
(*Saintfield and Carrickmannon*, Down & C.)

McHugh, Brendan, Very Rev, PE
Parochial House, Mullanhoe,
Ardboe, Dungannon,
Co Tyrone BT71 5AU
Tel 028-86737338
(Armagh, retired)

McHugh, Christopher, Very Rev, PP
Chaplain,
Grange Vocational School,
Sligo
Tel 071-9163100
(Elphin)

McHugh, Dominic, Very Rev Canon
79 Castle Street,
Ballymoney,
Co Antrim BT53 6JT
Tel 028-27662259
(*Ballymoney and Derrykeighan*, Down & C.)

McHugh, Laurence (CSSp)
Holy Spirit Missionary College,
Kimmage Manor, Dublin 12
Tel 01-4064300

McHugh, Patrick
3 Seafield Court,
60-64 Castle Avenue,
Clontarf, Dublin
(Kilmore, retired)

McHugh, Patrick, Very Rev
22 Rosehill, Sligo
(Elphin, retired)

McHugh, Patrick, Very Rev, PP
Castleblayney,
Co Monaghan
Tel 042-9740051
(Clogher)

McHugh, Patrick, Very Rev, PP
Parochial House, Termon,
Co Donegal
Tel 074-9139016
(*Termon*, Raphoe)

McHugh, Sean
Bohernasup, Ballina,
Co Mayo
(Killala, retired)

McHugh, Seán, PP
Spiddal, Co Galway
Tel 091-533155
(Galway)

McIldowney, Hugh
7 Riverdale Close,
Belfast BT11 9DH
Tel 028-90603042
(Down & C., retired)

McIlraith, Cormac
The Presbytery,
52 Booterstown Avenue,
Dublin
Tel 01-2882162
(Dublin)

McInerney, Declan
Our Lady of Lourdes,
Creagh, Ballinasloe,
Co Galway
Tel 090-9645080
(Clonfert)

McInerney, Michael, Very Rev, AP
Quin, Co Clare
Tel 065-6825649
(*Quin*, Killaloe)

McInerney, Thomas (OP)
St Mary's Priory, Tallaght,
Dublin 24
Tel 01-4048100

McIntyre, Raymond (SDB)
Vice-Rector & Bursar,
Salesian College,
Pallaskenry, Co Limerick
Tel 061-393313

McKay, Brian (OCarm)
Whitefriar Street Church,
56 Aungier Street, Dublin 2
Tel 01-4758821

McKay, Dermot, Very Rev, PP
Parochial House,
51 Victoria Road, Larne,
Co Antrim BT40 1LY
Tel 028-28273230/28273053
(*Larne*, Down & C.)

McKeever, Brendan (CP)
Chaplain,
Our Lady's Hospice,
Harold's Cross, Dublin 6W
Tel 01-4972101/ 4992000

McKeever, Des (SPS)
St Patrick's, Kiltegan,
Co Wicklow
Tel 059-6473600

McKeever, John, CC
Parochial House,
42 Abbey Street,
Armagh BT61 7DZ
Tel 028-37522802
(*Cooley*, Armagh)

McKeever, Joseph, Very Rev, PP
9 Newry Road, Crossmaglen,
Newry, Co Down BT35 9HH
Tel 028-30861208
(Armagh)

McKeever, Martin (CSsR)
President,
Alphonsian Academy,
Via Merulana 31, CP 2458,
00100 Rome, Italy
Tel 0039-06494901

McKeever, Michael, CC
Church Hill, Letterkenny,
Co Donegal
Tel 074-9137057
Ard Adhamhnáin,
Letterkenny, Co Donegal
Tel 074-9121208
(*Termon*, Raphoe)

McKenna, Dermot (SJ)
St Francis Xavier's,
Upper Gardiner Street,
Dublin 1
Tel 01-8363411

McKenna, Hugh (OFM)
Provincial, Franciscan Friary,
4 Merchant's Quay,
Dublin 8
Tel 01-6742500

McKenna, John F., CC
19 Ballagh Road, Clogher,
Co Tyrone BT76 0TQ
Tel 028-85548525
(*Clogher*, Clogher)

McKenna, John, Very Rev Canon
Baile na Buaile,
Daingean Ui Chuis,
Co Chiarrai
(Kerry, retired)

McKenna, John, Very Rev Canon, PP
Trillick, Omagh,
Co Tyrone BT78 3RD
Tel 028-89561350
(*Trillick*, Clogher)

McKenna, Joseph (Birmingham)
1 St Joseph's Villas,
Church Road, Bundoran,
Co Donegal
Tel 071-9841756
(Clogher, retired)

McKenna, Joseph (SM)
Cerdon, Marist Fathers,
St Mary's Road, Dundalk,
Co Louth
Tel 042-9334019

McKenna, Kevin, PEm
24 Glenroe Park, Dungiven,
Co Derry BT47 4PE
Tel 028-77743857
(Derry, retired)

McKenna, Liam (SJ)
St Francis Xavier's,
Upper Gardiner Street,
Dublin 1
Tel 01-8363411

McKenna, Owen (SMA)
SMA House,
82 Ranelagh Road,
Ranelagh, Dublin 6
Tel 01-4968162/3

McKenna, P. (MI)
St Camillus, Killucan,
Co Westmeath
Tel 044-74115

McKenna, Padraig, CC
St Joseph's, Carrickmacross,
Co Monaghan
Tel 042-9661231
(Carrickmacross, Clogher)

McKenna, Patrick, CC
Teconnaught,
2 Drumnaconagher Road,
Crossgar BT30 9AN
Tel 028-44830342
(*Crossgar (Kilmore),* Down & C.)

McKenna, Patrick, Very Rev, PP, VF
503 Ormeau Road,
Belfast BT7 3GR
Tel 028-90642446
(*Holy Rosary*, Down & C.)

McKenna, Robert, Very Rev, PE, AP
Parochial House,
26 Newtown Road,
Camlough, Newry,
Co Down BT35 7JJ
Tel 028-30830237
(*Bessbrook (Killeavy Lower),* Armagh)

McKenna, Seamus (IC)
St Patrick's, Upton,
Innishannon, Co Cork
Tel 021-4776268/4776923

McKenna, Seamus, BA, HDE
Cork Regional Marriage Tribunal,
The Lough, Cork
Tel 021-4963653
(Kerry)

McKeogh, Stephen (OCD)
St Joseph's Carmelite
Retreat Centre,
Termonbacca,
Derry BT48 9XE
Tel 028-71262512

McKeon, Austin, Rt Rev Mgr, PP
Tulsk, Castlerea,
Co Roscommon
Tel 071-9639005
(*Tulsk (Ogulla and Baslic),* Elphin)

McKeon, Seamus, Very Rev, PP
Aughnacliffe, Co Longford
Tel 043-6684118
(*Colmcille*, Ardagh & Cl.)

McKeown, Donal, Most Rev, DD
Titular Bishop of Killossy
and Auxiliary Bishop of
Down and Connor,
96 Downview Park West,
Belfast BT15 5HZ
Tel 028-90781642
(Down & C.)

McKeown, Noel (OP)
St Catherine's, Newry,
Co Down BT35 8BN
Tel 028-30262178

McKeown, Phelim, CC
Parochial House,
9 Chapel Road, Bessbrook,
Newry, Co Down BT35 7AU
Tel 028-30830272
(*Bessbrook (Killeavy Lower),* Armagh)

McKevitt, Brian (OP)
St Mary's Priory, Tallaght,
Dublin 24
Tel 01-4048100

McKiernan, Fintan, Very Rev, PP
56 Mary Street, Derrylin,
Co Fermanagh, BT92 9LA
Tel 028-67748315
(*Derrylin*, Kilmore)

McKiernan, Peter, Very Rev, PP
Knockbride, Bailieboro,
Co Cavan
Tel 042-9660112
(*Knockbride*, Kilmore)

McKiernan, Tom, Very Rev, PP
Visiting Chaplain,
St Mogue's College,
Bawnboy, Co Cavan
Tel 049-9523112
(Kilmore)

McKinlay, Denis, Very Rev, Adm
Parochial House,
91 Main Street,
Castlewellan,
Co Down BT31 9DH
Tel 028-43778259
(*Castlewellan (Kilmegan),* Down & C.)

McKinley, Patrick (Moderator)
68 Maplewood Road,
Springfield, Tallaght,
Dublin 24
Tel 01-8421551
(*Springfield*, Dublin)

McKinney, Anthony (OCarm)
Gort Muire, Ballinteer,
Dublin 16
Tel 01-2984014

McKinney, Liam, CC
Parochial House,
9a Newry Road,
Crossmaglen, Newry,
Co Down BT35 9HH
Tel 028-30868698
(*Crossmaglen (Creggan Upper),* Armagh)

McKinstry, Gordon
12 The Meadows,
Randalstown,
Co Antrim BT41 2JB
(Down & C., retired)

McKittrick, Brian, CC
The Presbytery, Celbridge,
Co Kildare
Tel 01-6288827
(*Celbridge*, Dublin)

McKnight, Bruno (OFMCap)
Capuchin Friary,
Church Street, Dublin 7
Tel 01-8730599

McLaughlin, Brian (CSSp)
Holy Spirit Missionary
College,
Kimmage Manor, Dublin 12
Tel 01-4064300

McLaughlin, Con, PP
Barrack Hill, Carndonagh,
Lifford, Co Donegal
Tel 074-9374104
Director,
Inishowen Pastoral Centre,
Carndonagh, Co Donegal
Tel 074-9374103
(Derry)

McLaughlin, Eamonn, CC
Parochial House,
Leitirmacaward, Co Donegal
Tel 074-9544102
(*Dungloe*, Raphoe)

McLaughlin, George
Chez Nous, Drumawier,
Greencastle, Co Donegal
(Derry, retired)

McLaughlin, Kevin (OMI)
Oblate Scholasticate,
St Anne's,
Goldenbridge Walk,
Inchicore, Dublin 8
Tel 01-4540841/4542955
52a/52b Bulfin Road,
Dublin 8
Tel 01-4531660
(*Inchicore, St Michael's*, Dublin)

McLaughlin, Michael, Very Rev, PP
Airfield, Inch, Ennis,
Co Clare
Tel 065-6839332
(*Inch and Kilmaley*, Killaloe)

McLaughlin, Pat (CSsR), CC
St Gerard's,
722 Antrim Road,
Newtownabbey,
Co Antrim BT36 7PG
Tel 028-90774833
(*St Gerard's*, Down & C.)

McLaughlin, Peter, PP
143 Melmount Road,
Sion Mills, Strabane,
Co Tyrone BT82 9EX
Tel 028-81658264
(*Sion Mills*, Derry)

McLaughlin, Pius (OFM)
Franciscan Friary,
Rossnowlagh,
Co Donegal
Tel 072-9851342

McLaverty, Anthony, Very Rev, CC
470 Falls Road,
Belfast BT12 6EN
Tel 028-90321102
(*St John's*, Down & C.)

McLaverty, George, Very Rev
518 Donegall Road,
Belfast BT12 6DY
(Down & C., retired)

McLoone, Francis, Very Rev, PP
Killymard, Co Donegal
Tel 074-9721929
(*Killymard*, Raphoe)

McLoone, John, Very Rev, PP
Frosses, Co Donegal
Tel 074-9736006
(*Inver*, Raphoe)

McLoughlan, H. (SMA)
African Missions,
Blackrock Road, Cork
Tel 021-4292871

McLoughlin, Christopher, Very Rev Canon
(priest in residence,
Tourlestrane Parish)
Kilmactigue, Aclare,
Co Sligo
Tel 071-9181007
(Achonry, retired)

McLoughlin, Denis (CP)
St Paul's Retreat,
Mount Argus, Dublin 6W
Tel 01-4992000

McLoughlin, Eugene (SMA), CC
St Joseph's,
Blackrock Road, Cork
Tel 021-4292871
(*St Joseph's (Blackrock Road),* Cork & R.)

McLoughlin, Eugene, Very Rev Canon, PP, VF
Parochial House,
Roscommon
Tel 090-6626298
(*Roscommon*, Elphin)

McLoughlin, Joseph (CSsR)
Mount Saint Alphonsus,
Limerick
Tel 061-315099

McLoughlin, Joseph (SAC), CC
The Presbytery, Corduff,
Blanchardstown, Dublin 15
(*Corduff*, Dublin)

McLoughlin, Michael, Very Rev, PP
Moycullen, Co Galway
Tel 091-555106
(*Moycullen*, Galway)

McLoughlin, Patrick (CSsR), CC
722 Antrim Road,
Newtownabbey,
Co Antrim BT36 7PG
Tel 028-90774833/4
(*St Gerard's*, Down & C.)

McLoughlin, Terence (OP)
St Mary's, The Claddagh,
Co Galway
Tel 091-582884

McMahon, Andrew, CC
St Paul's Presbytery,
Old Portadown Road,
Lurgan,
Co Armagh BT66 8RG
Tel 028-38326883
(*Shankill, St Paul's (Lurgan),* Dromore)

McMahon, Anthony, CC
Parochial House, Nenagh,
Co Tipperary
Tel 067-37134/086-8243801
(*Nenagh*, Killaloe)

McMahon, James (OSB)
Glenstal Abbey, Murroe,
Co Limerick
Tel 061-386103

McMahon, John, CC
Bridge Street,
Manorhamilton, Co Leitrim
Tel 071-9856987
(Kilmore)

McMahon, Joseph (OFM)
Adam & Eve's,
4 Merchant's Quay,
Dublin 8
Tel 01-6771128

McMahon, Joseph, BA, BD, HDE
President,
St Flannan's College,
Co Clare
Tel 065-6828019
(Killaloe)

McMahon, Padraig, Very Rev, Adm
Cathedral House, Mullingar,
Co Westmeath
Tel 044-9348338/9340126
(*Mullingar*, Meath)

McMahon, Richard (CSsR)
St Patrick's, Esker, Athenry,
Co Galway
Tel 091-844549

McMahon, Richard (CSsR), CC
Kiltulla, Athenry, Co Galway
Tel 091-848208
(*Kiltulla and Attymon,* Clonfert)

McMahon, Seamus (SM)
Australia

MacManuis, Clement (CSsR)
St Joseph's, Dundalk,
Co Louth
Tel 042-9334042/9334762

McManus, Frank, CC
Chaplain,
The Rock Welfare Home,
Ballyshannon,
Co Donegal
Tel 071-9851221
(Clogher)

McManus, John, (SPS), CC
10 Ashford, Monksland,
Athlone, Co Westmeath
Tel 090-6493262
(*Athlone, SS Peter and Paul's,* Elphin)

McManus, John, Very Rev
Lisbreen, 73 Somerton Road,
Belfast BT15 4DE
Tel 028-90776185
(Down & C., on leave)

McManus, Kevin (OSA), PP
St John's Priory,
Thomas Street,
Dublin 8
Tel 01-6770393

McManus, Michael, CC
Drum, Athlone,
Co Roscommon
Tel 090-6437125
(*Athlone, SS Peter and Paul's*, Elphin)

McManus, Patrick (Moderator)
34 Dollymount Grove,
Clontarf, Dublin 3
Tel 01-2889879
(*Dollymount*, Dublin)

McManus, Patrick (SSC)
St Columban's, Dalgan Park,
Navan, Co Meath
Tel 046-9021525

McManus, Thomas, Very Rev, PP
Corlough, Belturbet,
Co Cavan
Tel 049-9523122
(*Corlough and Drumreilly*, Kilmore)

McMenamin, Joseph (White Fathers)
Promotion Director,
Cypress Grove, Templeogue,
Dublin 6W
Tel 01-4055526

McMenamin, William, Very Rev Canon, PE
'St Columba's'
Meeting House Street,
Raphoe, Co Donegal
Tel 074-9144834
(Raphoe, retired)

McMorrow, Maurice, CC
Glenade, Kinlough,
Co Leitrim
Tel 071-9841461
(*Kinlough and Glenade*, Kilmore)

McMullan, Alex, Very Rev Canon
4 Irish Street, Killyleagh,
Co Down BT30 9QS
Tel 028-44828211
(*Killyleagh*, Down & C.)

McMullan, Anthony (OP)
St Malachy's, Dundalk,
Co Louth
Tel 042-9334179/9333714

McMullan, Brendan, Very Rev
26 Willowbank Park,
Belfast BT6 0LL
Tel 028-90794440
(Down & C., retired)

McMullan, Kevin, Very Rev, PP
418 Old Park Road,
Belfast BT14 6QF
Tel 028-90748148
(Down and C., retired)

McNaboe, Desmond (OFMCap), Very Rev,
Provincial Office,
12 Halston Street, Dublin 7
Tel 01-8733205
(*Halston Street and Arran Quay*, Dublin)

McNally, Albert, Very Rev, PP, VF
6 Hillside Avenue,
Dunloy BT44 9DQ
(Down and C., retired)

McNally, Andrew, Very Rev
c/o 8 Moneymore Road,
Magherafelt,
Co Derry BT45 6AD
(Armagh)

McNally, Brendan, Very Rev, PE
Parochial House,
Reaghstown, Ardee,
Co Louth
Tel 041-6855117
(Armagh, retired)

McNally, James, Very Rev, PE
14 Derrygarve Road,
Castledawson,
Co Derry BT45 8HA
Tel 028-79649998
(Armagh, retired)

McNamara, Austin, Very Rev, Adm
Cathedral House,
Cathedral Place, Limerick
Tel 061-414624/087-2589279
(*St John's*, Limerick)

McNamara, Brian, Very Rev Canon, Adm
Derrylester, Enniskillen,
Co Fermanagh
Tel 028-66348224
(*Killesher*, Kilmore)

McNamara, Cormac (SM)
Mexico

McNamara, David (CSsR)
Mount Saint Alphonsus,
Limerick
Tel 061-315099

McNamara, Donal, Very Rev Canon, PP, VF
St Munchin's, Clancy Strand,
Limerick
Tel 061-455635
(*St Munchin's and St Lelia's*, Limerick)

McNamara, Frank, Very Rev, PE
Portiuncula Nursing Home,
Multyfarnham,
Co Westmeath
(Meath, retired)

McNamara, Gerard, Very Rev, PP
Ballyduff Upper,
Co Waterford
Tel 058-60227
(*Ballyduff*, Waterford & L.)

McNamara, Gerard, Very Rev, PP
Bulgaden, Kilmallock,
Co Limerick
Tel 063-88005/087-2408998
(*Bulgaden/Martinstown*, Limerick)

McNamara, John (OCD)
St Joseph's Carmelite
Retreat Centre,
Termonbacca,
Derry BT48 9XE
Tel 028-71262512

McNamara, John, Very Rev, Adm
Parochial House,
Our Lady's Nativity Parish,
Old Hill, Leixlip, Co Kildare
Tel 01-8401661
(*Leixlip*, Dublin)

McNamara, Kevin (MSC)
Woodview House,
Mount Merrion Avenue,
Blackrock, Co Dublin
Tel 01-2881644

McNamara, Kevin (MSC), CC (pro-tem)
Killarney, Co Kerry
Tel 064-6631014
(*Killarney*, Kerry)

McNamara, Leslie
Columban Missionary Society,
Dalgan Park, Dublin Road, Navan, Co Meath
(Limerick)

McNamara, Liam, Very Rev Canon, PP
Ballybricken, Grange, Kilmallock, Co Limerick
Tel 061-351158
(*Ballybricken*, Cashel & E.)

McNamara, Martin (MSC)
Woodview House, Mount Merrion Avenue, Blackrock, Co Dublin
Tel 01-2881644

McNamara, Martin, Very Rev, PP
Kiltulla, Athenry, Co Galway
Tel 091-848021
(*Kiltulla and Attymon*, Clonfert)

McNamara, Oliver, CC
Annaghdown, Co Galway
Tel 091-791142
(*Corrandulla (Annaghdown)*, Tuam)

McNamara, Patrick (CSSp)
Spiritan House, 213 North Circular Road, Dublin 7
Tel 01-8389664/8683504

McNamara, Robert (CSsR)
Marianella/Liguori House, 75 Orwell Road, Dublin 6
Tel 01-4067100

McNamara, Thomas (SMA)
Religious Formation Programme, Loretto House, Dublin

McNamara, Walter (CSSp)
Holy Spirit Missionary College, Kimmage Manor, Dublin 12
Tel 01-4064300

McNamee, Ambrose (OCD)
The Abbey, Loughrea, Co Galway
Tel 091-841209

McNamee, Paul
c/o Bishop's House, Dublin Road, Carlow
(Kildare & L.)

McNeice, Damian, PC
149 Swords Road, Whitehall, Dublin 9
Tel 01-8372521
(*Larkhill-Whitehall-Santry*, Dublin)

McNeill, Peter C., Adm
58 Ballydrumman Road, Ballyward, Castlewellan, Co Down
Tel 028-40650207
(*Drumgooland and Dromara*, Dromore)

McNelis, Denis, Very Rev, PP
Parochial House, Laytown, Co Meath
Tel 041-9827258
(Meath)

McNerney, John
Chaplains' Residence, St Stephen's, UCD, Belfield, Dublin 4
Tel 01-2600715
(Dublin)

McNicholas, Gerald (SSC)
St Columban's Retirement Home, Dalgan Park, Navan, Co Meath
Tel 046-9021525

McNulty, James J. (CSSp)
St Mary's College, Rathmines, Dublin 6
Tel 01-4995760

McNulty, Thomas, CC
Parochial House, Grange, Carlingford, Co Louth
Tel 042-9376577
(*Armagh*, Armagh)

McPartlan, Peter, Very Rev, PP
Ballintemple, Ballinagh, Co Cavan
Tel 049-4337106
(*Ballintemple*, Kilmore)

McPartland, James, CC
St Patrick's Road, Wicklow Town, Co Wicklow
Tel 01-4540534
(*Wicklow*, Dublin)

McPhillips, James, CC
Killanny, Carrickmacross, Co Monaghan
Tel 042-9661452
(Clogher)

McQuaid, Macartan, Very Rev Canon
Chaplain, Emyvale, Co Monaghan
Tel 047-87221
(Clogher)

McQuillan, Ignatius, Rt Rev Mgr
(priest in residence)
60 Glenmore Park, Belt Road, Derry BT47 2JZ
Tel 028-91291758
(Derry, retired)

McShane, Dermot, Very Rev, PP
Bruckless, Co Donegal
Tel 074-9737015
(*Bruckless*, Raphoe)

McShane, Patrick, Very Rev Canon, PE
Tully, Donegal Town, Co Donegal
Tel 074-9740150
(Raphoe, retired)

McShane, Philip (OP)
St Mary's, Pope Quay, Cork
Tel 021-4502267

McSorley, Gerard, Rt Rev Mgr, PE
Ballybay, Co Monaghan
Tel 042-9741031
(*Ballybay*, Clogher)

McSweeney, Anthony, CC
Fethard, Co Tipperary
Tel 052-6131187
(*Fethard*, Cashel & E.)

McSweeney, Eustace (OFMCap)
Vicar, Capuchin Friary, Station Road, Raheny, Dublin 5
Tel 01-8313886

McSweeney, Myles, CC
Bandon, Co Cork
Tel 023-8865067
(*Bandon*, Cork & R.)

McSweeney, Patrick T., Very Rev Canon, PE
Nazareth House, Mallow, Co Cork
Tel 022-21561
(Cloyne, retired)

McTiernan, John, Very Rev, PP
Drumahaire, Co Leitrim
Tel 071-9164143
(*Drumahaire and Killargue*, Kilmore)

McTiernan, Sean (SPS)
St Patrick's, Kiltegan, Co Wicklow
Tel 059-6473600

McVeigh, Joseph, CC
Loughside Road, Garrison, Enniskillen, Co Fermanagh BT93 4AE
Tel 028-68659747
(*Belleek-Garrison*, Clogher)

McVeigh, Martin, Very Rev, PP
Parochial House, 9 Cavanakeeran Road, Pomeroy, Dungannon, Co Tyrone BT70 2RD
Tel 028-87758329
(*Pomeroy*, Armagh)

McVeigh, Patrick, Very Rev
3 Broughshane Road, Ballymena, Co Antrim BT43 7DX
(Down & C., retired)

McVerry, Peter (SJ)
Arrupe Community, 217 Silloge Road, Ballymun, Dublin 11
Tel 01-8420886
(Zam-Mal)

McWilliams, Luke, Very Rev, PP
Parochial House, 28 Chapel Road, Ballymena BT44 0RS
Tel 028-21771240
(*Cushendall*, Down and C.)

McWilliams, Patrick, Very Rev, PP
103 Roguery Road, Moneyglass, Toomebridge, Co Antrim BT41 3PT
Tel 028-79650225
(*Duneane*, Down & C.)

Meade, Bernard (CM)
St Paul's College, Raheny, Dublin 5
Tel 01-8318113

Meade, John (CSSp)
Rockwell College, Cashel, Co Tipperary
Tel 062-61444/087-9450163

Meade, Michael, PP
Parochial House, Donore, Drogheda, Co Louth
Tel 041-9823137
(*Donore*, Meath)

Meagher, Charles (SSC)
St Columban's, Dalgan Park, Navan, Co Meath
Tel 046-9021525

Meagher, John (OSA)
The Abbey, Fethard, Co Tipperary
Tel 052-31273

Meagher, Thomas F. (CSSp)
Holy Spirit Missionary College, Kimmage Manor, Dublin 12
Tel 01-4064300

Meaney, Anthony, CC
Parochial House, Ballycruttle Road, Downpatrick, Co Down BT30 7EL
Tel 028-44841213
(*Saul and Ballee*, Down & C.)

Medina, Nelson (OP)
St Saviour's, Upper Dorset Street, Dublin 1
Tel 01-8897610

Meehan, Conleth, CC
6 Allen Park Road, Stillorgan, Co Dublin
Tel 01-2880545
(*Mount Merrion*, Dublin)

Meehan, Dermot, Very Rev, PP
Swinford, Co Mayo
Tel 094-9252952
(Achonry)

Meehan, Francis (SMA)
SMA House, 82 Ranelagh Road, Ranelagh, Dublin 6
Tel 01-4968162/3

Meehan, Frank, Very Rev, PP
Shinrone, Co Offaly
Tel 0505-47167/087-2302413
(*Shinrone*, Killaloe)

Meehan, Patrick (SM)
Cerdon, Marist Fathers, St Mary's Road, Dundalk, Co Louth
Tel 042-9334019

Meehan, Patrick (SSC)
St Columban's Retirement Home,
Dalgan Park, Navan,
Co Meath
Tel 046-9021525

Meehan, Séamus, Very Rev, PP
Dungloe, Co Donegal
Tel 074-9521008
(*Dungloe*, Raphoe)

Meehan, William, Very Rev, PP
St Mary's, Irishtown,
Clonmel, Co Tipperary
Tel 052-6122954
(Waterford & L.)

Mehigan, Donal (OP)
St Saviour's,
Glentworth Street,
Limerick
Tel 061-412333

Melican, Michael (IC)
Rosminian House of Prayer,
Glencomeragh House,
Kilsheelan, Co Tipperary
Tel 052-33181

Melican, P. J. (SPS)
St Patrick's, Kiltegan,
Co Wicklow
Tel 059-6473600

Melody, Sean, Very Rev, PP
Sacred Heart Presbytery,
21 The Folly, Waterford
Tel 051-873759
(*Sacred Heart*, Waterford & L.)

Mercer, Vincent (OP)
Black Abbey, Kilkenny,
Co Kilkenny
Tel 056-7721279

Mernagh, Michael (OSA), CC
St Catherine's, Meath Street,
Dublin 8
Tel 01-4543356
(*Meath Street and Merchant's Quay*, Dublin)

Mernagh, Patrick, CF
McKee Barracks,
Blackhorse Avenue, Dublin 7
(Ferns)

Merrigan, Liam, Very Rev, PP
Drogheda Road,
Monasterevin, Co Kildare
Tel 045-525346
(Kildare & L.)

Meskell, Derek (CSsR)
Mount Saint Alphonsus,
Limerick
Tel 061-315099

Mhamwa, Thaddeus, PC
128 Roselawn Road,
Blanchardstown, Dublin 15
Tel 01-8219014
(*Blanchardstown*, Dublin)

Mikalonis, Ignacio (IVE), CC
Kilmyshall, Enniscorthy,
Co Wexford
Tel 053-9377188
(*Bunclody*, Ferns)

Mikalonis, Marco (IVE)
Kilmyshall, Enniscorthy,
Co Wexford
Tel 053-9377188
(*Bunclody*, Ferns)

Millar, George (SVD)
Maynooth, Co Kildare
Tel 01-6286391/2

Mills, Dermot (OMI), Co-PP
Our Lady of the Wayside Parish,
118 Naas Road, Dublin 12
Tel 01-4501040
(*Inchicore, St Michaels*, Dublin)

Milton, Raymond, Very Rev, PP
Knockcroghery,
Co Roscommon
Tel 090-6661127
(*Knockcroghery (St John's)*, Elphin)

Minniter, Anthony, Very Rev, PP
Ballindereen, Kilcolgan,
Co Galway
Tel 091-796118
(*Ballindereen*, Galway)

Minogue, James, Very Rev, AP
Castleconnell, Co Limerick
Tel 061-377166/087-6228674
(*Castleconnell*, Killaloe)

Mitchell, Francis, Adm
Tuam, Co Galway
Tel 093-24250
(Tuam)

Mitchell, James, Rev Dr
11 St Mary's Terrace, Galway
Tel 091-524411
(Galway, retired)

Mitchell, Kilian (OPraem)
Abbey of the Most Holy Trinity and St Norbert,
Kilnacrott, Ballyjamesduff,
Co Cavan
Tel 049-8544416

Mockler, John, CC
(study leave)
c/o Diocesan Office,
Social Service Centre,
Henry Street, Limerick
(Limerick)

Mohan, Mark, CC
Parochial House, St Patrick's,
Trim, Co Meath
Tel 046-9431251
(*Trim*, Meath)

Mohan, Richard, Rt Rev Mgr, Adm
Pettigo, Co Donegal
Tel 071-9861666
(*Pettigo*, Clogher)

Moley, John, Very Rev
24 Mallard Road,
Downpatrick,
Co Down BT30 6DY
(Down & C., retired)

Mollin, Matthew, Very Rev, PE
4 St Finbar, Maryfield,
Chapelizod, Co Dublin
Tel 01-6268851
(Meath, retired)

Molloy, Francis, Very Rev
Lurgan, Co Armagh
(Dromore, retired)

Molloy, John
Casailla 09-01-5825,
Guayaquil, Equador,
South America
Tel 00593-87504590
(Killaloe)

Molloy, John (SSC)
St Columban's Retirement Home,
Dalgan Park, Navan,
Co Meath
Tel 046-9021525

Molloy, Michael (SSC)
Society Archivist,
St Columban's,
Grange Road, Donaghmede,
Dublin 13
Tel 01-8476647

Molloy, Michael, Very Rev, PP
The Presbytery,
Ballydangan,
Athlone, Co Roscommon
Tel 090-9673539
(*Moore*, Tuam)

Molloy, Patrick (MHM)
Rector, St Joseph's House,
50 Orwell Park, Rathgar,
Dublin 6
Tel 01-4127700

Moloney, Bernard
Cahir Road, Cashel,
Co Tipperary
Tel 062-61443
(*Cashel*, Cashel & E.)

Moloney, Brendan, Very Rev, PP
Silvermines, Nenagh,
Co Tipperary
Tel 067-25864
(*Silvermines*, Killaloe)

Moloney, Dermot, Rt Rev Mgr, PP, VG
Crossboyne, Claremorris,
Co Mayo
Tel 094-9371824
(Tuam)

Moloney, Gerard (CSsR), PC
Marianella, 75 Orwell Road,
Dublin 6
Tel 01-4067212
(Editor, Redemptorist Communications),
Liguori House,
75 Orwell Road, Dublin 6
Tel 01-4067100/01-4922488

Moloney, Henry (CSSp)
Holy Spirit Missionary College,
Kimmage Manor, Dublin 12
Tel 01-4064300

Moloney, John J., Rt Rev Mgr, PE
50 Rathgar Road, Dublin 6
Tel 01-4971297
(Dublin, retired)

Moloney, Joseph, Very Rev, PE
Grove House, Vicar Street,
Tuam, Co Galway
(Tuam, retired)

Moloney, Leonard (SJ)
Headmaster,
Clongowes Wood College,
Naas, Co Kildare
Tel 045-868663/868202

Moloney, Michael, CC
Kiltegan, Co Wicklow
Tel 059-6473211
(*Rathvilly*, Kildare & L.)

Moloney, Raymond (SJ)
Milltown Park,
Sandford Road, Dublin 6
Tel 01-2698411/2698113

Molony, Raymond T., Very Rev Canon
Presbytery No. 2,
Thormanby Road,
Howth, Co Dublin
Tel 01-8322092
(Dublin, retired)

Monaghan, Stephen (CM), Very Rev
Superior, 11 Iona Drive,
Glasnevin, Dublin 9
Tel 01-8305238

Monahan, Finian (OCD)
The Abbey, Loughrea,
Co Galway
Tel 091-841209

Monahan, Fintan
Archbishop's House, Tuam,
Co Galway
Tel 093-24166
(Tuam)

Monahan, Patrick, CC
'Renvyle', Corrig Avenue,
Dun Laoghaire, Co Dublin
Tel 01-2802100
(*Dun Laoghaire*, Dublin)

Monahan, Paul (SMA), CC
The Presbytery, Neilstown,
Clondalkin, Dublin 22
Tel 01-4573546
(*Neilstown*, Dublin)

Monahan, Thomas (OP)
Provincial, Provincial Office,
St Mary's, Tallaght,
Dublin 24
Tel 01-4048118/4048112

Mongan, Gerard, CC
St Columba's Presbytery,
18 Pump Street,
Derry BT48 6JG
Tel 028-71262301
(*St Columba's, Long Tower (Templemore)*, Derry)

Monks, Frank (MI)
Superior,
St Camillus, Killucan,
Co Westmeath
Tel 044-74115

Monson, Eamon (SAC), Very Rev
St Benin's, Dublin Road, Shankill, Co Dublin
Tel 01-2824381

Montades, Rudy (SVD), CC
The Presbytery, City Quay, Dublin 2
Tel 01-6773706
(*City Quay*, Dublin)

Montague, Paul, CC
Ard Easmuinn, Dundalk, Co Louth
Tel 042-9334259
(Armagh)

Mooney, Desmond, CC
The Presbytery, 13 Tullygally Road, Legahory, Craigavon BT65 5BY
Tel 028-38343297
(*Moyraverty (Craigavon)*, Dromore)

Mooney, Oliver, Very Rev
Newry, Co Down
(Dromore, retired)

Mooney, Patrick, Very Rev, PP
The Parochial House, Glenamaddy, Co Galway
Tel 094-9659017
(Tuam)

Moore, Brian (CM), Very Rev
Provincial, Provincial Office, St Paul's, Sybil Hill, Raheny, Dublin 5
Tel 01-8510840/8510842

Moore, David
1A Rockstown Road, Carrickmore, Omagh, Co Tyrone, BT79 9BE
Tel 028-80760433
(Armagh)

Moore, Edward, Very Rev, PP
Allen, Kilmeague, Naas, Co Kildare
Tel 045-860135
(*Allen*, Kildare & L.)

Moore, Eoin (OCarm)
Terenure College, Terenure, Dublin 6W
Tel 01-4904621

Moore, Gerard, Co-PP
The Presbytery, St Mary's Parish, Sandyford, Dublin 18
Tel 01-8316219
(*Sandyford*, Dublin)

Moore, James, CC
Mallow, Co Cork
Tel 022-50626
(*Mallow*, Cloyne)

Moore, James, Very Rev, PP
Fintona, Omagh, Co Tyrone BT78 2NS
Tel 028-82841907
(*Fintona*, Clogher)

Moore, Kevin, Very Rev (*Moderator*)
122 Greencastle Road, Coolock, Dublin 17
Tel 01-8487657
(*Bonnybrook*, Dublin)

Moore, Michael (CSSp)
Rockwell College, Cashel, Co Tipperary
Tel 062-61444

Moore, Paschal, Very Rev, PP
Piltown, Co Kilkenny
Tel 051-643112/087-2408078
(*Templeorum*, Ossory)

Moore, Patrick (SPS)
St Patrick's, Kiltegan, Co Wicklow
Tel 059-6473600

Moore, Patrick B., Very Rev, PE
25 Thomastown Road, Dun Laoghaire, Co Dublin
(Dublin, retired)

Moore, Patrick, Very Rev, PP
Duagh, Listowel, Co Kerry
Tel 068-45102
(*Duagh*, Kerry)

Moore, Patrick, Very Rev, PP, VF
Parochial House, Castlepollard, Co Westmeath
Tel 044-9661126
(Meath)

Moore, Seamus, Very Rev, PE
8 Herbert Avenue, Dublin 4
Tel 01-2692501
(Dublin, retired)

Moore, Sean (CSsR)
Clonard Monastery, 1 Clonard Gardens, Belfast, BT13 2RL
Tel 028-90445950

Moore, Seán, Very Rev, PP
Parochial House, 290 Monaghan Road, Middletown, Co Armagh BT60 4HS
Tel 028-37568406
(*Middletown (Tynan)*, Armagh)

Moorhead, John, Very Rev, PP
Parochial House, Eglish, Birr, Co Offaly
Tel 057-9133010
(*Eglish*, Meath)

Morahan, Kieran (SMA)
Temporary diocesan work in Ireland
c/o African Missions, Provincial House, Feltrim, Blackrock Road, Cork
Tel 021-4292871

Morahan, Leo, Very Rev, PE
2 The Beeches, Louisburg, Co Mayo
Tel 098-66869
(Galway, retired)

Moran, Benedict (OP), Very Rev, PP
The Presbytery, St Aengus's, Balrothery, Tallaght, Dublin 24
Tel 01-4624038
(*Tallaght, Tymon North*, Dublin)

Moran, James (SJ)
Vice-Superior, 35 Lower Leeson Street, Dublin 2
Tel 01-6761248

Moran, John, CC
192 Navan Road, Dublin 7
Tel 01-8387902
(Dublin, retired)

Moran, Joseph, Very Rev Canon
Abbeybreaffey Nursing Home, Dublin Road, Castlebar, Co Mayo
(Tuam, retired)

Moran, Lorcan
Thomastown, Co Kilkenny
Tel 056-7793191
(Ossory)

Moran, Martin, Very Rev Canon, PP
Rosscahill, Co Galway
Tel 091-550106
(*Rosscahill (Killanin)*, Galway)

Moran, Noel, Very Rev
Lahard, Milltown, Co Kerry
(Kerry, retired)

Moran, Paddy, CC
1 Cedar Road, Wedgewood Estate Balally, Dublin 16
Tel 01-8380170
(*Balally*, Dublin)

Moran, Pat (OSA)
St Augustine's Priory, Washington Street, Cork
Tel 021-2753982

Moran, Willie (OCD)
Prior, The Abbey, Loughrea, Co Galway
Tel 091-841209

Morgan, Francis (OCSO)
Our Lady of Bethlehem Abbey, 11 Ballymena Road, Portglenone, Ballymena, Co Antrim BT44 8BL
Tel 028-25821211

Morgan, Liam, CC
Tinryland, Co Carlow
Tel 059-9131212
(*Tinryland*, Kildare & L.)

Moriarty, Declan
Sacred Heart Residence, Sybil Hill Road, Raheny, Dublin 5
(Dublin, retired)

Moriarty, Frank, Very Rev
Adare, Co Limerick
Tel 061-396177
(Limerick, retired)

Moriarty, James, Most Rev, DD
Bishop of Kildare and Leighlin, 68 Clontarf Road, Dublin 3
Tel 01-8054738
(Kildare & L.)

Moriarty, John (CSSp)
Holy Spirit Missionary College, Kimmage Manor, Dublin 12
Tel 01-4064300

Morris, Anthony (OP)
Holy Cross, Sligo, Co Sligo
Tel 071-9142700

Morris, Colm, PEm
Muff, Co Donegal
Tel 074-9384407
(Derry, retired)

Morris, Donal, Very Rev, Adm
(on study break)
c/o Diocesan Office, St Mary's, Sligo
(Elphin)

Morris, Fintan, CC
Kiltealy, Enniscorthy, Co Wexford
Tel 053-9255124
(*Ballindaggin*, Ferns)

Morris, John, Very Rev, PP
Solohead, Co Limerick
Tel 062-47614
(*Solohead*, Cashel & E.)

Morrissey, Michael (OCarm) CC
Carmelite Presbytery, Idrone Avenue, Knocklyon, Dublin 16
Tel 01-4941204/4944986
(*Knocklyon*, Dublin)

Morrissey, Robin, CC
1 Cathedral Terrace, Cobh, Co Cork
Tel 021-4813951
(Cloyne)

Morrissey, Thomas (SJ)
Manresa House, Dollymount, Dublin 3
Tel 01-8331352

Morrow, James (CSSp)
Holy Spirit Missionary College, Kimmage Manor, Dublin 12
Tel 01-4064300

Moss, Michael (FDP)
Sarsfield House, Sarsfield Road, Ballyfermot, Dublin 10
Tel 01-6266193/6266233

Mothersill, Joseph (OCarm)
Gort Muire, Ballinteer, Dublin 16
Tel 01-2984014

Motherway, Nicholas (SPS)
St Patrick's, Kiltegan,
Co Wicklow
Tel 059-6473600
Mowbray, Alan (SJ), PC
Gonzaga Jesuit Community,
Sandford Road,
Dublin 6
Tel 01-4972943
(*Milltown*, Dublin)
Moylan, John (SJ)
St Francis Xavier's,
Upper Gardiner Street,
Dublin 1
Tel 01-8363411
Moynihan, James, CC
Murrintown, Wexford
Tel 053-9139136
(*Piercestown*, Ferns)
Moynihan, Michael
The Presbytery, Castleisland,
Co Kerry
Tel 066-7141241
(Kerry)
Muchunu, Moses Muraya
Killarney, Co Kerry
Tel 064-6631014
(*Killarney*, Co Kerry)
Muckian, Patrick (SM)
Philippines
Mulcahy, Brian (CP)
St Paul's Retreat,
Mount Argus, Dublin 6W
Tel 01-4992000
Mulcahy, James, Very Rev, PE
St John's Pastoral Centre,
John's Hill, Waterford
Tel 051-858306
(Waterford & L., retired)
Mulcahy, Joseph (SPS)
St Patrick's, Kiltegan,
Co Wicklow
Tel 059-6473600
Mulcahy, Kevin, CC
Ballymacoda, Co Cork
Tel 024-98110
(*Ballymacoda and Ladysbridge*, Cloyne)
Mulcahy, Pat, Very Rev, PP
Lorrha, Nenagh,
Co Tipperary
Tel 0909-747009/
087-6329913
(*Dunkerrin*, Killaloe)
Mulcahy, Richard, Rt Rev
30 Knapton Road,
Dun Laoghaire,
Co Dublin
Tel 01-2804353
(Opus Dei)
Mulcahy, Thomas (MSC)
Myross Wood Retreat
House,
Leap, Skibbereen,
Co Cork
Tel 028-33118

Mulcahy, Timothy (OP), Very Rev
Prior, Holy Cross, Sligo,
Co Sligo
Tel 071-9142700
Muldowney, Peter, Very Rev
Ossory Diocesan Office,
James's Street, Kilkenny
Tel 056-7762448/056-7763753
(Ossory)
Mulhall, Brendan (CSsR), CC
Clonard Monastery,
1 Clonard Gardens,
Belfast BT13 2RL
Tel 028-90445950
Mulhern, Kevin (SMA)
Dromantine College,
Dromantine, Newry,
Co Down BT34 1RH
Tel 028-30821224
Mulholland, Patrick, Very Rev, PP
Parochial House, Portaferry,
Co Down BT22 1RH
Tel 028-42728234
(*Portaferry*, Down & C.)
Mulkerins, Bernard (SSC)
Director,
St Columban's Retirement
Home,
Dalgan Park, Navan,
Co Meath
Tel 046-9021525
Mulkerrins, Michael, Very Rev
Canon, PP
Renmore Avenue,
Renmore, Galway
Tel 091-751707
(*Renmore*, Galway)
Mullahy, Thomas (SMA)
African Missions,
Blackrock Road, Cork
Tel 021-4292871
Mullaly, Kevin
8 Finglaswood Road,
Finglas West, Dublin 11
Tel 01-8238354
(*Blanchardstown*, Dublin)
Mullan, Aidan, Rev, PP
19 Chapel Road, Dungiven,
Derry BT47 4RT
Tel 028-77741219
(*Dungiven*, Derry)
Mullan, Joseph, Very Rev, PP
St MacCullin's, Lusk,
Co Dublin
Tel 01-8438421
(*Lusk*, Dublin)
Mullan, Kevin, PP
257 Dooish Road,
Drumquin, Omagh,
Co Tyrone BT78 4RA
Tel 028-82831225
(*Drumquin*, Derry)

Mullan, Michael (LC)
Director,
Faith and Family Centre,
Dal Riada House,
Avoca Avenue, Blackrock,
Co Dublin
Tel 01-2889317
Vocations Director and
Regnum Lay Apostolate,
Novitiate,
Leopardstown Road,
Foxrock, Dublin 18
Tel 01-2955902
Mullan, Michael, CC
300 Drumsurn Road,
Limavady,
Co Derry BT49 0PX
Tel 028-77762165
(*Dungiven*, Derry)
Mullan, Patrick, PP
Stella Maris House, Eglinton,
Co Derry BT47 3EA
Tel 028-71810240
(*Faughanvale*, Derry)
Mullane, Denis, Very Rev, PP, VF
Kilcolman, Ardagh,
Co Limerick
Tel 069-60126
(*Coolcappa*, Limerick)
Mullaney, Michael
Ballycahill, Thurles,
Co Tipperary
Tel 0504-26080
(Cashel & E.)
Mullany, Francis (SSC)
St Columban's Retirement
Home,
Dalgan Park, Navan,
Co Meath
Tel 046-9021525
Mullan, Joseph, PP
49 Rathgar Road,
Dublin 6
Tel 01-4970039/0872326254
(*Rathgar*, Dublin)
Mullen, John (IC)
Clonturk House,
Ormond Road,
Drumcondra, Dublin 9
Tel 01-6877014
Mullen, Pearse (SSCC) PP
Sacred Hearts Presbytery,
St John's Drive,
Sruleen, Clondalkin,
Dublin 22
Tel 01-4570032
(*Sruleen*, Dublin)
Mulligan, Ben, Very Rev, PP
42 Corke Abbey, Little Bray,
Co Wicklow
Tel 01-2720224
(Dublin,retired)
Mulligan, Declan, CC
24 Downs Road, Newcastle,
Co Down BT33 0AG
Tel 028-43722401
(*Newcastle (Maghera)*, Down & C.)

Mulligan, John (SM)
Cerdon, Marist Fathers,
St Mary's Road, Dundalk,
Co Louth
Tel 042-9334019
Mulligan, Larry (OFM)
Franciscan Friary,
Liberty Street, Cork
Tel 021-4270302
Mulligan, Rory (SM)
Norway
Mulligan, Thomas, Very Rev, PP
Attymass, Ballina, Co Mayo
Tel 096-45095
(*Attymass*, Achonry)
Mulligan, Vincent (OMI)
Oblate House of Retreat,
Inchicore, Dublin 8
Tel 01-4534408/4541805
Mullin, Joseph, Very Rev
Canon, PP, VF
Lisoneill, Lisnaskea,
Co Fermanagh BT92 0JE
Tel 028-67721342
(Clogher)
Mullin, Seamus, Very Rev
Canon, AP
Miltown Malbay, Co Clare
Tel 065-7084003
(*Miltown Malbay*, Killaloe)
Mullins, Anthony, Very Rev
Diocesan Administrator,
Diocesan Office,
Social Services Centre,
Henry Street, Limerick
Dromin, Killmallock,
Co Limerick
Tel 063-31962
(*Dromin & Athlacca*, Limerick)
Mullins, Melvyn, Co-PP, Adm
192 Sundrive Road,
Dublin 12
Tel 01-4023307/6777480
(*Clogher Road*, Dublin)
Mullins, Michael, Very Rev, PP
St Anne's Presbytery,
Convent Hill, Waterford
Tel 051-855819
(*Ballybricken*, Waterford & L.)
Mullins, Patrick (OCarm)
Provincial Office and
Carmelite Community,
Gort Muire, Ballinteer,
Dublin 16
Tel 01-2984014
Mullins, Patrick, Very Rev, PP
Cummer, Tuam,
Co Galway
Tel 093-41427
(*Cummer (Kilmoylan and Cummer)*, Tuam)
Mulloy, Frank (CSSp)
Templeogue College,
Dublin 6W
Tel 01-4903909

Mulvaney, Martin, Very Rev, PP
Drumlion, Carrick-on-Shannon, Co Roscommon
Tel 071-9620415
(*Croghan*, Elphin)

Mulvaney, Martin, Very Rev, PP
Parochial House, Johnstown, Navan, Co Meath
Tel 046-9021731
(*Johnstown*, Meath)

Mulvany, Seamus, Very Rev, PP
Parochial House, Tubberclaire-Glasson, Athlone, Co Westmeath
Tel 090-6485103
(*Glasson*, Meath)

Mulvey, Anthony (CSsR)
St Joseph's, Dundalk, Co Louth
Tel 042-9334042/9334762

Mulvey, Patrick, Very Rev
25 Thomastown Road, Dun Laoghaire, Co Dublin
(Dublin, retired)

Mulvihill, Anthony, Very Rev, PP
Croagh, Rathkeale, Co Limerick
Tel 069-64185/087-9059348
(*Croagh and Kilfinny*, Limerick)

Mulvihill, Eamonn, Very Rev, PP
Fenit, Tralee, Co Kerry
Tel 066-7136145
(*Spa*, Kerry)

Mulvihill, William, CC
Parochial House, Collon, Co Louth
Tel 041-9826106
(*Ardee & Collon*, Armagh)

Mulvilhill, Michael (CSSp)
Holy Spirit Missionary College, Kimmage Manor, Dublin 12
Tel 01-4064300

Mundow, Sean, Very Rev, PP
77 Botanic Avenue, Dublin 9
Tel 01-8373455
(*Glasnevin*, Dublin)

Munnelly, Alan, CC
Glenhest, Newport, Co Mayo
Tel 098-41170
(*Lahardane (Addergoole)*, Killala)

Munnelly, Patrick, Very Rev, PP
Ardagh, Ballina, Co Mayo
Tel 096-31144
(Killala)

Munster, Ramon, Very Rev Canon, PP
Bundoran, Co Donegal
Tel 071-9841290
(*Bundoran*, Clogher)

Murchan, Michael, Very Rev, PE
Knightsbridge Nursing Home, Trim, Co Meath
(Meath, retired)

Murney, Peadar, Very Rev, PP
56 Auburn Road, Killiney, Co Dublin
Tel 01-2856660
(*Johnstown-Killiney*, Dublin)

Murphy O'Connor, Kerry, Ven Archdeacon, PP
The Presbytery, Turner's Cross, Cork
Tel 021-4312466
(*Turner's Cross*, Cork & R.)

Murphy, Aidan, Very Rev, PP
Parochial House, Termonfechin, Drogheda, Co Louth
Tel 041-9822121
(*Termonfechin*, Armagh)

Murphy, Alphonsus, Very Rev, PE
Carbury, Co Kildare
Tel 046-9553020
(Kildare & L., retired)

Murphy, Anthony (MHM)
c/o St Joseph's House, 50 Orwell Park, Rathgar, Dublin 6
Tel 01-4127700

Murphy, Barry, Adm
Parochial House, Brackenstown Road, Swords, Co Dublin
Tel 01-8020602
(*Brackenstown*, Dublin)

Murphy, Bernard (OCarm)
Whitefriar Street Church, 56 Aungier Street, Dublin 2
Tel 01-4758821

Murphy, Brendan, Very Rev, PP
Feenagh, Kilmallock, Co Limerick
Tel 063-85013/086-8094490
(*Feenagh and Kilmeedy*, Limerick)

Murphy, Brian (OSB)
Glenstal Abbey, Murroe, Co Limerick
Tel 061-386103

Murphy, Canice (OP)
St Saviour's, Bridge Street, Waterford
Tel 051-875061

Murphy, Colm, Very Rev, PP
Clongeen, Foulksmills, Co Wexford
Tel 051-565610
(*Clongeen*, Ferns)

Murphy, Conor (OMI)
170 Merrion Road, Ballsbridge, Dublin 4
Tel 01-2693658

Murphy, Cyril (SSC)
St Columban's Retirement Home, Dalgan Park, Navan, Co Meath
Tel 046-9021525

Murphy, Daniel, CC
Castlelyons, Co Cork
Tel 025-36196
(*Rathcormac*, Cloyne)

Murphy, Daniel (SMA)
African Missions, Blackrock Road, Cork
Tel 021-4292871

Murphy, David, CC
Caroreigh, Taghmon, Co Wexford
Tel 053-9134113
(Ferns)

Murphy, David, Adm
The Bungalow, Main Street, Clarinbridge, Co Galway
Tel 091-485777
(*Clarinbridge*, Galway)

Murphy, Denis (OP)
St Saviour's, Upper Dorset Street, Dublin 1
Tel 01-8897610

Murphy, Denis, Very Rev, PP
Tolerton, Ballickmoyler, Carlow
Tel 056-4442126
(*Doonane*, Kildare & L.)

Murphy, Edmund (OP)
Newbridge College, Droichead Nua, Co Kildare
Tel 045-487200

Murphy, Edward, Very Rev Canon, PE
Newtownbutler, Enniskillen, Co Fermanagh BT92 8JJ
Tel 028-67738640
(*Newtownbutler*, Clogher)

Murphy, Enda
Pontificio Collegio Irlandese, Rome, Italy
(Kilmore)

Murphy, Eoin
St Joseph's Church, 109 Linden Street, Saint John's, MI48879, USA
(Dublin)

Murphy, Francis, Very Rev, PP
Bree, Enniscorthy, Co Wexford
Tel 053-9247843
(*Bree*, Ferns)

Murphy, Gabriel, CC
Kiltimagh, Co Mayo
Tel 094-9381492
(Achonry)

Murphy, George, Very Rev, PP
Minane Bridge, Co Cork
Tel 021-4887105
(*Tracton Abbey*, Cork & R.)

Murphy, James (CSSp)
Holy Spirit Missionary College, Kimmage Manor, Dublin 12
Tel 01-4064300

Murphy, James (CSsR)
Mount Saint Alphonsus, Limerick
Tel 061-315099

Murphy, James (SJ)
Irish Jesuit Provincialate, Milltown Park, Sandford Road, Dublin 6
Tel 01-4987333

Murphy, James, CC
St Brigid's, Rosslare, Co Wexford
Tel 053-9132118
(*Tagoat*, Ferns)

Murphy, James, Very Rev, PP
St Canice's Presbytery, Dean Street, Kilkenny
Tel 056-7752991/ 087-2609545
(Ossory)

Murphy, Jason
(priest in residence)
Carrigans, Ballinagh, Co Cavan
(*Ballintemple*, Kilmore)

Murphy, Jeremiah (SAC)
'Homestead', Sandyford Road, Dundrum, Dublin 16
Tel 01-2956180/2954170

Murphy, Jerry (SSC)
St Mary's, Tang, Ballymahon, Co Longford
Tel 0906-432214

Murphy, Jerry, CC
St Mary's, Tang, Ballymahon, Co Longford
Tel 090-6432214
(*Drumraney*, Meath)

Murphy, John, CC
St Anne's, Strand Road, Portmarnock, Co Dublin
Tel 01-2697754
(*Portmarnock*, Dublin)

Murphy, John, Rt Rev Mgr
(priest in residence)
18 Rock Road, Lisburn, Co Antrim BT28 3SU
Tel 028-92648244
(*Hannahstown*, Down & C.)

Murphy, John, Very Rev Canon, PP, VF
Bailieboro, Co Cavan
Tel 042-9665117
(*Bailieboro*, Kilmore)

Murphy, John (OMI)
Oblate House of Retreat, Inchicore, Dublin 8
Tel 01-4534408/4541805

Murphy, Joseph (CSSp)
17 St Brigid's Park, Blacklion, Greystones, Co Wicklow
Tel 01-2874888

Murphy, Joseph (OFMCap)
Holy Trinity,
Fr Mathew Quay, Cork
Tel 021-4270827

Murphy, Joseph, Very Rev Mgr
Secretariat of State,
(Section for Relations with States),
00120 Vatican City
Tel 0039-0669883193
(Cloyne)

Murphy, Kyran (SPS)
On temporary diocesan work

Murphy, Laurence (OFM)
Franciscan Friary,
Friary Lane, Athlone,
Co Westmeath
Tel 090-6472095

Murphy, Laurence (SJ)
Clongowes Wood College,
Naas, Co Kildare
Tel 045-868663/868202

Murphy, Malachy, CC
Parochial House,
St Patrick Street,
Keady,
Co Armagh BT60 3TQ
Tel 028-37531246

Murphy, Malachy, Very Rev, Canon, PP
c/o 73 Somerton Road,
Belfast BT15 4DE
(Down & C., retired)

Murphy, Martin (IC)
Rosminian House of Prayer,
Glencomeragh House,
Kilsheelan, Co Tipperary
Tel 052-33181

Murphy, Martin (SSC)
St Columban's, Dalgan Park,
Navan, Co Meath
Tel 046-9021525

Murphy, Martin, Very Rev, PP
Drom, Thurles, Co Tipperary
Tel 0504-51196
(*Drom and Inch*, Cashel & E.)

Murphy, Michael
Youghal, Co Cork
Tel 024-92336
(*Youghal*, Cloyne)

Murphy, Michael (OFMCap)
Capuchin Friary,
Station Road, Raheny,
Dublin 5
Tel 01-8313886

Murphy, Michael J., Venerable Archdeacon
No. 1 Cathedral Place,
Killarney, Co Kerry
(Kerry, retired)

Murphy, Michael, CC
Robeen, Hollymount,
Co Mayo
Tel 094-9540026
(*Robeen*, Tuam)

Murphy, Michael, Very Rev Canon, PP
Ballyphehane, Co Cork
Tel 021-4965560
(*Ballyphehane*, Cork & R.)

Murphy, Michael, Very Rev, PP, VF
Parochial House, Kilcullen,
Co Kildare
Tel 045-481230
(*Kilcullen*, Dublin)

Murphy, Mícheál, Very Rev
c/o Bishop's House, Carlow
(Kildare & L.)

Murphy, Noel (CSSp)
Rockwell College, Cashel,
Co Tipperary
Tel 062-61444

Murphy, Pádraig, Very Rev, PP
Parochial House,
Ravensdale, Dundalk,
Co Louth
Tel 042-9371327
(Armagh)

Murphy, Patrick, Very Rev, PP
Parochial House, Mohill,
Co Leitrim
Tel 071-9631024
(*Mohill*, Ardagh & Cl.)

Murphy, Patrick, Very Rev, PP
Sneem, Co Kerry
Tel 064-6645141
(*Sneem*, Kerry)

Murphy, Patrick, Very Rev, PP
Templetuohy, Thurles,
Co Tipperary
Tel 0504-53114
(*Templetuohy*, Cashel & E.)

Murphy, Paul (OFMCap)
Capuchin Friary,
Church Street, Dublin 7
Tel 01-8730599

Murphy, Paul F., Very Rev, Adm
Ballynageeragh, Dunhill,
Co Waterford
Tel 051-396616
(*Dunhill*, Waterford & L.)

Murphy, Paul, Very Rev, PP
Parochial House,
Butlerstown, Co Waterford
Tel 051-384192
(*Butlerstown*, Waterford & L.)

Murphy, Peadar, Very Rev, PP
Aghabullogue, Co Cork
Tel 021-7334035
(*Aghabullogue*, Cloyne)

Murphy, Peter
National Chaplain,
Accord Catholic Marriage Care Service,
Columba Centre,
Maynooth, Co Kildare
Tel 01-5053107
(Dublin)

Murphy, Peter, Very Rev, PP, VF
Parochial House,
Hale Street, Ardee,
Co Louth
Tel 041-6850920
(*Ardee & Collon*, Armagh)

Murphy, Pierce, Very Rev
(priest in residence)
Borris,
Co Carlow via Kilkenny
Tel 059-9773128
(*Borris*, Kildare & L.)

Murphy, Seán, Very Rev, PP
Miltown Malbay, Co Clare
Tel 065-7084129
(*Miltown Malbay*, Killaloe)

Murphy, Thomas (SSC)
Superior General, Suite 504,
Tower 1, Silvercord,
30 Canton Road Tst,
Kowloon, Hong Kong SAR

Murphy, Thomas, Very Rev Canon, PP
Ballyragget, Co Kilkenny
Tel 056-8833123/
086-8130694
(Ossory)

Murphy, Timothy, Very Rev, PP
The Presbytery, Main Street,
Blessington, Co Wicklow
Tel 045-865442
(*Blessington*, Dublin)

Murphy, Vincent (SJ)
Clongowes Wood College,
Naas, Co Kildare
Tel 045-868663/868202

Murphy, William (CSSp)
Rockwell College, Cashel,
Co Tipperary
Tel 062-61444

Murphy, William, Most Rev, DD
Bishop of Kerry,
Bishop's House, Killarney,
Co Kerry
Tel 064-6631168
(Kerry)

Murray, Brendan (SSC)
St Columban's, Dalgan Park,
Navan, Co Meath
Tel 046-9021525

Murray, Brendan, Very Rev Canon
(priest in residence)
Apt 13 Downview Manor,
Belfast BT15 4JL
(*Holy Family*, Down & C.)

Murray, Declan (SJ)
Crescent College Comprehensive,
Dooradoyle, Limerick,
Tel 061-480920

Murray, Denis, Very Rev, PP
Carrigallen, Co Leitrim,
via Cavan
Tel 049-4339610
(*Carrigallen*, Kilmore)

Murray, Dermot (SJ)
Clongowes Wood College,
Naas, Co Kildare
Tel 045-868663/868202

Murray, Donal, Most Rev, DD
Former Bishop of Limerick,
Diocesan Office,
Social Service Centre,
Henry Street, Limerick
Tel 061-315856
(Limerick)

Murray, Francis, CC
46 Knockmoyle Road,
Omagh, Co Tyrone BT79 7TB
Tel 028-82242793
(Derry, retired)

Murray, Francis, Very Rev, PP
Ferbane, Co Offaly
Tel 090-6454380
(*Ferbane High Street and Boora*, Ardagh & Cl.)

Murray, Gerard, (SMA)
African Missions,
Blackrock Road, Cork
Tel 021-4292871

Murray, James
9 Hillcrest Manor,
Templeogue, Dublin 6W
(Dublin, retired)

Murray, James (OCarm), PP
Carmelite Presbytery,
Idrone Avenue, Knocklyon,
Dublin 16
Tel 01-4941204
(*Knocklyon*, Dublin)

Murray, James, CC
Carraroe, Sligo,
Co Sligo
Tel 071-9162136
(Elphin)

Murray, John, CC
Castlebar, Co Mayo
Tel 094-901253/21844
(*Castlebar (Aglish, Ballyheane and Breaghwy)*, Tuam)

Murray, John, Very Rev, PP
Parochial House,
9 Gortahor Road,
Rasharkin, Ballymona,
Co Antrim BT44 8SB
(*Rasharkin*, Down & C.)

Murray, Liam, Adm
St Mary's, Athlone,
Co Westmeath
Tel 090-6472088
(*Athlone*, Ardagh & Cl.)

Murray, Michael, CC
Belcarra, Castlebar, Co Mayo
Tel 094-9032006
(*Balla and Manulla*, Tuam)

Murray, Michael, Very Rev, PP
Parochial House,
Greencastle Road, Kilkeel,
Co Down BT34 4DE
Tel 028-41762242
(*Kilkeel (Upper Mourne)*, Down & C.)

Murray, P. J., Very Rev, PP
Maypole Hill, Dromore,
Co Down BT25 1BQ
Tel 028-92692218
(Dromore)

Murray, Patrick (MHM)
St Joseph's House,
50 Orwell Park, Rathgar,
Dublin 6
Tel 01-4127700

Murray, Patrick (SAC)
Droum, Gleinbeigh,
Co Kerry

Murray, Placid (OSB)
Glenstal Abbey, Murroe,
Co Limerick
Tel 061-386103

Murray, Raymond, Rt Rev
Mgr, PE
60 Glen Mhacaha,
Cathedral Road,
Armagh BT61 8AS
Tel 028-37510821
(Armagh, retired)

Murray, Senan (CSSp), CC
Askeaton, Co Limerick
Tel 061-392131
(*Askeaton and Ballysteen*,
Limerick)

Murray, Terence (OMI), Very
Rev, PP
Superior, The Presbytery,
Darndale, Dublin 17
Tel 01-8474547
(*Darndale*, Dublin)

Murray, Tom CC
Diocesan Offices,
St Michael's, Longford
Tel 043-3346432
(Ardagh & Cl.)

Murtagh, Brian (CSSp)
Spiritan Missionaries,
Ardbraccan, Navan,
Co Meath
Tel 046-9021441

Murtagh, Colm, Very Rev, PE
Parochial House, Kildalkey,
Co Meath
Tel 046-9546488
(Meath, retired)

Murtagh, Michael, CC
2 St Mary's Terrace, Arklow,
Co Wicklow
Tel 0402-41505
(*Arklow*, Dublin)

Murtagh, G. Michael, Very
Rev, PP
Parochial House,
Old Chapel Lane, Dunleer,
Co Louth
Tel 041-6851278
(*Dunleer*, Armagh)

Murtagh, John
Warrenpoint, Co Down
(Dromore, retired)

Murtagh, Liam, Very Rev
33 Grace Park Road,
Drumcondra, Dublin 9
(Dublin, retired)

Murtagh, Michael (CSsR)
Superior,
Clonard Monastery,
1 Clonard Gardens,
Belfast, BT13 2RL
Tel 028-90445950

Murtagh, Michael, CC
5 St Mary's Terrace, Arklow
Tel 0402-41505
(*Arklow*, Dublin)

Murtagh, Ray (SPS)
St Patrick's, Kiltegan,
Co Wicklow
Tel 059-6473600

Murtagh, Ronan
Ballymote Road,
Tubbercurry, Co Sligo
(Achonry)

Murtagh, William, Very Rev,
PE, AP
Parochial House,
Clogherhead, Drogheda,
Co Louth
Tel 041-9822224
(*Clogherhead*, Armagh)

Mutunzi, Eladius Leonard, PC
Presbytery 2, 6 Old Hill,
Leixlip, Co Kildare
Tel 01-6243673
(*Leixlip*, Dublin)

Myers, David (IC)
Provincial, Clonturk House,
Ormond Road,
Drumcondra, Dublin 9
Tel 01-6877014

## N

Nagle, Cathal
(Galway, retired)

Nagle, Joe (OFMCap)
Holy Trinity,
Fr Mathew Quay, Cork
Tel 021-4270827

Nallen, Michael
Aughoose, Ballina, Co Mayo
Tel 097-87990
(Killala)

Nallukunnel, Antony
(OFMConv), PP
Friary of the Visitation,
Fairview Strand, Dublin 3
Tel 01-8376000
(*Fairview*, Dublin)

Nally, John, Very Rev, PP
Parochial House,
Ballynacargy, Co Westmeath
Tel 044-9373923
(*Ballynacargy*, Meath)

Nash, Ger
Parochial House, Crusheen,
Ennis, Clare
Tel 065-6827113
(*Crusheen*, Killaloe)

Nash, Paul (OSB)
Glenstal Abbey, Murroe,
Co Limerick
Tel 061-386103

Nash, Tom (CSSp)
Community Leader,
Blackrock College,
Blackrock, Co Dublin
Tel 01-2888681

Naughten, Patrick
Woodford, Co Galway
Tel 090-9749010
(Clonfert, retired)

Naughton, John, Very Rev, PP
Eyrecourt, Ballinasloe,
Co Galway
Tel 090-9675148
(Clonfert)

Naughton, Joseph (CSsR)
St Joseph's, Dundalk,
Co Louth
Tel 042-9334042/9334762

Naughton, Richard, Very Rev,
PP, VF
Mountain Lodge,
132 Dublin Road, Newry,
Co Down BT35 8QT
Tel 028-30262174
(*Cloghogue (Killeavy
Upper)*, Armagh)

Naughton, Tom, CC
Midleton, Co Cork
Tel 021-4636704
(*Midleton*, Cloyne)

Navin, Charles, Very Rev
Tubber, Gort, Co Galway
Tel 091-63323
(Killaloe, retired)

Nawalaniec, Kaz
2 The Presbytery, Mahon,
Co Cork
Tel 021-4515460
(*Mahon*, Cork & R.)

Nealon, Edward (CSSp)
Spiritan Missionaries,
Ardbraccan, Navan,
Co Meath
Tel 046-9021441

Neary, Donal (SJ), Very Rev,
PP, VF
The Presbytery,
Upper Gardiner Street,
Dublin 1
Tel 01-8363411
(*Gardiner Street*, Dublin)

Neary, Michael, Most Rev, DD
Archbishop of Tuam,
Archbishop's House, Tuam,
Co Galway
Tel 093-24166
(Tuam)

Nechikattil, Pius (SSP)
Superior, Society of St Paul,
Moyglare Road, Maynooth,
Co Kildare
Tel 01-6285933

Needham, Gerard, Very Rev
Louisburgh, Co Mayo
(Tuam)

Neenan, Daniel, Rt Rev Mgr,
PP
1 Trinity Court,
Monaleen Road, Monaleen,
Limerick
Tel 061-330974/087-2208547
(Limerick)

Neeson, Patrick, Very Rev, PP
46 Blackstaff Road,
Ballycranbeg, Kircubbin,
Newtownards,
Co Down BT22 1AG
Tel 028-42738294
(*Kircubbin (Ardkeen)*, Down
& C.)

Nellis, Christopher, Very Rev,
PP
Parochial House, Armoy,
Ballymoney,
Co Antrim BT53 8RL
Tel 028-20751205
(*Armoy*, Down & C.)

Nestor, Dermot, Very Rev,
Co-PP
Parochial House,
Nutgrove Avenue,
Dublin 14
Tel 01-2985916
(*Churchtown*, Dublin)

Neville, Anthony, CC
Claddaghduff, Co Galway
Tel 095-44668
(*Inishbofin*, Tuam)

Neville, Edward (OFMCap)
Holy Trinity,
Fr Mathew Quay, Cork
Tel 021-4270827

Neville, James, Very Rev
Canon
Cedarville, Abbeyfeale,
Co Limerick
Tel 068-32884
(Limerick, retired)

Neville, Paddy (MHM)
St Joseph's House,
50 Orwell Park, Rathgar,
Dublin 6
Tel 01-4127700

Neville, Ronald, Very Rev, PE
213A Harold's Cross Road,
Dublin 6W
Tel 01-4974044
(Dublin, retired)

Nevin, Henry, (SDS), PP
Superior,
Our Lady of Victories,
Sallynoggin, Dun Laoghaire,
Co Dublin
Tel 01-2854667

Nevin, John (MHM)
St Mary's Parish,
25 Marquis Street,
Belfast BT1 1JJ
Tel 028-90320482
Tel 01-4789093

Newell, Eamonn (OFM)
Franciscan College,
Gormanston, Co Meath
Tel 01-8412203

Newell, Martin, Very Rev Canon, AP
Claran, Co Galway
Tel 093-35436
(*Headford (Killursa and Killower)*, Tuam)

Newman, John, Very Rev, PP
Monkstown, Co Cork
Tel 021-4863267
(*Monkstown*, Cork & R.)

Neylon, Finbarr, CC
(on sabbatical)
(*Cabra West*, Dublin)

Neylon, Sean, Very Rev, PP
Taghmaconnell, Ballinasloe, Co Galway
Tel 090-9683929
(*Taghmaconnell*, Clonfert)

Ndugwa, Severinus, PC
No. 2 Presbytery,
St Canice's Parish,
Finglas, Dublin 11
Tel 087-8180097
(*Finglas*, Dublin)

Ng'hwagi Lucas (SJ) (AOR)
St Francis Xavier's,
Upper Gardener Street,
Dublin 1
Tel 01-8363411

Nguekam, Rodrigue Marino (CSSp), CC
Church of the Transfiguration,
The Presbytery,
Bawnogue, Clondalkin,
Dublin 22
(*Clondalkin, Bawnogue*, Dublin)

Ngussa Jipandile, Nobert, PC
Presbytery No. 2, 6 Old Hill,
Leixlip, Co Kildare
Tel 01-6243673
(*Leixlip*, Dublin)

Nicholas, Michael (OFM)
Guardian,
Franciscan Friary,
Friary Lane, Athlone,
Co Westmeath
Tel 090-6472095

Niyoyita, Kizito (SJ)
Jesuit Community,
27 Leinster Road,
Rathmines, Dublin 6
Tel 01-4970250

Nohilly, Michael (SMA), Adm
Parke, Castlebar, Co Mayo
Tel 094-9031314
(*Parke (Turlough)*, Tuam)

Nohilly, Seamus (SMA)
Superior,
SMA House,
Claregalway, Co Galway
Tel 091-798880

Nolan, Brendan, Very Rev, PP
Our Lady's Island,
Broadway, Co Wexford
Tel 053-9131167
(Ferns)

Nolan, Brian (CM)
All Hallows Institute for Mission and Ministry,
Drumcondra, Dublin 9
Tel 01-8373745/6

Nolan, Brian (CSsR)
Mount Saint Alphonsus,
Limerick
Tel 061-315099

Nolan, Bryan, PC
21 Wheatfield Grove,
Portmarnock, Dublin
Tel 01-8038970
(*Portmarnock*, Dublin)

Nolan, Damien
1a Laghtagoona,
Corofin, Co Clare
Tel 065-6837178/
086-8396636
(*Corofin*, Killaloe)

Nolan, Denis, CC
The Presbytery, Rathnew,
Co Wicklow
Tel 0404-67488/087-2389594
(*Wicklow*, Dublin)

Nolan, Francis
St John's Presbytery,
Tralee, Co Kerry
Tel 066-7122522
(*Tralee, St John's*, Kerry)

Nolan, J. Michael, Rt Rev Mgr
26 Harmony Avenue,
Donnybrook, Dublin 4
(Dublin, retired)

Nolan, J., Very Rev
36 Ashfield, Greenville,
Listowel, Co Kerry
(Kerry, retired)

Nolan, James, Very Rev, PP
Davidstown, Enniscorthy,
Co Wexford
Tel 053-9233382
(*Davidstown and Courtnacuddy*, Ferns)

Nolan, John P., Very Rev, PP
Duncannon, New Ross,
Co Wexford
Tel 051-389118
(*Duncannon*, Ferns)

Nolan, Mark-Ephrem M. (OSB), Very Rev Dom
Superior,
Benedictine Monks,
Holy Cross Monastery,
119 Kilbroney Road,
Rostrevor,
Co Down BT34 3BN
Tel 028-41739979

Nolan, Martin (OSA)
St John's Priory,
Thomas Street,
Dublin 8
Tel 01-6770393

Nolan, Martin (SMA)
Dromantine College,
Dromantine, Newry,
Co Down BT34 1RH
Tel 028-30821224

Nolan, Placid (OP)
Holy Cross, Tralee,
Co Kerry
Tel 066-7121135/29185

Nolan, Robert, Very Rev, PP
Adamstown, Enniscorthy,
Co Wexford
Tel 053-9240512
(*Adamstown*, Ferns)

Nolan, Rory, CC
The Presbytery, Carlow
Tel 059-9131227
(*Cathedral, Carlow*, Kildare & L.)

Nolan, Seán, Very Rev, PP
St Joseph's, Emyvale,
Monaghan
Tel 047-87152
(*Errigal Truagh*, Clogher)

Nolan, Simon (OCarm)
Gort Muire, Ballinteer,
Dublin 16
Tel 01-2984014

Nolan, Tod, Very Rev, PP
Killererin, Barnderg,
Tuam, Co Galway
Tel 093-49222
(*Killererin*, Tuam)

Noonan, Bernard, Rt Rev Mgr, PP, VG
Moate, Co Westmeath
Tel 090-6481180
(*Moate and Mount Temple*, Ardagh & Cl.)

Noonan, James (OCD)
Provincial,
53 Marlborough Road,
Donnybrook, Dublin 4
Tel 01-6617163/6601832

Noonan, James (SPS), CC
Foynes, Co Limerick
Tel 069-65165
(*Shanagolden and Foynes*, Limerick)

Noonan, Joseph, Very Rev, PP
Adare, Co Limerick
Tel 061-396172/
087-2400700
(*Adare*, Limerick)

Noonan, Mark (CM), Very Rev
Phibsboro,
St Peter's, Dublin 7
Tel 01-8389708/8389841

Noonan, Michael, Very Rev, PE
Portarlington, Co Laois
Tel 057-8623431
(Kildare & L., retired)

Noonan, Michael, Very Rev, PP
The Presbytery, Raheen,
Limerick
Tel 061-301112/
087-6796217
(*Mungret/Crecora*, Limerick)

Noone, Cletus (OFM)
Franciscan Friary,
Ennis, Co Clare
Tel 065-6828751

Noone, Martin G., Very Rev, PP, VF
(*Moderator*)
St Mary's Prebytery,
Willbrook Road,
Rathfarnham,
Dublin 14
Tel 01-4954554
(*Rathfarnham*, Dublin)

Noone, Sean
The Presbytery,
Pollathomas,
Co Mayo
(Dublin, retired)

Noone, Thomas, Very Rev, PP
69 Griffith Avenue,
Dublin 9
Tel 01-2694522/8367904
(*Marino*, Dublin)

Norman, James, PC
Dun Bhríd,
64 Orwell Park Rise,
Dublin 6W
Tel 01-8376027
(*Willington*, Dublin)

Norris, Thomas, Very Rev
4109 Ocean Drive,
Corpus Christi,
Texas 78411, USA
(Ossory)

Norton, Gerard (OP)
Prior, St Mary's Priory,
Tallaght, Dublin 24
Tel 01-4048100

Norton, Michael, Very Rev, PE
Rosbercon, New Ross,
Co Wexford
Tel 051-420333/
087-2580496
(*Rosbercon*, Ossory)

Nowak, Krzysztof (S.Pol)
Jesuit Community,
27 Leinster Road,
Rathmines,
Dublin 6
Tel 01-4970250

Nugent, Andrew (OSB)
Glenstal Abbey, Murroe,
Co Limerick
Tel 061-386103

Nugent, Eugene, Rt Rev Mgr, DCL
Apostolic Nunciature,
Villa Roma,
Ivandry BP 650,
101 Antananarivo,
Madagascar
(Killaloe)

Nugent, Jack (CSSp)
Holy Spirit Missionary College,
Kimmage Manor,
Whitehall Road, Dublin 12
Tel 01-4064300

Nugent, Sean, Very Rev, PE
6 James Street, Clonmel,
Co Tipperary
Tel 052-6136862
(Waterford & L., retired)

Nugent, William (CSSp)
Holy Spirit Missionary College,
Kimmage Manor,
Dublin 12
Tel 01-4064300

Nulty, Denis, Very Rev, PP, VF
St Mary's Drogheda,
Co Louth
Tel 041-9834958
(Meath)

Nwaogwugwu, Cornelius (CM)
St Vincent's College,
Castleknock,
Dublin 15
Tel 01-8213051

Nwnkuna, Hyacinth (CSSp)
Blackrock College,
Blackrock,
Co Dublin
Tel 01-2888681
(*Blackrock*, Dublin)

Nyambe, Shoba, PC
87B St Stephen's Green,
Dublin 2
Tel 01-4759674
(*University Church*, Dublin)

Nyhan, Charles, CC
Cork Road, Carrigaline,
Co Cork
Tel 021-4371860
(*Carrigaline*, Cork & R.)

Nyland, P. J. (SDB)
Rector, Salesian House,
Warrenstown, Drumree,
Co Meath
Tel 01-8259894

## O

Ó Baoighill, Padraig, PP
Derrybeg, Letterkenny,
Co Donegal
Tel 074-9531310
Séiplineach,
Pobalscoil Ghaoth Dobhair,
Derrybeg, Letterkenny,
Co Donegal
Tel 074-9531040
(*Gweedore*, Raphoe)

Ó Baoill, Donnchadh, CC
Bun-a-leaca, Letterkenny,
Co Donegal
Tel 074-9531155
(*Gweedore*, Raphoe)

Ó Bréartúin, Liam S. (OCD)
53/55 Marlborough Road,
Dublin 4
Tel 01-6601832

Ó Brolcháin, Cormac (CSSp)
Blackrock College,
Blackrock, Co Dublin
Tel 01-2888681

Ó Cairbre, Padraig (SJ)
Director of Retreat House/Vice-Rector,
Manresa House,
Dollymount, Dublin 3
Tel 01-8331352

Ó Ceallaigh, Fiachra, Most Rev, DD, VG
Former Titular Bishop of Tre Taverne and Auxiliary Bishop of Dublin,
19 St Anthony's Road,
Rialto, Dublin 8
Tel 01-4537495
(Dublin)

Ó Ceannahbáin, Colm, Very Rev, PE
An Tulach,
Baile na hAbhann
(Tuam)

Ó Cochláin, Seosamh
Chaplain, University College,
Iona, College Road, Cork
Tel 021-4902703
(Cork & R.)

Ó Conaire, Máirtín (OCD)
The Abbey, Loughrea,
Co Galway
Tel 091-841209

Ó Conghaile, Eamon, CC
Tiernea, Lettermore,
Co Galway
Tel 091-551133
(*Carraroe (Kileen)*, Tuam)

Ó Cuill, Pádraig (OFMCap)
Capuchin Friary,
Church Street, Dublin 7
Tel 01-8730599

Ó Cuinn, Conall (SJ)
Milltown Park,
Sandford Road,
Dublin 6
Tel 01-2698411/2698113

Ó Cuív, Liam, Very Rev, Co-PP
Blakestown, Clonsilla,
Dublin 15
Tel 01-8210874
(*Blakestown*, Dublin)

Ó Dálaigh, Micheál, Very Rev Canon, PP
The Presbytery,
Curraheen Road, Cork
Tel 021-4343535
(*Curraheen Road*, Cork & R.)

Ó Dálaigh, Tadhg (MSC)
Woodview House,
Mount Merrion Avenue,
Blackrock, Co Dublin
Tel 01-2881644

Ó Dochartaigh, Michael, Very Rev
Ard an Aonaigh,
Killarney, Co Kerry
(Kerry, retired)

Ó Dochartaigh, Tadhg, Very Rev, PP
Firies, Killarney, Co Kerry
Tel 066-9764122
(*Firies*, Kerry)

Ó Dómhnaill, Rúairí, CC
The Presbytery, Ballymany,
Droichead Nua, Co Kildare
Tel 045-434069
(*Droichead Nua/Newbridge*, Kildare & L.)

Ó Donnchadha, Gearoid
'An tSaoirse', Fenit, Tralee,
Co Kerry
(Kerry, retired)

Ó Dúill, Piaras (OFMCap)
Capuchin Friary,
Church Street, Dublin 7
Tel 01-8730599

Ó Dúill, Séamus (SDS), CC
Cill Chiarain, Galway
Tel 095-33403
(*Carna (Moyrus)*, Tuam)

O Duláine, Connla (SJ)
St Ignatius Community & Church,
27 Raleigh Row, Salthill,
Galway
Tel 091-523707

Ó Fatharta, Pádraig (SPS)
St Patrick's, Kiltegan,
Co Wicklow
Tel 059-6473600

Ó Fearghaill, Fergus, DSS
Carlow College,
College Street, Carlow
Tel 059-9153200
(Kildare & L.)

Ó Fearraí, Cathal, Very Rev, PP, VF
Ballyshannon, Raphoe
Tel 071-9851295
(Ballyshannon, Raphoe)

Ó Fiannachta, Pádraig, Rt Rev Mgr
An Diseart, Green Street,
Dingle, Co Kerry
(Kerry, retired)

Ó Galláchóir, Nigel, CC
Dungloe, Co Donegal
Tel 074-9522194
Chaplain,
Rosses Community School,
Dungloe, Co Donegal
Tel 074-9521122
(Raphoe)

Ó Gallchóir, Colm, Very Rev, PP
Killybegs, Co Donegal
Tel 074-9731030
(*Killybegs*, Raphoe)

Ó Gallchóir, Seán, Very Rev, PP
Tory Island, Co Donegal
Tel 074-9135214
(*Gortahork*, Raphoe)

Ó Giolláin, Leon (SJ)
Chaplain's Room,
St Stephen's, UCD,
Belfield, Dublin 4
(Dublin)

Ó Griofa, Gearóid, Very Rev, PP
Gort, Co Galway
Tel 091-631055
(Galway)

Ó h-Ici, Liam, Very Rev, PP
Ovens, Co Cork
Tel 021-4871180
(*Ovens*, Cork & R.)

O Hanlon, Denis Luke (OCSO)
Mount Melleray Abbey,
Cappoquin, Co Waterford
Tel 058-54404

Ó hAodha, Donncha
Nullamore,
Richmond Avenue South,
Dublin 6
Tel 01-4971239
(Opus Dei)

Ó hIceadha, Tomás, Very Rev, AP
Ballyferriter West, Tralee,
Co Kerry
Tel 066-9156499
(*Ballyferriter*, Kerry)

Ó hÓbáin, Eanna (OCarm)
Terenure College, Terenure,
Dublin 6W
Tel 01-4904621

Ó Huallacháin, Maelísa (OFM)
Franciscan House of Studies,
Dún Mhuire, Seafield Road,
Killiney, Co Dublin
Tel 01-2826760

Ó Lainn, Máirtín, Very Rev
Carraroe, Co Galway
(Tuam, retired)

Ó Laoide, Caoimhín (OFM)
Franciscan Friary, Ennis,
Co Clare
Tel 065-6828751

Ó Loingsigh, Micheál, CC
Midleton, Co Cork
Tel 021-4631354
(*Midleton*, Cloyne)

Ó Longaigh, Seán, Very Rev, PP
Askeaton, Co Limerick
Tel 061-392249
(*Askeaton and Ballysteen*, Limerick)

O Maidín, Uinsean (OCSO)
Mount Melleray Abbey,
Cappoquin, Co Waterford
Tel 058-54404

Ó Máille, Padraig (SPS)
St Patrick's, 21 Leeson Park,
Dublin 6
Tel 01-4977897

Ó Maoldhomhnaigh, Conn, MA
Chaplain, Carlow College,
College Street, Carlow
Tel 059-9153200
(Kildare & L.)

Ó Mathúna, Tadhg, Canon, SP
2 Parochial House,
Blackrock, Cork
Tel 021-4358025
(*Blackrock*, Cork & R.)

Ó Móráin, Tadhg, Very Rev, PE
Cornamona, Claremorris, Co Galway
Tel 094-9548003
(Tuam, retired)

Ó Murchú, Ailbe (OFM)
Vicar, Franciscan College, Gormanston, Co Meath
Tel 01-8412203

Ó Murchú, Tomás, Adm
Riverstick, Kinsale, Co Cork
Tel 021-4771332
(*Clontead*, Cork & R.)

Ó Riain, Diarmaid (OFM)
Franciscan Friary, Clonmel, Co Tipperary
Tel 052-6121378

Ó Sabhaois, Ciaran (OCSO)
Mount Saint Joseph Abbey, Roscrea, Co Tipperary
Tel 0505-25600

Ó Sabhaois, Tomás, Very Rev Canon, PE
Avila Nursing Home, Convent Hill, Bessbrook, Newry, Co Down BT35 7AW
(Armagh, retired)

Ó Seasnain, Feidhlim
Franciscan Friary, Ennis, Co Clare
Tel 065-6828751

Ó Siochrú, Colm R., CC
The Presbytery, Kilmead, Athy, Co Kildare
Tel 050-726117
(*Narraghmore*, Dublin)

Ó Súilleabháin, Pádraig (MSC), PP
Parish House, Leap, Skibbereen, Co Cork
Tel 028-33177
(*Leap-Glandore*, Cork & R.)

Ó Tuathaigh, Antoin
c/o Diocesan Office, Social Service Centre, Henry Street, Limerick
(Limerick, retired)

O'Beirne, James, Very Rev
Moate, Co Westmeath
(Ardagh & Cl., retired)

O'Boyle, Aidan, CC
Crossmolina, Ballina, Co Mayo
(*Crossmolina*, Killala)

O'Boyle, John, Rt Rev Mgr
Diocesan Resource Centre, St Jarlath's College, Bishop's Street, Tuam, Co Galway
Tel 093-52284
(Tuam)

O'Boyle, Kevin, (SSC)
Seafield, Quilty, Co Clare

O'Boyle, Paul, Very Rev, PP
Clane, Naas, Co Kildare
Tel 045-868249
(*Clane*, Kildare & L.)

O'Bric, Ailbe, Very Rev, PP
Clerihan, Clonmel, Co Tipperary
Tel 052-6135118
(*Clerihan*, Cashel & E.)

O'Brien, Anthony (OCSO)
Mount Saint Joseph Abbey, Roscrea, Co Tipperary
Tel 0505-25600

O'Brien, Anthony, Very Rev, PP
Carrigtwohill, Co Cork
Tel 021-4883236
(*Carrigtwohill*, Cloyne)

O'Brien, Augustine (MSC)
'Croí Nua', Rosary Lane, Taylor's Hill, Galway
Tel 091-520960

O'Brien, Ben (OSA)
(priest in residence), St Augustine's Priory, New Ross, Co Wexford
Tel 051421237

O'Brien, Brendan J. (CSSp)
Holy Spirit Missionary College, Kimmage Manor, Dublin 12
Tel 01-4064300

O'Brien, Chris (OSM), Very Rev
Servite Priory, Benburb, Dungannon, Co Tyrone, BT71 7JZ
Tel 028-37548241

O'Brien, Christopher, Very Rev, PE
Haroldstown, Tobinstown, Tullow, Co Carlow
Tel 059-9161633
(Armagh, retired)

O'Brien, Daniel (MSC)
Myross Wood Retreat House, Leap, Skibbereen, Co Cork
Tel 028-33118

O'Brien, Declan, Very Rev, PP
St Mary's Parish, 160 Foster Street, PO Box 22, Dandenong, VIC 3175, Australia
Tel 03-9791-4611
(Cloyne)

O'Brien, Donal, Very Rev, PP
Ballyvourney, Co Cork
Tel 026-45042
(*Ballyvourney*, Cloyne)

O'Brien, Eamon, Very Rev
No. 5 Hopecroft, Main Street, Glenavy BT29 4LN
(Down & C., retired)

O'Brien, Eamonn
Church Road, Croom, Co Limerick
Tel 061-397213/087-0767521
(*Croom*, Limerick)

O'Brien, Eamonn, Very Rev, PE
Newbrook Nursing Home, Mullingar, Co Westmeath
(Meath, retired)

O'Brien, Francis, Very Rev, PP
81 Castle Street, Ballymoney, Co Antrim BT53 6JT
Tel 028-27662003
(*Ballymoney and Derrykeighan*, Down & C.)

O'Brien, Gerard, Very Rev, PP
Bornacoola, Carrick-on-Shannon, Co Leitrim
Tel 071-9638229
(*Bornacoola*, Ardagh & Cl.)

O'Brien, Gregory, Very Rev, PP
2 Rossmore Road, Templeogue, Dublin 6W
Tel 01-8385244
(*Willington*, Dublin)

O'Brien, Humbert (OP)
St Magdalen's, Drogheda, Co Louth
Tel 041-9838271

O'Brien, James
Sacred Heart Residence, Sybil Hill Road, Killester, Dublin 5
(Dublin, retired)

O'Brien, James, Rt Rev Mgr
Congregation for Divine Worship and the Discipline of the Sacraments, Vatican City 00120, Italy
Tel 003906-69884551
(Cloyne)

O'Brien, James, Very Rev
Feakle, Co Clare
Tel 061-924035/087-2665793
(*Feakle, Killanena and Flagmount*, Killaloe)

O'Brien, John
'The Knock', Danville, Bennettsbridge Road, Kilkenny
Tel 087-6430620
(Ossory, retired)

O'Brien, John
Elmfield Mews, Spawell Road, Wexford
(Ferns, retired)

O'Brien, John (OFM)
Franciscan Friary, Friary Lane, Athlone, Co Westmeath
Tel 090-6472095

O'Brien, John (SMA)
Superior, SMA House, 82 Ranelagh Road, Ranelagh, Dublin 6
Tel 01-4968162/3

O'Brien, John, Adm
Parochial House, 199 Navan Road, Dublin 7
Tel 01-2768191
(*Navan Road*, Dublin)

O'Brien, John, PP
Borris, Co Carlow via Kilkenny
Tel 059-9773128
(*Borris*, Kildare & L.)

O'Brien, John, Very Rev, PP
Parochial House, Oristown, Kells, Co Meath
Tel 046-9054124
(*Oristown*, Meath)

O'Brien, Jordan (OP), Very Rev, PP
Prior, St Saviour's, Glentworth Street, Limerick
Tel 061-412333
(*St Saviour's*, Limerick)

O'Brien, Joseph (OP), Very Rev
Prior, St Dominic's, Athy, Co Kildare
Tel 059-8631573

O'Brien, Joseph, Very Rev, PP
Abbey, Tuam, Co Galway
Tel 093-43510
(*Abbeyknockmoy*, Tuam)

O'Brien, Kennedy (SJ)
Minister, Gonzaga College, Sandford Road, Dublin 6
Tel 01-4972943

O'Brien, Kieran (OSA)
Duckspool House (Retirement Community), Abbeyside, Dungarvan, Co Waterford
Tel 058-23784

O'Brien, Kieran, CC
St John's Presbytery, Tralee, Co Kerry
Tel 066-7122522
(*Tralee, St John's*, Kerry)

O'Brien, Leonard, Rt Rev Mgr, PP, VG
The Presbytery, Clonakilty, Co Cork
Tel 023-8833165
(*Clonakilty and Darrara*, Cork & R.)

O'Brien, Liam, AP
Killorglin, Co Kerry
Tel 066-9761160
(*Killorglin*, Kerry)

O'Brien, Liam (MSC)
Woodview House, Mount Merrion Avenue, Blackrock, Co Dublin
Tel 01-2881644

O'Brien, Lorcan, Rt Rev Mgr, VG
4 Walnut Ave., Drumcondra, Dublin 9
Tel 01-8379253/8372496
(*Drumcondra*, Dublin)

O'Brien, Martin, Very Rev, PP
Newline, Tulla, Co Clare
Tel 065-6835117/087-2504075
(*Tulla*, Killaloe)

O'Brien, Michael
St Anne's Presbytery,
Convent Hill, Waterford
Tel 051-855819
(*Ballybricken*, Waterford & L.)

O'Brien, Michael, Very Rev
Nazareth House, Mallow,
Co Cork
(Cork & R., retired)

O'Brien, Ned (SAC)
Provincial House,
'Homestead',
Sandyford Road, Dundrum,
Dublin 16
Tel 01-2956180/2954170

O'Brien, Pat (MI)
(Chaplain to St Luke's
Hospital),
St Camillus,
South Hill Avenue,
Blackrock, Co Dublin
Tel 01-2882873

O'Brien, Pat (SPS), CC
Curate's House, Prosperous,
Co Kildare
Tel 045-868187
(*Prosperous*, Kildare & L.)

O'Brien, Pat, Very Rev, PP
Caherlistrane, Co Galway
Tel 093-55428
(*Caherlistrane (Donaghpatrick and Kilcoona),* Tuam)

O'Brien, Patrick, Very Rev
Canon, AP
Tuamgraney, Co Clare
Tel 061-921056
(*Bodyke*, Killaloe)

O'Brien, Patrick, Very Rev, PP
Kilanerin, Gorey,
Co Wexford
Tel 0402-37120
(*Kilanerin*, Ferns)

O'Brien, Peter, Very Rev
Kilfian, Killala, Co Mayo
Tel 096-32420
(*Kilfian*, Killala)

O'Brien, Seamus
Chaplain,
Mater Private Hospital,
Dublin 7
Tel 01-8858888
(Dublin)

O'Brien, Sean (MHM)
St Joseph's House,
50 Orwell Park, Rathgar,
Dublin 6
Tel 01-4127700

O'Brien, Terence (MSC)
Carrignavar,
Co Cork
Tel 021-4884044

O'Brien, Timothy, Very Rev,
PP
Carrigatoher, Nenagh,
Co Tipperary
Tel 067-31231
(*Youghalarra*, Killaloe)

O'Brien, Valentine (CSSp)
Holy Spirit Missionary
College,
Kimmage Manor, Dublin 12
Tel 01-4064300

O'Byrne, Christopher, Rt Rev
Mgr Canon, PE, AP
Parochial House,
12 Aughrim Road,
Magherafelt,
Co Derry BT45 6AY
Tel 028-79634038
(*Magherafelt and Ardtrea North*, Armagh)

O'Byrne, Christopher, Very
Rev, PP
Lawrencetown, Ballinasloe,
Co Galway
Tel 090-9685613
(*Lawrencetown and Kiltormer*, Clonfert)

O'Byrne, Gerard, Very Rev, PP
Rathangan, Co Kildare
Tel 045-524316
(*Rathangan*, Kildare & L.)

O'Byrne, Hugh, Very Rev, PP
Blackwater, Enniscorthy,
Co Wexford
Tel 053-9127118
(*Blackwater*, Ferns)

O'Byrne, John, AP
St Mary's,
Athlunkard Street,
Limerick
Tel 061-414092
(*St Mary's*, Limerick)

O'Byrne, John Bosco (OFM)
Franciscan Friary,
Liberty Street, Cork
Tel 021-4270302

O'Byrne, Michael, Very Rev,
PP
Kilmeaden, Co Waterford
Tel 051-384117
(*Portlaw*, Waterford & L.)

O'Byrne, Patrick, PE, CC
Daingean, Co Offaly
Tel 057-9344161
(*Daingean*, Kildare & L.)

O'Byrne, Patrick, Co-PP
No. 2 The Presbytery,
Mountview,
Blanchardstown, Dublin 15
Tel 01-4510986
(Mountview, Dublin)

O'Byrne, Patrick J., CC
188 Lower Kilmacud Road,
Kilmacud, Co Dublin
Tel 01-4510986
(*Mount Merrion*, Dublin)

O'Byrne, Simon (OFM)
Franciscan House of Studies,
Dún Mhuire, Seafield Road,
Killiney, Co Dublin
Tel 01-2826760

O'Byrne, Thomas, CC
(priest in residence)
Priest's House, Emo,
Portlaoise, Co Laois
Tel 057-8646517
(*Emo*, Kildare & L.)

O'Byrne, William, Very Rev, PP
Kill, Co Kildare
Tel 045-878008
(Kildare & L.)

O'Callagahan, Flor (OSA)
St Augustine's Priory,
Dungarvan,
Co Waterford
Tel 058-41136

O'Callaghan, Benedict
(OCarm)
Terenure College, Terenure,
Dublin 6W
Tel 01-4904621

O'Callaghan, Ciarán (CSsR)
Vicar-Superior, Liguori
House,
75 Orwell Road, Dublin 6
Tel 01-4067100

O'Callaghan, Denis, Rt Rev
Mgr, PE
Mallow, Co Cork
Tel 022-21112
(Cloyne, retired)

O'Callaghan, Donal
Muintir Mhuire,
Ballybutler, Ladysbridge,
Co Cork
Tel 024-98852
(Cloyne, retired)

O'Callaghan, Edward (OFM)
Vicar, Franciscan Friary,
Lady Lane, Waterford
Tel 051-874262

O'Callaghan, Enda (SJ)
St Ignatius Community &
Church,
27 Raleigh Row, Salthill,
Galway
Tel 091-523707

O'Callaghan, John (OSB)
Glenstal Abbey, Murroe,
Co Limerick
Tel 061-386103

O'Callaghan, John P.
Mount Carmel, Carriglea,
Halfway House, Waterford
Tel 051-382919
(Waterford & L., retired)

O'Callaghan, John, Very Rev,
PP
Drimoleague, Co Cork
Tel 028-31133
(*Drimoleague*, Cork & R.)

O'Callaghan, Kevin, Rt Rev
Mgr, PP, VG
No. 2 Presbytery,
Curnaheen, Cork
Tel 021-4346775
(*Ballineaspaig*, Cork & R.)

O'Callaghan, Liam (MSC)
Carrignavar, Co Cork
Tel 021-4884044

O'Callaghan, Liam (SMA)
SMA House, Wilton, Cork
Tel 021-4541069/4541884

O'Callaghan, Martin, Very Rev
Prof
c/o 73 Somerton Road,
Belfast BT15 4DE
(Down & C., retired)

O'Callaghan, Peadar, Very
Rev, PE
Suimhneas, Charleville,
Co Cork
Tel 086-8054040
(Cloyne, retired)

O'Carroll, Caimin, Very Rev
Canon, AP
Barefield, Ennis, Co Clare
Tel 065-6821190/
087-2521388
(*Doora and Kilraghtis*, Killaloe)

O'Carroll, Ciarán, Very Rev,
Adm, EV
87A St Stephen's Green,
Dublin 2
Tel 01-4589002
(*University Church*, Dublin)

O'Carroll, Gerard (SPS)
St Patrick's, Main Street,
Knock, Co Mayo
Tel 094-9388661

O'Ciarain, Peadar
Sons of Divine Providence,
Orione House,
13 Lower Teddington Road,
Hampton, Wick,
Kinston-upon-Thames,
KT1 4EU
(Dublin, retired)

O'Cochláin, Pádraig, Very Rev,
PP
The Presbytery, 5 The Lawn,
Finglas, Dublin 11
Tel 01-8343110
(*Finglas*, Dublin)

O'Conaire, Máirlín (ODC),
Adm
St Andrew's Church, Leitrim,
Loughrea, Co Galway
Tel 091-841758
(Clonfert)

O'Connell, Alphonsus (OCSO)
Mount Melleray Abbey,
Cappoquin, Co Waterford
Tel 058-54404

O'Connell, Anthony, Very Rev,
PP
Rathnure, Co Wexford
Tel 054-55122
(*Rathnure*, Ferns)

O'Connell, Chrysostom (OCSO)
Our Lady of Bethlehem Abbey,
11 Ballymena Road,
Portglenone, Ballymena,
Co Antrim BT44 8BL
Tel 028-25821211

O'Connell, Ciaran, Very Rev
Rector,
Pontifical Irish College,
Via Dei SS. Quattro 1,
00184, Roma

O'Connell, Con (MSC)
Grace Dieu Retreat House,
Tramore Road, Waterford
Tel 051-374417/37337

O'Connell, David, CC
The Presbytery,
Bandon, Co Cork
(*Bandon*, Cork & R.)

O'Connell, Denis (OMI)
Oblate House of Retreat,
Inchicore, Dublin 8
Tel 01-4534408/4541805

O'Connell, Gerard, CC
Irremore, Listowel, Co Kerry
Tel 068-40244
(*Lixnaw*, Kerry)

O'Connell, James (SM), Very Rev, Adm
Holy Family Parish, Dundalk,
Co Louth
Tel 042-9336301
(*Dundalk, Holy Family*, Armagh)

O'Connell, James, Very Rev, PP
Stradbally, Co Laois
Tel 057-8625132
(Kildare & L.)

O'Connell, Jim (MHM)
Rector, St Joseph's,
Freshford House, Kilkenny
Tel 056-7721482

O'Connell, Jimmy (SM), Adm
Superior, Holy Family Parish,
Parochial House, Dundalk,
Co Louth
Tel 042-9336301
(*Holy Family*, Armagh)

O'Connell, John, Very Rev, AP
Moyne, Thurles,
Co Tipperary
Tel 0504-45129
(*Templetuohy*, Cashel & E.)

O'Connell, John, Very Rev, DD
53 Ardmore Wood,
The Presbytery,
Herbert Road, Bray,
Co Wicklow
Tel 01-2867309
(Dublin, retired)

O'Connell, John, Very Rev, PE
Caragh, Naas, Co Kildare
Tel 045-875602
(*Caragh*, Kildare & L.)

O'Connell, John (Seán) (CSSp)
Holy Spirit Missionary College,
Kimmage Manor, Dublin 12
Tel 01-406 4300

O'Connell, Liam (SJ)
Superior,
Crescent College Comprehensive,
Dooradoyle, Limerick
Tel 061-480920

O'Connell, Martin (SPS)
St Patrick's, Kiltegan,
Co Wicklow
Tel 059-6473600

O'Connell, Michael (MSC)
MSC Mission Support Centre,
PO Box 23, Western Road,
Cork
Tel 021-4545704

O'Connell, Michael, Very Rev Canon, PE
Buttevant, Co Cork
(Cloyne, retired)

O'Connell, Pat (CSsR)
Marianella, 75 Orwell Road,
Dublin 6
Tel 01-4067100

O'Connell, Patrick (MHM)
Vice-Rector,
St Joseph's House,
50 Orwell Park, Rathgar,
Dublin 6
Tel 01-4127700

O'Connell, Philip, Very Rev, PP
Ballylongford, Co Kerry
Tel 068-43110
(*Ballylongford*, Kerry)

O'Connell, Raymond (OSM), Very Rev
Servite Priory, Benburb,
Dungannon,
Co Tyrone, BT71 7JZ
Tel 028-37548241

O'Connell, Seamus
St Patrick's College,
Maynooth, Co Kildare
Tel 01-6285222
(Kerry)

O'Connell, T. J.
Kent, England
(Clonfert)

O'Connell, Terry
c/o Diocesan Office,
Social Service Centre,
Henry Street, Limerick
(Limerick)

O'Connell, Tomás, CC
Cathedral Presbytery,
Thurles, Co Tipperary
Tel 0504-22229/22779
(*Thurles, Cathedral of the Assumption*, Cashel & E.)

O'Connell, Vincent (CSSp), PC
Hospital Chaplain,
Hermitage Medical Centre,
Old Lucan Road, Dublin 20
Tel 01-6260900/6266241
(*Palmerstown*, Dublin)

O'Connor, Alphonsus (OCSO)
Mellifont Abbey, Collon,
Co Louth
Tel 041-9826103

O'Connor, Anthony, Very Rev, PP
Glenmore, via Waterford,
Co Kilkenny
Tel 051-880213/087-2517766
(*Glenmore*, Ossory)

O'Connor, Benjamin
c/o Cloyne Diocesan Centre,
Cobh, Co Cork
Tel 021-4811430
(Cloyne)

O'Connor, Bernard (SSC)
St Columban's Retirement Home,
Dalgan Park, Navan,
Co Meath
Tel 046-9021525

O'Connor, Brendan
Ely University Centre,
10 Hume Street, Dublin 2
Tel 01-6767420
(Opus Dei)

O'Connor, Charles (OMI)
170 Merrion Road,
Ballsbridge, Dublin 4
Tel 01-2693658

O'Connor, Charles (SJ)
Milltown Park,
Sandford Road, Dublin 6
Tel 01-2698411/2698113

O'Connor, Christopher (MHM)
St Joseph's House,
50 Orwell Park, Rathgar,
Dublin 6
Tel 01-4127700

O'Connor, Christopher, Very Rev Dean, PE
Craughwell, Co Galway
Tel 091-846124
(Galway, retired)

O'Connor, Columba (OSA)
Duckspool House
(Retirement Community),
Abbeyside, Dungarvan,
Co Waterford
Tel 058-23784

O'Connor, Dan (MSC)
Carrignavar, Co Cork
Tel 021-4884044

O'Connor, Daniel J., Rt Rev Mgr, PP, VF
St Michael's Parochial House,
4 Eblana Avenue,
Dun Laoghaire, Co Dublin
Tel 01-2801505/
087-7425862
(*Dun Laoghaire*, Dublin)

O'Connor, Daniel, Very Rev Canon, PE
The Presbytery, Dungarvan,
Co Waterford
Tel 058-42381
(Waterford & L., retired)

O'Connor, David (CSSp)
Holy Spirit Missionary College,
Kimmage Manor, Dublin 12
Tel 01-4064300

O'Connor, Declan, Very Rev Canon, PP, VF
Listowel, Co Kerry
Tel 068-21188
(*Listowel*, Kerry)

O'Connor, Denis, (CSsR) CC
32 Auburn Drive,
Dublin 15
Tel 01-8214003
(*Castleknock*, Dublin)

O'Connor, Denis, Very Rev Dean, PE
2 Woodlawn,
Model Farm Road,
Ballineaspaig, Cork
Tel 021-4542972
(Cork & R., retired)

O'Connor, Dermot (CSsR)
St Patrick's, Esker, Athenry,
Co Galway
Tel 091-844549

O'Connor, Dermot (SJ)
Irish Jesuit Provincialate,
Milltown Park, Sandford Road, Dublin 6
Tel 01-4987333

O'Connor, Dominic (OP)
St Dominic's, Athy,
Co Kildare
Tel 059-8631573

O'Connor, Donal (SMA)
Retired in Ireland outside SMA houses

O'Connor, Donal, PP
The Presbytery, Beaufort
Co Kerry
Tel 064-6644128
(*Beaufort*, Kerry)

O'Connor, Eamonn, Very Rev, PP
Rooskey, Carrick-on-Shannon,
Co Roscommon
Tel 071-9638014
(*Kilglass*, Elphin)

O'Connor, Edward (SMA)
Vice-Superior,
African Missions,
Blackrock Road, Cork
Tel 021-4292871

O'Connor, Erill D., Very Rev Canon
14 Clare Road,
Drumcondra, Dublin 9
(Dublin, retired)

O'Connor, Fergus, Very Rev, (Opus Dei) PP
31 Herbert Avenue,
Dublin 4
Tel 01-2691825
(*Merrion Road*, Dublin)

O'Connor, Frank
c/o Limerick Diocesan Pastoral Centre,
St Michael's Courtyard,
Denmark Street, Limerick
Tel 061-400133
(Limerick)

O'Connor, Gerard, PP
Aglish, Cappoquin,
Co Waterford
Tel 024-96287
(*Aglish*, Waterford & L.)

O'Connor, Gerry (CSsR), CC
52 Elmdale Park,
Dublin 10
Tel 01-6233813
(*Cherry Orchard*, Dublin)

O'Connor, James (CSsR)
Mount Saint Alphonsus,
Limerick
Tel 061-315099

O'Connor, John (SAC), Very Rev, PP
Provincial Secretary,
St Benin's, Dublin Road,
Shankill, Co Dublin
Tel 01-2824425
(*Shankill*, Dublin)

O'Connor, John C., Very Rev
Director, Our Lady's Home,
68 Ard Na Va Road,
Belfast BT12 6FF
Tel 028-90325731/90242429
(Down & C.)

O'Connor, Joseph, PP
Parochial House,
Plumbridge, Omagh,
Co Tyrone BT79 8EF
Tel 028-81648283
(Derry, retired)

O'Connor, Kevin
Oblate House of Retreat,
Inchicore, Dublin 8
Tel 01-4534408/4541805

O'Connor, Laurence, Very Rev, PP
Ballycullane, New Ross,
Co Wexford
Tel 051-562123
(*Ballycullane*, Ferns)

O'Connor, Liam (OCSO)
Mount Saint Joseph Abbey,
Roscrea, Co Tipperary
Tel 0505-25600

O'Connor, Martin, Very Rev, PP
Ballindine, Co Mayo
Tel 094-9364423
(*Ballindine (Kilvine),* Tuam)

O'Connor, Michael (CSSp), CC
Presbytery No. 2,
Church Grounds,
Kill Avenue, Dun Laoghaire,
Co Dublin
Tel 01-2140863
(*Kill-O'-The-Grange*, Dublin)

O'Connor, Michael (OMI), Very Rev
(*Moderator*)
Oblate Fathers,
House of Retreat, Inchicore,
Dublin 8
Tel 01-454111
(*Inchicore, Mary Immaculate*, Dublin)

O'Connor, Michael G. (CSsR)
Mount Saint Alphonsus,
Limerick
Tel 061-315099

O'Connor, Michael, Very Rev
c/o St John's Pastoral Centre,
John's Hill, Waterford
(Waterford & L.)

O'Connor, Muiris, Very Rev, PP, VF
Ballybrown, Clarina,
Co Limerick
Tel 061-353711/086-6075628
(*Patrickswell/Ballybrown*, Limerick)

O'Connor, Padraig, Very Rev Canon, PP, VF
Mountbellew, Ballinasloe,
Co Galway
Tel 090-9679235
(*Moylough and Mountbellew*, Tuam)

O'Connor, Pat (CSsR)
Vicar, Clonard Monastery,
1 Clonard Gardens,
Belfast, BT13 2RL
Tel 028-90445950

O'Connor, Patrick, Very Rev, PP, VF
Parochial House, Athboy,
Co Meath
Tel 046-9432184
(Meath)

O'Connor, Peter, CC
10 Cranfield Place,
Sandymount, Dublin 4
Tel 01-6676438
(*Sandymount*, Dublin)

O'Connor, Peter, Very Rev, PP
12 Brookwood Grove,
Artane, Dublin 5
Tel 01-8312390
(*Artane*, Dublin)

O'Connor, Philip, Very Rev, PP
Parochial House, Dysart,
Mullingar, Co Westmeath
Tel 044-9226122
(*Dysart*, Meath)

O'Connor, Richard
c/o Diocesan Offices,
Killarney, Co Kerry
(Kerry)

O'Connor, Seamus (SSC)
St Columban's, Dalgan Park,
Navan, Co Meath
Tel 046-9021525

O'Connor, Sean
St John's College, Kilkenny
Tel 056-7756889
(Ossory)

O'Connor, Thomas, DD
St Patrick's College,
Maynooth, Co Kildare
Tel 01-6285222
(Meath)

O'Connor, Timothy (SPS)
On temporary diocesan work

O'Connor, Tom (OSCam)
St Camillus,
South Hill Avenue,
Blackrock, Co Dublin

O'Connor, Tom (SPS)
St Patrick's, Kiltegan,
Co Wicklow
Tel 059-6473600

O'Conor, Joe (SPS)
St Patrick's, Kiltegan,
Co Wicklow
Tel 059-6473600

O'Conor, Patrick (SSC), CC
Mulrankin, Co Wexford
Tel 053-9135166
(*Kilmore*, Ferns)

O'Cuilleanáin, Fionnbarra (SMA)
African Missions,
Blackrock Road, Cork
Tel 021-4292871

O'Cuiv, Shan, PC
c/o The Presbytery,
Clondalkin, Dublin 22
Tel 01-4573440
(*Clondalkin*, Dublin)

O'Dea, Francis, Very Rev, PP
Dromcollogher, Charleville,
Co Limerick
Tel 087-2443106
(*Dromcollogher/Broadford*, Limerick)

O'Dea, Tom
Ballynacally, Co Clare
Tel 065-6838135/
086-8107475
(*Ballynacally*, Killaloe)

O'Doherty, Bartie (SPS)
St Patrick's, Kiltegan,
Co Wicklow
Tel 059-6473600

O'Doherty, Colm, PP
16 Castlefin Road,
Castlederg,
Co Tyrone BT81 7EB
Tel 028-81671393
(*Castlederg*, Derry)

O'Doherty, Daniel, Very Rev, PE
Ballyheerin, Fanad,
Co Donegal
(Raphoe, retired)

O'Doherty, Donal, Very Rev Mgr, PE
Holy Cross,
Upper Kilmacud Road,
Dundrum, Dublin 14
Tel 01-2985264
(Dublin, retired)

O'Doherty, Kevin (SPS)
St Patrick's, Kiltegan,
Co Wicklow
Tel 059-6473600

O'Doherty, Kevin, Very Rev, PE
Falcarragh, Co Donegal
Tel 074-9165356
(Raphoe, retired)

O'Doherty, Kieran, Very Rev, PP, VF
34 Moneysharvin Road,
Swatragh, Maghera,
Co Derry BT46 5PY
Tel 028-79401236
(Derry)

O'Doherty, Michael, Very Rev Canon
No. 1 Lynch Heights,
Sun Hill, Killorglin,
Co Kerry
(Kerry, retired)

O'Doherty, Oliver, Very Rev
The Presbytery, Church Road, Nenagh,
Co Tipperary
(Killaloe, retired)

O'Doherty, Seán, Very Rev Canon, PP
Durrow, Portlaoise, Co Laois
Tel 057-8736156
(*Durrow*, Ossory)

O'Donnell, Anthony (SMA)
African Missions,
Blackrock Road, Cork
Tel 021-4292871

O'Donnell, Brian, CC
157 Glen Road, Maghera,
Co Derry BT46 5JN
Tel 028-79642359
(*Maghera*, Derry)

O'Donnell, Chris
Limerick Diocesan Pastoral Centre,
St Michael's Courtyard,
Denmark Street, Limerick
Tel 061-4001330
(Limerick)

O'Donnell, Christopher (OCarm)
Terenure College, Terenure,
Dublin 6W
Tel 01-4904621

O'Donnell, Columba (OSA)
Duckspool House
(Retirement Community),
Abbeyside, Dungarvan,
Co Waterford
Tel 058-23784

O'Donnell, Cornelius, Very Rev, PP
Rathcormac, Fermoy,
Co Cork
Tel 025-36286
(*Rathcormac*, Cloyne)

O'Donnell, Desmond (OMI)
Oblate House of Retreat,
Inchicore, Dublin 8
Tel 01-4534408/4541805

O'Donnell, Edward (SJ)
Gonzaga College,
Sandford Road, Dublin 6
Tel 01-4972943

O'Donnell, Edward, Very Rev, PP
42 Derryvolgie Avenue,
Belfast BT9 6FP
Tel 028-90665409
(*St Brigid's*, Down & C.)

O'Donnell, Gerard, Very Rev, PP
Geesla, Bangor, Ballina,
Co Mayo
Tel 097-86740
(*Kiltane*, Killala)

O'Donnell, Hugh (OFM)
Franciscan House of Studies,
Dún Mhuire, Seafield Road,
Killiney, Co Dublin
Tel 01-2826760

O'Donnell, Hugh (SDB), CC
Rinaldi House,
72 Sean McDermott Street,
Dublin 1
Tel 01-8363358
(*Sean Mc Dermott Street,* Dublin)

O'Donnell, James, CC
Bohermore, Cashel,
Co Tipperary
Tel 062-61409
(Cashel & E.)

O'Donnell, James, Rt Rev Mgr, AP
Macroom, Co Cork
Tel 026-41042
(*Macroom*, Cloyne)

O'Donnell, Joe, CC
Carnamuggagh Lower,
Letterkenny, Co Donegal
Tel 074-9122608
(*Aughaninshin*, Raphoe)

O'Donnell, John, Very Rev
9 Rockview, Blacklion,
Co Cavan
(*Killinagh and Glangevlin*, Kilmore)

O'Donnell, Louis (OSA)
St John's Priory,
Thomas Street,
Dublin 8
Tel 01-6770393

O'Donnell, Michael (MSC)
MSC Mission Support Centre,
PO Box 23, Western Road,
Cork
Tel 021-4545704

O'Donnell, Owen, Very Rev, PE
Parochial House, Dunamore,
Cookstown, Co Tyrone
Tel 028-86751216
(Armagh, retired)

O'Donnell, P.J.
c/o Diocesan Office,
Social Service Centre,
Henry Street, Limerick
(Limerick, retired)

O'Donnell, Pat, Very Rev, PP
Milltown, Co Kerry
Tel 066-9767312
(*Milltown*, Kerry)

O'Donnell, Patrick (CSsR)
Clonard Monastery,
1 Clonard Gardens,
Belfast, BT13 2RL
Tel 028-90445950

O'Donnell, Terence (IC)
Clonturk House,
Ormond Road,
Drumcondra, Dublin 9
Tel 01-6877014

O'Donoghue, Brendan, Very Rev Canon, AP
12 Tullyglass Square,
Shannon, Co Clare
Tel 061-361257/086-8308153
(*Shannon*, Killaloe)

O'Donoghue, Fergus (SJ)
35 Lower Leeson Street,
Dublin 2
Tel 01-6761248

O'Donoghue, James (MHM), CC
St Mary's, Marquis Street,
Belfast BT1 1JJ
Tel 028-90320482
(*St Mary's*, Down & C.)

O'Donoghue, James, CC
Holyford, Co Tipperary
Tel 062-71104
(*Kilcommon*, Cashel & E.)

O'Donoghue, James, CC
Kilsheelan, Clonmel,
Co Tipperary
Tel 052-6133292
(*Kilsheelan*, Waterford & L.)

O'Donoghue, Jim (MHM)
St Mary's Parish,
25 Marquis Street,
Belfast BT1 1JJ
Tel 028-90320482
(*St Mary's*, Down & C.)

O'Donoghue, Neville (SM)
St Columba's,
Church Avenue, Ballybrack,
Co Dublin
Tel 01-2858301

O'Donoghue, Patrick, CC
Pro-Cathedral House,
83 Marlborough Street,
Dublin 1
Tel 01-8745441
(*Pro-Cathedral*, Dublin)

O'Donoghue, Patrick, Most Rev, AP
The Presbytery, Bantry,
Co Cork
Tel 027-50082
(*Bantry*, Cork and R.)

O'Donoghue, Paul, CC
The Lough Presbytery,
St Finbarr's West, Cork
Tel 021-4322633
(*The Lough*, Cork & R.)

O'Donoghue, Sean (CSSp)
Holy Spirit Missionary College,
Kimmage Manor, Dublin 12
Tel 01-4064300

O'Donohoe, Joseph (OPraem)

O'Donohue, Neville (SM)
St Columba's,
Church Avenue, Ballybrack,
Co Dublin
Tel 01-2858301

O'Donohue, Patrick
Chaplain, NUI, Galway
Tel 091-495055/582179

O'Donohue, Vincent, Very Rev Canon, PE
18 Kilcrea Park,
Magazine Road,
Co Cork
Tel 021-4856881
(Cloyne, retired)

O'Donovan, Chris, AP
Lissavaird, Rosscarbery,
Co Cork
Tel 023-8834334
(*Rosscarbery and Lissavaird*, Cork & R.)

O'Donovan, Colman, Very Rev Canon, PE
1 Youghal Road, Midleton,
Co Cork
Tel 021-4621617
(Cloyne, retired)

O'Donovan, Con, Very Rev, PE
16 Deer Park Avenue,
St Joseph's Road, Mallow,
Co Cork
Tel 022-51948
(Cloyne, retired)

O'Donovan, Dan
Creagh, Ballinasloe,
Co Galway
Tel 090-9645080
(Clonfert)

O'Donovan, Ignatius (OSA)
St Augustine's Priory,
Shop Street,
Drogheda, Co Louth
Tel 041-9838409

O'Donovan, James, Very Rev Canon, PP
Ballinlough, Cork
Tel 021-4292296
(*Ballinlough*, Cork & R.)

O'Donovan, John
PO Box 897, Oldsmar,
Florida 34677, USA
(Killaloe)

O'Donovan, John, CC
The Presbytery,
Dunmanway, Co Cork
Tel 028-8845000
(*Dunmanway*, Cork & R.)

O'Donovan, John, Very Rev, PP
Parochial House,
Hattons Alley,
Blackpool, Cork
Tel 021-4501022
(*Blackpool/The Glen*, Cork & R.)

O'Donovan, Michael, Very Rev, PP
The Presbytery, Caheragh,
Co Cork
Tel 028-31126
(*Caheragh*, Cork & R.)

O'Donovan, Padraig (SSC)
St Columban's, Dalgan Park,
Navan, Co Meath
Tel 046-9021525

O'Donovan, Pat, CC
Monkstown, Co Cork
Tel 021-4863267
(*Monkstown*, Cork & R.)

O'Donovan, Paul (OFMCap)
Guardian,
St Francis Capuchin Friary,
Rochestown, Co Cork
Tel 021-4896244

O'Donovan, Raymond (OP)
Newbridge College,
Droichead Nua, Co Kildare
Tel 045-487200

O'Donovan, Tadhg
(priest in residence)
Mallow, Co Cork
(*Mallow*, Cloyne)

O'Donovan, William (OMI)
Oblate House of Retreat,
Inchicore, Dublin 8
Tel 01-4534408/4541805

O'Donovan, William, Very Rev, PP
Conna, Mallow, Co Cork
Tel 058-59138
(*Conna*, Cloyne)

O'Dowd, Gabriel, CC
The Presbytery,
St Margaret's, Finglas,
Dublin 11
Tel 01-8341009
(*Finglas*, Dublin)

O'Dowd, Sean (SPS), CC
Deerpark Road, Athlone,
Co Westmeath
Tel 090 6490575
(*Athlone, SS Peter and Paul's*, Elphin)

O'Driscoll, Aidan, Very Rev, PP
The Presbytery,
Upper Mayfield, Cork
Tel 021-4503116
(*Upper Mayfield*, Cork & R.)

O'Driscoll, Eamonn (OFM)
Guardian, Franciscan Friary,
Lady Lane, Waterford
Tel 051-874262

O'Driscoll, Fachtna (SMA)
Provincial, African Missions,
Provincial House, Feltrim,
Blackrock Road, Cork
Tel 021-4292871

O'Driscoll, Kieron, PP
Barrett's Hill, Ballinhassig,
Co Cork
Tel 021-4885104
(*Ballinhassig*, Cork & R.)
O'Driscoll, Liam, Canon, Adm
Diocesan Offices,
Redemption Road, Cork
Tel 021-4301717
Administrator
Church of the Most Precious Blood,
Clogheen, Co Cork
Tel 021-4392122
(Cork & R.)
O'Driscoll, Martin, Very Rev, PP
North Street,
Skibbereen, Co Cork
Tel 028-22878
(*Rath and the Islands*, Cork & R.)
O'Driscoll, Michael
Bushmount, Clonakilty,
Co Cork
Tel 023-33991
(Cork & R., retired)
O'Driscoll, Neil (SJ)
(residing elsewhere)
St Francis Xavier's,
Upper Gardiner Street,
Dublin 1
Tel 01-8363411
O'Driscoll, P.J., CC
Monument Hill, Fermoy,
Co Cork
Tel 087-6490381
(*Fermoy*, Cloyne)
O'Driscoll, Paul, CC
3 Stanhope Place, Athy
Tel 0402-32196
(*Athy*, Dublin)
O'Driscoll, Philip, CC
23 Barclay Court, Blackrock,
Co Dublin
Tel 01-2883329
(Dublin, retired)
O'Driscoll, Sean, CC
Ballyphehane, Co Cork
Tel 021-4310835
(*Ballyphehane*, Cork & R.)
O'Driscoll, Timothy (CSSp)
Holy Spirit Missionary College,
Kimmage Manor,
Whitehall Road, Dublin 12
Tel 01-4064300
O'Duill, Feargal (LC)
Vocations Director,
Leopardstown Road,
Foxrock, Dublin 18
Tel 01-2955902
O'Dwyer, Christy, Rt Rev Mgr, PP, VG
Diocesan Archivist,
Bohermore, Cashel,
Co Tipperary
Tel 062-61127
(*Cashel*, Cashel & E.)

O'Dwyer, John, Very Rev Dean, PP
Oranmore, Co Galway
Tel 091-794634
(*Oranmore*, Galway)
O'Dwyer, Michael (SAC), CC
9 Seaview Lawn, Shankill,
Co Dublin
Tel 01-2822277
(*Shankill*, Dublin)
O'Dwyer, Michael, Very Rev, PP, VF
Parochial House,
15 Moy Road, Portadown,
Co Armagh BT62 1QL
Tel 028-38350610
(*Portadown (Drumcree)*, Armagh)
O'Dwyer, Richard (SJ)
Irish Jesuit Provincialate,
Milltown Park,
Sandford Road, Dublin 6
Tel 01-4987333
O'Dwyer, Sean, Very Rev, PP
Parochial House, Cahir,
Co Tipperary
Tel 052-7441404
(*Cahir*, Waterford & L.)
O'Farrell, Ambrose (OP)
47 Leeson Park, Dublin 6
Tel 01-6602427
O'Farrell, Anthony (CSSp)
Holy Spirit Missionary College,
Kimmage Manor, Dublin 12
Tel 01-406 4300
O'Farrell, Donal (SSC)
St Columban's Retirement Home,
Dalgan Park, Navan,
Co Meath
Tel 046-9021525
O'Farrell, Eddie (CSSp)
Provincial Secretary,
Holy Spirit Provincialate,
Temple Park,
Richmond Avenue South,
Dublin 6
Tel 01-4975127/4977230
O'Farrell, Martin, Very Rev, PP
Aghadoe, Kinsaley Lane,
Malahide, Co Dublin
Tel 01-8461767
(*Kinsealy*, Dublin)
O'Farrell, Patrick, Very Rev, PP
Lisdowney, Ballyragget,
Co Kilkenny
Tel 056-8833138/
087-2353520
(*Lisdowney*, Ossory)
O'Farrell, Peter, CC
Cobh, Co Cork
Tel 021-4855983
(*Cobh*, St Colman's Cathedral, Cloyne)

O'Fearghail, Fearghus, PC
St Laurence O'Toole's
Presbytery, 49 Seville Place,
Dublin 1
Tel 01-8740796
(*Northwall, Seville Place*, Dublin)
O'Fearraí, Cathal, Very Rev, PP, VF
Ballyshannon, Co Donegal
(Raphoe)
O'Fearraigh, Brian, CC
Derrybeg, Letterkenny
Tel 074-9531947
Séiplineach, Pobalscoil
Chloich Cheannfhaola,
Falcarragh, Letterkenny,
Co Donegal
Tel 074-9135424/9135231
(Raphoe)
O'Flaherty, Michael
School of Law,
University of Nottingham,
University Park,
Nottingham NG7 2RD,
England
(Galway)
O'Flaherty, Séan, Rt Rev Mgr, PE
Parkmore, Castlegar,
Galway
Tel 091-764764
(Galway, retired)
O'Flynn, Ciaran (SPS)
On temporary diocesan work
O'Flynn, Finbarr, CC
Dungourney, Co Cork
Tel 021-4668406
(*Imogeela (Castlemartyr)*, Cloyne)
O' Flynn, Michael (CSsR)
St Patrick's, Esker, Athenry,
Co Galway
Tel 091-844549
O'Flynn, Silvester (OFMCap)
Guardian, Capuchin Friary,
Ard Mhuire, Creeslough,
Letterkenny, Co Donegal
Tel 074-9138005
O'Flynn, Thomas (OP)
St Mary's Priory, Tallaght,
Dublin 24
Tel 01-4048100
O'Gara, Frank (OCarm), PP
Terenure College, Terenure,
Dublin 6W
Tel 01-4904621
O'Gorman, Charles, Very Rev, PP
Blacklion, Co Cavan
Tel 071-9853012
(*Killinagh and Glangevlin*, Kilmore)
O'Gorman, Daniel, CC
Herbertstown, Hospital,
Co Limerick
Tel 061-385104
(Cashel & E.)

O'Gorman, Eamonn, Very Rev, PP
Seir Kieran, Clareen,
Birr, Co Offaly
Tel 0509-31080/087-2236145
(*Mooncoin*, Ossory)
O'Gorman, John, Very Rev, PP
Menlough, Ballinasloe,
Co Galway
Tel 090-9684818
(*Menlough (Killascobe)*, Tuam)
O'Gorman, Kevin (SMA)
St Patrick's College,
Maynooth
O'Gorman, Maurice, Very Rev, PP
Clashmore, Co Waterford
Tel 024-96110
(*Clashmore*, Waterford & L.)
O'Gorman, Patrick, Very Rev, PP
Golden, Co Tipperary
Tel 062-72146
(*Golden*, Cashel & E.)
O'Gorman, Tom
Cloughleigh Presbytery,
1 Shallee Drive,
Cloughleigh, Ennis, Co Clare
Tel 065-6840715
(*Ennis*, Killaloe)
O'Gorman, William, Very Rev, PP
Tournafulla, Co Limerick
Tel 069-81010/087-2580020
(*Tournafulla/Mountcollins*, Limerick)
O'Grady, Desmond (SJ)
Gonzaga College,
Sandford Road, Dublin 6
Tel 01-4972943
O'Grady, James, Very Rev, PP
Headford, Co Galway
Tel 093-35448
(Tuam)
O'Grady, Michael, CC
264 Howth Road, Killester,
Dublin 5
Tel 01-8533466
(*Killester*, Dublin)
O'Grady, Nicholas (CP)
St Paul's Retreat,
Mount Argus, Dublin 6W
Tel 01-4992000
O'Grady, Peter (OFM)
The Abbey, 8 Francis Street,
Galway
Tel 091-562518
O'Grady, Vincent (CSSp)
Holy Spirit Missionary College,
Kimmage Manor, Dublin 12
Tel 01-406 4300
O'Hagan, Eugene, Very Rev,
Lisbreen, 73 Somerton Road,
Belfast BT15 4DE
Tel 028-90776185
(Down & C.)

O'Hagan, Francis, PP
71 Duncrun Road,
Bellarena, Limavady,
Co Derry BT49 0JD
Tel 028-77750226
(*Magilligan*, Derry)

O'Hagan, Hugh J., Very Rev, PP
Parochial House,
31 Ballynafie Road,
Ahoghill BT42 1LF
Tel 028-25871351
(*Ahoghill*, Down & C.)

O'Hagan, Joseph, Very Rev Canon
Cabra, Hilltown
(Dromore, retired)

O'Hagan, Mark, Very Rev, Adm
St Patrick's Presbytery,
Roden Place, Dundalk,
Co Louth
Tel 042-9334648
(*Dundalk, St Patrick's*, Armagh)

O'Hagan, Martin, Very Rev, PP
71 North Street,
Newtownards,
Co Down BT23 4JD
Tel 028-91812137
(*Newtownards*, Down & C.)

O'Hagan, Patrick, PP
Parochial House, Moyville,
Co Donegal
Tel 074-9382057
(Derry)

O'Halloran, Giles (OSA)
St John's Priory,
Thomas Street, Dublin 8
Tel 01-6770393

O'Halloran, J.A., Very Rev Canon, PE
An Teaghlach Uilinn,
Moycullen, Co Galway
Tel 091-555444
(Galway, retired)

O'Halloran, James (SDB)
Rinaldi House,
72 Sean Mc Dermott Street,
Dublin 1
Tel 01-8363358

O'Halloran, Richard, CC
41 Lismore Park, Waterford
Tel 051-354034
(*St Paul's*, Waterford & L.)

O'Halloran, Tom, Very Rev
Borrisokane, Co Tipperary
Tel 067-27105
(Killaloe)

O'Hanlon, David
Pontifico Colegio Portugues,
Via Nicolo V,
2-00165 Roma, Italy
(Meath)

O'Hanlon, Denis, Very Rev, PP
Lisgoold
Tel 021-4642363
(*Carrigtwohill*, Cloyne)

O'Hanlon, Denis Luke (OCSO)
Mount Melleray Abbey,
Cappoquin, Co Waterford
Tel 058-54404

O'Hanlon, Francis, Very Rev, PP
Shannonbridge, Athlone,
Co Westmeath
Tel 090-9674125
(*Shannonbridge*, Ardagh & Cl.)

O'Hanlon, George, Very Rev Canon
(priest in residence)
62 Coolkeeran Road,
Armoy, Ballymoney,
Co Antrim BT53 8XN
Tel 028-20751121
(*Loughguile*, Down & C.)

O'Hanlon, Gerard (SJ)
25 Croftwood Park,
Cherry Orchard, Dublin 10
Tel 01-6267413

O'Hara, Emmet (SAC)
Pallottine College, Thurles,
Co Tipperary
Tel 0504-21202

O'Hara, Vincent (OCD)
Avila, Bloomfield Avenue,
Morehampton Road,
Dublin 4
Tel 01-6430200

O'Hare, Martin (SMA), CC
St Patrick's Presbytery,
Ballina, Co Mayo
Tel 096-71360
(*Ballina*, Killala)

O'Hare, Paddy (SM)
Japan

O'Hare, Peter, Very Rev, PP
16 Rossglas Road,
Killough,
Co Down BT30 7QQ
Tel 028-44841221
(*Killough (Bright)*, Down & C.)

O'Hea, James (SMA)
SMA House, Wilton, Cork
Tel 021-4541069/4541884

O'Hea, Jarlath (OCarm)
Whitefriar Street Church,
56 Aungier Street, Dublin 2
Tel 01-4758821

O'Herlihy, Pat (SSC)
No. 2 Presbytery,
Our Lady Crowned Church,
Mayfield Upper, Cork
Tel 021-4508610/

O'Higgins, Kevin (SJ)
Arrupe Community,
217 Silloge Road, Ballymun,
Dublin 9
Tel/Fax 01-8625345

O'Holohan, John (SJ)
St Francis Xavier's,
Upper Gardiner Street,
Dublin 1
Tel 01-8363411

O'Hora, Gerard, Very Rev
Cathedral Presbytery,
Ballina, Co Mayo
Tel 096-71365
(*Ballina*, Killala)

O'Horo, Michael, Very Rev, PP
Skreen, Co Sligo
Tel 071-9166629
(*Skreen and Dromard*, Killala)

O'Kane, David, CC
9 Church Street, Claudy,
Derry BT47 4AA
Tel 028-71337727
(*Claudy*, Derry)

O'Kane, Hugh (SMA), CC
(priest in residence)
53 Ballinlea Road,
Ballycastle,
Co Antrim BT54 6JL
Tel 028-20762498
(*Ballintoy*, Down & C.)

O'Kane, James, Very Rev, PP
Parochial House,
121 Dublin Road,
Kilcoo, Co Down BT34 5HP
Tel 028-40630314
(*Kilcoo*, Down and C.)

O'Kane, Patrick, PP
1 Aileach Road,
Ballymagroarty,
Derry BT48 0AZ
Tel 028-71267070
(Derry)

O'Kane, Peter, CC
Pontificio Collegio Irlandese,
Via Dei SS Quattro 1,
00184 Roma, Italy
(Derry)

O'Kane, Peter, Very Rev, PP
2A My Lady's Mile,
Holywood,
Co Down BT18 9EW
Tel 028-90422167
(*Holywood*, Down & C.)

O'Kane, Seamus
12 Gortinure Road,
Maghera,
Co Derry BT46 5RB
Tel 07989-946344
(Derry)

O'Keefe, Fergus (SJ)
Minister,
John Sullivan House,
56/56A Mulvey Park,
Dundrum, Dublin 14
Tel 01-2983978
Spiritual Director,
Lay Retreat Association of Saint Ignatius,
Milltown Park, Dublin 6
Tel 01-2951856

O'Keefe, John, CC
Birdhill, Killaloe,
Co Tipperary
Tel 061-379172
(Cashel & E.)

O'Keefe, Martin, CC
Glenisland, Castlebar,
Co Mayo
Tel 094-9024161
(*Islandeady*, Tuam)

O'Keeffe, Anthony (OFMCap)
St Francis Capuchin Friary,
Rochestown, Co Cork
Tel 021-4896244

O'Keeffe, Anthony, Very Rev Canon, PP, VF
Shanagolden, Co Limerick
Tel 069-60112/087-4163401
(*Shanagolden and Foynes*, Limerick)

O'Keeffe, Gerard (OP)
St Dominic's, Athy,
Co Kildare
Tel 059-8631573

O'Keeffe, John (OFM)
Collegio S. Isidoro,
Via degli Artisti 41,
00187 Roma, Italy
Tel +39-06-4885359

O'Keeffe, John (SJ)
Superior,
Campion House Residence,
28 Lower Hatch Street,
Dublin 2
Tel 01-6383990

O'Keeffe, John (SMA)
SMA House, Wilton,
Cork
Tel 021-4541069/4541884

O'Keeffe, John, Very Rev, AP
The Village Nursing Home,
Craughwell, Co Galway
Tel 091-777700
(Killaloe, retired)

O'Keeffe, Joseph
42 Nessan Court,
Church Road, Raheen,
Limerick
Tel 061-309151/086-3333539
(Limerick)

O'Keeffe, Joseph, Very Rev, PP
Burnfort, Mallow, Co Cork
Tel 022-29920
(*Mourne Abbey*, Cloyne)

O'Keeffe, Laurence, Very Rev, PP
Clifden Villa, Clifden,
Co Kilkenny
Tel 056-7726560/
087-2258443
(*Clara*, Ossory)

O'Keeffe, Martin (OMI)
The Presbytery, Glenisland,
Castlebar, Co Mayo
Tel 085-1086639

O'Keeffe, Patrick (CSsR)
St Patrick's, Esker,
Athenry, Co Galway
Tel 091-844549

O'Keeffe, Philip, Very Rev, PE
Kiliphilbeen, Ballynoe,
Mallow, Co Cork
Tel 058-59526
(Cloyne, retired)

O'Keeffe, Thomas, Very Rev
20 Glen Avenue,
The Park, Cabinteely,
Dublin 18
Tel 01-2853643/086-2646270
(Dublin, retired)

O'Keeffe, Tony
Chaplain, McKee Barracks,
Dublin 7
Tel 01-8388614
(Dublin)

O'Kelly, Francis (SSC)
St Columban's, Dalgan Park,
Navan, Co Meath
Tel 046-9021525

O'Kelly, Michael
(*Moderator)*
197 Kylemore Road,
Ballyfermot, Dublin 10
(*Ballyfermot*, Dublin)

O'Laoghaire, Sean, Very Rev,
PE
Paulstown, Gowran,
Co Kilkenny
Tel 059-9726104
(Kildare & L., retired)

O'Leary, Aidan (OSA)
St Augustine's Priory,
Grantstown, New Ross,
Co Wexford
Tel 051-561119

O'Leary, Alan, P
The Presbytery, Schull,
Co Cork
Tel 028-28171
(*Schull*, Cork & R.)

O'Leary, Anthony (CP)
St Gabriel's Retreat,
The Graan, Enniskillen,
Co Fermanagh
Tel 028-66322272

O'Leary, Brian (SJ)
Milltown Park,
Sandford Road, Dublin 6
Tel 01-2698411

O'Leary, Celestine (OCSO)
Mount Melleray Abbey,
Cappoquin, Co Waterford
Tel 058-54404

O'Leary, Con (SMA)
African Missions,
Blackrock Road, Cork
Tel 021-4292871

O'Leary, Denis J., Very Rev, PP
Bandon, Co Cork
Tel 023-8841728
(*Bandon*, Cork & R.)

O'Leary, Gerald, Very Rev, PP
Horeswood, Campile,
Co Wexford
Tel 051-388129
(*Horeswood and Ballykelly*,
Ferns)

O'Leary, Gerard, CC
Institute of St Anselm,
51-59 Norfolk Road,
Cliftonville,
Kent CT9 2EU, UK
(Kerry)

O'Leary, Gerard, Very Rev,
Adm, VF
Parochial House, Ballyhahill,
Co Limerick
Tel 069-82103/087-9378685
(*Loughill/Ballyhahill*,
Limerick)

O'Leary, John, Very Rev
175 Adams Street,
11E Brooklyn, NY 11208 USA
Tel 718-5107111
(Armagh)

O'Leary, Joseph
1-38-16 Ekoda, Nakanoku,
Tokyo, 16J0022 Japan
(Cork & R.)

O'Leary, Noel (SMA)
Superior,
Dromantine College,
Dromantine, Newry,
Co Down BT34 1RH
Tel 028-30821224

O'Leary, Oscar (OFM)
Franciscan Friary,
Liberty Street, Cork
Tel 021-4270302

O'Leary, Owen (SSC)
St Columban's, Dalgan Park,
Navan, Co Meath
Tel 046-9021525

O'Leary, Rory (OFM)
Franciscan Friary, Lady Lane,
Waterford
Tel 051-874262

O'Leary, Sean (CSSp)
Provincial Assistant,
Holy Spirit Provincialate,
Temple Park,
Richmond Avenue South,
Dublin 6f
Tel 01-4975127/4977230

O'Leary, Timothy, Very Rev
Canon, CC,
Mitchelstown, Co Cork
Tel 025-84088
(*Mitchelstown*, Cloyne)

O'Leary, Timothy, Very Rev,
PP
Glenroe, Kilmallock,
Co Limerick
Tel 063-86040
(*Glenroe and Ballyorgan*,
Limerick)

O'Leary, Oscar (OFM)
Franciscan Friary, Liberty
Street, Cork
Tel 021-4270302

O'Loan, Fergus (OCarm)
Whitefriar Street Church,
56 Aungier Street, Dublin 2
Tel 01-4758821

O'Loughlin, Declan
Parochial House, 30
Newline, Killeavy, Newry,
Co Down BT35 8TA
Tel 028-30889609
(Armagh)

O'Loughlin, Michael (SSC)
43 Moyland, Shanballa,
Loughville, Lahinch Road,
Ennis, Co Clare
Tel 065-6845321

O'Loughlin, Peadar (SSC)
St Columban's, Dalgan Park,
Navan, Co Meath
Tel 046-9021525

O'Loughlin, Peter, Very Rev,
PP
Kilmihil, Co Clare
Tel 065-9050016/
086-8250016
(*Kilmihil*, Killaloe)

O'Mahony, Anthony, CC
The Presbytery, Bantry,
Co Cork
Tel 027-50193
(*Bantry*, Cork & R.)

O'Mahony, Ambrose (OFM)
Franciscan Friary,
Liberty Street, Cork
Tel 021-4270302

O'Mahony, Bartholomew,
Very Rev, PP
Cork Road, Carrigaline,
Co Cork
Tel 021-4371684
(*Carrigaline*, Cork & R.)

O'Mahony, Brendan
(OFMCap)
Holy Trinity,
Fr Mathew Quay, Cork
Tel 021-4270827

O'Mahony, Damien, CC
1 Kilmorna Heights,
Ballyvolane, Cork
Tel 021-4550425
(*Blackpool/The Glen*, Cork &
R.)

O'Mahony, Dan Joe (OFMCap)
The Oratory,
Blanchardstown, Dublin 15
Tel 01-8200915/086-8090633
Capuchin Friary,
Station Road, Raheny,
Dublin 5
Tel 01-8313886
(*Laurel Lodge,
Carpenterstown*, Dublin)

O'Mahony, Dan, Very Rev, PP
Cloonacool, Tubbercurry,
Co Sligo
Tel 071-9185156
(*Tubbercurry*, Achonry)

O'Mahony, Denis, Very Rev
Canon
Killeagh, Farranfore,
Co Kerry
(Kerry, retired)

O'Mahony, Denis, Very Rev,
PP
Abbeydorney, Co Kerry
Tel 066-7135146
(*Abbeydorney*, Kerry)

O'Mahony, Dermot, Most Rev
DD
Titular Bishop of Tiava;
former Auxiliary Bishop of
Dublin,
19 Longlands, Swords,
Co Dublin
Tel 01-8401596
(Dublin)

O'Mahony, Donal, Very Rev
Canon, PP
Cloyne, Midleton, Co Cork
Tel 021-4652597
(*Midleton*, Cloyne)

O'Mahony, George, Very Rev,
PP
Ballincollig, Co Cork
Tel 021-4871206
(*Ballincollig*, Cork & R.)

O'Mahony, John K., Very Rev
Canon, AP
The Presbytery, Kinsale,
Co Cork
Tel 021-4773700
(*Kinsale*, Cork & R.)

O'Mahony, Joseph, CC
Macroom, Co Cork
Tel 026-61049
(*Macroom*, Cloyne)

O'Mahony, Kieran (OSA)
Augustinian Retreat Centre,
Old Court Road,
Dublin 16
Tel 01-4930932

O'Mahony, Michael A., CC
The Presbytery,
Skibbereen, Cork
(*Rath and the Islands*, Cork
& R.)

O'Mahony, Michael, CC
8 The Meadows,
Classis Lake, Ballincollig,
Co Cork
Tel 021-4877161
(*Ballincollig*, Cork & R.)

O'Mahony, Nicholas, Rt Rev
Mgr, PP, VG
Parochial House, Tramore,
Co Waterford
Tel 051-381525
(*Tramore*, Waterford & L.)

O'Mahony, Pat (SMA), CC
The Presbytery, Upper
Mayfield, Cork
Tel 021-4500828
(*Upper Mayfield*, Cork & R.)

O'Mahony, Patrick (SMA)
Temporary diocesan work in
Ireland

O'Mahony, Stephen
Chaplain to school,
Kiltimagh, Co Mayo
Tel 094-9381261
(*Kiltimagh (Killedan)*,
Achonry)

O'Mahony, Stephen, Very Rev, PP
Liscarroll, Mallow, Co Cork
Tel 022-48128
(*Churchtown (Liscarroll), Cloyne*)

O'Mahony, Thomas, Very Rev, PP
Parochial House, Skryne, Tara, Co Meath
Tel 046-9025152
(*Skryne*, Meath)

O'Malley, Donough, Very Rev Canon, PP
St Mary's, Athlunkard Street, Limerick
Tel 061-414092
(*St Mary's*, Limerick)

O'Malley, Eoin (OSM)
Servite Priory, Benburb, Dungannon, Co Tyrone BT71 7JZ

O'Malley, Michael
c/o Archbishop's House, Tuam
(Tuam)

O'Meara, Denis, Very Rev Canon
Beechwood House Nursing Home, Newcastlewest, Co Limerick
(Cashel & E., retired)

O'Meara, Donagh
Ballyheafey, Killaloe, Co Clare
Tel 061-376766/087-2322140
(Killaloe)

O'Meara, Michael, Very Rev, PP
Kinnity, Birr, Co Offaly
Tel 057-9137021/ 087-7735977
(*Kinnitty*, Killaloe)

O'Meara, Noel (CSSp)
St Michael's College, Ailesbury Road, Dublin 4
Tel 01-2189423

O'Melia, Joseph (OMI)
Oblate House of Retreat, Inchicore, Dublin 8
Tel 01-4534408/4541805

O'Moore, Maurice, Very Rev Canon, PE
6 Richmond Avenue, Monkstown, Co Dublin
Tel 01-2802186
(Dublin, retired)

O'Neill, Angelus (OFMCap), CC
Capuchin Friary, Church Street, Dublin 7
Tel 01-8474469
(*Halston Street and Arran Quay*, Dublin)

O'Neill, Arthur
1B Willow Court, Druid Valley, Cabinteely, Dublin 18
Tel 01-4508432
(*Cabinteely*, Dublin)

O'Neill, Charles
Colmanswell, Charleville, Co Limerick
Tel 063-89459
(Limerick, retired)

O'Neill, Daniel (MSC)
Carrignavar, Co Cork
Tel 021-4884044

O'Neill, Daniel (SMA)
SMA House, Claregalway, Co Galway
Tel 091-798880

O'Neill, Denis (SPS)
St Patrick's, 21 Leeson Park, Dublin 6
Tel 01-4977897

O'Neill, Donal, Very Rev
Bishop's House, Killarney, Co Kerry
Tel 064-6685313
(*Kilgarvan*, Kerry)

O'Neill, Eugene
(priest in residence)
4 Ballymacnab Road, Armagh, BT60 2QS
Tel 028-37531620
(*Killcluney*, Armagh)

O'Neill, Eugene, CC
142 Carnmoney Road, Newtownabbey, Co Antrim BT36 6JU
Tel 028-90832488
(*St Mary's on the Hill*, Down & C.)

O'Neill, Fergal, CC
10 Beechwood, Lissane, Clarecastle, Co Clare
087-6615975
(Killaloe)

O'Neill, Francis, Very Rev, PP
Ballyclough, Mallow, Co Cork
Tel 022-27650
(Cloyne)

O'Neill, Gerard (SDB)
Chaplain, Collins Barracks, Cork

O'Neill, Hugh (SJ)
Milltown Park, Sandford Road, Dublin 6
Tel 01-2698411/2698113

O'Neill, Ian, Very Rev, PP
Claregalway, Co Galway
Tel 091-798104
Diocesan Secretary, Diocesan Office, The Cathedral, Galway
Tel 091-563566
(Galway)

O'Neill, Joe, CC
c/o Bishop's House, Carlow
(Kildare & L.)

O'Neill, John, Very Rev Canon, PP, VF
Lisvernane, Aherlow Co Tipperary
Tel 062-56155
(*Galbally*, Cashel & E.)

O'Neill, Kevin, Rt Rev Mgr, BA, MSc Ed
President, Carlow College, College Street, Carlow
Tel 059 9153200
(Kildare & L.)

O'Neill, Míceál (OCarm)
Centro Internazionale S. Alberto, Via Sforza Pallavicini 10, 00193 Roma

O'Neill, Niall (SJ)
Crescent College Comprehensive, Dooradoyle, Limerick
Tel 061-480920

O'Neill, Pat
Ruan, Co Clare
Tel 065-6827799/ 086-2612124
(*Dysart & Ruan*, Killaloe)

O'Neill, Peter (SSC)
House Superior, St Columban's, Dalgan Park, Navan, Co Meath
Tel 046-9021525

O'Neill, Roger, CC
New Ross, Co Wexford
Tel 051-447081
(*New Ross*, Ferns)

O'Neill, Seamus (SPS)
Society Leader, St Patrick's, Kiltegan, Co Wicklow
Tel 059-6473600

O'Neill, Seamus (SSC)
20 Tobermore Road, Moykeenan, Draperstown, Co Derry BT45 7HG
Tel 048-79627206

O'Neill, Sean, PP, VF
Parochial House, 1 Rockstown Road, Carrickmore, Omagh, Co Tyrone BT79 9BE
Tel 028-80761207
(*Termonmaguirc (Carrickmore, Loughmacrory & Creggan)*, Armagh)

O'Neill, Sean, Very Rev, PE
'Iona', 3 St Colmcille's Park, Swords, Co Dublin
Tel 01-8404470
(Dublin, retired)

O'Rahelly, Edmond V., Very Rev, PP
Ballina, Co Tipperary
Tel 061-376178
(*Ballina*, Cashel & E.)

O'Regan, Kevin, CC
Ascension Presbytery, Gurranabraher, Cork
Tel 021-4303655
(*Gurranabraher*, Cork & R.)

O'Regan, Liam, Very Rev Canon, AP
'Carraigin', Moneygourney, Douglas, Cork
Tel 021-4363998
(*Douglas*, Cork & R.)

O'Regan, Michael (OSA)
St Augustine's Priory, Washington Street, Cork
Tel 021-2753982

O'Regan, Robert (SMA)
African Missions, Blackrock Road, Cork
Tel 021-4292871

O'Reilly, Anthony
Newry, Co Armagh
(Kerry)

O'Reilly, Arthur P., CC
285 Foreglan Road, Dungiven, Co Derry BT47 4PJ
Tel 028-71338261
(*Banagher*, Derry)

O'Reilly, Brendan (OCarm)
Carmelite Priory, Moate, Co Westmeath
Tel 090-6481160/6481398

O'Reilly, Brian (SVD)
Provincial, 133 North Circular Road, Dublin 7
Tel 01-8386743

O'Reilly, Brian, Very Rev, PP
Parochial House, Rathdrum, Co Wicklow
Tel 01-4599899
(*Rathdrum*, Dublin)

O'Reilly, Colm, Most Rev, DD
Bishop of Ardagh and Clonmacnois, St Michael's, Longford, Co Longford
Tel 043-3346432
(Ardagh & Cl.)

O'Reilly, Damian, Very Rev
Pro-Cathedral House, 83 Marlborough Street, Dublin 1
Tel 01-8745441
(*Pro-Cathedral*, Dublin)

O'Reilly, Desmond
St Charles Borromeo Parish, 7584 Center Parkway, Sacramento, California 95823, USA
(Dublin)

O'Reilly, F. X., Very Rev, PE
Portiuncula Nursing Home, Multyfarnham, Co Westmeath
(Meath, retired)

O'Reilly, Jimmy (SPS), CC
St Mary's Tower Hill, Portlaoise, Co Laois
Tel 057-8621671
(*Portlaoise*, Kildare & L.)

O'Reilly, Hugh (CSSp)
Holy Spirit Missionary College,
Kimmage Manor, Dublin 12
Tel 01-4064300

O'Reilly, John (OP), CC
St Mary's Priory,
The Claddagh, Galway
Tel 091-582884
(*St Mary's*, Galway)

O'Reilly, John, PP
Piercestown, Co Wexford
Tel 053-9158851
(*Piercestown*, Ferns)

O'Reilly, Joseph (IC)
Cottrell Lodge,
16A Ormond Road,
Drumcondra, Dublin 9
Tel 01-8572234
Provincial,
1 Grace Park Gardens,
Drumcondra, Dublin 9
Tel 01-8378314/8368730

O'Reilly, Kieran (SMA), Very Rev
Bishop of Killaloe,
Westbourne,
Ennis, Co Clare
Tel 065-6828638
(Killaloe)

O'Reilly, Leo, Most Rev, DD
Bishop of Kilmore, Bishop's House, Cullies, Co Cavan
Tel 049-4331496
(Kilmore)

O'Reilly, Martin, CC
4 Darling Street, Enniskillen, Co Fermanagh BT74 7DP
Tel 028-66322075
(*Enniskillen*, Clogher)

O'Reilly, Myles (SJ)
Rector, Gonzaga College,
Sandford Road, Dublin 6
Tel 01-4972943

O'Reilly, Oliver, CC
Parochial House, Shercock,
Co Cavan
Tel 042-9669127
(*Bailieboro (Killann)*, Kilmore)

O'Reilly, Paddy (OSA), CC
Parochial House,
St Helena's Drive,
Dublin 11
Tel 01-8343444
(*Rivermount*, Dublin)

O'Reilly, Paddy (SPS)
St Patrick's, Kiltegan,
Co Wicklow
Tel 059-6473600

O'Reilly, Peter, Very Rev Canon, PP
1 Darling Street, Enniskillen, Co Fermanagh BT74 7DP
Tel 028-66322627*f*
(*Enniskillen*, Clogher)

O'Reilly, Peter, Very Rev, Co-PP
231 Beech Park, Lucan,
Co Dublin
Tel 01-6281756
(*Lucan*, Dublin)

O'Reilly, Thomas, Very Rev, PP
Clonaslee, Co Laois
Tel 057-8648030
(Kildare & L.)

O'Riordáin, John J. (CSsR)
Mount Saint Alphonsus,
Limerick
Tel 061-315099

O'Riordan, Anthony (SJ)
134 Cosgrave Park,
Moyross, Limerick
Tel 061-451783/0879286945

O'Riordan, Anthony (SVD)
133 North Circular Road,
Dublin 7
Tel 01-8386743

O'Riordan, Conor (OP)
St Malachy's, Dundalk,
Co Louth
Tel 042-9334179/9333714

O'Riordan, Daniel, Rt Rev Mgr, PP, VG, VF
The Presbytery, Castleisland, Co Kerry
Tel 066-7141241
(Kerry)

O'Riordan, David, Very Rev, PP
Ladysbridge, Co Cork
Tel 021-4667173
(*Ballymacoda and Ladysbridge*, Cloyne)

O'Riordan, Eugene (SMA)
African Missions,
Blackrock Road, Cork
Tel 021-4292871

O'Riordan, Jeremiah, Very Rev, PP
Donoughmore, Co Cork
Tel 021-7337023
(*Donoughmore*, Cloyne)

O'Riordan, John C. (CSSp), Most Rev
Holy Spirit Missionary College,
Kimmage Manor, Dublin 12
Tel 01-4064300

O'Riordan, J.P. (CSsR), CC
Scala, Castlemahon House,
Castle Road, Cork
Tel 021-4358800
(*Blackrock*, Cork & R.)

O'Riordan, Jude (OFM)
Adam & Eve's,
4 Merchant's Quay,
Dublin 8
Tel 01-6771128

O'Riordan, Martin
Lisgoold, Co Cork
Tel 021-4642543
(Cloyne, retired)

O'Riordan, Timothy, Very Rev, PP
Abbeyside, Dungarvan,
Co Waterford
Tel 058-42036
(*Abbeyside*, Waterford & L.)

O'Riordáin, John J. (CSsR)
Redemptorists,
Mount St Alphonsus,
Limerick
Tel 061-315099

O'Rourke, Brendan (CSsR)
Superior, St Patrick's, Esker,
Athenry, Co Galway
Tel 091-844549

O'Rourke, Declan (OCSO)
Mount Melleray Abbey,
Cappoquin, Co Waterford
Tel 058-54404

O'Rourke, Denis (SPS)
Bursar General, St Patrick's,
Kiltegan, Co Wicklow
Tel 059-6473600

O'Rourke, John (OP)
Holy Cross, Tralee, Co Kerry
Tel 066-7121135/29185

O'Rourke, John, Very Rev, PP
Gortnahoe, Thurles,
Co Tipperary
Tel 056-8834128
(*Gortnahoe*, Cashel & E.)

O'Rourke, John, Very Rev, PP
Loughglynn, Castlerea,
Co Roscommon
Tel 094-9880007
(*Loughglynn*, Elphin)

O'Rourke, Kevin (SJ)
St Francis Xavier's,
Upper Gardiner Street,
Dublin 1
Tel 01-8363411

O'Rourke, Kieran, Very Rev, PP
Looscaun, Woodford,
Co Galway
Tel 090-9749100
(*Woodford*, Clonfert)

O'Rourke, Pat (SMA)
Superior,
Dromantine College,
Dromantine, Newry,
Co Down BT34 1RH
Tel 028-30821224

O'Rourke, Pat (LC), CC
24 Watermill Road, Raheny,
Dublin 5
Tel 01-8313232
(*Raheny*, Dublin)

O'Rourke, Sean
15 Seaview Park, Shankill,
Co Dublin
(Dublin, retired)

O'Saorai, Padraig
12 Ashville, Athy, Co Kildare
(Dublin, retired)

O'Shaughnessy, Anthony, Adm
73 Newtown Park, Leixlip,
Co Kildare
Tel 01-4931057
(*Confey*, Dublin)

O'Shaughnessy, Sean (CSSp)
Holy Spirit Missionary College,
Kimmage Manor, Dublin 12
Tel 01-4064300

O'Shaughnessy, Thomas F., (Team Assistant)
73 Annamoe Road, Dublin 7
Tel 01-8385626
(*Cabra*, Dublin)

O'Shea, A. B., Very Rev, PP
Sooey, Coola, via Boyle,
Co Sligo
Tel 071-9165144
(*Riverstown*, Elphin)

O'Shea, Colum P. (SMA)
Superior, African Missions,
Blackrock Road, Cork
Tel 021-4292871

O'Shea, Donagh (OP)
St Mary's Priory, Tallaght,
Dublin 24
Tel 01-4048100

O'Shea, Fintan (OFM)
3 The Millhouse, Steelworks,
Foley Street, Dublin 1

O'Shea, Henry (OSB)
Glenstal Abbey, Murroe,
Co Limerick
Tel 061-386103

O'Shea, John, Very Rev Canon, PP, VF
Convent Street, Abbeyfeale,
Co Limerick
Tel 068-31157/087-9708282
(*Abbeyfeale*, Limerick)

O'Shea, Kieran
Ballycallan, Co Kilkenny
Tel 056-7769564/
086-8272828
(Ossory)

O'Shea, Martin, Rt Rev Mgr, PP
5 St Assam's Road West,
Raheny, Dublin 5
Tel 01-8313806
(*Raheny*, Dublin)

O'Shea, Maurice, Very Rev, PP
6 Beechpark Lawn,
Castleknock, Dublin 15
Tel 01-8212967
(*Castleknock*, Dublin)

O'Shea, Michael, CC
9 Castletroy Heights,
Monaleen, Limerick
Tel 061-335764/087-9791432
(*Monaleen*, Limerick)

O'Shea, Michael, CC
The Presbytery,
12 School Street, Wexford
Tel 053-9122055
(*Wexford*, Ferns)

O'Shea, Philip, Very Rev, PP
Myshall, Co Carlow
Tel 059-9157635
(*Myshall*, Kildare & L.)

O'Shea, Thomas, Very Rev, PE, CC
Ballylinan, Athy, Co Kildare
Tel 059-8625261
(*Arles*, Kildare & L.)

O'Sullivan, Andrew (Moderator)
Parochial House,
St Mary's Parish,
Sandyford, Dublin 18
Tel 045-481222
(*Sandyford*, Dublin)

O'Sullivan, Anthony, Very Rev, PP
Brosna, Co Kerry
Tel 068-44112
(*Brosna*, Kerry)

O'Sullivan, Billy (priest in residence)
c/o Parochial House,
Ballincollig, Co Cork
Tel 021-4371206
(*Ballincollig*, Cork & R.)

O'Sullivan, Brendan, CC
The Presbytery, Longford
Tel 043-3346465
(*Longford*, Ardagh & Cl.)

O'Sullivan, Brian, PE
The Cottage, Glengara Park,
Glenageary,
Co Dublin
Tel 01-2360681
(Dublin, retired)

O'Sullivan, Brian (OSA)
Via Piemonte 60,
00187 Rome, Italy
Tel 00396-4203121

O'Sullivan, Denis (CSsR)
Mount Saint Alphonsus,
Limerick
Tel 061-315099

O'Sullivan, Denis (SMA)
SMA House, Wilton, Cork
Tel 021-4541069/4541884

O'Sullivan, Denis, Very Rev, PE
Monasterevin, Co Kildare
Tel 045-525351
(Kildare & L., retired)

O'Sullivan, Desmond L. (CSSp)
Holy Spirit Missionary College,
Kimmage Manor, Dublin 12
Tel 01-4064300

O'Sullivan, John (MSC)
Woodview House,
Mount Merrion Avenue,
Blackrock, Co Dublin
Tel 01-2881644

O'Sullivan, John (OSA)
St Augustine's,
Taylor's Lane,
Balyboden, Dublin 16
Tel 01-4241000

O'Sullivan, John K.
97 Kincora Avenue,
Clontarf, Dublin 3
(Dublin, retired)

O'Sullivan, John L. (CSSp)
Holy Spirit Missionary College,
Kimmage Manor,
Whitehall Road,
Dublin 12
Tel 01-4064300

O'Sullivan, John, Very Rev
6 Ferngrove Avenue,
Aghagallon,
Craigavon BT67 0HA
(Down & C., retired)

O'Sullivan, Kieran, Very Rev, PP
Adrigole, Bantry, Co Cork
Tel 027-60006
(*Adrigole*, Kerry)

O'Sullivan, Leo (OSA)
St Augustine's Priory,
O'Connell Street,
Limerick
Tel 061-415374

O'Sullivan, Leo (SPS)
St Patrick's, Kiltegan,
Co Wicklow
Tel 059-6473600

O'Sullivan, Liam (CSSp)
Holy Spirit Missionary College,
Kimmage Manor,
Dublin 12
Tel 01-4064300

O'Sullivan, Louis
Our Lady's Manor,
Bullock Castle, Dalkey,
Co Dublin
(Dublin, retired)

O'Sullivan, Michael (OSA)
St John's Priory,
Thomas Street,
Dublin 8
Tel 01-6770393

O'Sullivan, Michael (SJ)
John Austin House,
135 North Circular Road,
Dublin 7
Tel 01-8386768

O'Sullivan, Michael (White Fathers)
c/o Cypress Grove,
Templeogue, Dublin 6W
Tel 01-4055263/4055264

O'Sullivan, Noel, Very Rev Dr, PP
Glanmire, Co Cork
Tel 021-4866307
(*Glanmire*, Cork & R.)

O'Sullivan, Owen (OFMCap)
St Francis Capuchin Friary,
Rochestown, Co Cork
Tel 021-4896244

O'Sullivan, Padraig
Apt 1 The Presbytery,
Balbriggan,
Co Dublin
Tel 01-8491250
(*Balbriggan*, Dublin)

O'Sullivan, Patrick (CSsR)
Mount Saint Alphonsus,
Limerick
Tel 061-315099

O'Sullivan, Patrick, Very Rev (MSC), Adm
Leap, Co Cork
Tel 028-33177
(*Kilmacabea*, Cork & R.)

O'Sullivan, Patrick, Very Rev, PP
'Elm View', Roxboro Road,
Limerick
Tel 061-410846/087-2237501
(*Our Lady Queen of Peace*, Limerick)

O'Sullivan, Paul (OCD)
St Teresa's,
Clarendon Street, Dublin 2
Tel 01-6718466/6718127

O'Sullivan, Séan, AP
Lissarda, Crookstown, Cork
Tel 021-7336053
(*Kilmurry*, Cork & R.)

O'Sullivan, Teddy, Very Rev Canon, PP
Parochial House, Douglas
Co Cork
Tel 021-4891265
(*Douglas*, Cork & R.)

O'Sullivan, William (SMA)
African Missions,
Blackrock Road, Cork
Tel 021-4292871

O'Toole, Brian (CSSp)
St Mary's College,
Rathmines, Dublin 6
Tel 01-4995760

O'Toole, Colm (OCSO), Dom Abbot Emeritus,
Mount Saint Joseph Abbey,
Roscrea, Co Tipperary
Tel 0505-25600

O'Toole, Lorcan (CSSp)
Holy Spirit Missionary College,
Kimmage Manor, Dublin 12
Tel 01-4064300

O'Toole, Patrick (CSSp)
Spiritan Missionaries,
Ardbraccan, Navan,
Co Meath
Tel 046-9021441

O'Toole, Peter Baptist (OFM)
Franciscan Friary,
Lady Lane, Waterford
Tel 051-874262

O'Toole, Sean
The Presbytery, Sea Road,
Arklow, Co Wicklow
Tel 0402-32153.
(Dublin, retired)

O'Toole, Thomas, CC
Kilmacow, via Waterford,
Co Kilkenny
Tel 051-88529/087-2240787
(Ossory)

Ogbonna, Magnus (MSP) CC
St Patrick's Presbytery,
Roden Place, Dundalk,
Co Louth
Tel 042-9334648
(*Dundalk, St Patrick's*, Armagh)

Oladipo, Francis, PC
32 Earlsfort Road, Lucan,
Dublin 22
Tel 01-4572900
(*Lucan South*, Dublin)

Olden, Michael, Rt Rev Mgr, PE
'Woodleigh',
Summerville Avenue,
Waterford
Tel 051-874132
(Waterford & L., retired)

Olejnik, Krzysztof (SCHR), CC
191 Upper Newtownards Road,
Belfast BT4 3JB
Tel 028-90654157
(*St Colmcille's*, Down & C.)

Onwukeme, Victor (MSP), CC
Parochial House,
42 Abbey Street,
Armagh B61 7DZ
(Armagh)

Orr, Thomas, CC
Ballycanew, Gorey,
Co Wexford
Tel 053-9427184
(*Camolin*, Ferns)

Owen, John (SVD)
The Presbytery, City Quay,
Dublin 2
Tel 01-6773073
(*City Quay*, Dublin)

Owens, Finnian (OCSO)
Our Lady of Bethlehem Abbey,
11 Ballymena Road,
Portglenone, Ballymena,
Co Antrim BT44 8BL
Tel 028-25821211

Owens, Peter, PP
143 Andersonstown Road,
Belfast BT11 9BW
Tel 028-90615702
(*St Agnes'*, Down & C.)

Palmisano, Joseph (SJ) (NEN)
Campion House Residence,
28 Lower Hatch Street,
Dublin 2
Tel 01-6383990

Parker, Thomas (SSC)
St Columban's Retirement Home,
Dalgan Park, Navan,
Co Meath
Tel 046-9021525

Parokkaran, Martin (OCarm)
Carmelite Presbytery,
Idrone Avenue, Knocklyon,
Dublin 16
Tel 01-4941204
(*Knocklyon*, Dublin)

Parys, Bartlomiej (SVD)
Maynooth, Co Kildare
Tel 01-6286391/2

Patton, Gerard, Very Rev, PP
Parochial House,
Dundrum, Newcastle,
Co Down BT33 0LU
Tel 028-43751212
(*Dundrum and Tyrella*, Down & C.)

Pauly, Winifred (CSsR), CC
The Presbytery,
197 Kylemore Road,
Ballyfermot, Dublin 10
Tel 01-6264789

Payyapilly, Paul, AP
Church of the Most Precious Blood,
Clogheen, Co Cork
Tel 021-4392122
(*Clogheen (Kerry Pike)*, Cork & R.)

Pazhayakalam, Tony (CST), PC
Parochial House,
Brackenstown Road,
Swords, Co Dublin
Tel 01-8401188
(*Brackenstown*, Dublin)

Pecak Marek, CC
(priest in residence)
Midleton, Co Cork
Tel 021-4634027
(*Midleton*, Cloyne)

Peelo, Adrian (OFM)
Old Mission San Luis Rey,
4050 Mission Avenue,
Oceanside,
CA 92057-6497 USA

Pentony, Liam, Very Rev, CC
Parochial House, Dromiskin,
Dundalk, Co Louth
Tel 042-9382877
(*Darver and Dromiskin*, Armagh)

Peoples, William, Very Rev, PP
Donegal Town,
Co Donegal
Tel 074-9721026
(*Donegal Town*, Raphoe)

Pepper, Pierre, CC
Banagher, Co Offaly
Tel 090-6454309
(*Cloghan and Banagher*, Ardagh & Cl.)

Perrem, Leonard (OP)
St Mary's Priory, Tallaght,
Dublin 24
Tel 01-4048100

Perrotta, John (FDP)
Sarsfield House,
Sarsfield Road,
Ballyfermot, Dublin 10
Tel 01-6266193/6266233

Perry, Jim (SVD)
Maynooth, Co Kildare
Tel 01-6286391/2

Perumayan, Antony, CC
St Paul's Presbytery,
125 Falls Road,
Belfast BT12 6AB
Tel 028-90325034

Peyton, Patrick, Very Rev Canon, PP
Parochial House, Collooney,
Co Sligo
Tel 071-9167235
(Achonry)

Phair, John, Very Rev, PP
Rossinver, Co Leitrim
Tel 071-9854022
(*Ballaghameehan*, Kilmore)

Phelan, Richard, Very Rev Canon, PP
Kilmanagh, Co Kilkenny
Tel 056-7769116/
087-2843461
(*Ballycallan*, Ossory)

Philip, John (OSCam)
Chaplain,
Mater Hospital, Dublin
11 St Vincent St North,
Dublin 7

Philomin, Leo, Very Rev, (OMI) PP
The Presbytery, Darndale,
Dublin 17
Tel 01-8474547
(*Darndale-Belcamp*, Dublin)

Pierce, Pat (IC)
Rector,
Rosminian House of Prayer,
Glencomeragh House,
Kilsheelan, Co Tipperary
Tel 052-33181

Pierse, Thomas, Very Rev
32 Knockmoyle Estate,
Tralee, Co Kerry
(Kerry, retired)

Piert, John, Very Rev Canon, PC
The Presbytery, Johnstown,
Arklow,
Co Wicklow
Tel 0402-31112
(*Arklow*, Dublin)

Pinheiro, Reuben (OCarm)
Gort Muire, Ballinteer,
Dublin 16
Tel 01-2984014

Placek, Mariusz (OCarm)
Carmelite Friary, Kinsale,
Co Cork
Tel 021-772138

Planell, Francis
Harvieston,
Cunningham Road, Dalkey,
Co Dublin
Tel 01-2859877
(Opus Dei)

Plower, Thomas (MSC), Very Rev
Church of the Resurrection,
Headford Road, Galway
Tel 091-762883
(*Tirellan*, Galway)

Plunkett, Oliver, Very Rev, PP
Donaghmore, Co Limerick
Tel 061-313898/087-6593176
(*Donaghmore/Knockea*, Limerick)

Poland, James, Very Rev
Rostrevor, Co Down
(Dromore, retired)

Polke, Desmond
(priest in residence)
Parochial House, Castlefin,
Lifford, Co Donegal
Tel 074-9146251
(*Doneyloop*, Derry)

Pollack, James (IC)
Faughart Parish,
St Brigid's Kilcurry,
Dundalk, Co Louth
Tel 042-9334410

Poole, John (OMI)
Oblate House of Retreat,
Inchicore, Dublin 8
Tel 01-4534408/4541805

Poole, Joseph (CSSp)
Spiritan Community,
Ballintubber, Castlerea,
Co Roscommon
Tel 094-9655226

Porter, Michael, PP
Parochial House,
447 Victoria Road,
Ballymagorry, Strabane,
Co Tyrone BT82 0AT
Tel 028-718802274
(*Leckpatrick*, Derry)

Powell, Eric (SDS)
Our Lady of Victories,
Sallynoggin,
Dun Laoghaire, Co Dublin
Tel 01-2854667

Powell, Gerald, Very Rev, PP
4 Holymount Road, Gilford,
Craigavon,
Co Armagh BT63 6AT
Tel 028-40624236
(*Tullylish*, Dromore)

Powell, Oliver
Gort Ard University Residence,
Rockbarton North, Galway
Tel 091-523846
(Opus Dei)

Power, Anthony, CC
35 Grange Park Avenue,
Raheny, Dublin 5
Tel 01-8480244
(*Grange Park*, Dublin)

Power, Brian, Very Rev, PP
Dunmore East,
Co Waterford
Tel 051-383127
(*Killea (Dunmore East)*, Waterford & L.)

Power, Gregory, Very Rev, PE
St Mary's, Clonmel,
Co Tipperary
Tel 052-6182690
(Waterford & L., retired)

Power, John (OSA)
St Augustine's Priory,
New Ross, Co Wexford
Tel 051-421237
(Ferns)

Power, Joseph, Very Rev, PP
Kilrush, Bunclody,
Co Wexford
Tel 053-9377262
(Ferns)

Power, Liam, STL
Carlow College,
College Street, Carlow
Tel 059-9153200
(Kildare & L.)

Power, Liam, Very Rev, Adm
St John's Presbytery,
New Street, Waterford
Tel 051-874271
Communications Office,
St John's Pastoral Centre,
John's Hill, Waterford
Tel 051-874199
(*St John's*, Waterford & L.)

Power, Nicholas, Very Rev Canon
Moorfield, Rathaspeck,
Co Wexford
(Ferns, retired)

Power, Patrick (OFM), PP
Provincial Delegate,
St Anthony's Parish (English-Speaking Chaplaincy),
23/25 Oudstrijderslaan,
1950 Kraainem, Belgium
Tel +32-2-7201970

Power, Robert, Very Rev, Adm
Ardfinnan, Clonmel,
Co Tipperary
Tel 052-7466216
(*Ardfinnan*, Waterford & L.)

Power, Seamus, Very Rev, PE
'Sheen Lodge', Ennis Road,
Limerick
Tel 061-454841
(Limerick, retired)

Power, Thomas J., (MSC) PP
The Presbytery, Killinarden,
Tallaght, Dublin 24
Tel 01-4522251
(*Killinarden*, Dublin)

Power, William (CSsR)
Mount Saint Alphonsus,
Limerick
Tel 061-315099

Prendergast, Patrick, Very Rev, PP
Glenties, Co Donegal
Tel 074-9551117
(*Glenties*, Raphoe)

Prendiville, James, CC
The Presbytery, Hollywood (via Naas), Co Wicklow
Tel 045-864206
(*Ballymore Eustace*, Dublin)

Prendiville, William (OSA)
St Augustine's Priory,
O'Connell Street,
Limerick
Tel 061-415374

Previnth, Peter
(supply priest)
c/o Michael Casey
Parish House,
24 Killarney Street, Dublin 1

Price, Cathal, Very Rev, CC
54 Foxfield St John, Dublin 5
Tel 01-8323683
(*Kilbarrack-Foxfield*, Dublin)

Prior, Dermot
Virginia, Co Cavan
Tel 049-8547015
(*Virginia*, Kilmore)

Prior, Paul
Director of Formation,
St Patrick's College,
Maynooth, Co Kildare
(Kilmore)

Przanowski, Krzysztof, CC
St Mary's Athlone,
Co Westmeath
Tel 090-6472088

Purcell, Denis, CC
Cuffesgrange, Co Kilkenny
Tel 056-7729299/
087-1356687
(*Danesfort*, Ossory)

Purcell, Eamon
112 Hilltop,
St Patrick's Road, Limerick
Tel 061-413734
(*St Patrick's*, Limerick)

Purcell, Edmond (CSSp)
Rockwell College, Cashel,
Co Tipperary
Tel 062-61444

Purcell, Francis, Very Rev
St John's Presbytery,
Kilkenny
Tel 056-7721072/
086-6010001
(*St John's*, Ossory)

Purcell, James, CC
Rosegreen, Cashel,
Co Tipperary
Tel 062-61713
(*Cashel*, Cashel & E.)

Purcell, Richard (OCSO), Rt Rev Dom
Abbot,
Mount Saint Joseph Abbey,
Roscrea, Co Tipperary
Tel 0505-25600

Purcell, William
St Kieran's College, Kilkenny
Tel 056-7721086/087-6286858
(Ossory)

Pyburn, Daniel, PP
The Presbytery, Dromore,
Bantry, Co Cork
(*Bantry*, Cork & R.)

## Q

Queally, Peter (CSSp)
Rockwell College, Cashel,
Co Tipperary
Tel 062-61444

Queally, Peter, AP
Oiléan Cléire, Baltimore,
Co Cork
Tel 028-39103
(*Rath and the Islands*, Cork & R.)

Quealy, Patrick, Very Rev Canon, PE
Care Choice Dungarvan,
The Burgery,
Dungarvan, Co Waterford
Tel 058-40200
(Waterford & L., retired)

Quigley, Seán, PC
48 Aughrim Street, Dublin 7
Tel 01-8386176
(*Aughrim Street*, Dublin)

Quigley, Thomas, Very Rev, PP
Latton, Castleblayney,
Co Monaghan
Tel 042-9742212
(*Latton*, Clogher)

Quinlan, Brendan, Very Rev, PP
41 Cremore Heights,
St Canice's Road, Glasnevin,
Dublin 11
Tel 01-8573776
(*Ballygall*, Dublin)

Quinlan, John
36 Clogher Li,
Tralee, Co Kerry
Tel 066-7181367
(Kerry, retired)

Quinlan, John (SMA)
African Missions,
Blackrock Road, Cork
Tel 021-4292871

Quinlan, Leo, Very Rev
42A Strand Street, Skerries,
Co Dublin
(Dublin, retired)

Quinlivan, Brendan, Very Rev, PP
Scariff, Co Clare
Tel 061-921013/087-2736310
(Killaloe)

Quinn, Brian, Very Rev, PP
Ballyraine, Letterkenny,
Co Donegal
Tel 074-9127600
(*Aughaninshin*, Raphoe)

Quinn, Denis, CC
The Presbytery,
Kimberley Road, Greystones,
Co Wicklow
Tel 01-2877025
(*Greystones*, Dublin)

Quinn, Denis, Very Rev, PP
Falcarragh, Co Donegal
Tel 074-9135196
(*Falcarragh*, Raphoe)

Quinn, Desmond (SSC)
Assistant Bursar,
St Columban's, Dalgan Park,
Navan, Co Meath
Tel 046-9021525

Quinn, Edward (OMI) CC
The Prebytery, Darndale,
Dublin 17
Tel 01-8474599
(*Darndale-Belcamp*, Dublin)

Quinn, Frank (IC)
Clonturk House,
Ormond Road,
Drumcondra, Dublin 9
Tel 01-6877014

Quinn, James, Canon, CC
Taugheen, Claremorris,
Co Mayo
Tel 094-9362500
(*Crossboyne and Taugheen*, Tuam)

Quinn, John (SDB)
Vice-Rector, Rinaldi House,
72 Sean McDermott Street,
Dublin 1
Tel 01-8363358

Quinn, John, Very Rev, PP
Gortletteragh,
Carrick-on-Shannon,
Co Leitrim
Tel 071-9631074
(*Gortletteragh*, Ardagh & Cl.)

Quinn, John, Very Rev, PP
West Barrs, Glenfarne,
Co Leitrim
Tel 071-9855134
(*Glenfarne*, Kilmore)

Quinn, Ken
General Hospital,
Co Wexford
Tel 053-9142233
(Ferns)

Quinn, Michael, Very Rev, PP
Carracastle,
Ballaghaderreen,
Co Mayo
Tel 094-9254301
(*Carracastle*, Achonry)

Quinn, Michael, Very Rev, PP
Crosserlough, Co Cavan
Tel 049-4336122
(*Crosserlough*, Kilmore)

Quinn, Richard (CSSp)
11 Silchester Court,
Glenageary,
Co Dublin
Tel 01-2806375

Quinn, Seamus, CC
Belcoo, Enniskillen,
Co Fermanagh BT93 5FJ
Tel 028-66386225
(*Killeevan*, Clogher)

Quinn, Sean, Very Rev, PE, AP
Parochial House,
Dillonstown, Dunleer,
Co Louth
Tel 041-6863570
(*Togher*, Armagh)

Quinn, Seán, Very Rev, PP
Parochial House,
Louth Village, Dundalk,
Co Louth
Tel 042-9374285
(*Louth*, Armagh)

Quinn, Stephen
Carmelite Priory,
Boars Hill, Oxford OX1 5HB
(Down & C., retired)

Quinn, Tadhg, Very Rev, PP
St John the Apostle,
Knocknacarra, Galway
Tel 091-590059
(*St John the Apostle*, Galway)

Quirke, Brendan (OSA)
St John's Priory,
Thomas Street,
Dublin 8
Tel 01-6770393

Quirke, Ciary (SJ)
Manresa House,
Dollymount, Dublin 3
Tel 01-8331352

Quirke, Denis, Very Rev
Nicholas Place,
Bridge Street, Milltown,
Co Kerry
(Kerry, retired)

Quirke, Gerard, Very Rev, PP
Ballingarry, Thurles,
Co Tipperary
Tel 052-9154115
(*Ballingarry*, Cashel & E.)

Rabbitte, Peter, Very Rev Canon, PP
Lisdoonvarna, Co Clare
Tel 065-7074142
(*Lisdoonvarna and Kilshanny*, Galway)

Radley, William, Very Rev, PP
St Agatha's Parish Centre,
Headford, Killarney,
Co Kerry
Tel 064-7754008
(Kerry)

Rafferty, Colm (SSC)
126 Grove Road, Swatragh,
Co Derry BT46 5Q2
Tel 028-79401209

Rafferty, James (CM)
99 Cliftonville Road,
Belfast BT14 6JQ
Tel 028-90751771

Rafferty, Terence, Very Rev, PP
10 Barr Hill, Newry,
Co Down BT34 1SY
Tel 028-38821252
(Dromore)

Rafter, Roger (SAC)
Pallottine College, Thurles,
Co Tipperary
Tel 0504-21202

Raftery, Eamon (SMA)
St Vincent's College,
Castleknock, Dublin 15
Tel 01-8213051

Raftery, Gregory
An Der Tiefenriede 11, 3000,
Hanover 1, Germany
(Galway)

Raftery, Peter, (CSSp)
Templeogue College,
Templeville Road,
Dublin 6W
Tel 01-490 3909

Raftery, Thomas (CSSp)
Templeogue College,
Dublin 6W
Tel 01-4903909

Raftice, Robert, Very Rev Canon
Mount Carmel, Callan,
Co Kilkenny
Tel 056-7725301/7725553/086-0614682
(Ossory, retired)

Rainey, Sean (SSC)
St Columban's Retirement Home,
Dalgan Park, Navan,
Co Meath
Tel 046-9021525

Raleigh, Patrick (SSC)
Regional Vice-Director,
St Columban's, Dalgan Park,
Navan, Co Meath
Tel 046-9021525

Ralph, Joseph (OP)
St Catherine's,
Newry, Co Down BT35 8BN
Tel 028-30262178

Ramsbottom, Pat, Very Rev, PE
Gorman's Cottage,
Cooleragh, Co Kildare
Tel 045-890744
(Kildare & L., retired)

Randles, James A., Very Rev Canon, PE
Sacred Heart Residence,
Sybil Hill Road,
Raheny, Dublin 5
(Dublin, retired)

Reaume, Michael (SM)
St Columba's,
Church Avenue, Ballybrack,
Co Dublin
Tel 01-2858301

Reburn, Frank, CC
11 Millview Court,
Malahide, Co Dublin
Tel 01-8338575
(*Malahide*, Dublin)

Reddan, Michael (SVD)
Donamon Castle,
Roscommon
Tel 090-6662222

Reddan, Michael (SVD)
The Presbytery, John's Mall,
Birr, Co Offaly
Tel 087-7599789
(*Birr*, Killaloe)

Redmond, Noel (CSSp)
Templeogue College,
Dublin 6W
Tel 01-4903909

Redmond, Richard, CC
(Ballyduff) The Square,
Ferns, Enniscorthy,
Co Wexford
Tel 053-9366162
(*Ferns*, Ferns)

Redmond, Stephen (SJ)
Milltown Park,
Sandford Road,
Dublin 6
Tel 01-2698411/2698113

Redmond, Tim (SPS)
Editor, *Africa*,
St Patrick's, Kiltegan,
Co Wicklow
Tel 059-6473600

Reedy, Patrick (CSSp)
Templeogue College,
Dublin 6W
Tel 01-4903909

Regan, Christopher (OFM)
Franciscan Friary,
Liberty Street, Cork
Tel 021-4270302

Regan, Henry
Presbytery No. 1,
Church Grounds,
Kill Avenue, Dun Laoghaire,
Co Dublin
Tel 01-2800901
(Dublin, retired)

Regan, James (SPS)
Chaplains Residence,
Dublin Road, Longford
Tel 043-3346211
(Ardagh and Cl.)

Regan, Michael, Very Rev, PP
Carraig na bhFear, Co Cork
Tel 021-4884119
(*Carraig na Bhfear*, Cork & R.)

Regula, Robert (OP), CC
St Mary's Priory, Tallaght,
Dublin 24
Tel 01-4048100
(*Tallaght, St Mary's*, Dublin)

Reid, Alexander (CSsR)
Liguori House,
75 Orwell Road, Dublin 6
Tel 01-4067100

Reid, Desmond (CSSp)
St Coc's Church, Mill Lane
Kilcock, Co Kildare
Tel 01-6287277
(Kildare and L.)

Reidy, Denis, Very Rev Mgr, PE
Teach on tSagairt,
Main Street
Carrigtwohill, Co Cork
Tel 021-4533776
(*Carrigtwohill*, Cloyne)

Reidy, Raymond (SPS), CC
Church of the Resurrection,
Fethard Road, Clonmel,
Co Tipperary
Tel 052-6123239
(*Clonmel, SS Peter & Paul*, Waterford & L.)

Reihill, Seamus (SPS)
St Patrick's, Kiltegan,
Co Wicklow
Tel 059-6473600

Reilly, Anthony, Very Rev, PP
Parochial House,
Palmerstown, Dublin 20
Tel 01-6249323
(*Palmerstown*, Dublin)

Reilly, Eamon (OMI)
Oblate House of Retreat,
Inchicore, Dublin 8
Tel 01-4534408/4541805

Reilly, John, Very Rev, PP
Lahardane, Ballina, Co Mayo
Tel 096-51007
(*Lahardane*, Killala)

Reilly, Martin (SPS), CC
(on temporary diocesan work)

Reilly, Matthew (SSC)
St Columban's, Dalgan Park,
Navan, Co Meath
Tel 046-9021525

Reilly, Michael, PP
Belmullet, Co Mayo
Tel 097-81426
(*Belmullet*, Killala)

Reilly, Michael, Very Rev Canon, PP
Castlegar, Galway
Tel 091-751548
(*Castlegar*, Galway)

Reilly, Michael, Very Rev, PP
Lanesboro, Co Longford
Tel 043-3321166
(*Lanesboro*, Ardagh & Cl.)

Reilly, Michael, Very Rev, PP
Parochial House,
Bunninadden, Ballymote,
Co Sligo
Tel 071-9183232
(*Bunninadden (Kilshalvey, Kilturra and Cloonoghill)*, Achonry)

Reilly, Patrick (OPraem), CC
13 Seaview Park, Portrane,
Co Dublin
Tel 01-8436099
(*Donabate*, Dublin)

Reilly, Peter J., Very Rev, PP
Parochial House,
St Joseph's Parish,
East Wall, Dublin 3
Tel 01-8742320
(*East Wall*, Dublin)

Reilly, William
Casilla 09-01-5825,
Guayaquil, Ecuador
(Killala)

Reilly, William, Very Rev
Knock, Inverin, Co Galway
Tel 091-593122
(*Spiddal*, Tuam)

Relihan, Patrick, CC
Youghal, Co Cork
Tel 024-92456
(*Youghal*, Cloyne)

Revatto, Geoffrey (SSC)
St Columban's Retirement Home,
Dalgan Park, Navan,
Co Meath
Tel 046-9021525

Revatto, Thomas (SSC)
St Columban's Retirement Home,
Dalgan Park, Navan,
Co Meath
Tel 046-9021525

Reynolds, Brian (OP), CC
Droichead Nua, Co Kildare
Tel 045-431394
(*Droichead Nua/Newbridge*, Kildare & L.)

Reynolds, Gerard (CSsR)
Clonard Monastery,
1 Clonard Gardens,
Belfast BT13 2RL
Tel 028-90445950

Reynolds, Kenneth (OFMCap)
Holy Trinity,
Fr Mathew Quay, Cork
Tel 021-4270827

Reynolds, Kevin, (MHM) Very Rev
St Joseph's House,
50 Orwell Park,
Rathgar, Dublin 6
Tel 01-4127700

Reynolds, Michael B. (CSSp)
Holy Spirit Missionary College,
Kimmage Manor, Dublin 12
Tel 01-4064300

Reynolds, Patrick (CSsR)
The Presbytery,
103 Cherry Orchard Avenue,
Dublin 10
Tel 01-6267930
(*Cherry Orchard*, Dublin)

Reynolds, William (SJ), CC
The Presbytery,
Upper Gardiner Street,
Dublin 1
Tel 01-8363411
(*Gardiner Street*, Dublin)

Rice, Gerard, Very Rev, PE
Kilcloon, Co Meath
Tel 01-6286252
(*Kilcloon*, Meath)

Rice, Patrick, Very Rev Canon, PE
Little Sisters of the Poor,
Holy Family Residence,
Roebuck Road, Dundrum,
Dublin 14
(Dublin, retired)

Rice, Seamus, Very Rev, PE, AP
Parochial House,
89 Derrynoose Road,
Derrynoose,
Co Armagh BT60 3EZ
Tel 028-37531222
(Armagh)

Rice, Tony (CSsR)
St Joseph's, Dundalk,
Co Louth
Tel 042-9334042/9334762

Rigney, Liam, Very Rev, PP
Parochial House, Moyglare Road
Tel 01-8556474
(*Maynooth*, Dublin)

Riordan, Michael, Very Rev, AP
The Presbytery,
Togher, Cork
Tel 021-4316700
(*Togher*, Cork & R.)

Riordan, Patrick (SJ)
Irish Jesuit Provincialate,
Milltown Park,
Sandford Road, Dublin 6
Tel 01-4987333

Riordan, Ray (CSsR)
Cork University Hospital,
Wilton, Cork
Tel 021-4546400

Rivero, Rodrigo (OP)
St Mary's Priory, Tallaght,
Dublin 24
Tel 01-4048100

Roban, Myles (SSC)
10 Belfield Springs,
Enniscorthy, Co Wexford
Tel 0539237770

Roberts, Donal, Very Rev, PP
Macroom, Co Cork
Tel 026-21068
(*Macroom*, Cloyne)

Robinson, Denis (CSSp)
Holy Spirit Missionary College,
Kimmage Manor,
Dublin 12
Tel 01-4064300

Robinson, Denis, CC
The Presbytery,
Mourne Road, Dublin 12
Tel 01-4556199
(*Mourne Road*, Dublin)

Robinson, John, Very Rev, PP
Borris-in-Ossory, Portlaoise,
Co Laois
Tel 0505-41148/087-2431412
(*Borris-in-Ossory*, Ossory)

Roche, Donal (OP)
St Mary's Priory, Tallaght,
Dublin 24
Tel 01-4048100

Roche, Donal, Very Rev, PP
Parochial House,
Foxdene Avenue, Lucan,
Dublin 22
Tel 01-4056858
(*Lucan South*, Dublin)

Roche, Joseph, Very Rev, PP
*(priest in charge)*
Ardhan, Galway
Tel 091-635164
(*Ardhan*, Galway)
Parochial House, Kilchreest,
Loughrea, Co Galway
Tel 091-840859
(*Kilchreest/Castledaly*, Galway)

Roche, Luke, Very Rev, PP
Castlemaine, Co Kerry
Tel 066-9767322
(Kerry)

Roche, Simon (OP)
St Mary's, Pope Quay, Cork
Tel 021-4502267

Rochford, Seamus, Very Rev, PP
Emly, Co Tipperary
Tel 062-57103
(*Emly*, Cashel & E.)

Rocks, Ned (CSsR)
St Joseph's, Dundalk,
Co Louth
Tel 042-9334042/9334762

Rodgers, Jack (SPS)
St Patrick's, Kiltegan,
Co Wicklow
Tel 059-6473600

Rodgers, J. J., AP
Borrisokane, Co Tipperary
Tel 067-27140
(*Borrisokane*, Killaloe)

Rodgers, Michael (SPS)
Tearmann Spirituality Centre,
Brockagh, Glendalough,
Co Wicklow
Tel 0404-45208

Rodriguez, Paulino (MSC)
(Peru) c/o Parish Office,
Herbert Road, Bray,
Co Wicklow
Tel 01-2868413
(*Bray Holy Redeemer*, Dublin)

Rogan, Edward, Very Rev
Inver, Barnatra, Ballina,
Co Mayo
Tel 097-84598
(*Kilcommon-Erris*, Killala)

Rogan, Sean, Very Rev Canon, PP, VF
Parochial House,
54 St Patrick's Avenue,
Downpatrick,
Co Down BT30 6DN
Tel 028-44612443
(*Downpatrick*, Down & C.)

Rogers, Michael, Very Rev, PP
Parochial House,
25 Priestbush Road,
Whitecross,
Co Armagh BT60 2TP
Tel 028-37507214
(*Whitecross (Loughilly)*, Armagh)

Rogers, Patrick (CP)
St Paul's Retreat,
Mount Argus, Dublin 6W
Tel 01-4992000

Rogers, Thomas, Very Rev, PP
Holy Family Presbytery,
Luke Wadding Street,
Waterford
Tel 051-37527
(*Holy Family*, Waterford & L.)

Rohan, Joseph, CC
Ballycotton, Midleton,
Co Cork
Tel 021-4646726
(*Cloyne*, Cloyne)

Ronayne, James, Very Rev, PP
Clifden, Co Galway
Tel 095-21251
(*Clifden (Omey and Ballindoon)*, Tuam)

Rooney, Joe (SM)
England

Rooney, Joseph
(priest in residence)
45 Ballyholme Esplanade,
Bangor, Co Down BT20 5NJ
Tel 028-91465425
(*Bangor*, Down & C.)

Rooney, Joseph, JCL
Office of the Armagh
Regional Marriage Tribunal,
511 Ormeau Road,
Belfast BT7 3GS
Tel 028-90491990
(Down & C.)

Rooney, Liam (SCJ)
Parochial House,
St John Vianney,
Ardlea Road, Dublin 5
Tel 01-8474123
(*Ardlea*, Dublin)

Rooney, Noel, Very Rev, PP
279 Sunset Drive,
Cartron Point, Sligo
Tel 071-9142422
Chaplain,
Ballinode Vocational School,
Sligo
Tel 071-9147111
(Elphin)

Rosario, Ripon (SJ)
John Sullivan House
56/56A Mulvey Park,
Dundrum, Dublin 14
Tel 01-2983978

Rosbotham, Gabriel, CC
Cathedral Close, Ballina,
Co Mayo
Tel 096-71355
(*Ballina*, Killala)

Rosney, Arnold, CC
5 Drumgeely Avenue,
Shannon, Co Clare
Tel 061-471513/087-8598710
(*Shannon*, Killaloe)

Ross, Jim (SM)
Fiji

Ross, Michael (SDB)
Rector, Salesian House,
45 St Teresa's Road,
Crumlin, Dublin 12
Tel 01-4555605

Rothery, Colin, CC
43 Chestnut Grove,
Ballymount Road,
Dublin 24
Tel 01-4515570
(*Kilnamanagh-Castleview*, Dublin)

Router, Michael
Cullies, Cavan
Tel 049-75004
(Kilmore)

Rowan, Kevin, Adm
Parochial House, Ashford,
Co Wicklow
Tel 0404-40540
(*Ashford*, Dublin)

Ruane, Noel S. (SVD)
Donamon Castle,
Roscommon
Tel 090-6662222

Ruddy, Michael (SSCC)
Sacred Heart Presbytery,
St John's Drive, Clondalkin
Dublin 22
Tel 01-4570032

Rushe, Patrick, Very Rev Adm, VF
Holy Redeemer Parochial House,
Ard Easmuinn,
Dundalk, Co Louth
Tel 042-9334259
(*Dundalk, Holy Redeemer*, Armagh)

Russell, Thomas (OFM)
Vicar, Franciscan Friary,
Rossnowlagh, Co Donegal
Tel 072-9851342

Russell, William, Adm
Enniscouch,
Rathkeale, Co Limerick
Tel 069-63490/087-2272825
(*Rathkeale*, Limerick)

Ryan, Aidan, Very Rev, PP
Ballinahown, Athlone,
Co Westmeath
Tel 090-6430124
(Ardagh & Cl.)

Ryan, Aloysius (OCarm)
Carmelite Priory,
White Abbey, Co Kildare
Tel 045-521391

Ryan, Alphonsus (OFMCap)
Capuchin Friary,
Church Street, Dublin 7
Tel 01-8730599

Ryan, Anselm (OP)
St Saviour's, Bridge Street, Waterford
Tel 051-875061

Ryan, Anthony, Very Rev, PP
Parochial House, Doon, Co Limerick
Tel 061-380165
(*Doon*, Cashel & E.)

Ryan, Bill (OFMCap)
Chaplain, Bon Secours Hospital
Tel 01-8065300
(Dublin)

Ryan, Conor, Very Rev Canon, PP, VF
Castlefarm, Hospital, Co Limerick
Tel 061-383108
(*Hospital*, Cashel & E.)

Ryan, Damian, PP
Lourdes House, Childers Road, Limerick
Tel 061-467676
(*Our Lady of Lourdes*, Limerick)

Ryan, Daniel J.
c/o Archbishop's House, Thurles, Co Tipperary
(Cashel & E., retired)

Ryan, Denis, PE
1 Rossmore Road, Dublin 6W
(Dublin, retired)

Ryan, Derek (CSsR)
Clonard Monastery, 1 Clonard Gardens, Belfast, BT13 2RL
Tel 028-90445950

Ryan, Dermot
St Kiernan's College, Kilkenny
Tel 056-7721086
(Ossory)

Ryan, Edmund (SAC)
Pallottine College, Thurles, Co Tipperary
Tel 0504-21202

Ryan, Eugene (SSC)
St Columban's, Dalgan Park, Navan, Co Meath
Tel 046-9021525

Ryan, Fergal, Very Rev, PP
Cahirdaniel, Co Kerry
Tel 066-9475111
(*Cahirdaniel*, Kerry)

Ryan, Fergus (OP)
Convent of SS Xystus and Clement
Collegio San Clemente, Via Labicana 95, 00184 Roma
Tel 39-06-7740021

Ryan, Gerard (CSSp)
Holy Spirit Missionary College, Kimmage Manor, Whitehall Road, Dublin 12
Tel 01-4064300

Ryan, James (OFMCap)
Capuchin Friary, Ard Mhuire, Creeslough, Letterkenny, Co Donegal
Tel 074-9138005

Ryan, James, Rt Rev Mgr, AP
Bohermore, Cashel, Co Tipperary
Tel 062-61353
(*Cashel*, Cashel & E.)

Ryan, James, Very Rev
(priest in residence)
Cleariestown, Co Wexford
Tel 053-9139110
(Ferns, retired)

Ryan, John J., Very Rev, AP
Garryspillane, Kilmallock, Co Limerick
Tel 062-53189
(*Knocklong*, Cashel & E.)

Ryan, John, Very Rev, PP
Aghinagh, Coachford, Co Cork
Tel 026-48037
(*Aghinagh*, Cloyne)

Ryan, Joseph, CC
11 Palmerstown Court, Dublin 20
Tel 01-6268772
(*Ballyfermot Upper*, Dublin)

Ryan, Liam (OSA)
St Augustine's Priory, O'Connell Street, Limerick
Tel 061-415374

Ryan, Liam, Very Rev Canon, PP, VF
Moyglass, Fethard, Co Tipperary
Tel 052-9156244
(*Killenaule*, Cashel & E.)

Ryan, Liam, Very Rev, DD
Cappamore, Co Tipperary
(Cashel & E., retired)

Ryan, Liam, Very Rev, PE
Mondaniel, Fermoy, Co Cork
(Cloyne, retired)

Ryan, Martin (CSsR), CC
Presbytery 3, Most Sacred Heart Parish, Joseph's Road, Dublin 7
Tel 01-8385766

Ryan, Martin (OCarm)
Prior, Carmelite Priory, Moate, Co Westmeath
Tel 090-6481160

Ryan, Michael (OCSO)
Bolton Abbey, Moone, Co Kildare
Tel 059-8624102

Ryan, Michael (SSC)
112 The Sycamores, Freshford Road, Kilkenny
Tel 086-8977569

Ryan, Michael G., CC
Templemore, Co Tipperary
Tel 050431492
(*Templemore*, Cashel & E.)

Ryan, Michael J., Very Rev, PE
Clonmel Road, Cahir, Co Tipperary
Tel 052-7443004
(Waterford & L., retired)

Ryan, Michael, CC
Church Road, Templemore
Tel 0504-31492
(Cashel and E.)

Ryan, Michael, Rt Rev Mgr, PP, VG
Castlecomer, Co Kilkenny
Tel 056-4441262/086-3693863
(*Castlecomer*, Ossory)

Ryan, Noel (SPS)
St Patrick's, Kiltegan, Co Wicklow
Tel 059-6473600

Ryan, Patrick (OCSO)
Mount Melleray Abbey, Cappoquin, Co Waterford
Tel 058-54404

Ryan, Patrick J. (MHM)
St Joseph's House, 50 Orwell Park, Rathgar, Dublin 6
Tel 01-4127700

Ryan, Patrick J. (CSSp)
Holy Spirit Missionary College, Kimmage Manor, Dublin 12
Tel 01-4064300

Ryan, Patrick, Very Rev, PP
The Presbytery, Eadestown, Naas, Co Kildare
Tel 045-862187
(*Eadestown*, Dublin)

Ryan, Paul
c/o Killaloe Diocesan Office, Westbourne, Ennis, Co Clare
(Killaloe)

Ryan, Seamus, Very Rev, PP
St Matthew's, No. 1 Presbytery, Blackditch Road, Dublin 10
Tel 01-6265695
(*Ballyfermot Upper*, Dublin)

Ryan, Sean (SMA), CC
St Peter's Presbytery, 10 Fair Street, Drogheda, Co Louth
Tel 041-9838239
(*Drogheda*, Armagh)

Ryan, Thomas J., Very Rev, Canon PP, VF
Liscreagh, Co Limerick
Tel 061-386227
(*Murroe and Boher*, Cashel & E.)

Ryan, Thomas, Very Rev, CC
Gleneden, North Circular Road, Limerick
Tel 061-329448/087-2997733
(*Our Lady of the Rosary*, Limerick)

Ryan, Thomas, Very Rev, PP
5 Derravaragh Road, Caherdavin Park, Limerick
Tel 061-452790
(*Christ the King*, Limerick)

Ryan, Tom, Very Rev, PP
4 Dun na Rí, Shannon, Co Clare
Tel 061-364133/087-2349816
(*Shannon*, Killaloe)

Ryan, William, Very Rev Canon, PP, VF
Parochial House, Dungarvan, Co Waterford
Tel 058-42374
(*Dungarvan*, Waterford & L.)

Ryder, Andrew (SCI)
Sacred Heart Fathers, Fairfield, 66 Inchicore Road, Dublin 8
Tel 01-4538655

Ryder, John, PEm
16 Whitehouse Park, Duncrana Road, Derry
(Derry, retired)

Ryle, Sean (SSC)
St Columban's Retirement Home, Dalgan Park, Navan, Co Meath
Tel 046-9021525

## S

Sammon, Frank (SJ), CC
35 Lower Leeson Street, Dublin 2
Tel 01-6761248
(Zam-Mal)

Sandham, Denis (MI)
(Chaplain to Beaumont Hospital)
Superior, St Camillus, South Hill Avenue, Blackrock, Co Dublin
Tel 01-2882873

Scallon, Kevin (CM)
All Hallows Institute for Mission and Ministry, Drumcondra, Dublin 9
Tel 01-8373745/6

Scallon, Paschal (CM), Very Rev, Co-PP
St Peter's, Phibsboro, Dublin 7
Tel 01-8389708
(*Phibsboro*, Dublin)

Scanlan, Charles
Ballinwillin, Lismore, Co Waterford
Tel 058-54282
(Waterford & L.)

Scanlan, Liam V. (SPS)
St Patrick's, Kiltegan, Co Wicklow
Tel 059-6473600

Scanlan, Patrick, Very Rev, PP
Castletownroche, Co Cork
Tel 022-26188
(*Castletownroche*, Cloyne)

Scanlon, Columba (OFM)
Adam & Eve's,
4 Merchant's Quay, Dublin 8
Tel 01-6771128

Scanlon, Michael, Very Rev, PP
Cloghan, Birr, Co Offaly
Tel 090-6457122
(*Cloghan and Banagher*, Ardagh & Cl.)

Scanlon, Thomas (CP)
Passionist Retreat Centre,
Tobar Mhuire, Crossgar,
Co Down BT30 9EA
Tel 028-44830242

Scott, Michael (SDB) CC
Salesian House,
45 St Teresa's Road,
Crumlin, Dublin 12
Tel 01-4555605

Scott, Philip (OCSO)
Our Lady of Bethlehem Abbey,
11 Ballymena Road,
Portglenone, Ballymena,
Co Antrim BT44 8BL
Tel 028-25821211

Screene, Michael (MSC)
Leader, 'Croí Nua',
Rosary Lane, Taylor's Hill,
Galway
Tel 091-520960

Scriven, Richard, Very Rev, PP
The Rower, Thomastown,
Co Kilkenny
Tel 087-2420033
(Ossory)

Scully, Anthony, CC
89 Ballybough Road,
Dublin 3
Tel 01-8363451
(*North William Street*, Dublin)

Scully, Brendan (OFM)
Guardian,
Franciscan College,
Gormanston, Co Meath
Tel 01-8412203

Scully, Michael (SSC)
St Columban's Retirement Home,
Dalgan Park, Navan,
Co Meath
Tel 046-9021525

Scully, Patrick (SSC)
St Columban's Retirement Home,
Dalgan Park, Navan,
Co Meath
Tel 046-9021525

Scully, Thomas (OMI)
Oblate House of Retreat,
Inchicore, Dublin 8
Tel 014534408/4541805

Seaver, Patrick, CC
4 Glenview Terrace,
Farranshone, Limerick
Tel 061-328838
(*St Munchin's and St Lelia's*, Limerick)

Seery, Michael, Very Rev, PP
Parochial House,
115 Omagh Road,
Ballygawley,
Co Tyrone BT70 2AG
Tel 028-85568208
(*Ballygawley (Errigal Kieran)*, Armagh)

Serrage, Michael (MSC)
Leader & Director,
Grace Dieu Retreat House,
Tramore Road, Waterford
Tel 051-374417/373372

Sexton, Frank (OSA)
St Augustine's Priory,
O'Connell Street,
Limerick
Tel 061-415374

Sexton, John
(priest in residence)
Killargue, Drumahaire
Co Leitrim
Tel 071-9164131
(Kilmore)

Sexton, Pat, Very Rev, PP
5 Cottage Gardens,
Station Road, Ennis,
Co Clare
Tel 065-6840828/087-2477814
(Killaloe, retired)

Sexton, Peter (SJ)
House 27, Trinity College,
Dublin 2
Tel 01-8961260
(Dublin)

Sexton, Sean, Very Rev, PC
Kilnamona, Co Clare
Tel 065-6829570/087-2621884
(Killaloe)

Seymour, Tom, Very Rev, AP
Church Road, Nenagh,
Co Tipperary
Tel 067-31381/087-2889055
(*Nenagh*, Killaloe)

Shanahan, John, Very Rev, PP
Valentia Island, Co Kerry
Tel 066-9476104
(*Valentia*, Kerry)

Shanahan, Tom (OCD)
The Abbey, Loughrea,
Co Galway
Tel 091-841209

Shanka, Matthew (SAC)
Pallottine College, Thurles,
Co Tipperary
Tel 0504-21202

Shanley, Ciaran (CSSp)
Holy Spirit Missionary College,
Kimmage Manor, Dublin 12
Tel 01-4064300

Shannon, Declan, CC
St Mary's, Athlone,
Co Westmeath
Tel 090-6472088
(*Athlone*, Ardagh & Cl.)

Shannon, Richard, CC
42A Strand Street, Skerries,
Co Dublin
Tel 01-8106771
(*Skerries*, Dublin)

Sharkey, Liam
Ballyweelin, Rosses Point,
Co Sligo
(Elphin, retired)

Sharkey, Lorcan, Very Rev, PP
Cloghan, Lifford, Co Donegal
Tel 074-9133007
(*Cloghan*, Raphoe)

Shaughnessy, Bernard, CC
Coolarne, Turloughmore,
Co Galway
Tel 091-797626
(*Lackagh*, Tuam)

Sheary, Patrick (SJ)
Irish Jesuit Provincialate,
Milltown Park,
Sandford Road, Dublin 6
Tel 01-4987333

Sheedy, Cyril (CSSp)
Holy Spirit Missionary College,
Kimmage Manor, Dublin 12
Tel 01-406 4300

Sheedy, Michael, Very Rev, PP
Toler Street, Kilrush,
Co Clare
Tel 065-9051093
(*Kilrush*, Killaloe)

Sheehan, Anthony, CC
Doneraile, Co Cork
Tel 022-24120
(*Doneraile*, Cloyne)

Sheehan, Joseph (CSSp)
Holy Spirit Missionary College,
Kimmage Manor, Dublin 12
Tel 01-4064300

Sheehan, Martin, Very Rev, Adm
St Joseph's, Lauragh,
Killarney, Co Kerry
Tel 064-6683107
(*Tuosist*, Kerry)

Sheehan, Michael, CC
Parochial House,
11 Moy Road,
Portadown,
Co Armagh BT62 1QL
Tel 028-38332218
(*Portadown (Drumcree)*, Armagh)

Sheehan, Michael, Very Rev, Adm
St Patrick's Presbytery,
199 Donegall Street,
Belfast BT1 2FL
Tel 028-90324597
(*St Patrick's*, Down & C.)

Sheehan, Niall, CC
Cathedral Presbytery,
38 Hill Street, Newry,
Co Down BT34 1AT
Tel 028-30262586
(Dromore)

Sheehan, Patrick (MSC)
Woodview House,
Mount Merrion Avenue,
Blackrock, Co Dublin
Tel 01-2881644

Sheehan, Patrick, Very Rev Canon
'Shalom', Rossbeigh,
Glenbeigh, Co Kerry
(Kerry, retired)

Sheehan, Patrick, Very Rev, PP
The Presbytery,
Bell Steel Road, Poleglass,
Belfast BT17 0PB
Tel 028-90625739
(*The Nativity*, Down & C.)

Sheehan, Rory, Very Rev, PP
Parochial House,
111 Causeway Street,
Portrush,
Co Antrim BT56 8JE
Tel 028-70823388
(*Portrush*, Down & C.)

Sheehan, Ted
Springhill, Glanmire,
Co Cork
Tel 021-4866306
(*Glanmire*, Cork & R.)

Sheehy, James (SSC)
Ballinamuck West,
Dungarvan, Co Waterford
Tel 087-6126862

Sheehy, Richard, Very Rev, PP
52 Lower Rathmines Road,
Dublin 6
Tel 01-4975958
(*Rathmines*, Dublin)

Sheehy, Sean
(assistant priest)
Castlegregory, Co Kerry
Tel 066-7139145
(*Castlegregory*, Kerry)

Sheeran, James, CC
The Presbytery,
St Colmcille's Parish,
18 Aspen Road,
Kisealy Court,
Swords, Co Dublin
Tel 01-8187908
(*Swords*, Dublin)

Sheerin, Michael, Very Rev, PP
Parochial House,
Lobinstown, Navan,
Co Meath
Tel 046-9053155
(*Lobinstown*, Meath)

Sheil, Michael (SJ)
Rector,
Clongowes Wood College,
Naas, Co Kildare
Tel 045-868663/868202

Sheils, Patrick (CSsR)
Marianella, 75 Orwell Road, Rathgar, Dublin 6
Tel 01-4067100

Shelley, Padraig,
c/o Bishop's House, Carlow
(Kildare & L.)

Shen-yi Hssii, Matthew (SJ)
John Sullivan House, 56/56A Mulvey Park, Dundrum, Dublin 14
Tel 01-2983978

Sheppard, Jim, Very Rev
189 Carrigenagh Road, Ballymartin, Kilkeel, Co Down BT34 4GA
(Down & C., retired)

Sheridan, Christopher CC
7 Bayside Square East, Sutton, Dublin 13
Tel 01-8730700/8745441
(*Bayside*, Dublin)

Sheridan, Daniel, Very Rev, PP
Killeshandra, Co Cavan
Tel 049-4334179
(*Drumlane*, Kilmore)

Sheridan, Eamon (SSC)
General Council, 504, Tower 1, Silvercord, 30 Canton Road TST, Kowloon, Hong Kong SAR

Sheridan, James (CP)
St Paul's Retreat, Mount Argus, Dublin 6W
Tel 01-4992000

Sheridan, John-Paul, CC
Blackwater, Enniscorthy, Co Wexford
Tel 053-9129288
(Ferns)

Sheridan, Paddy, CC
Robeen, Hollymount, Co Mayo
Tel 094-9540026
(*Robeen*, Tuam)

Sheridan, Patrick (CP)
St Paul's Retreat, Mount Argus, Dublin 6W
Tel 01-4992000

Sherlock, Vincent, Very Rev
Kilmovee, Ballaghadereen, Co Roscommon
Tel 094-9649137
(Achonry)

Sherry, Richard, Rt Rev Mgr, DD, PE
No. 2 Presbytery, Stillorgan Road, Donnybrook, Dublin 4
Tel 01-2692102
(Dublin, retired)

Shevlin, James, Very Rev, PE, AP
Parochial House, Omeath, Co Louth
Tel 042-9375198
(*Carlingford and Clogherny*, Armagh)

Shibanada, Julius
Church of the Sacred Heart, Donnybrook, Dublin 4
(*Donnybrook*, Dublin)

Shiel, Patrick, Very Rev
74 Mount Drinan Avenue, Kinsealy, Downs, Swords, Co Dublin
(Dublin, retired)

Shiels, Michael, CC
No. 2 Presbytery, St Canice's Parish, Finglas, Dublin 11
Tel 087-8180097
(*Finglas*, Dublin)

Shiels, Joseph (SSC)
St Columban's Retirement Home, Dalgan Park, Navan, Co Meath
Tel 046-9021525

Shine, John, Rt Rev Mgr, AP
Priest's Road, Tramore, Co Waterford
Tel 051-381531
(*Tramore*, Waterford & L.)

Shine, Larry, (CSSp), CC
Ballyleague, Lanesboro, Co Longford
Tel 043-3321171
(*Ballagh*, Elphin)

Shire, Joseph, Very Rev, PP
Ballyagran, Kilmallock, Co Limerick
Tel 063-82028/087-6924563
(*Ballyagran and Granagh*, Limerick)

Shortall, Bryan (OFMCap), PP
Guardian, Capuchin Friary, Church Street, Dublin 7
(*Halston Street and Arran Quay*, Dublin)

Shortall, Michael, PC
87 Beechwood Lawns, Rathcoole, Co Dublin
Tel 01-4587187
(*Saggart*, Dublin)

Shorten, Kieran, Very Rev (OFMCap)
Vicar, Capuchin Friary, Ard Mhuire, Creeslough, Letterkenny, Co Donegal
Tel 074-9138005

Sikora, Krzysztof (SVD)
Donamon Castle, Roscommon
Tel 090-6662222
Polish Chaplain, Knock Shrine, Co Mayo
Tel 094-9388100
(Tuam)

Silke, John J., Very Rev Dean, PhD
'Stella Maris', Portnablagh, Co Donegal
Tel 074-9136122
(Raphoe, retired)

Silke, Leo (SMA)
SMA House, Wilton, Cork
Tel 021-4541069/4541884

Simpson, Michael, CC
Presbytery No. 2, Holy Family Parish, St Joseph's Road, Dublin 7
Tel 01-8339177
(*Aughrim Street*, Dublin)

Simson, Pierre (White Fathers)
Cypress Grove, Templeogue, Dublin 6W
Tel 01-4055263/4055264

Sinnott, John, Very Rev, PP
Enniscorthy, Co Wexford
Tel 053-9388559
(*Ballindaggin*, Ferns)

Sinnott, John, Very Rev, PP
Parochial House, Enniskerry, Co Wicklow
Tel 01-2863506
(*Enniskerry*, Dublin)

Sinnott, Patrick, CC
St Aidan's, Enniscorthy, Co Wexford
Tel 053-9235777
(*Enniscorthy, Cathedral of St Aidan*, Ferns)

Sinnott, Peter J., CC
No. 3 Presbytery, Castle Street, Dalkey, Co Dublin
Tel 01-2859212
(*Dalkey*, Dublin)

Sinnott, Thomas (MHM)
Midlands Prison, Dublin Road, Portlaoise, Co Laois
Tel 057-8672222
(Kildare & L.)

Sisti, Louis (SAC)
Provincial House, 'Homestead', Sandyford Road, Dundrum, Dublin 16
Tel 01-2956180/2954170

Siwek, Rafal, CC
The Presbytery, Cavan
Tel 049-4331404/4332269
(*Cavan*, Kilmore)

Skelly, Oliver, Very Rev, PP
Parochial House, Coole, Co Westmeath
Tel 044-9661191
(*Coole,* Meath)

Skinnader, John, CSSp,
St Michael's Parish, 4 Darling Street, Enniskillen, Co Fermanagh BT74 7DP
Tel 028-66322075
(Clogher)

Slater, Albert, CC
Keenagh, Ballina, Co Mayo
Tel 096-53018
(*Crossmolina*, Killala)

Slater, David (OSA)
St Augustine's Priory, Dungarvan, Co Waterford
Tel 058-41136

Slater, John (MHM)
St Joseph's House, 50 Orwell Park, Rathgar, Dublin 6
Tel 01-4127700

Slattery, Gerard
c/o Diocesan Office, Social Service Centre, Henry Street, Limerick
(Limerick)

Slattery, John, Very Rev, PP
Puckane, Nenagh, Co Tipperary
Tel 067-24105/087-2794577
(*Puckane*, Killaloe)

Slattery, Martin, Very Rev, AP
Apt 5, Luke Wadding Suites, Adelphi Wharf, Waterford
Tel 051-311561
(*Trinity Within and St Patrick's*, Waterford & L.)

Slattery, Sean, Very Rev, PP
Ballymacward, Ballinasloe, Co Galway
Tel 090-9687614
(*Ballymacward and Gurteen*, Clonfert)

Sleeman, Simon (OSB)
Glenstal Abbey, Murroe, Co Limerick
Tel 061-386103

Slevin, Paschal (OFM)
Franciscan House of Studies, Dún Mhuire, Seafield Road, Killiney, Co Dublin
Tel 01-2826760

Slevin, Peter (CM), Very Rev
President/Superior, St Vincent's College, Castleknock, Dublin 15
Tel 01-8213051

Slowey, Henry (CM)
St Vincent's College, Castleknock, Dublin 15
Tel 01-8213051

Stapor, Tomasz (SJ) (PME)
Jesuit Community, 27 Leinster Road, Rathmines, Dublin 6
Tel 01-4970250

Smith, Adrian (SM), Most Rev
Archbishop
Honiara, Solomon Islands

Smith, David (MSC)
Leader, Woodview House, Mount Merrion Avenue, Blackrock, Co Dublin
Tel 01-2881644

Smith, Declan, Very Rev, PP
Parochial House, Taghmon, Mullingar, Co Westmeath
Tel 044-9372140
(*Taghmon*, Meath)

Smith, Desmond (SMA)
Rathduff, Ballina, Co Mayo
Tel 096-21596
(*Backs*, Killala)
Smith, Kevin (OPraem), Rt Rev
Abbey of the Most Holy
Trinity and St Norbert,
Kilnacrott, Ballyjamesduff,
Co Cavan
Tel 049-8544416
Smith, Martin (SPS)
St Patrick's,
21 Old Cavehill Road,
Belfast BT15 5GT
Tel 028-90778696
Smith, Michael, Most Rev,
DCL, DD
Bishop of Meath,
Bishop's House,
Dublin Road, Mullingar,
Co Westmeath
Tel 044-9348841
(Meath)
Smith, Philip, Very Rev, PP
Parochial House, Ballymore,
Mullingar, Co Westmeath
Tel 044-9356212
(*Ballymore*, Meath)
Smith, Sean, CC
The Presbytery,
Newtownmountkennedy,
Co Wicklow
Tel 01-2819253
(*Kilquade*, Dublin)
Smith, Tom (OSCam)
St Camillus, Killucan
Co Westmeath
Smith, Tom (SPS)
St Patrick's, Kiltegan,
Co Wicklow
Tel 059-6473600
Smyth, Brendan, CC
Parochial House,
Glenavy Road, Crumlin,
Co Antrim BT29 4LA
Tel 028-94422278
(*Glenavy and Killead*, Down
& C.)
Smyth, Derek, CC
2 Kill Lane, Foxrock,
Dublin 18
Tel 01-2894734
(*Foxrock*, Dublin)
Smyth, Edward (OCD)
Prior,
53/55 Marlborough Road,
Donnybrook, Dublin 4
Tel 01-6601832
Smyth, James (SJ)
St Francis Xavier's,
Upper Gardiner Street,
Dublin 1
Tel 01-8363411
Smyth, Malachy (SSC)
Communications
Co-ordinator,
St Columban's,
Dalgan Park, Navan,
Co Meath
Tel 046-9021525
Smyth, Michael (MSC)
'Croí Nua', Rosary Lane,
Taylor's Hill, Galway
Tel 091-520960
Smyth, Patrick (OCarm)
Carmelite Priory,
White Abbey, Co Kildare
Tel 045-521391
Smyth, Patrick J. (SSC)
St Columban's Retirement
Home,
Dalgan Park, Navan,
Co Meath
Tel 046-9021525
Smyth, Ted (SPS)
St Patrick's, Kiltegan,
Co Wicklow
Tel 059-6473600
Smyth, Terry (OPraem)
Abbey of the Most Holy
Trinity and St Norbert,
Kilnacrott,
Ballyjamesduff, Co Cavan
Tel 049-8544416
Solma, Martin (SM)
Provincial, Provincial
Headquaters,
4425 West Pine Boulevard,
St Louis, MO 6308-2301,
USA
Tel 314-533-1207
Somers, James (SDB), CC
The Presbytery, Chapelizod,
Dublin 20
Tel 01-6264656
(*Chapelizod*, Dublin)
Somers, P. J. (SDB)
Curragh Camp, Co Kildare
Tel 045-441277
(*Curragh Camp*, Kildare & L.)
Sorahan, Jim, CC
Ballinamuck, Co Longford
Tel 043-3324110
(*Drumlish*, Ardagh & Cl.)
Spain, Michael (OCD)
St Teresa's,
Clarendon Street, Dublin 2
Tel 01-6718466/6718127
Spelman, Andrew (CM)
St Peter's, Phibsboro,
Dublin 7
Tel 01-8389708
Spelman, Joseph, Rt Rev Mgr
(priest in residence)
Collooney, Co Sligo
Tel 071-9167109
(Achonry, retired)
Spence, Michael, Very Rev
St Malachy's College,
36 Antrim Road,
Belfast BT15 2AE
Tel 028-90748285
(Down & C.)
Spillane, Edmund (IC)
Nursing Home
Spillane, Joseph (SPS), CC
Ballydehob, Co Cork
Tel 028-3711
(*Schull*, Cork & R.)
Spillane, Martin
Chaplain,
Tralee General Hospital,
Co Kerry
Tel 066-7126222
(Kerry)
Spillane, Martin (SPS)
On temporary diocesan
work
Spring, Finbar (OSA)
St Augustine's Priory,
Dungarvan,
Co Waterford
Tel 058-41136
Spring, Noel, Very Rev, PP
Ballybunion, Co Kerry
Tel 068-27102
(*Ballybunion*, Kerry)
St John, Paul (SVD), Very Rev,
Adm
The Presbytery, City Quay,
Dublin 2
Tel 01-6773706
(*City Quay*, Dublin)
Stack, Thomas, Very Rev Mgr,
PE
Apt 4, Maple Hall (adjoining
church),
Milltown, Dublin 6
Tel 01-2697613
(Dublin, retired)
Stafford, Patrick, Very Rev, PP
Glynn, Enniscorthy,
Co Wexford
Tel 053-9128115
(*Glynn*, Ferns)
Standún, Padraic, PP
Carna, Co Galway
Tel 091-595452
(*Carna*, Tuam)
Stankard, Edward, Rt Rev
Mgr, PP, VG
Cappatagle, Ballinasloe,
Co Galway
Tel 091-843017
(Clonfert)
Stanley, Cathal
(Leave of Absence)
Portumna
Tel 086-1052479
(Clonfert)
Stanley, Gerard, Very Rev, PP
Parochial House, Rathkenny,
Co Meath
Tel 046-9054138
(*Rathkenny*, Meath)
Stanley, James (CSsR)
Marianella, 75 Orwell Road,
Dublin 6
Tel 01-4067100
Stanley, Paddy (SM), CC
Holy Family Parish,
Parochial House,
Dundalk, Co Louth
Tel 042-9336301
(*Dundalk, Holy Family*,
Armagh)
Stapleton, Christy
c/o Diocesan Office,
Balinalee Road, Longford
(Ardagh & Cl.)
Stapleton, Jim (CSSp)
Holy Spirit Missionary
College,
Kimmage Manor, Dublin 12
Tel 01-4064300
Stapleton, John, Very Rev, PP
Killeigh, Co Offaly
Tel 057-9344161
(*Killeigh*, Kildare & L.)
Starken, Brian (CSSp)
Provincial Leader,
Holy Spirit Provincialate,
Temple Park,
Richmond Avenue South,
Dublin 6
Tel 01-4975127/4977230
Starkey, Hugh, Very Rev
Canon
(priest in residence)
Parochial House,
26 Tyrella Road, Ballykinlar,
Downpatrick BT30 8DF
Tel 028-44851221
(*Dundrum and Tyrella*,
Down & C.)
Staunton, Brendan (SJ)
St Francis Xavier's,
Upper Gardiner Street,
Dublin 1
Tel 01-8363411
Staunton, Fachtna (MHM)
St Joseph's, Freshford
House, Kilkenny
Tel 056-7721482
Staunton, Patrick (OCarm)
Assistant Provincial,
Provincial Office and
Carmelite Community,
Gort Muire, Ballinteer,
Dublin 16
Tel 01-2984014
Staunton, Ray (SM)
Chanel College, Coolock,
Dublin 5
Tel 01-8480655/8480896
Steblecki, Hilary (OFM)
Franciscan Friary, Killarney,
Co Kerry
Tel 064-6631334/6631066
Steed, Bernard (SSC)
St Columban's, Dalgan Park,
Navan, Co Meath
Tel 046-9021525
Steele, Joseph M. (CSSp)
Holy Spirit Missionary
College,
Kimmage Manor, Dublin 12
Tel 01-4064300
Steen, Brendan (CM)
St Paul's College, Raheny,
Dublin 5
Tel 01-8318113

Stenson, Alex, Rt Rev Mgr, PP
126 Furry Park Road,
Dublin 5
Tel 01-8333793
(*Killester*, Dublin)

Stevenson, Liam, Very Rev Canon, PP, VF
6 Scarva Road, Banbridge,
Co Down BT32 3AR
Tel 028-40662136
(*Seapatrick (Banbridge)*, Dromore)

Stevenson, Patrick, Very Rev, PP
The Presbytery, Crosshaven,
Co Cork
Tel 021-4831218
(*Crosshaven*, Cork & R.)

Stewart, Charles (OFMCap)
Capuchin Friary,
Ard Mhuire, Creeslough,
Letterkenny, Co Donegal
Tel 074-9138005

Stewart, John, Very Rev
27F Windsor Avenue,
Belfast BT9 6EE
(Down & C., retired)

Stokes, John, Very Rev
44 Carlton Court, Swords,
Co Dublin
(Dublin, retired)

Stokes, Tom (SM)
USA

Stone, Tom (OCD)
Avila, Bloomfield Avenue,
Morehampton Road,
Dublin 4
Tel 01-6430200

Strain, Paul, Very Rev, PP
Co-ordinator,
St Joseph's Centre for the Deaf,
321 Grosvenor Road,
Belfast BT12 4LP
Tel 028-40448211
Parish
470 Falls Road,
Belfast BT12 6EN
Tel 028-90321511
(*St John's*, Down & C.)

Stritch, Denis, Very Rev, PP
Meelin, Newmarket,
Co Cork
Tel 029-68007
(*Rockchapel and Meelin*, Cloyne)

Stuart, Gerard, Very Rev, PP
Parochial House, Ratoath,
Co Meath
Tel 01-8256207
(Meath)

Stuart, William (IC)
Clonturk House,
Ormond Road,
Drumcondra, Dublin 9
Tel 01-6877014

Sugrue, Patrick (CSsR)
St Joseph's, Dundalk,
Co Louth
Tel 042-9334042

Sullivan, Donal (IC)
Clonturk House,
Ormond Road,
Drumcondra, Dublin 9
Tel 01-6877014

Sullivan, Kevin
Abbeydorney, Co Kerry
Tel 066-7145639
(*Abbeydorney*, Kerry)

Sullivan, Patrick, CC
Glencar, Manorhamilton,
Co Leitrim
Tel 071-9855433
(*Manorhamilton*, Kilmore)

Sullivan, Paul (OCD)
St Teresa's,
Clarendon Street, Dublin 2
Tel 01-6718466/6718127

Supple, Michael D., Very Rev Canon
Apartment 8,
Giltown Lodge, Kilcullen,
Co Kildare
(Dublin, retired)

Surlis, Paul
1684 Albermarle Drive,
Crofton, Maryland 21114,
USA
Tel 001-410-4511459
(Achonry, retired)

Surlis, Tómas Very Rev, DD
St Nathy's College,
Ballaghaderreen,
Co Roscommon
Tel 094-9860010
(Achonry)

Susai, Jega (SVD)
Donamon Castle,
Roscommon
Tel 090-6662222

Swan, Colum, Very Rev, PE
32 Cherrygrove, Naas,
Co Kildare
Tel 045-856274
(Kildare & L., retired)

Swan, William
Pontifical Irish College,
Via de SS Quattro 1,
00184 Roma, Italy
(Ferns)

Sweeney, Dennis (IC)
Clonturk House,
Ormond Road, Drumcondra,
Dublin 9
Tel 01-8374840

Sweeney, Desmond, Very Rev, PE
17 Meadowvale, Ramelton
Tel 074-9151085
(Raphoe, retired)

Sweeney, Donal (OFMCap)
Vicar, Capuchin Friary,
Friary Street, Kilkenny
Tel 056-7721439

Sweeney, Donal, (OP), Very Rev, PP, Adm
St Mary's Priory, Tallaght,
Dublin 24
Tel 01-4048100
(*Tallaght, St Mary's*, Dublin)

Sweeney, Eugene, Very Rev, Adm
Parochial House,
42 Abbey Street,
Armagh BT61 7DZ
Tel 028-37522802
(*Armagh*, Armagh)

Sweeney, Gerard (SMA)
SMA House, Claregalway,
Co Galway
Tel 091-798880

Sweeney, Gerard, CC
Parochial House, Burt,
Lifford, Co Donegal
Tel 074-9368155
(*Fahan*, Derry)

Sweeney, Hugh, Very Rev, PP
Glenswilly, New Mills,
Letterkenny, Co Donegal
Tel 074-9137020
(*Glenswilly*, Raphoe)

Sweeney, James, CC
Ardaghey, Co Donegal
Tel 074-9736007
(Raphoe)

Sweeney, Michael, AP
Glenvar, Letterkenny,
Co Donegal
Tel 074-9150014
(Raphoe)

Sweeney, Oliver, Very Rev, PP
Poulfur, Fethard-on-Sea,
New Ross, Co Wexford
Tel 051-397048
(Ferns)

Sweeney, Owen, Rt Rev Mgr
54 Seabury,
Sudney Parade Avenue,
Dublin 4
Tel 01-2698878
(Dublin, retired)

Sweeney, Patrick, PC
13 Home Farm Road,
Drumcondra, Dublin 9
Tel 01-6264639
(*Ballymun Road*, Dublin)

Sweetman, John, Very Rev, PP
c/o Bishop's House,
PO Box 40, Wexford
Tel 053-9122177
(Ferns)

Swinburne, Robbie (SDB), CC
Salesian House, Milford,
Castletroy, Limerick
Tel 061-330268
(*Our Lady Help of Christians*, Limerick)

Symonds, Paul
2/4 Broughshane Road,
Ballymena,
Co Antrim BT43 7DX
Tel 028-25641515
(Down & C., on leave)

Szalaj, Kazimierz (SVD), CC
Donamon Castle,
Roscommon
Tel 090-6662222
(Tuam)

Szalwa, Marian (SCJ)
Parochial House,
St John Vianney,
Ardlea Road, Dublin 5
Tel 01-8474123
(*Ardlea*, Dublin)

Szymanski, Marcin (OP)
St Saviour's,
Upper Dorset Street,
Dublin 1
Tel 01-8897610

## T

Taaffe, Eugene, Very Rev, PP, VF
c/o The Presbytery Parish of Ss Peter and Paul,
Dublin Road,
Balbriggan, Co Dublin
Tel 01-8202544
(*Balbriggan*, Dublin)

Taaffe, Pat, AP
3 Cottage Garden,
Station Road, Ennis,
Co Clare
Tel 065-6891983/
086-1731070
(*Ennis*, Killaloe)

Talbot, Denis, Very Rev Canon, AP
Galbally, Co Tipperary
Tel 062-37929
(*Galbally*, Cashel & E.)

Talbot, Liam (SDS)
Our Lady of Victories,
Sallynoggin, Dun Laoghaire,
Co Dublin
Tel 01-2854667

Talty, Robert (OP)
St Mary's, Pope Quay, Cork
Tel 021-4502267

Tanham, Gerard, Very Rev, PP, VF
Parochial Place,
1 Stanhope Place,
Athy, Co Kildare
Tel 059-8631781/
087-2311947
(*Athy*, Dublin)

Tapley, Paul (OFMCap)
Capuchin Friary,
Friary Street, Kilkenny
Tel 056-7721439

Tarpey, Richard, Very Rev Canon, AP
Ennistymon, Co Clare
Tel 065-7071346
(*Ennistymon*, Galway)

Tarrant, Joseph, CC
Asdee, Co Kerry
Tel 068-41152
(*Ballylongford*, Kerry)

Taylor, Liam
St Patrick's, Ormonde Road, Kilkenny
Tel 056-7764400/ 086-8180954
(*St Patrick's*, Ossory)

Taylor, Paul, CC
Presbytery, Main Street, Celbridge, Co Kildare
Tel 01-6275874/086-3524530
(*Celbridge*, Dublin)

Teehan, Willie, Very Rev, PP
Templederry, Co Tipperary
Tel 0504-52988/087-2347927
Director, Nenagh Centre, Loreto House, Kenyon Street, Nenagh, Co Tipperary
Tel 067-31272
(*Killanave and Templederry*, Killaloe)

Terry, John, Very Rev Canon, PE
Terriville, Ballylanders, Cloyne, Co Cork
Tel 021-4646779
(Cloyne, retired)

Tessema, Workineh (Team Assistant)
The Presbytery, Holy Redeemer Parish, Herbert Road, Bray, Co Dublin
Tel 01-2868413
(*Bray Holy Redeemer*, Dublin)

Thankachan Njaliath, Paul, CC
Chaplain for Pastoral Care of the Syro Malabar Community in the Dublin Diocese, based in Tallaght
Tel 01-4510166
(Dublin)

Thennatil, Vinod Kurian
Cooleens, Glenconnor, Clonmel, Co Tipperary
Tel 052-25679
(*Clonmel, St Oliver Plunkett*, Waterford & L.)

Thettayil, Polachan (IC)
St Patrick's, Upton, Innishannon, Co Cork
Tel 021-4776268/4776923

Thompson, Declan (SPS), CC
Parochial House, Sallins, Co Kildare
Tel 045-897150
(*Sallins*, Kildare & L.)

Thompson, Peter (SMA)
Vice Superior and Bursar, Dromantine College, Dromantine, Newry, Co Down BT34 1RH
Tel 028-30821224

Thorne, Bernard (OSM)
Provincial, Servite Priory, Benburb, Dungannon, Co Tyrone BT71 7JZ
Tel 028-37548241

Thornton, Gerard (MSC)
Woodview House, Mount Merrion Avenue, Blackrock, Co Dublin
Tel 01-2881644

Thornton, Paul, CC
146 Seapark, Malahide, Co Dublin
(*Yellow Walls*, Malahide)

Thornton, Richard J. (CSSp)
Blackrock College, Blackrock, Co Dublin
Tel 01-2888681

Threadgold, Jeremiah
Sacred Heart Residence, Sybil Hill Road, Raheny, Dublin 5
(Dublin, retired)

Thynne, Eoin, HCF
McKee Barracks and St Bricin's Hospital, Dublin 7
Tel 01-6778502
(Dublin)

Tiernan, Paschal (OP)
Dominican Community, St Mary's Priory, Tallaght, Dublin 24
Tel 01-4048100

Tiernan, Peter, Very Rev, PP
Carrickedmond, Colehill, Co Longford
Tel 044-9357442
(*Carrickedmond and Abbeyshrule*, Ardagh & Cl.)

Tierney, Celsus, CC
Holy Cross Abbey, Holy Cross, Thurles, Co Tipperary
Tel 0504-43118
(Cashel & E.)

Tierney, Mark (OSB)
Glenstal Abbey, Murroe, Co Limerick
Tel 061-386103

Tierney, Philip (OSB)
Glenstal Abbey, Murroe, Co Limerick
Tel 061-386103

Tighe, James, Very Rev, CC
Elphin, Co Roscommon
Tel 071-9635131
(*Elphin*, Elphin)

Tighe, Paul, Rt Rev Mgr
Secretary of the Pontifical Council for Social Communications, Vatican City
(Dublin)

Timmons, Declan (OFM), CC
The Abbey, 8 Francis Street, Galway
Tel 091-562518
(Galway)

Timoney, Charles
Provincialate, Cypress Grove Road, Templeogue, Dublin 6W

Timoney, Gerald, Very Rev Canon, PE
Irvinestown, Enniskillen, Co Fermanagh BT94 1GD
Tel 028-68621329
(*Irvinestown*, Clogher)

Timoney, Martin
c/o Diocesan Office, Letterkenny, Co Donegal
(Raphoe)

Timoney, Pearse
The Presbytery, Ballygarvan, Co Cork
Tel 021-4888971
(*Ballinhassig*, Cork & R.)

Timoney, Senan (SJ)
Peter Faber House, 28 Brookvale Avenue, Belfast BT14 6BW
Tel 028-90757615

Timothy, Malcolm (OFM)
Franciscan College, Gormanston, Co Meath
Tel 01-8412203

Timpu, Eugene
Sean McDermott Street, Dublin 1
Tel 086-3266467
(*Sean McDermott Street*, Dublin)

Tinkasiimire, Rustico, PC
10 Finglaswood Road, Finglas, West Dublin 11
Tel 01-8341284
(*Finglas West*, Dublin)

Tinsley, Ambrose (OSB)
Glenstal Abbey, Murroe, Co Limerick
Tel 061-386103

Toal, Donal (SMA), Very Rev, PP
The Presbytery, Neilstown, Clondalkin, Dublin 22
Tel 01-4573546
(*Neilstown*, Dublin)

Tobin, Edmond, Very Rev, PE
Munroe, Rehill, Ballylooby, Cahir, Co Tipperary
Tel 052-7441975
(Waterford & L., retired)

Tobin, Martin, Very Rev, PP
Clogh, Castlecomer, Co Kilkenny
Tel 056-4442135/ 086-2401278
(*Clogh*, Ossory)

Tobin, Michael (OFMCap)
Capuchin Friary, Friary Street, Kilkenny
Tel 056-7721439

Tobin, Philip (OFMCap)
Capuchin Friary, Friary Street, Kilkenny
Tel 056-7721439

Tobin, Richard (CSsR)
St Joseph's, Dundalk, Co Louth
Tel 042-9334042/9334762

Toland, Liam, CC
Parochial House, 189 Carnlough Road, Broughshane, Co Antrim BT43 7DX
Tel 028-25684211
(*Braid*, Down & C.)

Toman, Gary
The Chaplaincy, 28 Elmwood Avenue, Belfast BT9 6AY
Tel 028-90669737
(Down & C.)

Toner, Michael C., Very Rev, PP
Parochial House, 114 Battlehill Road, Richhill, Co Armagh BT61 8QJ
Tel 028-38871661
(*Kilmore*, Armagh)

Toner, Terence, Very Rev, PP
Parochial House, Kilmessan, Co Meath
Tel 046-9025172
(*Kilmessan*, Meath)

Toner, Thomas, Rt Rev Mgr
43b Glen Road, Belfast BT11 8BB
Tel 028-90613949
(*St Teresa's*, Down & C.)

Toner, William (SJ)
25 Croftwood Park, Cherry Orchard, Dublin 10
Tel 01-6267413

Tonge, Ivan, Very Rev, PP
St Patrick's, 2 Cambridge Road, Dublin 4
Tel 01-8744236/8741625
(*Ringsend*, Dublin)

Tonna, Paul (SJ) (MAL)
St Ignatius Community & Church, 27 Raleigh Row, Salthill, Galway
Tel 091-523707

Toohey, Seamus, CC
7 Avondale Court, Blackrock, Co Dublin
Tel 01-2884043
(*Newtownpark*, Dublin)

Toomey, Michael
Priest's Road, Tramore, C Waterford
Tel 051-386642
(*Tramore*, Waterford & L.)

Torbitt, Hugh
c/o Diocesan Office, St Michael's, Longford
(Ardagh & Cl.)

Tormey, James, CC
130 Churchview Road, Ballybrack, Co Dublin
Tel 01-2851919
(*Ballybrack-Killiney*, Dublin)

Touhy, Séamus (OP)
St Mary's Priory, Tallaght, Dublin 24
Tel 01-4048100

Towey, Thomas, Very Rev, PP
Ballisodare, Co Sligo
Tel 071-9167467
(Achonry)

Townsend, Mark, PP
Daingean, Co Offaly
Tel 057-9362006
(*Daingean*, Kildare & L.)

Tracey, Finbarr (SVD)
133 North Circular Road, Dublin 7
Tel 01-8386743

Tracey, Liam (OSM)
Church of the Divine Word, Marley Grange,
25-27 Hermitage Downs, Rathfarnham, Dublin 16
Tel 01-4944295/4941064

Travers, Charles, Rt Rev Mgr, CC
1 Convent Court, Roscommon
Tel 090-6628917
(*Roscommon*, Elphin)

Travers, John (SMA)
Dromantine College, Dromantine, Newry, Co Down BT34 1RH
Tel 028-30821224

Travers, Vincent (OP)
Provincial, Provincial Office, St Mary's, Tallaght, Dublin 24
Tel 01-4048118/4048112

Treacy, Bernard (OP), Very Rev
Superior, 47 Leeson Park, Dublin 6
Tel 01-6602427

Treacy, John, CC
14 Heathervue Road, Riverview, Knockboy, Waterford
Tel 051-843207
(*SS Joseph and Benildus*, Waterford & L.)

Treacy, Pat, CC
Curates House, Convent Hill, Roscrea, Co Tipperary
Tel 0505-21370/087-9798643
(*Roscrea*, Killaloe)

Treanor, Eamon, Very Rev, PP
Parochial House, Kilsaran, Castlebellingham, Dundalk, Co Louth
Tel 042-9372255
(*Kilsaran*, Armagh)

Treanor, Martin, Very Rev, PP
Inniskeen, Dundalk, Co Louth
Tel 042-9378105
(*Inniskeen*, Clogher)

Treanor, Noel, Most Rev, DD
Bishop of Down and Connor, Lisbreen,
73 Somerton Road, Belfast, Co Antrim BT15 4DE
Tel 028-90776185
(Down & C.)

Treanor, Oliver
St Patrick's College, Maynooth, Co Kildare
Tel 01-6285222
(Down & C.)

Tremer, Gerard, Very Rev, PP, VF
Parochial House,
1 Convent Road, Cookstown, Co Tyrone BT80 8QA
Tel 028-86763370
(*Cookstown*, Armagh)

Trotter, Trevor (SSC)
Vicar General,
504, Tower 1, Silvercord,
30 Canton Road TST, Kowloon, Hong Kong SAR

Troy, Michael (OCarm)
Prior, Terenure College, Terenure, Dublin 6W
Tel 01-4904621

Troy, Ulic (OFM), Very Rev
Franciscan College, Gormanston, Co Meath
Tel 01-8412203

Tuffy, Muredach, CC
Director,
Newman Institute Ireland, Centre for Pastoral Care, Salmon Weir, Ballina, Co Mayo
Tel 096-72066
Parish
Rathduff, Ballina, Co Mayo
Tel 096-21596
(*Backs*, Killala)

Tully, Andrew
(on study leave)
c/o Bishops House, Co Cavan
(Kilmore)

Tumilty, Stephen (OP)
St Catherine's, Newry, Co Down BT35 8BN
Tel 028-30262178

Tuohy, David (SJ)
Dominic Collins' House Residence,
129 Morehampton Road, Dublin 4
Tel 01-2693075

Tuohy, Timothy, Very Rev, AP
Carrigoran Nursing Home, Newmarket on Fergus, Co Clare
(Killaloe, retired)

Tuohy, Tom (SM)
Replacement Army Chaplain, Dublin

Turley, Paul (CSsR)
Clonard Monastery,
1 Clonard Gardens, Belfast BT13 2RL
Tel 028-90445950

Twohig, David (OCarm)
Carmelite Presbytery, Idrone Avenue, Knocklyon, Dublin 16
Tel 01-4941204
(*Knocklyon*, Dublin)

Twohig, Terence (SSC)
St Columban's Retirement Home,
Dalgan Park, Navan, Co Meath
Tel 046-9021525

Twohig, Vivian, Very Rev, PP
Mullagh, Loughrea, Co Galway
Tel 091-843119
(*Mullagh and Killoran*, Clonfert)

Twomey, Bernard (OSA)
St Catherine's, Meath Street, Dublin 8
Tel 01-4543356
(*Meath Street and Merchants Quay*, Dublin)

Twomey, Donal (SPS)
St Patrick's, Kiltegan, Co Wicklow
Tel 059-6473600

Twomey, Jack (OFMCap)
St Francis Capuchin Friary, Rochestown, Co Cork
Tel 021-4896244

Twomey, Kieran, Very Rev, PP
Woodlawn, Model Farm Road, Ballineaspaig, Cork
Tel 021-4346818
(*Ballineaspaig*, Cork & R.)

Twomey, Patrick, Very Rev Canon, PE
Bellevue, Mallow, Co Cork
(Cloyne, retired)

Twomey, Vincent, D. (SVD)
Maynooth, Co Kildare
Tel 01-6286391/2

Tynan, Joseph, CC
Ballydavid, Littleton, Thurles, Co Tipperary
Tel 0504-44317
(*Moycarkey*, Cashel & E.)

Tynan, Sean, Very Rev
Laurel Lodge Nursing Home, Longford
(Ardagh & Cl., retired)

Tyndall, David
Cathal Brugha Barracks, Rathmines, Dublin 6
Tel 8046493
(Dublin)

Tyrrell, Gerard
Chaplaincy for Deaf People,
40 Lower Drumcondra Road, Dublin 9
Tel 01-8305744
(Dublin)

Tyrrell, Patrick (SJ)
(temporarily outside Ireland)
Irish Jesuit Provincialate, Milltown Park, Sandford Road, Dublin 6
Tel 01-4987333

Tyrrell, Paul, Co-PP
41 St Agnes Road, Crumlin, Dublin 12
Tel 01-6600075
(*Crumlin*, Dublin)

## U

Ubale, Linus, PC
58 Ticknock Park, Ticknock Hill, Rathfarnham, Dublin 14
Tel 01-2956414
(*Sandyford*, Dublin)

Ugwu, Stephen (OCD)
Avila, Bloomfield Avenue, Morehampton Road, Dublin 4
Tel 01-6430200

Urbanowski, Mariusz (SCHR)
4 Broughshane Road, Ballymena, Co Antrim BT43 7DX
Tel 028-25641515
(*Ballymena (Kirkinriola)*, Down & C.)

Uwah, Innocent
The Presbytery,
12 Coarse Moor Park, Straffan, Co Kildare
Tel 01-6012197/085-1404355
(*Celbridge*, Dublin)

## V

Van de Poll, Jan (SJ) (NER)
Manresa House, Dollymount, Dublin 3
Tel 01-8331352

Van Gucht, Koenraad (SDB), Very Rev, PP
Salesian House, Milford, Castletroy, Limerick
Tel 061-330268/330914
(*Our Lady Help of Christians*, Limerick)

Vaughan, Aidan (OFMCap)
Holy Trinity, Fr Mathew Quay, Cork
Tel 021-4270827

Vaughan, Denis
45 The Oaks, Maryborough Ridge, Douglas, Cork
(Cloyne, retired)

Vaughan, T. T. (SPS)
St Patrick's, Kiltegan, Co Wicklow
Tel 059-6473600

**W**

Wadding, George (CSsR)
Liguori House,
75 Orwell Road, Dublin 6
Tel 01-4067100

Wade, Thomas, Very Rev (SMA), PP
St Joseph's,
Blackrock Road, Cork
Tel 021-4292871
(*St Joseph's (Blackrock Road)*, Cork & R.)

Wafer, Andy (SSCC)
Coudrin House,
27 Northbrook Road,
Dublin 6
Tel 01-6473755/01-6686590

Waldron, Kieran, Very Rev Canon, PE
Devlis, Ballyhaunis, Co Mayo
Tel 094-9630246
(Tuam, retired)

Waldron, Paul, CC
The Presbytery, Dungarvan,
Co Waterford
Tel 058-42384
(*Dungarvan*, Waterford & L.)

Waldron, Peter, Very Rev Canon, PP
Keelogues, Ballyvary,
Co Mayo
Tel 094-9031009
(*Keelogues*, Tuam)

Walker, David (OP)
St Saviour's,
Upper Dorset Street,
Dublin 1
Tel 01-8897610

Wall, David (SSC)
St Columban's Retirement Home,
Dalgan Park, Navan,
Co Meath
Tel 046-9021525

Wall, John, Very Rev, PP
Annaduff,
Carrick-on-Shannon,
Co Leitrim
Tel 071-9624093
(*Annaduff*, Ardagh & Cl.)

Wall, John, Very Rev, PP
St Columba Parish House,
New Road, Clondalkin,
Dublin 22
Tel 01-4640441
(*Clondalkin*, Dublin)

Wall, Michael
Chaplain,
Mary Immaculate College of Education
Tel 061-204331
(Limerick)

Wall, Michael
Sacred Heart Residence,
Sybil Hill Road,
Raheny, Dublin 5
(Dublin, retired)

Wallace, Laurence, Very Rev, PP
Muckalee, Ballyfoyle,
Co Kilkenny
Tel 056-4441271/087-2326807
(Ossory)

Wallace, Matthew, Very Rev, PP
Holy Trinity Presbytery,
26 Norglen Gardens,
Belfast BT11 8EL
Tel 028-90590985/6
(*Holy Trinity*, Down & C.)

Walsh, Brendan, Very Rev, PP
Causeway, Co Kerry
Tel 066-7131148
(*Causeway*, Kerry)

Walsh, David (SPS)
Assistant Society Leader,
St Patrick's, Kiltegan,
Co Wicklow
Tel 059-6473600

Walsh, Des, Very Rev, PP
Turloughmore, Co Galway
Tel 091-797114
(*Lackagh*, Tuam)

Walsh, Donal, Very Rev
Tinnahinch,
Graiguenamanagh,
Co Kilkenny
Tel 059-9725550
(Ossory, retired)

Walsh, Eamonn, Most Rev, DD, VG
Titular Bishop of Elmham and Auxiliary Bishop of Dublin, Naomh Brid,
Blessington Road, Tallaght,
Dublin 24
Tel 01-4598032
(Dublin)

Walsh, Gearóid, Very Rev Canon, PP
Castletownbere, Co Cork
Tel 027-70849
(Kerry)

Walsh, James, Very Rev, PP
Kilmeena, Westport,
Co Mayo
Tel 098-41270
(*Kilmeena*, Tuam)

Walsh, James, Very Rev, PP
Oughterard, Co Galway
Tel 091-552290
(*Oughterard*, Galway)

Walsh, Jarlath (SMA)
SMA House, Wilton, Cork
Tel 021-4541069/4541884

Walsh, John
Mountdavid House, North Circular Road, Limerick
Tel 061-452063/087-2433488
(Limerick)

Walsh, John (OP)
Convent of SS Xystus and Clement,
Collegio San Clemente,
Via Labicana 95, 00184
Roma
Tel 39-06-7740021

Walsh, John (OSA)
Duckspool House
(Retirement Community),
Abbeyside, Dungarvan,
Co Waterford
Tel 058-23784

Walsh, John R., PP
Parochial House, Buncrana,
Co Donegal
Tel 074-9361393
(*Buncrana*, Derry)

Walsh, John, Very Rev, PE
Rath, Portlaoise, Co Laois
Tel 057-8626401
(Kildare & L., retired)

Walsh, John, Very Rev, PP
Aghamore, Ballyhaunis,
Co Mayo
Tel 094-9367024
(*Aghamore*, Tuam)

Walsh, John, Very Rev, PP
The Presbytery,
Frankfield, Cork
Tel 021-4361711
(*Frankfield-Grange*, Cork & R.)

Walsh, Joseph (OFM)
Adam and Eve's,
4 Merchant Quay,
Dublin 8
Tel 01-6771128

Walsh, Joseph, CC
Gortnahoe,
Thurles, Co Tipperary
Tel 056-8834867
(*Gortnahoe*, Cashel & E.)

Walsh, Kevin, CC
Dublin Road, Portlaoise,
Co Laois
Tel 057-8622301
(*Portlaoise*, Kildare & L.)

Walsh, Laurence (OCSO), Dom Prior,
Mount Saint Joseph Abbey,
Roscrea, Co Tipperary
Tel 0505-25600

Walsh, Liam (OP)
St Saviour's,
Upper Dorset Street,
Dublin 1
Tel 01-8897610

Walsh, Martin (SMA)
Retired in Britain

Walsh, Michael F., Very Rev, PE
Ballinard, Bonmahon
Co Waterford
Tel 051-292992
(Waterford & L., retired)

Walsh, Michael, Very Rev, PP
Parochial House,
Collinstown, Co Westmeath
Tel 044-9666326
(*Collinstown*, Meath)

Walsh, Michael, Very Rev, PE
Springlawn, Tubber, Moate,
Co Westmeath
Tel 090-6481141
(*Tubber*, Meath)

Walsh, Nicky (SPS)
St Patrick's, Kiltegan,
Co Wicklow
Tel 059-6473600

Walsh, Pádraig, CC
St Brendan's, Tralee,
Co Kerry
Tel 066-7125932
(*Tralee, St Brendan's*, Kerry)

Walsh, Pat
Priests House, Aliohill,
Enniskeane, Co Cork
(Cork & R., retired)

Walsh, Patrick (CSsR)
Mount Saint Alphonsus,
Limerick
Tel 061-315099

Walsh, Patrick (MSC)
Western Road, Cork
Tel 021-4804120

Walsh, Patrick J., Most Rev, DD
Bishop Emeritus of Down and Connor,
6 Waterloo Park North,
Belfast BT15 5HW
Tel 028-90778182
(Down & C.)

Walsh, Paul (CSSp)
Holy Spirit Missionary College,
Kimmage Manor, Dublin 12
Tel 01-406 4300

Walsh, Paul (SM)
London

Walsh, Pearse, CC
The Presbytery,
Kilmacanogue
Bray, Co Wicklow
Tel 01-4780616
(*Enniskerry*, Dublin)

Walsh, Richard (OP), CC
St Saviour's Priory, Kilbarry,
Waterford
Tel 051-376581
(*St Saviour's*, Waterford & L.)

Walsh, Sean (IC)
Clonturk House,
Ormond Road,
Drumcondra, Dublin 9
Tel 01-6877014

Walsh, Thomas (SMA), AP
Cathedral Presbytery, Cork
Tel 021-4304325
(Cork & R.)

Walsh, Vincent (SSC)
St Columban's Retirement Home,
Dalgan Park, Navan,
Co Meath
Tel 046-9021525

Walsh, William (CSSp)
Holy Spirit Missionary College,
Kimmage Manor,
Dublin 12
Tel 01-4064300

Walsh, William, Most Rev, DD
Bishop of Killaloe,
Westbourne, Ennis,
Co Clare
Tel 065-6828638
(Killaloe, retired)

Walsh, William, Very Rev, PP
8 Merval Crescent,
Clareview, Limerick
Tel 061-453026
(*Our Lady of the Rosary*, Limerick)

Walshe, Adrian, CC
Castleblayney,
Co Monaghan
Tel 042-9740027
(*Castleblayney*, Clogher)

Walshe, Stephen (CSSp), CC
St Anne's, Sligo
Tel 071-9145028
(*Sligo, St Anne's*, Elphin)

Walshe, Thomas, Very Rev, PP
Rosenallis, Portlaoise,
Co Laois
Tel 057-8628513
(*Rosenallis*, Kildare & L.)

Walton, James, CC
Templemore, Co Tipperary
Tel 0504-31225
(*Templemore*, Cashel & E.)

Walwa, Robert
15 Connawood Drive, Bray,
Co Wicklow
Tel 01-2829467
(*Bray St Peter's*, Dublin)

Ward, Alan, CF
Chaplain,
Finner Army Camp,
Ballyshannon, Co Donegal
Tel 071-9842294
(Clogher)

Ward, Andrew (OCSO)
Mellifont Abbey, Collon,
Co Louth
Tel 041-9826103

Ward, Bonaventure (OFM)
Franciscan Friary,
Lady Lane, Waterford
Tel 051-874262

Ward, Conor, Rt Rev Mgr
17 Prospect Lawn, The Park,
Cabinteely, Dublin 18
Tel 01-2898656
(*Cabinteely*, Dublin)

Ward, John
1 Chestnut Grove,
Ballymount Road,
Kingswood Heights, Dublin 24
Tel 01- 4515824
(Dublin, retired)

Ward, Michael, Very Rev Canon, PE
6 Augherainey Close,
Donaghmore, Dungannon,
Co Tyrone BT70 3HF
Tel 028-87761847
(Armagh, retired)

Ward, Pat, Very Rev, PP
Burtonport, Co Donegal
Tel 074-9542006
(*Burtonport*, Raphoe)

Ward, Paul, Very Rev, PP
Parochial House,
1 Bayside Square North,
Sutton, Dublin 13
Tel 01-8323150
(*Bayside*, Dublin)

Ward, Peter (CSsR)
Clonard Monastery,
1 Clonard Gardens,
Belfast BT13 2RL
Tel 028-90445950

Warrack, Colin (SJ)
Gonzaga College,
Sandford Road, Dublin 6
Tel 01-4972943

Warren, Ray (OMI)
Parochial House,
118 Naas Road, Dublin 8
Tel 01-4501040/087-2900468
(*Bluebell*, Dublin)

Waters, Ignatius (CP), CC
St Paul's Retreat,
Mount Argus, Dublin 6W
Tel 01-4992000
(*Mount Argus*, Dublin)

Watson, Noel, CC
No. 1 Presbytery, 4 Old Hill,
Leixlip, Co Kildare
Tel 01-6243718
(*Leixlip*, Dublin)

Watters, Brian, CC
79 Ivanhoe Avenue,
Carryduff, Belfast BT8 8BW
Tel 028-90817410
(*Drumbo*, Down & C.)

Watters, Enda (CSSp)
Holy Spirit Missionary College,
Kimmage Manor, Dublin 12
Tel 01-406 4300

Weakliam, David (OCarm), Very Rev, PP
Prior,
Whitefriar Street Church,
56 Aungier Street, Dublin 2
Tel 01-4758821

Welsh, Oscar (SMA)
Assistant Provincial Bursar,
African Missions,
Blackrock Road, Cork
Tel 021-4292871

Whearty, Roderick
St Fiacre's Gardens,
Bohernatownish Road,
Loughboy, Kilkenny
Tel 056-77701730
(*St Patrick's*, Ossory)

Whelan, Brian, CC
The Presbytery,
12 School Street, Wexford
Tel 053-9122055
(*Wexford*, Ferns)

Whelan, Edward, PE, CC
Ballon, Co Carlow
Tel 059-9159329
(*Ballon*, Kildare & L.)

Whelan, John (OSA)
St Augustine's Priory,
Galway
Tel 091-562524

Whelan, Joseph O. (MHM)
St Joseph's House,
50 Orwell Park, Rathgar,
Dublin 6
Tel 01-4127700

Whelan, Joseph, Very Rev, Co-PP
Parochial House,
Our Lady Queen of Peace,
Putland Road, Bray,
Co Wicklow
Tel 01-2988746
(*Bray, Putland Road*, Dublin)

Whelan, Marc (CSSp)
Holy Spirit Missionary College,
Kimmage Manor, Dublin 12
Tel 01-4064300

Whelan, Martin, CC
18 University Road, Galway
Tel 091-524875/563577
(Galway)

Whelan, Michael
c/o Archbishop's House,
Tuam
(Tuam)

Whelan, Michael (MSC)
Western Road, Cork
Tel 021-4804120

Whelan, Patrick (SMA)
SMA House, Claregalway,
Co Galway
Tel 091-798880

Whelan, Patrick A. (CSSp)
Holy Spirit Missionary College,
Kimmage Manor, Dublin 12
Tel 01-4064300

Whelan, Patrick, Very Rev, PP
St Patrick's Presbytery,
Forster Street, Galway
Tel 091-567994
(*St Patrick's*, Galway)

Whelan, Seamus (SPS)
St Patrick's, Kiltegan,
Co Wicklow
Tel 059-6473600

Whelan, Tom (CSSp)
Holy Spirit Missionary College,
Kimmage Manor,
Dublin 12
Tel 01-4064300

Whelan, Tom, PP
Templemore Road,
Cloughjordan,
Co Tipperary
Tel 0505-42266/087-2730299
(Killaloe)

White, Brian, CC
Grianán Mhuire,
Main Street, Blackrock,
Dundalk, Co Louth
Tel 042-9322244
(*Haggardstown and Blackrock*, Armagh)

White, Cornelius, Very Rev
Nazareth Home,
Dromahane, Mallow,
Co Cork
Tel 022-50486
(Cork & R., retired)

White, David, Very Rev, PP
Parochial House,
182 Garron Road,
Glenariffe,
Co Antrim BT44 0RA
Tel 028-21771249
(*Glenariffe*, Down & C.)

White, Jerry (SSCC)
Cootehill, Co Cavan
Tel 049-5552188

White, Laurence, Very Rev, Co-PP
Parochial House,
186 Clontarf Road,
Dublin 3
Tel 01-2862346
(*Clontarf, St John's*, Dublin)

White, Patrick
Training and Development Officer,
Youth Link Training Offices,
143 University Street,
Belfast BT7 1HP
Tel 028-90323217
(Down & C.)

White, Séamus, CC
Parochial House,
6 Circular Road,
Dungannon,
Co Tyrone BT71 6BE
Tel 028-87722631
(*Dungannon (Drumglass, Killyman and Tullyniskin)*, Armagh)

White, Thomas, Most Rev
6 Osborne Court, Seapoint Avenue, Blackrock,
Co Dublin
Tel 01-2806609
(Ossory)

Whiteford, Kieran, Very Rev, PP
Parochial House, Loughinisland, Downpatrick, Co Down BT30 8QH
Tel 028-44811661
(*Loughinisland*, Down & C.)

Whitmore, Fintan Brennan (OH)
Chaplain, Our Lady's Children's Hospital, Crumlin, Dublin 12
Tel 01-4096100
(Dublin)

Whitney, Ciaran, Very Rev, PP, VF
Chaplain, Post-Primary School, Strokestown, Co Roscommon
Tel 071-9633041
Parish
Strokestown, Co Roscommon
Tel 071-9633027
(Elphin)

Whittaker, Michael, Very Rev, PP
The Presbytery, Enfield, Co Meath
Tel 046-9541282
(*Enfield*, Meath)

Whittle, Joseph (SDB)
Kilcullen Road, Dunlavin, Co Wicklow

Whooley, Eoin, Very Rev, PP
Lislevane, Bandon, Co Cork
Tel 023-8846914
(*Barryroe*, Cork & R.)

Whyte, Daniel, Very Rev, PP, VF
53 Marlo Park, Bangor, Co Down BT19 6NL
Tel 078-12184624
(Down & C., retired)

Wickham, Anthony, Very Rev, PP
Clondrohid, Macroom, Co Cork
Tel 026-41014
(*Clondrohid*, Cloyne)

Williams, John (OSA)
St Augustine's, Taylor's Lane, Balyboden, Dublin 16
Tel 01-4241000

Williams, Patrick, Venreable Archdeacon, PE
Caherlohan, Tulla, Co Clare
(Tuam, retired)

Wilson, Desmond
6 Springhill Close, Belfast BT12 7SE
Tel 028-90326722
(Down & C., retired)

Wilson, John Rt Rev Mgr, Adm
Parochial House, Ballymore Eustace, Naas Co Kildare
(*Ballymore Eustace*, Dublin)

Winkle, Patrick, CC
Youghal, Co Cork
Tel 024-92270
(*Youghal*, Cloyne)

Winter, William, Very Rev PP
Banteer, Co Cork
Tel 029-56010
(*Banteer (Clonmeen)*, Cloyne)

Woods, Brendan (SJ)
Milltown Park, Sandford Road, Dublin 6
Tel 01-2698411/2698113

Woods, Daniel, Very Rev, PP
Kilcommon, Co Tipperary
Tel 062-78103
(*Kilcommon*, Cashel & E.)

Woods, Michael, Very Rev, PP
Parochial House, 40 Market Street, Tandagree, Co Armagh BT62 2BW
Tel 028-38840442
(*Tandragee (Ballymore and Mullaghbrack)*, Armagh)

Woods, Thomas, Rt Rev Mgr, DD
Newbrook Nursing Home, Mullingar, Co Westmeath
(Meath, retired)

Woods, Thomas, Very Rev
Edenville, Kinlough, Co Leitrim
(Kilmore, retired)

Wrenn, Timothy (SDB)
Our Lady of Lourdes Parish, Sean McDermott Street, Dublin 1
Tel 01-8363558

Wright, Colum, Very Rev, PP
10 Oaklands, Loughbrickland, Co Down BT32 3NH
Tel 028-40623264
(*Aghaderg*, Dromore)

Wright, John (OFMCap)
Guardian, Capuchin Friary, Station Road, Raheny, Dublin 5
Tel 01-8313886

Wynne, Owen (SCI)
Sacred Heart Fathers, Fairfield, 66 Inchicore Road, Dublin 8
Tel 01-4538655

## Y

Yilma, Gobezayehu Getachew, PC
287 South Circular Road, Rialto, Dublin 8
Tel 01-4539020
(*Rialto*, Dublin)

Young, Gerard, Co-PP
23 Oakdown Road, Dublin 14
Tel 01-8339666
(*Churchtown*, Dublin)

Young, Joseph
21 Marian Avenue, Janesboro, Limerick
Tel 061-405835
(Limerick)

Young, Patrick, Very Rev
Billis, Cavan
Tel 049-4372386
(Kilmore, retired)

Young, Richard (OCD)
St Joseph's, Berkeley Road, Dublin 7
Tel 01-8306356/8306336

Young, Robert, Very Rev, PP
The Presbytery, Kinsale, Co Cork
Tel 021-4774019
(*Kinsale*, Cork & R.)

Younge, Patrick (OFM)
Guardian, The Abbey, 8 Francis Street, Galway
Tel 091-562518

## Z

Zaggi, Douglas, PC
The Presbytery, St Brigid's Parish, Straffan, Co Kildare
Tel 01-6012197
(*Celbridge*, Dublin)

Zuribo, Aloysius
16 Ashfield Drive, Balbriggan, Co Dublin
Tel 01-8020602
(*Balbriggan*, Dublin)

# PARISH INDEX

*Where a parish has an alternative or historical name, both names are given e.g. Arney/Cleenish. In such cases the parish appears in the list in each form, i.e. Arney/Cleenish and Cleenish/Arney*

**D**

## E



## F



## G

**H**



**I**



**J**



**K**

## L



## M

# GENERAL INDEX

N



O

S